Second Edition

Criminology
in Canada

THEORIES, PATTERNS, AND TYPOLOGIES

Second Edition

Criminology in Canada

THEORIES, PATTERNS, AND TYPOLOGIES

Larry J. Siegel
University of Massachusetts at Lowell

Chris McCormick
St. Thomas University

THOMSON

NELSON

Australia   Canada   Mexico   Singapore   Spain   United Kingdom   United States

Criminology in Canada:
Theories, Patterns, and Typologies
Second Edition

by Larry J. Siegel and Chris McCormick

Editorial Director and Publisher:
Evelyn Veitch

Executive Editor:
Joanna Cotton

Marketing Manager:
Karen Howell

Developmental Editor:
Edward Ikeda

Production Editor:
Wendy Yano

Production Coordinator:
Hedy Sellers

Copy Editor:
Wendy Thomas

Creative Director:
Angela Cluer

Proofreader:
Wendy Thomas

Interior Design:
Ken Phipps

Interior Design Modifications:
Peter Papayanakis

Cover Design:
Ken Phipps

Cover Photo:
Karl Grupe/Photonica

Cover Design:
Ken Phipps

Compositor:
Janet Zanette

Indexer:
Edwin Durbin

Printer:
Phoenix Color

National Library of Canadian Cataloguing in Publication Data

Siegel, Larry J
    Criminology in Canada: theories, patterns, and typologies/Larry J. Siegel, Chris McCormick.—2nd ed.

Includes bibliographical references and indexes.
ISBN 0-17-616975-X

1. Criminology—Canada.
2. Crime—Canada. 3. Criminology.
I. McCormick, Christopher Ray, 1956– II. Title.

HV6025.S53 2002   364.971
C2002-901963-X

This book is dedicated to my children, Julie,
Andrew, Eric, and Rachel Siegel, and
to my wife, Theresa G. Libby.
–Larry J. Siegel

To my students.
–Chris McCormick

Contents

Preface

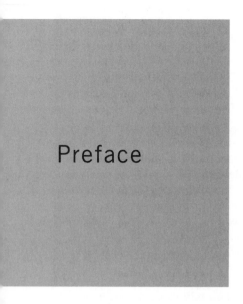

Since launching a massive search at a farm in Port Coquitlam, British Columbia, in early 2002, police were flooded with calls to a special tip line. The farm became the focus of one of the biggest investigations in the province's history. A joint task force involving the Vancouver police and the RCMP were investigating the disappearance of 50 women since 1983, possibly one of the largest serial homicide cases in the Western world. The missing women worked in the sex trade in the lower east side of Vancouver, and many of them were drug addicts. Many people had speculated for some time that a serial killer was behind the disappearances, but the search at the farm appeared to be a major break in the investigation; several weeks after the investigation was started, one of the owners of the farm was charged with the murder of two of the women who had disappeared. The police had been tipped to the farm two years earlier, but failed to act, some think because the victims were prostitutes.

Criminal acts capture public attention in a way that nothing else does. And yet our ability to determine the validity of those news stories, television documentaries, and magazine articles is compromised by the fact that most of us have little independent knowledge of crime. Unless you hang out with cops (or criminals) or study criminological theory and patterns of crime, more than likely what you know about crime is gleaned from the media.

The media do a good job reporting crime, but also seem to have an inordinate interest in notorious killers, serial murderers, drug lords, and sex criminals. Fraud and counterfeiting do not receive much attention unless the amounts involved are in the millions. It is not surprising, then, that many people are more concerned about violent crime than almost any other social problem. Most people worry to one degree or another about becoming victims of violent crime, having their houses broken into, or having their cars stolen. People alter their behaviour to limit the risk of victimization and question whether legal punishment alone can control criminal offenders. They are shocked at graphic news accounts of drive-by shootings, police brutality, and prison riots. They are fascinated by books, movies, and TV shows about law firms, clients, fugitives, and hardened killers.

Why do people behave the way they do? What causes one person to become violent and antisocial, while another channels his or her energy into work, school, and family? How can an at-risk kid in a high-crime neighbourhood who successfully resists the temptation of the streets be explained? What accounts for the behaviour of the multimillionaire who cheats on his or her taxes and engages in other fraudulent schemes? The former has nothing yet is able to resist crime; the latter has everything and falls prey to its lure. Is behaviour a function of personal characteristics, or upbringing and experience? Is it influenced by culture or environment? Or is it a combination of all these influences? This text addresses some of these difficult questions through a typology-based approach.

As a professor of criminology, I have taught over 1500 students in the last five years, probably half of those at the first-year level. To me what is important is communicating my interest in crime, law, and justice to my classes, inspiring my students with the same interest in the field that I have. My goal has always been to help students understand a very broad field in a way that's easy to understand. What could be more important or fascinating than a field of study that deals with such wide-ranging topics as the motivation for mass murder, the association between media violence and interpersonal aggression, the family's influence on drug abuse, and the history of organized crime? Criminology is a dynamic field, changing constantly with the release of major research studies, Supreme Court rulings, and governmental policy. Its dynamism and diversity make it an important and engrossing area of study. In this book I have sought to find examples and cases that make the field "come alive."

What makes criminology difficult, but also interesting, is that debates continue over the nature and extent of crime and the causes and prevention of criminality. Some people view criminals as society's victims who are forced to violate the law because of poverty and the lack of opportunity. Others view aggressive, antisocial behaviour as a product of mental and physical abnormalities that persist through the life course. Genetic, neurological, and physiological factors are also felt to influence criminality. Still another view is that crime is a function of the rational choice of greedy, selfish people who can only be deterred through the threat of harsh punishments. For these people there can be no treatment, only punishment. As new research uncovers factors that affect crime, the debate over the nature and cause of crime develops.

Debate also continues over how the criminal justice system should best treat known criminals. Should they be punished by being locked up? Or should they be given a second chance and diverted into alternative justice programs? Should crime control policy focus on punishment or rehabilitation, or even medical treatment? If the underlying cause is poverty, how could that be remedied? Many of these questions are tied to current events we learn about through the media. When two British children were accused of abducting and murdering a two-year-old child, the case sparked international outrage, fuelling the call for reforms to juvenile justice. When Melanie Carpenter was abducted from her place of work in Surrey, British Columbia, in broad daylight, there was sufficient public alarm that the dangerous offender legislation was amended. Similarly, when Georgina Leimonis was shot in a Toronto café, there were calls for the deportation of violent criminals.

Because interest in crime and justice is so great and so timely, this text is designed to review these ongoing issues and cover the field of criminology in an organized and comprehensive manner. It is meant as a broad overview of the field, designed to whet the reader's appetite and encourage further and more in-depth exploration. One of my graduating students told me she had kept this book in its first edition throughout university, using it as a reference beyond first year. That type of testimonial inspires me to keep on working with Larry Siegel in writing this book to suit student needs, while meeting my interest in communicating my enthusiasm for a rich, growing field of study.

TOPIC AREAS

The text is divided into three main sections or topic areas.

Section 1 provides a framework for studying criminology. Chapter 1 defines the field and discusses its most basic concepts: the definition of crime, the component areas of criminology, the history of criminology, criminological research methods, and the ethical issues that confront the field. Chapter 2 covers the criminal law and its functions, processes, defences, and reform. Much of this is generic to a justice system anywhere in the Western world, so it was important to add a Canadian face to the material. For example, the topic of wrongful convictions illustrates how mistakes can happen in even the most rationally organized system. There is also material on recent changes to the law, including stalking laws and community notification laws. Chapter 3 deals with the nature, extent, and patterns of crime, covering the various ways we know about crime in our society: police statistics, victimization surveys, and the media. In the recent past, commissions of inquiry have also become an independent and indepth source of knowledge about crime. New material is presented on gun control as well as the findings of an important new study that followed chronic juvenile offenders into their adulthood. In addition, new material on international crime rates is included. Chapter 4 is devoted to a relatively rare topic for a criminology text, the concept of victimization. This includes looking at the nature of victims, theories of victimization, and programs designed to help crime victims. A much expanded section on hate crime in Canada has been developed for this edition.

Section 2 contains six chapters that cover criminological theory. Why do people engage in criminal behaviour? These views include theories of criminal choice (Chapter 5); biological and psychological views (Chapter 6); structural, cultural, and ecological theories (Chapter 7); social process theories that focus on socialization and include learning and control (Chapter 8); and theories of social conflict (Chapter 9). Chapter 10 covers attempts by criminologists to integrate various theories into a unified whole. These chapters build on Section 1, but also prepare the foundation for the empirical topics discussed in the next section. Of particular interest are the material on closed circuit television in Chapter 5; real cases of sleepwalking used as a defence in Chapter 6; early research done at McGill University in the 1920s in Chapter 7; and research on ethnicity and criminality in Chapter 9.

Section 3 is devoted to the major forms of criminal behaviour. Chapters 11 to 14 cover violent crime, common theft offences, white-collar and organized crimes, and public order crimes, including sex offences and substance abuse. Each of these chapters has been updated from the first Canadian edition, using the latest criminal statistics (2001), and victimization surveys (1999). Throughout, recent Canadian research is highlighted and current topics keep the text fresh. The latest scandal on Bay Street, as well as the extent of fraud on eBay, can be found here.

The text has been carefully structured to cover relevant material in a comprehensive, balanced, and objective fashion.

FEATURES

Photos, charts, and figures are important pedagogical features for any text. Each chapter includes a chapter outline, a list of key terms contained in the chapter, and at least one boxed insert. These boxes contain a detailed discussion or reading of an important and intriguing topic, issue, or program. An extensive glossary provides concise definitions of key terms used throughout the text for quick reference.

Connections boxes are located in appropriate places throughout each chapter. These brief inserts link the material being currently discussed with relevant information located elsewhere in the text. Connections either expand on the subject matter or show how it can be applied to other areas or topics. In a book this comprehensive, they help organize and coordinate the material for quicker learning.

The World Wide Web is becoming an important academic research tool. Consequently, a supporting Web page is available that contains material that supplements the text. This feature will help students who either want to read supplementary material or want to use nontraditional sources in research. Every attempt has been made to supply Web site addresses that are contemporary and may be either Canadian or international. Some Web sites do expire; if this happens, try deleting the suffix, or search for the parent site.

NEW IN THIS EDITION

This second Canadian edition retains many of the same organizational features of the very successful first edition, with some notable differences.

A new feature, **Crime in the News**, looks at how the media cover crime by reproducing a news story. The media are important resources for our understanding of criminal justice. For example, in Chapter 6, a case from the media is highlighted in which a woman was given leniency after she stabbed her husband. Her defence? She was suffering from premenstrual syndrome, which compromised her ability to make good choices.

Another new feature to this edition is **Famous Canadian Criminals**, which uses cases from our past to illustrate principles from the text. For example, Chapter 4 highlights the case of Angelique Lyn Lavallee, a battered woman in a violent common-law relationship who killed her partner late one night by shooting him in the back of the head as he left her room. This case ultimately resulted in a decision by the Supreme Court of Canada (1990) that set the legal framework for what has become known as the "battered wife syndrome" defence. Justice Minister Alan Rock also agreed to consider extending that principle to some pre-1990 cases. In this case, we see the origin of an important doctrine of Canadian criminal justice, as well as consider the significance of gender in criminal cases.

Another new feature is **Thinking Like a Criminologist**, in which the student is asked to apply the reasoning from the chapter to a more applied criminal justice question. For example, in Chapter 12, to deter property crime, various measures are discussed that could prevent theft from households and cars. Can you think of other preventive measures after reading this chapter?

In addition, each chapter contains an important new section called **Culture, Gender, Ethnicity, and Criminology**, in which broader questions on the relationship between crime and the wider society are addressed. In Chapter 6, for example, some issues concerning the relation between the media and violence are discussed. Are the media implicated in influencing violent behaviour? Do the media simply reflect norms already existing in society? These are questions that are still open for discussion. In Chapter 4, gay-bashing is examined in some detail, and in Chapter 9 issues involving natives and the criminal justice system are highlighted.

ANCILLARY MATERIALS

Nelson provides a number of pedagogical supplements to help instructors use this text in their courses and to aid students in preparing for exams, including

- PowerPoint presentation software—new;
- a study guide—new;
- an Instructor's Resource Manual;
- a printed test bank;
- a computerized test bank;
- a book-specific Web site at www.siegelcriminology 2e.nelson.com for chapter links, quizzes, study tools, and more.

InfoTrac also comes with this text, a resource unique to Nelson, which provides online access to look up articles for your research, determine topics for group projects, and find study aids as well.

PERSPECTIVE

In this Canadian edition, I have made every effort to make the presentation of material interesting, balanced, and objective, and especially, as distinctly Canadian as possible. No single political or theoretical position dominates the text; instead, the many diverse views that are contained within criminology and that characterize its interdisciplinary nature are presented. The text analyzes the most important scholarly works and scientific research reports, while also presenting topical information on recent cases and events.

ACKNOWLEDGMENTS

Many people helped make this book possible. I have attempted to incorporate the suggestions of those who reviewed this edition and made suggestions, including

Les Samuelson (University of Saskatchewan)
James Euale (Sault College)
Scot Wortley (University of Toronto)
Oliver Stoetzer (Fanshawe College)
John F. Anderson (Malaspina University College)
Diane Symbaluk (Grant MacEwan College)

The list of those who helped with material or advice include those at Nelson. Many thanks to Joanna Cotton, Edward Ikeda, Ken Phipps, and Wendy Yano for their assistance. In particular, I would like to thank Larry Siegel (University of Massachusetts at Lowell) for producing such a great text from which to work.

In addition, I also thank copy editor Wendy Thomas and the following research and editorial assistants who helped in many ways to bring this text to its second edition: Robert Doiron, Mike Fleming, Rayna House, Lindsay Ross, and Peggy Scott.

Chris McCormick
Department of Criminology
St. Thomas University
Fredericton, New Brunswick
2002

Concepts of Crime, Law, and Criminology

How is crime defined? How much crime is there, and what are the trends and patterns in the crime rate? How many people fall victim to crime, and who is likely to become a crime victim? How did our system of criminal law develop, and what are the basic elements of crimes? What is the science of criminology all about? These are some of the core issues that will be addressed in the first four chapters of this text, providing a solid foundation for the chapters to come. Chapter 1 introduces students to the field of criminology: its nature, area of study, methodologies, and historical development. Concern about crime and justice has been an important part of the human condition for more than 5000 years, since the first criminal codes were set down in the Middle East. And while the scientific study of crime—criminology—is considered a contemporary science, it has existed for more than 200 years.

Chapter 2 introduces students to one of the key components of criminology: the development of criminal law. It discusses the social history of law, the purpose of the law and how it defines crime, and it briefly examines criminal defences and legal reform using prominent Canadian examples. The final two chapters of this section review the various sources of crime data to derive a picture of crime. Chapter 3 focuses on the nature and extent of crime, while Chapter 4 is devoted to victims and victimization. Important, stable patterns in the rates of crime and victimization indicate that these are not random events. The way crime and victimization are organized and patterned profoundly influences how criminologists view the causes of crime.

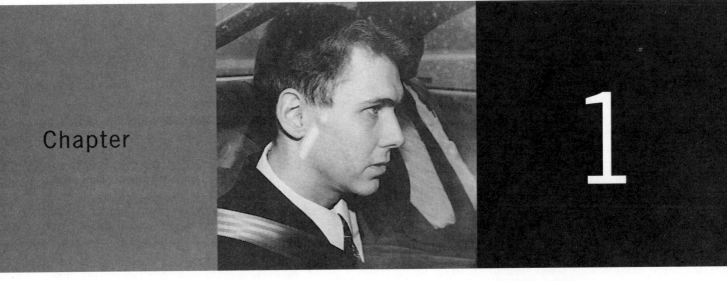

Chapter 1

Crime and Criminology

In July 1991, Niagara Region police identified the remains of a woman found dismembered and embedded in concrete in a lake to be those of 14-year-old Leslie Mahaffy. Two people were eventually convicted of her death and that of 15-year-old Kristen French: Karla Homolka and Paul Bernardo. In a controversial plea bargain, Homolka cooperated with the prosecution and testified against her former husband, and was sentenced to 12 years in jail. Bernardo received a life sentence for the two murders and was declared a dangerous offender for a string of serial rapes.

Details of the case were subject to a publication ban between the two separate trials of Homolka and Bernardo. However, this didn't prevent the public from finding out details of the case. In the United States, *The Washington Post* published a story and readers looked it up in public libraries; *The Buffalo News* also printed an article and Canadians drove across the border to buy it. Details of the crimes were posted on the Internet faster than news lists and discussion groups could be shut down. Media coverage quickly became a story only barely eclipsed in importance by the trials themselves. Were the media sensationalizing the case, or were they simply responding to the public's need to know? Was a ban necessary to guarantee fair trials for the accused? A December 1992 survey done by polling company Angus Reid reported that despite the media ban, 25 percent of Ontario residents had learned banned details of the trial. However, 35 percent weren't even aware of the case at all.

This case helps illustrate why crime and criminal behaviour have long fascinated people. Crime touches all

Convicted killers Paul Bernardo (see opener) and Karla Homolka are doing institutional time for their crimes: Bernardo was classified as a dangerous offender and incarcerated, while Homolka was given a 12-year sentence.

segments of society. Both the poor and desperate and the affluent engage in criminal activity. Crime occurs across racial, class, and gender lines. It involves some acts that shock the conscience and others that seem relatively harmless human foibles.

Criminal acts may be the work of strangers who prey on people they have never met, or they can involve friends and family members in **intimate violence**.[1] Regardless of whether crime is shocking or pardonable, there is still little consensus about its cause or what can be done to prevent it. What might compel a couple like Paul Bernardo and Karla Homolka to commit such crimes? They came from a community with tree-shaded parks, nice homes, and sports fields. The couple's wedding included a horse-drawn carriage. They were seen as a young couple with a bright future. Could such outrageous behaviour be better understood if it had been committed by indigent teens who were the product of bad neighbourhoods and dysfunctional homes? Could someone who was really "normal" ever commit such a horrible crime? Is it possible that if this couple were convicted and imprisoned for life this extreme punishment might deter others? Do the media have any responsibility in reporting such horrific crimes? Research indicates that habitually aggressive behaviour is often learned in homes in which children are victimized and parents serve as aggressive role models—learned violence then persists into adulthood.[2] Is it possible to overcome a predisposition to violence through the fear of punishment?

Crime stories such as this one take their toll on the public. At the time Paul Bernardo was being convicted for his crimes, about one-third of the Canadian population said that they do not feel safe walking alone in their own neighbourhood at night, and this fear was more likely to be expressed by women than men. While this fear is decreasing, due perhaps to the steady decrease in the crime rate, it is still out of proportion to one's actual risk of victimization. Forty-six percent of Canadians 15 years and over thought that crime had increased between 1988 and 1993, despite the fact that overall rates of victimization actually remained the same or decreased. The 1993 General Social Survey showed that 24 percent of Canadians were victims of crime in 1993, the same percentage of Canadians who were victims of crime in 1988. Canadians were in fact no more likely to be victims of assault, theft (either of personal or household property), vandalism, or break and enter in 1993 than they were five years previously. In a more recent poll conducted in Ottawa, 60 percent of people surveyed thought that the city's crime rate was worse than it was five years ago.[3]

The fact that the public overestimates the likelihood of crime in their own neighbourhood despite contradictory evidence from their own experience points to the influence of other factors in the public's knowledge of crime, such as the media. It suggests that people do not in fact rely on their own experience in assessing the likelihood of being a victim of crime. The public's fear may be exaggerated; however, we cannot simply dismiss this fear as irrational. While the fear of crime might be greater than a person's actual chance of becoming a victim of crime, that fear is usually derived from objective sources, such as the media. Fear has long-term effects, creating a negative view of the police and the courts, and an attitude favouring harsher punishments for offenders. The fear of crime also sets the larger social agenda; a poll conducted by the Council for Canadian Unity in 2000 found that more people favour putting resources into reducing crime than those favouring reducing poverty.[4]

Connections

Experts have suggested a variety of explanations for bizarre violent episodes such as serial homicide. While some focus on cultural factors, others lay the blame on psychological abnormality. Psychologists link violent behaviour to a number of psychological influences, including observational learning from violent TV shows, traumatic childhood experiences, mental illness, impaired cognitive processes, and a psychopathic personality structure. Chapter 6 reviews the most prominent of these prescriptions for violence.

Concern about crime and the need to develop effective measures to control criminal behaviour have spurred the development of the study of **criminology**. This academic discipline is devoted to the development of valid and reliable information about the causes of crime as well as crime patterns and trends. **Criminologists** use scientific methods to study the nature, extent, cause, and control of criminal behaviour. Unlike media commentators, whose opinions about crime can be coloured by personal experiences, biases, and values, criminologists attempt to bring objectivity and scientific methods to the study of crime and its consequences. Because of the threat of crime and the social problems it represents, the field of criminology has gained prominence as an academic area of study.

This chapter introduces criminology: how it is defined, its goals, and its history. It also addresses such questions as How do criminologists define crime? How do they conduct research? What ethical issues face those wishing to conduct criminological research?

What Is Criminology?

Criminology is the scientific approach to the study of criminal behaviour. In their classic definition, criminologists Edwin Sutherland and Donald Cressey state:

Criminology is the body of knowledge regarding crime as a social phenomenon. It includes within its scope the processes of making laws, of breaking laws, and of reacting toward the breaking of laws.... The objective of criminology is the development of a body of general and verified principles and of other types of knowledge regarding this process of law, crime, and treatment.[5]

Sutherland and Cressey's definition includes the most important areas of interest to criminologists: the development of criminal law and its use to define crime, the cause of law violations, and the methods used to control criminal behaviour. Also important is the use of the scientific method in criminology. Criminologists use objective research methods to pose research questions (hypotheses), gather data, create theories, and test the validity of theories. They use every method of established social science inquiry: analysis of existing records, experimental designs, surveys, historical analysis, and content analysis.

An essential part of criminology is the fact that it is an interdisciplinary science. Relatively few academic centres in Canada grant graduate degrees in criminology. Many criminologists have been trained in other fields, most commonly sociology but also criminal justice, political science, psychology, economics, and the natural sciences. While for most of the 20th century, criminology's primary orientation has been sociological, today it can be viewed as an integrated approach to the study of criminal behaviour. Although it combines elements from many other fields, the primary area of interest for criminologists is understanding the true nature of law, crime, and justice.

Criminology and Criminal Justice

In the late 1960s, interest in the so-called crime problem gave rise to the development of research projects aimed at understanding the way police, courts, and correctional agencies actually operated.[6] Similarly, reviews of criminal justice practice focused on the management of dangerous offenders and the protection of the public against violent crime. Eventually, academic programs devoted to studying the **criminal justice system** were opened in the United States, although in Canada criminology is largely studied from within sociology departments. There are only five university departments of criminology in Canada, at Simon Fraser, Ottawa, Montreal, Toronto, and St. Thomas universities.

Although the terms *criminology* and *criminal justice* may seem similar, and people often confuse the two, there are major differences between these fields of study. Criminology explains the etiology (origin), extent, and nature of crime in society, whereas criminal justice refers to the agencies of social control that handle criminal offenders. Whereas criminologists are mainly concerned with identifying the nature, extent, and cause of crime, criminal justice scholars are engaged in describing, analyzing, and explaining the behaviour of the agencies of justice—police departments, courts, and correctional facilities—and identifying effective methods of crime control.[7]

Because both fields are crime-related, they do overlap. Criminologists must be aware of how the agencies of justice operate and how they influence crime and criminals. Criminal justice experts cannot begin to design programs of crime prevention or rehabilitation without understanding something of the nature of crime. It is common, therefore, for criminal justice programs to feature courses on criminology and for criminology courses to evaluate the agencies of justice. Not surprisingly, these programs are often staffed by criminologists. Thus, these two fields not only coexist but help each other grow and develop.

Criminology and Deviance

Criminology is also sometimes confused with the study of deviant behaviour. However, significant distinctions can be made between these areas of scholarship. **Deviant behaviour** is behaviour that departs from social norms and that is subject to social control.[8] Included within the broad spectrum of deviant acts are behaviours that range from committing a violent crime to joining a nudist colony.

Crime and deviance are often confused, yet not all crimes are deviant or unusual acts, and not all deviant acts are illegal or criminal. For example, using recreational drugs such as marijuana may be illegal, but is it deviant? A significant percentage of youths have used or are using drugs, and three-quarters of Canadians surveyed think soft drugs should be allowed for individual use.[9] In Vancouver, a recent poll showed that support for decriminalizing marijuana increased from 47 to 57 percent in just three years.[10] After Ross Rebagliati was threatened with losing his gold medal in the snowboarding event at the 1998 Winter Olympics after testing positive for marijuana (which he denied using), public surveys showed more concern with the high-handedness of officials than with Rebagliati's purported marijuana use. Therefore, to argue that all crimes are behaviours that depart from the norms of society is probably erroneous. Conversely, many deviant acts are not criminal even though they may be shocking. For example, suppose a passerby observes a person drowning and makes no effort to save that victim. Although the general public would probably condemn the person's behaviour as callous, immoral, and deviant, no legal action could be taken, since citizens are not required by law to effect rescues. In sum, many criminal acts, but not all, fall within the concept of deviance. Similarly, some deviant acts, but not all, are considered crimes.

The relationship between crime and deviance is illustrated in Figure 1.1: Hagan's Varieties of Deviance. John Hagan, a prominent scholar who teaches in the Faculty of Law at the University of Toronto, developed a model depicting the relationship between crime and deviance along three dimensions: the evaluation of social harm, the level of agreement about the norm, and the severity of societal response. As Figure 1.1 shows, the most serious acts of deviance are also the least likely to occur; however, there is strong agreement over their harmfulness and the need for a serious societal response.[11]

Two issues that involve deviance are of particular interest to criminologists: (1) How do deviant behaviours become crimes? and (2) When should crimes be legalized? The first issue involves the historical development of law. Many acts that are legally forbidden today were once considered merely unusual or deviant behaviour. To understand the nature and purpose of law, criminologists study the process by which crimes are created from deviance. For example, the sale and possession of marijuana was legal in Canada until 1923 (in the United States until 1937), when it was prohibited under federal law by simply being added to the law prohibiting opium.[12] Despite being criminalized, however, marijuana still enjoys widespread popularity. Health Canada released a survey in 1989 estimating that 60 percent of Canadians between 20 and 44 years had used marijuana.[13]

Criminologists also consider whether outlawed behaviours have evolved into social norms and, if so, whether they should either be legalized or have their penalties reduced (**decriminalization**). For example, debate continues over assisted suicide, which is estimated to be widely but quietly practised.

Connections

Some of the drugs considered highly dangerous today were once sold openly and considered medically beneficial. For example, the narcotic drug heroin, now considered extremely addictive, was originally named in the mistaken belief that its painkilling properties would prove "heroic" to medical patients. The history of drug and alcohol abuse is discussed further in Chapter 14.

There is also frequent discussion about where to draw the line between behaviour that is merely considered deviant and unusual, and behaviour that is outlawed and criminal. For example, when does sexually oriented material cross the line from being merely suggestive to being pornographic? Can a line be drawn that separates sexually oriented materials into two groups, one that is legally acceptable and a second that is considered depraved or obscene? And, if such a line can be drawn, who gets to draw it? Conversely, if scientists show that a normative act, such as smoking or drinking, poses a

Figure 1.1   Hagan's varieties of deviance

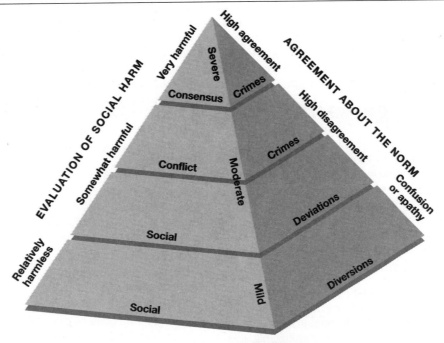

serious health hazard, should it be made illegal? Many recent efforts have been made to control morally questionable behaviour and restrict the rights of citizens to freedom of their actions. In a very controversial case, a British Columbia man was charged with the possession of violent, pornographic stories involving children. He argued that the law violated his freedom of expression and was acquitted. On appeal, the case eventually went to the Supreme Court of Canada, which ruled in January 2001 that John Robin Sharpe was deprived of his right to freedom of expression when police seized his pornography, as long as it was for his own personal use.

In sum, criminologists are concerned with the concept of deviance and its relationship to criminality. The shifting definition of deviant behaviour is closely associated with our concepts of crime. The relationship between criminology, criminal justice, and deviance is illustrated in Figure 1.2.

Figure 1.2   The relationship between criminology, criminal justice, and deviance

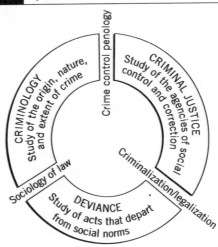

A Brief History of Criminology

The scientific study of crime and criminality is a relatively recent development. Although written criminal codes have existed for thousands of years, they were for the most part restricted to defining crime and setting punishments. What motivated people to violate the law remained a matter of conjecture.

During the Middle Ages, superstition and fear of satanic possession dominated thinking. People who violated social norms or religious practices were believed to be witches or possessed by demons. The prescribed method for dealing with the possessed was burning at the stake, a practice that survived into the 17th century. For example, between 1575 and 1590 Nicholas Remy, head of the Inquisition in the French province of Lorraine, ordered 900 sorcerers and witches burned to death; Peter Binsfield, the bishop of the German city of Trier, ordered the deaths of 6500 people. An estimated 100 000 people were prosecuted throughout Europe for witchcraft during the 16th and 17th centuries. Even those who questioned demonic possession advocated extremely harsh penalties as a means of punishing criminals and setting an example for others. Both violent and property crimes were often punished with execution.

Connections

The English common law is the immediate antecedent of the Canadian legal system, except for that of Quebec, which inherited the Napoleonic Code from France. Moreover, the influence of some of the earliest written codes, such as those of Hebrews and Babylonians, can still be detected. Chapter 2 traces the history of the law in some detail.

Classical Criminology

By the mid-18th century, social philosophers had begun to call for rethinking the prevailing concepts of law and justice. They argued for a more rational approach to punishment, stressing that the relationship between crimes and their punishment should be balanced and fair. This view was based on the prevailing philosophy of the time called **utilitarianism**, which emphasized that behaviour is purposeful and not motivated by supernatural forces. Rather than cruel public executions designed to frighten people into obedience or to punish those the law failed to deter, reformers called for a more moderate and just approach to penal sanctions. The most famous of these was Cesare Beccaria (1738–1794), an Italian aristocrat whose writings described both a motive for committing crime and methods for its control.

Beccaria believed that people want to achieve pleasure and avoid pain. Crimes must therefore provide some pleasure to the criminal. It follows that to deter or prevent crime, one must administer pain in an appropriate amount to counterbalance the pleasure obtained from crime. Beccaria's famous theorem was that

in order for punishment not to be in every instance, an act of violence of one or many against a private citizen, it must be essentially public, prompt, necessary, the least possible in the given circumstances, proportionate to the crimes, and dictated by the laws.[14]

During the Middle Ages, superstition and fear of satanic possession dominated thinking. People who violated social norms or religious practices were believed to be witches or possessed by demons. The prescribed method for dealing with the possessed was burning at the stake, a practice that survived into the 17th century. This painting, *The Trial of George Jacobs, August 5, 1692* by J.H. Matteson (1855), depicts the ordeal of Jacobs, a patriarch of Salem, Massachusetts. During the witch craze, he had ridiculed the trials, only to find himself being accused, tried, and executed.

The writings of Beccaria and his followers form the core of what today is referred to as **classical criminology**. As originally conceived in the 18th century, classical criminology theory had several basic elements:

1. In every society, people have free will to choose criminal or lawful solutions to meet their needs or settle their problems.
2. Criminal solutions may be more attractive than lawful ones because they usually require less work for a greater payoff.
3. People's choice of criminal solutions may be controlled by their fear of punishment.
4. The more severe, certain, and swift the punishment, the better able it is to control criminal behaviour.

The classical perspective influenced judicial philosophy during much of the late 18th and the 19th centuries. Prisons began to be used as a form of punishment, and sentences were geared proportionately to the seriousness of the crime. Capital punishment was still widely used but began to be employed for only the most serious crimes. The byword was "Let the punishment fit the crime."

During the 19th century, a new vision of the world challenged the validity of classical theory and presented an innovative way of looking at the causes of crime.

Nineteenth-Century Positivism

While the classical position held sway as a guide to crime, law, and justice for almost 100 years, during the late 19th century a new movement began that would challenge its dominance. **Positivism** developed as the scientific method began to take hold in Europe. This movement was inspired by new discoveries in biology, astronomy, and chemistry. If the scientific method could be applied to the study of nature, why not use it to study human behaviour? Auguste Comte (1798–1857), considered the founder of sociology, applied scientific methods to the study of society. According to Comte, societies pass through stages that can be grouped on the basis of how people try to understand the world in which they live. People in primitive societies consider inanimate objects as having life (for example, the sun is a god); in later social stages, people embrace a rational, scientific view of the world. Comte called this final stage the positive stage, and those who followed his writings became known as positivists.

The positivist tradition has two main elements. The first is the belief that human behaviour is a function of external forces that are beyond individual control. Some of these forces are social, such as the effect of wealth and class, while others are political and historical, such as war and famine. Other forces are more personal and psychological, such as an individual's brain structure and his or her biological makeup or mental ability. Each of these forces operates to influence human behaviour.

The second aspect of positivism is its use of the scientific method to solve problems. Positivists rely on the strict use of empirical methods to test hypotheses. That is, they believe in the factual, firsthand observation and measurement of conditions and events. Positivists would agree that an abstract concept such as "intelligence" exists because it can be measured by an IQ test. However, they would challenge a concept such as the "soul" because it is a condition that cannot be verified by the scientific method. The positivist tradition was spurred on by Charles Darwin (1809–1882), whose work on evolution encouraged the view that all human activity could be verified by scientific principles.

Positivist Criminology

If the scientific method could be used to explain all behaviour, then it was to be expected that by the mid-19th century "scientific" methods were being applied to understanding criminality. The earliest of these scientific studies were biologically oriented. Physiognomists, such as J.K. Lavater (1741–1801), studied the facial features of criminals to determine whether the shape of ears, nose, and eyes and the distance between them were associated with antisocial behaviour. Phrenologists, such as Franz Joseph Gall (1758–1828) and Johann Kaspar Spurzheim (1776–1832), studied the shape of the skull and bumps on the head to determine whether these physical attributes were linked to criminal behaviour. Phrenologists believed that external cranial characteristics dictate which areas of the brain control physical activity. Though their primitive techniques and quasi-scientific methods have been discredited, these efforts were an early attempt to apply a scientific approach to the study of crime.

By the early 19th century, abnormality in the human mind was being linked to criminal behaviour patterns. Philippe Pinel (1745–1826), one of the founders of French psychiatry, claimed that some people behave abnormally even without being mentally ill. He coined the phrase *manie sans delire* to denote what eventually was referred to as a psychopathic personality. In 1812 an American, Benjamin Rush (1745–1813), described patients with an "innate preternatural moral depravity."[15] Another early criminological pioneer, English physician Henry Maudsley (1835–1918), believed that insanity and criminal behaviour are strongly linked: "Crime is a sort of outlet in which their unsound tendencies are discharged; they would go mad if they were not criminals, and they do not go mad because they are criminals."[16] These early research efforts shifted attention to brain functioning and personality as the key to criminal behaviour.

Figure 1.3   **Phrenology head**

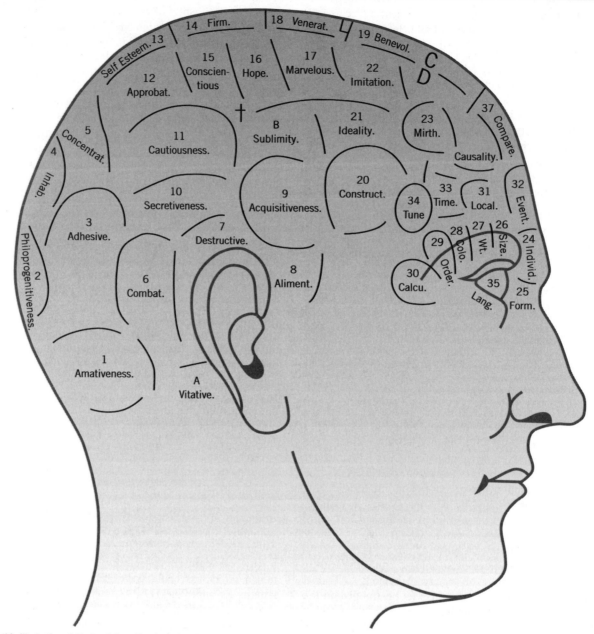

In this illustration of the head from the viewpoint of phrenology, we see the areas of the brain associated with various behaviours and emotions. Note in particular the "destructiveness centre" above the ear.

Cesare Lombroso and the Criminal Man

In Italy, Cesare Lombroso was studying the cadavers of executed criminals in an effort to scientifically determine whether law violators were physically different from people of conventional values and behaviour. Lombroso (1835–1909), known as the "father of criminology," was a physician who served much of his career in the Italian army. That experience gave him ample opportunity to study the physical characteristics of soldiers convicted and executed for criminal offences. Later, he studied inmates at institutes for the criminally insane at Pavia, Pesaro, and Reggio Emilia.

Lombrosian theory can be outlined in a few simple statements. First, Lombroso believed that serious offenders—those who engage in repeated assault- or theft-related activities—have inherited criminal traits. These "born criminals" have inherited physical problems that impel them into a life of crime. This view helped spur interest in a **criminal anthropology**.[17] Second, he held that born criminals suffer from **atavistic anomalies**—physically, they are throwbacks to more primitive times when people were savages. Thus, criminals supposedly have the enormous jaws and strong canine teeth common to carnivores and savages who devour raw flesh. In addition, Lombroso compared criminals' behaviour to that of the mentally ill and those suffering from certain forms of epilepsy. He concluded that criminogenic traits can be acquired through indirect heredity: from a "degenerate family with frequent cases of insanity, deafness, syphilis, epilepsy, and alcoholism among its members." Direct heredity—being related to a family of criminals—is the second primary cause of crime.

Lombroso's version of criminal anthropology was popularized in North America via articles and textbooks that adopted his ideas. He attracted a circle of followers who expanded on his vision of biological determinism. His work was very popular in Europe and in the United States. By the turn of the century, authors were already discussing "the science of penology" and "the science of criminology."

Connections

The theories of criminology that have their roots in Lombroso's biological determinism will be discussed in Chapter 6. Criminologists who today suggest that crime has a biological basis also believe that environmental conditions influence human behaviour. Hence, the term biosocial theory has been coined to reflect the assumed link between physical and mental traits, the social environment, and behaviour.

The Development of Sociological Criminology

At the same time that biological views were dominating criminology, another group of positivists were developing the field of sociology to scientifically study the major social changes that were then taking place in 19th-century society.

Sociology seemed an ideal perspective from which to study society. After thousands of years of stability, the world was undergoing a population explosion: The population, estimated at 600 million in 1700, had risen to 900 million by 1800. People were flocking to cities in ever-increasing numbers. Manchester, England, had 12 000 inhabitants in 1760 and 400 000 in 1850; during the same period, the population of Glasgow, Scotland, rose from 30 000 to 300 000. The development of such machinery as power looms had doomed cottage indus-

tries and given rise to a factory system in which large numbers of people toiled for extremely low wages. The spread of agricultural machines increased the food supply while reducing the need for a large rural workforce; the excess labourers further swelled the cities' populations. At the same time, political, religious, and social traditions continued to be challenged by the scientific method.

The foundations of sociological criminology can be traced to the works of L.A.J. (Adolphe) Quetelet (1796–1874) and Emile Durkheim (1858–1917).

L.A.J. Quetelet. Quetelet was a Belgian mathematician who began (along with André-Michel Guerry, from France) what is known as the cartographic school of criminology.[18] Quetelet, who made use of social statistics developed in France in the early 19th century (called the Comptes généraux de l'administration de la justice), was one of the first social scientists to use objective mathematical techniques to investigate the influence of social factors, such as season, climate, sex, and age, on the propensity to commit crime. Quetelet's most important finding was that social forces were significantly correlated with crime rates. Quetelet showed that the same lawlike mechanical regularity that could be observed in the heavens and in the world of nature also existed in the world of social facts.[19] Quetelet was a pioneer of sociologically oriented criminology. He identified many of the relationships between crime and social phenomena that still serve as a basis for criminology today.

Emile Durkheim. (David) Emile Durkheim (1858–1917) was one of the founders of sociology and a significant contributor to criminology.[20] His definition of crime as a normal and necessary social event has been more influential on modern criminology than any other.

According to Durkheim's vision of social positivism, crime is seen as normal because it has existed in every age, in both poverty and prosperity. Crime is an integral part of all healthy societies because it is virtually impossible to imagine a society in which criminal behaviour is totally absent. Such a society would almost demand that all people be and act exactly alike. The inevitability of crime is linked to the differences (heterogeneity) within society. Because people are so different from one another and use such a variety of methods and forms of behaviour to meet their needs, it is not surprising that some will resort to criminality. Even if "real" crimes were eliminated, human weaknesses and petty vices would be elevated to the status of crimes. As long as human differences exist, then, crime is inevitable and one of the fundamental conditions of social life. Fundamentally, it can serve as a symbolic reminder of the moral boundaries of society.

Crime, argued Durkheim, can also be useful and on occasion even healthy for a society to experience. The existence of crime implies that a way is open for social change and that the social structure is not rigid or inflexible. Put another way, if crime did not exist, it would mean that everyone behaves the same way and agrees totally on what is right and wrong. Such universal conformity would stifle creativity and independent thinking. Durkheim offered the example of the Greek philosopher Socrates, who, simply because he questioned the social order, was considered a criminal and sentenced to death for corrupting the morals of youth. When given the chance to flee to save his life, Socrates refused, saying that doing so would negate his ideal of standing up for what he believed. In addition, Durkheim argued that crime is beneficial because it calls attention to social ills. A rising crime rate can signal the need for social change and promote a variety of programs designed to relieve the human suffering that may have caused crime in the first place.

In *The Division of Labor in Society,* Durkheim described the consequences of the shift from a small, rural society, which he labelled "mechanical," to the more modern "organic" society with a large urban population, division of labour, and personal isolation. From this shift flowed **anomie,** or norm and role confusion, a powerful sociological concept that helps describe the chaos and disarray accompanying the loss of traditional values in modern society. Durkheim's research on suicide indicated that anomic societies maintain high suicide rates; by implication, anomie might cause other forms of deviance to develop.

The Chicago School and the McGill School

The primacy of sociological positivism was secured by research begun in the early 20th century by Robert Ezra Park (1864–1944), Ernest W. Burgess (1886–1966), Louis Wirth (1897–1952), and their colleagues in the Sociology Department at the University of Chicago. Known as the **Chicago School,** these sociologists pioneered research on the social ecology of the city and inspired a generation of scholars to conclude that social forces operating in urban areas create criminal interactions; some neighbourhoods become almost natural areas for crime.[21] These urban neighbourhoods maintain such a high level of poverty that critical social institutions, such as the school and the family, break down. The resulting social disorganization reduces the ability of social institutions to control behaviour, and the outcome is a high crime rate.

The Chicago School sociologists and their contemporaries focused on the functions of social institutions and how their breakdown influences behaviour. They pioneered the ecological study of crime—crime as a function of where one lives. Important works in the Chicago School tradition were *The Gang* (1927) by Frederic Thrasher, *The Ghetto* (1928) by Louis Wirth, *Gold Coast and Slum* (1929) by Harvey Zorbaugh, and *The Hobo* (1923) by Nels Anderson, a professor in the Sociology Department at the University of New Brunswick.

Less well known is the work of Carl Dawson and his colleagues at McGill University. Dawson, a native of Prince Edward Island and a graduate of Acadia University, studied at the University of Chicago before he went to Montreal to head up McGill's Social Work and Sociology Departments. He and his students studied the process of industrial development, transportation, poverty, ethnicity and immigration, housing, juvenile delinquency, welfare, and physiographic barriers to mobility. This work constituted a significant contribution to early sociology and criminology in Canada.[22]

Connections

The ecological approach of the Chicago School was very influential and was applied to the study of crime in various cities, such as Chicago, New York, and Montreal. In particular it became known for the concentric zone model of deviance, in which crime is found to be higher in the more socially disorganized areas of a city. For a more in-depth discussion of the work of Carl Dawson and the application of this approach to Montreal, see Chapter 7.

During the 1930s, another group of sociologists, influenced by psychology, began to add a social-psychological component to criminological theory. They concluded that the individual's relationship to important social processes, such as education, family life, and peer relations, is the key to understanding human behaviour. In any social milieu, children who grow up in a home wracked by conflict, attend an inadequate school, and associate with deviant peers become exposed to pro-crime forces. One position was that people learn criminal attitudes from older, more experienced law violators; another view was that crime occurs when families fail to control adolescent misbehaviour. Each of these views linked criminality to the failure of socialization.

By mid-century, most criminologists had embraced either the ecological or the socialization view of crime. However, these were not the only views of how social institutions influence human behaviour. In Europe, the writings of another social thinker, Karl Marx (1818–1883), had pushed the understanding of social interaction in another direction and sowed the seeds for a new approach in criminology.[23]

Conflict Criminology

Oppressive labour conditions prevalent during the rise of industrial capitalism convinced Marx that the character of every civilization is determined by its mode of production—the way its people develop and produce material goods. The most important relationship in industrial culture is between the owners of the means of production—the capitalist **bourgeoisie**—and the people who do the actual labour—the **proletariat.** The economic system determines all facets of human life; consequently, people's lives revolve around the means of production. The exploitation of the working class, Marx believed, would eventually lead to class conflict and the end of the capitalist system.

While Marx did not develop a theory of crime and justice, his writings were applied to legal studies by other social thinkers, including Ralf Dahrendorf, George Vold, and Willem Bonger.[24] Though these writings laid the foundation for a Marxist criminology, decades passed before Marxist theory had an important impact on criminology. The Vietnam War, the development of an anti-establishment counterculture movement in the 1960s, the civil rights movement, and the women's movement were all important events challenging the model of social consensus underlying the functionalism of the Chicago School. Young sociologists who became interested in applying Marxist principles to the study of crime began to analyze the social conditions that were felt to promote class conflict and crime. What emerged from this intellectual ferment was a conflict-oriented radical criminology of the 1970s that indicted the economic system for producing the conditions that support a high crime rate. The radical tradition has played a significant role in criminology ever since.

Criminology Today

The various schools of criminology developed over a 200-year period. Although they have undergone great change and innovation, each continues to have an impact on the field. For example, classical theory has evolved into rational choice and deterrence theories. Choice theorists today argue that criminals are rational and use available information to decide whether crime is a worthwhile undertaking; deterrence theory holds that this choice is structured by the fear of punishment.

Criminal anthropology has also evolved considerably. While criminologists no longer believe that a single trait or inherited characteristic can explain crime, some are convinced that biological and mental traits interact with environmental factors to influence all human behaviour, including criminality. Biological and psychological theorists study the association between criminal behaviour and such traits as diet, hormonal makeup, personality, and intelligence.

Sociological theories, tracing back to Quetelet and Durkheim, maintain that individuals' lifestyles and living conditions directly control their criminal behaviour. Those at the bottom of the social structure cannot achieve success and thus experience anomie, strain, failure, and frustration. This is referred to today as the structural perspective.

Some sociologists who have added a social-psychological dimension to their views of crime causation find that individuals' learning experiences and socialization directly control their behaviour. In some cases, children learn to commit crime by interacting with and modelling their behaviour after others they admire, while other criminal offenders are people whose life experiences have shattered their social bonds to society. This is called the social process perspective.

The writings of Marx and his followers continue to be influential. Today conflict criminologists still see social and political conflict as the root cause of crime. In their view, the inherently unfair economic structure of advanced capitalist countries is the engine that drives the high crime rate.

Criminology, then, has had a rich history that still exerts an important influence on the thinking of its current practitioners. These major perspectives are summarized in Figure 1.4.

Figure 1.4 The major perspectives of criminology. The focus is on *individual* (biological, psychological, and choice theories), *social* (structural and process theories), *political* and *economic* (conflict), and *multiple* (integrated) factors.

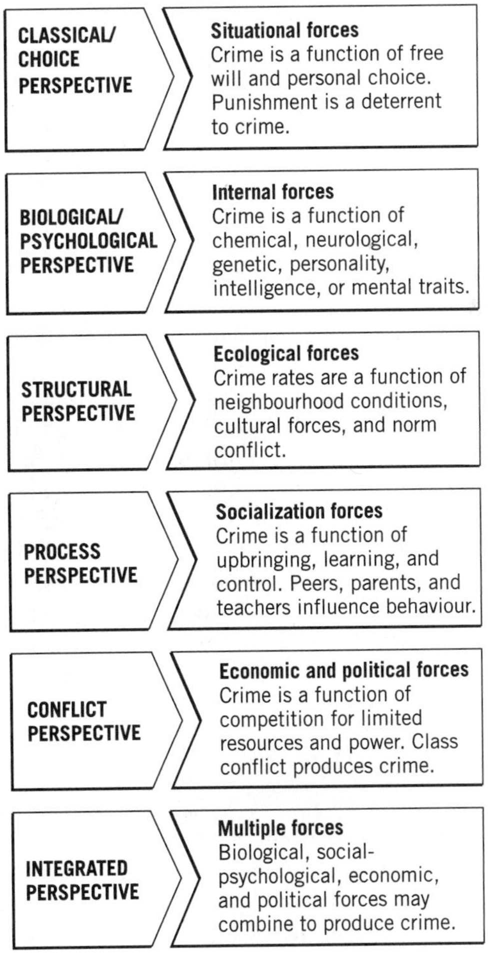

CLASSICAL/ CHOICE PERSPECTIVE
Situational forces
Crime is a function of free will and personal choice. Punishment is a deterrent to crime.

BIOLOGICAL/ PSYCHOLOGICAL PERSPECTIVE
Internal forces
Crime is a function of chemical, neurological, genetic, personality, intelligence, or mental traits.

STRUCTURAL PERSPECTIVE
Ecological forces
Crime rates are a function of neighbourhood conditions, cultural forces, and norm conflict.

PROCESS PERSPECTIVE
Socialization forces
Crime is a function of upbringing, learning, and control. Peers, parents, and teachers influence behaviour.

CONFLICT PERSPECTIVE
Economic and political forces
Crime is a function of competition for limited resources and power. Class conflict produces crime.

INTEGRATED PERSPECTIVE
Multiple forces
Biological, social-psychological, economic, and political forces may combine to produce crime.

What Criminologists Do: The Criminological Enterprise

Regardless of their background or training, criminologists are primarily interested in studying crime and criminal behaviour. As Marvin Wolfgang and Franco Ferracuti put it:

> A criminologist is one whose professional training, occupational role, and pecuniary reward are primarily concentrated on a scientific approach to, and study and analysis of, the phenomenon of crime and criminal behaviour.[25]

Within the broader arena of criminology are several subareas that, taken together, make up the **criminological enterprise**. Criminologists may specialize in a subarea in the same way that psychologists might specialize in a subfield, such as child development, perception, personality, psychopathology, or sexuality. Some of the more important criminological subareas are described in this section and are summarized in Figure 1.5.

Criminal Statistics

The subarea of criminal statistics involves measuring the amount and trends of criminal activity. How much crime occurs annually? Who commits it? When and where does it occur? Which crimes are the most serious? Criminologists interested in criminal statistics try to create valid and reliable measurements of criminal behaviour. For example, they create techniques to access the records of police and court agencies. They develop paper-and-pencil survey instruments and then use them with large samples of citizens to determine the percentage of people who actually commit crime and the number of law violators who escape detection by the justice system. They also develop techniques to identify the victims of crime to establish more accurate indicators of the "true" number of criminal acts—how many people are victims of crime and what percentage report crime to police. The study of criminal statistics is one of the most crucial aspects of the criminological enterprise because without valid and reliable data sources, efforts to conduct research on crime and create criminological theories would be futile.

Sociology of Law

The sociology of law is a subarea of criminology concerned with the role that social forces play in shaping criminal law and, conversely, the role of criminal law in shaping society. Criminologists study the history of legal thought in an effort to understand how criminal acts, such as theft, rape, and murder,

Figure 1.5 The criminological enterprise. These subareas constitute the field or discipline of criminology.

SUBAREA	PRIMARY FOCUS
CRIMINAL STATISTICS	**Gathering valid crime data** Devising new research methods Measuring crime patterns and trends
SOCIOLOGY OF LAW	**Determining the origin of law** Measuring the forces that can change laws and society
THEORY CONSTRUCTION	**Predicting individual behaviour** Understanding the cause of crime rates and trends
CRIMINAL BEHAVIOUR SYSTEMS	**Determining the nature and cause of specific crime patterns** Studying violence, theft, and organized, white-collar and public order crimes
PENOLOGY	**Studying the correction and control of criminal behaviour**
VICTIMOLOGY	**Studying the nature and cause of victimization** Aiding crime victims

evolved into their present form. Criminologists may also be asked to join in the debate when a new law is proposed to banish or control behaviour. For example, a debate has been raging over the legality of Napster, an on-line service, letting its estimated 64 million members worldwide share music in apparent violation of copyright law. What role should the law take in curbing the public's access to media and culture? Should society curb actions that some people consider illegal but by which no one is actually harmed? And how is harm defined: Is a child who reads a pornographic magazine "harmed"; is a company denied profits "harmed"; is the behaviour Napster allows any different than videotaping a documentary from the television, or taping a song from the radio or from a cassette owned by a friend?

Criminologists also partake in updating the content of the criminal law. The law must be flexible to respond to changing times and conditions. Computer fraud, airplane hijacking, theft from automatic teller machines, and illegally tapping into TV cable lines are acts that obviously did not exist when the criminal law was originally formed. Sometimes, the law must respond to new versions of traditional or common acts. For example, Sue

Rodriguez, who suffered from ALS (amytrophic lateral sclerosis), committed suicide in February 1994 after losing her bid for legally assisted suicide before the Supreme Court in December of 1992.[26] In the United States, Dr. Jack Kevorkian has made international headlines for helping people kill themselves by using his "suicide machine." How should the law respond to these controversial issues?

While there are some who believe that the actions of Rodriguez or Kevorkian are criminal, immoral, and socially harmful, many others are not quite so certain. Many Canadians felt great sympathy for Sue Rodriguez's plight, and before Kevorkian brought international media coverage to the issue there was no law banning second-party help in suicides. In response, Michigan passed legislation making it a felony to help anyone commit suicide.[27] Is assisted suicide the product of a care and concern for human suffering, or a callous criminal act? Should a law be passed that a majority of the general public disapproves of—a condition that makes the law virtually unenforceable? Conversely, should the criminal law be restricted to only those acts that are unpopular with the general public?

Theory Construction

A question that has intrigued criminologists from the first is why do people engage in criminal acts? Why, when they know their actions can bring harsh punishment and social disapproval, do they steal, rape, and murder? In short, why do people behave the way they do? Does crime have a social or an individual basis? Is it a psychological, biological, social, political, or economic phenomenon? Since criminologists bring their personal beliefs and backgrounds to bear when they study criminal behaviour, there are diverse theories of crime causation. Some criminologists have a psychological orientation and view crime as a function of personality, development, social learning, or cognition. Others investigate the biological correlates of antisocial behaviour and study the biochemical, genetic, and neurological linkages to crime. Sociologists look at the social forces producing criminal behaviour, including neighbourhood conditions, poverty, socialization, and group interaction.

Understanding the true cause of crime remains a difficult problem. Criminologists are still unsure why, given similar conditions, one person elects criminal solutions to his or her problems while another conforms to accepted social rules of behaviour. Further, understanding crime rates and trends has proved difficult: Why do rates rise and fall? Why are crime rates higher in some areas or regions than in others? Why do some groups seem more crime-prone than others? Is it possible that crime is relative to societal standards and thus a social construction created by the media, politicians, and social alarmists?

Criminal Behaviour Systems

The criminal behaviour systems subarea of criminology involves research on specific criminal types and patterns: violent crime, theft crime, public order crime, and organized crime. Numerous attempts have been made to describe and understand particular crime types. For example, Marvin Wolfgang's famous study, *Patterns in Criminal Homicide,* is considered a landmark analysis of the nature of homicide and the relationship between victim and offender.[28] Edwin Sutherland's analysis of business-related offences helped coin a new phrase—**white-collar crime**—to describe economic crime activities.[29]

The study of criminal behaviour also involves research on the links between different types of crime and criminals. This is known as crime typology. Unfortunately, typologies often disagree, so no standard exists within the field. Some typologies focus on the criminal, suggesting the existence of offender groups, such as professional criminals, psychotic criminals, occasional criminals, and so on. Others focus on the crimes, clustering them into such categories as property crimes, sex crimes, and so on.

Penology

The study of penology involves the correction and control of known criminal offenders. Penologists formulate strategies for crime control and then help implement these policies in "the real world." While the field of criminal justice overlaps this area, criminologists have continued their efforts to develop new crime-control programs and policies. Some criminologists view penology as involving rehabilitation and treatment. Their efforts are directed at providing behaviour alternatives for would-be criminals and treatment for individuals convicted of law violations. This view portrays the criminal as someone society has failed; someone under social, psychological, or economic stress; someone who can be helped if society is willing to pay the price. Others argue that crime can be prevented only through a strict policy of social control. They advocate such strict penological measures as capital punishment and mandatory prison sentences. Future penological research efforts seem warranted, since some criminal offenders continue to commit crimes after their release from prison (recidivate).

Connections

In recent years, criminologists have devoted ever-increasing attention to the victim's role in the criminal process. It has been suggested that individuals' lifestyles and behaviour may actually increase the risk that they will become crime victims. Some have suggested that living in a high-crime neighbourhood increases risk, while others point to the problems caused by associating with dangerous peers and companions. For a discussion of victimization risk, see Chapter 4.

Culture, Gender, Ethnicity, and Criminology

The Changing Face of International Crime Rates

People in many countries are justifiably concerned about crime, and most people view it as a major social problem. Let's briefly look at some of the recent patterns, in order to isolate some cultural differences.

North America

In 1988, a *Juristat* survey indicated that one-quarter of all Canadians felt unsafe walking at night in their own neighborhood. By 1993 this percentage had increased slightly, but by 1999 88 percent of people surveyed felt reasonably safe.

While women and men expressed similar levels of overall satisfaction with their safety, women were more fearful than men in specific situations:

- 64 percent women (29 percent men) felt worried while using public transportation alone after dark
- 29 percent women (12 percent men) reported being worried if they were home alone in the evening
- 18 percent women (6 percent of men) felt unsafe when walking alone in their area after dark

Fears about crime need not be related to the actual rate of victimization. For example, Canada has a relatively lower crime rate than other industrialized countries and it is becoming safer: For example, the homicide rate decreased 9 percent between 1995 and 1999; violent crimes decreased almost 2 percent, and property offences decreased 16 percent in the same period.

The crime rate has declined in recent years but the United States has led the world with its murder, rape, and robbery rates. For example, police statistics show that the murder rate was six times higher and the rape rate was about three times higher in the United States than in England and Wales. The United States also imprisons far more people than other countries. The percentage of the population sent to prison and jail in the United States exceeds that of such notoriously punitive countries as Singapore, Romania, and South Africa. There are a number of explanations for the high U.S. crime rate:

urban areas in which the poorest and wealthiest citizens reside in close proximity;

racism and discrimination;

failure of an underfunded educational system;

the troubled American family;

easy access to handguns;

and a culture that defines success in terms of material wealth.

Each of these factors may explain the disproportionate amount of violent crime in the United States.

Europe

In many nations there is a disturbing upswing in crime. For example, murder rates have sharply increased in England, Germany, and Sweden. Racial assaults and hate crimes have increased dramatically in Germany and England. The most recent data available indicate that robbery, assault, burglary, and motor vehicle theft rates are actually lower in the United States than they are in England and Wales: Robbery rates rose more than 81 percent in England and Wales between 1981 and 1995, but they fell 28 percent in the United States. Similarly, assault increased 53 percent in England and Wales but declined 27 percent in the United States; burglary doubled in England and Wales but fell by half in the United States.

The rate for the Netherlands was 32 percent, for France it was 25 percent, and for Switzerland it was 27 percent. England and Wales has a higher rate of repeat violent offences than the United States, and theft of personal property is almost twice as high in the Netherlands as in America.

In 2000, the official crime rate in England and Wales showed an average increase of 19 percent; and an increase of 38 percent for muggings in London. It was felt that a third of all property crime is committed to finance drug abuse. Responding to the crime problem, former Prime Minister Thatcher said in an address, "[The] permissive society is in fact no society at all. It is little more than a state of nature where the line between right and wrong is first blurred and then obliterated—a place where no one dares to say no. There can be no order without authority, and authority that is impotent or hesitant in the face of intimidation, crime and violence, cannot endure."

Some feel that the rising crime rate in England is due to less punitiveness, while the falling crime rate in the United States is due to an increase in punishment. However, it is difficult to know what is causing changes in the crime rate. In England in 1998 it was reported that changes in record keeping, including an end to the practice of counting a string of offences as one crime could create a 20 percent increase in the official rate. And in 2000 it was reported that police tend to downgrade crime by at least 20 percent, artificially decreasing the official rate. On the other hand, with 3000 fewer police on the beat, the early release of criminals from prison, and the decreased use of police stop and search techniques, would mean an increase in crime.

Eastern Europe and Asia

England is not alone in experiencing higher crime rates. Russia and the former Soviet republics have experienced an increase in large-scale organized crime gangs, who commonly use violence and intimidation. In 1998 it was reported that economic crimes increased 20 percent over the previous year, drug trafficking increased 16 percent, arms trafficking 29 percent, and banditry 52 percent. In other European nations, violence has been fuelled by a dramatic growth in the number of illegal guns smuggled into these countries from the former Soviet republics. Additionally, unrestricted immigration has brought newcomers who face cultural differences, lack of job prospects, and racism. Social and economic pressures, including unemployment and cutbacks in the social welfare system, have also contributed to increased violence. In the formerly communist countries in Eastern Europe, especially, weak law enforcement institutions, rapid changes in economic laws, deteriorating economic conditions, incomplete reforms, and destabilized social norms have contributed to rising criminality.

Increased criminal activity in Asia is also reported. For example, Japan, a nation that prides itself on low crime rates, has experienced an upsurge in juvenile crime. It is estimated that 45 percent of all crimes are committed by people under 20, about double the percentage in the United States. With so much Japanese crime committed by youths, and with the juvenile crime rate escalating, experts predict an overall increase in future crime rates.

However, Tokyo, the world's safest major city, suffers muggings at the rate of 40 per year per one million inhabitants, compared to New York City's rate of 11 000. Why is the Japanese crime rate so much lower than that of the United States, and of most developed nations? Japan's homicide rate is two to three times lower than the U.S. rate, and handgun murders in the United States are 200 times higher than Japan's. Robbery in Japan is about as rare as murder: 1.8 per 100 000 inhabitants, compared to America's rate of 205.4. The U.S. larceny rate is 4 times greater than Japan's, the rape rate is nearly 25 times greater, and the robbery rate is 140 times greater. Japan is still considered one of the safest countries in the world, but its crime rate is rising every year. Authorities say that organized crime and juvenile crime are the two biggest contributors to the increase. Criminologists report that violent crime is the highest in 23 years; in 1999 alone, incidents of rape, murder, arson, and assault showed an 11 percent per capita increase.

Juvenile delinquency is also increasing in Singapore; in fact, it more than doubled during the first half of the 1990s. Singapore and Japan are not the only Asian nations experiencing an upsurge in crime. Vietnamese authorities report a troubling increase in street crimes like burglary and theft. Many crimes are drug-related: Vietnam has an estimated 200 000 opium addicts, and almost 50 000 acres of land are now growing the poppies from which heroin is produced.

Although it is difficult to obtain accurate crime data from China, the world's largest nation seems to be cracking down on crime. In recent years Chinese courts annually sentenced more than 100 000 street criminals. Death sentences were doled out to 1000 criminals, and many thousands more were sentenced to life in prison. The current wave of punishment is a response to a significant increase in street crimes, including robberies and drug trafficking.

Violence rates are also increasing in other parts of the Americas. The homicide rate in Jamaica is 32 per 100 000; in Colombia homicide rates are close to 70 per 100 000, about 10 times the U.S. average! As in Asia and Europe, high regional murder rates are tied to the flourishing drug trade.

It is difficult to obtain international comparisons of crime rates, but they add immeasurably to our understanding of trends.

Source: Statistics Canada

Victimology

Two classics of criminology, one by Hans von Hentig and another by Stephen Schafer, first identified the critical role of the victim in the criminal process. These authors suggested that victim behaviour is often a key determinant of crime, that a victim's actions may precipitate or provide an opportunity for crime, and that the study of crime is not complete unless the victim's role is considered.[30]

The areas of particular interest in victimology include using victim surveys to measure the nature and extent of criminal behaviour, calculating the actual costs of crime to victims, creating probabilities of victimization risk, studying victim culpability or precipitation of crime, and designing services for the victims of crime. Victimology has taken on greater importance as more criminologists focus their attention on the victim's role in the criminal event.

How Do Criminologists View Crime?

Professional criminologists usually align themselves with one of several schools of thought or perspectives in their field. Each perspective maintains its own view of what constitutes criminal behaviour and what causes people to engage in criminality. This diversity of thought is not unique to criminology: Biologists, psychologists, sociologists, historians, economists, and natural scientists disagree among themselves about critical issues in their fields. It is not surprising that conflicting views exist within criminology, considering the multidisciplinary nature of the field. In fact, it is common for criminologists to disagree on the nature and definition of crime itself. A criminologist's choice of orientation or perspective depends in part on his or her definition of crime—the beliefs and research orientations of most criminologists are related to their conceptualization of crime. This section discusses the three most common concepts of crime used by criminologists.

The Consensus View of Crime

According to the consensus view, crimes are behaviours believed to be repugnant to all elements of society. The substantive criminal law, which sets out the definition of crimes and their punishments, reflects the values, beliefs, and opinions of society's mainstream. The term consensus is used because it implies that there is general agreement among a majority of citizens on what behaviours should be outlawed by the criminal law and henceforth viewed as crimes.

Several attempts have been made to create a concise, yet thorough and encompassing, consensus definition of crime. The eminent criminologists Edwin Sutherland and Donald Cressey have taken the popular stance of linking crime with the criminal law:

> Criminal behaviour is behaviour in violation of the criminal law.... [It] is not a crime unless it is prohibited by the criminal law [which] is defined conventionally as a body of specific rules regarding human conduct which have been promulgated by political authority, which apply uniformly to all members of the classes to which the rules refer, and which are enforced by punishment administered by the state.[31]

This approach to crime implies that its definition is a function of the beliefs, morality, and direction of the existing legal power structure. Note also their statement that the criminal law is applied "uniformly to all members of the classes to which the rules refer." This statement reveals the authors' faith in the concept of an ideal legal system that can deal adequately with all classes and types of people. While laws banning burglary and robbery are directed at controlling the neediest members of society, laws banning insider trading, embezzlement, and corporate price fixing are aimed at controlling the wealthiest. The reach of the criminal law should not be restricted to any single element of society.

The consensus model of crime is probably accepted by a majority of criminologists. Nonetheless, a number of its premises have been disputed, especially the idea that the law is applied uniformly. Let us now examine that issue in more depth.

The Conflict View of Crime

In opposition to the consensus view, the conflict view depicts society as a collection of diverse groups—owners, workers, professionals, students—who are in constant and continuing conflict. Groups able to assert their political power use the law and the criminal justice system to advance their economic and social position. Criminal laws, therefore, are viewed as acts created to protect the haves from the have-nots. Conflict criminologists often compare and contrast the harsh penalties exacted on the poor for their "street crimes" (burglary, robbery, and larceny) with the minor penalties the wealthy receive for their white-collar crimes (securities violations and other illegal business practices). While the poor go to prison for minor law violations, the wealthy are given lenient sentences for even the most serious breaches of law.

According to the conflict view, the definition of crime is controlled by wealth, power, and position and not by moral consensus or the fear of social disruption.[32] Crime, according to this definition, is a political concept designed to protect the power and position of the upper classes at the expense of the poor. Even laws prohibiting violent acts, such as rape and murder, may have political undertones: Banning violent acts ensures domestic tranquillity and guarantees that the anger of the poor and disenfranchised classes will not be directed at their wealthy capitalist exploiters. The conflict view of crime would include in a list of "real" crimes such things as violations of human rights owing to racism, sexism, and imperialism; unsafe working conditions, inadequate child care, inadequate opportunities for employment and education, and substandard housing and medical care; crimes of economic and political domination; pollution of the environment; price fixing; police brutality; and assassinations and war making.[33]

The Interactionist View of Crime

The interactionist view of crime traces its antecedents to the symbolic interaction school of sociology, first popularized by George Herbert Mead, Charles Horton Cooley, and W.I. Thomas.[34] This position holds that (1) people act according to their own interpretations of reality, according to the meaning things have for them;

(2) they learn the meaning of a thing from the way others react to it, either positively or negatively; and (3) they reevaluate and interpret their own behaviour according to the meaning and symbols they have learned from others.

According to this perspective, the definition of crime reflects the preferences and opinions of people who hold social power in a particular legal jurisdiction and who use their influence to impose their definition of right and wrong on the rest of the population. Criminals are individuals whom society chooses to label as outcasts or deviants because they have violated social rules. In a classic statement, sociologist Howard Becker argued: "The deviant is one to whom that label has successfully been applied; deviant behaviour is behaviour people so label."[35] Crimes are outlawed behaviours because society defines them that way and not because they are inherently evil or immoral acts.

Connections

Interactionists believe that society should intervene as little as possible in the lives of law violators lest they be labelled and stigmatized. Labelling theory, discussed in Chapter 8, is based on interactionist views and holds that the application of negative labels leads first to a damaged identity and then to a criminal career.

The interactionist view of crime is similar to the conflict perspective because they both suggest that behaviour is outlawed when it offends people who maintain the social, economic, and political power necessary to have the law conform to their interests or needs. However, unlike the conflict view, the interactionist perspective does not attribute capitalist economic and political motives to the process of defining crime. Instead, interactionists see the criminal law as conforming to the beliefs of "moral crusaders" or **moral entrepreneurs** who use their influence to shape the legal process in the way they see fit. Laws against pornography, prostitution, and drugs are believed to be motivated more by moral crusades than by capitalist sensibilities. Consequently, interactionists are concerned with shifting moral and legal standards. To the interactionist, crime has no meaning unless people react to it, labelling perpetrators as deviant and setting them on a course of sustained criminal activity. The one-time criminal, if not caught or labelled, can simply return to a "normal" way of life with little permanent damage—college students who try marijuana do not view themselves, nor do others view them, as criminals or drug addicts. Only when prohibited acts are recognized and sanctioned do they become important, life-transforming events.

Defining Crime

The consensus view of crime dominated criminological thought until the late 1960s. Criminologists devoted themselves to learning why lawbreakers violated the rules of society. The criminal was viewed as an outlaw who, for one reason or another, flouted the rules defining acceptable conduct and behaviour. In the 1960s, the interactionist perspective gained prominence. The rapid changes society was experiencing made traditional law and values questionable. Many criminologists were swept along in the social revolution of the 1960s and likewise embraced an ideology that suggested that crimes reflected rules imposed by a conservative majority on nonconforming members of society. During the 1970s, more radical scholars gravitated toward conflict explanations (see Figure 1.6).

Figure 1.6 | **The definition of crime affects how criminologists view the cause and control of illegal behaviour and shapes their research orientation**

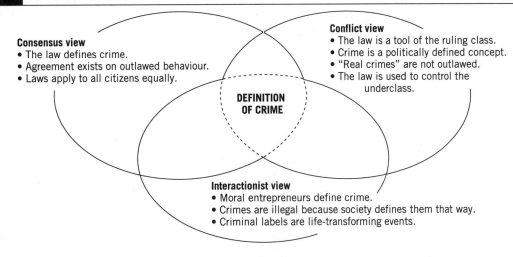

Consensus view
- The law defines crime.
- Agreement exists on outlawed behaviour.
- Laws apply to all citizens equally.

Conflict view
- The law is a tool of the ruling class.
- Crime is a politically defined concept.
- "Real crimes" are not outlawed.
- The law is used to control the underclass.

DEFINITION OF CRIME

Interactionist view
- Moral entrepreneurs define crime.
- Crimes are illegal because society defines them that way.
- Criminal labels are life-transforming events.

Today, each position still has many followers. This is important because criminologists' personal definitions of crime dominate their thinking, research, and attitudes toward their profession. Because they view crime differently, criminologists have taken a variety of approaches in explaining its causes and suggesting methods for its control. Considering these differences, it is possible to take elements from each school of thought to formulate an integrated definition of crime:

> Crime is a violation of societal rules of behaviour as interpreted and expressed by a criminal legal code created by people holding social and political power. Individuals who violate these rules are subject to sanctions by state authority, social stigma, and loss of status.

This definition combines the consensus view's position that the criminal law defines crimes with the conflict perspective's emphasis on political power and control and the interactionist view's concepts of stigma. Thus, crime as defined here is a political, social, and economic function of modern life.

Doing Criminology

Criminologists have used a wide variety of research techniques to measure the nature and extent of criminal behaviour. To understand and evaluate theories and patterns of criminal behaviour, it is important to develop some knowledge of how these data are collected. It is also important to understand the methods used in criminology, as this understanding provides insight into how professional criminologists approach various problems and questions in their field.

Survey Research

A great deal of crime measurement is based on analysis of survey data. Surveys include interviewing or questioning a group of subjects about the research topics under consideration. This method is also referred to as **cross-sectional research**, since it involves the simultaneous measurement of subjects in a sample who come from different backgrounds and groups (that is, a cross-section of the community). Most surveys involve sampling– selecting for study a limited number of subjects who are representative of entire groups sharing similar characteristics, called populations. For example, a criminologist might interview a sample of 500 people drawn from the population of 150 000 offenders that were under the supervision of correctional agencies in 1993 in Canada; in this case, the sample is meant to represent the entire population of inmates. Or a sample of burglary incidents could be taken from Toronto; here, the sample would hopefully represent all burglaries occurring

in Toronto. It is assumed that the characteristics of people or events in a carefully selected sample will be quite similar to those of the population at large.

Survey research can be designed to measure the attitudes, beliefs, values, personality traits, and behaviour of participants. Self-report surveys ask participants to describe in detail their recent and lifetime criminal activity; victimization surveys seek information from people who have been victims of crime; attitude surveys may measure the attitudes, beliefs, and values of various groups, such as prostitutes, students, drug addicts, police officers, judges, or juvenile delinquents.

The cross-sectional survey is one of the most widely used methods of criminological study. It is an excellent and cost-effective technique for measuring the characteristics of large numbers of people. Because questions and methods are standardized for all subjects, the distorting effect of the perceptions or biases of the person gathering the data is minimized. The statistical analysis of data from carefully drawn samples enables researchers to generalize their findings from small groups to large populations. Though surveys measure subjects at a single point in their life span, questions can elicit information on subjects' prior behaviour as well as their future goals and aspirations.[36]

Despite their utility, surveys are not without their problems. Since they typically involve a single measurement, they are of limited value in showing how subjects change over time. In addition, surveys have been criticized because they assume that subjects will be honest and forthright. Though efforts are usually made to ensure the validity of questionnaire items, it is difficult to guard against people who either deliberately lie and misrepresent information or are unsure of answers and give mistaken responses. Surveys of delinquents and criminals are especially suspect, as they rely on the willingness of a group of people not known for their candor about intimate and personal matters. Surveys are also limited when the area to be studied involves the way people interact with one another or other topics an individual may not be able to judge personally, such as how he or she is perceived by significant others. Despite these drawbacks, surveys continue to be an extremely popular method of gathering criminological data.

Longitudinal (Cohort) Research

Longitudinal (cohort) **research** involves the observation of a **cohort**—a group of people who share a like characteristic—over time. For example, researchers might select all girls born in Surrey, British Columbia, in 1970 and follow their behaviour patterns for 20 years. The research data might include their school experiences, arrests, hospitalizations, and information about their family life (divorces, parental relations). The subjects might be given repeated intelligence and physical exams; their diets could be monitored. Data could be collected directly from the subjects or without

Famous Canadian Criminals

Serial Homicide

$100,000 Reward

BRITISH COLUMBIA
Ministry of Attorney General

VANCOUVER POLICE DEPARTMENT

Missing Downtown Eastside Women

 File: 95-290934 SPENCE, Dorothy Born: 1962 Last Seen: 95-07-30 Reported Missing: 95-10-30

 File: 95-348364 MELNICK, Diana Born: 1975 Last Seen: 95-12-27 Reported Missing: 95-12-29

 File: 97-019529 HOLYK Tanya Born: 1975 Last Seen: 96-10-29 Reported Missing: 96-11-03

File: 97-158127 HENRY, Janet Born: 1961 Last Seen: 97-06-25 Reported Missing: 97-06-28

File: 96-022017 KOSKI, Kerri Born: 1959 Last Seen: 98-01-07 Reported Missing: 98-01-29

 File: 98-088486 DEVRIES, Sarah Born: 1969 Last Seen: 98-04-12 Reported Missing: 98-04-21

 File: 98-182514 EGAN, Sheila Born: 1978 Last Seen: 98-07-14 Reported Missing: 98-08-05

File: 95-303014 KNIGHT, Catherine Born: 1966 Last Seen: 95-04-?? Reported Missing: 95-11-11

File: 96-034215 GANZALEZ, Catherine Born: 1968 Last Seen: 95-03-?? Reported Missing: 96-02-07

 File: 97-061038 LANE, Stephanie Born: 1976 Last Seen: 97-01-10 Reported Missing: 97-03-11

File: 97-163182 WILLIAMS, Olivia Born: 1975 Last Seen: 96-12-06 Reported Missing: 97-07-04

File: 98-047919 HALL, Inga Born: 1952 Last Seen: 98-02-26 Reported Missing: 98-03-03

File: 98-095800 BECK, Cindy Louise Born: 1965 Last Seen: 97-09-?? Reported Missing: 98-04-30

 File: 98-209922 FREY, Marnie Born: 1973 Last Seen: 97-08-?? Reported Missing: 98-09-04

 File: 98-226384 HALLMARK, Helen Born: 1966 Last Seen: 97-06-15 Reported Missing: 98-09-23

 File: 98-286097 JARDINE, Angela Born: 1971 Last Seen: 98-11-10 Reported Missing: 98-12-06

 File: 99-008101 CREISON, Marcella Born: 1978 Last Seen: 98-12-27 Reported Missing: 99-01-11

 File: 92-172368 WATTLEY, Kathleen Born: 1959 Last Seen: 92-06-16 Reported Missing: 92-06-29

 File: 86-019762 ALLENBACH, Elaine Born: 1965 Last Seen: 86-03-13 Reported Missing: 86-04-11

File: 99-147110 YOUNG, Julie Born: 1967 Last Seen: 98-10-?? Reported Missing: 99-06-01

 File: 96-019193 PERKINS, Patricia Gay Born: 1956 Last Seen: **1978 Reported Missing: 96-01-22

 File: 90-301877 SOET, Ingrid Born: 1959 Last Seen: 89-08-26 Reported Missing: 90-10-01

File: 99-105703 BORHAVEN, Andrea Fay Born: 1972 Last Seen: 1997 Reported Missing: 99-05-18

 File: 98-261602 MURDOCK, Jacqueline Born: 1971 Last Seen: 97-08-14 Reported Missing: 98-10-30

File: 98-297035 GURNEY, Michelle Born: 1969 Last Seen: 98-12-11 Reported Missing: 98-12-22

 File: 99-039399 McDONELL, Jacquilene Born: 1976 Last Seen: 99-01-16 Reported Missing: 99-02-22

 File: 99-090895 COOMBES, Linda Jean Born: 1959 Last Seen: 93-11-?? Reported Missing: 1995

 File: 99-057168 WILLIAMS, Taressa Born: 1973 Last Seen: 98-07-01 Reported Missing: 99-03-17

 File: 99-089295 SMITH, Karen Born: 1964 Last Seen: 92-06-?? Reported Missing: 99-04-27

 File: 86-086028 RAIL, Sherry Lynn Born: 1956 Last Seen: 84-01-30 Reported Missing: 87-01-08

File: 91-281226 JANSEN, Rose Ann Born: 1949 Last Seen: 91-10-23 Reported Missing: 91-10-24

The Ministry of Attorney General and the Vancouver Police Board have authorized a reward of up to $100,000 for information leading to the arrest and conviction of the person or persons responsible for the unlawful confinement, kidnapping or murder of any or all of the listed women, missing from the streets of Vancouver. Upon the arrest and conviction of a person or persons responsible for the unlawful confinement, kidnapping or murder of any one or more of the women listed as missing in this reward poster, a reward will be decided by the Vancouver Police Board, in its sole discretion, and that decision is final, binding and not reviewable.

Only those people who come forward and volunteer information which is received by the Vancouver Police Department on or before May 1, 2001, will be eligible to receive a reward.

Any persons having information regarding the unlawful confinement, kidnapping or murder of any of the missing women listed in this poster are requested to communicate that information immediately to the Vancouver Police Department, Missing Persons Unit.

North America at:
1-800-993-8799 OR

In the Vancouver Area at:
(604) 717-3415 OR

Call your local police agency or You can remain anonymous and call:
669-TIPS

GREATER VANCOUVER CRIME STOPPERS

Additional details and larger photos are available on the Vancouver Police Department Web site at: **www.city.vancouver.bc.ca/police**

A poster released by the Vancouver Police implies a link between dozens of cases of missing women, many of whom are suspected to be prostitutes or drug addicts.

Canada's First Serial Killer?

Dr. Thomas Neill Cream, born in Glasgow and a graduate of McGill (1876), is estimated to have killed seven women in Great Britain and North America. Some think that he was Jack the Ripper, responsible for the murder of prostitutes. He worked occasionally as an abortionist, and at one point he was convicted of murder for adding strychnine to a patient's prescription.

Canada's Deadliest Serial Killer?

Michael Wayne McGray, 35, of Nova Scotia, pleaded guilty in 2000 to four counts of murder and implicated himself in 16 others. He testified that he found victims at random, driven by a "boiling urge" to kill. In 1991 he killed two gay men in Montreal, sparking fears of a serial murderer targeting homosexuals. As a child he was violently beaten by his father, and he himself became a bully, killing local dogs and cats. Sent to a reformatory, he was assaulted by guards; his criminal career eventually included sexual assault, break and enter, forgery, and dangerous driving. A psychiatrist diagnosed him as suffering from an extreme form of Tourette's syndrome.

A Deal with a Devil

Clifford Robert Olson had a criminal history that included breaking and entering, burglary, fraud, and theft. As a child he tormented neighbourhood dogs and cats. In 1981, his crimes became more serious, when he killed 11 children in British Columbia. Two weeks after the first murder he raped a teen prostitute, but when she went to the police they declined to press charges. In a widely criticized deal with the RCMP he was paid $100 000 in exchange for information about the murders and the location of six bodies police had been unable to find. In 1996 he applied under Section 745, the faint-hope clause, to have his 25-year parole ineligibility period reviewed.

The Terror of the Miramichi

Allan Legere, born in 1948, had a long history of crimes including peeping through windows, theft, and possession of stolen property. In 1989, he escaped from custody where he was being held for murder and went on a six-month crime spree. Between May and November 1989 he beat four people to death in New Brunswick. His was the first trial in Canada to use DNA evidence.

The Scarborough Rapist

Paul Bernardo, with the help of his wife Karla Homolka, was convicted in 1995 of killing teens Leslie Mahaffy and Kristen French. Both were held captive before being sexually assaulted and killed. Bernardo and Homolka were also implicated in the killing of Homolka's sister. Bernardo, who pleaded guilty to over 50 serial sexual assaults, was declared a dangerous offender, and pleaded guilty to over 50 serial sexual assaults. He had been interviewed by the police, who obtained a forensic sample, but it was months

before it was ever tested. His lawyer was subsequently charged with obstruction of justice for concealing a set of videotapes Bernardo made of his assaults.

Unknown

Vancouver police were looking for the killer or killers of over 50 sex trade workers missing from the streets. Going back as far as 1983,

they were missing from an area of the city known for drug dealing, addiction, homelessness, and violence. However, in early 2002, after an extensive investigation at a pig farm in Port Coquitlam, B.C., they charged a suspect with two murders, initially. More charges were later added.

their knowledge from schools, police, and other sources. If the research were carefully conducted, it might be possible to determine which life experiences, such as growing up in a broken home or failing at school, typically preceded the onset of crime and delinquency.

Since it is extremely difficult, expensive, and time-consuming to follow a cohort over time and since most of the sample do not become serious criminals, another approach is to take an intact cohort of known offenders and look back into their early life experiences by checking their educational, family, police, and hospital records; this format is known as a retrospective cohort study.[37]

To carry out cohort studies, criminologists frequently use records of social organizations, such as hospitals, schools, welfare departments, courts, police departments, and prisons. School records contain data on a student's academic performance, attendance, intelligence, disciplinary problems, and teacher ratings. Hospitals record incidents of drug use and suspicious wounds indicative of child abuse. Police files contain reports of criminal activity, arrest data, personal information on suspects, victim reports, and actions taken by police officers. Court records allow researchers to compare the personal characteristics of offenders with the outcomes of their court appearances—conviction rates and types of sentences. Prison records contain information on inmates' personal characteristics, adjustment problems, disciplinary records, rehabilitation efforts, and length of sentence served.

In one retrospective longitudinal survey, Cathy Spatz Widom wanted to study the effects of child abuse on a person's adult behaviour. Using court records, she compared a group of approximately 900 people who were reported to have been abused to a group of over 600 people with no reported abuse. Interviewing the subjects 15 years after their cases had been heard in court, she was able to determine that when all other possible factors were controlled, there was a connection between child abuse and juvenile delinquency. Being abused or neglected increased the likelihood of arrest as a juvenile by 53 percent, and as an adult by 38 percent.[38]

Connections

Some critical criminological research has been based on cohort studies. Some of the most important research has been conducted by University of Pennsylvania criminologist Marvin Wolfgang and his colleagues. Their findings have been instrumental in developing knowledge about the onset and development of a criminal career. Wolfgang's cohort research is discussed in Chapter 2.

Aggregate Data Research

In doing their research, criminologists also make use of large databases gathered by government agencies and research foundations, such as Statistics Canada data, employment data, reports from Correctional Services Canada, and so on. The most important of these sources are crime statistics compiled by Statistics Canada (the Canadian Centre for Justice Statistics) based on the Uniform Crime Reporting System. The UCR is an annual report that reflects the number of crimes reported by citizens to local police departments and the number of arrests made by police agencies in a given year. The UCR is probably the most important source of official crime statistics and will be discussed more completely in Chapter 3.

Aggregate data can be used to focus on the social forces that affect crime. They can tell us about the effect of overall social trends and patterns on the crime rate. For example, to study the relationship between crime and poverty, criminologists make use of data collected by Statistics Canada on income and the number of people on welfare and single-parent families in an urban area and then cross-reference this information with official crime statistics from the same locality. The implication that crime is correlated with poverty is not a simple one to explain, but preliminary data would establish whether a pattern exists. We would have to use a different technique, however, if we wanted to study corporate crime because crimes of the powerful are more carefully hidden.

Experimental Research

To conduct experimental research, criminologists manipulate or intervene in the lives of their subjects to see the outcome or effect the intervention has. True experiments usually have three elements: (1) random assignment of subjects; (2) a control or comparison group; and (3) an experimental condition. For example, experimental research might involve a sample of convicted offenders who have been sentenced to prison. Some of the sample, chosen at random, would be asked to participate in a community-based treatment program. A follow-up could then determine whether those placed in the community program were less likely to recidivate (repeat their offences) than those who served time in the correctional institution.

A quasi-experiment is undertaken when it is impossible to randomly assign subjects or manipulate conditions. For example, researchers may want to measure the effectiveness of a new law setting a lower blood alcohol threshold for impaired driving. Since this law will be federal, and thus uniform across Canada, the researchers will be more interested in how it is enforced by the police than in any interstate variation in the law as would be the case in the United States. Since they cannot ask police to randomly arrest drunk drivers, they can compare one province's enforcement patterns with those of nearby provinces that have more lenient impaired-driving enforcement programs. This type of offence is very sensitive to levels of police enforcement. While not a true experiment, this approach would give an indication of the effectiveness of law enforcement on drunk driving, since the provinces are comparable except for their enforcement programs. This has particular relevance when assessing whether a lower rate of impaired driving charges means that fewer people are driving drunk. Recent criticism targets enforcement programs as being weak or ineffective, making it seem that impaired driving is becoming less of a problem despite the fact that "drinking drivers account for only 1 percent of drivers on the road at night during the weekend, but they represent nearly half of all the fatal crashes at that time."[39]

Another approach, referred to as a time-series design, would be to record nationwide impaired driving arrest and fatality data for the months and years preceding and following passage of the legislation setting lower limits for impaired driving. The effectiveness of the new limits as a deterrent to impaired driving would be supported if a drop in the arrest and fatality rates coincided with the legislation's adoption.

Criminological experiments are relatively rare because they are difficult and expensive to conduct; they involve the manipulation of subjects' lives, which can cause ethical and legal roadblocks; and they require long follow-up periods to verify results. Nonetheless, they have been an important source of criminological data.

Observational and Interview Research

Sometimes criminologists focus their research on relatively few subjects, interviewing them in depth or observing them as they go about their activities. This research often obtains the kind of in-depth data absent in large-scale surveys. For example, a recent study by Claire Sterck-Elifson focused on the lives of middle-class female drug abusers. The 34 interviews she conducted provide insight into a group whose behaviour might not be captured in a large-scale survey. Sterck-Elifson found that these women were introduced to cocaine at first "just for fun": "I do drugs," one 34-year-old lawyer told her, "because I like the feeling. I would never let drugs take over my life."[40] Unfortunately, a number later lost control of their habit and suffered both emotional and financial stress.

In a recent study anonymously reviewed by one of the authors, a criminologist interviewed youths who lived on the street in Toronto. Using a technique called snowball sampling, he would interview one, then get that person to introduce him to more. As a result he was able to interview about 200 youths about their criminal activities; the information gathered was then related to the perceived inability of the subjects to succeed in legitimate jobs.

Another common criminological method is the first-hand observation of criminals to gain insight into their motives and activities. This may involve going into the field and participating in group activities, such as was done in William Whyte's famous study of a Boston gang, *Street Corner Society*.[41] Other observers conduct field studies but remain in the background, observing but not being part of the ongoing activity.[42]

Still another type of observation involves bringing subjects into a structured laboratory setting and observing how they react to a predetermined condition or stimulus. This approach is common in studies testing the effect of observational learning on aggressive behaviour, such as exposing subjects to violent films and observing their subsequent behavioural changes.[43] A set of studies have sought to determine a relationship between explicit sexually violent pornography and attitudes endorsing interpersonal violence against women. Many of these experimental studies have found that exposure to violent sexual material is related to a self-reported tendency to rape, the perception of rape victims as experiencing less trauma, and more callousness toward women in general. Because many of these studies were conducted in a laboratory setting, their generalizability may be limited.[44]

Criminology thus relies on many of the basic research methods common to other fields, including sociology, psychology, and political science. Multiple methods are needed to ensure that the goals of criminological inquiry can be achieved.

Ethical Issues in Criminology

A critical issue facing students of criminology is recognizing the field's political and social consequences. All too often, criminologists forget the social responsibility they bear as experts in the area of crime and justice. When acted on by government agencies, their pronouncements and opinions become the basis for sweeping social policy. The lives of millions of people can be influenced by criminological research data. We have witnessed many debates over gun control, capital punishment, and mandatory sentences. While some criminologists have successfully argued for social service, treatment, and rehabilitation programs to reduce the crime rate, others consider them a waste of time, suggesting instead that a massive prison construction program coupled with tough criminal sentences can bring the crime rate down. By presenting themselves as experts on law-violating behaviour, criminologists place themselves in a position of power; the potential consequences of their actions are enormous. Therefore, they must be aware of the ethics of their profession and be prepared to defend their work in the light of public scrutiny. Major ethical issues include what is to be studied, who is to be studied, and how studies are to be conducted.

Under ideal circumstances, when criminologists choose a subject for study, they are guided by their own scholarly interests, pressing social needs, the availability of accurate data, and other similar concerns. Nonetheless, in recent years some fear that a great influx of government and institutional funding has influenced the direction of criminological inquiry. In Canada the departments of Health and Welfare, Heritage Canada, and Justice, and the Office of the Solicitor General historically have been important sources of funding, while in the United States major sources of monetary support include the Justice Department's National Institute of Justice and the Office of Juvenile Justice and Delinquency Prevention. Private foundations also play an important role in supporting criminological research.

Though the availability of research money may

pay for or sponsor the research. One Canadian criminologist says there has been a major decline in academic justice policy research since 1987, with an increase in research hired out to consultants that is designed to satisfy the needs of civil servants and believes that "these developments augur poorly for informed public debate."[45]

A potential conflict of interest may arise when the institution funding research is itself one of the principal subjects of the research project. For example, governments may be reluctant to fund research on fraud and abuse of power by government officials. They may also exert a not-so-subtle influence on the criminologists seeking research funding: If criminologists are too critical of the government's efforts to reduce or counteract crime, perhaps they will be barred from receiving further financial help. This situation is even more acute when we consider that criminologists typically work for universities or public agencies and are under pressure to bring in a steady flow of research funds or to maintain the continued viability of their agency. Even when criminologists maintain discretion of choice, the direction of their efforts may not be truly objective.

A second major ethical issue in criminology concerns who is to be the subject of inquiries and study. Too often, criminologists have focused their attention on the poor and minorities while ignoring the middle-class criminal, white-collar crime, organized crime, and government crime. Critics have charged that by "unmasking" the poor and desperate, criminologists have justified any harsh measures taken against them. For example, a few social scientists have suggested that criminals have lower intelligence quotients than the average citizen and that because minority group members have lower-than-average IQ scores, their crime rates are high.[46] This was the conclusion reached in *The Bell Curve*, a popular though highly controversial book written by Richard Herrnstein and Charles Murray.[47] Such research is methodologically flawed and ideologically biased, but because it can selectively misrepresent data it can focus attention on the criminality of one group while ignoring others. For example, Alan Ryan says in *The Bell Curve Debate* that crime is mainly a male activity, and while a focus on IQ can explain male crime it cannot explain the difference in crime rates between women and men.[48] To the link between this type of the

they provide may later be used to prove the existence of significant racial differences in their self-reported crime rates. Should subjects be told what the true purpose of a survey is? Would such disclosures make meaningful research impossible? How far should criminologists go when collecting data? Is it ever permissible to deceive subjects to collect data?

Summary

Criminology is the scientific approach to the study of criminal behaviour and society's reaction to law violations and violators. It has a rich history in the utilitarian philosophy of Beccaria, the biological positivism of Lombroso, the social theory of Durkheim, and the political philosophy of Marx. It is an interdisciplinary field, with many of its practitioners originally trained as sociologists, psychologists, economists, political scientists, historians, and natural scientists. Included among the various subareas that make up the criminological enterprise are criminal statistics, the sociology of law, theory construction, criminal behaviour systems, penology, and victimology. Criminology and criminal justice are mutually dedicated to understanding the nature and control of criminal behaviour. The study of deviant behaviour also overlaps with criminology because many "deviant" acts, but not all, are violations of the criminal law.

In viewing crime, criminologists use one of three perspectives: the consensus view, the conflict view, or the interactionist view. The consensus view is that crime is illegal behaviour defined by the existing criminal law, which reflects the values and morals of a majority of citizens. The conflict view is that crime is behaviour created so that economically powerful individuals can retain their control over society. The interactionist view portrays criminal behaviour as a relativistic, constantly changing concept that reflects society's current moral values. According to the interactionist view, criminal behaviour is behaviour so labelled by those in power; criminals are people society chooses to label as outsiders or deviants.

Criminologists use a variety of research methods. These include cross-sectional surveys, longitudinal cohort studies, experiments, and observations. In doing research, criminologists must be concerned about ethical standards because their findings can have a significant impact on individuals and groups.

Thinking Like a Criminologist

John Douglas is a former FBI agent who has become an expert on a tool of detection called profiling. In his popular books *Mindhunter: Inside the FBI's Elite Serial Crime Unit* and *Sexual Homicide: Patterns and Motives*, he describes a "homicidal triad," a set of signs that predict the likelihood of a person's future violence; these signs include fire-setting, cruelty to animals, and bed-wetting.

Douglas applies behavioural patterns to crimes by looking at crime scene evidence, police reports, victim statements, and autopsy results. Being a successful profiler requires years of experience to be able to combine inductive reasoning applied to specific crime scene information with general trends observed from many similar crimes.

However, a problem in the investigation of serial homicide is the sharing of crime investigation information across jurisdictions, creating so-called linkage-blindness. Following several highly complex cases, such as the Clifford Olson case, it became apparent to the RCMP that a system to identify and track serial criminals was needed in Canada. Modelled on the FBI's system, the major crimes file was enhanced by a psychological profiler and in the 1990s became the Violent Crime Linkage Analysis System (ViCLAS), a truly national system. Input is based on details of victimology, modus operandi, forensics, and criminal behaviour. Data on homicides, sexual assaults, missing persons, unidentified bodies, and abductions are entered into the system. By 1997, approximately 20 000 cases were in the system and over 3000 links had been made between cases.

Key Terms

anomie
atavistic anomalies
bourgeoisie
Chicago school
classical criminology
cohort
criminal anthropology

criminal justice system
criminological enterprise
criminologists
criminology
cross-sectional research
decriminalization
deviant behaviour

intimate violence
longitudinal research
moral entrepreneurs
positivism
proletariat
utilitarianism
white-collar crime

See the book-specific website at www.siegelcriminology2e.nelson.com for additional chapter links, discussions, and quizzes.

Chapter

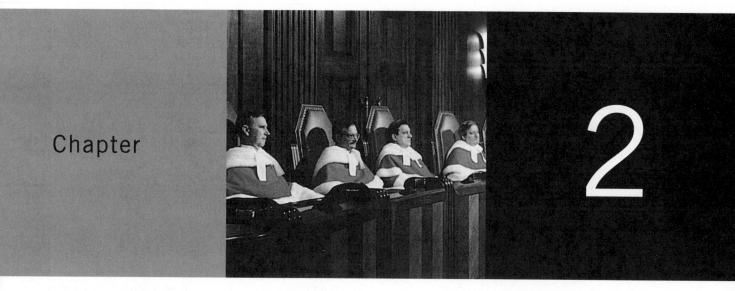

2

The Criminal Law and Its Process

The criminal law controls the definition and content of crime. Developed over many generations, it incorporates historical traditions, moral beliefs, and social values, as well as political and economic developments and conditions. The criminal law is a living concept, constantly evolving to keep pace with society. It governs the form and direction of almost all human interaction. Business practices, family life, education, property transfer, inheritance, the availability of certain drugs, and other common forms of social relations must conform to the rules set out by the legal code. Most important for our purposes, the law defines the behaviours that society labels as criminal. Consequently, it is important for students of criminology to have a basic understanding of the law and its relationship to crime and deviance. This chapter will review the nature and purpose of the law, chart its history, and discuss its elements.

The Origins of Law

We know that crimes and criminal behaviour were recognized in many early societies.[1] In preliterate societies, common custom and tradition (mores and folkways) were the equivalents of law. Each group had its own set of customs, which were created to deal with situations that arose in daily living. These customs would often be followed long after the reason for their origin was forgotten. Many customs had the force of law, and eventually some developed into formal or written law.

Early Legal Codes

The concept of crime was recognized in the earliest surviving legal codes. One of the first was developed in about 2000 B.C. by King Dungi of Sumer (an area that is part of present-day Iraq). Its content is known today because it was later adopted by Hammurabi (1792–1750 B.C.), the sixth king of Babylon, in his famous set of written laws today known as the **Code of Hammurabi**. Preserved on basalt rock columns, the code set out crimes and their correction. Punishment was based on physical retaliation, or **lex talionis** ("an eye for an eye"). The severity of punishment depended on class standing: For assault, slaves would be put to death; freemen might lose a limb.

Connections

Efforts are now being made to make punishments fit the crime. See Chapter 5 for more on the view that crime and punishment should be closely aligned.

Babylonian laws were strictly enforced by judges who were themselves controlled by advisers to the king. Such crimes as burglary and theft were common in ancient Babylon, and officials had to take their duties seriously. Local officials were expected to apprehend criminals. If they failed in their duties, they had to personally replace lost property; if murderers were not caught, the responsible official paid a fine to the deceased's relatives. It would seem inconceivable to hold police officers to such a standard today!

Another of the ancient legal codes still surviving is the **Mosaic Code** of the Israelites (1200 B.C.). According to tradition, God entered into a covenant or contract with the tribes of Israel in which they agreed to obey his law, as presented to them by Moses, in return for God's special care and protection. The Mosaic Code is not only the foundation of Judeo-Christian moral teachings, but it also is a basis for our present-day legal system: Prohibitions against murder, theft, perjury, and adultery precede by several thousand years the same laws found in our legal system.

Also surviving is the Roman law contained in the Twelve Tables (451 B.C.). The Twelve Tables were formulated by a special commission of ten men in response to pressure from the lower classes (plebeians). The plebeians believed that an unwritten code gave arbitrary and unlimited power to the wealthy classes (patricians) who served as magistrates. The original code was written on bronze plaques, which have been lost, but records of sections, which were memorized by every Roman male, survive. The remaining laws deal with debt, family relations, property, and other daily matters. Other notable ancient lawgivers through the centuries are Confucius (551–479 B.C., China), Mohammed (A.D. 570–632, Arabia), Solomon (873–933 B.C., Israel), and Lycurgus (9th century B.C., Greece); a list of important legal documents would certainly have to include the Koran (A.D. 652, Arabia).

The Dark Ages

The early formal legal codes were lost during the Dark Ages, which lasted for hundreds of years after the fall of Rome. During this period, superstition and fear of magic and satanic black arts dominated thinking.

Some attempts were made at regulating the definition and punishments of crime during the early feudal period. Those that still exist indicate that monetary payments were the main punishments for crimes. Some early German and Anglo-Saxon societies developed legal systems featuring compensation (**wergild**) for criminal violations. For example, under the legal code of the Salic Franks, killing a freedwoman of childbearing age was punished by wergild in the amount of 24 000 denars; if the woman was past childbearing age, the wergild was reduced to 8000 denars.

Guilt was determined by ordeals, such as having the accused place his or her hand in boiling water or hold a hot iron to see whether God would intervene and heal the wounds. It was also possible to challenge one's accuser to a duel, the outcome determining the legitimacy of the accusation (trial by combat). Guilt could be disputed with the aid of **oath-helpers**, groups of 12 to 25 people who would support the accused's innocence. Exhibit 2.1 presents an ordeal called the judgment of the glowing iron, a method of proof used in early Germanic law.

Despite such "reforms," up until the 18th century the systems of crime, punishment, law, and justice were chaotic. The law was controlled by the lords of the great manors, who tried cases according to local custom and rule. Although there was general agreement that such acts as theft, assault, treason, and blasphemy constituted crimes, the penalties on law violators were often arbitrary, discretionary, and cruel. Punishments included public flogging, branding, beheading, and burning. Peasants who violated the rule of their masters were violently put down. According to a 14th-century Norman chronicle, disobedient peasants or those who stole from their masters were treated harshly: Some had their teeth pulled out, others were impaled, had their eyes torn out, their hands cut off, their ankles charred; others were burned alive or plunged in boiling lead. Even simple wanderers and vagabonds were viewed as dangerous and subject to these extreme penalties.

Origins of Common Law

Because the ancient legal codes had been lost during the Middle Ages, the concept of law and crime was chaotic, guided by superstition and local custom. Slowly, in England, a common law developed that helped standardize law and justice. The English common law became the foundation for the legal systems of Canada and the United States.

Before the Norman Conquest in 1066, the legal system among the Anglo-Saxons in England was decentralized. Each county (shire) was divided into units called hundreds, which were groups of 100 families. Each hundred was further divided into groups of ten called tithings. Each tithing was responsible for maintaining order among themselves and dealing with disturbances, fires, wild animals, and so on. Therefore, the law varied in substance from county to county, hundred to hundred, and tithing to tithing.

Petty cases were tried by courts of the hundred group. More serious and important cases could be heard by an assemblage of local landholders, or by the local nobleman; if the act concerned spiritual matters, it could be judged by clergymen and church officials in courts known as ecclesiastics. The ecclesiastical courts were responsible for disciplining the clergy; ensuring church attendance and conformity to the rites of the Church of England; and controlling sexual morality and matrimonial disputes. In early Canadian society, Baptist church courts existed to enforce the moral rules of the faith. Between 1810 and 1880, for example, almost 8000 people were excluded from Maritime Baptist churches for crimes ranging from fornication to usury.[2]

Crime and Custom. Crimes during this period were viewed as personal wrongs, and compensation therefore was often paid to the victims. If payment was not made, the victims' families would attempt to forcibly collect damages or seek revenge. The result could be a blood feud between two families. The recognized crimes included treason, homicide, rape, property theft, assault (putting another in fear), and battery (wounding another). For

| Exhibit 2.1 | The Judgment of the Glowing Iron |

After the accusation has been lawfully made, and three days have been passed in fasting and prayer, the priest, clad in his sacred vestments with the exception of his outside garment, shall take with a tongs the iron placed before the altar; and, singing the hymn of the three youths, namely, "Bless him all his works," he shall bear it to the fire, and shall say this prayer over the place where the fire is to carry out the judgment: "Bless, O Lord God, this place, that there may be for us in it sanctity, chastity, virtue and victory, and sanctimony, humility, goodness, gentleness and plentitude of law, and obedience to God the Father and the Son and the Holy Ghost." After this, the iron shall be placed in the fire and shall be sprinkled with holy water; and while it is heating, he shall celebrate mass. But when the priest shall have taken the Eucharist, he shall adjure the man who is to be tried ... and shall cause him to take the communion. Then the priest shall sprinkle holy water above the iron and shall say: "The blessing of God the Father, the Son, and the Holy Ghost descend upon this iron for the discerning of the right judgment of God." And straightway the accused shall carry the iron to a distance of nine feet. Finally his hand shall be covered under seal for three days, and if festering blood be found in the track of the iron, he shall be judged guilty. But if, however, he shall go forth uninjured, praise shall be rendered to God.

Source: The Internet Medieval SourceBook

treasonous acts, the punishment was death. Theft during the Anglo-Saxon era could result in slavery for the thieves and their families. If caught in the act of fleeing with the stolen goods, the thief could be killed.

For many other acts, including both theft and violence, compensation could be paid to the victim. For example, even a homicide could be settled by paying wergild to the deceased's family, unless the crime was carried out by poison or ambush—in which case it was punished by death. Eventually, wergild was divided so that of the sum (bot) paid, part (wer) went to the king, and the remainder (wite) went to the victim or, in the case of death, the deceased's kin.

A scale of compensation existed for lesser injuries, such as the loss of an arm or an eye. Important persons, churchmen, and nuns received greater restitution than the general population, and they paid more if they were the criminal defendant (*wer* means "worth" and referred to what the person, and therefore the crime, was worth). The nobility began to see the value in the wer, and it became the predominant portion of the bot; it was the precursor of the modern-day criminal fine. To a great degree, criminal law was designed to provide an equitable solution to what was considered a private dispute.

Connections

Monetary compensation is used today as a criminal sanction. Criminal forfeiture is used to punish white-collar criminals, and for the seizure of goods obtained through organized crime. This is discussed further in Chapter 13.

The Norman Conquest. After the Norman Conquest in 1066, William the Conqueror, the Norman leader, did not immediately change the substance of Anglo-Saxon law. At the outset of William's reign, justice was administered as it had been in previous centuries. The church courts handled acts that might be considered sin, and the local manorial courts dealt with most secular violations. However, to secure control of the countryside and to ensure military supremacy over his newly won lands, William replaced the local tribunals with royal administrators, who dealt with the most serious breaches of the peace.

Because the royal administrators could not constantly be present in each community, a system was developed in which they travelled in a circuit throughout the land, holding court in each county several times a year. When court was in session, the royal administrator, or judge, would summon a number of citizens who would, on their oath, tell of the crimes and serious breaches of the peace that had occurred since the judge's last visit. The royal judge would then decide what to do in each case, using local custom and rules of conduct as his guide. If, for example, a local freeholder was convicted of theft, he

might be executed if those before him had suffered that fate for a similar offence. However, if in previous cases the thief had been forced to make restitution to the victim, then that judgment would be rendered in the current case. This system, known as **stare decisis** (Latin for "to stand by decided cases"), was used by the early courts to determine the outcome of future cases; courts were bound to follow the law established in previously decided cases (precedent) unless the law was overruled by a higher authority, such as the king or the pope.

The current English system of law came into existence during the reign of Henry II (1154–1189). Henry also used travelling judges, better known as circuit judges. These judges followed a specific route known as a circuit and heard cases that had previously been under the jurisdiction of local courts. Juries, which began to develop about this time, were groups of local landholders whom the judges called not only to decide the facts of cases but also to investigate the crimes, accuse suspected offenders, and even give testimony at trials. Gradually, royal prosecutors came into being. These representatives of the Crown submitted evidence and brought witnesses to testify before the jury. But not until much later was the accused in a criminal action allowed to bring forth witnesses to rebut charges; not until the 18th century were witnesses required to take oaths. Few formal procedures existed, and both the judge and the prosecutor felt free to intimidate witnesses and jurors when they considered it necessary. The development of these routine judicial processes heralded the beginnings of the common law.

The Common Law

As it is used today, the term **common law** refers to a law applied to all subjects of the land, without regard for geographic or social differences. As best they could, Henry's judges began to apply a national law instead of the law that held sway in local jurisdictions. This attempt was somewhat confused at first, as it had to take into account both local custom and the Norman conquerors' feudal law. However, as new situations arose, judges took advantage of legal uncertainty by either inventing new solutions or borrowing from the laws of European countries. During formal and informal gatherings, the circuit judges shared these incidents, talked about unique cases, and discussed their decisions, thus developing an oral tradition of law. Later, as cases began to be written about, more concrete examples of common-law decisions began to emerge. Together, these cases and decisions filtered through the national court system and eventually produced a fixed body of legal rule and principles. Thus, common law is judge-made law, or case law. It is the law found in previously decided cases. Crimes such as murder, burglary, arson, and rape are common-law crimes—they were initially defined and created by judges.

Common Law and Statutory Law

The common law was and still is the law of the land in England. In most instances, the common law retained traditional Anglo-Saxon concepts. For example, the common law originally defined murder as the unlawful killing of another human being with malice afore-thought.[3] By this definition, for offenders to be found guilty of murder, they must have (1) planned the crime and (2) intentionally killed the victim out of spite or hatred. However, this general definition proved inadequate to deal with the many situations in which one person took another's life. Over time, to bring the law closer to the realities of human behaviour, English judges added other forms of murder: killing someone in the heat of passion, killing someone out of negligence, and killing someone in the course of committing another crime, such as during a robbery. Each form of murder was given a different title (manslaughter, felony murder, and so on) and provided with a different degree of punishment. Thus, the common law was a constantly evolving legal code, based on legal decisions "from the ground up."

Connections

Common-law practices still guide modern legal codes. For example, murder statutes still retain different degrees of seriousness based on the intent of the actor. Each degree is correlated with a level of punishment commensurate with its seriousness. The degrees of murder and other definitional issues are discussed in Chapter 11.

In some instances, the creation of a new common-law crime can be traced back to a particular case. For example, an unsuccessful attempt to commit an illegal act was not considered a crime under early common law. The modern doctrine that criminal attempt can be punished under law can be traced directly back to 1784 and the case of *Rex v. Scofield*. In that case, Scofield was charged with having put a lit candle and combustible material in a house he was renting, with the intention of burning it down; however, his attempt was unsuccessful. Scofield defended himself by arguing that an attempt to commit a misdemeanour was not actually a crime. In rejecting this argument, the court stated: "The intent may make an act, innocent in itself, criminal; nor is the completion of an act, criminal in itself, necessary to constitute criminality."[4] After *Scofield*, attempt became a common-law crime, and today criminal attempt (called **inchoate crimes**) is defined as a crime in section 24 of the Canadian Criminal Code (CCC).

When the situation required it, the English Parliament enacted legislation to supplement the judge-made common law. Violations of these laws are referred to as statutory crimes. For example, in 1723 the Waltham Black Act punished offences against rural property with death, from the poaching of small game to arson if the criminal was armed or disguised.[5] Moreover, the act eroded the rights of the accused; it allowed the death sentence to be carried out without a trial if the accused failed to surrender when ordered to do so. The underlying purpose of the act was Parliament's desire to control the behaviour of peasants whose poverty forced them to poach on royal lands. In the Black Act, then, the British ruling class created a mechanism for protecting its property and position of social power.

Another example also illustrates how the law develops to protect the rights of the privileged. In 1812, the British government proposed a new capital offence, The Frame Breaking Act, which enabled people convicted of machine-breaking to be sentenced to death (see Figure 2.1). The law was in response to mill workers upset by changes occurring in the workplace: wage reductions, the use of unapprenticed workmen, and their own replacement by new weaving technology. The Army of Redressers, under the leadership of General Ned Ludd, broke into factories at night to destroy the new power looms. This is the origin of the term Luddite, which is used today to refer to someone who has an irrational hatred of technology.

More generally, statutory laws usually reflect existing social conditions, as they deal with issues of morality,

| Figure 2.1 | The British Parliaments acts against the Luddites |

WHEREAS,

Several EVIL-MINDED PERSONS have assembled together in a riotous Manner, and DESTROYED a NUMBER of

FRAMES,

In different Parts of the Country :

THIS IS

TO GIVE NOTICE

That any Person who will give Information of any Person to Person thus wickedly

BREAKING THE FRAMES

Shall, upon CONVICTION, receive

50 GUINEAS

REWARD.

And any Person who was actively engaged in RIOTING, who will impeach his Accomplices, shall, upon CONVICTION, receive the same Reward, and every Effort made to procure his Pardon.

☞ Information to be given to Messers. COLDHAM and ENFIELD.

Nottingham, March 29, 1812.

such as gambling, sexual activity, and drug-related offences. For example, early in the history of Canada and the United States, it was both legal and relatively easy to obtain narcotics, such as heroin, opium, and cocaine.[6] Their use became habits of the middle class. However, public and governmental concern arose over the use of narcotics by immigrants, such as the Chinese, who had come to Canada to build railroads and work in mines. By 1910, opium was outlawed in Canada.[7] However, as outlined in Chapter 14, there is a question as to whether laws regulating narcotics were in fact thinly disguised attempts to control Asian immigration into Canada.

We can see in the case of marijuana how the statutory law is subject to change. As the use of "pot" became widespread among the middle class in the 1960s, attitudes became more relaxed, and enforcement of the law has become more lax. In 1995, a Health Canada poll discovered that 69 percent of Canadians were against the prohibition of marijuana.

The Development of Law in Canada

Canada's unique legal system was not achieved overnight nor without conflict.[8] The Canadian criminal justice system has been strongly influenced by international practice and, in particular, the common law of England; it was codified in the first Canadian Criminal Code of 1892, which abolished common-law offences. The exception is Quebec, which falls under the civil Napoleonic code. As well, the geographic, economic, political and cultural attributes of early Canada have shaped our criminal justice system. Initially, Canada's size and the pattern of westward settlement resulted in cases of frontier justice, but by the time the west was opening up, defendants were being taken to the more established parts of Canada for trial. The spread of law enforcement and the development of a legal system was gradual, becoming more sophisticated and professional.

Pierre Berton describes the stark difference between the American city of Skagway, which was noted for is lawlessness, and Dawson in Canada, where crime and disorder were kept firmly in check by the North-West Mounted Police (NWMP). In part, their success has been attributed to the unorthodox methods they used, not enforcing some laws and making up others.[9]

Before Confederation in 1867 there was no standard criminal justice system in Canada. At stages during settlement, an infrastructure for justice existed in eastern Canada, while law was being administered by circuit judges in log buildings in western Canada. The military was the first to maintain law and order, especially in naval ports. But gradually, the reforms taking place in Europe had an impact in Canada, manifested in the construction of prisons designed as places of punishment, the training of professional police, and the declining use of the death penalty.

Crime control was eventually centralized in the federal government through the British North America Act. In the BNAA, the federal government was given the exclusive power to create criminal law (s. 91[27]); this is the source of statutory law. The provinces were to be responsible for the administration of justice (s. 92[14]). Generally, Parliament was given the authority to effect "peace, order and good government." Subordinate legislation can take the form of municipal bylaws, provincial department regulations, and orders in council.

The Police of Canada Act (1868) created the Dominion Police, and the North-West Mounted Police began in 1873. (Initially given jurisdiction only in the prairies, the force became the Royal Canadian Mounted Police in 1920.) With this, the pattern was set for the modern system of municipal and provincial police forces, with a federal police agency. In the prairie West, however, there was still no organized system of law enforcement by the time of Confederation. The Hudson's Bay Company was using its employees to enforce its own penal code. The North-West Mounted Police were sent to protect the "Indians" from the Americans and to bring the Queen's justice to a dangerous territory, becoming an instrument of federal economic policy and an important force in subjugating natives. Being a police force, the NWMP was able to use the criminal sanction and, in the name of law and order, repress political dissent, control the indigenous population, and maintain sovereignty.[10] Maintenance of order helped to encourage settlers, and in the process new markets were created for manufactured goods. The treatment of aboriginal Canadians by the NWMP is seen by some as benevolent, especially in contrast to the situation in the United States. There, a policy of genocide helped clear the territory for ranchers.

Connections

There has been much debate recently about the treatment of natives in the development of Canada. For more on this topic, see the discussion in Chapter 9.

Another important feature of the Canadian legal system is the federal Criminal Code. Before Confederation, the British system of common law was used for criminal prosecutions. The laws were generally adopted intact, but modified over time with judicial precedent and legislative amendments, creating substantial variation across the country. For example, incest was punishable by a severe prison sentence in some provinces but was not even a crime in others.[11]

All existing statute law was eventually consolidated, and most of the common law continued to apply to permit "elasticity." Some offences prohibited in the 1892 Criminal Code had their origin in 17th-century England; for example, offences against public order included inciting to mutiny, unlawful drilling (of soldiers), attending or promoting a prize fight, piracy, possessing a weapon at a public meeting, and pretending to practise witchcraft. Other previously included offences have since been repealed or amended, such as seducing a woman under promise of marriage, carnally knowing idiots, keeping a common bawdy-wigwam, injuring persons by furious driving, leaving holes in the ice unguarded, and abduction of heiresses. Some interesting laws still on the books in Canada are displayed in Table 2.1.

Common Law in Other Countries

In the United States, which also inherited the British tradition, the U.S. colonies under British rule were subject to the law handed down by English judges. After the colonies acquired their independence, they adapted and changed the English law to fit their needs. In many states, legislatures standardized such common-law crimes as murder, burglary, arson, and rape by putting them into statutory form. In other states, comprehensive penal codes were passed, thus abolishing the common-law crimes. Today few states allow prosecution for common-law violations.

Conversion to statutory law allowed for the modification and modernizing of common-law principles. As in England, whenever the common law proved inadequate to deal with changing social and moral issues, legislatures

Table 2.1	Outdated Canadian crimes

The Canadian Criminal Code includes laws defining the following activities as crimes. Some of them might surprise you.

- Duelling (section 71): It is an indictable offence to challenge or accept a challenge to fight a duel.
- Having a stink bomb (section 178): It is a summary offence for anyone except a peace officer to possess an offensive volatile substance.
- Trespassing at night (section 17): This is a summary, reverse onus offence, which means that the burden of proof lies on defendants to show they have lawful excuse to loiter or prowl.
- Pretending to practise witchcraft (section 365): It is a summary offence to fraudulently pretend to use witchcraft or sorcery; it is legal to be a witch.
- Falsely claiming royal warrant (section 413): It is a summary offence to claim that one's goods are made for the services of Her Majesty, a rarely prosecuted offence.

Figure 2.2	Sources of law

THE CANADIAN LEGAL SYSTEM

SOURCES

Formal Sources	Legal Sources	Literary Sources	Historical or Material Source
• Sovereign • State • Will of people • Etc.	• Legislation • Judicial precedent • Custom	*Authoritative* • Statutes • Law reports • Books of authority *Non-Authoritative* • Medieval chronicles • Periodicals • Other books	• Mercantile custom • Religious beliefs • Ideas of reasonableness • Natural justice • Conscience • Public policy • Roman/Canon law • Professional practice • Judicial opinion

LAW

SOURCE: As used in Gerald L. Gail, *The Canadian Legal System*, 3rd ed. (Toronto: Carswell, 1990).

could supplement it with statutes, creating new elements in the various state and federal legal codes.

The British common-law tradition was imposed not only on the American colonies but also on its other overseas possessions, including its African colonies. In some instances, this has created a dual legal system divided between traditional tribal law and British common law. An example is the conflict between traditional tribal and British common law in the African country of Sierra Leone.[12] Women in Sierra Leone are still considered the property of their fathers and later their husbands or heads of families. If a woman is raped, the case is usually brought to the customary courts, which handle complaints according to traditional tribal customs. If the accused is found to be guilty of sexual assault, referred to as "woman-damage," he will be forced to pay compensation to the victim's family. Because this is a property issue, consent of the victim is not important; the "damage" involves a trespass or misuse of "someone's property." The victim's story is usually accepted because the tribal custom is that a woman should confess a wrongful sexual act or else suffer divinely inspired ill fate and misfortune. After admitting guilt, the accused typically agrees to compensate either the husband or the victim's parents for the damage he caused. If the defendant refuses to admit guilt or pay damages, the case can be brought under the jurisdiction of the General Courts, which use British common law; the maximum penalty can be life in prison. Threat of complaint to the formal justice system is used as an incentive to settle the case according to tribal law and pay monetary penalties rather than face trial, conviction, and imprisonment. In Sierra Leone, British common law and the traditional tribal customs are often at cross-purposes. Yet the two systems can function together because each serves to maintain group norms.

Classification of Law

Law can be classified in a number of ways that can help us understand its nature and purpose. Three of the most important classifications are (1) crimes and torts, (2) indictable and summary offences, and (3) *mala in se* and *mala prohibitum*. Figure 2.3 shows the relationship between different types of law. These classifications are briefly described here.

Crimes and Torts

Law can be divided into two broad categories: criminal law and civil law. Civil law is all law other than criminal law and includes such legal areas as property law (the law governing transfer and ownership of property) and contract law (the law of personal agreements). Of all areas of the civil law, **tort law** (the law of personal wrongs and damage) is most similar in intent and form to the criminal law.

A tort is a civil action in which an individual asks to be compensated for personal harm. The harm may be either physical or mental and includes such acts as trespass, assault and battery, invasion of privacy, libel (false and injurious writings), and slander (false and injurious statements). A tort can occur when someone is injured by the actions of another. As the O.J. Simpson civil trial illustrated, someone can be sued for damages even if he or she has been acquitted of a criminal act (the reason being that the standards of evidence for a finding are lower in civil cases).

A tort may also occur when a behaviour is an indirect cause of injury—that is, when it sets off a chain of events that leads to injury or death. In 1990, for example, the families of two youths, James Vance and Raymond Belknap, who had attempted suicide in 1985 (one died and the other survived for several years) sued the heavy-metal rock group Judas Priest and CBS Records because they claimed the group had put the subliminal message "Do it" in its *Stained Class* album to effect "mind control" over the band's fans. The group was vindicated, in large part because the youths were shown to be self-destructive before the album was released, engaging in truancy and drug use. Since this was a U.S. case, the judge ruled that the band's recordings were not protected by the First Amendment right to free speech if indeed they had carried privacy-invading mind-control messages.[13]

Because some torts are similar to some criminal acts, a person can possibly be held both criminally and civilly liable for one action. For example, if one man punches another, it is possible for the assailant not only to be charged by the state with assault and battery—and imprisoned if found guilty—but to be sued by the victim in a tort action of assault in which he could be required to pay monetary damages.

Perhaps the most important similarity between criminal law and civil law is that they have a common purpose. Both attempt to control people's behaviour by setting limits on what acts are permissible; both accomplish this through state-imposed sanctions.

Of course, there are also several differences between criminal law and civil law. First, the main purpose of criminal law is to give the state the power to protect the public from harm by punishing individuals whose actions threaten the social order. In tort law, the harm or injury is considered a private wrong, and the main concern is to compensate individuals for harm done to them by others.

In a criminal action, the state initiates the legal proceedings by bringing charges and prosecuting the violator. The victim has little role. If it is determined that the criminal law has been broken, the state can impose punishment, such as imprisonment, probation (community supervision by the court), or a fine payable to the state.

Figure 2.3   Types of law

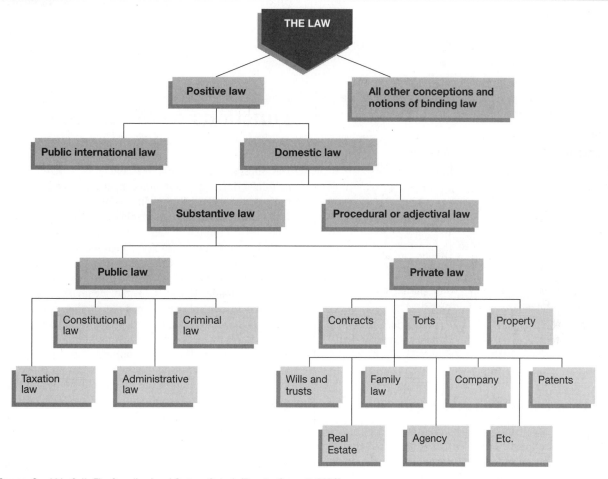

Source: Gerald L. Gall, *The Canadian Legal System*, 3rd ed. (Toronto: Carswell, 1990).

In a civil action, however, the injured person must initiate proceedings. In a successful action, the injured individual usually receives financial compensation for the harm done.

Another major difference is the burden of proof required to establish the defendant's liability. In criminal matters, the defendant's guilt must be proved beyond a reasonable doubt. In a civil case, the defendant is required to pay damages if, by a preponderance of the evidence, the trier of fact finds that he or she committed the wrong. According to this doctrine, while both parties may share some blame, the defendant is at fault if he or she contributed more than 50 percent to the cause of the dispute. Establishing guilt by a preponderance of the evidence is easier than establishing it beyond a reasonable doubt.[14] Table 2.2 summarizes the differences and similarities between crimes and torts.

Indictable and Summary Offences

In addition to being divided from civil law, criminal laws can be further classified as either indictable offences or offences punishable on summary conviction. The distinction is based on seriousness: An **indictable offence** is a serious offence such as murder (Section 231), while a **summary offence** such as loitering (Section 179 on vagrancy) is a minor or petty crime. The main differences involve procedure and penalty. Summary offences have a six-month limitation period on prosecution, they are heard in provincial court, and the maximum fine is $2000 and/or a six-month jail term.

On the other hand, indictable offences have no limitation period on prosecution and can result in much more serious penalties if the defendant is found guilty.[15] Indictable offences involve a choice of trial by judge or

Table 2.2	Comparison of criminal and tort law

SIMILARITIES

Both criminal and tort law seek to control behaviour.

Both laws impose sanctions.

Similar areas of legal action exist—for example, personal assault and control of white-collar offences, such as environmental pollution.

DIFFERENCES

Criminal Law	Tort Law
Crime is a public offence.	Tort is a civil or private wrong.
The sanction associated with a criminal law is incarceration or death.	The sanction associated with a tort is monetary damages.
The right of enforcement belongs to the state.	The individual brings the action.
The government ordinarily does not appeal.	Both parties can appeal.
Fines go to the state.	The individual receives compensation for harm done.
The standard of proof is "beyond a reasonable doubt."	Guilt is established by a preponderance of the evidence.

jury, and Section 625.1 of the Criminal Code includes the provision for a prehearing or preliminary inquiry to determine if there is admissible evidence that could result in a conviction in a full trial. Most preliminary inquiries are concluded in less than a day.

Mala in Se and Mala Prohibitum

It is also possible to classify crimes as *mala in se* or *mala prohibitum*. Some illegal acts, referred to as **mala in se** crimes, are rooted in the core values inherent in Western civilization. These "natural laws" are designed to control such behaviours as inflicting physical harm on others (assault, rape, murder), taking possessions that rightfully belong to another (larceny, burglary, robbery), or harming another person's property (malicious damage, trespass) that have traditionally been considered a violation of the morals of Western civilization.

Another type of crime, sometimes called statutory crime or **mala prohibitum** crime, involves violations of laws that reflect current public opinion and social values. In essence, statutory crimes are acts that conflict with contemporary standards of morality. Crimes are periodically created to control behaviours that conflict with the functioning of society. *Mala prohibitum* offences include drug use and possession of unlicensed handguns. While it

is relatively easy to link *mala in se* crimes to an objective concept of morality, it is much more difficult to do so if the acts are *mala prohibitum*. In adjudicating cases of obscenity, for example, the judge must take subjective community standards into account in deciding if something violates that provision of the code.

Functions of the Criminal Law

The substantive criminal law today is a written code defining crimes and their punishments. In Canada it is centralized under the jurisdiction of the federal government, while in the United States, individual states can develop their own criminal codes. This centralization enables greater social control in Canadian society and perhaps accounts for Canadians' higher respect for authority. Although criminal codes will have their differences, most use comparable terms, and the behaviours they are designed to control are often quite similar, especially in Western countries. Regardless of which culture or jurisdiction created them or when, criminal codes have several distinct functions. The most important of these include (1) providing social control, (2) discouraging revenge, (3) expressing public opinion and morality, (4) deterring criminal behaviour, and (5) maintaining the social order.

This idea of the "function" of the law is a political one, in that there is more than one model on the role of the law. From the consensus viewpoint (as discussed in Chapter 1), the law maintains social order because it reflects the interests of the majority. The conflict model, on the other hand, sees the law as a tool in the reproduction of the dominant social and economic order.[16]

Providing Social Control

The primary purpose of the criminal law is to control the behaviour of people within its jurisdiction. The criminal law is a written statement of rules to which people must conform their behaviour. Every society also maintains unwritten rules of conduct—ordinary customs and conventions referred to as **folkways** and universally followed behaviour called norms and morals, or **mores**. However, it is the criminal law that formally prohibits behaviours believed by those in political power to threaten societal well-being and that may challenge their own authority. For example, the criminal law incorporates centuries-old prohibitions against the following behaviours harmful to others: taking the possessions of another person, physically harming another person, damaging another person's property, and cheating another person out of his or her possessions. Similarly, the law prevents actions that challenge the legitimacy of the government, such as planning its overthrow, collaborating with its enemies,

Robert Latimer, convicted of killing his severely disabled daughter, was given a mandatory minimum sentence of 10 years in 2001, despite widespread controversy about his actions. Seventy percent of people polled by *The Globe and Mail* disagreed with the sentence.

and so on. Whereas violations of mores and folkways may be informally punished by any person, control of the criminal law is given to those in political power, administered and enforced by its agents.

Discouraging Revenge

By delegating enforcement to others, the criminal law controls an individual's need to seek revenge or vengeance against those who have violated his or her rights. By punishing people who infringe on the rights, property, and freedom of others, the law shifts the burden of retribution from the individual to the state. As Oliver Wendell Holmes stated, this prevents "the greater evil of private retribution."[17]

Although state retaliation may offend the sensibilities of many citizens, it is greatly preferable to a system in which people would have to seek justice for themselves.

Expressing Public Opinion and Morality

The criminal law also reflects constantly changing public opinions and moral values. *Mala in se* crimes, such as murder and forcible rape, are almost univer-

sally prohibited, but the prohibition of legislatively created *mala prohibitum* crimes, such as traffic law and gambling violations, changes according to shifting social conditions and attitudes. The criminal law is used to codify these changes. For example, if the government decides to criminalize certain behaviours, such as membership in an organized gang, it will amend the Criminal Code. The criminal law then has the power to define the boundaries of moral and immoral behaviour. Nonetheless, it has proved difficult to legally control public morality, because of the problems associated with (1) gauging the will of the majority, (2) respecting the rights of the minority, and (3) enforcing laws that many people consider trivial or self-serving.

The power of the law to express norms and values can be viewed in the development of the crime of **vagrancy** (the going about from place to place by a person who has no visible means of support and who, though able to work for his or her maintenance, refuses to do so). In a famous treatise, criminologist William Chambliss linked the historical development of the law of vagrancy to the prevailing economic interests of the ruling class. He argued that the original vagrancy laws were formulated in the 14th century after the bubonic plague had killed significant numbers of English peasants, threatening the labour-intensive feudal economy. The first vagrancy laws were aimed at preventing workers from leaving their estates to secure higher wages elsewhere. The laws punished migration, thereby mooring peasants to their manors and aiding wealthy landowners.[18]

In an opposing view of the social conditions that influenced the creation of vagrancy laws, Jeffrey Adler argues that early English vagrancy laws were less concerned with maintaining capitalism than with controlling beggars and relieving the overburdened public relief and welfare systems.[19] Adler suggests that early American vagrancy laws provided town officials with a mechanism to repel the moral threat to the community posed by vagrants, "sabbath breakers," paupers, and the wandering poor; economic demands had little to do with the content of the law. The current law on vagrancy in Canada is innocuous in comparison. Section 179 is a summary offence and is restricted to controlling those who support themselves by crime, but also those who have been convicted of any of several sexual offences and are found loitering near playgrounds or public bathing areas.

Deterring Criminal Behaviour

The criminal law's social control function is realized through its ability to deter potential law violators. The threat of punishment associated with violating the law is designed to prevent crimes before they occur. During the Middle Ages, public executions were held to drive this point home. And while we don't have public executions

Exhibit 2.2	The Decriminalization of Homosexuality in Canada

As a result of a case which went to the Supreme Court of Canada (*Klippert v. The Queen*, 1967 S.C.R. 822), Canadian legal history reached a turning point. The case was against Everett Klippert, a homosexual in a small community, well known to the police. Klippert had pleaded guilty in August 1965 to four charges of acts of gross indecency; his criminal record showed 18 similar convictions.

After Klippert's sentencing, the Crown applied to declare him a dangerous sexual offender, and Judge Sissons imposed a sentence of preventive detention. Two psychiatrists had testified that Klippert had never caused injury or pain to any individual, was unlikely to in the future, and would likely recommit the same offence with other consenting male adults; as well, his sexual orientation was viewed by the psychiatrists as incurable. Judge Sissons declared Klippert a dangerous sexual offender, and Klippert's appeal to the Court of Appeal of the Northwest Territories was dismissed. He appealed unsuccessfully to the Supreme Court of Canada.

In the Supreme Court decision, Chief Justice J. Cartwright and Mr. Justice Emmett Hall dissented, indicating that they would have allowed the appeal, and their reasons formed part of the government's political decision to decriminalize homosexuality. In response to Klippert's case, Pierre Trudeau made his now-famous comment that "the state has no place in the bedrooms of the nation," and two years later such discrimination and potential for persecution was abolished in Canada when homosexuality was decriminalized in 1969. The Criminal Law Amendment Act, 1968–69, amended the Criminal Code to exclude homosexuality between consenting adults (persons aged 21 years and older) from the provisions of the code regarding acts of gross indecency.

Source: Based on research by Peggy Scott

today, the impact of criminal law is felt through news accounts of long prison sentences that perform the function of **general deterrence**. That is, people are less likely to commit crimes when they know there will be a penalty attached. Clearly, such an idea is based on the assumption that crime is rational and thought out beforehand; it would not work for crimes of passion, committed in the heat of the moment.

The **specific deterrent** power of the criminal law is tied to the power it gives the state to sanction offenders. Whereas violations of folkways and mores are controlled informally, breaches of the criminal law are left to the jurisdiction of political agencies. Those violating mores and folkways can be subject to social disapproval, whereas criminal law violators alone are subject to physical coercion and punishment. Today, the most common punishments are fines, community supervision or probation, and incarceration in jails or prison. Canada last used the death penalty in 1962, and it was finally abolished in 1976.

Connections

The social control function of the criminal law assumes that crime is rational and that the threat of punishment will deter crime. This assumption is actually the subject of significant debate: If the criminal law can deter crime, why is there so much crime today? For the answer, see the discussion of general deterrence in Chapter 5.

Maintaining the Social Order

All legal systems are designed to support and maintain the boundaries of the social system they serve. In medieval England, the law protected the feudal system by defining an orderly system of property transfer and ownership. Laws in some socialist nations protect the primacy of the state by strictly curtailing profiteering and individual enterprise. Our own capitalist system is also supported and sustained by the criminal law. In a sense, the content of the criminal law is more a reflection of the needs of those who control the existing economic and political system than a representation of some idealized moral code. In our society, by meting out punishment to those who damage or steal property, the law promotes the activities needed to sustain an economy based on the accumulation of wealth. It would be impossible to conduct business through the use of contracts, promissory notes, credit, banking, and so on unless the law protected private capital. Maintaining a legal climate in which capitalism can thrive is an underlying goal of the criminal law. This is part of the conflict model of the law.

The criminal law has not always protected commercial enterprise; if one merchant cheated another, it was considered a private matter. Then in 1473, in the *Carrier's* case, an English court ruled that a merchant who held and transported merchandise for another was guilty of theft if he kept the goods for his own purposes.[20] Before the *Carrier's* case, the law did not consider it a crime for people to keep something that was already in their possession. Breaking with legal precedent, the British court recognized that the new English mercantile trade system could not be sustained if property rights had to be individually enforced. To this day, the substantive criminal law prohibits such business-related acts as fraud, embezzlement, and commercial theft.

The Legal Definition of a Crime

The media often tell us about people who admit at trial that they committed the act they are accused of but who are not found guilty of the crime. In most instances, this occurs because state or federal prosecutors have not proved that the defendant's behaviour falls within the legal definition of a crime. To fulfil the legal definition, all elements of the crime must be proved, including that there was a law defining the act as criminal.

For the state to prove that a crime occurred and that the defendant committed it, the prosecutor must show that the accused engaged in the guilty act, or *actus reus*, and had the *mens rea*, or intent to commit the act. The *actus reus* can be either an aggressive act, such as taking someone's money, burning a building, or shooting someone, or a failure to act when there is a legal duty to do so, such as a parent's neglecting to seek medical attention for a sick child. The *mens rea* (guilty mind) refers to an individual's state of mind at the time of the act or, more specifically, the person's intent to commit the crime. For most crimes, both the *actus reus* and the *mens rea* must be present for the act to be considered a crime. For example, if George decides to kill Bob and then takes a gun and shoots Bob, George can be convicted of the crime of murder, because both elements are present. George's shooting of Bob is the *actus reus*; his decision to kill Bob is the *mens rea*. However, if George only thinks about shooting Bob but does nothing about it, the element of *actus reus* is absent, and no crime has been committed. Let us now look more closely at these issues.

Actus Reus

As mentioned, the *actus reus* is the criminal act itself. For an act to be considered illegal, the action must be voluntary. For example, one person shooting another could certainly be considered a voluntary act. However, if the shooting occurs while the person holding the gun is having an epileptic seizure or a heart attack or is sleepwalking, he or she will not be held criminally liable, because the act is not voluntary. But if the individual knows he or she has such a condition and does not take precautions to prevent the act from occurring, the person could be held responsible for the criminal act. The central issue concerning voluntariness is whether the individual has control over his or her actions. For instance, in 1992 the Supreme Court of Canada upheld the acquittal of Kenneth Parks, who drove 23 kilometres and stabbed his mother-in-law to death. The trial judge ruled that he had been sleepwalking, which is not insanity as defined in law, and was thus acting involuntarily (non-insane

automatism). Had he been found guilty, he could have been jailed for life.[21]

Mens Rea

In most situations, for an act to constitute a crime it must be done with criminal intent—otherwise known as *mens rea*. Intent in the legal sense can mean carrying out an act intentionally, knowingly, and willingly. However, the definition also encompasses situations in which recklessness or negligence establishes the required criminal intent. Some crimes require specific intent, and others require general intent. The type of intent needed to establish criminal liability varies depending on how the crime is defined. Most crimes require a general intent, or an intent to commit the crime. Thus, when Ann picks Bill's pocket and takes his wallet, her intent is to steal. Specific intent, on the other hand, is an intent to accomplish a specific purpose as an element of the crime. It involves an intent in addition to the intent to commit the crime. For example, burglary is the breaking and entering of a dwelling house with the intent to commit a crime. The breaking and entering aspect requires a general intent; the intent to commit a theft is a specific intent.

Criminal intent also exists if the results of an action, though originally unintended, are substantially certain to occur. For example, Kim, out for revenge against her former boyfriend John, poisons the punch bowl at John's party. Before John has a drink himself, several of his guests die as a result of drinking the punch. Kim could be said to have intentionally killed the guests even though that was not the original purpose of her action. The law would hold that Kim or any other person should be substantially certain that the others at the party would drink the punch and be poisoned along with John.

The concept of *mens rea* also encompasses the situation in which a person intends to commit a crime against one person but injures another party instead. For instance, if Sam, intending to kill Larry, shoots at Larry but misses and kills John, Sam is guilty of murdering John, even though he did not intend to do so. Under the doctrine of **transferred intent**, the original criminal intent is transferred to the unintended victim.

Mens rea is also found in situations in which harm has resulted because a person has acted negligently or recklessly. Negligence involves a person's acting unreasonably under the circumstances. Criminal negligence is often found in situations involving drunken driving. If a drunken driver speeding and zigzagging across lanes hits and kills another person, criminal negligence exists. In the case of drunken driving, the law maintains that a "reasonable person" would not drive a car when drunk and thus unable to control the vehicle. The intent that underlies the finding of criminal liability for an unintentional act is known as **constructive intent**.

Strict Liability

Both the *actus reus* and the *mens rea* must be present before a person can be convicted of a crime. However, several crimes defined by statute do not require *mens rea*. The actor is guilty simply by doing what the statute prohibits; mental intent does not enter the picture. The Crown needs only to prove the *actus reus* of the offence, unless the accused can show they acted with due diligence, or proper care. These offences are known as **strict-liability crimes**, or public welfare offences, and generally apply to statutes other than the Criminal Code. Health and safety regulations, traffic laws, and narcotic control laws are strict-liability statutes. For example, a person stopped for speeding is guilty of breaking the traffic laws regardless of whether he or she had intended to go over the speed limit or had done it by accident, out of carelessness, or for any other reason. The underlying purpose of these laws is to protect the public; therefore, intent is not required. Offences of "absolute liability" cannot be defended against by showing a person acted with due diligence. However, in general these have been found to violate the Charter of Rights.

Connections

Many white-collar crimes such as pollution of the environment are considered strict liability. A person who is detected dumping toxic wastes is guilty of a crime; proving intent is usually not required. For an analysis of white-collar law enforcement, see Chapter 13.

Criminal Defences

When people defend themselves against criminal charges, they must refute one or more of the elements of the crime of which they have been accused. A number of approaches can be taken to criminal defence. First, defendants may deny the *actus reus* by arguing that they were falsely accused and that the real culprit has yet to be identified. Defendants may also claim that while they did engage in the criminal act they are accused of, they lacked the *mens rea* needed to be found guilty of the crime. If a person whose mental state is impaired commits a criminal act, it is possible for the person to excuse his or her law-violating actions by claiming he or she lacked the capacity to form sufficient intent to be held criminally responsible for the actions. Ignorance, insanity, and intoxication are among the types of excuse defences.

Another type of defence is that of justification. Here, the individual usually admits committing the criminal act but maintains that the act was justified and that he or she

therefore should not be held criminally liable. Among the justification defences are necessity, duress, self-defence, and entrapment.

Persons standing trial for criminal offences may defend themselves by claiming either that their actions were justified under the circumstances or that their behaviour can be excused by their lack of *mens rea*. If either the physical or mental elements of a crime cannot be proved, the defendant cannot be convicted. We will now examine some of these defences and justifications in greater detail.

Ignorance or Mistake

As a general rule, ignorance of the law is no excuse (CCC s. 19). However, courts have recognized that ignorance can be an excuse if the government fails to make enactment of a new law public or if the offender relied on an official statement of the law that was later deemed incorrect. Ignorance or mistake can be an excuse if it negates an element of a crime. For example, if Andrew purchases stolen merchandise from Eric but is unaware that the material was illegally obtained, he cannot be convicted of receiving stolen merchandise because he had no intent to do so. This is termed a "mistake of fact."

While ignorance or mistake has been used to excuse some crime, such as sexual relations with minor females, the law has since been changed. That section of the law setting the limits on "consent no defence" (CCC s. 150:1 [4,5]) says that a belief that the complainant was of legal age is not a defence unless the accused took all reasonable steps to ascertain the age of the complainant. A "mistake of law," on the other hand, in which the accused is not aware that he or she is breaking the law, can sometimes be a defence in a civil case, despite section 19.

Insanity

Insanity is a defence to criminal prosecution in which the defendant's state of mind negates their criminal responsibility. A successful insanity defence results in a verdict of "not guilty by reason of insanity." Insanity is a legal category and does not necessarily mean that persons using the defence are mentally ill or unbalanced, only that their state of mind at the time the crime was committed made it impossible for them to have the necessary intent to satisfy the legal definition of a crime. The accused cannot appreciate the quality of the act or understand that it was wrong. It is usually left to psychiatric testimony in court to prove a defendant is legally sane. Section 16 (4) of the Criminal Code states that everyone is presumed to be sane, and thus that the burden of proving insanity rests on the accused. Interestingly enough, the Supreme Court found in 1990 that this is a technical violation of the Charter.

It used to be the case that a person found to be not guilty by reason of insanity (NGRI) on conviction was automatically placed in indefinite custody of mental health authorities until diagnosed as sane. However, in *R. v. Swain* (1991), the Supreme Court of Canada ruled that indefinite sentences were a violation of the accused's constitutional rights. Sometimes, a person who was sane when he or she committed a crime became insane soon afterward. In that instance, the person receives psychiatric care until capable of standing trial and is then tried on the criminal charge, since the person actually had *mens rea* at the time the crime was committed. Being "fit to stand trial" includes, for example, being able to instruct a lawyer. The test used to determine whether a person is legally insane is based on the 1843 McNaughtan Rule (CCC s. 16).

The McNaughtan Rule. In 1843 an English court established the McNaughtan Rule. Daniel M'Naghten, believing Edward Drummond to be Sir Robert Peel, the prime minister of Great Britain, shot and killed Drummond (Peel's secretary). At his trial for murder, M'Naghten claimed that he could not be held responsible for the murder because his delusions had caused him to act. The jury agreed with M'Naghten and found him not guilty by reason of insanity.

Because of the importance of the people involved in the case, the verdict was not well received. The British House of Lords reviewed the decision and requested the court to clarify the law with respect to insane delusions. The court's response became known as the **McNaughtan Rule**:

> To establish a defence on the ground of insanity, it must be proved that at the time of the committing of the act the party accused was labouring under such a defect of reason from disease of the mind, as not to know the nature and quality of the act he was doing; or, if he did know, that he did not know he was doing what was wrong.[22]

Essentially, the McNaughtan Rule maintains that an individual is insane if he or she is unable to tell the difference between right and wrong because of some mental disability. The McNaughtan Rule is a widely used test for legal insanity; however, over the years it has attracted much criticism. First, great confusion has surfaced over such wording as "disease of the mind" and "know the nature and quality of the act." These phrases have never been properly clarified. Second, critics, mainly from the mental health profession, have pointed out that the rule is unrealistic and narrow in that it does not cover situations in which people know right from wrong but cannot control their actions.

The insanity defence has been the source of debate and controversy. Many critics of this defence maintain that inquiry into a defendant's psychological makeup is inappropriate at the trial stage; they would prefer that the issue be raised at the sentencing stage, after guilt has been determined. Opponents also charge that criminal responsibility is separate from mental illness and that the two should not be equated. It is a serious mistake, they argue, to consider criminal responsibility as a trait or quality that can be detected by a psychiatric evaluation. Moreover, it is felt that some criminals avoid punishment because they are erroneously judged by psychiatrists to be mentally ill. Conversely, some people who are found not guilty by reason of insanity because they suffer from a mild personality disturbance would have been incarcerated as mental patients far longer than they would have been imprisoned if they had been convicted of a criminal offence, which made it a dangerous defence.

Connections

One reason there are so few successful insanity pleas is that there may be relatively few insane criminals. The association between mental illness and crimes seems to be tenuous at best. For a discussion of this issue, see the sections in Chapter 6 on mental illness and crime.

Intoxication

Intoxication, which includes the taking of alcohol or drugs, is generally not considered a defence. However, there are two exceptions to this rule. First, an individual who becomes intoxicated by mistake, through force, or under duress can use involuntary intoxication as a defence. Second, voluntary intoxication is a defence when specific intent is needed and the person could not have formed the intent because of his or her intoxicated condition. For example, if a person breaks into and enters another's house but is so drunk that he or she cannot form the intent to commit a robbery, the intoxication is a defence against burglary but not against the breaking and entering. However, a recent change in the law makes it an offence to be that drunk. Bill C-72, "An Act to Amend the Criminal Code (Self-induced intoxication)," received royal assent on July 13, 1995, and amended the Criminal Code so people remained accountable for the violent acts they committed while intoxicated.

Duress

Duress is a defence to a crime when the defendant commits an illegal act because the defendant or a third person has been threatened by another with death or serious bodily harm if the act is not performed. For example, if Pete, holding a gun on Jerry, threatens to kill Jerry unless he breaks into and enters Bill's house, Jerry has a defence of duress for the crime of breaking and entering. This defence, however, does not cover the situation in which defendants commit a serious crime, such as murder or sexual assault, to save themselves or others. The reason for this exception is that the defence is based on the social policy that, when faced with two evils (harm to oneself or violating the criminal law), it is better to commit the lesser evil to avoid the threatened harm. In the situation of murder versus threatened harm, however, taking another's life is considered the greater of the two evils. The threat has to be immediate, and the accused cannot be a member of the group planning to commit the offence.

Necessity

The defence of necessity is applied in situations in which a person must break the law to avoid a greater evil caused by natural physical forces (storms, earthquakes, illness). This defence is available only when committing the crime is the lesser of two evils. For example, a person lacking a driver's licence is justified in driving a car to escape a fire. However, as the famous English case *Regina v. Dudley and Stephens* indicates, necessity does not justify the intentional killing of another.[23] In that case, three sailors and a cabin boy had been shipwrecked and were floating in the open seas in a lifeboat. After nine days without food and seven without water, two of the sailors, Dudley and Stephens, killed and ate the cabin boy. Four days later, the sailors were rescued. The court acknowledged that the cabin boy most likely would have died naturally because he was in the weakest condition, but nevertheless judged the killing unjustified.

In Canada a similar situation involved a man named Martin Hartwell, who piloted a plane that crashed in the Northwest Territories in 1972. Severely injured, he survived for 31 days, from November 8, when he crashed with three passengers, to December 9, when he was rescued. One passenger, a nurse, died on impact, and another, a pregnant woman needing surgery for a premature baby, was injured in the crash and died a few days later. A young boy suffering from acute appendicitis survived for three weeks, during which time the two ate corned beef, sugar cubes, snow, soap, and candles. During an inquest into events surrounding the crash it was revealed that the pilot had survived by resorting to cannibalism. It was not known whether criminal charges were ever preferred against the pilot, but his actions would certainly have fallen under the defence of necessity.[24]

Self-Defence

Self-defence involves a claim that the defendant's actions were a justified response to the provocative behaviour of the victim. Self-defence can be used to protect one's person or one's property.

An individual is justified in using force against another to protect himself or herself against unprovoked assault (CCC s. 34). When that happens, the person claims to have acted in self-defence and is therefore not guilty of the harm done. If the defendant was justified in using

In August 2000, tension erupted at the Burnt Church native reserve. In a standoff between the Department of Fisheries and Oceans and native fishers, the natives pressed for their demand to have their fishing rights recognized, rights that had been affirmed by the Supreme Court of Canada.

force, self-defence excuses such crimes as murder, manslaughter, and assault and battery. The law, however, has set limits as to what is reasonable and necessary self-defence. First, defendants must have a reasonable belief that they are in danger of death or great harm and that it is necessary for them to use force to prevent harm to themselves. For example, if Mary threatens to kill Jan but it is obvious that Mary is unarmed, Jan is not justified in pulling her gun and shooting Mary. However, if Mary, after threatening Jan, reaches into her pocket as if to get a gun and Jan then pulls her gun and shoots Mary, Jan could claim self-defence, even if it is discovered that Mary was unarmed. In this situation, Jan had a reasonable belief that harm was imminent and that it was necessary to shoot first to avoid injury to herself.

In 1990 the Supreme Court of Canada ruled that in the case of a battered woman the threat need not be imminent if it is part of a pattern of domestic violence (*R. v. Lavallee*, S.C.C. 852). Lynn Lavallee was a battered woman in a volatile relationship; she killed her partner late one night by shooting him in the back of the head as he left her room. The shooting occurred after an argument in which the appellant had been physically abused and was fearful for her life after being taunted with the threat that either she kill him or he would get her. This case created what has become known as the "battered woman syndrome," an area of law in which Canada is the leader.

Second, the amount of force used must be no greater than that necessary to prevent personal harm. For instance, if Steve punches Ben, Ben could not justifiably hit Steve with an iron rod. Ben could, however, punch Steve back if he believed Steve was going to continue punching. The rules concerning self-defence also apply to situations involving the defence of a third person. Thus, if a person reasonably believes that another is in danger of unlawful bodily harm from an assailant, the person may use the force necessary to prevent the danger. Using force to defend one's property from trespass or theft is allowable if the force is reasonable. This means that the use of force should be a last resort after requests to stop interfering with the property or legal action have failed. This is based on the social policy that human life is more important than property.

Entrapment

Entrapment is another defence that excuses a defendant from criminal liability. The entrapment defence is raised when the defendant maintains that law enforcement officers induced him or her to commit a crime. The defendant would not have committed the crime had it not been for trickery, persuasion, or fraud on the officers' part. In other words, if law enforcement officers plan a crime, implant the criminal idea in a person's mind, and pressure that

person into doing the act, the person may plead entrapment. However, the police cannot induce a person to break the law. This situation is different from that in which an officer simply provides an opportunity for the crime to be committed and the defendant is willing and ready to do the act. For example, if a plainclothes police officer poses as a potential customer and is approached by a prostitute, no entrapment has occurred. However, if the same officer approaches a woman and persuades her to commit an act of prostitution, the defence of entrapment is appropriate. Several Supreme Court cases have ruled that the police cannot randomly test a citizen's virtue.

The Canadian Charter of Rights and Freedoms

The Charter of Rights and Freedoms is the ultimate arbiter of law and legal rights in Canada. All laws must operate in such a way as not to violate the rights guaranteed

Culture, Gender, Ethnicity, and Criminology

What Happens When People Go Outside the Law, to Uphold the Law

In the middle of the afternoon on November 11, 1986, Stephen Kesler, his wife, and two daughters were working in their small store in Calgary when two men entered. One demanded that Mrs. Kesler fill a pillowcase with drugs. The other man removed $150 from the cash register. Kesler attacked him and chased him from the store with a shotgun. According to a witness, Kesler shouted at the fleeing robber to stop, but when he continued to run, Kesler shot him fatally in the back.

Kesler returned to the store to confront the other man who was armed with a .22. Five shots were fired, and Kesler was hit in the shoulder. Apparently out of ammunition, the man fled. Kesler chased him and began to beat him with the butt of his shotgun. Kesler was restrained by a passerby, and

the police arrived. He was charged with second-degree murder, but was eventually found not guilty, even though the prosecution argued that when the shot was fired, the accused was not preventing an assault on himself (Grayson 1992).

The idea of going outside the law in order to enforce social order is not new. Instead of asking why people deviate, perhaps it would be better to ask why people conform.

On the U.S. frontier, vigilantism was common in the absence of organized law enforcement. The localization of justice remains in the U.S. system today because most criminal law is a matter of state jurisdiction, and there is significant variation across the country. In Canada, however, the definition of offences against the criminal law is defined by the federal government; this enables a quick response to perceived threats to national security such as rebellions, riots, and political dissent.

When Canada was still a young country, the North West Mounted Police was an important force in maintaining order. However, before its arrival, the law had been administered in a different way. In the Yukon, for example, in the mid-1890s, law was administered in a process called the miners' meeting, an example of frontier justice. Anyone could air a grievance, criminal or civil, and the assembled parties reached a verdict and decided on the disposition in the case.

Palmer (1978) notes that in the 19th century people who violated certain standards of behaviour might be subject to various forms of "misrule." The offender might be seized, put on a donkey or wooden beam, and ridden about town or along a country road to the derision of the crowd. Physical beatings, tarrings and featherings, and even killings were not unheard of; an escalating pattern of violence across the

Canadas in the early 1800s led to a series of local bylaws outlawing the "charivari" as an outrageous act of barbarism. Palmer estimates that hundreds of such ritualized confrontations took place over the course of the 19th century and were common until the beginning of the 20th century.

It might be surprising to realize that Canadians and Americans are equally supportive of spontaneous vigilantism, even though Canada has the lower crime rate and Canadians have high confidence in their police. When individuals identify with the established order but resort to means that break the law in order to uphold the established order, they are called vigilantes. Given that spontaneous vigilantes may be the intended or actual victims of crimes and that juries frequently acquit those who can be viewed as meting out justice, it is clear that vigilantism might be seen as extra-legal, rather than simply outside the law. Even the police and juries are sometimes prepared to accept what some might feel to be excessive actions.

Paul Grayson (1992) summarizes five forms of vigilantism: crime-control vigilantism, practised against people who are believed to be violating the law; group-control vigilantism, which is by people in power against those who are revolting against that power; regime-control vigilantism, which is establishment violence designed to consolidate power; organized vigilantism, which is planned out in advanced; and spontaneous vigilantism, which occurs to prevent an immediately perceived threat. In all cases, it can be argued, vigilantism occurs to repair a break in the normative order.

These ritualized confrontations were quite often means of maintaining social control, but this might not necessarily be desirable in the 21st century. For example, Dobash and Dobash (1981) describe how misrules and charivaris were sometimes carried out against men who beat their wives. However, the intent was not to stop the violence but to set limits on the husband's right to discipline his wife. In this way the misrule upheld patriarchal relations between men and women. In France in the 18th century rituals for men who beat their wives were restricted to May. In England in the 19th century, wife beaters were subject to a parade of men, women, and children beating bells, kettles, and frying pans who proceeded to the house of the offending man, where they would chant rhymes and songs.

In the cuckold's court, men were ridiculed publicly if it was thought they were doing women's work, if they were henpecked, or cuckolded. Their crime was permitting an inversion of the proper roles men and women should occupy in a marriage. In Britain from 1500 for at least 200 years a woman could be subject to public ridicule if she was domineering or quarrelsome. Forced to wear a "scold's bridle" she would be paraded through the village. By the 20th century such ritual shamings and confrontations had pretty much disappeared. Conflict resolutions have been appropriated by the state, which reserves to itself the right to try an accused and subject them to punishment if found guilty. Regulation and surveillance have become part of the monopoly of the state.

Existing law does not recognize the legitimacy of retribution carried out by individual citizens. However, a large proportion of Canadians report qualified support for vigilantism. Given the objective differences in crime rates between Canada and the United States, it is not surprising that more Americans than Canadians feel threatened by the circumstances in which they live. However, the Canadian support is surprising.

In 1988, for example, Statistics Canada's survey on personal risk revealed that while only 21 percent of Canadians felt there had been an increase in crime in their area over the previous year, in 1989 a Gallup poll reported that 53 percent of Americans believed there had been an increase in crime in their area. Similarly, the 1989 U.S. General Social Survey revealed that 40 percent of Americans specified that they would be afraid to walk in areas around their neighbourhoods at night. A similar question asked by Statistics Canada in 1988 found that only 25 percent of Canadians would be afraid.

In a poll undertaken by Gallup in January 1985 just after the Kesler incident, 70 percent specified that such actions were "sometimes" justified and 8 percent "always" justified.

Sources: Russell P. Dobash, and R. Emerson Dobash, "Community Response to Violence Against Wives: Charivari, Abstract Justice and Patriarchy," *Social Problems* 28 (1981): 563–578; J. Paul Grayson, "Vigilantism in Canada and the United States," *Legal Studies Forum,* 16 (1992): 21–39; W.R. Morrison, *Showing the Flag: The Mounted Police and Canadian Sovereignty in the North, 1894-1925* (Vancouver: University of British Columbia Press, 1985); Bryan D. Palmer, "Discordant Music: Charivaris and Whitecapping in Nineteenth Century North America," *Labour* (1978), 3: np; Thomas Stone, "The Mounties as Vigilantes: Perceptions of Community and the Transformation of Law in the Yukon," *Law and Society Review* 14 (1979), Fall.

under the Charter. The impact of the Charter has been great. Because it guarantees rights to the individual that cannot be abridged except in unusual circumstances, these rights are said to be "inalienable." A person has a right to a lawyer, and appeals of convictions have been launched based on an accused person being denied access to legal advice. However, the Charter has been criticized for doing too much to protect the rights of individuals and not enough to protect society.

The Charter is included in the Constitution Act, which was repatriated from Britain in 1982. Rather than providing an extended discussion at this point, we will refer to the Charter and some its famous cases throughout this text. In *R. v. Stinchcombe* (1991), for example, it was ruled that the prosecution must give all the evidence gathered by the police to the defendant so that he or she can make a complete defence to the charges. This is known as **disclosure**, and it has become a fundamental

Table 2.3	Constitution Act 1982—Canadian Charter of Rights and Freedoms—Legal Rights

Whereas Canada is founded upon principles that recognize the supremacy of God and the rule of law ...

LIFE, LIBERTY AND SECURITY OF THE PERSON

7. Everyone has the right to life, liberty and security of the person and the right not to be deprived thereof except in accordance with the principles of fundamental justice.

SEARCH OR SEIZURE

8. Everyone has the right to be secure against unreasonable search or seizure.

DETENTION OR IMPRISONMENT

9. Everyone has the right not to be arbitrarily detained or imprisoned.

ARREST OR DETENTION

10. Everyone has the right on arrest or detention
    (a) to be informed promptly of the reasons therefor;
    (b) to retain and instruct counsel without delay and to be informed of that right; and
    (c) to have the validity of the detention determined by way of habeas corpus and to be released if the detention is not lawful.

PROCEEDINGS IN CRIMINAL AND PENAL MATTERS

11. Any person charged with an offence has the right
    (a) to be informed without unreasonable delay of the specific offence;
    (b) to be tried within a reasonable time;
    (c) not to be compelled to be a witness in proceedings against that person in respect of that offence;
    (d) to be presumed innocent until proven guilty according to law in a fair and public hearing by an independent and impartial tribunal;
    (e) not to be denied reasonable bail without just cause;
    (f) except in the case of an offence under military law tried before a military tribunal, to the benefit of trial by jury where the maximum punishment for the offence is imprisonment for five years or a more severe punishment;
    (g) not to be found guilty on account of any act or omission unless, at the time of the act or omission, it constituted an offence under Canadian or international law or was criminal according to the general principles of law recognized by the community of nations;
    (h) if finally acquitted of the offence, not to be tried for it again and, if finally found guilty and punished for the offence, not to be tried or punished for it again; and
    (i) if found guilty for the offence and if the punishment for the offence has been varied between the time of commission and the time of sentencing, to the benefit of the lesser punishment.

TREATMENT OR PUNISHMENT

12. Everyone has the right not to be subjected to any cruel or unusual treatment or punishment.

SELF-INCRIMINATION

13. A witness who testified in any proceedings has the right not to have any incriminating evidence so given used to incriminate that witness in any other proceedings except in a prosecution for perjury or for the giving of contradictory evidence.

INTERPRETER

14. A party or witness in any proceedings who does not understand or speak the language in which the proceedings are conducted or who is deaf has the right to the assistance of an interpreter.

principle of Canadian justice. The principle of disclosure figured largely in the discussion of the wrongful conviction of Donald Marshall, where it was found that the prosecution had evidence that could have been the basis for his release had it been known to the defence. In the case of Donald Marshall, a special provision in the Criminal Code was invoked and was instrumental in his eventual release. The statute is Section 690, by which the Minister of Justice can direct a new trial or appeal if it seems warranted. A group called the Association in Defence of the Wrongfully Convicted has played a very important role in securing reviews of wrongful convictions, as seen in the box "Famous Canadian Criminals."

Changing the Criminal Law

In recent years, many governments have been examining their substantive criminal law. Since the law, in part, reflects public opinion regarding various forms of behaviour, what was a crime 40 years ago may not be considered so today. The crime of possessing marijuana, for example, has been virtually decriminalized with penalties reduced to a fine instead of a prison sentence. In May 1999, Health Minister Allan Rock allowed people to apply to use marijuana for medicinal purposes. However, because there was no legal way to obtain the drug, it was inevitable that someone would be charged for growing it. In December 2000, an Alberta judge stayed a charge against Grant Krieger for cultivating marijuana. In April 2001, it was announced that Canada will become the only country in the world with a government-regulated system for using marijuana as medicine. The health minister denied that this was the thin edge of the wedge for legalizing marijuana. In 2001, the Supreme Court agreed to hear the case of Chris Clay, convicted of drug possession and trafficking. His argument: that marijuana laws are unconstitutional!

Other former criminal offences, such as gambling, have been almost totally legalized and all criminal penalties have been removed. With respect to some other laws, however, penalties have been toughened, especially for violent crimes such as rape and spousal assault.

In some instances, new criminal laws have been created to conform to emerging social issues. For example, **assisted suicide** has recently become the subject of legal debate in both Canada and the United States. In Michigan, reflecting what lawmakers believed to be prevailing public opinion, a statutory ban was passed in an effort to stop Dr. Jack Kevorkian from practising what he calls obitiatry, helping people take their lives.[25] A similar law in Canada was challenged in 1998, when Dr. Nancy Morrison, a respirologist at Victoria General Hospital in Halifax, Nova Scotia, was charged with ending the life of a terminally ill cancer patient after he had been taken off

life support.[26] Unlike Kevorkian, Morrison was eventually acquitted, an outcome that sheds doubt on the wisdom of such laws. Assisted suicide is but one of many emerging social issues that have prompted the call for change in the criminal law.

Connections

Euthanasia and assisted suicide are discussed in more detail in Chapter 14, where issues surrounding the rightful connection between the law and morality are debated.

Another area in which it is clear that the law is always evolving concerns what has come to be known as "stalking." The Canadian federal government and more than 25 U.S. states have enacted **stalking** statutes, which prohibit and punish acts described typically as "the willful, malicious and repeated following and harassing of another person."[27]

Stalking, or criminal harassment, was added to the Criminal Code in 1993; in 1999 5382 incidents of criminal harassment were reported to police, up 32 percent from 1996. Although stalking laws were originally formulated to protect women terrorized by former husbands and boyfriends, the laws have often been applied to people stalked by strangers or casual acquaintances. There has been criticism that the reaction to the perceived threat of stalking has been exaggerated and that stalking covers other behaviours that are already against the law, such as trespassing. However, others have argued that the gendered character of the crime has finally been recognized.

Community notification is a "quasi-legal" response to public concern about sexual predators moving into neighbourhoods. In Canada there is no general legal policy regarding whether the public should be warned about the release of sexual offenders, but in 2001 Ontario became the first province to develop a sex offender registry. Due to some high-profile cases, in 1996 the U.S. federal government passed legislation requiring that the general public be informed of the existence of convicted pedophiles in their midst.[28] Similarly, new laws have been passed to keep sexually dangerous individuals under control. For example, California's "sexual predator" law allows authorities to keep some criminals in custody even after their sentences are served. In Canada the Crown can apply on conviction, but before sentencing, to have an offender classified as a "dangerous offender" (CCC s. 753). This means that such offenders can be held in jail indefinitely. While there are fewer than 300 dangerous offenders in Canada, public concern is that they pose a very serious threat to public safety.

Related to societal concerns about dangerous sexual predators, in 2000 a National DNA Data Bank was launched in Canada, which enables judges to authorize

Famous Canadian Criminals

Wrongfully Convicted

David Milgaard was sentenced in 1970 to life imprisonment for murder; a second s.690 application was granted in 1991; a new trial was ordered by the Supreme Court of Canada in 1992 and the charges were then stayed. He was subsequently exonerated by DNA testing arranged by AIDWYC in 1997.

Donald Marshall Jr. was sentenced in 1971 to life imprisonment for murder; a s.690 application was granted in 1982; he was acquitted by the Nova Scotia Court of Appeal in 1983.

Wilson Nepoose was sentenced in 1987 to life imprisonment for murder; in 1991 a s.690 application resulted in his case being referred to the Alberta Court of Appeal; a new trial was ordered in 1992; a retrial was not proceeded with.

Wilfred Bcaulieu was sentenced in 1992 to three and a half years' imprisonment for two sexual assaults. A s.690 was allowed in 1996, his appeal was allowed by the Alberta Court of Appeal and an acquittal was subsequently entered in 1997.

Richard McArthur was sentenced in 1986 to life imprisonment for murder; a s.690 reference was granted in February, 1998; it was scheduled to be heard by the Alberta Court of Appeal in April 1999 at which time AIDWYC was advised an acquittal would be entered at the Crown's request.

Clayton Johnson was sentenced in 1993 to life imprisonment for murder; a s.690 application was filed by AIDWYC in March 1998; his case was referred to Nova Scotia Court of Appeal in September, 1998. Johnson was free on bail when he heard in 2002 that the Crown was dropping all charges.

Rejean Hinse was sentenced in 1964 to 15 years' imprisonment for armed robbery; he was acquitted by the Supreme Court of Canada in 1997 after being granted an extension of time to appeal.

Richard Norris was sentenced in 1980 to 23 months' imprisonment for sexual assault; he was acquitted in 1991 by the Ontario Court of Appeal after being granted an extension of time to appeal.

Michael McTaggart was sentenced in 1987 to five years' imprisonment for bank robbery convictions; a new trial was ordered by the Ontario Court of Appeal in 1990; the charges were withdrawn four months later.

Thomas Sophonow was sentenced in 1983 to life imprisonment for murder; he was reconvicted in 1985; an acquittal was entered in December 1985 by the Manitoba Court of Appeal. AIDWYC is working on DNA testing in his case.

Gregory Parsons was sentenced in 1994 to life imprisonment for murder; the Newfoundland Court of Appeal ordered a new trial in 1996; a stay of proceedings was entered in 1998 based on DNA testing; AIDWYC intervened before the Newfoundland Supreme Court on a Charter application to set aside the stay and have an acquittal entered; an acquittal was entered with the consent of the Crown in November 1998.

Guy Paul Morin was sentenced in 1992 to life imprisonment for murder; an acquittal was entered by the Ontario Court of Appeal in 1995 as a result of DNA testing.

Lierman Kagliek was sentenced in 1993 to 10 years' imprisonment for sexual assaults; the Court of Appeal in the Northwest Territories entered an acquittal in 1998 based on DNA findings.

Steven Truscott was sentenced to death in 1959 for capital murder; his sentence was commuted to life imprisonment in 1960; his conviction was upheld in 1967 after a Reference to the Supreme Court of Canada; AIDWYC is now preparing a s. 690 application on Truscott's behalf.

Donzel Young was sentenced in 1991 to life imprisonment for murder; a s.690 application was filed in 1995 by Young and AIDWYC; Young was murdered in prison in 1995; Mr. Justice Kaufman was appointed by the Minister to review the case. However, due to witnesses disappearing, his case is now in limbo.

The Association in Defence of the Wrongly Convicted (AIDWYC), founded in 1993, is dedicated to preventing wrongful convictions and reversing those that have already occurred. They believe these cases represent a small percentage of those wrongly convicted in Canada.

the collection of DNA samples from convicted offenders. DNA was first used in an RCMP investigation in 1989, and the trial of Alan Legere was the first to use DNA evidence.

So far in this section on changing laws, we have looked at crimes that are fairly familiar. Let us now look at an area of concern that has the potential to affect more

Exhibit 2.3	Quick Code: Criminal Harassment, Section 264, CCC

264(1) Criminal harassment

(1) No person shall, without lawful authority and knowing that another person is harassed or recklessly as to whether the other person is harassed, engage in conduct referred to in subsection (2) that causes that other person reasonably, in all the circumstances, to fear for their safety or the safety of anyone known to them.

264(2) Prohibited conduct

(2) The conduct mentioned in subsection (1) consists of
  (a) repeatedly following from place to place the other person or anyone known to them;
  (b) repeatedly communicating with, either directly or indirectly, the other person or anyone known to them;
  (c) besetting or watching the dwelling-house, or place where the other person, or anyone known to them, resides, works, carries on business or happens to be; or
  (d) engaging in threatening conduct directed at the other person or any member of their family.

264(3) Punishment

(3) Every person who contravenes this section is guilty of
  (a) an indictable offence and is liable to imprisonment for a term not exceeding five years; or
  (b) an offence punishable on summary conviction.

Source: R.S., 1985, c. C-46, s. 264; R.S., 1985, c. 27 (1st Supp.), s. 37; 1993, c. 45, s. 2.

people than most other crimes combined: high-tech crimes. A whole new breed of high-tech crimes are emerging that contain elements of fraud, theft, swindles, and false claims. These crimes are difficult to categorize because they can be committed by corporations and individuals, can be singular or ongoing, and can involve the theft of information, identity, resources, or funds. High-tech crimes cost consumers billions of dollars each year and will increase dramatically in the years to come. They are also difficult to detect and police. What are some of these emerging forms of white-collar crime?

Millions of people worldwide are on the Internet, and the number entering cyberspace is growing rapidly. Criminal entrepreneurs view this vast pool as a target for high-tech crimes. There have been a number of highly

publicized cases in which adults have solicited teenagers in Internet "chat rooms." Others have used the Internet to sell and distribute obscene material, prompting some service providers to censor or control sexually explicit material.

In March 2001, legislation was introduced to create tough penalties to rid the Internet of child pornography. The new crime of "Internet luring," with a maximum penalty of five years in prison, is in response to reports that pedophiles use Internet chat rooms and false identities to entice children away from their homes. The legislation makes it a crime to transmit child pornography on the Net, make child pornography available in cyberspace, or possess it for the purpose of transmitting it, making it available or exporting it. The offences all carry a maximum penalty of 10 years in prison.

Bogus get-rich-quick schemes, weight-loss scams, and investment swindles have also been pitched on the Internet. In some cases these fraudulent acts can be dangerous to clients. For example, in a 1995 case a Minnesota woman advertised the health benefits of "germanium" on an Internet provider, claiming that it could cure AIDS, cancer, and other diseases. Germanium products, however, have been banned because they cause irreversible kidney damage.[29]

Other future directions of the criminal law remain unclear; both expansions and contractions can be expected. Certain actions, such as crimes by corporations and political corruption, will be given more attention. Other offences, such as recreational drug use, may be reduced in importance or removed entirely from the criminal law system. In addition, changing technology will require modification in the criminal law. For example, such technologies as automated teller machines and cellular phones have already spawned a new generation of criminal acts involving "theft" of access numbers and cards and software piracy. As the "information highway" is laid down, as the nation's computer network advances, and as biotechnology produces new substances, the criminal law will be forced to address threats to the public safety that today are unknown. On the other hand, developments in technology, such as DNA testing and electronic monitoring, will change the way in which criminal investigation and punishment are carried out.

Connections

The criminal law must be constantly modified to include areas that only a few years earlier were unknown. Chapter 13 contains sections on technological crimes, including the emerging areas of computer crime.

Summary

The substantive criminal law is a set of rules that specifies the behaviour society has outlawed. The criminal law can be distinguished from the civil law on the basis that the former involves powers given to the state to enforce social rules, while the latter controls interactions between private citizens. The criminal law serves several important purposes: It represents public opinion and moral values, it enforces social controls, it deters criminal behaviour and wrongdoing, it punishes transgressors, and it banishes private retribution. It can also entrench the interests of the powerful and be used to resist social change. The criminal law used in Canada and the United States traces its origin to the English common law, which was formulated during the Middle Ages when King Henry II's judges began to use precedents set in one case to guide actions in another in a system called *stare decisis*.

In Canada's legal system, common-law crimes have been codified by lawmakers into the federal criminal code. Today, most crimes fall into the category of indictable offences—serious crimes usually punished by a prison term—or summary offences—minor crimes that carry a fine or a light jail sentence. The former include murder, rape, assault with a deadly weapon, and robbery; the latter include simple assault and the possession of small amounts of drugs.

Every crime has specific elements. In most instances, these elements include the *actus reus* (guilty act), which is the actual physical part of the crime (for example, taking money or burning a building), and the *mens rea* (guilty mind), which refers to the state of mind of the individual who commits a crime—more specifically, the person's intent to do the act.

At trial, accused individuals can defend themselves by claiming to have lacked *mens rea* and, therefore, not being responsible for the criminal actions. One type of defence is excuse for mental reasons, such as insanity, intoxication, necessity, or duress. Another defence is justification by reason of self-defence or entrapment. Of all defences, insanity is perhaps the most controversial. In most cases, persons using an insanity defence claim that they did not know what they were doing when they committed a crime or that their mental state did not allow them to tell the difference between right and wrong (the McNaughtan Rule). Insanity defences can also include the claims that the offender lacked the substantial capacity to conform his or her conduct to the criminal law. Regardless of the insanity defence used, critics charge that mental illness is separate from legal responsibility and that the two should not be equated. Supporters counter that the insanity defence allows mentally ill people to avoid penal sanctions.

The criminal law is undergoing constant reform. Some acts are being decriminalized—their penalties are being reduced—while laws are being revised to make penalties for some acts more severe. The law must confront social and technological change.

Thinking Like a Criminologist

The Canadian Parliament is considering passing some new laws designed to meet the changing social and economic landscape. The parliamentarians have asked you, a criminologist, to appear before the Justice Committee on Criminal Code reform in order to identify some of the emerging areas in which legal controls are needed. One area of concern is whether laws should be passed to control the use of the Internet: for example, regulating the sale of digital information, including data, text, images, sounds, computer programs, software, and databases. The fear is that unscrupulous entrepreneurs may use the Net to sell undesirable material such as pornography.

Would you advise Parliament to control the Net closely? What dangers might be presented by such an attempt at regulation? Is there a tradeoff between individual rights and social security?

Key Terms

actus reus
assisted suicide
Code of Hammurabi
common law
community notification
constructive intent
disclosure
duress
entrapment
folkways
general deterrence

indictable offence
insanity
inchoate crimes
lex talionis
mala in se
mala prohibitum
McNaughtan Rule
mens rea
mores
Mosaic Code
oath-helpers

specific deterrence
stalking
stare decisis
strict-liability crimes
summary offence
tort law
transferred intent
vagrancy
wergild

 See the book-specific website at www.siegelcriminology2e.nelson.com for additional chapter links, discussions, and quizzes.

Chapter

3

The Nature and Extent of Crime

How much crime is there? What are the patterns and trends in crime? Who commits crime? What is the nature of criminality? These are some of the most important questions in the study of criminology. Without such information, it would not be possible to formulate theories that explain the onset of crime or to devise social policies that facilitate its control or elimination.

In this chapter, data collected on criminal offences are reviewed in some detail and then used to provide an introductory summary of crime patterns and trends. These patterns are then described in more detail in Chapters 11 through 14. This chapter addresses a number of questions: Are crime rates increasing? What factors influence crime rate trends? Where and when does crime take place? What are the social and individual patterns that affect the crime rate? What effect do social class, age, gender, and race have on the crime rate? Finally, the chapter reviews the concept of criminal careers and what available crime data can tell us about the onset, continuation, and termination of criminality.

The above questions address the issue of how to explain crime. However, the factors that cause criminal behaviour are different from those forces that affect what we know about crime. One issue that will become apparent is that a "crime rate" does more than reflect the simple increase or decrease of crime. There are five reasons why crime rates change: (1) some crimes are **report-sensitive**, which means that the willingness of the public to report the crime determines whether or not we know about it; (2) **policing-sensitive** crimes reflect the level of police enforcement; (3) the rates for crimes that are **definition-sensitive** can change if the law does; and (4) **media-sensitive** crimes cause a "feedback loop" when they are publicized, changing the perceptions of the public and their willingness to report. And of course the fifth reason why crime rates change is that there really is a change in the number of crimes in society, which leads us to ask what factors are responsible.

In this first section of the chapter, we will look at the official statistics on crime and consider what they do and do not tell us about crime. In the second section, we will look at such factors as age and class and briefly consider how they might be causes of crime.

The Uniform Crime Report

The Canadian Centre for Justice Statistics (CCJS) has collected information on crime reported by the police every year since 1962 through the **Uniform Crime Report (UCR)** survey. This is an aggregate census based on nearly 100 percent compliance by 1800 separate police locations made up of about 420 different police forces across Canada. The UCR represents crimes substantiated through police investigation and is an invaluable base from which

to study crime in society. In 1984 the UCR was revised so that it could collect more detailed information on crime variables such as accused and victim characteristics (e.g., age, sex, alcohol and drug consumption, victim–offender relationship, and level of injury), and incident characteristics (e.g., location, time, secondary violations, and weapons). The first police departments to collect and report **incident-based data** were the Niagara Regional and Fredericton police departments. In the year 2000 Trend Database, information from 166 police agencies represents about 53 percent of the national volume of reported crime. As well as the two UCR surveys, the CCJS has collected detailed information on murder in the Homicide Survey since 1961.

Collecting the UCR

The methods used to compile the UCR are quite complex. Each month, police agencies report the **incidence** or number of crimes known to them to the Canadian Centre for Justice Statistics. This "crime count" is taken from records of all complaints of crime these agencies received from victims or from officers who discovered the infractions. This crime database represents only official knowledge about crimes, since some crimes are never detected, and some are not reported to the police. Various checks are performed on the validity of the crime statistics before the results are made public.

Whenever complaints of crime are determined, through investigation, to be unfounded or false, they are eliminated from the count. The number of offences known is then recorded in the aggregate statistics. This happens even if no one is arrested for the crime, or if stolen property is recovered, or if a prosecution is undertaken.

The UCR uses several terms to express crime data. First, the number of crimes reported to the police and arrests made are expressed as raw figures (for example, 536 murders occurred in 1999). Second, the **percentage change** in the amount of crime between years is computed (for example, the police reported crime dropped 1 percent in 2000). The percentage change is important, because it is a "soft indicator" of whether society is becoming more dangerous. In 2000, the property crime rate decreased 5 percent, and the violent crime rate increased 1 percent after seven years' decline.

The third, and perhaps most important, way of expressing crime data is the crime rate per 100 000 people. Calculating the **crime rate** involves dividing the total crimes by the population; this enables changes in the population to be ignored when looking at changes in crime. For example, when the UCR indicates that the murder rate was 2 in 1999, it means that 2 people in every 100 000 were murdered between January 1 and December 31 of 1999. Out of a population of 30.5 million people, 536 murders occurred. Therefore, the likelihood of a person being murdered is very low in Canada.

The standard way to display the incidence and rate of crime is to show all the crimes reported to the police that are felt to be **founded**—in other words, the information excludes false reports and is not weighted by the relative population. For example, Ontario had 187 murders in 1996, while Prince Edward Island had 1. However Ontario also had a far greater population base than Prince Edward Island, skewing the absolute number of crimes. When that is factored in, Prince Edward Island's murder rate is 1/100 000, and Ontario's is 2/100 000. The overall incidence of murder in Canada in 1999 was 536 cases, and the rate of murder was around 2 per 100 000 people.

Table 3.1 shows information about selected crimes in Canada. For example, the incidence of violent crime is low relative to the amount of property crime committed in Canada. In 2000 there were 2 593 580 total Criminal Code offences in Canada (including traffic), 301 857 of which were violent crimes (10 percent). Property crime, however, accounted for 1 251 667 offences, or 56 percent of all offences. "Other" Criminal Code offences such as prostitution and gaming accounted for almost three-quarters of a million more offences. It is apparent that abductions are few (751), while minor thefts (under $5000) were numerous (662 616).

As can be seen in Figure 3.1, the crime rate varies across Canada, with the lowest rate in the east and the highest in the western provinces. There has been little attempt to measure this phenomenon. Timothy Hartnagel suggests that provinces with a high rate of in-migration have higher rates of property and violent crime.[1] He believes that geographic mobility produces weakened informal social control. Large-scale changes in the economy combined with a rapid change in population are destabilizing.

In addition, police agencies report the total crimes that were cleared. To say that a crime is cleared does not mean that a person was cleared of suspicion, even though that would be the common meaning. Crimes are cleared in two ways: (1) when at least one person is arrested, charged, and turned over to the court for prosecution, or (2) by exceptional means, when some element beyond police control precludes the physical arrest of an offender (for example, the offender leaves the country). A case can be "cleared by charge" even if someone is not arrested, and a case can be "cleared otherwise" even if no charge is laid. The clearance rate for homicide was 74 percent in 2000, while a minor theft had a likelihood of being cleared 20 percent of the time. If 72 percent of violent offences and 22 percent of property violations were cleared, 38 and 78 percent, respectively, of crime and property violations go uncleared. In fact, the clearance rate underestimates the total number of crimes solved by the police, because most crimes are not reported to the authorities.

From the time a crime is reported to the police, the number of cases in the system drops as they move through the system. This process is called attrition, and the result is what criminologists call a crime funnel. The

Table 3.1	Incidence, rate, and clearance status of selected crimes, Canada, 2000		
	ACTUAL	**RATE**	**CLEARANCE STATUS (%)**
CRIMES OF VIOLENCE	**301 875**	**982**	**72**
Homicide	542	2	74
Sexual assault	24 049	78	65
Nonsexual assault	245 650	799	77
Abduction	751	2	56
Robbery	27 012	88	36
PROPERTY CRIME	**1 251 667**	**4 070**	**22**
Break and enter	293 416	954	17
Motor vehicle theft	160 268	521	12
Theft over $5000	21 381	70	17
Theft $5000 and under	662 616	2 155	20
Fraud	90 568	297	59
OTHER CRIMES	**800 384**	**2 603**	**45**
Prostitution	5 0361	16	87
Gaming and betting	242	1	77
Offensive weapons	15 306	50	74
TOTAL CRIMINAL CODE (excluding traffic)	**2 353 926**	**7 655**	**36**
DRUGS	**87 945**	**286**	**80**
TOTAL INCIDENTS	**2 593 580**	**8 434**	**40**

Source: *Canadian Crime Statistics 2000*, Statistics Canada 2001, Catalogue No. 85-205-XPE.

idea of a funnel illustrates the fact that the number of crimes detected and punished by the criminal justice system is lower than the number committed. Of the total crimes committed, only 37 percent are estimated to have been reported in 1999. The clearance rate is 73 percent for violent crimes, 27 percent for property crimes, and 47 percent for "other," giving a 37 percent clearance rate overall. In other words, out of a hundred crimes, 37 will be reported, and 14 will be solved. Perhaps 3 or 4 percent go to court and result in a conviction.

Violent crimes are more likely to be solved than property crimes, probably because police devote more resources to these more serious acts, because witnesses

Figure 3.1   **Crime rates by province and territory, 2000**

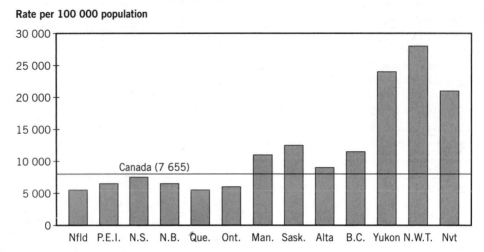

Rate per 100 000 population

SOURCE: Crime Statistics 2000, Statistics Canada, *The Daily,* July 19, 2001.

(including the victim) are available to identify offenders, and because, in many instances, the victim and offender were previously acquainted.

The Accuracy of the UCR

Despite the importance and wide use by criminologists of the UCR, its accuracy has been suspect. We'll address the five main areas of concern: reporting practices, law enforcement practices, legal definitions, media practices, and methodological problems.

Reporting Practices. One major concern of criminologists is that many serious crimes are not reported by victims to police and therefore do not become part of the UCR. This phenomenon means that crimes are report-sensitive. The reasons for not reporting vary. Some people do not have property insurance and therefore believe it is useless to report theft-related crimes. In other cases, the victim may fear reprisals from the offender's friends or family. In some cases people simply want to deal with it their way, whether that means forgetting it or getting revenge. The increase in levels of violence reported by women in recent years is probably due to an increase in the reporting of sexual assault and domestic violence against women. Between 1982 and 1991, the sexual assault rate more than doubled, compared to the rate for assault (63 percent), other violent offences (32 percent), and robbery (10 percent). The rate of sexual assault, as measured by Statistics Canada's 1993 Violence Against Women Survey, was 40 percent. The rates reported in the 1993 General Social Survey (16 percent) and again in 1999 (21 percent) were quite different.

The likelihood of crime victims reporting criminal incidents to the police varies from crime to crime.

Because of the difficulties posed by underreporting, victimization surveys are used to measure those crimes not reported to the police. The 1993 General Social Survey (GSS) showed that crime reports ranged from a low of 10 percent for sexual assault to a high of 68 percent for attempted break and enter. The average report rate for all household offences was 52 percent. The 1999 General Social Survey estimated that 78 percent of sexual assaults and 67 percent of household thefts were not reported to the police. That survey also showed that both women (8 percent) and men (7 percent) are victims of domestic violence.[2] Reasons for not reporting this crime include fear, shame, and the feeling that the victim is responsible. Some other reasons victims do not report crime to the police are because the victim believed the incident was "a private matter," that "nothing could be done," that the "victimization was not important enough," or because of the fear of revenge.[3] These findings indicate that the UCR data may significantly underrepresent the total number of annual criminal events.

Victimization surveys, also discussed later in this chapter, are now used in many countries to complement UCR data. The 2000 British Crime Survey (BCS) showed there were four and a half as many crimes reported by victims in the survey as were reported to the police.[4] The 2000 Scottish Crime Survey shows an official police crime rate 33 percent of that recorded in their study. The United States uses the National Crime Victimization Survey to supplement its UCR data.

Law Enforcement Practices. The way in which police departments record and report criminal and delinquent activity also affects the validity of UCR statistics. This means that some crimes are police-sensitive. This effect was recognized more than 40 years ago, when researchers

Connections

Victimization surveys are covered in more detail in Chapter 4. They have become a vitally important way of measuring the dark figures of crime—crimes that are is not reported to the police and thus that are not included in statistics.

found that the number of burglaries in New York City rose from 2726 to 42 491 between 1948 and 1952, and larcenies increased from 7713 to 70 949.[5] These increases were found to be related to the change from a precinct to a centralized reporting system for crime statistics.

Some local police departments make errors in UCR reporting, although the Canadian Centre for Justice Statistics does extensive checks on the data it receives. Of a more serious nature are allegations that police officials may deliberately alter reported crimes to improve their department's public image. Police administrators interested in lowering the crime rate may falsify crime reports, for example, by classifying a burglary as a nonreportable trespass. This was probably more of a problem in the past than today. Research published in 1983 found there were provincial differences in charge rates because of discretion on the part of the police.[6] Scott Wortley's work, discussed later in this chapter, looks at the effect of police discretion in the differential charge rates against nonwhites in Ontario.

Ironically, boosting police efficiency and professionalism may actually help increase crime rates. Higher crime rates may occur as departments adopt more sophisticated computer-aided technology and hire better-educated and better-trained employees. One study found that crime rates are significantly affected by the way law enforcement agencies process UCR data. As the number of unsworn (civilian) police employees assigned to dispatching, record keeping, and criminal incident reporting increased, so, too, did national crime rates. What appears to be a rising crime rate may have been an artifact of improved police record-keeping ability.[7] How law enforcement agencies interpret the definitions of crimes may also affect reporting practices. Some departments may define crimes loosely—for example, reporting a trespass as a burglary or an assault on a woman as an attempted rape—while others pay strict attention to guidelines. These reporting practices may help explain interjurisdictional differences in crime, especially in the past.[8] Patrick Jackson found, for example, that arson may be seriously underreported in the United States because many fire departments do not report to the FBI, and those that do define as accidental or spontaneous many fires that are probably set by arsonists.[9]

Such examples suggest that there are variations in how the police count crime. In addition, however, the way in which police enforce the law affects the crime rate as well. Crimes such as prostitution, drug crime, traffic offences, and crime on the Internet are sensitive to the level of policing, that is, the resources police devote to detecting the crime. Clearly, if the police go undercover they will be able to arrest far more prostitutes, johns, and pimps than if they wait for someone to report the crime to them.

However, it is difficult to know for certain how important variations in police charging practices are.[10] While the police have a lot of discretion in deciding whether to lay charges, the Crown, screening agencies, and alternative measures programs also affect the laying of charges in different jurisdictions. The simple development of zero-tolerance school violence policies has probably done a lot to increase the number of youths charged with nonsexual assault. This crime accounted for 73 percent of all youth violent offences in 2000.

Legal Definitions. Amendments to the Criminal Code in 1990 broadened the definition of arson to include mischief fires. Given that the cause was "unknown" in almost half of fires with losses of over $500 000, what counts as a "suspicious fire" has some latitude; this has seriously broadened the scope of arson and increased arson statistics.[11] Changes to the law and what comes under its scope also affect crime rates: Changes in the rates reflect changes in the legal definition of the crime. As Figure 3.2 shows, arson varied from approximately 30 to 40 incidents per 100 000 population from 1978 to 1990 except for a slight dip in 1989. Then it suddenly increased 17 percent between 1989 and 1990, solely because of a change in the definition of arson.

Interestingly, arson is a crime that is highly misunderstood. The popular misconception is that it is the work of a lone pyromaniac who likes to watch fires. However, some fires are set to collect insurance money, while others are set for revenge against a hated target. Arson is difficult to investigate, not because of the nature of the evidence, but because there is a high public tolerance for the crime.

An even more dramatic example of a definition-sensitive crime is sexual assault. Before 1983 a man could not be charged for sexually assaulting his wife. With the introduction of Bill C-127 in 1983, rape and indecent assault were replaced with sexual assault. Along with other changes designed to increase reporting, there was a subsequent increase in the number of men charged with the crime. Canada's sexual assault legislation was amended in 1988 to better deal with child sexual abuse, and in 1991 to include the concept of consent.

Other legislative changes which have affected criminal justice statistics are the Young Offenders Act (1984); Dangerous and Impaired Operation (1985), which allowed the police to take breath and blood samples; Property Value Limits (1985, 1995); and Bill C-68 (1997), which requires firearm owners to be licensed and to register their guns.

Media Practices. An additional factor to consider when looking at crime is the effect of the media. We often hear of seemingly random crimes, committed in public, by

| Figure 3.2 | Arson incidents 1978 to 1993 |

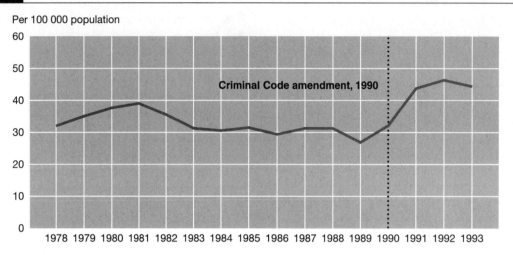

SOURCE: *Canadian Crime Statistics 1993.* Statistics Canada 1993, Catalogue No. 85–205, p. 50.

strangers against innocent victims. The current controversy over youth crime leads one to suspect that the public is being overexposed to a relatively infrequent type of crime. In 1996 7 percent of those charged with violent offences in Canada were youths, compared with almost 8 percent in 1995. The total number of youths charged with Criminal Code offences dropped further between 1996 and 1997, continuing a general decline since 1991. Youth property offences dropped dramatically at 12 percent, and violent offences for youths decreased 2 percent. However, there is a continuing feeling that youth crime is out of control and that "something must be done about it."

One way to explain the discrepancy between the reality of dropping rates of youth crime and the perception that youth crime is out of control is media coverage. The media may distort the frequency of youth crime, causing unease on the part of the public, much as we saw in Chapter 1 when we looked briefly at the fear of crime. As Table 3.2 shows, the type of youth crime cases the media report are not the same as those youths are charged with.

Youth courts in Canada have heard fewer cases in recent years compared with the early 1990s. This fact is consistent with the decline in police statistics mentioned above. In 1996, youth courts processed 110 065 cases, down 4 percent from 1992. Furthermore, the rate of property crime, a category that accounted for about half of all youth court cases, dropped 21 percent from 1992 to 1996. Violent crime increased by 2 percent over the five-year period, but mostly between 1992 and 1993. The most common crimes heard in youth court were theft of goods under $5000 and break and enter. Murder accounted for less than 1 percent of the cases heard in youth court.[12]

However, as we see in Table 3.2, while violent crimes accounted for 22 percent of the cases heard in Ontario's youth court, they represented 94 percent of stories about youth crime in the Toronto media. Property crime, which represented 50 percent of all youth court cases, appeared as the topic in only 5 percent of media stories. It seems clear that the public, who would have little knowledge of the types of cases in youth court, would get the message from the media that violent youth crime continued to be a large problem. This distorted media perception would affect the reported rates of youth crime and the public's willingness to press charges, and would eventually result in pressure on politicians to change the law. Figure 3.3 begins to map out this relationship. Where does the cycle end?

For many people, the Juristat series, a series of publications put out by the Canadian Centre for Justice Statistics, presents the only data available on crime. The work of creating official statistics about crime is different than that undertaken in producing academic research. Scientific reviewers are interested in the scientific merits of research. However, individuals in the CCJS try to strike a balance between "good news" and "bad news" stories about criminal justice.

The challenge for publications such as Juristat is to present its information in a way that makes it appealing to the media to report without misrepresenting the facts.[13] For example, the presentation of UCR statistics in the United States in the 1920s was designed to provide journalists with information about crime.[14] Today, the media influence the timing and wording of press releases, the type of statistics used, and the types of information presented. To make reporting easier, the CCJS employs an "information officer" who will provide the media with stories. It is quite often beyond the scope of a reporter's ability to question the production of statistical knowledge.[15]

Table 3.2	Comparing young offenders in the courts and the news, 1993–94	
	ONTARIO YOUTH COURT	**TORONTO NEWS**
Violent crime	11 004 (22%)	106 (94%)
Property crime	25 008 (50%)	6 (5%)
Other	8 942 (18%)	1 (1%)
YOA*	3 622 (7%)	—
Total	50 008 (100%)	113 (100%)

Note: Numbers may not add up to 100 percent due to missing categories.

* Statutory breaches of the Young Offenders Act

Source: Jane B. Sprott, "Understanding Public Views of Crime and the Youth Justice System," *Canadian Journal of Criminology* (July 1996): 271–90.

Figure 3.3	Crime as a topic

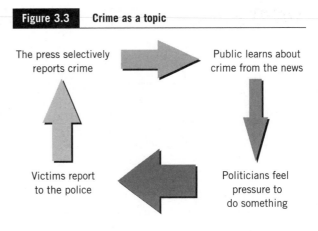

Methodological Problems. Methodological issues also raise questions about the usefulness and validity of the UCR. Among the most often cited are the following:

- The definition of a crime can change.
- Nonviolent crimes are underreported.
- Cases are screened as unfounded and founded.
- The notation "cleared by charge" may not be made in the month the offence was committed.
- Reports can sometimes vary in accuracy and completeness.
- If multiple crimes are committed by an offender, only the most serious is recorded.
- Each act is listed as a single offence for some crimes but not for others.[16]

What does the future hold for the UCR? The changes made in the form of the Revised UCR will enable better analysis of incidents and the characteristics of accused persons and their relationships to victims.

Self-Report Surveys

The problems associated with official statistics have led many criminologists to seek alternative sources of information to assess the true extent of crime patterns. In addition, official statistics do not say much about the personality, attitudes, and behaviour of individual criminals. They also are of little value in charting the extent of substance abuse in the population, because relatively few abusers are arrested. Criminologists have therefore sought additional sources to supplement and expand official data.

One commonly used alternative to official statistics is the **self-report survey**. Self-report studies are designed to allow participants to reveal information about their violations of the law. The studies have many formats. For example, the criminologist can approach people who have been arrested by police, or even prison inmates, and interview them about their illegal activities. Subjects can also first be telephoned at home and then mailed a survey form. Most often, self-report surveys are administered to large groups through a mass distribution of questionnaires. The names of subjects can be requested, but more commonly, they remain anonymous. The basic assumption of self-report studies is that the anonymity of the respondents and the promise of confidentiality backed by the academic credentials of the survey administrator will encourage people to accurately describe their illegal activities. Self-reports are viewed as another mechanism to get at the "dark figures of crime," the figures missed by official statistics.

The Focus of Self-Reports

Most self-report studies have focused on juvenile delinquency and youth crime, for two reasons.[17] First, the school setting makes it convenient to test thousands of subjects simultaneously, all of them with the means (pens, desks, time) to respond to a research questionnaire. Second, since school attendance is universal, a school-based self-report survey is an estimate of the activities of a cross-section of the community. Self-reports, though, are not restricted to youth crime and have been used to examine the offence histories of prison inmates, drug users, and other subsets of the population.

Self-reports make it possible to assess the number of people in the population who have committed illegal acts and the frequency of their law violations. They are particularly useful for assessing the extent of the national substance abuse problem, as most drug use goes undetected by police. And, because most self-report instruments also contain items measuring subjects' attitudes, values, personal characteristics, and behaviours, the data

Crime in the News

Man Gets 10 Years for Attack

Calgary. A man has been sentenced to 10 years in prison for attacking a bank machine user with a sledgehammer. Trevor Stang, 32,

was found guilty of aggravated assault after Jaafar Omar was hit over the head three times with a two-kg sledgehammer while trying to pay a gas bill at an automated teller. Stang then fled with $30 and Mr. Omar's car. "Mr. Omar

could've been anyone," said Justice Denis Hart. "Random violence ... strikes at the heart of a civilized society. Everyone is a potential victim, no one is immune."

National Post, May 12, 2001

obtained from them can be used for various purposes, such as testing theories, measuring attitudes toward crime, and computing the association between crime and important social variables, such as family relations, educational attainment, and income.

Self-reports provide a broader picture of the distribution of criminality than official data because they do not depend on the offender being apprehended. They also avoid the problem of "filtering out," which runs through official measures. They can be used to estimate the number of criminal offenders who are unknown to the police and who never figure in the official crime statistics, some of whom may even be serious or chronic offenders.[18] Since many criminologists believe that class, gender, and racial bias exists in the criminal justice system, self-reports allow evaluation of the distribution of criminal behaviour across racial, class, and gender lines. Their use enables criminologists to determine whether the official arrest data are truly representative of the offender population or whether they reflect bias, discrimination, and selective enforcement. For example, racial bias may be present if surveys indicate that blacks and whites report equal amounts of crime, but the official data indicate that minorities are arrested more often than whites. In sum, self-reports can provide a significant amount of information about offenders that cannot be found in the official statistics.

This source of information is used less in Canada than the United States. It was pioneered in the 1960s and has resulted in only a handful of studies.[19] The only one on adult criminals was conducted by the Institute for Social Research at York University and included self-report questions on crime in a study of public attitudes toward the law in Canada. However, a 1999 study was conducted by researchers from the University of Alberta and the University of Calgary and surveyed 2001 students aged 12 to 18 from 67 Alberta public and Catholic junior and senior high schools. Participants completed a questionnaire about their perceptions of youth crime, violence, and personal safety; victimization at school and away from school; the extent that they had engaged in delinquent behaviour; weapons possession at school; and their perceptions of and contact with the police and the criminal justice system.

In an another self-report study, this one done in 2000, the Centre for Addiction and Mental Health and the University of Montreal conducted the first national survey of alcohol and other drug use, called the Canadian Campus Survey (CCS). The survey was conducted in the fall of 1998, and collected responses from 7800 undergraduate students in 16 Canadian universities. Heavy drinking turned out to be of concern. Forty-seven percent of students reported using cannabis at some point in their lives. About 10 percent of students had used other illicit drugs during the previous year. This type of study demonstrates the value of self-report studies, where the behaviour in question is unlikely to be reported to the police, and for which there is no victim in the traditional sense. Various other drug use surveys done in Canada include those done by the Addiction Research Foundation and the Canadian Centre on Substance Abuse.

The Accuracy of Self-Reports

Though self-report data have had a profound effect on criminological inquiry, some important methodological issues have been raised about their accuracy. Critics of self-report studies suggest that it is unreasonable to expect people to candidly admit illegal acts. They have nothing to gain, and the ones taking the greatest risk are the ones with official records who may be engaging in the most criminality. On the other hand, some people may exaggerate their criminal acts, may forget some of them, or may be confused about what is being asked. Most surveys contain an overabundance of trivial offences—skipping school, running away, using a false ID—often lumped together with serious crimes to form a "total crime index." Consequently, comparisons between groups can be highly misleading. Nor can we be certain how valid self-report studies are, because we have nothing reliable to measure them against. Correlation with official reports is expected to be low, because the inadequacies of those reports were largely responsible for the development of self-reports in the first place. One study suggests that while official statistics show a declining youth crime rate, self-report and survey data show the opposite.[20]

Various techniques have been used to verify self-report data.[21] The "known group" method compares incarcerated youths with "normal" groups to see whether the former report more delinquency. Another approach is to use peer informants who can verify the honesty of a subject's answers. A typical approach is to ask youths if they have ever been arrested for or convicted of a delinquent act and then check their official records against their self-reported responses. A number of studies using this method have found a remarkable uniformity between self-reported answers and the official record. The conclusion of criminologists who evaluate self-report methodologies is that (a) the problems of accuracy in self-reports are "surmountable," (b) self-reports are more accurate than most criminologists believe, and (c) self-reports and official statistics are quite compatible.[22]

Connections

Criminologists suspect that a few high-rate offenders are responsible for a disproportionate share of all serious crime. Results would be badly skewed if even a few of these chronic offenders were absent or refused to participate in a schoolwide self-report survey. For more on the chronic offenders, see the discussion on page 76 of this chapter.

The "Missing Cases" Issue

Although these findings are encouraging, nagging questions still remain about the validity of self-reports. Even if 90 percent of a school population voluntarily participate in a self-report study, researchers can never know for sure whether the few who refuse to participate or are absent that day make up a significant portion of the school's population of persistent high-rate offenders. School surveys also fail to count incarcerated youth and dropouts, whose numbers may include some of the most serious offenders. Some research suggests that the "missing cases" in self-reports may be more crime-prone than the general population.[23]

It is also possible that self-reports are weakest in the one area in which they are most heavily relied on: measuring substance abuse.[24] Drug users may significantly underreport the frequency of their substance abuse. Gray and Wish surveyed a group of juvenile detainees and also tested them with urinalysis. They found that less than one-third of the kids who tested positively for marijuana also reported using it, while only 15 percent of those testing positive for cocaine admitted to having used it during the previous month. While this research involves a sample of incarcerated youth who might be expected to underreport drug use, the findings undercut the validity of self-report surveys.[25]

While self-reports are a widely used measure of criminal behaviour, their accuracy in determining the behaviour of two critical elements of the offending

population, chronic offenders and persistent drug abusers, may be limited. Just as there are systematic biases in police statistics, there are biases in self-report surveys as well, in that different populations report in different ways. However, an obvious conclusion is that this would certainly be an impractical method of counting crime.

Connections

Self-report data are used as the standard measure of the nation's youth drug population. When reading the results of national drug use surveys in Chapter 14, keep in mind this research on the validity of self-report surveys. Are heavy crack cocaine users likely to respond accurately to a self-report survey?

Victim Surveys

A third source of crime data is surveys that ask the victims of crime about their encounters with criminals. Because many victims do not report their experiences to the police, victim surveys are considered a method of getting at the dark figures of crime.

In Canada, the first survey of victims of crime was conducted in 1981 under the name of the Canadian Urban Victimization Survey (CUVS). This was a telephone survey of residents in major metropolitan areas, with questions in eight areas of victimization: sexual assault, robbery, assault, break and enter, motor vehicle theft, household property theft, personal theft, and vandalism. This survey also examined the victim's experience of crime, the reason victims decide to report or not report crimes to the police, and the perception of crime held by Canadians. The CUVS revealed that many crimes were not reported to the police. It also began to show the relationship between victim and offender that often underlies certain crimes such as sexual assault.

The CCJS also conducted surveys on criminal victimization as part of the General Social Survey in 1988, 1993, and 1999. The most recent survey involved telephone interviews with approximately 26 000 people. All respondents were asked about their experiences with criminal victimization and their opinions on a variety of justice-related topics. This included their fear of crime and their perceptions about the performance of the police, criminal courts, and prison and parole systems.

In the United States, a national survey of 10 000 households was conducted in 1966 as part of the President's Commission on Law Enforcement and the Administration of Justice. The commission was a groundbreaking attempt that brought many of the nation's leading law enforcement and academic experts together to develop a picture of the crime problem in the United States and how the criminal justice system responds to criminal behaviour. The survey indicated, as had the CUVS, that the number of criminal victimizations in the United States was far higher than previously believed and that many victims failed to report crime to the police, fearing retaliation or official indifference. This resulted in the National Crime Victimization Survey (NCVS) in 1973. Now, international comparisons can be made with the International Criminal Victimization Survey and the World Crime Surveys, both under the auspices of the United Nations.

Like the UCR and self-report surveys, victimization surveys may suffer from some methodological problems, so their findings must be interpreted with caution. Among the potential problems are

- Overreporting owing to victims' misinterpretation of events. For example, a lost wallet is reported as stolen, or an open door is viewed as a burglary attempt.
- Underreporting owing to embarrassment of reporting crime to interviewers, fear of getting in trouble, or simply forgetting an incident.
- Inability to record the personal criminal activity of those interviewed, such as drug use or gambling; murder is also not included, for obvious reasons.
- Sampling errors that produce a group of respondents who are not representative of the nation as a whole.
- Inadequate question format that invalidates responses. Some groups such as adolescents may be particularly susceptible to error because of question format.[26]

In 1992 the NCVS was redesigned to improve its validity, and in 1993 the Canadian General Social Survey was much improved from that of 1988. For example, in 1993 the word "rape" was left off the list of examples of an attack, and questions were asked instead about forced sexual activity. The change in wording resulted in far more sexual assaults being reported in the 1993 survey.

Connections

Not only do victim surveys provide indications of criminal incidents, but they can also be used to describe the individuals who are most at risk of being hurt by crime and where and when they are most likely to become victimized. Data from crime surveys are used in Chapter 4 to draw a portrait of the nature and extent of victimization in Canada.

Are Crime Statistics Sources Compatible?

Are the various sources of criminal statistics compatible? Each has its own strengths and weaknesses, and in general they are difficult to compare. The UCR is carefully tallied

and contains data on crime that the other data sources lack, yet it omits the many crimes that victims choose not to report to the police. The GSS does contain unreported crime and important information on the personal characteristics of victims, but the data consist of estimates made from relatively limited samples of the total population, so that even narrow fluctuations in the rates of some crimes can have a major impact on findings; it also relies on personal recollections that may be inaccurate. One common problem is "telescoping" events from the past, in which victims think that events happened more recently than they really did. The GSS does not include data on important crime patterns, including murder and drug abuse. In their favour, self-report surveys can provide information on the personal characteristics of offenders—their attitudes, values, beliefs, and psychological profile—that is unavailable from any other source. Yet, at their core, self-reports rely on the honesty of criminal offenders and drug abusers, a population not generally known for accuracy and integrity.

Despite these differences, a number of prominent criminologists have concluded that the data sources are more compatible than was first believed possible. While their tallies of crimes are certainly not in synch, the crime patterns and trends they record are often quite similar.[27] For example, all three sources are in general agreement about the personal characteristics of serious criminals (such as age and gender) and where and when crime occurs (such as urban areas, nighttime, and summer months).

While this finding may be persuasive, some criminologists still question the compatibility between the data sources and imply that they measure separate concepts (for example, reported crimes, actual crimes, and victimization rates). This ongoing academic debate punctuates the fact that interpreting crime data is often problematic. Because each source of crime data uses a different method to obtain results, differences will inevitably occur between them. These differences must be carefully considered when interpreting the data on the nature and trends in crime that follow.[28]

The following section considers different ways of displaying information about crime. This is an attempt to expand the idea there are alternative sources of information than official crime statistics.

Alternative Sources of Information

Commissions of Inquiry. So far, three major sources of crime data have been discussed: police reports, victim surveys, and self-reports. There is a fourth source of information, which has been overlooked in criminological inquiry: The commission of inquiry is almost unparalleled in its richness as a resource. Some recent notable examples are the Commission on Systemic Racism in the Ontario Criminal Justice System,[29] the Royal Commission on the Wrongful Incarceration of Donald Marshall Jr. in Nova Scotia,[30] the Report of the Task

Force on the Criminal Justice System and Its Impact on the Indian and Metis people of Alberta,[31] the Report of the Aboriginal Justice Inquiry (1991), the Report of the Saskatchewan Indian Justice Review Committee,[32] and the Report of the Commission of Inquiry Into the Shooting Death of Leo Lachance.[33]

Commissions of inquiry are appointed by provincial or federal governments. They are judicative or quasi-judicial, which means they have broad-ranging powers of investigation similar to a court's. They cannot establish individual criminal liability, but they have a broader mandate than a court trial. The information revealed in a commission of inquiry might have been undiscovered or not investigated by the police. Similarly it might not have been disclosed to victims or publicized in the media.

The commissions of inquiry mentioned above add significantly to our knowledge of the treatment of natives and ethnic minorities in the criminal justice system. As well, some inquiries have contributed to our knowledge of institutional child abuse, for example, the Mount Cashel Orphanage Inquiry.[34] The children in the orphanage, run by the Irish Christian Brothers, were wards of the welfare system and were subject to extreme physical and sexual abuse. Even though the police investigated in 1975, charges were not laid, under the direction of the Minister of Justice.

In Nova Scotia, Chief Justice Stratton of New Brunswick was appointed by the Minister of Justice to hold an investigation into sexual and physical abuse at various provincial schools and training centres. The Stratton Report found "a conspiracy of silence and inaction" existed at one school. The staff and administration did not believe the complaints of the residents and they did not take steps to address any allegations that they thought might have some veracity. Those in positions of trust "turned a blind eye and deaf ears and ... chose not to implicate themselves or their co-workers."[35]

Many other commissions of inquiry could be mentioned, from the inquiry into tainted blood to the Dubin inquiry on drug doping in professional sports. They are a fertile source of information on crime that might not have been brought to light in any other way.

Crisis Index for Justice. Another interesting attempt to measure the rate and impact of crime was the report released by the Mennonite Central Committee in Winnipeg, Manitoba, in 1997. Its report is a critique of Canada's criminal justice system.[36] The report was worded in a way that was clearly critical of a system that "responds to crime primarily by punishing offenders, yet virtually ignores the victims and communities hurt by crime." The report argues that simply increasing the amount of money spent on corrections has had little effect on the crime rate. As a way to stimulate debate on reform of the criminal justice system, the authors constructed a so-called crime index based on four measur-

able areas of criminal justice: the crime rate (overall and violent), the incarceration rate, spending per year on prisons, and the percentage of provincial corrections spending allocated to community corrections. Community corrections includes electronic monitoring, probation, services for victims and offenders, and alternative justice approaches. The report refers to studies that have found that such approaches improve rehabilitation and reintegration, and cost less in the bargain.

By ranking the provinces in relation to one another, the report maps the relative degree of crisis. Saskatchewan, with a similar crime rate to Nova Scotia's, spends 147 percent more on corrections and has a 94 percent higher rate of imprisonment. With the second-highest incarceration rate among developed Western nations, Canada annually spends four times more per prisoner than it does per university student! Prison accounts for 85 percent of the corrections budget in Ontario, 15 percent higher than Nova Scotia. On the other hand, Nova Scotia spends 24 percent of its corrections budget on community corrections, while Ontario spends half that, at 12 percent.

Official Crime Trends in Canada

Studies using official statistics have indicated a gradual increase in the crime rate between 1962 and 1996, even while taking the increase in population into account. Violent crime increased almost five times from a rate of 221 to 973 per 100 000 people, and property crime tripled from 1891 to 5192 per 100 000 people. Figure 3.4 indicates an overall increase in crime from 2771 to 8758 incidents per 100 000 people between 1962 and 1996.

Since 1991, however, the crime rate has decreased (3 percent in 1992, 5.3 percent in 1993, 4.8 percent in 1994, and 1 percent in 1995).[37] Some have argued that the drop in crime is a result of an increase in private security and new crime prevention measures such as proactive community policing.[38] However, there are probably other reasons as well.

Explaining Crime Trends

What factors produce increases or decreases in the crime rate, other than the general factors mentioned above? How can the recent decline in the violence rate be explained? A number of critical factors have been used to explain crime rate trends. Given the shift in crime rates happening in many countries, as Table 3.3 indicates, a few of the most important are discussed here.

Age. Criminologists see changes in the age distribution of the population as having had the greatest influence on recent violent crime trends. As a general rule, the crime rate follows the proportion of young males in the population. The postwar baby-boom generation reached their

Famous Canadian Criminals

A Man Who Abused Boys

FOR IMMEDIATE RELEASE
Edmonton Police Department
August 2, 2001
PUBLIC INFORMATION AND
WARNING

In the interest of public safety, the Edmonton Police Service is issuing the following warning: Karl Richard TOFT will be released from the Bowden Institution on Friday, August 3, 2001 after serving a sentence for numerous convictions for sexual assault, buggery and indecent assault. TOFT has received some Sex Offender treatment, however, he is still considered to be a risk of significant harm and a high risk Sex Offender.
His criminal convictions date back to 1992 for numerous sexual offenses perpetrated against male children aged 12 to 17 years of age, over an 18-20 year period. The Edmonton Police Service acknowledges that while Karl TOFT has received some Sex Offender Programming, and indications are that he has a

desire to seek further treatment, at this time the EPS still has serious concerns about his continued high risk to the community.
The Edmonton Police Service is issuing this information and warning after careful deliberation and consideration of all related issues, including privacy concerns, in the belief that it is clearly in the public interest to inform the members of the community about Karl Richard TOFT.
The Edmonton Police Service believes that his presence on the street poses a risk of significant harm to the health or safety of the public.
Members of the public are advised that the intent of this process is to enable citizens to take suitable precautionary measures. Releasing this information is NOT intended to encourage people to engage in any form of vigilante action.
Note: This information is released under the authority of the Freedom of Information and Protection of Privacy Act, S.A. 1994 c. F - 18.5

SOURCE: Bob Wilson/CP Picture Archive/Fredericton Daily Gleaner

Toft was released from Bowden Institution in August 2001. He had served two-thirds of a 13-year sentence and was automatically due for statutory release. He was to be released to a halfway house, but was instead sent to a psychiatric hospital. The last-minute change was prompted by public protests and an internal review. During the three decades he served as a guard he had access to children he exploited. A provincial compensation report says there could be as many as 1400 offences in total. When it was originally announced that he was to be released, Edmonton police issued a public alert that listed his convictions, his participation in a sex offender program, a physical description, and a photo. There were also concerns for his safety, as his life was also threatened by a former inmate. However, in a Law and Order Poll on August 28, 2001, 61 percent of those surveyed felt that Toft's personal safety should not be a reason to keep him in prison.

Karl Toft was employed as a guard at the New Brunswick Kingsclear Youth Training School. By his own admission he abused more than 200 boys under his care. He was convicted of 34 charges of sexual assault against 18 boys at his trial in 1992. He certainly ranks as one of the most notorious pedophiles in Canadian history. Karl Toft's crimes became known to the authorities in 1984, but he was not investigated

by the police until 1990 and the RCMP concluded that they would not pursue charges. In 1991 he was finally arrested and charged by the Fredericton city police. A commission of inquiry (the Miller Inquiry, 1995) heard testimony from 157 witnesses. It is alleged by some, and recorded in the inquiry's report, that there were provincial officials who knew of the abuse but did nothing about it.

teenage years in the 1960s, when the crime rate began a sharp increase. Since both the victims and perpetrators of crime tend to fall in the 18-to-25-year age category, the rise in crime reflected the age structure of society. With the "greying" of society in the 1980s and a decline in the

birth rate, it was not surprising that the overall crime rate stabilized between 1990 and 1995. Because the number of juveniles is likely to increase over the next decade, some criminologists fear that this will signal a return to escalating crime rates.[39]

| Figure 3.4 | Crime rates per 100 000 population, 1962-2000 |

Rate per 100 000 population

SOURCE: Crime Statistics 2000, Statistics Canada, *The Daily,* July 19, 2001.

In the *Juristat* report on crime in Canada for the year 2000, the youth crime rate increased by 1 percent, while the national crime rate decreased by 1 percent. Violent offences by youths increased 7 percent, while sexual assault by youths increased a shocking 18 percent. However, these figures might be influenced by bureaucratic processes. In some provinces, a youth can be recommended for alternative measures only at the post-charge stage. Thus, trying to divert more youths from formal court processes might result in more charges being laid initially. In addition, the total number of cases is quite low, and any change calculated as a percentage will thus seem higher. In 1999, 1422 youths were charged with sexual assault in Canada. This increased to 1686 cases in 2000, an absolute increase of 264, but a relative increase of 18 percent.[40] The general impression is that youth crime, and especially that committed by young women, is increasing in seriousness. However, whether this impression is supported by evidence is under debate.[41]

Race. There is also no simple relationship between race and crime. Any relationship that does exist is most likely a product of various factors, including constrained social opportunity, discrimination, and selective reporting and surveillance by the police. The Commission on Systemic Racism in the Ontario Criminal Justice System (Ontario 1995) was established in 1992 after black youths, angered by the killing of a young black man by the police, rioted. The commission's mandate was to make recommendations about the extent to which criminal justice practices, procedures, and policies in Ontario reflect systemic racism. The inquiry looked at the police, courts, and correctional institutions and found that blacks have a disproportionate chance of being charged and imprisoned in Ontario compared with whites. When charged with drug trafficking, blacks are 27 times more likely than whites to be held in pretrial detention, and about 20 times as likely

SOURCE: Mike Graston/Windsor Star

| Table 3.3 | Crime rates in Canada, United States, and England and Wales |

	1992	1993	1994	1995	1996
	(year-to-year percentage change in rate)				
Canada	–3%	–5%	–4%	–2%	–2%
United States	–3%	–2%	–1%	–1%	–3%
England/Wales	+5%	–2%	–5%	–3%	–2%

SOURCE: "Canadian Crime Statistics 1996," *Juristat* 17, (1997): 4.

to be imprisoned when found guilty. Blacks make up 3 percent of Ontario's population but 15 percent of the prison population. When defence counsel were asked if they perceived racial bias in the system, 67 percent of lawyers with clients substantially made up of racial minorities believed there were abuses in the bail system that were detrimental to their clients. They also made allegations of "trumped-up" multiple charges by the police, especially with street-level addicts who traffic in narcotics and who are more likely to come from a minority background.

We can also see in the statistics collected by Corrections Canada shown in Table 3.4 that race is an issue. Sixty-six percent of correctional inmates were Caucasian; 16.4 percent were aboriginal. Forty-two percent of inmates on the prairies were white, about two-thirds of the Canadian average; 43 percent were aboriginal, more than two and a half times the national average. Nationally, blacks make up 7 percent of inmates, but in Ontario they are 14 percent of the inmate population. The statistical overrepresentation of certain ethnic groups isn't a surprise, but the causes are not clear.[42] Thus, racism in the criminal justice system has become an important issue.

Natives and Crime. In a study called "Aboriginal Peoples in Canada," published by the Canadian Centre for Justice Statistics Profile Series, it is noted that according to the 1996 Census, about 800 000 people, or 3 percent of the total population of Canada, identified themselves as Aboriginal.[43] However, according to the 1999 General Social Survey, a disproportionate number—35 percent of the Aboriginal population—were victims of a crime in the year preceding the survey. This was much higher than the proportion of non-Aboriginal people (26 percent) who

were victimized in the same period. About 19 percent of the Aboriginal population reported being victimized two or more times in the previous 12 months, compared to 10 percent of the non-native population. Aboriginal people are more likely to be victims of violent crime, nearly three times more likely, than non-Aboriginal people are (307 versus 110 incidents per 1000 population). Furthermore, Aboriginal people are more likely to be victims of spousal violence. Approximately 20 percent of Aboriginal people reported being assaulted by their spouse, compared to 7 percent of non-Aboriginal people. Eighty percent of native women are victims of violence; death from violence occurs at a rate three times higher than that of non-native communities; and suicides among males is four times higher than the non-native rate.[44]

Aboriginal people are more likely to have contact with police, and for more serious reasons. For example, they were more likely to come into contact with the police: as victims of a crime (17 percent versus 13 percent), as witnesses to a crime (11 percent versus 6 percent) and by being arrested (4 percent versus 1 percent). Aboriginal people were also less satisfied with the police. They were less likely to rate the police as being approachable and easy to talk to (58 percent versus 67 percent), ensuring the safety of citizens (55 percent versus 63 percent), enforcing the laws (48 percent versus 61 percent), supplying information on ways to reduce crime (46 percent versus 55 percent), and responding promptly to calls (43 percent versus 50 percent).

The Economy. There is still debate over the effects the economy has on crime rates. Some criminologists believe that a poor economy actually helps lower crime rates. Unemployed parents are at home to supervise children and guard their homes. And because there is less money

Table 3.4	Percentage of incarcerated offenders by race and region on March 31, 1997								
RACE	**ATLANTIC**		**QUEBEC**		**ONTARIO**		**PRAIRIE**		**PACIFIC**	
	M	**F**	**M**	**F**	**M**	**F**	**M**	**F**	**M**	**F**
Caucasian	85.0	55.6	88.5	62.9	74.1	65.7	51.2	33.3	71.7	71.4
Aboriginal	6.1	11.1	3.5	3.2	4.9	9.8	38.3	48.1	18.6	20.0
Black	7.0	13.9	5.6	8.1	11.8	16.8	2.2	1.2	1.6	2.9
Asiatic	0.3	0.0	0.7	0.0	4.3	4.9	2.2	2.5	3.8	0.0
Other	0.7	2.8	1.6	0.0	3.4	1.4	2.6	6.2	3.7	0.0
Not stated	0.9	16.7	0.1	25.8	1.6	1.4	3.4	8.6	0.6	5.7
TOTAL (APPROXIMATE)	**100%**	**100%**	**100%**	**100%**	**100%**	**100%**	**100%**	**100%**	**100%**	**100%**

Based on an incarcerated offender population of 14,448, Offender Management System, CSC, March 31, 1997. Basic Facts about Corrections in Canada, Solicitor General, 1997: 19.

Exhibit 3.1	Quick Facts – General Profile of the Native Offender

- The Aboriginal population, at 800 000, represents about 3 percent of the Canadian population.
- In provincial jurisdiction, about 15 000 (15 percent) of offenders sentenced in 1998 were native.
- In federal jurisdiction, about 17 percent of inmates are native.
- About 12 percent of inmates are native males, and 17 percent are native females.
- Those in the 18-to-37 year-old age group make up 76 percent of Inuit offenders, 85 percent of Metis offenders, and 83 percent of Indian offenders.
- Sixty-five percent of aboriginal offenders had prior convictions.
- Natives are five times as likely to be convicted of serious assault as non-natives are.
- Natives are four times as likely to be victimized by crime as non-natives.
- The on-reserve rate of violence is five times higher than off-reserve.
- Almost 90 percent of Aboriginals report being victims of childhood or adult violence.
- One-third of those under 15 live in single-parent families.
- In Manitoba, natives represent 16 percent of 12- to 17-year-olds, but make up 71 percent of youths sentenced to custody.

Source: National Crime Prevention Centre, *Aboriginal Canadians: Violence, Victimization and Prevention*, Department of Justice, 2001; Nathalie L. Quann and Shelley Trevethan, *Police Reported Aboriginal Crime in Saskatchewan*, Statistics Canada, 2000.

to spend, a poor economy means that there are actually fewer valuables around worth stealing. It also seems unlikely that law-abiding, middle-aged workers will suddenly turn to a life of crime if they are laid off during an economic downturn.

However, it is possible that long-term periods of sustained economic weakness and unemployment may eventually affect crime rates. The long-term economic recession that occurred in the late 1980s may have produced a climate of hopelessness in North America's largest cities, which saw increased violence rates between 1985 and 1990. Teenage unemployment rates are especially high in urban areas that contain large at-risk populations. Canadian research shows an upturn in arson in times of economic recession.[45] Insurance fraud goes up when unemployment worsens, as well.

Social Malaise. As the level of social problems increases, so do crime rates. Increases in the number of single-parent families, in divorce and dropout rates, in nonrecreational drug use, and in teen pregnancies may also influence crime rates. Cross-national research indicates that child homicide rates are greatest in those nations that have the highest rates of so-called illegitimacy and teenage mothers.[46] This is a very controversial finding, because it neglects the social reasons for child poverty and also contributes to the invisibility of those teenage dads. As illegitimacy rates rise and social spending is cut, the rate of violent crime might trend upward. Social malaise may explain why some cities and regions have higher crime rates than others. Another controversial research finding published by the U.S. National Bureau of Economic Research maintained that legalized abortion in the early 1970s contributed to a lowering of the crime rate in the 1990s. The authors say that improved policing and better prisons, plus a strong economy, can account for only half of the 30 percent crime rate decline in the United States.[47]

Culture and Crime Rates. Some think that culture makes a difference as well. Take the example of Japan. Despite the fact that Japan is a large industrialized country whose population is jammed into overcrowded urban areas, its crime rate is extremely low compared with many of the Western countries. The fear of crime is relatively low in Japan, even though the Japanese news media focus a lot of attention on the few lurid and violent incidents that do occur. How can this difference be explained?

Cultural differences may play an important role in controlling crime in Japan. In North America, individualism and self-gratification are emphasized, and success is defined by material goods and possessions. To achieve an upper-class lifestyle, people are willing to engage in confrontations, increasing the likelihood of violence. In Japan, honour is the most important personal trait. Japan's homogeneous society has a written history that spans 14 centuries. The Japanese are deeply loyal to historical traditions, which provide a sense of moral order. They belong to a network of social groups that create a strong commitment to social norms. In contrast, America's melting pot society has not allowed the same sort of moral order or tradition to develop. The most important cultural norms in Japan are extraordinary patience when seeking change, a cooperative approach to decision making, extreme respect for seniority and age, and concern for society at the expense of the individual. Japanese customs that subordinate personal feelings for the good of the group produce fewer violent confrontations. Research by Rosemary Gartner and Robert Nash Parker shows that murder rates in Japan and Scotland have been unaffected by population trends because in these nations violence is considered shameful and a disgrace.[48]

Nowhere are obedience and respect more important in Japan than in relationships with family members and

Culture, Gender, Ethnicity, and Criminology

The Politics of Statistics

In 1989, an inspector with the Metro Toronto Police Department said that black people accounted for a disproportionate amount of street crime in the Jane-Finch area. While this area does have a high rate of crime, the fact that he linked it to an ethnic group provoked controversy. Similarly, in 1991, when a Metro Toronto police sergeant said that Vietnamese and Mainland Chinese immigrants committed a high percentage of the crime in the Asian community, he was publicly reviled and officially reprimanded. This was despite the fact that he himself was Chinese, and many people in the Chinese community supported him. In 1990 the Canadian Centre for Justice Statistics had proposed including statistics on the race of suspects and victims in its crime reports. The idea was quickly abandoned in the face of political pressure. Is this a matter of political correctness?

The criminal justice system already collects statistics, such as age and sex, identifiers that are beyond an individual's control. Furthermore, Correctional Services notes the race of an inmate on its admission forms. Such information is integral to an informed analysis of crime patterns and a criminal's treatment. Statistics on the proportion of natives in the criminal justice system, for example, show the extreme overrepresentation of natives in prison. In 1998–99, Aboriginals represented 3 percent of the general population in Canada, but 15 percent of the offenders in federal custody. Such disparities can alert us to socioeconomic conditions on reserves and possible bias on the part of the justice system. Some think the collection of this data shouldn't be abandoned just because it might be politically incorrect (Gabor 1994).

Statistics on race-related crime are routinely collected in the United States. American research has found that race is a strong predictor of criminal activity. The FBI reports that in 1999, 69 percent of those arrested were white and 29 percent were black. As of 2000, the U.S. Census Bureau estimated that 93 percent of the American population was white, and 13 percent was black. This means that blacks are overrepresented in arrest statistics, while whites are underrepresented relative to their proportion of the population. Blacks are more likely to be arrested for murder (52 percent), robbery (54 percent), and being in possession of stolen property (43 percent). However, they are less likely to be arrested for arson (24 percent), vandalism (22 percent), and driving under the influence (10 percent).

There are several reasons why the relationship between race and crime is underdeveloped in Canada (Hatt 1994; Johnston 1994; Wortley 1999). The first is found in the innate problem of crime statistics. Again, going back to U.S. statistics, while crime is underreported, 1986 FBI data indicate that 47 percent of violent crimes reported to the police were committed by blacks. However, when we go to alternative sources of information, the ratio of crimes committed by blacks goes down. The U.S. Department of Justice's victimization survey found that blacks were responsible for 24 percent of violent crimes, about half the official rate. Moreover, self-report surveys found no relationship between ethnicity and crime (Roberts and Gabor 1990; Roberts 1994). One conclusion that can be drawn from these data is that people are more likely to report to the police those crimes committed by ethnic minorities.

The second reason is the inherent difficulty of measuring race. Ethnicity is not homogeneous. Over 10 million people identified themselves as being from multiple ethnic origins in the 1996 census, a full 35 percent of Canada's population. As Haggerty (2001) points out, there are real problems in categorizing ethnicity. Is ethnicity a matter of skin colour, country of origin, or self-identification?

The third reason that the relationship between race and crime is not studied more is the possibility that racial information will be used to justify racism. Wortley and Brownfield (1996) found that blacks report a higher rate of stops and searches by police. In a survey of black, Chinese, and white residents of Toronto, blacks were most likely to perceive discrimination, an opinion that is reflected in their experiences (Wortley 1996). Forty-three percent of black males reported being stopped by the police, compared to 25 percent of whites, and 19 percent of Chinese. Four out of ten black respondents reported that they were treated unfairly, compared to 15 percent of Chinese and 10 percent of whites. Between 1986 and 1993, the number of whites incarcerated for drug trafficking increased 151 percent, while the number of blacks committed to detention increased 1164 percent (Wortley 1999). Research also shows that blacks are less likely to be granted bail (Ontario 1995). The "racialization" of crime, when an ethnic group becomes identified with criminal activity, is backed up by research. A survey conducted in Toronto in 1995 found that 45 percent of those surveyed believed there was a relationship between ethnicity and crime. Furthermore, two-thirds of those people thought that blacks committed more crime (Henry, Hastings, and Freer 1996).

In the early 1990s, after University of Western professor Phillippe Rushton published work relating race and crime (1987, 1988), a debate ensued in the *Canadian Journal of Criminology* (Roberts and Gabor 1990; Cernovsky and Litman 1993; Hatt 1994; Rushton 1994; Johnston 1994). Julian Roberts and Thomas Gabor of the University of Ottawa wrote how the overrepresentation of certain ethnic minorities in crime statistics was misleading and should not be construed as support for a genetic theory of crime (Roberts and Gabor 1990). Rushton had proposed a theory that blacks were less intelligent and law-abiding than whites or Asians. Roberts and Gabor argued there is a link between ethnicity and crime, but it is easily exaggerated and more often misunderstood. Blacks are underrepresented in tax fraud and securities violations, and arrests for white-collar crimes are much higher for whites. This debate over race is not new. The practice of assigning a racial category to offenders has a long history. Cesare Beccaria, for example, used a racial typology of criminals as part of his explanation for criminality. This points to how crime itself is not a homogeneous category. The relationship between ethnicity and crime is to some extent crime-specific.

When plans were underway to develop the incident-based UCR II crime survey in the late 1980s, it was recognized that there was a potential to significantly increase the amount of data available on crimes (September 3, 2001, Haggerty 2001). Specifically, it would be possible to trace links between crime and numerous contextual factors associated with the accused, including his or her ethnicity. The Canadian police community was a strong advocate for introducing racial variables. Such data would make it possible to better control the criminality of certain ethnic groups, as well as reveal systemic racism within the criminal-justice system. The common-sense demarcation of race chosen was European origin (white); South Asian; black; East/Southeast Asian; Central and South American; and Aboriginal. By 1991 police forces were providing the centre with data on racial origin, but after objections were raised by the Prime Minister's Office, the Privacy Commissioner of Canada, the media, and academics, the project was abandoned. One fear was that the police would assign criminals to ethnic groupings already perceived as being "criminogenic" and reinforce dominant stereotypes.

In fact, two commissions at the time advocated increasing the variety of statistics on the status of Aboriginals in criminal justice (Alberta 1991; Saskatchewan 1992). And other reports, including one on racism in the criminal justice system in Manitoba (Manitoba 1991), were damning in their conclusion that racism was systemic. The Commission of Inquiry that looked at the shooting of Leo Lachance (Saskatchewan 1993), concluded that a major obstacle in the investigation in the case was that racism was not seen to be an issue. The 1989 Royal Commission into the Wrongful Conviction of Donald Marshall Jr. was unequivocal in its finding that racism played a part in his miscarriage of justice (Nova Scotia 1989). So perhaps there are solid grounds for wanting to conduct research on the relationship between race, crime, and victimization.

Sources: Thomas Gabor, "The Suppression of Crime Statistics on Race and Ethnicity: The Price of Political Correctness," *Canadian Journal of Criminology*, 36 (1994): 153–163; Ken Hatt, "Reservations about Race and Crime Statistics," *Canadian Journal of Criminology*, 36 (1994): 164–66; J. Phillip Johnston, "Academic Approaches to Race–Crime Statistics Do Not Justify Their Collection," *Canadian Journal of Criminology*, 36 (1994):166–74; Scot Wortley, "A Northern Taboo: Research on Race, Crime, and Criminal Justice in Canada," *Canadian Journal of Criminology*, 41 (1999): 261–75; Scot Wortley, "Justice for All? Race and Perceptions of Bias in the Ontario Criminal Justice System — A Toronto Survey," *Canadian Journal of Criminology*, October 1996: 439–67; Scot Wortley and David Brownfield, "The Usual Suspects: Race, Age, and Gender Differences in Involuntary Police Contact," 48th Annual Conference of the American Society of Criminology, Chicago, 1996; Julian V. Roberts, "Crime and Race Statistics: Toward a Canadian Solution," *Canadian Journal of Criminology*, 36 (1994): 175–85; Julian V. Roberts and Thomas Gabor, "Lombrosian Wine in a New Bottle: Research on Crime and Race," *Canadian Journal of Criminology* 32 (1990): 291–313; J. Phillippe Rushton, "Population Differences in Rule-Following Behaviour: Race, Evolution and Crime," presented to the 39th Annual Meeting of the American Society of Criminology, 1987; J. Phillippe Rushton, "Race Differences in Behaviour: A Review and Evolutionary Analysis," *Personality and Individual Differences* 9 (1988): 1009–1024; J. Phillipe Rushton, "Race and Crime: A Reply to Roberts and Gabor," *Canadian Journal of Criminology*, 32 (1990): 315–34; J. Phillippe Rushton, "Race and Crime: A Reply to Cernovsky and Litman," *Canadian Journal of Criminology*, 36 (1994): 79–83; Nathalie L. Quann and Shelley Trevethan, *Police Reported Aboriginal Crime in Saskatchewan*, Statistics Canada, 2000; Zack Z. Cernovsky and Larry C. Litman, "Re-analyses of J.P. Rushton's Crime Data," *Canadian Journal of Criminology*, 35 (1993): 31–37; Thomas Gabor and Julian V. Roberts, "Rushton on Race and Crime: The Evidence Remains Unconvincing," *Canadian Journal of Criminology*, 32 (1990): 335; Frances Henry, Patricia Hastings, and Brian Freer, "Perceptions of Race and Crime in Ontario: Empirical Evidence from the Toronto and Durham Region," *Canadian Journal of Criminology*, October 1996: 46–476; Kevin Haggerty, *Making Crime Count* (Toronto: University of Toronto Press, 2001).

friends. Children owe parents total respect; younger siblings must obey older brothers and sisters; younger friends show reverence toward older acquaintances; and all show respect to the emperor. Bowing, a familiar Japanese custom, symbolizes this respect. The Japanese, then, are deterred from criminal behaviour not only because of moral principles of right and wrong but also to avoid embarrassment to self, family, or acquaintances. There are those who believe that this fear of shame is the key to the crime rate.[49] In Japan shameful acts are confronted in an effort to reintegrate offenders into society.

Although Japanese crime rates are low, what crime there is tends to involve organized criminal gangs. Youth in the bosozoku (hot-rodder) and "yankee" gangs flout conventional dress and speech codes so important in Japan. Members embrace an overtly macho behavioural code, featuring violence, reckless driving, and drug use. They may "graduate" into yakuza gangs, the huge organized crime groups that are responsible for a significant portion of all crimes in Japan. Yakuza engage in drug trafficking, extortion, gambling, and other criminal conspiracies. They are often hired by legitimate enterprises to "settle" labour disputes, close business deals, and collect debts. While membership in traditional organized crime families is on the wane in North America, the number of Japanese yakuza members has increased sharply.[50]

Connections

The link between the economy, social malaise, and the crime rate is important for criminological theory. If crime rates are higher in poor or distressed regions, there may be an association between poverty and crime. This is the assumption made by the social structure theorists, who are discussed in Chapter 7.

Guns. The availability of firearms, especially the proliferation of weapons in the hands of teens, may influence the crime rate. There is evidence that more guns than ever before are finding their way into the hands of young people, and concern that guns are too easily available. Bill C-68 was introduced to the legislature in 1995 as an attempt to control this problem. In 1996, 25 percent of those charged with robbery with a firearm were youths. Numbers in the United States are even higher,[51] which suggests that in at least some areas juvenile gun possession is all too prevalent and may in part be responsible for increasing violence rates.

Despite growing concern over firearms and crime in Canada, the percentage of violent crimes committed with a gun decreased from 6.5 percent to 4.8 percent between 1994 and 1998. Firearms were used in 34 percent of homicides, 29 percent of attempted murders, and 10 percent of aggravated assaults. Firearms were used in 37 percent of robberies, but have decreased to 18 percent in 1998.[52] In an exchange in the *Canadian Journal of Criminology*, Thomas Gabor (Ottawa) and Gary Mauser debated to what extent Canadians use firearms for self-protection. Mauser concluded that Canadians were three times more likely to use guns in self-defence than to commit violent crimes. Gabor's summary of the relevant research showed, however, that self-defence killings were outnumbered by the death of residents in the homes by 40 to 1. For example, if a gun is available, it increases the likelihood it will be used in a suicide.[53]

Drugs. Increasing drug use may affect crime rates. According to Alfred Blumstein, groups and gangs involved in the urban drug trade recruit juveniles because they work cheaply, are immune from heavy criminal penalties, and are "daring and willing to take risks."[54] Arming themselves for protection, these drug-dealing kids present a menace that persuades neighbourhood adolescents to arm themselves for protection. The result is an "arms race" that produces an increasing spiral of violence.

Some experts tie increases in the violent crime rate between 1980 and 1990 to the "crack cocaine" epidemic that swept North America's largest cities and the drug-trafficking gangs that fought over "drug turf." These well-armed gangs did not hesitate to use violence to control territories, intimidate rivals, and increase "market share." Washington, D.C., provides a dramatic example of the drug–crime relationship: In 1985, 21 percent of the homicides there were reported as drug-related; by 1988, 80 percent of the homicides were drug-related. With the waning of the crack epidemic (users are switching to heroin), violence seems to have subsided in New York City and other metropolitan areas where the crack epidemic was rampant.[55]

Connections

The drug-crime connection is a critical one for lawmakers. If drug use causes crime rates to increase, then the outright ban on drugs is warranted. If there is no drug-crime connection, efforts to legalize drug use might be justified. For sections on the drug-crime connection and the legalization issue, see Chapter 14.

Justice Policy. Some law enforcement experts have suggested that reduction in crime rates may be attributed to aggressive police practices that target "quality of life" crimes such as panhandling, graffiti, petty drug dealing, and loitering. By showing that even the smallest infractions will be dealt with seriously, aggressive police departments may be able to discourage potential criminals from committing even more serious crimes. This has been called the "broken windows" approach, discussed elsewhere in this book, which is oriented to reducing the "incivilities" experienced by neighbourhood residents. The interpretation of the results is a topic of debate, but the argument is that by reducing fear among residents, they become more involved in fighting crime.[56]

It is also possible that tough laws targeting drug dealing and repeat offenders with lengthy prison terms can have an effect on crime rates. The fear of punishment may inhibit some would-be criminals. Lengthy sentences also help boost the nation's prison population. It is possible that placing a significant number of potentially high-rate offenders behind bars helps stabilize crime rates.

Connections

While there is still a great deal of debate over the impact that incarcerating criminals has on the crime rate, most scholars dispute the idea that "locking 'em up" alone can bring crime rates down. New criminals are continually coming along to replace those behind bars. For more on this topic, see the sections in Chapter 5 on incapacitation.

What the Future Holds

It is always risky to speculate about the future of crime trends, since current conditions can change rapidly. But some criminologists have gone out on a limb to predict future patterns. Darrell Steffensmeier and Miles Harer's suggestion that violent crime would drop during the remainder of the 1990s as the baby boomers pass into middle and old age has proven true. The property crime rate will at first decline, then level off and begin rising toward the end of the decade as the baby-boomlet kids born in the early 1980s begin to hit their "peak" crime years. After the year 2000, both property and violent crimes are predicted to increase.[57] Steffensmeier and Harer consider the age structure of society to be the single most powerful influence on the crime rate. In a similar vein, criminologist James A. Fox predicts a significant increase in teen violence if current trends in the proportion of youths in society persist.[58]

Of course, such predictions are based on population trends and can be thrown off by changes in the economy, justice policy, drug use, gun availability, gang membership, and other sociocultural forces. Fox suggests that if social conditions worsen, teen homicide might increase even more. It is also possible that current national outrage over violent crime will help make violence so unpalatable that local residents will be willing to take drastic actions to reduce crime, including cooperating with the police and pressuring neighbourhood families to control their young.

Crime Patterns

What do the various sources of criminological statistics tell us about crime? What is known about the nature of crime and criminals? What trends or patterns exist in the crime rate that can help us understand the causes of crime?

Criminologists look for stable patterns in the crime rate to gain insight into the nature of crime. If crime rates are consistently higher at certain times, in certain areas, and among certain groups, this knowledge might be used to explain the onset or cause of crime. For example, if criminal statistics show that crime rates are consistently higher in poor neighbourhoods in large urban areas, then crime may be a function of poverty and neighbourhood decline. If, in contrast, crime rates are spread evenly across the social structure, there would be little evidence that crime has an economic basis; crime might then be linked to socialization, personality, intelligence, or some other trait unrelated to class position or income. What, then, are the main traits and patterns in crime statistics?

The Ecology of Crime

There seem to be patterns in the crime rate that are linked to temporal and ecological factors. Some of the most important of these factors are the day, season, and climate; temperature; the density of the population; and geographical region.

Day, Season, and Climate. Most reported crimes occur during the warm summer months of July and August. During the summer, teenagers, who usually have the highest crime levels, are out of school and have greater opportunity to commit crime. During warm weather, people spend more time outdoors, making themselves easier targets. Similarly, homes are left vacant more often during the summer, making them more vulnerable to property crimes.

Crime rates may also be higher on the first day of a month than at any other time. Potential criminals believe that government welfare and social security cheques arrive at this time and therefore increase such activities as breaking into mailboxes and accosting recipients on the streets. Also, people may have more disposable income at this time, and the availability of extra money may relate to behaviours associated with crime such as drinking, partying, gambling, and so on.[59]

Temperature. Although weather effects (that is, swings in temperature) may also influence violent crime rates, laboratory studies suggest that the association between temperature and crime resembles an inverted U-shaped curve: Crime rates increase with a rise in temperature and then begin to decline at some point when it may simply be too hot for any physical exertion. However, field studies indicate that the rates of some (such as domestic assault) but not all (such as rape) crimes continue to increase as temperatures rise. Research has shown that a long stretch of highly uncomfortable weather is related to increased homicide rates, indicating that the stress of long-term exposure to extreme temperatures may prove sufficiently acute to increase violence rates. In their study of temperature effects on assault, Ellen Cohn and James Rotton found evidence that the effect was highly significant, especially during the morning and evening hours: A person is four times as likely to be assaulted at midnight when temperatures exceed 30° than when they are at -20°! The research on this topic is certainly interesting to read.[60]

Population Density. Areas with low per capita crime rates tend to be rural—large urban areas have by far the highest violence rates. These findings are also supported by victim data.

Region. Definite differences are apparent in regional crime rates. Canada exhibits a pattern of rising crime rates from east to west, but there is little research on why this happens. Earlier in the chapter it was suggested that internal migration has resulted in weaker social control in western provinces. For many years, southern U.S. states also had significantly higher rates in almost all crime categories than were found in other regions of the country; these data convinced some criminologists that there was a southern subculture of violence. However, the western U.S. states now have the dubious distinction of having the highest crime and violence rates.

Social Class and Crime. A still unresolved issue in criminology is the relationship between social class and crime. Traditionally, crime has been thought of as a lower-class phenomenon. After all, people at the lowest rungs of the social structure have the greatest incentive to commit crimes. Those unable to obtain desired goods and services through conventional means may resort to theft and other illegal activities, such as selling narcotics, to obtain them; these activities are referred to as **instrumental crimes.** Those living in areas of poverty are also believed to engage in disproportionate amounts of **expressive crimes,** such as rape and assault, as a means of expressing their rage, frustration, and anger against society. Alcohol and drug abuse, common in poor areas, helps fuel violent episodes.[61]

Official statistics from the United States, where there has been more research on this topic than in Canada, indicate that crime rates in inner-city, high-poverty areas are generally higher than those in suburban or wealthier areas; for example, the highest homicide victimization levels are in deteriorated inner-city areas.[62] Studies using aggregate police statistics (arrest records) have consistently shown that crime rates in lower-class areas are higher than in wealthier neighbourhoods. Another "official" indicator of a class–crime relationship can be obtained through surveys of prison inmates, which consistently show that prisoners were members of the lower class and unemployed or underemployed in the years before their incarceration.

An alternative explanation for these findings is that the relationship between official crime and social class is a function of law enforcement practices and not actual criminal behaviour patterns. Police may devote more resources to poverty areas, and consequently, apprehension rates may be higher there. Similarly, police may be more likely to formally arrest and prosecute lower-class citizens than those in the middle and upper classes, which may account for the lower class's overrepresentation in the official statistics and the prison population. The third explanation is that crimes are class-related; that is, the rich are more likely to commit tax fraud, while the poor are more likely to commit welfare fraud.

Evidence for a Class–Crime Relationship. Self-report data have been used extensively to test the class–crime relationship. Surprisingly, early self-report studies conducted in the 1950s did not find a direct relationship between social class and youth crime. They found that socioeconomic class was related to official processing by police, court, and correctional agencies but not to the actual commission of crimes. In other words, while lower- and middle-class youth self-reported equal amounts of crime, the lower-class youth had a greater chance of getting arrested, convicted, and incarcerated and becoming official delinquents. In addition, factors generally associated with lower-class membership, such as broken homes, were found to be related to institutionalization but not to admissions of delinquency.[63]

For more than 20 years, a majority of self-report studies agreed that a class–crime relationship did not exist: If the poor possessed more extensive criminal records than the wealthy, it was because of differential law enforcement and not class-based behaviour differences. In what is considered to be the definitive work on this subject, Charles Tittle, Wayne Villemez, and Douglas Smith reviewed 35 studies containing 363 separate estimates concerning the relationship between class and crime.[64] They concluded that little if any support exists for the contention that crime is primarily a lower-class phenomenon. Consequently, Tittle and his associates argued that official statistics probably reflect class bias in the processing of lower-class offenders. The Tittle review is usually cited by criminologists as the strongest statement refuting the claim that the lower class is disproportionately criminal. In 1990, writing with Robert Meier, Tittle once again reviewed existing data (published between 1978 and 1990) on the class–crime relationship and again found little evidence that a consistent association could be found between class and crime.[65]

While convincing, this research has sparked significant debate over the validity of studies assessing the class–crime relationship. Many self-report instruments include trivial offences, such as using a false ID or drinking alcohol. Their inclusion may obscure the true class–crime relationship because affluent youth often engage in trivial offences, such as petty larceny, drug use, and simple assault. Those who support a class–crime relationship suggest that if only serious felony offences are considered, a significant association can be observed.[66] Those studies showing middle- and lower-class youths to be equally delinquent rely on measures weighted toward minor crimes (for example, using a false ID or skipping school); when serious crimes, such as burglary and assault, are used in the comparison, lower-class youths register as significantly more delinquent.[67]

The Class–Crime Controversy. The relationship between class and crime is an important one for criminological theory. If crime is related to social class, it follows that economic and structural factors, such as poverty and neighbourhood disorganization, are a significant cause of criminal behaviour.

One reason that a true measure of the class–crime relationship has thus far eluded criminologists is that the methods used to measure "class" vary widely. So many different indicators are used that findings are ambiguous. For example, David Brownfield found that some widely used measures of social class, such as father's occupation and education, are only weakly related to self-reported crime, while others, such as unemployment or membership on the welfare roles, are much stronger correlates of criminality.[68]

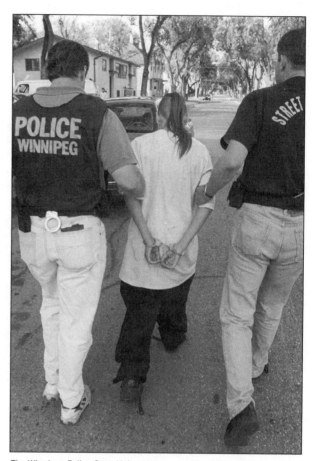

The Winnipeg Police Gang Unit arrests a member of the youth gang called Indian Posse in a big sweep in August 1995. It is estimated that the gang and the Manitoba Warriors have 1500 members in Winnipeg and have been connected to crimes such as murder, robbery, and drug dealing.

Connections

If class and crime are unrelated, the causes of crime must be found in factors experienced by members of all social classes—psychological impairment, family conflict, peer pressure, school failure, and so on. Theories that view crime as a function of problems experienced by members of all social classes are reviewed in Chapter 8.

It is also possible that the association between class and crime may be more complex than a simple linear relationship (the poorer you are, the more crime you commit). Age, race, and gender may all influence the connection between class and crime.[69] Some researchers speculate that exclusion from paid labour creates resentment and criminality in those who expect better treatment than they are getting; white females have had their expectations raised by the women's movement and expect greater occupational opportunities than minority females, whose vision is tempered by the economic reality of joblessness in minority neighbourhoods.[70] Considering these findings, it is not surprising that the true relationship between class and crime is difficult to determine. The effect may be obscured because its impact varies within and between groups.

Like so many other criminological controversies, the debate over the true relationship between class and crime will most likely persist. The weight of recent evidence seems to suggest that serious street and official crime is more prevalent among the lower classes, while less serious and self-reported crime is spread more evenly throughout the social structure.[71] Income inequality, poverty, and resource deprivation are all associated with the most serious violent crimes, including homicide and assault.[72] Nonetheless, while crime rates may be higher in lower-class areas, poverty alone cannot explain why a particular individual becomes a chronic violent criminal; if it could, the crime problem would be much worse than it is now.[73]

And of course class must be related by definition to professional and white-collar crime, about which more will be said later.

Age and Crime

There is general agreement that age is inversely related to criminality. Respected criminologists Travis Hirschi and Michael Gottfredson state, "Age is everywhere correlated with crime. Its effects on crime do not depend on other demographic correlates of crime."[74] Regardless of economic status, marital status, race, sex, and so on, younger people are more likely to commit crime than their older peers. Research indicates this relationship has remained stable across time periods ranging from 1935 to the present.[75] Official statistics tell us that young people are arrested at a disproportionate rate to their numbers in the population; victim surveys generate similar findings for crimes in which the age of the assailant can be determined.

The Age–Crime Controversy. The relationship between age and crime is of major theoretical importance because many existing criminological theories fail to adequately explain why the crime rate drops with age, which is referred to as **aging out**, or the **desistance phenomenon**. This theoretical failure has been the subject of considerable academic debate. One position, championed by Hirschi and Gottfredson, is that the relationship between age and crime is constant and that therefore the age variable is actually irrelevant to the study of crime. Because all people, regardless of their demographic characteristics (race, gender, class, family structure, domicile, work status, and so on), commit less crime as they age, it is not important to consider age as a factor in explaining crime. Even hard-core chronic offenders commit less crime as they age. Differences in offending rates for groups (for example, between males and females or between the rich and poor) that exist at any point in their respective life cycles will be maintained throughout their lives.[76]

Connections

Hirschi and Gottfredson have used their views on the age–crime relationship as a basis for their general theory of crime. This important theory holds that the factors that produce crime change little after birth and that the association between crime and age is a constant. For more on their views, see Chapter 10.

Those who oppose the above view of the age–crime relationship suggest that personal factors, such as gender and race, and social factors, such as lifestyle, economic situation, and peer relations, have a significant impact on the age–crime relationship. There are a number of reasons that criminal behaviour is not constant. Evolving patterns or cycles of criminal behaviour may be keyed to personal characteristics and lifestyle, including gender, race, and class. For example, gender seems to influence the age–crime association: The male-to-female crime ratio difference appears to decline with age. The female homicide rate peaks at age 20 and then continues at a stable but low rate throughout adulthood; in contrast, the male homicide rate is much higher but begins to drop after age 30.[77]

The likelihood of a long-term criminal career may be determined by the age at which offending commences. People who get involved in criminality at a very early age (**early onset**) and who gain official records will be the ones most likely to become chronic offenders. Research shows that preschoolers (under age five) who are labelled "troublesome" or "difficult" by parents are the ones most likely to become persistent offenders through their adolescence.[78] Their criminal behaviour is resistant to the aging-out process.

Desistance (aging out) may also be influenced by criminal specialization; crime types may peak at different ages and follow different trajectories. Crimes that provide significant economic gain, such as gambling, embezzlement, and fraud, are less likely to decline with maturity than are high-risk, low-profit offences, such as assault. People who are frequent cocaine and heroin users continue to commit criminal acts 10 years or more past the age when nonaddicts have terminated their criminal activity.[79]

Two Classes of Criminals? The population thus may contain different sets of criminal offenders, one or more groups whose criminality declines with age (as predicted by Hirschi and Gottfredson) and another whose criminal behaviour remains constant through their maturity.[80] The age–crime pattern may also undergo change; it has been noted that a greater proportion of violent criminal behaviour is concentrated among youthful offenders than it was 40 years ago (although the youth violence rate declined in 1995).

In sum, some criminologists view the relationship between crime and age as constant, while others believe that it varies according to offence and offender. This difference has important implications for criminological research and theory. If age is a constant, then the criminality of any group can be accurately measured at any single point in time. If, on the other hand, the relationship between age and crime varies, it would be necessary to conduct longitudinal studies that follow criminals over their life cycle to fully understand how their age influences their offending patterns.[81] John Hagan believes, then, that crime should be conceived of as a type of social event that takes on different meanings at different times in a person's life.[82] Various experiments have tried to deal with the problem of young offenders, such as boot camps and early intervention programs. In Scotland, the Freagarrach Project for persistent offenders (more than five offences) was able to achieve a 20 to 50 percent reduction in repeat offences. These youths had an average of 18 offences against them. Close counselling, education, exercise, and a system of rewards achieved more significant results than a simple prison sentence would achieve.

Disagreements over the relationship between age and crime, and what to do about it, have produced spirited debates in criminology and sponsored new research in such countries as the United States, Canada, Sweden, and Britain.[83] Clearly, more research is required on this important topic.

Why Does Aging Out Occur? Despite the debate raging over the relationship between age and crime, there is little question that the overall crime rate declines with age. Why does this phenomenon take place? One view is that there is a direct relationship between aging and desistance. As they mature, troubled youths are able to develop a long-term life view and resist the need for immediate gratification.[84] Gordon Trasler found that kids view teenage crime as "fun." Youths view their petty but risky and exciting crimes as a social activity that provides adventure in an otherwise boring and unsympathetic world. As they grow older, their life patterns are inconsistent with criminality; delinquents literally grow out of crime.[85]

James Q. Wilson and Richard Herrnstein argue that the aging-out process is a function of the natural history of the human life cycle. Deviance in adolescence is fuelled by the need for conventionally unobtainable money and sex and reinforced by close relationships with peers who defy conventional morality. At the same time, teenagers are becoming independent from parents and other adults who enforce conventional standards. They have a new sense of energy and strength and are involved with peers who are similarly vigorous and frustrated. Adulthood brings increasingly powerful ties to conventional society, not the least of which is the acquisition of a family. Adults also develop the ability to delay gratification and forgo the immediate gains that law violations bring; crime rates consequently decline with age.

> When you're a teenager, you're rowdy. Nowadays, you aren't rowdy. You know, you want to settle down because you can go to jail now. [When] you are a boy, you can be put into a detention home. But you can go to jail now. Jail ain't no place to go.[86]

Aging out of crime may also be influenced by the success or failure of interpersonal relationships. Children who are labelled antisocial by teachers, police, parents, and neighbours find they may have little choice but to remain committed to their criminal careers.[87] If, however, youngsters believe that they have little chance of achieving success, money, and happiness through crimes, they are more likely to desist.[88] As they mature, individuals may be influenced by their adult relationships. For example, people who maintain successful marriages are more likely to desist from antisocial behaviours than those whose marriages fail.[89]

Although most people age out of crime, some may find a criminal career a reasonable alternative. Yet even people who actively remain in a criminal career will eventually slow down as they age. Crime is too dangerous, physically taxing, and unrewarding, and punishments are too harsh and long-lasting, to become a long-term way of life for most people. The uniformity of maturational changes in the crime rate suggests to some that it must be part of a biological "evolutionary process."[90] By middle age, even the most chronic offenders often terminate criminal behaviour.

Connections

The belief that life events influence behaviour choices is at the core of life-course theories. They hold that as people and their social environment change, so do their criminal behaviour patterns. Theories of the criminal life course are discussed in Chapter 10.

Changing Demographics. The general decline in crime rates over the decade of the 1990s has coincided with the decreasing proportion of persons aged 15 to 24. This age group has the highest rate for committing crimes and being a victim of crime. In the year 2000, the Canadian Centre for Justice Statistics tells us that persons aged 15 to 24 years were 14 percent of the total population. Meanwhile, they accounted for 45 percent of those charged with property crimes, and 31 percent of persons charged with violent crimes. Figure 3.5 shows the trend in overall crime, and the official rate of 15-to-24-year-olds committing crime. Between 1962 and 1978, both lines show a constant increase. The overall crime rate climbed 158 percent while the rate of 15-to-24-year-olds increased by 34 percent. The overall rate of crime increased until 1991, while the rate of 15-to-24-year-olds declined. Since 1991, both measures have decreased: the general crime rate by 26 percent and that of 15-to-24-year-olds by 6 percent. Variations in the size of the high-risk age group have had some effect on the crime rate, but the extent of this influence is not clear. Adding to the debate is Steven Levitt's work on whether the changing age structure can explain changes in crime rates. He says that changing age demographics produce only about a 1 percent change in the amount of crime. While an increase in the number of youths is forecast within a decade, there will also be an increase in older adults as well, driving the trend downward.[91]

Gender and Crime

The three major forms of criminal statistics generally agree on the finding that male crime rates are probably much higher than those for females. However, women are more at risk of committing, and being victimized by, certain crimes, as shown in Exhibit 3.2.

Figure 3.5   **Crime rate and selected demographics**

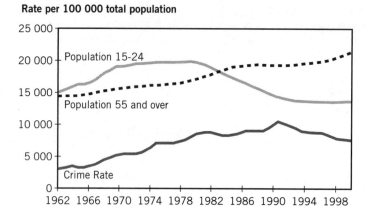

Rate per 100 000 total population

Note that the population 15-24 and population 55 and over lines refer to changes in population for these age groups and not changes in crime rates.
Source: Uniform Crime Reporting Survey, CCJS and Annual Demographic Statistics, 2000 Report.

Explaining Gender Differences: Biosocial Differences. How can the gender differences in the crime rate be explained? Early criminologists pointed to the emotional, physical, and psychological differences between males and females. They maintained that because females were weaker and more passive, they were less likely to commit crimes. The most widely cited evidence was contained in Cesare Lombroso's 1895 book, *The Female Offender*.[92] Lombroso argued that there was a small group of female criminals who lacked "typical" female traits of "piety, maternity, undeveloped intelligence, and weakness." In physical appearance as well as in emotionality, delinquent females appeared closer to men than to other women. Lombroso's theory became known as the **masculinity hypothesis**; in essence, a few "masculine" females were responsible for the handful of crimes committed by women.

Another early view of female crime focused on the supposed dynamics of sexual relationships. Female criminals were viewed as either sexually controlling or sexually naive, either manipulating men for profit or being manipulated by them. The female's criminality was often masked, because criminal justice authorities were reluctant to take action against a woman.[93] Referred to as the **chivalry hypothesis**, Pollack's view was that much of the criminality of females is hidden because of the generally protective and benevolent attitudes toward them in our culture.[94] In other words, police are less likely to arrest, juries less likely to convict, and judges less likely to incarcerate female offenders.

While these early writings are now seen as sexist and androcentric (male-centred), some criminologists still consider trait differences as a key determinant of crime rate differences. For example, some criminologists link antisocial behaviour to hormonal influences by arguing that male sex hormones (**androgens**) account for their

more aggressive behaviour and that gender-related hormonal differences can also explain the gender gap in the crime rate.[95]

Explaining Gender Differences: Socialization. By mid-century, it was common for criminologists to describe gender differences in the crime rate as a function of socialization. Textbooks explained the relatively low female crime rate by citing the fact that in contrast to boys, girls were supervised more closely and protected from competition.[96] The few female criminals were seen as troubled individuals, alienated at home, who pursued crime as a means of compensating for their disrupted personal lives.[97] The streets became a "second home" to girls whose physical and emotional adjustment was hampered by a strained home life, marked by such conditions as absent fathers, overly competitive mothers, and so on.

Connections

Gender differences in the crime rate may be a function of androgen levels because these hormones cause areas of the brain to become less sensitive to environmental stimuli, making males more likely to seek high levels of stimulation and to tolerate more pain in the process. Chapter 6's discussion of the biosocial causes of crime reviews this issue in greater detail.

Some experts continue to explain gender-based crime differences as a function of socialization. Most girls, they argue, are socialized to be less aggressive than boys; they are supervised more closely by parents. The majority of females learn to respond to provocation by feeling anxious and depressed, whereas boys are encour-

Exhibit 3.2	Quick Facts – Profile of Women and the Criminal Justice System

Based on the 1999 General Social Survey:

- Twenty-five percent of women and 27 percent of men report being victimized in the past year.
- Women are more likely to be victims of sexual assault (33/1000) than men (8/1000).
- Men are more likely to victims of robbery (12/1000) than women (7/1000).
- Men are more likely to be victims of assault (92/1000) than women 70/1000).
- Over 60 percent of victimizations against men and women are not reported to the police.
- Women report more difficulty (33 percent) than men (17 percent) in daily activities after victimization.
- Women knew their perpetrator (82 percent of the time) or were related (41 percent) or friends (41 percent).
- Strangers victimized women 18 percent of the time, compared to men (36 percent).
- Women are more likely to be murdered by a spouse (35 percent) than a man (3 percent).
- Sixty-five percent of women who were assaulted by a partner were victimized more than once.
- Women are a minority of offenders (17 percent of all adults).
- Women committed 22 percent of property crimes, and 17 percent of violent crimes.
- The most common charge against women is theft (25 percent adult women; 32 percent young women).
- Women are less likely to be found guilty (53 percent of the time) than men (63 percent).
- Females represented 21 percent of the youth court caseload.
- Female inmates are more likely to be younger, of Aboriginal descent, single, less educated, and unemployed.
- Drug-related offences account for 27 percent of federal and 13 percent of admissions to provincial facilities.

Source: *Women in Canada*, Canadian Centre for Justice Statistics Profile Series, Catalogue 85F0033MIE, June 2001.

discomfort.[98] Overall, women are much more likely to feel distressed than men, experiencing sadness, anxiety, and uneasiness. The relatively few females who commit violent crimes report having home and family relationships that are more troubled than those experienced by male delinquents.[99]

Explaining Gender Differences: Feminist Views. In the 1970s, several influential works, most notably Freda Adler's *Sisters in Crime* and Rita James Simon's *The Contemporary Woman and Crime*,[100] revolutionized the thinking on the cause of gender differences in the crime rate. Their research, which today is referred to as **liberal feminist theory**, focused attention on the social and economic role of women in society and its relationship to female crime rates. Both Adler and Simon believed that the traditionally lower crime rate for women could be explained by their "second-class" economic and social position. They further contended that as women's social roles changed and their lifestyles became more like those of males, the crime rates would converge. However, one researcher tried to discover whether gender convergence produced higher crime rates for women, but was unable to find a strong link.[101]

Criminologists, responding to the feminist research, began to refer to the "new female criminal." The rapid increase in the female crime rate during the 1960s and 1970s, especially in what had traditionally been male-oriented crimes (burglary, larceny), seemed to give support to the convergence model. In addition, self-report studies seem to indicate that (1) the pattern of female criminality, if not its frequency, is quite similar to that of male criminality, and (2) the factors that predispose male criminals to crime have an equal impact on female criminals.[102] The contributions of Adler and Simon encouraged other criminologists to assess the association among economic issues, gender roles, and criminality.

Connections

Critical criminologists view gender inequality as stemming from the unequal power of men and women in a capitalist society and the exploitation of females by fathers and husbands. Women are considered a "commodity" worth possessing, like land or money; female crime patterns can be explained by these exploitive power relationships. These views, referred to as Marxist or radical feminism, are considered more fully in Chapter 9.

aged to retaliate with aggression. While females get angry as often as males, many have been taught to blame themselves for harbouring such negative feelings. Females are therefore much more likely than males to respond to anger with feelings of depression, anxiety, fear, and shame. While females are socialized to fear that their anger will harm valued relationships, males react with "moral outrage," looking to blame others for their

Will the gender differences in the crime rate eventually dissolve? Are gender differences permanent and unchanging? Some criminologists find that gender-based crime rate differences remain significant and argue that the emancipation of women has had relatively little influence on female crime rates.[103] They dispute the idea that increases in the female arrest rate reflect economic or social changes brought about by the women's movement. For one thing, many female criminals come from the socioeconomic class least affected by the women's movement; their crimes seem more a function of economic inequality than women's rights. For another, the offence patterns of women are still quite different from those of men, who are still committing a disproportionate share of serious crimes, such as robbery, burglary, murder, and assault.[104] In the year 2000, women committed 15 percent of violent crimes in Canada, 16 percent of the assaults, 10 percent of the homicides, and 2 percent of the sexual assaults. In contrast, young women committed 25 percent of the violent crime, 29 percent of assaults, 12 percent of homicides, and 4 percent of sexual assaults. While this could be taken as gender convergence, much international research has failed to find an association between economic development and female crime rates.[105] That is, there is little evidence that nations undergoing economic development also experience increases in the female violence rate.

Perhaps it is too soon for criminologists to write off "the new female criminal." After all, though male arrest rates are still considerably higher than female rates, the female rates seem to be increasing at a faster pace.

It is possible, as Roy Austin claims, that convergence has been delayed by a slower-than-expected change in gender roles; the women's movement has not yet achieved its full impact on social life.[106] One reason is that while expanding their economic role, women have not abandoned their conventional role of taking care of family and home; women today are being forced to cope with added financial and social burdens. If gender roles are truly equivalent, crime rates may eventually converge; these changes appear to now be taking place.

Connections

The concept of relative deprivation refers to the fact that people compare their success to those they are in immediate contact with. Even if conditions improve, they may still feel like they are falling behind. A sense of relative deprivation, discussed in Chapter 7, may lead to criminal activity.

Criminal Careers

The crime data show that most offenders commit a single criminal act and upon arrest discontinue their antisocial activity. Others commit a few crimes of less serious nature. However, a small group of individuals accounts for a majority of all crimes committed. These persistent offenders are referred to as **career criminals,** or **chronic offenders.**

Delinquency in a Birth Cohort

The concept of the chronic or career offender is most closely associated with the research efforts of Marvin Wolfgang, Robert Figlio, and Thorsten Sellin.[107] In their landmark study, *Delinquency in a Birth Cohort,* official records were used to follow the criminal careers of a cohort of 9945 boys born in Philadelphia in 1945 from the time of their birth until they reached 18 years of age in 1963. Official police records were used to identify delinquents. About one-third of the boys (3475) had some police contact. The remaining two-thirds (6470) had none. Each delinquent's actions were given a seriousness weight score for every delinquent act.[108] The weighting of delinquent acts allowed the researchers to differentiate, for example, between a simple assault requiring no medical attention for the victim and a serious assault in which the victim needed hospitalization.

The best-known discovery of Wolfgang and his associates was the chronic offender. The cohort data indicated that 54 percent (1862) of the sample's delinquent youths were repeat offenders, while the remaining 46 percent (1613) were one-time offenders. However, the repeaters could be further categorized as nonchronic recidivists and chronic recidivists. The former consisted of 1235 youths who had been arrested more than once but fewer than five times and who made up 35.6 percent of all delinquents. The latter were a group of 627 boys arrested five times or more, who accounted for 18 percent of the delinquents and 6 percent of the total sample of 9945.

It was the chronic offenders (known today as "the chronic 6 percent") who were involved in the most dramatic amounts of delinquent behaviour; they were responsible for 5305 offences, or 51.9 percent of all offences. Even more striking was the involvement of chronic offenders in serious criminal acts. Of the entire sample, they committed 71 percent of the homicides, 73 percent of the rapes, 82 percent of the robberies, and 69 percent of the aggravated assaults.

Wolfgang and his associates found that arrest and court experience did little to deter the chronic offender. In fact, punishment was inversely related to chronic offending: The more stringent the sanctions chronic offenders received, the more likely they would be to engage in repeated criminal behaviour.

Birth Cohort II

The subjects who made up Wolfgang's original birth cohort were born in 1945. How have behaviour patterns changed in subsequent years? To answer this question, Wolfgang and his associates selected a new, larger birth cohort, born in Philadelphia in 1958, and followed them until their maturity.[109] The 1958 cohort was larger than the original, having more than 27 000 subjects, including 13 000 males and 14 000 females.

Although the proportion of delinquent youths was about the same as that in the 1945 cohort, those in the larger sample were involved in 20 089 delinquent arrests. Chronic offenders (five or more arrests as juveniles) made up 7.5 percent of the 1958 sample (compared with 6.3 percent in 1945) and 23 percent of all delinquent offenders (compared with 18 percent in 1945). Chronic female delinquency was relatively rare—only 1 percent of the females in the survey were chronic offenders.

Chronic male delinquents continued to commit more than their share of criminal behaviour. They accounted for 61 percent of the total offences and a disproportionate amount of the most serious crimes: 61 percent of the homicides, 76 percent of the rapes, 73 percent of the robberies, and 65 percent of the aggravated assaults. The chronic female offender was less likely to be involved in serious crimes.

It is interesting that as a group, the 1958 cohort were involved in significantly more serious crimes than the 1945 group. For example, their violent offence rate (149 per 1000 in the sample) was three times higher than the rate for the 1945 cohort (47 per 1000 subjects).

In the 1945 cohort chronic offenders dominated the total crime rate and continued their law-violating careers as adults. The newer cohort study is showing that the chronic offender syndrome is being maintained in a group of subjects born 13 years later than the original cohort and, if anything, more violent than that first group. Finally, the efforts of the justice system seem to have little preventive effect on the behaviour of chronic offenders: The more often a person was arrested, the more likely he or she was to be arrested again. For males, 26 percent of the entire group had one violent-offence arrest; of that 26 percent, 34 percent went on to commit a second violent offence, while 43 percent of the three-time losers went on to a fourth arrest, and so on.

Chronic Offender Research

Wolfgang's pioneering effort to identify the chronic career offender has been replicated by a number of other important research studies. Lyle Shannon also used the cohort approach to investigate career delinquency patterns.[110] D.J. West and D.P. Farrington's ongoing study of youths born in London has also shown that a small number of recidivists continue their behaviour as adults and that arrest and conviction have little influence on their behaviour other than to amplify the probability of their law violations: Youths with multiple convictions as juveniles tend to have multiple convictions as adults. The most important childhood risk factors associated with chronic offending include a history of troublesomeness, a personality that reveres daring behaviour, a delinquent

sibling, and a convicted parent. Farrington finds that the most chronic offenders could be identified by age 10 on the basis of personality and background features.[111]

In another important study, a sample was followed through adulthood to age 30.[112] Seventy percent of the "persistent" adult offenders had also been chronic juvenile offenders; they had an 80 percent chance of becoming adult offenders and a 50 percent chance of being arrested four or more times as adults. In comparison, subjects with no juvenile arrests had only an 18 percent chance of being arrested as an adult. The chronic offenders also continued to engage in the most serious crimes. Although they accounted for only 15 percent of the follow-up sample, the former chronic delinquents were involved in 74 percent of all arrests and 82 percent of all serious crimes, such as homicide, rape, and robbery.

The cohort follow-ups clearly show that chronic juvenile offenders continue their law-violating careers as adults, a concept referred to as the **continuity of crime**. Kids who are found to be disruptive and antisocial as early as age five or six are the ones most likely to exhibit stable, long-term patterns of disruptive behaviour through adolescence. They have measurable behavioural problems in such areas as learning and motor skills, cognitive abilities, family relations, and other areas of social, psychological, and physical functioning. Youthful offenders who persist are more likely to abuse alcohol, get into trouble while in military service, become economically dependent, have lower aspirations, get divorced or separated, and have a weak employment record.[113] Canadian research shows that aggressive children are more likely to feel unhappy and rejected. [114] Criminalizing their behaviour by lowering the age of criminal responsibility would do nothing to deal with the problems that might cause the behaviour in the first place.

Additional studies conducted in Europe, such as the Stockholm cohort project (Project Metropolitan, which contains 15 117 male and female subjects), indicates that criminal career development in Sweden follows many of the same patterns found in U.S. cohorts. Similarly, data from a sample of 411 males born in London found that the frequency of offending was predicted by early onset of antisocial behaviour, associating with deviant peers, certain personality traits (such as a low level of anxiety), poor school achievement, and dysfunctional family relations. Those delinquents who persisted into adulthood (ages 21 to 32) exhibited low IQs, substance abuse, chronic unemployment, and a low degree of commitment to school.[115] Further analysis of these data shows that the persistent offender group may be further subdivided into high- and low-rate offenders, with the former committing two or three times as many offences as the latter.[116] Punishment does little to deter their behaviour and, if anything, prompts escalation of their criminal activities.

Correctional Services Canada reports that of 14 091 male offenders incarcerated in 1997, 54 percent had no term of previous federal incarceration, 17 percent had one term, 11 percent had two, 7 percent had three, and 10 percent had more than three. Women were far more likely to have had no previous term of federal incarceration (75 percent), and less likely to have more than three (4 percent). Of provincial inmates, 83 percent had at least one prior conviction. In a "snapshot" of inmates done in 1996, it was found that 96 percent of those classified as high risk had previous convictions.[117]

In sum, research shows that a small group of offenders are responsible for a great deal of all crime. These youths begin their offending career at an extremely young age and persist into their adulthood.

Implications of the Chronic Offender Concept

The findings of the cohort studies and the discovery of the chronic offender have revitalized criminological theory. If relatively few offenders become chronic, persistent criminals, it is possible that they possess some individual trait that is responsible for their criminality. Most people exposed to troublesome social conditions, such as poverty, do not become chronic offenders; thus, it is unlikely that social conditions alone can cause chronic offending. If not, what does?

Traditional theories of criminal behaviour have failed to distinguish between chronic and occasional offenders. They have concentrated more on explaining why people begin to commit crime and paid scant attention to the reasons that people stop offending. The "discovery" of the chronic offender 25 years ago has forced criminologists to consider such issues as persistence and desistence in their explanations of crime; more recent theories account not only for the onset of criminality but also its termination. Why do most offenders "age out" of crime? Why do some persist into adulthood? Ongoing research efforts are now aimed at answering these critical questions.

The chronic offender concept has also raised questions about the treatment of known offenders: If we can identify chronic offenders, what should we do about them? How can chronic offenders be controlled if punishment actually escalates the frequency of their criminal activity? The chronic offender has thus become a central focus of crime control policy. Concern about repeat offenders has been translated into programs at various stages of the justice process.

Even more important has been the effect of the chronic offender on sentencing policy. Sentencing policies are increasingly designed to incapacitate serious offenders for long periods of time without hope of probation or parole. In the United States a mandatory sentence for vio-

Studies in Europe show that persistent chronic offenders account for a significant portion of all criminal acts. Frequency of offences has been associated with early onset of antisocial behaviour, association with deviant peers, personality disorders, poor school achievement, dysfunctional family relations, low IQ, substance abuse, chronic unemployment, and a low degree of commitment to school. Could these neo-Nazi youths based in Berlin be influenced by the same personal characteristics that promote and sustain chronic criminal offending?

lent or drug-related crimes in more than 30 states is commonly known as a "three strikes and you're out" policy. Whether such policies can be effective in reducing crime rates or are merely "get tough" measures designed to placate conservative voters still remains to be seen.

Summary

There are three primary sources of crime statistics: the Uniform Crime Report based on police data accumulated by the CCJS, self-reports of criminal behaviour, and victim surveys. All three sources tell us that there is quite a bit of crime in Canada and that until the early 1990s the amount of violent crime was increasing. Each data source has its strengths and weaknesses, and though quite different from one another, they actually agree on the nature of criminal behaviour. Commissions of inquiry are also a quasi-judicial source of information about crime that can provide detailed investigation of criminal issues.

The data sources show some stable patterns in the crime rate. Ecological patterns show that some areas of the country are more crime-prone than others, that there are seasons and times for crime, and that these patterns are quite stable. There is also evidence of a gender and age gap in the crime rate. Men usually commit more crime than women, and young people commit more crime than the elderly. The crime data show that people commit less crime as they age, but the significance and cause of this pattern is still not completely understood.

Similarly, there appear to be class patterns in the crime rate. However, it is still unclear whether these are true differences or a function of discriminatory law enforcement.

One of the most important findings from cohort research is the existence of the chronic offender, a repeat criminal responsible for a significant amount of all law violations. Chronic offenders begin their career early in life and, rather than aging out of crime, persist in their criminal behaviour into adulthood. The discovery of the chronic offender has led to the study of developmental criminology—why people persist, desist, terminate, or escalate their deviant behaviour.

One thing this chapter clearly shows is that we not only have to understand the reasons why crime occurs, but we need to be aware of what the statistics on crime reflect as well, because they seldom portray at face value the reality they purport to describe. Crime statistics can be an artifact of reporting practices, police enforcement, changing legal definitions of crime, and media representations.

Thinking Like a Criminologist

An assistant deputy minister in the federal Department of Justice has asked for your professional advice on how to reduce the threat of young offenders becoming chronic offenders. Some of the more conservative members of the government believe that juvenile delinquents who are punished harshly are less likely to recidivate than youths who receive lesser punishments, such as community corrections or probation.

The bureaucrat is unsure whether such an approach can reduce the threat of chronic offending. Can tough punishment produce deviant identities that lock kids in a criminal way of life? This would be counterproductive. On the other hand, will a strategy stressing punishment have relatively little impact if these are serious chronic offenders? You have been asked for your professional advice. You find it difficult, because you remember a lecture given by the Minister of Corrections, John Edwards, at St. Thomas University in 1996 in which he described the profile of the federal offender. Ninety-seven percent are male, most are single, and 75 percent have committed serious violent offences. Two-thirds of the admissions have done provincial time, and most have records going back into juvenile years. The average educational level of offenders is Grade 7, and 68 percent test out below Grade 8 in language and mathematics. More than half claim to have been abused as children, and three-quarters have unstable job histories. Does punishment begin to get at these underlying issues?

Key Terms

aging out
androgens
attrition
career criminals
chivalry hypothesis
chronic offenders
continuity of crime
crime rate

definition-sensitive crimes
desistance phenomenon
early onset
expressive crimes
founded
incidence
incident-based data
instrumental crimes

liberal feminist theory
masculinity hypothesis
media-sensitive crimes
percentage change
policing-sensitive crimes
report-sensitive crimes
self-report survey
Uniform Crime Report (UCR)

 See the book-specific website at www.siegelcriminology2e.nelson.com for additional chapter links, discussions, and quizzes.

Chapter

Victims and Victimization

4

For many years, crime victims were not considered an important topic for criminological study. Victims were viewed as the passive receptors of a criminal's anger, greed, or frustration; they were people considered to be in the "wrong place at the wrong time." In the late 1960s, a number of pioneering studies found that, contrary to popular belief, the victim's function is an important one in the crime process. Victims can influence criminal behaviour by playing an active role in the criminal incident—for example, when an assault victim initially insults and provokes his eventual attacker. Research efforts have found that victims can also play an indirect role in the criminal incident—for example, when people adopt a lifestyle that continually brings them into high crime areas.

The discovery that the victim plays an important role in the crime process has prompted the scientific study of the victim, or **victimology**; criminologists who focus their attention on the crime victim refer to themselves as **victimologists**. Victim studies have also taken on great importance because of concern for those injured in violent crimes or who suffer loss owing to economic crimes.

"Gutless politicians are only concerned for the rights of criminals" reads a protest sign outside the Just Desserts café in Toronto. The criticism became especially vehement after it was revealed that the suspect in the shooting at the café was not a Canadian citizen and had been convicted previously of violent offences. There was an outcry demanding that "aliens" who commit crimes should be deported.

The 1993 General Social Survey (GSS) in Canada indicates that 24 percent of Canadians were the victims of at least one crime in the previous year. An estimated two million households suffered from a break and enter, motor vehicle theft, theft of household property, or vandalism in 1992. The advantage of using the General Social Survey to measure victimization is that it enables us to count crimes not reported to the police.

In this chapter, the focus is on victims and their relationship to the criminal process. First, using available victim data, we analyze the nature and extent of victimization. We then turn to a discussion of the relationship between victims and criminal offenders, and we summarize the various theories of victimization. Finally, we look at how society has responded to the needs of victims and at the special problems they still face.

Problems of Crime Victims: Loss and Suffering

Being the target or a victim of rape, robbery, or assault is in itself a terrible burden and one that can have considerable long-term consequences.[1] The Insurance Board of Canada estimates that over $1 billion a year is paid in claims due to property crime and that theft is the cause of one-third of all homeowner claims paid. Between 1981 and 1985 police recovered stolen property in about 30 percent of the reported incidents. This recovery rate fell to 23 percent in the 1990s because of the shifting emphasis on policing violent crime.

However, property losses are only a small part of the toll that crime takes on victims. Productivity losses due to injury, medical costs, and the "value" that can be placed on psychological pain and emotional trauma also take their toll. As stated in a press release in June 1998 by the Solicitor General of Canada announcing a new $32-million crime prevention initiative:

> Crime in Canada has traditionally been dealt with primarily through reactive measures—the apprehension, sentencing, incarceration and rehabilitation of offenders. According to Statistics Canada estimates (1994–95), almost $10 billion a year is spent by governments on Canada's criminal justice system (i.e., police, courts and corrections). However, this amount represents a small portion of the total costs of crime. If the personal and physical costs—such as costs associated with pain and suffering of victims or lost productivity—are included, the annual cost of crime in Canada may be as high as $46 billion. Moreover, this figure does not include the cost of white collar crime, tax evasion or stock market manipulation.

There are other costs of crime that cannot be quantified. Crime hurts people and makes them feel unsafe; it decreases quality of life and changes the face of our communities. The ripple effects of crime are felt in a broad range of sectors including health, social services, education, labour and employment.

In order to prevent crime, action must take place at the community level. It is the people who live, work and play in a community who best understand their area's resources, problems, needs and capacities.

Another study, this in the United States, put the total value of all crime-related costs, including long-term suffering, trauma, and risk of death, at about $1800 per person.[2]

The problems associated with crime are not restricted to its costs. Victims are likely to suffer serious physical injury, often requiring medical treatment. And victims' suffering does not end when the attacker leaves the scene of the crime. They may suffer more "victimization" at the hands of the justice system. While the crime is still fresh in their minds, victims may be subjected to insensitive questioning by police, including innuendos or suspicion that the victim was somehow at fault. Victims may also

Table 4.1	Estimates of some of the costs of crime, 1993	
	CONSERVATIVE ESTIMATE ($BILLIONS)	MORE EXTENSIVE ESTIMATE ($BILLIONS)
Direct costs of victimization	4.73	13.58
Shattered lives	—	12.50
Policing and private security	9.10	12.60
Court and legal costs	0.98	0.98
Corrections costs	2.70	2.70
Total excluding shattered lives	17.50	29.90
Total including shattered lives	—	42.40

Source: Paul Brantingham and Stephen T. Easton, *Who Pays and How Much?* (Vancouver: Fraser Institute, 1998).

Connections

Some crimes are called "victimless" crimes, not because there is no one hurt in the process, but because they are defined by an agreement between two parties. See Chapter 14 for more on this definition of crime.

have difficulty learning what is going on in the case. In addition, their property is often kept for a long time as evidence and may never be returned, and their wages may be lost because of time spent testifying in court.

Time may be wasted when victims appear in court only to have their case postponed or dismissed. Furthermore, they may find that authorities are indifferent to their fear of retaliation if they cooperate in the offender's prosecution, and they may be fearful of testifying in court and being embarrassed by defence attorneys. Only a few courthouses have services onsite to assist victims appearing in court as witnesses.[3]

After the incident is over, the victim may suffer stress and anxiety, even when physical traumas and financial losses and the justice process have been forgotten. For example, women who were sexually and physically abused as children are more suicidal as adults than are nonabused females.[4] Those who suffered the pains of abuse also have significantly higher levels of homelessness; a history of physical and sexual abuse is especially common among homeless women, who also display symptoms of mental illness.[5] The long-term emotional trauma suffered by women in the aftermath of spousal assault is also well documented.[6] Spousal abuse victims suffer an extremely high prevalence of depression, post-traumatic stress disorder, anxiety disorder, and obsessive-compulsive disorder. Symptoms include nightmares, hyper arousal, and repression of the abuse.

In a report prepared for Canada's Solicitor General, Trevor Markesteyn documents how as a result of a nondomestic assault, such as being robbed, women generally suffer more than men, and the elderly experience more distress than the young. Many Canadians are victimized every year by robbery, and if the crime is marked by violence and loss of property, the psychological consequences can range from mild upset and anger to post-traumatic stress disorder. Virtually every victim experiences some emotional and/or behavioural reaction and 10 to 30 percent of robbery victims suffer severe short-term trauma. After six months the effects appear to diminish, but 5 to 10 percent of victims continue to suffer significant psychopathology. The effects last longer for victims of domestic violence, although this crime is seriously underreported and thus difficult to measure. Child abuse is also more pervasive than official statistics indicate, and children who are victims of physical assault will have problems such as noncompliance, tantrums and aggression, serious intellectual deficits, language delays, and interpersonal problems.[7]

Of course women are not the only ones who suffer in the aftermath of violence; male victims of violent attacks also suffer postcrime stress disorders. Viewing themselves from a male frame of reference, these victims express feelings of being weak and helpless. Also, whereas female victims tend to internalize and place the blame for their victimization on themselves, males are more likely to externalize blame, expressing anger toward their attackers.[8] One researcher points out in his work on life-story interviews with men incarcerated for violent offences that many of those who inflict violence on others have themselves been subjected to multiple forms of abuse.[9]

In short, the pain and suffering experienced by crime victims does not stop after the criminal incident is over. Many go through a fundamental life change, viewing the world more suspiciously and less as a safe, controllable, and meaningful place, becoming more likely to suffer psychological stress for extended periods of time.[10]

Some victims may find that the physical wounds received during a criminal incident haunt them for the rest of their lives, especially if they become physically disabled due to wounds sustained during episodes of violence. Many victims have no insurance, and treatment costs add to the overload on an overburdened health-care system.[11]

The Perception of the Risk of Being a Victim

In a national survey, 46 percent of Canadians 15 years and over thought that crime had increased between 1988 and 1993, despite the fact that overall rates of victimization had remained the same or decreased. During this time 24 percent of Canadians were victims of crime, the same percentage who were victims of crime in 1988. Researchers have found that Canadians were no more likely to be victims of assault, theft (either of personal or household property), vandalism, or break and enter in 1993 than they had been five years previously. The results of this victimization study raise questions about crime and the public's perception of risk.[12]

The fact that the public overestimates the likelihood of crime in their own neighbourhood, despite contradic-

tory evidence from their own experience, points to the influence of extraneous factors in the public's knowledge of crime. It would seem that people do not rely on their own experience in assessing the likelihood of being a victim of crime. Are members of the public overly concerned about crime? Is their fear totally out of fit with reality? Are the media responsible?

We can certainly find evidence of the media's distortions. In 1996, Statistics Canada reported a decrease in Canada's murder rate for the fourth year in a row. At the same time, however, television news had increased its coverage of murder stories, as we can see from Figure 4.1.[13] According to the National Media Archive's annual study of murder stories, coverage tended to focus on sensational murders–the Bernardo and Simpson trials each made up 18 percent of the CBC's murder stories in 1995. Furthermore, according to Statistics Canada, 16 percent of the murders in 1995 were committed by someone unknown to the victim, but on television the murders most likely to be reported are these random murders. While 83 percent of the murders committed in Canada are committed by a spouse or acquaintance of the victim, 54 percent of CBC and 66 percent of CTV coverage focused on random murders. Only 18 percent of CBC and 11 percent of CTV murder stories focused on murders committed by someone known to the victim.[14]

In the 1999 General Social Survey, however, only 29 percent of Canadians felt that crime had increased, showing that the public feels safer than they did in 1993. The fear of crime does not seem to adversely affect people's activities, as three out of four Canadians walk alone in their own neighbourhoods after dark, and fewer people felt worried being at home alone at night. Overall,

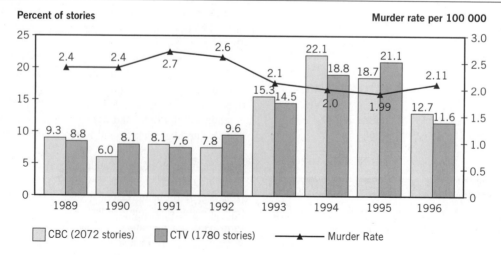

| Figure 4.1 | Television coverage of murder, 1989–1996 |

SOURCE: National Media Archive 1997: figure A

91 percent of Canadians reported being very or somewhat satisfied with their personal safety.[15]

It is reassuring that the fear of crime seems to be decreasing, yet we have to be conscious of how crime can be distorted in the media, because it has an effect on demands for police services, the public's perception of the courts, and how politicians develop programs to prevent and fight crime.[16]

Problems of Crime Victims: Antisocial Behaviour

In the 1996 film *Never Talk to Strangers*, a psychiatrist played by Rebecca DeMornay suspects that her new boyfriend (Antonio Banderas) is a killer. As the bodies begin to pile up, the audience begins to share her suspicions. In the film's surprise ending, we learn that DeMornay is the real killer. It seems her personality was irrevocably damaged when her father sexually abused her as a child and murdered her mother while she looked on.

There is growing evidence that the association between early victimization and later criminality is not merely the fictional subject of Hollywood films; people who are the victims of crime also seem more likely to commit crime themselves. For example, an analysis of juvenile court records from a metropolitan area in the U.S. midwest conducted by Tim Ireland and Cathy Spatz Widom found that child maltreatment was a significant predictor of future criminality. Having been abused or neglected increased the odds of being arrested as a juvenile and also of having at least one alcohol- or drug-related arrest in adulthood. The odds of adult arrest were 39 percent greater for maltreated than for nonabused adolescents.[17] Widom has referred to the phenomenon of child victims later becoming adult criminals as the **cycle of violence**.[18] In her early work Widom was cautious about generalizing her findings to the entire population, because the data obtained from juvenile court reflected only those cases that came to the attention of the authorities. Cases of abuse that were unreported might not exhibit the same pattern. However, despite this caution the cycle of violence thesis has become well accepted in the field and has become part of the popular lexicon as well.

The cycle of violence hypothesis is supported by research showing that young males are more likely to engage in violent behaviour if they were (1) the target of physical abuse and (2) exposed to interadult violence, especially if weapons were used.[19] The association between victimization and future behavioural difficulties is not limited to males; research efforts have found that females exposed to family violence may be even more likely to manifest behavioural and adjustment problems as they mature.[20]

Victimization thus presents financial, physical, and emotional strains that are difficult to overcome.

Connections

It has become common for Hollywood to depict women as psychopathic serial killers (*Friday the 14th, Black Widow, The Crush*). Are female serial killers common? Most research shows that movies aside, women are rarely involved in multiple murders. Chapter 11 reviews serial murder in some detail.

The Nature of Victimization

While criminologists depend largely on official statistics, victimization surveys are an important source of information about the nature and extent of victimization. The surveys were originally conceived as a way to estimate the distribution of unreported crime and use a highly sophisticated and complex sampling methodology to annually collect data from thousands of citizens. Statistical estimation techniques are then applied to the sample data to make estimates of victimization rates, trends, and patterns that occur in the entire population.

Victimization Surveys. In 1982 the Ministry of the Solicitor General conducted the Canadian Urban Victimization Survey, sampling 61 000 households in seven major Canadian cities: Vancouver, Edmonton, Winnipeg, Toronto, Montreal, Halifax/Dartmouth, and St. John's. The original purpose of this first victimization survey was to acquire information on the extent of crime between January 1 and December 31, 1981; the impact of victimization; public perception of crime and the criminal justice system; and public knowledge of crime prevention and compensation programs.[21] The results clearly showed that many offences were not reported to the police. Robberies, for example, were estimated to occur at a rate of 993 per 100 000 population, compared with the official police rate of 108 per 100 000![22]

The next Canadian victimization survey was conducted in 1988 as part of the General Social Survey. It was a telephone survey of about 10 000 Canadians 15 years of age and older; they were asked about their knowledge of victim services, perceived risk of victimization, and the number and kind of accidents and crimes respondents had been involved in during 1987. This national study included both urban and rural residents. Overall, it was estimated that there were 143 personal victimizations per 1000 people and 216 household incidents of victimization per 1000 people.[23] Two other victimization surveys have been conducted as part of the General Social Survey, in 1993 and 1999. They are discussed elsewhere in the book.

International patterns of victimization show that Canadians are relatively free from contact with crime compared with some countries, as shown in Table 4.2. With regard to car theft, Canada ranked sixth, seventh for burglary, and eighth for violent crime. In overall victimization, Canada's rate was lower than Australia, England and Wales, Netherlands, and Sweden. An alarming finding in the 2000 British Crime Survey was that while there was a 19 percent decrease in acquaintance-related violence, stranger-related violence increased 29 percent.

Some patterns in the victimization survey findings are stable and repetitive. These patterns are critical social facts because they indicate that victimization is not random but rather a function of personal and ecological factors. The stability of these patterns allows judgments to be made about the nature of victimization; policies can then be created that might eventually reduce the victimization rate. Who are victims? Where does victimization take place? What is the relationship between victims and criminals? Is there a difference in the report rate between crime that is **acquaintance-related** and that which is **stranger-related**? Answers to these questions can come from crime victimization surveys. In the following sections, some of the most important patterns and trends in victimization are discussed.

Connections

The importance of victimization will be more apparent in the context of other sources of information about crime. Chapter 3 presents an overview of major issues related to the measurement of crime.

Table 4.2	The profile of crime in different countries[1]					

(percentage of all offences: total = 100%): 2000 ICVS

	THEFTS FROM AND OF CARS	CAR VANDALISM	MOTORCYCLE AND BICYCLE THEFT	BURGLARY WITH ENTRY AND ATTEMPTS	ALL CONTACT CRIME[2]	THEFT OF PERSONAL PROPERTY
Australia	18	20	4	15	29	14
Belgium	14	23	15	17	19	13
Canada	20	15	10	13	27	15
Catalonia (Spain)	25	38	4	7	14	12
Denmark	14	13	26	13	21	12
England & Wales	19	23	6	12	30	10
Finland	11	16	19	6	36	13
France	23	31	6	8	24	9
Japan	8	26	40	13	11	2
Netherlands	12	26	21	10	19	12
Northern Ireland	20	25	10	11	22	11
Poland	21	23	10	10	20	16
Portugal	29	33	4	13	14	8
Scotland	16	30	6	9	28	12
Sweden	19	14	21	7	24	16
USA	20	22	7	15	20	16
Average	18	24	13	11	22	12

[1] Based on incidence rates. Percentages add to 100%.
[2] Based on robbery, sexual incidents, and assaults and threats.

Source: John von Kesteren, Pat Mayhew, Paul Nieuwbeerta, *Criminal Victimisation in Seven Industrialized Countries.* Key Findings from the 2000 International Crime Victims Survey. Research Policy number 187.

The Social Ecology of Victimization

The GSS survey data can tell us a lot about the social and demographic patterns of victimization: where, when, and how it occurs; or whether a victim's involvement in crime is random.

In Canada, the risk of personal injury increases from east to west, is higher for males than for females, and is lower for the elderly than the young. Neighbourhood characteristics influence the chances of victimization. Those living in urban areas have significantly higher rates of theft, sexual assault, and robbery than people living in nonmetropolitan, rural areas. Violent victimizations are more likely to be committed by strangers and in public than in times past. Robberies committed by strangers increased from 45 percent to 67 percent between 1988 and 1993, and assaults perpetrated by strangers increased from 26 percent to 38 percent in the same period.[24] According to the 1999 General Social Survey, however, 51 percent of robberies, and 25 percent of assaults were committed by strangers, down slightly from the 1993 proportions.

Victim Characteristics

A number of social and demographic characteristics distinguish victims from nonvictims. The most important of these factors are gender, age, social status, marital status, and location of residence. Table 4.3 shows victimization by social status, as well as age, location, gender, marital status, and lifestyle.

Gender. The GSS provides information on the background characteristics of the victims of crime, including gender. Men are more likely to be victims of robbery (12 victimizations per 1000 men versus 7 per 1000 for women) and assault (92 per 1000 for men, 70 per 1000 for women). Women are more likely to be victims of sexual assault (33 per 1000 for women, compared to 8 per 1000 for men) and theft (80 per 1000 for women, 71 per 1000 for men). Women's overall personal victimization was 189 per 1000 compared to 183 for men.

When men are the victims of violent crime, the perpetrator is usually a stranger. Women are much more likely to be attacked by a relative than men are; about two-thirds of all attacks against women are committed by a husband, boyfriend, family member, or acquaintance.[25] In two-thirds of sexual assaults, the victim is acquainted with her attacker. And as one researcher shows, women who violate the law are often prior victims of abuse.[26]

Gender is a significant factor in certain crimes, such as stalking and sexual assault. Women account for 78 percent of criminal harassment cases.[27] The way in which authorities deal with such crimes can be crucial. In the infamous Jane Doe case, the Metropolitan Toronto police failed to warn women that a serial rapist was committing crimes in their neighbourhood because they didn't want to alert the suspect. In 2000 a woman sued the same police force for $4.5 million in damages for failing to warn women in the city's north end that a sexual predator was attacking women in underground parking garages.

Age. Young people commit a greater proportion of certain crimes than other age groups. The Canadian Centre for Justice Statistics estimates that youths 16 to 24 years are responsible for 40 to 50 percent of victimizations.[28] And another researcher says that in the case of homicide these youths are especially likely to kill parents and other family members.[29] Moreover, because much crime is "intra-age" (within the same age group), youths themselves face a much greater victimization risk than older persons. Victim risk is highest in the 15 to 24 age group (405 per 1000), dropping abruptly to 262 incidents per 1000 between the ages of 25 and 34 years, as shown in Table 4.3. The elderly, who are thought of as being the helpless targets of predatory criminals, are actually much safer than young people, with a victimization rate of 12 per 1000.

According to these statistics, 37 percent of all personal crimes were committed against those between 15 and 24 (17 percent of the population). Moreover, 49 percent of sexual assaults and 57 percent of robberies, and 34 percent of robberies occurred in that age group. Those over 65 years of age (15 percent of the population) accounted for only 2 percent of total violations against the person.

The association between age and victimization may be bound up in the lifestyle shared by most young people. Adolescents often stay out late at night, go to public places, and hang out with other kids who have a high risk of criminal involvement. As was noted above, lifestyle is a significant factor in criminal victimization. Most adolescents aged 12 to 19 are attacked by offenders in the same age category, while a great majority of adults are victimized by adult criminals. Approximately 50 percent of victimizations occurred in or around a private residence, about 30 percent at a public institution such as a school, and about 20 percent in a public place such as a parking lot.

The home can be a dangerous place for children as well. Official statistics for 1994 show that 37 percent of all offenders in solved violent incidents against children under 12 were family members, and 25 percent were parents. Incidents in the home involving nonfamily members as offenders accounted for 63 percent of all offences, of which 16 percent were committed by strangers.[30] A more precise estimate of Canadian cases is difficult to cite, largely due to interprovincial inconsistencies in reporting. However, one survey estimated that more than 46 000 children in Ontario were suspected of being victims of abuse, which would be a rate of 21 per 1000 people or 2.1 percent.[31]

Table 4.3   Personal victimization rates, by victim characteristics, 1999[1]

Victim Characteristics	No. of Incidents (000s)						Rate per 1,000 population 15+					
	Total Personal Crimes	Theft Personal Property	Total Violent	Violent Sexual Assault	Robbery	Assault	Total Personal Crimes	Theft Personal Property	Total Violent	Sexual Assault	Violent Robbery	Assault
Total	4522	1831	2691	502	228	1961	186	75	111	21	9	81
Sex												
Females	2334	985	1349	410	81	858	189	80	109	33	7	70
Males	2188	845	1343	92	147	1103	183	71	112	8	12	92
Age (years)												
15-24	1661	620	1041	248	130	662	405	151	254	61	32	161
25-34	1161	445	716	126	46	544	262	101	162	28	10	123
35-44	891	370	520	74	—	427	170	70	99	14	—	81
45-54	539	242	297	43	—	230	128	58	71	10	—	55
55-64	173	97	76	—	—	64	64	36	28	—	—	24
65+ 97	56	41	—	—	—	27	16	12	—	—	—	—
Marital Status												
Married	1337	643	694	78	—	587	104	50	54	6	—	46
Common law	503	169	333	—	—	266	245	83	163	—	—	130
Single	2114	810	1303	291	165	846	347	133	214	48	27	139
Widow or widower	91	50	—	—	—	—	69	38	—	—	—	—
Separated or divorced	440	149	291	68	—	211	276	93	182	43	—	133
Don't know/Not stated	—	—	—	—	—	—	—	—	—	—	—	—
Main activity												
Working at a job	2590	1086	1504	235	95	1174	196	82	114	18	7	89
Looking at a job	147	—	118	—	—	79	327	—	263	—	—	175
A student	1149	488	661	145	87	429	384	163	221	49	29	143
Household work[2]	309	94	216	58	—	148	152	46	106	28	—	73
Retired	134	73	61	—	—	46	35	19	16	—	—	12
Other[3]	113	33	80	—	—	49	220	64	157	—	—	96
Don't know/Not stated	80	—	51	—	—	—	—	—	—	—	—	—

EVENING ACTIVITIES (# PER MONTH)

Less than 10	416	155	261	42	—	204	75	28	47	8	—	37
10-19	664	304	360	61	—	270	128	59	70	12	—	52
20-29	898	382	516	92	44	380	186	79	107	19	9	79
30+	988	1554	307	141	1105	305	119	187	37	17	133	
Don't know/Not stated	2542	—	—	-	-	—						

HOUSEHOLD INCOME ($)

0-14 999	360	88	272	61	—	181	254	62	192	43	—	127
15 000-29 999	557	189	368	70	—	279	194	66	128	24	—	97
30 000-39 999	412	164	249	46	—	189	174	69	105	20	—	80
40 000-59 999	825	348	477	82	—	361	199	84	115	20	—	87
60 000+	1226	559	667	92	60	515	193	88	105	14	9	81
Don't know/not stated	1141	484	658	151	71	435						

LOCATION OF HOME

Urban	3813	1573	2240	409	202	1629	199	82	117	21	11	85
Rural	709	257	451	94	—	332	138	50	88	18	—	65

Figures may not add to total due to rounding.
- nil or zero
— amount too small to be expressed
[1] Includes all incidents of spousal sexual and physical assault.
[2] Includes taking care of children and maternity/paternity leave.
[3] Includes long-term illness and volunteering.

Source: Statistics Canada, General Social Survey, 1999. Catalogue no. 85-002, Vol. 20, No. 10.

© "Personal Victimization Rates, by Victim Characteristics, 1999" from *Juristat*, 20, Catalogue No. 85-002.

In the United States, a survey conducted in 1979 by sociologists Richard Gelles and Murray Straus found that in a given year between 1.4 and 1.9 million children in the United States are subject to physical abuse by their parents. In addition to parent–child abuse, they found that 16 percent of the couples in their sample reported a violent act toward a spouse, 50 percent of multichild families reported attacks between siblings, and 20 percent had incidents in which children attacked parents.[32]

The U.S. National Committee to Prevent Child Abuse indicates that there was a 50 percent increase in cases of child abuse reported to police and social service agencies in 1995 compared to 1985.[33] It is uncertain whether this increase in reported abuse is a result of an increase in incidents or the result of greater public awareness of the problem, state efforts to encourage reporting, the proliferation of programs to prevent maltreatment, and expansion of the definition of abuse. Nonetheless, these data help explain in part why adolescents have a much greater victimization risk than adults.

Social Status. The poorest Canadians might be expected to be the most likely victims of crime, since one would think that they are more likely to live in areas that are crime-prone: inner-city, urban neighbourhoods. Indeed, the GSS shows that those households with incomes below $15 000 had a victimization rate of 254 per 1000, compared to the national average of 186 for personal crimes. The rate for violent crimes in this income category was 192 per 1000, compared to a national average of 111. The $60 000-and-over income group had the next highest victimization rate.

One fact that is particularly disturbing is that poverty increases the risk of child abuse. A 1998 report, *The Canadian Incidence Study of Reported Child Abuse and Neglect*, documents that 40 percent of child abuse cases stem from neglect, 19 percent from emotional maltreatment, 31 percent from physical abuse, and 10 percent from sexual abuse. Many of the children also suffered from depression and anxiety, and in three-quarters of the cases at least one parent suffered from drug abuse or domestic violence. Nearly half the families were led by a single parent, and 36 percent were collecting social assistance.[34]

While the poor are more likely to be the victims of assault, the wealthy are more likely to be the target of theft. Perhaps the affluent, who sport more expensive attire and drive better cars, earn the attention of thieves looking for attractive targets. Victim data suggest that thieves choose their targets carefully, selecting those who seem best able to provide them with a substantial haul. In contrast, the targets of violence, an expressive crime, are the nation's poorest people.

Marital Status. A traditional problem with crime statistics is that they provide little information on crime victims. Both the GSS and its predecessor the 1982 Canadian Urban Victimization Survey are not well designed to study violence against women in relationships. The CUVS, for example, failed to provide much information on wife abuse because subjects were not asked directly if their husbands or former partners had attacked them. It also failed to include nonphysical abuse in its scale of violence. However, both surveys do show that there is a significant underreporting of crime.

The General Social Surveys of 1988 and 1993 were designed to gather information on attacks by family members, although they still defined wife abuse narrowly as a physical crime. For these and other reasons, the incidence of wife assault reported by the GSS, at 15 per 1000 women (1.5 percent), is conservative. Statistics Canada's national survey of violence against women found that 30 percent of women currently or previously married had experienced at least one incident of abuse. The rate of assault was highest among young women—four times the national average and twice the national average in the lowest income group. With statistics like these it is obvious that we are only starting to understand the extent of violence against women in relationships.[35]

The 1999 GSS shows that the violent victimization rate was highest for those who are single (21 percent), with married (5 percent) and common-law partners (16 percent) lower. The relationship between marital status and victimization is probably influenced by age and lifestyle as well as by gender. Younger unmarried people go out in public more often and interact with high-risk peers, increasing their exposure to victimization. Total personal victimization rates for those who engaged in 30 or more evening activities a month was far higher than those with fewer than 10 (305 versus 75 per 1000). These data are evidence of the relationship between lifestyle and victimization risk. The accused was a family member in 27 percent of the cases, a friend or acquaintance in 36 percent, and a stranger in 26 percent.

In August 1996, British Columbia's Attorney General and Women's Equality Minister announced an updated policy on violence against women in relationships. Attorney General Ussal Dosanjh said, "The extent of violence against women in relationships is alarming, and our government is committed to stopping it.... Violence against women in relationships undermines the very foundations of our society." The renewed government action was to include

- establishing a central registry of protection orders to ensure police have access to accurate current information on peace bonds and civil restraining orders;
- enacting new legislation providing improved rights and services for victims;
- funding transition houses, counselling and assaultive men's treatment programs, and violence prevention and public education programs.

British Columbia's actions reflect those taken in many provinces and, despite criticisms, represent an effort to deal with an entrenched problem. There has been an attempt in recent years to assert that women are as violent as men, but most research shows that women usually suffer more in physical confrontations. As Yasmin Jiwani of the FREDA Centre for Research on Violence against Women and Children says, "In a country where 3.4 wives are murdered for every one husband killed, and where 98 percent of sexual assaults and 86 percent of violent crimes are committed by men; where women constitute 98 percent of spousal violence victims of sexual assault, kidnapping or hostage taking; and where 80 percent of victims of criminal harassment are women while 90 percent of the accused are men, it is startling that the GSS shows that the rates of spousal violence experienced by men and women were only slightly different–8 percent for women, and 7 percent for men in relationships five years prior.[36] There is clearly, then, a difficulty in measuring the problem of marital status and victimization.

Furthermore, when a spouse is killed, it is usually the woman; and when women kill, it is usually in self-defence. Jane Stafford shot her sleeping common-law husband as he lay passed out in his truck. The evidence at trial indicated that the deceased was domineering and abusive. The respondent testified that the deceased had threatened to kill all the members of her family, one by one, if she tried to leave him. On the night in question he had threatened to kill her son. After he passed out, Stafford got one of the many shotguns kept by her husband and shot him.[37]

It is only within the last 15 or so years that the Canadian courts have come to realize that standards for assessing the violence of women compared to that of men must be different in some situations. In 1982, when Jane Stafford was acquitted of killing her abusive husband, the Crown appealed. Rather than face another trial she pleaded guilty. While there was no explicit legal recognition of how her abuse could have led her to kill her husband, by 1990 the legal tide had changed. In a 1990 ruling, the Supreme Court of Canada decreed in the Lavallee case that battered women who kill their abusers, even if there was no immediate threat, could still claim self-defence in certain situations.

The Supreme Court said in its decision, "It is difficult for the lay person to comprehend the battered wife syndrome. It is commonly thought that battered women are not really beaten as badly as they claim, otherwise they would have left the relationship. Alternatively, some believe that women enjoy being beaten, that they have a masochistic strain in them." Luckily we have left such views behind and it is clear that the Supreme Court did not agree with these views.

Repeat Victimization

Does prior victimization enhance or reduce the chances of future victimization? It is possible that certain stable patterns of behaviour encourage victimization and that a few people who maintain them become "chronic victims" who are constantly the target of predatory crimes.

Most research efforts do in fact show that prior victimization is a strong predictor of future victimization: Individuals who have had prior victimization experiences have a significantly higher chance of future victimization than those who have remained nonvictims.[38] Research also shows that households that have experienced victimization in the past are the ones most likely to experience it again in the future.[39] Repeat victimizations are most likely to occur in areas with high crime rates and account for a significant portion of all criminal acts.

What factors predict chronic victimization? It is possible that some combination of personal and social factors encourages victimization risk. Most repeats occur soon after a previous crime has occurred, suggesting that such victims share some personal characteristic that makes them a magnet for predators.[40] For example, kids who are shy, physically weak, or socially isolated may be prone to being bullied in the schoolyard. David Finkelhor and Nancy Asdigian identified three specific types of characteristics that increase the potential for victimization:

1. Target vulnerability. The victims' physical weakness or psychological distress renders them incapable of resisting or deterring crime and makes them easy targets.
2. Target gratifiability. Some victims have characteristics that increase their risk because they have some quality, possession, skill, or attribute that an offender wants to obtain, use, have access to, or manipulate. Having attractive possessions such as a leather coat may make one vulnerable to predatory crime.
3. Target antagonism. Some characteristics increase risk because they arouse anger, jealousy, or destructive impulses in the offender. For example, young people whose style of dress is distinctive from the norm may be the targets of undeserved attacks in the street.[41]

Social, personal, and experiential factors may also interact to enhance chronic victimization. For example, boys who are bullied at school because they are depressed, shy, and withdrawn may become even more introverted after being victimized, increasing their chances for future victimization.[42]

Repeat victimization may also be a function of rational choice and offender decision making: Offenders "learn" the weaknesses of victims and use them over and over again. For example, when the abusive husband finds out that his battered wife will not call the police, he repeatedly victimizes her; when the police do not respond to reported hate crimes, the perpetrators learn they have little to fear from the law.[43]

Although an increasing number of violent crimes are committed by strangers, a surprising number of violent crime victims are either related to or acquainted with their attackers. The most obvious is sexual assault, where 68 percent of victims in 1999 reported that the

Famous Canadian Criminals

A Woman Who Killed

"In 1991 a charge of second degree murder was stayed against a Nelson, B.C., woman who blew away her husband with a shotgun while he was talking on the telephone. In 1992 a Brampton, Ont., housewife was acquitted of aggravated assault even though she drugged her husband, then cut off his penis while he slept."

So starts an article, "New Hope for Husband Murderers," from a 1995 issue of *Alberta Report*. The article deals with Justice Minister Allan Rock's decision to appoint a judge to review the cases of more than a dozen women convicted before 1990 of killing their abusive partners. The federal government would have the authority to release the women, shorten their sentences, or order new trials. This decision followed a 1990 Supreme Court of Canada ruling that set the legal framework for what has become known as the "battered wife syndrome" defence. Justice Minister Rock also agreed to consider extending that principle to some pre-1990 cases.

Angelique Lyn Lavallee was a battered woman in a violent common-law relationship who killed her partner late one night by shooting him in the back of the head as he left her room. They had had an argument and she was fearful for her life. He had frequently abused her and she had concocted excuses to explain her injuries. A psychiatrist with experience in treating battered wives prepared a psychiatric assessment of the appellant that was used to support her defence of self-defence. He explained her ongoing terror and her inability to

escape the relationship despite the violence and continuing pattern of abuse that put her life in danger. He testified that when Lavallee shot her partner it was the desperate act of a woman who sincerely believed she would be killed that night. Lavallee was acquitted on the grounds that she was psychologically trapped in an abusive relationship and hence that in order to protect herself she had the right to take steps that would not otherwise be tolerated. This differs from the traditional right of self-defence in that a woman can now legally murder her husband even though he is not directly threatening her safety. The jury acquitted the appellant but its verdict was overturned by a majority of the Manitoba Court of Appeal.

Ms. Lavallee did not testify but the statement she made to police on the night of the shooting was put in evidence. In it she described a party with friends: "Me and Wendy argued as usual and I ran in the house after Kevin pushed me. I was scared, I was really scared. I locked the door. Herb was downstairs with Joanne and I called for Herb but I was crying when I called him. I said, 'Herb come up here please.' Herb came up to the top of the stairs and I told him that Kevin was going to hit me, actually beat on me again. Herb said he knew and that if I was his old lady things would be different; he gave me a hug.... He went outside to talk to Kevin leaving the door unlocked. I went upstairs and hid in my closet from Kevin. I was so scared.... My window was open and I could hear Kevin asking questions about what I was doing and what I was saying. Next thing I know he was coming up the stairs for me.

He came into my bedroom and said, 'Wench, where are you?' And he turned on my light and he said, 'Your purse is on the floor' and he kicked it. Okay, then he turned and he saw me in the closet. He wanted me to come out but I didn't want to come out because I was scared. I was so scared. He grabbed me by the arm right there. There's a bruise on my face also where he slapped me. He didn't slap me right then, first he yelled at me then he pushed me and I pushed him back and he hit me twice on the right hand side of my head. I was scared. All I thought about was all the other times he used to beat me, I was scared, I was shaking as usual. The rest is a blank, all I remember is he gave me the gun and a shot was fired through my screen. This is all so fast. And then the guns were in another room and he loaded it the second shot and gave it to me. And I was going to shoot myself. I pointed it to myself, I was so upset. Okay, and then he went and I was sitting on the bed and he started going like this with his finger [the appellant made a shaking motion with an index finger] and said something like 'You're my old lady and you do as you're told' or something like that. He said, 'Wait till everybody leaves, you'll get it then' and he said something to the effect of 'either you kill me or I'll get you' — that was what it was. He kind of smiled and then he turned around. I shot him but I aimed out. I thought I aimed above him and a piece of his head went that way."

Source: Les Sillars, "New Hope for Husband Murders," *Alberta Report* 22 (1995), p. 18; *R. v. Lavallee*, [1990] 1 S.C.R.: 852; "Ministers Respond to Self-Defence Review," Department of Justice News Release, Ottawa, September 26, 1997.

assailant was an acquaintance. Similarly, a full 75 percent of assault victims reported that the offender was a family member, friend, or acquaintance. Only in robberies were a majority of the offences committed by a stranger (51 percent).

Connections

Efforts to understand the causes of the problems in native communities today focus on their wider relations with the dominant white society. In Chapter 9, issues of inequality and ethnicity are discussed in more detail.

Theories of Victimization

For most of its history, criminological theory has focused on the actions of the criminal offender, and the role of the victim was virtually ignored. The resultant focus has sometimes been called "offenderology."[44] Then a number of scholars noted that the victim is not a passive target in crime but someone whose behaviour can influence his or her own fate. Crime is seldom random or gratuitous, but an outcome of an organizational process that involves both victim and offender. One of the first criminologists to comment on the role that victims play was Hans Von Hentig. In the 1940s, his writings portrayed the crime victim as someone who "shapes and molds the criminal."[45] The criminal might be a predator, but the victim may have helped the offender by providing an opportunity for the crime to happen. Another pioneering victimologist, Stephen Schafer, focused on the victim's responsibility in the "genesis of crime."[46] Schafer found that some victims may have provoked or encouraged the criminal. These early works helped focus attention on the role of the victim in the crime problem and led to further research efforts that have sharpened the image of the crime victim. Today, there are a number of theories that attempt to explain the causes of victimization. We address three of these theories here: victim precipitation, lifestyles, and routine activities.

Victim Precipitation Theory

Is it possible that people cause their own victimization? According to the **victim precipitation** view, some people may actually initiate the confrontation that eventually leads to their injury or death. Victim precipitation can be either active or passive. We recognize that words like "willing prey" seem to blame the victim, but this theory tries to explain why some people become victims; it does not try to excuse the actions of the offender.

Abuse committed at residential and mission schools for Natives run by religious orders gained national prominence during the 1980s. Children told of being physically, emotionally, and sexually abused by priests and nuns after they had been forcibly taken from their families and transported hundreds of miles to schools where they were not allowed to speak their own languages. *Globe and Mail*, September 8, 1992, p. A6.

Active precipitation occurs when victims act provocatively, use threats or "fighting words," or even attack first. This model of victim-precipitated crime was first popularized by Marvin Wolfgang in his 1958 study of criminal homicide. He defined the term victim precipitation as follows:

> "Victim-precipitated" is applied to those criminal homicides in which the victim is a direct, positive precipitator in the crime. The role of the victim is characterized by his having been the first in the homicide drama to use physical force against his subsequent slayer. The victim-precipitated cases are those in which the victim was the first to show and use a deadly weapon, to strike a blow in an altercation—in short, the first to commence the interplay or resort to physical violence.[47]

Examples of a victim-precipitated homicide include the death of an aggressor in a barroom brawl or a wife who kills her husband after he attacks and threatens to kill her. Wolfgang found that 150, or 26 percent, of the 588 homicides in his sample could be classified as victim-precipitated. Clearly this applies more readily to violent crime than to property crime. In most cases where a victim precipitates a violent confrontation, he or she is more likely to suffer harm as a result than the person targeted.

Active Precipitation and Rape. Nowhere is the concept of victim precipitation more controversial than in the crime of rape. In 1971 Menachim Amir suggested that female victims often contribute to their attacks through a relationship with the rapist.[48] Amir's findings are controversial, because they divert our attention (and finding of blame) from the man to the woman. However, perhaps because of this controversy, it focuses our attention on court cases where the defendant is acquitted because the victim's actions are construed as consenting to sexual intimacy. Date rapes, which may at first start out as romantic though nonintimate relationships and then deteriorate into rape, are rarely treated with the same degree of punitiveness as stranger rapes. As law professor Susan Estrich claims in her book *Real Rape,*

> The force standard continues to protect, as "seduction," conduct which should be considered criminal. It ensures broad male freedom to "seduce" women who feel themselves to be powerless, vulnerable, and afraid. It effectively guarantees men freedom to intimidate women and exploit their weakness and passivity, so long as they don't "fight" with them, and it makes clear that the responsibility should be placed squarely on the women.[49]

While this (second) victimization is publicly condemned, there are still numerous instances of defendants being found not guilty because judges or juries believe that a sexual assault was victim-precipitated. In a highly publicized case in the Northwest Territories in 1989, the judge said, "The majority of rapes occur when the woman is drunk and passed out. A man comes along and sees a pair of hips and helps himself." In Alberta, a judge explained his acquittal of a man who sexually assaulted a young woman who was being interviewed for a job in this way: "The complainant did not present herself in a bonnet and crinolines, she was the mother of a six-month-old baby, and along with her boyfriend shared an apartment with another friend."[50] In another case, a mathematics professor at the University of New Brunswick was criticized for saying that "a girl who had sexual intercourse with a large number of boys would not suffer as a result of an unwanted sexual encounter.... When a boy invites a girl to his bedroom ... she should consider it an invitation for sexual intercourse."[51]

In such cases, saying that the victims "caused" the attack, or otherwise brought it on themselves, seems to confirm the suggestion:

> The male researcher finds his escape in victimology. He seeks the problem's cause in the behaviour of its victim, and goes on to persuade himself and the public at large that by changing that behaviour, the problem can be controlled. In this way, the study of victimology becomes the art of victim blaming.[52]

Such cases obviously involve "blaming the victim." However, perhaps the theory itself is "inadequately operationalized," suggests Ezzat Fattah, one of the early pioneers in the discipline of victimology.[53] In other words, if we specify that the interactions of victim and perpetrator involve asymmetrical relations of power which are exploited by the aggressor, it is apparent that the "blame" is on the latter.

Connections

Efforts to separate the causes of rape from the concept of victim precipitation have resulted in modification of rape laws in Canada, including the banning of testimony in court about the sexual history and reputation of the victim, and a ban on the publication of the identity of the victim in the news media, and a clearer definition of consent. This is discussed further in Chapter 11.

Passive Precipitation. Passive precipitation occurs when the victim exhibits some personal characteristic that unknowingly threatens or encourages the attacker. The threat can occur because of personal conflict, such as when two people are in competition over a job, promotion, love interest, or some other scarce and coveted commodity. Although the victim may never have met his or her attacker or even known of the attacker's existence, the attacker feels menaced and acts accordingly.[54]

In another scenario, the victim may belong to a group whose mere presence threatens the attacker's reputation, status, or economic well-being. For example, hate crime violence may be precipitated when immigrant group members move into a community to compete for jobs and housing; women in the workforce may be seen as threatening by insecure and emotionally unstable men, prompting sexual violence.

It is estimated that 40 organized hate groups are operating in Canada. In 1996, Justice Minister Allan Rock amended the section in the Canadian Criminal Code dealing with sentencing reform. According to this legislation, if a judge determined that hatred was the motivation in an attack, that could be considered an **aggravating** rather than a **mitigating** factor and thus require a more severe sentence. When this Bill was proposed in 1995, the Justice Minister was accused of promoting the special interests of homosexuals and had to defend the proposal by saying that he was not promoting a gay lifestyle.[55]

Introducing a law restricting assaults, threats, or other forms of violence based on intolerance would make society a safer place to live for all people. Such a law should not be seen as catering to the special interests of a select few but as an affirmation that we wish to live in a society free of hatred.

Research indicates that passive precipitation is related to power; if the target group can establish them-

---

Exhibit 4.1   Quick Code – Hate Crime

Section 718.2 A court that imposes a sentence shall also take into consideration the following principles:

(a) a sentence should be increased or reduced to account for any relevant aggravating or mitigating circumstances relating to the offence or the offender, and, without limiting the generality of the foregoing,

   (i) evidence that the offence was motivated by bias, prejudice or hate based on race, national or ethnic origin, language, colour, religion, sex, age, mental or physical disability, sexual orientation, or any other similar factor,

   (ii) evidence that the offender, in committing the offence, abused the offender's spouse or common-law partner or child,

   (iii) evidence that the offender, in committing the offence, abused a position of trust or authority in relation to the victim, or

   (iv) evidence that the offence was committed for the benefit of, at the direction of or in association with a criminal organization

shall be deemed to be aggravating circumstances....

Source: 1995, c. 22, s. 6; 1997, c. 23, s. 17; 2000, c. 12, s. 95.

---

selves economically or gain political power in the community, their vulnerability will diminish. They are now too formidable a target to attack and are no longer passive precipitators. For example, research shows that employed women in Canada were underrepresented as homicide victims, whereas unemployed women suffered higher homicide victimization rates.[56] By implication, gaining economic power reduced the victimization risk for women.

Whether active or passive, the concept of victim precipitation implies that in some but not all crimes, the offender's crime begins as a reaction to a victim's actions. The crime, as reaction, could not take place without action on the part of the victim. The victim's actions might consciously put him or her in harm's way, but the actions might be inadvertent as well. Routine activities theory, discussed later in this chapter, will explore this further. One important point, however, is that modern crime prevention programs involve making targets harder to victimize, which requires that the programs be victim centred.

The Extent of Hate Crime. There is no systematic collection of hate crime statistics in Canada, although the Centre for Justice Statistics is considering it. Research by Julian Roberts has found that hate crime in Canada occurs primarily on the basis of race (66 percent), religion

(23 percent), and sexual orientation (10 percent). Analyzing evidence obtained from the Montreal, Ottawa, and Toronto police, Roberts estimates that approximately 60 000 hate crimes are committed annually in Canada.[57] The Ottawa Police are one of a number of police forces that have established specialized hate/bias crime units. The Peel Regional police report 29 incidents of hate/bias motivated crime in 1999, most of which appeared motivated by race. In the United States, the FBI collects data on hate crimes under the Hate Crime Statistics Act of 1990. The most current data available (1999) indicate that almost 8000 hate crimes occur each year.[58] Race was the motivating factor in 55 percent of the cases, followed by religion (18 percent) and sexual orientation (18 percent). This is based on reports from over 12 000 law enforcement agencies.

In addition to what little official information on hate crime in Canada exists, some organizations do collect statistics. The League for Human Rights of B'Nai Brith has produced an annual report on the number of anti-Semitic incidents in Canada since 1982. As well, the 519 Church Street Community Centre in Toronto reported 116 hate incidents motivated by sexual orientation.

In 1999, for the first time, the General Social Survey measured self-reported hate crime victimization incidents at the national level.[59] The 1999 GSS sampled approximately 26 000 households, significantly more than the 10 000 sampled in 1988 and 1993. Of a reported 6 186 914 offences, 4 percent (272 732 incidents) were considered by the victim to be motivated by hate. Of all incidents classified as hate crimes, 77 percent were personal, and 64 percent of those were assaults. Whereas almost half (49 percent) of all hate crime incidents are assaults, less than one in five (18 percent) non-hate crime incidents are assaults. Race-ethnicity is the motivation in 43 percent of offences, and "other" (including religion and sexual orientation) in 37 percent of incidents. Most victims of hate crime incidents (92 percent) live in urban areas. Most incidents occur in commercial establishments and public institutions (30 percent) or on the street and in public places (27 percent). And whereas police-reported statistics indicated that for 30 percent of non-hate crimes, the perpetrator was a stranger, in almost half (46 percent) of all violent hate crime incidents, the offender was a stranger to the victim. Of the total number of incidents where victims believed the offence was hate-motivated, 45 percent were reported to the police, while 53 percent were not reported. This survey has added significantly to our understanding of hate crime in Canadian society.

Hate/bias crime is slowly being recognized as a widespread and serious problem and as a new category of violent personal crime.[60] This crime is displayed in violent acts directed toward a particular person or members of a group merely because the targets share a discernible racial, ethnic, religious, or gender characteristic or sexual orientation. Hate crimes can include the desecration of a house of worship or cemetery, harassment of a minority-group family that has moved into a previously all-white neighbourhood, or a racially motivated murder of an individual.[61] For example, in 1998 four skinheads on their way home from a neo-Nazi meeting outside Vancouver attacked an elderly Sikh caretaker and killed him. It is doubtful that this type of incident has become more common; however, the publicity surrounding such incidents has certainly increased, and with it the shock and revulsion felt by the public.

A number of conditions may directly or indirectly influence hate crime offending, such as the following:

- economic recessions, increased crime, and unemployment being blamed on minorities;
- the movement of minorities into an area, being seen as a threat to a traditional way of life;
- the desire to alleviate boredom;
- feelings of resentment for the economic or social success of minorities;
- historical animosities that have been transmitted from one generation to another;
- the belief that the actions of the offenders are condoned by the larger society or community.

Hate crimes usually involve convenient and vulnerable targets who are incapable of fighting back. For example, many incidents have been reported of teenagers attacking vagrants and the homeless in an effort to rid their town or neighbourhood of people they consider undesirable.[62]

Racial and ethnic minorities have also been the targets of attack. Well-publicized hate crimes directed against racial minorities include incidents like that in Bensonhurst, New York, in which gangs of white youths chased and killed black youths who wandered into their neighbourhoods.

The Roots of Hate. Why do people commit bias crimes? Research has found that hate crimes are generally spontaneous incidents motivated by the victims' walking, driving, shopping, or socializing in an area in which their attacker believes they do not belong.[63] Other reasons found for bias attacks were that the victim had moved into an ethnically distinct neighbourhood or had dated a member of a different racial or ethnic group. Although hate crimes are often unplanned, it was found that a majority of these crimes were serious incidents involving assaults and robberies. The researchers note that hate crimes involve at least some planning and are best categorized on the basis of their different motives.[64]

While hate crimes are often mindless attacks directed toward "traditional" minority victims, political and economic trends may cause violent attacks to be redirected. For example, hate crimes have increased against Asian Americans since September 11, 2001.

Lifestyle Theories

Some criminologists believe that people may become crime victims because they have a **lifestyle** that increases their exposure to criminal offenders. Both GSS and UCR data sources show that victimization risk is increased by such behaviours as being single, associating with young men, going out in public places late at night, and living in an urban area. Conversely, one's chances of victimization can be reduced by staying home at night, moving to a rural area, staying out of public places, earning more money, associating with young women, or getting married. The important point is that crime is not a random occurrence but rather in part a function of the behaviour and actions of its targets.

Criminality and victimization thus seem bound in an association in which the probability of crime depends on the activities of the potential victim.[65] Crime occurs because victims have a lifestyle that places them in jeopardy: A person's chances of being robbed by a stranger are much greater in downtown Montreal at 2 a.m. than in a locked farmhouse in rural Manitoba.

The likelihood of victimization is greatest among groups with high-risk lifestyles. For example, teens may have the greatest risk of victimization because their lifestyle places them in an at-risk location—the neighbourhood high school. That's where the most criminal element of the population, teenage males, congregate. In 1991 it was estimated that in 48 percent of nonsexual assaults against children, the accused was an acquaintance, especially in the case of male victims. Physical force was the most common weapon (81 percent of cases), and 60 percent took place in a public or open area.[66]

An adolescent's lifestyle continues to place him or her at risk after leaving the school grounds. Gary Jensen and David Brownfield found that kids who hang out with their friends and get involved in the "recreational pursuit of fun" face an elevated risk for victimization. For example, their friends may give them a false ID so they can go drinking; hanging out in bars places them at risk because many fights and assaults occur in places that serve liquor.[67]

Adolescents are not the only ones with high-risk lifestyles. A number of studies have found that the homeless population is extremely vulnerable to physical harm because they are constantly exposed to the criminal population in large urban areas. The homeless have a high victimization risk compared to the general population, and homeless victims tend to be more vulnerable in other ways: They are more likely to have a history of mental hospitalization, depression, and physical problems, including fainting and blackout spells.[68]

The Equivalent Group Hypothesis. The lifestyle view suggests that victims and criminals share similar characteristics because they are not actually separate groups and

Culture, Gender, Ethnicity, and Criminology

Heterosexual Panic or Homo-cide: The Extent of Hate Crime

Hate crime is slowly being recognized as a widespread and serious problem, and in recent years criminology and criminal justice professionals have begun studying the issue of hate crime in society. One group targeted for hate crimes is gay men and lesbians. Gay bashing has become an all too common occurrence, with incidents on the rise in Canada and the United States. In 1992 a public inquiry into the killings of 14 homosexual men in Montreal since 1989 became billed as an inquiry into discrimination against lesbians and gays. Toronto's Wellesley Hospital has created a program to help its emergency staff to be more sensitive and effective when caring for victims of gay bashing. A community survey conducted by 519 Church Street Community Centre showed that 78 percent of respondents had experienced verbal assaults and 50 percent had been threatened with physical violence.

A New Brunswick study on discrimination and violence against lesbians, gays, and bisexuals found that 82 percent of respondents had been verbally abused; 34 percent had been chased or followed; 10 percent had been spat upon; 19 percent had had their property damaged; 17 percent had had objects thrown at them; 18 percent had been punched, kicked, hit or beaten; and 23 percent had been harassed or assaulted by the police.

In a Nova Scotia study on homophobic abuse and discrimination, it was found that 72 percent of respondents had been verbally abused because of their actual or presumed sexual orientation; 42 percent had been threatened with violence; 33 percent had been chased or followed; 9 percent had been spat upon; 12 percent had their property damaged; 25 percent had objects thrown at them; 18 percent had been assaulted with a weapon, punched, kicked, or beaten; 16.5 percent had been harassed, and another 2 percent had been beaten, by the police.

In a survey of homophobic violence reported in the *Gay Times* (1996), one in three gay men and one in four lesbians said they had been bashed in the previous five years. For those under 18 years of age the figures for gay bashing were even higher. Avoidance techniques were adopted, such as not holding hands or kissing in public (88 percent), avoiding telling people they are gay (65 percent), and avoiding looking "obviously gay" (59 percent).

- In 1985, Kenn Zeller was murdered by five teenagers in a Toronto park: the teenagers had agreed to go to the park to "beat up a fag."
- In 1989, a gay AIDS activist, Joe Rose, was murdered on a crowded Montreal bus. A gang of about 15 youths boarded the bus, taunted him with shouts of "faggot," and stabbed him to death with scissors and knives.
- In 1992, Daniel Lacombe was killed in Montreal by a group of young adults who had decided to go out and beat up gays.
- At least 14 gay men were murdered in Montreal between 1989 and 1994 as a result of homophobic violence.

And then there's the link between gaybashing and homicide. The FBI reports that of the 17 murders reported among hate-motivated incidents, racial bias motivated 9 of the murders; sexual-orientation bias and ethnicity or national origin bias motive 3 each; and religious bias motivated 2. In the Matthew Shepard case, which galvanized public attention in 1998, two men were tried and found guilty for luring a gay man from a bar, pistol-whipping him, and leaving him to die tied to a fence. The defendants tried to argue that his sexual advances provoked them into a homosexual panic, and that they were just defending themselves.

Victor Janoff, a graduate researcher at Simon Fraser University, in his M.A. thesis in criminology, *Pink Blood: Queer-bashing in Canada*, provides a comprehensive overview of queer-bashing. The thesis analyzes the impact of violence on gays and lesbians and assembles evidence on the prevalence of homophobic violence in Canada. In an extensive series of interviews with police officers, community activists, victims, and prosecutors, he details over 300 incidents, including 85 homicides. In particular he highlights the problem of the "homosexual panic defence."

The "homosexual panic defence" is based on a theory that a homosexual proposition can cause a reaction akin to temporary insanity in a person with latent homosexual tendencies or in someone who has been abused. Usually, a homosexual advance is used as evidence of provocation in order to reduce the attacker's sentence, for example, from murder to manslaughter. The *Gay Times* reports that the defence of homosexual panic has been used in the United States at least 15 times in the last ten years to reduce charges from murder to manslaughter.

In a recent case in British Columbia, the Crown accepted a

plea of guilty of manslaughter from a person accused of murder, on the grounds that the person had been provoked by an aggressive homosexual assault. It appears that the court accepted the argument that a heterosexual man should be expected to react to an alleged homosexual advance with extreme violence. In another case, the Manitoba Court of Appeal said there can be no doubt that a homosexual advance may be provocation. However in Alberta, in a case where the defendant alleged that the victim had reached toward the accused as if to grab him, the Court of Appeal decided it would be impossible for a jury to conclude that an ordinary man's sensitivity to a homosexual approach should lead to anything more than annoyance.

Violence against homosexuals is on the rise in Australia, and in that country homosexual advances are often used by the defence as a provocation for murder. Since 1993 this defence has been used in 13 cases that resulted in death. Each year men are murdered in Australia because they are homosexual. Since 1990, the police have systematically recorded gay-hate related killings in New South Wales. Using data from the National Homicide Monitoring Program, the Australian Institute of Criminology has compared the victims and offenders in such homicides with other male homicides in New South Wales and found that the victims are generally older than other male homicide victims and are more likely to have been beaten to death. The offenders are much more likely to be younger than other homicide offenders, and more likely to be unemployed (82 percent) and unmarried (77 percent). In a 1998 report on the "homosexual advance defence," a working group from the Criminal Law Division recommends that this defence be excluded through legislation. Reviewing 13 cases between 1993 and 1998, they concluded that this defence had its basis in prejudice in the criminal justice system against gay men.

Sources: L. Still, "Homophobe Who Killed Gay Handed Five-year Sentence," *The Vancouver Sun*, June 29, 1995; D. Dahl, "Bias in the Criminal Justice System—The 'Homosexual Panic Defence'," *The Vancouver Sun*, December 28, 1995; *R. v. Ryznar*, [1986] 6 WWR 210 (Man CA); *R. v. Hansford* (1987), 55 CR (3d) 347 (Alta CA) at 363);

"Anti-Gay Crimes Are Reported on Rise in 5 Cities," *New York Times*, March 20, 1992, A12; "Gay Discrimination Focus of Probe," *The Globe and Mail*, November 15, 1993, p. A3; Jenny Mouzos and Sue Thompson, "Gay-Hate Related Homicides: An Overview of Major Findings in New South Wales," *Australian Institute of Criminology, Trends and Issues in Crime and Criminal Justice* 155, June 2000; Anne Vassal, John Fisher, Ralf Jürgens, Robert Hughes, "Gay and Lesbian Issues and HIV/AIDS: A Discussion Paper," Canadian HIV/AIDS Legal Network & Canadian AIDS Society, Montreal, 1997 http://www.aidslaw.ca/Maincontent/issues/gaylesbian/07p2bE.html; C. Petersen, "A Queer Response to Bashing: Legislating Against Hate," *Queen's Law Journal* 16 (1991; 237 at 246; S. Samis, "An Injury to One Is an Injury to All: Heterosexism, Homophobia and Anti-Gay/Lesbian Violence in Greater Vancouver," MA (Sociology) thesis, Simon Fraser University, 1994; Quebec Human Rights Commission; "Discrimination and Violence Encountered by Lesbian, Gay and Bisexual New Brunswickers," New Brunswick Coalition for Human Rights Reform, 1990; "Proud but Cautious: Homophobic Abuse and Discrimination in Nova Scotia," Nova Scotia Public Interest Research Group, 1994; Ellen Faulkner, *Anti-Gay/Lesbian Violence in Toronto: The Impact on Individuals and Communities*, Department of Justice Canada: Research and Statistics Division/Policy Sector. TR1997-5e (A Project of the 519 Church Street Community Centre Victim Assistance programme, 519 Church Street, Toronto, Ontario: p. 40.)

that in fact a criminal lifestyle exposes people to increased levels of victimization risk. The **equivalent group hypothesis** is supported by research showing that crime victims also self-report significant amounts of criminal behaviour. A number of studies have shown that adolescents who engage in delinquent behaviour or join gangs also face the greatest risk of victimization. For example, young victims of school crime were likely to strike back at other students in order to regain lost possessions or recover their self-respect.[69] In another study, it was found that the victims of violent assault were those most likely to become offenders themselves.[70] Similarly, an association has been found between participation in self-reported delinquent behaviour and personal victimization in such crimes as robbery and assault.[71] The conclusion seems to be that for personal victimizations, those most likely to be the victims of crime are those who have been most involved in crime.[72]

The criminal–victim connection may exist because the conditions that create criminality also predispose people to victimization. Both share similar lifestyle and residence characteristics. Some former criminals may later become targets because they are perceived as vulnerable: Criminal offenders are unlikely to call the police, and if they do, who will believe them? Some victims may commit crime out of frustration; others may use violence as a means of revenge, self-defence, or social control. Some may have learned antisocial behaviour as a consequence of their own victimization experiences, as in the case of abused children.[73] Research cited in one study showed that over 85 percent of female offenders had experienced physical and sexual violence both inside and outside the home, at the hands of parents, intimate partners, and strangers.[74]

The Proximity Hypothesis. Lifestyle theory implies that some people willingly put themselves in jeopardy by choosing high-risk lifestyles, or that some people become victims because they are forced to live in close physical proximity to criminals and are selected because they share similar backgrounds and circumstances.[75] One of the earliest formulations of this theory is that of Hindelang, Gottfredson, and Garofalo, who advanced the idea that association with and exposure to high-risk persons in high-risk locations at high-risk periods increase the incidence of the risk of crime.[76] For example, people who reside in socially disorganized "high-crime areas" have the greatest risk of coming into contact with criminal offenders, irrespective of their own behaviour or lifestyle. Thus, according to the **proximity hypothesis**, victims do not encourage crime; they are simply in the "wrong place at the wrong time."[77] Thus, there may be little reason for residents in lower-class areas to alter their lifestyle or take safety precautions, since personal behaviour choices do not in fact influence the likelihood of victimization.[78]

In this view, the probability of victimization is more dependent on where one lives than how one lives. People who risk exposure to criminals because they live in close proximity to them are at much greater risk of victimization than people who reside in less risky areas but have attractive, unguarded homes.[79] Neighbourhood crime levels are more important for determining the chances of victimization than individual characteristics. Even those people who exhibit high-risk traits, such as unmarried males, will increase their chances of victimization if they reside in a high-crime area.[80]

The Deviant Place Hypothesis. The **deviant place** hypothesis suggests that there are natural areas for crime, places in which crime flourishes regardless of the precautions taken by their residents. Rodney Stark has described these areas as poor, densely populated, highly transient neighbourhoods in which commercial and residential property exist side by side. The commercial property provides criminals with easy access to targets for theft crimes, such as shoplifting and larceny. Successful people stay out of these stigmatized areas; they are homes for "demoralized kinds of people" who are easy targets for crime: the homeless, the addicted, the mentally disabled, and the elderly poor.[81]

William Julius Wilson has described how people who can afford to leave dangerous areas do so and has noted that the ability to leave is related to race; "white flight" has become a familiar term in the United States.[82] More affluent people realize that criminal victimization can be avoided by moving to an area with greater law enforcement and lower crime rates. Because some residents are better able to flee inner-city high-crime areas, those left behind suffer higher victimization rates.

Which has the greatest influence on victimization risk, place of residence or lifestyle? Perhaps both victim lifestyle and place of domicile interact to produce crime and victimization rates. People who live in more affluent areas and take safety precautions significantly lower their chances of becoming crime victims. Residents of poor areas have a much greater risk of becoming victims because they live in areas with many motivated offenders; to protect themselves, they have to "try harder" to be safe than the more affluent. People who take chances, who live in high-risk neighbourhoods, and who are law violators themselves share the greatest risk of victimization. While victim behaviour cannot, of course, explain the onset of criminality, it can influence the occasion of crime. Although criminal motivation may be acquired early in life, the decision to commit a particular crime may depend on the actions and reactions of potential victims.

Routine Activities Theory

An important attempt to formally describe the conditions that produce victim risk is contained in the work of Lawrence Cohen and Marcus Felson and is referred to as **routine activities theory**.[83] Cohen and Felson assume that the motivation to commit crime is constant. In every society, there will always be some people who are willing to break the law for gain, revenge, greed, or some other motive. Consequently, the volume and distribution of **predatory crime** (violent crimes against the person and crimes in which an offender attempts to steal an object directly) are closely related to the interaction of three variables that reflect the routine activities of the typical Canadian lifestyle: the availability of **suitable targets** (such as homes containing easily saleable goods); the absence of **capable guardians** (such as police, homeowners, neighbours, friends, and relatives); and the presence of **motivated offenders** (such as a large number of unemployed teenagers). The presence of these components increases the likelihood that a predatory crime will take place: Targets are more likely to be victimized if they are poorly guarded and are exposed to a large group of motivated offenders (see Figure 4.2).

Cohen and Felson used the routine activities approach to explain the rise in the crime rate between 1960 and 1980. They note that the number of adult caretakers at home during the day (guardians) decreased because of increased female participation in the workforce; while mothers are at work and children are in day care, homes are left unguarded. Similarly, with the growth of suburbia and the decline of the traditional neighbourhood, the number of such familiar "guardians" as family, neighbours, and friends diminished. At the same time, the volume of easily transportable wealth increased, creating a greater number of available targets. In one study, Cohen linked burglary rates to the proliferation of a commodity easily stolen and disposed of: television sets.[84] Finally, with the baby-boom generation coming of age during the period 1960 to 1980, there was an excess of motivated offenders, and the crime rate increased in predicted fashion. The implication of this theory is that crime is not a product of social disorder, but of both prosperity and of the changing economy.

Crime and Everyday Life. A core premise of routine activities theory is that all things being equal, the greater the opportunity to commit crime, the higher the crime and victimization rate. According to Marcus Felson, crime has grown as society changed from a nation of small villages and towns to one of large urban environments. In a village not only could thieves be easily recognized, but the commodities they stole could be identified long after the crime occurred. Cities provided the critical population mass that allowed predatory criminals to hide and evade apprehension. After the crime, criminals could blend into the crowd and disperse their loot; in the modern city, the public transportation system provides a quick exit for escape.

As suburbs grew in importance, labour and family life moved away from the household, decreasing guardianship. The microwave, freezer, and automatic dishwasher freed adolescents from common household chores. Rather than help prepare the family dinner and wash dishes afterward, adolescents had the freedom to meet with their peers and avoid parental controls. As car ownership increased, teens had greater access to trans-portation outside of parental control. Greater mobility makes it impossible for neighbours to know whether a teen belongs in an area or is an intruder planning to commit a crime. Schools have become larger and more complex in modern society, providing an ideal site for crime. The many hallways and corridors prevent teachers from knowing who belongs where; spacious school grounds reduce teacher supervision. In the shopping mall strangers converge in large numbers and youths "hang out." The interior is filled with people, so drug deals can be concealed in the pedestrian flow. Stores have attractively displayed goods, encouraging shoplifting and employee pilferage. Substantial numbers of cars are parked in areas that make larceny and car theft virtually undetectable. Cars carrying away stolen merchandise have an undistinguished appearance; who notices people placing items in a car in a shopping mall lot? In addition, shoppers can be attacked in parking lots as they walk in isolation to and from their cars.

These changes in the structure of society helped increase and sustain crime rates into the early 1990s. The upshot is that rather than change people, crime prevention strategies must reduce the opportunity to commit crime.

Routine Activities and Lifestyle. Routine activities theory is similar to the lifestyle approach because it shows how

---

Figure 4.2   **Routine activity theory posits the interaction of three factors**

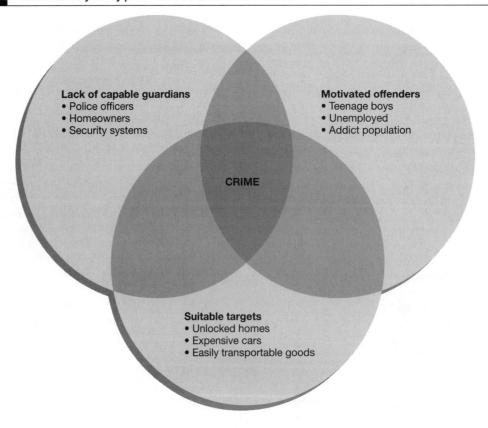

Lack of capable guardians
• Police officers
• Homeowners
• Security systems

Motivated offenders
• Teenage boys
• Unemployed
• Addict population

CRIME

Suitable targets
• Unlocked homes
• Expensive cars
• Easily transportable goods

routine living arrangements can affect victim risk: People who live in unguarded areas are going to be at the mercy of motivated offenders. Terance Miethe and Robert Meier argue that there is actually a great deal of congruence between the two theories, each relying on four basic concepts: (1) proximity to criminals; (2) time of exposure to criminals; (3) target attractiveness; and (4) guardianship.[85] For example, both routine activities theory and lifestyle theory would predict that (1) people who live in high crime areas (2) who go out late at night (3) carrying valuables such as an expensive watch (4) without friends or family to watch or help them increase their victimization risk.

Exhibit 4.2 is from a test that lets you rate your risk of being murdered, using known risk factors taken from executive security courses, police detectives, and security consultants. The test was developed by the Metro Nashville Police Department and includes questions on factors that affect assault rates. The key elements reflect the ideas discussed here, that the lifestyle and routine activities people engage in can put them at relative danger from crime.

Testing Routine Activities Theory. Numerous attempts have been made to substantiate the principles of routine activities theory.[86] Cohen and Felson maintain that certain personal characteristics increase the likelihood that people's routine activities will place them at a greater risk for victimization. These characteristics include being a young minority-group member, having a low socioeconomic status, living in an urban area, and being a single parent. Supporting this view, Michael Maxfield found that victimization was most common in homes composed of a single parent and several children. Single parents may be less able to protect their families and themselves from the most common predatory criminals: other family members and former loved ones.[87] Note that this implies that going out of the home may not be the best predictor of risk, given the characteristics of violence in the family, especially for women and children.

Homes that are well guarded are the least likely to be burglarized.[88] Rape rates are high in areas where socioeconomic distress results in divorce, unemployment, and overcrowded living conditions—factors that reduce the number of guardians and increase the number of potential offenders.[89] However, some empirical research has failed to find a relationship between property victimization and "guardianship," seeming to provide weak support for routine activities theory.[90] The routine activities view also suggests that lifestyle plays an important role in victimization risk. Those who maintain a high-risk lifestyle by staying out late at night and having frequent activity outside the home also run increased chances of victimization.[91] This was corroborated in the now-dated Greater Vancouver Victimization Survey conducted by Statistics Canada for the Solicitor General.[92] Interestingly, when Steven Messner and Kenneth Tardiff studied patterns of urban homicide, they found that lifestyles significantly influenced victimization: People who tended to stay at home were the ones most likely to be killed by family or friends.[93] James Lasley found that youths in Britain who stay out late at night and use excessive amounts of alcohol stand the greatest risk of becoming crime victims.[94] A connection has also been found between the developmental level of a society and the amount of theft that occurs, but there does not appear to be a relationship with homicide, which is a more conflict-linked expressive crime.[95]

Because of the uniformity of this supporting research, routine activities theory has become a very popular theory of victimization.

Is the Routine Activity Approach Valid? Not all criminologists support the routine activity model.[96] According to routine activities theory, the affluent should have a lower victimization risk than the poor because they have the means to purchase security. Yet affluence allows people to increase activity outside the home, and wealth makes a tempting target—factors that are also associated with greater risk. According to Birkbeck and LaFree, routine activities theory may explain why some people become victims, but it fails to explain whether others were first considered as potential targets and then discarded and if so, why that decision was made. Furthermore, the model does not explain why some people do not have a greater likelihood of victimization despite the presence of risk factors.[97]

It has also been suggested that routine activities theory overemphasizes the victim and overlooks offender differences. Why do offenders choose to commit crime? Offender motivation is assumed to be rational and offenders assumed to act from similar motives. However, it is unlikely that all offenders perceive criminal opportunity or the risk of apprehension in a similar fashion. Other researchers have suggested that peer group pressure and cultural norms exert pressure on potential offenders, guide their motivation, and influence their choices; routine activities theory, they conclude, neglects to account for the factors that shape criminal choice.[98] And finally, as mentioned before, the model is especially inadequate for measuring violence in the home, committed by acquaintances. We cannot assume, as does Felson, that women are less vulnerable because they spend more time with family members, given the high rates of assault and sexual abuse that occurs in families.[99]

Caring for the Victim

The GSS indicated that 24 percent of Canadians were victims of at least one crime in 1993, which represented no change since 1988. According to the 1999 General Social Survey (GSS) conducted by Statistics Canada, 25 percent of Canadians aged 15 and older were victims of at least one crime in the previous year. In Britain it is estimated

---

Exhibit 4.2   Rate Your Risk of Being Assaulted on the Street

The following test lets you rate your risk of being assaulted on the street. This test uses known risk factors taken from executive security courses, police detectives and security consultants. Some of the questions may seem unusual but they are all factors that affect aggravated assault statistics.

1. How much do you travel outside of the city where you live in one year?
   - You travel under 1,000 miles total.
   - You travel about 1,000 to 5,000 miles in U.S.
   - You travel in the U.S. more than 5,000 miles.
   - You travel worldwide.

2. When you fly
   - You fly by commercial carrier.
   - You regularly fly using small, foreign owned carriers.
   - You travel (fly, drive, etc.) with more than one suitcase and one carry-on type bag.

3. Security Techniques
   - You go to conventions or seminars in other cities even occasionally.
   - You wear a convention badge while out of the meeting room itself on such a trip.
   - You regularly wear your last name visible when you work.
   - You (or other family members) open the door of your home for visitors without positive identification.
   - You never open your door to strangers when you are unarmed.
   - You only open a door when armed.
   - Your mailbox doesn't lock.
   - You have a solid door without a "peephole" or way to view who is outside.
   - You have a lock on your bedroom door.

4. How much cash do you carry?
   - You rarely carry any cash.
   - You carry $20 to $50.
   - You carry $50 to $400.
   - You carry over $400.
   - You separate the money you need from other large denomination bills.

5. Credit and Bank Cards
   - How many credit cards do you carry?
   - How many major oil credit cards do you carry?
   - How many major credit cards do you carry (MasterCard, Visa, American Express, Carte Blanche, Discover, etc.)?
   - You carry one or more ATM cards.
   - You carry secret code numbers to cards written down (even though you might hide them).

   - You never use outside ATM (anytime teller machines) after dark. (Leave this blank if the ATM is at a police sub-station.)

6. Sundry Habits
   - How many acts of adultery have you committed (in the last two years)? Count each meeting during this marriage.
   - You are unmarried and you have dated a married person in the last year. How many dates have you had with this married person?
   - You are unmarried and you steadily cohabit with one person but you have dated on the sly in the last year.
   - Indicate your total number of partners.
   - You go to nightclubs and take home partners or go somewhere with them.
   - If so, are you male or female?
   - Do you ever use prostitutes?
   - Do you ever hitchhike or pick up hitchhikers?
   - Do you walk in public more than five times per month?
   - Do you generally walk at night with one or more companions?
   - Do you ever use cocaine, crack, uppers, downers or narcotics away from home on any occasion?
   - Do you ever get drunk in public to the point where your speech is even slightly slurred or your balance is affected?

7. On the Street
   - You visibly wear lots of gold chains when in public.
   - You wear rings, bracelets, or other jewelry worth over $2,000 while in public.
   - You wear an overcoat or full-length rain suit over a suit jacket in public.
   - You wear a natural fur in public.
   - Do you carry an umbrella or cane without necessity?
   - Do you walk with young children (age eight or under) or a dog?

8. Outings
   - Do you drive with any car door unlocked?
   - You have a remote starting device on your car.
   - You regularly commute by bus or subway.
   - You cannot change a car tire yourself — and you drive.
   - You drive (more than once a month) with an eighth of a tank of gas or less.
   - You carry a tire inflator/puncture sealant screw-on canister in your car.
   - You frequent the same gas station.
   - You work at a gas station, bar, fast food restaurant, or drive-in market.

- You are going camping or partying in a boat in the next year.
- There is no controlled access in and out of your work.

9. Other Factors
   - You are a black male between the ages of 14 and 26.
   - You are over 60 years old.
   - You can run over 300 m without stopping to walk.
   - You are a first-degree black belt or higher in any martial art (Karate, Judo, Tae Kwon Do, Kung Fu, etc.).

- You speak quietly when you talk.
- You are considered calm but assertive when you talk.
- You are afraid of guns and can't stand to touch one.
- You are commissioned to or otherwise legally carry a handgun.
- You always carry a handgun and you aren't commissioned or registered.
- You know others illegally carry firearms where you drink or gamble.

Source: http://www.nashville.net/~police/risk/beaten.html Rate Your Risk© Ken Pence1995

that the average person can expect to be the victim of a car theft once in his or her life; however, the risk of robbery is lower than that of being admitted to hospital as a psychiatric patient.[100] However, in the aftermath of crime a victim will suffer financial problems, mental stress, and physical hardship.[101] Dean Kilpatrick and his associates found that among 391 adult females in a southern city 75 percent had been victimized by crime at least once in their lives, including having been raped (25 percent) and sexually molested (18 percent). Disturbingly, 25 percent of the victims had developed post-traumatic stress syndrome, and their psychological symptoms had lasted for more than a decade after the crime occurred.[102] The long-term effect of sexual victimization can include years of problem avoidance, social withdrawal, and self-criticism.[103]

Helping victims cope is the responsibility of all of society. Law enforcement agencies, courts, and correctional and human service systems have come to realize that due process and human rights exist both for the defendant and for the victim of criminal behaviour.

The Government's Response

In 1998, Anne McLellan, Minister of Justice and Attorney General of Canada, and Andy Scott, Solicitor General of Canada, announced the details of a $32-million-a-year national crime prevention initiative aimed at developing community-based responses to crime, with an emphasis on children and youth, women, and Native people. This program is Phase II of the National Strategy on Community Safety and Crime Prevention. Phase I of the National Strategy, launched in 1994, established the National Crime Prevention Council, providing the framework for federal crime prevention efforts. Phase II aims to increase public safety for individuals and the community by providing Canadians with the knowledge, skills, and resources they need to enhance crime prevention in their communities. Part of the Safer Communities

Initiative is the Community Mobilization Program, which is to provide support to communities in developing comprehensive and sustainable approaches to crime prevention that deal with the root causes of crime.

Earlier, because of public concern over violent personal crime, a Task Force on Victims of Crime had been set up in the United States in 1982, which undertook an extensive study of crime victimization to determine how victims could be assisted.[104] Its most significant recommendation was that the victim should have the right to be present and be heard at all critical stages of the judicial proceedings. Other recommendations included protecting witnesses and victims from intimidation, requiring restitution in criminal cases, setting up programs of victim compensation, expanding victim–witness programs, requiring the use of victim impact statements at sentencing in federal criminal cases, and providing federal funding for state victim compensation and assistance projects.[105] With these acts, the U.S. federal government began to take action to address the plight of victims and make their assistance an even greater concern of the public and the justice system.

The following is a discussion of the most prominent forms of victim services in operation in Canada.

Victim Impact Statement

In 1986 the Canadian Department of Justice funded projects to test and evaluate victim impact statements (VIS) in six Canadian cities: Victoria, North Battleford, Winnipeg, Calgary, Toronto, and Montreal. The evaluations included measuring the effect of the statements on the criminal justice system, how satisfied the victim was with the program, and the success of project implementation. The overall evaluation of the VIS was positive. In 1988 Section 735 of the Criminal Code allowed victims to record a statement describing the physical injury, financial loss, and personal reactions to criminal victimization. The VIS would be introduced after conviction and prior to sentencing. While victim impact statements are most often used in cases involving interpersonal victimization, they can be used in conjunction with any offence; however, most victims choose not to participate.

There are notable differences in how each province organizes and implements the use of the VIS; however, it is generally agreed that they allow prosecutors and judges to experience the impact of crime more fully, and that they help victims recover from crime and reduce their feeling of powerlessness as participants in the criminal justice system. Chapter 22 of the Statutes of Canada on Sentencing Reform proclaimed in 1996 included the provision that victim impact statements be considered in sentencing.[106]

Victim Compensation

One agenda of victim advocates has been to lobby for legislation creating crime **victim compensation** programs.[107] As a result of such legislation, the victim can apply for compensation from the state to pay for damages associated with the crime. Each provincial compensation scheme is unique, however, and the amount of awards varies from $5000 to $30 000. While victims typically seek compensation in property crimes, the most common way victims receive compensation is through private insurance. Compensation may be made for medical and dental bills, loss of present and future wages, counselling, and in some cases for pain and suffering. In the case of death, the victim's survivors can receive aid for loss of support.

An important service of most victim programs is to familiarize clients with compensation options and help them apply for aid. The usual time limit for applying for compensation is one year, although this can be waived, as in cases of childhood victimization. Victims can be disqualified if they are found to have contributed to their injuries, to have provoked the offender, or to have been in the process of committing a criminal offence.

Court Services

A common victim program service involves helping victims deal with the criminal justice system. One approach is to prepare victims and witnesses by explaining court procedures: how to be a witness, how bail works, what to do if the defendant makes a threat. Lack of such knowledge can cause confusion, making some victims reluctant to testify in court proceedings. Many victim programs also provide transportation to and from court and counsellors who remain in the courtroom during hearings to explain procedures and provide support. While some courthouses have on-site services to aid witnesses, most do not. Court escorts are particularly important for elderly victims, the handicapped, victims of child abuse and assault, and those who have been intimidated by friends or relatives of the defendant.

In this context, pretrial safety for victims and their families needs to be ensured in court as well. This is achieved in part through the use of peace bonds, restraining orders, and provisions against communication with witnesses. There are also various legislated procedures to aid victims in testifying, such as publication bans to protect a victim's identity. The controversial "rape-shield" provisions to prevent evidence about a victim's sexual history and public exclusion orders in the case of child witnesses are especially important.[108] Victim services are funded in part by a victim fine surcharge of 15 percent of a fine; if there is no fine, the judge can set the amount up to $10 000.

Public Education

Some victim programs engage in public education that helps familiarize the general public with their services and with other agencies that help crime victims. In some instances these are primary education programs that teach methods of dealing with conflict without resorting to violence, such as school-based programs which present information on spousal and dating abuse, or discussions of how to reduce violent incidents.[109] Some victim assistance projects seek to help victims learn about victim compensation services and related programs. For example, CAVEAT (Canadians Against Violence) developed its educational programs based on information from victims of violence and current research. Their crime prevention workshops and forums examine both prevention and response strategies, such as increasing awareness of issues, learning prevention skills, and developing early identification and intervention strategies.

Other programs help employers understand the plight of employees who have been victims of crime. Because victims may miss work or suffer postcrime emotional trauma, they may need to be absent from work for extended periods of time. If employers are unwilling to give them leave, victims may refuse to participate in the criminal justice process. Being an advocate with employers and explaining the needs of victims is a service provided by more than half of all victim programs.

Crisis Intervention

Most victim programs make referrals for services to help victims recover from their ordeal. It is common to refer clients to the local network of public and private social service agencies that can provide emergency and long-term assistance with transportation, medical care, shelter, food, and clothing. In addition, some programs provide **crisis intervention** to victims, many of whom are feeling isolated, vulnerable, and in need of immediate services. Some programs offer counselling at the service's office, while others do outreach in victims' homes, at the crime scene, or in a hospital. No crime requires more crisis intervention efforts than rape and sexual assault. After years of rape being ignored by the justice system, increased sensitivity to this crime and its victims has spurred the opening of crisis centres around the country. These centres typically feature 24-hour-a-day emergency phone lines and information on police, medical, and court procedures. Some provide volunteers to assist the victim as her case is processed through the justice system. The growth of these services has been so explosive that services are now available in many major cities and college communities.[110] Some services maintain Web sites on the Internet as well.

Most rape crisis centres provide the following services to victims: (1) emergency assistance, including information, referral, and some support, usually over the telephone, and available 24 hours a day; (2) face-to-face crisis intervention, or accompaniment, usually provided in the hospital, police station, courts, or other public location, also available 24 hours a day; and (3) counselling, either one-on-one or in groups, in a varying number of sessions, often provided at the centre, usually scheduled, and limited to business hours and evenings.[111]

While crisis intervention has become widespread, child care for victims while in consultation or in court is less common.

Victim–Offender Reconciliation Programs

Victim–offender reconciliation programs use mediators to facilitate face-to-face encounters between victims and their attackers. The aim is to engage in direct negotiations that lead to restitution agreements and possibly reconciliation between the two parties involved.[112] Included in this innovation are alternative measures, or diversion programs. These exist for young offenders in all provinces, and for adults since 1996 in most provinces. In most cases charges are either stayed or not laid providing community service work is carried out. While they were at first designed to handle routine misdemeanours such as petty theft and vandalism, it is now common for these programs to hammer out restitution agreements in more serious incidents.

Connections

Reconciliation programs are based on the concept of restorative justice. Restorative justice rejects punitive correctional measures and instead suggests that crimes of violence and theft should be viewed as interpersonal conflicts that need to be settled in the community through noncoercive means. The theoretical roots of the restorative justice concept can be found in Chapter 9's discussion of "peacemaking criminology."

Victims' Rights

In an important article, Frank Carrington suggested in 1981 that crime victims have legal rights that should assure them basic services from the government, and many now do.[113] According to Carrington, just as the law guarantees that offenders have the right to counsel and a fair trial, society also has the obligation to ensure basic rights for law-abiding citizens. These rights range from adequate protection under the law from violent crimes, to victim compensation and assistance from the criminal justice system.

In 1988 the provincial and federal governments agreed on principles for the treatment of victims. Some of these principles are the following:

- Victims should be treated with courtesy and receive redress for the crime committed against them.
- Victims should receive information about their role in criminal justice proceedings and be asked what assistance they need.
- The victim and his or her family's safety should be ensured, and there should be an opportunity for their views about the impact of the crime to be heard.
- Criminal justice system personnel should be made sensitive to the needs of victims.[114]

The Province of Ontario posts a "Victim's Bill of Rights" (VBR) on its Public Law and Policy Division Web page.[115] The VBR received royal assent on December 14, 1995, and was proclaimed on June 11, 1996. It designates June 11 as the Annual Day of Commemoration for Victims of Crime and includes such items as

- a statement of principles supporting victims through the criminal justice process;
- improved access to information concerning services;
- provision for victims of sexual assault to be interviewed by officials of the same gender;
- provisions making it easier for victims to sue assailants in civil actions;
- the presumption that a victim of domestic assault or sexual assault has suffered emotional distress;
- legislative amendments to support child witnesses in civil proceedings;
- changes in and expansion of the Victims' Justice Fund.

Victim advocacy today is offered by an eclectic group of organizations, some independent, some government-sponsored, and some self-help. Advocates can be especially helpful when victims need to interact with the agencies of justice. For example, they can lobby police departments to keep investigations open and request the return of recovered stolen property. They can demand from prosecutors and judges protection from harassment and reprisals, such as making "no contact" a condition of bail. They can help victims make statements during sentencing hearings and probation and parole revocation procedures. Victim advocates can also interact with the news media, making sure that reporting is accurate and that victim privacy is not violated. Such groups can help victims with a variety of needs, not only legal but therapeutic and spiritual as well.

Self-Protection

Although the public is generally satisfied with the police, fear of crime and concern about community safety have prompted many people to become their own "police force" and take an active role in community protection and citizen crime control groups. The more crime in an area, the greater the amount of fear and the more likely residents will engage in self-protective measures.[116] As Leslie Kennedy of the University of Alberta points out, a significant number of crimes may not be reported to police simply because victims prefer to take matters into their own hands, although this shouldn't be taken to imply that they seek revenge.[117] Rosemary Gartner and Anthony Doob report that 70 percent of robbery victims and 64 percent of assault victims said they didn't report their victimization to the police because they "dealt with it another way."[118] However, attitudes supporting taking the law into one's own hands are probably more conservative in Canada than in the United States. For example, one of the authors of this text once saw a bumper sticker in Canada on a car from Texas and marvelled at its message: "Fight Crime. Shoot Back!"

One way in which this self-protection trend has manifested itself is in the concept of **target hardening**, or making one's home and business crime-proof through locks, bars, alarms, and other devices.[119] This approach is based in routine activities theory and places the onus on the victim to prevent crime. Many people have taken specific steps to secure their homes or place of employment, taking crime prevention measures such as installing a burglar alarm, participating in a neighbourhood watch program, or engraving valuables with an identification number. Other commonly used crime prevention techniques include building a fence or barricade at the entrance of a home or business; installing an intercom or phone to gain access to the building, as well as surveillance cameras, window bars, or warning signs; hiring a doorkeeper, guard, or receptionist in an apartment building; and obtaining dogs known for their ability to guard premises. The use of these measures is inversely proportional to perception of neighbourhood safety:

Connections

Target hardening is based on the idea of rational deterrence, that making a crime difficult to complete will make it unattractive to the instrumentalist criminal. For more on rational choice and deterrence theory, see Chapter 5.

People who fear crime are more likely to use crime prevention techniques, if they can afford it.

There is mounting evidence that people who engage in household protection are less likely to become victims of property crimes.[120] One study found that people who install burglar alarms are less likely to become burglary victims than those who forgo similar preventive measures.[121] When such measures are effective in deterring crime, what then occurs is crime **displacement**, where crime moves to weaker targets.[122]

Fighting Back

Some people take self-protection to its ultimate end and are prepared to fight back when they are attacked by criminals. How successful are victims when they fight back? Research indicates that victims who fight back often frustrate their attackers but also face increased odds of being physically harmed during the attack; for example, fighting back does decrease the odds of a rape being completed but increases the victim's chances of receiving other physical injuries.[123] This raises speculation that while resistance may draw the attention of bystanders and make the sexual assault physically difficult to complete, it can also cause offenders to escalate their violence. In the United States a federal survey found that robbery victims who fought back were less likely to experience completed crimes than passive victims, but they were also more likely to be injured during the robbery. The victims who escaped both serious injury and property loss were the ones who used the most violent responses to crime, such as a weapon, or the least violent, such as reasoning with their attackers. Those who fought back with their fists or who tried to get help were the most likely to experience both injury and theft.[124]

Armed victims are often ready and willing to use their guns against offenders—2.5 million times a year in the United States, where about one-third of households

WHY ARE GUYS LIKE THIS OUT ON THE STREETS?   BECAUSE GUYS LIKE *THESE* ARE CLOGGING UP THE JAILS:

RELEASED AFTER SLITTING A MAN'S THROAT; NOW SUSPECTED OF MURDERING FIVE PEOPLE   SERVING MINIMUM MANDATORY SENTENCE FOR GROWING A POT PLANT IN HIS CLOSET

SOURCE: Pete at wag@mtn.org.

contain guns.[125] It is estimated that armed victims kill 1500 to 2800 potential felons each year in the United States and wound between 8700 and 16 000. This research shows that victims kill far more criminals than the estimated 250 to 1000 killed annually by police in the United States.[126] One researcher has found that the risk of collateral injury is relatively rare and that potential victims should be encouraged to fight back; empirical research studies unanimously show that defensive gun use is associated with both lower rates of crime completion and lower rates of injury to the victim.[127]

In Canada, there are some supporters of an "armed citizenry," and some research done by Gary Mauser supports the view that Canadians do use guns for self-defence. The estimate is that Canadians use firearms to protect themselves between 60 000 and 80 000 times per year, and that 19 000 to 37 500 of these incidents involve defence against human threats.[128] Other criminologists such as Gary Green speculate that firearm ownership brings with it a number of problems, including accidental deaths and the use of stolen guns in other crimes.[129] The issue of gun control will be discussed in depth in later chapters.

Community Organization

Not everyone is capable of buying a handgun or semiautomatic weapon and doing battle with predatory criminals. Another approach has been for communities to organize on the neighbourhood level against crime. Citizens have been working independently and in cooperation with local police agencies in neighbourhood patrol and block watch programs. These programs organize local citizens in urban areas to patrol neighbourhoods, watch for suspicious people, help secure the neighbourhood, lobby for improvements (such as better lighting), report crime to police, put out community newsletters, conduct home security surveys, and serve as a source for crime information or tips, as in Crime Stoppers.[130]

While such programs are welcome additions to police services, there is little evidence that they have an appreciable effect on the crime rate. There is also concern that their effectiveness is spottier in low-income, high-crime areas, which are in the most need of crime prevention assistance.[131] Block watches and neighbourhood patrols seem more successful when they are part of general-purpose or multi-issue community groups, rather than when they focus directly on crime problems.

Another community-based program is National Night Out, an event involving citizens and law-enforcement agencies in both the United States and Canada. The program was created by the National Association of Town Watch, a nonprofit organization dedicated to developing crime and drug prevention programs, generating support and participation in local anti-crime programs, and strengthening neighbourhood spirits and police and community relations. Between the hours of 7 and 10 p.m., residents are urged to keep their porch lights on to warn criminals that neighbourhoods are fighting back against crime.

In sum, community crime prevention programs, target hardening, and self-defence measures are flourishing across North America. They are a response to the fear of crime and the perceived shortcomings of police agencies to ensure community safety. Along with private security, they represent attempts to supplement municipal police agencies and expand the "war on crime" to become a personal, neighbourhood, and community concern.

Summary

Criminologists now consider victims and victimization a major focus of study. More than 24 percent of Canadian citizens suffer from crime each year, and the social and economic costs of crime are in the billions of dollars. Like crime, victimization has stable patterns and trends. In general, victims of violent crime tend to be young, poor, single males living in large cities. Crime takes place more often at night in public places. However, many victimizations also occur in the home, and women and female children are often the target of intrafamilial violence. Many women who are killed are the victims of their husbands.

There are a number of theories of victimization. One view, called victim precipitation, contends that victims provoke criminals. Lifestyle theories suggest that victims put themselves in danger by engaging in high-risk activities, such as going out late at night, living in a high-crime area, and associating with high-risk peers. The routine activities theory maintains that a pool of motivated offenders exists and that they will take advantage of unguarded, suitable targets. The major theories of victimization are summarized in Table 4.4.

Numerous programs help victims by providing court services, economic compensation, public education, and crisis intervention. However, victims still complain about feeling victimized by the criminal justice system, whether that means being interviewed by unsympathetic police officers, being forced to wait for their court hearing in the same area of the courthouse as the defendant, not qualifying for legal aid, or not receiving compensation.

Rather than depend on the justice system, some victims have attempted to help themselves. In some instances, this self-help means community organization for self-protection. In other instances, victims have armed themselves and fought back against their attackers. There is evidence that fighting back reduces the number of completed crimes but is also related to victim injury. The development of victimology certainly adds to the complexity of studying the crime problem.

Table 4.4	Victim Theories	
THEORY	**MAJOR PREMISE**	**STRENGTHS**
Victim precipitation	Victims trigger criminal acts by their provocative behaviour. Active precipitation involves fighting words or gestures. Passive precipitation occurs when victims unknowingly threaten their attacker.	Explains multiple victimizations. If people precipitate crime, it follows that they will become repeat victims if their behaviour persists over time.
Lifestyle theories	Victimization risk is increased when people have a high-risk lifestyle. Placing oneself at risk by going to dangerous places results in increased victimization.	Explains victimization patterns in the social structure. Males, young people, and the poor have high victim rates because they have a higher-risk lifestyle than females, the elderly, and the affluent.
Equivalent group hypothesis	Criminals and victims are one and the same. Both crime and victimization are part of a high-risk lifestyle.	Shows that the conditions that create criminality also produce high victimization risk. Victims may commit crime out of a need for revenge or frustration.
Routine activities theory	Crime rates can be explained by the availability of suitable targets, the absence of capable guardians, and the presence of motivated offenders.	Can explain crime rates and trends. Shows how victim behaviour can influence criminal opportunity. Suggests that victim risk can be reduced by increasing guardianship and/or reducing target vulnerability.
Proximity hypothesis	People who live in deviant places are at high risk for crime. Victim behaviour has little influence over the criminal act.	Places the focus of crime on deviant places. Shows why people with conventional lifestyles become crime victims.

Thinking Like a Criminologist

The Solicitor General of Canada has asked you to prepare a report on the relationship between physical abuse and criminal acts among adolescents ages 10 to 18. As a result of the self-report survey you conduct, you are able to provide the following information:

Adolescents experiencing abuse or violence are at high risk of immediate and lasting negative effects on health and well-being. Of the high school students surveyed, an alarming one in five (21 percent) said they had been physically abused. Of the older students, ages 15 to 18, 29 percent said they had been physically abused. Younger students also reported significant rates of abuse: 17 percent responded "yes" when questioned whether they had been physically abused. Although girls were far less likely to report abuse than boys, 12 percent said they had been physically abused. Most abuse occurs at home; it occurs more than once; and the abuser is usually a family member. More than half of those physically abused had tried alcohol and drugs, and 60 percent had admitted to a violent act. Nonabused children were significantly less likely to abuse substances, and only 30 percent indicated they had committed a violent act.

What is your interpretation of the association between abuse and delinquency? What recommendations would you make about current discussions to reform the Youth Criminal Justice Act to make it more responsive to underlying factors that affect youth crime?

Key Terms

acquaintance-related crime
active precipitation
aggravating factor
capable guardians
crisis intervention
cycle of violence
deviant place hypothesis
displacement

equivalent group hypothesis
lifestyle
mitigating factor
motivated offenders
passive precipitation
predatory crime
proximity hypothesis
routine activities theory

stranger-related crime
suitable targets
target hardening
victim compensation
victim precipitation
victimologists
victimology

 See the book-specific website at www.siegelcriminology2e.nelson.com for additional chapter links, discussions, and quizzes.

Theories of Crime Causation

"An important goal of the criminological enterprise is to create valid and accurate theories of crime causation. Social scientists have defined theory as sets of statements that explain why and how several concepts are related. For a set of statements to qualify as a theory, we must be able to deduce some conclusions from it that are subject to empirical verification; that is, theories must predict or prohibit certain observable events or conditions."*

Criminologists have sought to collect vital facts about crime and interpret them in a scientifically meaningful fashion. By developing empirically verifiable statements, or hypotheses, and organizing them into theories of crime causation, they hope to identify the causes of crime.

Since the late 19th century, criminological theory has pointed to various underlying causes of crime. The earliest theories generally attributed crime to a single underlying cause: atypical body build, genetic abnormality, insanity, physical anomalies, and poverty. Later theories attributed crime causation to multiple factors: poverty, peer influence, school problems, and family dysfunction.

In this section, theories of crime causation are grouped into five chapters. Chapters 5 and 6 focus on theories based on individual traits. They hold that crime is either a free-will choice made by an individual, a function of personal psychological or biological abnormality, or both. Chapters 7 through 9 investigate theories based in sociology and political economy. These theories portray crime as a function of the structure, process, and conflicts of social living. Chapter 10 is devoted to theories that combine or integrate these various concepts into a cohesive, complex view of crime.

*Rodney Stark, *Sociology*, 2nd ed. (Belmont, Calif.: Wadsworth, 1987), p. 618.

Chapter

5

Choice Theory

Crime data tell us that criminality is a young man's game: Most offenders are young males who desist from crime as they mature; the bulk of adult offending is committed by relatively few persistent offenders. Why do these youths commit criminal acts? Furthermore, given that most young offenders age out or desist from crime, why do some continue to violate the law and risk apprehension, trial, and punishment well into adulthood?

To some criminologists, persistence is a function of personal choice. The decision to violate the law—commit a robbery, sell drugs, attack a rival, fill out a false tax return—is made for a variety of personal reasons, including greed, revenge, need, anger, lust, jealousy, thrill seeking, or vanity. The central issue is that the illegal act is a matter of individual decision making, a rational choice made after weighing the potential benefits and consequences of crime. The jealous suitor concludes that the risk of punishment is worth the satisfaction of "punching out" a rival; the greedy shopper considers the chance of apprehension by store detectives so small that she takes a "five-finger discount" on a new sweater; the drug dealer concludes that the huge profits he can earn from a single shipment of cocaine far outweigh the possible costs of apprehension. In the final analysis, people choose crime simply because it is rewarding, satisfying, easy, or fun.

This chapter will review the philosophical underpinnings of **choice theory**, which first appeared as **classical criminology**. Our discussion will then turn to more recent theoretical models that flow from the concept of choice. Because the central premise is that criminals are rational, their behaviour can be controlled or deterred by the fear of punishment. The phenomenon of desistence can then be explained by a growing and intense fear of punishment. These models include situational crime prevention, general deterrence theory, specific deterrence theory, and incapacitation. Finally, the chapter briefly reviews how choice theory has influenced policy making in the area of criminal justice.

The Development of Classical Theory

Theories of crime based on the rational decision making of motivated criminals can trace their roots to the classical school of criminology. As you may recall from Chapter 1, classical criminology was based on the works of Beccaria, Bentham, and other utilitarian philosophers. At its core are the following concepts:

- people choose all behaviour, including criminal behaviour;
- a violation of another person is a violation of the social contract;

- society must provide the greatest good for the greatest number;
- the law shouldn't try to legislate morality;
- people should be presumed innocent until proven guilty, with no torture;
- laws should be written out with punishments prescribed in advance;
- individuals give up some of their liberty in exchange for social protection;
- people are motivated by pain and pleasure;
- punishment should be limited to what is necessary to deter people from crime;
- punishment should be severe, certain, and swift;
- the law must be rational, transparent, and just, or is itself a crime;
- people's choices can be controlled by the fear of punishment; and
- severity, certainty, and swiftness of punishment are the most effective in controlling criminal behaviour.[1]

In keeping with his utilitarian views, Beccaria called for fair and certain punishment to deter crime. Because people are egotistical and self-centred, they must be goaded by the fear of punishment, which provides a tangible motive for them to obey the law and suppress the "despotic spirit" that resides in every person.

Beccaria felt that, to be effective, punishments must be proportional to their crimes. Without proportionality, people will not be deterred from committing more serious offences. For example, if both rape and murder were punished by death, a rapist would have little reason to refrain from killing his victim in order to eliminate the potential threat of the victim contacting the police and giving evidence in court.

Although some have questioned Beccaria's principles and motives, even his harshest critics recognize that he was one of the rare reformers to have an enduring influence on justice policy and a true criminological success story.[2] Beccaria's ideas and writings have inspired criminologists who believe that criminals choose to commit crime and that crime can be controlled by the judicious application of criminal punishments. The result has been a foundation for criminal justice which is still with us today.

Beccaria's vision has had a powerful influence on events in the criminal justice system.[3] The belief that punishment should fit the crime and that people should be punished proportionately for what they did and not to satisfy the whim of a capricious judge or ruler was widely adopted throughout Europe and North America. In Britain, philosopher Jeremy Bentham (1748–1833) helped popularize Beccaria's views in his writings on **utilitarianism**. According to this theory, actions are evaluated by their tendency to produce advantage, pleasure, and happiness and to avoid or prevent mischief, pain, evil, or unhappiness.[4] Bentham believed that the purpose of all law is to produce and support the total happiness of the community it serves. Since punishment is in itself harmful, its existence is justified only if it promises to prevent greater evil than it creates. Punishment, therefore, has four main objectives:

- to prevent all criminal offences;
- when it cannot prevent a crime, to convince the offender to commit a less serious one;
- to ensure that a criminal uses no more force than is necessary; and
- to prevent crime as cheaply as possible.

The most stunning example of how the classical philosophy of Beccaria and Bentham was embraced in Europe occurred in 1789, when France's postrevolutionary Constituent Assembly adopted these ideas in the Declaration of the Rights of Man:

> ... the law has the right to prohibit only actions harmful to society.... The law shall inflict only such punishments as are strictly and clearly necessary.... No person shall be punished except by virtue of a law enacted and promulgated previous to the crime and applicable to its terms.

Similarly, a prohibition against "cruel and unusual punishments" was incorporated into Canada's Charter of Rights and Freedoms, as Section 12: "Everyone has the right not to be subjected to any cruel and unusual treatment or punishment."

The use of torture and severe punishments was largely abandoned in the 19th century. The practice of incarcerating criminals and structuring prison sentences to fit the severity of the crime was a reflection of classical criminology. Although the proportionality demanded by Beccaria was often ignored by the legal system, the general theme of gearing punishment to deter crime was widely accepted.

By the end of the 19th century, the popularity of the classical approach began to decline, after 100 years of dominance, and by the mid-20th century this perspective was neglected by mainstream criminologists. During this period, positivist criminologists focused on the internal and external factors—poverty, low IQ, poor education, inadequate home life—believed to be the true cause of criminality. Since these conditions could not be easily curbed, the concept of punishing people for behaviours beyond their control seemed both foolish and cruel. Although classical principles still controlled the way police, courts, and correctional agencies operated, most criminologists rejected classical criminology as an explanation of criminal behaviour.

Choice Theory Emerges

Beginning in the mid-1970s, the classical approach began to enjoy a resurgence of popularity. The rehabilitation of known criminals, considered a cornerstone of positivist policy, came under attack. According to positivist criminology, if crime were caused by some social or psychological problem, such as poverty, crime rates could be reduced by providing good jobs and economic opportunities. A number of national surveys (the best known being Robert Martinson's "What Works?") failed to uncover examples of rehabilitation programs that prevented future criminal activity.[5] The book *Beyond Probation* went so far as to suggest that punishment-oriented programs could suppress future criminality much more effectively than those that relied on rehabilitation and treatment efforts.[6]

A significant increase in the reported crime rate, as well as serious disturbances in the nation's prisons, frightened the general public. To many criminologists, reviving the classical concepts of social control and punishment made more sense than futilely trying to improve entrenched social conditions or rehabilitate criminals using ineffectual methodologies.[7]

Beginning in the late 1970s, a number of criminologists began producing books and monographs expounding the theme that criminals are rational actors who plan their crimes, fear punishment, and deserve to be penalized for their misdeeds. In a 1975 book that came to symbolize renewed interest in classical views, *Thinking About Crime,* political scientist James Q. Wilson debunked the positivist view that crime is a function of external forces, such as poverty, that can be altered by government programs. Instead, he argued, efforts should be made to reduce criminal opportunity by deterring would-be offenders and incarcerating known criminals.

Persons who are likely to commit crime, Wilson maintained, lack inhibition against misconduct, value the excitement and thrills of breaking the law, have a low stake in conformity, and are willing to take greater chances than the average person. If they can be convinced that their actions will bring severe punishment, only the totally irrational will be willing to engage in crime. While incapacitating criminals should not be the sole goal of the justice system, such a policy does have the advantage of restraining offenders and preventing their future criminality without having to figure out how to change their attitudes or nature, a goal that has proved difficult to accomplish. Wilson made this famous, albeit cynical, observation:

> Wicked people exist. Nothing avails except to set them apart from innocent people. And many people, neither wicked nor innocent, but watchful, dissembling, and calculating of their chances, ponder our reaction to wickedness as a clue to what they might profitably do.[8]

Here Wilson seems to be saying that unless we react forcefully to crime, those "sitting on the fence" will get a clear message: Crime pays.

Coinciding with the publication of Wilson's book was a conservative shift in public policy in many Western countries. Political decision makers embraced ideas suggested by Wilson as a means of bringing the crime rate down, perhaps because they focused blame on the individual. These views have helped shape criminal justice policy for the past two decades.

Does Crime Pay? Rational offenders might be induced to commit crime if they perceive that crime pays more than they could possibly earn from a legitimate job. Crime pays if, taking into account the probability of arrest and the cost of punishment, the benefits of employment are lower than the expected benefits of theft. Does crime, in fact, pay?

To answer this question, James Q. Wilson and Allan Abrahams (1992) used a sample of incarcerated inmates to determine their perceived and actual "take" from crime. Wilson and Abrahams divided the group into mid- and high-rate offenders in one of six crime categories: burglary, theft, swindling, auto theft, robbery, and mixed offences predominantly involving drug sales.

Using crime loss estimates derived from the NCVS survey, Wilson and Abrahams found that mid-rate bur-

glars on average earn about 32 percent of what they could have earned in a legitimate job. High-rate burglars, who commit an average of 193 crimes per year, earn roughly what they would have earned from a job (but they spend more time behind bars). Even if free for the entire year, high-rate burglars would earn about the same as if they had held a job for the same period.

Crime profits are reduced by the costs of a criminal career: legal fees, bail bonds, loss of family income, and the psychic cost of a prison sentence. Given these costs, most criminals actually earn little from crime. Would you be willing to become a high-rate robber if you knew that you would be spending half your life in prison for an annual salary of under $15 000? In 1986 the average take for a gas station robbery was $300. Bank robberies, on the other hand, netted on average $2 500 in 1993, but the clearance rate was as high as 80 percent, with an even higher conviction rate.[9]

If crime pays so little, why are there so many criminals? There are a number of reasons criminals choose crime despite its relatively low payoff.

Famous Canadian Criminals

The Curious Career Choice of Edwin Alonzo Boyd

Edwin Alonzo Boyd, the son of a Toronto policeman, embarked on his career as a bank robber in September 1949. He undertook this first robbery on his own, taking in just over $2000. Sometimes he had a partner, Howard Gault, a former jail guard. Boyd's efforts were not always successful. In one robbery, the bank manager grabbed a gun and shot at Boyd, who had no choice but to run without the loot. Another time, Boyd was chased in his stolen car by a bank employee and just barely escaped.

Boyd was finally captured in 1951 and sent to Toronto's Don Jail, where he met Lennie "Tough Lennie" Jackson, another bank robber, and Willie "The Clown" Jackson, a small-time criminal. With another bank robber, Steve Suchan, the three escaped. Lennie had a wooden leg, in which he had hidden a hacksaw blade. Using the blade, they sawed through the bars, slid through the window, and

landed in an exercise yard below. They used bedsheets to make a rope that they then threw to the top of a wall and clambered up it to make their way to freedom. They went on a bank-robbing spree that included the biggest cash haul in Toronto's history. Short-lived at ten months, it was the stuff of exciting newspaper coverage.

It all came to an end in March 1952, when two police detectives, Edmund Tong and Roy Perry, pulled over a car. Tong had been on the trail of the Boyd gang but didn't know the black Mercury contained his sought-after quarry. Suchan and Lennie Jackson were inside. As Tong approached the suspect vehicle, he was gunned down, and Perry was wounded in the arm.

In response to the public outrage, a manhunt was quickly mounted. Suchan and Jackson were captured in Montreal but Boyd, who had had nothing to do with the murder, eluded capture for a while. He was arrested peacefully at his brother's house. The four soon found themselves back in the Don

Jail. Once again, they took advantage of Leonard Jackson's artificial foot – using it to hide a piece of metal, a file, and hacksaw blades. They made a key to their cell door with the metal and file and used the hacksaw blades to cut through the bars. Rewards totalling $26 000 were posted for their capture. After a huge manhunt, police captured the gang in an abandoned barn near Yonge Street and Sheppard Avenue. All four were convicted on charges of armed robbery and auto theft. Leonard Jackson and Steve Suchan were executed by hanging for the murder of Edmund Tong.

Alonzo Boyd was sentenced to life in prison, but was eventually paroled in 1966 and retired to a private life under a different name in British Columbia. William Jackson also served a lengthy jail term in the Kingston Penitentiary, before being released.

Sources: Brian Vallee, *Edwin Alonzo Boyd* (Toronto: Doubleday, 1998); torontopolice.on.ca/d32/history; tv.cbc.ca/lifeandtimes/bio1998/boyd.

One reason is that criminals tend to overestimate the money they can earn from crime. Wilson and Abrahams found that in some cases, criminals' estimates were more than 12 times higher than a realistic assessment of their earning potential. For example, burglars estimated they could earn $2674 per month from crime, while a more realistic figure is only $230! In 1992, when three young man robbed a McDonald's restaurant in Sydney River, Nova Scotia, they had convinced themselves they could get $200 000 from the robbery. For a take that was only a fraction of what they had estimated, they killed three people and received long prison sentences for their trouble.[10]

Some criminals believe they have no choice but to commit crime because legitimate work is unavailable. This may be another false assumption. About two-thirds of the inmates reported having been employed before they were imprisoned. Rather than being excluded from the job market, criminals seem to be relatively unsuccessful participants within it; they are underemployed, not unemployed.

Criminals are realistic about their long-term careers, believing that eventually everyone is caught and punished. However, they are overly optimistic about getting away with each individual crime. They believe that the odds of getting caught for a particular crime are rather small, and being impulsive, they take the short-term view that each particular crime is worth the risk; they may eventually get caught, but not this time.

Crime could be deterred if would-be criminals understood the true costs of committing crime and the relatively small payoff of a criminal career, but that does not usually occur, nor is there an easy way to make it happen.

From these roots, a more contemporary version of classical theory evolved that is based on intelligent thought processes and criminal decision making; it is today referred to as the rational choice approach to crime causation.[11]

The Concepts of Rational Choice

According to the rational choice approach, law-violating behaviour occurs when an offender decides to risk transgressing after considering both personal factors (such as need for money, revenge, thrills, and entertainment) and situational factors (how well a target is protected, the efficiency of the local police force). Before choosing to commit a crime, the reasoning criminal evaluates the risk of apprehension, the seriousness of expected punishment, the potential value of the criminal enterprise, and his or her immediate need for criminal gain.

The decision to commit a specific type of crime, then, is a matter of personal decision making based on weighing the available information. Conversely, the decision to forgo crime may be based on the criminal's perception that the economic benefits are no longer there or that the risk of apprehension is too great. For example, studies of residential burglary indicate that criminals will forgo activity if they believe a neighbourhood is well patrolled by police.[12] In fact, evidence exists that when police begin to concentrate patrols in a particular area of the city, crime rates tend to increase in adjacent areas that may be perceived by criminals as "safer" (referred to as **crime displacement**).[13]

Offence and Offender Specifications

Rational choice theorists view crime as both offence- and offender-specific.[14] **Offence-specific crime** refers to the fact that offenders will react selectively to the characteristics of particular offences. The decision of whether to commit an individual burglary, for example, might involve evaluating the target's likely cash yield; the availability of resources, such as a getaway car; and the probability of capture by police.

Offender-specific crime refers to the fact that criminals are not simply driven people who for one reason or another engage in random acts of antisocial behaviour. Before deciding to partake in crime, they analyze whether they have the prerequisites for committing a criminal act, including their skills, motives, needs, and fears. Criminal acts might be ruled out if the potential offenders perceive that they can reach a desired personal goal through legitimate means or if they are too afraid of getting caught.[15]

Note the distinction made here between crime and criminality.[16] Crime is an event; criminality is a personal trait. Criminals do not commit crime all the time, and even the most honest citizens may on occasion violate the law. Some high-risk people lacking opportunity may never commit crime, whereas given enough provocation or opportunity, a low-risk, law-abiding person may commit crime. What, then, are the conditions that promote crime and criminality?

Structuring Criminality. A number of personal factors condition people to choose criminality. Perceptions of economic opportunity may influence offending choices: Offenders are more likely to desist from crime if they believe that (1) their future criminal earnings will be relatively low, and (2) attractive and legal income-generating opportunities are available.[17] In this sense, making a rational choice is a function of perception of conventional alternatives and opportunities.

Fluctuations in the perceptions of risk over the life course may also influence behaviour choices. Neal Shover found that experienced criminals may turn from a life of crime when they develop a belief that the risks from crime are greater than its potential profit.[18] The veteran criminal has discovered the limitations of his or her powers and knows when to take a chance and when to be cautious. Thus, learning and experience may be important elements in the choice of crime.[19]

Personality and lifestyle also help structure criminal choices. According to sociologist Robert Agnew, those people who choose crime over conformity share a number of personal traits: (1) They perceive freedom of movement and lack of social constraints; (2) they have less self-control than other people and seem unaffected by fear of social control (that is, criminal punishment); and (3) they are typically under stress or facing some serious personal problem or condition that forces them to choose risky behaviour.[20]

Structuring Crime

The evidence indicates that the decision to commit crime, regardless of its substance, is structured by the choice of (1) where the crime occurs, (2) the characteristics of the target, and (3) the means (techniques) available for its completion.

Choosing the Place of Crime. Criminals appear to choose the place of crime. Bruce Jacobs's interviews with 40 active street dealers of crack cocaine showed that dealers carefully evaluated the desirability of their "sales area" before setting up shop.[21] Dealers considered the middle of a long block the best choice because they could see everything coming toward them from both directions; police raids could then be spotted ahead of time. Another tactic was to entice buyers of whom they were suspicious either into spaces between apartment buildings or into back lots to do drug deals. While the dealer may have lost the tactical edge of being on a public street, he gained a measure of protection because his confederates could watch over the operation and come to the rescue if the buyer tried to "pull something."

Choosing Targets. Evidence of rational choice may also be found in the way criminals locate their targets. Victimization data indicate that high-income households are the most likely targets of property crimes; in contrast, the wealthy are rarely the victims of violent crimes. It is unlikely that this pattern could be a random event.

Studies of both professional and occasional criminals also yield evidence that choosing targets is a rational event. Burglars seem to make prudent choices when they check to make sure that no one is home before they enter a residence. Some call ahead, while others ring the doorbell, preparing to claim they had the wrong address if someone answers. Some check to find out which families have star high-school athletes, since those that do are sure to be at the game, leaving their houses unguarded.[22] Others seek the unlocked door and avoid the one with a deadbolt; houses with dogs are usually considered off-limits.

Burglars indicate that they carefully choose their targets. Some avoid freestanding buildings because they can more easily be surrounded by police; others select targets that are known to do a primarily cash business, such as bars, supermarkets, and restaurants.[23] Burglars also report being sensitive to the activities of their victims. They note that homemakers often develop predictable behaviour patterns, which helps the burglars plan their crimes.[24] Burglars seem to prefer "working" between 9 a.m. and 11 a.m. and in mid-afternoon, when parents are either working or dropping off or picking up kids at school. Burglars avoid Saturdays because most families are at home; Sunday morning during church hours is considered a prime time for weekend burglaries. Bank robbers choose city banks over country banks, because of the ease of getting away. Some prefer banks near subway routes, while others prefer areas with heavy pedestrian traffic.

Learning Criminal Techniques. Criminals report learning the techniques of crime that help them avoid detection; for example, crack dealers learn how to "stash" crack cocaine in some undisclosed location so that they will not be forced to carry large amounts of product on their persons.

Females drawn into drug dealing tell how they have learned the "trade" in a businesslike manner:

> He taught me how to "recon" [reconstitute] cocaine, cutting and repacking a brick from 91 proof to 50 proof, just like a business. He treats me like an equal partner, and many of the friends are business associates. I am a catalyst.... I even get guys turned on to drugs.[25]

In sum, rational choice involves both the shaping of criminality and the structuring of crime. Personality, age, status, risk, and opportunity seem to influence the decision to become a criminal; place, target, and techniques help to structure crime.

Rational Choice and Routine Activities

Rational choice theory dovetails with **routine activities theory**, which maintains that along with a supply of motivated offenders, the absence of capable guardians and the presence of suitable targets determine crime and victimization rate trends.[26] Routine activities theory provides a **macro** view of crime, predicting how change in social and economic conditions influences the overall crime and victimization rates. In contrast, **rational choice theory** provides a **micro** view of why individual offenders decide to commit specific crimes. While not identical, these approaches agree that crime rates are a product of criminal opportunity: Increase the number of guardians, decrease the suitability of targets, or reduce the offender population, and crime rates should likewise decline; increase opportunity and reduce guardianship and crime rates should increase.

What are the connections between rational choice and routine activities?

Connections

In Chapter 4, routine activities theory discussed how victimization is patterned, not random or accidental. This theory gives a macro perspective on some of the causes of crime.

Suitable Targets. Research indicates that criminal choice is influenced by the perception of target vulnerability. As they go about their daily activities, travelling to school or work, potential criminals may encounter targets of illegal opportunity: an empty carport, an open door, an unlocked car, a bike left on the street. Corner homes, usually near traffic lights or stop signs, are more likely to be burglarized: Stop signs give criminals a legitimate reason to stop their cars and look for an attractive target. Secluded homes, such as those at the end of a cul-de-sac, surrounded by wooded areas, also make suitable targets.[27] Thieves also report being concerned about the convenience of their target. They are more apt to choose sites for burglaries and robberies that are familiar to them and that are located in easily accessible and open areas.[28]

Because criminals often go on foot or use public transportation, they are unlikely to travel long distances to commit crimes and are more likely to drift toward the centre of a city than to move toward outlying areas.[29] Garland White found that "permeable neighbourhoods," those with a greater than usual number of access streets from traffic arteries into the neighbourhood, are the ones most likely to have high crime rates.[30] This might lend credence to the idea of having "gated communities," where access is strictly controlled. It is possible that criminals choose these neighbourhoods for burglaries because they are familiar and well travelled, because they appear more open and vulnerable, and because they offer more potential escape routes. Here, we can see the influence of a routine activity on criminal choice: The more suitable and accessible the target, the more likely that crime will occur.[31]

Capable Guardians. Routine activity also implies that the presence of **capable guardians** may deter crime. Criminals tend to shy away from victims who are perceived to be armed and potentially dangerous. In a series of interviews conducted with career property offenders, Kenneth Tunnell found that burglars will avoid targets if they feel there are police in the area or if "nosy neighbours" might be suspicious and cause trouble.[32] And evidence is accumulating that predatory criminals are aware of law enforcement capability: Communities that enjoy the reputation of employing aggressive "crime-fighting" cops are less likely to attract potential offenders than areas perceived as having passive law enforcers.[33]

Guardianship can also involve passive or mechanical devices, such as security fences or burglar alarms. Research indicates that physical security measures can improve guardianship and limit offender access to targets.[34]

Motivated Criminals. Routine activities theory predicts that crime rates correspond to the number of **motivated criminals** in the population (that is, teenage males, drug users, unemployed adults). Rational offenders may be less likely to commit crimes if they believe they can achieve personal goals through legitimate means; in short, job availability reduces crime. In contrast, criminal motivation increases when there is a need to accumulate wealth; a rising cost of living has been associated with increasing criminal motivation.[35]

If crime is rational, criminal motivation should be reduced if potential offenders perceive alternatives to crime; in contrast, the perception of blocked legitimate opportunities should increase criminal motivation.

Connections

Lack of conventional opportunity is a persistent theme in sociological theories of crime. The frustration caused by a perceived lack of opportunity explains the high crime rates in lower-class areas. Chapter 7 sections on strain and cultural deviance theories provide an alternative explanation of how lack of opportunity is associated with crime.

Tunnell's career criminals said they committed crimes because they considered legitimate opportunities unavailable to people with their limited education and background. One offender told him:

> I tried to stay away from crime.... Nobody would hire me. I was an ex-con and I tried, I really tried to get gainful employment. There was nobody looking to hire me with my record. I went in as a juvenile and came out as an adult and didn't have any legitimate employment résumé to submit. Employment was impossible. So, I started robbing.[36]

Note how crime became the choice when legitimate alternatives were absent. In contrast, potential offenders who perceive legitimate alternatives, such as high-paying jobs, are less likely to choose crime.[37]

Interactive Effects. According to the routine activities approach, motivation, opportunity, and targets are interactive: The presence of any one factor encourages the others. Motivated criminals will not commit crime unless they have suitable targets available and the opportunity to attack them. Motivated offenders must also have the opportunity to commit crime; without opportunity, even the most driven will forgo criminality. The presence of guardians will deter even the most motivated offenders, rendering even the most attractive targets off-limits.

Figure 5.1 illustrates the interrelationship between opportunity, routine activities, and environmental factors.

Figure 5.1 shows that criminal opportunities (suitable victims and targets) abound in urban environments where facilitators (guns, drugs) are readily found. Environmental factors such as physical layout and cultural style may either facilitate or restrict criminal opportunity. Motivated offenders living in these urban "hot spots" continually learn about criminal opportunities from peers, the media, and their own perceptions. This information may either escalate their criminal motivation or warn them of its danger.[38]

Exhibit 5.1 shows three basic approaches to crime prevention, depending on the level of intervention required. Efforts to measure the interaction between opportunity, motivation, and crime show that the relationship is in fact significant. For example, Mark Warr found that kids who are attached to their parents and spend their weekends at home report little in the way of criminal motivation; lack of opportunity may reduce motivation.[39] Often-cited research by John Hagan indicates that kids whose family relationships are strained, distant, and unrewarding are more likely to become

Figure 5.1   **The opportunity structure for crime**

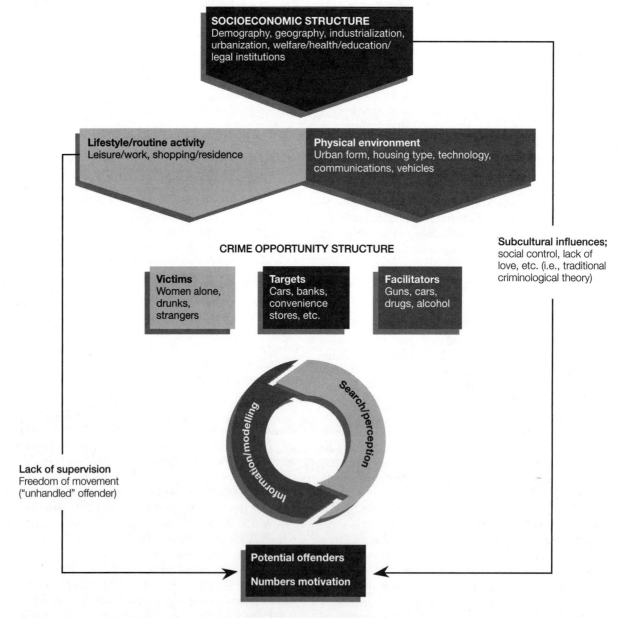

SOURCE: Ronald Clarke, "Situational Crime Prevention" in *Building a Safer Society: Strategic Approaches to Crime Prevention*, vol. 19 of *Crime and Justice, A Review of Research*, ed. Michael Tonry and David Farrington (Chicago University of Chicago Press, 1995), p. 103. Reprinted by permission.

Exhibit 5.1	Basic Approaches to Crime Prevention
Primary Prevention	Actions taken to reduce the occurrence of criminal acts, e.g., Neighbourhood Watch, Block Parents
Secondary Prevention	Detecting early signs of high-risk individuals or situations before a crime takes place, e.g., Mothers Against Drunk Driving
Tertiary Prevention	Intervention programs for youth or adult offenders to prevent further offences, e.g., community notification programs

attached to deviant peers, which in turn helps increase criminal motivation.[40]

In a nationally drawn sample of 1700 youths aged 18 to 26, researchers found that adolescents who spend a great deal of time socializing with peers in the absence of authority figures (riding around in cars, going to parties, going out at night for fun) are also the ones most likely to engage in deviant behaviours.[41] In the presence of "motivated peers," the lack of structure and guardianship leaves more opportunity for antisocial behaviours, including substance abuse, crime, and dangerous driving. These researchers found that participation in unstructured activities helps explain the association between crime rates and gender, age, and status: Teenage boys have the highest crime rates because they are the group most likely to engage in unsupervised socialization. Opportunity combined with lack of guardianship increases criminal motivation.

Mapping. Clearly, if crime is a rational choice and involves the assessment of guardianship, opportunity, and motivation, it can be mapped. For years statisticians have been measuring things to discover patterns in the social and natural worlds. Figure 5.2 shows the distribution of homicide in Division 51, Toronto, from 1990 to 1999. Producing such maps based on either police reports or calls for service enables the police to understand where the "hot spots" are, and where enforcement would be most effective.

Is Crime Rational?

Is crime rational? It is relatively easy to show that some crimes are the product of rational and objective thought, especially when they involve an ongoing criminal conspiracy centred on economic gain. When prominent

bankers in the U.S. savings and loan industry were indicted for criminal fraud, their elaborate financial schemes not only showed signs of rationality but exhibited brilliant, though flawed, financial expertise.[42] The stock market manipulations of Wall Street insiders such as Ivan Boesky and Michael Milken and the drug dealings of organized crime bosses demonstrate a reasoned analysis of market conditions, interests, and risks.

Connections

In Chapter 13, various criminal enterprises run by white collar professionals and involving corporate interests are discussed. Learn how workers are exposed to risks, how consumers are sold faulty products, and how environmental pollution is a cost of doing business.

Are Street Crimes Rational?

While it is not surprising that ongoing criminal conspiracies involving organized and white-collar crime exhibit rationality, what about common street crimes such as prostitution and petty theft? These would seem more likely to be random acts of criminal opportunity than well-thought-out, planned conspiracies. However, there is evidence that even these "unplanned" street crimes may also be the product of careful risk assessment, including environmental, social, and structural factors. Ronald Clarke and Patricia Harris found that auto thieves are highly selective in their choice of targets. If they want to strip cars for their parts, they are most likely to choose Volkswagens; if they want to sell the cars or keep them permanently, they choose Mercedes; for temporary use, Buicks are top-ranked.[43] Vehicle selection seems to be based on the cars' attractiveness and suitability for a particular purpose: German automobiles are selected for stripping because they usually have high-quality audio equipment that has good value on the second-hand market; thus, target selection seems highly rational.

Studies of prostitutes suggest that even these often desperate women make clear choices in their daily activities. For example, Lisa Maher's interviews with "street-level sex workers" in Brooklyn, New York, show that prices for sexual services are declining and that competition is increasing. Increasing drug use has produced an influx of women new to the street willing to charge little to support their habits. Despite fierce competition, more-experienced street workers still resist sex practices that compromise their chances of survival, such as sex without condoms, refuse to trade sex for drugs, and refuse to service clients they consider too dangerous or distasteful.[44] These activities show clear signs of rational choice.

Similarly, there is an attempt to influence johns in their choice of soliciting. Some jurisdictions confiscate johns' cars, and others require men to go to "john school"

Figure 5.2   **Homicides in Police Division 51, Toronto, 1990-99**

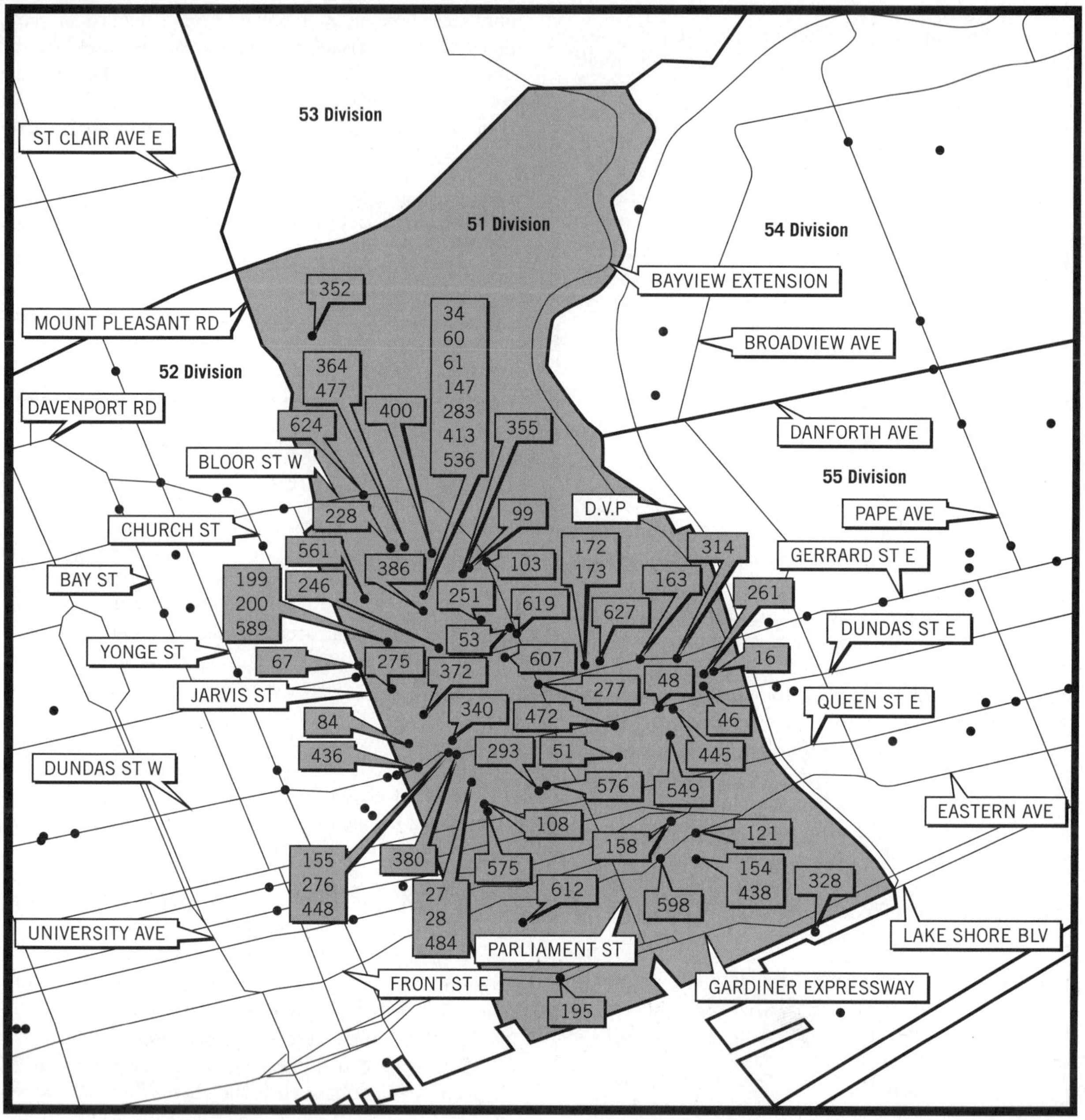

after conviction, where they learn more about the exploitation hidden in prostitution.

Is Drug Use Rational?

Is it possible that drug users and dealers, a group not usually associated with clear thinking, make rational choices? Research does in fact show that from its onset, drug use is controlled by rational decision making. Users report that they begin taking drugs when they believe that the benefits of substance abuse outweigh its costs—that is, drugs will provide an enjoyable, exciting, thrilling experience. Their entry into substance abuse is facilitated by their perception that valued friends and family members endorse and encourage drug use and abuse substances themselves.[45]

In adulthood, heavy drug users and dealers show signs of rationality and cunning in their daily activity. Bruce Jacobs found that they used specific techniques to avoid apprehension by police. They play what they call the "peep game" before dealing drugs, scoping out the territory to make sure the turf is free from anything out of place that may be a potential threat, such as police officers or rival gang members.[46] One crack dealer told Jacobs:

There was this red Pontiac sittin' on the corner one day with two white guys inside. They was just sittin' there for an hour, not doin' nothin'. Another day, diff'rent people be walkin' up and down the street you don't really recognize. You think they might be kin of someone but then you be askin' around and they [neighbours] ain't never seen them before neither. When ya' see strange things like that, you think somethin' be goin' on [and you don't deal].

Drug dealers also give careful consideration to whether they should deal alone or in groups: Large groups draw more attention from the police but can offer more protection. Drug-dealing gangs and groups can help divert the attention of police: If their drug dealing is noticed by detectives, a dealer can walk away or dispose of evidence while confederates distract the cops.

Patricia Morgan and Karen Ann Joe's three-city (San Francisco, San Diego, Honolulu) study of female drug abusers also found a great deal of rationality and careful decision making. One dealer who earns $50 000 per year told them:

I stayed within my goals, basically.... I don't go around doing stupid things. I don't walk around telling people I have drugs for sale, I don't have people sitting out in front of my house. I don't have traffic in and out of my house.... I control the people I sell to.[47]

Morgan and Joe found that these female dealers consider drug distribution a positive experience that provides them with economic independence, self-esteem, increased ability to function, professional pride, and the ability to maintain control over their lives. These women often seemed more like yuppies opening a boutique than out-of-control addicts:

I'm a good dealer. I don't cut my drugs, I have high-quality drugs insofar as it's possible to get high-quality drugs. I want to be known as somebody who sells good drugs, but doesn't always have them, as opposed to someone who always has them and sometimes the drugs are good.

Can Violence Be Rational?

While there is evidence that instrumental crimes, such as drug dealing and burglaries, are rational, is it possible that violent acts through which the offender gains little material benefit are the product of a reasoned decision-making process?

Evidence exists that even violent criminals are selective in their choice of suitable targets, picking people who are vulnerable and lack adequate defences. For example, robbery offenders are likely to choose victims who are vulnerable and have low coercive power—victims who do not pose any threat.[48] In their interview survey of violent felons, James Wright and Peter Rossi found that violent offenders avoid victims who may be armed and dangerous. About three-fifths of all felons surveyed were more afraid of armed victims than of police, about 40 percent had avoided a victim because they believed the victim was armed, and almost one-third reported that they had been scared off, wounded, or captured by armed victims.[49] Even serial murderers, outwardly the most irrational of all offenders, tend to pick their targets with care. Most choose victims who are either defenceless or cannot count on police protection: prostitutes, gay men, hitchhikers, children, hospital patients, the elderly, the homeless. Rarely do serial killers target weightlifters, martial arts experts, or any other potentially powerful person.[50]

A number of recent studies have found that even the most violent and lethal interactions seem to be motivated by rational thought and not unthinking rage. Scott Decker found that people most often killed acquaintances in disputes involving drug deals gone awry. Even in apparently senseless killings among strangers, the "real" motive was revenge for a prior dispute or disagreement among the parties involved (or their families).[51] Similarly, Richard Felson and Steven Messner found that many homicides were motivated by the offenders' desire to avoid retaliation from a victim they had assaulted or to avoid future prosecutions by getting rid of witnesses.[52] While some killings are the result of angry aggression, others seem to show signs of rational planning. So, while violent acts appear to be irrational, they also involve calculation of risk and reward.

The Seductions of Crime

The focus of rational choice theory is on the opportunity to commit crime and on how criminal choices are structured by the social environment. There will always be people willing and able to bypass the law, given the proper conditions and opportunity. Some irrational or mentally disturbed people may commit crimes without thought to potential hazard, but it seems likely that immediate or situational variables determine and guide most criminal behaviour: People commit crime when they view its outcome as beneficial.[53] For many, crime is attractive; it brings rewards, excitement, prestige, and other desirable outcomes without lengthy work or effort. Whether it is violent or profit oriented, crime has an allure that some people cannot resist.

Sociologist Jack Katz argues that there are in fact immediate benefits to criminality, which he labels the seductions of crime.[54] These situational inducements directly precede the commission of a crime and draw offenders into law violations. Someone challenges the "bad-ass" with a bump or a stare, and they vanquish their opponent with a beating. Youths want to maximize their pleasure by doing something exciting, so they break into and vandalize a school building.

According to Katz, choosing crime can help satisfy personal needs. For some people, shoplifting and vandalism are attractive because getting away with it is a thrilling demonstration of personal competence; monetary gain is not their primary motive. Even murder can have an emotional payoff. Killers behave like the avenging gods of mythology, choosing to have life-or-death control over their victims.

Katz finds that situational inducements created from emotional upheaval can also structure the decision to commit crime. When an individual is faced with humiliation, righteousness, arrogance, or ridicule, violent reactions seem a natural response. When someone is rebuked at a party because he or she is disturbing people, the person responds, "So, I'm acting like a fool, am I?" and goes on the attack. Public embarrassment leads to action: The person must "sacrifice" or injure the body of the victim to maintain his or her "honour."

A number of research studies have supported Katz's view that situational inducements play an important role in causing adolescent misbehaviour.[55] For example, people are most likely to be "seduced" if they fear neither the risk of apprehension nor its social consequences. People who fear either losing the respect of their peers or suffering legal punishments are the ones most likely to forgo the seductions of crime.[56]

We have been speaking of crime in its usual sense, as predatory, unwanted behaviour. What do we do about acts that are violations of the criminal law, but that are nonetheless accepted by everyone involved? In 1994, the government of Ontario implemented the Ontario Tobacco Control Act. This Act provided a graduated penalty structure of fines up to $25 000 for merchants who sold tobacco to minors. Nonetheless, 60 percent of retailers remained willing to sell to minors. This would clearly be an instrumental crime, where the threat of punishment would hold most weight. One study concluded that four factors influenced the retailer's decision to sell: time of day, his or her gender, his or her age, and his or her compliance with other regulations. This research clearly demonstrates the principles of rational choice theory.[57] However, how can illegal acts be prevented? That is the challenge, and the focus of the next section.

Eliminating Crime

It follows that if crime is rational and people choose to commit crime, then crime can be controlled or eradicated by convincing potential offenders that the choice of crime is a poor one, that it will not bring them rewards but instead pain, hardship, and deprivation. Evidence exists that jurisdictions with relatively low incarceration rates also experience the highest crime rates.[58] Perhaps "street smart" offenders know which areas offer the least threat and plan their crimes accordingly. A number of potential strategies flow from this premise:

1. Situational crime prevention is aimed at convincing would-be criminals to avoid specific targets. It relies on the doctrine that crime can be avoided if motivated offenders are denied access to suitable targets. When people install security systems in their homes or hire security guards, they are broadcasting the message: Guardianship is great here; stay away—the potential reward is not worth the risk of apprehension.
2. General deterrence strategies are aimed at making potential criminals fear the consequences of crime. The threat of punishment is aimed at convincing rational criminals that crime does not pay.
3. Specific deterrence refers to punishing known criminals severely so that they will never be tempted to repeat their offences. If choosing crime is rational, painful punishments should reduce its future allure.
4. Incapacitation strategies attempt to reduce crime rates by denying motivated offenders the opportunity to commit crime. If, despite the threat of law and punishment, some people still find crime attractive, the only way to control their behaviour is to take them out of society.

In the following sections, each of these crime reduction or control strategies based on the rationality of criminal behaviour is discussed in some detail.

Situational Crime Prevention

Rational choice theory suggests that because criminal activity is offence-specific, crime prevention—or at least crime reduction—should be achieved through policies that convince potential criminals to desist from criminal activities, delay their actions, or avoid a particular target. Table 5.1 presents 16 techniques for preventing crime, from target-hardening to facilitating compliance.

Criminal acts will be avoided if (1) potential targets are carefully guarded, (2) the means to commit crime are controlled, and (3) potential offenders are carefully monitored. Desperate people may contemplate crime, but only the truly irrational will attack a well-defended, inaccessible target and risk strict punishments. Crime prevention, then, can be achieved by reducing the opportunities people have to commit particular crimes, a practice known as **situational crime prevention**.

Situational crime prevention was first popularized in the United States in the early 1970s by Oscar Newman, who coined the term **defensible space** to signify that crime can be prevented or displaced through the use of residential architectural designs that reduce criminal opportunity, such as well-lit housing projects that maximize surveillance.[59] In 1971 C. Ray Jeffery wrote *Crime Prevention through Environmental Design*, in which he extended

Table 5.1	Sixteen techniques of situational crime prevention

INCREASING PERCEIVED EFFORT	INCREASING PERCEIVED RISKS	REDUCING ANTICIPATED REWARDS	INDUCING GUILT OR SHAME
1. Target hardening	5. Entry/exit screening	9. Target removal	13. Rule setting
Slug rejector devices	Automatic ticket gates	Removable car radio	Harassment codes
Steering locks	Baggage screening	Women's refuges	Customs declaration
Bandit screens	Merchandise tags	Phone card	Hotel registrations
2. Access control	6. Formal surveillance	10. Identifying property	14. Moral condemnation
Parking lot barriers	Burglar alarms	Property marking	"Shoplifting is stealing"
Fenced yard	Speed cameras	Vehicle licensing	Roadside speedometers
Entry phones	Security guards	Cattle branding	"Bloody idiots drink and thrive"
3. Deflecting offenders	7. Surveillance by employees	11. Reducing temptation	15. Controlling disinhibitors
Bus stop placement	Pay phone location	Gender-neutral phone lists	Drinking age laws
Tavern location	Park attendants	Off-street parking	Ignition interlock
Street closures	CCTV systems		Server intervention
4. Controlling facilitators	8. Natural surveillance	12. Denying benefits	16. Facilitating compliance
Credit card photo	Defensible space	Ink merchandise tags	Improved library checkout
Caller ID	Street lighting	PIN for car radios	Public lavatories
Gun controls	Cab driver ID	Graffiti cleaning	Trash bins

SOURCE: Ronald Clark and Ross Homel, "A Revised Classification of Situational Crime Prevention Techniques," 1996.

Newman's concepts and applied them to nonresidential areas, such as schools and factories.[60] According to this view, such mechanisms as security systems, deadbolt locks, high-intensity street lighting, and neighbourhood watch patrols should be able to reduce criminal opportunity.[61] In 1992 Ronald Clarke published *Situational Crime Prevention*, which compiled the best-known strategies and tactics to reduce criminal incidents.[62]

In Canada, Patricia Brantingham and Paul Brantingham of Simon Fraser University are undoubtedly leaders in research on situational crime prevention. They say that despite the claims of many programs, most crime prevention efforts have mixed success. Generic programs cannot address the diversity of criminal behaviour and need to be targeted toward specific social order problems. The motive for stealing a car for a joyride is different than that for stealing a car for parts. Therefore, the prevention strategy should also be different. In addition, assuming a rational basis for committing a crime might also overestimate the extent to which people consider legal consequences of their actions. It might also underestimate the demand for certain crimes, such as prostitution. Despite tough new laws making it easier for the police to deal with the buying and selling of sex, the overall volume of prostitution has remained relatively unchanged. Neighbourhood Watch programs are also very popular, but their main effect is probably to improve people's attitudes about their neighbourhoods. Situational variables such as traffic flow, pedestrian walkways, and public lighting become part of an environment that can enable or discourage crime.[63]

Crime Prevention Strategies

Criminologists have suggested a number of situational crime prevention efforts that might reduce crime rates. One approach is to create an overall strategy or plan to reduce crime in general. For example, Marcus Felson suggests that such a "total community" strategy might include some or all of the following elements:

- uniform school release schedules so that there is no doubt when kids belong in school and when they are truant; should be combined with effective truancy control efforts;
- after-school and weekend activities to keep kids under adult supervision;

- school lunch programs designed to keep kids in school and away from shopping areas;
- no-cash policies in schools to reduce kids' opportunity to either be targets or engage in the consumption of drugs or alcohol;
- shopping areas and schools kept separate;
- construction of housing to maximize guardianship and minimize illegal behaviour;
- encouragement of neighbourhood stability so that residents will be acquainted with one another;
- privatization of parks and recreation facilities so that people will be responsible for their area's security.[64]

Felson's suggestions are designed to reduce crime by limiting the access that members of a highly motivated offender group (high school kids) have to tempting targets. Crime maps show that robberies and vandalism occur close to urban high schools. Some features of the "total community strategy" are designed to eliminate specific crimes (for example, by youths), but mainly to reduce the overall crime rate.

Connections

Chapter 12 discusses many types of property crime, the total cost to society, and some tips on how to discourage it. For crimes of opportunity, especially, prevention measures are usually fairly inexpensive and uncomplicated.

Targeting Specific Crimes

Situational crime prevention can also involve developing tactics to reduce or eliminate a specific crime problem, such as shoplifting in an urban mall or street-level drug dealing. Recent research shows the utility of targeting specific subsets of the criminal population in reducing the level of crime overall. Operation Ceasefire in Boston, for example, is a successful problem-oriented policing intervention aimed at reducing youth homicides.[65] According to criminologists Ronald Clarke and Ross Homel, crime prevention tactics in use today generally fall in one of four categories: (1) increasing the effort needed to commit the crime; (2) increasing the risks of committing the crime; (3) reducing the rewards for committing the crime; and (4) inducing guilt or shame for committing the crime.

Some basic techniques and some specific methods that can be used to prevent auto crime are listed in Exhibit 5.2.

Some tactics designed to increase the offender's effort include target-hardening techniques, such as putting unbreakable glass on storefronts, locking gates, and fencing yards. Technological advances can be used to make it more difficult to commit crimes, such as having an owner's photo on credit cards to reduce the use of stolen cards. The development of new products, such as steering locks on cars, can make it more difficult to commit crimes. Empirical evidence indicates that the use of steering locks has helped reduce car theft in the United States, Britain, and Germany.[66] Another such study found that installing a locking device on cars that prevents inebriated drivers from starting the vehicle significantly reduced drunk-driving rates.[67]

It is also possible to increase the risks from committing crime by increasing the chances of apprehension. Improving surveillance lighting, creating neighbourhood watch programs, controlling building entrances and exits, installing burglar alarms and security systems, and increasing the number of private security officers and police patrols all may help reduce crime rates. However, research has not shown that two-officer patrols are better at catching burglars than single-officer units.[68] In her analysis of gasoline "drive-offs" from convenience stores, Nancy LaVigne found that removing signs from store windows, installing brighter lights, and instituting a pay-first policy can reduce the number of incidents of people filling their tanks and driving off without paying.[69]

Target reduction strategies are designed to reduce the value of crime to the potential criminal. These include making car radios removable so they can be kept at home at night, marking property so that it is more difficult to sell when stolen, and having gender-neutral phone listings to discourage obscene phone calls. Caller ID has resulted in significant reductions in the number of obscene phone calls because the telephone number of the party placing the call is displayed. The threat of exposure has had a deterrent effect on the number of obscene calls reported to police.[70] Tracking systems similar to global positioning systems help police locate and return stolen vehicles.

Inducing guilt or shame might include such techniques as setting strict rules that embarrass offenders,

Exhibit 5.2	Neighbourhood Watch Tips on Vehicle Security

In Canada, vehicle thefts occur every eight minutes.
- Never leave your vehicle unattended with the engine running.
- Never have an identification tag on your key ring that identifies your home address.
- Be careful if you hide a spare key in the car—thieves know where to look!
- Never leave wallets, credit cards, or valuables in the car; always lock them in the trunk.
- Mark your stereo and other equipment with your Operation Identification number.
- Mount stereos, cellular phones, CD players, etc., inconspicuously.
- Consider deterrent devices such as alarms and steering wheel locking mechanisms.
- When using a public garage or parking lot, park your car in a well-lit area.

SOURCE: http://neighbourhoodwatch.ottawa.com/vehicle.htm

such as publishing "John lists" in the newspaper to punish those arrested for soliciting prostitutes, or facilitating compliance by providing trash bins whose easy access might "shame" chronic litterers into using them. In 2000, a Canadian police officer recommended that drunk drivers be forced to have a large sign with the letter "D" placed on their car. This penalty for drunkenness hearkens back to the 1600s, when in Boston, for example, "Robert Coles was fyned ten shillings and enjoyned to stand with a white sheet of paper on his back whereon Drunkard shalbe written in great lres & to stand therewith soe longe as the Courte finde meete, fo abuseing himself shamefully with drinke" (www.getchwood.com).

Crime Discouragers

The success of situational crime prevention may also rest on the behaviour of people whose actions directly influence the prevention of crime; these are known as "crime discouragers." Discouragers can be grouped into three categories: guardians, who monitor targets (such as store security guards); handlers, who monitor potential offenders (such as parole officers and parents); and managers, who monitor places (such as homeowners and doormen). Marcus Felson notes that crime discouragers also have different levels of responsibility, ranging from highly personal involvement, such as homeowners protecting their house and parents controlling their children, to the most impersonal general involvement, such as a stranger who stops someone from shoplifting in the mall[71] (see Table 5.2).

Felson suggests that the concept of crime discouragement can be useful to plan situational crime prevention tactics. More effective crime reduction may occur if (1) managers are given tools to better monitor places,

(2) guardians are better equipped to protect targets, and (3) handlers are allowed to exert greater control over offenders. For example, a store clerk can enhance his or her discouragement role with a mirror to watch merchandise and a button to summon supervisory help. A handler will become more effective if supplied with hidden cameras and eavesdropping devices. Managers given greater supervisory powers will help reduce crime by exerting better control over their charges.

Ramifications of Situational Prevention

Although situational crime prevention seems plausible, it can also produce unforeseen and unwanted consequences. Preventing crime from occurring in one locale might do little to deter criminal motivation. People who desire the benefits of crime may choose alternative targets. Crime, then, is not prevented but deflected or displaced.[72] For example, increasing police patrols in one area may shift crimes to a more vulnerable neighbourhood. While crime displacement cannot be a solution to the general problem of crime, some evidence exists that deflection efforts can partially reduce the frequency of crime or produce less serious offence patterns.

There are six kinds of crime displacement:

- *Temporal.* Offenders perpetrate crimes at times seen as less risky.
- *Target.* Difficult targets are given up in favour of those easier to hit.
- *Spatial.* Offenders move from high-target areas to less protected areas.
- *Tactical.* Tactics are changed to get around security measures.

Table 5.2	Crime discouragers		
TYPES OF SUPERVISORS AND OBJECTS OF SUPERVISION			
LEVEL OF RESPONSIBILITY	**A. GUARDIANS** (MONITORING SUITABLE TARGETS)	**B. HANDLERS** (MONITORING LIKELY OFFENDERS)	**C. MANAGERS** (MONITORING AMENABLE PLACES)
1. Personal (owners, family, friends)	Student keeps eye on own bookbag	Parent makes sure child gets home	Homeowner monitors area near home
2. Assigned (employees with general assignment)	Store clerk monitors jewellery	Principal sends kids back to school	Doorman protects building
3. Diffuse (employees with general assignment)	Accountant notes shoplifting	School clerk discourages truancy	Hotel maid impairs trespasser
4. General (strangers, other citizens)	Bystander inhibits shoplifting	Stranger questions boys at mall	Customer observes parking structure

SOURCE: Marcus Felson, "Those Who Discourage Crime," in John Eck and David Weisburd, *Crime and Place* (Monsey, NY: Criminal Justice Press, 1995), p. 59. Reprinted by permission.

- *Perpetrator.* New offenders take the place of those who are apprehended.
- *Type of crime.* Offenders take up another type of crime if one type becomes too difficult to commit.[73]

As Thomas Gabor points out, the notion of displacement assumes an equilibrium—that if the flow of water is reduced in one area, it will spring up in another. However, crime might "spill over" from one area to the next, but not be the result of displacement. He suggests that offenders casually drift in and out of crime. The offender's willingness to commit crime does not necessarily translate into criminal behaviour if the opportunity is missing. Therefore, there might be a net preventive effect. [74]

There is also the problem of **extinction**: Crime reduction programs may produce a short-term positive effect, but benefits dissipate as criminals adjust to new conditions. They learn to dismantle alarms or avoid patrols; they may become motivated to try new offences they had previously avoided. For example, if every residence in a neighbourhood is provided with a foolproof burglar alarm system, motivated offenders might then turn to armed robbery, a riskier and more violent crime. However, for many offenders, the reduction of opportunity does not mean a choice between a blocked opportunity and the need to find it somewhere else. In addition, offenders are unlikely to turn to crimes they find morally repugnant, for example, from shoplifting to armed robbery.

While displacement and extinction may be a problem, a hidden benefit of situational crime prevention has been noted: **diffusion of benefits**.[75] Diffusion occurs when (1) efforts to prevent one crime cause the unintended prevention of another, and (2) crime control efforts in one locale reduce crime in other, nontarget areas.

Diffusion may be produced by two independent effects. Crime control efforts may deter criminals by causing them to fear apprehension. For example, video cameras set up in a mall to reduce shoplifting can also reduce property damage, because would-be vandals fear they are being caught on camera. One recent evaluation of a police program to crack down on drugs in targeted areas of Jersey City, New Jersey, also produced a reduction in public morals crimes.[76]

Another type of diffusion effect is called **discouragement**. By limiting one type of target, would-be lawbreakers may forgo other criminal activity because crime no longer pays. In studying the effect of drug enforcement programs that utilize enforcement of municipal codes and nuisance abatement laws, it was found that not only did drug dealing decrease in targeted areas but improvement was found in surrounding areas. The program most likely discouraged buyers and sellers who saw familiar hangouts closed. The sign that drug dealing would not be tolerated probably decreased the total number of people involved in drug activity even though they did not operate in the targeted area.[77]

General Deterrence

According to the rational choice view, motivated, rational people will violate the law if left free and unrestricted. Rational offenders want the goods and services crime provides without having to work for them; they will commit crime if they do not fear apprehension and punishment. The concept of **general deterrence** holds that crime rates will be influenced and controlled by the threat of criminal punishment. If people fear apprehension and punishment, they will not risk breaking the law. An inverse relationship should thus exist between crime rates and the certainty, severity, and celerity (speed) of legal sanctions. If, for example, the punishment for a crime is increased and if the effectiveness and efficiency of the criminal justice system in enforcing the law prohibiting that act are improved, the number of people engaging in that act should decline.

The factors of certainty, severity, and celerity may also influence one another. For example, if a crime—say, robbery—is punished severely but few robbers are ever caught or punished, it is likely that the severity of punishment for robbery will not deter people from robbing. On the other hand, if the certainty of apprehension and conviction is increased by modern technology, more efficient police work, or some other factor, even minor punishments might deter the potential robber. Do these factors actually affect the decision to commit crime and consequently general crime rates?

Certainty of Punishment

According to deterrence theory, if the probability of arrest, conviction, and sanctioning increases, crime rates should decline. Rational offenders will soon realize that the increased likelihood of being punished outweighs any benefit they perceive from committing crimes.

A few research efforts do in fact show an inverse relationship between crime rates and the certainty of punishment.[78] In one often-cited study of arrest probability, Charles Tittle and Alan Rowe concluded that if police could make an arrest in at least 30 percent of all reported crimes, the crime rate would significantly decline.[79]

While these results seem to support the deterrent effect of certainty of punishment, the relationship between certainty and crime rates is far from settled. Most efforts have found little relationship between the likelihood of being arrested or imprisoned and corresponding crime rates.[80]

One reason for this ambivalent finding is that the certainty of punishment–crime association may be both crime- and group-specific. For example, research by Jiang Wu and Allen Liska found the effect to be race-specific: African American arrest probability influences African

American offence rates alone, while white arrest probabilities affect white offending patterns. Wu and Liska conclude that in large cities the threat of arrest is communicated within neighbourhoods and has an independent effect on residents of each racial grouping.[81]

Some research efforts have found a crime-specific deterrent effect. For example, Edwin Zedlewski's research shows that increased certainty of arrest helps lower the burglary rate, while larceny rates remain unaffected by law enforcement efforts.[82] In Varma and Doob's analysis of the deterrence of tax evasion, they found that the certainty of being caught was a stronger deterrent than the size of the penalty. This lends more weight to certainty, than to the severity of the punishment.[83]

In corporate crime, punishment is far from certain. In July 1998, the Toronto Stock Exchange assessed a $4-million penalty against the brokerage firm First Marathon Securities Ltd. for failing to supervise its business operations and employees. Some of those employees were involved in a conflict of interest in the promotion of Cartaway Resources, one of the most spectacular stock flops in Canadian mining history. Because the employees were not properly supervised, they were able to act as promoters, underwriters, and investors in the stock. The fine, while embarrassing to the company, would not have a big impact on its estimated profit of $50 million per year. The Ontario Securities Commission, which oversees 80 percent of the country's capital market located in Ontario, had a budget of $20 million in 1997, and the "compliance" department had a staff of only six to oversee hundreds of companies.[84]

Connections

In cases we will look at in Chapter 13, the rewards for engaging in corporate criminality are too great, and the oversight too minimal, for crimes not to occur.

It is arguable that general deterrence is difficult in cases of corporate crime because quite often the penalties are administrative, not criminal. The Ontario Securities Commission is not a department of the criminal justice system, and it does not have the authority to lay criminal penalties. However, that may be about to change. Australia, the United States, Britain, and now Canada are considering changes to their Criminal Codes to make corporations more accountable for their actions. An important political issue in Canada is the expected amendments to the Criminal Code that will hold corporate managers criminally accountable for their actions. In the 1997 report into the Westray mine disaster, Mr. Justice Peter Richard said:

> The Government of Canada ... should introduce in the Parliament of Canada such amendments to legislation as are necessary to ensure that

corporate executives and directors are held properly accountable for workplace safety.[85]

In 2000, the NDP introduced a private member's bill which would have criminalized a company failing to take actions to prevent crimes occurring; however, it found little support.

The Effect of Police Actions. If the increased certainty of apprehension and punishment deters criminal behaviour, it follows that increasing the number of police officers on the street should be able to bring the crime rate down. Moreover, if these police officers are active and aggressive crime fighters, would-be criminals should be convinced that the risk of apprehension outweighs the benefits they can gain from crime.

There has been some debate as to whether the mere number of police officers on the street can bring the crime rate down. Some, such as David Bayley, have been skeptical that police presence is actually a crime deterrent.[86] Bayley's suspicions are justified by numerous studies that failed to show that increasing the number of police officers in a community can lower crime rates.

While these results are discouraging, the lack of association between police presence and crime rates may be a result of the difficulty in measuring a police–crime association. One problem is that at times when crime rates are high and increasing, communities begin to add police officers. The number of officers increases along with the crime rate, making it appear that adding police actually increases community crime rates! When crime rates go down, it may be due to other factors, such as a decrease in the number of young males in the population.

A recent, more sophisticated U.S. study solves some of these methodological problems. It found that adding police may actually reduce crime rates. It estimated that for every officer added, there would be 24 fewer crimes per year.[87] The study used aggregate state-level data in their analysis, so it is difficult to conclude that adding police would be beneficial in every community. Nonetheless, their research seems to indicate that adding police officers may in the long run provide a general deterrent effect.

Police Experiments. Some police departments have conducted experiments to determine whether increasing police activities or allocation of services can influence crime rates. In 1988, for example, Edmonton implemented a Neighbourhood Foot Patrol, consisting of 21 Neighbourhood Patrol Constables assigned to 21 neighbourhoods. This initiative in "community policing" identified city areas by repeat calls for service and occurrence data (crime incidents). The result was a comprehensive analysis of the effectiveness of reorganizing the police along a community policing model. It was found that community and police satisfaction increased, and calls for service went down.[88]

Several criminologists have developed a "tool kit" for the assessment of community policing by the practitioners themselves. Police and crime prevention organizations are accountable for the sound implementation, delivery, and success of their initiatives. Good evaluation is implemented from the very beginning, alongside the initiative, and allows for the adjustment of the initiative as need be.[89]

In another well-known experiment to evaluate the effectiveness of police patrols and the general deterrent effect of police activity, the Kansas City police department's 15 independent police beats or districts were divided into three groups.[90] The first retained a normal police patrol; the second (proactive) was supplied with two to three times the normal amount of patrol forces; and the third (reactive) eliminated its preventive patrol entirely, and police officers responded only when summoned by citizens to the scene of a crime. Surprisingly, data from the Kansas City study indicated that these variations in patrol techniques had little effect on the crime patterns in the 15 locales. The presence or absence of patrol forces did not seem to affect residential or business burglaries, auto thefts, larcenies involving auto accessories, robberies, vandalism, or other criminal behaviour. Variations in police patrol techniques appeared to have little effect on citizens' attitudes toward the police, their satisfaction with police, or their fear of future criminal behaviour.

Other police departments have instituted **crackdowns**—sudden changes in police activity designed to increase the communicated threat or actual certainty of punishment—to lower crime rates. Crackdowns can target specific neighbourhoods or specific offences, and their duration can range from a few weeks to several years and involve attempts to crack down on the "symptoms" of crime, the signs of public disorder that create fear. Initial and residual deterrent effects vary, sometimes based on factors outside the scope of the crackdowns themselves. For example, a police task force targets street-level narcotics dealers by using undercover agents and surveillance cameras in known drug-dealing locales. An analysis of 18 police crackdowns by Lawrence Sherman indicates that they may have an initial deterrent effect on controlling crime but they suffer diffusion over time.

These crackdowns illustrate what has become known as the "broken-windows approach," first developed by George Kelling, in which the police deal with what the public sees as symptoms of crime, such as urinating and sleeping in public, littering and loitering, graffiti, and being drunk in public.[91] Efforts to crack down on crime, whether conducted by the police or undertaken in some more informal means, can target specific neighbourhoods or specific offences. Their duration can range from a few weeks to several years. In an example from Toronto, police took a zero-tolerance approach to crime, targeting such minor offences as panhandling and urinating in public. This is similar to a crackdown on illegal parking and disorder in Washington, DC, and a similarly huge effort to reduce crime in New York's subways.[92]

Severity of Punishment

The introduction or threat of severe punishments should also bring the crime rate down. Some studies have found that increasing sanction levels can in fact control common criminal behaviours. For example, Gary Green has shown that they have an effect for at least one crime: using an illegal, unauthorized descrambler to obtain pay cable television programs.[93] Green first determined how many people out of a sample of 3500 were using a descrambler and avoiding payments to the local cable company. Threatening letters were sent to the 67 violators, conveying the general message that illegal theft of cable signals would be criminally prosecuted; the letter did not indicate that the subject's personal violation had been discovered. Green found that about two-thirds of the 67 violators reacted to the threat by desisting and trying to hide their crime by removing the illegal device; a six-month follow-up showed that the intervention had a long-lasting effect.

While the Green research shows that the threat of strict punishment can deter crime, there is little consensus that draconian sanctions alone can reduce criminal activities. H. Laurence Ross's analysis of the deterrent effects of anti–drunk-driving laws on motor vehicular violations is an example of the limited utility of sanctioning severity. Ross found that when laws are toughened, there is a short-term deterrent effect. However, because the likelihood of getting caught is relatively low, the impact of deterrent measures on alcohol-impaired driving is negligible over the long term.[94] In a later study, Ross, along with Richard McCleary and Gary LaFree, evaluated the effect of a new law in Arizona that mandated jail sentences for drunk-driving convictions; time series analysis indicated that the new law had little deterrent effect.[95]

Research has also been devoted to the effect that firearm sentencing laws have on violent crime rate. These laws provide expanded and mandatory sentences for felonies committed with guns. Some research efforts claim that these laws can lower crime rates, while others question their deterrent effect.[96] A recent study of firearm control by Thomas Marvell and Carlisle Moody suggests that these controls may reduce some crimes but that there is little evidence that they can reduce crime in general on a national level.[97]

In sum, despite the hope of those espousing a law and order agenda, there is little evidence that increasing the punishments for specific crimes can alone deter their occurrence.

The Special Case of Capital Punishment

It stands to reason that if punishment severity can have a deterrent effect on crime, fear of the death penalty, the ultimate legal deterrent, should significantly reduce murder rates. Because no one denies its emotional impact, failure of the death penalty to deter violent crime jeopardizes the validity of the entire deterrence concept. Various studies have tested the assumption that capital punishment deters violent crime. The research can be divided into three types: immediate impact studies, comparative research, and time series analysis.

Capital punishment was abolished in Canada in 1976, and the last executions were held in 1962. However, because over 65 percent of Canadians would like to see it reinstated, we will briefly look at the research to evaluate its effectiveness.

Immediate Impact Studies. If capital punishment is a deterrent, the reasoning goes, it should have the greatest impact after a well-publicized execution has taken place. Robert Dann began testing this assumption in 1935, when he chose five highly publicized executions of convicted murderers in different years and determined the number of homicides in the 60 days before and after each execution.[98] He found that each 120-day period had approximately the same number of homicides, as well as the same number of days on which homicides occurred. Dann's study revealed that an average of 4.4 more homicides occurred during the 60 days following an execution than during those preceding it, suggesting that the overall impact of executions might actually increase the incidence of homicide.

That executions may increase the likelihood of murder has been labelled the **brutalization effect**, suggesting that potential criminals model their behaviour after state authorities: If the government can kill its enemies, so can they.[99]

The findings of some criminologists have indicated that in the short run executing criminals can bring the murder rate down. David Phillips studied the immediate effect of executions in Britain from 1858 to 1914 and found a temporary deterrent effect based on the publicity following the execution.[100] A more contemporary (1950 to 1980) evaluation of executions in the United States by Steven Stack concluded that capital punishment does indeed have an immediate impact and that 16 well-publicized executions may have saved 480 lives.[101]

In sum, a number of criminologists find that executions actually increase murder rates, while others argue that their immediate impact can lower murder rates.

Comparative Research. Another type of research compares the murder rates in jurisdictions that have abolished the death penalty with the rates of those that have the death penalty. Using this approach, research shows that homicide rates and execution risks move independently of each other.[102] Having and using a death penalty has no deterrent effect on violent crime rates.

The failure to show a deterrent effect of the death penalty is not limited to cross-state comparisons. Research by Dane Archer, Rosemary Gartner, and Marc Beittel in 14 nations around the world found little evidence that countries with a death penalty have lower violence rates than those without; homicide rates actually decline after capital punishment is abolished, a direct contradiction to its supposed deterrent effect.[103]

Time Series Analysis. The development of econometric statistical analysis has allowed researchers to accurately gauge whether the murder rate changes when death penalty statutes are created or eliminated. The most widely cited study is Isaac Ehrlich's 1975 work, which made use of national crime and execution data.[104] According to Ehrlich, the perception of execution risk is an important determinant of whether one individual will murder another. As a result of his analysis, Ehrlich concluded that each execution per year in the United States would save seven or eight people from being victims of murder.

Ehrlich's research has been widely cited by advocates of the death penalty as empirical proof of the deterrent effect of capital punishment. However, subsequent research that attempted to replicate Ehrlich's analysis showed that his approach was flawed and that capital punishment is no more effective as a deterrent than life imprisonment.[105]

In sum, studies that have attempted to show the deterrent effect of capital punishment on the murder rate indicate that the execution of convicted criminals has relatively little influence on behaviour.[106] While it is still uncertain why the threat of capital punishment has failed as a deterrent, the cause may lie in the nature of homicide itself: Murder is often an expressive "crime of passion" involving people who know each other and who may be under the influence of drugs or suffering from the burdens of poverty.[107] These factors may either prevent or inhibit rational evaluation of the long-term consequences of an immediate violent act. Overall, it is probably safe to say that much murder is a **conflict-linked crime** not committed during the course of another crime.

The failure of the "ultimate deterrent" to deter the "ultimate crime" has been used by critics to question the validity of the general deterrence hypothesis that severe punishments will reduce crime rates. In general, there is little direct evidence that the severity of punishments alone can reduce or eliminate crime.

Perception and Deterrence

A core element of general deterrence theory is that people who believe that they are likely to be caught and severely punished will abstain from crime; thus, deterrence theory would be discredited if perceptions of future punishment have little or no effect on behaviour.[108]

Research measuring the association between the perception of punishment and deterrence has at best been inconclusive. Some efforts have found that the greater the perceived risk of apprehension, the less likely criminals are willing to risk crime.[109] However, others have found little association between fear of future punishments and criminal activity.[110] This would be especially true for "conflict-linked" crime.

Where deterrence has been found, it is the certainty and not the severity of punishment that seems to influence people.[111] A cross-sectional survey by Steven Klepper and Daniel Nagin found that people who believe they will be caught and subjected to criminal prosecution are less likely to engage in tax evasion.[112] Scott Decker and his associates found that the perceived risk of getting caught influenced active burglars, while the threat of severe punishments had relatively little deterrent effect.[113] These research efforts suggest that perceived risk of apprehension rather than punishment severity can deter active criminal offenders.

One criticism of this **perceptual deterrence** research is that it usually involves samples of noncriminals, such as college students, and crimes of minor seriousness, such as smoking marijuana. Experienced offenders, who are more criminally motivated and less committed to moral values, may be less likely to be deterred by the perception that they will be punished in the future.[114]

There are indications that experienced offenders are in fact the ones least threatened by the idea of future punishment.[115] Research by Eleni Apospori, Geoffrey Alpert, and Raymond Paternoster found that prior sanctions actually lower the perception that crime is a risky undertaking; criminals with the greatest number of prior convictions have the lowest fear of legal sanctions. Perhaps punishments were less fearsome than they had anticipated; only the most severe and draconian punishments seem to have any influence on experienced criminals.[116]

In sum, research measuring the perceptions of punishment seem in sync with studies using aggregate criminal justice data to determine deterrent effects. The certainty of punishment seems to have a greater influence on the choice of crime than the severity of punishment, and people who believe they are certain to be arrested and punished for a crime are less likely to break the law regardless of the severity of the punishment.[117] Nonetheless, there is little clear-cut evidence that either the perception or the reality of punishment can deter most crimes.

Informal Sanctions

Evidence is accumulating that the fear of **informal sanctions** may have a greater crime-reducing impact than the fear of formal legal punishments.

Informal sanctions occur when significant others, such as parents, peers, neighbours, and teachers, direct their disapproval, anger, and indignation toward an offender. If this happens, law violators run the risk of feeling shame, being embarrassed, and suffering a loss of respect.[118] Can the fear of public humiliation deter crime?

Research efforts have in fact established the influence of informal sanctions. In a national survey of almost 2000 subjects in the United States, Charles Tittle found that perception of informal sanctions was a more effective determinant of deterrence than perception of formal sanctions.[119] Tittle concluded that social control is rooted in how people perceive negative reactions from interpersonal acquaintances (family, friends), while formal sanctions (arrest, prison) are irrelevant to the general public. Tittle found that legal sanctions do no more than supplement informal control processes by influencing a small segment of "criminally inclined" persons.[120] If Tittle's conclusions are accurate, it also means that family and friends who don't react negatively to crime are facilitating it.

Other studies have also found that people who are committed to conventional moral values and believe crime to be "sinful" are unlikely to violate the law. Evidence from Britain shows that efforts to control drunk driving by shaming offenders produced a moral climate that helped reduce its incidence.[121] Perhaps the same moral effect can help reduce drug use in Canada.

Those fearful of being rejected by family and peers are also reluctant to engage in deviant behaviour.[122] Two factors seem to stand out: personal shame over violating the law and the fear of public humiliation if the deviant behaviour becomes public knowledge. A series of studies found that people who say that involvement in crime will cause them to feel ashamed are less likely to commit theft, fraud, and motor vehicular offences than those who report not feeling ashamed about crime.[123] People have been found to be more likely to respond to antilittering drives and anti–drunk-driving campaigns if the thought of being accused of littering or driving drunk makes them feel ashamed or embarrassed.[124] There is also evidence that women are much more likely to fear shame and embarrassment than men, a finding that may help explain gender differences in the crime rate.[125]

Other research has also found that fear of shame and embarrassment can be a powerful deterrent to crime.[126] One study found that spouse abusers were more afraid of social costs (for example, loss of friends and family disapproval) than they were of legal punishments (such as going to jail). The researchers found that in cases of wife assault the potential for self-stigma and personal humiliation was the greatest deterrent to crime.[127]

The effect of informal sanctions may vary according to the cohesiveness of community structure and type of crime. Informal sanctions may be most effective in highly unified areas where everyone knows one another and the crime cannot be hidden from public view. The threat of informal sanctions may also have the greatest influence on instrumental crimes, which involve planning, and not on impulsive or expressive criminal behaviours or those associated with substance abuse.[128]

This research seems to indicate that public education on the social cost of crime that stresses the risk of shame and humiliation may be a more effective crime-prevention tool than the creation and distribution of legal punishments; potential offenders may be deterred if they can be convinced that crime is sinful or immoral.[129]

CCTV and Public Surveillance

There is a lot of debate over whether to mount closed circuit television (CCTV) cameras in public places in an attempt to deter crime. While CCTV has been around for quite some time, it is just starting to emerge as a tool to monitor crime in public locations. CCTV can be either actively monitored (by a person watching in real time), and/or passively monitored (recorded). Although there is little analysis of the overall effectiveness of CCTV, the Scottish government's Central Research Unit analyzed CCTV surveillance in two cities, Ardrie and Glasgow. They concluded there had been 21 percent fewer offences in the two-year period after introduction of the cameras. Housebreaking, shoplifting, and theft from vehicles fell by 48 percent. Significantly, they concluded there was no displacement effect to non-monitored areas. [130]

Some believe, however, that CCTV does not have an effect on crime rates, but rather that falling crime rates are due to a downward trend in society as a whole. There is also criticism that even with video cameras rolling, there is still considerable judgment on the part of camera operators as to what gets reported. Determinations of who looks suspicious is solely dependent on the way the camera operators view what is going on.

England is at the forefront in using video surveillance, with their systems going back to 1986. However, Canada, France, Italy, Monaco, Russia, Spain, Ireland, and others are all increasing their use of CCTV. In the United States, about 75 percent of businesses use some form of CCTV to protect their premises.[131] The International Center for the Prevention of Crime estimates that delinquency in public areas can be reduced by up to 68 percent with the use of CCTV, but it has to be used in conjunction with a quick response by the police and video hardcopies have to be stored for future prosecution.[132] The type of surveillance (active or passive) also makes an important difference. Several Canadian studies show that unmonitored cameras are one of the least effective deterrents to robberies in banks and convenience stores. For example, the Peel Regional Police have concluded that closed circuit television is expensive to implement and is not a major deterrence. In order to be effective, CCTV has to be used in conjunction with other devices.

Some legal issues surround the use of CCTV surveillance techniques. First, there is the notion that such techniques will damage the image of the police by creating a "big brother" mentality. Second, there is fear that the recordings will be sold for their commercial value, violating the rights of those recorded on these tapes. In the United States, legal challenges have dealt with issues of privacy and the distinction between public and private places. The trend has been to allow surveillance so long as it does not occur in truly private areas and as long as its use has "helped" save money or lives. [133]

Video surveillance has been in use in Canada since about 1992, not only by law enforcement agencies, but by banks, libraries, restaurants, and convenience stores, and at industrial sites, offices, apartment buildings, and public transit stations. In 1995, 70 percent of all bank robberies in Canada were video-recorded, and CCTV surveillance tapes captured 75 percent of all crimes investigated by law enforcement or private security. CCTV video cameras in commercial areas have also been instrumental in helping to find missing persons.[134] In British Columbia, the use of CCTV systems is controlled by the Freedom of Information and Protection of Privacy Act, 1996. Some fear that acceptance of video surveillance may be the first step in a series of more intrusive surveillance techniques. There is a concern that once installed, CCTV systems will be used to serve a wide range of social control functions. Another concern is inadvertent "function creep" whereby a camera system installed to watch for criminal behaviour may end up being used as a tool to monitor performance.[135] Other criticisms include the fear that they may be a form of passive discrimination in which people are judged by the stereotypic image they portray without any consideration given to them as individuals.

However, those in favour of them claim that they help construct an image of a modern, efficient security system. For the most part, they are not thought of in the same light as traditional surveillance methods (such as the police).

Another criticism is that since the state is indirectly behind most public-space CCTV systems, the systems

How CCTV helps prevent crime. Many governments, police forces, and private businesses are using closed circuit television cameras to prevent crimes occurring, and identify suspects when they do. Parking lots, bank lobbies, convenience stores, hospitals, schools—when were you last on CCTV?

permit the state to maintain a high degree of control over its population.[136]

In conclusion, there is a difference of opinion as to the effectiveness of CCTV surveillance. Such systems reinforce the traditional view that violence takes place in the public sphere. However, they can be used as a tool to ensure the success of local economies by providing a safe place for businesses to set up and for consumers to gather. It seems that the evidence is not yet all in.

General Deterrence in Review

Some experts, such as Ernest Van Den Haag, believe that the purpose of the law and justice system is to create a "threat system."[137] That is, the threat of legal punishment should, on the face of it, deter lawbreakers through fear. Who among us can claim that they never had an urge to commit crime but were deterred by fear of discovery and its consequences? Nonetheless, the relationship between crime rates and deterrent measures is far less than choice theorists might expect. Despite efforts to punish criminals and make them fear crime, as we have seen there is little evidence that the fear of apprehension and punishment can reduce crime rates. How can this discrepancy be explained?

First, deterrence theory assumes a rational offender who weighs the costs and benefits of a criminal act before deciding on a course of action. There is reason to believe that in many instances, criminals are desperate people acting under the influence of drugs and alcohol or suffering from personality disorders. Surveys show a significant portion of all offenders, perhaps up to 80 percent, are substance abusers.[138] Chronic offender research indicates that a relatively small group of offenders commit a significant percentage of all serious crimes. Some psychologists believe that members of this select group suffer from an innate or inherited emotional state that renders them both (1) incapable of fearing punishment and (2) less likely to appreciate the consequences of crime.[139] It is likely that the threat of future punishment has little deterrent effect on these people.

Second, many offenders are members of what is referred to as the underclass—people cut off from society, lacking the education and skills they need to be in demand in the modern economy.[140] It may be unlikely that such desperate people will be deterred from crime by fear of punishment because, in reality, they perceive few other options for success.

Third, as Beccaria's famous equation tells us, the threat of punishment involves not only its severity but its certainty and speed. Our legal system is not very effective. Only 10 percent of all serious offences result in apprehension (since half go unreported and police make arrests in about 20 percent of reported crimes). Police routinely do not arrest suspects in personal disputes, even when they lead to violence, as in the case of wife assault.[141] As apprehended offenders are processed

Crime in the News

RCMP video surveillance: "Big Brother is watching": federal privacy watchdog

October 5, 2001
DENE MOORE Canadian Press

VANCOUVER (CP) - RCMP ran afoul of federal privacy laws when they set up a surveillance camera on a Kelowna, B.C., street, says Canada's privacy commissioner. In a report released Thursday that could have national implications, George Radwanski said the so-called crime camera in downtown Kelowna contravenes federal law.

But RCMP in Kelowna said Thursday they will continue to use the camera. . . .

The area where the $22,000 camera was mounted was marked with 11 signs informing people the area was monitored by video surveillance for law enforcement purposes.

The force stopped the continuous recording but continued to monitor the camera day and night.

The video recording kicks in when there is suspicious activity. . . .

In 1992, the Quebec privacy commissioner found that the city of Sherbrooke contravened that province's privacy laws by videotaping citizens' activities.

"If we cannot walk or drive down a street without being systematically monitored by the cameras of the state, our lives and our society will be irretrievably altered," Radwanski wrote.

"The Orwellian idea that 'Big Brother is watching' will have become no longer apocryphal, but a literal and permanent daily reality," Radwanski wrote in his seven-page decision.

The Vancouver police department has proposed setting up 23 cameras in the city's crime-ridden downtown eastside. London, Toronto and Winnipeg are considering them as well. . . .

The city says 80 per cent of residents support the surveillance cameras, "or safety cameras, as I like to call them," said Mayor Walter Gray.

The average person is caught on videotape up to a dozen times a day, experts say.

Copyright © 2001 National Post Online

through all the stages of the criminal justice system, the odds of their receiving serious punishment diminish. Thus, some offenders may believe that they will not be severely punished for their acts and consequently have little regard for the law's deterrent power.

As you may recall, only offenders who suffer the most severe and draconian sanctions are likely to fear future legal punishments. Raymond Paternoster found that adolescents, a group responsible for a disproportionate amount of crime, may be well aware that the juvenile court "is generally lenient in the imposition of meaningful sanctions on even the most serious offenders."[142] Research shows that even those accused of murder, the most serious of crimes, are often convicted of lesser offences and spend relatively short amounts of time behind bars.[143] Young offenders found guilty of murder in Canada face a maximum sentence of five years. In making their "rational choice," offenders may be aware that the deterrent effect of the law is minimal.

Fourth, in cases such as white-collar crime, it would seem that the rational deterrence of sanctions would be most likely to have an effect, since the crime is rationally calculated and planned; however, it is also likely that offenders perceive their actions as "normatively" acceptable within their subculture. In such an environment, it is the sanctions that would seem unfair and deviant to the offender, not the criminal actions.

Specific Deterrence

The general deterrence model focuses on future or potential criminals. In contrast, the theory of **specific** (also called special or particular) **deterrence** holds that criminal sanctions should be so powerful that known criminals will never repeat their criminal acts. For example, the drunk driver whose sentence is a large fine and a week in the county jail will, it is hoped, be convinced that the price to be paid for drinking and driving is too great to consider future violations; burglars who spend five years in a tough, maximum-security prison should find their enthusiasm for theft dampened.[144] In principle, punishment works if a connection can be established between the planned action and memories of its consequence. If these recollections are adequately intense, the action will be prevented or reduced in frequency.[145]

Does Specific Deterrence Deter Crime?

At first glance, specific deterrence does not seem to work, as a majority of known criminals are not deterred by their punishment. Chronic offender research indicates that a stay in a juvenile justice facility has little deterrent effect

on the likelihood that a persistent delinquent will become an adult criminal.[146] It comes as no surprise, then, that most prison inmates had prior records of arrest and conviction before their current offence. In 1997, Correctional Services Canada reported that 46.2 percent of incarcerated male offenders (6510 inmates), and 25.2 percent of female offenders (90 inmates), had served a previous term of federal incarceration.[147] And research done in the United States shows that about two-thirds of all convicted felons are rearrested within three years of their release from prison, and those who have been punished in the past are the most likely to recidivate.[148] Research also shows that offenders sentenced to prison have no lower rates of recidivism than those receiving community sentences for similar crimes. For example, white-collar offenders who received a prison sentence were as likely to recidivate as a matched group of offenders who received an alternative sanction.[149]

Some research efforts have actually shown that rather than reducing the frequency of crime, punishment increases reoffending rates.[150] It is possible that (1) punishment brings defiance rather than deterrence or (2) the stigma of apprehension helps lock offenders into a criminal career instead of convincing them to avoid one.

Connections

Theoretically, experiencing punishment should deter future crime. However, punishment stigmatizes people and "spoils" their identity, a turn of events that may encourage antisocial behaviour. The two factors may cancel each other out, helping to explain why punishment does not substantially reduce future criminality. The effects of stigma and negative labels are discussed further in Chapter 8.

There does exist some empirical research indicating that in a few instances, offenders who receive harsher punishments than their peers will be less likely to recidivate, or if they do commit crimes again, they will do so less frequently.[151] However, the consensus is that the association between crime and specific deterrent measures remains uncertain at best.

Pain Versus Shame

If current efforts at specific deterrence are less than successful, should new approaches be attempted? In their two widely discussed works on specific deterrence, criminologists Graeme Newman and John Braithwaite take opposing approaches to reforming criminals.

Newman embraces traditional concepts of specific deterrence.[152] However, he adds a new wrinkle in his provocative suggestion that society should return to the use of corporal punishment. He advocates the use of electric

Culture, Gender, Ethnicity, and Criminology

Deterrence and Domestic Violence

Is it possible to reduce the incidence of spouse abuse and domestic violence through mandatory arrest policies? Groundbreaking research that illustrates the specific deterrent effect of legal punishment was conducted in Minneapolis, Minnesota, by Lawrence Sherman and Richard Berk. They had police officers randomly assign treatments to the domestic assault cases they encountered on their beat. One approach was to give some sort of advice and mediation, another was to send the assailant from the home for a period of eight hours, and the third was to arrest the assailant. They found that when police took formal action (arrest), the chance of recidivism was substantially less than when they took less punitive measures, such as warning the offenders or ordering them out of the house for a cooling-off period. A six-month follow-up found that only 10 percent of the arrested group repeated their violent behaviour, compared with 19 percent of the advised group and 24 percent of the sent-away group. Sherman and Berk concluded that a formal arrest, the most punitive alternative, was the most effective means of controlling domestic violence, regardless of what happened to the offender in court. This research finding was considered highly significant, because it was one of the few instances in which a specific deterrent effect could be identified, and because it promised a solution to one of society's most intractable problems—wife abuse.

While the findings of the Minneapolis experiment seemed to affirm the effectiveness of specific deterrence, efforts to replicate the experimental design in other locales have so far failed to duplicate the original findings. In these other locales, formal arrest was not a greater deterrent to spouse abuse than warning or advising the assailant; in fact, in some cases, the frequency of domestic assaults increased after arrest. While there was an initial cooling-off period, in the long term resentment seemed to build in the offender. There are also indications that police officers in the original experiment failed to assign cases in a random fashion, which altered the experimental findings.

Despite these setbacks, it is still unclear whether the findings of the original Minneapolis experiment were invalid. An in-depth review of the replication studies concludes that the available information is still incomplete and inadequate for a definitive statement about the effect of arrest on spousal abuse.

It may thus be premature to dismiss the specific deterrent effect of arrest on spouse abuse. There are indications that specific deterrence policies can, under some circumstances, deter domestic abuse. One study showed that a period of short-term custody lasting about three hours may reduce recidivism; unfortunately, deterrent effects decayed over time. Evidence also exists that one subset of offenders—those with a greater stake in conformity—are more deterrable than those with little social commitment; deterrence seems to work with those who have more to lose, such as a high-paying job.

It is difficult to explain why the specific deterrent effect of arrest can be absent, decay over time, or only affect a subset of offenders (those married and employed). It is possible that offenders who suffer arrest are initially fearful of punishment but eventually replace fear with anger and violent intent toward their mate when their case does not result in severe punishment. However, the best we can say at the moment is that research on the effectiveness of prosecution of spousal abusers is ambiguous and indicates that more research needs to be done.

SOURCE: Lawrence Sherman and Richard Berk, "The Specific Deterrent Effects of Arrest for Domestic Assault," *American Sociological Review* 49 (1984): 261–72; Richard Berk and Phyllis J. Newman, "Does Arrest Really Deter Wife Battery? An Effort to Replicate the Findings of the Minneapolis Spouse Abuse Experiment," *American Sociological Review* 50 (1985): 253–62; Franklyn Dunford, "The Measurement of Recidivism in Cases of Spouse Assault," *Journal of Criminal Law and Criminology* 83 (1992): 120–36; J. David Hirschel, Ira Hutchinson, and Charles Dean, "The Failure of Arrest to Deter Spouse Abuse," *Journal of Research in Crime and Delinquency* 29 (1992): 7–33; J. David Hirschel and Ira Hutchinson, "Female Spouse Abuse and the Police Response: The Charlotte, North Carolina Experiment," *Journal of Criminal Law and Criminology* 83 (1992): 73–119; David Huizinga and Delbert Elliott, "The Role of Arrest in Domestic Assault: The Omaha Experiment," *Criminology* 28 (1990): 183–206; David Hirschel, Ira Hutchinson, Charles Dean, Joseph Kelley, and Carolyn Pesackis, *Charlotte Spouse Abuse Replication Project: Final Report* (Washington, DC: National Institute of Justice, 1990); Richard Berk, Gordon Smyth, and Lawrence Sherman, "When Random Assignment Fails: Some Lessons from the Minneapolis Spouse Abuse Experiment," *Journal of Quantitative Criminology* 4 (1989): 209–23; Joel Garner, Jeffrey Fagan, and Christopher Maxwell, "Published Findings from the Spouse Assault Replication Program: A Critical Review," *Journal of Quantitative Criminology* 11 (1995): 2–28; Lawrence Sherman, Janell Schmidt, Dennis Rogan, Patrick Gartin, Ellen Cohn, Dean Collins, and Anthony Bacich, "From Initial Deterrence to Long-Term Escalation: Short-Custody Arrest for Poverty Ghetto Domestic Violence," *Criminology* 29 (1991): 821–50; Anthony Pate and Edwin Hamilton, "Formal and Informal Deterrents to Domestic Violence: The Dade County Spouse Assault Experiment," *American Sociological Review* 57 (1992): 691–97; Richard Berk, Alec Campbell, Ruth Klap, and Bruce Western, "The Deterrent Effect of Arrest in Incidents of Domestic Violence: A Bayesian Analysis of Four Field Experiments," *American Sociological Review* 57 (1992): 698–708; Jeffrey Fagan, "Cessation of Family Violence: Deterrence and Dissuasion," in *Family Violence*, ed. Lloyd Ohlin and Michael Tonry (Chicago: University of Chicago Press, 1989), pp. 377–426.

shocks to punish offenders because they are over with quickly, they have no lasting effect, and they can easily be adjusted to fit the severity of a crime.

According to Newman, corporal punishment could be used as an alternative sanction to fill the gap between the severe punishment of prison and the nonpunishment of probation. Electric shocks can be controlled and calibrated to fit the crime. For violent crimes in which the victim was terrified and humiliated and for which a local community does not wish to incarcerate, a violent corporal punishment should be considered, such as whipping. In these cases, humiliation of the offender is seen as justifiably deserved. In sum, Newman embraces specific deterrence strategies if they can be relatively inexpensive, immediate, and individualized and leave no lasting disabilities. In 1994, when a young American boy was flogged in Singapore after he pleaded guilty to vandalizing property, an international debate was provoked over the value of corporal punishment.

Braithwaite's *Crime, Shame and Reintegration* takes a radically different approach.[153] Braithwaite notes that countries, such as Japan, in which conviction for crimes brings an inordinate amount of shame have extremely low crime rates. In Japan, prosecution of the criminal proceeds only when the normal process of public apology, compensation, and forgiveness by the victim breaks down.

Shame is a powerful tool of informal social control, as we have already discussed. Citizens in cultures in which crime is not shameful do not internalize an abhorrence for crime because when they are punished, they view themselves as merely "victims" of the justice system; their punishment comes at the hands of neutral strangers being paid to act. In contrast, shaming relies on the participation of victims. Imagine the deterrent effect of the "brank," shown in the picture.

Braithwaite divides the concept of shame into two distinct types. The most common form of shaming typically involves **stigmatization**. This form of shaming is an ongoing process of **degradation** in which the offender is branded as an evil person and cast out of society. Shaming can occur at a school disciplinary hearing or a criminal court trial. Harold Garfinkel called trials "degradation ceremonies." Bestowing stigma and degradation may have a general deterrent effect: It makes people afraid of social rejection and public humiliation. However, as a specific deterrent, stigma is doomed to failure, since people who suffer humiliation at the hands of the justice system "reject their rejectors" by joining a deviant subculture of like-minded people who, collectively, resist social control.

Braithwaite argues that crime control can be better achieved through a policy of **reintegrative shaming.** Here, disapproval is extended to the offenders' evil deed, while they are cast as respected people who can be reaccepted by society. A critical element of reintegrative shaming occurs when the offenders begin to understand and recognize their wrongdoing and shame themselves. To be reintegrative, shaming must be brief and controlled and then followed by "ceremonies" of forgiveness, apology, and repentance.

To prevent crime, Braithwaite charges, society must encourage reintegrative shaming. For example, women and men interested in reducing domestic violence may mount a crusade to shame spouse abusers.[154] Early rough justice in Canada was often used to control the excesses

The brank or scold's bridle was used in the 16th and 17th centuries. Also called a witch's bridle, it had a metal cage for the head and spikes to pierce the tongue. Some also had a bell, which would humiliate the "scold" as she was paraded through the streets in a cart. A scold was a troublesome woman who scolded her husband and wrangled with her neighbours. It was usually a husband who brought his wife to court, where a judge would decide if she was a public nuisance. Karen Farrington, *Dark Justice: A History of Punishment and Torture.* Toronto: Reed Consumer Books Limited, 1996.

of spousal abuse. In addition, an effort must be made to create pride in solving problems nonviolently, in caring for others, and in respecting the rights of women.

As you may recall, there is evidence that the fear of personal shame can have a general deterrent effect. It may also be applied to produce specific deterrence. Braithwaite and Stephen Mugford report on attempts to apply reintegrative shaming techniques with juvenile offenders in Australia. One program brings offenders together with victims (so that they can experience shame) and with close family members and peers (who help with reintegration).[155] Efforts like these can humanize a system of justice that today relies on repression and not forgiveness as the basis of specific deterrence.

Rethinking Deterrence

So far both specific and general deterrence strategies have not yielded the results predicted by choice theorists. While a few studies have shown expected effects, there is still little conclusive evidence that formal sanctions can convince would-be criminals to forgo their intended behaviour or convince experienced offenders that "crime does not pay."

Some criminologists have called for the reconceptualization of both specific and general deterrence.[156] They argue that these concepts should not be considered independent but rather interactive: Most people have had experience with the direct effect of punishment (specific deterrence) and the indirect effect of the fear of punishment (general deterrence). In addition, they may have experienced punishment avoidance, either getting away with crime themselves or knowing about others who have escaped detection or have been punished (vicarious deterrence). The total deterrent effect includes a combination of personal and vicarious experiences with punishment and its aftermath.

The two effects may cancel each other out, explaining in part the ambiguity of deterrent effects: An experienced criminal may instinctively fear apprehension, but his experience tells him that the law's "bark is worse than its bite." A person with criminal friends may find his or her fear of punishment diminished when the friends describe how easy it is to get away with crime. Empirical research shows that people are in fact influenced by both general and specific deterrent effects and that both work in concert to influence behaviour.[157] Stafford and Warr's views may help criminologists better understand the forces that promote deterrence so that the concept can be studied in a more rational fashion.

Incapacitation Strategies

It stands to reason that if more criminals were sent to prison, the crime rate should go down. Because most people age out of crime, the duration of a criminal career is limited. Placing offenders behind bars during their "prime crime" years should lessen their lifetime opportunity to commit crime. The shorter the span of opportunity, the fewer the number of offences they can commit over their life course; hence, crime is reduced.

This idea of seems logical, but does it work? For the past 20 years, there has been significant growth in the number and percentage of the population held in prison and jails; today, more than 1.5 million Americans and 34 000 Canadians are incarcerated. Between 1988 and 1998, Canada's prison population rose 24 percent. At 129 per 100 000 of the population, Canada's incarceration rate is not as high as the United States (645). However, it is above Australia and France (110), the United Kingdom (104), Germany (95), and Norway (84). Advocates of incapacitation suggest that this effort has been responsible for the overall stabilization and actual decline in crime rates in the 1990s. Others suggest that this association is illusory and that a stable crime rate is actually controlled by such factors as the size of the teenage population, the threat of tough new mandatory sentences, a healthy economy, the initiation of tougher gun laws, the end of the "crack epidemic," and the implementation of tough and aggressive policing strategies in large cities such as Montreal and Toronto.[158]

It is also possible that what appears to be an incapacitation effect may actually reflect the effect of some other legal phenomenon and not the fact that so many criminals are locked up. If, for example, the crime rate drops as more and more people are sent to prison, it would appear that incapacitation works. However, crime rates may really be dropping because potential criminals now fear punishment and are being deterred from crime. What appears to be an incapacitation effect may actually be an effect of general deterrence.[159]

Can Incapacitation Reduce Crime?

Research on the direct benefits of incapacitation has not shown that increasing the number of people behind bars or the length of their stay can effectively reduce crime. A number of studies have set out to measure the precise effect of incarceration rates on crime rates, and the results have not supported a strict incarceration policy. In an often-cited study using FBI index crime data to estimate the effect of imprisonment on crime rates, it was found that if the prison population were cut in half, the crime rate would most likely go up only 4 percent; if prisons were entirely eliminated, crime might increase 8 percent. Looking at this relationship from another perspective, if the average prison sentence were increased 50 percent, the crime rate might be reduced only 4 percent. One researcher concluded that prisons may be terribly unpleasant, psychologically destructive, and at times dangerous to life and limb, but there is no compelling evidence that imprisonment substantially increases (or decreases) the likelihood of criminal involvement.[160]

A similar study of prison rates and incapacitation estimated that a 50 percent reduction in average time served would result in a 4.6 percent increase in property crime and a 2.5 percent increase in violent crime, while another found that an increase in incarceration rates may actually lead to an increase in crime rates.[161]

A few studies have found an inverse relationship between incarceration rates and crime rates. Reuel Shinnar and Shlomo Shinnar's research on incapacitation in New York led them to conclude that a policy of mandatory prison sentences of five years for violent crime and three for property offences could reduce the reported crime rate by a factor of four or five.[162] Similarly, Stephan Van Dine, Simon Dinitz, and John Conrad estimated that a mandatory prison sentence of five years for any felony offence could reduce the murder, rape, robbery, and serious assault rates by 17 percent. A similar sentence limited to repeat felons would reduce the rate of these crimes by 6 percent.[163]

With these few exceptions, existing research indicates that the crime control effects of a strict incapacitation policy are modest at best.[164] The Solicitor General of Canada's position is that incarceration is limited as a deterrence, and that the best solution is to use alternative measures such as conditional sentencing, and try to return the offender to the community.

The Logic of Incarceration

Why hasn't an incarceration strategy worked? There is little evidence that incapacitating criminals will deter them from future criminality and even more reason to believe that they may be more inclined to commit crimes upon release. As you may recall, prison has few specific deterrent effects: The more prior incarceration experiences inmates had, the more likely they were to recidivate (and return to prison) within 12 months of their release.[165] Whatever reason they had to commit crime before their incarceration, there is little to suggest that a prison sentence will reduce those criminogenic forces. The criminal label precludes their entry into many legitimate occupations and solidifies their attachment to criminal careers.

The economics of crime suggest that if money can be made from criminal activity, there will always be someone to take the place of the incarcerated offender. New criminals will be recruited and trained, offsetting any benefit accrued by incarceration. Incarcerating established offenders may open new opportunities for competitors who were suppressed by the more experienced criminals. For example, the incarceration of organized crime members helped open drug markets to new gangs; the flow of narcotics into the country increased after organized crime leaders were imprisoned.

Incarceration may not work because the majority of criminal offences are committed by teens and very young adult offenders who are unlikely to be sent to prison for a single felony conviction. Incarcerated criminals, aging behind bars, are already past the age where they are "at risk" to commit crime. A strict incarceration policy may result in people being kept in prison beyond the time they are a threat to society while a new cohort of high-rate adolescents are on the street.

It is also expensive to maintain an incapacitation strategy. The "crime control system" in Canada costs about $2 billion each year. The combined cost of all justice spending was $10 billion in 1994–95, with policing (58 percent) and adult corrections (19 percent) taking the most money.[166] The average annual cost of keeping an adult offender in maximum security is $68 156! Even if incarceration could reduce the crime rate, the costs would be enormous. At a time of deficits and fiscal austerity, would taxpayers be willing to spend billions more on new prison construction and annual maintenance fees?

Selective Incapacitation: Three Strikes and You're Out

A more efficient incapacitation model is suggested by the "discovery" of the chronic career criminal. If in fact a relatively small number of people account for a relatively large percentage of the nation's crime rates, then an effort to incapacitate these few troublemakers might have a significant payoff. Some have suggested that a policy of **selective incapacitation** could be an effective crime-reduction strategy.[167] In a widely cited study of over 2000 inmates serving time for theft offences in California, Michigan, and Texas, Peter Greenwood found that the selective incapacitation of chronic offenders could reduce the rate of robbery offences by 15 percent and the inmate population by 5 percent.

According to Greenwood's model, chronic offenders can be distinguished on the basis of their offending patterns and lifestyle (for example, their employment record and history of substance abuse). Once identified, high-risk offenders would be eligible for sentencing enhancements that would substantially increase the time they serve in prison.

Another concept receiving widespread international attention is the "three strikes and you're out" policy now used in many U.S. states; it gives people convicted of three violent offences a mandatory life term without parole. This policy seems to offer an attractive solution to the problem of chronic offending and is being considered in Britain. Many states already have habitual offender laws that provide long (or life) sentences for repeat offenders. Some criminologists argue that such strategies, though attractive to the public, will not work, because (1) most "three-time losers" are at the verge of aging out of crime anyway, (2) current sentences for violent crimes are already severe, (3) an expanding prison population will drive up already high prison costs, (4) there would be racial disparity in sentencing, and (5) the police would be in danger because two-time offenders would violently resist a third arrest, knowing they face a life sentence.

In a meta-analysis of 50 studies dating from 1958 and involving 336 052 offenders, it was found that a prison sentence increased the likelihood of a repeat offence, compared to a community-based sanction. Also, there was some tendency for lower risk offenders to be more negatively affected by the prison experience. The conclusion was that prisons should not be used with the expectation of reducing criminal behaviour, and that the use of incarceration has enormous cost implications. However, they also feel that the primary justification of prison should be to incapacitate offenders (particularly, those of a chronic, higher risk nature) for reasonable periods and to exact retribution.[168]

Policy Implications of Choice Theory

From the origins of classical theory to the development of modern rational choice views, the belief that criminals choose to commit crime has had an important influence on the relationship between law, punishment, and crime. When police patrol in well-marked cars, it is assumed that their presence will deter would-be criminals. When the harsh realities of prison life are portrayed in movies and TV shows, the lesson is not lost on potential criminals. Nowhere is the idea that the threat of punishment can control crime more evident than in the implementation of tough, mandatory criminal sentences to control violent crime and drug trafficking.

Despite its questionable deterrent effect, severe penalties such as life imprisonment or capital punishment are also viewed as effective means of restricting criminal choice. Many observers are dismayed because people who are convicted of murder sometimes kill again when released on parole. One study of 52 000 incarcerated murderers found that 810 had been previously convicted of murder and had killed 821 people following their previous release from prison.[169] About 9 percent of all inmates on death row in the United States have had prior convictions for homicide; if they had been executed for their first offence, hundreds of people would be alive today.[170]

So while research on the core principles of choice theory and deterrence theories produces mixed results, there is little doubt that these models have had an important impact on crime prevention strategies.

The concept of criminal choice has also prompted the creation of justice policies referred to as **just desert**.[171] The just desert position can be summarized in these three statements:

1. Those who violate others' rights deserve to be punished.

2. We should not deliberately add to human suffering; punishment makes those punished suffer.
3. However, punishment may prevent more misery than it inflicts; this conclusion reestablishes the need for desert-based punishment.

This utilitarian view is the key to the desert approach: Punishment is needed to preserve the social equity disturbed by crime; nonetheless, the severity of the punishment should be commensurate with the seriousness of the crime. These principles were laid out by Cesare Beccaria more than 200 years ago and still form a foundation of our criminal justice system.

Desert theory is also concerned with the rights of the accused. It alleges that the rights of the person being punished should not be unduly sacrificed for the good of others (as with deterrence). The offender should not be treated as more (or less) **blameworthy** than is warranted by the character of his or her offence. For example, Von Hirsch asks the following question: If two crimes, A and B, are equally serious, but if severe penalties are shown to have a deterrent effect only with respect to A, would it be fair to punish the person who has committed crime A more harshly simply to deter others from committing the crime? Conversely, imposing a light sentence for a serious crime would be unfair, because it would treat the offender as being less blameworthy than he or she is. In sum, the just desert model suggests that retribution justifies punishment because people deserve what they get for past deeds. Punishment based on deterrence or incapacitation is wrong because it involves an offender's future actions, which cannot accurately be predicted. Punishment should be the same for all people who commit the same crime. Criminal sentences based on individual needs or characteristics are inherently unfair, as all people are equally blameworthy for their misdeeds.

The influence of Von Hirsch's views can be seen in sentencing models that give the same punishments to all people who commit the same type of crime.

Summary

Choice theory assumes that criminals carefully choose whether to commit criminal acts. These theories are summarized in Table 5.3. However, people are influenced by their fear of the criminal penalties associated with being caught and convicted for law violations. The more severe, certain, and swift the punishment, the more likely it is to control crime. The choice approach is rooted in the classical criminology of 18th-century social philosophers Cesare Beccaria and Jeremy Bentham.

The growth of positivist criminology, which stressed external causes of crime and rehabilitation of known offenders, reduced the popularity of the classical

Table 5.3	Choice theories	
THEORY	**MAJOR PREMISE**	**STRENGTHS**
Rational choice	Law-violating behaviour is an event that occurs after offenders weigh information on their personal needs and the situational factors involved in the difficulty and risk of committing a crime.	Explains why high-risk youths do not constantly engage in delinquency acts. Relates theory to delinquency control policy. It is not limited by class or other social variables.
Routine activities	Crime and delinquency are a function of the presence of motivated offenders, the availability of suitable targets, and the absence of capable guardians.	Can explain fluctuations in crime and delinquency rates. Shows how victim behaviour influences criminal choice.
General deterrence	People will commit crime and delinquency if they perceive that the benefits outweigh the risks. Crime is a function of the severity, certainty, and speed of punishment.	Shows the relationship between crime and punishment. Suggests a real solution to crime.
Specific deterrence	If punishment is severe enough, criminals will not repeat their illegal acts.	Provides a strategy to reduce crime.
Incapacitation	Keeping known criminals out of circulation will reduce crime rates.	Recognizes the role opportunity plays in criminal behaviour. Provides solution to chronic offending.

approach in the 20th century. However, in the late 1970s the concept of criminal choice once again became an important perspective of criminologists. Today, choice theorists view crime as offence- and offender-specific. Research shows that offenders consider their targets carefully before deciding on a course of action. By implication, crime can be prevented or displaced by convincing potential criminals that the risks of violating the law exceed the benefits.

Deterrence theory holds that if criminals are indeed rational, an inverse relationship should exist between punishment and crime. However, a number of factors confound the relationship. For example, if people do not believe they will be caught, even harsh punishment may not deter crime. Deterrence theory has been criticized on the grounds that it wrongfully assumes that criminals make a rational choice before committing crimes, it ignores the intricacies of the criminal justice system, and it does not take into account the social and psychological factors that may influence criminality. Research designed to test the validity of the deterrence concept has not indicated that deterrent measures actually reduce the crime rate.

Specific deterrence theory holds that the crime rate can be reduced if known offenders are punished so severely that they never commit crimes again. There is little evidence that harsh punishments actually reduce the crime rate. Incapacitation theory maintains that if deterrence does not work, the best course of action is to incarcerate known offenders for long periods of time so that they lack criminal opportunity. Research efforts have not provided clear-cut proof that increasing the number of people in prison—and increasing prison sentences—will reduce crime rates.

Choice theory has been influential in shaping public policy. The criminal law is designed to deter potential criminals and fairly punish those who have been caught in illegal acts. Some courts have changed sentencing policies to adapt to classical principles, and the correctional system seems geared toward incapacitation and special deterrence. The renewed interest in the use of the death penalty is testimony to the importance of classical theory.

Thinking Like a Criminologist

The Solicitor General has issued a request for proposals for a national survey of sentencing practices. The government is interested in recommendations about criminal punishment. Specifically, would the length of criminal sentences and the way they are served have an impact on crime rates? What could be gained by either increasing punishment or requiring inmates to spend more time behind bars before their release? Are we being too lenient or too punitive as a society? As someone who has studied choice theory, you have some ideas on how crime rates might be affected if the way we punished offenders was radically changed. Initially, you favour selective incapacitation. However, you come across research called "Deterrence and Homeless Male Street Youth" in the *Canadian Journal of Criminology* (1998) which causes you to question yourself. What it found is that while street youths fear legal sanctions, more serious offenders do not. Instead, their fear of punishment is reduced by their poverty. Drug use, and association with criminal peers, causes a lack of normative constraints. The more serious street youth offenders are immersed in a lifestyle where crime, drugs, and criminal peers feed off one another, isolating them from conventional society. What would you propose with regard to sentencing for this group of offenders?

Key Terms

blameworthy	discouragement	perceptual deterrence
brutalization effect	extinction	rational choice theory
capable guardians	general deterrence	reintegrative shaming
choice theory	informal sanctions	routine activities theory
classical criminology	instrumental crime	seductions of crime
conflict-linked crime	just desert	selective incapacitation
crackdowns	macro perspective	situational crime prevention
crime displacement	micro perspective	specific deterrence
defensible space	motivated criminals	stigmatization
degradation	offence-specific crime	target reduction strategies
diffusion of benefits	offender-specific crime	utilitarianism

See the book-specific website at www.siegelcriminology2e.nelson.com for additional chapter links, discussions, and quizzes.

Chapter

6

Trait Theories

Ageneration of Americans have grown up on films and TV shows that portray violent criminals as mentally deranged and physically abnormal. Beginning with Alfred Hitchcock's film *Psycho*, producers have made millions depicting the ghoulish acts of people who at first seem normal and even friendly but turn out to be demented and dangerous. Lurking out there are crazed babysitters (*The Hand That Rocks the Cradle*), frenzied airline passengers (*Turbulence*), deranged roommates (*Single, White Female*), psychotic tenants (*Pacific Heights*), demented secretaries (*The Temp*), unhinged police officers (*Maniac Cop*), irrational fans (*The Fan, Misery*), abnormal girlfriends (*Fatal Attraction*) and boyfriends (*Fear*), unstable husbands (*Sleeping with the Enemy*) and wives (*Black Widow*), loony fathers (*The Stepfather*) and mothers (*Friday the 13th, Part 1*), maniacal children (*The Good Son*), and psychotic teenaged admirers (*The Crush*). And no one can be safe when even the psychologists and psychiatrists who should be treating these disturbed people turn out to be demonic murderers themselves (*Silence of the Lambs, Dressed to Kill, Never Talk to Strangers*). Is it any wonder that we respond to a particularly horrible crime by saying of the perpetrator, "That guy must be crazy" or "She's a monster!"

Connections

Some critics have called for the strict regulation of movies, videos, and TV shows, believing that viewing them is harmful to their mostly adolescent audience. Does watching all these aggressive, crazed people cause viewers to act violently themselves? For more on this issue, see the in-depth discussion of media violence later in this chapter.

The view that criminals bear physical or mental traits that make them "different" and "abnormal" is not restricted to the moviegoing public. Since the 19th century, criminologists have suggested that biological and psychological traits may influence behaviour. It is believed that some personal trait must separate the deviant members of society from the nondeviant. These personal differences explain why, when faced with the same life situations, one person commits crime and becomes a chronic offender, while another attends school, church, and neighbourhood functions and obeys the laws of society. One person reacts to being cut off in traffic with "road rage," while another barely notices. All people may be aware of and even fear the sanctioning power of the law, but some are unable to control their urges and passions. The variations on this view of crime causation are referred to as **trait theories**, or sometimes constitutional theories.

Trait theorists do not suggest that a single biological or psychological attribute is adequate to explain all criminality. Rather, as common sense would suggest, each offender is considered unique, physically and mentally; consequently, there must be a unique explanation for each person's behaviour. Some may have inherited criminal tendencies; others are suffering from nervous system (neurological) problems; some may have a blood chemistry disorder that heightens their antisocial activity. Criminologists who focus on the individual thus see many explanations for crime because, in fact, there are many differences among criminal offenders.

Trait theorists are not overly concerned with legal definitions of crime; they do not try to explain why people violate particular statutory laws such as car theft or burglary. After all, these are artificial legal concepts based on arbitrary boundaries (speeding is a good example). Instead, trait theorists focus on basic human drives–aggression, violence, and impulsivity–that are linked to antisocial behaviour patterns. They also recognize that human traits alone do not produce criminality and that crime-producing interactions involve both personal traits–such as intelligence, personality, and chemical and genetic makeup–and environmental factors–such as family life, educational attainment, and neighbourhood conditions. While some people may have a predisposition toward aggression, environmental stimuli can either suppress or trigger antisocial acts. Physical or mental traits are, therefore, but one part of a large pool of environmental, social, and personal factors that account for criminality.

Trait theories have gained prominence recently because of what is now known about chronic recidivism and the development of criminal careers. If only a small percentage of all offenders go on to become persistent repeaters, it is possible that what sets them apart from the criminal population is an abnormal biochemistry, brain structure, or genetic makeup.[1] Even if criminals do "choose crime," the fact that some repeatedly make that choice could well be linked to their physical and mental makeup.

This chapter reviews the two major divisions of trait theory: the biological and the psychological.

Biological Trait Theory
Development of Biological Theories

Cesare Lombroso's work on the "born criminal" was a direct offshoot of the application of the scientific method to the study of crime. His identification of primitive atavistic anomalies was based on what he believed to be sound empirical research using established scientific methods.

Lombroso was not alone in the early development of biological theory. A contemporary of Lombroso's, Raffaele Garofalo (1852–1934), shared his belief that certain physical characteristics indicate a criminal nature. For example, Garofalo stated that among criminals "a lower degree of sensibility to physical pain seems to be

Connections

Biological explanations of criminal behaviour first became popular during the middle part of the 19th century with the introduction of positivism—the use of the scientific method and empirical analysis to study behaviour. Positivism was discussed in Chapter 1 in the context of the history of criminology.

demonstrated by the readiness with which prisoners submit to the operation of tattooing."[2] Enrico Ferri (1856–1929), another student of Lombroso's, believed that a number of biological and organic factors caused delinquency and crime.[3] However, he also added a social dimension to Lombroso's work and was a pioneer in the view that criminals should not be held personally or morally responsible for their actions, because forces outside their control cause criminality.

Advocates of the inheritance school traced the activities of several generations of families believed to have an especially large number of criminal members. The most famous of these studies involved the study of a "degenerate family" called the Jukes. Richard Dugdale's *The Jukes: A Study in Crime, Pauperism, Disease, and Heredity* (1875) traced the history of the Jukes over 150 years, a family responsible for a disproportionate amount of crime. Dugdale claimed to have proved the existence of hereditary criminality. As he said: "Fornication is the backbone of their habits, flanked on one side by pauperism, on the other by crime. The secondary features are prostitution, with its complement of bastardy, and its resultant neglected and miseducated childhood; exhaustion, with its complement intemperance and its resultant unbalanced minds; and disease with its complement extinction."[4]

A later attempt at criminal anthropology, the body-build or **somatype** school developed by William Sheldon, held that criminals manifest distinct physiques that make them susceptible to particular types of delinquent behaviour. Mesomorphs, for example, have well-developed muscles and an athletic appearance. They are active, aggressive, sometimes violent, and the most likely to become criminals. Endomorphs have heavy builds and are known for lethargic behaviour. Ectomorphs are tall, thin, and less social and more intellectual than the other types.[5]

The work of Lombroso and his contemporaries is regarded today as a historical curiosity, not scientific fact. Their research methodology has been discredited. They did not use control groups from the general population to compare results. Many of the traits they assumed to be inherited are not genetically determined. Many of the biological features they identified could be caused by deprivation in surroundings and diet. Even if most criminals shared certain biological traits, these traits might be products not of heredity but of some environmental condition, such as poor nutrition or health care. It is equally likely that only criminals who suffer from biological abnormality are caught and punished by the justice system. In his later writings, even Lombroso admitted that the born criminal was just one of many criminal types. Because of these deficiencies, the validity of individual-oriented explanations of criminality became questionable and for a time passed from the criminological mainstream.

Sociobiology. Biological explanations of crime fell out of favour in the early 20th century. During this period, criminologists became concerned about the sociological influences on crime, such as the neighbourhood, peer group, family life, and social status. The work of biocriminologists was viewed as methodologically unsound and generally invalid by the sociologists who dominated the field and who held the belief that biological factors were not important when attempting to understand human nature.[6]

But this situation changed. As Pierre van den Bergle put it in 1974:

> What seems no longer tenable at this juncture is any theory of human behaviour which ignores biology and relies exclusively on sociocultural learning.... Most social scientists have been wrong in their dogmatic rejection and blissful ignorance of the biological parameters of our behaviour.[7]

In the early 1970s, spurred by the publication of *Sociobiology* by Edmund O. Wilson, the biological basis for crime once again emerged into the limelight.[8] **Sociobiology** differs from earlier theories of behaviour in that it stresses that biological and genetic conditions affect the perception and learning of social behaviours, which in turn are linked to existing environmental structures. Sociobiologists view the gene as the ultimate unit of life that controls all human destiny. While the environment and experience do have an impact on behaviour, most actions are controlled by a person's "biological machine." Most important, sociobiology holds that people are controlled by the innate need to have their genetic material survive and dominate others. Consequently, they do everything in their power to ensure their own survival and that of others who share their gene pool (relatives, fellow citizens, and so forth). Even when they are altruistic and come to the aid of others, people are motivated by the belief that their actions will be reciprocated and that their gene survival capability will be enhanced.

Sociobiologists view biology, environment, and learning as mutually interdependent factors. Problems in one area can be altered by efforts in another. For example, people suffering from learning disorders can be given special tutoring to improve their reading skills. In this view, then, people are biosocial organisms whose personalities and behaviours are influenced by physical as well as environmental conditions.

| Exhibit 6.1 | Sheldon's Somatypes |

In the 1940s, an American psychologist named William Sheldon proposed the idea that body types were associated with personality characteristics. After studying 4000 photographs of college-age men, he drew some connections between body type and temperament. Specifically, he said there were three categories of human bodies: the endomorph, characterized by a preponderance of body fat; the mesomorph, characterized by a well-developed musculature; and the ectomorph, who had neither much muscle tissue nor body fat. He said that ectomorphic people tend to be quiet and reflective; mesomorphs are energetic; and endomorphic people are magnanimous and love to eat. Those three broad categories of body types, or "somatypes," play a minor role in modern psychology and criminology, but are still used in bodybuilding today. In Sheldon's words, "the somatype is intended as a kind of identification tag . . . a rather crude tool fashioned to reflect a basic

structural orderliness which can be perceived in human life." For example, consider the following:

Somatype 117 – Walking Sticks – Fragile stretched-out creatures with the utmost surface exposure in proportion to mass. . . . This extremely rare somatype (incidence 2 per ten thousand), with his extreme predominance of surface over mass, seems caught in a predicament of biological overexposure, and for such an organism the ordinary circumstances of social life may amount to chronic overstimulation. Hebephrenic psychopathy may be one natural response to such a situation. The 117 is more common in the mental hospitals than in the general population, and his diagnosis is usually hebephrenic schizophrenia. But also he is encountered more frequently on college campuses than in the general population, and there the diagnosis is sometimes Phi Beta Kappa.

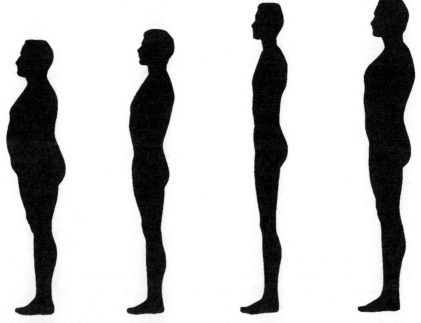

From left to right: endomorph, mesomorph, ectomorph, normal

Source: William Sheldon, *Atlas of Men. A Guide for Somatyping the Adult Male at All Ages* (New York: Harper and Brothers, 1954).

Although sociobiology has been criticized as methodologically unsound and socially dangerous, it has had a tremendous effect on reviving interest in finding a basis for crime and delinquency, because if biological (genetic) makeup controls human behaviour, it follows that it should also be responsible for determining whether a person chooses law-violating or conventional behaviour.

Modern Biological Theories. The influence of sociobiology helped revive interest in the biological basis of crime. Rather than view the criminal as a person whose behaviour is controlled by biological conditions determined at birth, modern biological trait theorists believe that physical, environmental, and social conditions work in concert to produce human behaviour. They assume that environmental forces can either "trigger" antisocial behaviour in people biologically predisposed to deviance, or conversely, if conditions are right, help mediate or offset the effects of biological predisposition.

Biological trait theory has several core principles.[9] First, it assumes that genetic makeup contributes significantly to human behaviour. Not all humans are born with equal potential to learn and achieve (**equipotentiality**). Whereas sociologically oriented criminologists say that all people are born equal and that thereafter their behaviour is controlled by social forces (parents, schools, neighbourhoods, friends), biosocial theorists argue that no two people are alike (with rare exceptions, such as identical twins) and that the combination of human genetic traits and the environment produces individual behaviour patterns.

Another critical focus of modern biological theory is the importance of brain functioning, mental processes, and learning. Social behaviour, including criminal behaviour, is learned. Each individual organism is believed to have a unique potential for learning. The physical and social environments interact to either limit or enhance an organism's capacity for learning. However, people learn through a process involving the brain and central nervous system, and learning is not controlled by social interactions but by biochemistry and cellular interaction. Learning can take place only when physical changes occur in the brain. There is a significant link, therefore, between behaviour patterns and physical or chemical changes that occur in the brain and nervous system.[10]

Some, but not all, biosocial theorists also believe that learning is influenced by instinctual drives. Developed over the course of human history, **instincts** are inherited, natural, and unlearned dispositions that activate specific behaviour patterns designed to reach certain goals. For example, people are believed to have a drive to "possess and control" other people and things; thus, some theft offences may be motivated by the instinctual need to possess goods and commodities. Rape and other sex crimes may be linked to the primitive instinctual drive males have to "possess and control" females.[11] However, such a theory shouldn't be taken as legitimating rape as natural.

The following subsections examine some of the more important subbranches or schools of thought within biological criminology (see Figure 6.1 for an overview).[12] First we will review the biochemical factors believed to affect the learning of proper behaviour patterns. Then we'll consider the relationship of brain function and crime, and we'll analyze current ideas about the association between genetic factors and crime. Finally, we will evaluate evolutionary views of crime causation.

Biochemical Conditions and Crime

Some trait theorists believe that biochemical conditions, including both those that are genetically predetermined and those acquired through diet and environment, con-trol and influence antisocial behaviour. This view of crime received national attention in 1979 when Dan White, the confessed killer of San Francisco mayor George Moscone and city councilman Harvey Milk, claimed his behaviour was precipitated by an addiction to sugar-laden junk foods.[13] Milk was the first openly gay councillor of San Francisco and was responsible for the city's first gay rights ordinance. White, a former police officer also on the city council, opposed Milk's political reforms. When White's "Twinkie defence" was supported by psychiatric evidence of hypoglycemia, the jury found him guilty of the lesser offence of diminished capacity manslaughter rather than first-degree murder. (White committed suicide after serving his prison sentence.)

Some of the more important biochemical factors that have been linked to criminality range from nutrition to hormones.

Nutritional Deficiencies. Biocriminologists maintain that minimum levels of vitamins and minerals are needed for normal brain functioning and growth, especially in the early years of life. If people with normal needs do not receive the appropriate nutrition, they will suffer from vitamin deficiency. If people have genetic conditions that cause greater-than-normal needs for certain vitamins and minerals, they are said to suffer from vitamin dependency. People with vitamin deficiency or dependency can manifest many physical, mental, and behavioural problems, including lower intelligence test scores.[14] Alcoholics often suffer from thiamine deficiency because of their poor diets and consequently are susceptible to the serious, often fatal Korsakoff's disease.[15]

Research conducted over the past decade shows that the dietary inadequacy of certain chemicals and minerals, including sodium, potassium, calcium, amino acids, monoamines, and peptides, can lead to depression, mania, cognitive problems, memory loss, and abnormal sexual activity.[16] Research studies examining the relationship between crime and vitamin deficiency and dependency have seemed to find a close link between antisocial behaviour and insufficient quantities of some B vitamins (B_3 and B_6) and vitamin C. In addition, studies have purported to show that a major proportion of all schizophrenics and children with learning and behaviour disorders are dependent on vitamins B_3 and B_6.

Sugar and Crime. Another suspected nutritional influence on behaviour is a diet especially high in carbohydrates and sugar.[17] For example, some recent research found that the way the brain processed glucose was related to scores on tests measuring reasoning power.[18] In addition, sugar intake levels have been associated with attention span deficiencies.

Diets high in sugar and carbohydrates have also been linked to violence and aggression. Stephen Schoenthaler conducted an experiment with 276 incarcerated youths to determine whether a change in the amount of sugar in their diet would have a corresponding

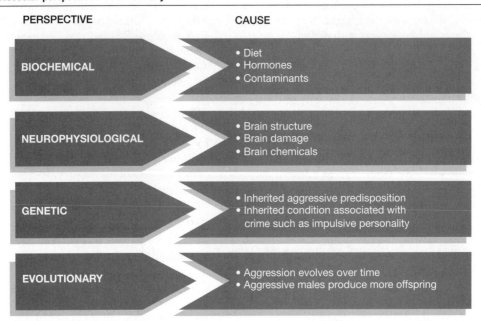

Figure 6.1 **Biosocial perspectives on criminality**

influence on their behaviour within the institutional setting.[19] In the experiment, several dietary changes were made: Sweet drinks were replaced with fruit juices, table sugar was replaced with honey, breakfast cereals high in sugar were eliminated, molasses was substituted for sugar in cooking, and so on. Schoenthaler found that these changes produced a significant reduction in disciplinary actions within the institution; the number of assaults, thefts, fights, and incidents of disobedience within the institution declined about 45 percent. It is important to note that these results were consistent when such factors as age, previous offence record, and race of the offender were considered.

These are but a few of the research efforts linking sugar intake to emotional, cognitive, and behavioural performance. While these results are impressive, a number of biologists have questioned this association, and some recent research efforts have failed to find a link between sugar consumption and violence.[20] In one important study, a group of researchers had 25 preschool children and 23 school-age children described as sensitive to sugar follow a different diet for three consecutive three-week periods. One diet was high in sucrose, the second substituted aspartame (Nutrasweet) as a sweetener, and the third relied on saccharin. Careful measurement of the subjects found little evidence of cognitive or behavioural differences that could be linked to diet. If anything, sugar seemed to have a calming effect on the children.[21]

In sum, while some research efforts allege a sugar–violence association, others suggest that many people who maintain diets high in sugar and carbohydrates are not violent or crime-prone and that in some cases sugar intake may actually reduce or curtail violent tendencies.[22]

Hypoglycemia. Hypoglycemia is a condition that occurs when glucose (sugar) in the blood falls below levels necessary for normal and efficient brain functioning. The brain is sensitive to the lack of blood sugar because it is the only organ that obtains its energy solely from the combustion of carbohydrates. Thus, when the brain is deprived of blood sugar, it has no alternative food supply to call on, and its metabolism slows down, impairing its function. Symptoms of hypoglycemia include irritability, anxiety, depression, crying spells, fatigue, insomnia, nervousness, mood swings, phobias, temper outbursts, headaches, and confusion.

Studies have linked hypoglycemia to outbursts of antisocial behaviour and violence. As early as 1943, D. Hill and W. Sargent linked murder to hypoglycemia, while other studies have related assaults and fatal sexual offences to hypoglycemic reactions.[23] Hypoglycemia has also been connected with a syndrome characterized by aggressive and assaultive behaviour, glucose disturbance, and brain dysfunction. Studies of jail and prison inmate populations have found a higher than normal level of hypoglycemia, and high levels of reactive hypoglycemia have been found in groups of habitually violent and impulsive offenders.[24]

Hormonal Influences. Criminologist James Q. Wilson, in his 1993 book *The Moral Sense,* concludes that hormones, enzymes, and neurotransmitters may be the key to understanding human behaviour. These chemicals help explain gender differences in the crime rate. Wilson writes that males are biologically and naturally more aggressive than females, while women are more nurturing of the young and more important for survival of the species.[25] Hormone levels also help explain the aging-out process: Levels of the principal male steroid hormone decline during the life cycle, which may explain why violence rates diminish over time.[26]

A number of biosocial theorists are now evaluating the association between violent behaviour episodes and hormone levels, and the findings suggest that abnormal levels of male sex hormones (**androgens**) do in fact produce aggressive behaviour.[27] A growing body of evidence suggests that hormonal changes are related to mood and behaviour and, concomitantly, that adolescents experience more intense mood swings, anxiety, and restlessness than their elders.[28] An association between hormonal activity and antisocial behaviour is suggested because rates of both factors peak in adolescence.

One area of concern has been **testosterone**, the most abundant androgen, which controls secondary sex characteristics, such as facial hair and voice timbre. Research conducted on both human and animal subjects has found that prenatal exposure to unnaturally high levels of androgens permanently alters behaviour. Girls who were unintentionally exposed to elevated amounts of androgens during their fetal development display an unusually high long-term tendency toward aggression; boys prenatally exposed to steroids that decrease androgen levels displayed decreased aggressiveness.[29] In contrast, samples of inmates indicate that testosterone levels are higher in men who committed violent crimes than in the other prisoners.[30] In 2001 the science journal *Nature* reported on a study showing that fish that watched two other males attack each other had higher levels of testosterone than fish that didn't watch the fighting. This shows that the body's biology both reacts to social behaviour and influences individual behaviour. The behaviour of people, of course, is much more influenced by culture and experience.[31]

How do hormone levels influence violent behaviours? Hormones cause areas of the brain to become less sensitive to environmental stimuli. Males, who possess high androgen levels, are more likely than females to need excess stimulation and to be willing to tolerate pain in their quest for thrills. Androgens are linked to brain seizures that, under stressful conditions, can result in emotional volatility. Androgens affect the brain structure itself, influencing the left hemisphere of the neocortex, the part of the brain that controls sympathetic feelings toward others. Some other physical reactions produced by hormones that have been linked to violence include the need to seek unusually high levels of environmental stimulation, impulsive emotional responses to stressful environmental encounters, and a rightward shift in neocortical functioning, which is less prone to reason or to respond to linguistic commands.[32]

Although some studies have been unable to demonstrate hormonal differences in samples of violent and nonviolent offenders, drugs that decrease testosterone levels are now being used to treat male sex offenders.[33] The female hormones estrogen and progesterone have been administered to sex offenders to decrease their sexual potency.[34] The long-term side effects of this treatment and their potential danger are still unknown. A problem with sex offenders is that most will have substance-abuse disorders, antisocial personality disorders, mood disorders, or psychological problems. The identification of the problem, then, is not a simple one.

Premenstrual Syndrome (PMS). Hormonal research has not been limited to male offenders. The suspicion has long existed that the onset of the menstrual cycle triggers excessive amounts of the female sex hormones, affecting antisocial, aggressive behaviour. During the 19th century "disordered menstruation" was often introduced as a factor in defending women on serious charges such as arson or homicide. Today this condition is commonly referred to as **premenstrual syndrome** (PMS).[35] The link between PMS and delinquency was first popularized by Katharina Dalton, whose studies of English women indicated that females are more likely to commit suicide and be aggressive and otherwise antisocial just before or during menstruation.[36] While the Dalton research is often cited as evidence of the link between PMS and crime, methodological problems make it impossible to accept her findings at face value, especially since the syndrome has been defined with up to 150 disparate symptoms.

Debate continues over any link between PMS and aggression. Some doubters, such as criminologist Julie Horney, argue that it is equally likely that the psychological and physical stress of aggression brings on menstruation and not vice versa.[37] In contrast, Diana Fishbein, a noted expert on biosocial theory, concludes that an association does in fact exist between elevated levels of female aggression and menstruation. Research efforts, she argues, show that (1) a significant number of incarcerated females committed their crimes during the premenstrual phase, and (2) at least a small percentage of women appear vulnerable to cyclical hormonal changes that make them more prone to anxiety and hostility.[38]

Only a few criminal trials in Canada, Britain, and the United States have successfully used PMS as a mitigating factor in a woman's defence and usually result in the defendant being required to receive hormone injections as a condition of the sentence.[39]

While the debate is ongoing, it is important to remember that the overwhelming majority of females who suffer anxiety and hostility prior to and during menstruation do not actually engage in violent criminal behaviour, so any link between PMS and crime is tenuous at best.[40]

Another mental disorder which is felt to be typically female is Munchausen's Syndrome by Proxy (MSBP), in which the mother either induces or fabricates illness in a child in order to achieve repeat contact with the health care system. The syndrome was identified in the late

Crime in the News

Woman's Syndrome Brings Leniency

Canadian Press – *Vancouver Sun*, February 10, 1987

London, Ont. – A woman who stabbed her husband in the back last year while suffering from premenstrual syndrome was placed on probation Monday because she couldn't get proper treatment in a correctional institution.

District Court Judge Joseph Winter suspended sentencing Marsali Edwards, 29, for three years.

"For what I am about to do, I am of course going to be severely criticized," Judge Winter said before passing sentence.

But he warned that his decision should not be viewed as a license for other women to repeat Edwards's actions.

Winter also ordered her to report regularly to a probation officer and to undergo treatment by a "competent, appropriate, knowledgeable medical practitioner other than a psychiatrist."

The case establishes a precedent in Canadian law for the use of premenstrual syndrome as a mitigating factor in sentencing people charged with violent crimes.

The disorder, which experts say affects 20 to 40 percent of women, has been blamed for a wide range of symptoms, including hostility, anxiety and depression to food cravings, acne and changes in hair texture.

It has been used in a few cases in the United States to win acquittals.

Winter stressed his sentence was also based on Edwards's background, which he described as "very unfortunate."

During a four-day trial last December, court was told Edwards was adopted at the age of three after being abused by her natural parents. During her adolescence, she ran away to marry a high school teacher who was three times her age.

The marriage lasted six months, after which she began living with Brian Edwards, 41.

Edwards, who later married her, was described as a "wife-beating drunk" by Winter, who said the man's alcohol problem was so severe that it caused him to be discharged from the Canadian Forces. That marriage also broke down, court was told.

1970s; however, there is little consensus as to what type of disorder it is.

Allergies. Allergies are defined as unusual or excessive reactions of the body to foreign substances.[41] For example, hay fever is an allergic reaction caused when pollen cells enter the body and are fought or neutralized by the body's natural defences. The result of the battle is itching, red eyes, and active sinuses.

Cerebral allergies cause an excessive reaction of the brain, whereas neuroallergies affect the nervous system. Cerebral allergies and neuroallergies are believed to cause the allergic person to produce enzymes that attack wholesome foods as if they were dangerous to the body. They may also cause swelling of the brain and produce sensitivity in the central nervous system, conditions linked to mental, emotional, and behavioural problems. Research indicates a connection between these allergies and hyperemotionality, depression, aggressiveness, and violent behaviour.[42]

Neuroallergy and cerebral allergy problems have also been linked to hyperactivity in children, which may portend antisocial behaviour and the labelling of children as potential delinquents. The foods most commonly involved in producing such allergies are cow's milk, wheat, corn, chocolate, citrus, and eggs; however, about 300 other foods have been identified as allergens. The potential seriousness of the problem has been raised by studies linking the average consumption of one suspected cerebral allergen—corn—to cross-national homicide rates.[43]

Environmental Contaminants. Dangerous quantities of copper, cadmium, mercury, and inorganic gases, such as chlorine and nitrogen dioxide, can now be found in the ecosystem. Research indicates that these environmental contaminants can influence behaviour. At high levels, these substances can cause severe illness or death; at more moderate levels, they have been linked to emotional and behavioural disorders.[44] Some studies have linked the ingestion of food dyes and artificial colours and flavours to hostile, impulsive, and otherwise antisocial behaviour in youths.[45] Lighting may be another important environmental influence on antisocial behaviour. Research projects have suggested that radiation from artificial light sources, such as fluorescent tubes and television sets, may produce antisocial, aggressive behaviour.[46]

A number of recent research studies have also linked lead to problem behaviours. Ingestion of lead may help explain why hyperactive children manifest conduct problems and antisocial behaviour.[47] Deborah Denno looked at the behaviour of more than 900 African American youths and found that lead poisoning was one of the most significant predictors of male delinquency and persistent adult criminality. Herbert Needleman and his associates tracked 300 boys from ages 7 to 11 and found that those who had high lead concentrations in their bones were much more likely to report attention problems, delinquency, aggressiveness, and poor language skills.[48] High lead ingestion is also related to lower IQ scores, a factor linked to aggressive behaviour.[49] Lead has also been linked to attention deficit disorder. In a presentation to a conference on pediatric medicine in 2000, Needleman reported research on 216 youths convicted in a juvenile court. The delinquent youths had higher levels of lead in their bones than in the control group. He said that elevated lead levels can lead to antisocial activities like bullying, vandalism, truancy, and shoplifting.

Neurophysiological Conditions and Crime

Some criminologists focus their attention on **neurophysiology**, or the study of brain activity. They believe that neurological and physical abnormalities are acquired as early as the fetal or perinatal stage or through birth delivery trauma and then control behaviour throughout the life span.[50]

The relationship between neurological dysfunction and crime first received a great deal of attention in 1968, when Charles Whitman, after killing his wife and his mother, barricaded himself in a tower at the University of Texas with a high-powered rifle and proceeded to kill 14 people and wound 24 others before he was killed by police. An autopsy revealed that Whitman suffered from a malignant brain tumour. Whitman had previously experienced uncontrollable urges to kill and had gone to a psychiatrist seeking help for his problems. He kept careful notes documenting his feelings and his inability to control his homicidal urges, and he left instructions for his estate to be given to a mental health foundation so it could study mental problems such as his own.[51]

Since the Whitman case, a great deal of attention has focused on the association between neurological impairment and crime. Various studies have indicated a relationship between impairment in brain functions (abstract reasoning, problem-solving skills, motor behaviour skills) and aggressive behaviour.[52]

Neurological Impairments and Crime. There are numerous ways to measure neurological functioning, including visual awareness tests, short-term auditory memory tests, and verbal IQ tests. These tests have been found to distinguish criminal offenders from noncriminal control groups.[53]

Probably the most important measure of neurophysiological functioning is the **electroencephalograph**. An EEG records the electrical impulses given off by the brain, commonly called brain waves, which can be recorded by electrodes placed on the scalp.[54] The frequency is given in cycles per second, measured in hertz (Hz), and usually ranges from 0.5 to 30 Hz.

In what is considered the most significant investigation of EEG abnormality and crime, a randomly selected group of 335 violent delinquents was divided into those who were habitually violent and those who had committed only a single violent act. While 65 percent of the habitually aggressive had abnormal EEG recordings, only 24 percent of the one-time offenders had recordings that deviated from the norm. When the records of individuals who had brain damage, were mentally retarded, or were epileptic were removed from the sample, the percentage of abnormality among boys who had committed a solitary violent crime was the same as that of the general population, about 12 percent. However, the habitually aggressive subjects showed a 57 percent abnormality.

Other research efforts have linked abnormal EEG recordings to antisocial behaviour in children. Although 5 to 15 percent of the general population have abnormal EEG readings, 50 to 60 percent of adolescents with known behaviour disorders display abnormal recordings.[55] Behaviours highly correlated with an abnormal EEG included poor impulse control, inadequate social adaptation, hostility, temper tantrums, and destructiveness.[56]

Studies of adults have associated slow and bilateral brain waves with hostile, hypercritical, irritable, nonconforming, and impulsive behaviour.[57] Psychiatric patients with EEG abnormalities have been reported to be highly combative and to suffer episodes of rage. Studies of murderers have shown that a disproportionate number manifest abnormal EEG recordings.[58] EEG analysis, then, shows that measures of brain activity are significantly associated with antisocial behaviour.

Minimal Brain Dysfunction. Minimal brain dysfunction (MBD) is related to an abnormality in cerebral structure. It is sometimes simply maladaptive behaviour that interrupts the lifestyle of an individual. However, in its most serious form, MBD has been linked to serious antisocial acts, an imbalance in the urge-control mechanisms of the brain, and chemical abnormality. The category of minimal brain dysfunction includes several abnormal behaviour patterns, such as dyslexia, visual perception problems, hyperactivity, poor attention span, temper tantrums, and aggressiveness. One type of minimal brain dysfunction is manifested through episodic periods of explosive rage. This form of the disorder is considered an important cause of such behaviour as spouse beating, child abuse, suicide, aggressiveness, and motiveless homicide. One perplexing feature of this syndrome is that people who are afflicted with it often maintain warm and pleasant personalities between episodes of violence.

Some studies measuring the presence of minimal brain dysfunction in offender populations have found that up to 60 percent exhibit brain dysfunction on psychological tests.[59] Criminals have been characterized as having dysfunction of the dominant hemisphere of the brain.[60] Researchers using brain wave data have predicted with 95 percent accuracy the recidivism of violent criminals.[61]

Attention Deficit/Hyperactivity Disorder. Many parents have noticed that their children do not pay attention to them—they run around and do things in their own way. Sometimes this inattention is a function of age; in other instances, it is a symptom of **attention deficit/ hyperactivity disorder** (AD/HD), in which a child shows a developmentally inappropriate lack of attention, impulsivity, and hyperactivity. The various symptoms of AD/HD are described in Table 6.1.

Between 3 and 5 percent of children, most often boys, are believed to suffer from this disorder, and it is the most common reason children are referred to mental health clinics. The condition has been associated with poor school performance, grade retention, placement in special needs classes, bullying, stubbornness, and lack of response to discipline.[62] These behaviour problems are sometimes misdiagnosed as AD/HD. Although the origins of AD/HD are still unknown, suspected causes include neurological damage, prenatal stress, and even food additives and chemical allergies; recent research has suggested a genetic link.

A series of research studies now link AD/HD, minimal brain dysfunctions (such as poor motor function), hyperactivity, and below-average written and verbal cognitive ability to the onset and sustenance of a delinquent career. Research suggests that youths who suffer both AD/HD and MBD and grow up in a dysfunctional family are the ones most vulnerable to chronic and persistent delinquency.[63] Others have found that the relationship between chronic delinquency and attention disorders may be mediated by school failure: Kids who are poor readers are the most prone to antisocial behaviour; many poor readers also have attention problems.[64]

This AD/HD–crime association is important because symptoms of AD/HD seem stable through adolescence into adulthood.[65] Early diagnosis and treatment of children suffering AD/HD may enhance their life chances. Today, the most typical treatment is doses of stimulants, such as Ritalin and Dexedrine, which help control emotional and behavioural outbursts.

Other Brain Dysfunctions. Other brain dysfunctions have been related to violent crime. Persistent criminality has been linked to dysfunction in the frontal and temporal regions of the brain, since they are believed to play an important role in the regulation and inhibition of human behaviour, including the formation of plans and intentions, and in the regulation of complex behaviours.[66] Brain lesions that occur at specific points of the neurological system, such as the auditory system, can have permanent effects on behaviour, and clinical evaluation of depressed and aggressive psychopathic subjects showed a significant number (more than 75 percent) had dysfunction of the temporal and frontal regions of the brain.[67]

Table 6.1	Symptoms of attention deficit/hyperactivity disorder

LACK OF ATTENTION

Frequently fails to finish projects

Does not seem to pay attention

Does not sustain interest in play activities

Cannot sustain concentration on schoolwork or related tasks

Is easily distracted

IMPULSIVITY

Frequently acts without thinking

Often "calls out" in class

Does not want to wait his or her turn in lines or games

Shifts from activity to activity

Cannot organize tasks or work

Requires constant supervision

HYPERACTIVITY

Constantly runs around and climbs on things

Shows excessive motor activity while asleep

Cannot sit still; is constantly fidgeting

Does not remain in his or her seat in class

Is constantly on the go like a "motor"

Source: Adapted from American Psychiatric Association, *Diagnostic and Statistical Manual of Mental Disorders*, 4th ed. (Washington, DC: American Psychiatric Press, 1994); also online at http://web.cs.mun.ca/~jamie/dsm4.html.

Tumours, Injury, and Disease. The presence of brain tumours has also been linked to a wide variety of psychological problems, including personality changes, hallucinations, and psychotic episodes. There is evidence that people with tumours are prone to depression, irritability, temper outbursts, and even homicidal attacks (as in the Whitman case). Clinical case studies of patients suffering from brain tumours indicate that previously docile people may undergo behaviour changes so great that they attempt to seriously harm their families and friends; when the tumour is removed, their behaviour returns to normal.[68] In addition to brain tumours, head injuries caused by accidents, such as falls or auto crashes, have been linked to personality reversals marked by outbursts of antisocial and violent behaviour.[69] Brain scans can show the presence of underlying trauma.

A variety of central nervous system diseases, including cerebral arteriosclerosis, epilepsy, senile dementia, Korsakoff's syndrome, and Huntington's chorea, have also been associated with memory deficiency, orientation loss, and affective (emotional) disturbances dominated by rage, anger, and increased irritability.[70]

Brain Chemistry and Crime. Neurotransmitters are chemical compounds that influence or activate brain functions. Those studied in relation to aggression include androgens, dopamine, norepinephrine, serotonin, monoamine oxidase, and GABA. Evidence exists that abnormal levels of these chemicals are sometimes associated with aggression. For example, several researchers have reported inverse correlations between serotonin concentrates in the blood and impulsive or suicidal behaviour. What this means is that people with histories of impulsive violence usually have a reduction in the function of the serotonin system. Recent studies of habitually violent Finnish criminals show that low serotonin levels are associated with poor impulse control and hyperactivity. Low levels of certain chemicals in the brain are also linked with increased irritability, sensation seeking, and depression.[71] Prozac, which is commonly prescribed for depression, is a serotonin enhancer.

Biocriminologist Lee Ellis has found that prenatal exposure of the brain to high levels of androgens can result in a brain structure that is less sensitive to environmental inputs. Affected individuals seek more intense and varied stimulation and are willing to tolerate more adverse consequences than individuals not so affected.[72] Such exposure also results in a rightward shift in brain functioning and a lessening of cognitive and emotional tendencies. This is similar to the hormonal research discussed above. It should not be surprising then that left-handers are disproportionately represented in the criminal population, since the movement of each hand tends to be controlled by the hemisphere of the brain on the opposite side of the body.

In another analysis, Ellis found that individuals with a low supply of the enzyme monoamine oxidase (MAO) engage in behaviours linked with violence and property crime, including defiance of punishment, impulsivity, hyperactivity, poor academic performance, sensation seeking and risk taking, and recreational drug use. Abnormal levels of MAO may explain both individual and group differences in the crime rate. For example, Ellis found that females have higher levels of MAO than males, a condition that may explain gender differences in the crime rate.[73]

Because this linkage has been found, it is not uncommon for violence-prone people to be treated with antipsychotic drugs that help control levels of neurotransmitters; these treatments are sometimes referred to as "chemical restraints" or "chemical straightjackets."

The brain and neurological system can also produce natural opiates, which are chemically similar to the narcotics opium and morphine. Perhaps the risk and thrills involved in crime cause the brain to produce increased amounts of these natural narcotics. The result is an elevated mood state, perceived as an exciting and rewarding experience that acts as a positive reinforcer to crime.[74] The brain then produces its own natural "high" as a reward for risk-taking behaviour. While some people achieve this high by rock climbing and skydiving, others engage in crimes of violence.

Arousal Theory. It has long been suspected that obtaining thrills is a motivator of crime. Adolescents may engage in such crimes as shoplifting and vandalism simply because they offer the attraction of "getting away with it"; delinquency is a thrilling demonstration of personal competence.[75] Is it possible that thrill seekers are people who have some form of abnormal brain functioning that directs their behaviour?

According to **arousal theory**, for a variety of genetic and environmental reasons, some people's brains function differently in response to environmental stimuli. People seek to maintain a preferred or optimal level of arousal. Too much stimulation leaves them anxious and stressed out; too little makes them feel bored and weary. There is, however, variation in the way people's brains process sensory input. Some nearly always feel comfortable with little stimulation, while others require a high degree of environmental input to feel comfortable. The latter group become "sensation seekers" who seek out stimulating activities, which may include aggressive, violent behaviour patterns.[76]

The factors that determine a person's optimal level of arousal are not fully determined. Suspected sources include brain chemistry (serotonin levels) and brain structure. For instance, some people have brains with many more nerve cells with receptor sites for neurotransmitters than others.

Connections

Jack Katz has written on the seductions of crime. Perhaps some people may be "seduced" into crime because the experience produces the "natural high" they crave. Katz's work is discussed in Chapter 5.

Genetics and Crime

Early biological theorists believed that criminality ran in families. Though research on deviant families, such as the Jukes and Kallikaks, is not taken seriously today, modern biosocial theorists are still interested in genetics. If some human behaviours are influenced by heredity, why not antisocial tendencies? Evidence exists that animals can be bred to have aggressive traits. Pit bulldogs, fighting bulls, and fighting cocks have been selectively mated to produce superior predators. Of course, no similar data are available for people, but a growing body of research is focusing on the genetic factors associated with human behaviour.[77] There is evidence, for example, that some personality traits, including extraversion, openness, agreeableness, and conscientiousness, are genetically determined.[78] There are also data suggesting that human traits associated with criminality have a genetic basis.[79] Personality conditions linked to aggression—such as psychopathy, impulsivity, and neuroticism—and psychopathology, such as schizophrenia, may be heritable.[80]

This line of reasoning was cast in the spotlight when Richard Speck, the convicted killer of eight nurses in Chicago, was said to have inherited an abnormal XYY chromosomal structure (XY is the normal sex chromosome pattern in males). There was much public concern that all XYYs were potential killers and should be closely controlled. Civil libertarians expressed fear that all XYYs could be labelled dangerous and violent regardless of whether they had engaged in violent activities.[81] When it was disclosed that neither Speck nor most violent offenders actually had an extra Y chromosome, interest in the XYY theory dissipated. However, the Speck case drew researchers' attention to looking for a genetic basis of criminal behaviour.

Is it possible that the tendency for crime and aggression is inherited? Since the Speck case, numerous researchers have carefully explored the heritability of criminal tendencies using a variety of techniques. The most commonly used approaches are twin studies and adoption studies.

Twin Studies. If, in fact, inherited traits cause criminal behaviours, twins should be quite similar in their antisocial activities. However, since twins are usually brought up in the same household and are exposed to the same set of social conditions, determining whether their behaviour was a result of biological, sociological, or psychological conditions would be difficult. Trait theorists have tried to overcome this dilemma by comparing identical, monozygotic (MZ) twins with fraternal, dizygotic (DZ) twins of the same sex. MZ twins are genetically identical, while DZ twins have only half their genes in common. If heredity does determine criminal behaviour, the MZ twins should be much more similar in their antisocial activities than the DZ twins.

The earliest studies conducted on the behaviour of twins detected a significant relationship between the criminal activities of MZ twins and a much lower association between those of DZ twins. A review of relevant studies conducted between 1929 and 1961 found that 60 percent of MZ twins shared criminal behaviour patterns (if one twin was criminal, so was the other), while only 30 percent of DZ twins were similarly related. These findings may be viewed as powerful evidence for a genetic

basis to criminality. More recent studies have supported these findings. Karl Christiansen studied 3586 male twin pairs and found a 52 percent similarity for MZ pairs and only 22 percent for DZ pairs. This result suggests that the MZ twins may share a genetic characteristic that increases the risk of their engaging in criminality.[82] Similarly, David Rowe and D. Wayne Osgood have analyzed the factors that influence self-reported delinquency in a sample of twin pairs and concluded that genetic influences actually have significant explanatory power.[83] Genetic effects have been found to be a significant predictor of problem behaviours in children as young as three years old.[84] While the behaviour of some twin pairs seems to be influenced by their environment, others displayed behaviour disturbances that could only be explained by their genetic similarity.[85]

The controversy over the heritability of crime still rages. On the one hand, opponents suggest that available evidence provides little conclusive proof that crime is genetically predetermined. Not all research efforts have found that MZ twin pairs are more closely related in their criminal behaviour than DZ or ordinary sibling pairs, and some have found only a small association.[86] On the other hand, one of the leading experts in this field, David Rowe, has recently reviewed the available research and concluded that individuals who share genes are alike in personality regardless of how they are reared; in contrast, he concluded, environment induces little or no personality resemblance in twin pairs.[87]

Adoption Studies. If the behaviour of adopted children is more similar to their biological parents than their adoptive parents, the idea of a genetic basis for criminality would be supported. If, on the other hand, adoptees are more similar to their adoptive parents than their biological parents, an environmental basis for crime would seem more valid.

Several studies indicate that some relationship may exist between biological parents' behaviour and the behaviour of their children, even when their contact has been infrequent.[88] In what is considered the most significant study in this area, Barry Hutchings and Sarnoff Mednick analyzed 1145 male adoptees born in Copenhagen, Denmark, between 1927 and 1941; of these, 185 had criminal records.[89] After following up on 143 of the criminal adoptees and matching them with a control group of 143 noncriminal adoptees, Hutchings and Mednick found that the criminality of the biological father was a strong predictor of the child's criminal behaviour. When both the biological and the adoptive fathers were criminal, the probability that the youth would engage in criminal behaviour greatly expanded: 25 percent of the boys whose adoptive and biological fathers were criminals had been convicted of a criminal law violation; only 13.5 percent of those whose biological and adoptive fathers were not criminals had similar conviction records.[90]

A more recent analysis of Swedish adoptees also found that genetic factors were highly significant. Boys who had criminal parents were significantly more likely to violate the law, while environmental influences were significantly less important. Nonetheless, having a positive environment, such as being adopted into a more affluent home, helped inhibit genetic predisposition.[91]

Evaluating Genetic Research. The findings of the twin and adoption studies give some tentative support to a genetic basis for criminality. However, those who oppose the genes–crime relationship point to the inadequate research designs and weak methodologies of supporting research. The newer, better-designed research studies, critics charge, provide less support than earlier, less methodologically sound studies.[92]

The genes–crime relationship is quite controversial since it implies that the propensity to commit crime is present at birth and cannot be altered. Rational choice theory would be irrelevant. It also raises moral dilemmas. If in utero genetic testing could detect a gene for violence, should a fetus be aborted? Should those holding a particular genetic makeup be followed and watched as a precautionary measure?

Evolutionary Views of Crime

Recent biosocial research has been on evolutionary factors in criminality.[93] As human beings have evolved, certain traits and characteristics have become ingrained and instinctual. These biosocial characteristics may be responsible for some crime patterns.

Gender differences in the violence rate have been explained by the evolution of mammalian mating patterns. Hypothetically, to ensure survival of the gene pool (and the species), it is beneficial for a male of any species to mate with as many suitable females as possible, as each can bear his offspring. In contrast, because of the long period of gestation, females require a secure home and a single, stable nurturing partner to ensure their survival. Because of these differences in mating patterns, the most aggressive males mate most often and have the greatest number of offspring. Therefore, over the history of the human species, aggressive males have had the greatest impact on the gene pool. The descendants of these aggressive males now account for the disproportionate amount of male aggression and violence.[94]

There are two general evolutionary theories of crime: r/k theory and the "cheater" theory.[95]

R/K Selection Theory. R/k theory holds that all organisms can be located along a continuum based on their reproductive drives. Those along one end reproduce rapidly whenever they can and invest little in their offspring, while those along the other end reproduce slowly and take care in raising their offspring. Males today "lean" toward r-selection, because they can reproduce faster without the need for investment in their offspring; females are k-selected, because they can have fewer offspring but give more care and devotion to them. K-oriented people should be more cooperative and sensitive to others, while r-oriented people should be more cunning and deceptive. Males therefore should be more criminal, and they are. Persons who commit violent crimes seem to exhibit r-selection traits, such as a premature birth, early and frequent sexual activity, neglect as a child, and a short life expectancy.

"Cheater Theory." The second evolutionary model, "cheater theory," suggests that a subpopulation of men has evolved with genes that incline them toward extremely low parental involvement. Sexually aggressive, they use their cunning to gain sexual conquests with as many females as possible. Because females would not willingly choose them as mates, they use stealth to gain sexual access, including such tactics as mimicking the behaviour of more stable males. They use devious and illegal means to acquire resources they need for sexual domination. Their deceptive reproductive tactics spill over into other endeavours, where their talent for irresponsible, opportunistic behaviour supports their antisocial activities. Deception in reproductive strategies is thus linked to a deceitful lifestyle.

Connections

The relationship between evolutionary factors and crime has just begun to be studied. Criminologists are now exploring how social oranizations and institutions interact with biological traits to influence personal decision making, including criminal strategies. See the sections on latent trait theories in Chapter 10 for more on the integration of biological and environmental factors.

Psychologist Byron Roth notes that cheater males may be especially attractive to those younger, less intelligent women who begin having children at an early age. State-sponsored welfare, claims Roth, removes the need for potential mates to have the resources needed to be stable providers and family caretakers. With the state meeting their financial needs, these less intelligent women are attracted to men who are physically attractive and flamboyant. Their fleeting courtship process produces children with low IQ, aggressive personalities, and little chance of proper socialization in father-absent families. Because the criminal justice system treats them leniently, argues Roth, sexually irresponsible men are free to prey on young girls. Over time, their offspring will supply an ever-expanding supply of cheaters who are both antisocial and sexually aggressive.

Evaluation of the Biological Branch of Trait Theory

Biosocial perspectives on crime raise some challenging questions for criminology. They have in turn been challenged by critics, who suggest they are racist and dysfunctional. If biology can explain the cause of street crimes, such as assault, murder, or rape, and if, as the official crime statistics suggest, the poor and minority-group members commit a disproportionate number of such acts, then by implication biological theory says that members of these groups are biologically different, flawed, or inferior.

Connections

Biosocial theory focuses on the violent crimes of the lower classes while ignoring the white-collar crimes of the upper and middle classes. That is, while it may seem logical to believe there is a biological basis to aggression and violence, it is more difficult to explain how insider trading and fraud are biologically related. For the causes of white-collar crime, see Chapter 13.

Biological explanations for the geographic, social, and temporal patterns in the crime rate are also problematic. Is it possible that more people are genetically predisposed to crime in western Canada than in the eastern provinces? Furthermore, biological theory ignores self-reports that indicate that almost everyone has engaged in some type of illegal activity in their lifetime. Crime is more widespread than criminal justice statistics would make it appear.

Biosocial theorists counter that their views are not deterministic. Rather than suggest that there are born criminals and noncriminals, they maintain that some people carry the potential to be violent or antisocial and that environmental conditions can sometimes trigger antisocial responses.[96] This would explain why some otherwise law-abiding citizens engage in a single antisocial act, and why some people with long criminal careers often engage in conventional behaviour. It also explains why geographic and temporal patterns occur in the crime rate: People who are predisposed to crime may simply have more opportunities to commit illegal acts in the summer in Vancouver and Toronto than in the winter in Gander, Newfoundland, and Nelson, British Columbia.

The biosocial view, then, is that behaviour is a product of interacting biological and environmental events.[97] For example, Avshalom Caspi and his associates found that girls who reach physical maturity at an early age are the ones most likely to engage in delinquent acts. This finding might suggest a relationship between biological traits (hormonal activity) and crime. However, the Caspi research found that the association may also have an environmental basis. Physically mature girls are the ones most likely to have prolonged contact with a crime-prone group: older adolescent boys.[98] Here, the combination of biological change, social relationships, and routine opportunities predicts crime rates.

The most significant criticism of biosocial theory has been the lack of adequate empirical testing. In most research efforts, sample sizes are relatively small and nonrepresentative. A great deal of biosocial research is conducted with samples of adjudicated offenders who have been placed in clinical treatment settings. Methodological problems make it impossible to determine whether findings apply only to offenders who have been convicted of crimes and placed in treatment or to the population of criminals as a whole.[99] In short, more research is needed to clarify the relationships proposed by biosocial researchers.

Psychological Trait Theories

The second branch of trait theory focuses on the mental aspects of crime, including the association between intelligence, personality, learning, and criminal behaviour.

In *The English Convict*, Charles Goring (1870–1919) used his "biometric method" to study the characteristics of 3000 English convicts. He found little difference in the physical characteristics of criminals and noncriminals but instead uncovered a significant relationship between crime and a condition he referred to as "defective intelligence." Goring believed that criminal behaviour was inherited and could therefore best be controlled by regulating the reproduction of families exhibiting such traits as "feeblemindedness, epilepsy, insanity, and defective social instinct."[100]

Gabriel Tarde (1843–1904) used a somewhat different psychological approach in his early research: He was the forerunner of modern-day learning theorists.[101] Unlike Goring, who viewed criminals as mentally impaired, Tarde believed people learn from one another through a process of imitation. Tarde proposed three laws of imitation to describe why people engaged in crime: First, individuals in close and intimate contact imitate one another's behaviour. Second, imitation spreads from the top down; consequently, youngsters imitate older individuals, paupers imitate the rich, peasants imitate royalty, and so on. Crime among young, poor, or low-status people is really their effort to imitate wealthy,

Connections

Chapter 1 discussed how some of the early founders of psychiatry tried to develop an understanding of the "criminal mind." Later theories suggested that mental illness and insanity were inherited and that deviants were inherently mentally damaged by reason of their inferior genetic makeup.

Famous Canadian Criminals

Kenneth Parks, Sleepwalker

In the early morning hours of May 24, 1987, 23-year-old Kenneth Parks drove 23 km and attacked his parents-in-law with a kitchen knife as they lay sleeping in their bed. His mother-in-law was killed and his father-in-law seriously injured. Immediately after the incident, he went to the police station and told the police, "I just killed someone with my bare hands. Oh my God, I just killed someone; I've just killed two people; my God, I've just killed two people with my hands; my God, I've just killed two people. My hands; I just killed two people. I killed them; I just killed two people; I've just killed my mother- and father-in-law. I stabbed and beat them to death. It's all my fault."

In a similar case in Arizona in 1999, a man named Scott Falater claimed he was sleepwalking when he stabbed his wife 44 times and pushed her body into the backyard swimming pool. In a police video he says that he is unaware why he is being questioned.

He claimed to have been sleepwalking during the crime. He had always been a deep sleeper and had a great deal of trouble waking up. Several members of his family also suffered from sleep problems such as sleepwalking, adult enuresis, nightmares, and sleeptalking. The year prior to the incident was particularly stressful. He worked ten hours a day as a project coordinator for Revere Electric. In addition, he had lost money betting on horse racing. When he stole $30 000 from his employer, he was dismissed and charged. His personal life suffered from all of this. His parents-in-law, with whom he got on well, were aware of the situation and supported him.

Kenneth Parks was charged with the first degree murder of Barbara Ann Woods and the attempted murder of Denis Woods. At the trial he presented a defence of automatism. The testimony of five expert witnesses called by the defence was not contradicted by the Crown. This evidence was that Parks was sleepwalking and that sleepwalking is not a neurological, psychiatric, or other illness. At issue was whether sleepwalking should be classified as non-insane automatism, which would result in an acquittal, or as a "disease of the mind" (insane automatism), leading to a special verdict of not guilty by reason of insanity. The trial judge presented only the defence of automatism to the jury, who acquitted Parks of first degree murder and then of second degree murder. The judge then acquitted Parks of attempted murder. Two subsequent appeals upheld his acquittal.

However, Scott Falater was not so lucky. He was convicted.

---

older, high-status people (for example, through gambling, drunkenness, accumulation of wealth).

Tarde's third law is the law of insertion: New acts and behaviours are superimposed on old ones and subsequently either reinforce or discourage previous customs. For example, drug taking may be a popular fad among college students who previously used alcohol. However, students may find that a combination of both substances provides even greater stimulation, causing the use of both drugs and alcohol to increase. Or a new criminal custom can develop that eliminates an older one—for example, train robbing has been replaced by truck hijacking. Tarde's ideas are quite similar to those of modern social learning theorists, who believe that both interpersonal and observed behaviour, such as watching a movie or television, can influence criminality.

Since the pioneering work of Tarde and Goring, psychologists, psychiatrists, and other mental health professionals have played an active role in formulating criminological theory. In trying to understand and treat abnormal mental conditions, psychologists have encountered clients whose behaviour falls within categories society has labelled as criminal, deviant, violent, and antisocial.

This section is organized along the lines of the predominant psychological views most closely associated with the cause of criminal behaviour; these perspectives are outlined in Figure 6.2. Some psychologists view antisocial behaviour from a psychoanalytic perspective. Their focus is on early childhood experience and its effect on personality. In contrast, behaviourists stress social learning and behaviour modelling as the keys to criminality. Cognitive theorists analyze human thought and perception and how they affect behaviour. Other psychologists are concerned about the influence of personality or intelligence on behaviour.

Psychodynamic Perspective

Psychodynamic or psychoanalytic psychology was originated by Viennese doctor Sigmund Freud (1856–1939) and has since remained a prominent segment of psychological theory.[102]

According to **psychodynamic theory**, the human mind performs three separate functions. The conscious mind is the aspect of the mind that people are most aware of—everyday thoughts. The preconscious mind contains elements of experiences that are out of awareness but can be

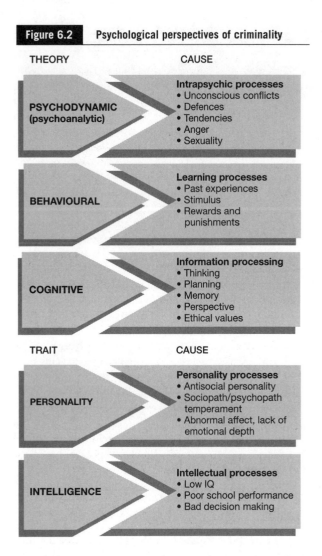

Figure 6.2   Psychological perspectives of criminality

THEORY / CAUSE

PSYCHODYNAMIC (psychoanalytic) — **Intrapsychic processes**
- Unconscious conflicts
- Defences
- Tendencies
- Anger
- Sexuality

BEHAVIOURAL — **Learning processes**
- Past experiences
- Stimulus
- Rewards and punishments

COGNITIVE — **Information processing**
- Thinking
- Planning
- Memory
- Perspective
- Ethical values

TRAIT / CAUSE

PERSONALITY — **Personality processes**
- Antisocial personality
- Sociopath/psychopath temperament
- Abnormal affect, lack of emotional depth

INTELLIGENCE — **Intellectual processes**
- Low IQ
- Poor school performance
- Bad decision making

brought back to consciousness at any time—memories, experiences. The unconscious part of the mind contains biological desires and urges that cannot readily be experienced as thoughts. Part of the unconscious contains feelings about sex and hostility, which people keep below the surface of consciousness by a process called **repression**.

Psychodynamic theory also holds that the human personality contains a three-part structure. The id, the primitive part of people's mental makeup, is present at birth; it represents unconscious biological drives for sex, food, and other life-sustaining necessities. The id follows the pleasure principle: It requires instant gratification without concern for the rights of others. The ego develops early in life, when a child begins to learn that its wishes cannot be instantly gratified. The ego is that part of the personality that compensates for the demands of the id by helping the individual guide his or her actions to remain within the boundaries of social convention. The ego is guided by what is practical by societal standards. The superego develops as a result of incorporating within the personality the moral standards and values of par-

ents, community, and significant others. It is the moral aspect of people's personalities; it passes judgments on their behaviour.

Human Development. The most basic human drive present at birth is eros, the instinct to preserve and create life. Eros is expressed sexually. Consequently, early in their development humans experience sexuality, which is expressed in the seeking of pleasure through various parts of the body. During the first year of life, a child attains pleasure by sucking and biting: the oral stage. During the second and third years of life, the focus of sexual attention is on the elimination of bodily wastes: the anal stage. The phallic stage occurs during ages four and five, as children focus their attention on their genitals. Males begin to have sexual feelings for their mother (the Oedipus complex) and girls for their father (the Electra complex). The latency stage begins at age six, and during this period, feelings of sexuality are repressed until the genital stage begins at puberty, which marks the beginning of adult sexuality.

If conflicts are encountered during any of these psychosexual stages of development, a person can become fixated at that point. For example, an infant who does not receive enough oral gratification during the first year of life is likely as an adult to engage in such oral behaviour as smoking, drinking, or drug abuse, or to be clinging and dependent in personal relationships. Thus, the root of adult behaviour problems can be traced to problems developed in the earliest years of life.

Psychodynamics of Abnormal Behaviour. According to the psychodynamic perspective, people who experience feelings of mental anguish and are afraid they are losing control of their personalities are said to be suffering from a **neurosis** and are referred to as neurotics. Those people who have lost total control and who are dominated by their primitive id are said to suffer from **psychosis** and are referred to as psychotics. Their behaviour may be marked by bizarre episodes, hallucinations, and inappropriate responses. According to the psychodynamic view, the most serious types of antisocial behaviour, such as murder, might be motivated by psychosis, while neurotic feelings would be responsible for less serious delinquent acts and status offences, such as petty theft and truancy.

Psychosis takes many forms, the most common being **schizophrenia**. Schizophrenics exhibit illogical and incoherent thought processes and a lack of insight into their behaviour. They may experience delusions and hallucinate. For example, they may see themselves as agents of the devil, avenging angels, or the recipients of messages from animals and plants. David Berkowitz, the "Son of Sam," exhibited these traits when he claimed that his killing spree began when he received messages from a neighbour's dog. Paranoid schizophrenics also suffer complex delusions involving wrongdoing or persecution, and they think everyone is out to get them. In a study of 50 stalkers, psychotic illness was associated with the stalking of strangers. Almost three-quarters of those who stalked strangers and acquaintances had a psychotic illness, while only 20 percent of those who were former sexual intimates were psychotic. Although there was no relationship between serious violence and psychosis, there was a strong relationship between violence and former sexual intimacy, as shown in Table 6.2.[103]

Psychosis and Crime. Freud did not spend much time theorizing about crime. He did link criminality to the unconscious sense of guilt a person retains because of his Oedipus complex or her Electra complex. He believed that in criminals, especially youthful ones, it is possible to detect a powerful sense of guilt that existed before the crime and is therefore not its result but its motive. It is as if the person is relieved to be able to fasten the unconscious sense of guilt onto something real and immediate.[104]

Other psychologists have used psychoanalytic concepts to link criminality to abnormal mental states produced by early childhood trauma. For example, Alfred Adler (1870–1937), the founder of individual psychology, coined the term **inferiority complex** to describe people who compensate for feelings of inferiority with a drive for superiority; controlling others may help reduce personal inadequacies. Erik Erikson (1902–1984) identified the **identity crisis**—a period of serious personal questioning young people undertake in an effort to determine their own values and sense of direction. Adolescents undergoing an identity crisis might exhibit out-of-control behaviour and experiment with drugs and other forms of deviance.

The psychoanalyst whose work is most closely associated with criminality is August Aichorn.[105] After examining many delinquent youths, Aichorn concluded that societal stress, though damaging, could not alone result in a life of crime unless a predisposition existed that prepared youths psychologically for antisocial acts. This mental state, which he labelled **latent delinquency**, is found in youngsters whose personality requires them to (1) seek immediate gratification (to act impulsively), (2) to consider satisfaction of their personal needs more important than relating to others, and (3)

to satisfy instinctive urges without consideration of right and wrong (that is, they lack guilt).

Psychodynamics of Criminal Behaviour. Since this early work, psychoanalysts have continued to view the criminal as an id-dominated person who suffers from the inability to control impulsive, pleasure-seeking drives.[106] Perhaps because they suffered unhappy experiences in childhood or had families that could not provide proper love and care, criminals suffer from weak or damaged egos that make them unable to cope with conventional society. Weak egos are associated with immaturity, poor social skills, and excessive dependence on others. People with weak egos may be easily led by antisocial peers into crime and drug abuse. Some offenders have undeveloped superegos and consequently lack internalized representations of those behaviours that are punished in conventional society; they commit crimes because they have difficulty understanding the wrongfulness of their actions.[107]

Personality conflict or underdevelopment may result in neurotic or psychotic behaviour patterns. There seems to be a link between abnormal personality and mental distress and disorder.[108] Offenders classified as neurotics (or conduct disorders) are driven by an unconscious desire to be punished for prior sins, either real or imaginary. They may violate the law to gain attention or punish their parents. In its most extreme form, criminality may be viewed as a form of psychosis that prevents offenders from appreciating the feelings of their victims or controlling their own impulsive needs for gratification.

Crime, then, is a manifestation of feelings of oppression and the inability of people to develop the proper defence mechanisms to keep these feelings under control. Criminality actually allows troubled people to survive by producing positive psychic results: It helps them feel free and independent, gives them the possibility of excitement and the chance to use their skills and imagination, provides them with the promise of positive gain, allows them to blame others for their predicament (for example, the police), and gives them a chance to rationalize their sense of failure ("If I hadn't gotten into trouble, I could have been a success").

Table 6.2	Violence, psychosis, and relationship to victim in stalkers		
	STRANGERS	**ACQUAINTANCES**	**FORMER SEXUAL INTIMATES**
Serious violence	25%	28%	78%
Psychotic illness	75%	72%	12%
Total = 50	subtotal = 12	subtotal = 18	subtotal = 18

Source: Frank R. Farnham, David V. James, and Paul Cantrell, "Association Between Violence, Psychosis, and Relationship to Victim in Stalkers," *The Lancet,* January 15, 2000: 199.

The psychodynamic model of the criminal offender depicts an aggressive, frustrated person dominated by events that occurred early in childhood.

Behavioural Theories

Behaviour theory maintains that human actions are developed through learning experiences. Rather than focus on unconscious personality traits or biological predispositions, behaviour theorists are concerned with the actual behaviours people engage in during the course of their daily lives. The major premise of behaviour theory is that people alter their behaviour according to the reactions they receive from others. Behaviour is supported by rewards and extinguished by punishments. Behaviour is constantly being shaped by life experiences. With criminal activity, the behavioural view is that crimes, especially violent acts, are learned responses to life situations that do not necessarily represent abnormal or morally immature responses.

Social learning is the branch of behaviour theory most relevant to criminology.[109] Social learning theorists, such as Albert Bandura, argue that people are not actually born with the ability to act violently but that they learn to be aggressive through their life experiences. These experiences include personally observing others acting aggressively to achieve some goal or watching people being rewarded for violent acts on television or in movies. People learn to act aggressively when, as children, they model their behaviour after the violent acts of adults. Later in life, these violent behaviour patterns persist in social relationships. The boy who sees his father repeatedly strike his mother is more likely to grow up to become a battering parent and husband.

Although social learning theorists agree that mental or physical traits may predispose a person toward violence, they believe that the activation of a person's violent tendencies is achieved by factors in the environment. The specific forms that aggressive behaviour takes, the frequency with which it is expressed, the situations in which it is displayed, and the specific targets selected for attack are largely determined by social learning. Their interpretations of behaviour, in turn, influence the way they learn from experiences. One adolescent who spends a weekend in jail for drunk driving may find it the most awful experience of her life, one that teaches her to never drink and drive; another may find it an exciting experience about which he can brag to his friends.

Social learning theorists view violence as something learned through a process called **behaviour modelling**. The most prominent models are family members. Bandura reports that studies of family life show that children who use aggressive tactics have parents who use similar behaviours when dealing with others. A second influence on the social learning of violence is provided by environmental experiences. People who reside in areas in which violence is a daily occurrence are more likely to act violently than those who dwell in low-crime areas where norms stress conventional behaviour. A third source of behaviour modelling is the mass media. Films and television shows commonly depict violence graphically. Moreover, violence is often portrayed as an acceptable behaviour, especially for heroes who never have to face legal consequences for their actions. For example, David Phillips found that the homicide rate increases significantly immediately after a heavyweight championship prizefight.[110]

What triggers violent acts? One idea is that a direct, pain-producing physical assault will usually trigger a violent response. Yet the relationship between painful attacks and aggressive responses has been found to be inconsistent. Whether people counterattack in the face of physical attack depends in part on their skill in fighting and their perception of the strength of their attackers. Verbal taunts and insults have also been linked to aggressive responses. People who are predisposed to aggression by their learning experiences are likely to view insults from others as a challenge to their social status and to react with violence. Still another violence-triggering mechanism is a perceived reduction in one's life conditions. Prime examples of this phenomenon are riots and demonstrations in poverty-stricken ghetto areas. Studies have shown that discontent also produces aggression in the more successful members of lower-class groups who have been led to believe they can succeed but have been thwarted in their aspirations. While it is still uncertain how this relationship is constructed, it is apparently complex. No matter how deprived some individuals are, they will not resort to violence. It seems evident that people's perceptions of their relative deprivation have differing effects on their aggressive responses.

In summary, social learning theorists have said that the following four factors help produce violence and aggression:

1. An event that heightens arousal, such as being provoked through physical assault or verbal abuse.
2. Aggressive skills learned from observing others, either personally or through the media.
3. Expected outcomes, or the belief that aggression will be rewarded, either in the form of reduced tension or anger, money, enhanced self-esteem, or the praise of others.
4. Consistency of behaviour with values, or the belief that aggression is justified and appropriate, given the circumstances of the current situation.

Cognitive Theory

One area of psychology that has received increasing recognition in recent years has been the **cognitive school**. Psychologists with a cognitive perspective focus on mental processes and how people perceive and mentally represent the world around them and solve problems. The pioneers of this school were Wilhelm Wundt (1832–1920), Edward Titchener (1867–1927), and William James (1842–1920). Today, there are several sub-areas within the cognitive area. For example, the moral development branch is concerned about the way people morally reason about the world, while the information-processing branch focuses on the way people process, store, encode, retrieve, and manipulate information to make decisions and solve problems.

Moral and Intellectual Development Theory. The moral and intellectual development branch of cognitive psychology is perhaps the most important for criminological theory. Jean Piaget (1896–1980), the founder of this approach, hypothesized that people's reasoning processes develop in an orderly fashion, beginning at birth and continuing until adolescence and older.[111] At first, during the sensorimotor stage, children respond to the environment in a simple manner, seeking interesting objects and developing their reflexes. By the fourth and final stage,

Culture, Gender, Ethnicity, and Criminology

The Media and Violence

On November 27, 1995, thieves ignited flammable liquid in a New York City subway token booth, seriously injuring the clerk. Their behaviour was virtually identical to a robbery scene in the film *Money Train* (with Wesley Snipes and Woody Harrelson), which had been released a few days before.

Do the media influence behaviour? Does broadcast violence cause aggressive behaviour in viewers? This has become a hot topic because of the persistent theme of violence on television and in films. Critics have called for drastic measures, ranging from banning TV violence to putting warning labels on heavy metal albums out of the fear that listening to hard-rock lyrics produces delinquency.

If there is a TV–violence link, the problem is alarming, given the amount of television watched by young people. Systematic viewing of TV begins at age two and a half and continues at a high level during the preschool and early school years. It has been estimated that children ages 2 to 5 watch TV for 28 hours per week; children ages 6 to 11, 24 hours per week; and teens, 23 hours per week. Marketing research indicates that adolescents aged 11 to 14 rent violent horror movies at a higher rate than any other age group; kids this age use older peers and

siblings and apathetic parents to gain access to R-rated films. Many households now have cable TV, which features violent films and shows. Even children's programming is saturated with violence. The average child views 8000 TV murders before finishing elementary school.

The fact that kids watch so much violent TV is not surprising, considering the findings of a well-publicized study conducted by researchers in 1995. Of the 161 television movies monitored (every one that aired that season), 23 raised concerns about their use of violence, a violent theme, a violent title, or the inappropriate graphic nature of a scene. Of the 118 theatrical films monitored (all that aired that season), 50 raised concerns about their use of violence.

Even some children's television shows feature "sinister combat" as the theme. The characters are usually happy to fight and frequently do so with little provocation. A University of Pennsylvania study found that children's programming contained an average of 32 violent acts per hour, 56 percent had violent characters, and 74 percent had characters who became the victims of violence.

In 1977 Ronald Zamora killed an elderly woman and then pleaded guilty by reason of insanity. Although his attorney claimed Zamora was addicted to TV violence

and could no longer differentiate between reality and fantasy, Zamora was found guilty. At least 43 deaths have been linked to the movie *The Deer Hunter*, which featured a scene in which a main character kills himself while playing Russian roulette for money.

John Hinckley, Jr., shot President Ronald Reagan as a result of his obsession with actres Jodie Foster, which developed aft he watched her play a prostitute the film *Taxi Driver*. Hinckley ha viewed the film at least 15 time In October 1993, a five-year-old Ohio boy set a fire that caused death of his two-year-old sister. boy's mother charged that the youth had been influenced by t MTV show *Beavis and Butt-He* whose cartoon heroes started fires and chanted "Fire is good." MTV responded to the public outcry over the incident by moving the show's broadcast time from 7 p.m. to 10:30 p.m. A national survey conducted in the wake of the controversy found that almost 80 percent of the public believes that violence on TV can cause violence "in real life."

Psychologists believe that media violence does not in itself cause violent behaviour, because if it did, there would be millions of daily incidents in which viewers imitated the aggression they saw on TV or in movies. The concern is that media violence contributes to aggression. There are several explanations for the effects of television and film violence on behaviour:

- Media violence can provide aggressive "scripts" that children store in memory. Repeated exposure to these scripts can increase their retention and lead to changes in attitudes. Exposure to violent displays of any type could provide cues leading to the retrieval of these and other scripts and to the emission of aggressive behaviour.
- Observational learning occurs when the violence seen on television is copied by the child viewer. Children learn to be violent from television in the same way that they learn cognitive and social skills from their parents and friends.
- Television violence increases the arousal levels of viewers and makes them more prone to act aggressively. Studies measuring the galvanic skin response of subjects—a physical indication of arousal based on the amount of electricity conducted across the palm of the hand—show that viewing violent TV shows led to increased arousal levels in young children.
- Television violence promotes attitude changes, which can then result in behaviour changes. Watching television violence promotes such negative attitudes as suspiciousness and the expectation that the viewer will become involved in violence. Attitudes of frequent television viewers toward aggression become positive when they see violence as a common and socially acceptable behaviour.
- Television violence helps already aggressive youths justify their behaviour. It is possible that, instead of

causing violence, television helps violent youths rationalize their behaviour as a socially acceptable and common activity.

- Television violence may disinhibit aggressive behaviour, which is normally controlled by other learning processes. Disinhibition takes place when adults are viewed as being rewarded for violence and when violence is seen as socially acceptable. This contradicts previous learning experiences in which violent behaviour was seen as wrong.

In laboratory experiments, groups of subjects have been exposed to violent TV shows and their behaviour compared to control groups who viewed nonviolent programming. Observations have also been made in playgrounds, on athletic fields, and in residences. Other experiments require subjects to answer attitude surveys after watching violent TV shows. Still another approach is to use aggregate measures of TV viewing; for example, the number of violent TV shows on the air during a given time period is compared with crime rates during the same period.

Most evaluations of experimental data indicate that watching violence on TV is correlated with aggressive behaviours or at least has a short-term impact on behaviour. Subjects who view violent TV shows are likely to begin aggressive behaviour almost immediately.

Although this evidence is persuasive, the relationship between media and violence is still unproven. A number of critics argue that the evidence simply does not support the claim that watching TV or movies and listening to heavy metal music is related to antisocial behaviour. Simon Singer found that teenage heavy metal fans were no more delinquent than nonlisteners.

Candace Kruttschnitt and her associates found that an individual's exposure to violent TV shows is only weakly related to subsequent violent behaviour. There is also little evidence that areas that experience the highest levels of violent TV viewing also have rates of violent crime that are above the norm.

Millions of children watch violence every night yet fail to become violent criminals. If violent TV shows caused interpersonal violence, there should be few ecological and regional patterns in the crime rate, of which there are many. Put another way, how can regional differences in the violence rate be explained considering the fact that people all across the nation watch the same TV shows and films?

Critics also assert that experimental results are inconclusive and short-lived. People may have an immediate reaction to viewing violence on TV, but aggression is quickly extinguished once the viewing ends. Experiments that show a correlation between aggression and TV fail to link the association with actual criminal behaviours, such as rape or assault. The experimental results indicate that violent media have an immediate impact on people with a preexisting tendency toward crime and violence. But do kids who act more aggressively after watching violent TV later grow up to become rapists and killers?

Some would argue that violent TV shows be controlled. One answer would be to have government regulators limit the content of programs or restrict times that violent shows may be aired (for example, after children's bedtimes). The TV industry and the film industry now place advisory warnings on shows that have objectionable content. Parents can now purchase a "V-Chip" to screen out violent or objectionable programming on their televisions.

While such practices may help guide some parents, they do little to restrict TV watching when children are home alone. And what about the local news or football game? For example, Garland White, Janet Katz, and Kathryn Scarborough found that when the local football team wins, violent assaults on women increase; sports dominance may trigger feelings of power and control, which results in sexual aggression in males. This research received nationwide attention and prompted antibattering public service announcements during the 1997 Super Bowl. If such findings

are valid, it is unlikely that those concerned with media violence can engineer a ban of pro football games on television.

Sources: UCLA Center for Communication Policy, *Television Violence Monitoring Project* (Los Angeles, CA, 1995); Associated Press, "Hollywood Is Blamed in Token Booth Attack," *Boston Globe*, November 28, 1995, p. 30; Garland White, Janet Katz, and Kathryn Scarborough, "The Impact of Professional Football Games upon Violent Assaults on Women," *Violence and Victims* 7 (1992): 157–71; Simon Singer, "Rethinking Subcultural Theories of Delinquency and the Cultural Resources of Youth," paper presented at the annual meeting of the American Society of Criminology, Phoenix, AZ, November 1993; Albert Reiss and Jeffrey Roth, eds., *Understanding and Preventing*

Violence (Washington, DC: National Academy Press, 1993); Reuters, "Seventy-Nine Percent in Survey Link Violence on TV and Crime," *Boston Globe*, December 19, 1993, p. 17; Scott Snyder, "Movies and Juvenile Delinquency: An Overview," *Adolescence* 26 (1991): 121–31; Steven Messner, "Television Violence and Violent Crime: An Aggregate Analysis," *Social Problems* 33 (1986): 218–35; Candace Kruttschnitt, Linda Heath, and David Ward, "Family Violence, Television Viewing Habits, and Other Adolescent Experiences Related to Violent Criminal Behaviour," *Criminology* 243 (1986): 235–67; Jonathan Freedman, "Television Violence and Aggression: A Rejoinder," *Psychological Bulletin* 100 (1986): 372–78; Wendy Wood, Frank Wong, and J. Gregory Chachere, "Effects of Media Violence on Viewers' Aggression in Unconstrained Social Interaction," *Psychological Bulletin* 109 (1991): 371–83.

the formal operations stage, they have developed into mature adults who can use logic and abstract thought.

Lawrence Kohlberg applied the concept of moral development to issues in criminology.[112] He found that people travel through stages of moral development, during which their decisions and judgments on issues of right and wrong are based on different reasoning. It is possible that serious offenders have a moral orientation that differs from that of law-abiding citizens. Kohlberg's stages of development are

Stage 1: Right is obedience to power and avoidance of punishment.

Stage 2: Right is taking responsibility for oneself, meeting one's own needs, and leaving to others the responsibility for themselves.

Stage 3: Right is being good in the sense of having good motives, having concern for others, and "putting yourself in the other person's shoes."

Stage 4: Right is maintaining the rules of a society and serving the welfare of the group or society.

Stage 5: Right is based on recognized individual rights within a society with agreed-upon rules—a social contract.

Stage 6: Right is an assumed obligation to principles applying to all humankind—principles of justice, equality, and respect for human life.

As we can see, the person travels through levels of increasing abstraction, extending personal rights to others, and then to all society. Kohlberg thus classified people according to the stage at which their moral development ceased to grow.

In studies conducted by Kohlberg and his associates, criminals were found to be significantly lower in their moral judgment development than noncriminals of the same social background.[113] Since his pioneering efforts, researchers have continued to show that criminal offenders are more likely to be classified in the lowest levels of moral reasoning (stages 1 and 2), while noncriminals have reached a higher stage of moral development.

Recent research indicates that the decision not to commit crimes may be influenced by one's stage of moral development. People at the lowest levels report that they are deterred from crime because of their fear of sanctions; those in the middle consider the reactions of family and friends; those at the highest stages refrain from crime because they believe in duty to others and universal rights.[114]

Moral development theory suggests that people who obey the law simply to avoid punishment or who have outlooks mainly characterized by self-interest are more likely to commit crimes than those who view the law as something that benefits all of society and who sympathize with the rights of others. Higher stages of moral reasoning are associated with conventional behaviours, such as honesty, generosity, and nonviolence. It is certainly abstract to consider the "general good" a matter of one's ultimate self-interest.

Information Processing. When cognitive theorists who study information processing try to explain antisocial behaviour, they do so in terms of perception and analysis of data. When people make decisions, they engage in a sequence of thought processes. They first encode information so that it can be interpreted. They then search for

Does watching violent TV and movies cause kids to act in an aggressive fashion? While laboratory observations suggest a media–violence link, there is less evidence that such an association occurs in the "real world." Millions of kids watch violence every day, yet few become violent criminals. It is possible, however, that watching violent TV shows can reinforce a preexisting predisposition to commit aggressive behaviour, thereby increasing the incidence of violent crime.

Connections

The deterrent effect of informal sanctions and feelings of shame discussed in Chapter 5 may hinge on the level of a person's moral development. The lower one's state of moral development, the less impact informal sanctions may have. If moral development increases, informal sanctions may be better able to control crime.

a proper response and decide on the most appropriate action; finally, they act on their decision.[115]

According to this approach, violence-prone people may be using information incorrectly when they make decisions. One reason is that they may be relying on mental "scripts" learned in childhood that tell them how to interpret events, what to expect, how they should react, and what the outcome of the interaction should be.[116] Hostile children may have learned improper scripts by observing how others react to events; their own parents' aggressive and inappropriate behaviour would have considerable impact. Violence becomes a stable behaviour because the scripts that emphasize aggressive responses are repeatedly rehearsed as the child matures.

Violence-prone kids see people as more aggressive than they actually are and as intending them ill when there is no reason for alarm. As these children mature, they use fewer cues than most people to process information. Some use violence in a calculating fashion as a means of getting what they want; others react in an overly volatile fashion to the slightest provocation. Aggressors are more likely to be vigilant, on edge, or suspicious. When they attack victims, they may believe they are defending themselves, even though they are misreading the situation.[117]

Information-processing theory has been used to explain date rape. Sexually violent males believe that when their dates say no to sexual advances, the women are really "playing games" and actually want to be taken forcefully.[118] This type of attitude is self-justifying, of course.

Treatment based on information processing acknowledges that people are more likely to respond aggressively to a provocation when thoughts intensify the insult or otherwise stir feelings of anger. Cognitive therapists attempt to teach explosive people to control aggressive impulses by viewing social provocations as problems demanding a solution rather than as insults requiring retaliation. Programs are aimed at teaching problem-solving skills that may include listening, following instructions, joining in, and using self-control. Treatment interventions based on learning social skills are relatively new, but there are some indications that this approach can have long-term benefits for reducing criminal behaviour.

Mental Illness and Crime

Each of the schools of psychology has a unique approach to the concept of mental abnormality. Psychoanalysts view mental illness as a retreat from unbearable stress and conflict; cognitive psychologists link it to thought disorders and overstimulation; behaviour theorists might look to environmental influences, such as early family experiences and social rejection. Regardless of the cause of mental illness, is there a link between it and crime?

A great deal of early research efforts found that many offenders who engage in serious, violent crimes suffer from some sort of mental disturbance. James Sorrells's well-known study of juvenile murderers found that many homicidal youths could be described as hostile, explosive, anxious, and depressed.[119] Likewise, in a study of 45 males accused of murder, Richard Rosner and his associates found that 75 percent could be classified as having some mental illness, including schizophrenia.[120] Abusive mothers have been found to have mood and personality disorders and a history of psychiatric diagnoses.[121]

There is some indication that those who are diagnosed as mentally ill are more likely to violate the law than the mentally sound are. Substance abuse among the mentally ill is significantly higher than that among the general population.[122] Furthermore, the diagnosed mentally ill appear in arrest and court statistics at a rate disproportionate to their presence in the population.[123]

Despite this evidence, some question remains as to whether, as a group, the mentally ill are any more criminal than the mentally sound. The mentally ill may be more likely to withdraw or harm themselves than to act aggressively toward others.[124] Research conducted in New York shows that on release, prisoners who had prior histories of hospitalization for mental disorders were less likely to be rearrested than those who had never been hospitalized.[125] And other research reports that the great majority of known criminals are not mentally ill.

While these research efforts give only tentative support to the proposition that mental disturbance or illness can be an underlying cause of violent crime, it is still possible that some link exists. The existing data suggest that certain symptoms of mental illness are connected to violence, including the feelings that others were wishing the person harm, that their mind was dominated by forces beyond their control, and that thoughts were being put into their head by others.[126] It is also likely that people suffering from other psychological disorders such as substance abuse, psychopathy, and neuroticism are the ones most at risk for chronic criminal behaviour.[127] Interest in this topic continues to influence research.

Personality and Crime

Personality can be defined as the reasonably stable patterns of behaviour, including thoughts and emotions, that distinguish one person from another. One's personality reflects a characteristic way of adapting to life's demands and problems. The way people behave is a function of how their personality enables them to interpret life events and make appropriate behavioural choices. Can the cause of crime be linked to personality? This issue has always caused significant debate.[128] In their early work, Sheldon Glueck and Eleanor Glueck identified a number of personality traits they believed characterized antisocial youth:[129]

self-assertiveness	sadism
defiance	lack of concern for others
extroversion	feeling unappreciated
ambivalence	distrust of authority
impulsiveness	poor personal skills
narcissism	mental instability
suspicion	hostility
destructiveness	resentment

Several other research efforts have attempted to identify criminal personality traits.[130] For example, Hans Eysenck identified two personality traits that he associated with antisocial behaviour: extroversion-introversion and stability-instability. Extreme introverts are over-aroused and avoid sources of stimulation, while extreme extroverts are unaroused and seek sensation. Introverts are slow to learn and be conditioned; extroverts are impulsive individuals who lack the ability to examine their own motives and behaviours. Those who are unstable, a condition that Eysenck calls neuroticism, are anxious, tense, and emotionally unstable.[131] People who are both neurotic and extroverted lack self-insight, are impulsive and emotionally unstable, and are unlikely to have reasoned judgments of life events. While extrovert neurotics may act self-destructively—for example, by abusing drugs—more stable people will be able to reason that such behaviour is ultimately harmful and life-threatening. Eysenck believes that the direction of the personality is controlled by genetic factors and is heritable.

A number of other personality deficits in criminals are hyperactivity, impulsiveness, short attention spans, conduct disorders, anxiety disorders, and depression. These traits make them prone to problems ranging from psychopathology to drug abuse, sexual promiscuity, and violence.[132] As a group, people who share these traits are believed to have a character defect referred to as the **antisocial, sociopathic, or psychopathic** personality. Although these terms are often used interchangeably, some psychologists do distinguish between sociopaths and psychopaths by suggesting that the former are a product of a destructive home environment, while the latter are a product of a defect or aberration within themselves.[133]

The Antisocial Personality. Some but not all serious violent offenders may have a disturbed character structure commonly called psychopathy, sociopathy, or antisocial

Connections

The Glueck research is representative of the view that antisocial people maintain a distinct set of personal traits that makes them particularly sensitive to environmental stimuli. Once dismissed by mainstream criminologists, the Gluecks' views, reviewed in Chapter 10's section of life-course theories, still influence contemporary criminological theory.

personality. Psychopaths have a low level of guilt and anxiety and persistently violate the rights of others. Although they may exhibit superficial charm and above-average intelligence, this surface often masks a disturbed personality that makes them incapable of forming enduring relationships with others and continually involves them in such deviant behaviours as violence, risk taking, substance abuse, and impulsivity.

From an early age, the psychopath's home life was filled with frustrations, bitterness, and quarrelling. Consequently, throughout life, he or she is unreliable, unstable, demanding, and egocentric. Psychopaths are risk-taking sensation seekers who are constantly involved in a variety of antisocial behaviours. They have been described as grandiose, egocentric, manipulative, forceful, and coldhearted, with shallow emotions and the inability to feel empathy with others, remorse, or anxiety over their misdeeds. They are also able to rationalize their behaviour so that it appears warranted, reasonable, and justified.

Considering these personality traits, it is not surprising that studies show that psychopaths are significantly more criminal-prone, and that psychopaths continue their criminal careers long after other offenders burn out or age out of crime. Psychopaths are continually in trouble with the law and therefore are likely to wind up in penal institutions. It has been estimated that up to 30 percent of all inmates can be classified as psychopaths or sociopaths, but a more realistic figure is probably 10 percent; not all psychopaths become criminals, and, conversely, most criminals are not psychopaths.

What Causes Psychopathy? Although psychologists are still not certain of the causes of psychopathy, a number of factors are believed to contribute to the development of a psychopathic or sociopathic personality. Some experts focus on family experiences, suggesting that the influence of an unstable parent, parental rejection, lack of love during childhood, and inconsistent discipline may be related to psychopathy. Early childhood experiences seem quite important. Children who lack the opportunity to form an attachment to a mother figure in the first three years of life, who suffer sudden separation from the mother figure, or who see changes in the mother figure are the most likely to develop sociopathic personalities. Psychopathy may also be related to personal traits. Attention deficit/hyperactive disorder kids are more likely to suffer from conduct problems in childhood.

Psychopaths may also suffer from lower than normal levels of arousal. If psychopathy is caused by damage to the frontal and temporal lobes, psychopaths may need greater-than-average stimulation to bring them up to comfortable levels (similar to the arousal theory discussed earlier in this chapter). Research shows that antisocial individuals are often sensation seekers who desire a hedonistic pursuit of pleasure, an extroverted lifestyle, partying, drinking, and a variety of sexual partners. The desire for this stimulation may originate in their physical differences.

It is possible that psychopaths have a "low fear quotient" that inhibits their fear of punishment. All people have a natural or innate fear of certain stimuli—spiders, snakes, fires, strangers. Psychopaths fall on the low end of the fearfulness continuum. The normal socialization process depends on the current punishment of antisocial behaviour inhibiting future transgressions. Someone who does not fear punishment is simply harder to socialize.

Psychopaths may have ineffective coping mechanisms for dealing with negative stimuli and may be less capable of regulating their activities than other people. While nonpsychopaths may become anxious and afraid when facing the prospect of committing a criminal act, psychopaths in the same circumstances feel no such fear. These reduced anxiety levels result in impulsive and inappropriate behaviour, apprehension, and incarceration. Psychologists have attempted to treat patients diagnosed as psychopaths by giving them adrenaline, which increases their arousal levels.

Antisocial Personality and Chronic Offending. The antisocial personality concept seems to jibe with what is known about chronic offending. In a recent paper, Lawrence Cohen and Bryan Vila argue that chronic offending should be conceived as a continuum of behaviour at whose apex lies the most extremely dangerous and predatory criminals. As many as 80 percent of these high-end chronics exhibit sociopathic behaviour patterns. Though making up about 4 percent of the male population and less than 1 percent of the female population, they are responsible for half of all the serious felony offences committed annually. Not all high-rate chronics are sociopaths, but enough are to support a strong link between personality dysfunction and long-term criminal careers.

Should people diagnosed as psychopaths be separated and treated even if they have not yet committed a crime? Should psychopathic murderers be spared the death penalty because they lack the capacity to control their behaviour? These are difficult questions, ones which will probably not go away.[134]

Research on Personality. Since maintaining a deviant personality has been related to crime and delinquency, numerous attempts have been made to devise accurate measures of personality and determine whether they can predict antisocial behaviour. Two types of standardized personality tests have been constructed. The first are projective techniques that require a subject to react to an ambiguous picture or shape by describing what it represents or by telling a story about it. The Rorschach inkblot test and the Thematic Apperception Test are examples of two widely used projective tests. Such tests are given by clinicians trained to interpret responses and categorize them according to established behavioural patterns. While these tests were not used extensively, some early research found that delinquents and nondelinquents could be separated on the basis of their personality profiles.[135]

The second frequently used method of psychological testing is the personality inventory. This type of test requires subjects to agree or disagree with groups of questions in a self-administered survey, such as the Minnesota Multiphasic Personality Inventory (MMPI).[136] In one study, the MMPI was given to a sample of ninth-grade boys and girls in Minneapolis and it was found that the scores had a significant relationship to later delinquent involvement.[137]

Despite the time and energy put into using the MMPI and other scales to predict crime and delinquency, the results have proved inconclusive. Three surveys of the literature of personality testing found inconclusive evidence that personality traits could consistently predict criminal involvement.[138] While some law violators may suffer from an abnormal personality structure, there are also many more whose personalities are indistinguishable from the norm. Efforts to improve the MMPI have resulted in a new scale with, it is hoped, improved validity.[139]

Are Some People Crime-Prone? Interest in the personality characteristics of criminals has been increasing. Because the most commonly used scales have not been very successful in predicting criminality, psychologists have turned to other measures, including the Multidimensional Personality Questionnaire (MPQ), to assess such personality traits as control, aggression, alienation, and well-being. Research has found that such scales can show how personality is linked to delinquency, and that these measures are valid across genders, races, and cultures.[140] This research indicates that adolescent offenders who are crime-prone respond to frustrating events with strong negative emotions, feel stressed and harassed, and are adversarial in their interpersonal relationships. Crime-prone people tend to experience states such as anger, anxiety, and irritability. They are also predisposed to weak personal constraints and have difficulty controlling impulsive behaviour urges. Because they are both impulsive and aggressive, crime-prone people are quick to take action against perceived threats.

Evidence that personality traits predict crime and violence is important because it suggests that the root cause of crime can be found in the forces that influence human development at an early stage in the life course. If these results are valid, rather than focus on job creation and neighbourhood improvement, crime control efforts might be better focused on helping families raise children who are reasoned and reflective and enjoy a safe environment.

Intelligence and Crime

A number of the early criminologists maintained that many delinquents and criminals have below-average intelligence and that low IQ is a cause of their criminality. They believed criminals to be inherently substandard in intelligence and thus naturally inclined to commit more crimes than more intelligent persons. Furthermore, it was thought that if authorities could determine which individuals had low IQs, they might identify potential criminals before they could commit socially harmful acts.

Because social scientists had a captive group of subjects in juvenile training schools and penal institutions, they began to measure the correlation between IQ and crime by testing offenders. These inmates were used as a test group on which numerous theories about intelligence were built, leading ultimately to the nature versus nurture controversy that is still going on today.

Canada's Experiment with Eugenics. In the early part of the 20th century, acting on the idea that IQ is related to delinquency, several provincial governments passed laws in an attempt to weed out undesirable characteristics, a practice known as "negative eugenics." Alberta passed its Sexual Sterilization Act and created a Provincial Eugenics Board in 1928. This law was in force until 1972. British Columbia's law was passed in 1933 and existed until 1973. Ontario and Quebec only narrowly missed passing such laws under opposition by the Roman Catholic Church. In 1965, Leilana Muir sued the Alberta government for involuntary sterilization in 1959, and for falsely categorizing her as a moron under this law. She had been physically abused by her mother, and abandoned at the Provincial Training School for Mental Defectives at the age of 11. British Columbia sterilized at least 200 people, and Alberta sterilized almost 3000 people for mental defects. In total, almost 5000 people with disabilities were approved for sterilization. Female youths underwent tubal ligations or hysterectomies for "menstrual management," while males had vasectomies or were castrated. The Eugenics Board acted arbitrarily and falsely—who can imagine approving such procedures on children? In 1997, when Ms. Muir sued again, she was awarded $750 000 in compensation, but the Alberta government refused to award the other victims. In 1999, it agreed to an $82-million settlement to 247 victims. The belief that mental illness, mental disability, and criminality were inherited was one born from poorly constructed evolutionist thinking and has since been discounted.

Nature Theory. Nature theory argues that intelligence is largely determined genetically and that low intelligence as demonstrated by a low IQ score is linked to behaviour, including criminal behaviour. When the newly developed IQ tests were administered to inmates of prisons and juvenile training schools in the first decades of the 20th century, the nature position gained support because a large proportion of the inmates scored low on the tests. Henry Goddard found during his studies in 1920 that many institutionalized persons were what he considered "feebleminded" and concluded that at least half of all juvenile delinquents were mental defectives.[141] In 1926, William Healy and Augusta Bronner tested groups of delinquent boys in Chicago and Boston and found that 37 percent were subnormal in intelligence. They concluded that delinquents were five to ten times more likely to be mentally deficient than normal boys.[142] These and other early studies were embraced as proof that low IQ scores indicated potentially delinquent children and that a correlation existed between innate low intelligence and deviant behaviour. Intelligence tests were believed to measure the inborn genetic makeup of individuals, and many criminologists accepted the idea that individuals with substandard IQs were predisposed toward delinquency and adult criminality.

Nurture Theory. The rise of culturally sensitive explanations of human behaviour in the 1930s led to the nurture school of intelligence. According to this theory, intelligence must be viewed as partly biological but primarily sociological. Nurture theorists discredited the notion that persons commit crimes because they have low IQs. Instead, they postulated that environmental stimulation from parents, relatives, social contacts, schools, peer groups, and innumerable others create a child's IQ level and that low IQs result from an environment that also encourages delinquent and criminal behaviour. Thus, if low IQ scores are recorded among criminals, these scores may reflect the criminals' cultural background, not their mental ability.

Studies challenging the IQ–crime assumption began to appear as early as the 1920s. In 1926 John Slawson studied 1543 delinquent boys in New York institutions and compared them with a control group of New York City boys.[143] He found that although 80 percent of the delinquents achieved lower scores in abstract verbal intelligence, they were about normal in mechanical aptitude and nonverbal intelligence. These results indicated the possibility of cultural bias in portions of the IQ tests. He also found no relationship among the number of arrests, the types of offences, and IQ.

In 1931, Edwin Sutherland evaluated IQ studies of criminals and delinquents and noted discrepancies believed to reflect testing methods rather than differences in the mental ability of criminals.[144] Sutherland's research all but put an end to the belief that crime is caused by feeblemindedness; the IQ–crime link was all but forgotten in the criminological literature.

Rediscovering IQ and Criminality. Although the alleged IQ–crime link had been dismissed by mainstream criminologists, it became an important area of study once again when respected criminologists Travis Hirschi and Michael Hindelang published a paper linking the two variables.[145] After reexamining existing research data, they concluded that "the weight of evidence is that IQ is more important than race and social class" for predicting criminal and delinquent involvement. Rejecting the notion that IQ tests are race- and class-biased, they concluded that major differences exist between criminals and noncriminals within similar racial and socioeconomic class categories. Their position is that low IQ increases the likelihood of criminal behaviour through its effect on school performance. That is, youths with low IQs do poorly in school, and school failure and academic incompetence are highly related to delinquency and later to adult criminality.

Other research supports these conclusions,[146] although in *Crime and Human Nature*, James Q. Wilson and Richard Herrnstein feel that the IQ–crime link is an indirect one: Low intelligence leads to poor school performance, which enhances the chances of criminality.[147] They concluded, "A child who chronically loses standing in the competition of the classroom may feel justified in settling the score outside, by violence, theft, and other forms of defiant illegality."

The IQ–crime relationship has also been found in cross-national studies.[148] However, the issue is still a matter of significant debate. A number of recent studies have found that IQ level has negligible influence on criminal behaviour.[149] And a recent evaluation of existing knowledge on intelligence conducted by the American Psychological Association concluded that the strength of an IQ–crime link is "very low."[150] In contrast, *The Bell Curve*, Richard Herrnstein and Charles Murray's influential albeit controversial book on intelligence, comes down firmly on the side of an IQ–crime link. Their extensive summary of the available literature shows that people with low IQs are more likely to commit crime, get caught, and be sent to prison. Conversely, at-risk kids with higher IQs seem to be protected from becoming criminals. They conclude that criminal offenders have an average IQ of 92, about 8 points below the mean; chronic offenders score even lower than the "average" criminal. And to those skeptics who suggest that only low-IQ criminals get caught, they counter with data showing little difference in IQ scores between self-reported and official criminals.[151]

It is unlikely that the IQ–criminality debate will be settled in the near future. Measurement is beset by many methodological problems. The well-documented criticisms suggesting that IQ tests are race- and class-biased would certainly influence the testing of the criminal population, who are beset with a multitude of social and economic problems. Even if it can be shown that known offenders have lower IQs than the general population, it is difficult to explain many patterns in the crime rate: Why are males more criminal than females (are females three times smarter than males)? Why do crime rates vary by region, time of year, and even weather patterns? Why does aging out occur? IQ does not increase with age—why should crime rates fall? There are critical theoretical problems with such an approach as well: Various issues that are ignored include the role of the police in enforcing the law and their use of discretion, the ability of the law to reinforce social inequality, and so on. These issues are discussed in Chapter 9 on Social Conflict Theory.

Social Policy Implications

For most of the 20th century, biological and psychological views of criminality have had an important influence on crime control and prevention policy. These views can be seen in primary prevention programs that seek to treat personal problems before they manifest themselves as crime, such as family therapy organizations, substance abuse clinics, and mental health associations. Referrals to these resources are made by teachers, employers, courts, welfare agencies, and others. It is assumed that if a

person's problems can be treated before they become overwhelming, some future crimes will be prevented. Secondary prevention programs provide such treatment as psychological counselling to youths and adults after they have violated the law. Attendance in such programs may be a mandatory requirement of a probation order, part of a diversionary sentence, or aftercare at the end of a prison sentence.

Connections

The law recognizes the psychological aspects of crime when it permits the insanity plea as an excuse for criminal liability or when it allows trial delay because of mental incompetency. See Chapter 2 for more on the insanity defence.

Biologically oriented therapy is also being used in the criminal justice system. Programs have altered diet, changed lighting, compensated for learning disabilities, treated allergies, and so on.[152] What is more controversial has been the use of mood-altering chemicals, such as lithium and benzodiazepines to control the behaviour of antisocial individuals. Another practice that has elicited

Is it nature or nurture? Even if some aspects of intelligence are inherited, there seems little question that those children who are raised in an environment lacking in economic resources and parental support will fail to maximize their intellectual potential. The mother here is going to college while on welfare in order to better support herself and her child. Is it the responsibility of society to provide resources sufficient to enable all youth to achieve their rightful share of intellectual development?

outcries of concern is the use of brain surgery to control antisocial behaviour, for example to control their sex drives. Critics have argued, however, that these procedures are without scientific merit.[153]

Some criminologists view biologically oriented treatments as a key to solving the problem of the chronic offender. They argue that a number of inherited physical traits that cause disease have been successfully treated with medication after their genetic code has been broken; why not, then, a genetic solution to crime?[154]

Whereas such biological treatment is a relatively new phenomenon, it has become commonplace since the 1920s to offer psychological treatment to offenders before, during, and after a criminal conviction. For example, since the 1970s pretrial programs have sought to divert offenders into nonpunitive rehabilitative programs designed to treat rather than punish them. Based on some type of counselling regime, diversion programs are commonly used with first offenders, nonviolent offenders, and so on. At the trial stage, judges often order psychological profiles of convicted offenders for planning a treatment program. Should they be kept in the community? Do they need a more secure confinement to deal with their problems? If correctional confinement is called for, inmates are commonly evaluated at a correctional centre to measure their personality traits or disorders. Correctional facilities almost universally require inmates to participate in some form of psychological therapy: group therapy, individual analysis, transactional analysis, and so on. Parole decisions may be influenced by the prison psychologist's evaluation of the offender's adjustment.

Summary

The earliest positivist criminologists were biologists. Led by Cesare Lombroso, these early researchers believed that some people manifested primitive traits that made them born criminals. Today, that research is debunked because of poor methodology, testing, and logic. Biological views fell out of favour in the early 20th century, but in the 1970s criminologists again turned to the study of the biological basis of criminality. For the most part, the effort has focused on the causes of violent crime. Interest has entered on several areas: (1) biochemical factors, such as diet, allergies, hormonal imbalances, and environmental contaminants (such as lead); (2) neurophysiological factors, such as brain disorders, EEG abnormalities, tumours, and head injuries; and (3) genetic factors, such as the XYY syndrome and inherited traits. There is also an evolutionary branch, which holds that changes in the human condition that have taken thousands of years to evolve may help explain crime rate differences.

Table 6.3 reviews the biological and psychological theories of criminal behaviour.

Psychological attempts to explain criminal behaviour have their historical roots in the concept that all criminals are insane or mentally damaged. This position is no longer accepted. Today, there are three main psychological perspectives. The psychodynamic view says that aggressive behaviour is linked to personality conflicts developed in childhood. However, according to behavioural and social learning theorists, criminality is a learned behaviour: Children who are exposed to violence and see it rewarded may become violent as adults. In contrast, cognitive psychologists are concerned with human development and how people perceive the world. They see criminality as a function of improper information processing or moral development.

Psychological traits, such as personality and intelligence, have been linked to criminality. One important subject of study has been the psychopath, a person who lacks emotion and concern for others. The controversial issue of the relationship of IQ to criminality has been resurrected once again with the publication of studies purporting to show that criminals have lower IQs than noncriminals. Psychologists have developed standardized tests with which to measure personality traits. One avenue of research has been to determine whether criminals and noncriminals manifest any differences in their responses to test items.

Table 6.3	Biological and psychological theories

THEORY	MAJOR PREMISE	STRENGTHS
BIOLOGICAL		
Biochemical	Crime, especially violence, is a function of diet, vitamin intake, hormonal imbalance, or food allergies.	Explains irrational violence. Shows how the environment interacts with personal traits to influence behavior.
Neurological	Criminals and delinquents often suffer brain impairment, as measured by the EEG. Attention deficit disorder and minimum brain dysfunction are related to antisocial behaviour.	Explains irrational violence. Shows how the environment interacts with personal traits to influence behaviour.
Genetic	Criminal traits and predispositions are inherited. The criminality of parents can predict the delinquency of children.	Explains why only a small percentage of youth in a high-crime area become chronic offenders.
Evolutionary	As the human race evolved, traits and characteristics have become ingrained. Some of these traits make people aggressive and predisposed to commit crime.	Explains high violence rates and aggregate gender differences in the crime rate.
PSYCHOLOGICAL		
Psychodynamic	The development of the unconscious personality early in childhood influences behaviour for the rest of a person's life. Criminals have weak egos and damaged personalities.	Explains the onset of crime and why crime and drug abuse cut across class lines.
Behavioural	People commit crime when they model their behaviour after others they see being rewarded for the same acts. Behaviour is reinforced by rewards and extinguished by punishment.	Explains the role of significant others in the crime process. Shows how family life and media can influence crime and violence.
Cognitive	Individual reasoning processes influence behaviour. Reasoning is influenced by the way people perceive their environment and by their moral and intellectual development.	Shows why criminal behaviour patterns change over time as people mature and develop their moral reasoning. May explain the aging-out process.

Thinking Like a Criminologist

In our culture, we believe that people should not be blamed for actions that are beyond their control. There is the sense that a person cannot be legally responsible if he or she cannot meet certain tests. An obvious test of competence is cognitive, that is, is there a criminal intent. Thus the McNaughtan rule (1843) says that every man is to be presumed to be sane, and that to establish an insanity defence, it must be proved that, at the time of the committing of the act, the party accused was suffering from a disease of the mind that meant he or she did not to know the nature of the act being committed; or if he or she did know it, there was no knowledge that it was wrong. Used in this way, the definition seems overly restrictive and psychiatric. As a criminologist with expertise of trait theories of crime, do you think this goes far enough in explaining aberrant behaviour?

Key Terms

androgens

antisocial personality

arousal theory

attention deficit/hyperactivity
 disorder (AD/HD)

behaviour modelling

behaviour theory

cognitive school

electroencephalograph (EEG)

equipotentiality

hypoglycemia

identity crisis

inferiority complex

instincts

latent delinquency

minimal brain dysfunction (MDB)

neurophysiology

neurosis

personality

premenstrual syndrome (PMS)

psychodynamic theory

psychopathy

psychosis

r/k theory

repression

schizophrenia

social learning

sociobiology

sociopathy

somatype

testosterone

trait theories

See the book-specific website at www.siegelcriminology2e.nelson.com for additional chapter links, discussions, and quizzes.

Chapter

7

Social Structure Theories

Motivations for crime do not result simply from the flaws, failures, or free choices of individuals. A complete explanation of crime ultimately must consider the sociocultural environments in which people are located.[1]

Sociology has been the primary focus used in criminology since early in the 20th century. In the United States, the primacy of sociological criminology was secured by research begun by Robert Ezra Park (1864–1944), Ernest W. Burgess (1886–1966), Louis Wirth (1897–1952), and their colleagues in the Sociology Department at the University of Chicago. Known as the **Chicago School**, these sociologists pioneered research work on the social ecology of the city and inspired a generation of scholars to conclude that social forces operating in urban areas create criminal interactions; some neighbourhoods become "natural areas" for crime.

Connections

As you may recall from Chapter 1, sociological positivism can be traced to the works of Quetelet, Comte, and Durkheim. The work of Durkheim will be reviewed again in this chapter in the sections on anomie theory.

In 1915, Robert Ezra Park called for anthropological methods of description and observation to be applied to urban life.[2] He was concerned about how neighbourhood structure develops, how isolated pockets of poverty form, and what social policies could be used to alleviate urban problems. Later, Park, with Ernest Burgess, studied the social ecology of the city and found that some neighbourhoods form **natural areas** of wealth and affluence, while others suffer poverty and disintegration.[3] Regardless of their race, religion, or ethnicity, the everyday behaviour of people living in these areas is controlled by the social and ecological climate.

Over the next 20 years, Chicago School sociologists carried out an ambitious program of research and scholarship on urban topics, including criminal behaviour patterns. Such works as Harvey Zorbaugh's *The Gold Coast and the Slum*, Frederick Thrasher's *The Gang*, and Louis Wirth's *The Ghetto*[4] are classic examples of objective, highly descriptive accounts of urban life. Their influence was such that most criminologists have been trained in sociology, and criminology courses are routinely taught in departments of sociology. In fact, in Canada there are only five distinct departments of criminology at the university level.

Sociological Criminology

There are many reasons why sociology has become the predominant approach of criminologists in this century. First, it has long been evident that varying patterns of criminal behaviour exist within the social structure. Some geographic areas are more prone to violence and serious theft-related crimes than others. Criminologists have attempted to discover why such patterns exist and how they can be eliminated. Explanations of crime as an individual-level phenomenon fail to account for these consistent patterns in the crime rate. If violence, as some criminologists suggest, is related to chemical or chromosome abnormality, how can ecological differences in the crime rate be explained? It is unlikely that all people with physical anomalies live in one section of town or in one area of the country. There has been a heated national debate over the effects of violent TV shows on adolescent aggression. Yet adolescents in cities and towns with widely disparate crime rates all watch the same shows and movies, ranging from St. John's, Newfoundland, to Vancouver, British Columbia. How can crime rate differences in these areas be explained? If violence has a biological or psychological origin, should it not be distributed more evenly throughout the social structure?

Sociology is concerned with social change and the dynamic aspects of human behaviour. It follows transformations in cultural norms and institutions and the subsequent effect they have on individual and group behaviour. These concepts are useful today because the changing structure of postmodern society continues to have a tremendous effect on intergroup and interpersonal relationships.[5] A reduction in the influence of the family has been accompanied by an increased emphasis on individuality, independence, and isolation. Weakened family ties have been linked to crime and delinquency.[6]

Another important social change has been rapid advances in technology and its influence on the social system. People who lack the requisite social and educational training have found that the road to success through upward occupational mobility has become almost impossible. Even today, in one of the most industrialized countries in the world, most children grow up to occupy the same social class position as their parents. Lack of upward mobility may make drug dealing and other crimes an attractive solution to socially deprived but economically enterprising people. Recent evidence shows that adults who are only marginally employed are the ones most likely to commit certain types of crime; thus, the quality of employment and not merely unemployment influences criminality.[7]

Connections

The association between crime and economic class has been muddied by the ambiguous relationship between unemployment and crime. Crime rates sometimes go up during periods of full employment and drop during periods of relatively high unemployment. In addition, Chapter 13 discusses another type of class-linked crime: elite or white-collar crime.

Sociology's stress on intergroup and interpersonal transactions also promotes it as a source for criminological study. Criminologists believe that understanding the dynamics of interactions between individuals and important social institutions, such as their families, their peers, their schools, their jobs, criminal justice agencies, and the like, is important for understanding the cause of crime.[8] The relationship of one social class or group to another or to the existing power structure that controls the nation's legal and economic system may also be involved in criminality. Sociology is concerned with the benefits of positive human interactions and the costs of negative ones. Crime is itself an interaction and therefore should not be studied without considering the interactions of all participants in a criminal act: the law violator, the victim, the law enforcers, the lawmakers, and social institutions.

To summarize, concern about the ecological distribution of crime, the effect of social change, and the interactive nature of crime itself has made sociology the foundation of modern criminology. This chapter reviews sociological theories that emphasize the relationship between social status and criminal behaviour. In Chapter 8, the focus will shift to theories that emphasize socialization and its influence on crime and deviance; Chapter 9 covers theories based on the concept of social conflict.

Economic Structure and Crime

It is probably fair to say that all societies are characterized by social stratification, but we don't expect it in an affluent one. Social strata are created by the unequal distribution of wealth, power, and prestige. Social classes are segments of the population whose members have a relatively similar portion of desirable things and who share attitudes, values, norms, and an identifiable lifestyle. Social classes are also characterized by similar levels of control over the process of production, which influences their life chances. In our society, it is common to identify people as upper-, middle-, and lower-class citizens, with a broad range of economic variations existing within each group. The upper-upper class is reserved for a small number of exceptionally well-to-do families who maintain enormous financial and social resources. The lower class consists of those people who live in poverty, which includes the working poor.

A new shift is occurring in the distribution of poverty. For the first time, the elderly are better off than working-class people. Programs such as universal medical care and social security coupled with private pensions have improved the lifestyle of retirees. At the same time, the young have been hit hard: a large proportion of Canada's children now live in poverty, a frightening reality despite the United Nations' designation of Canada as being "the best country to live in the world." Another ominous sign is the polarization of the economy: The wealthy have increasingly amassed an ever greater share of total income, while the middle class and poor have seen their economic health decline. The 1990s, for example, saw real wages decline dramatically, by almost 10 percent.

Inequality

Lower-class slum areas are scenes of inadequate housing and health care, disrupted family lives, underemployment, and despair. Members of the lower class also suffer in other ways. They are more prone to depression, less likely to have achievement motivation, and less likely to put off immediate gratification for future gain. Some are driven to desperate measures to cope with their economic plight.

Members of the lower class are constantly bombarded with a flood of advertisements linking material possessions to self-worth, but they are often unable to attain desired goods and services through conventional means. Although they are members of a society that extols material success above any other, they are unable to satisfactorily compete for such success with members of the upper classes.

The social problems found in lower-class slum areas in the United States have been described as an "epidemic" that spreads like a contagious disease, destroying the inner workings that enable neighbourhoods to survive; they become "hollowed out."[9] As neighbourhood quality decreases, the probability that residents will develop problems sharply increases. Adolescents in the worst neighbourhoods have the greatest risk of dropping out of school and becoming teenage parents.

The disabilities suffered by the lower-class citizen are particularly acute for racial minorities. Blacks and Native people in Canada have a mean income level significantly lower than that of whites and an unemployment rate markedly higher. Although many of the urban poor are white, minorities are overrepresented within the poverty classes.

Economic problems are not the only ones faced by racial minorities. Native Canadians, for example, have a much shorter life span than whites. This pattern is even more pronounced in the United States, where racial segregation and isolation of poor African Americans and Hispanics in urban areas is increasing.[10]

In 1966, sociologist Oscar Lewis argued that the crushing lifestyle of slum areas produces a "culture of poverty" passed from one generation to the next.[11] The **culture of poverty** is marked by apathy, cynicism, helplessness, and mistrust of social institutions, such as schools, government agencies, and the police. This mistrust prevents slum dwellers from taking advantage of the meagre opportunities available to them. Lewis's work was the first of a group that described the plight of **at-risk** children and adults. In 1970 Gunnar Myrdal described a worldwide **underclass** cut off from society, its members lacking the education and skills in demand in modern society.[12]

In this picture of a "ghetto," we see the conditions in which some people live. Does this provide an "enriched" environment in which to grow up and escape poverty and crime, or a "deprived" one in which crime prospers?

Are the Poor "Undeserving"?

Despite all our technological success, the fact that a significant percentage of citizens are either homeless or living in areas of concentrated poverty is an important social problem. The media frequently focus on the distress suffered by homeless and poverty-stricken families. Yet some observers view impoverished people as somehow responsible for their own fate, the so-called undeserving poor; if they tried, the argument goes, they could "improve themselves."[13] Over 50 percent of all Canadians see poverty as a personal failure.

This conclusion is baseless. It is a sad fact that poverty is becoming ever more concentrated among minority groups forced to live in physically deteriorated, inner-city neighbourhoods that have high crime, poor schools, and excessive mortality, and that they are more likely to suffer social ills than poor people living in more affluent communities.[14] People living in poor urban areas suffer higher rates of unemployment, are more dependent on welfare, and are more likely to live in single-parent households than equally indigent people who reside in more affluent areas. The burden of living in these high-poverty areas, then, goes beyond merely "being poor." Under these conditions, self-help and upward mobility are highly problematic. The barriers to getting ahead are not personal, but systemic.

Community effects may be particularly damaging on children. Adolescents residing in areas of concentrated poverty are more likely to suffer in their cognitive development, sexual and family formation practices, school attendance habits, and transition to employment. Lack of education and family stability makes them poor candidates for employment.

These findings suggest that the poor confront obstacles far greater than the mere lack of financial resources, in that they are ill-prepared to take advantage of employment opportunities even in favourable labour markets.

The fact that many of the underclass are children who can expect to spend all their life in poverty is probably the single most important problem facing the nation today.

Unemployment and Crime

The social structure approach links crime to economic deprivation. It follows that if people do not hold jobs, they will be more likely to turn to crime as a means of support. If jobs are available, crime rates should go down. People who hold jobs should be less criminal than the unemployed. Is this assumption valid? Is there a relationship between crime and unemployment?

Despite the logic of this proposition, little clear-cut evidence exists linking unemployment and crime rates. The crime rate has risen dramatically during times of relative economic prosperity, such as the 1960s. Crime and unemployment are not only weakly related, but one relationship among many. Although criminals have poorer work records than noncriminals, there is little indication that changing market conditions cause them to renounce crime and choose legitimate earning opportunities. Crime rates in cities and states are slightly linked to labour market conditions, but the relationship between them is tenuous.

A routine activities theorist (Chapter 5) might suggest that the weaker-than-expected relationship between crime and unemployment rates can be explained by the fact that while joblessness increases the motivation to commit crime, it simultaneously decreases the opportunity to gain from criminal enterprise. During periods of economic hardship, potential victims have fewer valuable items in their possession and guard those valuables more closely. Parents who are unemployed can be at home to supervise their children, reducing the opportunity for the kids to commit crime; teenagers have higher crime rates than any other age group. These results should not be unexpected. Crime rates are highest among adolescents who are not yet part of the workforce and are unlikely to be directly affected by employment rates.

When individual offenders are the unit of analysis, an unemployment–crime link is more readily observed. Unemployed individuals are more likely to commit crime than the employed. Surveys of adult inmates show that many were unemployed and underemployed before their incarceration; median income of both male and female inmates was below the poverty level. It is possible that on an individual level, unemployment increases crime because it reduces people's stake in conformity. By severing attachments to co-workers and reducing parents' ability to be breadwinners, unemployment reduces the attachment people have to conventional institutions and their ability to exert authority over their children. While this view is persuasive, it is also possible that unemployed offenders stand a greater chance of being detected, convicted, and incarcerated than the employed. Nonetheless, the fact that known offenders are often underemployed or unemployed is generally supportive of a crime–unemployment relationship.

There are a number of possible explanations for the rather weak crime–unemployment association. It may be that only extremely high unemployment rates are associated with crime. As you may recall, crime rates peaked in the 1930s during the Great Depression. It is possible that only such a long and sustained period of economic chaos can affect crime rates. Recent short-term fluctuations in the economy may be of too short a duration to have a measurable effect.

The unemployment–crime relationship may also be offence-specific, helping in part to explain the weaker than expected association. Unemployment seems to have the greatest influence on opportunistic property crimes, such as burglary, and the least on violent assaultive crimes, which may be motivated by noneconomic factors, such as rage, jealousy, or substance abuse.

It is also possible that the crime–unemployment relationship travels a different path than expected: Rather than joblessness motivating people to commit crime, it is possible that criminal behaviour excludes offenders from the workplace. Put another way, an early experience with delinquent behaviour and drug abuse may later result in protracted unemployment as an adult. John Hagan explains this relationship as a function of social embeddedness: the process by which early behaviour patterns become stable, lifelong habits and tendencies. Hagan found that kids with early criminal experiences, whose friends are delinquent and whose parents are convicted criminals become embedded in behaviours that result in later adult unemployment. The chain of events runs from having criminal friends and parents, engaging in delinquency, and gaining police and court contacts to losing the opportunity for meaningful employment as adults. Embeddedness in a deviant lifestyle is contrasted with the establishment of roots in a conventional one: Youths who get early work experience, who make contacts, and who learn the ropes of the job market establish the groundwork for a successful career. Hagan concludes: "Criminal youths are embedded in contexts that isolate them from the likelihood of legitimate adult employment."

So, is there an association between crime and unemployment? The data suggest that these two variables are interrelated, but it may be that crime causes unemployment and not that the unemployed become criminals.

Branches of Social Structure Theory

Considering the deprivations suffered by the lower class, it is not surprising that a disadvantaged economic class position has been viewed by many criminologists as a primary cause of crime. This view is referred to here as social structure theory. As a group, social structure theories suggest that forces operating in deteriorated lower-class areas push many of their residents into criminal behaviour patterns. These theories consider the existence of unsupervised teenage gangs, high crime rates, and social disorder in slum areas as major social problems.

Lower-class crime is often the violent, destructive product of youth gangs and marginally employed young adults. Although members of the middle and upper classes also engage in crime, social structure theorists have traditionally viewed middle-class crime or white-collar crime as being of relatively lower frequency, seriousness, and danger to the general public. This view is changing as criminology develops a better approach to the study of corporate crime. The "real crime problem" as traditionally defined is seen to be a lower-class phenomenon, beginning in youth and continuing into young adulthood.

Most social structure theories focus on the law-violating behaviour of youth. They suggest that the social forces that cause crime begin to affect people while they are relatively young and continue to influence them throughout their life. Although not all youthful offenders become adult criminals, many begin their training and learn criminal values as members of youth gangs and groups.

Social structure theorists challenge those who would suggest that crime is an expression of psychological imbalance, biological traits, insensitivity to social controls, personal choice, or any other individual-level factor. They argue that people living in equivalent social environments seem to behave in a similar, predictable fashion. If the environment did not influence human behaviour, crime rates would be distributed equally across the social structure, which they are not. Because crime rates are higher in lower-class urban centres than in middle-class suburbs, social forces must be operating in urban areas that influence or control behaviour.[15]

There are three independent yet overlapping branches within the social structure perspective: social disorganization theory, strain theory, and cultural deviance theory, as outlined in Figure 7.1.

Social disorganization theory focuses on the conditions within the urban environment that affect crime rates. A disorganized area is one in which institutions of social control, such as the family, commercial establishments, and schools, have broken down and can no longer carry out their expected or stated functions. Indicators of social disorganization include high unemployment and school dropout rates, deteriorated housing, low income levels, and large numbers of single-parent households. Residents in these areas experience conflict and despair, and antisocial behaviour flourishes.

Strain theory, the second branch of social structure theory, holds that crime is a function of the conflict between the goals people have and the means they can use to legally obtain them. Strain theorists argue that

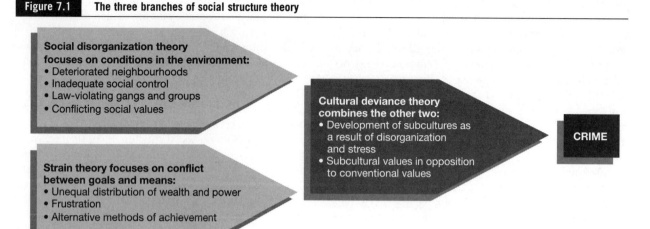

Figure 7.1   The three branches of social structure theory

Social disorganization theory focuses on conditions in the environment:
- Deteriorated neighbourhoods
- Inadequate social control
- Law-violating gangs and groups
- Conflicting social values

Strain theory focuses on conflict between goals and means:
- Unequal distribution of wealth and power
- Frustration
- Alternative methods of achievement

Cultural deviance theory combines the other two:
- Development of subcultures as a result of disorganization and stress
- Subcultural values in opposition to conventional values

CRIME

while social and economic goals are common to people in all economic strata, the ability to obtain these goals is class-dependent. Most people desire wealth, material possessions, power, prestige, and other life comforts. Members of the lower class are unable to achieve these symbols of success through conventional means. Consequently, they feel anger, frustration, and resentment, which is referred to as strain. Lower-class citizens can either accept their condition and live out their days as socially responsible, if unrewarded, citizens, or they can choose an alternative means of achieving success, such as theft, violence, or drug trafficking.

Cultural deviance theory, the third variation of structural theory, combines elements of both strain and social disorganization. According to this view, because of strain and social isolation, unique lower-class cultures develop in disorganized neighbourhoods. These independent **sub-cultures** maintain a unique set of values and beliefs that are in conflict with conventional social norms. Criminal behaviour is an expression of conformity to lower-class subcultural values and traditions and not a rebellion against conventional society. Subcultural values are handed down from one generation to the next in a process called **cultural transmission.**

While distinct in critical aspects, each of these three approaches has at its core the view that socially isolated people, living in disorganized neighbourhoods, are the ones most likely to experience crime-producing social forces. We will now examine each branch of social structure theory in some detail.

Social Disorganization Theory

Social disorganization theory links crime rates to neighbourhood ecological characteristics. Crime rates are elevated in highly transient, "mixed-use" (residential and commercial properties exist side by side) or "changing neighbourhoods" in which the fabric of social life has become frayed. These localities are unable to provide essential services, such as education, health care, and proper housing, and experience significant levels of unemployment, single-parent families, and families on welfare and aid to dependent children (see Figure 7.2).

Social disorganization theory views crime-ridden neighbourhoods as ones in which residents are trying to leave at the earliest opportunity. Common sources of control, such as the family, school, business community, social service agencies, are weak and disorganized. Personal relationships are strained because neighbours are constantly moving. Constant resident turnover weakens communications and blocks attempts at solving neighbourhood problems or establishing common goals.[16]

Concentric Zone Theory

Social disorganization theory was popularized by the work of two Chicago sociologists, Clifford R. Shaw and Henry McKay, who linked life in transitional slum areas to the inclination to commit crime. Shaw and McKay began their pioneering research in Chicago during the early 1920s while working for a state-supported social service agency.[17] They were heavily influenced by the thoughts of the Chicago School sociologists Ernest Burgess and Robert Park, who had pioneered the ecological analysis of urban life.

Shaw and McKay began their analysis during a period in the city's history that was typical of the transition taking place in many other urban areas. Chicago had experienced a mid-19th-century population expansion, fuelled by a dramatic influx of foreign-born immigrants. Congregating in the central city, the newcomers occupied the oldest housing.

Physically deteriorating sections of the city soon developed. This condition prompted the city's wealthy, established citizens to become concerned about the moral

Figure 7.2 Social disorganization theory

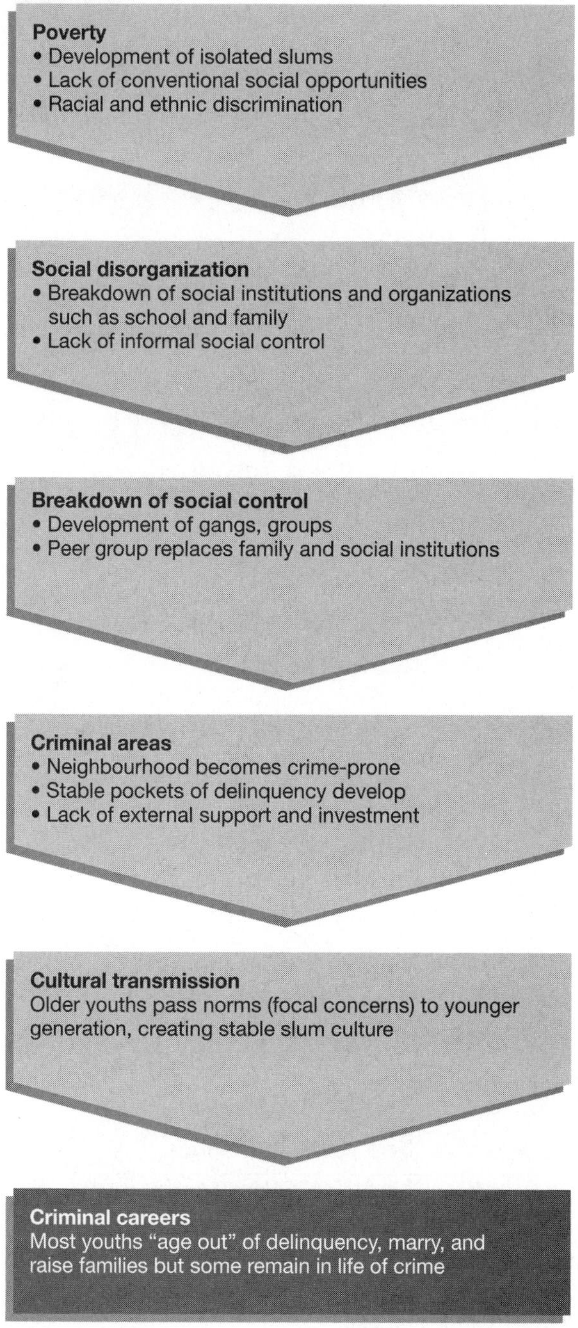

Poverty
- Development of isolated slums
- Lack of conventional social opportunities
- Racial and ethnic discrimination

Social disorganization
- Breakdown of social institutions and organizations such as school and family
- Lack of informal social control

Breakdown of social control
- Development of gangs, groups
- Peer group replaces family and social institutions

Criminal areas
- Neighbourhood becomes crime-prone
- Stable pockets of delinquency develop
- Lack of external support and investment

Cultural transmission
Older youths pass norms (focal concerns) to younger generation, creating stable slum culture

Criminal careers
Most youths "age out" of delinquency, marry, and raise families but some remain in life of crime

trialization, urbanization, immigration, and increased geographic and social mobility.

Transitional Neighbourhoods. Shaw and McKay explained crime and delinquency within the context of the changing urban environment and ecological development of the city. They saw that Chicago had developed into distinct "natural areas," some affluent and others wracked by extreme poverty. The transitional areas had high rates of population turnover and were incapable of inducing residents to remain and defend the neighbourhood against criminal groups.

Low rents in these areas attracted newly arrived immigrants from Europe who congregated in these **transitional neighbourhoods**. Their children were torn between being assimilated into a new culture and abiding by the traditional values of their parents. Informal social control mechanisms that had restrained behaviour in the "old country" or rural areas were disrupted. These slum areas were believed to be the spawning grounds of young criminals.

In transitional slum areas, successive changes in the composition of population, the disintegration of traditional cultures, divergent cultural standards, and the gradual industrialization of the area resulted in dissolution of neighbourhood culture and organization. The continuity of conventional neighbourhood traditions and institutions was broken. The effectiveness of the neighbourhood as a unit of control and as a medium for the transmission of the moral standards of society was greatly diminished. High population turnover impeded the establishment of common values and norms. Children growing up in these areas had little access to the cultural heritages of conventional society. For the most part, the organization of their behaviour took place through participation in the spontaneous play groups and organized gangs that developed in these areas. The values they developed were then passed down through succeeding generations through cultural transmission. Frederic Thrasher documents this well in his 1927 classic *The Gang*.

Concentric Zones. Shaw and McKay identified the areas in Chicago that had excessive crime rates. Using a model of analysis pioneered by Ernest Burgess, they noted that distinct ecological areas had developed in the city, comprising a series of five concentric circles, or zones, and that there were stable and significant differences in interzone crime rates (see Figure 7.3 for how Thrasher adapted this in his study of city gangs). The areas of heaviest concentration of crime appeared to be the transitional inner-city zones, where large numbers of foreign-born citizens had recently settled. The zones farthest from the city's centre had correspondingly lower crime rates. Analysis of these data indicated a surprisingly stable pattern of criminal activity in the five ecological zones over a 65-year period.

Shaw and McKay concluded that in transitional neighbourhoods, multiple cultures and diverse values, both conventional and deviant, coexist. Kids growing up

fabric of Chicago society. The belief was widespread that immigrants from Europe were crime-prone and morally dissolute. In fact, local groups were created with the very purpose of "saving" the children of poor families from moral decadence.[18] It was popular to view crime as the province of inferior racial and ethnic groups, but as we can see, this belief was rooted in the anxiety over social changes altering the face of 20th-century society: indus-

Figure 7.3   Thasher's concentric zone map of Chicago gangland

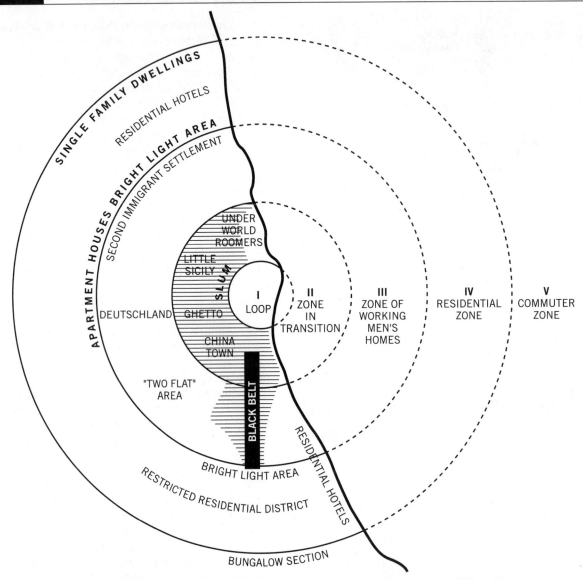

SOURCE: Frederic M. Thrasher, *The Gang: A Study of 1,313 Gangs in Chicago* (Chicago: University of Chicago Press, 1927), p. 24.

in the street culture often find that adults who have adopted a deviant lifestyle, such as the gambler, pimp, or the drug dealer, are the most financially successful people in the neighbourhood. Required to choose between conventional and deviant lifestyles, many slum kids opt for the latter. They join with like-minded youths and form law-violating gangs and cliques. The development of teenage law-violating groups is an essential element of youthful misbehaviour in slum areas. Because of their deviant values, slum youths often come into conflict with existing middle-class norms, which demand strict obedience to the legal code. Consequently, a **value conflict** occurs that sets the delinquent youth and his or her peer group even further apart from conventional society. The result is a fuller acceptance of deviant goals and behav-

iour. Shut out of conventional society, neighbourhood street gangs become fixed institutions, recruiting new members and passing on delinquent traditions from one generation to the next.

Shaw and McKay's statistical analysis confirmed their theoretical suspicions. They found that even though crime rates changed, the highest rates were always in zones I and II (central city and transitional areas). The areas with the highest crime rates retained high rates even when over time families moved out to the suburbs and the ethnic composition changed (in this case, from German and Irish to Italian and Polish).[19]

The Legacy of Shaw and McKay. Social disorganization concepts originally articulated by Shaw and McKay have remained prominent within criminology for more than 75 years. The most important is that crime is a creature of the destructive ecological conditions in urban slums. Criminals were not, as some criminologists of the time believed, biologically inferior, intellectually impaired, or psychologically damaged. Crime was a constant fixture in a slum area regardless of the racial or ethnic identity of its residents.

Since the basis of their theory was that neighbourhood disintegration and slum conditions are the primary causes of criminal behaviour, Shaw and McKay paved the way for the many community action and treatment programs developed in the last half-century. Shaw was the founder of one very influential community-based treatment program, the Chicago Area Project.

Another important feature of Shaw and McKay's work is that it depicted both adult criminality and delinquent gang memberships as a normal response to the adverse social conditions in urban slum areas. Their findings mirror Durkheim's concept that crime can be normal and useful.

Despite these noteworthy achievements, the validity of Shaw and McKay's findings has been subject to challenge. Some have faulted their assumption that neighbourhoods are essentially stable, while others have found their definition of social disorganization confusing.[20] The most important criticism, however, concerns their use of police records to calculate neighbourhood crime rates. A zone's high crime rate may be a function of the level of local police surveillance and may therefore obscure interzone crime rate differences. Numerous studies indicate that police use extensive discretion when arresting people and that social status is one factor that influences their decisions. It is likely that people in middle-class neighbourhoods commit many criminal acts that never show up in official statistics, while people in lower-class areas face a far greater chance of arrest and court adjudication.[21] Thus, the relationship between environment and crime rates may be a reflection of police behaviour and not criminal behaviour.

These criticisms aside, the Shaw–McKay theory provides a valuable contribution to our understanding of the causes of criminal behaviour. By introducing a new variable—the ecology of the city—into the study of crime, the authors paved the way for succeeding generations of criminologists to focus on the social influences on criminal and delinquent behaviour.

The Social Ecology School

During the 1970s, criminologists were influenced by several critical analyses of social disorganization theory that presented challenges to its validity. During this period, theories with a social psychological orientation, stressing offender socialization within the family, school, and peer group, dominated the criminological literature.

Connections

If social disorganization causes crime, why are the majority of low-income people law abiding? To explain this anomaly, some sociologists have devised theoretical models suggesting that individual socialization experiences mediate the effect of environmental influences. These theories will be discussed in Chapter 9.

Despite its "fall from grace," the social disorganization tradition was kept alive by "area studies" showing that such ecological conditions as substandard housing, low income, and unrelated people living together predicted a high incidence of delinquency.[22]

Then in the 1980s, a group of criminologists began to revive concern about the effects of social disorganization.[23] These modern-day **social ecologists** have developed a "purer" form of structural theory that stresses the relation of community deterioration and economic decline to criminality while placing less emphasis on value conflict. In the following sections, some of the more recent social ecological research is discussed in some detail.

Community Deterioration. A growing body of literature indicates that crime rates are associated with community-level indicators of social disorganization, including disorder, poverty, alienation, disassociation, and fear of crime.[24] Neighbourhoods that are deteriorated and have a high percentage of deserted houses and apartments experience high crime rates; abandoned buildings serve as a "magnet for crime."[25] Areas in which houses are in poor repair, boarded up, and burned out and whose owners are best described as "slumlords" are also sites of the highest violence rates and gun crime.[26] The percentage of people living in poverty and the percentage of broken homes are strongly related to neighbourhood crime rates.[27] Gangs flourish in deteriorated neighbourhoods, adding to the crime rate. In one Chicago area study, G. David Curry and Irving Spergel found that gang homicide rates were associated with such variables as the percentage of the neighbourhood living below the poverty line, the lack of mortgage investment in a neighbourhood, the unemployment rate, and the influx of new immigrant groups; these factors are usually found in disorganized areas.[28]

The relationship between community deterioration and crime is found in many countries. Cross-national research conducted in Scandinavia found a clear link between crime and measures of social disorganization.[29] Socially disorganized neighbourhoods in Great Britain experience the highest amounts of crime and victimization. Communities characterized by sparse friendship networks, unsupervised teenage peer groups, and low organizational participation also had the greatest amounts of criminality. The social disorganization model,

Culture, Gender, Ethnicity, and Criminology

Carl Dawson and the McGill School

Carl Addington Dawson was born in 1887 in Augustine Cove, Prince Edward Island. He studied sociology at Acadia University in the 1890s, and then served as pastor of a Baptist church in Lockeport, Nova Scotia. Acadia was one of the first universities to offer courses in sociology, which was seen by urban reformers, settlement-house workers, and social-gospel ministers as a way to deal with the problems of urbanization and industrialization.

Dawson did not think that social reform was the best way to improve social conditions, but he believed that research and investigation of urban communities and their institutions would provide the insight to create a better society. Many churches were convinced that sin was not so much a product of an individual's shortcomings as it was a condition forced on that person by his or her position in society. The Baptists, for example, talked about improving the social environment as a way of preventing the production of criminals; they advocated prison reform, prohibition, and justice to native Canadians. They argued for inner-city missions, protection for children, and women's rights. Prohibitionists in Nova Scotia were motivated by a desire to eliminate the roots of human unhappiness, to create a society in which crime, disease, and social injustice would not exist.

Dawson had studied at Chicago and was brought to McGill University to research the problems of post-war Montreal. He was hired as the director of the School of Social Work, then became head of the first department of sociology in Canada in 1924. The new science of sociology gave the observer the

opportunity to understand the forces that led to social fragmentation and social cohesion. Human ecology combined ideas borrowed from plant and animal ecology, physiology, and cultural anthropology. This became the framework within which all McGill sociology courses were taught, and the frame of reference for all research projects undertaken by Dawson, his colleagues, and his students throughout the 1920s and 1930s.

Sociologists turned primarily to biology for guidelines because, among other things, they found in that discipline suggestions for explaining the flux that characterized human society. Existence was a struggle for survival, yet all beings were bound up in a web of relations with other beings, not because they were bound to the physical environment alone. Higher life-forms succeeded the lower ones by "invading" an area and forcing the inhabitants to settle in a zone on the rim of its original habitat. This would create instability until an equilibrium was attained, especially as centres of dominance emerged at focal points in transportation and communication.

Dawson saw society as an order that transcended its individual members, and the ultimate end of the evolutionary process was to establish an equilibrium and a harmonious social order. In keeping with his training, he chose not to focus on social pathology but rather to investigate the broader structure of the city and the way in which it moulded the behaviour and institutions of its inhabitants. His research was into *ordinary* areas, to "problemize the unproblematical," to ascertain through careful observation the social changes that were caused by advances in communication and transportation.

The city, he said, was an organism, with a centre of dominance—the business sector—around which were arranged a number of zones in concentric circles, their use and occupants varying with the value of the land and the distance from the centre. Each zone was divided into "natural areas," marked off from each other by natural or artificial boundaries and distinguished by their own characteristic institutions and populations. Inhabitants were "sifted" to these areas by a selective process, and their attitudes and behaviour were shaped by it. He and his students looked at industrial development, transportation innovations, immigration, housing, labour organization, crime, juvenile delinquency, family disorganization, welfare work, and child labour. They plotted railroad property, industrial and commercial frontage, parks, boulevards, and physiographic barriers on maps of the city.

At the turn of the century, only about one-third of the province's population were urban dwellers, but by 1928 Montreal had become the fifth largest city in North America. Its port, industries, and services drew migrants and immigrants by the thousands every year. Electric streetcars, first introduced in 1892, contributed to the expansion of the city and enabled thousands of workers to move out of the city's inner core into the numerous residential neighbourhoods and suburbs that were springing up all around the city. While the main tendencies of expansion radially from the centre held true for Montreal, its topographic features distorted the concentric circles in a kidney shape around Mont Royal, as shown in Figure 7.4.

As the city grew, business institutions that had been located near the river encroached on the residential district, where the old walled town of Ville Marie once stood. The St. Antoine district, on the verge of becoming a slum in the 1920s, had been created by the expansion of the business section. The area's more successful residents had already moved above the hill and to the west. The part of Montreal that experienced the most disruption as the business centre expanded was Dufferin district, a neighbourhood that lay in the city's transitional zone.

Robert Percy, an M.A. student who undertook the study of the area, found that the Dufferin district became a slum at the turn of the century, when the commercial sector of Montreal expanded and a flood of Asian and European immigrants poured into the city. Its boundaries were invaded by machine shops, warehouses, and light manufacturing. The more successful among the English, Irish, Scottish, and French families who lived in the district departed, and their vacated homes were remodelled into flats and occupied by the less prosperous.

While stable residential neighbourhoods were well equipped with churches and schools, Dufferin district did not have many such institutions, and rescue missions first made their appearance in Dufferin district in the 1890s. This was the disorganized physical environment, where there was constant noise, dirt, stimulation, vice, and despair.

Although the work of Carl Dawson and his students has been overshadowed by the Chicago School, it represents an important period in Canadian criminology, an attempt to apply scientific principles to the study of the natural organization of crime.

Muriel Bernice McCall and the study of social disorganization. Muriel McCall was one of the first to graduate with an M.A. in Sociology from McGill. In her 1928 thesis, McCall says that the population of any great city is heterogeneous rather than homogeneous. In the area of transition, "they are crowded together for the most part in cheap boarding houses under most unsatisfactory conditions. They are casual by nature and by choice preferring work as lackeys and porters or even bootblacks to employment of a more permanent nature. Their sense of moral right and wrong is practically lacking. When they do enter into any legal marriage relationship they regard it very lightly. They are ready to air their troubles on the slightest provocation and therefore contribute a great deal of disintegration."

On the other hand, "the fourth zone is the habitat of the upper middle and professional classes. Private ownership of a home and restrictions upon how and where it shall be built appear here for the first time. The homes in Westmount and in Notre Dame de Grace are homes of this kind. Small lawns appear in front of the house and some attempt is made to have the exterior of the home as attractive as the interior. There are children but the families tend to be small and

the care of them is often left to nurse maids hired for the purpose. Husband and wife are on an equality of footing. Father has his club and mother has hers. If they find it impossible to get any enjoyment out of being together there are always a multiplicity of other activities ready to claim them."

Sources: I am indebted to Marlene Shore for an excellent overview to this neglected period in Canadian criminological history, in *The Science of Social Redemption: McGill, the Chicago School, and the Origins of Social Research in Canada*, Toronto: University of Toronto Press, 1987. Also, Carl Dawson, "Research and Social Action," *Social Welfare* 5, 1923: 93–5; S.D. Clark, "Sociology in Canada: An Historical Overview," *Canadian Journal of Sociology* 1, 1975; V.A. Tomovic, "Sociology in Canada: An Analysis of Its Growth in English Language Universities, 1908–1972," Ph.D. thesis, University of Waterloo 1975; E.R. Forbes, "Prohibition and the Social Gospel in Nova Scotia," *Acadiensis* 1, 1971; John S. Moir, "*The Canadian Baptist* and the Social Gospel Movement, 1879–1914," in Jarold K. Zeman, ed., *Baptists in Canada: A Search for Identity Amidst Diversity*, Burlington: G.R. Welsh, 1980; C.A. Dawson, "Human Ecology," in *The Fields and Methods of Sociology*, ed. L.L. Bernard, New York: Ray Lang and Richard Smith, 1934; C.A. Dawson, "The City as an Organism. With Special Reference to Montreal," in *McGill University Publications*, 13 (1926); Wilfrid Emmerson Israel, "The Montreal Negro Community," M.A. thesis, McGill, 1928; Muriel Bernice McCall, "A Study of Family Disorganization in Canada," M.A. thesis, McGill, 1928; Wilfrid Emmerson Israel, "The Montreal Negro Community," M.A. thesis, McGill, 1928; Margaret Millicent Wade, "A Sociological Study of the Dependent Child," M.A. thesis, McGill, 1931.

then, has the power to explain crime rates in countries with similar socioeconomic conditions.[30]

Employment Opportunities. The relationship between unemployment and crime is unsettled: Aggregate crime rates and aggregate unemployment rates seem weakly related. Yet high unemployment may have crime-producing effects in particular neighbourhoods or areas.

Shaw and McKay found that areas wracked by poverty also experience social disorganization.[31]

Research indicates that neighbourhoods that provide few employment opportunities for youths and adults are the most vulnerable to predatory crime. Unemployment helps destabilize households, and unstable families are the ones most likely to contain children who put a premium on violence and aggression as a means of dealing

| Figure 7.4 | A Kidney-Zone Map of Social Differentiation in Montreal |

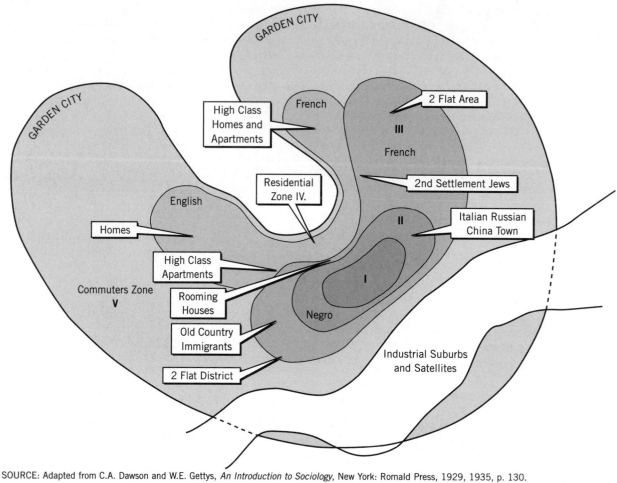

SOURCE: Adapted from C.A. Dawson and W.E. Gettys, *An Introduction to Sociology*, New York: Romald Press, 1929, 1935, p. 130.

with limited opportunity. Crime rates increase when large groups or cohorts of people of the same age compete for relatively scant resources.[32]

Limited employment opportunities also reduce the stabilizing influence of parents and other adults, who once counteracted the allure of youth gangs.[33] Even the most deteriorated neighbourhoods have a surprising degree of familial and kinship strength. Yet the consistent pattern of crime and neighbourhood disorganization that follows periods of high unemployment can neutralize their social control capability.

Community Fear. Disorganized neighbourhoods suffer social and physical incivilities—rowdy youth, trash and litter, graffiti, abandoned storefronts, burned-out buildings, littered lots, strangers, drunks, vagabonds, loiterers, prostitutes, noise, congestion, angry words, dirt, and stench. The presence of such incivilities helps convince residents of disorganized areas that their neighbourhood is dangerous and that they face a considerable chance of becoming crime victims. Not surprisingly, when crime

rates are actually high in these disorganized areas, fear levels undergo a dramatic increase.[34] Perceptions of crime and victimization produce neighbourhood fear.[35]

Fear becomes most pronounced in areas undergoing rapid and unexpected racial and age-composition changes, especially when they are out of proportion to the rest of the city.[36] Fear can become contagious. People tell others of their personal involvement with victimization, spreading the word that the neighbourhood is getting dangerous and that the chance of future victimization is high.[37] People dread leaving their homes at night and withdraw from community life. Not surprisingly, people who have already been victimized are more fearful of the future than those who have escaped crime.[38]

When fear grips a neighbourhood, business conditions begin to deteriorate, population mobility increases, and a "criminal element" begins to drift into the area. Fear helps produce more crime, as people decrease their level of "ownership" and stay off the street, increasing the chances of victimization, producing even more fear, in a never-ending loop.

Connections

Chapter 5's discussion of choice theory mentioned that communities characterized by "broken windows" had higher crime rates.

Siege Mentality. One unique aspect of community fear is the development of a **siege mentality**, in which the outside world is considered the enemy out to destroy the neighbourhood.[39] The siege mentality results in mistrust of critical social institutions, including business, government, and schools. Government officials seem arrogant and haughty. Residents become self-conscious, worried about respect, and sensitive to anyone who disrespects or "disses" them. When police ignore crime in poor areas, or when they are violent and corrupt, anger flares and people take to the streets and react in violent ways.

In 1992, after the Rodney King verdict acquitting four police officers in Los Angeles, people rioted as far away as Toronto, a city that certainly has less minority and police conflict than Los Angeles, but there was concern that blacks were getting injured and killed by police in Canada. There has long been tension between the police and ethnic minorities in large Canadian cities, where immigration has swelled the numbers of the non-white population.

Population Turnover. In our industrial society, urban areas undergoing rapid structural changes in racial and economic composition also seem to experience the greatest change in crime rates. Recent studies recognize that change and not stability is the hallmark of inner-city areas. A neighbourhood's residents, wealth, and density are constantly changing. Even disorganized neighbourhoods acquire new identifying features. Some may become multiracial, while others become racially homogeneous; some areas become stable and family-oriented, while in others, mobile, never-married people predominate.

As areas decline, residents flee to safer, more stable localities. Those who can't leave because they cannot afford to live in more affluent communities face an even greater risk of victimization. Because of racial differences in economic well-being, those "left behind" are all too often members of minority groups. Those who can't move find themselves surrounded by a constant influx of new residents. High population turnover can have a devastating effect on community culture because it interrupts communication and information flow.[40] A culture may develop that dictates standards of dress, language, and behaviour to neighbourhood youth that are in opposition to those of conventional society. All these factors are likely to produce increasing crime rates.

Community Change. Social ecologists have attempted to chart the change that undermines urban areas. Urban areas may have life cycles, which begin with the building of residential dwellings, followed by a period of decline with marked decreases in socioeconomic status and increases in population density. Later stages in this life cycle include changing racial or ethnic makeup, population thinning, and finally a renewal stage in which obsolete housing is replaced and/or upgraded (gentrification). There are indications that areas undergoing such change experience increases in their crime rates.[41] Communities go through cycles in which neighbourhood deterioration precedes increasing rates of crime and delinquency.[42] Those communities most likely to experience a rapid increase in antisocial behaviour contain large numbers of single-parent families and unrelated people living together. These areas have gone from having owner-occupied to renter-occupied units and have an economic base that has lost semiskilled and unskilled jobs. These ecological disruptions strain existing social control mechanisms and inhibit their ability to control crime and delinquency.

A large body of research shows that changing lifestyles in urban neighbourhoods, including declining economic status, increasing population, and racial shifts, are associated with increased neighbourhood crime rates, and even areas adjoining neighbourhoods undergoing racial change will experience corresponding increases in their own crime rates.[43] This phenomenon may reflect community reaction to perceived racial and class conflict. In changing neighbourhoods, adults support the law-violating behaviour of youths and encourage them to protect their property and way of life by violently resisting newcomers.

Poverty Concentration. One aspect of community change may be the concentration of poverty in deteriorated neighbourhoods. While poverty rates or unemployment may not be direct causes of crime, the most deteriorated areas even within the context of the slum seem to have much higher crime rates than more stable lower-class environments. Working and middle-class families flee inner-city poverty areas, resulting in a **concentration effect** in which elements of the most disadvantaged population are consolidated in urban ghettos. As the working and middle classes move out, they take with them their financial and institutional resources and support. Businesses are disinclined to locate in poverty areas; banks become reluctant to lend money for new housing or businesses.

Areas marked by concentrated poverty become isolated and insulated from the social mainstream and more prone to criminal activity. Gangs also concentrate in these areas, bringing with them a significant increase in criminal activity.[44] The concentration effect contradicts, in some measure, Shaw and McKay's assumption that crime rates increase in transitional neighbourhoods. Today the areas that may be the most crime-prone may be stable, homogeneous areas whose residents are "trapped" in public housing and urban ghettos. Ethnically and racially isolated areas maintain the highest crime rates.[45]

Weak Social Controls. Most neighbourhood residents share the common goal of living in a crime-free area. Some communities have the power to regulate the behaviour of their residents through the influence of community institutions, such as the family and school. Other neighbourhoods, experiencing social disorganization, find that efforts at social control are weak and attenuated. When community social control efforts are blunted, crime rates increase, further weakening neighbourhood cohesiveness in a never-ending cycle.

Neighbourhoods maintain a variety of agencies and institutions of social control. Some operate on the primary or private level and involve peers, families, and relatives. These sources exert informal control by either awarding or withholding approval, respect, and admiration. Informal control mechanisms include direct criticism, ridicule, ostracism, desertion, and physical punishment.[46] Communities also use internal networks and local institutions to control crime. Sources of institutional social control include businesses, stores, schools, churches, and social service and volunteer organizations.

Stable neighbourhoods are also able to arrange for external sources of social control. For example, community organizations and local leaders may have sufficient political clout to get funding for additional law enforcement personnel. The presence of police sends a message that the area will not tolerate deviant behaviour. Criminals and drug dealers avoid such areas and relocate to easier and more appealing targets.[47]

As neighbourhood disadvantage increases, its level of informal social control decreases.[48] In areas where social control remains high, children are less likely to become involved with deviant peers and to engage in problem behaviours. Since the population is transient in disorganized areas, interpersonal relationships remain superficial; social institutions such as schools and churches cannot work effectively in a climate of alienation and mistrust. In these areas, the absence of local political power limits access to external funding and police protection. Without money from the outside, the neighbourhood lacks the ability to "get back on its feet."[49]

Social control is also weakened because unsupervised peer groups and gangs, which flourish in disorganized areas, disrupt the influence of neighbourhood control agents.[50] Children who live in disorganized neighbourhoods find that involvement with conventional social institutions, such as schools and afternoon programs, is blocked; they are instead at risk for recruitment into gangs and law-violating groups.[51]

Social Altruism. The inverse of communities that provide weak social controls are those that provide strong social supports for their members. Residents teach one another that they have moral and social obligations to their fellow citizens; children learn to be sensitive to the rights of others and respect differences. In contrast, less altruistic communities stress individualism and self-interest.

Areas that place a greater stress on caring for fellow citizens seem, not surprisingly, less crime-prone than those that emphasize self-reliance. In an important survey, Mitchell Chamlin and John Cochran found that social altruism (which they define as the ratio of contributions given to the United Way charity by area income levels) is inversely related to crime rates.[52] More generous and caring areas are also relatively crime-free. Their findings can be interpreted in two ways: (1) crime rates are lower in altruistic areas; (2) well-funded charities help lower crime rates by providing a secure safety net for "at-risk" families.

Taken in sum, the writings of the social ecology school show that (1) social disorganization produces criminality and (2) the quality of community life, including levels of change, fear, incivility, poverty, and deterioration, has a direct influence on an area's crime rate. It is not some individual property or trait that causes some people to commit crime but the quality and ambience of the community in which they reside.

Strain Theory

Inhabitants of a disorganized inner-city area feel isolated, frustrated, left out of the economic mainstream, hopeless, and eventually angry and enraged. What effect do these feelings have on criminal activities?

Criminologists who view crime as a direct result of lower-class frustration and anger are referred to as strain theorists. They believe that while most people share similar values and goals, the ability to achieve personal goals is stratified by socioeconomic class. Strain is limited in affluent areas because educational and vocational opportunities are available. In socially disorganized areas, however, strain occurs because legitimate avenues for success are all but closed. To relieve strain, indigent people may be forced to either use deviant methods to achieve their goals, such as theft or drug trafficking, or reject socially accepted goals outright and substitute other, more deviant goals, such as being tough and aggressive (see Figure 7.5).

Anomie Theory

The roots of strain theories can be traced to Emile Durkheim's notion of anomie (from the Greek *a nomos*, "without norms"). According to Durkheim, an anomic society is one in which rules of behaviour, called *norms*, have broken down or become inoperative during periods of rapid social change. Anomie is most likely to occur in societies that are moving from a preindustrial model held together by traditions, shared values, and unquestioned beliefs. In industrial societies, which are highly developed and dependent on the division of labour, people are connected by their interdependent needs for one another's services and production. This shift in traditions and values creates social turmoil. Established norms begin to erode and lose meaning, a theme we saw also arises in disorganization theory. If a division occurs between what the population expects and what the economic and productive forces of society can realistically deliver, a crisis situation develops that can manifest itself in normlessness, or anomie.

Anomie undermines society's social control functions. Every society works to limit people's goals and desires. If a society becomes anomic, it can no longer establish and maintain control over its population's wants and desires. Since people find it difficult to control their appetites, their demands become unlimited. Under these circumstances, obedience to legal codes may be strained, making alternative behaviour choices, such as crimes, inevitable.

Durkheim's ideas were applied to criminology by sociologist Robert Merton in his theory of anomie.[53] Merton used a modified version of the concept of anomie to fit social, economic, and cultural conditions found in modern society. He found that two elements of culture

Famous Canadian Criminals

Women Who Kill Their Children

Prior to the 20th century, killing an infant was classed as murder and the current conception of postpartum depression did not exist. In the 18th century, the main offence under which women were charged was concealment of birth. And if a "bastard" child was born dead, it was assumed that the mother had killed the baby. Given the circumstances juries were often unwilling to convict. In 1867, infanticide was formally added as a form of murder, and in 1948, the current understanding of infanticide having a mental component came into effect. However, even before that change, it was commonly understood that some women lived lives of desperation that might result in them killing their babies. Contraception had been criminalized, abortion was not legally available, and single mothers were seen as deviant. Homes where unwed mothers could have their babies and give them up for adoption were common.

Consider the case of Marie McCabe, who in 1880 came to Canada with the help of a charitable organization. When she was six her mother died, and her father suffered an industrial accident. The nine children were placed in an orphanage, but only

Crime in the News

Concealment of Birth
Globe and Mail 1881
Mr. Fenton stated that he did not wish to press the charge against Mrs. Phair, and he did not think that anything could be proved against her.

Mrs. Phair was then discharged.

Mr. Murphy, on behalf of Emma Phair, said that he would withdraw the plea of not guilty, and put in one of guilty. He would also ask to be allowed to call witnesses to testify to the character borne by the defendants.

A number of witnesses were called, and all gave the unfortunate girl an excellent character, stating that she was a hard-working, quiet girl, and the sole support of her mother.

The Magistrate reserved judgment to the 21st.

This finished the business, and the Court rose.

Marie and her sister survived. Working as a chambermaid in a Quebec City hotel, she became pregnant by a local businessman, who promptly abandoned her. The local city welfare officials and private charity sources refused to help her, even after her child was born. In desperation she struck a deal with a family who agreed to keep her and the baby, and then adopt the child at the age of one.

However the deal was not a happy one, and when the baby was four months old, she abandoned it in a cistern, where it drowned. The corpse was discovered six months later, and she was charged by the police. She pled guilty at the coroner's inquest and then at the trial. She was sentenced to death

in 1883; however public concern suddenly appeared, and her case was trumpeted in the local newspaper. Calls for her clemency resulted in the commutation of her death penalty, and she was eventually released in 1889.

Today, it is recognized that emotional imbalance, as well as social situations, have an effect on the mother. Very few cases of infanticide come forward in any year, and they are treated very differently now than they were in the past.

Sources: I am indebted to Frank Anderson's *A Dance with Death: Canadian Women on the Gallows, 1754–1954* (Saskatoon: Fifth House, 1996). Also Helen Boritch, *Fallen Women: Female Crime and Criminal Justice in Canada* (Toronto: ITP Nelson, 1997).

Figure 7.5   The basic components of strain theory

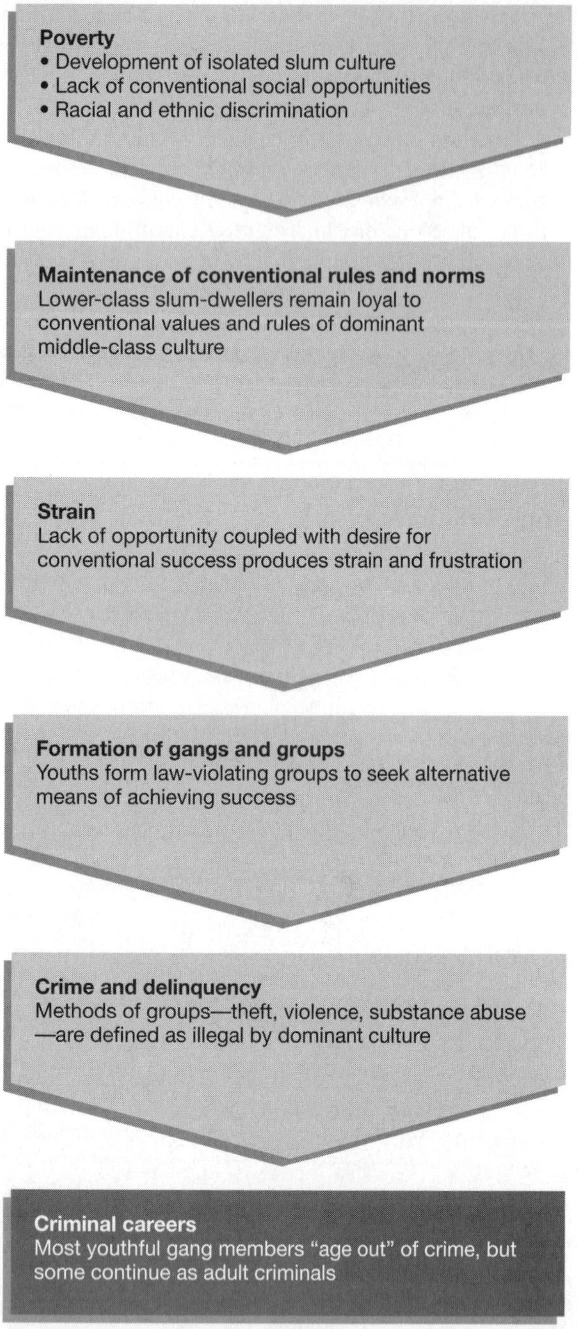

Poverty
- Development of isolated slum culture
- Lack of conventional social opportunities
- Racial and ethnic discrimination

Maintenance of conventional rules and norms
Lower-class slum-dwellers remain loyal to conventional values and rules of dominant middle-class culture

Strain
Lack of opportunity coupled with desire for conventional success produces strain and frustration

Formation of gangs and groups
Youths form law-violating groups to seek alternative means of achieving success

Crime and delinquency
Methods of groups—theft, violence, substance abuse—are defined as illegal by dominant culture

Criminal careers
Most youthful gang members "age out" of crime, but some continue as adult criminals

interact to produce potentially anomic conditions: culturally defined goals and socially approved means for obtaining them. For example, modern societies stress the goals of acquiring wealth, success, and power, and the socially permissible means of achieving those goals, which include hard work, education, and thrift.

Merton argued that the legitimate means to acquire wealth are stratified across class and status lines. Consequently, those with little formal education and few economic resources soon find that they are denied the ability to legally acquire wealth, the preeminent success symbol.

When socially desirable goals are uniform throughout society and access to legitimate means is bound by class and status, a strain occurs among those who are locked out of the legitimate opportunity structure. Consequently, they may develop criminal or delinquent solutions to the problem of attaining goals.

Social Adaptations. Merton argued that some people have inadequate means of attaining success, and others who do have the means reject societal goals as being unsuited to them. Table 7.1 shows Merton's diagram of the hypothetical relationship between social goals, the means for getting them, and the individual actor.

Conformity occurs when individuals both embrace conventional social goals and have the means at their disposal to attain them. In a balanced, stable society, this is the most common social adaptation. If a majority of its people did not practise conformity, the society would cease to exist.

Innovation occurs when an individual accepts the goals of society but rejects legitimate means or is incapable of attaining them through such means. Many people desire material goods and luxuries but lack the financial ability to attain them. The resulting conflict forces them to adopt innovative solutions to their dilemma: They steal, sell drugs, or extort money. Of the five adaptations, innovation is most closely associated with criminal behaviour.

If successful, innovation can have serious, long-term social consequences. Criminal success helps convince otherwise law-abiding people that innovative means work better and faster than conventional ones. The prosperous drug dealer's expensive car and flashy clothes give out the message that crime pays. "The process thus enlarges the extent of anomie within the system," claims Merton, "so that others, who did not respond in the form of deviant behaviour to the relatively slight anomie which they first obtained, come to do so as anomie is spread and is intensified."[54] This explains why crime is created and sustained in certain low-income ecological areas.

Ritualism occurs when social goals are lowered in importance and means are elevated. Ritualists gain pleasure from the practice of traditional ceremonies that have neither a real purpose nor a goal. The strict set of manners and customs in religious orders, feudal societies, clubs, and college fraternities encourage and appeal to ritualists. Ritualists should have the lowest level of criminal behaviour because they have abandoned the success goal that is at the root of criminal activity.

Retreatists reject both the goals and the means of society. Merton suggested that people who adjust in this fashion are "in the society but not of it." Included in this category are "psychotics, outcasts, vagrants, vagabonds, tramps, chronic drunkards, and drug addicts." Because

Table 7.1	Merton's typology of individual modes of adaptation		
Modes of Adaptation		**Cultural Goals**	**Institutionalized Means**
I.	Conformity	+	+
I.	Innovation	+	−
II.	Ritualism	−	+
V.	Retreatism	−	−
V.	Rebellion	±	±

Source: Robert Merton, "Social Structure and Anomie," in *Social Theory and Social Structure* (Glencoe, IL: Free Press, 1957).

such people are morally or otherwise incapable of using both legitimate and illegitimate means, they attempt to escape their lack of success by withdrawing, either mentally or physically. These behaviours are often both deviant and criminal, despite their lack of social harm, because withdrawing is itself deviant.

Rebellion involves substituting an alternative set of goals and means for conventional ones. Revolutionaries who wish to promote radical change in the existing social structure and who call for alternative lifestyles, goals, and beliefs are engaging in rebellion. Rebellion may be a reaction against a corrupt and hated government or an effort to create alternative opportunities and lifestyles within the existing system.

Evaluation of Anomie Theory. According to anomie theory, social inequality leads to perceptions of anomie. To resolve the goals–means conflict and relieve their sense of strain, some people innovate by stealing or extorting money, others retreat into drugs and alcohol, others rebel by joining revolutionary groups, while still others get involved in ritualistic behaviour by joining a religious cult.

Merton's view of anomie has been one of the most enduring and influential sociological theories of criminality. By linking deviant behaviour to the success goals that control social behaviour, anomie theory attempts to pinpoint the cause of the conflict that produces personal frustration and consequent criminality. By acknowledging that society unfairly distributes the legitimate means to achieving success, anomie theory helps explain the existence of high-crime areas and the apparent predominance of delinquent and criminal behaviour among the lower class. By suggesting that social conditions, not individual personalities, produce crime, Merton greatly influenced the directions taken to reduce and control criminality during the last half of the 20th century.

A number of questions are left unanswered by anomie theory.[55] Merton did not explain why people differ in their choice of criminal behaviour. Why does one anomic person become a mugger, while another deals drugs? Anomie may be used to explain differences in crime rates, but it cannot explain why most young criminals desist from crime as adults. Does this mean that perceptions of anomie dwindle with age? Is anomie short-lived?

Critics have also suggested that people pursue a number of different goals, including educational, athletic, and social success. Juveniles may be more interested in immediate goals, such as having an active social life or being a good athlete, than long-term "ideal" achievements, such as monetary success. Achieving these goals is not a matter of social class alone; other factors, including athletic ability, intelligence, personality, and family life, can either hinder or assist goal attainment.[56] Anomie theory also assumes that all people share the same goals and values, which is false.[57] Because of these and other criticisms, the theory of anomie, along with other structural theories, fell into a period of decline for almost 20 years.

Anomie Reconsidered. Like other views of criminality that stressed the influence of the social structure, strain theories fell out of favour when criminologists turned their attention to social psychological views of criminality. However, in the 1990s there has been a resurgence of interest in strain and anomie. Many may feel anomic because of the economic displacement brought on by a shifting economy. The "truly disadvantaged" in society

There is growing concern about so-called squeegee kids, who walk up to cars stopped in traffic and clean their windows. Despite the lack of evidence of any association with squeegee kids and crime, people are threatened by the tattoos, clothing, and hairstyle of these kids, who are often homeless. Cities such as Vancouver, Winnipeg, and Toronto have either passed or are considering bylaws limiting public panhandling in an effort to control the "squeegees."

seem at grave risk to both normlessness and high crime rates. In addition, some researchers have begun to reexamine original concepts and have found that with more precise measurements, perceptions of anomie are in fact associated with participation in criminal activity. Thus some of the early criticism of Merton may have been based on inadequate research results.[58] Important cross-cultural research efforts have also linked anomic conditions to criminality, indicating that anomie is not unique to culture.[59]

Criminologists are now producing newer versions of Merton's visionary concepts. Some of these work on the macro level, saying that the success goal integrated within North American society influences the nature and extent of the aggregate crime rate. There are also micro-level versions of the theory, which suggest that individuals who experience anomie are more likely to commit crime than those who are immune to feelings of strain or goal conflict. Examples of both of these views are discussed next.

Institutional Anomie Theory

The macro-level version of anomie theory views antisocial behaviour as a function of cultural and institutional influences in society, related to the success goals so pervasive in contemporary Western culture. This North American dream is both a goal and a process. As a goal, the Dream involves the accumulation of material goods and wealth. As a process, it involves both socialization to the pursuit of material success and the belief that prosperity is an achievable goal in one's culture. Anomic conditions occur because the desire to succeed at any cost drives people apart, weakens the collective sense of community, fosters ambition, and restricts the desirability of other kinds of achievement, such as a "good name" and respected reputation.

That we are conditioned to succeed "at all costs" should come as no surprise. Business people hold esteemed positions in society. What is distinct about modern North American society, according to Messner and Rosenfeld, and what most likely determines high national crime rates, is that anomic conditions have been allowed to "develop to such an extraordinary degree."[60]

Why does anomie pervade our culture? Perhaps institutions that might otherwise control the exaggerated emphasis on financial success have been rendered powerless or obsolete. There are three reasons social institutions have been undermined:

- Noneconomic functions and roles have been devalued. Performance in other institutional settings—the family, school, or community—is assigned a lower priority than the goal of financial success.
- When conflicts emerge, noneconomic roles become subordinate to and must accommodate economic roles. The schedules, routines, and demands of the workplace

take priority over those of the home, the school, the community, and other aspects of social life.
- Economic language, standards, and norms penetrate into noneconomic realms. Economic terms become part of the common vernacular: people want to get to the "bottom line"; spouses view themselves as "partners" who "manage" the household. Retired people say they want to "downsize" their household. Rather than paint the kitchen ourselves, we ask whether we should "outsource" the job. Corporate leaders run for public office promising to "run the country like a business."

The relatively high crime rates in Western society can be explained at the cultural level by the Dream mythology, which ensures that people will desire material goods that cannot always be achieved by legitimate means. Anomie becomes a norm, and extralegal means (crime) become a strategy for attaining material wealth. At the institutional level, the dominance of economic concerns weakens the informal social control exerted by the family, church, and school. These institutions have lost their ability to regulate behaviour and have instead become a conduit for promoting material success. For example, schools are not evaluated for conveying knowledge but for their ability to train students to get high-paying jobs.

Social conditions reinforce each other in a never-ending loop: Culture determines institutions and institutional change influences culture. Thus, crime rates may rise in a healthy economy because national prosperity heightens the attractiveness of monetary rewards, encouraging people to gain financial success by any means possible, including illegal ones, while reducing the importance of social institutions to exert social control.

Some research supports the idea of institutional anomie and shows that poverty rates are associated with crime rates. However, this relationship depends on the strength of institutional controls: Areas with high levels of church membership, lower levels of divorce, and high voter turnouts also enjoy lower crime rates. Strong institutional controls (family, church, and polity), they find, may counteract the influence of economic deprivation, a finding in sync with institutional-anomie theory.[61]

This version of anomie builds on Merton's macro-level views by trying to explain why the success goal has reached such a place of prominence in Western culture. The message "to succeed by any means necessary" has become a national maxim.

Relative Deprivation Theory

Criminologists have long assumed that **income inequality** increases both perceptions of strain and crime rates. Sharp divisions between the rich and poor create an atmosphere of envy and mistrust. According to John Braithwaite, those societies in which income inequality flourishes are especially demeaning to the poor. Criminal motivation is fuelled by both perceived humiliation and the right to humiliate a victim in return.[62]

If income inequality causes strain, it stands to reason that crime rates will be highest in areas where the affluent and indigent live in close proximity. This is referred to as **relative deprivation**. This view is most closely associated with sociologists Judith Blau and Peter Blau.[63] Their relative deprivation theory combines concepts specified in anomie with those also found in social disorganization models.

According to the research, lower-class people who feel deprived because of their race or class and who reside in urban areas that also house the affluent eventually develop a sense of injustice and discontent. The poor learn to distrust a society that has nurtured social inequality and blocked any chance of their legitimate advancement. Constant frustration produces pent-up aggression, hostility, and, eventually, violence and crime.[64] This collective sense of **social injustice**, directly related to income inequality, develops in communities in which the poor and wealthy live in close proximity. Thus the relatively deprived justifiably feel enraged and vent their hostility in criminal behaviour. The relatively enriched also feel threatened, but they retreat to gated communities.

Adolescents raised in inner-city poverty areas will experience this crime-producing frustration, since their neighbourhoods are usually located in the same metropolitan area as some of the most affluent neighbourhoods. Relative deprivation is felt most acutely by those youths who suffer racial and economic deprivations that place them in a lower status than other urban residents.[65] Wage inequality may motivate young males to enter the drug trade, an endeavour that increases the likelihood they will become involved in violent crimes.[66]

Testing Relative Deprivation. Research shows that crime rates do in fact increase under conditions of relative deprivation, as when contiguous neighbourhoods become polarized along class lines.[67] A number of research efforts have found that income inequality predicts violent and general area crime rates, even during times of improvement in income level and educational attainment.[68] This finding is important because it shows that crime rates can increase during times of relative affluence and declining unemployment rates: Groups whose standard of living may be improving might find that they are still losing ground in comparison with other groups. It is the perception of "relative deprivation" and not absolute poverty level that ushers in higher crime rates.

While some research efforts have failed to find a crime–inequality effect, the weight of the evidence supports relative deprivation, and it remains an important concept for understanding area crime rates.

Is Relative Deprivation "Relative"? The theory of relative deprivation holds that people living in deteriorated urban areas who lack proper health care, decent clothing, and adequate shelter, and who reside in close proximity to those who enjoy the benefits of higher social position, will inevitably resort to such crimes as homicide, robbery, and aggravated assault.[69] Is this view restricted to the lower classes, or can it also be responsible for crimes of the affluent? In other words, is relative deprivation "relative"?

It is possible that even the most affluent North Americans will feel strain when they fail to achieve "unlimited goals."[70] That is, no matter what their level of affluence, people may perceive strain because the goals they set for themselves are so lofty that they can never be achieved. The affluent may suffer when their expected standard of living or economic security declines. Research indicates that residing in an economically integrated neighbourhood harms the children of the more affluent families, producing greater dropout rates and more out-of-wedlock births among the prosperous than the indigent.[71]

Some affluent people may feel relatively deprived when they compare their accomplishments with those of their even more socially successful peers. The relatively affluent may then use illegal means to satisfy their own "unrealistic" success goals. Nikos Passas has described this phenomenon:

> Upper-class individuals ... are by no means shielded against frustrations, relative deprivation and anomia created by a discrepancy between cultural ends and available means, especially in the context of industrial societies, where the ends are renewed as soon as they are reached.[72]

Perhaps some of the individuals involved in the Bay Street securities scandals or Wall Street insider-trading cases felt "relatively deprived" and socially frustrated when they compared the paltry few millions they had already accumulated with the hundreds of millions held by the "truly wealthy," whom they envied.

There is some evidence that as economic inequality decreases between ethnic groups, white crime rates increase. Although whites maintain a distinct advantage in power and resources, some perceive the economic progress made by ethnic minorities as a step backward for themselves. Feelings of relative deprivation result in the rise of white power groups and in higher crime rates. Crime rates rise when lower-class whites begin to feel relatively less privileged than lower-class minorities. Many countries have experienced waves of anti-immigrant violence, for example. These research efforts support the relative deprivation model and indicate it may be more complex than originally thought.

General Strain Theory

Sociologist Robert Agnew's **general strain theory (GST)** differs from the previously discussed theoretical models because of its focus on the micro-level, or individual, effects of strain and not the macro-level (social) effects. While Merton tried to explain social class differences in the crime rate, Agnew tries to explain why individuals who feel stress and strain are more likely to commit crimes. Agnew also attempts to offer a more general explanation of criminal activity among all elements of society rather than restrict his views to lower-class crime.[73]

Multiple Sources of Stress. Agnew suggests that criminality is the direct result of **negative affective states**, such as anger, frustration, and adverse emotions, that come in the wake of negative and destructive social relationships. He finds that negative affective states are produced by a variety of sources of strain:

1. *Strain caused by the failure to achieve positively valued goals.* This category of strain, similar to what Merton referred to in his theory of anomie, is a result of the disjunction between aspirations and expectations. This type of strain occurs when a youth aspires to wealth and fame but, lacking financial and educational resources, assumes that such goals are impossible to achieve.

2. *Strain caused by the disjunction of expectations and achievements.* Strain can also be produced when a disjunction exists between expectations and achievements. When people compare themselves to peers who seem to be doing a lot better financially or socially (such as making more money or getting better grades), even those doing relatively well feel strain. For example, they may get into college but not into a prestigious school, like some of their friends. Perhaps they are not being treated fairly because the "playing field" is tilted against them. "Other kids have connections," they say. Perceptions of inequity may result in many adverse reactions, ranging from running away from its source to lowering the benefits of others through physical attacks or vandalism of their property.

3. *Strain as the removal of positively valued stimuli from the individual.* Strain may be the result of the loss of a positively valued stimulus from the individual. For example, the loss of a girlfriend or boyfriend can produce strain, as can the death of a loved one, moving to a new neighbourhood or school, and the divorce or separation of parents. The loss of positive stimuli may lead to delinquency as the adolescent tries to prevent the loss, retrieve what has been lost, obtain substitutes, or seek revenge against those responsible for the loss.

4. *Strain as the presentation of negative stimuli.* Strain may also be caused by the presence of negative stimuli. Included within this category are such pain-inducing social interactions as child abuse and neglect, crime victimization, physical punishment, family and peer conflict, school failure, and stressful life events ranging from verbal threats to air pollution.

While these sources of strain are independent of one another, they may overlap and be cumulative in practice. For example, insults from a teacher may be viewed as an unfair application of negative stimuli, which interferes with academic aspirations. The greater the intensity and frequency of strain experiences, the greater their impact and the more likely they are to cause delinquency.

Each type of strain will increase the likelihood of experiencing such negative emotions as disappointment, depression, fear, and, most important, anger. Anger increases perceptions of injury and of being wronged. It produces a desire for revenge, energizes individuals to take action, and lowers inhibitions; violence and aggression seem justified if one has been wronged and is righteously angry.

Because it produces these emotions, strain can be considered a predisposing factor for crime when it is chronic and repetitive and creates a hostile, suspicious, and aggressive attitude. Individual strain episodes may serve as a situational event or trigger that produces criminality, such as when a particularly stressful event ignites a violent reaction (see Figure 7.6).

Coping with Strain. Agnew recognizes that not all people who experience strain eventually become criminals. Some are able to marshal their emotional, mental, and behavioural resources to cope with the anger and frustration produced by strain. Some defences are cognitive, as individuals may be able to rationalize frustrating circumstances. Not getting the career they desire is "just not that important"; they may be poor, but the "next guy is worse off," and if things didn't work out, they "got what they deserved." Others seek behavioural solutions: They run away from adverse conditions or seek revenge against those who caused the strain. Others will try to regain emotional equilibrium with techniques ranging from physical exercise to drug abuse.

The general strain theory acknowledges that the ability to cope with strain varies with personal experiences over the life course. Kids who lack economic means are less likely to cope than those who have sufficient financial resources at their command. Personal temperament, prior learning of criminal attitudes and behaviours, and association with criminal peers who reinforce anger are among other factors affecting the ability to cope with strain. Coping with strain may also be influenced by the source of strain. When individuals can identify a target to blame for their problems, they are more likely to respond with retaliatory action ("Joe stole my girl by lying about me, so I beat him up!"). When individuals internalize blame, they are less likely to engage in criminal behaviour ("I lost my girlfriend because I was unfaithful; it's all my fault"). Sometimes the source of strain is difficult to pinpoint ("I feel depressed because my parents got divorced"). This last type of strain is ambiguous and unlikely to produce an aggressive response.[74]

Strain and Criminal Careers. How does GST explain both chronic offending and the stability of crime over the life course? GST recognizes that certain people have traits that may make them particularly sensitive to strain. These include having a difficult temperament, being overly sensitive or emotional, having a low tolerance for adversity, and having poor problem-solving skills. These traits, linked to aggressive and antisocial behaviour, seem to be stable over a person's life cycle.[75]

Connections

As you may recall, cohort studies show that criminal behaviour begins early in life, then remains stable over the life course. Considering that strain-producing interactions are not constant, explaining the stability of chronic offending is an important task for general strain theory. Chronic offending is discussed in Chapter 3.

Aggressive people who have these traits are likely to have poor interpersonal skills and are more likely to be treated negatively by others; their combative personalities make them feared and disliked. They are likely to live in families whose caretakers share similar personality traits. They are also more likely to reject conventional peers and join deviant groups. Such individuals are more likely to be subject to a high degree of strain over the course of their lives.

Crime peaks during late adolescence because this is a period of social stress caused by the weakening of parental supervision and the development of relationships with a diverse peer group. Many kids going through the trauma of family breakup and frequent changes in family structure find themselves under stress and react with involvement in precocious sexuality and substance abuse. For example, research shows that young girls of any social class are more likely to bear out-of-wedlock children if they themselves experienced an unstable family life.[76]

As they mature, their expectations may increase, and some kids are unable to meet academic and social demands. Adolescents are concerned about their standing with peers. Those deficient in these areas may become social outcasts, another source of strain. In adulthood, crime rates drop because these sources of strain are reduced. New sources of self-esteem emerge, and adults seem more likely to bring their goals in line with reality.

Evaluating GST. Agnew's work is quite important because it both clarifies the concept of strain and directs future research agendas. It also adds to the body of literature describing how social and life history events influence offending patterns. Because sources of strain vary over the life course, so, too, should crime rates, and they do.

Connections

Explaining continuity and change in offending rates over the life course has become an important goal of criminologists. Chapter 10's analysis of latent trait and life-course theories outlines the recent thinking on this topic.

Figure 7.6   Elements of general strain theory (GST)

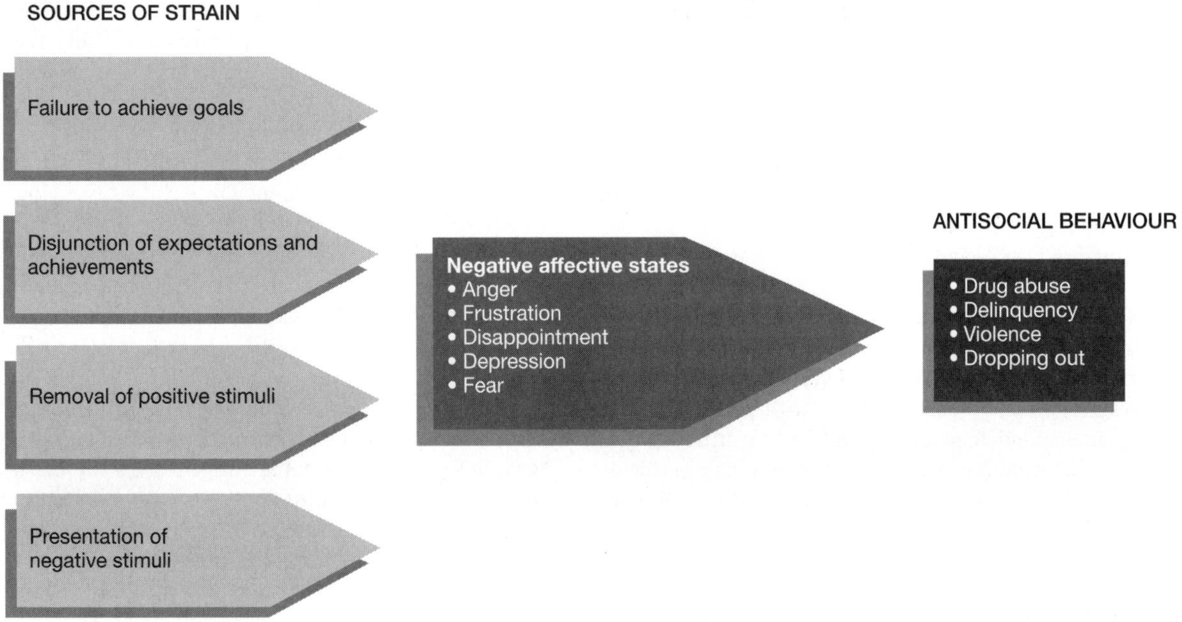

SOURCES OF STRAIN

- Failure to achieve goals
- Disjunction of expectations and achievements
- Removal of positive stimuli
- Presentation of negative stimuli

Negative affective states
- Anger
- Frustration
- Disappointment
- Depression
- Fear

ANTISOCIAL BEHAVIOUR
- Drug abuse
- Delinquency
- Violence
- Dropping out

There is also empirical support for GST. Recent research of this theory using longitudinal survey data found that adolescents who score high on scales measuring perceptions of strain labelled "life hassles" (for example, "My classmates do not like me," adults and friends "don't respect my opinions") and "negative life events" (being a victim of crime, the death of a close friend, serious illness) are also the ones most likely to engage in crime.[77]

Independent research efforts have concurred with this vision of strain. Some show that indicators of strain—family breakup, unemployment, moving, feelings of dissatisfaction with friends and school—are positively related to criminality.[78] Middle-class youth who drop out of school are more likely to engage in criminal behaviour than lower-class dropouts. It is possible that removing this "positive stimulus" has a greater strain effect on those who are expected to succeed because of their class position than those who already perceive more limited economic opportunities.[79]

Adolescents who report feelings of stress and anger are more likely to interact with delinquent peers and engage in criminal behaviours.[80] Persistent drug abusers report feeling a great deal of "life stress" and also associate with peers who are themselves substance users.[81] In some cases, this interaction may actually help them reduce strain and anxiety; criminality may serve as an effective "coping" mechanism that helps relieve feelings of anger and resentment. For example, they may reduce feelings of strain by lashing out at others, by stealing, or by vandalizing property.[82]

GST and Gender. One problem with GST is that it fails to adequately explain gender differences in the crime rate. Compared to males, females experience as much or more strain, frustration, and anger, yet their crime rate is much lower. Is it possible that gender differences exist either in the relationship between strain and criminality or in the ability to cope with the effects of strain? In an important study, John Hoffman and S. Susan Su show that stress influences both males and females equally: stressful life events have a similar impact on delinquency and drug abuse among both males and females.[83]

If stress is experienced equally by males and females and produces criminal behaviour in both males and females, how can the much greater male crime rate be explained? It is possible that females use different coping mechanisms to deal with strain. Psychologist Lisa Broidy suggests that even when presented with similar types of strain, males and females respond with a different constellation of negative emotions.[84] Females may be socialized to be "overcontrolled" to internalize stress, blaming themselves for their problems; males can relieve strain by striking out at others and deflecting criticism with aggression. Only those females who face overwhelming stress, then, may succumb to criminality. When women experience peaks of stress, their traditional coping mechanisms may be overwhelmed; they then lash out with anger amounting to rage. Women experiencing peaks of stress may be even more likely than men to explode with episodes of extreme uncontrolled violence.[85]

Cultural Deviance Theory

The third branch of social structure theory combines the effects of social disorganization and strain to explain how people living in deteriorated neighbourhoods react to social isolation and economic deprivation. Because their lifestyle is draining, frustrating, and dispiriting, members of the lower class create an independent subculture with its own set of rules and values. While middle-class culture stresses hard work, delayed gratification, formal education, and being cautious, the lower-class subculture stresses excitement, toughness, risk taking, fearlessness, immediate gratification, and "street smarts." The lower-class subculture is an attractive alternative because the urban poor find it impossible to meet the behavioural demands of middle-class society. Unfortunately, subcultural norms often clash with conventional values. Slum dwellers are forced to violate the law because they obey the rules of the deviant culture with which they are in close and immediate contact (see Figure 7.7).

Conduct Norms

The concept that the lower class develops a unique culture in response to strain can be traced to Thorsten Sellin's classic 1938 work, *Culture Conflict and Crime*, a theoretical attempt to link cultural adaptation to criminality.[86] Sellin's main premise was that criminal law is an expression of the rules of the dominant culture. The content of the law, therefore, may create a clash between conventional, middle-class rules and ethnic minorities and the lower class who are excluded from the social mainstream. These groups maintain their own set of **conduct norms**—rules governing the day-to-day living conditions within these subcultures. However, in a complex society, the number of different groups people belong to—family, peer, occupational, and religious—can be quite large. A conflict of norms exists when divergent rules of conduct govern the specific life situation in which a person may find him- or herself. For example, **culture conflict** occurs when the rules expressed in the criminal law clash with the demands of group conduct norms. To make his point, Sellin cited the case of a Sicilian father in New Jersey who killed the 16-year-old seducer of his daughter and then expressed surprise at being arrested; he had merely defended his family honour in a traditional way. Conduct norms are universal; they are not the product of one group, culture, or political structure.

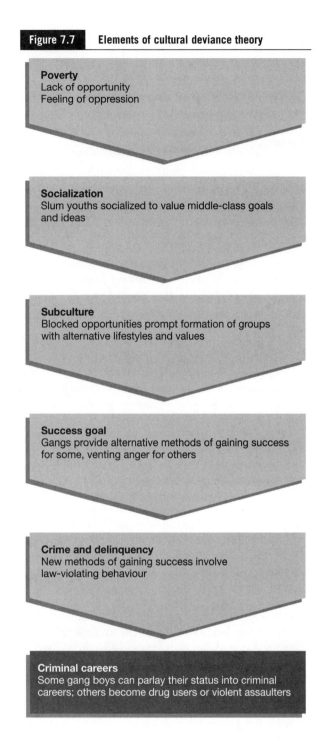

Figure 7.7 Elements of cultural deviance theory

Poverty
Lack of opportunity
Feeling of oppression

Socialization
Slum youths socialized to value middle-class goals and ideas

Subculture
Blocked opportunities prompt formation of groups with alternative lifestyles and values

Success goal
Gangs provide alternative methods of gaining success for some, venting anger for others

Crime and delinquency
New methods of gaining success involve law-violating behaviour

Criminal careers
Some gang boys can parlay their status into criminal careers; others become drug users or violent assaulters

Focal Concerns

In his classic 1958 paper, "Lower-Class Culture as a Generating Milieu of Gang Delinquency," Walter Miller identified the unique value system that defines lower-class culture.[87] Obedience to these **focal concerns** dominates life among the lower class. There is not necessarily a rebellion against middle-class values; rather, these values have evolved specifically to fit conditions in poor areas. The major lower-class focal concerns include the following:

1. *Trouble.* Getting into trouble includes such behaviour as fighting, drinking, and sexual misconduct. In lower-class communities, people are evaluated by their actual or potential involvement in trouble-making activity. Dealing with trouble can confer prestige, as when a man gets a reputation for being able to handle himself well in a fight. Not being able to handle trouble, and having to pay the consequences, can make a person look foolish and incompetent.
2. *Toughness.* Lower-class males want local recognition of their physical toughness. They refuse to be sentimental or soft and instead value physical strength, fighting ability, and athletic skill. Those who cannot meet these standards risk getting a reputation for being weak, inept, and effeminate.
3. *Smartness.* Members of the lower-class culture want to maintain an image of being "street-wise" and savvy, using their "street smarts," and having the ability to "out-con" the opponent. Although formal education is not admired, knowing essential survival techniques, such as gambling, conning, and out-smarting the law, is a requirement.
4. *Excitement.* Another important feature of the lower-class lifestyle is the search for fun and excitement to enliven an otherwise drab existence. The search for excitement may lead to gambling, fighting, getting drunk, and sexual adventures. In between, the lower-class citizen may simply "hang out" and "be cool."
5. *Fate.* Lower-class citizens believe their lives are in the hands of strong spiritual forces that guide their destinies, whether it's getting lucky, finding good fortune, or hitting the jackpot.
6. *Autonomy.* A general concern exists in lower-class cultures about personal freedom and autonomy. Being independent of authority figures, such as the police, teachers, and parents, is required; losing control is an unacceptable weakness, incompatible with toughness.

According to Miller, clinging to lower-class focal concerns promotes behaviour that often runs afoul of the law. Toughness may mean displaying fighting prowess; street smarts lead to drug deals; excitement may result in drinking, gambling, or drug abuse. It is this obedience to the prevailing cultural demands of lower-class society, and not alienation from conventional society, that causes urban crime.

These views of a lower-class subculture formed by strain inspired a number of formal theories that predicted the onset of gang delinquency in lower-class areas. The two best known are the theory of delinquent subcultures and the theory of differential opportunity.

Theory of Delinquent Subcultures

Albert Cohen first articulated the theory of delinquent subculture in his classic 1955 book, *Delinquent Boys*.[88] Cohen's central position was that the delinquent behaviour of lower-class youths is actually a protest against the norms and values of the middle-class culture. Because social conditions make them incapable of achieving success legitimately, lower-class youths experience a form of culture conflict that Cohen calls **status frustration**. As a result, many of them join gangs and engage in behaviour that is nonutilitarian, malicious, and negativistic.

Cohen viewed the delinquent gang as a separate subculture, possessing a value system directly opposed to that of the larger society. He described the subculture as one that takes its norms from the larger culture but turns them upside down. The delinquent's conduct is normal in the context of the subculture precisely because it is deviant according to the norms of the larger cultures.

According to Cohen, the development of the delinquent subculture is a consequence of socialization practices found in the ghetto or slum environment. Deficient socialization renders lower-class kids unable to achieve conventional success. Cohen suggests that lower-class parents are incapable of teaching children the necessary techniques for entering the dominant middle-class culture. Developmental handicaps suffered by lower-class kids include lack of education, poor speech and communication skills, and inability to delay gratification. These children lack the basic skills necessary to achieve social and economic success in a demanding "credentialist" society. (Incidentally, this link between social class and achievement is one that is debated in the sociology of education as well.)

Middle-Class Measuring Rods. One significant handicap that lower-class children face is the inability to positively impress authority figures, such as teachers, employers, or supervisors. In modern society, these positions tend to be held by members of the middle class, who have difficulty relating to the lower-class youngster. Cohen calls the standards set by these authority figures middle-class measuring rods. The conflict and frustration lower-class youths experience when they fail to meet these standards is a primary cause of delinquency.

Lower-class youths who have difficulty adjusting to the middle-class measuring rods of one institution may find themselves prejudged by others. The ratings are reviewed and magnified by records and the informal exchanges of information that commonly occur among institutions. A school record may be reviewed by juvenile court authorities, a juvenile court record may be opened by the military, and a military record can influence the securing of a job. A person's status and esteem in the community are largely determined by the judgments that most often reflect the traditional values of mainstream society.[89] Negative evaluations become part of a permanent file that follows an individual for the rest of his or her life. When he or she wants to improve, evidence of prior failures is used to discourage advancement.

The Formation of Deviant Subcultures. Cohen said that lower-class boys who suffer rejection by middle-class decision makers usually elect to join one of three existing subcultures: the corner boy, the college boy, or the delinquent boy.

The corner boy role is the most common response to middle-class rejection. The corner boy is not a chronic delinquent but may be a truant who engages in petty offences, such as precocious sex and recreational drug abuse. His main loyalty is to his peer group, on which he depends for support, motivation, and interest. His values, therefore, are those of the group with which he is in close personal contact. He is well aware of his failure to achieve the standards of the "dream," retreats into the comforting world of lower-class peers, and eventually becomes a stable member of the neighbourhood, holding a menial job, marrying, and remaining in the community.

The college boy embraces the cultural and social values of the middle class. Rather than scorning middle-class measuring rods, he actively strives to be successful by those standards. Cohen views this type of youth as one who is embarking on an almost hopeless path, since he is ill-equipped academically, socially, and linguistically to achieve the rewards of middle-class life.

The delinquent boy adopts a set of norms and principles in direct opposition to middle-class values. He engages in short-run hedonism, living for today and letting "tomorrow take care of itself." Delinquent boys strive for **group autonomy**. They resist efforts by family, school, or other sources of authority to control their behaviour. They may join a gang because it is perceived as autonomous, independent, and the focus of "attraction, loyalty, and solidarity." Frustrated by their inability to succeed, these boys resort to a process Cohen calls **reaction formation**. Symptoms of reaction formation include overly intense responses that seem disproportionate to the stimuli that trigger them. For the delinquent boy, this takes the form of irrational, malicious, and unaccountable hostility to the norms of respectable middle-class society, causing them to overreact to any perceived threat or slight. They sneer at the college boy's attempts at assimilation and scorn the corner boy's passivity. The delinquent boy is willing to take risks, violate the law, and flout middle-class conventions.

Cohen's work helps explain the factors that promote and sustain a delinquent subculture. By introducing the concepts of status frustration and middle-class measuring rods, Cohen makes it clear that social forces and not individual traits promote and sustain a delinquent career. By introducing the corner boy–college boy–delinquent boy triad, he helps explain why many lower-class youths fail to become chronic offenders: There is more than one social path open to poor youth.[90] His work is a skilful integration of strain and social disorganization theories and has become an enduring element of the criminological literature.

Strain and Street Youths. In their application of strain theory, Stephen Baron and Leslie Kennedy look at the growing problem of youths under the age of 24 who have left school and hang out on the street. This population is usually under- or unemployed, with no permanent housing. Their lives are characterized by poverty and hunger, and their lack of employment leaves them subject to a number of social problems including street crime.

For many of these youths, criminal activity is the primary way to gain material wealth. If blocked opportunity is a key to understanding crime, we can see that relative deprivation leads these youths to harbour feelings of resentment, despair, and frustration which may lead to criminal behaviour. The culturally produced feelings of failure and rejection lead to a sense of relative deprivation and thwarted ambition in a culture where the idea is that hard work is the way to get ahead. Youths in this situation gravitate together and develop a new frame of reference in which status is attained and alternative routes to financial success organized. Together they attempt to develop new norms, new standards, and new criteria for success that are more readily achieved.

Baron and Kennedy's study of 200 homeless male youths took place in the downtown business core of a city bordered by the local skid row. The area contained a mix of commercial and financial establishments surrounded by bars, pawnshops, hotels, shelters, detox centres, rooming houses, rundown residential units, and abandoned buildings.

Respondents reported an average legal income of $335 a month in the previous year: The average respondent reported more than 1600 offences in the prior 12 months, mostly for selling illegal drugs. They also reported an average of 348 property offences and 48 robberies throughout the year (thefts from cars, shoplifting, and break and enters).

The youths reported that their failure to find employment destroyed their motivation and made them less likely to think that lawbreaking is wrong: "Because I could make more money selling drugs than working for five bucks an hour"; "'Cause I don't feel guilty about it cause I hate flipping burgers. If you're going to have a job you might as well be doing something you like, like robbing people." Crime not only gave them money, but also provided a structure to their day and a sense of doing something.[91]

Theory of Differential Opportunity

In their well-known work *Delinquency and Opportunity*, Richard Cloward and Lloyd Ohlin also combine strain and social disorganization principles into a portrayal of a gang-sustaining criminal subculture.[92]

Cloward and Ohlin found that in delinquent subcultures, delinquent activity is a requirement for "fitting in." Youth gangs are an important part of the delinquent subculture. While not all illegal acts are committed by gang youths, they are the source of much criminal behaviour. Delinquent gangs spring up in disorganized areas where youths lack the opportunity to gain success through conventional means. True to strain theory principles, Cloward and Ohlin portray slum kids as individuals who want to conform to middle-class values but lack the means to do so: Reaching out for socially approved goals under conditions that made it impossible to achieve them may become a prelude to deviance.

Differential Opportunities. The centrepiece of the Cloward and Ohlin theory is the concept of **differential opportunity**. According to this concept, people in all strata of society share the same success goals; however, those in the lower class have limited means of achieving those goals. People who perceive themselves as failures within conventional society will seek alternative or innovative ways to gain success. People who conclude that there is little hope for advancement by legitimate means may join with like-minded peers to form a gang. Gang members provide the emotional support to handle the shame, fear, or guilt they may develop while engaging in illegal acts. Delinquent subcultures reward them in a way that conventional society cannot hope to duplicate. The youth who is considered a failure at school and is only qualified for a menial job at a minimum wage can earn thousands of dollars plus the respect of his or her peers by joining a gang and engaging in drug deals or armed robberies.

Cloward and Ohlin recognized that the opportunity for success in either conventional or criminal careers is limited. In stable areas, adolescents may be recruited by professional criminals, drug traffickers, or organized crime groups. Unstable areas cannot support flourishing criminal opportunities. In these socially disorganized neighbourhoods, adult role models are absent and young criminals have few opportunities to join established gangs or learn the fine points of professional crime. Cloward and Ohlin's most important finding, then, is that all opportunities for success, both illegal and conventional, are closed for the most "truly disadvantaged" youth.

Because of differential opportunity, kids are likely to join one of three types of gangs:

1. *Criminal gangs.* Criminal gangs exist in stable, but poor areas in which close connections among adolescent, young adult, and adult offenders create an environment for successful criminal enterprise. Youths are recruited into established criminal gangs that provide a training ground for a successful criminal career. Gang membership provides a learning experience in which the knowledge and skills needed for success in crime are acquired. During this "apprenticeship stage," older, more experienced members of the criminal subculture

hold youthful "trainees" on tight reins, limiting activities that might jeopardize the gang's profits (for example, engaging in nonfunctional, irrational violence). Over time, new recruits learn the techniques and attitudes of the criminal world and how to "cooperate successfully with others in criminal enterprises." To become a fully accepted member of the criminal gang, novices must prove themselves reliable and dependable in their contacts with their criminal associates and be "right guys." They are introduced to the middlemen of the crime business—drug importers, fences, pawnshop operators—and also to legal connections—crooked police officers and shady lawyers—who can help them gain their freedom in the rare instances when they are apprehended.

2. *Conflict gangs.* Conflict gangs develop in communities unable to provide either legitimate or illegitimate opportunities. These highly disorganized areas are marked by transient residents and physical deterioration. Crime in this area is individualistic, unorganized, petty, poorly paid, and unprotected. There are no successful adult criminal role models from whom youths can learn criminal skills. When such severe limitations on both criminal and conventional opportunity intensify frustrations of the young, violence is used as a means of gaining status. The stereotype of the conflict gang member is the swaggering gang tough who fights with weapons to win respect from rivals and engages in unpredictable and destructive assaults on people and property. Conflict gang members must be ready to fight to protect their own and their gang's integrity and honour. By doing so, they acquire a "rep," which provides them with a means for gaining admiration from their peers and consequently helps them develop their own self-image. Conflict gangs represent a way of securing

According to Cloward and Ohlin's theory of differential opportunity, those who perceive themselves as failures within conventional society or who conclude that there is little hope for advancement by legitimate means may join with like-minded peers to form a gang.

access to the scarce resources for adolescent pleasure and opportunity in underprivileged areas.

3. *Retreatist gangs.* Retreatists are double failures, unable to gain success through legitimate means and unwilling to do so through illegal ones. Some retreatists have tried crime or violence but are too clumsy, too weak, or too scared to be accepted in criminal or violent gangs. They then "retreat" into a role on the fringe of society. Members of the retreatist subculture constantly search for ways of getting high—alcohol, pot, heroin, unusual sexual experiences, music. They are always "cool," detached from relationships with the conventional world. To feed their habits, retreatists develop a "hustle"—pimping, conning, selling drugs, and committing petty crimes. Personal status in the retreatist subculture is derived from peer approval.

Analysis of Differential Opportunity Theory. Cloward and Ohlin's theory is important because of its integration of cultural deviance and social disorganization variables and its recognition of different modes of criminal adaptation. The fact that criminal cultures can be supportive, rational, and profitable seems to be a more realistic reflection of the actual world of the criminal gang than Cohen's original view of purely negativistic, destructive criminal youths who oppose all social values. Cloward and Ohlin's tripartite model of urban delinquency also relates directly to the treatment and rehabilitation of delinquents. While other social structure theorists portray delinquent youths as having values and attitudes in opposition to middle-class culture, Cloward and Ohlin suggest that many delinquents share the goals and values of the general society but lack the means to obtain success. This position suggests that delinquency prevention can be achieved by providing youths with the means for obtaining the success they truly desire without the need to change their basic attitudes and beliefs.

In the United States, the nation with perhaps the most gangs and the best information about them, the 1992 National Assessment of Gang Activity surveyed police departments in the largest cities and found that 91 percent (72 cities) reported the presence of youth gangs involved in criminal activity. Data from these cities along with data collected from 29 smaller cities and 11 county jurisdictions showed a total of 4881 gangs with 249 324 members. A 1994 replication of this survey indicated that there are 8625 to 16 643 gangs containing between 378 807 and 555 181 members (the lower-range figures are conservative estimates, while the upper range is a statistical estimate derived by using more liberal techniques). It was estimated that gang members commit between 437 066 and 580 331 crimes each year, and that gang activity is significantly higher today than ever before and that gang membership was, if anything, accelerating in the 1990s.[93]

Another survey of "gang cities" conducted throughout the 1990s by Malcolm Klein found that 94 percent of the 189 U.S. cities with populations of 100 000 or more and 800 to 900 of smaller cities with populations of 10 000 to 100 000 have gang problems. Combining these would create a total of more than 1000 gang locations. While smaller cities have relatively few gang members, averaging slightly more than 100, almost half of the larger cities report having 500 or more members, including 14 cities with more than 4000 gang members. Los Angeles alone has more than 1000 gangs! Klein's estimate of 500 000 gang members coincides with the National Assessment's.[94]

Connections

Chapter 13 looks at gangs in Canada and their relationship to ethnic minorities.

Why has gang activity increased? One compelling reason may be the involvement of youth gangs in the distribution and sale of illegal drugs, replacing traditional organized crime families as the dominant supplier of illegal substances. The introduction of the relatively cheap cocaine derivative crack, which provides a powerful, albeit short-term high, helped open new markets in the drug trade.[95]

Gang formation may be the natural consequence of the evolution of Western society from a manufacturing economy to a low-wage service economy.[96] The modern city, which traditionally required a large population base for its manufacturing plants, now faces incredible economic stress as these plants shut down. In this uneasy economic climate, gangs form and flourish in areas where the moderating influence of successful adult role models and stable families declines and where adolescents face constrained choices and weak social controls.[97] Gang activity provides members with a stable income stream in an otherwise unproductive urban marketplace. From this perspective, youth gangs are a response to the glooming of the economy.

The rise of gang memberships in a declining industrial market and the development of drug profits as an alternative or innovative method of financial success are social conditions predicted by opportunity theory. The prevalence of gang activity in urban North American society provides staunch support for the social structure approach.

Evaluation of Social Structure Theories

The social structure approach has significantly influenced both criminological theory and crime-prevention strategies. Its core concepts seem valid in view of the high crime and delinquency rates and gang activity occurring in the deteriorated inner-city areas of large cities. The public's image includes roaming bands of violent teenage gangs, drug users, prostitutes, muggers, and similar frightening examples of criminality. All of these are present today in urban areas.

Each branch of the general structural model supports and amplifies others. Some theorists, such as Robert Sampson and William Julius Wilson, suggest that these concepts are actually interdependent.[98] Factors that cause strain, such as lack of access to legitimate economic opportunities and economic inequality, also produce social disorganization. Stress leads to alcohol abuse and unprotected sex outside marriage, causing an increase in impaired households, dysfunctional families, urban hostility, and the deterioration of informal social controls. Only government assistance can reduce stress in urban areas, thereby lowering crime rates.

Critics of the approach charge that we cannot be sure that it is lower-class culture itself that promotes crime and not some other force operating in society. Critics of this approach deny that residence in urban areas is alone sufficient to cause people to violate the law.[99] They counter with the charge that lower-class crime rates may be an artifact of bias in the criminal justice system. Lower-class areas seem to have higher crime rates because residents are arrested and prosecuted by agents of the justice system who, as members of the middle class, exhibit class bias.[100] Class bias is often coupled with discrimination against minority-group members, who have long suffered at the hands of the justice system.

Even if the higher crime rates recorded in lower-class areas are valid, it is still true that most members of the lower class are not criminals. The discovery of the chronic offender indicates that a significant majority of people living in lower-class environments are not criminals and that a relatively small proportion of the population commits most crimes. If social forces alone could be used to explain crime, how can we account for the vast number of urban poor who remain honest and law-abiding? Given these circumstances, it is tempting to say that law violators must be motivated by some individual mental, physical, or social process or trait.[101]

It is also questionable whether a distinct lower-class culture actually exists. Several researchers have found that gang members and other delinquent youths seem to value middle-class concepts, such as sharing, earning money, and respecting the law, as highly as middle-class youths. Criminologists contend that lower-class youths value education as highly as middle-class students do.[102] Opinion polls can also be used as evidence that most lower-class citizens maintain middle-class values. People in the lowest income brackets also want tougher drug laws, more police protection, and greater control over criminal offenders. These opinions seem similar to conventional middle-class values rather than representative of an independent, deviant subculture.

While this evidence contradicts some of the central ideas of social structure theory, the discovery of stable patterns of lower-class crime, the high crime rates found in disorganized inner-city areas, and the rise of teenage gangs and groups support a close association between crime rates and social class position.

Social Structure Theory and Social Policy

Social structure theory has had a significant influence on social policy. If the cause of criminality is viewed as a separation between lower-class individuals and conventional goals, norms, and rules, it seems logical that alternatives to criminal behaviour can be provided by giving those who are deprived opportunities a chance to share in the rewards of conventional society.

One approach is to give indigent people direct financial aid through welfare and aid to dependent children. Research shows that crime rates are reduced when families receive supplemental income through public assistance payments.[103]

Efforts have been made to reduce crime rates by directly applying concepts suggested by social structure theories to social policy. Crime prevention efforts based on social structure precepts can be traced back to the Chicago Area Project, supervised by Clifford R. Shaw. This program attempted to organize existing community structures to develop social stability in otherwise disorganized slums. The project sponsored recreation programs for children in the neighbourhoods, including summer camping. It campaigned for community improvements in such areas as education, sanitation, traffic safety, physical conservation, and law enforcement. Project members also worked with police and court agencies to supervise and treat gang youth and adult offenders. In a 25-year assessment of the project, Solomon Kobrin found that it was successful in demonstrating the feasibility of creating youth welfare organizations in high-delinquency areas.[104] The project also made a distinct contribution to ending the isolation of urban males from the mainstream of society.

Social structure concepts have been a critical ingredient in social reform projects, particularly those that called for an all-out attack on the crime-producing structures of poor areas. The cornerstone of the U.S. War on Poverty's crime-prevention effort was called Mobilization for Youth (MFY). It was designed to serve multiple purposes: provide teacher training and education to help educators deal with the problem youth, create work opportunities through a youth job centre, organize neighbourhood councils and associations, provide street workers to deal with teen gangs, and set up counselling services and assistance to neighbourhood families. Subsequent War on Poverty programs included the Job Corps; VISTA (the urban Peace Corps); Head Start and Upward Bound (educational enrichment programs); Neighbourhood Legal Services; and the largest community organizing effort, the Community Action Program.

Across Canada, more than 100 Head Start projects have been instituted for natives. Designed as an early intervention strategy, and funded by more than $20 million annually, these projects are designed to increase self-esteem and develop a positive sense of self. This initiative is described in more detail in Chapter 8, on process theories.

War on Poverty programs were sought to reduce crime by developing a sense of community pride and solidarity in poverty areas and providing educational and job opportunities for crime-prone youths. As history tells us, the programs failed. However, federal and state funding often fell into the hands of middle-class managers and community developers and not the people it was designed to help. Managers were accused of graft and corruption. Community organizers engineered rent strikes, lawsuits, and protests which angered government officials and convinced them that financial backing of such programs should be ended. Rather than appeal to the political power structure, program administrators alienated it.

Since then, times have become more conservative. Instead of a total community approach to solving the crime problem, the tendency has been to adopt more selective crime-prevention policies. Some programs, such as Head Start and Neighbourhood Legal Services, have continued to help people; nonetheless, this attempt to change the very structure of society must be judged a noble failure.

A cornerstone of all these programs has been providing job opportunities for at-risk youth on the assumption that there is an inverse association between employment and crime.

Summary

Sociology has been the main orientation of criminologists because they know that crime rates vary among elements of the social structure, that society goes through changes that affect crime, and that social interaction relates to criminality. Social structure theories suggest that people's places in the socioeconomic structure of society influence their chances of becoming a criminal. Poor people are more likely to commit certain crimes because they are unable to achieve monetary or social success in any other way. Social structure theory has three schools of thought: social disorganization, strain, and cultural deviance theory (summarized in Table 7.2).

Table 7.2	Social structure theories	
THEORY	**MAJOR PREMISE**	**STRENGTHS**
SOCIAL DISORGANIZATION THEORY Shaw and McKay's concentric zone theory	Crime is a product of transitional neighbourhoods that manifest social disorganization and value conflict.	Identifies why crime rates are highest in slum areas. Points out the factors that produce crime. Suggests programs to help reduce crime.
Social ecology theory	The conflicts and problems of urban social life and communities, including fear, unemployment, deterioration, and siege mentality, influence crime rates.	Accounts for urban crime rates and trends.
STRAIN THEORY Anomie theory	People who adopt the goals of society but lack the means to attain them seek alternatives, such as crime.	Points out how competition for success creates conflict and crime. Suggests that social conditions and not personality can account for crime. Can explain middle- and upper-class crime.
General strain theory	Strain has a variety of sources. Strain causes crime in the absence of adequate coping mechanisms.	Identifies the complexities of strain in modern society. Expands on anomie theory. Shows the influences of social events on behaviour over the life course.
Institutional anomie theory	Material goals pervade all aspects of American life.	Explains why crime rates are so high in American culture.
Relative deprivation theory	Crime occurs when the wealthy and poor live in close proximity to one another.	Explains high crime rates in deteriorated inner-city areas located near more affluent neighbourhoods.
CULTURAL DEVIANCE THEORY Sellin's culture conflict theory	Obedience to the norms of their lower-class culture puts people in conflict with the norms of the dominant culture.	Identifies the aspects of lower-class life that produce street crime. Adds to Shaw and McKay's analysis. Creates the concept of culture conflict.
Miller's focal concern theory	Citizens who obey the street rules of lower-class life (focal concerns) find themselves in conflict with the dominant culture.	Identifies the core values of lower-class culture and shows their association to crime.
Cohen's theory of delinquent gangs	Status frustration of lower-class boys, created by their failure to achieve middle-class success, causes them to join gangs.	Shows how conditions of lower-class life produce crime. Explains violence and destructive acts. Identifies conflict of lower class with middle class.
Cloward and Ohlin's theory of opportunity	Blockage of conventional opportunities causes lower-class youths to join criminal, conflict, or retreatist gangs.	Shows that even illegal opportunities are structured in society. Indicates why people become involved in a particular type of criminal activity. Presents a way of preventing crime.

Social disorganization theory suggests that poor urban dwellers violate the law because they live in areas in which social control has broken down. The origin of social disorganization theory can be traced originally to the work of Clifford R. Shaw and Henry D. McKay, who concluded that disorganized areas marked by divergent values and transitional populations produce criminality. This research was also conducted at McGill University in Canada, as part of a larger process of social reform. Modern social ecology theory looks at such neighbourhood issues as community fear, unemployment, siege mentality, and deterioration.

Strain theories comprise the second branch of the social structure approach. They view crime as a result of the anger people experience over their inability to achieve legitimate social and economic success. Strain theories hold that most people share common values and beliefs, but the ability to achieve them is differentiated throughout the social structure. The best-known strain theory is Robert Merton's theory of anomie, which describes what happens when the means people have at their disposal are not adequate to satisfy their goals. Steven Messner, Richard Rosenfeld, and Robert Agnew have extended this theory by showing that strain has multiple sources.

Cultural deviance theories hold that a unique value system develops in lower-class areas. Lower-class values approve of such behaviours as being tough, never showing fear, and defying authority. People perceiving strain will bond together in their own groups or subcultures for support and recognition. Albert Cohen links the formation of subcultures to the failure of lower-class citizens to achieve recognition from middle-class decision makers, such as teachers, employers, and police officers. Richard Cloward and Lloyd Ohlin have argued that crime results from lower-class people's perception that their opportunity for success is limited. Consequently, youths in low-income areas may join criminal, conflict, or retreatist gangs.

Thinking Like a Criminologist

You have been seconded to a position in Toronto on a community liaison initiative. The mayor informs you the municipal government wants to initiate a demonstration project to show that government can reduce poverty, crime, and drug abuse. The government has the cooperation of the Toronto police force, in particular its Community Crime Prevention Council. They also have $200 000 in startup funding from the federal government.

The area chosen for development is a large inner-city neighbourhood in this city of over 3 million people. The chosen area suffers from a disorganized community structure, poverty, and hopelessness. Predatory delinquent gangs run free and terrorize local merchants and citizens. The school system has failed to provide opportunities and educational experiences sufficient to dampen enthusiasm for gang recruitment. Stores, homes, and public buildings are deteriorated and decayed. There is little remaining commercial enterprise. An uneasy truce exists between the varied ethnic and racial groups that populate the area. Residents feel little can be done to bring the neighbourhood back to life. Merchants are afraid to open stores, and there is little outside development from major retailers or manufacturers. People who want to start their own businesses find that banks will not lend them money.

One of the biggest problems has been the large housing projects that were developed in the 1960s. These are now overcrowded and deteriorated. Police are actually afraid to enter the buildings unless they arrive with a SWAT team. Several officers have been killed in the line of duty there over the last decade. Each building is controlled by a gang whose members demand tribute from the residents.

You are asked to propose an urban redevelopment program that can revitalize the area and eventually bring down the crime rate. You can bring any public or private element to bear on this overwhelming problem. You can also ask private industry to help in the struggle, promising them tax breaks for their participation. What programs do you feel could break the cycle of urban poverty?

Key Terms

at-risk

Chicago School

concentration effect

conduct norms

cultural deviance theory

cultural transmission

culture conflict

culture of poverty

differential opportunity

focal concerns

general strain theory (GST)

group autonomy

income inequality

natural areas

negative affective states

reaction formation

relative deprivation

siege mentality

social disorganization theory

social ecologists

social injustice

social structure theory

status frustration

strain theory

subcultures

transitional neighbourhoods

underclass

value conflict

See the book-specific website at www.siegelcriminology2e.nelson.com for additional chapter links, discussions, and quizzes.

Chapter

Social Process Theories

8

Many criminologists question whether a person's place in the social structure can alone control the onset of criminality. After all, the majority of people residing in the nation's most deteriorated urban areas are law-abiding citizens who hold conventional values and compensate for their lack of social standing and financial problems by working hard, living frugally, and keeping an eye to the future. Conversely, self-report studies tell us that many members of the privileged classes engage in theft, drug use, and other crimes.

Even if it is assumed that all criminals come from the lower classes (which they don't), it is evident that the great majority of even the poorest Canadians do not commit criminal acts even though they may have a great economic incentive to do so.[1]

Neighbourhood deterioration and disorganization alone cannot explain why one person embarks on a criminal career while another, living in the same environment, obeys the law, gets an education, and seeks legitimate employment.[2] Relatively few delinquent offenders living in the most deteriorated areas remain persistent, chronic offenders; most desist despite the continuing pressure of social decay. Some other social forces, then, must be at work to explain why the majority of at-risk individuals do not become persistent criminal offenders.

To explain these contradictory findings, attention has focused on social-psychological processes and interactions common to people in all segments of the social structure. **Social process theories** hold that criminality is a function of individual **socialization**. They draw attention to the interactions people have with the various organizations, institutions, and processes of society. As they pass through the life cycle, most people are influenced by the direction of their familial relationships, peer group associations, educational experiences, and interactions with authority figures, including teachers, employers, and agents of the justice system. If these relationships are positive and supportive, they will be able to succeed within the rules of society; if these relationships are dysfunctional and destructive, conventional success may be impossible and criminal solutions may become a feasible alternative.

Social process theories share one basic concept: All people, regardless of their race, class, or gender, have the potential to become delinquents or criminals. Although members of the lower class may have the added burdens of poverty, racism, poor schools, and disrupted family lives, these social forces may be counteracted by positive peer relations, a supportive family, and educational success. In contrast, even the most affluent members of society may turn to antisocial behaviour if their life experiences are intolerable or destructive.

Social process theorists thus focus their attention on the socialization of youths and attempt to identify the developmental factors—family relationships, peer influences, educational attainment, self-image development—that if supportive can lead to a successful life but if destructive or dysfunctional can result in antisocial behaviours and a career in crime.

The influence of social process theories has endured because the relationship between social class and crime is still uncertain. Most residents of inner-city areas refrain from criminal activity, and few of those who do commit crimes remain persistent, chronic offenders in their adulthood. If poverty were the sole cause of crime, indigent adults would be as criminal as indigent teenagers. Following a thorough review of the most recent research, Charles Tittle and Robert Meier still found the association between economic status and crime "problematic"; class position alone cannot explain crime rates.[3]

A number of research studies show that even in the most deteriorated areas, it is the quality of interpersonal interactions with parents, peers, and schools that controls criminality; income and environment alone cannot determine behaviour.[4] If this research is valid, socialization and not structure may be the key to understanding crime.

Connections

Chapter 3's analysis of the class–crime relationship showed why class–crime is still a hotly debated topic. While serious criminals may be disproportionately found in lower-class areas, self-report studies show that criminality cuts across class lines. The discussion of drug use in Chapter 14 also shows that many members of the middle class engage in recreational substance abuse, an indication that many law violators are not economically motivated.

Social Processes and Crime

Criminologists have long studied the critical elements of socialization to determine how they contribute to the development of a criminal career. Prominent among these elements are the family, the peer group, and school.

Family Relations

Evidence that parenting factors may play a critical role in determining whether individuals misbehave as children and even later as adults is one of the most replicated findings in the deviance literature.[5]

Family relationships have for some time been considered a major determinant of behaviour.[6] Youths who grow up in a household characterized by conflict and tension, where parents are absent or separated, or where familial love and support are lacking will be susceptible to the crime-promoting forces in the environment.[7] Even those children living in so-called high-crime areas will be better able to resist the temptations of the streets if they receive fair discipline, care, and support from parents who provide them with strong, positive role models.[8] Nonetheless, living in a disadvantaged neighbourhood places a terrific strain on family functioning, especially in single-parent families experiencing social isolation from relatives, friends, and neighbours. Kids who are raised within such distressed families are at risk for delinquency.[9] The relationship between family structure and crime is critical when the high rates of divorce and single parenthood are considered.

At one time, growing up in a broken home was considered a primary cause of criminal behaviour. However, many criminologists today discount the association between family structure and the onset of criminality, claiming that family conflict and discord are more important determinants of behaviour than family structure.[10] Not all experts, though, discount the effects of family structure on crime. James Q. Wilson and Richard Herrnstein claim that even if single mothers (or fathers) can make up for the loss of a second parent, it is simply more difficult to do so and the chances of failure increase.[11] Single parents may find it difficult to provide adequate supervision. There is evidence that children who live with single parents receive less encouragement and less help with schoolwork. They may be more prone to rebellious acts, such as running away and truancy.[12] Children in two-parent households are more likely to want to go on to college than kids in single-parent homes; poor school achievement and limited educational aspirations have been associated with delinquent behaviour.[13]

Because their incomes are reduced in the aftermath of marital breakup, many divorced mothers are forced to move to residences in deteriorated neighbourhoods; disorganized neighbourhoods place children at risk for crime and drug abuse.[14] Nor does remarriage seem to mitigate the effects of divorce on youths: Children living with a step-parent exhibit as many problems as youths in divorce situations and considerably more problems than those who are living with both biological parents.[15] There is also little evidence that children of divorce improve over time; family disruption has unmistakable long-term effects.

Other family factors considered to have predictive value for criminal behaviour include inconsistent discipline, poor supervision, and the lack of a warm, loving, supportive parent–child relationship.[16] Children who have warm and affectionate ties to their parents report greater levels of self-esteem beginning in adolescence and extending into their adulthood; high self-esteem is inversely related to criminal behaviour.[17] Parental deviance has also been linked to a child's criminal behaviour. Children growing up in homes where parents suffer from mental impairment are at risk for delinquency.[18] Even at age two, the children of drug abusers exhibit personality defects such as excessive anger and negativity.[19] Kids whose parents abuse drugs are more likely to become persistent substance abusers than the children of nonabusers.[20] John Laub and Robert Sampson have found evidence that the children of parents who engage in criminality and substance abuse are more likely to engage in law-violating behaviour than the offspring of conventional parents.[21]

There is also a suspected link between child abuse, neglect, sexual abuse, and crime.[22] A number of studies show a significant association between child maltreatment and serious self-reported and official delinquency, even when controlling for gender, race, and class.[23] Victims of child abuse are more likely to mature into abusing and violent adults than nonvictims are.[24] Child abuse is most prevalent among families living in socially disorganized neighbourhoods, explaining in part the association between poverty and violence.[25]

The effect of the family on delinquency has also been observed in other cultures. For example, research on Chinese families shows that those who provide firm support inhibit delinquency, whereas families who experience parental deviance are more likely to contain youths involved in antisocial behaviours.[26]

Connections

The age-graded theory of Sampson and Laub is discussed more fully in Chapter 10. While deviant parents may encourage offending, Sampson and Laub believe that life experiences can either encourage crime-prone people to offend or conversely aid them in their return to a conventional lifestyle.

Educational Experience

Adolescent achievement in the school and educational process has also been linked to criminality. Studies show that children who do poorly in school, lack educational motivation, and feel alienated are the most likely to engage in criminal acts.[27] A recent analysis of the findings of 118 studies of educational achievement found academic performance to be a significant predictor of crime and delinquency. Although white children and males seem more deeply influenced by school failure, all children who fail in school offend more frequently, commit more serious and violent offences, and persist in their offending into adulthood.[28]

Schools help contribute to criminality when they label problem youths, setting them apart from conventional society. One method of stigmatization is the "track system" that identifies some students as college-bound and others as academic underachievers or potential dropouts.[29] Recent research indicates that many school dropouts, especially those who have been expelled, face a significant chance of entering a criminal career.[30] In contrast, doing well in school and developing feelings of attachment to teachers have been linked to resistance to crime.[31]

It is not surprising that the school system has been the subject of criticism concerning its methods, goals, and objectives. The provinces' educational systems are underfunded and understaffed. Reading and math ability levels are in question. These trends do not bode well for the crime rate. Most important, surveys indicate that a lot of youth crime occurs within the schools themselves.

Peer Relations

Psychologists have long recognized that the peer group has a powerful effect on human conduct and can have a dramatic influence on decision making and behaviour choices.[32] Peer influence on behaviour has been recorded in many cultures and may be a universal norm.[33]

Early in children's lives, parents are the primary source of influence and attention. Between the ages of 8 and 14, children begin to seek out a stable peer group; both the number and variety of friendships increase as children go through adolescence. Soon, friends begin to have a greater influence over decision making than parents.[34] By their early teens, children report that their friends give them emotional support when they are feeling bad and that they can confide intimate feelings to peers without worrying about their confidences being betrayed. As they go through adolescence, children form **cliques**, small groups of friends who share activities and confidences. They also belong to **crowds**, loosely organized groups of children who share interests and activities. While clique members share intimate knowledge, crowds are brought together by mutually shared activities, such as sports, religion, or hobbies. Although bonds in this "wider circle of friends" may not be intimate, kids learn a lot about themselves and their world while navigating through these relationships.[35] Popular youths can be members of a variety of cliques and crowds. In later adolescence, peer approval has a major impact on socialization.

The most popular youths do well in school and are socially astute. In contrast, children who are rejected by their peers are more likely to display aggressive behaviour and disrupt group activities through bickering or other antisocial behaviour.[36] Peer relations, then, are a significant aspect of maturation.

Peers exert a powerful influence on youths and pressure them to conform to group values. Peers guide children and help them learn to share and cooperate, cope with aggressive impulses, and discuss feelings they would not dare bring up at home. With peers, youths can compare their own experiences and learn that others have similar concerns and problems; they realize they are not alone. It should come as no surprise, then, that much adolescent criminal activity begins as a group process.[37]

Delinquent peers can exert tremendous influence on behaviour, attitudes, and beliefs.[38] In every level of the social structure, youths who fall in with a "bad crowd" become more susceptible to criminal behaviour patterns.[39] Deviant peers help provide friendship networks that support delinquency and drug use.[40] Riding around, staying out late, and partying with deviant peers provide youths with the opportunity to commit deviant acts.[41] And because delinquent friends tend to be "sticky" (once acquired, they are not easily lost), peer influence may continue through the life span.[42] Some kids join more than one group, playing a leadership role in one, being a follower in another. And even though many groups are short-lived and transitory, being exposed to so many deviant influences in multiple groups may help explain why deviant group membership is highly correlated with personal offending rates.[43]

Institutional Involvement and Belief

People who hold high moral values and beliefs, who have learned to distinguish right from wrong, and who regularly attend religious services should also eschew crime and other antisocial behaviours. Religion binds people together and forces them to confront the effect their behaviour has on others; committing crimes would violate the principles of all organized religions.

An oft-cited study by Travis Hirschi and Rodney Stark found that, contrary to expectations, the association between religious attendance or belief and delinquent behaviour patterns was negligible and insignificant.[44] However, more recent research reached an opposing conclusion: Attendance at religious services has a significant negative impact on crime. Interestingly, the Evans research shows that participation is a more significant inhibitor of crime than the mere holding of religious beliefs and values.[45] And cross-national research shows that countries with high rates of church membership and attendance have lower crime rates than less "devout" nations.[46]

Connections

Arousal theory would also predict that church attendance is inversely correlated with crime rates, because criminals are people who need large amounts of stimulation and would not be able to sit through religious services. See Chapter 6 for more on arousal theory.

Branches of Social Process Theory

To many criminologists, the elements of socialization just described are the chief determinants of criminal behaviour. According to this view, people living in even the most deteriorated urban areas can successfully resist inducements to crime if they have a good self-image, have learned moral values, and have the support of their parents, peers, teachers, and neighbours. The girl with a positive self-image who is chosen for a college scholarship, has the warm, loving support of her parents, and is viewed as someone "going places" by friends and neighbours is less likely to adopt a criminal way of life than another adolescent who is abused at home, who lives with criminal parents, and whose bond to the school and peer group is shattered because she is labelled a "troublemaker."[47]

Like social structure theory, the social process approach has several independent branches (see Figure 8.1). The first branch, **social learning theory**, suggests that people learn the techniques and attitudes of crime from close and intimate relationships with criminal peers; crime is a learned behaviour. The second branch, **control theory**, maintains that everyone has the potential to become a criminal but that most people are controlled by their bond to society; crime occurs when the forces that bind people to society are weakened or broken. The third branch, **labelling theory**, says that people become criminals when significant members of society label them as such and they accept those labels as a personal identity.

Put another way, social learning theory assumes that people are born "good" and learn to be "bad"; control theory assumes that people are born "bad" and must be controlled in order to be "good"; labelling theory assumes that whether "good" or "bad," people are controlled by the reactions of others. Each of these independent branches will be discussed separately.

Social Learning Theory

Social learning theorists find that crime is a product of learning the norms, values, and behaviours associated with criminal activity. Social learning can involve the actual techniques of crime—how to hot-wire a car or roll a joint—as well as the psychological aspects of criminality—how to deal with the guilt or shame associated with illegal activities.

This section briefly reviews the three most prominent forms of social learning theory: differential association theory, differential reinforcement theory, and neutralization theory.

Connections

In the late 19th century, Gabriel Tarde's theory of imitation held that criminals imitate "superiors" they admire and respect. Learning theory also focuses on the influence of significant others. Tarde's work, discussed in Chapter 6, is thus a precursor to modern learning theories.

Figure 8.1   **The complex web of social processes that control human behaviour**

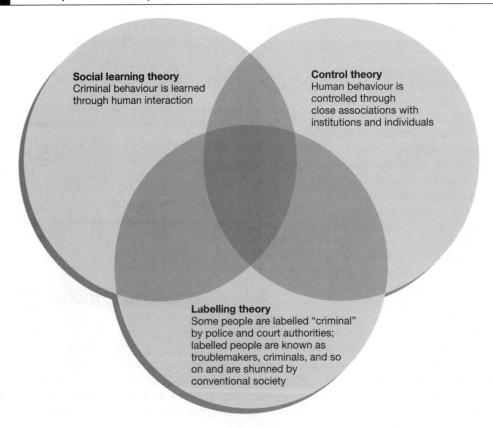

Social learning theory
Criminal behaviour is learned through human interaction

Control theory
Human behaviour is controlled through close associations with institutions and individuals

Labelling theory
Some people are labelled "criminal" by police and court authorities; labelled people are known as troublemakers, criminals, and so on and are shunned by conventional society

Differential Association Theory

Edwin H. Sutherland (1883–1950), considered a preeminent criminologist, first put forth the **differential association (DA) theory** in 1939 in his text *Principles of Criminology.*[48] The final form of the theory appeared in 1947. When Sutherland died in 1950, his work was continued by his longtime associate Donald Cressey. The latter was so successful in explaining his mentor's efforts that DA remains one of the most enduring explanations of criminal behaviour.

Sutherland's research on white-collar crime and professional theft led him to dispute the notion that crime is a function of the inadequacy of people in the lower classes.[49] To Sutherland, criminality stemmed from neither individual traits nor socioeconomic position; instead, he believed it to be a function of a learning process that could affect any individual in any culture.

A few ideas are basic to the theory of differential association.[50] Crime is a politically defined construct. It is defined by government authorities who are in political control. In societies wracked by culture conflict, the definition of crime may be inconsistent and consequently rejected by some groups of people. Put another way, people may vary in their relative acceptance of criminal and noncriminal definitions. The acquisition of behaviour is a social learning process, not a political or legal process. Skills and motives conducive to crime are learned as a result of contacts with pro-crime values, attitudes, and definitions and with other patterns of criminal behaviour.

Principles of Differential Association. The basic principles of differential association are as follows:[51]

1. *Criminal behaviour is learned.* This statement differentiates Sutherland's theory from prior attempts to classify criminal behaviour as an inherent characteristic of criminals. By suggesting that delinquent and criminal behaviour is learned, Sutherland said that it can be classified in the same manner as any other learned behaviour, such as writing, painting, or reading. It is not a matter of mere imitation.
2. *Criminal behaviour is learned in interaction with other persons in a process of communication.* Sutherland believed that illegal behaviour is learned actively. An individual does not become a law violator simply by living in a criminogenic environment or by manifesting personal characteristics, such as low IQ or family problems, associated with criminality. Instead, criminal and deviant behaviour is learned in association with individuals who serve as teachers and guides to crime. Thus, criminality cannot occur without the aid of others.
3. *The principal part of the learning of criminal behaviour occurs within intimate personal groups.* People's contacts with their most intimate social companions—family, friends, peers—have the greatest influence on their learning of deviant behaviour and attitudes. Relationships with these individuals affect the interpretation of everyday events. For example, children who grow up in homes where parents abuse alcohol are more likely to view drinking as being socially and physically beneficial.[52] Social support for deviance helps people overcome social controls so that they can embrace criminal values and behaviours. The intimacy of these associations far outweighs the importance of any other form of communication, such as movies or television.
4. *Learning criminal behaviour includes learning the techniques of committing the crime,* which are sometimes complicated and sometimes simple, and learning the specific motives, rationalizations, and attitudes. Because criminal behaviour is like any other learned behaviour, the actual techniques of criminality must be acquired and learned. Young delinquents learn from their associates the proper way to pick a lock, shoplift, and obtain and use narcotics. In addition, novice criminals must learn to use the proper terminology for their acts and then acquire "proper" reactions to law violations. For example, getting high on marijuana and learning the proper way to smoke a joint are behaviour patterns usually acquired from more experienced companions. Moreover, criminals must learn how to react properly to their illegal acts—when to defend them, rationalize them, and show remorse for them.
5. *The specific direction of motives and drives is learned from perceptions of various aspects of the legal code as being favourable or unfavourable.* Since the reaction to social rules and laws is not uniform across society, people constantly come into contact with others who maintain different views on the utility of obeying the legal code. When definitions of right and wrong are extremely varied, people experience what Sutherland calls culture conflict. The attitudes toward criminal behaviour of the important people in an individual's life influence the attitudes that he or she develops. The conflict of social attitudes is the basis for the concept of differential association.
6. *A person becomes a criminal when he or she perceives that there are more benefits than unfavourable consequences to violating the law* (see Figure 8.2). According to Sutherland's theory, individuals become law violators when they are in contact with persons, groups, or events that have more definitions favourable toward criminality and are isolated from counteracting forces. A definition favourable toward criminality occurs, for example, when a person is exposed to friends sneaking into a theatre to avoid paying for a ticket or talking about the virtues of getting high on drugs. A definition unfavourable toward crime occurs when friends or parents demonstrate their disapproval of crime. Of course, neutral behaviour, such as reading a book, exists. It is neither positive nor negative with respect to law violation.

Figure 8.2   **Differential association theory assumes that criminal behaviour will occur when the definitions for crime outweigh the definitions against crime.**

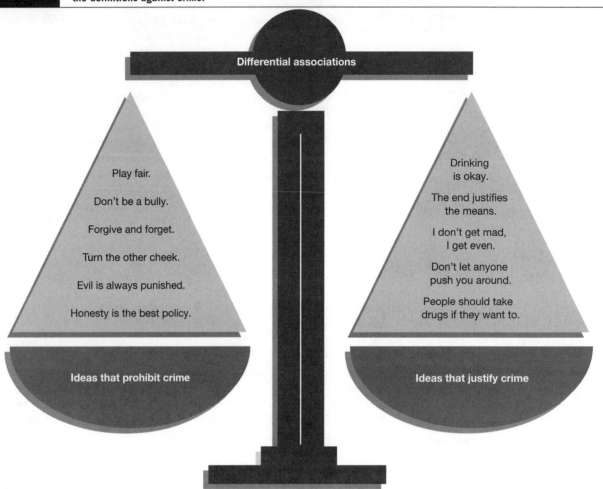

Differential associations

Play fair.

Don't be a bully.

Forgive and forget.

Turn the other cheek.

Evil is always punished.

Honesty is the best policy.

Ideas that prohibit crime

Drinking is okay.

The end justifies the means.

I don't get mad, I get even.

Don't let anyone push you around.

People should take drugs if they want to.

Ideas that justify crime

Cressey argues that this behaviour is important, "especially as an occupier of the time of a child so that he is not in contact with criminal behaviours during the time he is so engaged in the neutral behaviour."[53]

7. *Differential associations may vary in frequency, duration, priority, and intensity.* Whether a person learns to obey the law or to disregard it is influenced by the quality of social interactions. Those interactions of lasting duration have greater influence than those that are more brief. Similarly, frequent contacts have greater effect than rare and haphazard contacts. Furthermore, contacts made early in life probably have a greater and more far-reaching influence than those developed later on. Finally, the prestige of the individual or groups from whom definitions are learned is important. For example, the influence of a father, mother, or trusted friend far outweighs the effect of more socially distant figures.

8. *While criminal behaviour is an expression of general needs and values, it is not excused by those general needs and values,* since noncriminal behaviour is also an expression of the same needs and values. This principle suggests that the motives for criminal behaviour cannot logically be the same as those for conventional behaviour. Sutherland rules out such motives as desire to accumulate money or social status, personal frustration, or low self-concept as causes of crime, since they are just as likely to produce noncriminal behaviour, such as getting a better education or working harder on a job. It is only the learning of deviant norms through contact with an excess of definitions favourable toward criminality that produces illegal behaviour.

In sum, DA theory holds that people learn criminal attitudes and behaviour while in their adolescence from close and trusted relatives and companions. A criminal career develops if learned antisocial values and behaviours are not at least matched or exceeded by conventional attitudes and behaviours. Criminal behaviour is learned in a process similar to learning any other human behaviour.

Testing Differential Association. Despite the importance of DA theory, research devoted to testing its assumptions has been relatively sparse. It has proven difficult to conceptualize the principles of the theory so that they can be empirically tested. For example, social scientists find it difficult to evaluate such vague concepts as "definition toward criminality." It is also difficult to follow people over time, establish precisely when definitions toward criminality begin to outweigh prosocial definitions, and determine whether this imbalance produces criminal behaviour.

However, one important area of research is the friendship patterns of delinquent youths. Differential association implies that criminals maintain close and intimate relations with deviant peers.[54] In a classic work, James Short surveyed institutionalized youths and found that they had maintained close associations with delinquent youths prior to their law-violating acts.[55] Similarly, Albert Reiss and A. Lewis Rhodes found an association between delinquent friendship patterns and the probability that a youth would commit a criminal act.[56]

Studies have also found that law violators maintain close relationships with deviant peers.[57] For example, Mark Warr found that antisocial kids who maintain delinquent friends over a long duration are much more likely to persist in their delinquent behaviour than those without such peer support.[58] However, Warr discovered that recently cultivated friendships had a greater influence on criminality than friends acquired earlier in life, a finding that contradicts DA's emphasis on the "priority" of criminal influences.

DA principles seem especially relevant as an explanation of the onset of substance abuse and a career in the drug trade; learning proper techniques and attitudes from an experienced user or dealer appears to be a requirement.[59] In his interview study of low-level drug dealers, Kenneth Tunnell found that many novices were tutored by a more experienced dealer who helped them make connections with buyers and sellers. One told him:

> I had a friend of mine who was an older guy and he introduced me to selling marijuana to make a few dollars. I started selling a little and made a few dollars. For a young guy to be making a hundred dollars or so, it was a lot of money. So I got kind of tied up in that aspect of selling drugs.[60]

Tunnell found that making connections is an important part of the dealer's world. It does not seem surprising that research shows that adolescent drug users are likely to have intimate relationships with a peer friendship network that supports their substance abuse.[61]

Another approach to assessing DA theory tests the assumption that people who have assimilated procrime attitudes are also the ones most likely to engage in criminal activity.[62] These findings have been observed in cross-cultural research. In one study conducted in Hong Kong, Yuet-Wah Cheung and Agnes M.C. Ng found that DA items were the most significant predictor of delinquent behaviour in a sample of 1139 secondary-school students. They conclude that deviant youths may be imitating friends' behaviour or attempting to "keep up appearances" by yielding to group pressure.[63]

While these findings are persuasive, self-report research in support of DA must be interpreted with caution. Since subjects are usually asked about their peer relations, learning experiences, perceptions of differential associations, and criminal behaviours simultaneously, it is impossible to determine whether differential associations were the cause or the result of criminal behaviour. While it is possible that youths learn about crime and then commit criminal acts, it is also possible that experienced delinquents and criminals seek out like-minded peers after they engage in antisocial acts and that the internalization of deviant attitudes follows, rather than precedes, criminality.[64]

To answer critics, researchers must develop more valid measures of differential associations.[65] One possibility is that longitudinal analysis might be used to measure subjects repeatedly over time to determine whether those exposed to excess definitions toward deviance eventually become deviant themselves. Even then, it is difficult to show whether people who continually break the law develop a group of like-minded peers who support their behaviour, rather than a process in which "innocent" people are "seduced" into crime by exposure to the deviant attitudes of more criminal peers.[66]

To remedy this problem, future research may be directed at creating more accurate means with which to test the theory's basic principles.[67] A more valid approach may be to follow a cohort over time to assess the impact of criminal friends and associations: Does repeated exposure to excess definitions toward deviance escalate deviance through the life course? For example, some recent research found that adolescents who acquire criminal friends are also the ones most likely to eventually engage in criminal behaviour—a finding that supports DA. Warr notes that criminal friends are "sticky"; once gotten, they are hard to shake. They help lock people into antisocial behaviour patterns through the life course. In fact, people who maintain deviant friendships and close relationships with deviant peers are the ones most likely to persist in their offending careers.[68] Deviant friends help counteract the crime-reducing effects of the aging-out process.[69]

Analysis of Differential Association Theory. Misconceptions about DA theory have tended to produce unwarranted criticism of its principles and meaning.[70] For example, some criminologists claim that the theory is concerned solely with the number of personal contacts and associations a delinquent has with other criminal or delinquent offenders.[71] If this were true, and we pushed the idea to the extreme, those most likely to become criminals would be police, judges, and correctional authorities, since they are constantly associating with criminals. Sutherland stressed "excess definitions toward criminality," not mere association with criminals. Personnel of the juvenile justice system do have extensive associations with criminals, but these are more than counterbalanced by their associations with law-abiding citizens.

Another misconception is that definitions toward delinquency are acquired from learning the values of a deviant subculture, that criminals are people properly socialized into a deviant subculture.[72] However, Ronald Akers argues that while it is true that some people become criminals because they have been "properly" socialized into a deviant culture, individuals can also embrace criminality because they have been improperly socialized into the normative culture.[73]

Although DA stresses an excess of definitions toward delinquency, it does not specify that they must come solely from lower-class criminal sources. This distinguishes Sutherland's work from social structure theories. Outwardly law-abiding middle-class parents can encourage delinquent behaviour by their own drinking, drug use, or family violence. And both middle- and lower-class youths are exposed to media images that express open admiration for violent heroes, such as those played by Arnold Schwarzenegger or Jean-Claude Van Damme, who take the law into their own hands. The influence of differential association is not affected by social class, supporting Sutherland's belief that deviant learning can affect middle-class as well as lower-class youths.[74]

There are, however, a number of valid criticisms of Sutherland's work. It fails to explain why one youth who is exposed to delinquent definitions eventually succumbs to them while another, living under the same conditions, avoids them.[75] It also fails to account for the origin of delinquent definitions. How did the first "teacher" learn delinquent attitudes and definitions in order to pass them on? Another apparently valid criticism of DA is that it assumes criminal and delinquent acts to be rational and systematic. This ignores spontaneous and wanton acts of violence and damage that appear to have little utility or purpose, such as the isolated psychopathic killing, which is virtually unsolvable because of the killer's anonymity and lack of criminal associations.

The most serious criticism of DA theory concerns the vagueness of its terms, which makes its assumptions difficult to test. For example, what constitutes an "excess of definition toward criminality"? How can we determine whether an individual actually has a procriminal imbalance of these definitions? It is simplistic to assume that all criminals have experienced a majority of definitions

toward criminality and all noncriminals, a minority of them. Unless the terms used in the theory can be defined more precisely, its validity remains a matter of guesswork.

Despite these criticisms, DA theory maintains an important place in the study of criminal behaviour. For one thing, it provides a consistent explanation of all types of delinquent and criminal behaviour. Unlike the social structure theories discussed previously, it is not limited to the explanation of a single facet of antisocial activity, such as lower-class gang activity. The theory can also account for the extensive criminal behaviour found even in middle- and upper-class areas, where youths may be exposed to a variety of procriminal definitions from such sources as overly opportunistic parents and friends. And the research which suggests that criminal friends are "sticky" indicates that differential associations might be one of the keys to explaining deviance through the life course.

Differential Reinforcement Theory

Differential reinforcement (DR) theory (also called social learning theory) is another attempt to explain crime as a type of learned behaviour. First proposed by Ronald Akers in collaboration with Robert Burgess, it is a version of the social learning view that combines differential association concepts with elements of psychological learning theory.[76]

According to Akers, the same process is involved in learning both deviant and conventional behaviour. People neither learn to be "all deviant" or "all conforming" but rather strike a balance between the two opposing poles of behaviour. The balance is usually stable but can undergo revision over time.[77]

A number of learning processes shape behaviour. Direct conditioning or differential reinforcement occurs when behaviour is either rewarded or punished during interaction with others. Differential association involves learning from direct or indirect interaction with others. Imitation occurs from observational learning experiences, such as from watching TV and films. People also learn cognitive definitions, which are attitudes that are favourable or unfavourable toward a behaviour and can either stimulate or extinguish that behaviour.

Behaviour is reinforced when positive rewards are gained or when punishment is avoided (negative reinforcement). It is weakened by negative stimuli (punishment) and loss of reward (negative punishment). Whether deviant or criminal behaviour is begun or persists depends on the degree to which it has been rewarded or punished and the rewards or punishments attached to its alternatives.

People learn to evaluate their own behaviour through interaction with significant others and groups in their lives. These groups control sources and patterns of reinforcement, define behaviour as right or wrong, and provide behaviours for observational learning. The more individuals learn to define their behaviour as justified, rather than as undesirable, the more likely they are to engage in it. For example, kids who hook up with a drug-abusing peer group, whose members value drugs and alcohol, encourage their use, and provide opportunities to observe people abusing substances, will be encouraged through this social learning experience to use drugs themselves.

Akers's theory posits that the principal influence on behaviour is from "those groups which control individuals' major sources of reinforcement and punishment and expose them to behavioural models and normative definitions."[78] The important groups are the ones with which a person is in differential association—peer and friendship groups, schools, churches, and similar institutions. Within the context of these critical groups, "deviant behaviour can be expected to the extent that it has been differentially reinforced over alternative behaviour ... and is defined as desirable or justified."[79] Once people are initiated into crime, their behaviour can be reinforced by exposure to deviant behaviour models, association with deviant peers, and lack of negative sanctions from parents or peers. The deviant behaviour, originated by imitation, is sustained by social support. It is possible that differential reinforcements help establish criminal careers and are a key factor in explaining persistent criminality.

The principles of differential reinforcement have been subject to empirical review by Akers and other criminologists.[80] In an important test of his theory, Akers and his associates surveyed 3065 male and female adolescents on drug- and alcohol-related activities and their perception of variables related to social learning and DR. Included were the respondents' perception of esteemed peers' attitudes toward drug and alcohol abuse, the number of people they admired who actually used controlled substances, and whether people they admired would reward or punish them for substance abuse. Akers found a strong association between drug and alcohol abuse and social learning variables: Kids who believed they would be rewarded for deviance by those they respect were the ones most likely to engage in deviant behaviour.[81]

Akers has also found that the learning experience continues within a deviant group as behaviour is both influenced by and exerts influence over group process. For example, kids may learn to smoke because of social reinforcement by peers; over time, one's smoking influences friendships and peer group memberships.[82]

Differential reinforcement theory is an important view of the cause of criminal activity. It considers how both the effectiveness and content of socialization condition crime. Because not all socialization is positive, it accounts for the fact that negative reinforcements can produce criminal results. This jibes with research showing that parental deviance is related to adolescent antisocial behaviour.[83] Akers's work also fits well with rational choice theory because they both suggest that people learn the techniques and attitudes necessary to commit crime. Criminal knowledge is gained through experience. After considering the outcome of their past experiences, potential offenders decide which criminal acts will be profitable and which are dangerous and should be avoided.[84] Why do people make rational choices about crime? Because they have learned to balance risks against the potential for criminal gain.

Neutralization Theory

Neutralization theory is identified with the writings of David Matza and Gresham Sykes.[85] They also view the process of becoming a criminal as a learning experience. However, while learning theorists such as Sutherland and Akers dwell on the learning of techniques, values, and attitudes necessary for performing criminal acts, Sykes and Matza maintain that most delinquents and criminals hold conventional values and attitudes but master techniques that enable them to neutralize these values and drift back and forth between illegitimate and conventional behaviour. One reason is the subterranean value structure of society. **Subterranean values** are the morally tinged influences that have become entrenched in the culture but are publicly condemned by "right thinking" members of society. They exist side by side with conventional values and while condemned in public may be admired or practised in private, such as viewing pornographic videos. In contemporary culture it is common to hold both subterranean and conventional values; few people are "all good" or "all bad."

Matza argues that even the most committed criminals and delinquents are not involved in criminality all the time; they also attend schools, family functions, and religious services. Their behaviour can be conceived as falling along a continuum between total freedom and total restraint. This process, which he calls **drift**, refers to the movement from one extreme of behaviour to another, resulting in behaviour that is sometimes unconventional, free, or deviant and at other times constrained and sober.[86] Learning techniques of neutralization allows a person to temporarily "drift away" from conventional behaviour and get involved in more subterranean values and behaviours, including crime and drug abuse.[87]

Techniques of Neutralization. Sykes and Matza suggest that offenders develop a distinct set of justifications for their law-violating behaviour.

Sykes and Matza base their theoretical model on several observations.[88] First, criminals sometimes voice a sense of guilt over their illegal acts. If a stable criminal value system existed in opposition to generally held values and rules, criminals would be unlikely to exhibit any remorse for their acts, other than regret at being apprehended. Second, offenders frequently respect and admire honest, law-abiding persons. Really honest persons are often revered; if for some reason such persons are accused of misbehaviour, the criminal is quick to defend their integrity. Those admired may include sports figures, priests and other clergy, parents, teachers, and neighbours. Third, criminals draw a line between those whom they can victimize and those whom they cannot. Members of similar ethnic groups, churches, or neighbourhoods are often off-limits. This practice implies that criminals are aware of the wrongfulness of their acts. Why else limit them? Finally, criminals are not immune to the demands of conformity. Most criminals frequently participate in many of the same social functions as law-abiding people, such as school, church, and family activities.

Because of these factors, Sykes and Matza conclude that criminality is the result of the neutralization of accepted social values through the learning of a standard set of techniques that allow people to counteract the moral dilemmas posed by illegal behaviour.[89] Their research helped Sykes and Matza identify the following **techniques of neutralization:**

1. *Denial of responsibility.* Offenders claim their unlawful acts were simply not their fault. The acts resulted from forces beyond their control or were accidents.
2. *Denial of injury.* In denying the wrongfulness of an act, criminals are able to neutralize illegal behaviour. For example, stealing is viewed as borrowing; vandalism is considered mischief that has gotten out of hand.
3. *Denial of victim.* Criminals can maintain that the victim of crime "had it coming." Vandalism may be directed against a disliked teacher or neighbour; homosexuals may be beaten up by a gang because their behaviour is considered offensive. Denying the victim makes it morally acceptable for the criminal to commit such crimes as vandalism when the victims cannot be sympathized with or respected.
4. *Condemnation of the condemners.* An offender views the world as a corrupt place with a dog-eat-dog code. Since police and judges are on the take, teachers show favouritism, and parents take out their frustrations on their kids, it is ironic and unfair for these authorities to condemn his misconduct. By shifting the blame to others, criminals are able to repress the feeling that their own acts are wrong.
5. *Appeal to higher loyalties.* Novice criminals often argue that they are caught in the dilemma of being loyal to their own peer group while at the same time attempting to abide by the rules of the larger society. The needs of the group take precedence over the rules of society because the demands of the former are immediate and localized.

In sum, the theory of neutralization presupposes a condition in which such slogans as "I didn't mean to do it," "I didn't really hurt anybody," "They had it coming to them," "Everybody's picking on me," and "I didn't do it for myself" are used by people to neutralize unconven-

tional norms and values so they can drift into criminal modes of behaviour (see Figure 8.3).

Testing Neutralization Theory. A valid test of neutralization theory would have to be able to show that a person first neutralized his or her moral beliefs and then drifted into criminality. Otherwise, it could be argued that people who commit crime later make an attempt at rationalizing their behaviour. It is also possible that criminals and non-criminals have different moral values and that neutralizing them is therefore unnecessary.[90] The validity of the Sykes-Matza model depends on showing that all people share similar moral values and must neutralize them first to engage in criminal behaviour.

Despite this limitation, several attempts have been made to empirically verify the assumptions of neutralization theory.[91] Recent survey research by Robert Agnew indicates that delinquents do not value or condone violent behaviour and that they use neutralizations such as "It is all right to physically beat up people who call you names" to justify their aggressive activities.[92] Research also shows that institutionalized youths excuse deviant behaviours to a significantly greater degree than the general population does.[93] These findings indicate that people who commit criminal acts also have learned to rationalize their guilt. One study found that psychotherapists accused of sexually exploiting their clients also express neutralizations for their behaviour. Some blame the victim for "seducing them"; others claim there was little injury caused by the sexual encounter; still others seek scapegoats to blame for their actions.[94]

Are Social Learning Theories Valid?

Social learning theories make a significant contribution to our understanding of the onset of criminal behaviour. Nonetheless, the general learning model has been subject to some criticism. One complaint is that learning theorists fail to account for the origin of criminal definitions. How did the first "teacher" learn criminal techniques and definitions? Who came up with the original neutralization technique?

Learning theories also imply that people systematically learn techniques that allow them to be active and successful criminals, but they fail to adequately explain spontaneous and wanton acts of violence and damage and other expressive crimes that appear to have little utility or purpose. Is it possible that a random shooting is caused by an excess of deviant definitions? It is estimated that about 70 percent of all people arrested were under the influence of drugs and alcohol when they committed their crime. Do addicts pause to neutralize their moral inhibitions before mugging a victim? Do drug-involved kids stop to consider what they have "learned" about moral values?[95]

Despite these criticisms, learning theories maintain an important place in the study of delinquent and criminal behaviour. Unlike social structure theories, they are not limited to explaining a single facet of antisocial activity—for example, lower-class gang activity; they may be used to explain criminality across class structures. Even corporate executives may be exposed to a variety of procriminal definitions and learn to neutralize moral constraints. Social learning theories can be applied to a wide assortment of criminal activity.

Social Control Theories

Social control theories maintain that all people have the potential to violate the law and that modern society presents many opportunities for illegal activity. Criminal activities, such as drug abuse and car theft, are often exciting pastimes that hold the promise of immediate reward and gratification. Considering the attractions of crime, the question control theorists pose is "Why do people obey the rules of society?" To a choice theorist, the answer is fear of punishment; to a structural theorist,

obedience is a function of having access to legitimate opportunities; to a learning theorist, obedience is acquired through contact with law-abiding parents and peers. In contrast, control theorists argue that people obey the law because behaviour and passions are being controlled by internal and external forces. Some have self-control manifested in a strong moral sense that renders them incapable of hurting others and violating social norms. Some maintain self-control because they have a **commitment to conformity**—a real, present, and logical reason to obey the rules of society.[96] Perhaps they believe that getting caught in a criminal activity will hurt a dearly loved parent or jeopardize their chance at a college scholarship, or perhaps they feel that their job will be forfeited if they get in trouble with the law. In other words, all of a person's behaviour is controlled by their attachment and commitment to conventional institutions, individuals, and processes. If that commitment is absent, they are free to violate the law and engage in deviant behaviour; the "uncommitted" are not deterred by the threat of legal punishments.[97]

Figure 8.3 **Techniques of neutralization**

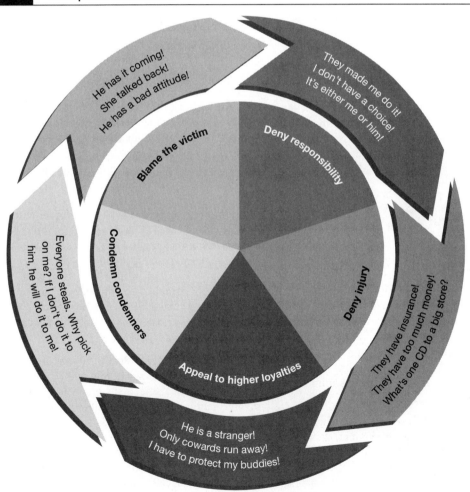

Self-Concept and Crime

Early versions of control theory speculated that low self-control is a product of weak self-concept and poor self-esteem. Youths who feel good about themselves and maintain a positive attitude are able to resist the temptations of the streets; a positive self-esteem helps kids control temptations toward delinquency. As early as 1951, Albert Reiss described how delinquents had weak "ego ideals" and lacked the "personal controls" to produce conforming behaviour.[98] Others noted that youths who believe criminal activity will damage their self-image and their relationships with others will be most likely to conform to social rules; they have a commitment to conformity. In contrast, those less concerned about their social standing are free to violate the law.[99]

Empirical research indicates that an important association between self-image and delinquency may in fact exist.[100] Howard Kaplan found that youths with poor self-concepts are the ones most likely to engage in delinquent behaviour and that successful participation in criminality helped raise their self-esteem.[101] Youths who perceive self-rejection ("I feel I do not have much to be proud of"; "I certainly feel useless at times") are the ones most likely to engage in deviant behaviours.[102] Youths who maintain both the lowest self-image and the greatest need for approval are the ones most likely to seek self-enhancement from delinquency.[103]

Why does low self-esteem lead to criminality? It is possible that to improve self-image people will make decisions that ultimately prove harmful. Kids who are having problems in school realize that they will feel much better if they can escape teachers' critical judgments by dropping out and joining a gang whose members value their cunning and their fighting ability. Ultimately, however, this is a self-defeating strategy, which is likely to hurt the long-term success of the individual.

Containment Theory

In an early effort to describe how self-image controls criminal tendencies, Walter Reckless and his associates argued that youths growing up in even the most criminogenic areas can insulate themselves from crime if they have sufficiently positive self-esteem. He called the individual's ability to resist criminal inducements **containments**, the most important of which are a positive self-image and "ego strength."[104] Kids with these traits can resist crime-producing "pushes and pulls." Here are some of the crime-producing forces that a strong self-image counteracts:

1. *Internal pushes.* Internal pushes include such personal factors as restlessness, discontent, hostility, rebellion, mental conflict, anxieties, and need for immediate gratification.
2. *External pressures.* External pressures are adverse living conditions that influence deviant behaviour, such as poverty, unemployment, minority status, and limited opportunities.
3. *External pulls.* External pulls are represented by deviant companions, membership in criminal subcultures or other deviant groups, and such influences as mass media and pornography.

Reckless and his associates made an extensive effort to validate the principles of containment theory. In a series of studies analyzing the school setting, they concluded that the ability of youths to resist crime depends on their maintaining a positive self-image in the face of environmental pressures toward delinquency. Despite the success Reckless and his associates had in verifying their containment approach, their efforts have been criticized for lack of methodological rigour, and the validity of containment theory has been disputed.

Reckless's version of control theory was a pioneering effort that set the stage for subsequent theoretical developments, following the idea that people are "controlled" by their feelings about themselves and others with whom they are in contact. In general then, control theory maintains that while all people perceive inducements to crime, some are better able to resist them than others.

Social Control Theory

Social control theory, originally articulated by Travis Hirschi in his influential 1969 book *Causes of Delinquency*, replaced containment theory as the dominant version of control theory.[105]

Hirschi linked the onset of criminality to the weakening of the ties that bind people to society. Hirschi assumed that all individuals are potential law violators but are kept under control because they fear that illegal behaviour will damage their relationships with friends, parents, neighbours, teachers, and employers. Without these social ties or bonds, and in the absence of sensitivity to others, a person is free to commit criminal acts. Hirschi did not portray society as containing competing subcultures with unique value systems. Most people are aware of the prevailing moral and legal code. He suggested, however, that in all elements of society, people vary in their responses to conventional social rules and values. Among all ethnic, religious, racial, and social groups, people whose bond to society is weak may fall prey to crime.

Elements of the Social Bond. Hirschi argued that the social bond a person maintains with society is divided into four main elements: attachment, commitment, involvement, and belief (see Figure 8.4).

Attachment refers to a person's sensitivity to and interest in others.[106] Psychologists believe that without a sense of attachment, a person becomes a psychopath and loses the ability to relate coherently to the world. The acceptance of social norms and the development of a social conscience depend on attachment to and caring for other human beings. Hirschi saw parents, peers, and schools as the important social institutions with which a person should maintain ties. Attachment to parents is the most important. Without attachment to family, feelings of respect for others in authority are unlikely to develop.

Commitment involves the time, energy, and effort expended in conventional lines of action. It embraces such activities as getting an education and saving money for the future. If people build up a strong involvement in life, property, and reputation, they will be less likely to engage in acts that will jeopardize their positions. Conversely, lack of commitment to conventional values may foreshadow a condition in which risk-taking behaviour, such as crime, becomes a reasonable behaviour alternative.

Heavy involvement in conventional activities leaves little time for illegal behaviour. Hirschi believes that involvement—in school, recreation, and family—insulates a person from the potential lure of criminal behaviour, while idleness enhances it.

People who live in the same social setting often share common moral beliefs; they may adhere to such values as sharing, sensitivity to the rights of others, and admiration for the legal code. If these beliefs are absent or weakened, individuals are more likely to participate in

According to Hirschi, potential law violators are normally kept under control because they fear that illegal behaviour will damage their social relationships. Without such social ties, a person may feel free to commit criminal acts. Kids who commit crimes with their friends may appear attached, but they actually have few emotional commitments to their deviant peers.

Famous Canadian Criminals

A Fateful Turn in the Promising Life of Bruce Curtis

In 1982, Bruce Curtis, a promising 18-year-old student from Middleton, Nova Scotia, shot and killed the mother of his friend Scott Franz. Bruce was an excellent student and valedictorian of his graduating class, and he was to enter Dalhousie University in the fall. He had been raised in a loving and caring family and was expected to do well with his life. What went wrong?

In July, he had accepted an invitation to visit his friend in New Jersey. The visit quickly turned sour, as Scott's parents argued incessantly. The stepfather had a history of abuse, and he had been drinking heavily. To escape the violence, the boys walked the streets and sat in the park. When they returned home late that night

they decided to sleep downstairs on the couch. Fearing further violence, they took two high-calibre rifles from where Scott's stepfather had hidden them. Early in the morning, hearing a shot, Bruce leapt up and went into the hallway where he collided with Scott's mother. The gun went off and killed her. The other shot he had heard was Scott shooting his stepfather, allegedly in self-defence. For some reason they didn't phone the police. They cleaned up the house and took the bodies to a park, where they dumped them in a ravine.

They were eventually captured by the police and charged with murder. During the trial it was revealed that Scott had not shot his father in self-defence, as he had said, but while he had been lying down in bed. Following what some felt was an unjust trial, Bruce received a 20-year sentence for aggravated manslaughter, while

Scott received 20 years for murder in exchange for testifying against his friend. Bruce continued to maintain that his shooting of Franz's mother was an accident, but there was to be no leniency.

After Bruce was incarcerated in 1983 in New Jersey's Bordentown Youth Correction Centre, his family undertook a long campaign to have him returned to Canada to serve out his sentence. Despite a general international agreement between the United States and Canada to allow such transfers, New Jersey's governor balked at allowing it. However, finally in 1988, Bruce Curtis was transferred to a Canadian prison. The following year he was placed on day parole, having served almost seven years of a 20-year term.

Source: *Journey Into Darkness: The Bruce Curtis Story*, a film directed by Graeme Campbell.

Figure 8.4   Elements of the social bond

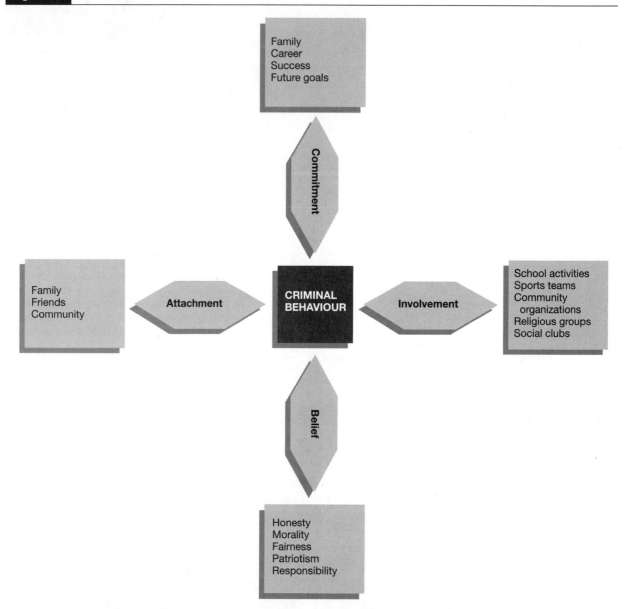

antisocial acts. It is the interrelationship of elements of the social bond that controls subsequent behaviour. For example, people who feel kinship and sensitivity to parents and friends should be more likely to adopt and work toward legitimate goals. On the other hand, a person who rejects social relationships probably lacks commitment to conventional goals. Similarly, people who are highly committed to conventional acts and beliefs are more likely to be involved in conventional activities.

Testing Social Control Theory. One of Hirschi's most significant contributions was his attempt to test the principal hypotheses of social control theory. He administered a detailed self-report survey to a sample of over 4000 junior and senior high school students in Contra Costa County, California.[107] He found considerable evidence to support the control theory model:

- Youths who were strongly attached to their parents were less likely to commit criminal acts.
- Commitment to conventional values, such as striving to get a good education and refusing to drink and "cruise around," was related to conventional behaviour.
- Youths involved in conventional activity, such as homework, were less likely to engage in criminal behaviour. Youths involved in unconventional behaviour, such as smoking and drinking, were more delinquency-prone.
- Delinquent youths maintained weak and distant relationships with people. Nondelinquents were attached to their peers.

- Delinquents and nondelinquents shared similar beliefs about society.

Hirschi's data lent important support to the validity of social control theory. Only in rare instances did his findings contradict the theory's most critical assumptions.

Supporting Research. Because of its importance and influence on criminology, social control theory has been the focus of numerous research efforts. Associations between indicators of attachment, belief, commitment, and involvement with measures of delinquency have tended to be positive and significant.[108] Research indicates that evidence of family detachment, including intrafamily conflict, abuse of children, and lack of affection, supervision, and family pride, are predictive of delinquent conduct.[109] Youths who are detached from the educational experience are at risk of criminality.[110] Lack of attachment to family, peers, and school has been found to predict delinquency in cross-cultural samples of youths.[111]

Other research efforts have shown that positive beliefs are related to criminality. That is, children who are involved in religious activities and hold conventional religious beliefs are less likely to become involved in substance abuse.[112] Similarly, youths who are involved in conventional leisure activities, such as supervised social activities and noncompetitive sports, are less likely to engage in delinquency.[113]

Canadian research has supported the general finding of social control theory.[114] In an important study of youths in Edmonton, Alberta, parental attachment was the strongest predictor of delinquent or law-abiding behaviour. Teens who are attached to their parents may develop the social skills that equip them both to maintain harmonious social ties and to escape life stresses such as school failure.[115]

Opposing Views. More than 70 published attempts have been made to corroborate social control theory by replicating Hirschi's original survey techniques.[116] While there has been significant empirical support for Hirschi's work, there are also those who question some or all of its elements.

One significant criticism concerns Hirschi's contention that delinquents are detached loners whose bond to their family and friends has been broken. Some critics have questioned whether delinquents (1) do in fact have strained relations with family and peers and (2) may in fact be influenced by close relationships with deviant peers and family members. A number of research efforts show that delinquents maintain relationships with deviant peers and are influenced by members of their deviant peer group.[117] However, delinquents may not be "lone wolves" whose only personal relationships are exploitive; their friendship patterns seem quite close to those of conventional youths.[118] For example, research shows that young male drug abusers maintained even more intimate relations with their peers than nonabusers

did; illicit drug abuse can be used to predict strong social ties and high levels of intimacy.[119]

Hirschi made little distinction in the importance of the elements of the social bond. For example, research shows that high levels of involvement, which Hirschi suggested should reduce delinquency, may actually increase delinquent behaviour. We could speculate that the more kids are involved in unsupervised, and possibly illegal, behaviours outside the home, the less contact they have with parental supervision and the greater the opportunity they have to commit crime.[120] Research with younger children found that the concepts of "involvement" and "belief" had relatively little influence over behaviour patterns.[121]

Hirschi's conclusion that any form of social attachment is beneficial, even to deviant peers and parents, has also been disputed. For example, Michael Hindelang found that attachment to delinquent peers escalated rather than restricted criminality.[122] Furthermore, youths attached to drug-abusing parents are more likely to become drug users themselves.[123] And in another important study in Edmonton, this one of dropouts, Leslie Samuelson, Timothy Hartnagel, and Harvey Krahn found that attachment to deviant peers helped motivate dropouts to commit crime and helped facilitate their delinquent acts.[124] Finally, attachment to delinquent friends is a powerful predictor of delinquency, strong enough to overcome the controlling effect of positive family relationships.[125]

There is some question as to whether social control theory can explain all modes of criminality or is restricted to particular groups or forms of criminality. When Marvin Krohn and James Massey surveyed 3065 junior and senior high school students, they found that control variables were better able to explain female delinquency than male delinquency, and minor delinquency (such as alcohol and marijuana abuse) than more serious criminal acts.[126] Other school-based research also found gender differences, in that social control variables were more predictive of female than male behaviour.[127] Perhaps girls are more deeply influenced by the quality of their bond to society than are boys.

Social bonds also seem to change over time. For example, in a sample of 12-, 15-, and 18-year-old boys, researchers found age differences in the perceptions of the social bond: Mid-teens are surprisingly likely to be influenced by their parents and teachers; boys in the other two age groups are more deeply influenced by their deviant peers.[128] This finding can be attributed to the problems of mid-adolescence, in which there is a great need to develop "psychological anchors" to conformity. It is possible, then, that at one age level, weak bonds (to parents) lead to delinquency, while at another, strong bonds (to peers) lead to delinquency.

The most severe criticism of social control theory has been levelled by sociologist Robert Agnew, who claims that Hirschi miscalculated the direction of the relationship between criminality and a weakened social bond.[129] While Hirschi's theory projects that a weakened bond leads to delinquency, Agnew suggests that the chain of events may flow in the opposite direction: Kids who break the law find that their bond to parents, schools, and society eventually becomes weak and attenuated. Other studies have also found that weakened social bonds are a consequence of criminality, not the reverse.[130]

These criticisms aside, the weight of the existing empirical evidence is supportive of control theory, and it has emerged as one of the preeminent theories in criminology.[131] For many criminologists, it is perhaps the most important way of understanding the onset of criminal misbehaviour.[132]

Connections

Although his work has achieved a prominent place in the criminological literature, Hirschi, along with Michael Gottfredson, has restructured his concept of control by integrating biosocial, psychological, and rational choice theory ideas into a General Theory of Crime. Because this theory is essentially integrated, it will be discussed more fully in Chapter 10.

Labelling Theory

Labelling theory explains criminal career formation in terms of destructive social interactions and encounters. Its roots are in the symbolic interaction theory of sociologists Charles Horton Cooley, George Herbert Mead, and Herbert Blumer.[133] **Symbolic interaction theory** holds that people communicate via symbols—gestures, signs, words, or images that stand for or represent something else. People interpret symbolic gestures from others and incorporate them into their self-image. Symbols are used by others to let people know how well they are doing and whether they are liked or appreciated. How people view reality, then, depends on the content of the messages and situations they encounter, the subjective interpretation of these interactions, and how they shape future behaviour. In this view, there is no simple objective reality. People interpret the actions of others, and this interpretation defines meaning. Because interpretation changes over time, so does the meaning of concepts and symbols.

Labelling theory picks up on these concepts of interaction and interpretation.[134] Throughout their lives, people are given a variety of symbolic labels in their interactions with others. These labels imply a variety of behaviours and attitudes; labels thus help define not just one trait but the whole person. For example, people labelled "insane" are also assumed to be dangerous, dishonest, unstable, violent, strange, and otherwise unsound. Valued labels, including "smart," "honest," and "hard worker," which suggest overall competence, can improve self-image and social standing. Research shows that people who are labelled with one positive trait, such as being physically attractive, are assumed to maintain others, such as intelligence and competence.[135] In contrast, negative labels, including "troublemaker," "mentally ill," and "stupid," help **stigmatize** their targets and reduce their self-image.

Both positive and negative labels entail the subjective interpretation of behaviour: A "troublemaker" is someone whom people label as "troublesome"; there need not be any objective proof or measure indicating that the person is actually a troublemaker. Although a label may be a function of rumour, innuendo, or unfounded suspicion, its adverse impact can be immense.

If a devalued status is conferred by a significant other—a teacher, police officer, elder, parent, or valued peer—the negative label may cause permanent harm to the target. Being perceived as a **social deviant** may affect their treatment at home, at work, at school, and in other social situations. Kids may find that their parents consider them a "bad influence" on younger brothers and sisters. School officials may limit them to classes for people with behaviour problems. Adults labelled "criminal," "ex-con," or "drug addict" may find their eligibility for employment severely restricted. And, of course, if the label is bestowed as the result of conviction for a criminal offence, the labelled person may be subject to official sanctions ranging from a mild reprimand to incarceration.

Connections

Fear of stigma has prompted efforts to reduce the impact of criminal labels through such programs as pretrial diversion and community treatment programs. In addition, some criminologists have called for noncoercive "peacemaking" solutions to interpersonal conflict. This peacemaking or restorative justice movement is reviewed in Chapter 9.

Beyond these immediate results, labelling advocates maintain that, depending on the visibility of the label and the manner and severity with which it is applied, a person will have an increasing commitment to a deviant career. "Thereafter he may be watched; he may be suspect ... he may be excluded more and more from legitimate opportunities."[136] Labelled persons may find themselves turning to others similarly stigmatized for support and companionship. Isolated from conventional society, they may identify themselves as members of an outcast group and become locked into a deviant career.

Because stigmatization is an interactive process, labelling theorists blame criminal career formation on the social agencies originally designed for its control. Institutions such as the police, courts, and correctional agencies, which label advocates, produce the stigmas that are so harmful to the very people they are trying to help, treat, or correct. Rather than reduce deviant behaviour, for which they were designed, such label-bestowing institutions actually help maintain and amplify criminal behaviour (see Figure 8.5).

Crime and Labelling Theory

Labelling theorists use an interactionist definition of crime. As sociologist Kai Erickson argued, "Deviance is not a property inherent in certain forms of behaviour, it is a property conferred upon those forms by the audience which directly or indirectly witnesses them."[137] This definition was amplified by Edwin Schur, who stated:

Human behaviour is deviant to the extent that it comes to be viewed as involving a personally discreditable departure from a group's normative expectation, and it elicits interpersonal and collective reactions that serve to "isolate," "treat," "correct" or "punish" individuals engaged in such behaviour.[138]

Crime and deviance, therefore, are defined by the social audience's reaction to people and their behaviour and the subsequent effects of that reaction; they are not defined by the moral content of the illegal act itself. Labelling theory argues that such crimes as murder, rape, and assault are only bad or evil because people label them as such. After all, the difference between an excusable act and a criminal one is often a matter of legal definition, which changes from place to place and from year to year. A killing can be a murder, an execution, an accident, self-defence, or a legitimate act in war. Labelling theorists would argue that such acts as abortion, marijuana use, possession of a handgun, and gambling have been legal at some points and places in history and illegal at others. Howard Becker refers to people who create rules as **moral entrepreneurs**. In a famous statement in his book *The Outsiders*, he summed up their effect as follows:

Social groups create deviance by making rules whose infractions constitute deviance, and by applying those rules to particular people and labelling them as outsiders. From this point of view, deviance is not a quality of the act a person commits, but rather a consequence of the application by others of rules and sanctions to an "offender." The deviant is one to whom the label has successfully been applied; deviant behaviour is behaviour that people so label.[139]

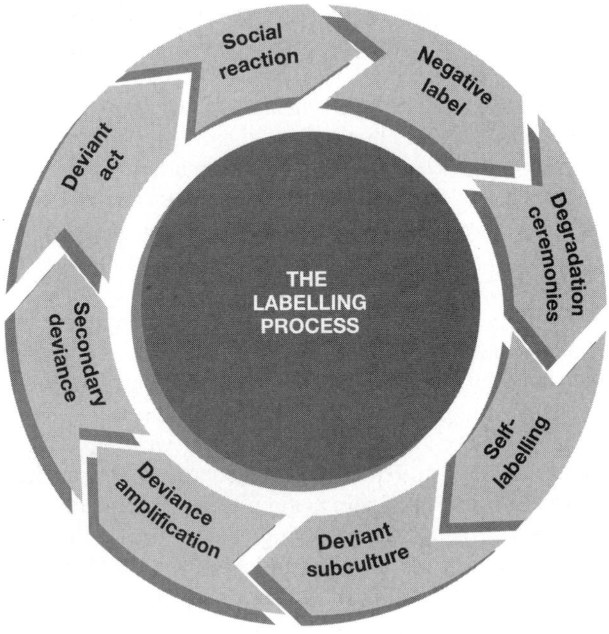

Differential Enforcement

An important principle of labelling theory is that the law is differentially applied, benefitting those who hold economic and social power and penalizing the powerless. Labelling theorists argue that the probability of being brought under the control of legal authority is a function of a person's race, wealth, gender, and social standing. Studies indicate that police officers are more likely to arrest males, minority-group members, and those in the lower class and to use their discretionary powers to give beneficial treatment to more favoured groups.[140] Similarly, minorities and the poor are more likely to be prosecuted for criminal offences and receive harsher punishments when convicted.[141] This evidence is used to support the labelling concept that personal characteristics and social interactions are actually more important variables in the criminal career formation process than the mere violation of the criminal law.

Labelling theorists also argue that the content of the law reflects power relationships in society. White-collar crimes are most often punished by a relatively small fine and rarely result in prison sentences, but long prison sentences are given to those convicted of "street crimes," such as burglary or car theft.[142] In sum, a major premise of labelling theory is that the law is differentially constructed and applied. It favours the powerful members of society who direct its content and penalizes people whose actions represent a threat to those in control.[143]

Figure 8.5   The labelling process

THE LABELLING PROCESS

Social reaction
Negative label
Degradation ceremonies
Self-labelling
Deviant subculture
Deviance amplification
Secondary deviance
Deviant act

Becoming Labelled

Labelling theorists are not especially concerned with explaining why people originally engage in acts that result in their being labelled.[144] Labelling theorists would not dispute any of the previously discussed theories of the onset of criminality: Crime may be a result of greed, personality, social structure, learning, or control. Labelling theorists' concern is with criminal career formation and not the origin of criminal acts.

It is, however, consistent with the labelling approach to suggest that the less personal power and fewer resources a person has, the greater the chance he or she will become labelled. In this view, a person is labelled deviant primarily as a consequence of the **social distance** between the labeller and the person labelled. Race, class, and ethnic differences between those in power and those without influence the likelihood of labelling. For example, a poor or minority-group teenager may run a greater chance of being officially processed for criminal acts by police, courts, and correctional agencies than a wealthy white youth would.

Of course, not all labelled people have chosen to engage in label-producing activities, such as crime. Some labels are bestowed on people for behaviours over which they have little control. Negative labels of this sort include "mentally unbalanced" and "mentally deficient." The probability of being labelled may depend on the visibility of the person in the community, the tolerance of the community for diversity, and the person's own power to combat labels.

Consequences of Labelling

Criminologists are most concerned with two effects of labelling: the creation of stigma and the effect on self-image. The labelled deviant becomes a social outcast who may be prevented from enjoying higher education, well-paying jobs, and other social benefits. Labelling theorists consider public condemnation an important part of the label-producing process. It may be accomplished in such "ceremonies" as a hearing in which a person is found to be mentally ill or a trial in which an individual is convicted of crime. A public record of the deviant acts causes the denounced person to be ritually separated from a place in the legitimate order and placed outside the world occupied by citizens of good standing. Harold Garfinkle has called transactions that produce irreversible, permanent labels "successful degradation ceremonies."[145]

Beyond these immediate results, the label tends to redefine the whole person. For example, the label "ex-con" may create in people's imaginations a whole series of behaviour descriptions—tough, mean, dangerous, aggressive, dishonest, sneaky—that a person who has been in prison may or may not possess. People begin to react to the "master status" of the label and what the

label signifies and not to the actual behaviour of the person who bears it. This is referred to as retrospective reading, a process in which the past of the labelled person is reviewed and reevaluated to fit his or her current outcast status. For example, boyhood friends of an assassin or killer are interviewed by the media and report that the suspect was withdrawn, suspicious, and negativistic as a youth. Now we can understand what prompted his current behaviour; the label must certainly be accurate.[146]

Labels become the basis of personal identity. As the negative feedback of law enforcement agencies, parents, friends, teachers, and other figures amplifies the force of the original label, stigmatized offenders may begin to reevaluate their own identities. If they are not really evil or bad, they may ask themselves, why is everyone making such a fuss about them? Frank Tannenbaum, a labelling theory pioneer, referred to this process as the **dramatization of evil.** With respect to the consequences of labelling delinquent behaviour, Tannenbaum stated:

> The process of making the criminal, therefore, is a process of tagging, defining, identifying, making conscious and self-conscious; it becomes a way of stimulating, suggesting and evoking the very traits that are complained of. If the theory of relation of response to stimulus has any meaning, the entire process of dealing with the young delinquent is mischievous insofar as it identifies him to himself or to the environment as a delinquent person. The person becomes the thing he is described as being.[147]

Primary and Secondary Deviance

One of the more well-known views of the labelling process is Edwin Lemert's concept of primary and secondary deviance.[148]

According to Lemert, **primary deviance** involves norm violations or crimes that have little influence on the actor and can be quickly forgotten. For example, a college student takes a "five-finger discount" at the campus bookstore. He successfully steals a textbook, uses it to get an A grade in a course, goes on to graduate, is admitted into law school, and later becomes a famous judge. Because his shoplifting goes unnoticed, it is a relatively unimportant event that has little bearing on his future life.

In contrast, **secondary deviance** occurs when a deviant event comes to the attention of significant others or social control agents who apply a negative label. The newly labelled offender then reorganizes his or her behaviour and personality around the consequences of the deviant act. The shoplifting student is caught by a security guard and expelled from college. With his law school dreams dashed and future cloudy, his options are limited; people who know him say he "lacks character," and he begins to share their opinion. He eventually becomes a drug dealer and winds up in prison. One little act begins a slippery slide.

To be successful, secondary deviance involves resocialization into a deviant role. The labelled person is transformed into one who "employs his behaviour or a role based upon it as a means of defence, attack, or adjustment to the overt and covert problems created by the consequent social reaction to him."[149] Secondary deviance produces a deviance amplification effect. Offenders feel isolated from the mainstream of society and become firmly locked into their deviant role. They may seek out others similarly labelled to form deviant subcultures or groups. Ever more firmly enmeshed in their deviant role, they are locked into an escalating cycle of deviance, apprehension, more powerful labels, and identity transformation. This is the core of labelling theory, that deviance is a process in which one's identity is transformed. Efforts to control the offenders, whether by treatment or punishment, simply help solidify them in their deviant role.

A number of attempts have been made to formulate theories of deviant career formation using a labelling perspective. Following are discussions of two such efforts.

General Theory of Deviance

One theoretical model that draws on labelling theory concepts is Howard Kaplan's general theory of deviance. This model begins with the assumption that people who cannot conform to social group standards face negative sanctions. They are considered failures either because they lack desirable physical, social, or psychological traits or because they fail to behave according to group expectations.

Those exposed to negative social sanctions experience **self-rejection** and a lower self-image. The experience of self-rejecting attitudes ("At times, I think I am no good at all") results in both a weakened commitment to conventional values and behaviours and the acquisition of motives to deviate from social norms. Facilitating this attitude and value transformation is the bond social outcasts form with similarly labelled peers.[150] Membership in a deviant subculture involves conforming to group norms that conflict with those of conventional society. Deviant group membership then encourages criminality and drug abuse.

Deviant behaviours that defy conventional values can serve a number of purposes. Some acts are defiant, designed to show contempt for the source of the negative labels, while others are planned to distance the target from further contact with the source of criticism (for example, an adolescent runs away from critical parents).[151]

Kaplan has found in adolescents that social sanctions lead to self-rejection, deviant peer associations, and eventual deviance amplification.[152] This model is important because it accounts for the creation of labels, their impact

According to Lemert's theory, if these kids are caught and labelled as "druggies," they may become secondary deviants, taking on an identity associated with their negative label, and enter a life of crime. If their actions go undetected, their behaviour remains primary and their drug use remains nothing more than an easily forgotten youthful indiscretion.

on self-image, and the long-term effect they have on criminal careers. Negative sanctions also have a labelling effect if they help undermine conventional relationships and encourage deviant peer group memberships.

Differential Social Control

Karen Heimer and Ross Matsueda propose a version of labelling theory that also leans on control theory concepts; they call this the theory of differential social control.[153]

Agreeing with the labelling perspective, Heimer and Matsueda find that self-evaluations reflect actual or perceived appraisals made by others. Kids who view themselves as delinquents are giving an inner voice to their perceptions of how parents, teachers, peers, and neighbours feel about them. Kids who believe that others view them as antisocial or troublemakers expect to be suspected and then rejected. Labelled youths may then join with similarly outcast delinquent peers who facilitate their behaviour. Eventually, antisocial behaviour becomes habitual and automatic. This is a self-fulfilling prophecy.

Tempering or enhancing the effect of this **reflective role-taking** are informal and institutional social control processes. Families, schools, peers, and the social system can either help control kids and dissuade them from crime or encourage and sustain their deviance. When these groups are dysfunctional, such as when parents use drugs, they encourage, rather than control, antisocial behaviour.

Empirical research supports the core of the model. **Reflected appraisal** as a rule violator has a significant effect on delinquency: Kids who believe that their parents and friends consider them deviants and troublemakers are the ones most likely to engage in delinquency. In another analysis, kids with "damaged" self-images are the ones most likely to engage in risk-taking behaviours, such as delinquency; self-image, influenced and directed by social interaction and approval, controls the content of behaviour.[154]

This work is important because it is an alternative to "traditional" labelling theory that focuses on social control and symbolic interaction.

Research on Labelling Theory

Research on labelling theory can be classified into two distinct categories. The first focuses on the characteristics of offenders who are chosen for labels. Labelling theory maintains that these offenders should be relatively powerless people who are unable to defend themselves against the negative labelling. The second type of research attempts to discover the effects of being labelled. People who are labelled view themselves as deviant and commit increasing amounts of criminal behaviour.

Who Gets Labelled? It is widely believed that poor and powerless people are victimized by the law and justice system and that labels are not equally distributed across class and racial lines. Although substantive and procedural laws govern almost every aspect of the criminal justice system, discretionary decision making controls its operation at every level. From the police officer's decision on whom to arrest, to the prosecutor's decisions on whom to charge and for how many and what kind of charges, to the court's decision on whom to release or on whom to permit bail, to the judge's decision on the length of the sentence, discretion works to the detriment of minorities.[155] A meta-review of 30 years of research on minorities in the juvenile justice system found that race bias adversely influences decision making.[156]

Connections

In Chapter 9 we look at some of the ways in which the powerless are discriminated against by the criminal justice system, and how it is necessary to develop a critical perspective to analyze that process. In a multicultural society, ethnic discrimination is a very important topic.

There is also evidence that those in power try to streamline the labelling process by discounting or ignoring the "protestations of innocence" made by suspects accused of socially undesirable acts, such as child abuse. Leslie Margolin found that people accused of child abuse were routinely defined as "noncredible" when they denied accusations of abuse and were only believed when they confessed their guilt. In contrast, victims were believed when they made accusations but were considered "noncredible" when they claimed the suspect was innocent.[157]

While these arguments are persuasive, little definitive evidence exists that the justice system is inherently unfair and biased. Procedures such as arrest, prosecution, and sentencing seem to be more often based on legal factors, such as prior record and crime seriousness, than personal characteristics, such as class and race.[158] These findings do little to support labelling theory.

The Effects of Labelling. However, there is empirical evidence that negative labels actually have a dramatic influence on the self-image of offenders, leading to self-labelling and deviance amplification.[159]

Parents do in fact negatively label their children who suffer a variety of problems, including antisocial behaviour and school failure.[160] This process is important because once labelled as troublemakers, adolescents begin to reassess their self-image. Parents who label their kids as troublemakers promote deviance amplification, because labelling causes parents to become alienated from their child; negative labels reduce a child's self-image and increase delinquency.[161]

There is also evidence that repeat and intensive official labelling does in fact produce self-labelling and damaged identities.[162] Kids labelled troublemakers in school are the ones most likely to drop out; dropping out has been linked to delinquent behaviour.[163] Another study found that male drug users labelled as addicts by social control agencies eventually became self-labelled and increased their drug use.[164] Lawrence Sherman found a limited labelling effect for people arrested in domestic violence cases: People with a low "stake in conformity"—that is, who were jobless and unmarried—increased offending after being given official labels.[165] This could be seen as a mischievous or perverse effect.

Labelling and Criminal Careers. Until recently, scant attention has been paid to the fact that stigmatization and negative labels may sustain chronic offending and criminal careers.[166] In fact, the very definition of a chronic offender is a person who has been arrested and therefore labelled multiple times in his or her offending career.

There is some empirical evidence that labelling plays an important role in persistent offending. While labels may not cause adolescents to initiate criminal behaviours, experienced delinquents are significantly more likely to continue offending if they believe that their parents and peers view them in a negative light.[167] Labelling thus may help sustain criminality over time.

In sum, there is considerable evidence that people who are labelled by parents, schools, and the criminal justice system stand a good chance of getting involved in deviance. It is still unclear, however, whether this outcome is actually a labelling effect or the product of some other personal and social factors that also caused the labelling to occur.

Is Labelling Theory Valid?

Labelling theory has been the subject of significant academic debate. Those who criticize it point to its inability to specify the conditions that must exist before an act or individual is labelled deviant—that is, why some people are labelled while others remain "secret deviants."[168] Critics also charge that labelling theory fails to explain differences in crime rates; if crime is a function of stigma and labels, why are crime rates higher in some parts of the country at particular times of the year?[169] Labelling theory also ignores the onset of deviant behaviour (that is, it fails to ask why people commit the initial deviant act) and does not deal with the reasons delinquents and criminals decide to forgo a deviant career.[170]

In addition, others have questioned labelling theory's claims that deviance is relative—that virtually no act is universally considered criminal behaviour.

They would argue that some crimes, such as rape and homicide, are universally sanctioned.[171] Furthermore, they would argue that crime is situationally motivated and depends more on ecological and personal conditions than labels and stigma.[172] Some charge that it all too often focuses on "nuts, sluts, and perverts" and ignores the root causes of crime.[173]

With the "discovery" of the chronic offender, it was believed that labelling theory would receive renewed interest as an explanation of chronic offending, because the chronic offender is defined as someone who has been repeatedly labelled by the justice system.[174] While this idea is intriguing, it, too, has met with criticism.[175] In an in-depth analysis of research on the crime-producing effects of labels, Charles Tittle found little evidence that stigma produces crime.[176] Tittle claims that many criminal careers occur without labelling, that labelling often comes after, rather than before, chronic offending, and that criminal careers may not follow even when labelling takes place. There is growing evidence that the onset of criminal careers occurs early in life and that those who go on to a "life of crime" are burdened with so many social, physical, and psychological problems that negative labelling may be a relatively insignificant event.[177]

While criticisms of labelling theory have reduced its importance in the criminological literature, its utility as an

Sometimes people are able to successfully organize to resist deviant labels. One technique is to appropriate the label and use it proudly, like the word "gay." Another is to proclaim that there is in fact nothing deviant about the behaviour. Here, Delwin Vriend (right) gets a congratulatory kiss from his partner at a rally in Edmonton after the Supreme Court of Canada ruled in Vriend's favour, forcing the Alberta government to amend its human rights code to include sexual orientation.

explanation of crime and deviance should not be dismissed. Here are some other features of the labelling perspective that are important contributions to the study of criminality:[178]

1. The labelling perspective identifies the role played by social control agents in the process of crime causation. Criminal behaviour cannot be fully understood if the agencies and individuals empowered to control and treat it are neglected.
2. Labelling theory recognizes that criminality is not a disease or pathological behaviour. It focuses attention on the social interactions and reactions that shape individuals and their behaviour.
3. Labelling theory distinguishes between criminal acts (primary deviance) and criminal careers (secondary deviance) and shows that these concepts must be interpreted and treated differently.

Labelling theory is also important because of its focus on interaction and the situation of crime. Rather than view the criminal as a robotlike creature whose actions are predetermined, it recognizes that crime is often the result of complex interactions and processes. The decision to commit crime involves the actions of a variety of people, including peers, the victim, the police, and other key characters. Labels may expedite crime because they guide the actions of all parties in criminal interactions. Actions deemed innocent when performed by one person are considered provocative when engaged in by another labelled as a deviant. Similarly, labelled people may be quick to judge, take offence, or misinterpret behaviour because of past experience. They experienced conflict in the past, so why not now?

An Evaluation of Social Process Theory

The branches of social process theory—social learning, social control, and labelling—are compatible because they suggest that criminal behaviour is part of the socialization process. Criminals are people whose interactions with critically important social institutions and processes—the family, schools, the justice system, peer groups, employers, and neighbours—are troubled and disturbed. Although there is some disagreement about the relative importance of those influences and the form they take, there seems to be little question that social interactions shape the behaviour, beliefs, values, and self-image of the offender. People who have learned deviant social values who find themselves detached from conventional social relationships, or who are the subject of stigma and labels from significant others will be the most likely to fall prey to the attractions of criminal behaviour. These

negative influences can affect people in all walks of life, beginning in their youth and continuing into adulthood. The major strength of the social process view is the vast body of empirical data showing that delinquents and criminals are indeed people who grew up in dysfunctional families, who had troubled childhoods, and who failed at school, at work, and in marriage. Prison data show that these characteristics are typical of inmates.

While persuasive, these theories have trouble accounting for some of the patterns and fluctuations in the crime rate. If social process theories are valid, for example, people in the western provinces must be socialized differently than those in the eastern provinces, since these latter regions have much lower crime rates. How can the fact that crime rates are lower in October than in July be explained if crime is a function of learning or control? How can social processes explain why criminals escalate their activity or why they desist from crime? Once a social bond is broken, how can it be "reattached"? Once crime is "learned," how can it be "unlearned"?

Social Process Theory and Social Policy

Social process theories have had a major influence on social policy making since the 1950s. Learning theories have greatly influenced concepts of treatment of the criminal offender. Their effect has been felt mainly by young offenders, who are viewed as being more salvageable than "hardened" criminals. Advocates of the social learning approach argue that if people become criminal by learning definitions and attitudes toward criminality, they can "unlearn" them by being exposed to definitions toward conventional behaviour. This philosophy has been used in numerous treatment facilities, which often use group interaction sessions to attack the criminal behaviour orientations held by residents (being tough, using alcohol and drugs, believing that school is for "sissies"), while promoting conventional lines of behaviour (going straight, saving money, giving up drugs). It is common today for residential and nonresidential programs to offer such treatment programs. They teach kids to say no to drugs, to forgo delinquent behaviour, or to stay in school. It is even common for celebrities to return to their old neighbourhood to tell kids to stay in school or off drugs. After Ben Johnson was banned from international competition for using steroids, for example, he gave talks to school kids on the value of being drug-free. If learning did not affect behaviour, such exercises would be futile.

Control theories have also influenced criminal justice and other social policy making. Programs have been developed to improve people's commitments to conventional lines of action, to create and strengthen bonds early

Culture, Gender, Ethnicity, and Criminology

The Head Start Program

Head Start is probably the best-known effort to help lower-class youths achieve proper socialization and, in so doing, reduce their potential for future criminality.

Head Start programs were first instituted in the United States in the 1960s as part of the War on Poverty. In the beginning, Head Start was a two-month summer program, providing comprehensive programming and promoting physical health and enhanced mental processes. It worked to improve social and emotional development, self-image, and interpersonal relationships. Preschoolers were provided with an enriched educational environment to develop their learning and cognitive skills. They were given the opportunity to use materials that middle-class children take for granted— pegs and pegboards, puzzles, toy animals, and so forth.

Today, services have been expanded beyond the two-month summer program. Over 1300 centres with 36 000 classrooms in the United States service 740 000 children and their families. Learning experiences appropriate to the child's age and development focus on reading books, understanding cultural diversity, and the expression of feelings and play with their peers. Students are guided in developing gross and fine motor skills and self-confidence. Health care is also an issue, and most children enrolled in the program receive comprehensive health screening, physical and dental examinations, and appropriate follow-up. Many programs provide meals and in so doing help children receive proper nourishment.

Head Start programs now serve parents in addition to their preschoolers. Some programs allow parents to enroll in classes that cover parenting, literacy, nutrition, domestic violence prevention, and other social issues. Social services, health, and education services are also available. Some controversy has surrounded the success of the Head Start program. In 1970, an evaluation of the Head Start effort found no evidence of lasting cognitive gains on the part of the participating children. Initial gains seemed to evaporate during the elementary school years, and by the third grade the performance of the Head Start children was no different from that of their peers.

While disappointing, this evaluation focused on IQ levels and not whether social competence improved. More recent research has produced dramatically different results. One report found that by age five, children who experienced the enriched day care offered by Head Start averaged more than 10 points higher on their IQ scores than their peers who did not participate in the program. Other research that carefully compared Head Start children with similar youths who did not attend the program found that the former made significant intellectual gains. Head Start children were less likely to have been retained in a grade or placed in classes for slow learners; they outperformed peers on achievement tests; and they were more likely to graduate from high school. Head Start kids also make strides in nonacademic areas: They had better health, immunization rates, and nutrition, and they had enhanced emotional characteristics after leaving the program.

Research also shows that the Head Start program can have important psychological benefits for the mothers of participants, such as decreasing depression and anxiety and increasing feelings of life satisfaction. While findings in some areas may be tentative, they are all in the same direction: Head Start enhances school readiness and has enduring effects on social competence.

If, as many experts believe, there is a close link between school performance, family life, and crime, programs such as Head Start can help some potentially criminal youths avoid problems with the law. By implication, their success indicates that programs that help socialize youngsters can be used to combat urban criminality.

In Canada, the federal Aboriginal Head Start program is aimed at children two to five years of age and focuses on school readiness, healthy living, language and cultural identity. This program is oriented to high-risk children: those in single parent families, with special needs, with incomes less than $1000, or with caregivers with low education.

Over 70 percent of the children came from families where the parents had Grade 12 or less. Children identified as high risk were less likely to have both parents in the same household, and were more likely to have a history of family violence. Other relevant factors were parents with histories of drug or alcohol abuse or who were survivors of residential school. In a 1998 evaluation report, success was reported at identifying those with risk factors, in retention through the whole program, and in addressing their needs.

in life before the onset of criminality. The educational system has been the scene of numerous programs designed to improve basic skills and create an atmosphere in which youths will develop a bond to their schools. The Head Start program is one the largest and best-known attempts to solidify social bonds.

Control theories' focus on the family has been put into operation in programs designed to strengthen the bond between parent and child. Other programs attempt to "repair" bonds that have been broken and frayed. Examples of this approach are the career, work furlough, and educational opportunity programs being developed in the nation's prisons. These programs are designed to help inmates maintain a stake in society so they will be less willing to resort to criminal activity on their release.

Labelling theorists caution against too much intervention. Rather than ask social agencies to attempt to rehabilitate people having problems with the law, they argue that "less is better." Put another way, the more institutions try to "help" people, the more these people will be stigmatized and labelled. For example, a special education program designed to help problem readers may cause them to be labelled by themselves and others as slow or stupid; a mental health rehabilitation program created with the best intentions may cause clients to be labelled as crazy or dangerous.

The influence of labelling theory can be viewed in the development of diversion and restitution programs. Diversion programs are designed to remove both juvenile and adult offenders from the normal channels of the criminal justice process by placing them in programs designed for rehabilitation. For example, a college student whose drunk driving causes injury to a pedestrian may, before a trial occurs, be placed for six months in an alcohol treatment program. If he successfully completes the program, charges against him will be dismissed. Often, they offer counselling; vocational, educational, and family services; and medical advice. Another label-avoiding innovation that has gained popularity is restitution. Rather than face the stigma of a formal trial, an offender is asked to either pay back the victim of the crime for any loss incurred or do some useful work in the community in lieu of receiving a court-ordered sentence.

Despite their good intentions, stigma-reducing programs have not met with great success. Critics charge that they substitute one kind of stigma for another—for instance, attending a mental health program in lieu of a criminal trial. In addition, diversion and restitution programs usually screen out violent offenders and repeat offenders. Finally, there is little hard evidence that the recidivism rate of people who have attended alternative programs represents an improvement over the rate of people who have been involved in the traditional criminal justice process.

Summary

Social process theories view criminality as a function of people's interaction with various organizations, institutions, and processes in society. People in all walks of life have the potential to become criminals if they maintain destructive social relationships. Social process theory has three main branches: Social learning theory stresses that people learn how to commit crimes; control theory analyzes the failure of society to control criminal tendencies; and labelling theory maintains that negative labels produce criminal careers. These theories are summarized in Table 8.1.

The social learning branch of social process theory suggests that people learn criminal behaviours much as they learn conventional behaviour. Differential association theory, formulated by Edwin Sutherland, holds that criminality is a result of a person's perceiving an excess of procrime definitions over definitions that uphold conventional values. Ronald Akers has reformulated Sutherland's work using psychological learning theory. He calls his approach differential reinforcement theory. Sykes and Matza's theory of neutralization stresses youths' learning of behaviour rationalizations that enable them to overcome societal values and norms and engage in illegal behaviour.

Control theories maintain that all people have the potential to become criminals but that their bonds to conventional society prevent them from violating the law. Walter Reckless's containment theory suggests that a person's self-concept aids his or her commitment to conventional action. Travis Hirschi describes the social bond as containing elements of belief, commitment, attachment, and involvement. Weakened bonds allow youths to become active in antisocial behaviour.

Labelling theory holds that criminality is promoted by becoming negatively labelled by significant others. Such labels as "criminal," "ex-con," and "junkie" serve to isolate people from society and lock them into lives of crime. Labels create expectations that the labelled person will act in a certain way; so-labelled people are always watched and suspected. Eventually, these people begin to accept their labels as personal identities, locking them further into lives of crime and deviance. Edwin Lemert has said that people who accept labels are involved in secondary deviance.

Social process theories have had a great influence on social policy. They have controlled treatment orientations as well as community action policies.

Table 8.1	Social process theories		
THEORY	**MAJOR PREMISE**	**STRENGTHS**	
Differential association theory	People learn to commit crime from exposure to antisocial definitions.	Explains onset of criminality. Explains the presence of crime in all elements of social structure. Explains why some people in high-crime areas refrain from criminality. Can apply to adults and juveniles.	
Differential reinforcement theory	Criminal behaviour depends on the person's experiences with rewards for conventional behaviours and punishment for deviant ones. Being rewarded for deviance leads to crime.	Adds learning theory principles to differential association. Links sociological and psychological principles.	
Neutralization theory	Youths learn ways of neutralizing moral restraints and periodically drift in and out of criminal behaviour patterns.	Explains why many delinquents do not become adult criminals. Explains why youthful law violators can participate in conventional behaviour.	
CONTROL THEORIES			
Containment theory	Society produces pushes and pulls toward crime. In some people, they are counteracted by internal and external containments, such as a good self-concept and group cohesiveness.	Brings together psychological and sociological principles. Can explain why some people are able to resist the strongest social pressure to commit crime.	
Control theory	A person's bond to society prevents him or her from violating social rules. If the bond weakens, the person is free to commit crime.	Explains the onset of crime; can apply to both middle- and lower-class crime. Explains its theoretical constructs adequately so they can be measured. Has been empirically tested.	
LABELLING THEORY			
Labelling theory	People enter into law-violating careers when they are labelled for their acts and organize their personalities around the labels.	Explains the role of society in creating deviance. Explains why some juvenile offenders do not become adult criminals. Develops concepts of criminal careers.	
General theory of deviance	People exposed to negative labels experience self-rejection, which causes them to bond with social outcasts.	Considers the relationship between negative labels, self-image, and personal relations.	
Differential social control	Social rejection leads to self-fulfilling prophecy. Weak social controls encourage deviance.	Considers the role of social control in the labelling process.	

Thinking Like a Criminologist

The government of Ontario is considering a bill that requires the names of people convicted of certain offences, such as vandalism, soliciting a prostitute, or nonpayment of child support, to be posted in local newspapers under the heading "For Shame." Those who favour the bill cite the fact that in Boston men arrested for soliciting prostitutes are forced to clean streets. In Dallas shoplifters are made to stand outside stores with signs stating their misdeeds. In some states convicted sex offenders have been required to put signs on their lawn stating their offence.

Members of the Canadian Civil Liberties Union have opposed the idea, stating, "It's simply needless humiliation of the individual." They argue that public shaming is inhumane and further alienates criminals who already have little stake in society, further ostracizing them from the mainstream. For the one-time offender, shaming damages their reputation and puts them at risk of further offending.

This "liberal" position is challenged by those who believe that convicted lawbreakers have no right to conceal their crimes from the public. Shaming penalties seem attractive as cost-effective alternatives to imprisonment. These critics ask what could be wrong with requiring a teenage vandal to personally apologize at the school and wear a shirt with a big "V" on it while cleaning up the mess. Similarly, drunk drivers should have a big "D" placed on their car. If you do something wrong, they argue, you should have to pay the consequences. You have been asked to address the Justice Committee on the issue of whether shaming could deter crime. What would you say?

Key Terms

cliques

commitment to conformity

containments

control theory

crowds

differential association (DA) theory

differential reinforcement (DR) theory

dramatization of evil

drift

labelling theory

moral entrepreneurs

neutralization theory

primary deviance

reflected appraisal

reflective role-taking

secondary deviance

self-rejection

social control theory

social deviant

social distance

social learning theory

social process theories

socialization

stigmatize

subterranean values

symbolic interaction theory

techniques of neutralization

  See the book-specific website at www.siegelcriminology2e.nelson.com for additional chapter links, discussions, and quizzes.

Chapter

9

Social Conflict Theory

It would be unusual to pick up the morning paper and not see headlines loudly proclaiming renewed strife between countries, between union negotiators and management attorneys, between citizens and police authorities, or between outspoken feminists and reactionary males protecting their turf. The world is filled with conflict. Conflict can be destructive when it leads to war, violence, and death; it can be functional when it results in positive social change. Criminologists who view crime as a function of social and economic conflict are aligned with a number of schools of thought, referred to as the conflict, critical, Marxist, or radical schools of criminology (see Figure 9.1).

The goal of social conflict theorists is to explain crime within economic and social contexts and to express the connections among social class, crime, and social control.[1] Social conflict theorists are concerned with such issues as the role government plays in creating a criminogenic environment; the relationship of personal or group power in controlling and shaping the criminal law; the role of bias in the operations of the justice system; and the relationship between a capitalist free-enterprise economy and crime rates.

Conflict theorists view crime as the outcome of class struggle. Conflict works to promote crime by creating a social atmosphere in which the law is a mechanism for

| **Figure 9.1** | **The branches of social conflict theory** |

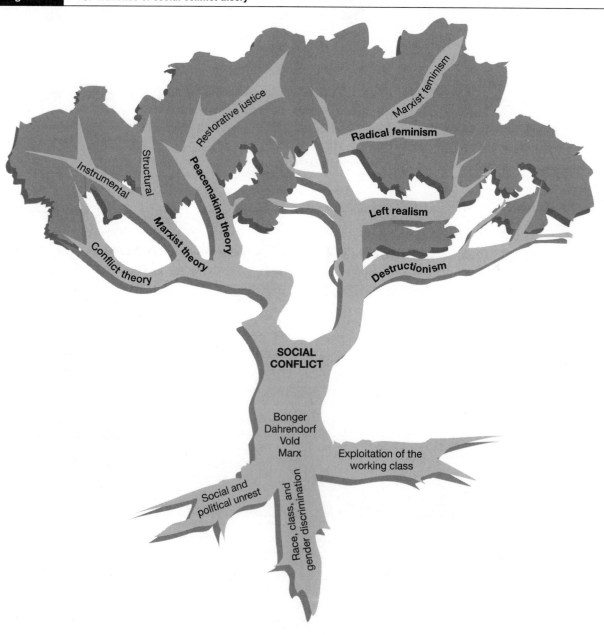

controlling dissatisfied, have-not members of society while maintaining the position of the powerful. That is why crimes that are the province of the wealthy, such as illegal corporate activities, are sanctioned much more leniently than those, such as burglary, that are considered lower-class activities.

Theorists who use this perspective reject the notion that law is designed to maintain a tranquil and fair society and that criminals are malevolent people who wish to trample the rights of others. Conflict theorists consider such acts as racism, sexism, imperialism, unsafe working conditions, inadequate child care, substandard housing, pollution of the environment, and war as the "true crimes." The crimes of the helpless—burglary, robbery, and assault—are more expressions of rage over unjust conditions than actual crimes.[2]

This chapter reviews criminological theories that allege that criminal behaviour is a function of conflict, a reaction to the unfair distribution of wealth and power in society. The social conflict perspective has several independent branches. One, generally referred to as **conflict theory**, assumes that crime is caused by the intergroup conflict and rivalry that exist in every society. A second branch focuses more directly on the crime-producing traits of capitalist society; the various schools of thought in this area of scholarship include critical, radical, and Marxist criminology.[3] Other sections are devoted to feminist, new realist, and peacemaking criminology.

Connections

As you may recall from Chapter 1, the philosophical and economic analysis of Karl Marx forms the historical roots of the conflict perspective of criminology.

Marxist Thought

Karl Marx lived in an era of unrestrained capitalist expansion.[4] By 1850, the tools of the Industrial Revolution, mechanized factories, the use of coal to drive steam engines, and modern transportation had become regular features of society. Production had shifted from cottage industries to large factories. Industrialists could hire workers on their own terms, and conditions in their factories were atrocious. Trade unions that promised workers salvation from these atrocities were ruthlessly suppressed by owners and government agents.

Marx had found his early career as a journalist interrupted by government suppression of the newspaper where he worked because of its liberal editorial policy. He then moved to Paris, where he met Friedrich Engels (1820–1895), who would become his friend and economic patron. By 1847 Marx and Engels had joined with a group of primarily German socialist revolutionaries known as the Communist League.

Productive Forces and Productive Relations

Marx focused his attention on the economic conditions of the capitalist system. He believed its development had turned workers into a dehumanized mass who lived an existence that was at the mercy of their capitalist employers. Young children were sent to work in mines and factories from dawn to dusk. People were being beaten down by a system that demanded obedience and cooperation and offered little in return. These oppressive conditions led Marx to conclude that the character of every civilization is determined by the way its people develop and produce material goods.

Production has two components: (1) productive forces, which include such things as technology, energy sources, and material resources; and (2) productive relations, which are the relationships that exist among the people producing goods and services. The most important relationship in industrial culture is between the owners of the means of production and the people who do the actual labour. Throughout history, society has been organized this way—master-slave, lord-serf, and now capitalist-proletarian. According to Marx and Engels, capitalist society is subject to the development of a rigid class structure: the capitalist bourgeoisie at the top, and the working proletariat who actually produce goods and services, at the bottom.

In Marxist theory, the term *class* does not refer to an attribute or characteristic of a person or a group; rather, it denotes position in relation to others. Thus, it is not necessary to have a particular amount of wealth or prestige to be a member of the capitalist class; it is more important to have the power to exploit others economically, legally, and socially. The political and economic philosophy of the dominant class influences all aspects of life. Consciously or unconsciously, artists, writers, and teachers bend their work to the whims of the capitalist system. Thus, the economic system controls all facets of human life; consequently, people's lives revolve around the means of production.[5]

Marx believed that societies and their structures are not stable but can change through slow evolution or sudden violence. Historically, such change occurs because of contradictions present in a society. These contradictions are antagonisms or conflicts between elements in the existing social arrangement that in the long run are incompatible with one another. If these social conflicts are not resolved, they tend to destabilize society, leading to social change.

Marx on Crime

Marx did not write a great deal on the subject of crime, but he mentioned it in a variety of passages scattered throughout his writing. He viewed crime as the product of law enforcement policies akin to a labelling process theory.[6] He also saw a connection between criminality and the inequities found in the capitalist system. He stated: "There must be something rotten in the very core of a social system which increases in wealth without diminishing its misery, and increases in crime even more rapidly than in numbers."[7]

However, Marx's collaborator, Friedrich Engels, did spend some time on the subject in his work *The Condition of the Working Class in England in 1844*.[8] Engels portrayed crime as a function of social demoralization—a collapse of people's humanity reflecting a decline in society. Workers, demoralized by capitalist society, are caught up in a process that leads to crime and violence. Workers were social outcasts, ignored by the structure of capitalist society and treated as brutes.[9] Left to their own devices, working people commit crime because their choice is a slow death of starvation or a speedy one at the hands of the law. The brutality of the capitalist system turns workers into animal-like creatures without a will of their own.

Developing a Social Conflict Theory of Crime

The writings of Karl Marx and Friedrich Engels greatly influenced the development of social conflict thinking. Although Marx himself did not write much on the topic of crime, his views on the relationship between the economic structure and social behaviour deeply influenced other thinkers. Conflict theory was first applied to criminology by two distinguished scholars in particular, Willem Bonger and George Vold.

The Contribution of Willem Bonger

Willem Bonger was born in 1876 in Holland and committed suicide in 1940, rather than submit to Nazi rule. He is famous for his Marxist/socialist concepts of crime causation, which were first published in 1916.[10]

Bonger believed that crime is social and not biological in origin and that, with the exception of a few special cases, it lies within the boundaries of normal human behaviour. The response to crime is punishment—the application of penalties considered more severe than spontaneous moral condemnation. It is administered by those in political control—that is, by the state. No act is naturally immoral or criminal. Crimes are antisocial acts that reflect current morality. Since the social structure is changing continually, ideas of what is moral and what is not change continually. A rapidly changing morality is common in modern society.

Bonger believed that society is divided into have and have-not groups, because of the system of production

that is in force. In every society that is divided into a ruling class and an inferior class, penal law serves the will of the former. Even though criminal laws may appear to protect members of both classes, hardly any act is punished that does not injure the interests of the dominant class. Crimes are thus considered to be antisocial acts because they are harmful to those who have the power at their command to control society.

Bonger argued that attempts to control law violations through force are a sign of a weak society. The capitalist system, characterized by extreme competition, is held together by force rather than consensus. The social order is maintained for the benefit of the capitalists at the expense of the population as a whole. Bonger argued that all people desire wealth and happiness. Unfortunately, in a capitalist society people can enjoy luxuries and advantages only if they possess large amounts of capital. People are encouraged by capitalist society to be egoistic, caring only for their own lives and pleasures and ignoring the plight of the disadvantaged. As a consequence of this environment, Bonger claimed, people have become more egoistic and more capable of crime than if the system had developed under a socialist philosophy.

Although the capitalist system makes both the proletariat and the bourgeoisie crime-prone, only the former are likely to become officially recognized criminals. The key to this problem is that the legal system discriminates against the poor by legalizing the egoistic actions of the wealthy. Upper-class individuals (the bourgeoisie) will commit crime if (1) they have an opportunity to gain an illegal advantage and (2) their lack of moral sense enables them to violate social rules. It is the drive toward success at any price that pushes wealthier individuals toward criminality. Recognized, official crimes are a function of poverty. The relationship can be direct, as when a person steals to survive, or indirect, as when poverty kills the social sentiments in each person and between people.

It is not the absolute amount of wealth that affects crime but its distribution. If wealth is distributed unequally through the social structure and people are taught to equate economic advantage with superiority, those who are poor and therefore inferior will be crime-prone. The economic system will intensify any personal disadvantage people have—for example, psychological problems—and increase their propensity to commit crime.

Bonger concluded that almost all crime will disappear if society progressed to a form where property was distributed based on "each according to his needs." If this stage of society cannot be reached, a residue of crime will always remain. If socialism can be achieved, then remaining crimes will be of the irrational psychopathic type caused by individual mental problems. Bonger's writing continues to be one of the most often-cited sources of Marxist thought.

In formulating their views, today's conflict theorists also rely heavily on the writings of pioneering social thinker Ralf Dahrendorf,[11] who believed that every society is based on the coercion of some of its members by others.[12] Dahrendorf did not speak directly to the issue of crime, but his model of conflict serves as a pillar of modern conflict criminology.

The Contribution of George Vold

Although Bonger contributed its theoretical underpinnings, social conflict theory was actually adapted to criminology by George Vold.[13] In arguing that crime can be explained by social conflict, Vold said that laws are created by politically oriented groups who seek the assistance of the government to help them defend their rights and protect their interests. If a group can marshal enough support, a law will be created to hamper and curb the interests of some opposing group. Vold wrote, "The whole political process of law making, law breaking and law enforcement becomes a direct reflection of deep-seated and fundamental conflicts between interest groups and their more general struggles for the control of the police power of the state." Every stage of the process—from the passage of the law, to the prosecution of the case, to the relationships between inmate and guard, parole agent and parolee—is marked by conflict.

Vold found that criminal acts are a consequence of direct contact between forces struggling to control society. Although their criminal content may mask their political meaning, closer examination of even the most basic violent acts often reveals political undertones. Vold's model cannot be used to explain all types of crime. It is limited to situations in which rival group loyalties collide. It cannot explain impulsive, irrational acts unrelated to any group's interest.

Modern Conflict Theory

Conflict theory came into criminological prominence during the 1960s. Self-report studies were suggesting that crime and delinquency were much more evenly distributed through the social structure than had been indicated by the official statistics.[14] If this was true, then middle-class participation in crime was going unrecorded, while the lower class was the subject of discriminatory law enforcement practices.

Criminologists began to view the justice system as a mechanism to control the lower class and maintain the status quo, rather than as the means of dispensing fair and evenhanded justice.[15] The publication of important labelling perspective works, such as Lemert's *Social Pathology* and Becker's *Outsiders*, also contributed to the development of the conflict model.[16] Labelling theorists rejected the notion that crime is morally wrong and called for the analysis of the interaction among crime,

criminal, victim, and social control agencies. Others said labelling theory spent too much time studying "nuts, sluts and perverts."[17]

Because they felt the labelling perspective was apolitical, a group of criminologists began to produce scholarship and research directed at (1) identifying "real" crimes in society, such as profiteering, sexism, and racism; (2) evaluating how the criminal law is used as a mechanism of social control; and (3) turning the attention of citizens to the inequities in society.[18] One of these sociologists, David Greenberg, comments on the scholarship that was produced:

> The theme that dominated much of the work in this area was the contention that criminal legislation was determined not by moral consensus or the common interests of the entire society, but by relative power of groups determined to use the criminal law to advance their own special interests or to impose their moral preferences on others.[19]

This movement was aided by the general and widespread social and political upheaval of the late 1960s and early 1970s. These forces included anti-Vietnam War demonstrations, counterculture movements, and various forms of political protest. Conflict theory flourished within this framework, since it provided a systematic basis for challenging the legitimacy of the government's creation and application of law. The crackdown on political dissidents by agents of the federal government, the prosecution of draft resisters, and the like all seemed designed to maintain control in the hands of political powerbrokers.

Conflict Criminology

In the early 1970s, conflict theory began to have a significant influence on criminological study. Several influential scholars abandoned the criminological mainstream and adopted a conflict orientation. William Chambliss and Robert Seidman wrote the well-respected treatise *Law, Order and Power*, which documented how the justice system operates to protect the rich and powerful. After closely observing the system's operations, Chambliss and Seidman drew this conclusion:

> To maintain the existing legal system requires a choice. That choice is between maintaining a legal system that serves to support the existing economic system with its power structure and developing an equitable legal system accompanied by the loss of "personal freedom." But the old question comes back to plague us: Freedom for whom? Is the black man who provides such a ready source of cases for the welfare workers, the mental hospitals, and the prisons "free"? Are

the slum dwellers who are arrested night after night for "loitering," "drunkenness," or being "suspicious" free?[20]

We can observe in Chambliss and Seidman's writing some of the common objectives of conflict criminology: to describe how the control of the political and economic system affects the administration of criminal justice; to show how the definitions of crime favour those who control the justice system; and to analyze the role of conflict in contemporary society. Their scholarship also reflects another major objective of conflict theory: to show how justice in society is skewed so that those who deserve to be punished the most (wealthy white-collar criminals whose crimes cost society millions of dollars) are actually punished the least, while those whose crimes are relatively minor and committed out of economic necessity (petty, underclass thieves) receive the stricter sanctions.[21]

Power Relations. Another motive of conflict theory is to describe the criminogenic influence of social and economic power—the ability of persons and groups to determine and control the behaviour of others. The unequal distribution of power produces conflict; conflict is rooted in the competition for power. Power is the means by which people shape public opinion to meet their personal interests. According to the conflict view, crime is defined by those in power; laws are culturally relative and not bound by any absolute standard of right and wrong.[22] The power to control people is exemplified by the relationship between the justice system and minorities.

The subtle and not-so-subtle ways the justice system victimizes ethnic minorities has been well documented.[23] Socioeconomic conditions that favour whites create an environment in which minority people commit crimes that get them processed by the system. Discretionary decisions by law enforcement officers have them charged with more serious offences; they are less likely to be advised to speak to a lawyer; they are shunted into the criminal courts and not diversion programs. Busy public defenders too often short-shrift their clients into plea bargains that assure early criminal records; and they are more likely to be encouraged to plead guilty. Health-care workers and teachers are quick to report suspected violent acts to the police, resulting in frequent and early arrests of minority adults and youths. Police departments routinely use policies of searching, questioning, and detaining ethnic males in an area if a violent criminal has been described as nonwhite. And media accounts create the image of pervasive minority group criminality by mentioning race when it concerns a black or Native suspect, but not when it concerns a white suspect. When this stereotyping is coupled with unfair treatment, those in power further alienate minorities from the mainstream, perpetuating a class- and race-divided society. It is not surprising, then, that surveys show that members of minority groups are much more likely to perceive "criminal injustice" than whites are.[24]

The Social Reality of Crime. Richard Quinney is one of the most influential conflict theorists. He integrated his beliefs about power, society, and criminality into a theory he referred to as the **social reality of crime**. The theory's six propositions are contained in Table 9.1.[25] According to Quinney, criminal definitions (law) represent the interests of those who hold power in society. Where conflict exists between social groups—for example, the wealthy and the poor—those who hold power will create laws to benefit themselves and hold rivals in check. So the rather harsh punishments for property crime in North America are designed to help those who already have wealth keep it in their possession; in contrast, the lenient sanctions attached to corporate crimes are designed to give the already powerful a free hand at economic exploitation.

Quinney wrote that the formulation of criminal definitions is based on such factors as (1) changing social conditions; (2) emerging interests; (3) increasing demands that political, economic, and religious interests be protected; and (4) changing conceptions of public interest. In his sixth statement on the social reality of crime, Quinney pulled together the ideas he developed in the preceding five: Concepts of crime are controlled by the powerful, and the criminal justice system works to secure the needs of the powerful. When people develop

A Mohawk calling himself Kadahfi leads demonstrators onto the Oka golf course. Plans to expand the golf course triggered the Oka crisis in 1990. (*Mail Star*, July 12, 1995: C16)

Culture, Gender, Ethnicity, and Criminology

Native People in Canada

- In the 1930s Native workers were used at Port Radium to bag and haul uranium ore; they were not allowed to use the "white" showers to clean themselves of the poison.
- A Native woman taken to a Vancouver Island residential school in the 1950s when she was six years old suffered 12 years of degradation, abuse, and rape.
- In 1989 Ontario's task force on policing and race relations heard testimony from Native people about beatings, racial slurs, and neglect from police on northern reserves.
- In 1993 six Innu children were found in an unheated shack in Davis Inlet, sniffing gasoline and saying that they wanted to die.
- Militant loggers from the Listuguj reserve in Quebec blockaded a road for three weeks in the summer of 1998 in a protest to improve Aboriginal logging rights.
- In 2001, two Saskatchewan police officers were convicted of abandoning Native men outside of Saskatoon in the middle of the winter without proper clothing.

Stories like these are just the tip of the iceberg in the study of relations between Native people and the Canadian criminal justice system. Research into the issue could take many directions. We could look at the socioeconomic conditions of Native people in Canada: the poverty rates they experience, the higher than normal rate of suicide, the violence and despair that is felt by those living in isolated reserves and in large cities. We could also question why Native people are overrepresented in prisons in western Canada; why

they are more likely to experience discrimination from the police; and why they are more likely to be advised to plead guilty and be sent to prison than whites.

We need only look at the case of Donald Marshall, Jr., for a prominent and clear example of how Native people are treated by the justice system. On May 28, 1971, Marshall, a 17-year-old Micmac, and Sandy Seale, a 17-year-old black teenager, were walking through Wentworth Park in Sydney, Nova Scotia. There they met Roy Ebsary and Jimmy MacNeil. When they asked Ebsary for money, he responded by fatally stabbing Seale and wounding Marshall. The police officers who responded to the incident did not cordon off the crime scene, search the area, or question witnesses. The sergeant of detectives subsequently accused Marshall of stabbing Seale during an argument and pressured two youths to claim that they had witnessed the attack. Information from Jimmy MacNeil was discounted by the police, as was that provided by Ebsary's daughter. Marshall was charged with murder and spent 11 years in jail for a murder he didn't commit. The RCMP reopened the case in 1982. Then justice minister Jean Chrétien referred the case to the Nova Scotia Court of Appeal, which acquitted Marshall in 1983 but concluded that he was partly to blame for his misfortune. In 1989, a Royal Commission investigating the wrongful conviction and incarceration of Donald Marshall, Jr., concluded that the criminal justice system had failed him at every turn.

The commission's seven-volume report did not whitewash problems in the criminal justice system; it commissioned research to show that Native and black minorities were discriminated

against by the system. In this larger context, what happened to Donald Marshall was certainly not an isolated case.

While Native people have been ill treated in the past for certain crimes, they are now pitted against the justice system in a way that brings laws based on rights into question.

In 1999, Donald Marshall was in the news again in another case that put Native people in conflict with the law on different grounds, when the Supreme Court of Canada heard a case on appeal from Nova Scotia. In 1993 in a case called *R. v. Marshall* [1999, 3 S.C.R.] Marshall had been charged and convicted of three offences set out in the federal fishery regulations: "the selling of eels without a licence, fishing without a licence and fishing during the close season with illegal nets." Marshall freely admitted that he had caught and sold 463 pounds of eels worth $787.10 without a licence and with a prohibited net within close times, but argued that he possessed a treaty right to catch and sell fish under the treaties of 1760–61. In its decision, the Supreme Court overturned the two lower court decisions. It specifically concluded that prohibitions on catching, retaining, and selling fish without a licence, and on fishing during the close time, as set out in Maritime Provinces Fishery Regulations were inconsistent with the treaty rights of Native people.

The federal government, through its Department of Fisheries and Oceans, subsequently set out to negotiate interim agreements with Native bands throughout the maritime region, but the Burnt Church reserve decided to develop its own management scheme and fish for lobster independently. The DFO declared that the Native people were acting "in defiance of the law" and moved in. With the RCMP looking on, the DFO, with their boats and helicopters, conducted surveillance and seized traps and gear. Native people are now more likely to challenge discrimination in the criminal justice system, and to press for their rights under historic treaties. However, change will be slow.

SOURCE: Royal Commission on the Donald Marshall, Jr., Prosecution, *Digest of Findings and Recommendations* (Province of Nova Scotia: King's Printer, 1989); *R. v. Marshall*, Supreme Court of Canada 1999.

behaviour patterns that conflict with these needs, the agents of the rich—the justice system—define them as criminals. Because of their reliance on power relations, criminal definitions are a constantly changing set of concepts that mirror the political organization of society. Law is not an abstract body of rules that represents an absolute moral code. Law is an integral part of society, a force that represents a way of life and a method of doing things. Crime is a function of power relations and an inevitable result of social conflict. Criminals are not simply social misfits but people who have come up short in the struggle for success and are seeking alternative means of achieving wealth, status, or even survival.[26] Consequently, law violations can be viewed as political or even quasi-revolutionary acts.[27]

Connections

Quinney has changed his theoretical outlook over his long and distinguished career. He is now a leader of the Zen-inspired peacemaking movement, which seeks to remove violence and coercion from the criminal justice system and promotes healing or "restorative justice." See the section on peacemaking later in this chapter.

Norm Resistance. Other writers have made influential contributions to the formation of a general conflict criminology. Austin Turk wrote that authority relationships are inevitable and that they produce social conflict. Authorities in society dominate and are in conflict with those who are controlled by, but have little ability to control, the law. Conflict is inherent in this superior–subordinate relationship because both groups have their own sets of cultural norms (those that express ideals and values) and social norms (actual group behaviours). Interaction between authorities and subjects eventually produces **norm resistance**, or open conflict between the two groups, which can take on a number of different forms. The probability of norm resistance is highest under certain conditions:

1. Authorities and subjects are both strongly committed to their cultural norms, which are in opposition to each other.
2. Subjects receive social support from their peers. People with group support will be resistant to authority or change.

| Table 9.1 | Propositions of the social reality of crime |

1. Crime is a definition of human conduct that is created by authorized agents in a politically organized society.
2. Criminal definitions describe behaviours that conflict with the interests of the segments of society that have the power to shape public policy.
3. Criminal definitions are applied by the segments of society that have the power to shape the enforcement and administration of criminal law.
4. Behaviour patterns are structured in segmentally organized society in relation to criminal definitions, and within this context, persons engage in actions that have relative probabilities of being defined as criminal.
5. Conceptions of crime are constructed and diffused in the segments of society by various means of communication.
6. The social reality of crime is constructed by the formulation and applications of criminal definitions, the development of behaviour patterns to criminal definitions, and the construction of criminal conceptions.

SOURCE: Adapted from Richard Quinney, *The Social Reality of Crime* (Boston: Little, Brown, 1970), pp. 15–23.

3. Subjects lack sophistication. People who are sophisticated, who can accurately assess the strengths and weaknesses of their opponents, will be better able to avoid conflict with authorities.[28]

Research on Conflict Theory

Research efforts designed to test conflict theory seem quite different from those that evaluate consensus models. Similar methodologies are often used, but conflict-centred research places less emphasis on testing the hypotheses of a particular theory and instead attempts to show that conflict principles hold up under empirical scrutiny. Areas of interest include comparing the crime rates of members of powerless groups with those of members of the elite classes, examining the operation of the justice system to uncover bias and discrimination, and attempting to chart the historical development of criminal law and identify laws created to preserve the power of the elite classes at the expense of the poor.

Conflict theorists maintain that social inequality creates the need for people to commit some crimes, such as burglary and larceny, as a means of social and economic survival, and to commit others, such as assault, homicide, and drug use, as a means of expressing rage, frustration, and anger. Conflict theorists point to data showing that crime rates vary according to indicators of poverty and need. For example, a comparison of homicide rates with infant mortality rates over a 50-year period (since the latter variable is an efficient measure of poverty) found that the two rates were significantly interrelated.[29] Other data collected by ecologists show that crime is strongly related to measures of social inequality, such as income level, deteriorated living conditions, and relative economic deprivation.[30]

Another area of conflict-oriented research focuses on the operations of the criminal justice system: Does it operate as an instrument of class oppression or as a fair and evenhanded social control agency? Some conflict researchers have found evidence of class bias. For example, U.S. state jurisdictions with significant levels of economic disparity were also the most likely to have the largest number of police shooting fatalities. These data suggest that police act more forcefully in areas where class conflicts create the perception that extreme forms of social control are needed to maintain order.[31] Similarly, an examination of criminal cases processed by the Chicago criminal courts found that members of powerless, disenfranchised groups are the most likely to receive prejudicial sentences in criminal courts.[32] Other research efforts have shown that both white and black offenders are more likely to receive stricter sentences in criminal courts if their personal characteristics (single, young, urban, male) give them the appearance of being a member of the **dangerous classes**.[33]

Conflict theorists also point to studies showing that the criminal justice system is quick to take action when the victim of crime is wealthy, white, and male but uninterested when the victim is poor, nonwhite, and female, indicating how power positions affect justice.[34] It is not surprising, then, that Thomas Arvanites's analysis of national population trends and imprisonment rates shows that as the percentage of minority-group members increases, the imprisonment rate does likewise.[35] This outcome may be a function of society becoming "less tolerant of nonwhite populations and/or feeling more threatened by them." Data showing racial and class discrimination by the justice systems support conflict theory.[36]

One reason for such displays of discrimination may be the attitudes of decision makers. For example, Michael Leiber has shown that justice professionals who express racist values are also more punitive and believe that courts should be stricter and that the death penalty is an effective deterrent.[37] In another study, race was found to have varying and subtle effects on decision making in the juvenile justice system.[38] Critical thinkers would argue that there must be a thorough rethinking of the role and purpose of the criminal justice system, giving the powerless a greater voice to express their needs and concerns, if these inequities are to be addressed.[39] There is also a need to test more of the ideas of conflict theories, for example, police–citizen encounters in domestic disputes, and whether these are affected by social class.[40]

Analysis of Conflict Theory

Conflict theorists attempt to identify the power relations in society and draw attention to their role in promoting criminal behaviour. The aim is to describe how class differentials produce an ecology of human behaviour that favours the wealthy and powerful over the poor and weak. To believe their view, we must reject the consensus view of crime, which states that law represents the values of the majority, that legal codes are designed to create a just society, and that by breaking the law criminals are predators who violate the rights of others. To a conflict theorist, the criminal law is a weapon used by the affluent to maintain their dominance in the class struggle. This view certainly has its critics. Some criminologists consider the conflict view "naive," suggesting instead that crime is a matter of rational choice made by offenders motivated more by greed and selfishness than poverty and hopelessness.[41]

Critics also point to data indicating only a weak relationship between indicators of economic factors and crime rates; such data indicate that crime is less likely to be a function of poverty and class conflict than a product of personal needs, socialization, or some other related factor.[42] For example, while Arvanites's research found that race influenced imprisonment, he found little clear-cut evidence that economic factors, such as unemployment rates or poverty levels, influenced crime rates.[43]

Similarly, studies of the criminal justice process, including police discretion, criminal court sentencing, and correctional policy, have not all found indicators of class or race bias, an outcome predicted by conflict theory.[44] An examination of the prison sentences of 10 488 inmates in three southeastern U.S. states concluded that socioeconomic status was unrelated to the length of prison terms assigned by the courts.[45] Sentencing decisions in California also found little evidence of race bias; African Americans were neither more likely to be sent to prison than white offenders nor to receive longer prison terms.[46] Evidence that the justice system is not class- and race-biased refutes conflict theory and supports consensus, traditional criminology.

Cross-cultural research also indicates that crime rates are not reduced when a free-market system is replaced by a less competitive economic model. One analysis of crime in the African country of Tanzania found that when the free enterprise system was replaced by a socialist system, the crime rate actually increased. New crimes, such as theft by public servants and corruption, appear to increase in response to government policies establishing socialism.[47]

Despite these critiques, conflict theory has had an important niche in the criminological literature. However, more radical versions of the general conflict model have become predominant, and attention is now turned to these more critical versions of social conflict theory.

Marxist Criminology

Above all, Marxism is a critique of capitalism.[48] Marxist criminologists view crime as a function of the capitalist mode of production: Capitalism produces haves and have-nots, each engaging in a particular branch of criminality.[49] In a capitalist society, those in political power also control the definition of crime and the emphasis of the criminal justice system.[50] Consequently, the only crimes available to the poor, or proletariat, are the severely sanctioned "street crimes": rape, murder, theft, and mugging. Members of the middle class, or petit bourgeoisie, cheat on their taxes and engage in petty corporate crime (employee theft), acts that generate social disapproval but are rarely punished severely. The wealthy bourgeoisie are involved in acts that should be described as crimes but are not—racism, sexism, and profiteering. Though there are regulatory laws to control business activities, these are rarely enforced, and violations are lightly punished. Laws regulating corporate crime are really window dressing designed to impress the working class with how fair the justice system really is. In reality, the justice system is the equivalent of an army that defends the owners of property in their ongoing struggle against the workers.[51]

The Development of a Radical Criminology

The development of radical theory can be traced to the National Deviancy Conference (NDC), formed in 1968 by a group of British sociologists. With about 300 members, this organization sponsored several national symposiums and dialogues. Members came from all walks of life, but at its core was a group of academics who were critical of the positivist criminology being taught in British and American universities. More specifically, they rejected the conservative stance of criminologists and their close financial relationship with government funding agencies. Originally, the NDC was not a Marxist-oriented group but rather investigated the concept of deviance from a labelling perspective. It called attention to ways in which social control might actually be a cause of deviance rather than a response to antisocial behaviour.

Many conference members became concerned about the political nature of social control. A schism developed within the NDC, with one group clinging to the now conservative interactionist/labelling perspective and the second embracing Marxist thought. Then, in 1973, radical theory was given a powerful academic boost when British scholars Ian Taylor, Paul Walton, and Jock Young published *The New Criminology*.[52] This brilliant work was a thorough and well-constructed critique of existing concepts in criminology and a call for development of new criminological methods. That book, and its successor, *Critical Criminology*, became the standard resource for scholars critical of both the field of criminology and the existing legal process.

While these events were transpiring in Britain, a small group of scholars in the United States began to follow a new radical approach to criminology. The locus of the radical school was the criminology program at the University of California, where Marxist scholars such as Anthony Platt, Paul Takagi, and Herman and Julia Schwendinger were located. Marxist scholars at other academic institutions included Richard Quinney (originally a conflict theorist), William Chambliss, Steven Spitzer, and Barry Krisberg. These radicals were influenced by the widespread social ferment during the late 1960s and early 1970s. The war in Vietnam, prison struggles, and the civil rights and feminist movements produced a climate in which criticism of the ruling class seemed a natural by-product. Mainstream, positivist criminology was criticized as being overtly conservative, progovernment, and antihuman. Critical criminologists scoffed when their fellow scholars used statistical analysis of computerized data to describe criminal and delinquent behaviour. As Barry Krisberg has written,

> Many of our scientific heroes of the past, upon rereading, turned out to be racists or, more generally, apologists for social injustice. In response to the widespread protests on campuses and throughout society, many of the contemporary giants of social science emerged as defenders of the status quo and vocally dismissed the claims of the oppressed for social justice.[53]

Marxists did not meet with widespread approval at major universities. Rumours of purges were common during the 1970s, and the criminology school at Berkeley was eventually closed for what many believe were political reasons. Even today, conflict exists between critical thinkers and mainstream academics. The prestigious Harvard Law School and other law centres have been the scenes of conflict and charges of purges and tenure denials because some professors held critical views of law and society. While some isolated radicals are tolerated if "they could not cause much trouble," the majority have been heavily victimized by what David Friedrichs refers to as "academic McCarthyism."[54]

In the ensuing years, new branches of a radical criminology were developing in the United States and Canada. In the early 1980s, the left realism school was started by scholars affiliated with the Middlesex Polytechnic and the University of Edinburgh in Great Britain. In the United States, scholars influenced in part by the pioneering work of Dennis Sullivan and Larry Tifft created the peacemaking movement.[55] At the same time, feminist scholars began to apply critical analysis to the relationship between gender, power, and criminality. These movements (discussed later in this chapter) have coalesced into a rich and complex criminological tradition.

Fundamentals of Marxist Criminology

As a general rule, Marxist criminologists ignore formal theory construction, with its heavy emphasis on empirical testing. They scoff at the objective "value-free" stance of mainstream criminologists and instead argue that there should be a political, ideological basis for criminological scholarship.[56] Crime and criminal justice must be viewed in a historical, social, and economic context. Leftist criminologists use the conflict definition of crime as a political concept designed to protect the power and position of the upper classes at the expense of the poor. As you may recall, some but not all radicals would include in a list of "real" crimes such acts as violations of human rights due to racism, sexism, and imperialism and other violations of human dignity and physical needs and necessities. Part of the radical agenda, then, is to make the public aware that these behaviours "are crimes just as much as burglary and robbery."[57]

The nature of a society controls the direction of its criminality; criminals are not social misfits but rather a product of the society and its economic system in which they reside. Capitalism has always produced a relatively high level of crime and violence.[58] According to Michael Lynch and W. Byron Groves, three implications follow from this view:

1. Each society will produce its own types and amounts of crime.
2. Each society will have its own distinctive ways of dealing with criminal behaviour.
3. Each society gets the amount and type of crime that it deserves.[59]

This analysis tells us that criminals are not a group of outsiders who can be controlled by an increased law enforcement presence. Criminality is a function of the social and economic organization of society. To control crime and reduce criminality is to end the social conditions that promote crime.

Economic Structure and Surplus Value

While no single view or theory defines Marxist criminology today, its general theme is the relationship between crime and the ownership and control of private property in a capitalist society.[60] That ownership and control, according to sociologist Gregg Barak, is the principal basis of power in capitalist society.[61] Social conflict is fundamentally related to the historical and social distribution of productive private property and surplus value (profit). Destructive social conflicts inherent within the capitalist system cannot be resolved unless that system is destroyed or ended.

One important aspect of the capitalist economic system is the effect of **surplus value**. This term refers to the value resulting from production when the cost of labour is less than the cost of the goods it produces. The excess value or profit can either be reinvested or used to enrich the owners. To increase the rate of surplus value, workers can be made to work harder for less pay, be made more efficient, or be replaced by "labour-saving" machines or technology. Therefore, economic growth does not have the same benefits for all elements of the population and in the long run may produce the same effect as a depression or recession!

As the rate of surplus value increases, more people are displaced from productive relationships, and the size of the "marginal" population swells. As corporations "downsize" to increase profits, high-paying labour and managerial jobs are lost to computer-driven machinery. Displaced workers are forced into service jobs at minimum wage. Many become temporary employees without benefits or a secure position.

As more people are thrust outside the economic mainstream (marginalization), a larger portion of the population is forced to live in areas (structural locations) conducive to crime. Once people are marginalized, commitment to the system declines, producing another criminogenic force: a weakened bond to society.[62]

The effect of surplus value is not unique to Canada and the United States. Crime and violence have escalated in former socialist republics that have converted to free-market economies. As well, an opposite change, from socialism to capitalism, can also drive crime rates higher. Both China and the former Soviet Union have experienced an upsurge in gang activity as they embrace market economies; Russia may now have a murder rate higher than that of the United States.[63]

While some form of these themes can be found throughout Marxist writing, there are actually a number of schools of thought within the radical literature. Some of these different approaches are discussed in further detail in the following sections.

Instrumental Marxism

One group of Marxists are referred to as instrumentalists. They view the criminal law and criminal justice system solely as an instrument for controlling the poor, have-not members of society; the state is the "tool" of the capitalists.

According to the instrumental view, capitalist justice serves the powerful and rich and enables them to impose their morality and standards of behaviour on the entire society. Under capitalism, economic power enables its holders to extend their self-serving definition of illegal or criminal behaviour to encompass those who might threaten the status quo or interfere with their quest for ever-increasing profits.[64] For example, the concentration of monetary assets in large firms becomes the political power needed to control the tax laws and limit the firms' tax liabilities.[65]

The poor, according to this branch of Marxist theory, may or may not commit more crimes than the rich, but they certainly are arrested and punished more often. Under the capitalist system, the poor are driven to crime because a natural frustration exists in a society in which affluence is well publicized but unattainable. When class conflict becomes unbearable, frustration can spill out in riots, such as the one that occurred in Los Angeles on April 29, 1992, and was described as a "class rebellion of the underprivileged against the privileged."[66]

Because of class conflict, a deep-rooted hostility is generated among members of the lower class toward a social order they are not allowed to shape or participate in.[67] Instrumental Marxists charge that conventional criminology identifies the social conditions that cause crime. However, the focus on family structure, intelligence, peer relations, and school performance serve to keep the lower classes servile by showing why they are more criminal, less intelligent, and more prone to school failure and family problems than the middle class. **Demystification** involves the identification of the destructive intent of capitalist-inspired and -funded criminology. The goal of criminology should be to explicate the rule of law in capitalist society and show how it works to preserve ruling-class power. The essence of instrumental Marxist theory can be summarized in the following statements:

- Society is based on an advanced capitalist economy.
- The state is organized to serve the interests of the dominant economic class.
- Criminal law is an instrument of the state to maintain the existing social and economic order.
- Crime control occurs through institutions and agencies established and administered by an elite.
- The contradictions of advanced capitalism require that the subordinate classes remain oppressed by whatever means necessary, especially through the coercion and violence of the legal system.

- Only with the collapse of capitalist society and the creation of a new society, based on socialist principles, will there be a solution to the crime problem.[68]

Concepts of Instrumental Marxism. Legal relations underpin the infrastructure that is required by a capitalist mode of production. The legal system is designed to guard the position of the owners (bourgeoisie) at the expense of the workers (proletariat). Legal relations maintain the family and school structure so as to secure the labour force. Even common-law crimes, such as murder and rape, are implemented to protect capitalism. According to the Schwendingers, the basic laws of the land (such as constitutional laws) are based on the conditions that reproduce the class system as a whole. Laws are aimed at securing the domination of the capitalist system. However, the system may at times secure the interests of the working class, for example, when laws are created that protect collective bargaining. Yet legal relations maintain patterns of individualism and selfishness and, in so doing, perpetuate a class system characterized by anarchy, oppression, and crime.[69]

Privilege. Barry Krisberg has linked crime to the differentials in **privilege** that exist in capitalist society. Crimes are created by the powerful to further their domination. Crimes deflect attention from the violence and social injustice the rich inflict on the masses to keep them subordinate and oppressed. Privilege is the possession of that which is valued by a particular social group in a given historical period. Privilege includes such rights as life, liberty, and happiness; such traits as intelligence, sensitivity, and humanity; and such material goods as monetary wealth, luxuries, land, and the like. The effective use of violence and coercion is the major factor in determining which social group ascends to the position of defining and holding privilege.[70]

Other Marxist scholars have called for a review of the role of the professional criminologist. For example, Anthony Platt has charged that criminologists have helped support state repression with their focus on poor and minority-group criminals:

> Criminology has serviced domestic repression. . . . This system has been used to repress and maintain the powerlessness of poor people, people of colour, and young people. In the past, we have been constrained by a legal definition of crime which restricts us to studying and ultimately helping to control only legally defined "criminals." We need a more humanistic definition of crime, one which reflects the reality of a legal system based on power. . . . A human rights definition of crime frees us to examine imperialism, racism, sexism, capitalism, exploitation, and other political or economic systems which contribute to human misery. . . .[71]

Michael Lynch observes that instrumental Marxist theory may be limited because it is based on assumptions that are incorrect: that law and justice always operate in the interests of the ruling class; that members of the ruling class "conspire" to control society; that what benefits one member of the ruling class benefits them all. In reality, some laws benefit the lower classes, and capitalists compete with one another rather than conspire.[72] Because of these deficiencies, some radicals have turned from instrumental theory and embraced structural Marxism.

Structural Marxism

Structural Marxists disagree with the view that the relationship between law and capitalism is unidimensional, always working for the rich and against the poor.[73] Law is not the exclusive domain of the rich, but it is used to maintain the long-term interests of the capitalist system and control members of any class who pose a threat to its existence. If law and justice were purely instruments of the capitalist class, why would laws controlling corporate crimes, such as price fixing, false advertising, and illegal restraint of trade, have been created and enforced? To a structuralist, the law is designed to keep the capitalist system operating in an efficient manner, and anyone, capitalist or proletarian, who "rocks the boat" is targeted to be sanctioned. For example, antitrust legislation is designed to prevent any single capitalist from dominating the system and preventing others from "playing the game." One person cannot get too powerful at the expense of the economic system as a whole.

One of the most highly regarded structural Marxist approaches is Stephen Spitzer's Marxian theory of deviance.[74] He finds that law in the capitalist system defines as deviant (or criminal) any person who disturbs, hinders, or calls into question any of the following:

- Capitalist modes of appropriating the product of human labour (for example, when the poor steal from the rich)
- The social conditions under which capitalist production takes place (for example, when some people refuse or are unable to perform wage labour)
- Patterns of distribution and consumption in capitalist society (for example, when people use drugs for escape and transcendence, rather than sociability and adjustment)
- The process of socialization for productive and non-productive roles (for example, when youths refuse to be schooled or deny the validity of family life)
- The ideology that supports the functioning of capitalist society (for example, when people become proponents of alternative forms of social organization)

Among the many important points Spitzer makes is that capitalist societies have special ways of dealing with

Protests are one way the public has to communicate their disapproval in a democratic society. However, sometimes these protests are not seen as legitimate. In 2001 protestors massed in Quebec City to demonstrate against the Free Trade Summit. One of their weapons of choice: a teddy-bear launching catapult! The police responded with tear gas and rubber bullets.

those who oppose its operation. One mechanism is to normalize formerly deviant or illegal acts by absorbing them into the mainstream of society—for example, through legalizing abortions. Conversion involves co-opting deviants by making them part of the system—for example, a gang leader may be recruited to work with younger delinquents. Containment involves segregating deviants into isolated geographic areas so that they can easily be controlled—for example, by creating a ghetto. Finally, Spitzer believes that capitalist society actively supports some criminal enterprises, such as organized crime, so that they can provide a means of support for groups who might otherwise become a burden on the state.

Research on Marxist Criminology

Marxist criminologists rarely use standard social science methodologies.[75] Marxists believe that the research conducted by mainstream liberal/positivist criminologists is designed to unmask the weak and powerless members of society so they can be better dealt with by the legal system—a process called correctionalism. They are particularly offended by purely empirical studies, such as those showing that minority-group members have lower IQs than the white majority or that the inner city is the site of the most serious crime while middle-class areas are relatively crime-free.

While uncommon, empirical research is not considered totally incompatible with Marxist criminology, and there have been some important efforts to quantitatively test its fundamental assumptions.[76] For example, Alan Lizotte has shown that the property crime rate reflects a change in the level of surplus value; the capitalist system's emphasis on excessive profits accounts for the need of the working class to commit property crime.[77]

Despite these few exceptions, Marxist research tends to be historical and analytical. Social trends are interpreted to understand how capitalism has affected human interaction.

Famous Canadian Criminals

Louis Riel (1844–1885), Métis leader

In 1869 the newly confederated Dominion of Canada was in the process of purchasing Rupert's Land from the Hudson's Bay Company. Because of this purchase, the Métis of Manitoba became worried about their land rights and the preservation of their culture. As a result, they proclaimed a provisional government, which they called the National Committee, and appointed as its secretary Louis Riel, a young Métis lawyer. During the Red River Rebellion of 1869, an armed group representing the Committee seized Upper Fort Garry and ordered the lieutenant-governor of the North-West Territory not to enter the Territory. In addition, Riel issued a "Declaration of the People of Rupert's Land and the North-West" and became head of the provisional government of Red River.

In an attempt to overthrow Riel, a group of men travelled from Portage la Prairie to Fort Garry, but they were captured and imprisoned. The Métis tried and sentenced one of the men, Thomas Scott, to death for insubordination in captivity and executed him by firing squad. Responding to appeals from a bishop, they then released the remaining prisoners. After land negotiations were completed between the federal government and the Métis, the government sent a military force on a "mission of peace" to Red River. Riel, fearing its true purpose, fled to the United States.

Although the federal government preferred that Riel stay in the United States—the province of Ontario considered him a murderer—his supporters in Manitoba and Quebec persuaded him to run for election in Canada. He was elected a member of Parliament three times, but when he attempted to take his seat in 1874, he was expelled from the House of Commons on the motion of a member from Ontario. In 1875, he was exiled from British possessions for five years. In the winter of 1878-79, Riel tried to assemble a coalition of Métis and

Photo used courtesy of Saskatchewan Archives Board

Indians to invade western Canada, but Poundmaker and Sitting Bull refused. He even wrote to Ulysses S. Grant, asking for his help in an invasion of western Canada. In 1884, he was asked to become political leader of a Métis movement in Saskatchewan, and the North-West Rebellion ensued. He seized a church at Batoche in 1885 but after less than two months of fighting he surrendered.

He was taken to Regina rather than stand trial before a 12-member mixed race jury in Winnipeg. His six-member jury was English, white, and Protestant. The Canadian Criminal Code did not yet exist, so the charge was laid under the British Statute of Treasons. Riel pleaded not guilty to the charge of treason although his lawyer wanted him to plead insanity. On August 1, 1885, he was found guilty with a recommendation for mercy. After appeals to the Manitoba Court of Appeal and to the Privy Council in London failed, Riel was hung on November 16, 1885. The Métis dream was over.

Relations between the Northwest Mounted Police and the Native residents eroded after the establishment of the federal Department of Indian Affairs in the early 1880s and the official policy of total assimilation and segregation on reserves.

Sources: http://library.usask.ca/northwest/background/riel.htm; *Canadian Encyclopedia* (Toronto: McClelland and Stewart, 1988).

Marxists investigate both macro-level issues, such as how the accumulation of wealth affects crime rates, and micro-level issues, such as the effect of criminal interactions on the lives of individuals living in a capitalist society. Of particular importance to Marxist critical thinkers is the analysis of the historical development of capitalist social control institutions, such as criminal law, police agencies, courts, and prison systems.

Crime, the Individual, and the State. Marxists devote considerable attention to the study of the relationships among crime, victims, the criminal, and the state. Two common themes emerge: (1) Crime and its control are a function of capitalism, and (2) the justice system is biased against the working class and favours upper-class interests. Marxian analysis of the criminal justice system is designed to identify the often-hidden processes that exert control over people's lives. It seeks an understanding of how conditions, processes, and structures became as they are today, and how behaviour comes to be defined as criminal or delinquent in society.[78] It might be to show how sentencing in a juvenile court is a function of social class;[79] how power relationships help undermine any benefit the lower class gets from sentencing reforms;[80] how the justice system is class biased;[81] or the relationship between capitalism and rape.[82] Critical research of this sort is designed to reinterpret commonly held beliefs about society within the framework of Marxist social and economic ideas.[83] The goal is not to prove statistically that capitalism causes crime but rather to show that it creates an environment in which crime is inevitable. Marxist research is humanistic, situational, descriptive, and analytical rather than statistical, rigid, and methodological.

Historical Analysis. A second type of Marxist research focuses on the historical background of commonly held institutional beliefs and practices. One aim is to show how changes in the criminal law corresponded to the development of capitalist economy. For example, Michael Rustigan analyzed historical records to show that law reform in 19th-century England was largely a response to pressure from the business community to make the punishment for property law violations more acceptable.[84] In a similar vein, Rosalind Petchesky has explained how the relationship between prison industries and capitalism evolved during the 19th century, while Paul Takagi has described the rise of state prisons as an element of centralized state control over deviants.[85]

Another topic of importance to Marxist critical thinkers is the development of modern police agencies. Since police often play an active role in putting down labour disputes and controlling the activities of political dissidents, their interrelationships with capitalist economics is of particular importance to Marxists. Prominent examples of research in this area include Stephen Spitzer and A.T. Scull's discussion of the history of private police and Dennis Hoffman's historical analysis of police excesses in the repression of an early union, the International Workers of the World (popularly known as the Wobblies).[86] Sidney Harring has provided one of the more important analyses of the development of modern policing, showing how police developed as an antilabour force that provided muscle for industrialists at the turn of the century.[87]

Critique of Marxist Criminology

Marxist criminology has met with a great deal of criticism from some members of the criminological mainstream.[88] In turn, radicals have accused mainstream criminologists of being culprits in the development of state control over individual lives and "selling out" their ideals for the chance to receive government funding.

Mainstream criminologists have also attacked the substance of Marxist thought. Some argue that Marxist theory is a simple rehash of the old tradition of helping the underdog, such as Robin Hood stealing from the rich to help feed the poor.[89] In reality, they might claim, most theft is for luxury, not survival. Moreover, they dispute the idea that the crimes of the rich are more reprehensible and less understandable than those who live in poverty. Criminality and immoral behaviour occur at every social level, but the relatively disadvantaged contribute disproportionately to crime and delinquency rates.[90]

Other critics charge that Marxists ignore all the varied prestige and interest groups that exist in a pluralistic society and focus almost unilaterally on class differentials.[91] They might scoff, for example, at critical thinkers who charge that efforts by the government to create social reforms are disguised attempts to control the underclass. Is it logical to believe that giving people more rights is a trick to allow greater control to be exerted over them? "People are more powerful with the right to a jury than without it.... The rights of free speech, free press, free association, public trial, habeas corpus, and governmental petition extended substantial power to colonials... who had previously been denied them."[92] The problems of Marxist theory are summarized in the following statements:

- Marxist criminologists refuse to confront the problems and conflicts of socialist countries, such as the gulags and purges of the Soviet Union under Stalin.
- Capitalism is blamed for every human vice. "After class explains everything, after the whole legal order is critiqued, after all predatory and personal crime is attributed to the conditions and reproduction of capitalism, there is nothing more to say."[93]
- Marxist criminology does little to explain the criminality existing in states that have abolished private ownership of the means of production, such as Cuba.
- Marxists overlook distinctions that exist between people in different classes.
- Marxists attempt to explain issues that are obvious. The revelation that politicians are corrupt and businesspeople greedy comes as a shock to no one.

Crime in the News

"Police Should Find Real Crimes to Solve in Halifax"

by Parker Barss Donham (Sunday Daily News) found at www.rabble.ca October 31, 2001

A police review board that fails to condemn police violations of civil liberties emboldens police to intrude even further upon the rights of citizens.

Last week, the Nova Scotia Police Review Board endorsed a Halifax Regional Police strip search of thirty-four citizens working at a dance. The police had a warrant, based on a dubious informant, to search the dance hall for a bottle of ecstasy pills supposedly hidden in the ceiling. When they found nothing, the cops proceeded to strip search everyone present.

The board justified this humiliating excess on the grounds that "the only logical" possibility was that someone present had hidden the drugs on their person — patently false, given that the strip search turned up no ecstasy. The board declined to consider whether the charter protection against arbitrary search and seizure applied.

A stupid ruling begets stupider police thinking.

Sunday's *Daily News* canvassed legal opinion as to what people should do if police with a warrant to search a public building demand to strip everyone inside.

Most of the lawyers said citizens needn't comply with a search demand unless they are arrested, and they can't be arrested without reasonable and probable

grounds they have committed an offence. The lawyers suggested citizens ask politely whether they are under arrest, and if not, decline to submit.

"Then you'd probably get placed under arrest," said police spokeswoman Sgt. Brenda Zima. "Certainly, that's not something we would encourage. It's not advisable, put it that way."

In other words, the mere assertion of one's constitutional rights may provoke arrest.

"That's an outrageous statement by a spokesperson for a police department in a democratic society," said Dalhousie law professor Archie Kaiser. "If you stand by your right to be left alone, you are somehow doing something suspicious." . . .

- Marxists suspect even those practices and freedoms that most people cherish as the cornerstones of democracy (right to trial, free press, religious freedom, and so on).

In response, Marxist scholars charge that critics rely on "traditional" variables, such as "class" and "poverty," in their analysis of radical thought. While important, these concepts do not reflect the key issues in the structural and economic process. In fact, like crime, they, too, may be the outcome of the capitalist system.[94]

Although radical criminologists dispute criticisms, they have also responded by creating new theoretical models that incorporate Marxist ideas in an innovative manner. In the following section, we discuss some recent forms of radical theory in some detail.

New Directions in Critical Criminology

Increasingly, mainstream criminology has been criticized for focusing too much on crimes committed by working-class, poor, or unemployed people. They are the most easy to subject to surveillance, and they are the least likely to know their rights. On the other hand, critical criminology looks at crimes of the powerful, and how

crime is a consequence of unequal power relations in society. In particular, left realism explains and measures street crime and proposes short-term solutions.

Left Realism

Some radical scholars are now addressing the need for the left to respond to the increasing power of right-wing conservatives. They are troubled by the emergence of a strict "law and order" philosophy that places crime control above due process. As shown in the Crime in the News box, there is a tendency to think that anything is justified in the war against crime, even if it violates a person's rights. At the same time, they find the focus of most left-wing scholarship—the abuse of power by the ruling elite—too narrow. It is wrong, they argue, to ignore the problem of inner-city gang crime and violence, which all too often targets indigent people.[95] Those who share these concerns are referred to as left realists.[96]

Left realism is most often connected to the writings of British scholars John Lea and Jock Young. In their well-respected 1984 work *What Is to Be Done about Law and Order?* they rejected the utopian views of "idealistic" Marxists who portray street criminals as revolutionaries.[97] They took the "realistic" approach that street criminals prey on the poor and disenfranchised, thus making them doubly abused, first by the capitalist system and then by members of their own class.

Exhibit 9.1	Basic Principles of Left Realism

- Crime is a symbol of the antisocial nature of capitalism.
- The relationship between the police and the public determines the efficacy of policing.
- The relationship between the victim and the offender determines the impact of crime.
- The relationship between the state and the offender is a major factor in recidivism.
- Relative deprivation leads to discontent; discontent plus lack of political solutions leads to crime.
- Local crime surveys provide the best measure of crime because national surveys may be irrelevant in any one area.
- Anti-crime strategies should be short term and avoid easy "crime control" solutions, such as more police.

Lea and Young's view of crime causation borrows from conventional sociological theory and closely resembles the relative deprivation approach. As they put it, "The equation is simple: relative deprivation equals discontent; discontent plus lack of political solution equals crime."[98]

Left realists argue that crime victims in all classes need and deserve protection; crime control reflects community needs. They do not view police and the courts as inherently evil tools of capitalism whose tough tactics alienate the lower classes. These institutions would in fact offer life-saving public services if their use of force could be reduced and their sensitivity to the public increased.[99] Another approach is **preemptive deterrence**, in which community organization efforts eliminate or reduce crime before it becomes necessary to use police forces. If the number of **marginalized** youth (those who feel they are not part of society and have nothing to lose by committing crime) could be reduced, delinquency rates would decline.[100]

To left realists Martin Schwartz and Walter DeKeseredy, street crime is "real"; the fear of violence among the lower classes has allowed the right wing to seize "law and order" as a political issue.[101] Gangs are not made up of "Robin Hoods," revolutionaries who steal from the rich. Most gang kids prey on members of their own race and class and are happy to keep the proceeds for themselves. According to Schwartz and DeKeseredy, gang kids may be the "ultimate capitalists," hustling their way to obtain the coveted symbols of success.[102]

Although the implementation of a socialist economy would help eliminate the crime problem, left realists recognize that something must be done in the meantime to control crime under the existing capitalist system. To create crime control policy, left realists welcome not only

radical ideas but build on the work of strain theorists, social ecologists, and other "mainstream" views. Community-based efforts seem to hold the most promise as crime control techniques.

Left realism has been critiqued by radical thinkers as legitimizing the existing power structure: By supporting the existing definitions of law and justice, it suggests that the "deviant" and not the capitalist system is the cause of society's problems. Is it not advocating the very institutions that "currently imprison us and our patterns of thought and action?"[103] In rebuttal, a left realist would charge that it is unrealistic to speak of a socialist state lacking a police force or system of laws and justice; the Criminal Code does in fact represent public opinion.

Radical Feminist Theory

Like so many theories in criminology, most of the efforts of radical theorists have been devoted to explaining male criminality.[104] To remedy this theoretical lapse, a number of feminist writers have attempted to explain the cause of crime, gender differences in the crime rate, and the exploitation of female victims from a radical feminist perspective. Scholars in this area can usually be described as holding one of two related philosophical orientations: Marxist feminism or radical feminism.

Marxist Feminism. The first group of writers can be described as **Marxist feminists**, who view gender inequality as stemming from the unequal power of men and women in a capitalist society. They view gender inequality as a function of the exploitation of females by fathers and husbands; women are considered a "commodity" worth possessing, like land or money.[105] The origin of gender differences can be traced to the development of private property and male domination over the laws of inheritance.[106]

Marxist feminists link criminal behaviour patterns to the gender conflict created by the economic and social struggles common in postindustrial societies. James Messerschmidt has made important contributions to understanding the roots of gender conflict. In *Capitalism, Patriarchy, and Crime*, he argues that capitalist society is marked by both patriarchy and class conflict. Capitalists control the labour of workers, while men control women both economically and biologically.[107] This "double marginality" explains why females in a capitalist society commit fewer crimes than males: They are isolated in the family and have fewer opportunities to engage in elite deviance (white-collar and economic crimes), and they are also denied access to male-dominated street crimes. For example, powerful males will commit white-collar crimes, as will powerful females. However, the female crime rate is restricted because of the patriarchal nature of the capitalist system.[108] Since capitalism renders women powerless, they are forced to commit less serious, nonviolent, self-destructive crimes, such as abusing drugs.

Powerlessness also increases the likelihood that women will become the target of violent acts.[109] Lower-class males are shut out of the economic opportunity structure. One way to improve their self-image is through acts of machismo that may involve violence or abuse of women. It is not surprising to find that a significant percentage of female victims are attacked by a spouse or intimate partner.

In his book *Masculinities and Crime*, Messerschmidt expands on these themes.[110] He suggests that in every culture males try to emulate what is considered "ideal" masculine behaviours. In Western culture this means being authoritative, in charge, combative, and controlling. Failure to adapt to these roles leaves men feeling effeminate and unmanly. Their struggle to dominate women to prove their manliness is called **doing gender**. Crime is a good way for men to "do gender" because abusers believe it separates them from the weak and allows them to demonstrate physical bravery.

Radical Feminism. In contrast, **radical feminists** view the cause of female crime as originating with the onset of male supremacy (patriarchy), the subsequent subordination of women, male aggression, and the efforts of men to control females sexually.[111] They focus on the social forces that shape women's lives and experiences to explain female criminality.[112] For example, radical feminists attempt to show how the sexual victimization of girls is a function of male socialization because so many young males learn to be aggressive and exploitive of women. Males seek out same-sex peer groups for social support and find within them encouragement for the exploitation and sexual abuse of women. On college campuses, peers encourage sexual violence against women defined as "teasers," "pickups," or "sluts"; a code of secrecy then protects the aggressors from retribution.[113] Sexual and physical exploitation triggers a reaction among young girls. They may run away or abuse substances, which is labelled deviant or delinquent behaviour.[114] In a sense, the female criminal is a victim herself.

The radical perspective is supported by a national survey in the United States conducted by the Centre for Research on Women at Wellesley College, which found that 90 percent of adolescent girls are sexually harassed in school, almost 30 percent report having been pressured to "do something sexual," and 10 percent said they were forced to do something sexual.[115]

According to the radical feminist view, exploitation acts as a trigger for the onset of delinquent and deviant behaviour. When female victims run away and abuse substances, they may be reacting to abuse at home and at school. Their attempts at survival are then labelled deviant or delinquent; victim blaming is not uncommon.

Research by Jane Siegel and Linda Meyer Williams shows that a significant number (86 percent) of girls who had been sent to the emergency room to be treated for sexual abuse later reported engaging in physical fighting as a teen or as an adult; many of these abused girls later formed a romantic attachment with an abusive partner. Clearly many girls involved in delinquency, crime, and violence have themselves been the victims of violence in their youth and later as adults.[116]

The Wellesley survey of sexual harassment found that teachers and school officials ignore about 45 percent of complaints made by female students. They found that some school officials responded to reports of sexual harassment by asking the young victim, "Do you like it?" and saying, "They must be doing it for a reason." Because agents of social control often choose to ignore reports of abuse and harassment, young girls may feel trapped and desperate.

Even within the radical feminist movement there are important differences. For example, some feminist scholars charge that the movement focuses on the problems and viewpoints of white, middle-class, heterosexual women without taking into account the special interests of lesbians and women of colour.[117]

How the Justice System Penalizes Women. Radical feminists have also indicted the justice system and its patriarchal hierarchy as contributing to the onset of female delinquency. From its inception, the juvenile justice system has viewed the great majority of female delinquents as sexually precocious girls who have to be brought under control. Writing on the "girl problem," Ruth Alexander has described how working-class young women desiring autonomy and freedom in the 1920s were considered delinquents and placed in reformatories. Lacking the ability to protect themselves from the authorities, these young girls were considered outlaws in a male-dominated society because they flouted the very narrow rules of appropriate behaviour that were applied to females in this Victorian society. Girls who rebelled against parental authority or who engaged in sexual behaviour deemed inappropriate were incarcerated to protect them from a career in prostitution.[118] In fact young women were much more likely to be prosecuted for sexual promiscuity under the Juvenile Delinquent's Act than young men, even though they had to be promiscuous with someone.

In a similar vein, a study of the early Los Angeles Juvenile Court found that in 1920 so-called delinquency experts identified young female "sex delinquents" as a major social problem that required a forceful public response. Civic leaders who were concerned about immorality mounted a eugenics and social hygiene campaign that identified the "sex delinquent" as a moral and sexual threat to society and advocated a policy of eugenics or sterilization to prevent these inferior individuals from having children. Los Angeles responded by hiring the first female police officers in the nation to deal with girls under arrest and female judges to hear girls' cases in juvenile court; it also established a female detention centre and a girls' reformatory.

When those 1920 juvenile court records were evaluated, they found that the majority of delinquent girls were petitioned for either suspected sexual activity or behaviour that placed them at risk of sexual relations. Despite the limited seriousness of these charges, the majority of girls were detained before their trials, and while in Juvenile Hall, all were given a compulsory pelvic exam. Girls adjudged sexually delinquent on the basis of the exam were segregated from the merely incorrigible girls to prevent moral corruption. Those testing positive for venereal disease were confined in the Juvenile Hall hospital for usually from one to three months. More than 29 percent of these female adolescents were eventually committed to custodial institutions.[119]

The judicial victimization of female delinquents has continued. A well-known feminist writer, Meda Chesney-Lind, has written extensively on the victimization of female delinquents by agents of the juvenile justice system.[120] She found that police in Honolulu, Hawaii, were likely to arrest female adolescents for sexual activity and to ignore the same behaviour among male delinquents. Some 74 percent of the females in her sample were charged with sexual activity or incorrigibility, but only 27 percent of the boys faced the same charges. Moreover, the court ordered physical examinations in over 70 percent of the female cases, but only about 15 percent of the males were forced to undergo this embarrassing procedure. Girls were also more likely to be sent to a detention facility before trial, and the length of their detention averaged three times that of the boys. Finally, a higher percentage of females than males were institutionalized for similar delinquent acts. Chesney-Lind explains her data by suggesting that because female adolescents have a much narrower range of acceptable behaviour than male adolescents, any sign of misbehaviour in girls is seen as a substantial challenge to authority and to the viability of the double standard of sexual inequality. Female delinquency is viewed as relatively more serious than male delinquency and therefore is more likely to be severely sanctioned.

Power-Control Theory. John Hagan and his associates have created a radical-feminist model that uses gender differences to explain the onset of criminality. The most significant statements of these views are contained in a series of scholarly articles and are expanded in Hagan's 1989 book, *Structural Criminology*.[121] Hagan's view is that crime and delinquency rates are a function of two factors: (1) class position (power), and (2) family functions (control).[122] The link between these two variables is that within the family, parents reproduce the power relationships they hold in the workplace. The class position

and work experiences of parents influence the criminality of children. A position of dominance at work is equated with control in the household.

In families that are **paternalistic**, fathers assume the traditional role of breadwinners, while mothers have menial jobs or remain at home to supervise domestic matters. Within the paternalistic home, mothers are expected to control the behaviour of their daughters while granting greater freedom to sons. In such a home, the parent–daughter relationship can be viewed as a preparation for the "cult of domesticity," which makes girls' involvement in delinquency unlikely, while boys are freer to deviate because they are not subject to maternal control. Consequently, male siblings exhibit a higher degree of delinquent behaviour than their sisters.

On the other hand, in **egalitarian** families—those in which the husband and the wife share similar positions of power at home and in the workplace—daughters gain a kind of freedom that reflects reduced parental control. These families produce daughters whose law-violating behaviour mirrors their brothers'. Ironically, these kinds of relationships also occur in female-headed households with absent fathers. Similarly, Hagan and his associates found that when both fathers and mothers hold equally valued managerial positions, the similarity between the rates of their daughters' and sons' delinquency is greatest.

By implication, middle-class girls are the most likely to violate the law because they are less closely controlled than their lower-class counterparts. And in homes in which both parents hold positions of power, girls are more likely to have the same expectations of career success as their brothers. Consequently, siblings of both sexes will be socialized to take risks and engage in other behaviour related to delinquency. Power-control theory, then, implies that middle-class youth of both sexes will have higher overall crime rates than their lower-class peers (although lower-class males may commit the more serious crimes).

Power-control theory has received a great deal of attention in the criminological community because it encourages a new approach to the study of criminality, one that includes gender differences, class position, and the structure of the family. While its basic premises have not yet been thoroughly tested, some critics have questioned its core assumption that power and control variables can explain crime.[123] More specifically, critics fail to replicate the finding that upper-class kids are more likely to deviate than their lower-class peers or that class and power interact to produce delinquency.[124] In response, Hagan and his colleagues suggest that these views are incorrect and that power-control theory retains its power to significantly add to our knowledge of the causes of crime.[125] Despite their assurances, empirical testing may produce further refinement of the theory. For example, Kevin Thompson found few gender-based supervision and behaviour differences in worker-, manager-, or owner-dominated households.[126] However, parental supervision practices were quite different in families headed by the chronically unemployed, and these findings conformed to the power-control model. The Thompson research indicates that the concept of class used by Hagan may have to be reconsidered: Power-control theory may actually explain criminality among the truly disadvantaged and not the working class.

Deconstructionism

A number of radical criminologists have used **deconstructionism** as a tool for analysis. This focuses on the critical analysis of communication and language in legal codes.[127] Rules and regulations are analyzed to determine whether they contain language and content that institutionalizes relations of power: gender, ethnicity, and social class.

Deconstructionists rely on various types of discourse analysis, such as **semiotics**, to conduct their research efforts. This means using language as signs that indicate more than the mere meaning of words. There are many signs or language groupings in operation today. For example, sports rely very heavily on the use of signs, and to become a sports "expert" means becoming familiar with terminology such as "blitzing the quarterback" and a "hat trick." These terms convey meaning that is far greater than the words themselves and provide images to sports fans familiar with the signs that would be lost on others.

Deconstructionists believe that language is value-laden and contains the same sorts of inequities present in the rest of the social structure. Concerns with materialism and social inequality appear in the content of the law and control its direction. Capitalism puts a price tag on all merchandise. Law, legal skill, and justice are "commodities" that can be bought and sold like any other.[128]

Restorative Justice

As an outgrowth of critical criminology, **restorative justice** is based on a social rather than a legal view of crime. Restorative justice views crime as an injury to personal and community relations rather than as an abstract legal violation against society.

According to the legal view, "society" consists of (1) formal institutions and (2) individuals. Society is defined as an aggregation of people over which the state has jurisdiction. Legally, this aggregation is assumed to possess the social qualities of a group: common meanings and values, sustained interaction, and symbolic bonds. In the restorative view, in contrast, society, because of its bureaucratic nature, is not capable of manifesting such social qualities. It is only in smaller, less formal, and more cohesive social groups, such as families, congregations, residential communities, that such qualities are found. Therefore, the potential for restoring social relations damaged by crime is to be found not in the state but in social groups, in the community.

Restorative justice is in opposition to the adversary system. Without the capacity to restore damaged social relations, society's response to crime has been almost exclusively punitive. The potential of punitive state sanctions, whether they are intended to simply punish, deter, or induce treatment, necessitates an adversarial system of justice as an insurance against the infliction of undeserved punishment. In attempting to ensure equal protection under the law, the procedural design of the adversarial system purposely limits consideration of the unique personal and social qualities of particular crimes. As a result of its preoccupation with the protection of individual rights, the adversarial system encourages the accused to deny, justify, or excuse their actions, thereby precluding the acceptance of responsibility. In addition, the central role of trained professionals in the adversarial process (prosecution and defence attorneys) severely limits the possibility of direct exchanges between the victim and offender. Because the adversaries are narrowly defined as the "accused" and the "state," little or no consideration can be given to community concerns and participation. Restorative justice is a direct response to the inadequacies of the adversarial process.

Restorative justice is guided by three essential principles: (1) community ownership of conflict (including crime), (2) material and symbolic reparation for victims and community, and (3) social reintegration of the offender. The restorative process begins by redefining crime in terms of a conflict among the offender, the victim, and affected constituencies (families, schools, workplaces, and so on). Therefore, the resolution take place within the context in which the conflict originally occurred rather than transferred to a specialized institution that has no social connection to the community or group from which the conflict originated. By maintaining "ownership" or jurisdiction over the conflict, the community is able to express its shared outrage about the offence. This approach allows for shared community outrage to be directly communicated to the offender. The victim is also given a chance to voice his or her story, and the offender can directly communicate his or her need for social reintegration and treatment.

The restoration process depends on a conception of the law as a discussion that is cohesive rather than punitive and disruptive. This encourages people to discuss the problems in their social life which are typically manifested in interpersonal conflict. The restoration process involves an informal communicative exchange among the victim, the offender, and the community. Although restorative processes differ in structure and style, their discourse generally includes a recognition of the injury to personal and social relations, a determination and acceptance of responsibility (ideally accompanied by a statement of remorse), a commitment to both material and symbolic (e.g., an apology) reparation, and a determination of community support and assistance for both victim and offender. The intended result of the restorative process is to repair injuries suffered by the victim and the community while ensuring reintegration of the offender.

Although there is widespread agreement among proponents of restorative justice as to what constitutes restoration, a clear division exists among those who believe that restorative justice can be achieved within the context of the existing social structure and those who contend that significant social structural change must occur for the true potential of restorative justice to be realized. The former argue that the social qualities of the group can be recreated within such processes as family group conferencing, victim–offender reconciliation, and sentencing circles. The latter suggest that such social qualities cannot be effectively recreated; rather, they must exist prior to the restorative process.

The effectiveness of restorative justice ultimately depends on the stake a person has in the community (or a particular social group). Persons who do not value their membership in the group will be unlikely to accept responsibility, show remorse, or repair the injuries caused by their actions. Existing restorative justice programs, such as mediation programs, will be unable to effectively reach those persons who are disengaged from all community institutions. Therefore, the relative effectiveness of existing restorative justice programs provides us with a measurement of the need for structural change.[129]

Peacemaking Criminology

> Suffering has risen out of disunity and separation from the embracing totality, and it can be ended only with the return of all sentient beings to a condition of wholeness.[130]

One of the newer movements in radical theory is **peacemaking criminology**. To members of the peacemaking movement, the main purpose of criminology is to promote a peaceful and just society. Rather than standing on empirical analysis of data sets, peacemaking draws its inspiration from religious and philosophical teachings ranging from Quakerism to Zen.

Peacemakers view the efforts of the state to punish and control as crime-encouraging rather than crime-discouraging. These views were first articulated in a series of books with an anarchist theme written by Larry Tifft and Dennis Sullivan more than 15 years ago.[131] In his foreword to Sullivan's *The Mask of Love*, Larry Tifft writes:

> The violent punishing acts of the state and its controlling professions are of the same genre as the violent acts of individuals. In each instance

these acts reflect an attempt to monopolize human interaction.[132]

Sullivan recognizes the futility of correcting and punishing criminals in the context of our conflict-ridden society:

> The reality we must grasp is that we live in a culture of severed relationships, where every available institution provides a form of banishment but no place or means for people to become connected, to be responsible to and for each other.[133]

The writings imply that mutual aid rather than coercive punishment is the key to a harmonious society. Today, advocates of the peacemaking movement, such as Harold Pepinsky and Richard Quinney, try to find humanist solutions to crime and other social problems.[134] Rather than punishment and prison, they advocate such policies as mediation and conflict resolution. This is closely related to the theoretical and applied principles of restorative justice.

Summary

Social conflict theorists view crime as a function of the conflict that exists in society. Social conflict has its theoretical basis in the works of Karl Marx, as interpreted by Willem Bonger and George Vold. Conflict theorists suggest that crime in any society is caused by class conflict. Laws are created by those in power to protect their rights and interests. All criminal acts have political undertones. Richard Quinney has called this concept the social reality of crime. One of conflict theory's most important premises is that the justice system is biased and designed to protect the wealthy. Research has not been unanimous in supporting this point.

Marxist criminology views the competitive nature of the capitalist system as a major cause of crime. The poor commit crimes because of their frustration, anger, and need. The wealthy engage in illegal acts because they are used to competition and because they must do so to keep their positions in society. Marxist scholars have attempted to show that the law is designed to protect the wealthy and powerful and to control the poor, have-not members of society. Branches of radical theory include instrumental Marxism and structural Marxism (see Table 9.2 for a summary of these theories).

Research on Marxist theory focuses on how the system of justice was designed and how it operates to further class interests. Quite often, this research uses historical analysis to show how the capitalist classes have exerted their control over the police, courts, and correctional agencies. Both Marxist and conflict criminology have been heavily criticized by consensus criminologists.

Table 9.2	Social conflict theories		
THEORY	**MAJOR PREMISE**	**STRENGTHS**	
Conflict theory	Crime is a function of class conflict. The definition of the law is controlled by people who hold social and political power.	Accounts for class differentials in the crime rate. Shows how class conflict influences behaviour.	
Marxist theory	The capitalist means of production creates class conflict. Crime is a rebellion of the lower class. The criminal justice system is an agent of class warfare.	Accounts for the associations between economic structure and crime rates.	
Instrumental Marxist theory	Criminals are revolutionaries. The real crime is sexism, racism, and profiteering.	Broadens the definition of crime and demystifies or explains the historical development of law.	
Structural Marxist theory	The law is designed to sustain the capitalist economic system.	Explains the existence of white-collar crime and business control laws.	
Radical feminist theory	The capitalist system creates patriarchy, which oppresses women.	Explains gender bias, violence against women, and repression.	
Left realism	Crime is a function of relative deprivation; criminals prey on the poor.	Represents a compromise between conflict and traditional criminology.	
Deconstruction	Language controls the meaning and use of the law.	Provides a critical analysis of meaning.	
Peacemaking	Peace and humanism can reduce crime; conflict resolution strategies can work.	Offers a new approach to crime control through mediation.	

During the 1990s, new forms of conflict theory emerged. Feminist writers drew attention to the influence of patriarchal society on crime; left realism took a centrist position on crime by showing its rational and destructive nature; peacemaking criminology brought a call for humanism to criminology; and deconstructionism looked at the symbolic meaning of law and culture.

Thinking Like a Criminologist

A local school board has just announced a plan to have police officers patrol schools daily with drug-sniffing dogs. Despite the lack of evidence that there is a drug problem, the dogs will be sniffing lockers, gym bags, and people. If any drugs are found, criminal charges may be filed against students who get caught. You are a lawyer and a member of the British Columbia Civil Liberties Association. Concerned students come to you for advice. They want you to answer the following questions:

1. Are civil liberties being violated? If so, which ones? Provide some details.

2. What type of legal or other action would you advise your clients to take? Estimate their chances of success.

Source: Adapted from "Legal rights: Search and seizure," www.bccla.org/rightstalk/legal.html.

Key Terms

conflict theory

dangerous classes

deconstructionism

demystification

doing gender

egalitarian

left realism

marginalization

Marxist feminists

norm resistance

paternalistic

peacemaking criminology

preemptive deterrence

privilege

radical feminists

restorative justice

semiotics

social reality of crime

structural Marxists

surplus value

 See the book-specific website at www.siegelcriminology2e.nelson.com for additional chapter links, discussions, and quizzes.

Chapter

10

Integrated Theories

Whereas early criminologists readily embraced the theoretical work of their colleagues, modern criminologists have tended to be specialized; they classify themselves as choice, conflict, labelling, control, or some other kind of theorist.[1] As a result, criminological theory ranges from the most radical (Marxist, conflict, and deconstructionist theory) to the most conservative (rational choice and trait theory) views. The ideological differences among these positions create a gulf that sometimes seems impossible to bridge, especially when advocates are dismissive of competing viewpoints. Recently, however, to derive a more powerful explanation of crime, some criminologists have begun integrating these individual factors into multifactor theories that attempt to blend seemingly independent concepts into complex explanations of criminality.

A number of reasons account for the current popularity of integrated theory. One is practical: The development of large, computerized databases and software that facilitate statistical analysis now makes theory integration practical. Criminologists of an earlier era simply did not have the tools to conduct the sophisticated computations necessary for theory integration.

The other reason is substantive. Single-factor theories focus on the onset of crime; they tend to divide the world simply into criminals and noncriminals, those who have a crime-producing condition and those who do not. For example, people who feel anomie become deviant, while those who do not remain law-abiding; people with high testosterone levels are violent, while people with low levels are not.

Connections

The issue of age and crime and the "desistance" phenomenon was discussed in Chapter 3. This means crime rates peak in the teenage years and then decline over the life course. Explaining this decline has become an important focus of criminology.

The view that people can be classified as either criminals or noncriminals and that this status is stable over the course of a person's life is now being challenged. Criminologists today are concerned not only with the onset of criminality but with its termination: Why do people age out or desist from crime? If, for example, criminality is a function of intelligence, as some criminologists claim, why do most delinquents fail to become adult criminals? It seems unlikely that intelligence level increases as young offenders mature. If the onset of criminality can be explained by intelligence level, then some other factor must explain its termination.

It has also become important to chart the natural history of a criminal career. Why do some offenders escalate their criminal activities, while others decrease or limit their

Connections

As you may recall from Chapter 3, the Philadelphia cohort studies conducted by Wolfgang and his associates identified the existence of a relatively small group of chronic offenders who committed a significant amount of all serious crimes and persisted in criminal careers into their adulthood.

law violations? Why do some offenders specialize in a particular crime, while others become generalists? Why do some criminals reduce criminal activity and then resume it once again? Research now shows that some offenders begin their criminal career at a very early age while others begin at a later point in their lives. How can early- and late-onset criminality be explained?[2] This approach is sometimes referred to as **developmental criminology.**

Integrated theories have also helped focus on the chronic or persistent offender. Single-factor theories have trouble explaining why only relatively few of the many individuals exposed to criminogenic influences in the environment actually become chronic offenders.

For example, structural theories make a convincing case for a link between crime and social variables such as neighbourhood disorganization and cultural deviance. It is more difficult for these theories to explain why only a few adolescents in the most disorganized areas mature into chronic offenders. Why do so many underprivileged youths resist crime despite their exposure to social disorganization and cultural deviance? There may be more than a single reason that one person engages in criminal behaviour and another, living under similar circumstances, can avoid a criminal career.

By integrating a variety of ecological, socialization, psychological, biological, and economic factors into a coherent structure, criminologists are attempting to answer these complex questions. This chapter summarizes these integrated theories.

Overview of Integrated Theories

Integrated theories can be divided into three groups on the basis of their view of human development and change: multifactor theories, latent trait theories, and life-course theories.

The earliest integrated theories are referred to as **multifactor theories.** These theories suggest that social, personal, and economic factors each exert influence on criminal behaviour. Multifactor theories combine the influences of variables that have been used in structural, socialization, conflict, choice, and trait theories.

The multifactor approach helps criminologists explain both criminal career formation and desistence from crime: Although many youths are at risk to crime, relatively few face the complete set of hazards that result in a criminal career, including an impulsive personality, a dysfunctional family, a disorganized neighbourhood, deviant friends, and school failure. For example, a model based on the concept of latent traits could explain the flow of crime over the life cycle. This model would assume that a number of people in the population have a personal attribute or characteristic that controls their inclination or propensity to commit crimes.[3] This disposition or **latent trait** may be present at birth or established early in life and remains stable over time. Suspected latent traits include defective intelligence, impulsive personality, and genetic abnormalities. Those who carry these latent traits are in danger of becoming career criminals, while those who lack them are a much lower risk. Latent traits should affect the behaviour choices of all people equally, regardless of their gender or personal characteristics.[4]

The positive association between past and future criminality detected in the cohort studies of career criminals may reflect the presence of underlying criminogenic traits. That is, if low IQ causes delinquency in childhood, it should also cause the same people to offend as adults, since intelligence is usually stable over the life span. Similarly, people who are antisocial during their adolescence are the ones most likely to be persistent criminals throughout their life span.

Because latent traits are stable, fluctuations in offending over time reflect criminal opportunities and not the propensity to commit crime. For example, assume that a stable latent trait such as low IQ causes some people to commit crime. Teenagers have more opportunity to commit crime than adults of equal intelligence; therefore, adolescent crime rates are higher. As they mature, low-IQ teens will commit less crime because they have fewer criminal opportunities. While the propensity to commit crime is stable, the opportunity to commit crime fluctuates. Latent trait theories thus integrate concepts usually associated with trait theories (personality and temperament) with rational choice theories (criminal opportunity and suitable targets).

Another approach that has emerged is **life-course theory**. In contrast to the latent trait view, life-course theories hold that the propensity to commit crimes is not stable and does change over time; it is a developmental process.

According to life-course theory, some career criminals may desist from crime for a while, only to resume their activities at a later date. Some commit offences at a steady pace, while others escalate their rate of criminal involvement. Offenders may specialize in one type of crime or become generalists who commit a variety of illegal acts. Criminals may be influenced by family matters, financial needs, and changes in lifestyle and interests. While latent traits may be important, they alone neither control the direction of criminal careers nor ensure that criminal acts are predetermined at birth or soon afterward.

Life-course theories also recognize that as people mature, the factors that influence their behaviour change.[5] At first, family relations may be most influential; in later adolescence, school and peer relations predominate; in adulthood, vocational achievement and marital relations may be the most critical. For example, some antisocial kids who are "in trouble" throughout their adolescence may manage to find stable work and maintain intact marriages as adults; these life events help them desist from crime. In contrast, the less fortunate who develop arrest records and get involved with the "wrong crowd" can find only menial jobs and are at risk for criminal careers. Social forces that are critical at one stage of life may have little meaning or influence at another.

Connections

Social process theories lay the foundation for assuming that peer, family, educational, and other interactions that vary over the life course influence behaviours. See the first few sections of Chapter 8 for a review of these issues.

These three views share some common ground.[6] They indicate that a criminal career must be understood as a passage along which people travel, that it has a beginning and an end, and that events and life circumstances influence the journey. The factors that affect a criminal career may include structural factors, such as income and status; socialization factors, such as family and peer relations; biological factors, such as size and strength; psychological factors, including intelligence and personality; and opportunity factors, such as free time, inadequate police protection, and a supply of easily stolen merchandise. Life-course and multifactor theories tend to stress the influence of changing interpersonal and structural factors (that is, people change along with the world they live in); latent trait theories assume that it is not people but criminal opportunities that change (that is, people do not change, but the opportunity to commit crime does).

These perspectives differ in their view of human development: Do people change, as life-course theories suggest, or are they stable, constant, and changeless, as the latent trait view indicates? Is there a dominant key that controls human destiny, or are there multiple influences on human behaviour? Are the social and personal factors that influence people stable, or do they change as a person matures?

In the remainder of the chapter, we discuss some of the most important integrated theories that address the development and sustenance of a criminal career in some detail.

Multifactor Theories

Multifactor theories integrate a range of variables into a cohesive explanation of criminality. Unlike the latent trait view, these theories recognize that factors that appear later in life, such as peer relations, exert an important influence on people.

Efforts to create multifactor theories are not new. Over two decades ago, Daniel Glazer combined elements of differential association with choice and control theory in his differential anticipation theory.[7] Glazer's version asserts: "A person's crime or restraint from crime is determined by the consequences he anticipates from it."[8] According to Glazer, people commit crimes whenever and wherever the expectations of gain exceed the expectations of losses (rational choice). This decision is tempered by the quality of their social bonds and their relationships with others (control theory), as well as their prior learning experiences (learning theory).

Attempts have been made to integrate such social process concepts as learning, labelling, and control with structural and other variables. A few prominent examples of integrated theory are discussed next.

The Social Development Model (SDM)

In their social development model (SDM), Joseph Weis, Richard Catalano, J. David Hawkins, and their associates have attempted to integrate social control, social learning, and structural models (see Figure 10.1).[9]

According to the **social development model (SDM)**, a number of community-level "risk factors" make some people susceptible to the development of antisocial behaviours. For example, the quality of community organization influences the child's risk of developing antisocial behaviour—social control is less effective when the frontline socializing institutions are weak in disorganized areas. In a low-income, disorganized community, families are under great stress, educational facilities are inadequate, fewer material goods are available, and respect for the law is weak. Because crime rates are high, there are greater opportunities for law violation, putting even more strain on the agencies of social control.

As a child matures within his or her environment, elements of socialization control the developmental process. Preexisting risk factors are either reinforced or neutralized through socialization. Children are socialized and develop bonds to their family through four processes:

1. Perceived opportunities for involvement in activities and interactions with others
2. The degree of involvement and interaction
3. The skills to participate in these interactions
4. The reinforcement (feedback) they perceive for their participation

To control the risk of antisocial behaviour, a child must maintain **prosocial bonds**. These bonds are developed within the context of a family life, which not only provides prosocial opportunities but reinforces them by offering consistent positive feedback. Parental attachment, then, has the power to affect a child's behaviour throughout the life course, determining both school experiences and personal beliefs and values. For those with strong family relationships, school will be a meaningful experience marked by academic success and commitment to education. Youths in this category are more likely to develop conventional beliefs and values, become committed to conventional activities, and form attachments to conventional others.

Children's antisocial behaviour also depends on the quality of their attachments to others. If they remain unattached or develop attachments to deviant others, their own behaviour may become antisocial. Unlike Hirschi's control theory, which assumes that all attachments are beneficial, SDM suggests that interaction with antisocial peers and adults promotes participation in delinquency and substance abuse over the life course.[10] Whereas Hirschi maintains that early family attachments are the key determinants of future behaviour, SDM suggests that later involvement in prosocial or antisocial behaviour determines the quality of attachments. Those adolescents who perceive opportunities and rewards for antisocial behaviour will form deep attachments to deviant peers, will become committed to a delinquent way of life, and will develop antisocial values and behaviour. In contrast, those who perceive opportunities and rewards for prosocial behaviour will take a different path, getting involved in conventional activities, forming attachments to prosocial others, and developing beliefs in the moral order.

The SDM thus holds that commitment and attachment to conventional institutions, activities, and beliefs work to insulate youths from the criminogenic influences of their environment; the prosocial path inhibits deviance by strengthening bonds to prosocial others and activities.

Many of the core assumptions of SDM have been tested empirically, and their validity has been verified.[11] The path predicted by SDM seems an accurate picture of the onset and continuation of delinquency and drug abuse. For example, research indicates that both social learning and control-bonding factors play an important role in predicting gang membership.[12] The SDM has also guided treatment interventions that promote the development of strong bonds to family and school and help kids use these bonds to resist any opportunity or motivation to take drugs and engage in delinquent behaviours.[13]

Elliott's Integrated Theory

Another attempt at theory integration has been proposed by Delbert Elliott and his colleagues David Huizinga and Suzanne Ageton of the Behavioral Research Institute in

Figure 10.1 The social development model of antisocial behaviour

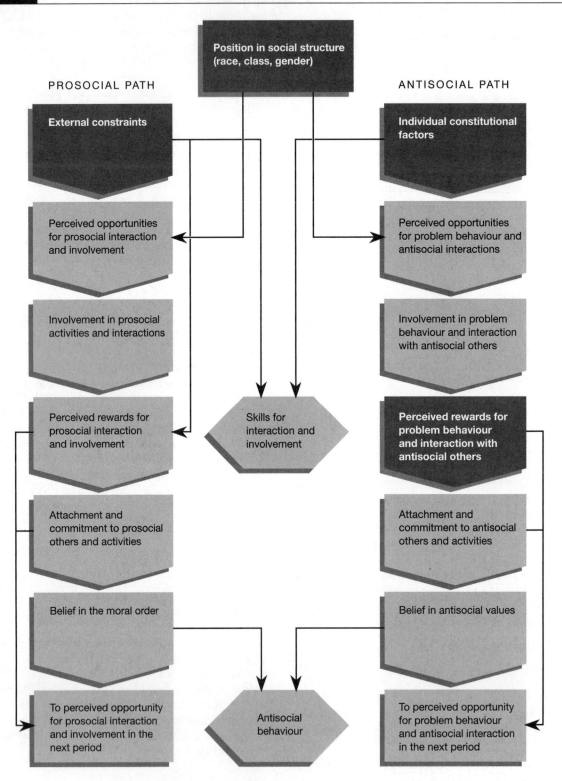

SOURCE: Adapted from Seattle Social Development Project.

Boulder, Colorado.[14] Their view combines the features of strain, social learning, and control theories into a single theoretical model.

According to the Elliott view (see Figure 10.2), adolescents who live in socially disorganized areas (A) and who are improperly socialized at home (B) face a significant risk of perceiving strain (C); perceptions of strain then lead to weakened bonds with conventional groups, activities, and norms (D). Weak conventional bonds and high levels of perceived strain lead some youths to reject conventional social values (E) and seek out and become bonded to deviant peer groups (F). From these delinquent associations come positive reinforcements for delinquent behaviours; delinquent peers help provide role models for antisocial behaviour (G). Attachment to delinquent groups, when combined with weak bonding to conventional groups and norms, leads to a high level of delinquent behaviour and drug abuse (H).

Social Factors. The picture Elliott and his colleagues draw of the teenage delinquent is not dissimilar to the one drawn by the SDM, with the addition of the concept of strain. Living in a disorganized neighbourhood, feeling hopeless and unable to get ahead, and becoming involved in petty crimes eventually lead to a condition in which conventional social values are weakened. Concern for education, family relations, and respect for the social order are weakened. A deviant peer group becomes an acceptable substitute; consequently, the attitudes and skills that support delinquent tendencies are amplified. The result is early experimentation with drugs, and delin-

quency becomes a way of life. Note how both the SDM and the Elliott integrated theory assume that involvement with delinquent friends increases the risk of criminal involvement.

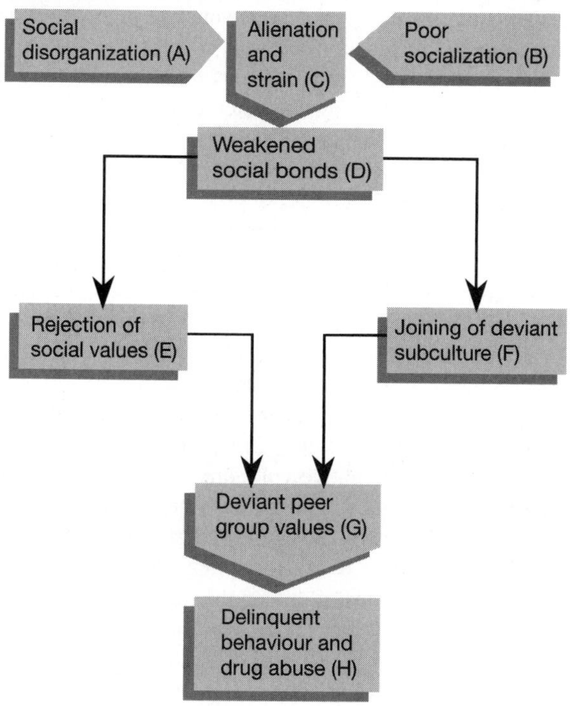

Testing Integrated Theory. Elliott and his colleagues tested their theoretical model with data taken from a national survey of approximately 1800 youths interviewed annually over a three-year period. With only a few minor exceptions, the results supported their integrated theory. One difference was that some subjects reported developing strong bonds to delinquent peers even if they did not reject the values of conventional society. Elliott and his colleagues interpret this finding as suggesting that youths living in disorganized areas may have little choice but to join with law-violating youth groups, since conventional groups simply do not exist. Elliott also found that initial experimentation with drugs and delinquency predicted both joining a teenage law-violating peer group and becoming involved with additional delinquency.

In another national survey of more than 1000 youths who had been interviewed annually over a three-year period,[15] it was found that bonding to a delinquent peer group escalates involvement in criminal activity.[16]

Integrated Structural Marxist Theory

Not all multifactor views of crime rely solely on mainstream concepts. One theory that has been developed integrates conflict concepts with structural and process factors: the **integrated structural Marxist theory**, illustrated in Figure 10.3.[17]

According to this model, crime is a result of socialization within the family. Family relationships marked by conflict and despair are the forerunner of criminal careers. However, in addition, those family relations are influenced by the quality of one's work experience.[18] Wage earners who occupy an inferior position in the economic hierarchy will experience negative relationships with their supervisors and employers. This creates strain and alienation within the family setting, especially if there is inconsistent and overly punitive discipline. Juveniles who live in such an environment will become alienated from their parents and experience adjustment problems in school. Youths growing up in a family headed by parents who are at the bottom of workplace control structures are also the ones most likely to go to underfunded schools, do poorly on standardized tests, and be placed in slow learning tracks; each of these factors has been correlated with delinquent behaviour.

Negative social relations at home and at school result in feelings of alienation and strain. These are reinforced by associations with groups of similarly alienated peers. These peer groups can be oriented toward patterns of violent behaviour, or to economic crime.

According to integrated structural theory, it is naive to believe that a crime control policy can be formulated

Figure 10.2   Elliott's Integrated Theory

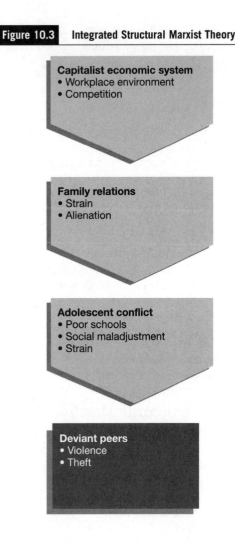

| Figure 10.3 | Integrated Structural Marxist Theory |

Capitalist economic system
• Workplace environment
• Competition

Family relations
• Strain
• Alienation

Adolescent conflict
• Poor schools
• Social maladjustment
• Strain

Deviant peers
• Violence
• Theft

without regard for its root causes. Coercive punishments or misguided treatments cannot be effective unless the core relationships with regard to material production are changed. Those who produce goods must be given greater opportunity and power to shape their lives and the lives of their families. Research is generally supportive of these core principles.[19]

The Latent Trait Approach

The second main approach considered here, latent trait theory, assumes that some latent trait or condition, in most cases present at birth or soon after, can account for the onset of criminality. Thereafter, the propensity for crime remains stable throughout the person's life, when social forces and opportunity can influence the likelihood of crime. People age out of crime because as they mature there are simply fewer opportunities to commit crime and greater inducements to remain "straight."

Some of the suspected traits linked to crime include biosocial factors such as attention deficit disorder and psychological traits such as impulsivity. Yet almost all biosocial and psychological advocates recognize the multidimensionality of crime. For example, as biosocial theorist Lee Ellis maintains, (1) the physical-chemical functioning of the brain is responsible for all human behaviour, (2) brain function is controlled by genetic and environmental factors, and (3) environmental influences on brain function encompass both physical (drugs, chemicals, and injuries) and experiential (social) factors. Ellis finds that all three components of modern biocriminology (biochemistry, genetics, and neurology) work in concert with social and experiential factors to control crime.[20]

Here we discuss in some detail two integrated theories that assume that crime is a function of a latent trait.

Connections

Individual-level factors seem ideally suited for a role in theory integration because, as noted in Chapter 6, it is evident that alone they cannot explain crime rate patterns and changes.

Crime and Human Nature

One of the most widely read and analyzed works in the criminological literature is James Q. Wilson and Richard Herrnstein's book *Crime and Human Nature*.[21] These social scientists make a convincing argument that personal traits, such as genetic makeup, intelligence, and body build, may outweigh the importance of social variables as predictors of criminal behaviour. Wilson and Herrnstein therefore propose an integrated theory of criminality that includes elements of biosocial makeup, personality, rational choice, and structure and social process.

Accordingly, all human behaviour, including criminality, is determined by its perceived consequences. A criminal incident occurs when an individual chooses criminal over conventional behaviour (referred to as "noncrime") after weighing the potential gains and losses of each. Crime, then, is a function of rational choice. According to Wilson and Herrnstein, "the larger the ratio of net rewards of crime to the net rewards of noncrime, the greater the tendency to commit the crime."[22]

The rewards for crime can include material gain, sexual gratification, revenge, and peer approval. The consequences can include pangs of conscience, victim reprisals, social disapproval, and the threat of legal punishment. Although crime's negative consequences may deter some would-be criminals, their impact may be neutralized by the fact that these consequences are typically distant threats, whereas the rewards of crime are immediate and current. The rewards for choosing noncrime are also gained in the future: If you "stay clean," someday people will learn to respect you, your self-image and reputation will improve, and you may achieve happiness and freedom.

Of course, one can never be quite sure of the rewards of either crime or noncrime. The burglar hoping for the "big score" may instead experience arrest, conviction, and incarceration; people who "play it straight" may find that their sacrifice does not get them to the place in society they desire.

Choosing Crime or Noncrime. The choice between crime and noncrime is quite often a difficult one. Criminal choices are reinforced by the desire to obtain basic rewards—food, clothing, shelter, sex—or learned goals—wealth, power, status—without having to work and save for them. Even if an individual has been socialized to choose noncrime, crime can be an attractive alternative, especially if any potential negative consequences are uncertain and delayed far into the future. By analogy, cigarette smoking is common because its consequences are distant and uncertain, while taking cyanide is rare because the effects are immediate and certain.

Integrating Social and Individual Traits. This model is integrative because it assumes that both biological and psychological traits influence the crime–noncrime choice. There is a close link between a person's decision to choose crime and such biosocial factors as low intelligence, body type, genetic influences, and possessing an autonomic nervous system that responds too quickly to stimuli. Psychological traits, including an impulsive personality and low intelligence, also determine the potential to commit crime.[23] Having these traits will not by itself guarantee that a person will become a criminal; however, all things being equal, those who have them will be more likely to choose crime over noncrime.

This model doesn't ignore the influence of social factors on criminality. A turbulent family life, school failure, and membership in a deviant teenage subculture also have a powerful influence on criminality. Thus, biosocial, psychological, and social conditions, working in concert, can influence thought patterns and, eventually, individual behaviour patterns. For example, intelligence level is an important determinant of criminal behaviour choice, and its influence is mediated by a social variable, school performance: A child who chronically loses standing in the competition of the classroom may feel justified in settling the score outside by violence, theft, and other forms of defiant illegality. School failure enhances the rewards for crime by engendering feelings of unfairness. In addition, failure in school predicts, to a substantial degree, failure in the marketplace. For someone who stands to gain little from legitimate work, the rewards of noncrime are relatively weak. Failure in school, therefore, not only enhances the rewards for crime, but it predicts weak rewards for noncrime.[24]

In this viewpoint, harsh punishment is not the answer to the crime problem. Strengthening the besieged family and helping it orient children toward noncrime solutions to their problems is seen as a better solution.

The family, regardless of its composition, can help a child cultivate character, conscience, and respect for the moral order. Similarly, schools can help by teaching the benefits of accepting personal responsibility and, within limits, helping students understand what constitutes "right conduct."

Research tends to support this model, although it has been criticized for questionable measurement techniques and observer bias.[25] This work represents a dramatic attempt to integrate two of the most prominent theoretical movements in the study of criminality.

General Theory of Crime

In an important work, *A General Theory of Crime,* Michael Gottfredson and Travis Hirschi have modified and redefined some of the principles articulated in Hirschi's social control theory by integrating the concepts of control with those of biosocial, psychological, routine activities, and rational choice theories.[26]

The Act and the Offender. In their **general theory of crime (GTC)**, Gottfredson and Hirschi consider the criminal offender and the criminal act as separate concepts (see Figure 10.4). On the one hand, criminal acts, such as robberies or burglaries, are illegal events or deeds that people engage in when they perceive them to be advantageous. For example, burglaries are typically committed by young males looking for cash, liquor, and entertainment; the crime provides "easy, short-term gratification."[27] Even if the number of offenders remains constant, crime rates may fluctuate because of the presence or absence of criminal opportunities. This aspect of the theory relies on concepts similar to rational choice and routine activities theories: People commit crime when it promises rewards with minimum threat of pain or punishment. If targets are well protected by effective guardians, crime rates will diminish.

On the other hand, criminal offenders are people predisposed to commit crimes. They are not robots who commit crime without restraint; their days are also filled with conventional behaviours, such as going to school, parties, concerts, and church. But given the same set of criminal opportunities, criminogenic people have a much higher probability of violating the law than noncriminals do.

Connections

In his original version of control theory discussed in Chapter 8, Hirschi focused on the social controls that attach people to conventional society; in this new work, he concentrates on self-control as a stabilizing force. The two views are connected, however, because both social control (or social bonds) and self-control are acquired through early experiences with effective parenting.

| Figure 10.4 | The General Theory of Crime |

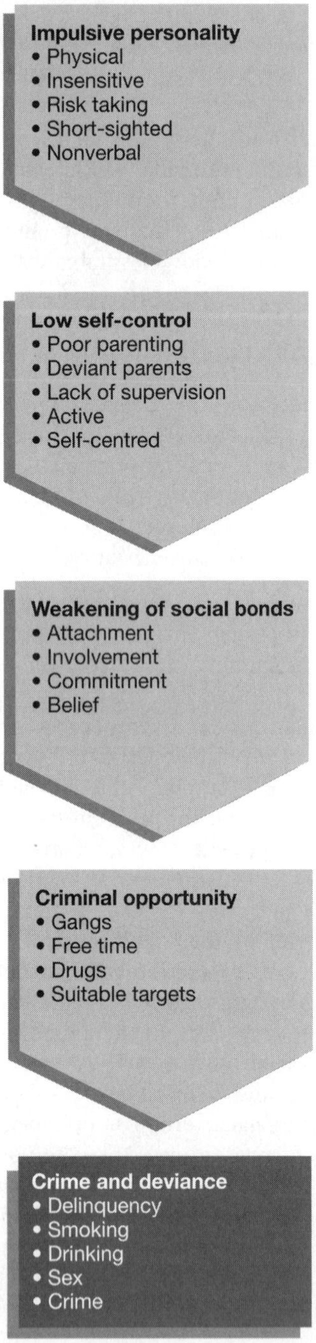

Impulsive personality
• Physical
• Insensitive
• Risk taking
• Short-sighted
• Nonverbal

Low self-control
• Poor parenting
• Deviant parents
• Lack of supervision
• Active
• Self-centred

Weakening of social bonds
• Attachment
• Involvement
• Commitment
• Belief

Criminal opportunity
• Gangs
• Free time
• Drugs
• Suitable targets

Crime and deviance
• Delinquency
• Smoking
• Drinking
• Sex
• Crime

By recognizing that there are stable differences in people's propensity to commit crime, the general theory adds a biosocial element to the concept of social control. Individual differences are stable over the life course and so is the propensity to commit crime; it is only opportunity that changes.

What Makes People Crime-Prone? What, then, causes people to become excessively crime-prone? The explana-tion for differences in the tendency to commit criminal acts can be found in a person's level of **self-control**. People with limited self-control tend to be impulsive, making them less sensitive, physical (rather than mental), risk-taking, short-sighted, and nonverbal.[28] They have a "here and now" orientation and refuse to work for distant goals; they lack diligence, tenacity, and persistence in a course of action. People who are impulsive tend to lack self-control. They are adventuresome, active, physical, and self-centred. As they mature, they have unstable mar-riages, jobs, and friendships.[29] People lacking self-control are less likely to feel shame if they engage in deviant acts and more likely to find these acts pleasurable.[30]

Criminal acts are attractive to these people because they provide easy and immediate gratification: "money without work, sex without courtship, revenge without court delays."[31] Because those with low self-control enjoy risky, exciting, or thrilling behaviours with imme-diate benefits, they are more likely to enjoy criminal acts that require stealth, danger, agility, speed, and power than conventional acts, which demand long-term study and cognitive and verbal skills.

Considering their desire for easy pleasures, it should come as no surprise that people lacking in self-control will also engage in noncriminal behaviours that provide them with immediate and short-term gratification, such as smoking, drinking, gambling, and illicit sexuality.[32]

What causes people to lack self-control? The origins of poor self-control are felt to be linked to inadequate child-rearing practices. Parents who refuse or are unable to monitor a child's behaviour, to recognize deviant behav-iour when it occurs, and to punish that behaviour will pro-duce children who lack self-control. Kids who are not attached to their parents, who are poorly supervised, and whose parents are criminal or deviant themselves are the most likely to develop poor self-control. In a sense, lack of self-control is a "natural occurrence" that will happen in the absence of steps taken to stop its development.[33]

Low self-control develops early in life and remains stable into and through adulthood.[34] Considering the continuity of criminal motivation, we might question the utility of the juvenile justice system and of giving special treatment to delinquent offenders. Why separate youthful and adult offenders legally, when the source of their criminality is essentially the same?[35]

Self-Control and Crime. The principles of self-control theory can be used to explain all varieties of criminal behaviour and all the social and behavioural correlates of crime. That is, such widely disparate crimes as burglary, robbery, embezzlement, drug dealing, murder, rape, and insider trading all stem from a deficiency of self-control. Likewise, gender, racial, and ecological differences in the crime rate can be explained by discrepancies in self-con-trol. Put another way, if the male crime rate is higher than the female crime rate (which it is), the discrepancy can be explained by the fact that males have lower levels of self-control.

Unlike other theoretical models that are limited to explaining narrow segments of criminal behaviour (such as theories of teenage gang formation), Gottfredson and Hirschi argue that self-control applies equally to all crimes, ranging from murder to corporate theft. For example, rates of white-collar crime remain quite low because people lacking in self-control rarely attain the position necessary to commit those crimes. However, relatively few white-collar criminals lack self-control in the manner rapists and burglars lack self-control. As well, people become less crime-prone as they age. While the criminal activity of low-self-control individuals also declines, they maintain an offence rate that remains consistently higher than those with strong self-control.

Supporting Evidence for the GTC. Several research efforts have been conducted that support this theoretical viewpoint. One approach identifies indicators of impulsiveness and self-control and determines whether scales measuring these factors correlate with measures of criminal activity.[36] For example, both male and female drunk drivers were found to be impulsive individuals who manifest low self-control.[37] Research on violent recidivists indicates that they can be distinguished from other offenders on the basis of their impulsive personality structure.[38] Studies of incarcerated youths show that they enjoy risk-taking behaviour and hold values and attitudes that suggest impulsivity.[39] Kids who take drugs and commit crime have been shown to be impulsive and enjoy engaging in risky behaviours.[40] In one recent study, low self-control was able to predict deviant behaviour (cutting class and drinking) among a sample of college students.[41] And a similar analysis of self-report data found that the quality of parental supervision influenced both self-control and subsequent deviant behaviour.[42] One study of Canadian youth found that kids with an "egocentric personality" develop weak social ties and are more likely to engage in delinquency and unconventional behaviours.[43]

Other recent studies have noted that low self-control may interact with criminal opportunity in the decision to commit crimes.[44] It is possible that the causal chain flows from (1) an impulsive personality to (2) lack of self-control to (3) the withering of social bonds to (4) the opportunity to commit crime and delinquency to (5) deviant behaviour.[45]

Analyzing the General Theory of Crime. Gottfredson and Hirschi's general theory provides answers to many of the questions left unresolved by Hirschi's original single-factor control model. By integrating the concepts of criminality and crime, Gottfredson and Hirschi help explain that even people who lack self-control can escape criminality, if they lack criminal opportunity. People who are at risk because they have an impulsive personality may forgo criminal careers because they have noncriminal opportunities that satisfy their impulsive needs: They enroll in tennis lessons; they go to church; they join the Boy Scouts; they enter the military; they have great athletic ability and make the team. In contrast, if the opportunity is strong enough, even those people with relatively strong self-control may be tempted to violate the law; the incentives to commit crime may overwhelm self-control.

Integrating criminal propensity and criminal opportunity can explain why the so-called "good kid," who has a strong school record and positive parental relationships, gets involved in drugs or vandalism or why the corporate executive with a spotless record gets caught up in business fraud. Even a successful executive may find his or her self-control inadequate if the potential for illegal gain runs into the tens of millions. It is also possible, as Michael Benson and Elizabeth Moore contend, that the fear of failure, and not the mere desire for excessive profits, overwhelms an affluent businessperson's self-control. During tough economic times, the impulsive manager who fears dismissal may be tempted to circumvent the law to improve the bottom line.[46]

Although the general theory seems persuasive, several questions and criticisms remain unanswered, including the following.[47]

1. *Tautological.* The theory involves circular reasoning: How do we know when people are impulsive? When they commit crimes! Are all criminals impulsive? Of course, or else they would not have broken the law![48] However, impulsivity is not in itself a propensity to commit crime but a condition that inhibits people from appreciating the long-term consequences of their behaviour. If given the opportunity, they are more likely to indulge in criminal acts than the nonimpulsive.[49] Therefore, impulsivity and criminality are not equivalent concepts. Some impulsive people may channel their reckless energies into noncrime activity, such as trading on the commodities markets or real estate speculation, and make a legitimate fortune.

2. *Personality disorder.* Saying someone lacks self-control implies that he or she suffers from a personality defect that makes him or her impulsive and rash. Psychologists have long sought evidence of a "criminal personality,"[50] yet it has proved elusive. There is still no conclusive proof that criminals can be distinguished from noncriminals on the basis of personality alone.

3. *Ecological differences.* GTC also fails to address ecological patterns in the crime rate. For example, if crime rates are higher in Vancouver than in London, Ontario, are Vancouverites more impulsive than Londoners? Can these differences be explained solely by variation in criminal opportunity? Little effort has been made to account for the influence of culture, ecology, economy, and so on in criminality.

Crime rate differences may simply reflect criminal opportunity, as areas have different levels of effective law enforcement, stricter laws, and higher levels of guardianship. Opportunity is controlled by economy and culture.

4. *Individual differences.* Although distinct gender differences in the crime rate exist, there is little evidence that males are more impulsive than females. Similarly, can racial differences in crime be explained as a failure of child-rearing practices in minority families?[51] We can't overlook issues of institutional racism, poverty, and relative deprivation, which have been shown to have a significant impact on crime rate differentials.

5. *Moral beliefs.* The general theory also ignores the moral concept of right and wrong, or "belief."[52] Does this mean that learning and assimilation of moral values have little effect on criminality? Belief is a central concept of social bond theory, but not control theory.

6. *Do people change?* The general theory assumes that people do not change; it is opportunity that changes. Is it possible that human personality and behaviour patterns remain little altered over the life course? Research indicates that factors that help control criminal behaviour, such as peer relations and school performance, vary over time. Factors that have a controlling effect in early adolescence may fade and be replaced by others.[53] For example, having delinquent peers encourages future criminality, and the propensity to commit crimes is influenced by peer relations that develop in adolescence.[54] As children mature, peer influence over delinquent behaviour choices continues to grow; in contrast, the GTC suggests that the influence of friends should be stable and unchanging.[55]

   Changing life circumstances, such as starting and leaving school, abusing substances and getting "straight," and starting or ending personal relationships, all have an influence on the frequency of offending.[56] People are more likely to commit crimes when using illegal drugs and less likely when they are living with a spouse. These findings contradict self-control theory, which assumes that criminality is independent of personal relationships.

6. *Cross-cultural differences.* There is evidence that criminals in other countries do not lack self-control, indicating that GTC may be culturally limited.[57] Behaviour that may be considered imprudent and risky in one culture may be socially acceptable in another and therefore cannot be explained by a "lack of self-control."[58]

While these questions remain, the strength of the general theory lies in its scope and breadth; it attempts to explain all forms of crime and deviance, from lower-class gang delinquency to sexual harassment in the business community.[59] By integrating concepts of criminal choice, criminal opportunity, socialization, and personality, deviant behaviour may originate at the same source. The GTC remains one of the key developments of modern criminological theory.

Life-Course Theories

What causes the onset of criminality? What sustains a criminal career over a person's life course? A number of themes are now emerging. One is that the seeds of a criminal career are planted early in life. Research now shows that kids who will later become delinquents begin their deviant careers at a very early (preschool) age.[60] Studies of narcotics addicts show that the earlier the onset of substance abuse, the more frequent, varied, and sustained the addict's criminal career.[61]

Another theme is the **continuity of crime:** The best predictor of future criminality is past criminality. Kids who are repeatedly in trouble during adolescence are the ones who will still be antisocial as adults. Criminal activity beginning early in the life course is likely to be sustained, because these offenders seem to lack the "social survival skills" necessary to find work or develop the interpersonal relationships needed to allow them to "drop out" of crime.[62]

The third of the integrated approaches considered here, life-course theory, sees criminality as multidimensional, having multiple roots: maladaptive personality traits, educational failure, and dysfunctional family relations. Criminality, according to this view, cannot be attributed to a single cause, nor does it represent a single underlying tendency.[63]

Life-course theorists conclude that multiple social, personal, and economic factors can influence criminality and that as these factors change over time, so, too, does criminal involvement.[64] As people make important transitions in their life—from child to adolescent, from adolescent to adult, from unwed to married—the nature of their social interactions changes and so, too, does their behaviour. Children whose socialization is ineffective because of improper, maladaptive parenting later build on this improper interactional style and engage in behaviour that leads them to be rejected by their peers and to experience academic failure.[65] They then turn to deviant

Connections

As you may recall from Chapter 3, a great deal of research has been conducted on the relationship of age and crime and the activities of chronic offenders. This body of scholarship has prompted interest in the life cycle of crime. It is also buttressed by social process theories, as discussed in Chapter 8.

peers from whom they learn new forms of antisocial behaviour. Early childhood family conflicts and lack of a strong bond with parents open the door for social conflict in later adolescence.[66]

The Glueck Research

One of the cornerstones of the recent life-course research lies in renewed interest in the research efforts of Sheldon and Eleanor Glueck. While at Harvard University in the 1930s, they popularized research on the life cycle of delinquent careers. In a series of longitudinal research studies, they followed the careers of known delinquents to determine the factors that predicted persistent offending.[67] They made extensive use of interviews and records in their elaborate comparisons of delinquents and nondelinquents.[68]

This research was a precursor of the life-course school, focusing on early onset of delinquency as a harbinger of a criminal career: "The deeper the roots of childhood maladjustment, the smaller the chance of adult adjustment." Offending careers were also stable: Children who are antisocial early in life are the ones most likely to continue their offending careers into adulthood.

A number of personal and social factors are related to persistent offending, the most important of which are family relations, such as the quality of discipline and emotional ties with parents. The adolescent raised in a large, single-parent family of limited economic means and educational achievement was the one most vulnerable to delinquency.

As well as looking at social variables, biological and psychological traits such as body type, intelligence, and personality, were found to play a role too. Children with low intelligence, with a background of mental disease, and with a powerful physique (mesomorphs) were the ones most likely to become persistent offenders.

This research was ignored for nearly 30 years as the study of crime and delinquency shifted almost exclusively to the social and social-psychological factors (poverty, neighbourhood deterioration, socialization) that formed the nucleus of structural and process theories.

Life Course Emerges

During the past decade, the Glueck "legacy" was "rediscovered" as a way to study criminal careers.[69] It has revived the interest in asking some basic questions about how a criminal career unfolds over a person's life cycle:[70]

1. Why do people begin committing antisocial acts?
2. Why do some stop or desist, while others continue or persist?
3. Why do some escalate the severity of their criminality—that is, go from shoplifting to drug dealing to armed robbery—while others deescalate and commit less serious crime as they mature?
4. If some terminate their criminal activity, what, if anything, causes them to begin again?
5. Why do some criminals specialize in certain types of crime, while others are generalists engaging in a garden variety of antisocial behaviour?

A number of key research efforts have found that criminogenic influences change and develop over time. In studies on delinquency prevention, it has been found that poor parental discipline and monitoring is key to the onset of criminality in early childhood. Then, in middle childhood, social rejection by conventional peers and academic failure sustained antisocial behaviour. In later adolescence, commitment to a deviant peer group created a "training ground" for crime. Kids who are improperly socialized by unskilled parents are the ones most likely to rebel by wandering the streets with their deviant peers.[71] While the onset of a criminal career is a function of poor parenting skills, its maintenance and support are connected to social relations that emerge later in life.[72] Similar results have been obtained from longitudinal analyses of elementary school–age boys that indicate that early onset is correlated with social withdrawal, depression, deviant peers, and family problems, while later onset (at ages 13 or 14) is related to low educational motivation.[73]

From these and similar efforts has emerged a view of crime that incorporates personal change and growth. The factors that produce crime and delinquency at one point in the life cycle may not be relevant at another; as people mature, the social, physical, and environmental influences on their behaviour are transformed.

In the following sections, we review some of the more important concepts associated with the life-course perspective and discuss three prominent life-course theories.

Is There a Problem Behaviour Syndrome?

Most criminological theories portray crime as the result of social problems rather than their cause. For example, learning theorists view a troubled home life and deviant friends as precursors of criminality; structural theorists maintain that acquiring deviant cultural values leads to criminality. In contrast, the life-course view is that criminality may best be understood as one of many social problems faced by at-risk youth. Criminality may be part of a **problem behaviour syndrome (PBS)**, a group of antisocial behaviours that cluster together and typically involve family dysfunction, substance abuse, smoking, precocious sexuality and early pregnancy, educational underachievement, suicide attempts, sensation seeking, and unemployment.[74] People who suffer from one of these conditions typically exhibit symptoms of the rest.[75] All varieties of criminal behaviour, including violence, theft, and public order crimes, may be part of a generalized PBS, indicating that all forms of antisocial behaviour have similar developmental patterns.[76]

Those who suffer PBS are prone to have a range of social problems, from abusing drugs to being accident-prone to requiring more health care and hospitalization than the general population.[77] PBS has been linked to personality (for example, rebelliousness and low ego), family problems (interfamily conflict, parental mental disorder), and educational failure (school rejection).[78] Kids who suffer PBS, including drug use, delinquency, and precocious sexuality, display symptoms at a very early age.[79]

Many examples support the existence of PBS. A survey of students in grades 6, 9, and 12 showed that children who experienced physical and sexual abuse at the hands of parents or other adults were also likely to have eating disorders (binge eating, purging, anorexia) and increased levels of cigarette smoking, alcohol consumption, stress, anxiety, hard-drug use, and suicidal thoughts.[80] Other research links family violence to a variety of family and environmental problems that seem to cluster together: low income, single parent, residence in an isolated poor area, lack of family support or resources, racism, and prolonged exposure to poverty.[81]

In one important study showing the nature of PBS, a sample of 400 youths were measured repeatedly over a six-year cycle. Behaviours that clustered together included delinquency, substance abuse, school misconduct and underachievement, precocious sexual behaviour, violence, suicide, and mental health problems.[82] Problem behaviours were also found to be stable: Subjects who experienced multiple problems at age 15 continued to experience them at age 21. In a subsequent analysis of adolescent misbehaviour, PBS might involve one of several clusters of behaviour, including drug "specialists," crime specialists, and "generalists" who engage in both delinquency and drug abuse. Generalists are the most likely to suffer PBS, displaying higher levels of psychological problems, a lack of control, and lower emotional stability.[83]

So problem behaviours—including violence, drug abuse, and theft—may cluster in a number of ways, affecting people as they mature from adolescence into adulthood.[84] The interconnection of problem behaviours should increase the risk of teenage pregnancy, AIDS, and other sources of social distress that require a combination of behaviours (sex, drug use, violence).

The Course of Criminal Careers

Life-course theorists recognize that there may be more than a single road travelled by career criminals: Some may specialize in violence and extortion; some may be involved in theft and fraud; others may engage in a variety of criminal acts. Some offenders may begin their career early in life, while others are "late bloomers" who begin committing crime at the age when most people desist.

Pathways to Crime. Are there different pathways to crime? In a study of a longitudinal cohort,[85] three distinct paths to a criminal career are identified (see Figure 10.5):

1. The **authority conflict pathway** begins at an early age with stubborn behaviour and defiance of parents. This leads to defiance (doing things one's own way, refusing to do things, disobedience) and then to authority avoidance (staying out late, truancy, running away).

2. The **covert pathway** begins with minor underhanded behaviour (lying, shoplifting) that leads to property damage (setting fires, vandalism) and eventually escalates to more serious forms of criminality, ranging from joyriding, pocket picking, larceny, and fencing to passing bad cheques, using bad credit cards, stealing cars, dealing drugs, and breaking and entering.

3. The **overt pathway** consists of an escalation of aggressive acts beginning with aggression (annoying others, bullying) leading to physical (and gang) fighting and on to violence (attacking someone, strongarming, forced theft).

This research indicates that each of these paths may lead to a sustained deviant career. Some youths enter two and even three paths simultaneously: They are stubborn, lie to teachers and parents, are bullies, and commit petty thefts. These are the adolescents most likely to become

| Figure 10.5 | Pathways to crime |

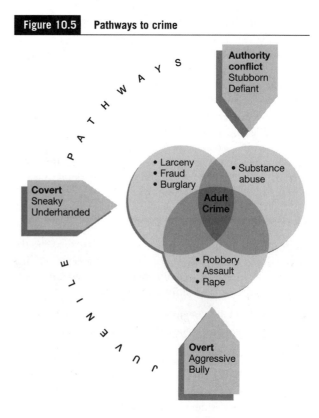

Culture, Gender, Ethnicity, and Criminology

Violent Female Criminals

Why do some people become persistent offenders while others desist from crime? Are the paths taken by males and females similar? While considerable research is now being devoted to gender differences in the crime rate, little has been done to chart the life course of violent female street criminals. To correct this oversight, research by Deborah Baskin and Ira Sommers and by Henry Brownstein and his associates used interviews with violent female felons in New York, providing considerable insight into the formation and maintenance of a criminal career.

They found that about 60 percent of violent female offenders begin their criminal career at a very early age; about half reported regular fighting as early as 10 years old, and about 40 percent reported that they regularly left home carrying a weapon. In contrast, the other 40 percent reported that they did not engage in fighting until much later, not until they had left school. Because of the clear time differential in when these females began their criminal careers, Baskin and Sommers conducted an independent analysis of the early- and late-onset offenders.

The women in both groups suffered from severe social and emotional problems. All were likely to have been raised in single-parent families and to have received little parental supervision. Both groups experienced physical and sexual abuse at the hand of a parent or guardian and were likely to have witnessed abuse between their guardians. Almost half were raised in households that relied on public welfare. More than half had a parent who was either a substance abuser or who had been

incarcerated sometime during his or her childhood.

Women in the early-onset group could be distinguished by the severity of their childhood problems. They were the ones most likely to reside in areas with high concentrations of poverty and to have family histories of psychiatric problems requiring hospitalization. They were more likely to be truant, leave school early, and associate with delinquent peers while in school. They also were more likely to be placed in a juvenile detention centre.

The major distinction between the groups, however, could be found in the scale and direction of their offending careers. While both groups were drug users, early-onset women began abusing substances two years ahead of the late-onset group. The early-onset group were involved in a variety of crimes, including serious robberies, assaults, and burglaries, even before they became involved with drug use. In contrast, the later-onset group were involved mostly in nonviolent crimes, such as shoplifting and prostitution, up until they began taking drugs. The violent offending of the latter group was thus clearly part of a drug–crime connection. In contrast, the violent behaviour of the early-onset women was part of a generalized PBS.

A number of research studies support these findings. Helene Raskin White and Stephen Hansell found that girls who begin using alcohol early in life are the ones most likely to be aggressive and violent in their later years. Although women are less likely to be aggressive than men, early alcohol abuse was a much stronger predictor of female than male violence. Henry Brownstein and his associates conducted interviews with 215

women convicted of murder. Most of these women told a familiar story: The most violent had histories of juvenile violence, drug abuse, and personal victimization. The researchers found that 65 percent had participated in some violent activity and 64 percent claimed to have seriously harmed someone when they were growing up; 58 percent had been the victim of serious physical harm, and 49 percent had been sexually abused. These women had a long-term commitment to crime, beginning in early childhood and continuing through their use of deadly violence in their adulthood. Brownstein also focused on the behaviour of 19 women who had killed in the context of drug dealing. Some of these acts were motivated by economic interests, while others were motivated out of their relationship with a man—killing on behalf of a man or out of fear of a man.

These research efforts support the life-course view: Events in these women's adult lives shaped the direction of their offending careers. The researchers found that there are in fact different pathways to a crime and that both environmental and serendipitous life circumstances (such as meeting the wrong man) influence offending. These conclusions support a life-course view and repudiate the latent trait approach.

Sources: Deborah Baskin and Ira Sommers, "Females' Initiation into Violent Street Crime," *Justice Quarterly* 10 (1993): 559–81; Helene Raskin White and Stephen Hansell, "The Moderating Effects of Gender and Hostility on the Alcohol–Aggression Relationship," *Journal of Research in Crime and Delinquency* 33 (1996): 450–70; Henry Brownstein, Barry Spunt, Susan Crimmins, and Sandra Langley, "Women Who Kill in Drug Market Situations," *Justice Quarterly* 12 (1995): 473–98.

persistent offenders as they mature. While some persistent offenders may specialize in one type of behaviour, others engage in a variety of criminal acts and antisocial behaviours. For example, they may start out cheating on tests and bullying kids in the schoolyard, then move on to take drugs, commit a burglary, steal a car, and then shoplift from a store.

Adolescent-Limited Offenders and Life-Course Persisters. In addition to taking different paths to criminality, people may begin their journey at different times in their life. Some are precocious, beginning their criminal careers at an early age; others are late bloomers who stay out of trouble until their teenage years. Some offenders may peak at an early age, while others persist into their adulthood. Research now shows that there are a number of types or "classes" of criminal careers that seem to reflect changes in the life course.[86]

Whereas the prevalence and frequency of antisocial behaviour peaks in adolescence and then diminishes for most offenders (these offenders are **adolescent-limited**), a small group of life-course persistent deviants offend well into their adulthood.[87] Life-course persistents combine family dysfunction with severe neurological problems that predispose them to antisocial behaviour patterns. These afflictions can be the result of maternal drug abuse, poor perinatal nutrition, or exposure to toxic agents such as lead. Those afflicted may have lower verbal ability, which inhibits reasoning skills, learning ability, and school achievement. During their youth, adolescent-limited delinquents mimic the behaviour of these more troubled teens but reduce the frequency of their offending as they mature at around age 18.[88]

Research also shows that kids who mature faster (**pseudomaturity**) have a greater chance of becoming life-course persisters. The earlier an adolescent engages in substance abuse and sexuality or suffers emotional distress, the more likely he or she will be involved in adult deviance.[89]

Early Versus Late Onset. While most life-course persisters are "early starters," some begin their offending career in late adolescence, after age 14. These "late starters" are also at high risk for adult criminality regardless of what age they began their offending careers.[90]

Why do some people enter a path to crime later rather than sooner? Research shows that early-starter adolescents experience (1) poor parenting, which leads them into (2) deviant behaviours and then (3) involvement with delinquent groups. In contrast, late starters follow a somewhat different path: (1) poor parenting leads to (2) identification with a delinquent group and then into (3) deviant involvement. By implication, adolescents who suffer poor parenting and are at risk for deviant careers can avoid criminality if they can bypass involvement with delinquent peers.[91]

Additional research efforts have found that early- and late-onset offenders take different paths into crime and are influenced by different life factors. Criminal peers exert a greater influence on the late bloomers than their more precocious peers. Late starters thus seem to be influenced by their peer group interaction, a factor that develops and expands as an adolescent travels the life course.[92] In a study of incarcerated criminals, early starters were more likely to be the victim of child abuse than later starters were. In addition, criminal punishments seemed to have a greater deterrent effect on early starters. It is possible that early starters learn from their experiences and become more cunning criminals, increasing their offending rates while avoiding detection.[93]

The discovery that people begin their criminal careers at different ages and follow different paths and trajectories of offending gives important support for the life-course view. If all criminals have a singular latent trait that makes them crime-prone, it would be unlikely that these variations in criminal careers would be observed. It is difficult to explain such concepts as "late onset" and "adolescent-limited behaviour" from the perspective of latent trait theory.

An ongoing effort has been made to track persistent offenders over their life course.[94] The early data seem to support what is already known about delinquent-criminal career patterns: Early onset predicts later offending, there is continuity in crime (juvenile offenders are the ones most likely to become adult criminals), and chronic offenders commit a significant portion of all crimes.[95]

Based on these findings, a number of systematic theories that account for the onset, continuance, and desistance from crime have been formulated. In the following sections, we discuss three life-course theories in some detail.

Farrington's Theory of Delinquent Development

One of the most important of the cohort longitudinal studies tracking persistent offenders is the Cambridge Study in Delinquent Development, which followed the offending careers of 411 London boys born in 1953.[96] This study was directed by David Farrington and is one of the most serious attempts to isolate the factors that predict the continuity of criminal behaviour throughout the life course. Using self-report data, in-depth interviews, and psychological testing, the boys were interviewed eight times over a period of 24 years, beginning at age 8 and continuing to age 32.[97]

The Cambridge study is important because it shows the same patterns found in other research: the existence of chronic offenders, the continuity of offending, and early onset leading to persistent criminality. Farrington found that the traits present in persistent offenders can be observed as early as age eight. The chronic criminal, typically a male, has been born into a low-income, large family headed by parents who have criminal records and

Famous Canadian Criminals

The Socialite Who Bought a Gun

On January 21, 1995, Earl Joudrie, a Calgary business tycoon, was leaving his condo after an emotional meeting with his wife. He'd confirmed his intention to seek a divorce. Suddenly, he was stunned by a "whack across his back which felt like a...two by four." He fell to the ground where Dorothy Joudrie pumped five more shots into him. She was "cold and controlled," he testified, "like a person I had never known." At her trial for attempted murder Mrs. Joudrie relied on the controversial defence of automatism, a robot-like state in which she was unaware of her actions. Her lawyer, Noel O'Brien, based his argument on a ruling by Canadian Supreme Court Justice Bertha Wilson: "The mental state of an accused at the critical moment she pulls the trigger cannot be understood except in terms of the cumulative effect of months or years of brutality." The brutality had occurred more than a decade earlier, but had resulted in hospitalization on three previous occasions, leaving her nose broken, her eyes blackened, and her ribs bruised.

Mrs. Joudrie was found not criminally responsible by reason of mental disorder and was required to attend the Alberta Hospital Edmonton (AHE) for assessment by the Provincial Board of Review to determine if she were a significant

threat to public safety. Initially, this was to be a mere formality, but the hospital board decided to keep her in hospital for further testing, and while she was there, she was assaulted by a patient who broke her nose. She was confined to the mental hospital for five months, before being set free in 1996 by Alberta's provincial review board. The ruling meant she was no longer considered a threat.

She also spent a month at the Betty Ford alcohol treatment centre in California, followed by 11 days in Calgary's Foothills Hospital where she was diagnosed with Grave's Disease (a thyroid condition) as well as lymphatic cancer. Restrictions were placed on her travel and she was not allowed to drink alcohol. She said of her five months in the mental hospital

that it "was punishment, there was no therapy, there was no treatment, and no compassion." She also said, "What got me out of the mental hospital was the fact that I had the money to fight the system. I want to speak up for the people who aren't so fortunate." Mrs. Joudrie and her lawyer credit her release to the fact that her money purchased the best legal and psychiatric specialists available. Others inside have lost hope, and they didn't have $50 000 for psychiatrists and doctors to prove they weren't a threat.

Having recovered from surgery for her cancer, Mrs. Joudrie was looking forward to resuming her extensive charity work, her golf and bridge, and "trying to make a difference with others less fortunate" than herself. After a difficult life, she died in February 2002.

Sources: Canadian Press, October 20, 1998; Kevin Udahl, "The 'Scariest Place In The World': How Dorothy Joudrie's Money Rescued Her From Hell," *Alberta Report*, November 16, 1998; Mary Nemeth, "A Turbulent and Troubled Life Laid Bare," *Maclean's*, May 13, 1996; Randy Olson, "Courts Confront the Question of Free Will," *Alberta Report/Western Report*, April 24, 1995; Les Sillars, "Unequal Before the Law?", *Alberta Report/Western Report*, March 6, 1995; Mary Nemeth, "Dorothy Joudrie's 'Nightmare' Ends," *Maclean's*, May 20, 1996; Les Sillars, "Until Fists, Alcoholism and Betrayal Do Us Part," *Alberta Report/Western Report*, May 20, 1996; Joe Woodward "Behind Robo-wife Stands Tyranny," *Alberta Report/Western Report*, May 27, 1996.

with delinquent older siblings. The future criminal receives poor parental supervision, including the use of harsh or erratic punishment and child-rearing techniques; his parents are likely to divorce or separate.

The chronic offender tends to associate with friends who are also future criminals. By age eight, he is already exhibiting antisocial behaviour, including dishonesty and aggressiveness. At school, he tends to have low educa-

tional achievement and is restless, troublesome, hyperactive, impulsive, and often truant.

After leaving school at age 18, the persistent criminal tends to maintain a relatively well-paid but low-status job and is likely to have an erratic work history and periods of unemployment. Deviant behaviour is specialized, as the typical offender commits property offences, such as theft and burglary, and engages in violence, vandalism, drug use, excessive drinking, drunk driving, smoking, reckless driving, and sexual promiscuity. This is evidence of a generalized problem behaviour syndrome. Chronic offenders are more likely to live away from home and have conflict with their parents. They wear tattoos, go out most evenings, and enjoy hanging out with groups of their friends. They are much more likely than nonoffenders to get involved in fights, to carry weapons, and to use them in violent encounters. The frequency of offending reaches a peak in the teenage years (about 17 or 18) and then declines in the 20s, when the offender "settles down."

By the time he reaches his 30s, the former delinquent is likely to be separated or divorced from his wife and to be an absent parent. His employment record remains spotty, and he moves often to rental units rather than owner-occupied housing. His life is still characterized by evenings out, heavy drinking and substance abuse, and more violent behaviour than his contemporaries'. Because the typical offender provides the same kind of deprived and disrupted family life for his own children that he experienced, the social experiences and conditions that produce delinquency are carried on from one generation to the next.

Nonoffenders and Desisters. Farrington has also identified factors that predict the discontinuity of criminal offences: People who exhibit these factors have a background that puts them at risk to crime, but they either are able to remain nonoffenders or begin a criminal career but later desist. The factors that "protect" high-risk youth from even beginning a criminal career include having a personality that renders them somewhat shy, having few friends (at age eight), having a nondeviant family, and being highly regarded by their mother. Shy kids with few friends avoid damaging relationships with other adolescent boys and are therefore able to avoid criminality.

What caused offenders to desist? Holding a relatively good job helps reduce criminal activity. Unemployment seems to be related to the escalation of theft offences, but violence and substance abuse are unaffected by unemployment. In a similar vein, getting married also helps diminish criminal activity. However, finding a spouse who is also involved in criminal activity and has a criminal record increases criminal involvement.

Physical relocation also helps some offenders desist. Leaving the city and going to a more rural or suburban area was linked to reductions in criminal activity. Relocation forces offenders to sever ties with co-offenders.

Although employment, marriage, and relocation helped offenders desist, not all found the key to success. At-risk youth who managed to avoid criminal convictions were unlikely to avoid other social problems. Rather than becoming prosperous homeowners with flourishing careers, they tended to live in unkempt homes and have

large debts and low-paying jobs. Desisters were more likely to remain single and live alone: Youths who experience social isolation at age 8 also experience it at age 32.

Theoretical Modelling. Farrington's theoretical model of criminality is as follows:

1. Childhood factors predict a continuity of teenage antisocial behaviour and adult dysfunction.
2. Personal and social factors are associated with criminal propensity. Kids who suffer economic deprivation, poor parenting, and an antisocial family and have personalities marked by impulsivity, hyperactivity, and attention deficit disorder are the most likely to become delinquent.
3. Adolescents who have criminogenic tendencies are motivated or "energized" to offend by their desire for material goods, excitement, and status with peers. Boys from less affluent families are unable to achieve these goals through legitimate means so they tend to commit offences.
4. Life events influence behaviour, and family life is critical to a deviant career. Adolescents exposed to effective child rearing, including consistent discipline and close supervision, build up internal inhibitions against offending in a social learning process. In contrast, this same learning process causes kids raised in antisocial families to develop dysfunctional beliefs and behaviour.
5. The chance of offending in any particular situation depends on the perception of the costs and benefits of crime and noncrime alternatives. More impulsive boys are more likely to offend because they are less likely to consider possible future consequences.
6. Factors that encourage criminality at one period during the life course may inhibit it in another. Being nervous and withdrawn and having few friends is negatively related to adolescent and teenage offending but positively related to adult social dysfunction.
7. Adult criminal behaviour is predicted by external and internal behaviours. External behaviours include engaging in violence and getting arrested and convicted for crimes. Internalizing behaviours include psychiatric disorders, substance abuse, nervousness, and social isolation.

This theory suggests that experiences over the life course shape the direction and flow of behaviour choices. People are not controlled by a single, unalterable latent trait. This life-course theory is age-graded. Although there may be continuity in offending, the factors that predict criminality at one point in the life course may not be the ones that predict criminality at another. While most adult criminals began their career in childhood, life events may help some children forgo criminality as they mature.

Interactional Theory

Terence Thornberry has also proposed an age-graded view of crime that he calls **interactional theory** (see Figure 10.6).[98]

Thornberry says that the onset of crime can be traced to a deterioration of the social bond during adolescence, marked by a weakened attachment to parents, low commitment to school, and lack of belief in conventional values. This view recognizes structural variables, for example, that growing up in a socially disorganized area will also create the greatest risk of a weakened social bond and subsequent delinquency. The onset of a criminal career is supported by residence in a social setting in which deviant values and attitudes can be learned and reinforced by delinquent peers.

Interactional theory also holds that serious delinquent youths form belief systems that are consistent with their deviant lifestyle. They seek out the company of other kids who share their interests, who are likely to reinforce their beliefs about the world, and who support their delinquent behaviour. According to interactional theory then, delinquents seek out a criminal peer group in the same fashion that chess buffs look for others who share their passion for the game—hanging out with other chess players helps improve their game. Similarly, deviant peers do not turn an otherwise "innocent" boy into a delinquent. They support and amplify the behaviour of kids who have already accepted a delinquent way of life; they support and amplify offending patterns.

The key idea here is that causal influences are bidirectional. Weak bonds lead kids to develop relationships with deviant peers and get involved in high-rate delinquency. Frequent delinquency involvement further weakens bonds and makes it difficult to reestablish conventional ones. Delinquency-promoting factors tend to reinforce one another and sustain a chronic criminal career.

Interactional theory is considered age-graded because it incorporates an element of the **cognitive perspective** in psychology: As people mature, they pass through different stages of reasoning and sophistication.[99] In this way, criminality is a developmental process that takes on different meaning and form as a person matures. The causal process is a dynamic one that develops over a person's life.[100] During early adolescence, attachment to the family is the single most important determinant of whether a youth will adjust to conventional society and be shielded from delinquency. By mid-adolescence, the influence of the family is replaced by the world of friends, school, and

David Farrington's longitudinal research found that the persistent offender was typically a male who began his criminal career as a property offender. Here we see a looter robbing a dépanneur in Montreal. Others stole about 15 cases of beer while a stunned cashier stood helplessly behind the counter. Looters threw beer bottles to break the store's window. Customers emerged wearing metal baskets to protect their heads before police took control of the scene. Does the explanation for this behaviour lie in socialization, poor parental supervision, or erratic punishment and child-rearing techniques?

| Figure 10.6 | Overview of the interactional theory of delinquency |

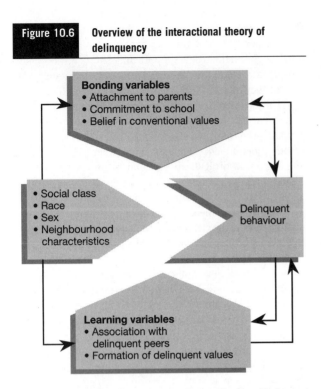

SOURCE: Terence Thornberry, Margaret Farnsworth, Alan Lizotte, and Susan Stern, "A Longitudinal Examination of the Causes and Correlates of Delinquency," working paper No. 1, Rochester Youth Development Study (Albany, NY: Hindelang Criminal Justice Research Center, 1987), p. 11.

youth culture. In adulthood, a person's behavioural choices are shaped by his or her place in conventional society and his or her own nuclear family.

One test of this model is to look at youths who will be followed through their offending careers.[101] Preliminary results support interactional theory hypotheses, including the deviance-amplifying powers of associating with a delinquent peer group.[102] Associating with delinquent peers does in fact increase delinquent involvement because the peer group reinforces antisocial behaviour.[103] As delinquent behaviour escalates, kids are more likely to seek out deviant friends. These friends reinforce delinquent beliefs (thinking it is okay to commit crimes). In contrast, conventional youths seek out friends equally conforming who then reinforce their prosocial lifestyle. As this process unfolds over the life course, antisocial kids will become part of a deviant peer network that will reinforce their behaviour; conventional youths will, in turn, be reinforced by their conventional friends.[104]

Similar patterns have been found for family and school relations: Delinquency is related to weakened attachments to family and the educational process; delinquent behaviour further weakens the strength of the bonds to family and school.[105] Other researchers have supported an interactional relationship between criminal behaviour and moral values (antisocial behaviour weakens moral beliefs and weakened beliefs encourage criminality).[106]

Life events can make even high-risk youths resilient to delinquency. Kids who grow up in indigent households with unemployment, high mobility, and parental criminality and who are placed in the care of social service agencies can resist delinquent involvements if they have prosocial life experiences. Among those encounters developed in later adolescence that enable kids to resist delinquency are forming a commitment to school, developing an attachment to teachers, and establishing the goal of a college education; scoring high on reading and math tests is also associated with prosocial behaviours.[107]

In sum, interactional theory suggests that criminality is part of a dynamic social process and not simply an outcome of that process. Although crime is influenced by social forces, it also influences these processes and associations to create behavioural trajectories toward increasing law violations for some people.[108] In so doing, the interactional theory integrates elements of social disorganization, social control, social learning, and cognitive theory into a powerful model of the development of a criminal career.

Sampson and Laub's Age-Graded Theory

If there are various pathways to crime and delinquency, are there trails back to conformity? In an important work, *Crime in the Making*, Robert Sampson and John Laub identify the turning points in a criminal career.[109] In this life-course perspective, they say that the stability of delinquent behaviour can be affected by events that occur later in life, even after a chronic delinquent career has been undertaken. They agree with Gottfredson and Hirschi that formal and informal social controls restrict criminality and that the onset of crime begins early in life and continues over the life course. They disagree that once this course is set, nothing can impede its progress.

Laub and Sampson reanalyzed the data originally collected by the Gluecks more than 40 years ago. Using modern statistical analysis made possible by computers, they found evidence supportive of the life-course view. They have found that children who enter delinquent careers are those who have trouble at home and at school and maintain deviant friends—findings not dissimilar from earlier research on delinquent careers.

Turning Points in Crime. Laub and Sampson's most important contribution has been identifying the life events that enable adult offenders to desist from crime (see Figure 10.7). Two critical **turning points** are marriage and career. For example, adolescents who are at risk to crime are able to live "normal" or conventional lives if they can find good jobs or achieve successful careers. Their success may hinge on a "lucky break": They may encounter employers who are willing to give them a chance despite their record.

When they achieve adulthood, even adolescents who had significant problems with the law are able to desist

Figure 10.7   Sampson and Laub's Age-Graded Theory

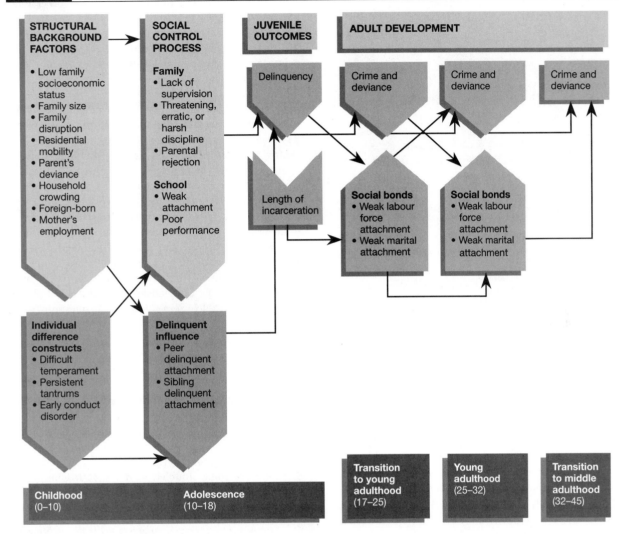

SOURCE: Robert Sampson and John Laub, *Crime in the Making* (Cambridge, MA: Harvard University Press, 1993), pp. 244–45.

from crime if they can become attached to a spouse who supports and sustains them even when the spouse knows they had gotten into trouble when they were younger. Happy marriages are life-sustaining, and marital quality improves over time (as people work less and have fewer parental responsibilities); people who are married even tend to live longer.[110] Research also shows that children who grow up in two-parent families are more likely to later have happier marriages than children who are the product of divorced or never-married parents.[111] This finding suggests the marriage–crime association may be intergenerational: If people with marital problems are more crime-prone, their children will also suffer a greater long-term risk of marital failure and antisocial activity. People who cannot sustain secure marital relations or who are failures in the labour market are less likely to desist from crime.

Social Capital. Social scientists recognize that people build social capital—positive relations with individuals and institutions that are life-sustaining. In the same manner that building financial capital improves the chances for personal success, building social capital supports conventional behaviour and inhibits deviant behaviour. For example, a successful marriage creates social capital when it improves a person's stature, creates feelings of self-worth, and encourages people to take a chance on the individual. A successful career inhibits crime by creating a stake in conformity; why commit crime when you are doing well at your job? The relationship is reciprocal: If a person is chosen as an employee, he or she will return the "favour" by doing the best job possible; if the person is chosen as a spouse, he or she blossoms into a devoted partner. In contrast, moving to a new city reduces social capital by closing people off from long-term relationships.[112]

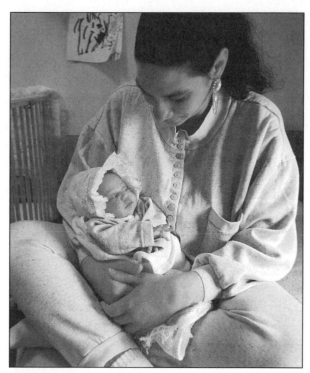

According to Sampson and Laub, building social capital helps inhibit the onset of criminality. Some treatment programs put these views into action, for example, by helping addicted homeless mothers become drugfree and develop marketable skills.

Sampson and Laub's research indicates that building social capital and strong social bonds reduces the likelihood of long-term deviance. This finding suggests that, in contrast to latent trait theories, events that occur in later adolescence and adulthood do in fact influence the direction of delinquent and criminal careers. Life events can either help terminate or sustain deviant careers. For example, getting arrested and punished may have little direct effect on future criminality, but it can help sustain a criminal career because it reduces the chances of employment and job stability, two factors that are directly related to crime.[113]

Testing Age-Graded Theory. There are several indicators that the age-graded theory is a valid criminological theory. At-risk youth with a history of delinquent behaviours have been found to desist if they later improve their peer relations, do better in school, and make effective use of their leisure time. Once begun, a delinquent career can be reversed if life conditions improve, an outcome predicted by age-graded theory.[114] Evidence shows that men who are unemployed or underemployed report higher criminal participation rates than employed men; men released from prison on parole who obtain jobs are less likely to recidivate than those who lack or lose employment.[115] There is also evidence that substance abusers who maintain a successful marriage in their 20s and

become parents are the ones most likely to mature out of crime.[116] Employment and marriage are two cornerstones of age-graded theory. In one recent study, it was found that delinquents who enter the military, serve overseas, and receive GI Bill benefits between ages 17 and 25 also enhance their occupational status and economic well-being; clearly, military service is a turning point in the life course.[117]

Other social scientists have attempted to directly test the principles of age-graded theory. In one survey effort, Raymond Paternoster found that people who are self-centred and present-oriented are less likely to accumulate social capital and more prone to commit criminal acts. In contrast, people who have accumulated social capital are unwilling to risk damage to that investment and therefore less likely to commit crime. Because behaviour is influenced by considerations of future punishment, as social capital increases the risk of crime decreases. This supports the life-course model (Laub and Sampson) while contradicting one of the key assumptions of the latent trait approach of Gottfredson and Hirschi.[118] While change is possible, some important questions need answering:

1. Why do some kids change while others resist?
2. Why do some people enter strong marriages while others fail?
3. What is it about a military career that helps reduce future criminality?
4. Does the connection between military service and desistance suggest universal military service as a crime-prevention alternative?
5. Why are some troubled youths able to conform to the requirements of a job or career while others cannot?

Some recent research suggests a further avenue for study. In an in-depth case study of a female crack dealer, it is shown that social capital, family, friends, education, marriage, and employment can also aid in a "successful" career as a crack dealer. The addict's own crack consumption was kept under control, and she remained competent as a "manager," keeping her family life and drug dealing separate.[119]

Summary

Recently, criminologists have been combining elements from a number of different theoretical models into integrated theories of crime, outlined in Table 10.1. One approach is to use multiple factors derived from a number of structural and process theories. Examples of this approach include the social development model and Elliott's integrated theory, both of which hold that social position controls life events. The social development

Table 10.1	Integrated Theories	
THEORY	**MAJOR PREMISE**	**STRENGTHS**
Multifactor Theories		
Social development model (SDM)	Weak social controls produce crime. A person's place in the structure influences his or her bond to society.	Combines elements of social structural and social process theories. Accounts for variations in the crime rate.
Elliott's integrated theory	Strained and weak social bonds lead youths to associate with and learn from deviant peers.	Combines elements of learning strain and control theories.
Integrated structural theory	Delinquency is a function of family life, which is in turn controlled by the family's place in the economic system.	Explains the relationship between family problems and delinquency in terms of social and economic conditions.
Latent Trait Theories		
General theory	Crime and criminality are separate concepts. People choose to commit crime when they lack self-control. People lacking self-control will seize criminal opportunities.	Integrates choice and social control concepts. Identifies the difference between crime and criminality.
Human nature theory	People choose to commit crime when they are biologically and psychologically impaired.	Shows how physical traits interact with social conditions to produce crime. Can account for noncriminal behaviour in high-crime areas. Integrates choice and developmental theories.
Life-Course Theories		
Farrington's theory of delinquent development	Personal and social factors control the onset and stability of criminal careers.	Makes use of data collected over a 20-year period to substantiate hypothesis.
Interactional theory	Criminals go through lifestyle changes during their offending career.	Combines sociological and psychological theories.
Age-graded theory	As people mature, the factors that influence their propensity to commit crime change. In childhood, family factors are critical; in adulthood, marital and job factors are key.	Shows how crime is a developmental process that shifts in direction over the life course.

model suggests that living in a disorganized area helps weaken social bonds; Elliott's theory holds that strain leads to weakened bonds. Both theories find that weakened bonds lead to the development of deviant peer group associations. In another variation, integrated structural theory, Colvin and Pauly add conflict variables to structural and process factors.

Latent trait theories hold that some underlying condition present at birth or soon after controls behaviour. Suspect traits include low IQ, impulsivity, and personality structure. This underlying trait explains the continuity of offending because once present, it remains with a person throughout his or her life. The latent trait theories developed by Gottfredson and Hirschi and by Wilson and Herrnstein both integrate choice theory concepts: People with latent traits choose crime over noncrime. The opportunity for crime mediates their choice.

Life-course theories argue that events that take place over the life course influence criminal choices. The cause of crime is constantly changing as people mature. At first, the nuclear family influences behaviour; during adolescence, the peer group dominates; in adulthood, marriage and career are critical. There are a variety of pathways to crime: Some kids are sneaky; others are hostile; and still others, defiant. Crime may be part of a garden variety of social problems, including health, physical, and interpersonal troubles. Important life-course theories have been formulated by Terence Thornberry, David Farrington, and John Laub and Robert Sampson.

Thinking Like a Criminologist

Luis Francisco is the leader of a Hispanic gang in Montreal. He was convicted of murder in 1998 and sentenced to life imprisonment.

Luis Francisco's life has been filled with displacement, poverty, and chronic predatory crime. The son of a prostitute in Haiti, at the age of nine he was sent to prison for robbery. He had trouble in school, and teachers described him as having attention problems; he dropped out in the seventh grade. On his 19th birthday in 1980, he immigrated to Canada and soon after became a member of the Montreal criminal gang Latin Kings. He shot and killed his girlfriend in 1981 and was not apprehended until 1984. Sentenced to nine years for second-degree manslaughter, Luis Francisco ended up in a maximum security prison in Manitoba, where he started a prison chapter of his gang. As King Blood, Francisco ruled his gang in and out of prison. Disciplinary troubles erupted when some Kings were stealing from the organization. Infuriated, King Blood phoned his street lieutenants and ordered their termination. The RCMP, who had been monitoring his communications, arrested 35 gang members. Thirty-four pleaded guilty; only Francisco insisted on a trial, where he was found guilty of conspiracy to commit murder.

Explain Luis's behaviour patterns from a developmental view. How would a latent trait theorist explain his escalating criminal activities?

Key Terms

adolescent-limited

authority conflict pathway

cognitive perspective

continuity of crime

covert pathway

developmental criminology

early onset

general theory of crime (GTC)

integrated structural Marxist theory

interactional theory

latent traits

life-course theory

multifactor theories

overt pathway

problem behaviour syndrome (PBS)

prosocial bonds

pseudomaturity

social capital

social development model (SDM)

turning points

 See the book-specific website at www.siegelcriminology2e.nelson.com for additional chapter links, discussions, and quizzes.

Crime Typologies

Regardless of why people commit crime in the first place, their actions are defined by law as falling into particular crime categories, or typologies. Criminologists often seek to group individual criminal offenders or behaviours so they may be more easily studied and understood. These are referred to as offender typologies.

In this section, crime patterns are clustered into four typologies: violent crime (Chapter 11); economic crimes involving common theft offences (Chapter 12); economic crimes involving white-collar criminals or criminal organizations (Chapter 13); and public order crimes, such as prostitution and drug abuse (Chapter 14). This format groups criminal behaviours by their focuses and consequences: bringing physical harm to others; misappropriating other people's property; and violating laws designed to protect public morals.

Typologies can be useful in classifying large numbers of criminal offences or offenders into easily understood categories. This text has grouped offences and offenders on the basis of their (1) legal definitions and (2) collective goals, objectives, and consequences.

Chapter

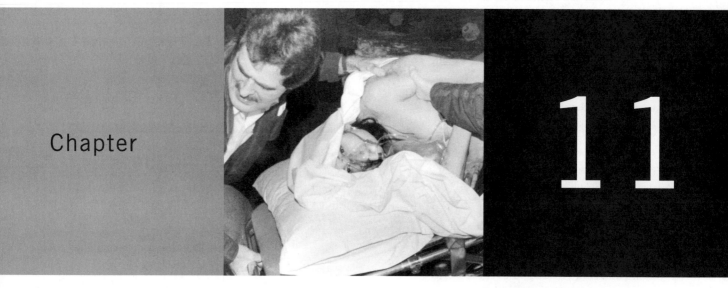

11

Violent Crime

In our society people are afraid of becoming crime victims, and they are altering their lifestyle in an effort to remain safe. They are bombarded with TV news stories and newspaper articles featuring grisly accounts of mass murder, child abuse, and serial rape. These accounts may be an unfortunate reflection of the harsh realities of modern life: Despite recent declines, violence rates have risen in the last 30 years. The rate of violence in the United States exceeds that of any other industrialized nation, and even Canada is not the "peaceable kingdom" everyone would like to think it is.[1]

Many people have personally experienced violence or have a friend who has been victimized; almost everyone has heard about someone being robbed, beaten, or killed; riots and violent protests have recently made the headlines; hate crime has become a common phrase; and assassination has claimed the lives of political, religious, and social leaders all over the world.

Because of events such as these, the public believes that government should take a "get-tough" approach to violent crime, especially when the perpetrators are young offenders. In addition to the generally held perception that the Young Offenders Act, currently being revised by the federal government, is too lenient, public opinion polls also indicate that 69 percent of Canadians favour the return of the death penalty, ranging from a high of 76 percent in the Prairies to 64 percent in the Maritimes.[2] In the United States the Supreme Court has made teenage criminals over the age of 16 eligible for the death penalty.[3] Many people believe that society is becoming more violent and that things are not like they were in the "good old days." Longing for the serenity of earlier days may be inappropriate when we consider that violence has been a long-standing feature of social life. Perhaps we are just hearing more highly publicized accounts of violent crime.

Some experts suggest that violence originates in a relatively small number of inherently violence-prone individuals who themselves may have been the victims of physical violence or of physical or psychological abnormalities. Other social scientists consider violence and aggression inherently human traits that can affect any person at any time. Still others believe that there are violence-prone subcultures within society whose members value force, routinely carry weapons, and consider violence to have an acceptable place in social interaction.[4]

Connections

As you may recall from Chapter 6, biosocial theorists link violence to a number of biological irregularities, including but not limited to genetic influences and inheritance, the action of hormones, the functioning of neurotransmitters, brain structure, and diet. Psychologists link violent behaviour to observational learning from violent TV shows, traumatic childhood experiences, low intelligence, mental illness, impaired cognitive processes, and abnormal (psychopathic) personality structure.

This chapter surveys the nature and extent of violent crime. First, we briefly review some hypothetical causes of violence. Then, we turn our attention to specific types of interpersonal violence: rape, homicide, assault, and robbery. Finally, we look at political violence, state-sponsored violence, and terrorism.

The Roots of Violence

What causes people to behave violently? There are a number of competing explanations for violent behaviour. A few of the most prominent are discussed below.

In 1984, Denis Lortie opened fire in Quebec's National Assembly with a machine gun, killing 3 and wounding 13 others; he pleaded guilty by reason of insanity.

On December 6, 1989, a male gunman killed 14 women and wounded 12 others at the École Polytechnique in Montreal. After his suicide, a statement found on his body blamed feminists for spoiling his life. The "Montreal Massacre" sparked an annual day of mourning and crystallized in many minds the link between gender and violence.[5]

In 1992, Valery Fabrikant walked into Concordia University's engineering department and killed three professors; the university had previously asked the police not to approve his gun permit.

On March 13, 1995, an ex–Boy Scout leader named Thomas Hamilton took four high-powered rifles into the primary school of the peaceful Scottish town of Dunblane and slaughtered 16 children and their teacher. This horrific crime shocked the British Isles into passing strict controls on all guns and totally outlawing handguns.

Bizarre outbursts such as these cry out for explanations. These acts of mass violence exacerbate our worst fears that we could be victimized by brutal, random crime committed by strangers in public places. Fear of crime distorts the experience of living in modern society. And the fear is not totally groundless.

Canada has a homicide rate higher than most Western societies (2.1 homicides per 100 000 people compared to England's 0.8, for example). There are high levels of violence in Aboriginal communities (with a suicide rate three times higher than the general population, and a violent crime rate three and a half times the national rate). Our society can't prevent the victimization of women and children, and we have many instances of police and prison violence.

Personal Traits

Some see a link between violence and personal traits. More than 35 years ago, Laura Bender examined convicted juveniles who had killed their victims and concluded that they suffered from abnormal electroencephalogram readings, learning disabilities, and psychosis.[6]

Famous Canadian Criminals

"The Killer"

Few people would have otherwise recognized his name. He was a loser. He had been unable to keep a girlfriend, and was not able to enter the military because of his apparent mental instability and antisocial personality. But, on December 6, 1989, Marc Lepine dressed in his military fatigues, hid his guns under his long coat, and made his way to the Ecole Polytechnique. There he went into a classroom and ordered all the men out, after which he shot the women students, cursing them for being feminists. Then he walked through the school, systematically shooting women, until he finally turned the gun on himself. Was he a madman, or is he part of the wider continuum of violence against women? Was this act an isolated one, or is it the extreme end of everyday misogyny?

In a letter found on his body he said he had decided to kill women for being feminist, for ruining his life. He had tried to enter the Polytechnique as a student, but when he was turned down, he blamed this on feminists too. He admired Denis Lortie for going into the legislature and shooting politicians, and wished he could emulate him.

When the Montreal Massacre happened in 1989, the initial reaction was incredulity, mixed with anger. It was difficult to understand how this could happen on several levels. How could a person be in possession of such weapons? Why did the police take so long to respond? Why did he single out the women?

The Women Victims

Genevieve Bergeron, 21, civil engineering

Helene Colgan, 23, mechanical engineering

Nathalie Croteau, 23, mechanical engineering

Barbara Daigneault, 22, mechanical engineering

Anne-Marie Edward, 21, chemical engineering

Maud Haviernick, 29, environmental design

Barbara Maria Klucznik, 31, materials

Maryse Laganiere, 25, Poly budget department

Maryse Leclair, 23, engineering materials

Anne-Marie Lemay, 27, mechanical engineering

Sonia Pelletier, 28, mechanical engineering

Michele Richard, 21, engineering materials

Annie St-Arneault, 23, mechanical engineering

Annie Turcotte, 21, engineering materials

For many, this event has come to symbolize wider patterns of violence against women in society.

When Suzanne Lapointe-Edward speaks about what happened to her daughter, she refuses to use his name – she calls him "the killer." She believes that the media made Lepine an anti-hero, while the women have become nameless victims. Lapointe-Edward lectures on campuses across the country to promote action and healing with respect to violence against women. She has also played a key role in obtaining stricter gun control legislation in Canada.

The context of violence is that women tend to be killed by men they know. Of 84 women killed in 2000, the accused were family members 43 percent, and acquaintances 23 percent, of the time. They also withstand repeated assaults before they go to the police. Of over 56 000 women who were victims of non-sexual assault, family members were accused 50 percent of the time, and acquaintances 35 percent. What was different that night in Montreal was the explicit misogyny, that these women were selected because of their gender, even though they had done nothing to "him," did not know him, and certainly had done nothing to deserve what happened.

Not all men are violent, but most violence is committed by men. It is a fact that is hard to overlook. However, men and women have joined together in trying to overcome a legacy of gendered violence, and work for change.

Sources: *After the Montreal Massacre*, 1990, National Film Board documentary; Elizabeth Stanko, *Everyday Violence* (London: Pandora, 1990); "Media Literacy: Ten Years Later, Media Still Don't Get the Montreal Massacre," Judy Rebick, CBC Straight From the Hip, December 12, 1999; Canadian Crime Statistics 2000, Canadian Centre for Justice Statistics 2001.

More recent research has found that murderous youths suffered signs of major neurological impairment (such as abnormal EEGs, multiple psychomotor impairment, and severe seizures), low intelligence as measured on standard IQ tests, a psychotic close relative, and psychotic symptoms such as paranoia, illogical thinking, and hallucinations.[7] Similarly, studies of male batterers indicate that abnormal personality structure, including depression, borderline personality syndrome, and psychopathology, are associated with various forms of spousal and family abuse.[8] However, there are other theories as well.

Figure 11.1   Sources of Violence

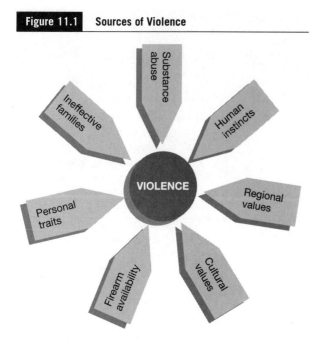

Ineffective Families

In August 1990, residents of Gainesville, Florida, were shocked when five young students were brutally murdered. Newspaper accounts told how the victims had been stabbed dozens of times, raped and their mutilated bodies posed in sexually suggestive positions.[9] A 35-year-old drifter named Danny Harold Rolling was arrested and convicted for committing these horrible crimes. On March 24, 1994, after 13 days of testimony, a jury recommended Rolling be sentenced to death. During the sentencing phase, Rolling had pleaded for mercy and claimed that his behaviour was a result of the emotional and physical abuse he had suffered at the hands of his father. His mother, a native of Shreveport, Louisiana, submitted a videotape backing his claim of abuse and ended it by stating, "Take me, I'm the one that had to have failed him somewhere."

Research linking violence to either ineffective, abusive, or inadequate parenting shows that parents reinforce a child's coercive behaviour by failing to set adequate limits or use proper and consistent discipline. Absent or deviant parents, inconsistent discipline, and lack of supervision have all been linked to persistent violent offending.[10]

Research carried out by the Canadian Centre for Justice Statistics confirms a similar pattern. As part of the National Longitudinal Survey of Children and Youth, over 20 000 children are interviewed every two years until they are 25 years of age. A key finding is that children who are exposed to fighting in the home are more

likely to be physically aggressive themselves. Figure 11.2 shows that almost three times as many children who witness violence are likely to be violent compared to those who aren't witnesses to violence. There is also a direct relationship between seeing violence; being hyperactive, anxious, or depressed; and committing property crimes.

Abused Kids. A number of research studies have found that individuals who were clinically diagnosed as abused in childhood later engaged in violent delinquent behaviour at a rate greater than that of unabused children.[11] Samples of convicted murderers contain a high percentage of seriously abused youths.[12] The abuse–violence association has been a factor in a number of cases in which parents have been killed by their children, as has sexual abuse in father (patricide) and mother (matricide) killings.[13] Children who are physically punished are the ones most likely to physically abuse a sibling and later engage in spouse abuse and other forms of criminal violence.[14]

The Brutalization Process. Case studies of violent criminals show that antisocial careers are created in a series of stages that begin with brutal episodes during early adolescence. The first stage is the **brutalization process**, during which abusive parents or caretakers cause the young victim to develop a belligerent, angry demeanour. When confronted at home, at school, or on the street,

Figure 11.2   Child behavioural outcomes in homes where children witnessed violence

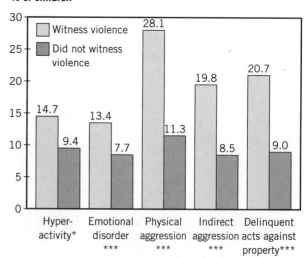

% of children

* Chi-square = < .05; df = 1
*** Chi-square = < .001; df = 1

Those who fell within the bottom 10% of the scale were considered to have behavioural problems.

Source: Statistics Canada, National Longitudinal Survey of Children and Youth, 1998-1999

Source: *Juristat* 21, 6, 2001

these belligerent youths respond with violent performance of angry, hostile behaviour. The success of their violent confrontations provides them with a sense of power and achievement. In the virulency stage, the emerging criminals develop a violent identity that makes them feared; they enjoy intimidating others. This process takes now-violent youths full circle, from being the victim of aggression to being its initiator; they are now the same person they grew up despising, ready to begin the process with their own children.[15]

While a significant amount of evidence has shown the association between abuse and violent crime, it is also true that many offenders have not suffered abuse and that many abused youths do not grow up to become persistent adult offenders.[16]

Evolutionary Factors/Human Instinct

It is also possible that violent responses and emotions are actually inherent in all humans, needing only the right spark to trigger them. Sigmund Freud believed that human aggression and violence were produced by instinctual drives.[17] Freud maintained that humans have two opposing instinctual drives that interact to control behaviour. **Eros**, the life instinct, drives people to self-fulfilment and enjoyment; while **thanatos**, the death instinct, produces self-destruction. Thanatos can be expressed externally (as violence and sadism) or internally (as suicide, alcoholism, or other self-destructive habits).

A number of biologists and anthropologists have also speculated that instinctual violence-promoting traits may be common to the human species as a whole. Aggression and violence are the results of instincts inborn in all animals, including human beings. Konrad Lorenz developed this theory in his famous book *On Aggression*,[18] where he argued that aggressive energy is produced by inbred instincts independent of environmental forces. In the animal kingdom, aggression usually serves a productive purpose—for example, it leads members of grazing species to spread out over available territory to ensure an ample food supply and the survival of the fittest.

Lorenz felt that humans have some of the same aggressive instincts as animals but without the inhibitions against fatal violence that members of lower species usually maintain. That is, among lower species, aggression is rarely fatal; when a conflict occurs, the winner is determined through a test of skill or endurance. This inhibition against killing members of their own species protects animals from self-extinction. Humans lack this inhibition against fatal violence.

Evolutionary theories in criminology suggest that violent behaviour may have become instinctual because of the long-term influences of reproductive behaviour: Males who are sexually aggressive are the ones most likely to produce children; their offspring will carry genes that support aggression. Over time male aggression has become predominant.[19]

Cultural Values

Explanations of the cause of violent behaviour that focus on the individual offender fail to account for larger patterns of violence in society. Is interpersonal violence more common in large, urban, inner-city areas than in other kinds of communities? Are violent crime rates linked to socially disorganized areas? Are there other social forces in operation that encourage violent crime?[20]

Subculture of Violence. To explain the existence of areas and groups with disproportionately high violence rates, Marvin Wolfgang has suggested the existence of a subculture of violence.[21] The subculture's norms are separate from society's central, dominant value system. Even though the subculture's members share some of the values of the dominant culture, violence has become legitimate as a way to solve conflicts.[22]

Ganging. Empirical evidence shows that violence rates are highest in urban areas where subcultural values support teenage gangs whose members typically embrace the use of violence.[23] Gang members are more likely to own guns and other weapons than nongang members; they are also more likely to have peers who are gun owners and more likely to carry guns outside the home.[24] Gang violence may be initiated for a variety of reasons: It enables new members to show toughness during initiation ceremonies; it can be used to retaliate against rivals for actual or perceived grievances; it is a response when graffiti is defaced by rivals; and it is used to protect turf from incursions by outsiders.[25] Research indicates that gang-related killings have increased significantly in recent years.[26] In Canada, increasing attention is being paid to Chinese and Vietnamese gangs as well as to outlaw motorcycle gangs.[27]

Regional Values

Some criminologists have suggested that regional values promote violence.[28] Research in the Southern United States attributed high homicide rates to a culture that stresses a frontier mentality, mob violence, night riders, personal vengeance, and easily available firearms. Southerners are also thought to place greater emphasis on personal honour and to own more firearms.[29] Not all criminologists have agreed with these conclusions.[30]

Police data and the results of victimization surveys in Canada show that the western provinces have a higher overall rate of violent crime. This pattern is consistent over the years for both property and violent crime. Provincial variations have been attributed to differences in age, sex, urban concentration, and social disorganization. Research explaining this phenomenon is as yet inconclusive.[31]

However Leslie Kennedy and Robert Silverman suggest that crime rates increase from low rates in the east and gradually increase in a westward direction due to relative disadvantage. That is, crime is likely to be higher in the west because there is a broader range between the haves and the have-nots, leading to greater feelings of animosity between the two groups. In areas of absolute disadvantage, as in much of eastern Canada, there is little animosity because there is little difference among individuals.[32]

Substance Abuse

It has also become common to link violence to substance abuse. Drug abuse influences violence in three ways: through the actual effects of the drugs, out of the need to obtain drugs, and in relation to drug trafficking.[33]

The relationship may be **psychopharmacological** when it is the direct consequence of ingesting mood-altering substances. Drugs such as PCP and amphetamines may produce violent and aggressive behaviours. Alcohol abuse has also been associated with all forms of violence, especially since drinking reduces cognition and the ability to communicate.[34]

Drug ingestion may result in economic compulsive behaviour when drug users resort to violence to gain funds to support their habit. In an intake survey conducted by Corrections Canada of over 6000 offenders entering federal institutions between 1994 and 1996, 48 percent admitted having used a drug on the day of their offence, and 30 percent said they had used cocaine in the six months prior to arrest. The U.S. Drug Use Forecasting (DUF) survey shows that up to 80 percent of all people arrested for violent crimes test positively for drugs.[35] Surveys of American prison inmates show that a significant majority report being under the influence of drugs and alcohol at the time they committed their last criminal offence.[36]

A bond between violent crime and substance abuse is also forged by the activities of drug trafficking gangs whose members both sell and use drugs. Many drug-related deaths are motivated by drug trafficking and interpersonal conflict brought on by drug abuse; relatively few people are killed by drug users trying to get drug money.[37]

Firearm Availability

While firearm availability is not in itself a cause of violence, it is certainly a facilitating factor: A petty argument can escalate into a fatal encounter if one party or the other has a handgun. In Canada, 42 percent of all homicides involved shootings in 1961, but this dropped to 31 percent in 1999. Handguns are used in over half of all firearm homicides.[38] The United States has a huge surplus of guns and most firearms (80 percent) used in crimes are stolen or obtained through illegal or unregulated transactions. The Uniform Crime Reports indicate that more than half of all American murders and 40 percent of all robberies involve a firearm.[39]

Handguns are a major cause of death for police officers killed in the line of duty, and the presence of firearms in the home has been found to significantly increase the risk of suicide, regardless of how carefully the guns were secured or stored.[40] As Exhibit 11.1 shows, 81 percent of all firearm deaths in Canada are suicides. In the United States assaults and violence among family members and other intimates are 12 times more likely to result in death if a handgun is used than if the attacks do not involve firearms.[41]

Connections

Some criminologists have focused on "violent" business or corporate crimes, such as the release of toxic pollutants into the environment. Because these latter acts are linked to business organizations, they will be covered in the sections on corporate crime in Chapter 13.

While gun control is a hotly debated topic in Canada, changes to the law in the form of Bill C-51 in 1979, Bill C-17 in 1991, and Bill C-68 in 1995 have created many obstacles to acquiring a gun: firearm acquisition certificate screening, penalties for gun-related offences, strengthened prohibition orders, provisions for safe handling and storage, and so on. Following the Montreal Massacre, carbines and high-capacity magazines became restricted. It is arguable that these legal changes have resulted in the lower rate of firearm homicides.

So far, we have reviewed a few of the factors suspected to be causes of violent crime. In the remainder of the chapter, we turn our attention to the individual acts that make up violent crime in our society. When violence is directed toward strangers, it is said to be **instrumental**—designed to improve the financial or social position of the criminal, such as through an armed robbery. This is also **crime-related violence**. In contrast, **expressive violence** is designed to vent rage, anger, or frustration, as when a romantic triangle results in a murder. This is called conflict-related violence.

Among the common-law violent crimes are rape, murder, assault, and robbery. There are also newly recognized forms of violence directed at specific targets. Included within this category are workplace crimes. In addition, violent, politically motivated crimes are commonly referred to as acts of terrorism.

Sexual Assault

Rape is defined by the common law as "the carnal knowledge of a female forcibly and against her will."[42] It is one of the most loathed, misunderstood, and frightening of crimes. Under traditional common-law definitions, rape

---

Exhibit 11.1 | Quick Facts about Weapons and Violent Crime, 1995

- Homicide is the violent crime that most frequently involves the use of weapons.[1]
- Firearm use in spousal homicides declined from 36 percent to 28 percent between 1985 and 1995.[2]
- Only 2 percent of all violent crime victims encountered firearms.
- Thirty-one percent of assault victims encountering knives sustained major injury, compared with 16 percent facing guns.
- From 1991 to 1995 the proportion of firearm deaths involving handguns increased from 29 to 50 percent.
- From 1991 to 1995, rates declined for homicide (26 percent) and for firearm homicide (39 percent).
- Canadians have 3.1 million rifles, 2.3 million shotguns, and 1 million handguns (estimated, 1990).
- Suicides accounted for 81 percent of all firearm deaths.
- Types of weapons used in violent incidents were similar for adults or youths.
- Handguns are more common in homicides in large urban areas.

SOURCE: "Weapons and Violent Crime," *Juristat* 17 (1997).

[1] 1st degree, 2nd degree, manslaughter, and infanticide
[2] registered marriages, common-law unions, separated, and divorced

---

Exhibit 11.2 | Quick Code: Sexual Assault Law in Canada before 1983

- 143. A male person commits rape when he has sexual intercourse with a female person who is not his wife,
  a. Without her consent, or
  b. With her consent if the consent
     i. Is extorted by threats or fear of bodily harm,
     ii. Is obtained by personating her husband, or
     iii. Is obtained by false and fraudulent representations as to the nature and quality of the act

SOURCE: C. Boyle, "Sexual Assault: A Case Study of Legal Policy Options," in *Canadian Criminology: Perspectives on Crime and Criminality*, ed. M. Jackson and C. Grifiths (Toronto: Harcourt Brace, 1991), p. 101.

---

nologists favour keeping the term "rape" for its traditional shock value. The campaign to alert the public to the seriousness of rape, to initiate help for victims, and to change legal definitions to facilitate the prosecution of rape offenders has increased the rate of sexual assault because victims feel less reluctant to come forward and report the crime to the police.

History of Rape

Rape has been known throughout history. In early civilization, rape was a common occurrence. Men staked a claim of ownership on women by forcibly abducting and raping them. This practice led to males' solidification of power and their historical domination of women. In fact, in her book *Against Our Will*, Susan Brownmiller says that the criminalization of rape occurred only after the development of a monetary economy.[46] Thereafter, the violation of a virgin caused an economic hardship on her family, who expected a significant dowry for her hand in marriage. In Babylonian and Hebraic law, the rape of a virgin was a crime punishable by death. However, if the victim was a married woman, both she and her attacker were considered equally to blame. Unless her husband chose to intervene, the victim and her attacker were put to death.

During the Middle Ages, it was a common practice for ambitious men to abduct and rape wealthy women in an effort to force them into marriage. The practice of "heiress stealing" illustrates how feudal law gave little thought or protection to women and equated them with property. It was only in the late 15th century that forcible sex was outlawed, and then only if the victim was of the nobility; raped peasant women and married women were

involved nonconsensual sexual intercourse performed by a male against a female he is neither married to nor cohabitating with.[43] Until 1983, Canadian law concerning rape contained a clause that provided an exemption for husbands accused of raping their wives. This was removed in 1983 under a series of sweeping changes to sexual assault laws. The situation is different in some countries, however. In 1993, for example, Italy's Supreme Court accepted a husband's argument that he raped his wife in order to save their marriage.[44]

In the traditional criminological literature rape was often viewed as a sexual offence. Even today, some men view rape as a sexual act, including one Tennessee judge who in 1994 released an accused rapist after stating that all he needed was a girlfriend and telling the public defender's office to arrange for a dating service.[45]

Criminologists now consider rape to be a violent, coercive act of aggression, and so the term has been changed to "sexual assault." Some feminists and crimi-

not considered rape victims until well into the 16th century. The Christian condemnation of sex during this period was also a denunciation of women as evil, having lust in their hearts and redeemable only by motherhood. A woman who was raped was almost automatically suspected of contributing to her attack.

Sexual Assault and the Military

In 1998 allegations began to surface of sexual assault in the Canadian military. While such stories are perhaps not new, what was shocking were accounts of women going to their superior or commanding officers only to have their complaints discounted. They were told that nothing could be done, or it was suggested that they were to blame for the incidents. A scandal in the United States was especially disturbing because it involved drill instructors, who are given almost total control over the lives of young female recruits, who depend on them for support and nurturing.[47]

The link between the military and rape is inescapable. Rape has been associated with armies and warfare, as conquering armies have considered rape of their enemies' women one of the spoils of war. Among the ancient Greeks, rape was socially acceptable and well within the rules of warfare. During the Crusades, even knights and pilgrims, bound by vows of chivalry and Christian piety, raped as they marched toward Constantinople.

The belief that women are part of the spoils of war has continued through the ages, from the Crusades to the war in Vietnam. The systematic rape of Bosnian women by Serbian army officers during the civil war in the former Yugoslavia horrified the world. These crimes seemed even more atrocious because they seemed part of an official policy of genocide. Reports from Haiti also indicate that rape of politically involved women became a norm in the wake of the 1991 military coup that ousted President Jean-Bertrand Aristide.[48]

Incidence of Sexual Assault

How many sexual assaults occur each year, and what is known about rape patterns? According to the Canadian Centre for Justice Statistics, there were a total of 24 049 sexual assaults in 2000, for a rate of 78 per 100 000 people, a drop of 14 percent since 1996. This crime has a lower clearance rate than for crimes of violence in general, but this might be due to the fact that the rate of sexual assault reported to the police has continued to increase over the years.[49]

Population density influences the rape rate: Metropolitan areas have a rape rate significantly higher than rural areas. Nonetheless, urban areas have experienced a much higher drop in rape reports than rural areas. Rape is also a warm-weather crime, usually occur-

Exhibit 11.3	The Violence Index

- Percentage of female assault victims attacked by a current or estranged partner: 43
- Percentage of male assault victims attacked by a female partner: 3
- Percentage of female homicide victims killed by a current or estranged partner: 38
- Number of female victims of violent crime per 1000 population: 77; of males: 90
- Percentage of homicide victims who are male: 66
- Percentage of those charged with violent crime who are male: 91
- Percentage of those charged with all serious crime who are male: 90
- Percentage of spousal assault charges laid against men: 93
- Percentage of wife assault occurring during a first pregnancy: 40
- Percentage of wife assault occurring while children are present: 50
- Percentage of battered women who say partner also battered their children: 26
- Percentage of women who say they have been sexually harassed at work: 37
- Average number of minutes reported between sexual assaults: 17

SOURCE: Salem Alaton, "The Violence Index," *The Globe and Mail*, December 5, 1992, p. D1.

ring during July and August, with the lowest rates occurring during December, January, and February.

These data must be interpreted with caution, because sexual assault is frequently underreported by victims. It is estimated that in Canada less than 10 percent of sexual assault victims report the crime to the police.[50] Many people fail to report sexual assaults because they are embarrassed, they believe nothing could be done, or they somehow blame themselves. In a well-known major U.S. study on date rape, researchers found that only 27 percent of the women whose sexual assault met the legal definition of rape thought of themselves as rape victims.[51]

Official data probably reflect reporting practices rather than crime trends.[52] Chapter 3 refers to this phenomenon as a report-sensitive crime. Some victim surveys indicate that at least 20 percent of adult women, 15 percent of college-aged women, and 12 percent of adolescent girls have experienced sexual abuse or assault sometime during their lifetime, so it is evident that both the official and victimization statistics significantly undercount rape.[53] In Canada 39 percent of women over 18 years of age report having experienced sexual assault in their adult lifetime, 5 percent in the previous year.[54] An independent study of sexual contact between physicians and patients conducted by the Ontario College of Physicians and Surgeons estimated that the rate of sexual abuse by doctors was nearly 10 percent.[55]

As Exhibit 11.3 shows, there is a large continuum of violence against women in our society, ranging from date rape and sexual assault to wife abuse and domestic violence. The fact that such crimes are examples of **gendered violence** should be obvious from the proportion of female victims and male offenders.

Types of Rapists

Some rapes are planned, others are spontaneous; some focus on a particular victim, while others occur during the commission of another crime, such as a burglary.[56] Some rapists are one-time offenders, while others engage in multiple or serial rapes. Some attack their victims without warning ("blitz rapes"), others try to "capture" their victims by striking up a conversation or by offering them a ride, and still others use a personal relationship to gain access to their target.[57]

One of the best-known attempts to classify the personality of rapists was made by psychologist A. Nicholas Groth, an expert on the classification and treatment of sex offenders. According to Groth, every rape encounter contains three elements: anger, power, and sexuality.[58] Consequently, rapists can be classified according to one of these dimensions:

- The anger rape occurs as a discharge of pent-up anger and rage. The rapist uses brutality to hurt his victim as much as possible; the sexual aspect of rape may have been an afterthought. Often the anger rapist acts on the spur of the moment after an upsetting incident has caused him conflict, irritation, or aggravation. The woman is usually physically beaten, and thus more likely to receive sympathy from her peers, relatives, and the justice system and less likely to be accused of precipitating the attack.
- The power rape involves an attacker whose goal is sexual conquest, and he uses only the amount of force necessary to achieve his objective. The power rapist wants to be in control and to have women at his mercy. It is not sexual gratification that drives the power rapist, but personal insecurities about heterosexuality and manhood. The victim is usually younger than the rapist, and the lack of evidence of physical violence may reduce the support given the victim by family and friends.
- The sadistic rape involves aggression, and the victim might be abused, degraded, or tortured. Victims are usually related to a personal characteristic he wants to harm or destroy. This type of rape victim needs psychiatric care long after her physical wounds have healed.

It is estimated that about 55 percent of rapists are of the power type; about 40 percent, the anger type; and about 5 percent, the sadistic type. The key issue is that rape is a crime of violence and not a sexual act. Rape involves a violent criminal offence in which a predatory criminal chooses to attack a victim. It might be committed during the course of another crime, or be caused by intense anger toward women; but it is almost always a gendered crime committed by men against women.[59]

Types of Rape

In their studies, criminologists usually divide rapes into two broad categories: stranger-to-stranger rapes and acquaintance rapes. Whereas the former involve people who have never met before the rape, the latter involve someone known to the victim, even family members and friends. So-called date rape involves a sexual attack during a courting relationship.

It is difficult to estimate the ratio of rapes involving strangers to those in which victim and assailant were in some way acquainted, as women are more reluctant to report acts involving acquaintances. By some estimates, about 50 percent of rapes involve acquaintances.[60] However, the Violence Against Women Survey carried out by Statistics Canada in 1993 placed the percentage of stranger sexual assaults at only 19 percent.[61] Typically there is felt to be a 90 : 10 ratio of acquaintance- to stranger-related sexual assaults.

Date Rape. Official crime data from the 1995 UCR indicated that 26 percent of sexual assaults against women involved family members, 21 percent involved strangers, and 6 percent were unknown. However, by far the largest category were sexual assaults against women committed by acquaintances, fully 48 percent. Similarly, in 1999, 26 percent involved family members, 14 percent were committed by strangers, 5 percent were unknown, and fully 55 percent involved acquaintances.[62] These are conservative numbers; because women are less likely to report crimes involving acquaintances, it is possible that acquaintance rapes constitute the bulk of sexual assaults. One disturbing trend of rape involves people who are in some form of courting relationship; this is referred to as **date rape.**

There is no single form of date rape. Some incidents occur on first dates, others after a relationship has been developing, and still others after the couple have been involved for some time. The male partner may feel he has invested so much time and money in his partner that he is owed sexual relations or that sexual intimacy is an expression that the involvement is progressing.[63]

A survey of Canadian college women found that about one-third of young women had experienced an episode of physical, verbal, or psychological sexual coercion; 25 percent said they had unwanted sexual relations during the previous year.[64]

The incidence of date rape may be even higher than surveys indicate because many victims blame themselves and do not recognize the incident as a rape, saying, for example, "I should have fought back harder," "I should not have gotten drunk." Some victims do not report because they do not view their experiences as a "real rape," which they believe involves a strange man "jumping out of the bushes"; others are embarrassed or frightened.[65]

To fight back, some campus women's groups have taken to writing on bathroom walls the names of men accused of date rape and sexual assault, as a way to alert potential victims to the danger they faced from men whom they might have considered trustworthy friends.[66]

Another disturbing phenomenon is campus gang rape, in which a group of men will attack a defenceless or inebriated victim; another trend is the growing number of women reporting that they have been raped while sedated by the date rape drug rohypnol.[67]

Marital Rape. Research indicates that many women are raped each year by their husbands as part of an overall pattern of spousal abuse. Spousal rapes are often accompanied by brutal and sadistic beatings and have little to do with normal sexual interests.[68]

As noted above, until recently, a legally married husband could not be charged with raping his wife; this was referred to as the **marital exemption**. The origin of this legal doctrine can be traced to the 16th-century pronouncement of Matthew Hale, England's chief justice, who wrote: "The husband cannot be guilty of rape committed by himself upon his lawful wife, for by their mutual matrimonial consent and contract the wife hath given up herself in this kind unto the husband which she cannot retract."[69] The marital exemption was abolished in Canada in 1983 and has also been abolished in Israel, Scotland, and New Zealand.[70] In 1980 only three U.S. states had laws against marital rape; today almost every state recognizes marital rape as a crime.

The Cause of Rape

What factors predispose some men to commit rape? The answers formulated by criminologists are almost as varied as the kinds of rape itself. However, most explanations can be grouped into a few consistent categories.

Evolutionary/Biological Factors. One explanation for rape focuses on the evolutionary/biological aspects of the male sexual drive, that forcible sexual contact may have served the purpose of maximizing offspring. Some believe that

males still have a natural sexual drive that encourages them to have intimate relations with as many women as possible.[71] Men who are sexually aggressive will have the reproductive edge over their more passive peers. In contrast, women are more cautious and want to choose stable partners who seem willing to make a long-term commitment to child rearing. This difference produces sexual tension that causes men to use forceful copulatory tactics, especially when the chances of punishment are quite low. Rape is bound up with sexuality as well as violence because the act involves the "drive to possess and control others to whom one is sexually attracted."[72]

Male Socialization. In contrast to the evolutionary biological view, some researchers argue that rape is a function of male socialization. In this way, rape is not a deviant act but a masculine one.[73] Boys are taught to be aggressive, forceful, tough, and dominating. Males are taught to dominate at the same time that they are led to believe that females want to be dominated. If males learn to separate their sexual feelings from needs for love and affection, and are socialized to be the aggressors, then male virginity and sexual inexperience are marks of shame. Similarly, sexually aggressive women frighten some men and cause them to doubt their own masculinity. Sexual insecurity may lead some men to commit rape to bolster their self-image and masculine identity.

If rape is an expression of male anger and devaluation of women and not an act motivated by sexual desire, it follows that men socialized into traditional sex-role stereotypes are more likely to be sexually aggressive.

Connections

Recall that in Chapter 9 Messerschmidt described how the need to prove one's masculinity helped men to justify their abuse of women. Men who are sexually violent need to prove that they are not effeminate.

Psychological Views. Another view is that rapists are suffering from some type of personality disorder or mental illness. Research shows that a significant percentage of incarcerated rapists exhibit psychotic tendencies, while many others have hostile and sadistic feelings toward women.[74]

Social Learning. Another explanation for rape is that men learn to commit rapes much as they learn any other behaviour. Some men are influenced by watching violent or pornographic films featuring women who are beaten, raped, or tortured.[75] In one case, a 12-year-old Providence, Rhode Island, boy sexually assaulted a 10-year-old girl on a pool table after watching TV coverage of a case in which a woman was similarly raped (the incident was made into a film, *The Accused*, starring Jodie Foster).[76]

This view is explored further in Chapter 14, where the issue of pornography and violence is analyzed in greater detail. Most research does not show that watching "porno films" is linked to sexual violence, but there may be a link between sexual aggression and viewing movies with sexual violence as their theme.

Sexual Motivation. Most current views of rape hold that it is a violent act and not sexually motivated. Yet, there might still be a sexual motive from some rapes:[77] While older criminals may be raping for motives of power and control, younger offenders are seeking sexual gratification as well.

In sum, while criminologists are still at odds over the precise cause of rape, there is evidence that it is the product of a number of social, cultural, and psychological forces.[78] Although some experts view rape as a normal response to an abnormal environment, others view it as the product of a disturbed mind and deviant life experiences.

Rape and the Law

Women who are sexually assaulted are reluctant to report the crime to the police because of the sexist fashion in which rape victims are often treated by police, prosecutors, and court personnel. There is also the possible invasion of a woman's privacy when a rape case is tried in court. In the past police were reluctant to make arrests and courts to convict in cases in which a woman was not beaten seriously or in which she had previously known her attacker. Laws made rape so difficult to prove that women believed the chances of their attacker being convicted were insufficient to warrant their participation in the prosecutorial process.

However, in the last 15 years, research indicates that police and the courts may have become more sensitive to the plight of rape victims and are now just as likely to investigate "acquaintance" rapes as they were "aggravated" rapes involving multiple offenders, weapons, and victim injuries. More than in the past, the justice system is willing to take all rape cases seriously and not ignore those in which the victim and attacker had a prior relationship or those that did not involve serious injury.[79]

Proving Rape. Proving guilt in a rape case is extremely challenging for prosecutors. First, some male psychiatrists and therapists still maintain that women fantasize about rape and therefore may falsely accuse their alleged attackers. Some judges also fear that women may charge men with rape because of jealousy, false proposals of marriage, or pregnancy.[80]

Sexism in society has created a cultural suspicion of women. Consequently, there is often an attempt to shift the burden to the woman to prove she has not provoked or condoned the rape. Although the law does not recognize it, jurors are sometimes swayed by the insinuation that the rape was victim-precipitated; thus, the blame is shifted from rapist to victim. To get a conviction, prosecutors must establish that the act was forced and violent and that no question of voluntary compliance exists. The legal consequences of rape often reflect archaic legal traditions along with inherent male prejudices and suspicions.

Rape represents a major legal challenge to the criminal justice system.[81] One issue is the concept of **consent.** Proving victim dissent is not a requirement in any other violent crime (robbery victims do not have to prove they did not entice their attacker by flaunting expensive jewellery), yet in rape cases defence counsel can try to create a reasonable doubt about the woman's credibility under Sections 265.4 and 276.1 of the Criminal Code. A defence attorney might try to introduce suspicion in the minds of the jury that the woman may have consented to the sexual act and later regretted her decision. Conversely, it is difficult for a prosecuting attorney to establish that a woman's character is so impeccable that the absence of consent is a certainty. Such distinctions are important in rape cases, because male jurors may be sympathetic to the accused if the victim is portrayed as unchaste.[82]

Law Reform. Because of the difficulty victims have had in receiving justice in rape cases, sexual assault legislation in Canada has undergone significant change since 1983. Efforts for reform have included changing the language of statutes, dropping the conditions of recent complaint and corroboration, and developing **shield laws,** which protect women from being questioned about their sexual history unless it is judged to have a direct bearing on the case. This is quickly becoming an international standard.[83]

In addition to requiring evidence that consent was not given, the common law of rape required **corroboration** that the crime of rape actually took place. This involved the need for independent or third-party evidence from police officers, physicians, and witnesses that the accused was actually the person who committed the crime, that sexual penetration took place, and that force was present and consent absent. In the past this requirement shielded rapists from prosecution in cases where the victim delayed reporting the crime or in which physical evidence had been compromised or lost.[84] Current law does not require corroboration, intercourse, or a complaint to be filed immediately.

Furthermore, in the early 1990s, consent was legally defined as required, and not possible where the victim was too drunk to know what she was doing. Section 273.1 of Canada's Criminal Code requires that sexual activity be voluntary. No consent is obtained, where

(a) the agreement is expressed by someone else;

(b) the complainant is incapable of consenting to the activity;

(c) the accused induces the complainant to engage in the activity by abusing a position of trust, power or authority;

(d) the complainant expresses, by words or conduct, a lack of agreement to engage in the activity; or

(e) the complainant, having consented to engage in sexual activity, expresses, by words or conduct, a lack of agreement to continue to engage in the activity.

Therefore, sexual assault laws outlaw any type of forcible or nonconsensual sex, including homosexual rape. However, research shows that the credibility of sexual assault victims is still more likely to be challenged in court than the testimony of victims of nonsexual assault.[85]

Linda Coates, a psychologist analyzing sexual assault cases, found that judges tend to characterize this crime as erotic and romantic rather than violent. She found that the new consent laws are not being applied uniformly, and that only when the victim would take action to resist an unwanted advance would the Court recognize lack of consent.[86]

Clearly, more efforts are needed to improve the prosecution rate in sexual assault cases.

Murder

To prove that murder has been committed with malice, prosecutors must prove that the accused intentionally desired the death of the victim. Express or actual malice is the state of mind assumed to exist when someone kills another person in the absence of any apparent provocation. Implied or constructive malice is considered to exist when a death results from negligent or unthinking behaviour; even though the perpetrator did not wish to kill the victim, the killing was the result of an inherently dangerous act and therefore is considered murder.

Degrees of Murder

Murder is defined in the common law as "the unlawful killing of a human being with malice aforethought." Exhibit 11.4 details some facts about homicide in Canada.

There are different levels or degrees of homicide.[87] This categorization came about with the abolition of capital punishment in 1976. Murder in the first degree occurs when a person kills after premeditation and deliberation. **Premeditation** means that the killing was considered beforehand and suggests that it was motivated by more than a simple desire to engage in an act of violence, or an act of impulse. The planning implied by this definition need not be a long, drawn-out process but may be an almost instantaneous decision to take another's life.

Exhibit 11.4	**Quick Facts about Homicide in Canada, 1999**

- Police departments reported 536 homicides in Canada in 1999, the lowest rate since 1967.

- Shooting is the most common technique (30 percent), followed by stabbing (27 percent), beating (23 percent), and strangulation (10 percent).

- Fire (2 percent), shaken baby syndrome (1 percent), and poisoning (1 percent) are the least common.

- Homicide rates are lowest in the Atlantic provinces, at 21 percent of the national average.

- Canada's largest urban areas had 63 percent of the population, and 63 percent of the nation's homicides.

- Acquaintances accounted for 49 percent of solved homicides, 35 percent by family members, and 15 percent by strangers.

- In 80 percent of the cases of a murder of a child under 12 years, the killer is a parent.

- The father is more than 2.3 times as likely to be the killer of a child than the mother.

- Stranger-related homicides remained stable over ten years, at between 10 and 16 percent of the total.

- Spousal-related homicides account for one out of every six solved homicides.

- The greatest risk of being a homicide victim is during the first two years of life.

- Natives account for 3 percent of the population, but 19 percent of those accused of homicide, and 14 percent of homicide victims.

- Youths represent 8 percent of the population, and commit 10 percent of the homicides.

- Almost one-third of all homicides occur during the commission of another offence.

SOURCE: "Homicide in Canada 1999," *Juristat* 20 (9), 2000.

Second-degree murder requires the actor to have malice aforethought but not premeditation or deliberation. Second-degree murder occurs when a person's disregard for the victim or the desire to inflict serious bodily harm on the victim results in the loss of life. It can include malice.

An unlawful homicide without malice is called manslaughter. Voluntary or non-negligent manslaughter refers to a killing committed in the heat of passion or during a sudden quarrel considered to have provided sufficient provocation to produce violence; while intent may be present, malice is not. Involuntary or negligent manslaughter refers to a killing that occurs when a person's acts are negligent and without regard for the harm they may cause others. Most involuntary manslaughter cases involve motor vehicle deaths, as when a drunk driver causes the death of a pedestrian. However, people can be held criminally liable for the death of another in any instance where their disregard of safety causes the death.

The Nature and Extent of Murder

It is possible to track murder rate trends over time with the aid of UCR data. The Homicide Survey details information on all homicide offences in Canada since 1961. Homicide is a relatively rare crime in Canada. Since 1975 the overall homicide rate has decreased. In 1999 there were 536 homicides, compared to an average of 639 in the 1980s. In comparison, the FBI reported over 16 000 homicides in the United States in 1999. The rate of homicide in the United States was 5.8 per 100 000, while in Canada it was 1.8 per 100 000. While the homicide rate dropped in the 1990s in Canada, the rate of youths accused in homicides remained stable.[88]

What else do the official crime statistics tell us about murder today? Murder victims tend to be males over 18 years of age. Murder, like many crimes, tends to be an intraracial crime, committed by people against members of their own ethnic group. Most homicides involve a single victim, and most (75 to 85 percent) are solved by the police. Few people are killed by a stranger, and most are killed during a conflict (57 percent), not during the course of another crime. Youths (12 to 17) accounted for 9 percent of all accused persons, and males represented two-thirds of homicide victims and 90 percent of all accused, patterns that have proved consistent over time.[89]

Today, few people would deny that some relationship exists between social and ecological factors and murder. This section explores some of these factors.

Murderous Relations

One factor that has received a great deal of attention from criminologists is the relationship between the murderer and the victim. Most criminologists generally agree that murders can be separated into those involving strangers—typically stemming from a felony attempt, such as a robbery or drug deal—and acquaintance homicides involving disputes between family, friends, and acquaintances. It is believed that the quality of relationships and interpersonal interactions may thus influence murder.

Connections

Chapter 4's discussion of victim precipitation mentioned the argument made by some criminologists that murder victims helped create the "transaction" that led to their death.

Spousal Relations. Women are three times more likely to be killed by their mates than are men. In Canada in 1999, half of all female victims and only 6 percent of male victims were killed by someone they had an intimate relationship with. However, whereas the number of unmarried men killed by their partners declined, the rate of women killed by the men they lived with had increased dramatically. The speculation is that men kill their spouses because they fear losing control and power. Because people who live together without marriage have a legally and socially more "open" relationship, it is possible that males in such relationships are more likely to feel loss of control and exert their power with the use of violence. In contrast, research indicates that females who kill their mates do so after suffering repeated violent attacks.[90]

Women Who Kill. Statistics Canada data show that while child killing represents a small proportion of the total number of homicides in Canada, it represents the largest proportion of killing done by women (24 percent). Infanticide is usually committed by very young women (69 percent are under 21 years old), and the vast majority of accused (70 percent) are single. Finally, 67 percent of these women have been classified as mentally ill.[91]

Children Who Kill. Researchers who have looked at cases of youths committing homicide have developed five categories of homicide for youths: parents, siblings, other family, friends, and no relationship. They demonstrated that the rate of homicide committed by youths rises as they approach 18 years of age, and most of the homicides involved only one offender and one victim. Moreover, the number of victims rises as social distance between victim and offender increases. The most common method of homicide for youths is guns, followed by knives. The most common targets are friends and acquaintances. Seventy percent of all homicides committed by youths in Canada are theft-related. Contrary to predictions, it was found that young children are more likely to use guns than are older children. Also, younger children's victims are more likely to be family members, whereas older children are more likely to kill in the commission of other crimes and are more likely to kill strangers.[92]

Stranger Relations. The number of stranger homicides seems to be on the increase. Under what circumstances do stranger homicides occur? In a study of homicide in the United States, it was found that stranger homicides were most often "felony murders," which occur during rapes, robberies, and burglaries, and the rest were random acts of urban violence that fuel public fear. A homeowner tells a motorist to move his car because it is blocking the driveway, an argument ensues, and the owner gets a pistol and kills the motorist; a young boy kills a store manager because, he says, "Something came into my head to hurt the lady."[93]

How do such murderous relations develop between two people who have never before met? David Luckenbill studied murder transactions to determine whether particular patterns of behaviour are common to the transaction between killer and victim.[94] He found that many homicides take a sequential form: The victim made what the offender considered an offensive move; the offender typically retaliated in a verbal or physical manner; an agreement to end things violently was forged with the victim's response; the battle ensued, leaving the victim dead or dying; the offender's escape was shaped by his or her relationship to the victim or the reaction of the audience, if any.

On the other hand, research by Leslie Kennedy and Robert Silverman found that the elderly are likely to be the victims of theft-based homicide, by strangers, in their homes. The bulk of crimes against the elderly take place in their homes, in the midst of a robbery. Even though routine activities theory would suggest that the elderly are least likely to be victimized by homicide, in cases of household theft, they stand a high risk. This is because it is usually the house that is the intended victim of the crime, and the elderly are victimized because criminals are unaware that they are in the house.[95]

Youths living on the street, however, experience violence certainly as a result of the activities they engage in, and almost as a part of their culture.[96]

Homicide Networks

While some murders may be the result of wanton violence by a stranger, others involve a social interaction between two or more people who know each other and whose destructive social interaction leads to the death of one party.[97] Although on the surface these deaths seem senseless, they often mask a deeper underlying cause: revenge, dispute resolution, jealousy, bad drug deals, racial bias, threats to identity or status (for example, someone who is a "badass" has his authority challenged).[98] Perpetrators and victims may be joined in a "homicide network" that links victims, suspects, and witnesses together.

It is often the case that a prior act of violence, motivated by profit or greed, generates revenge killings. The instigator of one criminal act becomes the victim in another. Those individuals who are most isolated from conventional society and who have the least confidence in the criminal justice system are those most likely to seek "street justice." Witness the ongoing battle between the Hells Angels and the Rock Machine motorcycle gangs in Quebec. The combatants take the victimization of family and friends seriously, setting up a murderous exchange with the people they feel are responsible.[99]

Types of Murderers

Other forms of stranger homicides take a toll on society. **Thrill killings** involve impulsive violence motivated by the killer's decision to kill a stranger as an act of daring or recklessness.

Gang killings involve members of gangs who make violence part of their group activity. Some of these gangs engage in warfare over territory or control of the drug trade; in drive-by shootings, enemies are killed and strangers are caught in the crossfire.

Cult killings occur when members of religious cults, some of which are devoted to satanism, are ordered to kill by their leaders. On some occasions, the cult members are ordered to kill peers who are suspected of deviating from the leaders' teachings. Other crimes involve random violence against strangers either as a show of loyalty or because of the misguided belief that the strangers are a threat to the cult's existence. In Matamoros, Mexico, police uncovered the grave of a 21-year-old U.S. college student who had served as a human sacrifice for members of a Mexican drug ring that practised *palo mayombe,* a form of black magic; killing the youth was believed to bring immunity from bullets and criminal prosecution.[100]

In 1994 bodies were recovered in homes belonging to the Order of the Solar Temple cult in Switzerland and Montreal. Some members of the apocalyptic cult were murdered, while others committed suicide. The cult combined teachings from medieval orders such as the Knights Templar, but there is evidence that the leaders appropriated their followers' wealth for their own personal gain. Police speculated that the cult's leaders were involved in an international money-laundering and arms-smuggling operation as well.

Some murders blamed on the influence of Satan are not carried out by members of an organized group but rather are perpetrated by individuals who have visions of the Devil telling them to kill. In 1993 a 15-year-old Houston boy killed his mother after hearing the Devil tell him to "kill all the Christians"; law enforcement officials linked the boy's passion for heavy metal music to the crime.[101]

Serial Murder

Donald Harvey was described as neat, pleasant, outgoing, and remarkably normal by those who knew him best. However, his co-workers in a Cincinnati-area hospital where he worked as a nurse's aide referred to Harvey as the "angel of death" because so many patients died in his ward. Their fears convinced a local TV station to conduct an investigation that resulted in Harvey's arrest and conviction on multiple murder charges. Harvey pleaded guilty to killing at least 21 patients and 3 other people; he claims to have killed 28 others, although he cannot remember details of their deaths. Harvey claims that he was a mercy killer who "gained relief for the patients"; prosecutors described him as a thrill seeker whose behaviour was triggered by his sexual ambivalence.[102]

This type of crime is referred to as serial murder. Some serial murderers, such as Theodore Bundy and the

Culture, Gender, Ethnicity, and Criminology

The Death of James Bulger

On February 12, 1993, the security cameras at a shopping centre near Liverpool, England, recorded two-year-old James Bulger being abducted by two strangers. He was taken on a long, aimless walk, cruelly tortured, sexually abused, beaten to death, and abandoned on the railroad tracks. Jon Venables and Robert Thompson, his murderers, were ten years old. When arrested and questioned, they each denied their role in the murder and blamed the other.

Jon's psychological profile showed that he was generally well behaved but sometimes hyperactive. His mother thought that Jon was the victim of bullies at school. However, Jon's parents had repeatedly split up and reunited, undermining the family as a source of stability. Jon seemed to have low self-esteem and was defensive about his family. He had a history of self-inflicted violence, banging his head against the wall, and cutting himself with scissors. He was also destructive at school. Both his siblings had developmental problems, and his parents had histories of clinical depression. His mother had on occasion physically and verbally assaulted Jon.

Robert's psychological profile showed that he was intelligent and had no sign of mental illness or

Preacher spells out Britain's moral decline

By Victoria Combe, Churches Correspondent

THE American evangelist Morris Cerullo yesterday took two full-page adverts in broadsheet newspapers, costing more than £40,000, to outline Britain's "rapid moral and spiritual decline". . . .

Mr Cerullo claimed Britain's laws, formerly a model of Christian principles for other governments, had been "eroded" since the 1960s by "atheists, rationalists and confused spiritual leaders". . . .

Listing disasters such as Hillsborough, Lockerbie and the Jamie Bulger killing, he said Britain was in a state of "rapid decline morally, spiritually and materially". [The] British people want political leaders who tell them the truth. Men and women who live honestly. They want unconfused Church leaders. "The nation wants men of integrity who lead by what God of the Bible has to say, not what they think may be politically acceptable." . . .

Electronic Telegraph, Monday, July 29, 1996.

depression. However, he was often assaulted by his older brothers and alcoholic mother. His father beat his wife and eventually abandoned the family. Both his mother and father came from abusive families. One of his brothers had been placed in protective services after he had been abused. Another was a thief, and another was an arsonist and suspected of sexually abusing young children.

An important issue in the trial was whether the boys knew the difference between right and wrong. The concept of "doli incapax" was established to protect innocent children from punishment and dates back to Roman law. If a child cannot grasp the consequences of his or her actions, he or she is legally incapable of wrongdoing. Jon and Robert's teachers and psychiatrists testified that they believed the defendants knew the severity of their crime. The interviews recorded by the police also revealed that they understood the charges against them.

The judge addressed the boys: "The killing of James Bulger was an act of unparalleled evil and barbarity. This child of two was

taken from his mother on a journey of over two miles and then, on the railway line, was battered to death without mercy. Then his body was placed across the railway line so it would be run over by a train in an attempt to conceal his murder. In my judgment your conduct was both cunning and very wicked."

With their conviction for the murder of James Bulger, Jon Venables and Robert Thompson became the youngest convicted murderers in Britain for 250 years. Their original sentence of 15 years was overturned when the European Court of Human Rights decreed in 1999 that the boys had not received a fair trial and mandated their release after eight years in jail. In a newspaper phone poll 96 percent of the British public protested that the boys had been released. Because of the public outcry over the killing, Jon and Robert have been given false identities for their own safety.

Sources: Blake Morrison, "Children of Circumstance," *The New Yorker*, February 14, 1994, pp. 48-60; www.crimelibrary.com; "Justice for James," at http://www.jamesbulger.co.uk/; Electronic Telegraph; various other media sources.

Australian race-car driver and photographer Christopher Wilder, roam the country killing at random. Others terrorize a city, such as the Los Angeles–based Night Stalker; the Green River Killer, who is believed to have slain more than four dozen young women in Seattle; and the Hillside Stranglers, Kenneth Bianchi and Angelo Buono, who tortured and killed 10 women in the Los Angeles area. Others, such as Donald Harvey and Milwaukee cannibal Jeffrey Dahmer, kill so cunningly that many victims are dispatched before the authorities even realize the deaths can be attributed to a single perpetrator.[103]

Serial killers operate over a long period of time and can be distinguished from the **mass murderer** who kills many victims in a single, violent outburst, such as Thomas Hamilton's outburst in Dunblane, Scotland, or James Huberty's murder of 21 people in a McDonald's restaurant in San Ysidro, California.

Types of Serial Murderers. Research shows that serial killers have long histories of violence, beginning in childhood with the targeting of other children, siblings, and small animals.[104] They maintain superficial relationships with others, have trouble relating to the opposite sex, and have guilt feelings about their interest in sex. Despite these commonalities, there is no single distinct type of serial killer.

Such factors as mental illness, sexual frustration, neurological damage, child abuse and neglect, smothering relationships with mothers, and childhood anxiety have been suggested as possible causes. However, most experts view serial killers as sociopaths who from early childhood demonstrated bizarre behaviour, such as torturing animals; who enjoy killing; who are immune to their victims' suffering; and who, when caught, bask in the media limelight. However, Philip Jenkins's study of serial murder in England identified one group of offenders who had no apparent personality problems until late in their lives, were married and respectable, and even had careers in the armed services and police.[105]

Ronald Holmes and James DeBurger have studied serial killers and found that they can be divided into at least four types:

1. Visionary killers. These psychotic murders are committed in response to some inner voice or vision that demands that some person or category of persons be killed.
2. Mission-oriented killers. Their murders are motivated to rid the world of a particular type of person they consider undesirable, such as prostitutes.
3. Hedonistic killers. These are thrill-seeking murderers who get excitement and sometimes sexual pleasure from their acts.
4. Power/control-oriented killers. These murderers enjoy having complete control over their victims.[106]

Other types of serial killers include the sadistic child killer, who gains sexual satisfaction from torturing and killing children; the psychopathic killer, who is motivated by a character disorder that results in his or her being unable to experience feelings of shame, guilt, sorrow, or other "normal" human emotions; and professional hit killers, who assassinate complete strangers for economic, political, or ideological reasons (terrorists and organized crime figures fall within this category).[107]

When the Serial Killer Is a Woman. An estimated 10 to 15 percent of serial killers are women. A study of 14 female serial killers found a pattern of distinct gender differences.[108] For instance, males were much more likely than females to use extreme violence and torture. Men tracked or stalked their victims, while women were more likely to lure victims to their death.

Female killers were somewhat older than their male counterparts and were abusers of both alcohol and drugs. Women were diagnosed as having histrionic, manic-depressive, borderline, dissociative, and antisocial personality disorders; men were more often diagnosed as having antisocial personalities.

The profile of the female serial killer that emerges is a person who smothers or poisons someone she knows. During childhood, she suffered from an abusive relationship in a disrupted family. Female killers' education levels are below average, and if they work, it is in a low-status position.

Controlling Serial Killers. Serial killers come from diverse backgrounds. So far, law enforcement officials have been at a loss to control random killers who leave few clues, constantly change their whereabouts, and have little connection to their victims. Catching serial killers is often a matter of luck. In the 1980s, because of a series of high-profile serial homicides that encompassed multiple jurisdictions, it became clear that there needed to be a better way for the police to share information. The proposed "automated case linkage system" was called ViCLAS (Violent Crime Linkage Analysis System). The idea was that it would help local law enforcement officials profile cases and identify potential suspects. It was modelled on the computerized information service developed by the FBI and U.S. Justice Department called Violent Criminal Apprehension Program (VICAP), which gathers information and matches offence characteristics on violent crimes around the country.[109] This way, crimes can be compared to determine whether they are the product of a single culprit.

Efforts to control serial killers take on greater importance when the rate of increase of this crime is considered. Philip Jenkins has studied serial killing over the past 50 years and reports an upsurge since the 1960s. In addition, the number of victims per criminal and the ferocity and savagery of the killings also seem to be increasing. Jenkins attributes this increase to a variety of influences, ranging from a permissive, drug-abusing culture to a mental health system so overcrowded that potentially dangerous people are released without supervision into an unsuspecting world.[110]

Assault

In 1995 the Canadian Centre for Justice Statistics reported almost 180 000 assaults, a rate of about 601 per 100 000 inhabitants. Assaults have a clearance rate of about 80 percent, and the majority of the protagonists are male.

Assault in the Home

One of the most frightening aspects of assaultive behaviour today is the incidence of violent attacks in the home. Exhibit 11.5 displays some facts about violence against children. Criminologists are now aware that intrafamily violence is an enduring social problem in our society. One area of intrafamily violence that has received a great deal of media attention is **child abuse**. This term describes any physical or emotional trauma to a child for which no reasonable explanation, such as an accident or ordinary disciplinary practices, can be found.[111]

Child abuse can result from actual physical beatings administered to a child by hands, feet, weapons, belts, sticks, burning, and so on. Another form of abuse results from neglect—not providing a child with the care and shelter to which he or she is entitled. It is difficult to estimate the actual number of child abuse cases, since so many incidents are never reported to the police.

In Canada 6 percent of the victims of violent crime are children under 12, while 20 percent are aged 12 to 19. In general, boys and girls are equally likely to be the victims of violent crimes. However, boys are more likely to be the victims of homicide, while girls are more likely to be sexually abused.[112] Over one million children a year in the United States are subject to physical abuse from their parents.[113] Physical abuse was found to rarely be a one-time event, and children of all ages suffer abuse.

Another aspect of the abuse syndrome is **sexual abuse**—the exploitation of children through rape, incest, and molestation by parents or other adults. It is difficult to estimate the incidence of sexual abuse. Many allegations of sexual impropriety have been made against religious figures such as priests and Boy Scout leaders.[114] Many Canadian organizations that use the services of volunteers now have their applications screened by the police for a criminal record, often paid by the applicant.

In an attempt to gauge the extent of the problem, one survey of women in the San Francisco area found that 38 percent had experienced intrafamilial or extrafamilial sexual abuse by the time they reached 18.[115] A survey of Minnesota students in grades 6, 9, and 12 found that about 2 percent of the males and 7 percent of the females had experienced incest, while 4 percent of the males and 13 percent of the females had suffered extrafamilial sexual abuse. Other research indicates that up to one in five girls suffers sexual abuse.[116]

While these results are disturbing, they most likely underestimate the incidence of sexual abuse. It is difficult

Exhibit 11.5	Quick Facts about Violence Against Children, 1994

- Children under 12 make up 16 percent of the population, but account for 71 percent of sexual offence victims.*
- Of victims under 12, boys were 58 percent of the homicide victims.
- Of victims under 12, girls were 72 percent of the sexual assault victims.
- When children under 12 were victimized, the perpetrator was usually an adult.
- The estimated rate of abuse and neglect is 21 cases per 100 children.
- In violent incidents against children under 12, 37 percent of assailants were family members, 40 percent friends, and 16 percent strangers.
- Parents kidnapped/abducted boys (43 percent), girls (25 percent); friends kidnapped/abducted boys (19 percent), girls (35 percent).
- Kidnapping/abduction by parents (33 percent), acquaintances (28 percent), strangers (25 percent).
- Eleven percent of violent incidents involving children and youths occurred on school property.
- Seven percent of persons charged with prostitution-related offences were youths 12 to 19 years of age.

* Includes sexual assault levels I, II, and III (28 percent), and sexual interference, invitation to sexual touching, sexual exploitation, and incest (43 percent).

SOURCE: "Children and Youths as Victims of Violent Crime," *Juristat* 15 (1995).

to get people to answer questions about youthful sexual abuse, and many victims either were too young to understand their abuse or have repressed their memory of the incidents. Children, the most common target, may be inhibited because parents are reluctant to admit abuse occurred. One study found that 57 percent of children referred to a clinic because they had sexually transmitted diseases claimed not to have been molested despite this irrefutable physical evidence. Parental response significantly influences reporting abuse: Kids whose caretakers admitted the possibility of abuse were 3.5 times more likely to report abuse than those whose parents denied any possibility that their child was a victim.[117]

The growing incidence of sexual abuse is of particular concern when its long-term impact is considered. Abused kids experience a long list of symptoms, including fear, posttraumatic stress disorder, behaviour problems, sexualized behaviour, and poor self-esteem. The amount of force used, its duration, and its frequency are all related to the extent of the long-term effects and the length of time needed for recovery.[118]

Causes of Child Abuse

Why do parents physically assault their children? Such maltreatment is a highly complex problem with neither a single cause nor a readily available solution. It cuts across ethnic, religious, and socioeconomic lines. Abusive parents cannot be categorized by sex, age, or educational level; they come from all walks of life.[119]

One factor that has been associated with systematic child abuse is familial stress. Abusive parents are unable to cope with life crises—divorce, financial problems, alcohol and drug abuse, poor housing conditions. This inability leads them to maltreat their children. A higher rate of assault on children occurs among lower economic classes; however this doesn't mean that lower-class parents are more abusive than those in the upper classes. First, low-income people are often subject to greater levels of environmental stress and have fewer resources to deal with it. Second, cases of abuse among poor families are more likely to be dealt with by public agencies and therefore are more frequently counted in official statistics.[120]

Other characteristics that are related are the presence of a step-parent in the household, young parents, poor parenting skills, marital violence, alcohol or drug abuse, large family size, poverty, unemployment, and disability in the child.[121]

Two other factors have a direct correlation with abuse and neglect. First, parents who themselves suffered abuse as children tend to abuse their own children; second, isolated and alienated families tend to become abusive. A cyclical pattern of family violence seems to be perpetuated from one generation to another within families. Evidence indicates that a large number of abused and neglected children grow into adolescence and adulthood with a tendency to engage in violent behaviour. The behaviour of abusive parents can often be traced to negative experiences in their own childhood—physical abuse, lack of love, emotional neglect, incest, and so on. These parents become unable to separate their own childhood traumas from their relationships with their children. They also often have unrealistic perceptions of the appropriate stages of childhood development. Thus, when their children are unable to act "appropriately"—when they cry, throw food, or strike their parents—the parents may react in an abusive manner: "A fussy baby can be the lighted match."[122]

Parents also become abusive if they are isolated from friends, neighbours, or relatives who can provide a lifeline in times of crisis. Potentially or actually abusing parents live in states of alienation from society, cut off from contact with other people in the neighbourhood. Many abusive and neglectful parents describe themselves as highly alienated from their families and lacking close relationships with people who could provide help and support in stressful situations.

Public concern about child abuse has led to the development of programs designed to prevent and deter it. The reporting of child abuse by doctors, social workers, and other such persons is mandated by law. As well, Human Resources Development Canada (HRDC) has implemented a National Longitudinal Study of Children that will follow 25 000 children as they grow to adulthood, in order to develop a database of information about child welfare in Canada (mentioned earlier in this chapter).

Spouse Abuse

On the evening of June 23, 1993, John Wayne Bobbitt came home and, according to his wife, Lorena, committed a marital rape. Afterward, while he slept, Lorena used a 12-inch kitchen knife to slice off two-thirds of his penis, which she then threw into a field. Police officers were able to recover it, and it was reattached in a 9 1/2-hour operation. The case drew reporters from around the United States; observers at the scene described representatives of the media as a "herd of buffaloes," backing into cars and falling in ditches.

Bobbitt was later tried and acquitted on charges of sexual assault stemming from the alleged rape. Claiming that her actions were a result of the rape and earlier abuse, Lorena was found not guilty on a charge of malicious wounding, by reason of insanity, on January 21, 1994. No longer considered a threat (at least to anyone other than her former husband), she was released from Virginia's Central State Hospital on February 28, 1994.[123]

Although highly publicized, this case is misleading: Spouse abuse overwhelmingly involves a physical assault in which a wife is injured by a husband.[124] There are indeed some cases of husband battering, but they typically involve a defensive measure taken by a previously abused spouse. According to criminologists Martin Schwartz and Walter DeKeseredy, the presentation of women as violent helps maintain the dominance of men in marital relations.[125]

Connections

In Chapter 4, the case of Lynn Lavallee is considered in relation to victimization theory.

Spouse abuse has occurred throughout recorded history. During the Roman era, men had the legal right to beat their wives for attending public games without permission, drinking wine, or walking outdoors with their faces uncovered, while adultery was punishable by death.

However, by the 4th century, excessive violence on the part of husband or wife could be used as sufficient grounds for divorce. During the early Middle Ages, love and marriage became separated. The ideal woman was protected and cherished, and the wife was guarded jealously and could be punished severely for violations of duty. A husband was expected to beat his wife for "misbehaviours" and might himself be punished by neighbours in the cuckold's court if he failed to do so.

By the mid-19th century, severe wife beating had fallen into disfavour, and accused wife beaters were subject to public ridicule. Nonetheless, limited chastisement was still the rule. By the close of the 19th century, laws had been passed in England and the United States outlawing wife beating. Yet the long history of husbands' domination of their wives' lives made physical coercion difficult to control. Until recent times, the subordinate position of women in the family was believed to give husbands the legal and moral obligation to manage their wives' behaviour. Even after World War II, there is evidence of English courts finding domestic assault to be a reasonable punishment for a wife who had disobeyed her husband.[126] These ideas form the foundation of men's traditional physical control of women and have led to severe cases of spousal assault.

Merlin Brinkerhoff and Eugene Lupri, in their study of family violence, began from the assumption that family violence is not uncommon, but indeed, a factor of many familial relationships. They found that both women and men are the agitators of violence, and that many times the abuse goes unreported. Furthermore, it was found that if there was one violent episode, it was likely violence would occur time and time again. Violent couples came from all socio-economic classes, and occupational/educational attainment had an insignificant role in predicting interspousal violence.[127]

The Nature and Extent of Spouse Abuse. It is difficult to estimate the extent of spouse abuse today. In a U.S. survey, 16 percent of surveyed families had experienced husband-to-wife assaults. In Canada, Statistics Canada's national Survey on Violence Against Women estimated that 29 percent of women who have ever been married have been assaulted. The rate was highest in British Columbia (36 percent) and lowest in Newfoundland (17 percent). In cases of previous marriages, 48 percent of the women had been assaulted, while 15 percent of currently married women reported being assaulted.[128] Nor is violence restricted to the postmarital stage of domestic relations. In a national survey of college students, more than 20 percent of the females had experienced violence during their dating and courtship relationships.[129]

What are the characteristics of the wife assaulter? The traits commonly found include the following:[130]

- Excessive alcohol abuse
- Hostility and dependency based on resentment and sexual inadequacy
- Excessive brooding over a wife's behaviour, however trivial
- Belief that society approves of wife assault, as justification of assault
- Being under economic stress
- Given to a sudden burst of anger after a verbal dispute
- Having served in the military
- Having been battered as children

Is Spouse Abuse Intergenerational? While it is generally agreed that child abuse is intergenerational, do the same patterns apply to spouse abuse? Although there is little conclusive evidence that spouse abusers grew up in homes where spouses were abused, some research indicates that abused children later act abusively toward their own children and their spouses.[131]

There are a number of views on why this phenomenon occurs. One is that children learn the role of parent/spouse through observation, and those who grow up in abusive households believe that harsh parenting and violent behaviour are "normal" in the typical family. A second view is that harsh parenting teaches kids that it is often necessary to hit those you love, spouses as well as children. A third view is that harsh and incompetent parenting produces children with many behavioural problems, including child, spouse, and substance abuse. This variation on problem behaviour syndrome suggests that people who have experienced abusive, incompetent parenting are also more likely to use drugs, commit crimes, and engage in a variety of antisocial behaviours, including persistent child and spouse abuse. The relationship between deviant behaviour and physical punishment is a constant across race, ethnic origin, and socioeconomic status.

A growing amount of support is being given to battered women. Shelters for assaulted wives are springing up around the country, and laws are being passed to protect a wife's interests. Police departments have made enforcement of domestic abuse laws a top priority with the so-called presumptive arrest policy. In Nova Scotia, for example, the 1992 directive of the Solicitor General's office has made it clear that "the police officer is to lay a charge where there are reasonable grounds to believe an offence has been committed." It is essential that this problem be brought to public light and controlled.

Robbery

The common-law definition of **robbery** is the taking or attempting to take anything of value from the care, custody, or control of a person or persons by force or threat of force or violence and/or by putting the victim in fear. A robbery is different from theft and becomes a crime of violence because it involves the use of force to obtain money or goods. The violence need not be severe or cause injury. Robbery is punished severely because the victim's life is put in jeopardy; the amount of force used and not the value of the items taken determines the level of punishment.

As with other violent crimes, it is useful to compare U.S. with Canadian statistics. In 1996 about 540 000 robberies were reported to police in the United States, for a rate of 220 per 100 000 population. In Canada in 1996, there were 6 646 "robberies with firearms," 10 322 "with other offensive weapons," and 14 274 "other" for a total of 31 242 incidents. The combined rate for robbery in Canada for 1996 was 104 per 100 000 residents, less than half the U.S. rate.[132]

The Ecology of Robbery

The ecological pattern for robbery is similar to that of other violent crimes. Robbery is most often a public crime—that is, fewer robberies occur in the home (6 percent) than in public places (37 percent), such as parking lots (5 percent), streets (28 percent), and open areas (4 percent). Commercial areas, including bars, restaurants, hallways, and office buildings, accounted for 44 percent of all robberies in 1995. The public nature of robbery has greatly influenced people's behaviour. Most people believe that large cities suffer the most serious instances of violent crimes, such as robbery, and, not surprisingly, many people have moved out of inner-city areas into suburban communities for this reason.

Robber Typologies

Attempts have been made to classify and explain the nature and dynamics of robbery.[133] Among the patterns identified are

- Robbery of persons who work in places where money changes hands, such as banks, or valuable goods are sold, such as jewellery stores
- Robbery in an open area, such as muggings or purse snatchings, in the street and parking lots, on public transit, and in open areas
- Robbery on private premises, such as breaking into homes (a small percentage of total robberies)
- Robbery in the aftermath of a chance meeting, such as a bar or a party
- Robbery after previous association of some duration between the victim and offender.

Robbers can also be categorized into the following specialties:[134]

- Professional robbers manifest a long-term commitment to crime as a source of livelihood and are committed to robbing because it is direct, fast, and very profitable. Planning and skill are the trade-

marks of the professional robber. Operating in groups in which assigned roles are the rule, professionals usually steal large amounts from commercial establishments.
- Opportunist robbers steal to obtain small amounts of money when an accessible and vulnerable target presents itself, such as cab drivers, drunks, and the elderly if the robbers need some extra spending money for clothes or other elements of their lifestyle. They are usually youths who do not plan their crimes, operate within juvenile gangs, are seldom organized, and spend little time discussing weapon use, getaway plans, or other strategies.
- Addict robbers steal to support their drug habits. They have a low commitment to robbery because of its danger but commit theft because it supplies needed funds. The addict is less likely to plan crime or use weapons than the professional robber but is more cautious than the opportunist. Targets are chosen on the basis of risk.
- Alcoholic robbers steal because of their excessive consumption of alcohol, usually to get some money to buy liquor. Alcoholic robbers have no real commitment to robbery as a way of life. They plan their crimes randomly and give little thought to victim, circumstance, or escape; for that reason, they are the most likely to be caught.

As these typologies indicate, the typical armed robber is unlikely to be a professional who carefully studies targets while planning a crime. People walking along the street, convenience stores, and gas stations are much more likely to be the target of robberies than banks or other highly secure environments. Robbers, therefore, seem to be diverted by modest defensive measures, such as having more than one clerk in a store or locating stores in strip malls rather than in stand-alone isolation.[135]

Evolving Forms of Violence

Assault, rape, robbery, and murder are traditional forms of interpersonal violence. However, as data become available, criminologists have recognized new categories within these crime types, such as serial murder, date rape, and hate crime. In this section we briefly discuss a new crime concern—workplace violence.

Connections

Hate crimes are another "newly discovered" form of violence, discussed in the context of passive precipitation theory in Chapter 4 on victimization.

Workplace Violence

In August 1992, after a long history of disciplinary problems and increasingly erratic behaviour, Dr. Valery Fabrikant walked into the engineering department at Concordia University and opened fire, killing three people and wounding two others. The reason given for his behaviour was that he had been denied a tenure position at the university.[136]

On April 6, 1999, a former employee at the Ottawa bus terminal took a high-powered rifle to work and shot five employees. Although it is alleged that he had a history of mental illness, he selected parts department employees only.

It has become commonplace to read of irate employees or former employees attacking co-workers or sabotaging machinery and production lines. Workplace violence is now considered the third leading cause of occupational injury or death in the United Sates.[137]

Who engages in workplace violence? The typical offender is a middle-aged white male who faces losing his job. The fear of economic ruin is especially strong in businesses where long-term employees fear job loss because of automation and reorganization. In contrast, when younger workers kill, it is usually while committing a robbery or other felony. The common name for this type of mass violence is "going postal," due to some high-profile shootings by postal employees.

Another trigger may be leadership styles. Some companies have authoritarian management styles that demand performance above all else from employees. Managers who are unsympathetic and unsupportive may help trigger workplace violence.

Not all workplace violence is caused by an injustice triggered by management. There have been incidents in which co-workers have been killed because they refused a romantic relationship with the assailant or had reported him for sexual harassment; others have been killed because they got a job the assailant coveted. There have also been cases of irate clients and customers who kill because of poor service or perceived slights.[138]

There are also a variety of responses to workplace "provocations." Some former employees attack supervisors to punish the company that dismissed them, a form of murder by proxy. Disgruntled employees may attack family members or friends, ignoring the actual cause of their rage and frustration. Others are content with sabotaging company equipment; computer data banks are particularly vulnerable to tampering. Over time, if there is an unresolved conflict, it may be compounded by some other events that eventually cause an eruption.

In his study of workplace violence in British Columbia's healthcare industry, Neil Boyd found that many instances of workplace violence are not formally reported. Using worker's compensation data for 1991, he found that more than 70 percent of nurses in British Columbia reported some form of violence at work, and 20 percent of these involved physical injury from an attack. Female workers were far more prone to violence at work than are males, but that might be due to the fact that 80 percent of workers in healthcare are female. The geographic location is also important, as upscale neighbourhoods are not nearly as conducive to violent outbursts as are "down and out" neighbourhoods. Boyd speculates that cutbacks have increased workload and tensions and have decreased the standard of medical care expected by many patients.[139]

Can workplace violence be controlled? A dispute resolution approach may help provide the control necessary to stave off the rising tide of workplace violence. Some researchers argue for a human resources approach, with aggressive job retraining and continued medical coverage in case of layoffs and due process guarantees to thwart unfair terminations.

Political Violence and Terrorism

In addition to interpersonal violence and street crime, violent behaviour also involves acts that have a political motivation, including terrorism. Political crime has been with us throughout history. It is virtually impossible to find a history book of any society that does not record the existence of political criminals.[140]

It is often difficult to separate political from interpersonal crimes of violence. For example, if a group robs a bank to obtain funds for its revolutionary struggles, should the act be treated as a political crime or as a common bank robbery? In the 1960s, the FLQ robbed banks and credit unions to finance its revolutionary activity in Quebec. Was this terrorism or bank robbery? Does the definition of a crime as political depend on the legal response the act evokes from those in power?

To be a political crime, an act must carry with it the intent to disrupt and change the government and must not merely be a simple common-law crime committed for reasons of greed or egotism. Those who violate the law because they believe their actions will ultimately benefit society are caught in the dilemma of knowing their actions may be wrong and harmful but believe these actions are necessary to create the changes they fervently desire.

One aspect of political violence that is of great concern to criminologists is **terrorism**. Because of its complexity, an all-encompassing definition of terrorism is difficult to formulate, although most experts agree that it generally involves the illegal use of force against innocent people to achieve a coercive political objective.[141]

Terrorism, then, is a type of political crime that emphasizes violence as a mechanism to promote change. Whereas other political criminals may engage in such acts as demonstrating, counterfeiting, selling secrets, spying, and the like, terrorists make systematic use of murder and destruction or the threat of such violence to terrorize individuals, groups, communities, or governments into conceding to the terrorists' political demands.[142] However, not all terrorist actions are aimed at political change; some terrorists may desire economic or social reform, for example, by attacking women wearing fur coats or sabotaging property during a labour dispute. Terrorism must also be distinguished from conventional warfare because it requires secrecy and clandestine operations to exert social control over large populations.[143]

The term *terrorist* is sometimes used interchangeably with *guerrilla*. The latter term, meaning "little war," developed out of the Spanish rebellion against French troops after Napoleon's invasion of the Iberian peninsula in 1808. Guerrillas are often located in rural areas, and the objects of their attacks include the military, the police, and government officials.[144] However, guerrillas can often become quite effective military organizations, as the Russians found out in their attempt to occupy Afghanistan in the 1980s.

Historical Perspective on Terrorism

Acts of terrorism have been known throughout history. Terrorism became widespread at the end of the Middle Ages, when political leaders were subject to assassination by their enemies. The word *assassin* is derived from an Arabic term meaning "hashish eater" and refers to members of a drug-using Moslem terrorist organization that carried out plots against prominent Christians and other religious enemies.[145] At a time when rulers were absolute despots, terrorist acts were viewed as one of the only means of gaining political rights.

At times, European states encouraged terrorist acts against their enemies. For example, Queen Elizabeth I empowered John Hawkins and Francis Drake to carry out attacks against the Spanish fleet. These privateers would have been considered pirates had they not operated with government approval. American privateers operated against the British during the Revolutionary War and the War of 1812. As you can see, history can turn terrorists into heroes, depending on which side wins.

The term *terrorist* became popular during the French Revolution. From the fall of the Bastille on July 14, 1789, until July 1794, thousands suspected of counterrevolutionary activity went to their deaths on the guillotine. While most victims of the French Reign of Terror were revolutionaries who had been denounced by rival factions, thousands of members of the hated nobility lived in relative tranquillity. The end of the terror was signalled by the death of its prime mover, Maximilien Robespierre, on July 28, 1794. He was executed on the same guillotine to which he had sent almost 20 000 people to their deaths.

In the hundred years after the French Revolution, terrorism continued around the world. The Hur Brotherhood in India was made up of religious fanatics who carried out terrorist acts. In Eastern Europe, the Internal Macedonian Revolutionary Organization campaigned against the Turkish government, which controlled its homeland (Macedonia became part of the former Yugoslavia). Similarly, the protest of the Union of Death Society, or Black Hand, against the Austro-Hungarian Empire's control of Serbia led to the group's assassination of Archduke Franz Ferdinand, an act that triggered the beginning of World War I. The Irish Republican Army developed around 1916 and kept up a steady battle with British forces from 1919 to 1923, culminating in the southern part of Ireland's gaining independence.

Between the world wars, right-wing terrorism existed in Germany, Spain, and Italy. Russia was the scene of left-wing revolutionary activity, leading to the death of the czar in 1917 and the rise of the Marxist state. During World War II, resistance to the Germans was common throughout Europe; these terrorists are now, of course, considered heroes. In Palestine, Jewish terrorist groups—the Haganah, Irgun, and Stern Gang, whose leaders included Menachim Begin, who later became prime minister—waged war against the British to force them to allow Jewish survivors of the Holocaust to settle in their traditional homeland. Today, Palestinian and Islamic terrorist groups carry out violent political action against the Israeli state.

Forms of Terrorism

Today, the term *terrorism* is used to describe many behaviours and goals. We will briefly describe some of the more common forms.[146]

Revolutionary Terrorism. Revolutionary terrorists use violence as a tool to invoke fear in those in power and their supporters. The ultimate goal is to replace the existing government with a regime that holds acceptable political views. Terrorist actions, such as kidnapping, assassination, and bombing, are designed to draw repressive responses from governments trying to defend themselves. These responses help revolutionaries expose, through the skilled use of media coverage, the government's inhumane nature. The original reason for the government's harsh response may be lost as the effect of counterterrorist activities is felt by uninvolved people.

In Europe, a Marxist group called the Marxist Baader-Meinhoff group in Germany conducted a series of robberies, bombings, and kidnappings in the 1980s. With the reunification of Germany, terrorist actions were believed over. Yet on April 1, 1991, its successor, the Red Army Faction, claimed "credit" for assassinating Detlev Rohwedder, the head of the government agency charged with rebuilding the East German economy.[147] In Italy, the Red Brigade kidnapped and executed a former Italian president, Albert Moro, and abducted James Dozier, a U.S. general, who was later rescued by security forces.[148]

As mentioned above, in the Middle East, the Palestine Liberation Organization has been active in directing terrorist activities against Israel and its western allies. While the PLO has reached accommodation with Israel in preparation for Palestinian political control of the West Bank and the Gaza Strip, splinter groups have broken from the PLO, including the Abu Nidal group, the Popular Front for the Liberation of Palestine, Hamas, and the Iranian-backed Hezbollah group, to continue the conflict. When the World Trade Center in New York City was bombed in 1993, the group responsible was demonstrating its hatred of U.S. policies in the Middle East. And again, on September 11, 2001, when the World Trade Center towers were brought down by hijacked airliners, it was a middle eastern group, Al-Qaeda, headed by Islamic extremist and millionaire Osama bin Laden, which was held responsible.

There have been numerous tragic incidents, but several stand out because of the large loss of life: Agents of the pro-Iranian Islamic Jihad used a truck bomb to blow up the U.S. Marine compound in Beirut, Lebanon, on April 18, 1983, killing 241; Libyan agents are the main suspects in the Christmas Day, 1988, bombing of Pan Am Flight 103 over Lockerbie, Scotland, which left 270 dead; and the August 7, 1998, bombings of U.S. embassies in Kenya and Sudan by agents of Osama bin Laden killed at least 250 and injured over 4000.[149] The attacks on September 11 killed approximately 5000 people.

Political Terrorism. In April 1996, after an 11-month federal investigation had resulted in their indictment on fraud charges, members of the U.S. Freemen movement held federal officers at bay in a month-long standoff before surrendering in Jordan, Montana. Heavily armed, the Freemen are one of many right-wing groups who have conducted or plan to conduct antigovernment activities in the United States. Their peaceful surrender prevented another in a long line of bloody engagements between federal agents and right-wing militants, such as the 1992 siege at Ruby Ridge, Idaho, or the infamous standoff in Waco, Texas, that resulted in the fiery deaths of followers of Branch Davidian leader David Koresh.[150]

Political terrorism is directed at people or groups who oppose the terrorists' political ideology or whom the terrorists define as "outsiders" who must be destroyed. Political terrorists in the United States tend to be heavily armed groups organized around such themes as white supremacy, Nazism, militant tax resistance, and religious revisionism. Identified groups include or have included the Aryan Republican Army, Aryan Nation, and Posse Comitatus, as well as the traditional Ku Klux Klan organizations. Some of these groups have formed their own churches; for example, the Church of Jesus Christ Christian claims that Jesus was born an Aryan rather than a Jew and that white Anglo-Saxons are the true "chosen" people. Some groups have conducted common-law crimes such as bank robberies to fund their activities, which might include bombings and other terror tactics.[151] The Oklahoma City bombing may have been the most tragic example of such activities.

Nationalistic Terrorism. Nationalistic terrorism is designed to promote the interests of minority ethnic or religious groups that (they feel) have been persecuted under majority rule. In India, Sikh radicals use violence for the purpose of recovering what they believe to be lost homelands. Sikh militants were responsible for assassinating Indian prime minister Indira Gandhi on November 6, 1984, in retaliation for the government's storming of their Golden Temple religious shrine in June 1984.[152] In

The World Trade Center towers collapse after a terrorist attack on September 11, 2001.

Egypt, fundamentalist Moslems have attacked foreign tourists in an effort to wreck the tourist industry, topple the secular government, and turn Egypt into an Islamic state.[153] In Algeria, fundamentalist Muslim groups have waged a decade-long battle against the government. On February 2, 1997, 50 militants armed with axes decapitated 31 people in the city of Medea.[154] The best-known nationalistic terrorist group operating today is the Provisional Irish Republican Army (IRA), which is dedicated to unifying Northern Ireland with the Republic of Ireland under home rule.

A Canadian nationalist terrorist group, the Front de liberation du Quebec (FLQ), planted bombs, robbed banks, and raided military armouries for weapons in the 1960s. They had suspected links with the Black Panthers, Cuba's revolutionary government, and radical groups in Algeria. On October 5, 1970, James Cross, a British trade official, was kidnapped by the FLQ. They demanded $500 000, the release of political prisoners, and safe passage to Cuba. The Quebec premier refused to negotiate and asked the federal government to send in troops. On October 10, Quebec cabinet minister Pierre Laporte was also abducted and murdered a week later. The imposition of the War Measures Act resulted in the arrest without warrant of 450 people, of which few were ever charged with a crime. When asked to justify his use of such extreme legal measures to fight terrorism, Prime Minister Pierre Trudeau said: "There's a lot of bleeding hearts who don't like to see people with helmets and guns . . . but it is more important to keep law and order in society." [155]

Nonpolitical Terrorism. Terrorist activity also involves groups that espouse a particular social or religious cause and use violence to address their grievances and not to topple governments. For example, anti-abortion groups have sponsored demonstrations at abortion clinics, and some members have gone so far as to attack clients, bomb offices, and kill doctors who perform abortions.

Animal rights organization members have harassed and thrown blood at people wearing fur coats. It has also become common for environmental groups to resort to terror tactics to sabotage their enemies' ability to harm the environment. One of the biggest targets is the livestock and research animal–producing industry. Members of such groups as the Animal Liberation Front (ALF) and Earth First! acknowledge making attacks against ranches and packing plants. ALF members free animals, such as by raiding turkey farms before Thanksgiving and rabbit farms before Easter.[156]

State-Sponsored Terrorism. State-sponsored terrorism occurs when a repressive government regime forces its citizens into obedience, oppresses minorities, and stifles political dissent. Death squads and the use of government troops to destroy political opposition parties are often associated with Latin American political terrorism.[157]

Some governments have been accused of using terrorist-type actions to control political dissidents. For example, in the first 18 months of its deployment, members of the Haitian National Police allegedly executed 15 political opponents of the regime.[158]

Much of what we know about state-sponsored terrorism comes from the efforts of human rights groups. London-based Amnesty International maintains that tens of thousands of people continue to become victims of security operations that result in disappearances and extrajudicial executions.[159] Political prisoners are now being tortured in about 100 countries, people have disappeared or are being held in secret detention in about 20 countries, and government-sponsored death squads operate in more than 35. Countries known for encouraging violent control of dissidents include Brazil, Colombia, Guatemala, Honduras, Peru, Iraq, and the Sudan. When Tupac Amaru rebels seized and held hostages at the Japanese ambassador's villa in Peru on December 17, 1996, Amnesty International charged that

Crime in the News

Police in Montreal defuse 150-pound bomb in car

By Clair Balfour, Globe and Mail Reporter
July 13, 1970
Montreal—A Volkswagen, converted into a mobile bomb, was discovered and defused behind the head office of the Bank of Montreal in the St. James Street financial district of Montreal early yesterday.

With its cargo of 150 pounds of dynamite it was the biggest of

four bombs investigated by city and district police in 48 hours. One went off and killed a man on Saturday as he drove on Metropolitan Boulevard, which carries the Trans-Canada Highway across the north side of Montreal.

Montreal police received a call at 12:55 a.m. yesterday about the car behind the bank. Police said the car contained a bomb composed of two sticks of dynamite wired to a clock set for 4:15 a.m. The 150 pounds of explosives were

in a case in the car and police said the small bomb would have triggered the case.

Sgt. Bob Cote of the Montreal police department's technical squad, said his men had a difficult time in disengaging the timing device.

The bomb, one of the largest dismantled by the city's bomb squad, would have leveled the building and caused considerable damage to the surroundings.

A soldier stands guard at Parliament Hill as security was stepped up because of terrorist kidnappings in Montreal during the PLQ Crisis October 13, 1970.

the action came in response to a decade-long campaign of human rights violations by national security forces and extensive abuses against opposition groups. Between January 1983 and December 1992 Amnesty International documented at least 4200 cases of people who had "disappeared" in Peru following detention by the security forces. Thousands more were killed by government forces in extrajudicial executions, including some 500 people in 19 separate massacres.[160]

Human Rights Watch, reporting on state-sponsored terrorism around the world, has charged that serious human rights violations, including disappearances, torture, and extrajudicial executions, persist at alarming levels in Guatemala one year after a human rights advocate rose to the presidency.[161]

Another form of state-sponsored terrorism, notes criminologist Ronald Kramer, is **structural violence**, which involves the physical harm caused by the unequal distribution of wealth. Structural violence involves a set of social conditions from which flows poverty, disease, hunger, malnutrition, poor sanitation, premature death, and high infant mortality.[162]

It is also possible for state-sponsored terrorism to be directed at people and governments outside the state's borders. Particularly disturbing is the possibility that some "outlaw" state such as Libya or North Korea will carry out a nuclear-based attack against a nation viewed as the enemy.[163] While special expertise is needed to build such a bomb, there are enough disaffected scientists available to provide the know-how to build an effective device. There are so many existing nuclear bombs in the hands of unstable Eastern European states that nuclear terrorists might be able to purchase what they need to build a bomb, as is allegedly the case with Osama bin Laden. Since 1990 there have been a half-dozen cases involving the theft and transportation of nuclear material and other cases involving people who made offers to agents to sell material not yet in their possession. While these are the known cases, it is impossible to know whether client states have already purchased enriched uranium or plutonium. If the New York Trade Center had been attacked with a low-yield nuclear device rather than chemical explosives, both towers would have collapsed and as many as 50 000 people would have been killed. Instead, it was airliners flown by hijackers armed with box-cutters that ultimately brought them down.

The most extreme form of state-sponsored terrorism occurs when a government seeks to wipe out a minority group within the jurisdiction it controls, referred to as **genocide**. The Holocaust during World War II is the most notorious example of genocide, but more recent atrocities have taken place in Cambodia, Rwanda, and Bosnia.

The Extent of Terrorism

According to the United States Department of State, the number of international terrorist incidents has decreased in recent years (296 in 1996). However, Iran, Iraq, Libya, North Korea, and Cuba continue their policy of giving material, logistic, and financial support to the groups that are committing terrorism.

Who Is the Terrorist?

Terrorists engage in criminal activities, such as bombings, shootings, and kidnappings. What motivates these individuals to risk their lives and those of innocent people? One view is that terrorists hold ideological beliefs that prompt their behaviour. At first, they have heightened perceptions of oppressive conditions–they feel relative deprivation.[164] Then they begin to recognize that these conditions can be changed by an active government reform effort that is not forthcoming. The terrorists conclude that they must resort to violence to encourage change.

The violence need not be aimed at a specific goal. Rather, terror tactics must contribute to setting in motion a series of events that enlist others in the cause and lead to long-term change. Successful terrorists must believe that their "self-sacrifice" outweighs the guilt created by committing a violent act that harms innocent people.

Terrorism, therefore, requires violence without guilt. The cause justifies the need for violence.[165]

According to Austin Turk, terrorists tend to come from upper- rather than lower-class backgrounds.[166] This was clearly the case in the September 11, 2001, hijackings. This may be because the upper classes can produce

Culture, Gender, Ethnicity, and Criminology

Genocide

The most extreme form of political violence is genocide—the attempt to eliminate a whole group of people defined by their race, religion, ethnicity, or political beliefs. Genocidal episodes have included the destruction of European Jews by the Nazis during the Holocaust, the killing of the Armenians in Turkey at the beginning of the 20th century, the annihilation of native tribes during the Spanish conquest of Latin America, and the "ethnic cleansing" that occurred during the recent wars in the former Yugoslavia.

A framework for understanding how these unimaginable outbreaks of political mass murder can occur in a civilized society would include conditions that have preceded the onset of genocide in Western society, such as the following:

- Difficult life conditions. The basic physical and material needs of society are not being met, and social groups lack a sense of positive identity, effectiveness, and control.
- Scapegoating. A group is identified as the cause of life's problems. Scapegoating helps affirm group identity by diminishing individual and group responsibility for life problems.
- New ideology. Ideologies emerge that offer the hope of a better life. People are given hope that if they join together and fulfil the ideology, success and riches will be at hand. The scapegoated group is seen as a

roadblock to its fulfilment.
- Devaluation. Members of a scapegoated group are devalued or considered lesser humans who can be harmed at will. Harmful behaviour changes the perpetrators, making them increasingly prone to act aggressively.
- "Just world" thinking. As members of the scapegoated group are harmed, both the perpetrators and bystanders begin to believe that the people who suffer deserve their fate.
- Commitment. As harm increases, so does commitment to group process and ideology. The more harm they cause their targets, the less likely perpetrators will be willing to change the course of their actions.
- Passive bystanders. Only bystanders, both within and outside the society, can exert pressure to stop the evolution toward group violence. For some reason, both groups remain passive, affirming the perpetrators' belief that they are right to victimize the outcast group.
- Authority orientation. Groups that have a strong and unquestioning respect for authority are more prone to group violence, and less likely to oppose destructive policies suggested by leaders. Security depends on obedience or the submission of the self to state authorities.
- Monolithic culture. A limited set of cultural values inhibits

intergroup relations, nonmembers are kept from important cultural and professional offices and from the legal process they could use to speak out against or halt destructive practices.
- Group self-concept. A shared belief that one's group is either superior or inferior (weak and vulnerable) is a precursor for genocidal impulses. Life's difficulties become more frustrating when they conflict with a group's feelings of superiority. Frustrated feelings of superiority combined with feelings of weakness and vulnerability lead to the embrace of destructive ideologies and scapegoating.
- History of aggression. Some cultures have a long history of violence and aggression. Using aggressive tactics to solve problems thus may seem normal, appropriate, and even desirable.

How does this model fit 20th-century genocides such as the Holocaust? The Germans had a long history of violence and aggression. Their culture was monolithic and featured such values as loyalty, obedience, and order. Life conditions in Germany were difficult after World War I, and the Jews were scapegoated as responsible for the economic catastrophe that followed. The Nazi ideology promised a better tomorrow that would elevate the Germans as the "purest" race and suggested that conditions could be improved by eliminating lesser races. The Nazi ideology was appealing with its emphasis on the superiority of the German people, nationalism, and unquestioning obedience to a leader.

Because the Jews were relatively successful, it was easy to portray them as dishonest and manipulative, enhancing their devalued status. Although there was a progression of anti-Semitic actions after Hitler came to power, nonaligned Germans distanced themselves from Jews, and the rest of the world stood idly by, attending the Berlin Olympics in 1936. American corporations conducted business in Germany throughout the 1930s. These conditions provoked an escalating round of violence that eventually led to genocide and mass destruction.

By setting out the factors that support genocide, we can get some insight into how the risk of political mass murder can be avoided. For example, societies must stress inclusion rather than exclusion, such as by including education about other cultures in school curriculums in order to lay a groundwork for understanding and acceptance.

Source: Ervin Staub, "Cultural-Societal Roots of Violence," *American Psychologist* 51 (1996): 117–32; *The Roots of Evil: The Origins of Genocide and Other Group Violence* (New York: Cambridge University Press, 1989).

people who are more politically sensitive, articulate, and focused in their resentments. Since their position in the class structure gives them the feeling that they can influence society, upper-class citizens are more likely to seek confrontations with authorities. Class differences are also manifested in different approaches to political violence. The violence of the lower class is more often associated with spontaneous expressions of dissatisfaction, manifested in collective riots and rampages and politically inconsequential acts. Higher-class violence tends to be more calculated and organized and uses elaborate strategies of resistance. Revolutionary cells, campaigns of terror and assassination, logistically complex and expensive assaults, and writing and disseminating formal critiques, manifestos, and theories are typically acts of the socially elite.

Upper-class political terrorism has been manifested in the death squads operating in Latin America and Asia. These vigilantes use violence to intimidate those opposing the ruling party. One graphic example of these terrorist activities occurred in Sri Lanka on October 5, 1989, when a death squad made up of members of the ruling party's security forces beheaded 18 suspected members of the antigovernment People's Liberation Front and placed the heads around a pond at a university campus.[167]

Responses to Terrorism

Governments have tried various responses to terrorism. Law enforcement agencies have infiltrated terrorist groups and turned members over to police. Rewards have been given for information leading to the arrest of terrorists, as was the case with the FLQ. "Democratic" elections have been held to discredit terrorists' complaints that the state is oppressive. Counterterrorism laws have been passed to increase penalties and decrease political rights. The United States, probably the biggest target of terrorist attacks, has antiterrorist legislation providing jurisdiction over terrorist acts committed abroad against U.S. citizens and punishing the killing of foreign officials and politically protected persons. In 1996 the U.S. Antiterrorism and Effective Death Penalty Act was signed into law banning fundraising to support terrorist organizations. It also allowed U.S. officials to deport terrorists from American soil, and to bar terrorists from entering the United States in the first place. Its other provisions include

- Requiring plastic explosives to contain chemical markers so that criminals who use them can be tracked down and prosecuted
- Increasing controls over biological and chemical weapons
- Toughening penalties over a range of terrorist crimes
- Banning the sale of defence goods and services to countries that are not "cooperating fully" with U.S. antiterrorism efforts.

In Canada, as a result of the events of September 11, Bill C-36 and Bill C-42 were speedily passed through Parliament. Among other powers, the first gave the police broad new powers of arrest without warrant, increased the period for which a person could be detained, and enabled the government to place a ban on the release of information related to terrorist investigations. As an omnibus bill, it included acts to amend the Criminal Code, the Official Secrets Act, the Canada Evidence Act, the Proceeds of Crime (Money Laundering) Act, and other acts. Bill C-42 gave the federal government the power to designate an area vital to national security, after which the military could compel everyone to leave and seal it off. These two bills came under heavy fire for violating civil rights. The U.S. antiterrorism bill is called the Patriot Act. Given the ability of the FBI to monitor Internet traffic, civil libertarians fear that there will be increasing violations of civil rights.[168]

Despite the development of antiterrorism statutes in North America and Europe, most politically motivated acts are prosecuted as common-law crimes. In Canada it is probably easier to deport someone under immigration law than it is to detain them under the new antiterrorism legislation.

Some countries have specially trained antiterrorist squads. The U.S. military, for example, has created the renowned Delta Force, made up of members from the four service areas. Delta Force activities are generally secret, but it is known that the force saw action in Iran (1980), Honduras (1982), Sudan (1983), and during the Grenada invasion (1983), and it was prepared to take action against the hijacking of the ship *Achille Lauro* in 1985. The American government's counter-revolutionary study, Project Camelot, had a branch studying the secession movement in Quebec.

Any attempts to meet force with force are fraught with danger. If the government's response is retaliation in kind, it could provoke increased terrorist activity—for revenge or to gain the release of captured comrades. Of course, a weak response may be interpreted as a licence for terrorists to operate with impunity. The U.S. government bombed Libya in 1986, in an attempt to convince its leader, Colonel Muammar Quaddafi, to desist from sponsoring terrorist organizations. While the raid made a dramatic statement, preventing terrorism is a task that so far has stymied the governments of most nations.

Summary

It seems that modern people live in an extremely violent time, with new forms of violence being identified and publicized more than ever before. Among the various explanations for violent crimes are personal traits, ineffective families, the presence of a subculture of violence that stresses violent solutions to interpersonal problems, substance abuse, and the availability of firearms.

There are many types of interpersonal violent crime. Sexual assault has been known throughout history, and at one time it was believed that a woman was as guilty as her attacker for her rape. At present, it is estimated that less than 10 percent of all sexual assaults are reported to police each year; the true number is probably much higher. Rape is an extremely difficult charge to prove in court.

Murder is the unlawful killing of a human being with malice. There are different degrees of murder, and punishments vary accordingly. One important characteristic of murder is that the victim and criminal often know each other. This has caused some criminologists to believe that murder is a victim-precipitated crime. Murder victims and offenders tend to be young and male.

Assault is another serious interpersonal violent crime. One important type of assault is that which occurs in the home, including child abuse and spouse abuse. It has been estimated that many children are abused by their parents each year, and a significant proportion of families report husband–wife violence. There is also a trend toward violence between dating couples on university and college campuses.

Robbery involves theft by force, usually in a public place. Types of offenders include professional, opportunist, addict, and alcoholic robbers.

Political violence is another serious problem. Many terrorist groups exist, at both the national and international levels. Hundreds of terrorist acts are reported each year in the United States alone. There are political terrorists, nationalists, and state-sponsored terrorists.

Violence is an important topic facing our society today, and the tasks of criminology are to identify and explain it and to work toward solutions. It is also our task to show that because we live in an information age, we are also more sensitive to reports of violent crime as well.

Thinking Like a Criminologist

The provincial government has hired you to prepare a report on what used to be called "statutory rape," that is, sex with underage youth. The government is concerned because of the growing number of underage girls who have been impregnated by adult men. Studies reveal that many teenage pregnancies result from affairs that underage girls have with older men, with age gaps ranging up to 10 years. The girl typically drops out of school and goes on welfare. Some outraged parents want the provincial government to more strictly enforce the law.

However, some critics suggest that implementing statutory rape laws to punish males who have relationships with minor girls does not solve the problems of teenage pregnancies and out-of-wedlock births. Liberals dislike the idea of using criminal law to solve social problems because it does not provide for the girls and their young children and focuses only on punishing offenders.

In contrast, conservatives fear that such laws give the state power to prosecute people for victimless crimes, thereby adding to the government's ability to control people's private lives. Not all cases involve much older men, and critics ask whether we should criminalize the behaviour of 17-year-old boys and their 15-year-old girlfriends.

As a criminologist with expertise on rape and its effects, what would you recommend regarding implementation of the law?

Key Terms

brutalization process	gang killings	robbery
child abuse	gendered violence	sexual abuse
consent	genocide	shield laws
corroboration	instrumental violence	structural violence
crime-related violence	marital exemption	terrorism
cult killings	mass murderer	thanatos
date rape	murder	thrill killings
eros	premeditation	
expressive violence	psychopharmacological	

 See the book-specific website at www.siegelcriminology2e.nelson.com for additional chapter links, discussions, and quizzes.

Chapter

12

Property Crimes

As a group, **economic crimes** can be defined as acts in violation of the criminal law designed to bring financial reward to an offender. In our society, the range and scope of criminal activity motivated by financial gain is tremendous. Self-report studies show that property crime among the young of every social class is widespread, although officially youths make up only 4 percent of property offences known to the police. Official statistics indicate that of the 2.4 million offences in Canada in 2000, 53 percent were property crimes. We know that corporate and other white-collar crimes are commonplace; political scandals indicate that even high government officials can be suspected of criminal acts.

Whereas average citizens may be puzzled and enraged by violent crimes, believing them to be both senseless and cruel, they often view economic crimes with a great deal more ambivalence. While it is true that society generally disapproves of crimes involving theft and corruption, the public seems quite tolerant of "gentlemen bandits," even to the point of admiring such figures. They pop up as characters in popular myths and legends—Robin Hood, Jesse James, Bonnie and Clyde, Edwin Alonzo Boyd. They are the semiheroic subjects of books and films, such as *48 Hours, Pulp Fiction*, and *Heat*.

How can such ambivalence toward criminality be explained? For one thing, tolerance toward economic criminals may be prompted by the fact that, if self-report surveys are accurate, almost every citizen has at some time been involved in economic crime. Even people who would never consider themselves criminals may have at one time engaged in petty theft, cheated on their income tax, stolen a textbook from a college bookstore, or pilfered from their place of employment. Consequently, it may be difficult for society to condemn economic criminals without feeling hypocritical.

People may also be more tolerant of economic crimes because they never seem to seriously hurt anyone—banks are insured, large businesses pass along losses to consumers, stolen cars can be easily replaced. The true pain of economic crime often goes unappreciated. Convicted offenders, especially businesspeople who commit white-collar crimes involving millions of dollars, are often punished rather lightly. We fail to realize how great the cost of economic crime is. In Nova Scotia, for example, a GPI Atlantic study found that crime costs an estimated $550 million a year in economic losses to victims, which includes public spending on police, courts and prisons, and private spending on burglar alarms, security guards, electronic surveillance, and theft insurance. This amounted to $600 per person in 1997. When unreported crimes such as insurance fraud are added, the cost is $1.2 billion a year, or $1250 per person. And this is lower than the national average!

This chapter is the first of two that review the nature and extent of economic crime in our society. It is divided into two principal sections. The first deals with the concept of professional crime and focuses on different types of professional criminals, including the **fence**, a buyer and seller of stolen merchandise. Then the chapter turns to a discussion of common theft-related offences, often referred to by criminologists as **street crimes**. These crimes include the major forms of common theft: larceny, theft by false pretences, and embezzlement. Included within these general offence categories are such common crimes as auto theft, shoplifting, and credit card fraud. Then the chapter discusses a more serious form of theft—**burglary,** or break and enter—that involves forcible entry into a person's home or place of work for the purpose of theft. Finally, the crime of **arson** is discussed briefly. In Chapter 13, attention will be given to white-collar crimes and economic crimes that involve organizations devoted to criminal enterprise.

A Brief History of Theft

Theft is not a phenomenon unique to modern times; the theft of personal property has been known throughout recorded history. The Crusades of the 11th century inspired peasants and downtrodden noblemen alike to leave the shelter of their estates to prey on passing pilgrims.[1] Not surprisingly, Crusaders felt it within their rights to appropriate the possessions of any infidels, Greeks, Jews, or Moslems, that they happened to encounter during their travels. By the 13th century, returning pilgrims, not content to live as serfs on feudal estates, gathered in the forests of England and the Continent to poach on game that was the rightful property of their lord or king and, when possible, to steal from passing strangers. By the 14th century, many of such highwaymen and poachers were full-time livestock thieves, stealing great numbers of cattle and sheep. Interestingly enough the origin of the vagrancy statutes are rooted in the need to control people who wandered about, with no lawful occupation, who preyed on travellers.

The 15th and 16th centuries brought hostilities between England and France in what has come to be known as the Hundred Years' War. Foreign mercenary troops fighting for both sides roamed the countryside, and loot and pillage were viewed as a rightful part of their pay. Theft became more professional with the rise of the city and the establishment of a permanent class of propertyless urban poor.[2] By the 18th century, three separate groups of property criminals were active. In the larger cities, such as London and Paris, groups of skilled thieves, pickpockets, forgers, and counterfeiters operated freely. As noted in the Culture feature below, some of the earliest organized police operated in London.

Thieves congregated in **flash houses**, which were public meeting places, often taverns, that served as headquarters for gangs. Here, deals were made, crimes plotted, and the sale of stolen goods negotiated. The second group of thieves were the smugglers, who moved freely in sparsely populated areas and transported goods without bothering to pay tax or duty. The third group were the poachers, who lived in the country and supplemented their diet and income with game that belonged to a landlord. By the 18th century, professional thieves in the larger cities had banded together into gangs to protect themselves, increase the scope of their activities, and help dispose of stolen goods.

Sometimes the difference between cop and criminal was difficult to see. Jack Wild, perhaps London's most famous thief, and thief taker, perfected the process of buying and selling stolen goods and gave himself the title of "Thief-Taker General of Great Britain and Ireland." Before he was hanged, Wild controlled numerous gangs and dealt harshly with any thief who violated his strict code of conduct.[3] During this period, individual theft-related crimes began to be defined by the common law. The most important of these categories are still used today.

Modern Thieves

There are hundreds of thousands of property and theft-related crimes that occur each year. In 1999, almost 700 000 thefts under $5000, and more than 300 000 break and enters were committed in Canada. Most are committed by occasional criminals who act opportunistically, who do not view themselves as committed career criminals; other theft-offenders are in fact skilled, professional criminals. The following sections review these two orientations toward property crime.

Occasional Criminals

Although criminologists are not certain, they suspect that the great majority of economic crimes are the work of amateur criminals whose decision to steal is spontaneous and whose acts are unskilled, unplanned, and haphazard. These would not involve the threat of violence, and many occur at domestic residences. Almost four in ten accused

Culture, Gender, Ethnicity, and Criminology

Catching Thieves in 18th-Century England

By the 18th century, the Industrial Revolution had lured thousands from the English countryside to work in the factory towns. The swelling population of urban poor, whose minuscule wages could hardly sustain them, resulted in increased crime rates. In the London area, law enforcement was provided by thief takers—organized groups of private police who earned a living by catching wanted thieves and collecting rewards for their capture. Between 30 and 40 thief takers were active in London by the mid-18th century.

Most thief takers started as prison turnkeys, constables, court bailiffs, or other minor court officers. They were called "monied police" because they made a living not only from catching and informing on criminals but also from receiving stolen property, stealing, intimidating others, perjuring themselves, and committing blackmail. Typically corrupt, they often relieved their

prisoners of money and stolen goods and made additional income by accepting hush money, giving perjured evidence, swearing false oaths, and operating extortion rackets. Petty debtors were especially easy targets for those who combined thief taking with the keeping of alehouses and taverns. The health and safety of incarcerated prisoners was entirely at the whim of the keepers/thief takers, who were free to charge what their prisoners could pay for board and other necessities. Court bailiffs, who also acted as thief takers, were the most passionately detested legal profiteers. They seized debtors and held them in small lockups, where they forced their victims to pay exorbitant prices for food and lodging.

Thief takers' use of violence was notorious. Among the most infamous violent thief takers was the rascal Jack Wild. He pursued thieves bearing arms and was prepared to maim or kill in order to gain his objectives. Wild was willing to take punishment as well as dish it out. Before he was hanged in

1725, Wild had two fractures in his skull, and his bald head was covered with silver plates. He had 17 wounds in various parts of his body from swords, daggers, and gunshots, and his throat had been cut in the course of his duties.

Henry Fielding, the famed author of *Tom Jones*, along with Saunders Welch and Sir John Fielding, sought to clean up the thief-taking system. As an appointed city magistrate in 1748, Fielding operated his own group of monied police from Bow Street in London, directing and deploying them throughout the city and its environs, deciding which cases to investigate and what streets to protect. His agents were carefully instructed on their legitimate powers and duties. Fielding's "Bow Street Runners" were a marked improvement over the earlier monied police because their administrative structure improved record keeping and investigative procedures. But Fielding's forces were not adequate, and by the 19th century state police officers were needed.

in thefts are youths, and most thefts are of goods with a value under a thousand dollars.

It is likely that millions of theft-related crimes occur each year, and most are not reported to police agencies. In 1999 the General Social Survey (Canada's national victimization study) found that 35 percent of theft of personal property, 32 percent of household theft, and 60 percent of motor vehicle theft are reported to the police.[4] This represents a 5 percent decline in reporting since 1993. Of those crimes not reported, 59 percent were not felt to be not important enough, and 50 percent felt that the police couldn't do anything.

School-age youths who commit thefts are unlikely to enter into a criminal career and their behaviour drifts between conventional and criminal behaviour. Added to the pool of amateur thieves are the millions of adults whose behaviour may occasionally violate the criminal law, such as shoplifters, pilferers, and tax cheats, but whose main source of income comes from conventional means and whose self-identity is noncriminal. Added together, their behaviours form the bulk of theft crimes.

According to routine activity theory, occasional property crime occurs when there is an opportunity or **situational inducement** to commit crime.[5] Opportunities are available to members of all classes, but members of the upper class have the opportunity to engage in the more lucrative business-related crimes of price fixing, bribery, embezzlement, and so on, which are closed to the lower classes. Therefore, lower-class individuals are overrepresented in street crime. Situational inducements are short-run influences on a person's behaviour that increase risk taking. These include psychological factors, such as financial problems, and social factors such as peer pressure. Seasonality contributes to the opportunity to commit crime, with almost 10 percent more crime occurring in the summer than the winter. Opportunity and situational inducements are not the cause of crime; rather, they are the occasion for crime—hence, the term **occasional criminal**. Some criminologists agree that such criminals develop a sensitivity to opportunities for theft.[6]

It seems evident that opportunity and inducements are not randomly situated. Consequently, the frequency of occasional property crime varies according to age, class, sex, and so on. Young persons, single women, high-income earners, urbanites, and homeowners are at greatest risk.[7]

Occasional offenders are not professional criminals, nor do they make crime their occupation. They do not rely on skills or knowledge to commit their crimes, they do not organize their daily activities around crime, and they are not committed to crime as a way of life. Occasional criminals have little group support for their acts. Unlike professionals, they do not receive informal, peer group support for their crimes. In fact, they will deny any connection to a criminal lifestyle and instead view their transgressions as being "out of character." They may see

their crimes as being motivated by necessity. For example, they were only "borrowing" the car the police caught them with; they were going to pay back the store they stole merchandise from. Because of the lack of commitment, occasional offenders may be the most likely to respond to the general deterrent effect of the law.

Professional Criminals

In contrast, **professional criminals** make a significant portion of their income from crime. Professionals do not delude themselves with the belief that their acts are impulsive, one-time efforts, nor do they use elaborate rationalizations to excuse the harmfulness of their action ("Shoplifting doesn't really hurt anyone"). Consequently, professionals pursue their craft with vigour, attempting to learn from older, experienced criminals the techniques that will earn them the most money with the least risk. Although their numbers are relatively few, professionals engage in crimes that produce the greater losses to society and perhaps cause the more significant social harm.

Professional theft traditionally refers to nonviolent forms of criminal behaviour that are undertaken with a high degree of skill for monetary gain and that exploit interests tending to maximize financial opportunities and minimize the possibilities of apprehension. The most typical forms include pocket picking, burglary, shoplifting, forgery and counterfeiting, extortion, sneak theft, and confidence swindling.[8]

Relatively little is known about the career patterns of professional thieves and criminals. From the literature on crime and delinquency, three patterns emerge: Youths come under the influence of older, experienced criminals who teach them the trade; juvenile gang members continue their illegal activities at a time when most of their peers have "dropped out" to marry, raise families, and take conventional jobs; youths sent to prison for minor offences learn the techniques of crime from more experienced thieves. For example, Harry King, a professional thief, relates this story of his entry into crime after being placed in a shelter-care home by his recently divorced mother:

> It was while I was at this parental school that I learned that some of the kids had been committed there by the court for stealing bikes. They taught me how to steal and where to steal them and where to sell them. Incidentally, some of the "nicer people" were the ones who bought bikes from the kids. They would dismantle the bike and use the parts: the wheels, chains, handlebars, and so forth.[9]

There is some debate in criminology over who may be defined as a professional criminal. In his classic works, Edwin Sutherland used the term to refer only to thieves who do not use force or physical violence in their crimes and live solely by their wits and skill.[10] However, some criminologists use the term to refer to any criminal who identifies with a criminal subculture, who makes the bulk of his or her living from crime, and who possesses a degree of skill in his or her chosen trade.[11] Thus, one can become a professional safecracker, burglar, car thief, or fence. Some criminologists would not consider drug addicts who steal to support their habit as professionals; they lack skill and therefore are amateur opportunists, rather than professional technicians. However, professional criminals who take drugs might still be considered under the general pattern of professional crime. If the sole criteria for being judged a professional criminal is using crime as one's primary source of income, then many drug users would have to be placed in the professional category.

Sutherland's Professional Criminal. What we know about the lives of professional criminals has come to us through their journals, diaries, autobiographies, and first-person accounts given to criminologists. The best-known account of professional theft is Edwin Sutherland's recording of the life of a professional thief or con man, Chic Conwell, in Sutherland's classic book, *The Professional Thief.*[12] This concept of professional theft has two critical dimensions. First, professional thieves engage in limited types of crime, which are described in Figure 12.1.

The second requirement to establish professionalism as a thief is the exclusive use of wits, front (a believable demeanor), and talking ability. Manual dexterity and physical force are of little importance. Thieves who use force or who commit crimes that require little expertise are not considered worthy of the title "professional." Professional areas of activity include such "heavy rackets"

as bank robbery, car theft, burglary, and safecracking. Sutherland and Conwell's criteria for professionalism are thus weighted heavily toward con games and trickery and give little attention to common street crimes.

Professional thieves must acquire status in their profession. Status is based on their technical skill, financial standing, connections, power, dress, manners, and wide knowledge. In their world, "thief" is a title worn with pride. Sutherland and Conwell also argue that professional thieves share feelings, sentiments, and behaviours. Of these, none is more important than the code of honour of the underworld; even under threat of the most severe punishment, a professional thief must never inform (squeal) on his or her fellows.

Sutherland and Conwell view professional theft as an occupation with much the same internal organization as that characterizing such legitimate professions as advertising, teaching, or police work. They conclude that a person can be a professional thief only if received as such by other professional thieves.

Professional Criminals: The Fence. Some experts have argued that Sutherland's view of the professional thief may be outdated because modern thieves often work alone, are not part of a criminal subculture, and were not tutored early in their careers by other criminals.[13] However, some recent research efforts show that the principles set down by Sutherland still have value for understanding the behaviour of one contemporary criminal: the professional fence, a person who earns his or her living solely by buying and reselling stolen merchandise.

The fence's critical role in criminal transactions has been recognized since the 18th century. Fences act as intermediaries who purchase stolen merchandise, ranging from diamonds to outboard motors, and then resell it to merchants who market the goods to legitimate customers. Much of what is known about fencing comes from three in-depth studies of individual fences by Carl Klockars, Darrell Steffensmeier, and Marilyn Walsh.[14]

Klockars examined the life and times of one successful fence who used the alias "Vincent Swaggi." Through 400 hours of listening to and observing Vincent, Klockars found that this highly professional criminal had developed techniques that made him almost immune to prosecution. During the course of a long and profitable career in crime, Vincent spent only four months in prison. He stayed in business in part because of his sophisticated knowledge of the law of stolen property: To convict someone of receiving stolen goods, the prosecution must prove that the accused was in possession of the goods and knew that the goods had been stolen. Vincent had the skills to make sure that these elements could never be proved. Also helping Vincent stay out of the law's grasp were the close working associations he maintained with society's upper classes, including influential members of the justice system. Vincent helped them purchase items at below-cost, bargain prices. He also helped authorities recover stolen goods and therefore remained

Figure 12.1 **Sutherland's Typology of Professional Thieves**

Pickpocket ("cannon")

Sneak thief from stores, banks, and offices ("heel")

Shoplifter ("booster")

Jewel thief who substitutes fake gems for real ones ("pennyweighter")

Thief who steals from hotel rooms ("hotel prowl")

Confidence game artist

Thief in rackets related to confidence games

Forger

Extortionist from those engaging in illegal acts ("shakedown artist")

Source: Edwin Sutherland and Chic Conwell, *The Professional Thief* (Chicago: University of Chicago Press, 1937).

Exhibit 12.1 | **Quick Code: Possession of Stolen Property**

Section 354. (1) Every one commits an offence who has in his possession any property or thing or any proceeds of any property or thing knowing that all or part of the property or thing or of the proceeds was obtained by or derived directly or indirectly from
(a) the commission in Canada of an offence punishable by indictment; ...

Section 355. Every one who commits an offence under section 354
(a) is guilty of an indictable offence and is liable to imprisonment for a term not exceeding ten years, where the subject-matter of the offence is a testamentary instrument or the value of the subject-matter of the offence exceeds five thousand dollars; ...

[Other relevant sections: 356, 357, 358, 359, and 360]

Source: *Pocket Criminal Code* (Scarborough, ON: Carswell, 1995).

in their good graces. Klockars's work strongly suggests that fences customarily cheat their thief-clients and at the same time cooperate with the law.

Darrell Steffensmeier studied the fence Sam Goodman, who lived in a world similar to Vincent Swaggi's. He also purchased stolen goods from a wide variety of thieves and suppliers, including burglars, drug addicts, shoplifters, dockworkers, and truck drivers. According to Sam, to be successful, a fence must meet the following conditions:

1. *Upfront cash.* All deals are cash transactions, so one must always have an adequate supply of ready cash on hand.
2. *Knowledge of dealing: learning the ropes.* The fence must be schooled in knowledge of the trade, including developing a "larceny sense"; learning to "buy right" at acceptable prices; being able to "cover one's back" and not get caught; finding out how to make the right contacts; and knowing how to "wheel and deal" and create opportunities for profit.
3. *Connections with suppliers of stolen goods.* The successful fence is able to engage in long-term relationships with suppliers of high-value stolen goods who are relatively free of police interference. The warehouse worker who pilfers is a better supplier than the narcotics addict, who is more likely to be apprehended and talk to the police.
4. *Connections with buyers.* The successful fence must have continuing access to buyers of stolen merchandise who are inaccessible to the common thief.
5. *Complicity with law enforcers.* The fence must work out a relationship with law enforcement officials, who invariably find out about the fence's operations. Steffensmeier found that to stay in business, the fence must either bribe officials with good deals on

merchandise and cash payments or act as an informer who helps police recover particularly important merchandise and arrest thieves.

Marilyn Walsh found that fences handle a tremendous number of products, from televisions to cigarettes, stereo equipment, watches, autos, and cameras.[15] In dealing their merchandise, fences operate through many legitimate fronts, including art dealers, antique stores, furniture and appliance retailers, remodelling companies, salvage companies, trucking companies, and jewellery stores. When deciding what to pay the thief for goods, the fence uses a complex pricing policy. Professional thieves who steal high-priced items are usually given the highest amounts, about 30 to 50 percent of the wholesale price. For example, furs valued at $5000 may be bought for $1200. However, the amateur thief or drug addict who is not in a good bargaining position may receive only ten cents on the dollar.

Fencing seems to contain many of the elements of professional theft as described by Sutherland: Fences live by their wits, never engage in violence, depend on their skill in negotiating, maintain community standing based on connections and power, and share the sentiments and behaviours of their fellows. The only divergence between Sutherland's thief and the fence is the code of honour; it seems likely that the fence is much more willing to cooperate with authorities than are most other professional criminals.

In a striking twist on an old trade, fencing stolen merchandise has now hit the World Wide Web, as described in the following Crime in the News feature. According to the National Fraud Information Center, online auction frauds account for 78 percent of all frauds and cost over $300 each.

The Nonprofessional Fence

Professional fences are the ones who have attracted the attention of criminologists. Yet like other forms of theft, fencing is not dominated by professional criminals alone; a significant portion of all fencing is performed by amateur or occasional criminals. The guy who steals an outboard motor and sells it out of the back of a truck in the parking lot of a coffee shop is unlikely to be making that his steady occupation (and is most likely to get caught).

Using data collected in interviews with convicted thieves, fences, and people who bought stolen property, Paul Cromwell, James Olson, and D'Aunn Avary discovered that novice burglars, such as juveniles and drug addicts, often find it so difficult to establish relationships with professional fences they turn instead to nonprofessionals to unload their stolen goods.[16]

One type of occasional fence is the part-timer who, unlike professional fences, has other sources of income. Part-timers are often "legitimate" businesspeople who integrate the stolen merchandise into their regular stock. For example, the manager of a local video store buys

Crime in the News

"eBay: Den of Thieves?"

By Laura Lorek
Interactive Week, ZDNet News
May 14, 2001
Crooks looking to unload stolen goods are increasingly turning to eBay to find buyers and reap some quick cash.

In the past few years, police have busted at least three major fencing rings on eBay in which burglars and thieves from Boston, Chicago and Jackson, Mich., used the online auction marketplace to sell thousands of dollars worth of jewelry, electronics, coin collections, baseball cards, designer clothes and household goods.

In late February, Chicago investigators nabbed two Marshall Field's window dressers who allegedly stole more than $2 million in high-end merchandise and then posted the stolen items for sale on eBay. The thieves stole a slew of pricey items, including $5,000 purses, $3,000 men's suits, $1,500 sweaters, computers, jewelry and even a $450 cashmere baby blanket and then posted the merchandise on eBay's auction site for sale to the highest bidder.

In June 2000, two men in the Boston area were arrested for burglarizing more than 100 homes and selling the stolen goods - baseball cards, collectors' edition coins, jewelry and silverware - on the popular auction site.

And in August 1999, two men from Jackson, Mich., were charged with selling stolen goods on eBay. They sold at least $19,000 worth of shoplifted merchandise, including digital cameras, fishing lures and radios, to buyers around the globe.

Kevin Pursglove, spokesman at eBay, said the San Jose company and its shoppers would have little reason to suspect that a particular item up for bid was stolen. Pursglove said eBay has 22 million items up for bid each day, which generate more than $22 million in daily sales. With that amount of traffic, there is no way to completely police all commerce, he said.

"With the overall level of e-commerce activity on eBay, problems like this are minuscule," Pursglove said. eBay limits its liability by calling itself a "venue."

Caveat Emptor

"We are not involved in the actual transaction between buyers and sellers," according to eBay's user agreement. "As a result, we have no control over the quality, safety or legality of the items advertised."

eBay does insure goods up to $200 with a $25 deductible, and it offers an escrow service by which a seller is not paid until the bidder has inspected his or her purchase.

Of course, fencing stolen goods is not a new crime. But before the rise in popularity of online auctions, thieves had few options to dispose of stolen goods quickly. They often dumped them at pawnshops for much less than they were worth.

Police said criminals usually collect only 25 cents on the dollar when they pass off fenced material. But on an auction site like eBay, a bidding war can result in much higher profits.

However, selling stolen goods on eBay and other Internet auction sites is a very risky proposition. Instead of anonymously fencing stolen goods in a pawn shop for a handful of cash, the criminals are creating a paper trail that is easy to trace, said Angela Bell, spokeswoman at the FBI.

However, selling stolen goods online is a cybercrime some experts believe could become more common and more sophisticated.

In 1997, the Federal Trade Commission received about 100 complaints about fraud through online auction sites. Last year, the FTC recorded 10,700 online auction fraud complaints making Internet auctions the biggest source of online consumer complaints.

stolen VCRs and tapes and rents them along with his legitimate merchandise. An added benefit is that profit on these items is not reported for tax purposes.

Some merchants become actively involved in theft either by specifying the merchandise they want the burglars to steal or by "fingering" victims. Some businessmen sell merchandise to people and then describe the customers' homes and vacation plans to known burglars so they can steal it back!

Some amateur fences barter stolen goods for services rendered. These "associational fences" typically have legitimate professional dealings with known criminals and include bail bonds agents, police officers, and attor-

neys. One lawyer bragged of getting a $12 000 Rolex watch from one client in exchange for legal services. Bartering for stolen merchandise avoids taxes and becomes a transaction in the "underground economy."

"Neighbourhood hustlers" buy and sell stolen property as one of many ways they make a living; they keep some of the booty for themselves and sell the rest in the neighbourhood. These deal makers are familiar figures to neighbourhood burglars looking to get some quick cash.

"Amateur receivers" can be complete strangers approached in a public place by someone offering a great deal on valuable commodities. It is unlikely that anyone buying a $500 stereo for $200, or a diamond ring for $50

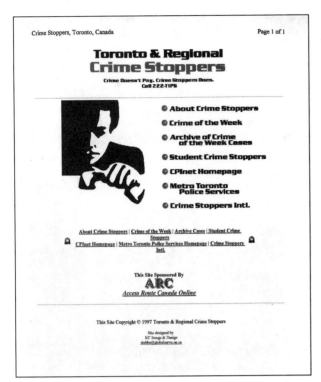

Crime Stoppers, Toronto, Canada   Page 1 of 1

Toronto & Regional
Crime Stoppers
Crime Doesn't Pay. Crime Stoppers Does.
Call 222-TIPS

- About Crime Stoppers
- Crime of the Week
- Archive of Crime of the Week Cases
- Student Crime Stoppers
- CPInet Homepage
- Metro Toronto Police Services
- Crime Stoppers Intl.

About Crime Stoppers | Crime of the Week | Archive Cases | Student Crime
Stoppers
CPInet Homepage | Metro Toronto Police Services Homepage | Crime Stoppers
Intl.

This Site Sponsored By
ARC
Access Route Canada Online

This Site Copyright © 1997 Toronto & Regional Crime Stoppers
Site designed by
KC Image & Design
stobbs@globalserve.on.ca

The Toronto and Regional CrimeStoppers is one of dozens of similar programs across the country responsible for recovering millions in stolen property every year. Recently, they redesigned their website to incorporate their new logo.

cash, would not suspect that it had been stolen. Some amateur receivers make a habit of buying merchandise at reasonable prices from a "trusted friend." Research indicates that the nonprofessional fence may account for a great deal of criminal receiving. It shows that both professional and amateur thieves have their own niche in the crime universe.

Criminologists and legal scholars recognize that common theft offences fall into several categories linked together because they involve the intentional misappropriation of property for personal gain. In some cases, as in fencing, the property is bought from another who is in illegal possession of the goods. In the case of embezzlement, burglary, and larceny, the property is taken through stealth, while in others, such as bad cheques, fraud, and false pretences, it is obtained through deception. Some of the major categories of common theft offences are discussed in the rest of this chapter in some detail.

Theft

Theft, or as it is sometimes called, larceny, was one of the earliest common-law crimes created by English judges to define acts in which one person took for his or her own use the property of another.[17] At common law, **larceny**

was defined as "the trespassory taking and carrying away of the personal property of another with intent to steal." Most jurisdictions have incorporated the common-law crime of larceny in their legal codes. Today, definitions of larceny often include such familiar acts as shoplifting, passing bad cheques, and other theft offences that do not involve using force or threats on the victim or forcibly breaking into a person's home or place of work. (The former is robbery; the latter, break and enter.)

As originally construed, larceny involved only taking property that was in the possession of the rightful owners. For example, it would have been considered larceny for someone to go secretly into a farmer's field and steal a cow. Thus, the original common-law definition required a "trespass in the taking"; this meant that for an act to be considered larceny, goods must have been taken from the physical possession of the owner.

In creating this definition of larceny, English judges were more concerned with disturbance of the peace than they were with thefts. They reasoned that if someone tried to steal property from another's possession, the act could eventually lead to a physical confrontation and possibly the death of one party or the other. Consequently, the original definition of larceny did not include crimes in which the thief had come into the possession of the stolen property by trickery or deceit. For example, if someone entrusted with another person's property decided to keep it, it was not considered larceny.

The growth of manufacturing and the development of the free enterprise system required greater protection for private property. The pursuit of commercial enterprise often required that one person's legal property be entrusted to a second party; therefore, larceny evolved to include the theft of goods that had come into the thief's possession through legitimate means.

To get around the element of "trespass in the taking," English judges created the concept of **constructive possession**. This legal fiction applied to situations in which persons voluntarily and temporarily gave up custody of their property but still believed that the property was legally theirs. For example, if a person gave a jeweller her watch for repair, she would still believe she owned the watch, although she had handed it over to the jeweller. Similarly, when a person misplaces his wallet and someone else finds it and keeps it, although identification of the owner can be plainly seen, the concept of constructive possession makes the person who has kept the wallet guilty of larceny.

Theft Today

Statistics Canada separates theft into two classes according to the value of the goods involved: theft over and under $5000. The former involves small amounts of money or property and accounts for the majority of thefts in Canada. The latter is more likely to be punished by a

Culture, Gender, Ethnicity, and Criminology

How Capitalism Influences Rape

Herman and Julia Schwendinger's classic study of rape provides an excellent example of Marxian critical analysis. The Schwendingers wanted to find out why women who are raped often feel guilty about their role in the rape experience. They believe a rape victim frequently experiences guilt because she has been raised in a sexist society and has internalized discriminatory norms. Women have traditionally been viewed as the weaker sex, dependent on persons in authority, such as parents or husbands. For a long time rape was seen as a property crime, against a woman's husband or father.

This dependency originates historically in unequal socioeconomic conditions that are related to family life in capitalist society. During the early stages of capitalism, families underwent strain when industry demanded a labour force of men, only infrequently supplemented by single women. The role of father was strained as men were separated from their households. The woman's role became more narrowly defined as child bearer and child raiser. The limited economic role of women helped define them as dependents.

Married women, especially, were viewed as nonproductive, since they did not participate in commodity markets and earn money.

In reality, women's household productivity must be viewed as an essential contribution to the family and the economy, yet their work often goes unappreciated by husbands and the rest of society. Since the housewife produces only for family use, her labour is unpaid, and she is totally dependent on her husband's wage for access to the commodities necessary for the family's existence. Because she has been socialized into dependency by the capitalist system, a woman's sense of self-worth may be more responsive to the evaluations of other persons. Furthermore, negative evaluations, such as those created by a rape experience, are likely to be turned inward by the woman, creating unwarranted self-recrimination and remorse.

The family is not the only culprit in this transaction. Schools and the mass media further reinforce dependency by teaching boys and girls in school to "look down on women." Textbooks stereotype the woman's role; girls are depicted as helpless and frightened. Vocational tests provide fewer opportunities for girls. In media presentations, women are usually depicted as housewives and mothers. When women are

portrayed on television commercials, they seem "concerned mainly with clean floors and clean hair—housework and their personal appearance."

Although women have made great advances, their labour is often in low-paid, low-mobility occupations. Consequently, their appearance in the labour force often does little to improve their economic dependency. It is for these reasons that women often blame themselves for being raped. The Schwendingers imply that women feel they have "let down" the people they depend on when they are trapped in a rape encounter. A woman's own sense of inadequacy leads to self-blame for the attack and prevents her from focusing on the true culprits: the rapist and the capitalist system whose economic structure results in a rape-producing climate. The Schwendingers' research approach illustrates the Marxian analysis of social process, and the effect of material economic conditions. Maybe it is not accident then that rape was traditionally seen as a crime of property.

SOURCES: Herman Schwendinger and Julia Schwendinger, *Rape and Inequality* (Newbury Park, CA: Sage, 1983); idem, "Rape Victims and the False Sense of Guilt," *Crime and Social Justice* 13 (1980): 4–17.

---

sentence in prison. In Canada in 1999, there were 22 478 thefts over $5000, and 679 095 thefts under $5000. Of the latter, 9 percent were bicycles, 13 percent were a result of shoplifting, and 40 percent were from motor vehicles.

Theft is the most common criminal offence, about 66 percent of all property crime in Canada. It was estimated to have cost $3 billion in 1993, the costliest property crime in our society.[18] Theft has increased 1 percent a year since 1979. As society becomes more affluent and mobile and people spend less time at home, guardianship decreases and opportunities for theft continue to increase.[19]

Shoplifting

Shoplifting is a common form of theft that involves the taking of goods from retail stores. Usually, shoplifters try to snatch goods—jewellery, clothes, records, appliances—when store personnel are otherwise occupied and hide the goods on their person. The "five-finger discount" is an extremely common form of crime; losses from shoplifting are measured in the billions of dollars each year.[20] Retail security measures add to the already high cost of this crime, which is passed on to the consumer. Shoplifting incidents have increased dramatically in the past 20 years,

Exhibit 12.2	Quick Facts about Theft in Canada

- In 1999 theft was the largest property crime category, at 67 percent of the total.
- Of thefts with a value under $5000 in 1999, 40 percent were from motor vehicles.
- In 1999 theft was lowest in Newfoundland (36 percent of the national average over $5000, 63 percent under $5000).
- British Columbia is 183 percent of the national average under $5000; and Saskatchewan is 128 percent of the national average over $5000.
- The 15 to 24 age group is nine times as likely to be victimized as the 65-plus age group.
- In 1993–94 "theft under" accounted for 78 percent of youth court theft cases; 64 percent were found guilty.
- Those earning $60 000 are twice as likely to be victimized as the $15 000 to $30 000 income group.
- The highest theft rate occurs in June to August, the lowest in December to February.
- Of all adults charged for theft over and under $5000, 74 percent were males.
- The clearance rate for having stolen goods was 90 percent in 1999.
- In 1999, the most likely single item to be stolen was a motor vehicle (21 percent); firearms were the least likely (0.1 percent).
- A motor vehicle was most likely to be stolen from a parking lot (43 percent), rather than a residence (18 percent).
- Thefts were highest from commercial establishments (29 percent in both categories).
- The rate of personal theft in 1999 was 17 percent higher than in 1993.

Sources: *Canadian Crime Statistics 1999*, Canadian Centre for Justice Statistics; Sandra Besserer and Catherine Trainor, "Criminal Victimization in Canada, 1999," *Juristat* 20 (2000); Dianne Hendrick, "Theft," in *Crime Counts: A Criminal Event Analysis*, ed. Leslie W. Kennedy and Vincent F. Sacco (Toronto: ITP Nelson, 1996).

Exhibit 12.3	Quick Code: Theft

Section 322. (1) Every one commits theft who fraudulently and without colour of right takes, or fraudulently and without colour of right converts to his use or to the use of another person, anything, whether animate or inanimate, with intent,

    (a) to deprive, temporarily, or absolutely, the owner of it, ...

Section 334. Except where otherwise provided by law, every one who commits theft

    (a) is guilty of an indictable offence and liable to imprisonment for a term not exceeding ten years, ...

[Other relevant sections: sections 323, 324, 326, 327, 328, 329, 330, 331, 332, 338, 356]

Source: *Pocket Criminal Code* (Scarborough, ON: Carswell, 1995).

and retailers now expect an annual increase of 10 to 15 percent. Some studies estimate that about one in every nine shoppers steals from department stores. Moreover, the increasingly popular discount stores have a minimum of sales help and depend on highly visible merchandise displays to attract purchasers, all of which makes them particularly vulnerable to shoplifters.

The Shoplifter. The classic study of shoplifting was conducted by Mary Owen Cameron.[21] She found that about 10 percent of all shoplifters were professionals who derived the majority of their income from shoplifting. Sometimes called **boosters** or **heels**, professional

shoplifters intend to resell stolen merchandise to pawnshops or fences, usually at half the original price.

The majority of shoplifters are actually amateur pilferers, called **snitches** in thieves' argot. Snitches are usually respectable persons who do not conceive of themselves as thieves but are systematic shoplifters who steal merchandise for their own use. They are not simply seized by an uncontrollable urge to take something that attracts them, they come equipped to steal. Usually, snitches who are arrested have never been apprehended before. For the most part, they are people who lack the kind of criminal experience that suggests extensive association with a criminal subculture.

Criminologists view shoplifters as people who are likely to reform if apprehended. Cameron reasoned that because snitches are not part of a criminal subculture and do not think of themselves as criminals, they are deterred by an initial contact with the law. Getting arrested has a traumatic effect on them, and they will not risk a second offence.[22] While this argument seems plausible, some criminologists argue that apprehension may have a labelling effect that inhibits deterrence and results in repeated offending. Youths who had been previously apprehended for shoplifting have been deterred by official processing.[23]

Shoplifting continues to be a serious problem. Many stores have installed elaborate security devices to combat shoplifting, but the growth of this type of larceny has continued.

Controlling Shoplifting. One major problem associated with combating shoplifting is that many customers who observe pilferage are reluctant to report it to security agents. Store employees themselves often hesitate to get involved in apprehending a shoplifter. For example, in a controlled experiment, Donald Hartmann found that customers observed only 28 percent of staged shoplifting incidents that had been designed to get their attention.[24] Furthermore, less than one-third of people who said they had observed an incident reported it to store employees.

In another controlled experiment using staged shoplifting incidents, Erhard Blankenburg found that less than 10 percent of shoplifting was detected by store employees and that customers appeared unwilling to report even serious cases.[25] (In March of 1998, PBS aired an experiment about pickpocketing on the street; while this is not an example of shoplifting, what is important is that not one passerby intervened to prevent the crime.) Even in stores with an announced policy of full reporting and prosecution, only 70 percent of the shoplifting detected by employees was actually reported to managers, and only 5 percent was prosecuted. According to this study, foreigners, adults, and blue-collar workers were disproportionately represented among those officially punished. It is also likely that a store owner's decision to prosecute shoplifters will be based on the value of the goods stolen, the nature of the goods stolen, and the manner in which the theft was realized. For example, shoplifters who planned their crime by using a concealed apparatus, such as a bag pinned to the inside of their clothing, were more apt to be prosecuted than those who had impulsively put merchandise into their pockets.[26]

To aid in the arrest of shoplifters in the United States, a number of states have passed merchant privilege laws that are designed to protect retailers and their employers from litigation stemming from improper or false arrests of suspected shoplifters.[27] These laws protect but do not immunize merchants from lawsuits. They require that arrests be made on reasonable grounds or probable cause, detention be of short duration, and store employees or security guards conduct themselves in a reasonable fashion.

Prevention Strategies. Retail stores are now initiating a number of strategies designed to reduce or eliminate shoplifting.

Target removal strategies involve using dummy or disabled goods on display while having the "real" merchandise kept under lock and key. For example, audio equipment with missing parts is displayed, and only after purchase are the necessary components installed. Some stores sell from a catalogue while keeping merchandise in stockrooms. In one incident at the Bay, a shopper stole a box from a display which he believed to contain a VCR, but unfortunately it was full of bricks. He was caught when he returned it for a refund.

Target hardening strategies involve locking goods into place or having them monitored by electronic systems. Clothing stores may use racks designed to prevent large quantities of garments from being slipped off easily.

Situational measures place the most valuable goods in the least vulnerable places, use warning signs to deter potential thieves, and have closed-circuit cameras. Goods

Exhibit 12.4	How to Stop Shoplifting: Some Useful Tips

- Train employees to watch for suspicious behaviour, such as a shopper loitering over a trivial item. Have them keep an eye out for shoppers wearing baggy clothes, carrying their own bag, or using some other method to conceal products taken from the shelf.
- Develop a call code. When employees suspect that a customer is shoplifting, they can use the call to bring store management or security to the area.
- Products on lower floors face the greatest risk. Relocate the most tempting targets to upper floors.
- Use smaller exits and avoid placing the most expensive merchandise near these exits.
- Design routes within stores to make theft less tempting and funnel customers toward cashiers.
- Place service departments (credit and packaging) near areas where shoplifters are likely to stash goods. Extra supervision reduces the problem.
- Avoid creating corners where there are no supervision sight lines in areas of stores favoured by young males. Restrict and supervise areas where electronic tags can be removed.

Sources: Marcus Felson, "Preventing Retail Theft: An Application of Environmental Criminology," *Security Journal* 7 (1996): 71–75; Marc Brandeberry, "$15 Billion Lost to Shoplifting," *Today's Coverage*, A Newsletter of the Grocers Insurance Group, Portland, OR, 1997.

may be tagged with devices that give off an alarm or spray a dye if they are taken out of the shop.

Exhibit 12.4 describes some of the steps retail insurers recommend to reduce the incidence of shoplifting.

Private Justice. Efforts to control the spread of shoplifting have prompted some commercial enterprises to establish highly sophisticated loss prevention units to combat would-be criminals. In an investigation of the loss prevention unit of a large national retail chain, researchers uncovered a private justice system that works parallel to but independent of the public justice system. Private security officers have many law enforcement powers also granted to municipal police officers, including arrest of suspects and search and seizure.[28]

In some stores, shoplifters may be required to compensate store owners for the value of the goods they attempted to steal, costs incurred because of their illegal acts, and punitive damages. Some major Canadian retailers practise this form of "cost recovery" but with some controversy, especially when the parents of a youth who steals are sued. However, store detectives do use the civil damage route to defray the costs of their operation.

The researchers found that the availability of civil damages had important effects on decision making. Store owners go after the more affluent shoplifters for civil recovery and ship the poor to the public criminal justice system for prosecution.

Auto Theft

It is estimated that motor vehicle theft affected one in ten households in 1993. In 2001, the Canadian Coalition Against Insurance Fraud estimated that over 450 cars are stolen in Canada every day, one every three minutes. One-third of all Criminal Code property offences in 1999 involved the theft of a car or of property from a car. That does not include trucks, motorcycles or "other." One in a hundred vehicles was reported stolen, and losses from motor vehicle thefts, thefts from motor vehicles, and vandalism against motor vehicles amounted to $1.6 billion in 1993.[29] In contrast, credit card fraud cost $55 million, and bank robberies $3.5 million!

The cost of auto theft is estimated to be $1 billion per year. Thirty years ago 95 percent of the cars were recovered, but this has dropped to 72 percent today. This means that in the past the typical car thief was out for a joyride; today, however, the car is stolen for resale or to be chopped into parts.[30]

A number of attempts have been made to categorize the various forms of auto theft.[31] One of the most detailed of these typologies uncovered five categories of auto theft transactions:

1. *Joyriding.* Many car thefts are motivated by teenagers' desire to acquire the power, prestige, sexual potency, and recognition associated with an automobile. Joyriders do not steal cars for profit or gain but to experience, even briefly, the benefits associated with owning an automobile.
2. *Short-term transportation.* Auto theft for short-term transportation is similar to joyriding. It involves the theft of a car simply to go from one place to another. In more serious cases, the thief may drive to another city or province and then steal another car to continue the journey.
3. *Long-term transportation.* Thieves who steal cars for long-term transportation intend to keep the cars for their personal use. Usually older than joyriders and from a lower-class background, these auto thieves may repaint and otherwise disguise cars to avoid detection.
4. *Profit.* Auto theft for profit is, of course, motivated by hope for monetary gain. At one extreme are highly organized professionals who resell expensive cars after altering their identification numbers and falsifying their registration papers. At the other end of the scale are amateur auto strippers, who steal batteries, tires, and wheel covers to sell them or reequip their own cars.
5. *Commission of another crime.* A small portion of auto thieves steal cars to use in other crimes, such as robberies and thefts. This type of auto thief desires both mobility and anonymity.

At one time, joyriding was the predominant motive for auto theft, and most cars were taken by relatively affluent, white, middle-class teenagers looking for excitement.[32] Youths still represent 40 percent of those charged with motor vehicle theft in 1999. However, there appears to be a change in this pattern: Fewer cars are being taken today while, concomitantly, fewer stolen cars are being recovered. Part of the reason is the increase in the number of professional car thieves who are linked to "chop shops," export rings, or both. Export of stolen vehicles has become a global problem, and the emergence of capitalism in Eastern Europe has increased the demand for Western-made cars.[33]

In 2001, the international police agency, Interpol, reported that more than three million cars are stolen in the world annually. The value of vehicles stolen from 45 countries in Europe, North America, Africa, and Asia is estimated at $21 billion U.S. per year. Interpol's Automated Search Facility database for stolen motor vehicles contains records for more than 2.5 million stolen cars from 59 countries, and is used by police forces worldwide to track stolen vehicles. The secretary general of Interpol alleges that profits from smuggling stolen cars is used to fund terrorist organizations.[34] Apparently, high-ranking members of the Hezbollah, an Iranian-backed terrorist group, favour the $70 000 Lincoln Navigator, quite often stolen in Ontario!

Which Cars Are Taken Most? Car thieves show signs of rational choice when they make their target selections. Today luxury cars and utility vehicles are in greatest demand. Several years ago, the Ford Mustang GT was the most popular two-door model stolen according to the Vehicle Information Centre of Canada, with over twice the claim frequency of the two-door Volkswagen Golf. In the United States, the Toyota Camry tops the list, while the Jeep Grand Cherokee only makes number 20. Older Japanese models are apparently more valuable because of the interchangeability of their parts.

Car models that have been in production for a few years without many design changes stand the greatest risk of theft. Camrys made between 1988 and 1991 are an attractive theft choice, because these models have parts that are most valued in the secondary market. Luxury cars, on the other hand, typically experience a sharp

Connections

Chapter 4 discusses the rational choice view of car theft. As you may recall, cars with expensive radios and parts are more often the target of rational thieves.

Crime in the News

Auto Theft

Dealership owner's vehicle stolen at Montreal airport

By Laverne Stewart, The Daily Gleaner

Parking his truck at the airport in Montreal cost Gerry Oleary a lot more than he expected.

When the Fredericton car dealership owner returned to Dorval Airport following a trip to Haiti recently, he discovered his $50 000, white GMC four-wheel-drive 2001 truck had been stolen from the airport's long-term parking lot.

His insurance company charges his car dealership a $10 000 deductible on claims on stolen cars.

In the hope of getting the truck back, Oleary is now offering a $5 000 reward.

The model is a popular vehicle in Russia and the Middle East. With less than 2 000 kilometres on it, the truck is exactly what organized car theft operations are looking for, according to Montreal police.

As the vehicle was fully loaded and came with an expensive security system, Oleary said he was surprised thieves were able to circumvent the alarm system without being detected.

"How do you get into a truck with an alarm system on it? The alarm systems on these trucks are really sensitive, so you have to be really good to get into these things," Oleary said.

Doug Hurley, commander of the property crimes unit with the Montreal Police Department, said thieves are able to break into such vehicles with little effort.

"They know the alarm systems as well or better than the car manufacturers," Hurley said.

The department's records indicate 222 vehicles were stolen from Dorval Airport last year. Organized criminals are behind most of the car thefts at the airport, Hurley said.

Typically, Hurley said, those crime rings use large containers to ship the stolen vehicles overseas from the port in Montreal.

Daily Gleaner, August 15, 2001: B1.

---

decline in their theft rate soon after a design change. Enduring models are also in demand because older cars are more likely to be uninsured, and demand for stolen used parts is higher for these vehicles.

According to the International Crime Survey of 1992, the risk of having a motor vehicle stolen in Canada was 1.1 percent, and of having something stolen from a car 7.2 percent. Canada ranked highest in car vandalism at 9.2 percent (65 percent cars, 23 percent trucks, and 7 percent snowmobiles).

The economics of auto theft are interesting. The Insurance Board of Canada estimates that an organized theft ring will pay between $150 and $500 for a stolen Jeep Grand Cherokee. The Vehicle Identification Number from a wrecked model purchased for $2000 will be placed on the stolen SUV for a cost between $500 and $1500. It can then be sold "legitimately" in another jurisdiction to an unsuspecting buyer for about $45 000, creating a profit of about $40 000. If it is sold in Eastern Europe, the profit could be as high as $95 000!

Carjacking. You may have read about gunmen approaching a car and forcing the owner to give up the keys; in some cases, people have been killed when they reacted too slowly. This type of auto theft has become common enough that it has its own name, **carjacking**.[35] This is considered to be a type of robbery because it involves the use of force.

Carjacking is a new form of crime that some have dubbed "urban terrorism." Such high-profile crime attracts widespread media coverage. In Florida, for example, the killing of tourists in out-of-state rental cars received international attention several years ago. In another form of carjacking, called the "bump and grab," cars are stolen when they are hit from behind and the driver pulls off to the side of the road.

In another form of urban terrorism, called a "home invasion," armed robbers force their way into a home while the residents are there and extort money by force.[36] Such crimes strike at the heart of our safest places, our homes, and cause a lot of concern, some would say unnecessary concern. Figure 12.2 shows the risk of carjacking compared with other life events.

Combating Auto Theft. Because of its commonality and high loss potential, auto theft has been a target of situational crime prevention efforts. Ronald Clarke and Patricia Harris have outlined some of the methods being tried to combat auto theft.[37] One approach has been to increase the risk of apprehension. Information hotlines offer rewards for information leading to the arrest of car thieves. Another approach has been to place fluorescent decals on windows that indicate that the car is never used between 1 and 5 a.m.; if police spot a car with the decal being operated during this period, they know it is stolen. Cars have also been equipped with radio transmitters. The

| Figure 12.2 | Carjacking compared to risks of other life events |

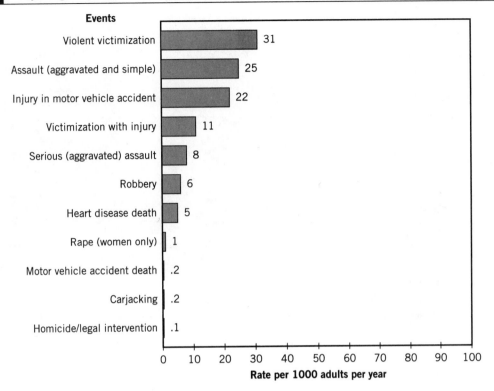

Source: Highlights from 20 Years of Surveying Crime Victims, October 1993, NCJ-144525. Online: http://www.ojp.usdoj.gov/bjs/pub/ascii/c.txt (U.S. Department of Justice)

LOJACK system involves a tracking device installed in the car that gives off a signal enabling the police to pinpoint its location.

Other prevention efforts involve making it more difficult to steal cars. Publicity campaigns have been directed at encouraging people to lock their cars. Ironically enough, the most common method of stealing a car is by using the keys (43 percent).[38] Most cars are stolen in Canada with their keys in them. Parking lots have been equipped with theft-deterring closed-circuit TV cameras and barriers. Manufacturers have installed more sophisticated steering-column locking devices and other security systems that make theft harder. Improved security measures such as lighting and patrols probably deter auto crime, but also only displace it to other areas.[39]

A study by the Highway Loss Data Institute (HLDI), however, found that most car theft prevention methods, especially alarms, have little effect on theft rates. The most effective methods appear to be devices that immobilize a vehicle by cutting off the electrical power needed to start the engine. Or alternately, you could just have a car that nobody would want to steal.

False Pretences/Fraud

The crime of **false pretences**, or **fraud**, involves a wrongdoer's misrepresenting a fact to cause a victim to willingly give his or her property to the wrongdoer, who keeps it.[40] The definition of false pretences was created by the English Parliament in 1757 to cover an area of law left untouched by larceny statutes. The first false pretences law punished people who "knowingly and designedly by false pretense or pretenses, [obtained] from any person or persons, money, goods, wares or merchandise with intent to cheat or defraud any person or persons of the same."[41] False pretences differs from traditional larceny because the victims willingly give their possessions to the offender, and the crime does not, as does larceny, involve a "trespass in the taking." An example of false pretences would be an unscrupulous merchant selling someone a chair by claiming it to be an antique but knowing all the while that it is a cheap copy. Another example would be a phony healer selling a victim a bottle of coloured sugar water as an "elixir" that would cure a disease. There are many types of fraud, including confi-

Famous Canadian Criminals

Albert Johnson Walker

After his company defrauded 30 clients of over $3 million from pension and investment funds, Albert Walker, a financial adviser, fled to England in 1990 with his daughter Sheena, 15. With an arrest warrant issued for him in Woodstock, Ontario, he was soon on Interpol's most wanted list, described as possibly dangerous. If he had stayed in Canada, he would have faced more than three dozen fraud-related charges. He was also facing charges of money-laundering.

When Walker was arrested in 1996 in a tiny village northwest of London, he been living with his daughter and her two children for two years. However he was not living under his own name, but that of David Davis. His daughter posed as his wife, Noel Davis. The paternity of the children was described as "unknown."

Through his personal secretary he had met and befriended a man

When Albert Walker, left, fled Canada, he took his daughter Sheena, right, with him. Walker was sought by Interpol for defrauding clients of over $3 million in pension and investment funds.

named Ronald Platt and arranged to use his identity in exchange for money. However, in 1996, he killed Platt and dumped his body in the ocean, assuming his identity once and for all. Police were able to trace his whereabouts on the day Platt was killed from information retrieved from his global positioning satellite (GPS) device. In 1998, he was found guilty of murder.

In 2000, he appeared in court to ask for a transfer to a Canadian prison, but was flatly turned down by the federal government.

Albert Johnson still faces a number of charges in Canada. However, he is unlikely to face them any time soon. This was a fraud of magnificent proportions, made possible because of his privileged position.

---

dence games. Exhibit 12.5 illustrates some facts and trends about fraud in Canada in recent years.

Confidence games are run by swindlers whose goal is to separate a victim (or sucker) from his or her hard-earned money. These "con games" usually involve getting a "mark" interested in some get-rich-quick scheme, which may have illegal overtones. The criminal's hope is that when victims lose their money, they will either be too embarrassed or too afraid to call the police. There are hundreds of varieties of con games. The most common is called the pigeon drop.[42] A package or wallet containing money is "found" by a con man or woman. A passing victim is stopped and asked for advice about what to do, since the wallet contains no identification. Another "stranger," who is part of the con, approaches and enters the discussion. The three decide to split the money. But first, to make sure everything is legal, one of the swindlers goes off to consult a lawyer. On returning, he or she says that the lawyer claims the money can be split up, but each party must prove he or she has the means to reimburse the original owner, should one show up. The victim is then asked to give some good-faith money for the lawyer to hold. When the victim goes to the lawyer's

office to pick up a share of the loot, he or she finds the address bogus and the money gone.

In the 1990s con games were appropriated by corrupt telemarketers, who contacted people, typically elderly, over the phone to bilk them out of their savings. The FBI estimates that illicit telephone pitches cost Americans some $3 to $40 billion a year, and in Canada $80 to 100 million.[43] In one scam, a salesman tried to get $500 from a 78-year-old woman by telling her the money was needed as a deposit to make sure she would get the $50 000 cash she had supposedly won in a contest. In another scheme a Las Vegas–based telephone con game used the name Feed America Inc. to defraud people out of more than $1.3 million by soliciting donations for various causes, including families of those killed in the Oklahoma City bombing. The Phone Busters unit of the Ontario Provincial Police estimates that one Canadian per week loses more than $5000 in such schemes. Some common telemarketing scams are detailed in Exhibit 12.6.

With the growth of direct-mail marketing and 1-900 telephone numbers that charge callers over $2.50 per minute for conversations with what are promised to be beautiful and willing sex partners, a flood of new confidence games may be about to descend on the public. In all, about 64 percent of fraud offences were cleared in 1995–most likely a small percentage of all swindlers, scam artists, and frauds.

Insurance fraud is an underresearched, but highly fraudulent area of activity. In a study conducted for the Insurance Board of Canada's investigative division by a team at St. Francis Xavier University, it was determined that of more than 4000 closed claims, 26 percent of personal injury claims were fraudulent. Opportunistic fraud, such as inflating medical expenses, was the most common type. The rate is highest in Ontario, and lowest in Alberta. It also tends to be higher in major cities and metropolitan areas.

In 2001, an organized ring of 25 people were sued for staging car accidents, allegedly defrauding the Insurance Corporation of British Columbia of $400 000. They would stage the accidents between 9.30 p.m. and midnight, in an area where there would be no witnesses, and then submit claims for about $30 000.

Bad Cheques

Another form of fraud is the cashing of a bank cheque, to obtain money or property, that is knowingly and intentionally drawn on a nonexistent or underfunded bank account. In general, for a person to be guilty of passing a bad cheque, the bank the cheque is drawn on must refuse payment, and the cheque casher must fail to make the cheque good within ten days after finding out the cheque was not honoured. Cheque fraud accounted for 68 percent of all reported frauds in 1979. By 1993 this had declined to 50 percent, and in 1999 to 33 percent. This form of fraud has a high clearance rate, usually around 65 to 70 percent, higher than that for most forms of property crime (23 percent).

The best-known study of cheque forgers was conducted by Edwin Lemert.[44] He found that the majority of cheque forgers–he called them naive cheque forgers–are amateurs who do not believe their actions will hurt anyone. Most naive cheque forgers come from middle-class backgrounds and have little identification with a criminal subculture. They cash bad cheques because of a financial crisis that demands an immediate resolution–perhaps they have lost money at the racetrack and have some pressing bills to pay. Lemert refers to this condition as closure. Naive cheque forgers are often socially isolated people who have been unsuccessful in their personal relationships. They are risk-prone when faced with a situation that is unusually stressful for them. The willingness of stores and other commercial establishments to cash cheques with a minimum of fuss to promote business encourages the cheque forger to risk committing a criminal act.

Not all cheque forgers are amateurs. Lemert found that a few professionals–whom he calls **systematic forgers**–make a substantial living by passing bad cheques. However, professionals constitute a relatively

---

Exhibit 12.5	Quick Facts about Fraud in Canada

- In 1999, 90 568 cases of fraud were reported to the police, with a clearance rate of 59 percent.
- Cheque fraud outnumbered credit card fraud 3 to 1 in 1995; but narrowed to 1.5 to 1 in 1999.
- Twenty-nine out of 100 women were charged with fraud compared to 6 out of 100 for break and enter.
- The fraud rate in Quebec and Ontario was the lowest in Canada, 76 percent of the national average; the highest rate was the Prairies, 114 percent of the national average.
- Youths were charged with only 7 percent of total fraud offences; the median age of offenders was 29 years.
- Primary locations are businesses (53 percent), banks (28 percent), and individuals (6 percent).
- The elderly are most often victimized by telephone fraud.
- Credit card counterfeiting is the fastest growing fraudulent crime.
- The cost of fraud is over $3 billion annually.
- Insurance fraud costs about $1 300 000 000 per year, representing 10 to 15 percent of auto, household, and commercial claims.

Sources: *Canadian Crime Statistics* 1995, 1999, Canadian Centre for Justice Statistics; Derek E. Janhevich, "The Changing Nature of Fraud in Canada," *Juristat* 18 (1998); Derek Paul McPhie, "Fraud," in *Crime Counts: A Criminal Event Analysis*, ed. Leslie W. Kennedy and Vincent F. Sacco (Toronto: ITP Nelson, 1996).

---

small segment of the total population of cheque forgers. It is difficult to know the total number of cheque forgeries committed each year or the amounts involved, but it is estimated that the 15 000 known incidents in 1993 resulted in a total loss of almost $100 million. Stores and banks may choose not to press charges, since the effort to collect the money due them is often not worth their while. It is also difficult to separate the true cheque forger from the neglectful shopper.

Credit Card Theft

The use of stolen credit cards has become a major problem in Canadian society. It has been estimated that credit card companies sustained an $84-million loss due to credit card fraud in 1996. Almost 78 000 credit card files were open in 1996, with over 18 000 of those stolen credit cards. Fully 24 percent of credit cards used fraudulently were lost or stolen. Counterfeit or forged cards accounted for over 30 percent of fraud cases in 1995–96, as reported by the Canadian Bankers' Association.[45]

Most credit card abuse is the work of amateurs who acquire stolen cards through theft or mugging and then

---

Exhibit 12.6   Telemarketing Scams

1. *The Prize Scam:* The caller tells you that you have won a valuable prize, or prizes, but you must first submit a payment for any of a variety of reasons, such as taxes, transportation, customs, insurance, or legal fees. Response: When you're a winner, you don't have to pay for your prize. Don't send them any money in advance.

2. *The Lottery Scam:* The caller wants you to be part of a syndicate, or group, to buy a large number of lottery tickets, usually for foreign lotteries, in order to better your chances of winning. They sometimes claim to be able to decrease the odds, from millions to one, down to as low as ten or even six to one, thereby making you almost a sure winner. Response: No matter what the caller says, the odds per ticket remain the same: millions to one. Also, your community benefits only from lotteries based here. Don't buy lottery tickets from a telephone solicitation.

3. *The Advance Fee Loan Scam:* This usually starts with an advertisement for an easy loan appearing in a local newspaper. The victim's credit history likely prohibits them from getting a loan from a bank. They call the number in the ad and are told they're approved for the amount they seek. However, the lending representative tells the victim that an advance fee is required, usually about 10 percent of the amount to be borrowed. Response: It is illegal, in Ontario, to require an advance fee for a loan. Don't deal with any lender who charges a fee, in advance, for a loan—report them to the Ministry of Consumer and Corporate Relations, Ontario.

4. *Vacation Scams:* The caller offers incredible savings, and sometimes even free travel or accommodation, to popular destinations. Certificates are issued, in the victim's name, appearing to represent a perceived reservation. Response: Remember, "You don't get something for nothing." If you try to take advantage of this golden opportunity you will undoubtedly end up paying what you would have anyway, had you made the travel arrangements yourself—that's if you are fortunate, and actually get a room worth staying in. Don't buy a vacation pitch; when travelling, deal with a reputable agent.

5. *Charity Scams:* The caller appears to be soliciting for what is clearly a worthy cause, and the name sounds similar to an easily recognized charity, so their "cause" seems "worthy." Response: There are so many causes that it is almost impossible to know them all—don't try. True charitable causes are worthwhile and should be supported. You should carefully select the causes you wish to support, look them up in the phone book (real organizations will always have their phone numbers listed), call and arrange to have your contribution sent directly. This approach ensures that your entire donation goes to the cause you wish to support; none of it is held back by a middleman. Don't send money to any "charity" with which you are not completely familiar.

6. *Police/Fire-fighter Magazines:* These operations focus on small businesses. The caller wants you to advertise in the magazine, purporting to support a police or fire department. Response: We don't know of any police or fire department that supports a magazine. Don't pay for advertising in these publications, if your goal is to support your police or fire department; your money simply supports the people who run the magazine, the circulation of which is almost non-existent.

---

use them for two or three days. However, professional credit card rings may be getting into the act. For example, in Los Angeles members of a credit card gang got jobs as clerks in several stores, where they collected the names and credit card numbers of customers. Gang members bought plain plastic cards and had the names and numbers of the customers embossed on them. The gang created a fictitious wholesale jewellery company and applied for and received authorization to accept credit cards from the customers. The thieves then used the phony cards to charge nonexistent jewellery purchases on the accounts of the people whose names and card numbers they had collected. The banks that issued the original cards honoured over $200 000 in payments before the thieves withdrew the money from their business account and left town.

Embezzlement

The crime of **embezzlement** was observed in early Greek culture when, in his writings, Aristotle alluded to theft by road commissioners and other government officials.[46] It was first codified into the law by the English Parliament during the 16th century to fill a gap in the larceny law.[47] Until then, to be guilty of theft a person had to take goods from the physical possession of another (trespass in the taking). However, as explained earlier, this definition did not cover instances in which one person trusted another and wilfully gave that person temporary custody of his or her property. For example, in everyday commerce, store clerks, bank tellers, brokers, and merchants gain lawful possession but not legal ownership of other people's money.

Embezzlement occurs when someone who is so trusted with property fraudulently converts it, that is, keeps it for his or her own use or the use of others. Embezzlement can be distinguished from fraud on the basis of when the criminal intent was formed. Most U.S. courts require that a serious breach of trust must have occurred before a person can be convicted of embezzlement. The mere act of moving property without the owner's consent, or damaging it or using it, is not considered embezzlement. However, using it up, selling it, pledging it, giving it away, or holding it against the owner's will is held to be embezzlement.

Although it is impossible to know how many embezzlement incidents occur annually, the FBI found that only 15 200 people were arrested for embezzlement in 1995—probably an extremely small percentage of all embezzlers. In the United States, the number of people arrested for embezzlement has increased 22 percent since 1986, indicating that (1) more employees are willing to steal from their employers, (2) more employers are willing to report instances of embezzlement, or (3) law enforcement officials are more willing to prosecute embezzlers.

Break and Enter

Under common law, the crime of **break and enter**, sometimes called burglary, is defined as "the breaking and entering of a dwelling house of another in the nighttime with the intent to commit a felony within." Burglary is considered a much more serious crime than larceny or theft, since it often involves entering another's home, a situation in which the threat of harm to occupants is great. Even though the home may be unoccupied at the time of the burglary, the potential for harm to the occupants is considered very serious.

The legal definition of burglary has undergone considerable change since its common-law origins. When first created by English judges during the late Middle Ages, laws against burglary were designed to protect people whose home might be set upon by wandering criminals. Including the phrase "breaking and entering" in the definition protected people from unwarranted intrusions; if an invited guest stole something, it would not be considered a burglary. Similarly, the requirement that the crime be committed at nighttime was added because evening was considered the time when honest people might fall prey to criminals.[48]

The Extent of Break and Enter

The definition of burglary includes any unlawful entry into a structure to commit an indictable offence. Break and enter is categorized into three subclasses: those against businesses, residences, and other. According to the UCR, about 320 000 break and enters occurred in 1999. Break and enter represented 26 percent of property crimes in 1993 and 25 percent in 1999 and have fallen in recent years. Most burglaries (62 percent) were of residences; 26 percent were business-related. Break and enter victims suffered losses of about $3 billion in 1993, with an average loss of about $3000.

The GSS reported that 5 percent of Canadian households were victimized by break and enter in 1995 and that slightly less than that were victims of household theft. The difference between the UCR and GSS statistics is explained by the fact that 32 percent of all break and enter and 57 percent of all household theft victims did not report the incident to police in 1993. However, similar to the UCR, the GSS indicates that the number of burglaries declined.

Those most likely to be burglarized are living in urban areas and in private houses.

Careers in Burglary

Great variety exists within the ranks of burglars. Many are crude thieves who, with little finesse, will smash a window and enter a vacant home or structure with minimal preparation. However, because it involves planning, risk, and skill, burglary has been a crime long associated with professional thieves. To become a skilled practitioner of burglary, the would-be burglar must learn the craft at the side of an experienced burglar. For example, Francis Hoheimer, an experienced professional burglar, has described how Oklahoma Smith educated him in the craft of burglary when the two were serving time in the Illinois State Penitentiary. Among Smith's recommendations are

> Never wear deodorant or shaving lotion; the strange scent might wake someone up. The more people there are in a house, the safer you are. If someone hears you moving around, they will think it's someone else.... If they call, answer in a muffled sleepy voice.... Never be afraid of dogs, they can sense fear. Most dogs are friendly; snap your finger, they come right to you.[49]

Despite his elaborate preparations, Hoheimer spent many years in confinement, so perhaps his advice is not the best.

Burglars on the Job

Burglars must "master" the skills of their "trade," learning to spot environmental cues that "nonprofessionals" fail to notice.[50] These are novices, journeymen, and professionals, described below. In an important book, *Burglars on the Job*, Richard Wright and Scott Decker describe the working conditions of active burglars.[51] Most are motivated by the need for cash in order to get high; they want to enjoy the good life, "keeping the party going," without the need for working. While, as Exhibit 12.9 shows, they approach their "job" in a rational, workmanlike fashion,

| Exhibit 12.7 | Quick Facts about Break and Enter in Canada |

- Break and enters (B&E) were the second most frequent kind of property crime in 1999, at 25 percent.
- This crime accounts for 14 percent of all Criminal Code incidents reported to the police.
- There were 318 448 reported cases in 1999, with a report rate of 65 percent.
- The majority of adult suspects (94 percent) charged with B&E in 1999 were male, while 38 percent of those charged overall were youths.
- Sixty percent of victims knew the perpetrator in 1993: acquaintance/friend (38 percent), ex/spouse (17 percent), family (5 percent).
- Main locations included private residences (65 percent), businesses (17 percent).
- A TV, stereo, or VCR is the single item most often stolen (17%).
- One in 16 residences had a B&E in 1996, an increase from 1991; overall property crime decreased.
- Break and enters cost the insurance industry $299 million in 1999.
- In 1993 4 percent of victims were faced with firearms, 90 percent by weapons, force, or threats.
- The clearance rate for break and enters in 1999 was 17 percent; for property crimes in general 23 percent.

Sources: *Canadian Crime Statistics* 1995, 1999, Canadian Centre for Justice Statistics; "Canadian Crime Statistics, 1996," *Juristat* 17 (1997); Rosemary Gartner and Anthony N. Doob, "Trends in Criminal Victimization: 1988–1993," *Juristat* 14 (1994); Peter Greenberg, "Break and Enter," in *Crime Counts: A Criminal Event Analysis*, ed. Leslie W. Kennedy and Vincent F. Sacco (Toronto: ITP Nelson, 1996).

their lives are controlled by their culture and environment. Unskilled and uneducated, urban burglars make the choices they do because they have had few conventional opportunities for success.

The Good Burglar. Neal Shover has studied the careers of professional burglars and uncovered the existence of a particularly successful type—the good burglar.[52] This is a characterization applied by professional burglars to colleagues who have distinguished themselves as burglars. Characteristics of the good burglar include (1) technical competence, (2) maintenance of personal integrity, (3) specialization in burglary, (4) financial success at crime, and (5) ability to avoid prison sentences.

Shover found that to receive recognition as good burglars, novices must develop four key requirements of the trade. First, they must learn the many skills needed to commit lucrative burglaries. This process may include learning such techniques as how to gain entry into homes and apartment houses, select targets with high potential payoffs, choose items with a high resale value, properly open safes without damaging their contents, and use the proper equipment, including cutting torches, electric saws, explosives, and metal bars. Second, the good burglar must be able to team up to form a criminal gang. Choosing trustworthy companions is essential if the obstacles to completing a successful job—police, alarms, secure safes—are to be overcome. Third, the good burglar must have inside information. Without knowledge of what awaits them inside, burglars can spend a tremendous amount of time and effort on empty safes and jewellery boxes. Finally, the good burglar must cultivate fences or buyers for stolen wares. Once the burglar gains access to people who buy and sell stolen goods, he or she must also learn how to successfully sell these goods for a reasonable profit.

The process of becoming a professional burglar is similar to the process Sutherland described in his theory of differential association. A person becomes a good burglar through learning the techniques of the trade from older, more experienced burglars. During this process, the older burglar teaches the novice how to handle such requirements of the trade as dealing with defence attorneys, bail bond agents, and other agents of the justice system. Consequently, the opportunity to become a good burglar is not open to everyone. Apprentices must be known to have the appropriate character before they are taken under the wing of the "old pro." Usually, the opportunity to learn burglary comes as a reward for being a highly respected juvenile gang member, from knowing someone in the neighbourhood who has made a living at burglary, or, more often, from having built a reputation for being solid while serving time in prison.

| Exhibit 12.8 | Quick Code: Break and Enter |

Section 348. (1) Every one who
(a) breaks and enters a place with intent to commit an indictable offence therein,
(b) breaks and enters a place and commits an indictable offence therein, or
(c) breaks out of a place after
  (i) committing an indictable offence therein, or
  (ii) entering the place with intent to commit an indictable offence therein, is guilty of an indictable offence and liable
(d) to imprisonment for life, if the offence is committed in relation to a dwelling-house, or
(e) to imprisonment for a term not exceeding fourteen years, if the offence is committed in relation to a place other than a dwelling-house ...
[Other relevant sections: 321, 349, 350, 351, 352]

Source: *Pocket Criminal Code* (Scarborough, ON: Carswell, 1995).

Exhibit 12.9   How Burglars Approach Their "Job"

- Targets are often acquaintances.
- Drug dealers are a favoured target because they have lots of cash and drugs, and victims aren't going to call police.
- Tipsters help the burglars select attractive targets.
- Some stake out residences to learn the occupants' routine.
- Many burglars approach a target masquerading as workmen, such as carpenters or housepainters.
- Most avoid occupied residences, considering them high-risk targets.
- Alarms and elaborate locks do not deter burglars but tell them there is something inside worth stealing.
- Some call the occupants from a pay phone: if the phone is still ringing when they arrive, they know no one is home.
- After entering a residence, their anxiety turns to calm as they first turn to the master bedroom for money and drugs. They also search kitchens, believing that some people keep money in the mayonnaise jar!
- Most work in groups, one serving as a lookout while the other(s) ransack the place.
- Some dispose of goods through a professional fence; others try to pawn the goods, exchange the goods for drugs, or sell them to friends and relatives. A few keep the stolen items for themselves, especially guns and jewellery.

Source: Richard Wright and Scott Decker, *Burglars on the Job: Streetlife and Residential Break-In*s (Boston, MA: Northeastern University Press, 1994).

The Burglary "Career Ladder." In interviewing 30 active burglars in Texas, researchers found that burglars go through stages of career development.[53] They begin as young novices who learn the trade from older, more experienced burglars, often siblings or relatives. Novices will continue to get this tutoring as long as they can develop their own markets (fences) for stolen goods. After their education is over, novices enter the journeyman stage, characterized by forays in search of lucrative targets and by careful planning; they develop reputations as experienced, reliable criminals. Finally, they become professional burglars when they have developed advanced skills and organizational abilities that give them the highest esteem among their peers; they plan and execute their crimes after careful deliberation.

The Texas burglars also displayed evidence of rational decision making. Most seemed to carefully evaluate potential costs and benefits before deciding to

According to the rational choice approach discussed in Chapter 5, burglars make rational and calculated decisions before committing crimes. If circumstances and culture dictate their activities, can their decisions be considered a matter of choice?

---

commit crime. There is evidence that burglars follow this pattern in their choice of burglary sites. Burglars show preference for corner houses because they are easily observed (surveillability) and offer the maximum number of escape routes. Other issues are occupancy and accessibility. They look for houses that show evidence of long-term care and wealth. Although people may erect fences and other barriers to deter burglars, these devices may actually attract crime because they are viewed as protecting something worth stealing: If there were nothing valuable inside, why go to so much trouble to secure the premises?[54]

The researchers also found that many burglars had serious drug habits and that their criminal activity was in part aimed at supporting their substance abuse.

Repeat Burglary. To what extent do burglars strike the same victim more than once? Research suggests that burglars may in fact return to the "scene of the crime" in order to repeat their offences. One reason is that many burgled items are deemed indispensable (such as televisions and VCRs), so it is safe to assume they will be quickly replaced.[55] Some have articulated why burglars would most likely try to hit the same target more than once:

- It takes less effort to burgle a home or apartment known to be a suitable target than an unknown or unsuitable one.
- The burglar is already aware of the target's layout.
- The ease of entry of the target has probably not changed, and escape routes are known.
- The lack of protective measures and the absence of nosy and intrusive neighbours, which made the first burglary a success, have probably not changed.
- Goods were observed that could not be taken out the first time.[56]

Chapter 4 discussed repeat victimization. As you may recall, it is common for particular people and places to be the target of numerous predatory crimes.

The Female Burglar

Despite the interest shown in the careers of both residential burglars and the female offender in general, relatively little is known about female burglars. Although most break and enter burglars apprehended by the police are male, about 6 percent, or 1400, are adult females.

To address this issue, researchers interviewed 18 females, ranging in age from 15 to 51, who were actively engaged in residential burglary. For comparison, 87 male burglars were also interviewed. They found that female burglars had offending patterns quite similar to those of males. In addition to burglary, both groups engaged in other thefts, such as shoplifting and assault. The major difference was that male burglars also engaged in auto theft, while females shunned this form of larceny.[57]

Another difference was that while females always worked with a partner, about 39 percent of the males said they seldom worked with others. Males also began their offending careers at an earlier age than females. About half of all females had been involved in fewer than 20 burglaries, while only 28 percent of males reported as few as 20 lifetime burglaries. Considering they start earlier and commit more crimes, it is not surprising that males had a much greater chance of doing time (26 percent) than females (6 percent).

There were also many similarities between the two groups. A majority of both male and female burglars reported substance abuse problems, including cocaine, heroin, and marijuana use. About 47 percent of the females considered themselves addicts, and 72 percent said they drank alcohol before they committed crimes; males reported less addiction, drug use, and alcohol abuse than females.

Female burglars who worked as accomplices committed burglaries because they felt compelled or pressured to commit crimes because of a relationship with another, more dominant person, typically a boyfriend or husband. Accomplices got into crime because they lacked legitimate employment, were drug dependent, or had alcohol problems. Accomplices exercised little control over their crimes and commonly acted as a lookout or driver.

In contrast, partners, who made up two-thirds of the sample, were involved in planning and carrying out the crimes because they enjoyed both the reward and the excitement of burglary. In planning their crimes, partners displayed many of the characteristics of the rational criminal: They helped spot targets and planned entries. As one female burglar stated:

> That's one reason why we got so many youngsters in jail today. I see this, so let's go make a hit. No, no, no. If they see this and it looks good, then it's going to be there for a while. So the point is, you have to case it and make sure you know everything. I want to know what time you go to work, the time the children go to school. I know there's no one coming home for lunch. So plan it with somebody else. We'll take the new dishwasher, washing machine, and this other stuff. We just put it in the truck. Do you know

when people rent a truck, nobody ever pays that any attention? They think you're moving [but] only if you rent a truck. Now if you bring it out of there and put it in the car, that's a horse of another colour.

Once the burglary began, partners carried out all forms of crime-related tasks, including gaining entry, searching the house, and disposing of the stolen merchandise.

In conclusion, most female burglars maintain roles and identities quite similar to those of their male colleagues. While some gender-based differences are evident (males more often work alone; women almost always work with others), both male and female burglars actively plan crimes for many of the same reasons. This research shows that for the majority of both male and female burglars, criminal careers may be a function of economic need and role equality, a finding that supports a feminist view of crime. It also illustrates that repeat criminals use rational choice in planning their activities.

Arson

Arson is the wilful and malicious burning of a home, public building, vehicle, or commercial building. UCR statistics for 1999 show there were 12 763 arsons known to the police. This is a very difficult crime to solve, with a clearance rate under 20 percent. Of those charged, 45 percent were adult males, and male youths accounted for an additional 37 percent.

There are several motives for arson. Juveniles may get involved in starting fires for various reasons as they mature. Juvenile firesetters fall into three general groups.[58] The first is made up of children under seven years of age. Generally, fires started by these children are the result of accidents or curiosity. In the second group are children ranging in age from 8 to 12. Although the firesetting of some of these children is motivated by curiosity or experimentation, a greater proportion of their firesetting represents underlying psychosocial conflicts. The third group comprises adolescents between the ages of 13 and 18. These youths tend to have a long history of undetected fire play and fire-starting behaviour. Their current firesetting episodes are usually the result of either psychosocial conflict and turmoil or intentional criminal behaviour.

Studies show that juvenile arsonists can be classified in one of four categories:

1. *The "playing with matches" firesetter.* This is the youngest fire starter, usually between the ages of four and nine, who sets fires because parents are careless with matches and lighters. Proper instruction on fire safety can help prevent fires set by these young children.

2. *The "crying for help" firesetter.* This type of firesetter is a 7- to 13-year-old who turns to fire to reduce stress caused by family conflict, divorce, death, or abuse. These youngsters have difficulty expressing their feelings of sorrow, rage, or anger and turn to fire as a means of relieving stress or getting back at their antagonists.

3. *The "delinquent" firesetter.* Some youths set fire to school property or surrounding areas to retaliate for some slight experienced at school. These kids may break into the school to vandalize property with friends and later set a fire to cover up their activities.

4. *The "severely disturbed" firesetter.* This youngster is obsessed with fires and often dreams about them in "vibrant colours." This is the most disturbed type of juvenile firesetter and the one most likely to set numerous fires with the potential for death and damage.[59]

Adult arson may also be a function of severe emotional turmoil. Some psychologists view fire starting as a function of a disturbed personality, and thus as a mental health problem and not a criminal act.[60]

It is alleged that arsonists often experience sexual pleasure from starting fires and then observing their destructive effects. While some arsonists may be sexually aroused by their activities, there is little evidence that most arsonists are psychosexually motivated.[61] It is equally likely that fires are started by angry people looking for revenge against property owners or by teenagers out to vandalize property.

Other arsons are set by "professional" arsonists who engage in arson for profit. This is often related to arson fraud, in which a business owner burns his or her property, or hires someone to do it, to escape financial problems.[62] Over the years, investigators have found that businesspeople are willing to become involved in arson to collect fire insurance or for various other reasons, including but not limited to

- obtaining money during a period of financial crisis;
- getting rid of outdated or slow-moving inventory;
- destroying outmoded machines and technology;
- paying off legal and illegal debt;
- relocating or remodelling a business, as when a theme restaurant has not been accepted by customers;
- taking advantage of government funds available for redevelopment;
- applying for government building money, pocketing it without making repairs, and then claiming that fire destroyed the "rehabilitated" building;
- planning bankruptcies to eliminate debts, after the merchandise supposedly destroyed was secretly sold before the fire;
- eliminating business competition by burning out rivals;
- using extortion schemes to demand that victims pay or the rest of their property will be burned;

Throughout the 1990s hundreds of mysterious burnings of churches have occurred. It is as yet undetermined whether the fires are part of a coordinated plot or are individual acts of arson. In 1998 in Toronto, Christ Church St. James, one of the oldest black churches in Canada, was gutted by fire set by an individual arsonist.

- solving labour-management problems; arson may be committed by a disgruntled employee;
- concealing another crime, such as embezzlement.

Some recent technological advances may help prove that many alleged arsons were actually accidental fires. There is now evidence of an effect called flashover in which, during the course of an ordinary fire, heat and gas

---

Exhibit 12.10 Quick Facts about Arson in Canada

- In 1990 57 people were killed and 551 injured in fires costing $244 million.
- Arson is an underreported crime, but 12 763 incidents were reported in 1999.
- The percentage of arson cases in which an accused was identified has dropped from 30 percent in 1974 to 21 percent in 1991, to 19 percent in 1999.
- Fifty percent of all fires with losses over $500 000 in 1989 had an unknown cause.
- The peak for arson in the 1980s coincided with an economic recession.
- Adults accounted for 55 percent of all arson charges in 1999, 82 percent being male.
- The most favoured locations are homes (31 percent) and commercial locations (20 percent).
- Arson was redefined in 1990, with the maximum penalty increased to life in prison.
- Arson is a difficult crime to investigate.

Sources: *Canadian Crime Statistics*, 1995, 1999, Canadian Centre for Justice Statistics; Lee Wolff, "Arson in Canada," *Juristat* 12 (1992); John L. McMullan and Peter D. Swan, "Social Economy and Arson in Nova Scotia," *Canadian Journal of Criminology* 31 (1989), pp. 281–308.

Exhibit 12.11 | **Quick Code: Arson**

Section 433. Every person who intentionally or recklessly causes damage by fire or explosion to property, whether or not that person owns the property, is guilty of an indictable offence and liable to imprisonment for life where

(a) the person knows that or is reckless with respect to whether the property is inhabited or occupied

(b) the fire or explosion causes bodily harm to another person.

[Other relevant sections: 434, 435, 436, 437]

Source: *Pocket Criminal Code* (Scarborough, ON: Carswell, 1995).

---

at the ceiling of a room can reach 1093°C. This causes clothes and furniture to burst into flame, duplicating the effects of arsonists' gasoline or explosives. It is possible that many suspected arsons are actually the result of flashover.[63] On the other hand arson is a difficult crime to investigate and prosecute because of the tendency on the part of the public to see arson as a "victimless" crime, or to feel compassion for the defendant.

Summary

Economic crimes are designed to bring financial reward to the offender. The majority of economic crimes are committed by opportunistic amateurs. However, economic crime has also attracted professional criminals. Professionals earn the bulk of their income from crime, view themselves as criminals, and have skills that aid them in their lawbreaking. Edwin Sutherland's classic book *The Professional Thief* is perhaps the most famous

portrayal of professional crime. According to Sutherland and his informant, professionals live by their wits and never resort to violence. A good example of the professional criminal is the fence who buys and sells stolen merchandise. There are also occasional thieves whose skill level and commitment fall below the professional level.

Common theft offences include larceny, fraud, embezzlement, and burglary. These are common-law crimes, created by English judges to meet social needs. Theft involves taking the legal possessions of another, divided into theft over and under $5000. The crime of false pretences, or fraud, is similar to larceny because it involves the theft of goods or money, but it differs because the criminal tricks victims into voluntarily giving up their possessions. Embezzlement is another larceny crime. It involves people taking something that was temporarily entrusted to them, such as bank tellers taking money out of the cash drawer and keeping it for themselves. Newer larceny crimes have also been defined to keep abreast of changing social conditions: passing bad cheques, stealing or illegally using credit cards, shoplifting, stealing autos to sell on the international underground market, and Internet fraud.

Burglary, a more serious theft offence, was defined in the common law as the "breaking and entering of a dwelling house of another in the nighttime with the intent to commit a felony within." Today, the definition of burglary includes theft from any structure at any time of day. Because burglary involves planning and risk, it attracts professional thieves. The most competent have technical competence and personal integrity, specialize in burglary, are financially successful, and avoid prison sentences.

Arson is another serious property crime. Although many arsonists are teenage vandals, professional arsonists specialize in burning commercial buildings for profit.

Thinking Like a Criminologist

To reduce the risk of loss during the Christmas holidays, the Association of Household Insurers suggests that you don't display presents where they can be seen from a window or doorway and put gifts in a safe place before leaving the house or taking a trip. Moreover, closing drapes or blinds during even short trips away from home is a good habit.

It is important to trick burglars into believing someone is home. If you are away, they suggest having lights on timers, stopping mail and newspaper delivery, and arranging,

if possible, to have the walkways shovelled and have a car parked in the driveway as additional security measures. Other suggestions include installing a good dead bolt lock with at least a one-inch throat into a solid wood or steel door that fits securely into a sturdy frame, keeping doors locked, putting a chain-link fence around a yard, getting a dog, and having police inspect the house for security. Putting a mannequin in a chair by the window might be a good idea too. Also, buy a weighted safe deposit box to secure items that

can't be replaced, and engrave your driver's licence number and province of residence on your property to give police a way to contact you if your home is burglarized and the stolen items are later found.

Con artists may take advantage of people's generosity during the holidays by making appeals for nonexistent charities. Always ask for identification from solicitors.

As a criminologist, can you come up with any new ideas that the association failed to cover?

Key Terms

arson

boosters

break and enter

burglary

carjacking

confidence games

constructive possession

economic crimes

embezzlement

false pretences

fence

flash houses

fraud

heels

larceny

occasional criminals

professional criminals

situational inducement

snitches

street crimes

systematic forgers

 See the book-specific website at www.siegelcriminology2e.nelson.com for additional chapter links, discussions, and quizzes.

Chapter

13

Crimes of Power:
White-Collar, Corporate,
and Organized Crime

In contrast to the previous chapter, the second component of economic crime involves illegal business activity. In this chapter, we divide these crimes of illicit entrepreneurship into the categories of white-collar crime, corporate crime, and organized crime. **White-collar crime** involves illegal activities of people within institutions whose acknowledged purpose is personal profit and gain through legitimate business transactions, whereas the beneficiary of **corporate crime** is the organization itself. **Organized crime** involves illegal activities of people and organizations whose purpose is profit and gain through illegitimate business enterprise. Organized crime and white-collar crime are linked here because, as criminologist Dwight Smith argues, enterprise and not crime is the governing characteristic of both phenomena:

> White-collar crime is not simply a dysfunctional aberration. Organized crime is not something ominously alien to the ... economic system. Both are made criminal by laws declaring that certain ways of doing business, or certain products of business, are illegal. In other words, criminality is not an inherent characteristic either of certain persons or of certain business activities but rather, an externally imposed evaluation of alternative modes of behaviour and action.[1]

According to this definition, business enterprise can be viewed as a spectrum of acts ranging from the most "saintly" to the most "sinful."[2] Although "sinful" organizational practices may be desirable to many consumers (for example, the sale of narcotics) or an efficient way of doing business (such as the dumping of hazardous wastes), society has seen fit to regulate or outlaw these behaviours. Organized crime and the crimes of business are the results of a process by which political constraints are based on economic activity.

White-collar and organized crime share some striking similarities. The sale of illegal goods and services to customers who know they are illegal shows the overlap between criminal and business enterprise. For example, an organized crime family is an association of businesspeople who join to further their business careers, an association that allows them to cultivate contacts and be in a position to take advantage of "good deals" offered by more experienced players. The criminal group settles disputes between members, who, after all, cannot take their problems to court.[3]

Organized crime involves individuals or groups whose marketing techniques (threat, extortion, smuggling) and product lines (drugs, sex, gambling, loansharking) have been outlawed. White-collar crimes include the use of illegal business practices (embezzlement, price fixing, bribery, and so on) to merchandise what are ordinarily legitimate commercial products.

Surprising to some, all the crimes discussed here can involve violence. While the use of force and coercion by

Exhibit 13.1	**Quick Facts about the Cost of Corporate Crime in Canada**

- Between 1972 and 1981 more than 10 000 Canadians died from injuries received on the job.
- In Canada there are about 500 homicide victims per year, but about 15 000 die from corporate inaction.
- Failure to remit payroll deductions costs society more than bank robbery, extortion, and kidnapping.
- Occupational deaths are the third leading cause of death after heart disease and cancer.
- Hundreds of thousands of workers are exposed to radioactive and chemical pollutants every year.
- In 1993 the Canadian Union of Public Employees estimated that 61 percent of workers were victimized by violence in the previous two years, 43 percent said no action was taken after a violent incident.
- The Canadian Labour Congress (1993) reports that deaths from workplace disease are largely uncompensated.
- Of those killed in fatal workplace accidents, 97 percent are men and 3 percent are women.
- Women are at risk of reproductive health hazards due to exposure to toxic substances during pregnancy.

Sources: John L. McMullan, *Beyond the Limits of the Law: Corporate Crime and Law and Order* (Halifax: Fernwood, 1992); Desmond Ellis and Walter DeKeseredy, *The Wrong Stuff: An Introduction to the Sociological Study of Deviance*, 2nd ed. (Scarborough, ON: Allyn and Bacon, 1996); Brian MacLean, ed., *The Political Economy of Crime* (Scarborough, ON: Prentice Hall, 1986).

organized crime members has been popularized in the media and therefore comes as no shock, that white-collar and corporate crimes may result in the infliction of pain and suffering seems more astonishing. Yet experts claim that 200 000 or more occupational deaths occur each year and that "corporate violence" annually kills and injures more people than all street crimes combined.[4]

It is also possible to link organized and white-collar crime because some criminal enterprises involve both forms of activity. Organized criminals may seek out legitimate enterprises to launder money, diversify their sources of income, increase their power and influence, and gain and enhance respectability.[5] Otherwise, legitimate businesspeople may turn to organized criminals to help them with problems of an economic nature (such as breaking up a strike or dumping hazardous waste products), stifle or threaten competition, and increase their influence. The distinction between organized crime and white-collar and corporate criminals may often become blurred.

Some forms of white-collar crime may be more like organized crime than others.[6] While some corporate executives cheat to improve their company's position in the business world, others are motivated purely for personal gain. It is this latter group, people who engage in ongoing criminal conspiracies for their own profit, that most resembles organized crime.[7]

White-Collar Crime

In the late 1930s, the distinguished criminologist Edwin Sutherland first used the term *white-collar crime* to describe the criminal activities of the rich and powerful. He defined white-collar crime as "a crime committed by a person of respectability and high social status in the course of their occupation."[8]

As Sutherland saw it, white-collar crime involved conspiracies by members of the wealthy classes to use their position in commerce and industry for personal gain without regard to the law. All too often, these actions were handled by civil courts, since injured parties were more concerned with recovering their losses than seeing the offenders punished criminally. Consequently, Sutherland believed, the great majority of white-collar criminals did not become the subject of criminological study. Yet their crimes were costly: The financial cost of white-collar crime is certainly many times greater than all the crimes that are customarily regarded as the "crime problem." However, the financial loss from white-collar crime, great as it is, seems less important than the damage to social relations. White-collar crimes violate trust: the trust between consumers and corporations, between clients and professionals, between citizens and their government. This violation of trust thereby lowers social morale and produces disorganization on a large scale. Other crimes produce relatively little effect on social institutions or social organization.[9]

Redefining White-Collar Crime

Although Sutherland's work is considered a milestone in criminological history, his focus was on corporate criminality. Since then there has been some disagreement over the precise definition of white-collar crime. Sutherland's major concern was the crimes of the rich and powerful, but modern criminologists have broadened their definition of white-collar crime. Herbert Edelhertz described it as "an illegal act or series of illegal acts committed by nonphysical means and by concealment or guile to obtain money or property or to avoid the payment or loss of money or property or to obtain business or personal advantage."[10] This definition encompasses almost any type of nonviolent property crime, even crimes with little connection to business enterprise.[11] In contrast, a recent symposium of experts on white-collar crime formulated the following definition:

White-collar crime consists of the illegal or unethical acts that violate fiduciary responsibility or public trust, committed by an individual of organization, usually during the course of legitimate occupational activity by persons of high or respectable social status for personal or organizational gain.[12]

This definition recognizes the focus on crimes of the upper class by limiting white-collar crimes to people with "respectable social status."

Today's definition of white-collar crime usually includes all individuals who use the marketplace for their criminal activity. This definition encompasses middle-income Canadians as well as corporate titans.[13] As criminologist Gilbert Geis put it, "White-collar crimes can be committed by persons in all social classes."[14]

Included within recent views of white-collar crime are such "middle-class" acts as income tax evasion, credit card fraud, and bankruptcy fraud. These are also sometimes called professional or elite deviance. Other white-collar criminals use their positions of trust in business or government to commit crimes. Their activities might include pilfering, soliciting bribes or kickbacks, and embezzlement. Some white-collar criminals set up businesses for the sole purpose of victimizing the general public. They engage in land swindles (for example, representing swamps as choice building sites), securities thefts, medical or health frauds, and so on. In addition to acting as individuals, some white-collar criminals become involved in criminal conspiracies designed to improve the market share or profitability of their corporations. This type of white-collar crime, which includes antitrust violations, price fixing, and false advertising, is also known as corporate crime.

State-corporate crime is illegal or socially injurious actions resulting from cooperation between governmental and corporate institutions.[15] Ronald Kramer and Raymond Michalowski charge that the explosion of the *Challenger* space shuttle on January 28, 1986, was the result of a state-corporate crime involving the cooperative and criminally negligent actions of the National Aeronautics and Space Administration and Morton Thiokol, Inc., the shuttle builder.

The White-Collar Crime Problem

It is difficult to estimate the extent and influence of white-collar crime on victims, because all too often those who suffer the consequences of white-collar crime are ignored by victimologists.[16] Some experts place its total monetary value in the hundreds of billions of dollars, far outstripping the expense of any other type of crime. For example, an **occupational crime** such as the loss due to employee theft from businesses alone amounts to billions of dollars per year.[17] The accounting firm KPMG's inves-

Mining's dam problem. A bulldozer plus a gap in the tailings dam at Boliden's minesite in the south of Spain, where five million cubic metres of sludge poured onto nearby farms.

tigation and security unit does an annual survey of Canada's 1000 largest companies. In 1997, 57 percent of respondents said they had been defrauded in the last year by their own employees. Inflated expense accounts, false invoices, and personal use of company supplies were estimated to cost an average of $1.3 million. A 1998 KPMG survey of 5000 U.S. businesses, agencies and nonprofit organizations showed an average loss of $624 000 from cheque fraud by employees, twice as much as reported in 1994. However, it must be noted that poor security often left companies open to fraud.

Beyond their monetary costs, white-collar crimes often involve damage to property and loss of human life. Violations of safety standards, pollution of the environment, and industrial accidents due to negligence can be classified as corporate violence. It is estimated that in the United States, corporate crime annually results in 20 million serious injuries, including 110 000 people who become permanently disabled, and 30 000 deaths. The potential impact ranges from acute environmental catastrophes such as the collapse of a dam to the chronic effects of diseases resulting from industrial pollution.[18]

In a similar vein, sociologist Gilbert Geis charges that white-collar crime is actually likely to be much more serious than street crime:

It destroys confidence, saps the integrity of commercial life and has the potential for devastating destruction. Think of the possible results if nuclear regulatory rules are flouted or if toxic wastes are dumped into a community's drinking water supply.[19]

The public has begun to recognize the seriousness of white-collar crimes and demand that they be controlled. People are coming to see white-collar crimes—such as a judge taking a bribe to give a light sentence, a doctor cheating on medical insurance claims, and a factory owner knowingly disposing of waste in a way that pollutes the water supply—as being more serious than a person stabbing another with a knife or stealing property worth $10 000 from outside a building.[20] While their acts are serious, white-collar criminals generally face monetary fines and relatively short sentences; judges and prosecutors are sometimes reluctant to incarcerate offenders who do not fit the image of "common criminals."

International White-Collar Crime

White-collar crime is not a uniquely North American phenomenon. It occurs in other countries as well, such as the corruption of office by government agents. In China, cases of corruption account for a high percentage of all cases of economic crime. Despite the fact that the penalty for corruption is death, most of the people involved in corruption and bribery are state personnel, including some high-ranking officials.[21] In the late 1980s there were no more than 10 000 corruption cases each year; by 1996 there were six times as many. One reason may be the increase in government-sponsored businesses, which now number more than 500 000 and are growing exponentially.[22]

China is not alone in experiencing organizational crimes. In Thailand crime and corruption are skyrocketing; top executives of the Bangkok Bank of Commerce are believed to have absconded with billions in depositors' money.[23] It is suspected that North American companies are also the targets of white-collar criminals overseas. Agents have been inserted into companies abroad to steal trade secrets, confidential procedures, and "intellectual property" such as computer programs and technology. The cost is somewhere between a conservative $50 billion and an astounding $240 billion a year.[24]

Offences perpetrated against the European Community (EC) can be grouped into four categories:[25]

1. *Corporate crime*, whereby legitimate companies or organizations, in the course of their usual business, cheat the EC, a crime fostered in part by a strongly competitive environment
2. *Government crime*, which includes illegal acts committed by government officials or with their knowledge and support, as well as those that lead to cover-ups of other persons' crimes
3. *Occupational crime*, which involves people making extra money by bending or breaking the rules, due perhaps to financial straits or other business-related problems
4. *Organized/professional crime*, which involves people or groups of people whose primary source of income is illegal[26]

Crimes within these categories amount to billions in losses each year. For example, fraud in the agricultural sector, which ranges from evasion of taxes and deceitful claims to phantom operations and false or forged documentation, may amount to $8 billion per year.[27]

Components of White-Collar Crime

White-collar crimes represent a range of behaviours, involving individuals acting alone or within a business structure. The victims can be the general public, the organization that employs the offender, or a competing organization. One of the best known typologies was created by Marshall Clinard and Richard Quinney, who divide white-collar crime into occupational and corporate categories. Occupational categories include offences committed by individuals in the course of their occupation and by employees against their employers. The second category, corporate crime, is "the offenses committed by corporate officials for the corporation and the offenses of the corporation itself."[28]

Herbert Edelhertz adds to this model, dividing white-collar criminality into four categories:

1. *Ad-hoc violations.* Committed episodically for personal profit, such as welfare fraud or tax cheating
2. *Abuses of trust.* Committed by a person in a place of trust in an organization against the organization; for example, embezzlement, bribery, or taking kickbacks
3. *Collateral business crimes.* Committed by organizations to further their business interests; for example, antitrust violations, or the concealment of environmental crimes
4. *Con games.* Committed for the sole purpose of cheating clients; for example, fraudulent land sales, sales of bogus securities, or sales of questionable tax shelters[29]

The accompanying item, Famous Canadian Criminals, details some of the activity of Christopher Horne, who committed an outrageous fraud while at RBC Securities. In a case on a grander scale, German financier Wolfgang Stolzenberg of Montreal-based Castor Holdings is alleged to have been involved in a 15-year Ponzi scheme, a pyramid scam in which money raised from new investors was used to pay off earlier investors. He is facing 41 counts of fraud and conspiracy and is alleged to have defrauded investors of some $200 million in the $1.5-billion bankruptcy of Castor Holdings Ltd. in 1992. It is the

Exhibit 13.2	A Typology of Corporate Crime
Victim	Crime
Consumer	false advertising, harmful products, price gouging, abuse of credit information
Environment	pollution, resource mismanagement, destruction of way of life
Worker	unsafe work conditions, pension fund abuse, failure to pay legal wages
Competitors	price-fixing, illegal takeovers, industrial espionage, corruption, and influence peddling
State	fraudulent billing, tax evasion, bribing politicians, illegal exporting of products

Sources: Adapted from John L. McMullan, *Beyond the Limits of the Law: Corporate Crime and Law and Order* (Halifax: Fernwood, 1992); C. Goff and C. Reasons, "Organizational Crimes against Employees, Consumers, and the Public," in *The Political Economy of Crime: Readings for a Critical Criminology*, ed. B. Maclean (Scarborough, ON: Prentice Hall, 1986); Desmond Ellis and Walter DeKeseredy, *The Wrong Stuff: An Introduction to the Sociological Study of Deviance*, 2nd ed. (Scarborough, ON: Allyn and Bacon, 1996).

The High Life of Christopher Horne

In 1996, RBC Dominion Securities Inc. was fined $250 000 for failing to properly supervise former vice-president and stockbroker Christopher Horne. Horne was a Toronto-based broker who defrauded elderly clients of millions of dollars over a ten-year period. Horne had quit his job with RBC Dominion Securities in 1994, but in 1996, he was charged with fraud and theft. The Royal Bank, which owned RBC Dominion, reimbursed over $5 million to his victims. In addition, it paid $21 000 in investigation costs.

Horne had misappropriated millions of dollars from client accounts, channelling the money into the Toronto and Grand Cayman bank accounts of a shell company, International Haven Services, which he had founded in Panama City in 1980. Horne had sat on the board of the Art Gallery of Ontario and used his ill-gotten gains to finance his own incredible art collection, estimated to be worth over $4 million. Horne was sentenced to five years in prison in August 1996.

Crime in the News — How Corporate Criminals Hide Their Money

"Nauru gets tough on illicit banking"
by Adrian Humphreys
The government of the world's smallest republic, branded a gangster's paradise because of its lax banking laws, says international pressure can be eased now that it has strengthened anti-money laundering regulations.

The Republic of Nauru amended legislation on banking and corporate secrecy in a bid to avoid sanctions by the Financial Action Task Force (FATF), an agency supported by about 30 countries, Mathew Batsiua, the island's Chief Secretary, said yesterday.

Nauru is a desolate South Pacific island of 24 square kilometres and with a population of 12,088. Money laundering specialists say the island is home to more shell corporations and banks than people. For years, its use by the Russian mafia, tax dodgers and other gangsters to hide money has enraged banks, police and tax collectors around the world. However, attempts to shame the tiny country into tightening regulations have failed.

National Post, December 8, 2001: A16.

Horne's collection of paintings, photographs, and sculptures was seized by the accounting firm of Coopers & Lybrand, appointed by the court to liquidate his assets to pay back creditors.

The Cayman Islands is a tax haven where individuals and corporations pay no taxes and benefit from absolute secrecy (for clean money). The Bahamas is another tax haven with no personal or corporate taxes. It is well established, with more than 400 banks and $320 billion U.S. on deposit. More than 44 000 offshore companies are registered there. Because of its unique financial position, money laundering is a problem there.

second-largest fraud investigation ever conducted by the Royal Canadian Mounted Police, after the inquiry into the failure of mining company Bre-X Minerals Ltd.

Types of White-Collar Crime

Edelhertz's typology captures the diverse nature of white-collar criminality and illustrates how both individuals and institutions can be the victims and offenders of a white-collar crime. Here we will use a typology created by criminologist Mark Moore to organize the analysis of white-collar crime.[30] That typology consists of seven elements, ranging from an individual using a business enterprise to commit theft-related crimes, to an individual using his or her place within a business enterprise for illegal gain, to business enterprises collectively engaging in illegitimate activity. While any typology is artificial

and no single one may be sufficient to encompass the complex array of acts that the term usually denotes, the analysis of white-collar crime here is meant to be so broad and inclusive that it contains the areas commonly considered important for criminological study.[31]

The seven categories of white-collar crime are (1) stings and swindles, (2) chiselling, (3) individual exploitation of institutional position, (4) influence peddling and bribery, (5) embezzlement and employee fraud, (6) client frauds, and (7) corporate crime.

Stings and Swindles

The first category of white-collar crime is **swindling**, or stealing through deception by individuals who have no continuing institutional or business position and whose entire purpose is to bilk people out of their money. Offences in this category range from door-to-door sale of

Connections

In Chapter 12 the crime of fraud was discussed in the context of individual-level crimes that involve con games. Although similar, swindles here involve organizations that are devoted to fleecing the public.

---

faulty merchandise to the passing of millions of dollars in counterfeit stock certificates to established brokerage firms. If caught, white-collar swindlers are usually charged with common-law crimes, such as embezzlement or fraud.

Financial Swindles. Although swindlers are often considered petty thieves, swindles can run into millions of dollars.[32]

The collapse of the Bank of Credit and Commerce International (BCCI) is a swindle that cost depositors billions of dollars. BCCI was the world's seventh-largest private bank, with assets of about $23 billion. Investigators believe that bank officials made billions in loans to confederates who had no intention of repaying them. BCCI officers also used false accounting methods to defraud depositors. Its officers helped clients, such as Colombian drug cartel leaders and dictators Saddam Hussein and Ferdinand Marcos, launder money, finance terrorist organizations, and smuggle illegal arms. U.S. Drug Enforcement Administration officials were able to compile a list of 379 cases in which BCCI laundered money for narcotics traffickers.[33] After the bank was shut down, hundreds of millions of dollars were spent to pay auditors to liquidate the bank's holdings. For example, English liquidators alone were paid $360 million in fees between 1991 and 1994.[34]

The Canadian impact of this crime was felt in the approximately $107 million invested by Canadians in the bank, only a quarter of which was insured by the Canada Deposit Insurance Corporation (CDIC). Assets of the Bank of Credit and Commerce Canada were seized by Canada's top financial regulator, the Superintendent of Financial Institutions, in July 1991, after concerns were raised over its mounting loan losses and its poor internal financial controls.

Despite the notoriety of such cases, investors continue to bite at bogus investment schemes promising quick riches, as we will see in other examples in this chapter. In 1997, the economy of Albania was virtually wiped out in a gigantic Ponzi scheme.

Religious Swindles. One of the most cold-blooded swindles is an investment scam that uses religious affiliations to steal from trusting investors. In the best-known case, TV evangelist Jim Bakker was convicted of defrauding followers of $3.7 million when he oversold lodging guarantees, called "lifetime partnerships," at his Heritage USA religious retreat. The jury found that Bakker had diverted

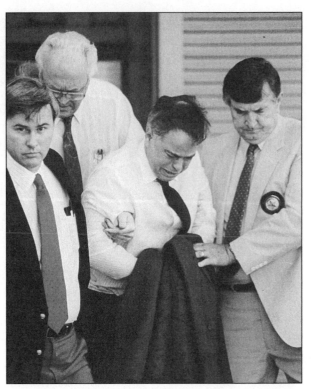

In the best-known case involving a religious swindle, TV evangelist Jim Bakker was convicted of defrauding followers of $3.7 million when he oversold "lifetime partnerships" at his Heritage USA religious retreat.

ministry funds for personal use while knowing that his PTL ministry was in financial trouble. He bought vacation homes in California and Florida, a houseboat, expensive cars, and unusual luxuries, such as an air-conditioned dog house. Bakker had sold hotel rooms to 153 000 people yet built only 258 rooms to accommodate them.[35] Bakker was sentenced to 45 years in prison, later reduced on appeal, and he was released from prison in 1996.

The Bakker case is not unique. The North American Securities Administrators Association estimates that swindlers using fake religious identities bilk thousands of people out of $100 million per year.[36] Swindlers take in worshippers of all persuasions: Jews, Baptists, Lutherans, Catholics, Mormons, and Greek Orthodox have all fallen prey to religious swindles. How do religious swindlers operate? Many join close-knit churches and establish a position of trust that enables them to operate without the normal investor skepticism. Some use religious television and radio shows to sell their product. Others place verses from the scriptures on their promotional literature to comfort hesitant investors. Religious swindles are tough to guard against because they are promoted in the same manner as legitimate religious fund-raising efforts and rely on the faithfuls' trust in those who devote themselves to doing charitable work.

Chiselling

Chiselling, the second category of white-collar crime, refers to cheating an organization, its consumers, or both on a regular basis. Chisellers may be individuals looking to make quick profits in their own businesses or employees of large organizations who decide to cheat on obligations to customers or clients by doing something contrary to either the law or company policy. Chiselling may involve charging for bogus auto repairs, cheating customers on home repairs, short-weighting (intentionally tampering with the accuracy of scales used to weigh products) in supermarkets or dairies, or fraudulently selling securities at inflated prices. It may even involve illegal use of information about company policies that have not been disclosed to the public. The secret information can be sold to speculators or used to make money in the stock market. Use of the information is in violation of the obligation to keep company policy secret.

Corporations can engage in large-scale chiselling when they misrepresent products or alter their content. The Beech-Nut Nutrition Corporation paid a $2-million fine for illegally selling a product labelled "apple juice" that was nothing more than sweetened water. Despite enforcement efforts, it is estimated that 10 percent of all fruit juices use illegal additives.[37]

Professional Chiselling. It is not uncommon for professionals to use their positions to chisel clients. Pharmacists have been known to alter prescriptions or substitute low-cost generic drugs for more expensive name brands. One study found that pharmacists who were business-oriented—and therefore stressed merchandising, inventory turnover, and the pursuit of profit at the expense of professional ethics—were the ones most inclined to chisel customers.[38]

The legal profession has also come under fire because of the unscrupulous behaviour of some of its members. In the 1970s the Watergate hearings, which revealed the unethical behaviour of high-ranking government attorneys, prompted the American Bar Association to require that all law students take a course in legal ethics. This action is needed, since lawyers chisel clients out of millions of dollars each year in such schemes as forging signatures on clients' compensation cheques and tapping escrow accounts and other funds for personal investments.[39] Special funds are often set up by bar associations to reimburse chiselled clients.

Securities Fraud. Chiselling can also take place in the commodity and stock markets. On an individual level, the **churning** of a client's account by an unscrupulous stockbroker involves repeated, excessive, and unnecessary buying and selling of stock with either the intent to defraud the client or in wilful disregard of the client's investment interest.[40]

An important organization that deals with stock market regulation in Canada is the Toronto Stock Exchange. This is a nonprofit organization governed by a 15-member board. While activities of the TSE are overseen by the Ontario Securities Commission, the TSE is a self-governing organization that enforces its own rules and regulations. The exchange investigates rules regarding insider trading or market manipulation, among others. The Vancouver Stock Exchange especially has been plagued with allegations of professional improprieties involving stock trading, and a former premier of British Columbia was once investigated for insider trading.

In 1989 the U.S. federal government's long-term probe of commodity futures trading on the Chicago Board of Trade resulted in many prominent brokers being indicted under racketeering and other statutes.[41] The brokers were alleged to have engaged in prearranged trading in which two or more brokers agree to buy and sell commodity futures among themselves without offering the orders to other brokers for competitive bidding; "front running," in which brokers place personal orders ahead of a large customer's order to profit from the market effects of the trade; and "bucketing," or skimming customer trading profits.[42]

Another form of securities fraud involves using one's position of trust to profit from inside business information. The information can then be used to buy and sell securities, giving the trader an unfair advantage over the general public. Another twist on the exploitation of a business position involves using deceptive practices to buy and sell shares in publicly traded companies.

Securities fraud can occur in a variety of situations. For example, it has been illegal for corporate employees with direct knowledge of market-sensitive information to use that information for their own benefit—for example, buying stock in a company they have learned will be taken over by the larger concern for whom they are employed. In recent years, the definition of **insider trading** has been expanded to include employees of financial institutions, such as law or banking firms, who misappropriate confidential information on pending corporate actions to purchase stock or give the information to a third party so that party may buy shares in the company. Courts have ruled that such actions are deceptive and in violation of security trading codes.[43]

Interpretations of what constitutes insider trading vary widely. To many, the "hot tip" is the bread and butter of stock market speculators, and the point when a tip becomes a criminal act is often fuzzy. In the most celebrated insider trading cases, billionaires Ivan Boesky and Michael Milken, two of Wall Street's most prominent **arbitrage** experts, were convicted and sentenced to prison. Arbitragers speculate on the stock of companies that are rumoured to be takeover targets by other firms and hope to make a profit on the difference between current stock prices and the price the acquiring company is willing to pay. Boesky used inside information on such deals as the merger negotiations between International Telephone and Telegraph and Sperry Corporation, and Coastal Corporation's takeover of American Natural Resources. Possession of this information allowed Boesky to profit in the millions; he received a three-year prison sentence, was barred from dealing in securities, and was ordered to pay $100 million in penalties. Milken was indicted (with the help of information provided by Ivan Boesky) on 98 counts of security fraud, pleaded guilty to six relatively minor counts, and received a harsh ten-year prison sentence and a billion-dollar fine; his sentence was later reduced because of his cooperation with authorities in other cases.[44]

Individual Exploitation of Institutional Position

Another type of white-collar crime involves individuals exploiting their power or position in organizations to take advantage of other individuals who have an interest in how that power is used. For example, a fire inspector who demands that the owner of a restaurant pay him to be granted an operating licence is abusing his institutional position. In most cases, this type of offence occurs when the victim has a clear right to expect a service and the offender threatens to withhold the service unless an additional payment or bribe is forthcoming.

Exploitation in Government. Throughout history, various political and government figures have been accused of using their positions to profit from bribes and kickbacks.[45] Political leaders have used their position to control and profit from the city's police force. Politicians have used their offices to buy and sell political favours.

The use of political office for economic gain is tempting. On the local level, scandals can emerge involving liquor licence board members, food inspectors, and fire inspectors wanting "consideration."[46] Even powerful politicians have been implicated in corrupt practices. In 1998, Conservative senator Michel Cogger was sentenced to pay a $3000 fine and do 120 hours of community work for peddling his influence to a Montreal businessman between 1986 and 1988. In the United States in 1996, former representative Dan Rostenkowski pleaded guilty to two federal corruption charges in return for a 17-month prison sentence and a $100 000 fine.[47]

Exploitation in Industry. Exploitation can also occur in private industry. It is common for purchasing agents in large companies to demand a piece of the action for awarding contracts to suppliers and distributors. In one such case, a J.C. Penney employee received $1.4 million from a contractor who eventually did $23 million of business with the company.[48] In another case, a pur-

chasing agent for the American Chiclets division of Warner-Lambert (maker of Dentyne, Chiclets, Trident, and Dynamints) received a $300 000 kickback from the makers of the wire racks on which the gum products are displayed in supermarkets.[49]

In some foreign countries, soliciting bribes to do business is a common, if not expected, practice. Not surprisingly, U.S. businesses have complained that stiff penalties for bribery give foreign competitors the edge over them. In European countries, such as Italy and France, giving bribes to secure contracts is perfectly legal, and in Germany corporate bribes are actually tax-deductible. Some government officials will solicit bribes to allow firms to do business in their countries. In one incident, the medical supply firm Baxter International is alleged to have bribed Arab officials to do business in Arab nations after it had been placed on a blacklist for owning a plant in Israel.

Influence Peddling and Bribery

Sometimes individuals holding an important institutional position sell power, influence, and information to outsiders who have an interest in influencing or predicting the activities of the institution. Offences within this category include government employees taking kickbacks from contractors in return for awarding them contracts they could not have won on merit, or outsiders bribing government officials who might sell information about future government activities. Influence peddling may not be directed solely at personal enrichment and can also involve securing a favoured position for one's political party or interest group. Political leaders have been convicted of securing bribes to obtain funds to rig elections and allow their party to control state politics.[50]

One major difference distinguishes influence peddling from exploitation of an institutional position. Exploitation involves forcing victims to pay for services to which they have a clear right, while influence peddlers and bribe takers use their institutional positions to grant favours and sell information to which their co-conspirators are not entitled.

Influence Peddling in Government. In 1995, a scandal erupted in Canada over alleged kickbacks in the airline industry. It was alleged that former prime minister Brian Mulroney, along with a former premier of Newfoundland, Frank Moores, had accepted payments from a private company in return for procuring a lucrative contract with the federal government to buy passenger airplanes. A Bavarian middleman, Franz Schreiber, had set up a shell company, International Airlines, to attempt to influence Air Canada to purchase the Airbus 330. In a *Fifth Estate* documentary on the CBC, it was alleged that $20 million was paid in kickbacks. The allegations were never proved, and the federal government was forced to pay out a settlement of $1 million to Mulroney when he sued it.

In 1981, FBI agents, working with a convicted swindler, Melvin Weinberg, posed as wealthy Arabs looking for favourable treatment from high-ranking politicians. The agents said they wished to obtain U.S. citizenship and receive favourable treatment in business ventures. As a result of this "sting," several office holders were indicted, including a U.S. senator, who was convicted of accepting an interest in an Arab-backed mining venture in return for promising to use his influence to obtain government contracts.[51] At trial, the prosecution played videotapes showing the senator meeting with federal undercover agents, boasting of his influence in the government, saying he would talk to the U.S. president about the business venture, and promising to seek immigration help for the bogus sheik.

In another case, senior officials at the Pentagon were found to have received hundreds of thousands of dollars in bribes for ensuring the granting of contracts for military clothing to certain manufacturers. The corruption was so pervasive that the military found it difficult to locate sufficient replacement manufacturers who were not involved in the scandal. More than $1 billion worth of contracts were suspended. The scandal touched some of the largest defence contractors in the United States, including Raytheon, Litton Industries, and Lockheed.[52]

In the mid-1980s officials at the U.S. Department of Housing and Urban Development (HUD) used their power to dispense huge grants to political figures, a number of whom were later convicted of taking bribes and defrauding the government. One woman siphoned off $5 million from the sale of repossessed homes, the largest individual theft of U.S. government funds in history.[53]

In Louisiana, the state insurance commissioner was convicted in 1991 on money laundering, conspiracy, fraud, and for taking $2 million in bribes in return for regulatory favours.[54]

Corruption in the Criminal Justice System. Agents of the criminal justice system have also gotten caught up in official corruption, a circumstance that is particularly disturbing because society expects a higher standard of moral integrity from people empowered to uphold the law and judge their fellow citizens. The credibility of the justice process is critically weakened when officials who hold power over other people engage in criminal behaviour.

In 2001, the RCMP was called in to investigate the drug squad of Toronto's police. Officers were suspected of corruption and the theft of money from the squad's "fink fund." The way the fraud worked was that the officers would send out users to buy drugs from traffickers, and then write out search warrants based on the users' information. However, they would attribute the source as a police informant and requisition money to pay them, but pocket the cash instead. More than a hundred court cases were compromised as a result; several officers were charged but the charges were subsequently stayed.

This example shows how the police are particularly vulnerable to charges of corruption. In New York, the **Knapp Commission** found that police corruption was widespread, ranging from patrol officers accepting small gratuities from local businesspeople to senior officers receiving payoffs in the thousands of dollars from gamblers and narcotics violators.[55] The commission found that construction firms made payoffs to have police ignore violations of city ordinances, such as double parking, obstruction of sidewalks, and noise pollution. Bar owners paid police to allow them to operate after hours or to give free rein to the prostitutes, drug pushers, and gamblers operating on their premises. Drug dealers allowed police to keep money and narcotics confiscated during raids in return for their freedom.

In 1993 New York City empowered the **Mollen Commission** to investigate corruption among city police. The commission found that a relatively small number of officers were immersed in a pattern of violence, coercion, theft, and drug dealing. Testifying before the commission to gain a reduced sentence on a narcotics charge, one officer told of "shaking down" drug dealers, brutalizing innocent citizens, and intimidating fellow officers to force their silence. Protected by the police officer code of secrecy, these cops were able to purchase luxury homes and cars with the profits from their illegal thefts, extortion, and drug sales.[56]

While such efforts are important, it will be difficult to eradicate police corruption without changing the social context of policing. Police operations must be made more visible, and the public must be given freer access to police operations. It is also possible that some of the vice-related crimes the police now deal with might be decriminalized or referred to other agencies. The decriminalization of drugs, for example, would lower the pressure placed on individual police officers and help relieve their moral dilemmas, such as whether it is really wrong to take money from drug dealers or gamblers.

Influence Peddling in Business. Politicians, police, and officials are not the only ones accused of bribery; business has had its share of scandals. In the 1970s, revelations were made that multinational corporations regularly made payoffs to foreign officials and businesspeople to secure business contracts. Gulf Oil executives admitted paying $4 million to the South Korean ruling party; Burroughs Corporation admitted paying $1.5 million to foreign officials. McDonnell-Douglas Aircraft Corporation was indicted for paying $1 million in bribes to officials of Pakistani International Airlines to secure orders.[57]

Despite legal changes, corporations that deal in foreign trade have continued to give bribes to secure favourable trade agreements.[58] In 1995, for example, several former executives of the Lockheed Aircraft Corporation pleaded guilty to bribery in the sale of transport aircraft to the Egyptian government.[59]

Embezzlement and Employee Fraud

The fifth type of white-collar crime involves individuals' use of their positions to embezzle company funds or appropriate company property for themselves. Here, the company or organization that employs the criminal, rather than an outsider, is the victim of the white-collar crime. This is sometimes called occupational crime.

Blue-Collar Fraud. Employee theft can reach all levels of the organizational structure. Blue-collar employees have been involved in systematic theft of company property, commonly called **pilferage**. The techniques of employee theft are quite varied:

- Piece workers zip up completed garments into their clothing and take them home.
- Cashiers ring up lower prices on single-item purchases and pocket the difference.
- Clerks sell untagged sale merchandise at its original cost, pocketing the difference.
- Receiving clerks obtain duplicate keys to storage facilities and return after hours to steal.
- Truck drivers make fictitious purchases of fuel, splitting the gains with the truck stop.
- Some employees simply hide items in garbage pails or incinerators or under trash heaps until they can be retrieved later.[60]

In one study, about 35 percent of employees surveyed reported involvement in pilferage.[61] Employee theft can be explained by factors related to the work setting, such as job dissatisfaction and the workers' belief they were being exploited by employers or supervisors. Employers, on the other hand, attributed employee fraud to economic conditions and declining personal values. It is difficult to determine the value of goods taken by employees, but it has been estimated that pilferage accounts for 30 percent to 75 percent of all shrinkage and amounts to losses of billions of dollars annually.[62]

Management Fraud. Blue-collar workers are not the only employees who commit corporate theft. Management-level fraud is also quite common. Such acts include (1) converting company assets for personal benefit; (2) fraudulently receiving increases in compensation (such as raises or bonuses); (3) fraudulently increasing personal holdings of company stock; (4) retaining one's present position within the company by manipulating accounts; and (5) concealing unacceptable performance from stockholders.[63] An example of management fraud is employees overstating company profits, while understating costs. If bonuses are tied to company profits, then management strikes it rich.[64]

A serious violation of the public trust occurred in the Bre-X scandal in 1996, involving insider trading, stock manipulation, and management fraud on a scale hardly ever accomplished in Canadian society, as shown in Exhibit 13.3.

Employee fraud seems widespread. A survey of 300 U.S. companies by the national accounting firm of KPMG Peat Marwick found that 75 percent reported having fallen prey to employee fraud during the previous 12 months; the estimated total loss was $250 million.[65]

The most significant cases of management fraud in U.S. history occurred in the savings and loan industry, discussed below. This was fraud on a massive scale, certainly beyond anything seen in Canada. However, in 1985 the Canadian Commercial Bank of Canada (CCB), and the Northland Bank the following year, collapsed because of unacceptable financial practices. The Canada Deposit Insurance Corporation estimated the total loss from the collapse of the CCB to be almost $250 million.

A Case-in-Point: The Savings and Loan Scandal. For more than a decade, the owners and managers of some of America's largest savings and loan banks swindled investors, depositors, and the public out of billions of

---

Exhibit 13.3	**The Bre-X Scandal**

In March 1997, Mike de Guzman, the top geologist of the Bre-X mine in Busang, Indonesia, leapt to his death from a helicopter. De Guzman had been credited with helping Calgary-based Bre-X discover what was believed to be the world's biggest gold deposit at the Busang mine.

The site was alleged to contain 200 million ounces of gold. However, suspicions surfaced that Bre-X's core samples had been "salted" with alluvial gold to contaminate the samples and increase the gold content. Tests conducted by Barrick Gold, a Toronto-based gold mining corporation, in 1996 showed no gold in 148 out of 150 samples. When news leaked out that the massive gold discovery was a fraud, Bre-X shares dropped substantially from a high of $286.50 in September 1996; they had risen rapidly as positive reports from Bre-X influenced investors to snap up shares. Shortly after, trading in the company was halted by regulators at the Toronto Stock Exchange until an independent audit of drilling tests was completed.

The executive chief geologist of the company, Jon Felderhof, was sued for $3 billion by Bre-X's receiver-manager, Deloitte and Touche. Felderhof is believed to have made at least $70 million trading in Bre-X stock. The total amount acquired by company insiders was estimated to be on the order of $150 million. It is estimated that 40 000 Canadian investors lost over $3 billion investing in Bre-X, dreaming that they could make that lucky strike.

Source: Glen Whelon, "Felderhof Hit by Suit," *Calgary Sun*, December 31, 1997; Sandra Roubin, "Bre-X Board Told in Late 1996 Tests Showed No Busang Gold," *Financial Post*, April 13, 1998.

dollars. The fraud cost $500 billion, 1700 banks collapsed, and criminal activity was a central factor in 70 to 80 percent of these cases.

How could crimes of this magnitude have been committed? In 1980, the U.S. federal government allowed the S&Ls to expand their business operations beyond residential housing loans, so they could get involved in high-risk commercial real estate lending. They were allowed to compete for deposits with commercial banks by offering high interest rates. The S&Ls also made deals with brokerage firms to sell high-interest certificates of deposit, encouraging investors to pour billions of dollars into banks they had never seen.

Surprisingly, the government insured all deposits. Even if crooked owners offered outlandish interest rates to attract deposits and then lent them to shady business-people, the federal government guaranteed that depositors could not lose money. Given this green light, the S&Ls made irresponsible and fraudulent loans, and losses began to mushroom. The first type of violation involved risky loans to commercial real estate developers, sometimes involving kickbacks.

A second criminal activity was collective embezzlement, siphoning off funds for personal gain. For example, Erwin Hansen took over Centennial Savings and Loan of California in 1980 and threw a Christmas party for 500 friends and guests that cost $148 000 and included a ten-course, sit-down dinner, roving minstrels, court jesters, and pantomimes. Hansen travelled extensively around the world in the bank's private airplanes, purchased antique furniture at the S&L's expense, and refurbished his home at a cost of over $1 million. Before it went bankrupt, the bank bought a fleet of luxury cars and an extensive art collection. The commissioner of the California Department of Savings and Loans said in 1987, "The best way to rob a bank is to own one."

Other practices involved outright fraud. Land was sold or "flipped" between conspirators, driving up the assessed evaluation. The overpriced land could then be sold to or mortgaged by a friendly bank owned by a co-conspirator for far more than it was worth. One loan broker bought a piece of property in 1979 for $874 000, flipped it, and sold it two years later to an S&L he had bought for $55 million. Another method was reciprocal lending in which bank insiders would lend each other money that was never paid back and then trade the bad loans back and forth to delay discovery of the fraud.

In the aftermath of these white-collar crimes, owners tried to cover up their crimes by shady accounting practices or fabricated income statements, some of them respected businesspeople with political connections. For example, the collapse of Denver-based Silverado Banking Savings and Loan cost taxpayers $1 billion, and President George Bush's son Neil was on Silverado's board of directors. Neil Bush was called to testify before the House Banking Committee on his relationships with two developers who owed the bank considerable sums.

One had given Bush $100 000 to invest with the condition that they share in the profits but not the losses. Even Neil Bush admitted, "I know it sounds a little fishy."

The crimes were also difficult to detect because they involved acts of business out of the public view. Much of the fraud revolved around seemingly innocent loans and mortgages made to associates for investment purposes. Of course, the investments later turned out to be worthless, and the bank and its stockholders were left accountable. Because the government guarantees deposits, it was forced to take over the banks and reorganize their assets. Bank examiners were taken in because the S&L managers had made numerous cash contributions to politicians and used these connections to establish their legitimacy.

The S&L crisis was a result of the unregulated finance capitalism that dominated the U.S. economy in the 1980s. Because nothing is produced or sold, financial institutions are ripe for fraud. Their business is the manipulation of money, and the line between smart business practices and white-collar crime is often thin. However, between 1988 and 1992, more than 3200 defendants had been charged, 2600 convicted, and 1700 sent to prison.[66]

Client Frauds

A sixth component of white-collar crime is theft by a client from an organization that advances credit to its clients. Included in this category are insurance fraud, credit card fraud, welfare and medical insurance fraud, and tax evasion. The estimate is that about 2 percent of welfare recipients cheat the federal government. In 2001, it was made public that Customs routinely makes available its lists of people crossing the border to Employment Canada, so that the latter can check to see who is not "available for work."

These offences are grouped together because they involve theft from organizations that have many individual clients who may take advantage of their positions of trust to steal from the organizations.

Health-Care Fraud. Client frauds may be common even among upper-income people.[67] Some physicians have been caught cheating the federal government out of Medicare or Medicaid payments, such as the Toronto area chiropractor caught billing the government in 1996 for $65 000 in services he never delivered. Other abusive practices include such techniques as "ping-ponging" (referring patients to other physicians in the same office), "gang visits" (billing for multiple services), and "steering" (directing patients to particular pharmacies).

Of a more serious nature are fraudulent acts designed to cheat both the government and the consumer, such as billing for services not actually rendered, billing in excessive amounts, setting up kickback schemes, and providing false identification on reimbursement forms. For example, a 1997 undercover operation in

New York State netted 20 professionals who were fraudulently overbilling insurance companies. One doctor saw a patient 11 times and billed for 150 office visits; another treated a patient once and sent in 90 claims. One of the chiropractors was secretly videotaped coaching a patient on how to fake injuries when examined by physicians evaluating his insurance claim.[68] Doctors involved in these schemes are liable to criminal prosecution under the law, and the dollar losses are astronomical.[69]

Bank Fraud. Bank fraud can encompass such diverse schemes as "cheque kiting" (see Exhibit 13.4), cheque forgery, false statements on loan applications, money laundering, sale of stolen cheques, bank credit card fraud, unauthorized use of automatic teller machines (ATMs), auto title frauds, and illegal transactions with offshore banks. For example, a car dealership would commit bank fraud by securing loans on titles to cars it no longer owns. Or a real estate owner would be guilty of bank fraud if he or she obtained a false appraisal on a piece of property with the intention of obtaining a bank loan in excess of the property's real worth.

Tax Evasion. Another important aspect of client fraud is tax evasion. This is a particularly challenging area for criminological study, since (1) so many citizens regularly underreport their income, and (2) it is often difficult to separate honest error from deliberate tax evasion.

To prove tax fraud, the government must find that the taxpayer either underreported income or did not report taxable income. A second element of tax fraud is "wilfulness" on the part of the tax evader. Finally, the government must show that the taxpayer has purposely attempted to evade or defeat a tax payment.

Tax evasion is a difficult crime to prosecute. It is often hard to prove the difference between a careless mistake and wilful fraud. However, the temptation is there, such as construction workers who provide services under the table and off the books.[70]

In Canada the value of the underground economy is estimated to be between 5 and 15 percent of the GNP, or $36 to $100 billion. In the United States the IRS estimates that more than $120 billion in taxes go uncollected each year because individuals fail to report all their income; nearly a third of that amount is from self-employed workers, including professionals, labourers, and door-to-door salespeople.[71]

If the temptation is high, the likelihood of getting caught is low. In the United States, for example, the number of tax audits declined from 8 percent in 1980 to about 2 percent currently.[72] Computer models are used to target anomalies. Despite some well-publicized cases involving the wealthy, such as a $16-million judgment against singer Willie Nelson and the prosecution and conviction of multimillionaire Leona Helmsley, the IRS has been accused of targeting middle-income taxpayers and ignoring the upper classes and large corporations.

Exhibit 13.4	Cheque Kiting

Cheque kiting is a scheme whereby a client with accounts in two or more banks takes advantage of the time required for cheques to clear to obtain unauthorized use of bank funds. For example, a person has $5000 on account in a bank and cashes a cheque for $3000 from an account in another bank in which he has no funds. The bank cashes the cheque because he is already a customer. He then closes his account before the cheque clears or writes cheques on his account that total $5000 and are cleared because he has funds in his account. In some instances, the kiter expects the bank to cover a withdrawal before a cheque is presented to another bank for collection: He simply wants a short-term interest-free loan. Others have no intention of ever covering the transaction but instead want to take cash out of the system after building accounts to artificially high amounts. Kiting can be a multimillion-dollar offence involving cheques written and deposited in banks in two or more provinces and sometimes among banks in multiple countries.

Corporate Crime

The final component of white-collar crime involves situations in which corporate representatives wilfully violate the laws that restrain these institutions from doing social harm. This is also known as corporate or organizational crime.

Interest in corporate crime first emerged in the early 1900s, when a group of writers, known as the muckrakers, targeted the unscrupulous business practices of John D. Rockefeller, Andrew Carnegie, J.P. Morgan, and other corporate business leaders.[73] In a 1907 article, sociologist E.A. Ross described the "criminaloid," a business leader who, while enjoying immunity from the law, victimized an unsuspecting public. However, it was Edwin Sutherland who focused theoretical attention on corporate crime when he began his research on the subject in the 1940s.[74]

Corporate crimes are socially injurious acts committed by companies to further their business interests, as can be seen from some of the examples in Exhibit 13.5 and in Exhibit 13.2. The target of their crimes can be the general public, the environment, or even their company's workers. They can range from the thousands of women with immune system disorders from breast implants, to the 26 miners who died in the Westray coal mine. In a current case, Firestone Tire is being sued after more than a hundred people have been killed when the tread separated from their tires causing their vehicles to crash, a problem which could have been fixed for as little as 90 cents.

What makes these crimes unique is that the corporation is a legal fiction, not an individual. In reality, it is

---

Exhibit 13.5 | Quick Facts on Cases of Corporate Crime

- In 1987 the ferry *Herald of Free Enterprise* sank in the English Channel, killing 200; the bow doors had not been properly secured because proper safety measures had been rejected as too costly.
- In the early 1970s Reed Paper, a processing plant in Dryden, Ontario, dumped 9000 kilograms of mercury into a nearby river, causing extensive brain damage among members of the Grassy Narrows Ojibwa band.
- Between 1958 and 1978 it is estimated that the cost of overcharging by the major oil companies cost Canadians $12 billion; the reason was lack of competition and price fixing.
- The Sydney Steel Corporation in Cape Breton is estimated to have released emissions 6000 percent above allowable standards; 700 000 tons of toxic materials in the tar ponds resist all attempts at cleanup or cover-up.
- In 1982 the Ocean Ranger sank off the coast of Newfoundland, killing all 84 people on board; among other problems, safety standards were inadequate.
- In 1992 the Westray coal mine in Plymouth, Nova Scotia, exploded, killing 26 miners; safety standards were lax and unenforced by government inspectors.

Sources: M. Clarke, *Business Crime* (Cambridge: Polity Press, 1990); Russell Mokhiber, *Corporate Crime and Violence: Big Business, Power and the Abuse of the Public Trust* (San Francisco: Sierra Club, 1988); Laureen Snider, *Bad Business: Corporate Crime in Canada* (Scarborough, ON: Nelson, 1993).

---

company employees or owners who commit corporate crimes and who ultimately benefit through career advancement or greater profits. Some of the acts included in the category of corporate crime are price fixing and illegal restraint of trade, false advertising, and the use of company practices that violate environmental protection statutes. The variety of crimes contained within this category is great, and the damage they cause vast. The following subsections will examine some of the most important offences.

Illegal Restraint of Trade and Price Fixing. Restraint of trade involves a contract or conspiracy designed to stifle competition, create a monopoly, artificially maintain prices, or otherwise interfere with free market competition.

A good example of restraint of trade is **price fixing**. There are four forms this act usually takes.[75] The first is predation, in which large firms agree among themselves to sell their products below market prices to drive out weaker firms, and thus reduce competition. A second

scheme is identical bidding, where the competitors agree to submit identical bids for each contract, above what would have been expected if collusion had not occurred. Purchasing agents use their discretion to choose among bidders; however, identical bidding usually ensures all vendors of getting a share of the market without losing any profitability. Or the market might be divided into territories within which only one member of the conspiring group is permitted a low bid. The remaining conspirators either refrain from bidding or give artificially high bids. Rotational bidding involves a conspiracy in which the opportunity to submit a winning bid for a government or business contract is rotated among the institutional bidders. The conspirators meet in advance and determine who will give the low bid. The winning bid is, of course, higher than it should be, since the losers have all submitted abnormally high bids. Close coordination among the bidders is essential; therefore, these schemes usually involve only a few large firms.

False Claims and Advertising. Executives in even the largest corporations are sometimes caught in the position in which the expectation of ever-increasing profits demand that sales be increased at any cost. At times, executives respond to this challenge by making claims about their product that cannot be justified by its actual performance. However, the line between clever, aggressive sales techniques and fraudulent claims is a fine one in business, but a large one morally. It is not fraudulent to show a delivery service vehicle taking off into outer space. However, it is illegal to knowingly and purposely advertise a product as possessing qualities that the manufacturer realizes it does not have. In 1991 the Food and Drug Administration seized all the Citrus Hill orange juice stored in a Minneapolis warehouse. It seems that the third-largest-selling breakfast drink in the United States had billed itself as "pure squeezed," "100 percent pure," and "fresh," despite the fact that it was made from concentrate.[76]

Orange juice might seem like a minor example. However, what if a car manufacturer claims that its cars get higher gas mileage than it really does, or if mouthwash can cure colds, or if a store advertises products which are unavailable? The list is endless.[77]

In the pharmaceutical industry, false advertising has a long history.[78] It has been common for medicines to be advertised as cure-alls for previously incurable diseases. Such medicines include alleged cures for cancer and arthritis and drugs advertised to give energy and sexual potency. The problem often arises because several competing companies market similar products and the key to successful sales is believed to be convincing the public that one product is superior to the rest. The intense drive for profits leads to the falsification of data and unethical sales promotions.[79]

It is difficult for authorities to police such violations of the public trust. The most serious consequence is usually an

Crime in the News

Corporate Disregard for Human Life

"Lessons of the Ford/Firestone scandal: Profit motive turns consumers into road kill"
By Anthony D. Prince
The year was 1981, the case was encaptioned *Grimshaw v. Ford Motor Company* and at issue was the auto giant's liability for permanently disfiguring burns and other severe injuries sustained by a 13-year-old boy named Richard Grimshaw who barely escaped a flaming Ford Pinto with his life. The driver, Mrs. Lilly Gray, was dead within days of the fiery rear-end collision. A California jury subsequently returned a $126 million civil judgment for young Richard; the Pinto was seared into the national consciousness as a symbol of corporate greed in America.

Rejecting safety designs costing between only $1.80 and $15.30 per Pinto, Ford had calculated the damages it would likely pay in wrongful death and injury cases and pocketed the difference. In a cold and calculating "costs/benefits" analysis, Ford projected that the Pinto would probably cause 180 burn deaths, 180 serious burn injuries, 2,100 burned vehicles each year. Also, Ford estimated civil suits of $200,000 per death, $67,000 per injury, $700 per vehicle for a grand total of $49.5 million. The costs for installing safety features would cost approximately $137 million per year. As a result, the Pinto became a moving target, its unguarded fuel tank subject to rupture by exposed differential bolts shoved into it by rear-end collisions at speeds of as little as 21 miles per hour. Spewing gasoline into the passenger compartment, the car and its passengers became engulfed in a raging inferno.

Only months before, an Elkhart, Indiana County, prosecutor had, for the first time in history, filed homicide charges against Ford Motor Company for the deaths of three Indiana girls in another Pinto rear-end collision. Ultimately, however, District Attorney Michael Cosentino, whose entire budget for the prosecution was $20,000, was no match for millions of dollars worth of corporate legal talent brought in by Ford. Cosentino could not even prevent the trial-court judge from systematically excluding Ford crash-test films and other inculpatory evidence. Yet, while an acquittal was a foregone conclusion, a precedent was established for criminally charging a product manufacturer in the death of a consumer.

As the Ford SUV/Firestone-Bridgestone tire scandal continues to dominate the headlines 20 years after *Grimshaw and the People of Indiana v. Ford Motor Company*, the only law to which these corporate giants seem beholden is the "law of maximum profits." At last count, more than 100 deaths worldwide have been directly attributed to Firestone tire failures and dozens more to fatal rollover accidents involving the top-heavy Ford Explorer, one of the best-selling vehicles in history. . . .

Far from being the exception, Firestone and Ford are only the most recent examples of the rule. The list is long and not pretty. In the 1970s, the Dalkon Shield, A.H. Robbins' toxic intrauterine device, cut a swath of death and injury to the reproductive systems of tens of thousands of women. In the 1980s, the carcinogenic poisoning of Woburn, Massachusetts, was still a buried secret until Jonathan Harr's book *A Civil Action* and the subsequently released movie starring John Travolta told the sordid story of W.R. Grace Corporation's thirst for profits at the expense of children's lives. Add to the list of victims the millions of asbestos insulators, coal miners, textile workers and addicted cigarette smokers whose life-breath is choked off every minute of every day all in pursuit of the almighty dollar.

Anthony Prince is an Oakland, Calif. product liability attorney and former union safety committeeman.

Excerpted from an article in the People's Tribune (Online Edition), Vol. 26 No. 11 / November, 2000; P.O. Box 3524, Chicago, IL 60654, http://www.lrna.org. For free electronic subscription, email pt-dist@noc.org with "Subscribe" in the subject line.

order that the company refrain from using the advertising or that it withdraw the advertising claims. Criminal penalties for false claims are rarely given.

Environmental Crimes. Much attention has been paid to the intentional or negligent environmental pollution caused by many large corporations. There are many types of environmental crimes. Some corporations have endangered the lives of their own workers by maintaining unsafe conditions in their plants and mines, or exposing workers to hazardous materials while on the job. For example, the asbestos industry was inundated with lawsuits after environmental scientists found a close association between exposure to asbestos and the development of cancer.

A second type of environmental crime committed by large corporations is illegal pollution of the environment. Sometimes pollution involves individual acts caused by negligence on the part of the polluter. Two cases stand out. The first was the leaking of methyl isocynate from a Union Carbide plant in Bhopal, India, on December 3, 1984. Estimates of the death toll range from 1400 to 10 000 people; another 60 000 were injured. Union Carbide later reported that the plant had not been operating safely and should have been closed. The firm blamed the negligence on local officials who were running the plant.[80] The second case occurred when the tanker *Exxon Valdez* ran aground on a reef off the coast of Alaska on March 24, 1989, dumping 11 million gallons of crude oil and fouling 700 miles of shoreline. On March 13, 1991, Exxon agreed to pay $1 billion in criminal and civil fines rather than face trial; this is the largest amount paid as a result of environmental pollution to date.[81] However, when the spill first occurred, the U.S. government announced that it would not pursue charges because it could not afford to; Exxon was then the largest multinational in the world, with an annual budget exceeding that of most countries.

Some recent environmental disasters in the news illustrate the fine line between an accident and a crime. At the Canadian-owned Los Frailes mine in Spain, five billion litres of toxic mine waste spilled through a break in a mine tailings pond in April 1998. Boliden Ltd. announced it would clean up the waste, which contaminated thousands of hectares of farming land. Environmentalists accused the company of failing to properly maintain the reservoir and of firing an engineer who had predicted the disaster. In 1996 the Canadian-owned Omai gold mine in Georgetown, Guyana, was the site of a massive cyanide spill from a tailings pond. The Omai mine was developed by Canadian Robert Friedland, who had been sued by the U.S. government for a massive environmental spill of cyanide at the Summitville gold mine in Colorado. He also developed the Voisey's Bay nickel mine in Labrador, and the assets from this sale to Inco were briefly seized by a U.S. court to pay for Summitville. Could these disasters have been prevented with adequate environmental safeguards; are these companies beyond the reach of the law; are they more likely to happen in poor countries heavily dependent on resource extraction?

Considering the uncertainties of federal budget allocations, there is some question whether environmental legislation can be enforced well enough to deter environmental crime. Lack of effective regulation was certainly an issue at the Westray mine. It is possible that solutions to environmental problems must be found at the local level.

High-Tech Crime

The Moore typology of white-collar crime is a useful way of organizing traditional methods of entrepreneurial crime. However, a whole new breed of high-tech crimes are emerging that contain elements of fraud, theft, swindles, and false claims. The crimes are difficult to categorize because they can be committed by corporations and individuals, can be singular or ongoing, and can involve the theft of information, resources, or funds. High-tech crimes cost consumers billions of dollars each year and will most likely increase dramatically in the years to come. They are also difficult to detect and police.

Internet Crimes

Millions of people worldwide are on the Internet, and the number entering cyberspace is growing rapidly. Criminal entrepreneurs view this vast pool as a target for high-tech crimes, and not only of individuals. It is estimated that the capacity to commit mass victimizations simultaneously is near.

There have been a number of highly publicized cases in which adults have solicited teenagers in Internet chat rooms. Others have used the Internet to sell and distribute obscene material, prompting some service providers to censor or control sexually explicit material. Recent controversy erupted over an Internet service provider who allowed right-wing hate groups to publish Web pages on the Internet.

Bogus get-rich-quick schemes, weight-loss scams, and investment swindles have also been pitched on the Internet. In some cases these fraudulent acts can be dangerous to clients. For example, in a 1995 case a Minnesota woman advertised the health benefits of "germanium," claiming that it could cure AIDS, cancer, and other diseases. Germanium products have been banned, however, because they cause irreversible kidney damage. [82]

Computer Crimes

Computer-related thefts are a new trend in employee theft and embezzlement. The widespread use of computers to record business transactions has encouraged some people to use them for illegal purposes. Computer crimes generally fall into five categories:[83]

1. Theft of services, or using the computer for unauthorized purposes
2. Use of data in a computer system for personal gain
3. Unauthorized use of computers employed for financial processing to obtain assets
4. Theft of property by computer for personal use or conversion to profit
5. Making the computer itself the object of a crime, such as spreading a computer virus

While most of these crime types involve using computers for personal gain, the last category typically encompasses activities that are motivated more by malice than profit. Computer criminals are typically motivated by (1) revenge for some perceived wrong, (2) a need to exhibit their technical prowess and superiority, (3) a desire to highlight the vulnerability of computer security systems (so that they will be hired as consultants), (4) a need to spy on other people's private financial and personal information (computer voyeurism), and (5) the desire to assert a philosophy of open access to all systems and programs.[84]

Types of Computer Crime. Several common techniques are used by computer criminals. In fact, theft via computers has become so common that experts have created their own jargon to describe theft styles and methods:

1. *The Trojan horse.* One computer is used to reprogram another for illicit purposes
2. *The salami slice.* An employee sets up a dummy account, and a small amount is subtracted from customers' accounts and added to the account of the thief
3. *"Super-zapping."* Employees use a maintenance program to order the system to issue cheques to his or her private account
4. *The logic bomb.* A virus program is secretly attached to the company's computer system
5. *Impersonation.* An unauthorized person uses the identity of an authorized computer user to access the computer system
6. *Data leakage.* A person illegally obtains data from a computer system by leaking it out in small amounts

A different type of computer crime involves the installation of a virus in a computer system. A virus is a program that disrupts or destroys existing programs and networks. All too often, this high-tech vandalism is the work of "hackers," who consider their efforts to be "pranks." In one well-publicized case, a 25-year-old computer whiz named Robert Morris unleashed a program that wrecked a nationwide electronic mail network. His efforts netted him three years' probation, a $10 000 fine, and 400 hours of community service.[85]

Shift magazine estimates that the number of computer viruses that exist in the world today is in excess of 56 000. This doubled between 1999 and 2000. In 1998, the first major Internet virus, the Morris worm, infected more than 6000 computers. In 2000, the Love Bug worm infected over 15 million computers. It is believed that 40 people were involved in writing the Love Bug; it cost almost $14 billion worth of damage. With the growth of the Internet, the ability to spread these viruses has grown. In 1999 it took about three days for the Melissa macro virus to spread to over 10 million computers worldwide.

An accurate accounting of computer crime will probably never be made, since so many offences go unreported. Sometimes company managers refuse to report the crime to police lest they display their incompetence to stockholders and competitors.[86] In other instances, computer crimes go unreported because they involve such "low-visibility" acts as copying computer software in violation of copyright laws.

The Cause of White-Collar Crime

When Ivan Boesky pleaded guilty to one count of security fraud, he agreed to pay a civil fine of $100 million, the largest at that time in Securities Exchange Commission (SEC) history. Boesky's fine was later superseded by Michael Milken's fine of more than $1 billion. How, people asked, can people with so much disposable wealth get involved in a risky scheme to produce even more?

Many offenders feel free to engage in business crime because they can easily rationalize its effects. Some convince themselves that their actions are not really crimes, because the acts involved do not resemble street crimes. For example, a banker who uses a position of trust to lend an institution's assets to a company he secretly controls may see himself as doing shrewd business, not a criminal act. Or a pharmacist who chisels customers on prescription drugs may rationalize that behaviour by thinking that it does not really hurt anyone. Further, some businesspeople feel justified in committing white-collar crimes because they believe that government regulators do not really understand the business world or the problems of competing in the free enterprise system. Even when caught, many white-collar criminals cannot see the error of their ways. Some white-collar criminals believe that everyone violates business laws, so it is not so bad if they do so themselves. Rationalizing or "neutralizing" greed is a common trait of white-collar criminals not unlike those other criminals use.

Greedy or Needy?

Greed is not the only motivation for white-collar crime; need also plays an important role. Executives may tamper with company books because they feel the need to keep or improve their jobs, satisfy their egos, or support their children. Blue-collar workers may pilfer because they need to keep pace with inflation or buy a new car. Many white-collar crimes involve relatively trivial amounts: Women convicted of white-collar crime typically work in lower-echelon positions, and their acts seem motivated more out of economic survival than greed and power.[87] Sometimes perhaps, even people in the upper echelons of the financial world, such as Ivan Boesky, may be working from a more basic emotional insecurity.[88]

A well-known study of embezzlers by Donald Cressey illustrates how embezzlement is caused by what is called a "nonshareable financial problem."[89] This condition may be the result of offenders' living beyond their means, perhaps piling up gambling debts; offenders feel they cannot

Figure 13.1 Westray Mine Disaster Map

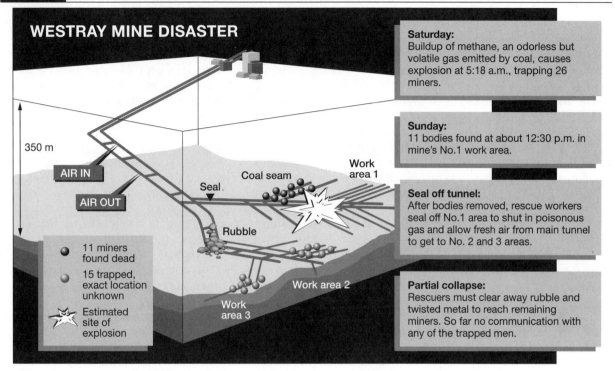

Source: *The Toronto Star*, May 11, 1992, p. A1.

let anyone know about such financial problems without ruining their reputations. The door to solving personal financial problems through criminal means is opened by the rationalizations society has developed for white-collar crime: "Some of our most respectable citizens got their start in life by using other people's money temporarily"; "in the real estate business, there is nothing wrong with using deposits before the deal is closed"; "all people steal when they get in a tight spot." Offenders use these and other rationalizations to resolve the conflict they experience over engaging in illegal behaviour. Rationalizations allow offenders' financial needs to be met without compromising their values.

There are a number of more formal theories of white-collar crime. In the following sections we examine two of the more prominent ones in detail.

Corporate Culture Theory

The corporate culture view is that some business organizations promote white-collar criminality in the same way that lower-class culture encourages the development of juvenile gangs and street crime. According to the corporate culture view, some business enterprises cause crime by placing excessive demands on employees while at the same time maintaining a business climate tolerant of employee deviance. New employees learn the attitudes and techniques needed to commit white-collar crime from their business peers in a learning process reminiscent of the way Edwin Sutherland described how gang boys learn the techniques of drug dealing and burglary from older youths through differential association.

A number of attempts have been made to use corporate culture and structure to explain white-collar crime. For example, Ronald Kramer argues that business organizations will encourage employee criminality if they encounter serious difficulties in attaining their goals, especially making profits. Some organizations will create cost-reduction policies that inspire lawbreaking and corner cutting to become norms passed on to employees. When new employees balk at violating business laws, they are told informally, "This is the way things are done here, don't worry about it." A business's organizational environment, including economic, political, cultural, legal, technological, and interorganizational factors, influences the level of white-collar crime. If market conditions are weak, competition intense, law enforcement lax, and managers willing to stress success at any cost, conditions for corporate crime are maximized.[90]

This is analogous to the cultural deviance approach suggesting that crime occurs when obedience to subculture norms and values causes people to break the rules of conventional society. However, cultural deviance theory was originally directed at lower-class slum boys, not business executives. However, the same crime-producing forces may be operating among both socioeconomic groups.

Exhibit 13.6	The Tragedy of Westray

In 1987 the Nova Scotia government was looking for someone to take over the stalled Westray mine located in Plymouth, in Pictou County. Clifford Frame of Curragh Mining Company agreed to develop the mine, despite studies pointing out the dangers inherent in the mine, such as the spontaneous combustion of high concentrations of methane gas.

A deal brokered between provincial and federal politicians and Frame was announced three days before the provincial election in 1988. Westray was to receive $85 million in the form of a federal loan guarantee, plus a $12-million provincial loan. A lucrative 15-year contract was signed with Nova Scotia Power, despite the fact that there was cleaner, cheaper coal to be found elsewhere.

Between February 1991 and April 1992, Labour Department inspection reports show that the mine's owners were cautioned about methane gas levels, improper storage of flammable materials, and the use of unauthorized equipment. However, no charges were laid. Despite cave-ins and a roof collapse, mining began in 1991. In November of that year changes were made to the mine's design without the knowledge or approval of the Department of Natural Resources.

On May 19, 1992, at 5:20 a.m., when a methane explosion ignited a buildup of coal dust in the mine, 26 miners were killed. The RCMP launched a criminal investigation, and a provincial inquiry was commissioned to determine whether neglect contributed to the disaster. In October, the Nova Scotia Department of Labour charged Curragh and four mine managers with 52 violations of the Occupational Health and Safety Act; the maximum penalty was $10 000. In November 1992, the Nova Scotia Supreme Court quashed the inquiry, and in December the safety charges were dropped so as to not interfere with the RCMP investigation. In April 1993, Curragh and two underground managers were charged with manslaughter and criminal negligence, but the charges were thrown out of court three months later for being too vague. The charges were relaid, but Curragh went into receivership, reducing the number of defendants to two.

In February 1995, the criminal trial began, but four months later the proceedings were stayed by the judge, who ruled that the prosecution did not properly disclose evidence. In December the Nova Scotia Court of Appeal subsequently quashed the appeal, and the likelihood that anyone would face criminal charges was looking increasingly grim. In March 1997 the Supreme Court of Canada upheld the new trial order.

By 1998, six years had elapsed since the explosion. The Nova Scotia government had announced that it would not pursue criminal charges, Curragh was bankrupt, and Frame would not testify before the provincial inquiry. The inquiry's report, based on 17 000 pages of oral testimony, was released, citing extensive problems with government regulation. The John T. Ryan Trophy Committee of the Canadian Institute of Mining, Metallurgy and Petroleum, which declared the Westray mine the safest colliery in Canada a month before it exploded, announced that it would adopt measures to ensure companies do not fudge accident statistics. The miners' families decided that they must move on, and the province announced that it would dismantle the Westray minehead.

Sources: Shaun Comish, *The Westray Tragedy: A Miner's Story* (Halifax: Fernwood, 1993); Dean Jobb, Calculated Risk: Greed, Politics, and the Westray Tragedy (Halifax: Nimbus, 1994); The Westray Story: A Predictable Path to Disaster, Report of the Westray Mine Public Inquiry (Halifax, 1997); newspaper archives.

Corporate Climate. The noted Australian sociologist John Braithwaite has promoted the corporate culture view in his writings on white-collar crime.[91] According to this model, businesspeople in any society may find themselves in a situation where their organization's stated goals cannot be achieved through conventional business practices; their opportunities are blocked. In a capitalist society, up-and-coming young executives may find that their profit ratios are below par. Under such moments of stress, entrepreneurs may find that illegitimate opportunities are the only solution to their problem. So when a government official is willing to take a bribe to overlook costly safety violations, the bribe is gratefully offered. Or when insider trading can increase profits, the investment banker leaps at the chance to engage in it. But how can traditionally law-abiding people overcome the ties of conventional law and morality?

Braithwaite believes that organizational crime is a function of the corporate climate, flourishing in corporations that contain an ongoing employee subculture that resists government regulation and socializes new workers in the skills and attitudes necessary to violate the law. For example, junior executives may learn from their seniors how to meet clandestinely with their competitors to fix prices. When governmental agencies are viewed as uncooperative, untrustworthy, and resistant to change, corporations will be more likely to develop clandestine, law-violating subcultures. A positive working relationship with their governmental overseers will reduce the need for a secret, law-violating infrastructure to develop. Illegal corporate behaviour can exist only in secrecy; public scrutiny brings the "shame" of a criminal label to people whose social life and community standing rests on their good name and character.

Shame of Discovery. The shame of discovery has an important moderating influence on corporate crime. Its source may be external: the general community, professional or industry peers, or government regulatory agencies. The source of shame and disapproval can also be internal. Many corporations have stated policies that firmly admonish employees to obey the rule of law. For example, it is common for corporations to encourage whistle-blowing by co-workers and to sanction workers who violate the law and cause embarrassment. In a sense, corporations that maintain an excess of definitions unfavourable to violating the law will be less likely to contain deviant subcultures and concomitantly less likely to violate business regulations. In contrast, corporate crime thrives in organizations that isolate people within spheres of responsibility, where lines of communication are blocked, and in which deviant subcultures are allowed to develop with impunity.

Those holding the corporate culture view would view the savings and loan scandal as prime examples of what happens when people work in organizations whose cultural values stress profit over fair play, in which government scrutiny is limited and regulators are viewed as the enemy, and in which senior members encourage newcomers to believe that greed is good.

The Self-Control View

Not all criminologists agree with the corporate culture theory. Travis Hirschi and Michael Gottfredson take exception to the idea that white-collar crime is a product of the corporate culture.[92] If that were true, there would be much more white-collar crime than actually exists, and white-collar criminals would not be embarrassed by their misdeeds, as most seem to be. Instead, Hirschi and Gottfredson maintain, the motives that produce white-collar crimes are the same as those that produce any other criminal behaviours; the desire for relatively quick, relatively certain benefit, with minimal effort. As you may recall, their general theory of crime holds that criminals lack self-control. White-collar criminals are people with low self-control who are inclined to follow momentary impulses without consideration of the long-term costs of such behaviour. White-collar crime is relatively rare because business executives tend to hire people with self-control, thereby limiting the number of potential white-collar criminals. Data show that the demographic distribution of white-collar crime is similar to that for other crimes. For example, gender, race, and age ratios are the same for such crimes as embezzlement and fraud as they are for street crimes, such as burglary and robbery.

Business executives and corporate executives seem to be people who would have above-average self-control.[93] There is some independent evidence that white-collar criminals are often repeat offenders. They also share many characteristics with street criminals (such as being impulsive and egocentric), although they begin their careers later in life and offend at a slower pace.[94]

Even if this view is accurate, it is possible that white-collar offenders manifest a wide range of self-control. The level of offenders' self-control may determine the path they take to crime. People with low self-control impulsively commit fraud and other crimes to pursue their own self-interest; these are most like common criminals. Others with high self-control pursue "ego gratification in an aggressive and calculating fashion"; they are the products of the "greed is good" philosophy. In the middle are offenders who take advantage of criminal opportunities to satisfy an immediate personal need; in them, self-control becomes overwhelmed by special problems. In this view, self-control is a variable and not a constant, which interacts with need and opportunity to produce white-collar crimes.[95]

Controlling White-Collar Crime

Conflict theorists argue that, unlike lower-class street criminals, white-collar criminals are rarely prosecuted and, when convicted, receive relatively light sentences.[96] Physicians who engage in medical insurance fraud are rarely prosecuted, and when they are, judges are reluctant to severely punish them. As one official told them, "When we convicted a guy, I wanted to see him do hard time. But what the hell, seeing what's going on in prisons these days and things like that, I think to put one of these guys in prison for hard time doesn't make any sense."[97] An analysis of 477 corporations found that only one in 10 serious and one in 20 moderate violations resulted in sanctions.[98] When white-collar statutes are enforced, the tendency is to investigate, prosecute, and penalize small, powerless businesses while treating the market leaders more leniently.[99]

There are a number of reasons for the leniency afforded white-collar criminals. Although white-collar criminals may produce millions of dollars of losses and endanger human life, some judges believe they are not "real criminals" but businesspeople just trying to make a living. Businesspeople often seek legal advice and are well aware of the loopholes in the law. If caught, they can claim that they had sought legal advice and believed they were in compliance with the law. White-collar criminals are often considered nondangerous offenders because they usually are respectable, older citizens who have families to support. These "pillars of the community" are not seen in the same light as a teenager who breaks into a drugstore to steal a few dollars. Their public humiliation at being caught is usually deemed punishment enough; a prison sentence seems unnecessarily cruel.

Judges and prosecutors may identify with the white-collar criminal based on shared background and worldviews.[100] Still another factor complicating white-collar crime enforcement is that many legal business and governmental acts seem as morally tinged as those made illegal by government regulation. For example, the U.S. Air Force forced a general to step down for mismanaging the manufacture of a C-17 cargo plane, which accrued $1.5 billion in cost overruns, and included funnelling $450 million in illegal payments to the contractor, McDonnell Douglas.[101] Despite their questionable morality and ethics, these acts were not treated as crimes. Yet when compared with other business practices made illegal by government regulation, such as price fixing, the distinctions are hard to see. It may seem unfair to prosecutors and judges to penalize some government and business officials for actions not too dissimilar from those applauded on Bay Street or in the *Financial Post*.[102]

Finally, some corporate practices that result in death or disfigurement are treated as civil actions in which victims receive monetary damages. The best-known case involved the A.H. Robins Company's Dalkon Shield intrauterine device, which caused massive trauma to hundreds of thousands of women, including pelvic disease, infertility, septic abortions, and a suspected 20 deaths. The company went bankrupt and set up a multibillion-dollar trust for the survivors.[103] More recently, a number of drug companies, including Bristol Myers Squibb, set up a similar trust fund to compensate victims who suffered because their products used in breast implant surgery were deemed defective and dangerous. In 1997 the leading U.S. tobacco companies agreed to set up a multibillion-dollar trust to compensate smokers and their families for illness and death related to smoking. Although these cases involve much more serious injury than, say, insider trading, they are not considered criminal matters.

White-Collar Law Enforcement Systems

The detection of white-collar crime is primarily in the hands of government administrative departments, inspectorates, commissions, and agencies.[104] Usually, the decision to pursue criminal rather than civil violations is based on the seriousness of the case and the perpetrator's intent, actions to conceal the violation, and prior record.

Culture, Gender, Ethnicity, and Criminology

Why the Mounties Can't Get Their Man

Over the past 30 years, Canada has been the setting for some spectacular frauds: John C. Doyle and Canadian Javelin; Lenny Rosenberg, Bill Player, and Ontario's $500-million Cadillac Fairview apartment flip; the collapse of the Principal Group of companies in Alberta; and, most recently, the Bre-X gold stock scam. Some of the swindles have been stunningly well-planned and daringly executed. Toronto stockbroker Christopher Horne, for example, built a world-class art collection with money he embezzled from clients. Montreal-based Castor Holdings sucked as much as $1.8 billion from victims around the world in a 15-year Ponzi scheme, a pyramid scam where money raised from new investors was used to pay off earlier investors.

Toronto has achieved a dubious new distinction. It is regarded by many experts in the justice field as the North American capital of organized criminal fraud, surpassing even such hotbeds of white-collar crime as south Florida, Houston, Orange County in California, and the suburbs of New York City. Extradition laws that make it difficult to expel white-collar crooks are part of the problem. Cutbacks in the justice system have forced compromises in both law enforcement and prosecution. Crown attorneys across the country have been given extraordinary powers to pick and choose the cases they want to prosecute, and police forces have been redeploying their resources to address the vocal concerns of various interest groups. These factors, combined with Canada's lax banking and securities laws, tough privacy legislation, increasing constitutional restrictions on the police, and a disinclination by politicians to declare all-out war on white-collar crime, have created fertile ground for fraudulent business practices to flourish.

Some experts say that the conditions are close to ideal. "If a fraud is committed against a bank or a Fortune 500 company, the police aren't interested," says Toronto forensic accountant Tedd Avey. "The big companies are on their own. All the police want to deal with are investment scams, widows and orphans and, perhaps, government as victims." Twenty years ago, Avey recalls, the RCMP was internationally renowned for its success in putting fraud artists behind bars. "Today," he says, "criminals know it's pretty well open season in Canada. They know they're not going to go to jail."

Others agree. "There's so much fraud that the police can't keep up," says Pat McKernan, a commercial crime officer who left the Mounties in 1995 and now is the head of security for Western Canada at Imperial Oil Ltd. in Calgary. And a veteran RCMP officer, who is still with the force and asked for anonymity, says that if a crook wants to commit fraud, "Canada is the place to come and do it." Added the Mountie: "Over the years, we have lost the ability and will to investigate fraud. As a result, the criminals have no fear of the police. It's a terrible situation."

So what are the authorities doing to combat white-collar crime? The answer, according to police and civilian experts, is that financially strapped police forces across the country—following the lead of the RCMP—are getting out of the commercial crime investigation business. Metropolitan Toronto police, sources told *Maclean's*, have a two-year backlog of fraud investigations—and will not even look at scams involving less than $1 million....

Over the years, the RCMP has attempted to adjust to the changing demands of its political masters. It has made itself less militaristic, promoted bilingualism, opened its ranks to women, recruited members of visible minorities, hired civilians for non-policing jobs, decentralized administration and operations, and embraced advanced technology. It has even learned to act more like a business, generating revenue for the government by, among other things, confiscating the assets of drug dealers and other criminals.

Despite its efforts to modernize, however, the RCMP keeps running up against one immutable fact—there are not enough resources available for the force to carry out its panoply of federal, provincial and municipal policing tasks, let alone keep pace with today's sophisticated criminals. Since 1992, the number of RCMP officers has declined 4.2 per cent, to 14,997 from 15,661, while the population has grown 6.3 per cent. And over the same period, far from seeing an increase in their annual budget—$1.8 billion this year—the Mounties have had to absorb cutbacks of $173 million.

Wages have been frozen for five years, with the result that RCMP officers now earn barely half as much as their counterparts in U.S. federal police agencies. Because the force will not pay housing allowances, even Mounties with 20 years' experience find they cannot afford to live in high-cost centres like Vancouver and Toronto. Restrictions on overtime are so tight that in some places policing has become essentially a 9 to 5 operation. Police sources say that in Hamilton, shift changes and a ban on overtime caused the RCMP to refuse to respond in two cases—one involving the sale of guns, the other a cocaine shipment....

The part of the RCMP's operations that has been most affected by budget cuts and policy changes is the investigation of white-collar crime. In the mid-1960s, partly in response to a series of gruesome murders in Quebec linked to a phoney bankruptcy scheme—a case known as the "limepit murders"—the Mounties pioneered a new approach to commercial crime investigation. Until then, fraud had generally been treated as a civil matter. But when it was evident that organized crime was making inroads into the business world, the RCMP felt it had to establish a powerful presence.

As a result, the Mounties created the specialized Commercial Crime Branch, which quickly attracted some of the force's best and brightest investigators. Widely copied in other countries, the elite branch had some high-profile successes in the late 1960s and 1970s. As a result of its investigations, the criminal-infested Canadian Stock Exchange in Montreal was shut down, and charges were brought against leading businessmen and companies in the patronage and fraud scandals related to the

dredging of the Hamilton harbour and the licensing of airport kiosks called Sky Shops.

In 1997, however, the branch was downgraded and incorporated into a much larger operation called Federal Services, which has borne the brunt of the budget cutbacks. Commercial crime investigators, especially, are starved for resources and manpower. This year, the Mounties will spend just $36.7 million investigating commercial crime of all types in all parts of the country. That is barely 2 per cent of the RCMP's overall budget and less than half of the amount—$83 million—that Canadian businesses lost last year to just one form of commercial crime: credit-card fraud.

The Mounties have largely taken themselves out of the business of investigating white-collar crime—except where the government itself is the victim or there is money to be recovered for the treasury. Today, if a corporation is targeted by criminals, it has little choice but to hire forensic accountants and other private investigators—at rates that can run as high as $600 per hour—to root out the crooks. Sonny Saunders, director of corporate security at the Royal Bank of Canada, says that budget cutbacks have caused most police forces in Canada to give low priority to fraud investigations. "Violent crime takes priority," Saunders said. "I don't think anybody would argue against that. But it means increasingly that most corporations are going to do their own fraud investigations. Every day there seems to be more and more withdrawal of police services."

For better or worse, Canada now has a two-tier system of law enforcement: the Mounties look after the interests of the state, and businesses look after themselves.

Source: Paul Palango, "Mountie Misery," *Maclean's*, July 28, 1997, pp. 10–15.

Any evidence of criminal activity is then sent to the appropriate department for investigation. Some agencies, such as a provincial department of labour, have their own investigators. Usually, enforcement is reactive (generated by complaints) rather than proactive (involving ongoing investigations or the monitoring of activities). In Canada, the RCMP has made enforcement of white-collar laws one of its top three priorities (along with combating foreign counterintelligence and organized crime).

There is evidence that prosecutors will pursue white-collar criminals more vigorously if they are part of a team effort that includes a network of law enforcement agencies.[105] However, local prosecutors might not consider white-collar crimes particularly serious. They are more willing to prosecute cases if the offence caused substantial harm and other agencies failed to take action. Relatively few prosecutors participate in interagency task forces designed to investigate white-collar criminal activity. Local prosecutors often believe that the criminal law should be used against corporate offenders and that tougher criminal penalties would improve corporate compliance with the law.

The number of prosecutors who believe that upper-class criminals are not above the law is growing. While their findings were encouraging, Michael Benson and colleagues also found that the funds and staff needed for local white-collar prosecutions are often scarce. Crimes considered more serious, such as drug trafficking, usually take precedence over corporate violations. Coordination is uncommon, and there is relatively little resource sharing. It is likely that concern over the environment may encourage local prosecutors to take action against those who violate state pollution and antidumping laws.

Corporate Policing

White-collar crime law enforcement is often left to business organizations themselves. However, corporate structures can be crime facilitative or crime inhibiting. Corporations spend hundreds of millions of dollars each year on internal audits that help unearth white-collar offences. According to Stuart Traub, corporate enforcement strategies can take a variety of forms:

- *Security strategies* involve employing contract security personnel and private police officers who guard merchandise and conduct surveillance in sensitive areas. Passive security measures include use of badges, passes, key cards, and checkpoints to restrict access to merchandise. Closed-circuit TV and other monitoring devices are used for surveillance.
- *Screening and education strategies* involve using preemployment screening and background checks to weed out potential problems. Personality and integrity tests help screen applicants. Stores are teaching employees how to spot theft and the best ways to report problems.

- *Whistle-blowing strategies* involve creating "hotlines" in which employees can report theft anonymously without fear of repercussions. Third-party firms may be called in to maintain hotlines because employees may be reluctant to report fellow workers to their own employer.[106]

In that last item we see the importance of protecting employees who blow the whistle on their firm's violations. Many jurisdictions have passed laws protecting workers from being fired if they testify about violations.[107] Without such help, the hands of justice are tied.

White-Collar Control Strategies: Compliance

The prevailing wisdom, then, is that many white-collar criminals avoid prosecution and that those who are prosecuted receive lenient punishments. What efforts have been made to bring violators of the public trust to justice? White-collar enforcement typically involves two strategies designed to control organizational deviance: compliance and deterrence.[108]

Compliance strategies aim for law conformity without the necessity of detecting, processing, or penalizing individual violators. They seek cooperation and self-policing within the business community and attempt to create conformity by providing economic incentives to companies to obey the law. Compliance systems depend on the threat of economic sanctions or civil penalties (referred to as economism) to control corporate violators, such as prosecuting securities violations.

One method of compliance is to set up administrative agencies to oversee business activity, with legislation spelling out penalties for violating regulatory standards. This approach has been used to control environmental crimes, for example, by levying heavy fines based on the quantity and quality of pollution released into the environment.[109] A recent case involved a lawsuit brought against the Sherwin-Williams paint company for a long-time pattern of dumping dangerous chemicals into the sewers on Chicago's South Side.[110]

In another form of economism, people and businesses are sometimes barred from receiving government contracts if they are found to have engaged in fraudulent practices, such as bribing public officials.[111]

While it is difficult to gauge the effectiveness of compliance, research indicates that strict enforcement of regulatory laws can reduce violations of illegal or dangerous business practices. For example, strict enforcement of penalties under the Occupational and Safety Health Act can significantly reduce workplace injuries.[112]

In sum, compliance strategies attempt to create a marketplace incentive to obey the law; for example, the more a company pollutes, the more costly and unprofitable that pollution becomes. Compliance strategies limit individual blame, and also avoid stigmatizing and "shaming" businesspeople by focusing on the act, rather than the actor, in white-collar crime.[113]

Compliance systems are not applauded by all criminologists. Some experts point out that economic sanctions have limited value in controlling white-collar crime because economic penalties are imposed only after crimes have occurred, require careful governmental regulation, and often amount to only a slap on the wrist.[114] Compliance is particularly difficult to achieve if the federal government adopts a pro-business, antiregulation policy that encourages economic growth by removing controls over business. It is also difficult to achieve when multinational corporations have sufficient resources to not only resist prosecution but also to use the courts to their own advantage.

It is also possible for corporations hit with fines and regulatory fees to pass the costs on to consumers in the form of higher prices or reduced services. Shareholders who had little to do with the crime may see their stock dividends cut or share prices fall.[115]

The fines and penalties involved in compliance strategies may be of little import for a company doing billions in annual business. When a large brokerage Canadian company like First Marathon is fined millions of dollars, that represents a small fraction of its total revenue. Similarly, when Baxter International was banned from bidding on new federal contracts for one year because it had deceived U.S. government purchasing agents, the punishment was a blow to its corporate reputation, but its total annual revenue still amounted to $8.5 billion. While humiliating, the ban affects a relatively small amount of the company's business.[116]

Because of these conditions, some criminologists maintain that the punishment of white-collar crimes should contain a retributive component similar to that used in common-law crimes. White-collar crimes, after all, are immoral activities that have harmed social values and deserve commensurate punishment.[117] Furthermore, corporations can get around economic sanctions by moving their rule-violating activities overseas, where legal controls over injurious corporate activities are lax or nonexistent.[118]

White-Collar Control Strategies: Deterrence

Deterrence strategies involve detecting criminal violations, determining who is responsible, and penalizing them to deter future violations. Punishment serves as a warning to potential violators who might break rules if other violators had not already been penalized. Deterrence systems are oriented toward apprehending violators and punishing them rather than creating conditions that induce conformity to the law.

Deterrence strategies should and have worked, since white-collar crime by its nature is a rational act whose perpetrators are extremely sensitive to the threat of criminal sanctions. There are numerous instances in which prison sentences for corporate crimes have produced a significant decline in white-collar activity; and the perceptions of detection and punishment for white-collar crimes appear to be a powerful deterrent to future law violations.[119]

Punishing White-Collar Criminals. There have been dramatic examples of deterrence strategies used by federal and state justice systems to prevent white-collar crime. It is not extraordinary to hear of corporate officers receiving long prison sentences in conjunction with corporate crimes.[120] Corporate executives have even been charged with murder because of the actions of their companies.[121] In other cases, prosecution fails, as in the Westray mine explosion.

Are such stiff penalties the norm, or are they infrequent instances of government resolve? A survey conducted by the U.S. Bureau of Justice Statistics reviewed enforcement practices in nine states and found that (1) white-collar crimes account for about 6 percent of all arrest dispositions, (2) 88 percent of all those arrested for white-collar crimes were prosecuted, and (3) 74 percent were subsequently convicted in criminal court. The survey also showed that while 60 percent of white-collar criminals convicted in state courts were incarcerated (a number comparable to the punishment given most other kinds of offenders), relatively few white-collar offenders (18 percent) received a prison term of more than a year.[122]

Is the Tide Turning? This new "get tough" deterrence approach appears to be affecting all classes of white-collar criminals. While the prevailing wisdom is that the affluent corporate executive usually avoids serious punishment, research indicates that high-status offenders are more likely to be punished than previously believed.[123] This research seems to indicate that public displeasure with highly publicized white-collar crimes may be producing a backlash resulting in more frequent use of prison sentences. Governments may be going overboard in their efforts to punish white-collar criminals, especially for crimes that are the result of negligent business practices rather than intentional criminal conspiracy.[124] Nonetheless, relatively few white-collar offenders are prosecuted, and when they are convicted many escape serious punishment.

Organized Crime

The second branch of organizational criminality is organized crime, defined as ongoing criminal enterprise groups whose ultimate purpose is personal economic gain through illegitimate means. In this case, a structured enterprise system is set up to supply consumers on a continuing basis with merchandise and services banned by the criminal law but for which a ready market exists: prostitution, pornography, gambling, and narcotics—the classic victimless crimes. The system may even resemble a legitimate business run by an ambitious executive officer, with assistants, staff attorneys, and accountants.[125]

Because of its secrecy, power, and fabulous wealth, a great mystique has grown up about organized crime. Legendary leaders, such as Al Capone, have been the subjects of books and films. The famous *Godfather* films popularized organized crime figures, and the media all too often glamorize them.[126] Most citizens believe that organized criminals are capable of taking over legitimate business enterprises if given the opportunity. Almost everyone is familiar with such synonyms as the mob, underworld, Mafia, wiseguys, syndicate, or La Cosa Nostra. Although most of us have neither met nor seen members of organized crime families, we feel sure that they exist, and most certainly, we fear them. This section briefly defines organized crime, reviews its history, and discusses its economic effect and control.

Characteristics of Organized Crime

A precise description of the characteristics of organized crime is difficult to formulate, but we can identify some of its general traits:

- *Organized crime is a conspiratorial activity*, involving the coordination of numerous people in the planning and execution of illegal acts or in the pursuit of a legitimate objective by unlawful means. Organized crime requires a commitment by primary members, although individuals with specialized skills may be brought in as needed.
- *Organized crime has economic gain as its primary goal*, although power and status may also be motivating factors. Economic gain is achieved through maintaining a near monopoly on illegal goods and services, including drugs, gambling, pornography, and prostitution.
- Organized crime activities also encompass seemingly legitimate activities, such as laundering illegal money through legitimate businesses, land fraud, and computer crimes.
- Organized crime employs predatory tactics, such as intimidation, violence, and corruption. It appeals to greed to accomplish its objectives and preserve its gains.
- Organized crime's conspiratorial groups are quick and effective in controlling and disciplining their members, associates, and victims. The individuals involved know that any deviation from the rules of the organization will evoke a prompt response from the other participants. This response may range from a reduction in rank and responsibility to a death sentence.

- Organized crime is not synonymous with the Mafia, which is actually a common stereotype of organized crime. Although several families in the organization called the Mafia are important components of organized crime activities, they do not hold a monopoly on underworld activities.
- Organized crime does not include terrorists dedicated to political change. Although violent acts are a major tactic of organized crime, the use of violence does not mean that a group is part of a confederacy of organized criminals.

Activities of Organized Crime

What are the main activities of organized crime? The traditional sources of income are derived from providing illicit materials and using force to enter into and maximize profits in legitimate businesses.[127] Most organized crime income comes from narcotics distribution, loan-sharking, and prostitution. In the United States annual gross income from criminal activity might top $50 billion, more than 1 percent of the gross national product; some estimates put gross earnings as high as $90 billion, outranking most major industries in the United States.[128] Moreover, additional billions come from gambling, theft rings, and other illegal enterprises, such as control over the pornography industry.[129]

In some cases, organized criminals have infiltrated labour unions, taking control of their pension funds and dues.[130] Hijacking of shipments and cargo theft are other sources of income, as are the fencing of high-value items. In recent years, they have branched into computer crime and other white-collar activities.

Organized Crime and Legitimate Enterprise

Outside of criminal enterprises, additional billions are earned by organized crime figures who force or buy their way into legitimate businesses and use them for profit. Businesses most likely to be affected are low technology (such as garbage collection), have uniform products, and operate in rigid markets where increases in price will not result in reduced demand. In addition, industries most affected by labour pressure are highly susceptible to takeovers because a mob-controlled work stoppage would destroy a product or interfere with meeting deadlines. Organized criminals today become involved in legitimate enterprise in five ways: (1) business activity that supports illegal enterprise by providing a front; (2) predatory exploitation, where protection money is demanded; (3) organization of monopolies or cartels to limit competition; (4) unfair advantages gained by such practices as manipulation of labour unions and corruption of public officials; and (5) illegal manipulation of legal vehicles, particularly stocks and bonds.[131]

These traits show how organized crime is more like a business enterprise than a confederation of criminals seeking to merely enhance their power.[132] Thus, controlling organized crime today involves a cooperative relationship among big business, politicians, and racketeers.

The Concept of Organized Crime

The term *organized crime* conjures up images of strong men in dark suits, machine-gun-toting bodyguards, rituals of allegiance to secret organizations, and professional gangland killings. These images have become part of what criminologists refer to as the **alien conspiracy theory** concept of organized crime. This is the belief that organized crime is a direct offshoot of a criminal society, the Mafia, that first originated in Italy and Sicily and now controls racketeering in major U.S. cities. In Canada, the parallel would be the concern about Chinese Triads and Vietnamese gangs in Toronto and Vancouver. A major premise of the alien conspiracy theory is that the Mafia is centrally coordinated by a national committee that settles disputes, dictates policy, and assigns territory.[133] Not all criminologists believe in this narrow concept of organized crime, and many view the alien conspiracy theory as a figment of the media's imagination.[134] Instead, they characterize organized crime as a group of ethnically diverse gangs or groups who compete for profit in the sale of illegal goods and services or who use force and violence to extort money from legitimate enterprises. These groups are not bound by a central national organization but act independently on their own turf.

Alien Conspiracy Theory: The Development of a Syndicate

According to the alien conspiracy theory, organized crime really consists of a national syndicate of Italian-dominated crime families that call themselves La Cosa Nostra. The major families have a total membership of about 1700 men inducted into organized crime families, and another 17 000 associates who are criminally involved with syndicate members.[135]

The first "organized" gangs consisted of Irish immigrants who made their home in the slum districts of New York City.[136] The Forty Thieves, considered the first New York gang with a definite, acknowledged leadership, were muggers, thieves, and pickpockets on the Lower East Side of Manhattan from the 1820s to just before the Civil War. Around 1890, Italian immigrants began forming gangs modelled after the Sicilian crime organization known as the Mafia; these gangs were called the Black Hand. Prohibition created a multimillion-dollar bootlegging industry overnight. Gangs vied for a share of the business,

and bloody wars for control of rackets and profits became common. However, the problems of supplying liquor to thousands of illegal drinking establishments (speakeasies) required organization and an end to open warfare.

The end of Prohibition required a new source of profits, and narcotics sales became the mainstay of gangland business, along with selling information on horse racing, which helped create a national network of gang-dominated bookmakers. After World War II, organized crime families began using their vast profits from liquor, gambling, and narcotics to buy into legitimate businesses, such as entertainment, legal gambling in Cuba and Las Vegas, hotel chains, jukebox concerns, restaurants, and taverns. By paying off politicians, police, and judges and by using blackmail and coercion, organized criminals became almost immune to prosecution. The machine-gun-toting gangster had given way to the businessman-racketeer. Gang activity has expanded into legitimate businesses, challenging some of the traditional stereotypes.

The Mafia Myth

Some charge that the Cosa Nostra version of organized crime is fanciful, and that the alien conspiracy theory is too heavily influenced by media accounts.[137]

The challenges to the alien conspiracy theory have produced alternative views of organized crime. For example, Philip Jenkins studied organized crime in Philadelphia and found little evidence that it was controlled by an Italian-dominated crime family.[138] Sociologist Alan Block has argued that organized crime is both a loosely constructed social system, composed of relationships binding professional criminals, politicians, law enforcers, and various entrepreneurs. In contrast, the social world of organized crime is often chaotic because of the constant power struggle between competing groups.

Some criminologists view the world of professional criminals as one shaped by the political economy. Madams, drug distributors, bookmakers, and so on are workers in the world of illegal enterprise. This view of organized crime is revisionist since it portrays mob activity as a quasi-economic enterprise system swayed by social forces and not a tightly knit, unified cartel dominated by ethnic minorities carrying out European traditions. This world of organized crime is dominated by business leaders, politicians, and union leaders who work hand in hand with criminals. Moreover, the violent, chaotic social world of power struggles does not lend itself to a tightly controlled syndicate.

Organized Crime Groups

Many now view organized crime as a loose confederation of ethnic and regional crime groups, bound together by a commonality of economic and political objectives. There are four or five main organized crime groups in

Canada.[139] They commit a variety of offences, as shown in Figure 13.2.

Asian-based Organized Crime. These groups are extensively involved in trafficking cocaine and ecstasy; the production, trafficking, and exporting of marijuana; and the importation and distribution of Southeast Asian heroin. They are also involved in large-scale illegal migrant smuggling operations, to Canada and into the United States. Based primarily in Vancouver, Calgary, Edmonton, Toronto, and Montreal, these groups include criminal youths and members of street gangs. They are involved in home invasions, kidnapping, theft, shoplifting, prostitution, assaults, illegal gambling, loan-sharking, and the production and distribution of counterfeit currency, software, manufactured goods, and credit and debit cards. They are also involved in the laundering of criminal proceeds and the investment of laundered money into legitimate businesses.

East European-based Organized Crime. Groups from Eastern Europe continue to expand their activities in Canada, particularly in the larger urban centres of Ontario, Quebec, British Columbia, and Atlantic Canada. They are well-connected to established criminal organizations around the world and exploit technology to commit sophisticated financial and Internet-based frauds. For a decade, Canada has experienced the growth of organized crime groups from the former Soviet Union. These groups engage in crimes ranging from petty theft to sophisticated fraud. Using legitimate business ventures as fronts for their illegal activities, the most frequently reported criminal activities include financial frauds, prostitution, theft, contraband smuggling, illicit drug impor-

tation, vehicle theft and illegal export (remember those stolen SUVs?), and money laundering. Credit card "skimming," e-commerce site hacking, and fraudulent credit card purchases are examples of activity they engage in, all of which are made easier by the Internet.

Traditional (Italian-based) Organized Crime. The traditional organized crime associated with Italy remains a threat and includes the Sicilian mafia, which has ties to other Sicilian clans in Venezuela, the United States, and Italy. They participate in joint criminal ventures, such as importing illegal narcotics, laundering drug proceeds, drug trafficking, illegal gaming, extortion, and loan-sharking. Illegal gaming activities include backroom gambling, sports betting, and illegal video lottery gaming terminals. Profits from these criminal activities are invested in both legitimate commercial enterprises as well as their on-going criminal operations.

Outlaw Motorcycle Gangs. Motorcycle gangs use violence to accomplish their goals; they associate with street gangs and other organized crime groups and are involved in money laundering, intimidation, assaults, attempted murder, murder, fraud, theft, counterfeiting, loan-sharking, extortion, prostitution, escort agencies, strip clubs, illegal booze cans, and the possession and trafficking of illegal weapons, stolen goods, contraband, alcohol, and cigarettes. Members of the Hells Angels continue to be involved in the importation and trafficking of cocaine, the cultivation and exportation of high-grade marijuana and, to a lesser extent, the production and trafficking of methamphetamine, the trafficking of ecstasy and other synthetic illicit drugs. The Hells Angels are the largest and most criminally active outlaw motorcycle gang in the country.

Figure 13.2   **Crimes committed by organized crime groups in Canada**

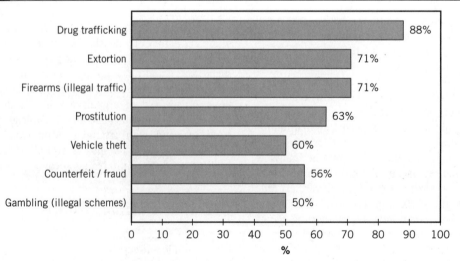

Source: Canadian Centre for Justice Statistics, Organized Crime Activity in Canada, 1998: Results of a "Pilot" Survey of 16 Police Services.

One important recent change in organized crime is the interweaving of ethnic groups. Asian racketeers and Native gangs now collaborate or compete with the more traditional groups, such as the Hells Angels, overseeing the distribution of drugs, prostitution, and gambling in a symbiotic relationship with old-line racketeers. Since 1970, Russia and other Eastern European countries have cooperated with Mafia families in narcotics trafficking, fencing of stolen property, money laundering, and other "traditional" organized crime schemes.[140]

In Winnipeg, the Manitoba Warriors and the Indian Posse are ethnic gangs based in the most impoverished areas and are involved in all the traditional areas of organized crime. Have these newly emerging groups achieved the same level of control as traditional crime families? Some experts argue that minority gangs will have a tough time developing the network of organized corruption, which involves working with government officials and unions, that traditional crime families enjoyed.[141]

Part of the evolution of organized crime is created by patterns of law enforcement. Pressure on traditional organized crime figures have encouraged the Hells Angels motorcycle club to step into the vacuum, to become the leading distributor of narcotics in Canada and the United States. A recent series of bombings erupted in Montreal as part of a turf war between the Hells Angels and the Rock Machine, another motorcycle gang. Chinese criminal gangs have taken over the dominant role in New York City's heroin market from the traditional Italian-run syndicates.[142] In Canada, Chinese Triad gangs traditionally relied on extortion as a source of illegal wealth, extending their activity to include the sale of drugs. One reason for their persistence is their cell structure; unlike the hierarchical structure of the traditional Mafia, using cells ensures that no one member of the criminal organization knows the whole picture.

Overall it is estimated that organized crime generates over $20 billion a year in Canada, half from the sale of drugs alone, and includes such activities as auto thefts, money laundering, smuggling, fraud, prostitution, and violent crime. Organized crime has also moved into such innovative lines of work as selling restricted weapons, providing access to illicit toxic waste dumps, and selling high-technology secrets. Most experts now agree that it is simplistic to view organized crime as a national syndicate that controls illegitimate rackets, ignoring the variety of gangs and groups, their membership, and their relationship to the outside world.[143] Mafia-type groups may play a major role in organized crime, but they are by no means the only ones that can be considered organized criminals.[144]

Organized Crime Abroad

Many countries confront the problem of organized criminal gangs. The Cali and Medellin drug cartels in Colombia are world famous for both their vast drug traf-

ficking profits and their unflinching use of violence to achieve their objectives. When Pablo Escobar, the head of the Medellin cartel, was captured and killed by police and soldiers on December 2, 1993, experts predicted that drug smuggling would increase with the shift of the cocaine trade to the control of the smoother and more businesslike Cali cartel.[145]

Japan also has a long history of organized criminal activity by Yakuza gangs. In 1993 officials of the Kirin Brewery, Japan's largest beer maker, resigned after allegations were made that they paid over 33 million yen in *sokaiya* (extortion money) to racketeers who threatened their business.[146] In China, organized gangs use violence to enforce contracts between companies, serving as an alternative to the legal system. They also help smuggle many of the 100 000 mainland Chinese who enter the United States each year. In June 1993, a Chinese ship packed with illegal immigrants foundered off the coast of New York, and ten of them drowned.[147]

Russia has been beset by organized crime activity since the breakup of the Soviet Union. As of 1993, an estimated 3000 criminal gangs were active in Russia. Bloody shoot-outs have become common as gangs attempt to stake out territory and extort businesses. In one incident, an auto dealership was attacked and two security guards killed when the owner failed to pay "protection money."[148]

Computer and communications technology has fostered international cooperation among crime cartels. East European and Russian gangs sell arms seized from the former Soviet Army to members of the Sicilian Mafia; Japanese and Italian mob members have met in Paris; drug money from South America is laundered in Canada and England.

Controlling Organized Crime

George Vold argues that the development of organized crime parallels early capitalist enterprises. Organized crime uses ruthless and monopolistic tactics to maximize profits; it is also secretive and protective of its operations and defensive against any outside intrusion.[149] Consequently, controlling its activities is extremely difficult, and little has been done to combat organized crime until fairly recently.

One measure aimed directly at organized crime in the United States was the (1970) Organized Crime Control Act, the so-called **Racketeer Influenced and Corrupt Organization Act**. RICO did not create new categories of crimes but rather new categories of offences in racketeering activity, such as murder, kidnapping, gambling, arson, robbery, bribery, extortion, and narcotic violations and such federally defined crimes as bribery, counterfeiting, transmission of gambling information, prostitution, and mail fraud.

From 1985 to 1987 many major organized crime figures were indicted, convicted, and imprisoned, including John Gotti. Some of these convictions are now in question because of allegations that the FBI secretly uses mobsters as informants to gain warrants.

In Canada attempts to control organized crime include Bill C-69, which gives the police more power to seize goods suspected of being purchased with the proceeds of crime. Section 312 of the Canadian Criminal Code itself makes it an offence to possess anything derived indirectly or directly from an indictable offence. During the confrontation between rival bike gangs in Montreal, a joint police task force (the RCMP and the Montreal Urban Community Police) made significant arrests and seized explosive devices, including 1000 sticks of dynamite. In addition, the Canadian Security Intelligence Service (CSIS) has asked that the $1000 bill be eliminated and that the movement of large sums of money be reported by financial institutions.

New developments in the enforcement of laws designed to control organized crime include police anti-drug-profiteering units and the integrated proceeds of crime units. A joint Canada–U.S. agreement on sharing the proceeds of crime was signed in 1995, and in 1998 a discussion paper was released by the federal solicitor general on how to control money laundering. In 1994 a money-laundering operation was broken in Montreal with cooperation from American authorities, and police seized almost $1 million. Some provincial police organizations have their own anti-biker squads, and the Witness Protection Act was designed to encourage witnesses to come forward with reports on crime. The National Action Plan to Combat Smuggling was launched in 1994, and $2 billion of smuggled goods were confiscated.

The Future of Organized Crime

Indications are that the traditional organized crime syndicates are in decline.[150] Active government enforcement policies have reduced by one-half the membership in organized crime from what it was 20 years ago; a number

---

Exhibit 13.7   The Fight Against Organized Crime

The Organized Crime Impact Study, commissioned by the Department of the Solicitor General in 1988, indicated that

- the Canadian illicit drug market is between $7 and $10 billion each year
- securities fraud and telemarketing scams cost Canadians at least $5 billion each year
- between $5 and $17 billion is laundered in Canada each year
- as many as 16 000 people may be smuggled into Canada every year
- the production and sale of counterfeit products - clothing, software, and pharmaceuticals - may cost Canadians over $1 billion each year
- the illegal smuggling of tobacco, alcohol, and jewellery may cost up to $1.5 billion in government tax revenues.

In recent years, the federal government, the provinces and territories, and the police have undertaken steps against organized crime, including

- the Anti-Smuggling Initiative (1994), to provide resources for the RCMP, Justice, and the Canada Customs and Revenue Agency to target smuggling and distribution networks at the border; it has led to 17 000 smuggling-related charges resulting in fines in excess of $113 million, and $118 million in evaded taxes and duties has been identified
- the Witness Protection Program Act (1996), a national program to protect those who risk their lives to assist police investigations

- the Solicitor General Canada and Justice Canada organizing a National Forum on Organized Crime (1996), to bring the police, federal and provincial governments, the private sector, the legal community, and academics together
- five Regional Coordinating Committees and a National Coordinating Committee on Organized Crime (1997) providing a foundation for further cooperation to combat organized crime
- Integrated Proceeds of Crime units (1997), which combine the resources of RCMP, local and provincial police officers, Canada Customs and Revenue Agency officers, Crown counsel and forensic accountants to target organized crime groups and seize their assets, over $110 million so far
- legislative amendments to the Criminal Code (1997), to make participation in a criminal organization an indictable offence, punishable by up to 14 years in prison
- the Solicitor General providing $115 million to the RCMP (1999) to modernize the Canadian Police Information Centre (CPIC), the computerized information system for Canadian law enforcement, to improve information-sharing with other law enforcement, provincial, and federal databases

Source: Solicitor General of Canada
(http://www.sgc.gc.ca/efact/eorgcrime.htm)

of organized crime's highest-ranking leaders have been imprisoned. Additional pressure comes from newly emerging ethnic gangs that want to "muscle in" on traditional syndicate activities, such as drug sales and gambling. For example, Chinese Triad gangs have been active in the drug trade, loan-sharking, and labour racketeering. Other ethnic crime groups include black and Colombian drug cartels and the Sicilian Mafia.

White, ethnic, inner-city neighbourhoods, once the locus of Mafia power, have been reduced in size as families have moved to the suburbs. Organized crime groups have consequently lost their political and social base of operations. In addition, the "code of silence," which served to protect Mafia leaders, is now being broken regularly by younger members who turn informer rather than face prison terms. For example, the reign of John Gotti, the most powerful mob boss in New York, was ended by testimony given at his murder trial by his one-time ally Sammy "The Bull" Gravano.

Jay Albanese, a leading expert on organized crime, predicts that pressure by the federal government will encourage organized crime figures to engage in "safer" activities, such as credit card and airline ticket counterfeiting and illicit toxic waste disposal. Instead of running illegal enterprises, established families may be content with financing younger entrepreneurs and channelling or laundering profits through their legitimate business enterprises. There may be greater effort among organized criminals in the future to infiltrate legitimate business enterprises to obtain access to money for financing and the means to launder illicitly obtained cash. Labour unions and the construction industry have been favourite targets in the past.[151]

While these actions are considered a major blow to Italian-dominated organized crime cartels, they are unlikely to stifle criminal entrepreneurship. As long as vast profits can be made from selling narcotics, producing pornography, or taking illegal bets, many groups stand ready to fill the gaps and reap the profits of providing illegal goods and services.

Summary

White-collar and organized criminals are similar because they both use ongoing illegal business enterprises to make personal profits. There are several types of white-collar crime. Stings and swindles involve the use of deception to bilk people out of their money. Chiselling customers, businesses, or the government on a regular basis is a second common type of white-collar crime. Surprisingly, many professionals engage in chiselling offences. Other white-collar criminals use their positions in business and the marketplace to commit economic crimes, involving illegal payments, embezzlement and employee pilferage and fraud, client fraud, and influence peddling and bribery. Further, corporate officers sometimes violate the law to improve the position and profitability of their businesses, which might include price fixing, false advertising, and environmental offences. More recently, computers have been used to commit high-tech crimes.

So far, little has been done to combat white-collar crimes. Most offenders do not view themselves as criminals and therefore do not seem to be deterred by criminal statutes. Although thousands of white-collar criminals are prosecuted each year, their numbers are insignificant compared with the magnitude of the problem. The government has used various law enforcement strategies to combat white-collar crime. Some involve deterrence, which uses punishment to frighten potential abusers. Others involve compliance strategies, which create economic incentives to obey the law.

The demand for illegal goods and services has produced a symbiotic relationship between the public and an organized criminal network. Organized crime supplies alcohol, smuggled tobacco, gambling, drugs, prostitutes, and pornography to the public. It is immune from prosecution because of public apathy and because of its own strong political connections. Organized criminals used to be white ethnics—Jews, Italians, and Irish—but today African Americans, Hispanics, Asians, and other groups have become included in organized crime activities. The old-line "families" are more likely to use their criminal wealth and power to buy into legitimate businesses.

There is debate over the control of organized crime. Some experts believe there is a national crime cartel that controls all activities. Others view organized crime as a group of disorganized, competing gangs dedicated to extortion or to providing illegal goods and services. Efforts to control organized crime have been stepped up. But as long as there are vast profits to be made, illegal enterprises will continue to flourish.

Thinking Like a Criminologist

People who commit computer crime are found in every segment of society. They range in age from 10 to 60, and their skill level runs from novice to professional. They are otherwise average people, not supercriminals possessing unique abilities and talents. Any person of any age with even a little skill is a potential computer criminal. Most studies indicate that employees represent the greatest threat to computers. Almost 90 percent of computer crimes against businesses are inside jobs. Ironically, as advances continue in remote data processing, the threat from external sources will probably increase. With the networking of systems and the adoption of more user-friendly software, the sociological profile of the computer offender may change. For example, computer criminals may soon be members of organized crime syndicates. They will use computer systems to monitor law enforcement activities. In the 21st-century organized crime family, the recruit will have to develop knowledge of the equipment used for audio surveillance of law enforcement communications: computers with sound card or microphone, modems, and software programs for the remote operation of the systems.

Which theories of criminal behavior best explain the actions of computer criminals, and which ones fail to account for computer crime?

Key Terms

alien conspiracy theory

arbitrage

churning

compliance

corporate crime

deterrence

insider trading

Knapp Commission

Mollen Commission

occupational crime

organized crime

pilferage

price fixing

Racketeer Influenced and Corrupt Organization Act (RICO)

swindling

white-collar crime

See the book-specific website at www.siegelcriminology2e.nelson.com for additional chapter links, discussions, and quizzes.

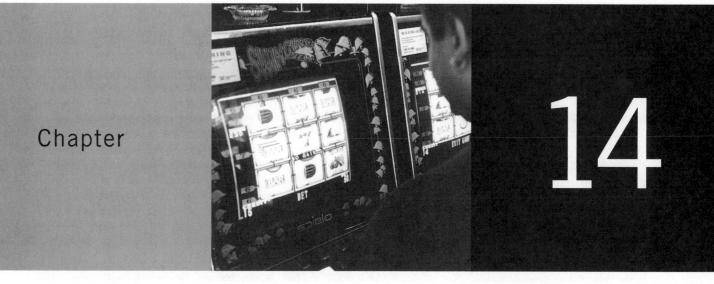

Chapter

Public Order Crimes: Legislating Morality

14

Gillian Guess had been a member of the jury in the murder trial of Peter Gill and five other men in 1995. Three years later, she was on trial herself for her conduct in that jury. During her trial the Crown attorney said she had openly flirted with Gill, sat in the jury box in a manner that allowed Gill to look up her skirt, had a sexual relationship with the accused, and then swayed the jury, resulting in Gill's acquittal. During the controversial trial, Ms. Guess maintained a Web site where she compared her prosecution to a witchhunt. She denounced the RCMP for recording her sexual encounters with Gill and regularly briefed the media despite warnings by the judge.[1]

Gillian Guess became the first person in North America to be convicted for obstructing a jury by having a relationship with an accused. Was it possible for her to act impartially while having an affair? Or is it possible that her behaviour was irrelevant, that the jury acquitted Gill on the basis of the evidence regardless of Guess's actions? Was this even a simple legal issue, or was it a matter of moral impropriety?

It has long been the custom for societies to ban or limit behaviours that are *believed* to run contrary to social norms, customs, and values. These behaviours are often referred to as **public order crimes** or **victimless crimes**, although the latter term can be misleading.[2] Public order crimes sometimes include acts that interfere with the operations of society and the ability of people to function efficiently, but more often than not, they simply offend our moral sense of how people should act. Put

Culture, Gender, Ethnicity, and Criminology

Results of the Great Canadian Moral Scruples Challenge

The Scruples Challenge is based on a telephone survey conducted in the summer of 1996. The study was commissioned by the Canadian Coalition Against Insurance Fraud, an organisation composed of consumer advocates, police and fire services, and private and public insurers.

The survey measured Canadians' attitudes toward insurance fraud in fourteen different ethical dilemmas. Participants were asked what they would do in those scenarios, and what they thought other people would do in the same situations.

The survey showed that younger people are less likely to behave ethically than older people. In some instances people in Atlantic Canada were more likely to behave ethically than people in other parts of the country. However, in general, class, education, and religion did not make a difference.

One of the most interesting results of the survey was the gap between what people said they would do and their perception of what others would do. For example, if a friendly bank teller accidentally gives you an extra $100, what would you do? Eighty-three percent of Canadians said they would give the money back. However, 12 percent said they would keep the extra money.

In another scenario, a bank machine gives a customer $20 more than it records on the bank receipt. Not surprisingly, 53 percent of Canadians said they would return the extra $20 to the bank, but in the phone poll, 28 percent thought that 70 percent of other Canadians would keep the money.

Two friends are discussing their home businesses. One asks the other to make a copy of an expensive piece of computer software. The self-report survey says that 37 percent of Canadians would refuse to copy the software. However, 24 percent would copy the software with no question asked, 12 percent would copy the software, but tell him it's wrong, and 23 percent would let him use their computer. In the phone poll, 52 percent of Canadians would give away a copy of the software, and they felt that 68 percent of other Canadians would do the same.

Let's take a couple more examples. For instance, a car mechanic does extra work on a car after an accident and includes the cost on the insurance bill. An honest 47 percent of Canadians said they would pay for the repairs and report the body shop, while 27 percent would take the car "as is." Nine percent would pay extra for the repairs, but not tell the insurance company, while 13 percent would refuse to sign the form releasing the car from the body shop.

In the phone poll, 25 percent of Canadians said they would go along with the mechanic and take the car "as is," and they felt that 72 percent of other Canadians would simply take the car.

Finally, a man is on leave from work because of an injury requiring a neck brace. When a colleague drops in on him, he finds the man is not wearing the brace and is doing heavy yard work. Fifty percent of Canadians said they would tell him he's wrong, while 20 percent would do nothing, and think less of him. Nineteen percent would report the co-worker, and 6 percent would call Crime Stoppers.

In the phone poll, 40 percent of Canadians said they would confront their colleague, but felt that only 14 percent of other Canadians would do the same.

What happens when you compare these results to your ethical standards? What do they tell you about the standards of Canadians?

another way, while such common-law crimes as rape or robbery are considered *mala in se*, inherently evil and wrong, there are also *mala prohibitum* crimes, which are behaviours outlawed because they conflict with social policy, moral sensibilities, and current public opinion.

Statutes designed to uphold public order usually prohibit the manufacture and distribution of morally questionable goods and services such as erotic material, commercial sex, and mood-altering drugs. They may also ban acts that some people holding political power consider morally tinged, such as abortion, marijuana use, or assisted suicide. These acts are controversial in part because otherwise law-abiding citizens often engage in them. Laws against such activities are controversial because they represent the selective prohibition of desired goods, services, and behaviours. However, as the Great Canadian Moral Scruples Challenge shows, the line between good and bad behaviour is often a grey one.

This chapter is divided into four main sections. The first briefly discusses the relationship between law and morality. The second deals with public order crimes of a sexual nature. The third focuses on drug and alcohol abuse. A final section discusses emerging issues, such as the decriminalization of gambling and euthanasia.

Law and Morality

The legislation of moral issues has been a continual source of frustration for lawmakers. There is little debate that the purpose of the criminal law is to protect society and reduce social harm. When a store is robbed or a child assaulted, it is relatively easy to condemn the social harm done the victim. It is, however, more difficult to sympathize with or even identify the victim of "immoral" acts, such as pornography or prostitution, in which the parties may be willing participants. If there is no victim, can there be a crime? Should acts be made illegal merely because they violate prevailing moral standards? If so, who defines morality? The absolute letter of the law might be unrealistically strict.

Should a person be punished for providing a service other people are willing to pay for? If people willingly put up the money to purchase sexual services, it hardly seems possible that these clients could be considered crime victims. Many, but not all, prostitutes willingly engage in sexual activity for money, and their income is far higher than they would have earned in "legitimate jobs." Although "immoral," should a prostitute and his or her clients be considered criminals for engaging in this "victimless crime"?

To answer this question, we might first consider whether there is actually a "victim" in so-called victimless crimes. Some participants may have been coerced or forced into their acts and are therefore its "victims." For example, opponents of pornography charge that women involved in "adult films" are dehumanized and turned into

objects and commodities.[3] Research on prostitution shows that many young runaways and abandoned children are coerced into a life on the streets, where they are cruelly treated and held as virtual captives.[4] While less than 20 percent of prostitutes are juveniles, a majority of street prostitutes interviewed had become sex trade workers before the age of 18.[5]

Even if public order crimes do not actually harm their participants, perhaps society as a whole should be considered the victim of these crimes. Is the community harmed when an adult bookstore opens or a brothel is established? Does this send out a message that a neighbourhood is in decline? Does it help educate children that deviance is to be tolerated and profited from?

On the other hand, when consenting behaviour between adults is criminalized, it sends out a message that repression is an acceptable way to enforce conformity. People quite often feel that the state has no business regulating the private sexual relationships of consenting adults.[6]

Debating Morality

Some scholars argue that acts such as pornography, prostitution, and drug use erode the moral fabric of society and therefore should be punished by law, because "one of the functions of the criminal law [is] to give expression to the collective feeling of revulsion toward certain acts, even when they are not very dangerous."[7] In his classic

A "game" unfolds nightly on the streets and alleys of downtown Canadian cities—a picture of prostitution which masks the hidden world of pimps and johns.

statement on the function of morality in the law, Sir Patrick Devlin stated:

> Without shared ideas on politics, morals, and ethics no society can exist. . . . If men and women try to create a society in which there is no fundamental agreement about good and evil, they will fail; if having based it on common agreement, the argument goes, the society will disintegrate. For society is not something that is kept together physically; it is held by the invisible bonds of common thought. If the bonds were too far relaxed, the members would drift apart. A common morality is part of the bondage. The bondage is part of the price of society; and mankind, which needs society, must pay its price.[8]

According to this view, victimless crimes are prohibited because the criminal law must express public morality.[9]

Some argue that basing criminal definitions on moral beliefs is an impossible task: Who defines morality? Are we not punishing differences rather than social harm? If morals are really the expression of the majority, does that mean they should be the basis for regulating the conduct of all? Are photographs of nude children by famed photographer Robert Mapplethorpe art or obscenity? As U.S. Supreme Court Justice William O. Douglas so succinctly put it, "What may be trash to me may be prized by others."[10]

In the Puritan society of Salem, Massachusetts, women were burned at the stake as witches because their behaviour seemed strange or different. In Africa today, female circumcision is performed to ensure virginity, remove sexual sensation, and make girls suitable for marriage. Critics of this practice consider it to be an act of mutilation and torture, while others argue that this ancient custom should be left to the discretion of the indigenous people who consider it part of their culture. Can an outsider define the morality of another culture?[11] Or, in a democracy, should a majority dictate how all should live?[12]

Joseph Gusfield says that outlawing acts because they are immoral shows the moral superiority of those who condemn the acts over those who commit them. The legislation of morality "enhances the social status of groups carrying the affirmed culture and degrades groups carrying that which is condemned as deviant."[13] Legislating morality thus creates insiders who are normal and outsiders who are deviant.

Criminal or Immoral?

It is possible that acts that most of us deem highly immoral are not criminal. There is no law against lust, gluttony, avarice, spite, or envy, although they are considered some of the "seven deadly sins." Nor is it a crime in most jurisdictions to ignore the pleas of a drowning person, even though such callous behaviour is considered immoral.

Violations of conventional morality may also be tolerated because they serve a useful social function. Watching sexually explicit films can release tension; immoral behaviour may provide benefits to legitimate enterprises.[14]

Some acts also seem well intentioned, but are still considered criminal, such as killing a loved one who is suffering from an incurable disease (euthanasia); stealing to feed a poor family; or marrying many women (polygamy), even though it may conform to religious beliefs.[15]

It might be possible to settle this argument by saying that immoral acts become crimes if they are harmful to the public. Yet some acts that cause social harm are legal, such as the use of tobacco and alcohol, and driving vehicles that can accelerate to over 160 km/h. More people die each year from alcohol-, tobacco-, and auto-related deaths than from all drug-related deaths combined. Should drugs be legalized and fast cars outlawed?

Even if an act were outlawed simply because it caused social harm, the law might prove difficult or impossible to enforce if the public was divided. For example, assisted suicide may be against the law because it causes "social harm," but prosecutors have failed to gain convictions in assisted suicide cases because so many people view it as a humanitarian act and refuse to convict people. Although Sue Rodriguez failed in her request to the Supreme Court of Canada for legal assisted suicide, many people were sympathetic to her cause.

Vigilante Justice

Canada doesn't have the "wild west" history of the United States, where "vigilance committees" were set up in boom towns to pursue cattle rustlers and stagecoach robbers. However, there is a largely unknown history of "popular justice" in early Canada, as discussed in Chapter 2. These vigilantes held to a strict standard of morality, punishing moral transgressions such as sexual deviance, drunkenness, severe wife beating, and adultery. The popularity of such vigilante movements diminished with the growth of state institutions and the development of the police.[16]

The avenging vigilante is an important part of North American popular culture, "do gooders" who take it on themselves to enforce the law, battle evil, and personally deal with those whom they consider immoral. From Superman to Captain Canada, the righteous **vigilante** is expected to go on **moral crusades** without authorization from legal authorities. Members of special interest groups are also ready to do battle for moral decency. Popular targets of moral crusaders are abortion clinics, pornographers, gun dealers, and logging companies. What else but moral issues could explain the thousands of acts of violence against abortion clinics over the last 30 years?

Howard Becker has labelled people who go on moral crusades in order to control the definition of morality **moral entrepreneurs**. These rule creators operate with an absolute certainty that their way is right and that any means are justified to get their way; "the crusader is fervent and righteous, often self-righteous."[17]

Moral crusades are often directed against people clearly defined as evil by one segment of the population. For example, anti-"smut" campaigns may attempt to ban the books of a popular author from the school library or prevent a "controversial" figure from speaking at the local college. One way for moral crusaders to accomplish their goal is to prove to all who will listen that some unseen or hidden trait makes their targets truly evil. This moral crusade polarizes people into "bad guys" and "good guys," creating a climate in which those categorized as "good" are deified, while the "bad" are demonized.[18] Mothers Against Drunk Driving, for example, are currently lobbying to have the legal limit for blood alcohol reduced from .08 percent to .05 percent, claiming they have the support of 66 percent of Canadians because of what they have "seen on the road."

Categorizing people as all good or all bad creates crime control policies that may be overly punitive. For example, the death penalty is justified if murderers are "bad guys"–unrepentant monsters who commit serial murders and mutilate their victims. If, instead, murderers were viewed as "good guys"–the disturbed victims of child abuse and neglect–it would be out of the question to consider the death penalty.

Enforcement of morally tinged statutes has become a significant problem for law enforcement agencies. In Vancouver, several stores selling marijuana paraphernalia have been raided, and pipes and seeds were seized under Section 462.2 of the Criminal Code.[19] However, if laws governing morally tinged behaviour such as marijuana use are enforced too vigorously, local authorities are branded as reactionaries who waste time on petty issues. If the authorities are confiscating marijuana destined for alleviating the pain of the sick, they risk being seen as insensitive. If, on the other hand, police agencies ignore public order crimes, they are accused of being soft on immorality and social degeneracy. "Society would be a lot better off," the argument goes, "if the cops cracked down on 'those people.'" Who "those people" are and what should be done about them is a matter of great public debate.

Let us now turn to specific examples of public order crimes.

Illegal Sexuality

One type of public order crime relates to what conventional society considers to be deviant sexual practices. Among these outlawed practices are paraphilia, prostitution, and pornography. Laws controlling these behaviours have been the focus of much debate.

Paraphilia

On October 21, 1996, more than 250 000 Belgians took to the streets to protest what they considered the government's inept handling of a case involving the deaths of four children, allegedly at the hands of a pedophile ring led by a convicted rapist, Marc Dutroix. Two of the victims (eight-year-old girls) had been imprisoned and molested for months in Dutroix's home. They starved to death when he was arrested and sent to jail on an unrelated charge. Other children had been kidnapped, raped, tortured, and sold into sexual slavery by the ring.[20]

The case of pedophile Marc Dutroix is an extreme example of sexual abnormality, or **paraphilia**, sexual practices involving recurrent sexual urges focused on (1) nonhuman objects (underwear, shoes, leather); (2) humiliation or the experience of receiving or giving pain (sadomasochism, bondage); or (3) children or others who cannot grant consent.[21] Some paraphilias, such as wearing clothes normally worn by the opposite sex (transvestitism), can be engaged in by adults in the privacy of their homes and do not involve a third party. Others, however, present a risk of social harm and are subject to criminal penalties, such as exposure of genitals in public (indecent exposure, Section 173 CCC) and sexual interference with a person under the age of 14 (Section 153 CCC). Voyeurism is handled under trespassing (Section 177 CCC) or stalking (Section 264 CCC).

Paraphilias that involve unwilling or underage victims show that quite often the victim and offender are likely to have had a prior relationship as family members, intimates, or acquaintances. Based on police-recorded incident data for 2000, family members were involved in 23 percent of sexual assaults and 29 percent of other sexual offences. Acquaintances committed 48, and 40 percent, respectively. Twenty percent of all sexual assaults and 43 percent of "other sexual offences" involved a child under 12 years of age. These statistics point to a sex offender who is older than other violent offenders, heterosexual, and more likely to be related to or known by the victim and thus exploiting a position of authority.[22]

This picture of the sex offender is very different than an earlier one. Believe it or not, in the 1950s and 1960s in Canada hundreds of suspected gay men and lesbians lost their jobs, were demoted from high security positions in the Canadian civil service, or were purged from the military. Many were also interrogated and followed by the RCMP. By the late 1960s the RCMP had collected the names of 9000 suspected lesbians and gay men.[23] There was also government-funded research into a means to detect homosexuals–this was known as the "fruit machine." However, homosexuality was dropped from the list of deviant sexualities of the Canadian Psychological Association in the late 1970s.

Famous Canadian Criminals

The Case of Everett Klippert

In 1965, during an investigation into a case of arson, a man named Everett Klippert told the police he was homosexual. At the time, however, a man having sex with men was categorized as "gross indecency" under the criminal law. Sentenced to three years in prison, he was interviewed by two psychiatrists who concluded that Klippert fitted under Canada's law respecting dangerous sexual offenders, simply because he was likely to repeat his behaviour. As a result, Klippert was incarcerated for life, a sentence confirmed by the Supreme Court of Canada in 1967.

Reaction to the judgment was swift. An editorial in the *Toronto Star* called the decision "a return to the Middle Ages," and Pierre Elliott Trudeau, then Justice Minister, said that "the state has no place in the bedrooms of the nation."

Two years later, in 1969, the country debated Bill C-150, an omnibus bill dealing with a variety of offences, from gross indecency to abortion to gambling. The bill decriminalized homosexuality by suggesting that sexual acts between consenting adults, when performed in private, became legal. The bill caused heated debate in the House of Commons. John Diefenbaker, recorded in the Hansard Debates of January 27, 1969, said, "I am opposed to these homosexuality amendments. I think they are wrong. . . . I know there is no individual more subject to intimidation and threat by the U.S.S.R. as it endeavours to obtain information detrimental to the security of Canada than those who are believed to be homosexuals."

Pierre Elliot Trudeau said, "It's certainly the most extensive revision of the Criminal Code since the 1950s and, in terms of the subject matter it deals with, I feel that it has knocked down a lot of totems and over-ridden a lot of taboos and I feel that in that sense it is new. It's bringing the laws of the land up to contemporary society .... The view we take here is that there's no place for the state in the bedrooms of the nation.... What's done in private between adults doesn't concern the Criminal Code. When it becomes public, this is a different matter, or when it relates to minors, this is a different matter."

On July 20, 1971, Everett Klippert was released from prison.

Sources: www.aidslaw.ca/Maincontent/issues/gaylesbian/07p2bE.html; Anne Vassal, John Fisher, Ralf Jürgens, Robert Hughes, *Gay and Lesbian Issues and HIV/AIDS, A Discussion Paper*, Canadian HIV/AIDS Legal Network and Canadian AIDS Society, Montreal, July 1997; Owen Wood, The Fight for Gay Rights: Canada Timeline, CBC News Online.

Prostitution

Prostitution has been known for thousands of years. The earliest record of prostitution appears in ancient Mesopotamia, where priests engaged in sex to promote fertility in the community. All women were required to do temple duty, and passing strangers were expected to make donations to the temple after enjoying its services.

Modern commercial sex appears to have its roots in ancient Greece, where Solon established licensed brothels in 500 BC. The earnings of Greek prostitutes helped pay for the temple of Aphrodite. Famous men openly went to prostitutes to enjoy intellectual, aesthetic, and sexual stimulation.

Although some early Christian religious leaders, such as St. Augustine and St. Thomas Aquinas, were tolerant of prostitution, this attitude disappeared after the Reformation. Martin Luther advocated the abolition of prostitution, and Lutheran doctrine depicted prostitutes as emissaries of the devil who were sent to destroy the faith.[24]

In more recent times, prostitution was tied to the rise of English brewery companies during the early 19th century. Saloons controlled by the companies employed prostitutes to attract patrons and encourage them to drink.

Today, there are many variations of prostitution, but in general, **prostitution** can be defined as the consensual exchange of sex for money, and money for sex. This exchange, in itself, is not illegal in Canada, although it is virtually impossible to transact without breaking some part of the law. For example, Section 213 of the Canadian Criminal Code (CCC) makes it illegal to either ask for or offer a money–sex exchange, in public. In other words, this law makes it an offence to be either the buyer or the seller, the prostitute or the client. This law has been challenged on constitutional grounds, in that it violates the constitutionally protected right to communication; however, the Supreme Court ruled that the law is a "reasonable infringement" on civil liberties, because of the nuisance caused by the public solicitation of sex for money.[25]

The definition of the offence of prostitution is sexually neutral, since prostitutes can, of course, be straight or gay, male or female. Other sections of the code include "Keeping a common bawdy-house" (Section 210 CCC), "Transporting person to bawdy-house" (Section 211 CCC), and "Procuring," otherwise known as pimping (Section 212 CCC). The most usual offence for which a person is charged under prostitution law is Section 213, "Communicating for the purposes of prostitution."

Crime in the News

The "Fruit Machine"

Privy Council, NRC backed "fruit machine"

By Dean Bibby, Canadian Press
April 24, 1992
The federal government's "fruit machine," intended to root out homosexuals in the civil service, was one of the most bizarre medical devices ever developed with taxpayers' money.

An individual peered into the narrow opening of a large box in which sometimes lewd pictures from magazines were shown. A camera recorded pupil size as each new image was flashed.

In one hand, the subject clutched a small mesh bag of anhydrous silica gel and anhydrous cobalt chloride. Around one finger was an aluminum ring that used a cadmium selemide photocrystal to record blood flow electronically.

The contraption drew on a grab-bag of poorly tested medical theories that nevertheless got support from the National Research Council, the Health and Welfare Department, and Privy Council.

The brains behind the machine was Robert Wake, a psychologist at Carleton University in Ottawa who used a 1962 sabbatical to launch the project. . . .

To identify gays, Wake proposed reading a list of "homosexual words" to an individual who was holding a mesh bag of crystals. Only a gay person would be stimulated to sweat, he reasoned. The so-called homosexual word list that Wake compiled included circus, bagpipe, blind, camp, fish, sew, house, and restaurant.

Exhibit 14.1	Quick Code on Prostitution

213. (1) Every person who in a public place or in any place open to public view
    (a) stops or attempts to stop any motor vehicle,
    (b) impedes the free flow of pedestrian or vehicular traffic or ingress to or egress from premises adjacent to that place, or
    (c) stops or attempts to stop any person or in any manner communicates or attempts to communicate with any person for the purpose of engaging in prostitution or of obtaining the sexual services of a prostitute is guilty of an offence punishable on summary conviction.
(2) Definition of "public place"
(2) In this section, "public place" includes any place to which the public have access as of right or by invitation, express or implied, and any motor vehicle located in a public place or in any place open to public view.

Source: Criminal Code of Canada

In 1990, Metropolitan Toronto Police charged *NOW* magazine with "communication for the purposes of prostitution," because some of its classified advertising offered sexual services for sale. The charges were laid by morality bureau officers despite the lack of official approval by the attorney general's office, and were subsequently dropped.[26]

Following are the conditions usually present in a commercial sexual transaction:

- Activity that has sexual significance for the customer: intercourse, exhibitionism, sadomasochism, oral sex

- Economic transaction: money or drugs are exchanged for the activity
- Emotional indifference: the interaction has nothing to do with affection[27]

Incidence of Prostitution. The Uniform Crime Reports for 2000 indicate that there were 5036 prostitution offences, 90 percent of which were for communication. Of adults charged, only 49 percent were male, despite the fact that one prostitute will service hundreds of different clients each year. The clearance rate is 87 percent, displaying the fact that prostitution is a "policing-sensitive" crime. As Figure 14.1 shows, probation and fines account for 69 percent of the sanctions given to males, and 54 percent of those given to women. Males, however, are much less likely to receive a jail sentence (3 percent) than are women (39 percent).

Types of Prostitution. There are several types of prostitutes. Those who work the streets in plain sight of police, citizens, and customers are referred to as hustlers, hookers, or streetwalkers. Although glamorized by the Julia Roberts character in the film *Pretty Woman* (who winds up with multimillionaire Richard Gere), streetwalkers are considered the least attractive, lowest-paid, most vulnerable men and women in the profession. Streetwalkers wear bright clothing and makeup, and take their customers to hotels or cars.[28] Streetwalkers are most likely to be members of ethnic or racial minorities who live in poverty. Many are young runaways who gravitate to major cities to find a new and exciting life and escape from sexual and physical abuse at home.[29] Of all prostitutes, streetwalkers have the highest incidence of drug abuse and larceny arrests.

Bar girls (B-girls) spend their time in bars, drinking and waiting to be picked up by customers. B-girls work

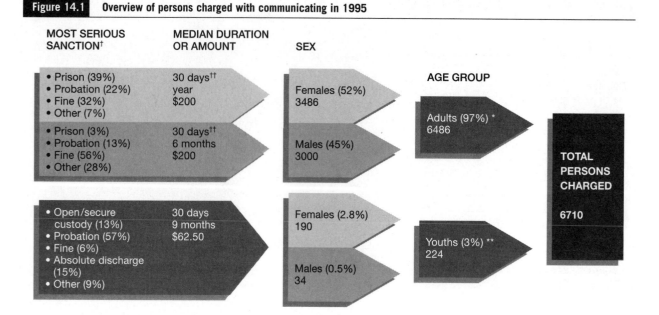

Figure 14.1   Overview of persons charged with communicating in 1995

* Persons aged 18 and over.
** Persons aged 12 to 17. Many youths are diverted to social service agencies in lieu of being charged.
† Adult court cases: Adults convicted of this offence in 1993 and 1994 (1993/94 and 1994/95 fiscal years in Ontario). Excludes New Brunswick, Manitoba and British Columbia; coverage is incomplete for Newfoundland, Nova Scotia, and Quebec. Youth court cases: Youths convicted in Canada in 1993/94 and 1994/95 fiscal years.
†† Based on cases where the sentence duration was known.

Source: Statistics Canada, *Juristat* 17 (2) (1997).

out an arrangement with the bartender so they are served diluted drinks or water coloured with dye or tea, for which the customer is charged an exorbitant price. It is common to find B-girls in towns with military bases and large transient populations.

Brothels flourished in the 19th and early 20th centuries. They were large establishments, usually run by **madams,** that housed several prostitutes. The madam employs and supervises the prostitutes, and her cut is usually 40 to 60 percent of the prostitutes' earnings. The madam's role may include recruiting women into prostitution and socializing them in the "trade."[30] The madam attracts prostitutes and customers, works out understandings with police authorities, and pacifies neighbours.

The aristocrats of prostitution are **call girls.** They charge customers up to $1500 per night and may net over $100 000 per year. Some gain clients through employment in escort services, while others develop independent customer lists. Many call girls come from middle-class backgrounds and service upper-class customers. Working exclusively via telephone "dates," call girls get their clients by word of mouth or by making arrangements with bellhops, cab drivers, and so on. They either entertain clients in their own apartments or make "outcalls" to clients' hotels and apartments. Call girls are

at risk by being alone with strangers, so they might request the business cards of their clients to make sure they are dealing with "upstanding citizens."[31]

In the adult entertainment zones of large cities, one might find "rap booths."[32] Here, the prostitute and her customer occupy booths that are separated by a glass wall, and they talk via telephone for as long as the customer is willing to pay. The more money he spends, the more she engages in sexual banter and disrobing. There is no actual touching, and sex is through masturbation.

In the 1980s, surveys found that some female prostitutes have substance abuse problems, and use prostitution as a method to support their drug habits. Not all drug-addicted prostitutes barter sex for drugs, but those who do report more frequent drug abuse and physical violence than other prostitutes.[33]

Some sex trade work is based in **massage parlours,** where oral sex and manual stimulation are common. Photography studios and model and escort services are other possible covers for commercial sex. Stag party girls will service all-male parties and groups by putting on shows and having sex with participants. In years past, many hotels had live-in prostitutes, while today's hotel prostitute makes a deal with the bell captain or manager to refer customers to her for a fee.

Becoming a Prostitute. Why does someone turn to prostitution? Both male and female prostitutes often come from troubled homes marked by extreme conflict and hostility, where divorce, separation, or death has split the family.[34] Many prostitutes were initiated by family members into sex as young as 10 to 12 years of age and have long histories of sexual exploitation and abuse.[35]

Conflict with school authorities, poor grades, and drug abuse are often factors in the prostitute's life.[36] Other personal characteristics include growing up in a slum neighbourhood, living in a broken home, being a member of a gang, seeing prostitutes, and unemployment. There is no evidence that people become prostitutes because of psychological problems. Money, drugs, and survival seem to be greater motivations.

Pimps may convince girls by flattery and promises, but relatively few kidnap or coerce kids into prostitution. It is more likely that friends or relatives introduce kids into prostitution.[37]

Child Prostitution. Child prostitution is now a worldwide problem. Girls from Latin America are being sold for sex in Europe and the Middle East. Southeast Asian girls wind up in Northern Europe and the Middle East, and Russian and Ukrainian girls are sold in Hungary, Poland, and the Baltic States. In Asia an estimated one million children are part of the sex trade. Thailand is the leader, but child prostitution is a growing problem in India, Bangladesh, and the Philippines. Sex tours are a common practice in these nations, and the United Nations has called for sanctions to punish operators. Canada now has laws to prosecute sex tourism with minors. In some poor Asian nations such as Thailand, most young girls are forced into prostitution because they are indigent.

Pimps. A pimp derives part or all of his livelihood from the earnings of a prostitute. The pimp helps steer customers to the prostitute, stays on the alert for and deals with police, posts bail, and protects his prostitutes from unruly customers. Pimps can pick up established "working girls" or they can "turn out" young girls who have never been in "the life." Occasionally, but not as often as the media would like us to believe, they pick up young runaways, buy them clothes and jewellery, and turn them into street prostitutes.

The role of the pimp is changing. The decline of the brothel, the development of independent prostitutes, and the control of prostitution by organized crime have decreased the number of full-time pimps. Many prostitutes are drug-dependent, and in some areas drug dealers have replaced pimps as the controlling force in prostitution.[38] Even when a prostitute has a pimp, the relationship is often short-lived and unstable. Pimps are often reluctant to work with younger prostitutes today because they face more severe legal penalties if caught running juveniles and because they consider juveniles unstable and untrustworthy.[39]

Johns. It is primarily men who buy the sexual services of both male and female prostitutes, although there is very little research on the topic. Just as in the real world of prostitution, the men are virtually invisible as attention is focused on the female prostitute. They tend to be between the ages of 20 and 40 years, usually married, and heterosexual even if they pick up young men. Their reasons for seeking out prostitutes are as varied as the desire for discreet sex to wanting sexual services they are unable to obtain elsewhere.[40]

Legalize Prostitution? Prostitution is typically considered a minor offence, punishable by a fine or a short jail sentence. In some jurisdictions johns who are arrested must attend "john school," where they have to listen to the stories of women forced to work in prostitution. John schools originated in San Francisco in 1995, and today over a dozen john school programs operate successfully in Canada. They focus on educating offenders on the legal ramifications of prostitution, the health risks, and the effects of prostitution on women. In 1999 a john school was started in Vancouver, operated by the John Howard Society. The school is a pre-charge diversion program. Offenders arrested in the course of police undercover sting operations for communication are screened by police and offered the option of attending a Prostitution Offender Program class. The cost of attending is $400, and during the day the john will hear various speakers including community members, legal experts, ex-sex trade workers, police officers, and health professionals.

For some feminists, women are victims of male dominance, and in patriarchal societies prostitution is a clear example of gender exploitation.[41] For other feminists, prostitution should be a matter of free choice.[42] Advocates of both sides argue that the penalties for prostitution should be reduced. Decriminalization would relieve already desperate women of the additional burden of severe legal punishment.

Pornography

The term **pornography** derives from the Greek *porne*, meaning "prostitute," and *graphein*, meaning "to write." Pornographic books, magazines, and films that depict explicit sex acts are widely available.

One problem of controlling pornography is its relation to **obscenity**, defined as "deeply offensive to morality or decency... designed to incite to lust or depravity."[43] Police and law enforcement officials can legally seize only material that is judged obscene. But who is to judge what is obscene? For example, the novel *Tropic of Cancer* by Henry Miller was banned in the United States because it was considered obscene, but today it is considered a work of great literary value. Allowing individual judgments on what is obscene makes a constitutional guarantee of free speech unworkable.

Opponents of pornography argue that pornographers exploit their models, who may include underage children or victims of physical and psychological coercion.

Child Pornography Rings. Many of the "hard-core" pictures that find their way into the hands of collectors are the work of pornographic groups or rings, adults who join together to exploit children and adolescents for sex. In a study of 55 child pornography rings, the typical one contained from three to eleven children, predominantly males, some of nursery-school age. The adults who controlled the ring used a position of trust to recruit the children and then continued to exploit them through a combination of material and psychological rewards.

Solo sex rings involve several children and a single adult, usually male, who uses a position of trust (counsellor, teacher, Boy Scout leader) to recruit children into sexual activity. Transition rings are impromptu groups set up to sell and trade photos and sex, whereas syndicated rings are well-structured and create extensive networks of customers who desire sexual services.[44] The sexual exploitation by these rings can cause the children to suffer from headaches and loss of appetite to genital soreness, vomiting, and urinary infections. Psychological problems include mood swings, withdrawal, edginess, and nervousness. Exploited children were prone to such acting-out behaviour as setting fires and becoming sexually focused in the use of language, dress, and mannerisms.

Does Pornography Cause Violence? An issue critical to the debate over pornography is whether viewing it produces sexual violence or assaultive behaviour against women. This debate was given added interest when serial killer Ted Bundy claimed his murderous rampage was fuelled by reading pornography.

What evidence exists that viewing sexually explicit material has an effect on behaviour? In 1970, a U.S. national commission on pornography could find no clear relationship between pornography and violence.[45] Twenty years later, another commission called for legal attacks on hard-core pornography and condemnation of all sexually related material but also found little evidence that obscenity per se is a cause of antisocial behaviour.[46]

How can we account for this surprisingly insignificant association? In Denmark, research showed that the rate of sex offences actually declined shortly after pornography was decriminalized in 1967.[47] Other research found that convicted rapists and sex offenders report less exposure to pornography than a control group of non-offenders.[48]

It is possible that viewing prurient material may have the unintended side effect of satisfying erotic impulses that otherwise might result in more sexually aggressive behaviour. While some criminologists believe there is a relationship between pornography and rape,[49] the evidence is inconclusive. However, there is evidence that people exposed to violent material are likely to be sexually aggressive toward female victims.[50] It is felt that violent pornography leads to a greater acceptance of rape myths and violence against women, and more tolerance of sexual aggression.

Laboratory experiments have found that men exposed to violence in pornography are more likely to act aggressively toward women.[51] This finding is especially distressing because it is common for adult-only books and films to have sexually violent themes, such as rape, bondage, and mutilation.[52]

Pornography and the Law. In Canada it is an offence to publish or circulate any obscene "thing" (Section 163 CCC), where "obscenity" is defined as the undue exploitation of sex and crime, horror, cruelty, and violence. The key question is whether the material violates community standards. There is seemingly a high level of tolerance for adult nudity in magazines, but not for pictures of adult-child sex.

In the case cited above, in which *NOW* magazine was charged for running sex ads in its business personals section, there was a lot of community support for the magazine and little for the actions of the police. Similarly, in Halifax in 1998, some police officers took it on themselves to contact businesses that advertised in *The Coast* about the purported obscenity of the "Savage Love" advice column. The column had been investigated by the morality section in 1996 and found not to be obscene, but this didn't prevent the police from trying to enforce what they thought were community standards.

The punishment of pornographers often creates moral and legal dilemmas, as in the posthumous 1990 exhibition of photographer Robert Mapplethorpe in Cincinnati. The exhibition was heavily criticized by conservative politicians because it contained images of nude children and men in homoerotic poses. Obscenity charges were brought against its director, but he was found not guilty. The actions taken against the Mapplethorpe exhibit brought protests from artists and performers, and civil libertarians who fear government control over art, music, and theatre.

Obviously, a plebiscite cannot be held to determine the community's attitude for every trial concerning the sale of pornography. Works that are considered obscene in Orillia might be considered acceptable in Toronto.

Controlling Sex for Profit

Sex for profit predates Western civilization, and law enforcement crusades can make sex-related goods and services a relatively scarce commodity, driving up prices. The threat of government regulation may also convince some participants in the sex-for-profit industry to police themselves. Fear of government control probably influences mainstream sex magazines to alter their content rather than risk provoking public officials.

Technological change will provide the greatest challenge to those seeking to control the sex-for-profit industry. Adult movie theatres are closing as people are able to buy or rent tapes in their local video stores and play them in the privacy of their homes. Adult CD-ROMs are now a staple of the computer industry. Internet sex services (cybersex) include live, interactive stripping and sexual activities. The government has moved to control the broadcast of obscene films via satellite and other technological innovations. On February 15, 1991, Home Dish Only Satellite Networks, Inc. was fined $150 000 for broadcasting pornographic movies to its 30 000 clients throughout the United States; it was the first case to involve prosecution for the illegal use of satellites to broadcast obscene films.[53] Police have also moved to control Internet-based pornography.[54]

Substance Abuse

The problem of substance abuse is widespread in modern societies. Large urban areas are beset by drug-dealing gangs, drug users who engage in crime to support their habits, and alcohol-related violence. Rural areas such as the coast of the Atlantic provinces are important staging centres for the transshipment of drugs across the country, and the production of synthetic drugs and marijuana farming are important parts of the underground economy.[55]

Another indication of the concern about drugs is simply the volume of cases, although as with prostitution, this is also a product of police enforcement. In 1999 there were almost 88 000 drug crimes known to the police, 75 percent of which were for cannabis (69 percent for possession). Like most criminal offences, the rate of drug offences is higher in western Canada than in eastern Canada but has been dropping steadily over the last two decades.

The drug problem, for the most part, is another type of victimless crime. In fact, the Canadian Centre on Substance Abuse (CCSA) says penalties for marijuana possession have done nothing to enhance public safety and health and recommends that possession be decriminalized. This is one side of the debate over whether drug use should be seen as a private matter and drug control simply government intrusion into people's private lives. These people would support **decriminalization**. Furthermore, legalization could reduce the profit of selling illegal substances and drive suppliers out of the market.[56] Others see these substances as dangerous, believing that the criminal activity of users makes the term "victimless" nonsensical. Still another position favours limited regulation: that the possession and use of all drugs and alcohol should be legalized but that the sale and distribution of drugs should be heavily penalized. This would punish those profiting from drugs and would enable users to be helped without fear of criminal punishment.

When Did Drug Use Begin?

The use of chemical substances to change reality and provide stimulation, relief, or relaxation has gone on for thousands of years. Mesopotamian writings indicate that opium was used 4000 years ago—it was known as the "plant of joy."[57] The ancient Greeks knew of drug use, and during the Crusades the Arabs were using marijuana. In the Western hemisphere, natives of Mexico and South America chewed coca leaves for endurance and used "magic mushrooms" in their religious ceremonies.[58] In fact, coca leaf aids in the uptake of oxygen in the thin air of the Peruvian Andes. Drug use was also accepted in Europe well into the 20th century. Recently uncovered pharmacy records circa 1900 to 1920 showed sales of cocaine and heroin solutions to members of the British royal family. Winston Churchill, then a member of Parliament, bought a cocaine solution while staying in Scotland in 1912.[59]

In the early years of Canada and the United States, opium and its derivatives were easily obtained. Opium-based drugs were adopted for use in various patent medicine cure-alls. Morphine was used extensively to relieve the pain of wounded soldiers. By the turn of the century many citizens were opiate users.

Several factors precipitated the stringent drug laws that are in force today. The rural religious creeds of the 19th century—for example, those of the Methodists, Presbyterians, and Baptists—emphasized individual human toil and self-sufficiency while designating the use of intoxicating substances as an unwholesome surrender to the evils of urban morality. Religious leaders were thoroughly opposed to the use and sale of narcotics. The medical literature of the late 1800s began to designate the use of morphine and opium as a vice, a habit, an appetite, and a disease. Late 19th- and early 20th-century police literature described drug users as habitual criminals. Moral crusaders in the 19th century defined drug use as evil and urged lawmakers to outlaw the sale and possession of drugs. Some well-publicized research efforts categorized drug use as highly dangerous.[60] Drug use was also associated with the foreign immigrants who were recruited to work in factories and mines and brought with them their national drug habits. Early antidrug legislation appears to be tied to prejudice against immigrating ethnic minorities.[61]

In Canada, large numbers of Asian immigrants had begun to arrive in the early 1880s, brought in as cheap labour by industrialists as a way to diffuse the growing power of the organized trade unions. In general, Asian workers were paid anywhere from one-half to two-thirds what European workers received. Because many of these workers were single men who planned on returning to their home country, they tended to keep to themselves. Their habits of gambling and opium smuggling, although legal in Canada, were nonetheless frowned upon as

The film *Reefer Madness* (1936) came to symbolize the danger of marijuana: the life of a promising young man brought to ruin, madness, and murder.

immoral. By 1907 many of these workers were no longer needed for large construction projects and they began to compete more directly for other jobs. This created political and labour unrest. In 1907 the Asiatic Exclusion League and its supporters rioted in downtown Vancouver. An estimated 20 000 people caused extensive damage to the shops of Chinese and Japanese people.

Deputy Minister of Labour William Lyon Mackenzie King was appointed to investigate and settle Chinese property damage claims. He discovered the use of opium among the Chinese population and decided that the only means of eliminating the civil unrest was to eliminate the Chinese. He based his report, "The Need for the Suppression of Opium Traffic in Canada," on sensational newspaper stories depicting the ruin of white women caused by opium use. Under the sponsorship of Mackenzie King, the Opium Narcotic Act of 1908 criminalized opium, and in 1911, the Opium and Drug Act expanded the list of prohibited drugs, made simple use and possession of the prohibited drugs an offence, and widened police powers of search and seizure.[62]

In 1920, one year before Mackenzie King became prime minister of Canada, the Opium and Drug Branch was established by the Department of Health and was put in charge of enforcing narcotics legislation. As well, *Maclean's* magazine ran a series of articles in the early 1920s about the illicit drug trade in Canada. These articles were written by Emily Murphy, a police magistrate and judge of the Juvenile Court in Edmonton, under the pen name of "Janey Canuck"; they were later compiled into a larger book entitled *The Black Candle*. The articles that Murphy wrote were biased and sensational. In one oft-quoted section, a Los Angeles County Chief of Police is quoted as saying that

> persons using this narcotic smoke the dry leaves of the plant, which has the effect of driving them completely insane. The addict loses all sense of moral responsibility. Addicts to this drug, while under its influence are immune to pain. While in this condition they become raving maniacs and are liable to kill or indulge in any forms of violence to other persons, using the most savage methods of cruelty without, as said before, any sense of moral responsibility.

When *The Black Candle* was released in 1922, it aroused public opinion and resulted in pressure on the government to create stricter drug laws. Cannabis hemp was made illegal under the Opium and Narcotic Drug Act of 1923 with seemingly little discussion. The film *Reefer Madness* in 1936 further reinforced this opinion. It was not until the LeDain Commission of 1969–1971 that marijuana was recommended for decriminalization.

Alcohol and Its Prohibition

The history of alcohol and the law has also been controversial and dramatic. At the turn of the century, a drive was mustered to prohibit the sale of alcohol. The **temperance movement** was fuelled by the belief that the purity of agrarian culture was being destroyed. The growth of the city was viewed as a threat to the lifestyle of people living on farms and in villages. The Anti-Saloon League led by Carrie Nation, the Women's Temperance Union, and the Protestant clergy of the Baptist, Methodist, and Congregationalist faiths viewed the growing city, filled with newly arriving Irish, Italian, and Eastern European immigrants, as centres of degradation and wickedness. The propensity of these ethnic people to drink heavily was viewed as the main force behind their degenerate lifestyle.[63]

Prohibition turned out to be a failure. Organized crime was only too happy to supply illicit liquor. Law enforcement agencies were inadequate, and officials were more than likely to be corrupted by wealthy bootleggers. The smuggling of alcohol from Canada into the United States was especially lucrative. However, one unanticipated con-

Crime in the News

The Sinking of the *I'm Alone*

For more than a day the United States Coast Cutter *Dexter*, with others, pursued the British schooner *I'm Alone*, admitted to be a rum-runner that had long laughed at the vigilance of the marine enforcers of prohibition. The captain of the felonious craft had refused to heave to. On Friday night she was shelled copiously. The sea was rough. The Coast Guard is righteously rough in the discharge of its function. Only one man on the refractory schooner was lost, and he fell overboard. The sinking occurred over 200 miles from the Louisiana coast. The prime question is where it began. The pursuers assert that she was within ten or eleven miles of the coast and therefore legally subject to seizure. The captain of the *I'm Alone* that he was anchored fourteen or fifteen miles offshore when first hailed by the cutter.

Here we draw near the "twelve mile limit," a modern expression of the older formula in leagues and embalmed for revenue and prohibition purposes. In the treaty of 1924 between Great Britain and the United States the rights of boarding, search and seizure outside of our territorial waters shall not be exercised at a greater distance from the coast of the United States than can be traversed in one hour by the vessel suspected of endeavoring to commit the offense. . . .

New York Times, March 29, 1929

sequence of Prohibition in Canada between 1921 and 1929 was the growth of provincial police forces.[64]

Commonly Used and Abused Drugs

A wide variety of drugs are available to drug abusers, only some of which are addicting. Various effects include hallucinations, depression, relaxation, and exhilaration. These drugs are controlled by the Food and Drugs Act and the Narcotic Control Act. Following are some of the most widely used illegal drugs.[65]

Anesthetics. Anesthetic drugs are nervous system depressants, blocking nervous system transmissions. They act on the brain to produce a generalized loss of sensation, or unconsciousness. The most widely abused anesthetic drug is phencyclidine (PCP), or "angel dust." PCP can be sprayed on marijuana and smoked, or it can be drunk or injected. PCP is an animal tranquillizer and causes hallucinations.

Volatile Liquids. Volatile liquids are easily vaporized and inhaled. They include lighter fluid, paint thinner, cleaning fluid, and model airplane glue. The psychological effect is a short-term sense of excitement and euphoria followed by disorientation, slurred speech, and drowsiness. Amyl nitrate ("poppers") is sold in capsules that are broken and inhaled, used during sexual activity to prolong and intensify the experience.

Barbiturates. These hypnotic-sedative drugs depress the central nervous system into a sleeplike condition. Prescribed by doctors as sleeping pills, on the illegal market they are called "downers" and are known by the colour of the capsules—"reds" (Seconal), "blue dragons" (Amytal), and "rainbows" (Tuinal). They create relaxed, sociable, and good-humoured feelings, but are probably the major cause of drug overdose deaths.

Tranquillizers. Tranquillizers have the ability to reduce anxiety, easing tension. Ampazine, Thorazine, Pacatal, and Sparine are used to control the mentally ill who suffer from psychoses, aggressiveness, and agitation. Valium, Librium, Miltown, and Equanil are used by the average citizen to combat anxiety, tension, fast heart rate, and headaches. These mild tranquillizers are easily obtained by prescription. However, increased dosages can lead to addiction, and withdrawal can be painful and hazardous.

Amphetamines. "Uppers" are synthetic drugs that stimulate the central nervous system to produce elevated blood pressure, increased breathing rate, and elevated mood. Psychological effects include increased confidence, euphoria, fearlessness, impulsivity, and appetite loss. Uppers include Benzedrine ("bennies"), Dexedrine ("dex"), Dexamyl, Bephetamine ("whites"), and Methedrine ("meth," "speed," "crystal meth," "ice"). Speed is the most widely used and the most dangerous. Swallowed in pill form or injected, long-term heavy use can result in exhaustion, anxiety, prolonged depression, and hallucinations.

Cannabis (Marijuana). "Pot," "grass," "ganja," "maryjane," or "dope" is produced from the leaves of *Cannabis sativa*, a hemp plant grown throughout the world. Hashish is made from resin from the female plant. Various effects include changes in auditory and visual perception of time and space, excitement, drowsiness, and increased appetite. Marijuana is not addicting, and it has been decriminalized in Canada for medical use. A contender for the leadership of the Progressive Conservative party in 1998 was the Rev. Michael Baldasaro, who champions the legalization of marijuana, which he calls the "tree of life."[66]

Hallucinogens. Hallucinogens, either natural or synthetic, produce vivid distortions of the senses without greatly disturbing the viewer's consciousness. Some produce hallucinations, while others cause psychotic behaviour. One common hallucinogen is mescaline, which occurs naturally in the peyote, a small cactus that grows in Mexico and the southwestern United States. Mescaline produces vivid hallucinations, a feeling of depersonalization, and out-of-body sensations. Alkaloid compounds, either natural or made in the laboratory, include DMT, morning glory seeds, and psilocybin. Transformed into D-lysergic acid diethylamide-25 (LSD), this substance (800 times more potent than mescaline) stimulates cerebral sensory centres to produce visual hallucinations, intensifies hearing, increases sensitivity, and induces euphoria.

Cocaine. Cocaine is an alkaloid derivative of the coca leaf first isolated in 1860 by Albert Niemann of Gottingen, Germany. Originally considered a medicinal breakthrough that could relieve fatigue and depression, it was endorsed by psychologists such as Sigmund Freud, and used in popular patent medicines. When pharmacist John Styth Pemberton first brewed his new soft drink in 1886, he added cocaine to act as a "brain tonic" and called the drink Coca-Cola; this secret ingredient was taken out in 1906.

When its addictive qualities and dangerous side effects became apparent, cocaine's use was controlled by such legislative bills as Ontario's "Anti-Cocaine Bill," an Act to amend the Pharmacy Act of 1908. However, not only was there growing awareness of the dangerous effects of cocaine; physicians and pharmacists were trying to control "medications" in a wider climate of moral reform. For example, in a flyer issued by the Children's Aid Society of Montreal, there is the claim that

> the cocaine habit must be stamped out of Canada. It is undermining our boyhood and cutting away the moral fibre of our girls. It is turning our young people into criminals and imbeciles. ... Will YOU help the Children's Aid Society fight cocaine? You can do so by asking your clergyman to preach about it, by writing to your member of parliament. ...[67]

Until the 1970s, cocaine remained an underground drug—the property of artists, jazz musicians, beatniks, and jet-setters. Cocaine produces euphoria, laughter, restlessness, and excitement. Overdoses cause delirium, increased reflexes, violent manic behaviour, and respiratory failure. Cocaine can be sniffed, or "snorted," into the nostrils or injected. Mixing cocaine and heroin is called "speedballing"; this practice is highly dangerous and is alleged to have killed comedian John Belushi. When cocaine is treated with a liquid to remove the hydrochloric acid, the resultant "freebase" is dissolved in a solvent such as ether and crystallized. Crushed and smoked, it produces a high more powerful than cocaine

Figure 14.2 **Major cannabis trafficking routes into Canada, 1993**

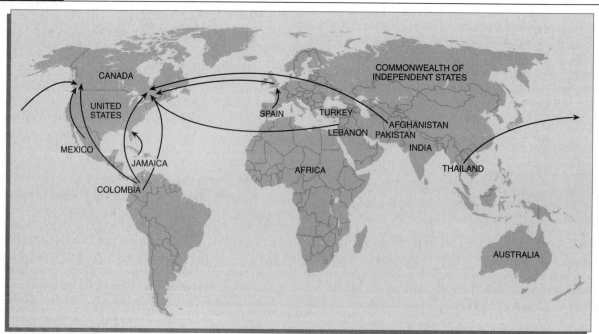

SOURCE: *RCMP National Drug Intelligence Estimate*, 1994 (Ottawa: Minister of Supply and Services, 1994).

but it is dangerous to make since it involves highly flammable products. The creation of "crack cocaine" also involves using ammonia or baking soda to remove the hydrochlorides and create a crystalline form of cocaine base that can then be smoked.[68]

The use of crack and other cocaine derivatives is not widespread. In 1993, for example, the RCMP seized less than 3 kg of crack in Ontario, while almost 3000 kg of cocaine were seized by police in Canada overall.[69] However, because crack cocaine is relatively cheap, it is concentrated among the poor and lower classes, who are susceptible to this powerful and relatively inexpensive drug. Between 1993 and 1995 the percentage of students reporting the use of crack cocaine increased from 0.5 percent to 1.9 percent, hardly an epidemic.[70] So while crack may not be the national epidemic among the middle class as some thought it would turn into, its use has had a powerful effect in the inner city.[71]

Narcotics. These drugs produce insensibility to pain, relieve anxiety, and create sedation. Users experience euphoria, reduced fear, apprehension, and tension. Narcotics can be injected under the skin or into a muscle, or directly into the bloodstream (mainlining).

The most common narcotics are derivatives of opium, a drug produced from the opium poppy flower. The Chinese popularized the habit of smoking or chewing opium extract to produce euphoric feelings. Morphine (from Morpheus, the Greek god of dreams), a derivative of opium, is about ten times as strong and is used legally by physicians to relieve pain. Heroin was first produced as a painkilling alternative to morphine in 1875 because, although 25 times more powerful, it was considered non-addictive by its creator, Heinrich Dreser. The drug's name derives from the fact that it was originally considered heroic because of its painkilling ability.

Heroin is today a commonly used narcotic, although less than 2 percent of all drug offences are for heroin. Dealers cut it with neutral substances such as sugar (lactose), and is often only 1 to 4 percent pure. Users can rapidly build up a tolerance, so larger doses or a changed method of ingestion are needed. Withdrawal symptoms include irritability, depression, extreme nervousness, pain in the abdomen, and nausea. Heroin abuse is generally considered a lower-class phenomenon, although a fair number of middle- and upper-class users exist, such as physicians.[72] The popularity of heroin in the 1990s has been linked to its relatively low cost, ready supply, and the effect of government efforts to control other substances such as crack cocaine. The drug of choice seems to be shifting from crack to heroin. While the popularity of heroin is increasing among the middle class, it is still common to associate heroin addiction with minority youths in lower-class, inner-city neighbourhoods.

Other opium derivatives include codeine, Dilaudid, Percodan, and Prinadol. Synthetics include Demerol, Methadone, Nalline, and Darvon.

Steroids. Anabolic steroids are used to gain muscle bulk and strength for athletics and bodybuilding. Although not physically addicting, steroids are dangerous because of the significant health problems associated with long-term use: liver ailments, tumours, hepatitis, kidney problems, sexual dysfunction, hypertension, and depression. Finally, steroid users often share needles, which puts them at high risk for contracting the AIDS virus.

After Canadian sprinter Ben Johnson tested positive for steroid use at the 1988 Olympic games, the Dubin Inquiry found widespread use of steroids among professional athletes, who use performance-enhancing drugs to stay competitive.[73] In 1998, a scandal rocked the Tour de France bicycle race after athletes were tested for banned substances, including synthetic hormones.

Designer Drugs. Designer drugs are chemical substances made and distributed in relatively small batches that induce mood-altering effects. They include MDMA ("ecstasy"), which combines an amphetamine-like rush with hallucinogenic experiences; the hallucinogens DMT and 2c-B or "Nexus"; and the steroid substitute GHB, which causes drowsiness.

Alcohol. Although the sale and purchase of alcohol is legal today, excessive alcohol consumption is considered a major substance abuse problem.

The cost of alcohol abuse is quite high. In 1992 almost 7000 deaths were attributed to alcohol in Ontario alone. Alcohol-related deaths accounted for almost 10 percent of all deaths in the province. The bulk of these deaths were indirectly related to alcohol consumption: for example, 110 homicides and 295 suicides out of 5685 deaths. In addition, 490 deaths resulted from motor vehicle accidents indirectly related to alcohol.[74]

Alcohol reduces tension, diverts worries, enhances pleasure, improves social skills, and transforms experiences for the better.[75] However, higher doses act as a sedative and depressant. Long-term use has been linked with depression, heart disease, and cirrhosis of the liver. And while many people think that drinking stirs their romantic urges, the weight of the scientific evidence indicates that alcohol decreases sexual response.[76] Moderate drinking has been linked to a reduced probability of heart attack.[77]

The Extent of Substance Abuse

Surveys. In surveying drug use, relying on self-report evidence is subject to error. This is true for any crime, but especially for those with high social disapproval levels. Drug users may boastfully overinflate the extent of their substance abuse, underreport out of fear, or simply be unaware or forgetful.

Another problem is that surveys can overlook important segments of the drug-using population: for example, people who are homeless, in prison, in drug rehabilitation clinics, or in AIDS clinics, as well as those who refuse to participate in the interviews. A survey can miss kids who are institutionalized and those who have dropped out of school.[78] A number of studies indicate that serious abusers underreport drug use in surveys.[79]

While these weaknesses are troubling, surveys that are administered often, in a consistent fashion, can "smooth out" sources of inaccuracy over time. That is, the effects of overreporting and underreporting and of missing subjects should have a consistent effect in every survey year.

Patterns. Despite a continuing effort to control it, the use of mood-altering substances persists. Despite the media attention given to the incidence of drug abuse, there is controversy over the extent of drug use. National surveys show that drug use is not substantially greater than it was two decades ago. Drug possession offences declined during the 1980s, except for cocaine, which tripled from 1985 to 1991. By 1996 drug offences were up, but almost 70 percent of that increase was for marijuana, which is very sensitive to police enforcement.[80]

The continued trend in drug abuse among adolescents indicates that the drug problem has not gone away and may be on the increase. When drug use declined in the 1980s, one reason may have been changing perceptions about the harmfulness of drugs, such as cocaine and marijuana; as people come to view these drugs as harmful, they tend to use them less. Considering the widespread publicity linking drug use, needle sharing, and the AIDS virus, it comes as no surprise that people began to see drug taking as dangerous and risky. In the 1990s, however, the perceived risk of drugs was on the decline.

In a survey of almost 5000 Manitoba high school students, about 40 percent smoked tobacco, 81 percent had drunk alcohol in the past year, and 33 percent drank once a week or more. Of those who drink, 30 percent do so in cars, and 15 percent at school. About 38 percent of students used cannabis, the commonly used drug. In Ontario, a 1999 survey on student drug use conducted by the Centre for Addiction and Mental Health showed that alcohol use had increased to 67 percent since 1993, cannabis use had more than doubled to 29 percent, and 28 percent of students smoked tobacco.[81]

Overall, research shows that when drug use declines, youths report greater disapproval of drug use among their friends, and peer pressure may contribute to lower use rates. In the 1990s the number of youths disapproving of drugs has declined (although a majority still disapprove); with lower disapproval has come increased usage. It should come as no surprise that a cohort of young people who perceive little peer rejection for drug use, who consider drugs risk-free and easily available, and whose parents either ignore or condone drug use will increase the frequency of their substance abuse.

Drug-Involved Youths Who Continue to Commit Crimes as Adults. Although about two-thirds of substance-abusing youths continue to use drugs after they reach adulthood, about half desist from other criminal activities. Those who persist in both substance abuse and crime as adults tend to come from poor families, have other criminals in the family, do poorly in school, start using drugs and committing delinquent acts at a young age, and have few opportunities in late adolescence to participate in legitimate and rewarding adult activities.

Some evidence also exists that these drug-using persisters have low nonverbal IQs and poor physical coordination. Nonetheless, there is still little scientific evidence to indicate why some drug-abusing kids drop out of crime while others remain active into their adulthood.

Smugglers. Smugglers import drugs into the country. They are generally middle-aged men who have strong organizational skills, established connections, capital to invest, and a willingness to take large business risks. There is a constant flow in and out of the business as some sources become the target of law enforcement activities, new drug sources become available, older smugglers become dealers, and former dealers become smugglers.

Adult Predatory Drug Users Who Are Frequently Arrested. Many users who begin abusing substances early in their adolescence will continue in drugs and crime in adulthood. Getting arrested, doing time, using multiple drugs, and committing predatory crimes is a way of life for them. They have few skills, did poorly in school, and have a long criminal record. They specialize in robberies, burglaries, thefts, and drug sales. They filter in and out of the justice system and will begin committing crimes as soon as they are released.[82]

Adult Predatory Drug Users Who Are Rarely Arrested. Some drug users commit hundreds of crimes each year but are rarely arrested. Known for their calculated violence, they plan their crimes carefully. They often work with partners and are more likely to use recreational drugs, such as coke and pot, than the more addicting heroin or opiates. Some may become high-frequency users and risk apprehension and punishment. But for the lucky few, their criminal careers can stretch for up to 15 years without interruption by the justice system.

AIDS and Drug Use

There is a link between drug use and the risk of contracting HIV.[83] Since monitoring of the spread of AIDS began in 1981, about one-fourth of all adult AIDS cases reported to the Centers for Disease Control in Atlanta have occurred among intravenous (IV) drug users.[84]

In Canada the percentage of HIV positive cases among injection drug users reached its peak in 1997 at 34 percent. In comparison, cases attributable to heterosexual contact range around 17 percent, and around 40 percent can be traced to homosexual contact. Women are more likely to be exposed through injection drug use (IDU) than men. In 2000, of 226 HIV positive females, 40 percent or 42 cases were due to IDU. In 2000, of 1085 HIV positive males, 17 percent or 73 cases were due to IDU. [85]

One reason for the AIDS–drug use relationship is the widespread habit of needle sharing among IV users.[86] Many users share needles, and while some use bleach as a disinfectant, the majority ignore this safety precaution.

Because the AIDS virus is spread through blood transfer, the sharing of HIV-contaminated needles is the primary mechanism for transmitting AIDS among the drug-using population. Any attempt to control drugs by outlawing the sale of hypodermic needles has the unfortunate consequence of promoting needle reuse and sharing. Consequently, legal jurisdictions have developed outreach programs to help these drug users; others have made an effort to teach users how to clean their needles and syringes; some have gone so far as to provide addicts with sterile needles.[87]

Drug users also have a significant exposure to AIDS because they tend to have multiple sex partners, some of whom may be engaging in prostitution to support a drug habit.[88] What further complicates the link between prostitution, drug use, and HIV is that women are more likely to contract it from men than men from women. This was especially true in the early 1990s, when the main risk for women was heterosexual sex; however by 2000, the main risk was injection drug use.[89]

In Vancouver's downtown eastside, a "public health emergency" has been declared among the area's estimated 6000 to 10 000 heroin addicts, who live in poor housing, share needles, and engage in prostitution. In 1993, 356 people died of drug overdoses at the peak of the epidemic. More alarming, however, is that the area's HIV transmission rate of 19 percent is the highest rate in the developed world. A recent survey found that 40 percent of the HIV-positive addicts were still lending needles despite needle exchange programs. British Columbia's chief coroner has proposed that the federal government decriminalize heroin so that the issue can be dealt with in a medical rather than a criminal manner; however, there is little widespread support for such an idea.[90]

While the threat of AIDS may be having an impact on the drug-taking behaviour of recreational and middle-class users, drug use may be increasing among the poor, high-school dropouts, and other disadvantaged groups.

The Cause of Substance Abuse

What causes people to abuse drugs? Although there are many views on the causes of drug use, most can be characterized as seeing the onset of an addictive career as either an environmental or a personal matter.

Subcultural View. Those who view drug abuse as having an environmental basis concentrate on lower-class addiction. Because many drug abusers are poor, the onset of drug use can be tied to devalued identities, low self-esteem, poor socioeconomic status, and the high level of mistrust, negativism, and defiance found in lower socio-economic areas.

Youths living in depressed areas, where feelings of alienation and hopelessness run high, often come in contact with established drug users, who teach them that narcotics provide an answer to their feelings of personal inadequacy and stress.[91] Perhaps the youths will join with peers to learn the techniques of drug use and receive social support for their habit and involving them in the drug use subculture.[92] Furthermore, upward mobility is available to only a few because of the deterioration of the manufacturing economy.[93]

Psychodynamic View. Yet not all drug abusers reside in lower-class slum areas; the problem of middle-class substance abuse is very real. Consequently, some experts have linked substance abuse to emotional problems that can strike people in any economic class. This explanation of substance abuse suggests that drugs help youths control or express unconscious needs and impulses. Drinking alcohol may also be associated with dependence and depression. A young teen may resort to drug abuse to reduce the emotional turmoil of adolescence, or to cope with troubling impulses. Research has found that addicts suffer personality disorders characterized by a weak ego, low frustration tolerance, anxiety, and fantasies of omnipotence.

Some research also shows an association between mental illness and drug abuse.[94]

Genetic Factors. It is also possible that substance abuse has a genetic basis. The biological children of alcoholics reared by nonalcoholic adoptive parents more often develop alcohol problems than the biological children of the adoptive parents.[95] Studies comparing alcoholism among identical twins and fraternal twins have found that the degree of concordance (both siblings behaving identically) is twice as high among the identical twin groups. However, identical twins are more likely to be treated similarly than fraternal twins are and therefore are more likely to be influenced by environmental conditions.

Taken as a group, people whose parents were alcoholic or drug dependent have a greater chance of developing a problem than children of nonabusers do. Nonetheless, most children of abusing parents do not become drug dependent themselves, suggesting that even if drug abuse is heritable, environment and socialization plays a role in the onset of abuse.[96]

Social Learning. Social psychologists suggest that drug abuse patterns may also result from the observation of parental drug use. Parental drug abuse begins to have a damaging effect on children as young as two years old, especially when parents manifest drug-related personality problems such as depression or poor impulse control.[97]

People who learn that drugs provide pleasurable sensations may be the most likely to experiment with illegal substances; a habit may develop if the user experiences lower anxiety, fear, and tension levels.[98] Having a history of family drug and alcohol abuse has been found to be a characteristic of violent teenage sexual abusers.[99] Heroin abusers report an unhappy childhood, which included harsh physical punishment and parental neglect and rejection.[100]

Drinking with an adult present, presumably a parent, was also a significant precursor of future substance abuse and delinquency.[101]

Problem Behaviour Syndrome (PBS). For many people, substance abuse is just one of many problem behaviours. Longitudinal studies show that drug abusers are maladjusted, alienated, and emotionally distressed.[102] A deviant lifestyle begins early in life and is punctuated with criminal relationships, a family history of substance abuse, educational failure, alienation, and low commitment to religious values. A recent meta-analysis of PBS research found support for the connection among problem drinking and drug abuse, delinquency, precocious sexual behaviour, school failure, family conflict, and other similar social problems.[103]

Rational Choice. Some people choose to use drugs and alcohol because they want to enjoy their effects: get high, relax, improve creativity, escape reality, increase sexual responsiveness. Adolescent alcohol abusers believe that getting high will make them powerful, increase their sexual performance, and facilitate their social behaviour; they care little about negative future consequences.[104] Research on middle-class, drug-abusing women shows that most were introduced by friends or lovers in the context of just having some fun.[105]

Substance use/abuse, then, may be a function of the rational belief that drugs can be of benefit to the user. The decision to use drugs involves evaluating personal consequences (addiction, disease, legal punishment) and the expected benefits of drug use (peer approval, positive affective states, heightened awareness, relaxation).[106]

Constructionist. Not all theories of drugs and crime start from the presupposition that drug use is automatically bad or that it leads to crime. The social constructionist position looks at how drug use is portrayed as evil, and who is in a position to influence the ideological characterization of drugs. In the example discussed above with regard to the criminalization of opium, labour leaders and politicians were able to trade upon racism against Asians prevalent in British Columbia society to successfully outlaw opium at the turn of the century. The criminalization of cocaine around the same time turned on a fear promoted by police officers and religious leaders that black men addicted to cocaine were corrupting white women. People who are able to influence public opinion in such a manner are called **claimsmakers.**[107]

In sum, there are many views of why people take drugs, and no one theory has proved to be an adequate explanation of all forms of substance abuse. However, research does show that drug users tend to suffer a variety of family and socialization difficulties, have addiction-prone personalities, and are generally at risk for many other social problems.[108]

Drugs and Crime

One reason for the criminalization of particular substances is the association believed to exist between drug abuse and crime. Many criminal offenders have extensive experience with drug use, and drug users do in fact commit an enormous amount of crime. Alcohol abuse has also been linked to criminality and appears to be an important precipitating factor in domestic assault and homicide cases.[109] Arrestees who test positive for drugs are also more likely to recidivate than nonusers.[110]

While the drug–crime connection is powerful, it is still uncertain whether the relationship is causal, as many users had a history of criminal activity before the onset of their substance abuse.[111] As well, many people use drugs recreationally without ever committing other crimes. If drug use is not a cause of crime, perhaps it can amplify the frequency and seriousness of criminality.[112]

Research Methods

Two approaches have been used to study the relationship between drugs and crime. One has been to survey known addicts to assess the extent of their law violations; the other has been to survey known criminals to see whether they were or are drug users.

User Surveys. Numerous studies have examined the criminal activity of drug users. They show that people who take drugs have extensive involvement in crime. Alcohol abuse has been linked to serious, violent offending patterns: People with long histories of drinking are also more likely to report violent offending patterns. While research indicates that drug use is not an initiator of crime (since many users had committed crime before turning to drugs), there was strong evidence that the amount and value of crime increased proportionately with the frequency of the subjects' drug involvement.[113]

Surveys of Known Criminals. The second method used to link drugs and crime is testing known criminals to determine the extent of their substance abuse. A survey of prison inmates disclosed that most (80 percent) had engaged in a lifetime of drug and alcohol abuse, more than one-third claimed to have been under the influence of drugs when they committed their last offence, and about 62 percent claimed to have used a major drug, such as heroin, cocaine, PCP, or LSD, on a regular basis before their

Famous Canadian Criminals

The High Life of Brian O'Dea

In 1975, Brian O'Dea, a marijuana smuggler, and a pilot flew a decrepit DC-6 to a town in Colombia, where they were to pick up eight tonnes of high-grade pot. Shortly before touchdown, the plane's nose gear failed, and the four-engine aircraft plunged through a fence and into a field of cacti. When the plane took off again, it was with one less engine.

When they were about a mile out over the water, a second engine died, and they crash-landed in the water.

After he was picked up by U.S. authorities, he received a ten-year sentence for importing marijuana into the United States. This was only one dramatic incident in a life lived outside the law.

By February 2001, out of jail and wanting to put his criminal past behind him, O'Dea decided to try his hand at a different career. He placed an ad in the *National Post* featuring the fact that he had been a marijuana smuggler and showing how this had given him business experience. The response was phenomenal. His ad circulated on the Internet, drawing mail from Egypt, China, and Australia. Talent agents, script brokers, and movie producers called from New York, Los Angeles, and Vancouver. His face turned up in the *Financial Times* and the *National Enquirer*. He appeared on "Good Morning America" and Court TV. *Playboy* wanted an interview. So did the *Wall Street Journal*.

There were a few job offers, too, though mostly from cold-call sales outfits and people operating on the fringes of the law. One man asked O'Dea to join what he described as an "offshore organ-transplant" business.

He has survived a troubled childhood, a cocaine addiction and numerous encounters with the world's

Employment Wanted

Former Marijuana Smuggler
Having successfully completed a ten-year sentence, incident-free, for importing 75 tons of marijuana into the United States, I am now seeking a legal and legitimate means to support myself and my family.

<u>Business Experience</u> - Owned and operated a successful fishing business - multi-vessel, one airplane, one island and processing facility. Simultaneously owned and operated a fleet of tractor-trailer trucks conducting business in the Western United States. During this time I also co-owned and participated in the executive level management of 120 people worldwide in a successful pot smuggling venture with revenues in excess of US$100 million annually. I took responsibility for my own actions, and received a ten-year sentence in the United States while others walked free for their cooperation.

<u>Attributes</u> - I am an expert in all levels of security; I have extensive computer skills, am personable, outgoing, well-educated, reliable, clean and sober. I have spoken in schools to thousands of kids and parent groups over the past ten years on *"the consequences of choice"*, and received public recognition from the RCMP for community service. I am well-traveled and speak English, French and Spanish. References available from friends, family, the U.S. District Attorney, etc.

Please direct replies to
Box 375, National Post Classified,
1450 Don Mills, ON, M3B 3R5

most dangerous drug lords. He has served time in federal penitentiaries in Canada and the United States and lived to tell his story. Now he needs a job, and telling that story is turning out to be it.

Part of O'Dea's new life is as a motivational speaker for the Congress of Canadian Student Associations to talk about his journey into the drug world.

At a Conference Centre in downtown Calgary, this is what he might say: "Good morning, I'm Brian O'Dea. For much of my life, if you'd asked me my name I would have told you something different. I'm going to teach you how to smuggle drugs. I ended up with way too much money and way too few brains, and way too big a coke habit ... that's what cocaine is. It wants everything from you, and it takes it."

O'Dea was born in St. John's, Newfoundland, in 1948. When he

was 11, his parents enrolled him in St. Bonaventure's school, a Roman Catholic institution run by the Christian Brothers. O'Dea says he endured two years of sexual abuse at the hands of a senior staff member there, a fact he kept to himself until he was 40. He downplays the impact, but admits it affected his sense of self-worth. He became a people-pleaser, often stealing from his parents to impress his friends.

By the time he reached his second year of university, in 1968, at St. Mary's in Halifax, O'Dea was using the tuition money his parents gave him to buy marijuana and hashish. Soon, he started dealing for most of his income. Within a couple of years, he was circumventing his expensive Toronto suppliers by taking buying trips to Britain. In 1972, when he mailed himself a half-kilogram of hash from England through the mail,

Canada Customs intercepted the package and notified the RCMP. He received 18 months.

Eighteen hours after his release from prison, O'Dea booked a ticket to Bogotá, Colombia, and bought 55 grams of coke. That was the first of many trips to Colombia. But by the end of the 1970s, a string of failures had driven him to the brink of bankruptcy.

Then an old acquaintance came to him with news of an abandoned shipyard on Anacortes Island, near Seattle, that was an ideal landing spot for marijuana shipments. With William and Christopher Schaffer, two brothers from Los Angeles with legendary marijuana-growing connections, O'Dea undertook what turned out to be a lucrative marijuana smuggling business.

O'Dea started by creating SeaCal Fisheries, an Alaska-based salmon-packing company, to land, vacuum-pack, and conceal the marijuana among its boxes of fresh fish. He hired five tractor-trailer units under the auspices of a friend's company to pick up the pot in Washington State and transport

it to California. And to ensure that every state trooper and weigh-scale operator on U.S. Interstate 5 should believe his company was legitimate, he set up a phantom roofing company to provide his trucks with cargo and waybills. For 12 months, one of his semis drove up and down the highway with the same load of cedar shingles, just to create cover.

The first load of dope arrived on Forrester Island, a speck of rock off southern Alaska, on Aug. 25, 1986, and made its way south without a hitch. According to prosecutors, the organization made more than $26-million from the deal. The second shipment ran into trouble. A disgruntled former group member had alerted the U.S. Drug Enforcement Agency (DEA) to the group's plans. U.S. authorities and RCMP were watching as the shipment arrived off Alaska with 42 tonnes of marijuana.

Although the DEA and RCMP continued to have O'Dea and his outfit under observation, they were not able to get concrete evidence. In 1989, however, the U.S.

Attorney's office in Seattle started squeezing confessions out of deckhands from O'Dea's boats, gradually working its way up the chain of command. "There was no way," says O'Dea, "they were going to walk away from $100-million worth of drugs."

By the time DEA officers arrived, in April 1990, to search his house, O'Dea was living in a spartan apartment, surviving on fruit juice and natural foods. He had sworn off drugs and alcohol and dedicated his life to good works. The turning point had come on the eve of his 40th birthday, he says, when he suffered a near-fatal drug overdose.

When he reflects on the changes in his life, he believes nothing he did was morally wrong. "I think the laws against marijuana are bad laws. So how do you change bad laws? Through Parliament? No way. Bad laws only get changed if somebody breaks them."

Source: Charlie Gillis, "You're Gonna Love This," *National Post*, December 8, 2001.

arrest.[114] These data support the view that a strong association exists between substance abuse and serious crime.

The drug–crime relationship may thus be explained in three ways: Some may commit crime to support a drug habit; others may become violent while under the influence of drugs or alcohol, which lower inhibitions and increase aggression levels; or the drug–crime connection may be a function of the violent world of drug distributors, who regularly use violence to do business.[115]

In sum, research testing both the criminality of known narcotics users and the narcotics use of known criminals produces a strong association between drug use and crime. Even if the crime rate of drug users were actually half that reported in the research literature, users would be responsible for a significant portion of total criminal activity.

The Cycle of Addiction

The drug–crime connection may also be mediated by the amount of drugs that users require and their ability to

support their habit through conventional means. Occasional users are people just beginning their addiction, who use small amounts of narcotics and whose habit can be supported by income from conventional jobs. In contrast, stabilized users have learned the skills needed to purchase and process larger amounts of drugs. Their addiction enables them to maintain their normal lifestyles, although they may turn to drug dealing to create contacts with drug suppliers. Full-time working people involved in drugs actually commit more crime than those not in the labour force. Employment, then, does little to reduce their criminal activity.[116]

If stable users make a "big score," perhaps through a successful drug deal, they may significantly increase their drug use and become free-wheelers. Their increased narcotics consumption then destabilizes their lifestyle, destroying family and career ties. Addiction is not a unidimensional process. There are various stages in the career of a hard-drug user, and criminal activity may vary according to the user's drug lifestyle. Perhaps crime is a "drug facilitator," enabling addicts to increase their drug consumption according to the success of their criminal careers.

Drugs and the Law

Both Canada and the United States first initiated legal action to curtail the use of some drugs early in the 20th century. Canada criminalized opium before 1910; in the United States, the 1914 Harrison Narcotics Act restricted the importation, manufacture, sale, and dispensing of narcotics. Marijuana was criminalized in Canada in 1923, and in the United States the Marijuana Tax Act of 1937 required registration and payment of a tax by all persons who imported, sold, or manufactured marijuana.

In later years, other federal laws were passed to clarify existing drug statutes and revise penalties. For example, psilocybin, a chemical component of some mushrooms, was criminalized in 1982 in Canada. This is a good example of the social constructionist position, in which the reaction defines the crime. Although no research has demonstrated a link between the consumption of psilocybin and the commission of crime, it is classified as a restricted drug under the Food and Drug Act (FDA). The FDA and the Narcotic Control Act (NCA) give the state wide-sweeping power to control the recreational use of drugs. For example, section 10 of the NCA gives the police the power to enter any place other than a house without a warrant if they believe narcotics are on the premises.

Sometimes police are accused of enforcing drug laws too zealously. In 1971 a Royal Commission was established in Vancouver under the Public Inquiries Act to inquire into the circumstances surrounding a police intervention at a marijuana "smoke-in." The inquiry established that the police officers had acted with unwarranted and excessive force when they charged a peaceful crowd with horses and riot gear.[117]

Alcohol Abuse

While drug control laws have been enacted on both the federal and provincial levels, provincial legislatures have also acted to control alcohol-related crimes. One of the more serious problems is the alarming number of highway fatalities linked to drunk driving. Governments are beginning to create more stringent penalties for drunk driving, although interprovincial variation means that seven provinces have seizure measures (measures enabling the police to seize cars) while three do not. Many provinces also prohibit the driving of cars after a criminal offence.

One caution in interpreting the success of drug control programs such as those designed to control drunk driving is that they are sensitive to levels of enforcement; if the number of roadside checks is reduced, the number of offences will appear to drop, although it might simply reflect the level of policing.

Connections

In Chapter 3 we talked about how crime rates can reflect changes in actual crimes, in levels of reporting by the public, and in reaction to policing activity.

Drug Control Strategies

Substance abuse remains a major social problem. Politicians looking for a campaign issue can take advantage of the public's fear of drug addiction by calling for a "war on drugs."[118] Yet can illegal drug use be eliminated or controlled?

A number of drug control strategies have been tried with varying degrees of success. Some are aimed at deterring drug use by stopping the flow of drugs into the country, apprehending and punishing dealers, and cracking down on street-level drug deals. Others focus on preventing drug use by educating potential users to the dangers of substance abuse ("just say no") and by organizing community groups to work with the at-risk population in their area. Still another approach is to treat known users so they can control their addictions.

Source Control

One approach to drug control is to deter the sale and importation of drugs through the systematic apprehension of large-volume drug dealers. Destroying overseas crops and arresting members of drug cartels in Central and South America, Asia, and the Middle East, where drugs are grown and manufactured, is known as source control. However, drug lords are willing and able to fight back through intimidation, violence, and corruption when necessary. The drug cartels do not hesitate to use violence and assassination to protect their interests. The United States invaded Panama with 20 000 troops in 1989 to stop its leader, General Manuel Noriega, from dealing cocaine, and then tried to suppress evidence that the CIA had been involved in cocaine smuggling itself.

The amount of narcotics produced each year is so vast that even if three-quarters of the opium crop were destroyed, the Canadian market would still require only a small portion of the remainder to sustain its drug trade.[119] Because drug users in North America and Europe are able and willing to pay more for drugs than anyone else in the world, if the supply were reduced, whatever drugs existed would find their way to the country. In Canada almost 8000 kg of marijuana and 72 000 kg of hashish were seized in 1993; 30 percent of this marijuana is produced within Canada.

Adding to control problems is the fact that the drug trade is an important source of revenue for many countries, and destroying the drug trade would undermine the economies of Third World nations. People in Peru, Bolivia, Colombia, Burma, Thailand, and Laos are engaged in cultivating and processing drugs. And even if the government of one nation is willing to cooperate in vigorous drug suppression efforts, suppliers in other nations, eager to cash in on the seller's market, would be encouraged to turn more acreage over to coca or poppy production.

The difficulty of source control is illustrated by the pursuit, capture, and slaying on December 2, 1993, of alleged billionaire drug lord Pablo Escobar. His Medellin drug cartel at one time controlled over 80 percent of the cocaine imported into North America; *Forbes* magazine included him in its annual list of billionaires. While he was in hiding, his drug empire had been replaced by that of his competitors, the Cali cartel. When the Colombian government put pressure on the drug cartels, even more powerful Mexican organizations emerged to take over the drug trade. In 1997 Mexico's government announced that it had arrested General Jesus Guttierrez Rebello, its top antinarcotics enforcer, for his suspected links to drug traffickers.[120]

Eradication efforts in one country may also encourage crop development in another. For example, the Bolivian government's voluntary coca eradication program surpassed its annual target in 1996, kept cultivation levels from significantly expanding, and reduced potential coca leaf production by 12 percent. Unfortunately, this decline was more than offset by a 32 percent increase in both coca cultivation and potential coca leaf production in Colombia, despite an aggressive aerial eradication program by Colombian enforcement authorities. Colombian coca cultivation has nearly tripled since 1987, and source control efforts have convinced the Colombian drug cartels of the importance of controlling all facets of cocaine production at home.[121]

The drug trade remains a dynamic force, with its wealth, power, and organization equal to or even exceeding the resources of many national governments. Hundreds of tonnes of cocaine flow to North America, Western Europe, Latin America, Asia, Africa, and the countries of the former Soviet Union. The lines between cocaine and heroin-consuming countries are blurring. Colombian cocaine syndicates have established distribution centres on virtually every continent, and recently, large Mexican drug organizations have gained control of much of the cocaine traffic formerly dominated by the Colombians.

Synthetic drugs have been gaining in popularity over the last decade. Methamphetamines (MDMA or "ecstasy") may be displacing cocaine as the stimulant of choice on the world drug market. Mexico is one of the principal suppliers, but there are centres of methamphetamine production in Poland, Japan, Burma, and the Philippines.

Law Enforcement Strategies

Law enforcement efforts have also been directed at intercepting drug supplies as they enter the country. Border patrols and military personnel using sophisticated hardware have been involved in massive interdiction efforts. Yet Canada's borders are so vast and unprotected that meaningful interdiction is impossible. Furthermore, home-grown marijuana and laboratory-made drugs, such as "ice," LSD, and PCP, could become the drugs of choice. Even now, their easy availability and relatively low cost are increasing their popularity among the at-risk population.

Law enforcement agencies have tried to direct efforts at large-scale drug rings. However, the long-term consequence has been to decentralize drug dealing and encourage younger independent dealers to become major suppliers. Since it is difficult to infiltrate and prosecute drug-dealing gangs, some nontraditional groups have broken into the drug trade. For example, the Hells Angels motorcycle club has become one of the primary distributors of cocaine and amphetamines.[122] Police can also target, intimidate, and arrest street-level dealers and users in an effort to make drug use so much of a hassle that consumption is cut back and the crime rate reduced. Approaches that have been tried include "reverse stings" in which undercover agents pose as dealers to arrest users who approach them for a buy. Police have attacked fortified crack houses with heavy equipment to breach their defences. Special police task forces have used undercover operations and drug sweeps to discourage both dealers and users.[123]

Police have also used "asset forfeiture" laws to seize the assets of known dealers. Under Section 462.37 of the Criminal Code, property can be seized if it is believed to have been derived from the proceeds of crime. Because the wealth generated from drug sales can be so immense, it is necessary to make it seem legitimate. Buying real estate, investing in legitimate businesses, and transferring money internationally are all preferred methods of hiding illegally gained wealth. Such methods of concealing the proceeds of crime, called "money laundering," require sophisticated expertise.

While some street-level enforcement efforts have had success, others are considered failures. Drug sweeps have clogged courts and correctional facilities with petty offenders while proving a costly drain on police resources. There are also suspicions that a displacement effect occurs: Stepped-up efforts to curb drug dealing in one area or city simply encourage dealers to seek out friendlier "business" territory.[124] However, once in a while, law enforcement strategies do succeed: In the summer of 1998 the RCMP busted the Cuntrera-Caruana crime empire in Montreal. Described by some as the largest, most powerful drug-smuggling and money-laundering organization in the world, the Cuntrera-Caruanas acted as middlemen between the Colombians and the Mafia.[125]

Community Strategies

Another type of drug control effort relies on the involvement of local community groups to lead the fight against drugs.

Citizen-sponsored programs attempt to restore a sense of community in drug-infested areas, to reduce fear, and to promote conventional norms and values.[126] These efforts can be classified into one of four distinct categories.[127] The first involves law enforcement efforts, which may include block watches, cooperative police–community efforts, and citizen patrols. Some of these citizen groups are nonconfrontational, willing to simply observe or photograph dealers, take down their licence plate number, then notify police. On occasion, telephone hotlines have been set up to take anonymous tips on drug activity. Other groups engage in confrontational tactics that may even include citizens' arrests. Some of these community-based efforts are home-grown, while others attract outside organizations, such as the Guardian Angels. Area residents have gone so far as contracting with private security firms to conduct neighbourhood patrols.

Another tactic is to use the civil justice system to harass offenders. Landlords have been sued for owning properties that house drug dealers; neighbourhood groups have formed and scrutinized drug houses for building code violations. Information acquired from these various sources is turned over to local authorities, such as police and housing agencies, for more formal action.

In community-based treatment efforts citizen volunteers participate in self-help support programs, such as Narcotics Anonymous or Cocaine Anonymous. Other programs provide youths with martial arts training, dances, and social events as an alternative to the drug life. Healing centres and treatment facilities, often organized around a theme such as Native healing, also operate to counter the effects of drug abuse.

Community drug prevention efforts are designed to enhance the quality of life, improve interpersonal relationships, and upgrade the neighbourhood's physical environment. Activities might include the creation of drug-free school zones, demonstrations and marches to publicize the drug problem, and better police protection or tougher laws passed. Residents have cleaned up streets, fixed broken street lights, and planted gardens in empty lots to broadcast the message that they have local pride and do not want drug dealers in their neighbourhood.

Community crime-prevention efforts seem appealing, but there is little conclusive evidence that they are an effective drug control strategy. Most residents do not participate in programs, and they tend to work best in stable, middle-income areas.[128] While these findings are discouraging, some studies have also found the opposite: that deteriorated areas can sustain successful antidrug programs.[129]

Drug Testing Programs

Drug testing of private employees, government workers, and criminal offenders is believed to prevent people from involvement in substance abuse. Employees are tested to enhance on-the-job safety and productivity. In some industries, such as mining and transportation, drug testing is considered essential because abuse can pose a threat to the public. Business leaders have been enlisted in the fight against drugs. Mandatory drug-testing programs in government and industry are common.

Drug testing is not without legal controversy, however. In 1991 the Canadian Civil Liberties Association filed a complaint with the Canadian Human Rights Commission over the Toronto-Dominion Bank's drug-testing policy. New bank employees were required to submit to a drug test within 48 hours of being offered a job; refusal to do so would be grounds for dismissal. Despite blasting the bank's policy as intrusive and an invasion of privacy, a federal human rights tribunal ruled in 1994 that the practice was not discriminatory. In 1998, however, the Canadian Federal Court of Appeal ruled that the Toronto-Dominion Bank's policy of testing new employees for drugs constituted a violation under the Human Rights Act. Key to the Federal Court of Appeal's decision in 1998 was that drug addiction is a disease and thus protected under the Human Rights Act, and that there was no demonstrable evidence that finding traces of drugs in a person's system meant their performance on the job would be affected.[130]

In 1995 it was reported that doctors and nurses working in neonatal units of Toronto hospitals were surreptitiously testing infants' hair for traces of cocaine. Acting on suspicion of mothers' drug use, staff sent samples to the Hospital for Sick Children for analysis, and positive results were sent to the Children's Aid Society. The director of the clinical pharmacology and toxicology program at the Hospital for Sick Children was quoted as saying that physicians had a right to know such information. The co-chairperson of the reproductive technology committee of the National Action Committee on the Status of Women criticized the practice as an invasion of the mother's privacy.[131]

Legalization

Despite the massive effort to control drugs through prevention, deterrence, education, and treatment strategies, the fight against substance abuse has not proved successful. It is difficult to get people out of the drug culture because of the enormous profits involved in the drug trade: 500 kg of coca leaves worth $4000 to a grower yields about 8 kg of street cocaine valued at about $300 000.

Considering these problems, some commentators have called for the legalization or decriminalization of restricted drugs. Legalization is warranted, according to Ethan Nadelmann, because the use of mood-altering substances is customary in almost all human societies; people have always wanted, and will find ways of obtaining, psychoactive drugs.[132] Banning drugs serves to create networks of manufacturers and distributors, many of whom use violence as part of their standard operating procedures. While some may charge that drug use is immoral, Nadelmann questions whether it is really any worse than the unrestricted use of alcohol and cigarettes, both of which are addicting and unhealthful. Far more people die each year because they abuse these legal substances than are killed in drug wars or from abusing illegal substances.

Prohibition failed to stop the flow of alcohol in the 1920s while at the same time increasing the power of organized crime. When drugs were legal and freely available earlier in this century, the proportion of people using drugs was not much greater than today; most users managed to lead normal lives, probably because of the legal status of their drug use.[133]

If drugs were legalized, the argument goes, price and distribution could be controlled by the government. This would reduce addicts' cash requirements, thus crime rates would go down, as users would no longer need the same cash flow to support their habit. Drug-related deaths would decline because government control would reduce needle sharing and the spread of AIDS, and drugs would not be cut with a variety of other substances. Legalization would also destroy the drug-importing cartels and gangs. Since drugs would be bought and sold openly, the government would reap a tax windfall from taxes on the sale of drugs and the income taxes paid by drug dealers on profits that have been part of the hidden economy. Of course, drug distribution would be regulated, like alcohol, keeping it out of the hands of adolescents, public servants such as police and airline pilots, and known felons. Those who favour legalization point to the Netherlands as a country that has legalized drugs and remains relatively crime-free.[134]

However, if drugs were legalized and freely available, drug users might significantly increase their daily intake. In countries such as Iran and Thailand, where drugs are cheap and readily available, the rate of narcotics use is quite high. Historically, the availability of cheap narcotics has preceded drug use epidemics, as was the case when British and American merchants sold opium in 19th-century China.[135]

Efforts to control legal use would backfire. If juveniles, criminals, and members of other at-risk groups were forbidden to buy drugs, would not that create an underground market almost as vast as the current one? If the government tried to raise money by taxing legal drugs, as it now does for liquor and cigarettes, might that not encourage drug smuggling to avoid tax payments?

What effect would a policy of partial decriminalization (for example, legalizing small amounts of marijuana) have on drug use rates? Would a get-tough policy help "widen the net" of the justice system and actually deepen some youths' involvement in substance abuse? Can society provide alternatives to drugs that will reduce teenage drug dependency?[136]

The various efforts at drug control are summarized in Figure 14.3.

Figure 14.3 **Strategies for controlling drugs**

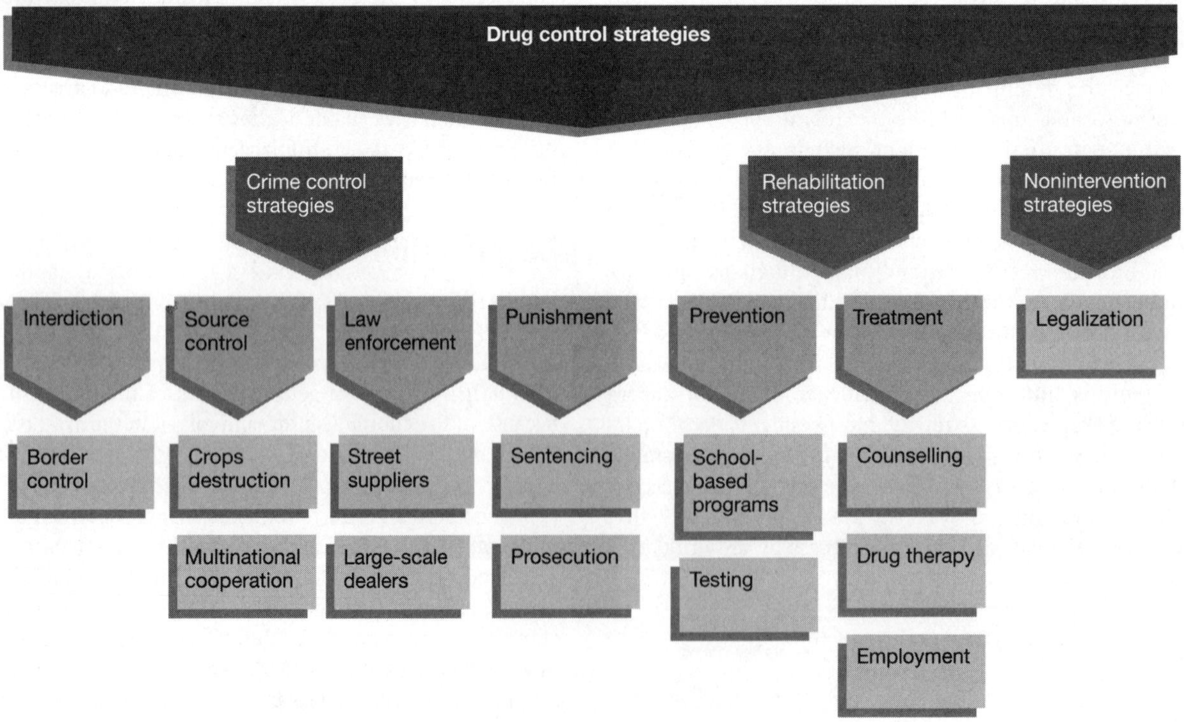

SOURCE: As used in Gerald L. Gail, *The Canadian Legal System*, 3rd ed. (Toronto: Carswell, 1990).

Emerging Issues

A chapter on the legislation of morality would not be complete without looking at issues that have become the focus of debate in contemporary society. Euthanasia and gambling are two examples of such issues.

Euthanasia

Euthanasia tests the moral resolve of a society interested in protecting human rights while also respecting human dignity. There are two different types of euthanasia: passive and active; the difference is whether a patient is capable of making a decision to end his or her life. In Quebec in 1991, Nancy B petitioned the court to allow her doctor and the hospital to disconnect her life-support equipment. The judge said he had to respect the patient's right to choose to discontinue treatment and ruled that doing so would not make the physician guilty of euthanasia.[137] However, when Sue Rodriguez petitioned the Supreme Court of Canada in 1993 for the right to assisted suicide, her request was denied. In 1997 a Halifax doctor named Nancy Morrison was charged with first-degree murder when she gave a patient suffering from terminal cancer an injection to ease his pain. Because this charge requires proof of premeditation, it was subsequently thrown out of court for lack of evidence.

Gambling

Gambling is a good example of decriminalization, in which the law gradually changes to allow a behaviour that was prohibited in the past. A hundred years ago, gambling was illegal in Canada. In 1900 an exemption was granted for religious and charity bazaars to hold small raffles under $50. This charitable exemption opened the door for gambling in Canada. In 1910 an amendment was passed allowing parimutuel betting at fairs in order to encourage horse breeding, and in 1952 games of chance were allowed at agricultural fairs to promote the rural economy.

Lotteries were legalized in 1969, and a national lottery helped finance the 1976 Olympic games in Montreal. In 1979 the federal government withdrew from lottery sales, and by 1985 exclusive control over lotteries had passed to the provinces. Lotteries are regulated by provincial Crown monopolies, such as the Atlantic Lottery Commission, and revenues flow into the provincial organizations where they are to be used for the benefit of all citizens. In 1989, the Nova Scotia Lottery Commission reported over $26 million in revenue from the Atlantic Lottery Commission.

Casinos came on the scene in the late 1980s and early 1990s. By 1995, Quebec, Ontario, and Manitoba had large casinos, while Alberta, British Columbia, Nova Scotia, and Saskatchewan allowed video lottery terminals. Provincial governments can realize huge profits from legalized gambling: The Windsor casino, for example, was expected to generate over $200 million in profits in its first year, while Montreal's casino made over $70 million in its first six months.[138]

Canadians spend hundreds of dollars per year per capita on gambling. Since this is an average figure, the actual amount a gambler spends every year may be far higher. People also tend to underreport the amount they spend on gambling because of the perceived stigma attached to it. In all provinces, people spend the most on lotteries, followed by bingo, horseracing, and other forms of gaming.

In 1994, Statistics Canada estimated that gambling accounted for about 4 percent of total provincial revenue, millions more than gathered through corporate taxes.[139]

Lotteries are regulated under Section 207 of the Criminal Code, which gives provinces the lawful right to "manage a lottery scheme," as shown in Exhibit 14.2. The Criminal Code also prohibits keeping a common gaming or betting house (Section 201), betting or bookmaking (Section 202), placing bets on behalf of others (Section 203), promoting lotteries (Section 206), and cheating at play (Section 209), among others. A new concern is whether the law can adapt to handle the increasing interest in gambling on the Internet, where overhead costs are low and the potential for profits is high.

There is a lot of controversy over the link between gambling and crime. When the Nova Scotia government announced that it was going to open a casino in Halifax, there was widespread opposition on the part of the police and citizens' and church groups. Three government commissions advised against it, and 40 000 people signed petitions in opposition. Police predicted an increase in prostitution, drug abuse, organized crime, and other spinoff crimes from gambling.[140] Such opposition is not unusual: for example, in Alberta, a series of plebiscites were held in 1998 on whether communities could prohibit VLTs; in British Columbia, citizens rejected a casino in 1994.

Research has shown that the social costs of gambling are high. Problem gamblers tend to have a high involvement in other drug and alcohol abuse, and to have higher rates of suicide, absenteeism from work, lower productivity, and higher rates of job loss due to gambling. Problem and pathological gamblers tend to turn to crime to support their habits, such as stealing from work and from friends and family. While men are more likely to be problem gamblers than women, women gamblers are more likely to be young, single, and unemployed and to have less than a high school education. Women are "escape" gamblers, and men are "excitement" gamblers.

The amount spent on lottery tickets per household varies by social class. In 1996, 52 percent of households with incomes under $20 000 bought lottery tickets compared with 77 percent of those with incomes over $60 000. However, low-income households spent

Exhibit 14.2	Quick Code: Permitted Lotteries

207. (1) Notwithstanding any of the provisions of this Part relating to gaming and betting, it is lawful

(a) for the government of a province, either alone or in conjunction with the government of another province, to conduct and manage a lottery scheme in that province, or in that and the other province, in accordance with any law enacted by the legislature of that province;

(b) for a charitable or religious organization, pursuant to a licence issued by the Lieutenant Governor in Council of a province or by such other person or authority in the province as may be specified by the Lieutenant Governor in Council thereof, to conduct and manage a lottery scheme in that province if the proceeds from the lottery scheme are used for a charitable or religious object or purpose;

(c) for the board of a fair or of an exhibition, or an operator of a concession leased by that board, to conduct and manage a lottery scheme in a province where the Lieutenant Governor in Council of the province or such other person or authority in the province as may be specified by the Lieutenant Governor in Council thereof has

(i) designated that fair or exhibition as a fair or exhibition where a lottery scheme may be conducted and managed, and

(ii) issued a licence for the conduct and management of a lottery scheme to that board or operator;

(d) for any person, pursuant to a licence issued by the Lieutenant Governor in Council of a province or by such other person or authority in the province as may be specified by the Lieutenant Governor in Council thereof, to conduct and manage a lottery scheme at a public place of amusement in that province if

(i) the amount or value of each prize awarded does not exceed five hundred dollars, and

(ii) the money or other valuable consideration paid to secure a chance to win a prize does not exceed two dollars....

Source: Criminal Code of Canada

1.2 percent of their income on lotteries, compared with 0.3 percent for the highest-income category. A survey of the Montreal casino found that the typical visitor was from Montreal (85 percent), had a high-school education (47 percent), and had a household income of under $40 000 (48 percent).

Summary

Public order crimes are acts considered illegal because they conflict with social policy, accepted moral rules, and public opinion. There is usually great debate over public order crimes. Some charge that they are not really crimes at all and that it is foolish to legislate morality. Others view such morally tinged acts as prostitution, gambling, and drug abuse as harmful and therefore subject to public control.

Prostitution is a sex-related public order crime that has been practised for thousands of years. There are several kinds of prostitutes, including streetwalkers, B-girls, and call girls. Studies indicate that most prostitutes come from poor, troubled families and have abusive parents. However, there is little evidence that prostitutes are emotionally disturbed, addicted to drugs, or sexually abnormal. Although prostitution is legal, society and its law enforcement agents make it virtually impossible to practise.

Pornography involves the sale of sexually explicit material intended to sexually excite paying customers. The depiction of sex and nudity is not illegal, but it does violate the law when it is judged obscene. Obscenity is a legal term that today is defined as material offensive to community standards. Thus, each local jurisdiction must decide what pornographic material is obscene. A growing problem is the exploitation of children in obscene materials. There is no hard evidence that pornography is related to crime or aggression, but data suggest that sexual material with a violent theme is related to sexual violence by those who view it.

Substance abuse is another type of public order crime. Debate continues over the legalization of drugs, usually centring on such nonaddicting drugs as marijuana. However, the federal government outlaws a wide variety of drugs, including narcotics, amphetamines, barbiturates, cocaine, hallucinogens, and marijuana. One of the main reasons for the continued ban on drugs is their relationship to crime. Numerous studies have found that drug addicts commit enormous amounts of property crime.

Alcohol is another commonly abused substance. Although it is legal to possess, it, too, has been linked to crime. Drunk driving and deaths caused by drunk drivers are growing national problems. Many strategies are used to control substance abuse, ranging from source control to treatment. So far, no single method seems effective. While legalization is debated, the facts that so many people already take drugs and that drug abuse is associated with crime make legalization unlikely in the near future.

Gambling is one of the more interesting "victimless crimes" discussed in this chapter because it illustrates the process of decriminalization. As governments come to depend more and more on income from gaming revenues, it will become an expanding province-run business.

| Figure 14.4 | "Lottery Play is Tied to Household Income" |

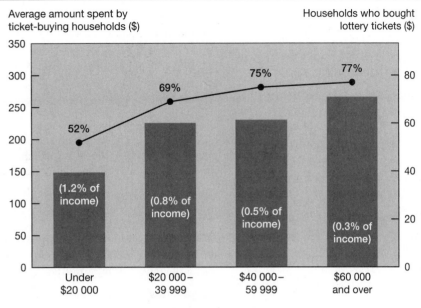

Thinking Like a Criminologist

According to data from a 1997 national school survey, high school boys who have been physically or sexually abused are at least twice as likely as nonabused boys to drink, smoke, or use drugs. The survey was an in-class questionnaire completed by 3162 boys in grades 5 to 12 at a nationally representative sample of 265 public, private, and parochial schools from December 1996 to June 1997. The survey included roughly equal samples of adolescent boys in grades 5 to 8 and 9 to 12. All responses were weighted to reflect grade, region, race and ethnicity, and gender.

Thirteen percent of boys in grades 9 to 12 said that they had been physically or sexually abused. Thirty percent of abused boys reported that they drank frequently, and 34 percent reported that they had used drugs in the past month, compared to 16 percent and 15 percent, respectively, of nonabused boys. Abused boys were also nearly three times more likely to smoke frequently (27 percent versus 10 percent).

As a criminologist, what would be your interpretation of these data? What is the association between child abuse and substance abuse?

Key Terms

brothels

call girls

claimsmakers

crack cocaine

decriminalization

designer drugs

madams

massage parlours

moral crusades

moral entrepreneurs

obscenity

paraphilia

pornography

prostitution

public order crimes

temperance movement

victimless crimes

vigilante

 See the book-specific website at www.siegelcriminology2e.nelson.com for additional chapter links, discussions, and quizzes.

GLOSSARY

absolute deterrent   A legal control measure designed to totally eliminate a particular criminal act.

access control   A crime prevention technique that stresses target hardening through security measures, such as alarm systems, that make it more difficult for criminals to attack a target.

accountability system   A way of dealing with corruption by making superiors responsible for the behaviour of their subordinates.

acquaintance-related crime   Similar to intimate violence, in some crimes there is a prior relationship between the offender and the victim; date rape is such a crime.

acquittal   Release or discharge, especially by verdict of a jury.

active precipitation   The view that the source of many criminal incidents is the aggressive or provocative behaviour of victims.

actual offences   This is the number of crimes reported to the police, minus those the police believe are unfounded.

actus reus   An illegal act. The *actus reus* can be an affirmative act, such as taking money or shooting someone, or a failure to act, such as failing to take proper precautions while driving a car.

addict   A person with an overpowering physical and psychological need to continue taking a particular substance or drug by any means possible.

addiction-prone personality   The view that the cause of substance abuse can be traced to a personality with a compulsion for mood-altering drugs.

adjudication   The determination of guilt or innocence; a judgment concerning criminal charges. Most offenders plead guilty as charged. The remainder are adjudicated by a judge and a jury or by a judge alone, and others are dismissed.

adolescent-limited   In the life-course view of crime, this refers to the fact that the prevalence and frequency of antisocial behaviour for most offenders peak in adolescence and then diminish.

adversary system   The procedure used to determine truth in the adjudication of guilt or innocence in which the defence (advocate for the accused) is pitted against the prosecution (advocate for the state), with the judge acting as arbiter of the legal rules. Under the adversary system, the burden is on the state to prove the charges beyond a reasonable doubt. This system of having the two parties publicly debate has proved to be the most effective method of achieving the truth regarding a set of circumstances. (Under the accusatory, or inquisitorial, system, which is used in continental Europe, the charge is evidence of guilt that the accused must disprove, and the judge takes an active part in the proceedings.)

affidavit   A written statement of fact, signed and sworn to before a person having authority to administer an oath.

age of onset   Age at which youths begin their delinquent careers. Early onset of delinquency is believed to be linked with chronic offending patterns.

aging out   The process by which individuals reduce the frequency of their offending behaviour as they age. It is also known as spontaneous remission, because people are believed to spontaneously reduce the rate of their criminal behaviour as they mature. Aging out is thought to occur among all groups of offenders.

aggravating factor   Some circumstances make the crime seem more serious in the eyes of others; in hate crime, for example, racism makes an assault a more serious offence and can result in a harsher sentence.

aggregate data   Data collected on groups of people rather than individuals. A good example of aggregate data is the Uniform Crime Reports; although the number of criminal incidents that occur in a given area can be counted, little data are provided on the offenders who commit the crimes or the circumstances in which they occurred. (Self-report surveys are usually considered individual-level data, since subjects' responses can be examined on a case-by-case basis.)

aggressive preventive patrol   A patrol technique designed to suppress crime before it occurs.

alien conspiracy theory   The view that organized crime was imported from Europe and that crime cartels have a policy of restricting their membership to people of their own ethnic background.

alienation   A mental condition marked by normlessness and role confusion, created by a lack of control over one's situation. A part of both strain theory and Marxist criminology.

alternative sanctions   The group of punishments falling between probation and prison; "probation plus." Community-based sanctions, including house arrest and intensive supervision, serve as alternatives to incarceration.

American Dream   The stereotype that anyone can make it through hard work and perseverance and that social factors are irrelevant to material success. Canadians call it this, too.

androgens   Male sex hormones, linked to criminality.

anaesthetics   Drugs used as nervous system depressants. Local anaesthetics block nervous system transmissions; general anaesthetics act on the brain to produce a generalized loss of sensation, stupor, or unconsciousness.

anger rape   A rape motivated by the rapist's desire to release pent-up anger and rage.

anomie   A condition produced by normlessness. Because of rapidly shifting moral values, the individual has few guides to what is socially acceptable. According to Merton, anomie is a condition that occurs when personal goals cannot be achieved by available means.

antisocial personality   Synonymous with psychopath, the antisocial personality is characterized by a lack of normal responses to life situations, the inability to learn from punishment, and violent reactions to nonthreatening events.

appeal   A review of lower-court proceedings by a higher court. Appellate courts do not retry the case under review. Rather, the transcript of the lower-court case is read by the appellate judges, who determine the legality of lower-court proceedings. When appellate courts reverse lower-court judgments, it is usually because of "prejudicial error" (deprivation of rights), and the case is remanded for retrial.

appellate courts   Courts that reconsider a case that has already been tried to determine whether the measures used complied with accepted rules of criminal procedure and were in line with the Constitution.

arbitrage   The practice of buying large blocks of stock in companies that are believed to be the target of corporate buyouts or takeovers.

argot   A unique language used in subcultures such as prison culture.

arousal theory   A view of crime suggesting that people who have a high arousal level seek powerful stimuli in their environment to maintain an optimal level of arousal. These stimuli are often associated with violence and aggression. Sociopaths may need greater than average stimulation to bring them up to comfortable levels of living; this need explains their criminal tendencies.

arraignment   The step in the criminal justice process at which the accused are read the charges against them, asked how they plead, and advised of their rights. Possible pleas are guilty, not guilty, *nolo contendere*, and not guilty by reason of insanity.

arrest   The taking of a person into the custody of the law, the legal purpose of which is to restrain the accused until he or she can be held accountable for the offence at court proceedings. The legal requirement for an arrest is probable cause. Arrests for investigation, suspicion, or harassment are improper and of doubtful legality. The

police have the responsibility to use only the reasonable physical force necessary to make an arrest. The summons has been used as a substitute for arrest.

arrest warrant   A written court order by a magistrate authorizing and directing that an individual be taken into custody to answer criminal charges.

arson   The intentional or negligent burning of a home, structure, or vehicle for criminal purposes such as profit, revenge, insurance fraud, or crime concealment; different than the traditional stereotype of the pyromaniac.

Aryan Brotherhood   A white supremacist subculture.

assembly-line justice   The view that the justice process resembles an endless production line that handles most cases in a routine and perfunctory fashion.

assisted suicide   The practice of seeking help in committing suicide; not legal in Canada.

at-risk   In Oscar Lewis's work, Lewis argued that the lifestyle of slum areas produces a "culture of poverty" passed from one generation to the next, marked by apathy, cynicism, helplessness, and mistrust of social institutions, making each generation more prone to criminality.

atavistic traits   According to Lombroso, the physical characteristics of born criminals that indicate they are throwbacks to animals or primitive people.

attention deficit/hyperactivity disorder (AD/HD) A condition in which a child shows a developmentally inappropriate lack of attention, impulsivity, and hyperactivity.

attorney general   The senior federal prosecutor and cabinet member who heads the Justice Department.

attrition   This refers to the "wearing away" of or decrease in cases as they make their way through the criminal justice system; the number of cases investigated by the police that ever result in convictions is a small percentage of the total.

authoritarian   A personality type that revolves around blind obedience to authority.

authority conflict pathway   The path to a criminal career that begins with early stubborn behaviour and defiance of parents.

bail   The monetary amount for or condition of pretrial release, normally set by a judge at the initial appearance. The purpose of bail is to ensure the return of the accused at subsequent proceedings. If the accused is unable to make bail, he or she is detained in jail. The prosecutor must show cause for denying bail.

bail bonding   The business of providing bail to needy offenders, usually at an exorbitant rate of interest.

base penalty The model sentence, which can be enhanced or diminished to reflect aggravating or mitigating circumstances.

behaviour modelling The belief that in modern society, aggressive acts are usually modelled after three principal sources: family members, environmental experiences, and the mass media.

behaviour theory The approach that holds the view that human actions are developed through a variety of learning experiences over the course of a lifetime.

behaviourism The branch of psychology concerned with the study of observable behaviour rather than unconscious motives. It focuses on the relationship between particular stimuli and people's responses to them.

beyond a reasonable doubt Degree of proof required for conviction of a defendant in criminal and juvenile delinquency proceedings. It is less than absolute certainty but more than high probability. If there is doubt based on reason, the accused is entitled to the benefit of that doubt by acquittal.

blameworthy The amount of culpability or guilt a person maintains for participating in a particular criminal offence.

blue curtain According to William Westly, the secretive, insulated police culture that isolates the officer from the rest of society.

booking The administrative record of an arrest listing the offender's name, address, physical description, date of birth, and employer; the time of arrest; the offence; and the name of arresting officer. Photographing and fingerprinting of the offender are also part of booking.

boosters A professional shoplifter; see *heel*.

boot camp A short-term militaristic correctional facility in which inmates undergo intensive physical conditioning and discipline.

bot Under Anglo-Saxon law, the restitution paid for killing someone in an open fight.

bourgeoisie In Marxist theory, the owners of the means of production; the capitalist ruling class.

break and enter Breaking into a house to commit theft.

broken windows The term used to describe the role of the police as maintainers of community order and safety.

brothel A house of prostitution, typically run by a madam who sets prices and handles "business" arrangements.

brutalization effect The belief that capital punishment creates an atmosphere of brutality that enhances rather than deters the level of violence in society. The death

penalty reinforces the view that violence is an appropriate response to provocation.

brutalization process According to Athens, the first stage in a violent career during which parents victimize children, causing them to develop a belligerent, angry demeanour.

burden of proof Duty of proving disputed facts on the trial of a case. The duty commonly lies on the person who asserts the affirmative of an issue and is sometimes said to shift when sufficient evidence is furnished to raise a presumption that what is alleged is true.

burglary Breaking into and entering a home or structure for the purposes of committing a felony.

call girls Prostitutes who make dates via the phone and then service customers in hotel rooms or apartments. Call girls typically have a steady clientele that is made up of repeat customers.

Canadian Centre for Justice Statistics The branch of Statistics Canada that collects, analyzes, and publishes crime statistics. It also publishes *Juristat*.

Canadian Urban Victimization Survey (CUVS) The first victimization survey in Canada, conducted in 1982. Among its findings was that crime has a very low report rate to the police.

capable guardians In routine activities theory, the presence of police, homeowners, neighbours, friends, and relatives can have a deterrent effect on crime; these are the "capable guardians."

capital punishment The use of the death penalty to punish transgressors, not used in Canada.

career criminal A person whose criminality is like a career and who repeatedly violates the law. They devote many aspects of their life to criminality and commit a large portion of the total amount of crime in a community.

carjacking A new form of crime, where a car is stolen while the person is driving it; it has a low likelihood of occurring but a high news value.

Carriers case The 15th-century case that defined the law of theft and reformulated the concept of taking the possessions of another.

certiorari Literally, "to be informed of, to be made certain in regard to."

challenge for cause Removing a juror because he or she is biased, has prior knowledge about a case, or otherwise is unable to render a fair and impartial judgment in a case.

chancery court A court created in 15th-century England to oversee the lives of high-born minors who were orphaned or otherwise could not care for themselves.

charge   In a criminal case, the specific crime the defendant is accused of committing.

Chicago School   A type of sociological research begun in the early 20th century by Robert Ezra Park, Ernest W. Burgess, Louis Wirth, and their colleagues in the Sociology Department at the University of Chicago. These sociologists pioneered research on the social ecology of the city and the study of urban crime. The Canadian counterpart was called the McGill School, under the direction of Charles Dawson, a former Baptist minister.

child abuse   Any physical, emotional, or sexual trauma to a child for which no reasonable explanation, such as an accident, can be found. Child abuse can also be a function of neglecting to give proper care and attention to a young child.

chivalry hypothesis   The idea that low female crime and delinquency rates are a reflection of the leniency with which police treat female offenders.

choice theory   The school of thought holding that people will engage in delinquent and criminal behaviour after weighing the consequences and benefits of their actions. Delinquent behaviour is a rational choice made by a motivated offender who perceives that the chances of gain outweigh any perceived punishment or loss.

chronic offender   According to Wolfgang, the small percentage of delinquent offenders who are arrested five or more times before they are 18, and who stand a good chance of becoming adult criminals; such offenders are responsible for more than half of all serious crimes.

chronicity   State of being a chronic recidivist.

churning   A white-collar crime in which a stockbroker makes repeated trades to fraudulently increase his or her commissions.

civil law   All law that is not criminal, including torts (personal wrongs), contract, property, maritime, and commercial law.

claimsmakers   An important concept in media analysis, where it is assumed that there are people located to significantly influence the social construction of crime images.

classical criminology   The theoretical perspective suggesting that (1) people have free will to choose criminal or conventional behaviours; (2) people choose to commit crime for reasons of greed or personal need; and (3) crime can be controlled only by the fear of criminal sanctions.

classification   The procedure in which prisoners are categorized on the basis of their personal characteristics and criminal history and then assigned to an appropriate institution.

clearance rate   This is the percentage of crimes reported to the police, which are determined to be founded, which are then solved or cleared away by the police.

cliques   In the study of peer relations, small groups of friends who share activities and confidences; see *crowds*.

cocaine   The most powerful natural stimulant, derived from the coca leaf. Its use produces euphoria, laughter, restlessness, and excitement. Overdoses can cause delirium, increased reflexes, violent manic behaviour, and possible respiratory failure.

Code of Hammurabi   The first written criminal code developed in Babylonia about 2000 BC.

cognitive school   A theory that studies the perception of reality and of the mental processes required to understand the world we live in.

cohort   A sample of subjects whose behaviour is followed over a period of time.

Commission on Systemic Racism in the Ontario Criminal Justice System   Reporting in 1995, this commission studied complaints that racism was a pervasive problem in the way police and courts worked.

commitment to conformity   In control theory, this is a logical reason to obey the rules of society.

common law   Early English law, developed by judges, that incorporated Anglo-Saxon tribal custom, feudal rules and practices, and the everyday rules of behaviour of local villages. Common law became the standardized law of the land in England and eventually formed the basis of the criminal law in Canada and the United States.

community notification laws   Recent legislative efforts that require convicted sex offenders to register with local police when they move into an area or neighbourhood.

community policing   A police strategy that emphasizes fear reduction, community organization, and order maintenance rather than crime fighting.

community service restitution   An alternative sanction that requires an offender to work in the community at such tasks as cleaning public parks or helping handicapped children in lieu of incarceration.

community treatment   The actions of correctional agencies that attempt to maintain the convicted offender in the community, instead of a secure facility; includes probation, parole, and residential programs.

compensation   Financial aid awarded to the victims of crime to repay them for their loss and injuries.

complaint   A sworn allegation made in writing to a court or judge that an individual is guilty of some designated (complained of) offence. This is often the first legal document filed regarding a criminal offence. The complaint can be taken out by the victim, the police officer, the district attorney, or another interested party. Although the complaint charges an offence, an indictment or information may be the formal charging document.

compliance   A white-collar enforcement strategy that encourages law-abiding behaviour through both the threat of economic sanctions and the promise of rewards for conformity.

concentration effect   This occurs when working- and middle-class families flee inner-city poverty areas, taking with them their financial and institutional resources and support elements, leaving the most disadvantaged population consolidated in urban ghettos.

concurrent sentences   Literally, running sentences together. Someone who is convicted of two or more charges must be sentenced on each charge. If the sentences are concurrent, they begin the same day and are completed after the longest term has been served.

confidence games   A form of fraud.

conflict-linked crime   An example of this type of crime would be murder, which is often an expressive crime of passion involving people who know each other and who may be under the influence of drugs or suffering from the burdens of poverty. These factors may either prevent or inhibit rational evaluation of the long-term consequences of an immediate violent act.

conduct norms   Behaviours expected of social group members. If group norms conflict with those of the general culture, members of the group may find themselves described as outcasts or criminals.

conflict theory   An approach that holds the view that human behaviour is shaped by socioeconomic inequality and that those who maintain social power will use it to further their own needs.

conjugal visit   A prison program that allows inmates to receive private visits from their spouses for the purpose of maintaining normal interpersonal relationships.

consecutive sentences   Prison sentences for two or more criminal acts that are served one after the other.

consensus view of crime   The belief that the majority of citizens in a society share common ideals and work toward a common good and that crimes are acts that are outlawed because they conflict with the rules of the majority and are harmful to society.

consent   The lack of which is a legal element in the charge of sexual assault; cannot be extinguished by drunkenness.

consent decree   Decree entered by consent of the parties. Not properly judicial sentence but in the nature of a solemn contract or agreement of the parties that the decree is a just determination of their rights based on the real facts of the case, if such facts are proved.

constable   The peacekeeper in early English towns, who organized citizens to protect the territory and conduct the night watch.

constructive intent   The finding of criminal liability for an unintentional act that is the result of negligence or recklessness.

constructive possession   In the crime of larceny, willingly giving up temporary physical possession of property but retaining legal ownership.

containments   According to Reckless, internal and external factors and conditions that help insulate youths from delinquency-promoting situations. Most important of the internal containments is a strong self-concept, while external containments include positive support from parents and teachers.

continuance   A judicial order to continue a case without a finding, to gather more information or allow the defendant to begin a community-based treatment program.

continuity of crime   The view that crime begins early in life and continues throughout the life course. Thus, the best predictor of future criminality is past criminality.

contract system (attorney)   Providing counsel to indigent (poor) offenders by having attorneys under contract to handle all (or some) legal aid cases.

contract system (convict)   The system used earlier in the last century in which inmates were leased out to private industry to work.

control theory   An approach that looks at the ability of society and its institutions to control, manage, restrain, or direct human behaviour, sometimes called social control theory.

convict subculture   The separate culture in the prison that has its own set of rewards and behaviours. The traditional culture is now being replaced by a violent gang culture.

conviction   A judgment of guilt; a verdict by a jury, a plea by a defendant, or a judgment by a court that the accused is guilty as charged.

co-offending   Committing criminal acts in groups. It is believed that a significant number of delinquent and criminal acts involve more than one offender.

corner boy   According to Cohen, a role in the lower-class culture in which young men remain in their birth neighbourhood, acquire families and menial jobs, and adjust to the demands of their environment.

corporal punishment   The use of physical chastisement, such as whipping or electroshock, to punish criminals.

corporate crime   White-collar crime involving a legal violation by a corporate entity, such as price fixing, restraint of trade, or hazardous waste dumping. It can also include large corporations and their efforts to control the marketplace and earn huge profits through unlawful bidding, unfair advertising, monopolistic practices, or other illegal means.

corpus delicti   The body of crime, made up of the *actus reus* and *mens rea*.

corrections   The agencies of justice that take custody of offenders after their conviction and are entrusted with their treatment and control.

corroboration   Before 1983 it was required that someone alleging sexual assault have someone corroborate, or back up, their claim; no longer required.

court administrator   The individual who controls the operations of the courts system in a particular jurisdiction; he or she may be in charge of scheduling, juries, judicial assignment, and so on.

court-leet   During the Middle Ages, the local hundred or manor court that dealt with most secular violations.

court of last resort   A court that handles the final appeal on a matter. The Supreme Court of Canada is the official court of last resort for criminal matters.

courtroom work group   The phrase used to denote that all parties in the adversary process work together to settle cases with the least amount of effort and conflict.

courts of limited jurisdiction   Courts that handle misdemeanours and minor civil complaints.

covert pathway   A path to a criminal career that begins with minor underhanded behaviour and progresses to fire starting and theft.

crack cocaine   A smokable form of purified cocaine that provides an immediate and powerful high.

crackdown   The concentration of police resources on a particular problem area, such as street-level drug dealing, to eradicate or displace criminal activity.

crime   A violation of societal rules of behaviour (criminal legal code) created by people holding social and political power. Individuals who violate these rules are subject to sanctions by state authority, social stigma, and loss of status.

crime control   A model of criminal justice that emphasizes the control of dangerous offenders and the protection of society. Its advocates call for harsh punishments, such as the death penalty, as a deterrent to crime.

crime displacement   An effect of crime prevention efforts in which efforts to control crime in one area shift illegal activities to another.

crime fighter   A police style that stresses dealing with hard crimes and arresting dangerous criminals.

crime rate   This number is derived by calculating the ratio of crimes in the whole population; usually expressed as per 100 000 people, it gives the criminologist a sense of the relative likelihood of crime occurring.

crime-related violence   When the violence is committed during the course of another crime, usually between strangers; see conflict-related violence.

criminal anthropology   Early efforts to discover a biological basis of crime through measurement of physical and mental processes; associated with Cesare Lombroso and the biological positivists.

criminal justice system   The complete institutional process of decision-making from the initial investigation or arrest by police to the eventual release of the offender and his or her reentry into society; the various sequential criminal justice stages through which the offender passes: police, courts, corrections.

criminal law   The body of rules that define crimes, set out their punishments, and mandate the procedures in carrying out the criminal justice process.

criminal sanction   The right of the state to punish people if they violate the rules set down in the Criminal Code; the punishment connected to commission of a specific crime.

criminological enterprise   This refers to the totality of criminology, even though there are many fields or subareas of study.

criminology   The scientific study of the nature, extent, cause, and control of criminal behaviour.

criminologist One who brings objectivity and method to the study of crime and its consequences; also see *criminology*.

crisis intervention   A form of program provided to victims of crime, many of whom are feeling isolated, vulnerable, and in need of immediate services; might involve counselling.

cross-examination   The process in which the defence and the prosecution interrogate witnesses during a trial.

cross-sectional research   Surveys that use data that derive from all age, race, gender, and income segments of the population being measured simultaneously. Since people from every age group are represented, age-specific crime rates can be determined. Proponents believe that this is a sufficient substitute for the more expensive longitudinal approach that follows a group of subjects over time to measure crime rate changes.

crowds   In the study of peer relations, loosely organized groups of children who share interests and activities; see *cliques*.

Crown attorney   The prosecutor who is charged with bringing offenders to justice and enforcing the laws of the country.

cruel and unusual punishment   Physical punishment that is far in excess of that given to people under similar circumstances and is therefore banned, e.g., capital punishment in Canada.

culpable   Referring to a wrongful act that does not involve malice. It connotes fault rather than guilt.

cult killings   When members of religious cults, some of which are devoted to devil worship, are ordered to kill as part of the cult's rituals; examples might include Jonestown, Guyana, or the Solar Temple cult.

cultural deviance theory   This is a variation of structural theory that combines elements of both strain and social disorganization. According to this view, because of strain and social isolation, unique lower-class subcultures develop in disorganized neighbourhoods that maintain a set of values and beliefs that are in conflict with conventional social norms. Criminal behaviour is an expression of conformity to lower-class subcultural values.

cultural transmission   The concept that conduct norms are passed down from one generation to the next so that they become stable within the boundaries of a culture. Cultural transmission guarantees that group lifestyle and behaviour are stable and predictable.

culture conflict   According to Sellin, a condition brought about when the rules and norms of an individual's subcultural affiliation conflict with the role demands of conventional society.

culture of poverty   The view that people in the lower class of society form a separate culture with its own values and norms that are in conflict with conventional society; the culture is self-maintaining and ongoing.

cycle of violence   Research in this area describes a phenomenon of child victims becoming adult criminals later in life due to their early experiences.

dangerous classes   An idea in conflict theory that personal characteristics (single, young, urban, male) linked to the so-called dangerous classes can result in harsher treatment in the criminal justice system.

date rape   A form of sexual assault that occurs between acquaintances; it has the lowest level of reporting.

deadly force   The ability of the police to kill suspects if they resist arrest or present a danger to an officer or the community. The police cannot use deadly force against an unarmed fleeing felon.

decarceration   A correctional philosophy that stresses the "least restrictive alternative possible" for removing as many people from secure detention as possible and making use of community alternatives.

deconstructionism   A modern approach that focuses on the critical analysis of communication and language in legal codes. Rules and regulations are analyzed to determine whether they contain language and content that forces racism or sexism to become institutionalized.

decriminalization   Reducing the penalty for a criminal act but not actually legalizing it.

defendant   The accused in criminal proceedings.

defence attorney   The counsel for the defendant in a criminal trial who represents the individual from arrest to final appeal.

defensible space   The principle that crime prevention can be achieved through modifying the physical environment to reduce the opportunity individuals have to commit crime.

definition-sensitive crimes   This is a category of crimes that are sensitive to legislative activity; gambling, for example, has steadily been decriminalized in the 20th century by a loosening of criminal sanctions around gaming.

degenerate anomalies   According to Lombroso, the primitive physical characteristics that make criminals animalistic and savage.

degradation   This form of shaming is an ongoing process in which the offender is branded as an evil person and cast out of society. This is a practice of exclusion that is very ritualistic and can occur at a school disciplinary hearing or a criminal court trial.

deinstitutionalisation   The movement to remove as many offenders as possible from secure confinement and treat them in the community.

demystification   The process by which conflict theorists unmask the true purpose of the capitalist system's rules and laws.

desert-based sentences   Sentences in which the length is based on the seriousness of the criminal act and not the personal characteristics of the defendant or the deterrent impact of the law; punishment is based on what people have done and not on what they or others may do in the future.

designer drugs   Chemical substances made and distributed in relatively small batches that induce mood-altering effects.

desistance phenomenon   The process in which crime rate declines with the perpetrator's age; synonymous with the aging-out process.

detective   The police personnel assigned to investigate crimes after they have been reported, to gather evidence, and to identify the perpetrator.

detention   Holding an offender in secure confinement before trial.

determinate sentence   A fixed term of incarceration, such as three years' imprisonment. Determinate sentences are felt by many to be too restrictive for rehabilitative purposes; the advantage is that offenders know how much time they have to serve, that is, when they will be released.

deterrence   The act of preventing crime before it occurs by means of the threat of criminal sanctions. Deterrence involves the perception that the pain of apprehension and punishment outweighs any chances of criminal gain or profit.

developmental criminology   A branch of criminology that examines change in a criminal career over the life course. Developmental factors include biological, social, and psychological change. Among the topics of developmental criminology are desistance, resistance, escalation, and specialization.

deviant behaviour   Behaviour that departs from the social norm.

deviant place hypothesis   Otherwise known as the proximity hypothesis, this means that some people are more susceptible to crime because of the areas they live in or frequent.

differential association theory   According to Sutherland, the principle that criminal acts are related to a person's exposure to an excess amount of anti-social attitudes and values.

differential opportunity   The idea that those who see themselves as failures within conventional society and who feel that there is little hope for advancement by legitimate means may join with like-minded peers to form a gang. This association provides the opportunity and socialization requisite to committing crime.

differential reinforcement theory   In social learning theory, the attempt to explain crime as a type of learned behaviour, combining a focus on differential association with elements of psychological learning.

diffusion of benefits   An effect that occurs when an effort to control one type of crime has the unexpected benefit of reducing the incidence of another.

direct examination   The questioning of one's own (prosecution or defence) witness during a trial.

directed verdict   The right of a judge to direct a jury to acquit a defendant because the state has not proven the elements of the crime or otherwise has not established guilt according to law.

disaggregate   Analyzing the relationship between two or more independent variables while controlling for the influence of a third dependent variable. For example, looking at the relationship between conviction for murder and the likelihood of a death sentence disaggregated by race would entail separate analysis of the sentencing outcomes of whites and blacks convicted of first-degree murder.

disclosure   A principle established in *R. v. Stinchcombe* (1991), which ruled that the prosecution must give all the evidence gathered by the police to the defendant in order to make a complete defence to the charges.

discouragement   An effect that occurs when an effort made to eliminate one type of crime also controls others because it reduces the value of criminal activity by limiting access to desirable targets.

discretion   The use of personal decision-making and choice in carrying out operations in the criminal justice system. For example, police discretion can involve the decision to make an arrest, while prosecutorial discretion can involve the decision to accept a plea bargain.

displacement   Heavy law enforcement in one area, for example, might only serve to drive crime to another, less well-enforced area, thus making it ineffective overall as a policing strategy; however politically, sometimes people just don't want crime in their neighbourhood.

disposition   For juvenile offenders, the equivalent of sentencing for adult offenders. The theory is that disposition is more rehabilitative than retributive. Possible dispositions may be to dismiss the case, release the youth to the custody of his or her parents, or place the offender on probation.

disputatiousness   In the subculture of violence, it is considered appropriate behaviour for a person who has been offended to seek satisfaction through violent means.

diversion   An alternative to criminal trial usually featuring counselling, job training, and educational opportunities.

DNA profiling   The identification of criminal suspects by matching DNA samples taken from them with specimens found at crime scenes.

doing gender   In masculinity studies, this refers to how Western culture emphasizes being authoritative, in charge, combative, and controlling. Failure to adapt these roles leaves men feeling effeminate and unmanly. Their struggle to dominate women to prove their manliness is called doing gender.

double bunking   The practice of holding two or more inmates in a single cell because of prison overcrowding.

double marginality   According to Alex, the social burden black police officers carry by being both minority group members and law enforcement officers.

dramatization of evil   In Tannenbaum's pioneering study of labelling, this refers to the process where the reaction to deviance sets up a feedback effect that the individual internalizes.

drift   According to Matza, the view that youths move in and out of delinquency and that their lifestyles can embrace both conventional and deviant values.

drug courier profile   A way of identifying drug runners based on their personal characteristics; police may stop and question individuals based on the way they fit the characteristics contained in the profile.

due process The constitutional principle based on the concept of the primacy of the individual and the complementary concept of limitation on governmental power; a safeguard against arbitrary and unfair state procedures in judicial or administrative proceedings. Embodied in the due process concept are the basic rights of a defendant in criminal proceedings and the requisites for a fair trial. These rights and requirements have been expanded by appellate court decisions and include (1) timely notice of a hearing or trial that informs the accused of the charges against him or her; (2) the opportunity to confront accusers and to present evidence on the accused's own behalf before an impartial jury or judge; (3) the presumption of innocence under which guilt must be proven by legally obtained evidence and the verdict must be supported by the evidence presented; (4) the right of an accused to be warned of constitutional rights at the earliest stage of the criminal process; (5) protection against self-incrimination; (6) assistance of counsel at every critical stage of the criminal process; and (7) the guarantee that an individual will not be tried more than once for the same offence (double jeopardy).

duress This is one of the grounds that excuse an accused from responsibility from an act, if it can be shown that they were forced or compelled by someone else to commit a criminal act.

Durham rule A definition of insanity used in New Hampshire that required that the crime be excused if it was a product of a mental illness.

early onset A term that refers to the assumption that a criminal career begins early in life and that people who are deviant at a very young age are the ones most likely to persist in crime.

economic compulsive behaviour Behaviour that occurs when drug users resort to violence to gain funds to support their habit.

economic crime An act in violation of the criminal law that is designed to bring financial gain to the offender.

economism The policy of controlling white-collar crime through monetary incentives and sanctions.

egalitarian Where there is an equal sharing of authority and power, for example, between the two partners in a family.

ego identity According to Erikson, ego identity is formed when persons develop a firm sense of who they are and what they stand for.

electroencephalogram (EEG) A device that can record the electronic impulses given off by the brain, commonly called brain waves.

embedded Becoming entrenched in a delinquent way of life, thereby reducing any chances of future success in the marketplace.

embezzlement A type of larceny that involves taking the possessions of another (fraudulent conversion) that have been placed in the thief's lawful possession for safekeeping, such as a bank teller misappropriating deposits or a stockbroker making off with a customer's account.

enterprise syndicate An organized crime group that profits from the sale of illegal goods and services, such as narcotics, pornography, and prostitution.

entrapment A criminal defence maintaining that the police originated the criminal idea or initiated the criminal action.

entrepreneur One willing to take risks for profit in the marketplace.

equipotentiality View that all individuals are equal at birth and are thereafter influenced by their environment.

equity The action or practice of awarding each his or her just due; sanctions based on equity seek to compensate individual victims and the general society for their losses due to crime.

equivalent group hypothesis The lifestyle view that victims and criminals share similar characteristics because they are not actually separate groups and that in fact a criminal lifestyle exposes people to increased levels of victimization risk.

eros Freud maintained that humans have two opposing instinctual drives that interact to control behaviour: *eros,* the life instinct, which drives people to self-fulfilment and enjoyment, and *thanatos,* the death instinct, which produces self-destruction.

***ex post facto* laws** Laws that make an act criminal after it was committed or that retroactively increase the penalty for a crime; for example, an *ex post facto* law could change shoplifting from a summary to an indictable offence and penalize offenders with a prison term, even though they had been apprehended six months prior. Such laws are unconstitutional.

exclusionary rule The principle that prohibits using evidence illegally obtained in a trial.

excuse A defence to a criminal charge in which the accused maintains he or she lacked the intent to commit the crime (*mens rea*).

expressive crimes Crimes that have no purpose except to accomplish the behaviour at hand, such as shooting someone.

expressive violence Violence that is designed not for profit but to vent anger or frustration.

extinction The phenomenon in which a crime prevention effort has an immediate impact that dissipates as criminals adjust to new conditions.

extraversion A personality trait marked by impulsivity and the inability to examine motives and behaviour.

false pretenses Illegally obtaining money, goods, or merchandise from another by fraud or misrepresentation.

Federal Bureau of Investigation (FBI) The arm of the U.S. Justice Department that investigates violations of U.S. federal law, gathers crime statistics, runs a comprehensive crime laboratory, and helps train local law enforcement officers.

femicide The killing of a woman, in use since the 18th century.

fence A buyer and seller of stolen merchandise.

filicide The killing of one's child.

fixed time rule A policy in which people must be tried within a stated period after their arrest.

flash houses In the 18th century, skilled thieves and pickpockets congregated in public meeting places, often taverns, that served as headquarters for gangs.

flat or fixed sentencing A sentencing model mandating that all people who are convicted of a specific offence and who are sent to prison must receive the same length of incarceration.

focal concerns According to Miller, the value orientations of lower-class cultures; features include the needs for excitement, trouble, smartness, fate, and personal autonomy.

folkways Generally followed customs that do not have moral values attached to them, such as not interrupting people when they are speaking.

foot patrols Police patrols that take officers out of cars and put them on a walking beat to strengthen ties with the community.

forfeiture The seizure of personal property by the state as a civil or criminal penalty; used in Canada to enforce narcotics legislation since the mid-1980s.

founded This is the percentage of crimes reported to the police that they believe to be real; otherwise known as actual.

fraud Taking the possessions of another through deception or cheating, such as selling a person a desk that is represented as an antique but is known to be a copy.

free will The idea that people are in charge of their own destinies and are free to make personal behaviour choices unencumbered by environmental controls; the opposite of determinism. Choice theories are based on the concept of free will.

functionalism The sociological perspective that suggests that each part of society makes a contribution to the maintenance of the whole. Functionalism stresses social cooperation and consensus of values and beliefs among a majority of society's members.

furlough A correctional policy that allows inmates to leave the institution for vocational or educational training, for employment, or to maintain family ties.

gang killings An example would be when teenage gangs make violence part of their group activity, engaging in warfare over territory or control of the drug trade.

gendered violence The concept that some forms of violence tend to be committed against women, by men, e.g., sexual assault.

general deterrence A crime control policy that depends on the fear of criminal penalties. General deterrence measures, such as long prison sentences for violent crimes, are aimed at convincing the potential law violator that the pains associated with crime outweigh its benefits.

general intent Actions that on their face indicate a criminal purpose, such as breaking into a locked building or trespassing on someone's property.

General Social Survey An annual survey conducted by Statistics Canada. The Crime Cycle has been administered in 1988, 1993, and 1999. It measures the rate of criminal victimization, independent of police statistics. It is similar to the National Crime Victimization Survey (NCVS) in the United States.

general strain theory A micro-level, or individual, analysis of the effects of strain and how individuals who feel stress and strain are more likely to commit crimes.

general theory of crime In Gottfredson and Hirschi's GTC model, the earlier elements of social control theory are integrated with the concepts of biosocial, psychological, routine activities and rational choice theories.

genocide An extreme form of state-sponsored terrorism when a government seeks to wipe out a minority group within the jurisdiction it controls.

gentrification A process of reclaiming and reconditioning deteriorated neighbourhoods by refurbishing depressed real estate and then renting or selling the properties to upper-middle-class professionals.

good faith exception The principle of law holding that evidence may be used in a criminal trial even though the search warrant used to obtain it is technically faulty, if the police acted in good faith and to the best of their ability when they sought to obtain it from a judge.

graffiti Inscription or drawing made on a wall or structure. Used by delinquents for gang messages and turf definition.

grass eaters A term used for police officers who accept payoffs when their everyday duties place them in a position to be solicited by the public.

greenmail The process by which an arbitrager buys large blocks of a company's stock and threatens to take over the company and replace the management. To ward off the threat to their positions, members of management use company funds to repurchase the shares at a much higher price, creating huge profits for the corporate raiders.

group autonomy Delinquent boys are said to adopt a set of norms and principles in direct opposition to middle-class values, which espouses engaging in short-run hedonism, living for today and letting "tomorrow take care of itself." Delinquent boys strive for group autonomy and resist efforts by family, school, or other sources of authority to control their behaviour.

habeas corpus The request that the detained person be produced; see *writ of habeas corpus.*

habitual criminal statutes Laws that require long-term or life sentences for offenders who have multiple felony convictions. In recent times, Canada has replaced it with the dangerous offender (DO) designation, and the long-term offender (LTO) classification.

halfway house A community-based correctional facility that houses inmates before their outright release so that they can become gradually acclimatized to conventional society.

hallucinogens Drugs, either natural or synthetic, that produce vivid distortions of the senses without greatly disturbing the viewer's consciousness. Some produce hallucinations and others cause psychotic behaviour in otherwise normal people.

hate crimes Acts of violence or intimidation designed to terrorize or frighten people considered undesirable because of their race, religion, ethnic origin, or sexual orientation. This is an example of passive victim precipitation.

hearsay evidence Testimony that is not firsthand but relates information told by a second party.

heel A professional shoplifter; see *booster.*

heroin The most dangerous commonly used drug made from the poppy plant. Users rapidly build a tolerance for it, fuelling the need for increased doses in order to feel a desired effect.

homicide The killing of a man or woman, a term in use since the 12th century.

homophobia The fear and dislike of homosexuals; studies in masculinity see it as part of an inferiority complex or lack of security in the traditional stereotypical male role model.

hot spots of crime The locations of a significant portion of all police calls. These hot spots include taverns and housing projects.

hue and cry In medieval England, the policy of self-help used in villages demanding that all respond if a citizen raised a hue and cry to get their aid.

hundred In medieval England, a group of 100 families who were responsible for maintaining the order and trying minor offences.

hypoglycaemia Some trait theorists believe that biochemical conditions, including both those that are genetically predetermined and those acquired through diet and environment, control and influence antisocial behaviour; in this case, criminality is influenced by a deficiency of sugar.

identity crisis A psychological state, identified by Erikson, in which youths face inner turmoil and uncertainty about life roles.

impulsivity According to Gottfredson and Hirschi's general theory, the trait that produces criminal behaviour; impulsive people lack self-control.

incapacitation The policy of keeping dangerous criminals in confinement to eliminate the risk of their repeating their offence in society.

inchoate crimes Incomplete or contemplated crimes such as solicitation or criminal attempts.

incidence The number of crimes reported to the police in a given time period.

incident-based data Compared to the aggregate (UCR) crime information, since 1988 incident-based data give the criminologist a more complete picture of such factors as the relationship between the offender and the victim, location, and the level of violence used.

income inequality The basic principle that differences in personal income create structural inequalities in society that might be at the root of crime.

indictable offence A serious offence that carries a serious penalty, as compared to a summary offence.

indigent Needy and poor or lacking the means to provide a living; sometimes used as a standard to define the need for legal aid.

inevitable discovery A rule of law stating the evidence that would be independently discovered can be used in a court of law, even though it was obtained in violation of legal rules and practices.

infanticide The killing of a child under one year of age by a woman suffering from postpartum depression.

inferiority complex A term used to describe people who compensate for feelings of inferiority with a drive for superiority; controlling others may help reduce personal inadequacies.

informal sanctions These may have a greater crime-reducing impact than the fear of formal legal punishments and occur when significant others, such as parents, peers, neighbours, and teachers, direct their disapproval, anger, and indignation toward an offender. This is a form of public humiliation.

information   Like an indictment, a formal charging document. The prosecuting attorney makes out the information and files it in court. Probable cause is determined at the preliminary hearing, which is public and attended by the accused and his or her attorney.

inhalants   Vapours from lighter fluid, paint thinner, cleaning fluid, and model airplane glue sniffed to reach a drowsy, dizzy state, sometimes accompanied by hallucinations.

initial appearance   The state in the justice process during which the suspect is brought before a magistrate for consideration of bail, usually within 24 hours.

inmate social code   The informal set of rules that govern inmates.

inmate subculture   The loosely defined culture that pervades prisons and has its own norms, rules, and language.

insanity   A legal defence maintaining that a defendant was incapable of forming criminal intent because he or she suffered from a defect of reason or mental illness.

insider trading   Illegal buying of stock in a company based on information provided by someone who has a fiduciary interest in the company, such as an employee or an attorney or accountant retained by the firm.

instincts   The view held by biosocial theorists is that learning is influenced by instinctual drives.

instrumental Marxist theory   The view that capitalist institutions, such as the criminal justice system, have as their main purpose the control of the poor to maintain the hegemony of the wealthy.

instrumental crimes   Those unable to obtain desired goods and services through conventional means may resort to theft and other illegal activities, such as the sale of narcotics, to obtain them.

instrumental violence   Violence designed to improve the financial or social position of the criminal.

integrated structural theory   In this approach, it is felt that a crime control policy cannot be formulated without regard for its root causes. Coercive punishments or misguided treatments cannot be effective unless the core relationships of material production are changed.

interactional theory   The idea that interaction with institutions and events during the life course determines criminal behaviour patterns; crimogenic influences evolve over time.

interactionist perspective   The view that one's perception of reality is significantly influenced by one's inter-

pretations of the reactions of others to similar events and stimuli.

interrogation   The method of accumulating evidence in the form of information or confessions from suspects; questioning that has been restricted because of concern about the use of brutal and coercive methods and to protect against self-incrimination.

interstitial area   In criminology, a space or separation in the social fabric; an interstitial area encourages the formation of gangs.

intimate violence   A form of violent behaviour that occurs in a context of familiarity, such as wife abuse or child abuse.

investigation   An inquiry concerning suspected criminal behaviour for the purpose of identifying offenders or gathering further evidence to assist the prosecution of apprehended offenders.

just desert   The philosophy of justice that asserts that those who violate the rights of others deserve to be punished. The severity of punishment should be commensurate with the seriousness of the crime.

justice model   A philosophy of corrections that stresses determinate sentences, abolition of parole, and the view that prisons are places of punishment and not rehabilitation.

justification   A defence to a criminal charge in which the accused maintains that his or her actions were justified by the circumstances and therefore he or she should not be held criminally liable.

juvenile delinquency   Participation in illegal behaviour by a minor who falls under a statutory age limit.

juvenile justice system   Court proceeding for youths within the juvenile age group. Under the paternal (*parens patriae*) philosophy, juvenile procedures are informal and nonadversary, invoked for the juvenile offender rather than against him or her; a petition instead of a complaint is filed; courts make findings of involvement or adjudication of delinquency instead of convictions; and juvenile offenders receive dispositions instead of sentences. The philosophy remains one of diminishing the stigma of delinquency and providing for the youth's well-being and rehabilitation rather than seeking retribution.

Knapp Commission   A public body that led an investigation into police corruption in New York and uncovered a widespread network of payoffs and bribes.

labelling   The process by which a person becomes fixed with a negative identity, such as "criminal" or "ex-con," and is forced to suffer the consequences of outcast status.

labelling theory   Theory that views society as creating deviance through a system of social control agencies that designate certain individuals as deviants. The stigmatized individual is made to feel unwanted in the normal social order. Eventually, the individual begins to believe that the label is accurate, assumes it as a personal identity, and enters into a deviant or criminal career.

landmark decision A decision handed down by the Supreme Court that becomes the law of the land and serves as a precedent for similar legal issues.

larceny Usually known as theft, the taking of property unlawfully is one of the oldest common law crimes.

latent delinquency The idea that there must be a mental predisposition that prepares youths psychologically for antisocial acts.

latent trait A stable feature, characteristic, property, or condition, present at birth or soon after, that makes some people crime prone over the life course.

learning disabilities Neurological dysfunctions that prevent people from learning.

left realism A branch of conflict theory that holds that crime is a real social problem experienced by the lower classes and that lower-class concerns about crime must be addressed by criminologists.

legalization The removal of all criminal penalties from a previously outlawed act.

lex talionis In the Code of Hammurabi, punishment was based on physical retaliation, or an eye for an eye.

liberal feminist theory This is an approach that focuses attention on the social and economic role of women in society and its relationship to female crime rates.

life course theory An approach that looks at the study of changes in criminal offending patterns over a person's entire life. Are there conditions or events that occur later in life that influence the way people behave or is behaviour predetermined by social or personal conditions at birth?

life history A research method that uses the experiences of an individual as the unit of analysis, such as using the life experience of an individual gang member to understand the natural history of gang membership.

lifestyle In some theories, the lifestyle of the victim is seen as an important factor in the likelihood of a crime being committed against them. An example might be the number of times they go out per month or the people they hang around with.

longitudinal (cohort) research Research that tracks the development of a group of subjects over time.

lower courts A generic term referring to those courts that have jurisdiction over summary offences and conduct preliminary investigations of indictable charges.

McGill School Work done at McGill University in the Departments of Sociology and Social Work, under the direction of Carl Dawson. This work uses an environmental model of succession and parallels (and predates some of) the work undertaken by the more widely known Chicago School.

McNaughtan Rule In 1843 an English court established that Daniel McNaughtan could not be held responsible in a case of murder because his delusions had caused him to act. This underlies the principle of criminal responsibility, that an accused cannot be held legally liable for his or her act if he or she does not know what he or she is doing or cannot distinguish right from wrong.

macro perspective A large-scale view of a situation or event takes into account contextual, social, and economic reasons, for example, to explain the phenomenon. This is relevant to such theories as Marxism and functionalism.

madam The traditional name for a woman who ran a brothel; more common today is the male pimp.

mala in se Refers to acts that are outlawed because they violate basic moral values, such as rape, murder, assault, and robbery.

mala prohibitum Refers to acts that are outlawed because they clash with current norms and public opinion, such as tax, traffic, and drug laws.

mandatory sentence A statutory requirement that a certain penalty shall be set and carried out in all cases on conviction for a specified offence or series of offences.

marginalization When people are forced outside the economic mainstream, a larger portion of the population is forced to live in areas more conducive to crime. Once this happens, commitment to the system declines, producing another criminogenic force: a weakened bond to society.

marijuana (*Cannabis sativa*) A hemp plant grown throughout the world. Its main active ingredient is tetahydrocannabinol (THC), a mild hallucinogen that alters sensory impressions.

marital exemption The practice in some places of prohibiting the prosecution of husbands for the rape of their wives.

Marxist feminists In this approach, gender inequality stems from the unequal power of men and women in a capitalist society, and gender inequality is a function of the exploitation of females by fathers and husbands. The origin of gender differences can be traced to the development of private property and male domination over the laws of inheritance. Marxist feminists link criminal behaviour patterns to the gender conflict created by the economic and social struggles common in postindustrial societies.

masculinity hypothesis The view that women who commit crimes have biological and psychological traits similar to those of men.

mass murderer   One who kills a large number of people in a single incident.

massage parlours   The more hidden side of prostitution includes seemingly legitimate businesses where men can buy sex under the guise of massage therapy.

matricide   The murder of a mother by her son or daughter.

meat eaters   A term used to describe police officers who actively solicit bribes and vigorously engage in corrupt practices.

media-sensitive crimes   This is a category of crimes that is sensitive to manipulation by the media; serial homicide, for example, is relatively rare, but gets incredible exposure in the media and thus increases public fear.

medical model   A view of corrections holding that convicted offenders are victims of their environment who need care and treatment to be transformed into valuable members of society.

mens rea   Guilty mind. The mental element of a crime or the intent to commit a criminal act.

methadone   A synthetic narcotic used as a substitute for heroin in drug-control efforts.

micro perspective   A small-scale view of events, looking at interaction to explain how and why things happen.

middle-class measuring rods   According to Cohen, the standards by which teachers and other representatives of state authority evaluate lower-class youths. Because they cannot live up to middle-class standards, lower-class youths are bound for failure, which gives rise to frustration and anger at conventional society.

minimal brain dysfunction   MBD is related to an abnormality in cerebral structure, an abruptly appearing maladaptive behaviour that interrupts the lifestyle and life flow of an individual linked to serious antisocial acts, an imbalance in the urge-control mechanisms of the brain, and chemical abnormality.

mitigating factor   Unlike an aggravating factor, this serves to make the crime appear less serious to other people; for example, it is now widely accepted that abused people might react more extremely than other people when threatened, based on the perception that their lives are at risk. These class of circumstances might serve to make the sentence lighter, or might serve as an entire defence.

Mollen Commission   An investigation unit set up to inquire into police corruption in New York in the 1990s.

monetary restitution   A sanction requiring that convicted offenders compensate crime victims by reimbursing them for out-of-pocket losses caused by the crime. Losses can include property damage, lost wages, and medical costs.

moral crusades   Efforts by interest-group members to stamp out behaviour they find objectionable. Typically, moral crusades are directed at public order crimes, such as drug use or pornography.

moral entrepreneurs   Interest groups that attempt to control social life and the legal order in order to promote their own personal set of moral values.

mores   Customs or conventions regarded as essential to a community, which are often at the basis of criminal law.

Mosaic Code   By tradition, the covenant between God and the tribes of Israel in which they agreed to obey his law, as presented to them by Moses, in return for God's special care and protection.

motivated criminals   The potential offenders in a population. According to rational choice theory, crime rates will vary according to the number of motivated offenders.

Mount Cashel Orphanage Inquiry One of two inquiries into abuse at the school run by the Christian Brothers in Saint John's, Newfoundland. It became the benchmark for many subsequent inquiries.

multifactor theories   The attempt to integrate individual factors and independent concepts into complex, coherent explanations of criminality.

murder   Colloquially refers to the killing of one person by another; homicide is separated into the categories of first and second-degree murder, manslaughter, and infanticide.

murder transaction   The concept that murder is usually a result of behaviour interactions between the victim and the offender.

National Crime Survey (NCVS) The ongoing victimization study conducted jointly by the Justice Department and the U.S. Census Bureau that surveys victims about their experiences with law violation.

natural areas Pioneering research in sociology conducted at the Chicago School and the McGill School looked at the social ecology of the city and how social forces operating in urban areas create criminal interactions resulting in some neighbourhoods becoming natural areas for crime.

negative affective states   According to Agnew, the anger, depression, disappointment, fear, and other adverse emotions that derive from strain.

neighbourhood policing   A style of police management that emphasizes community-level crime-fighting programs and initiatives.

neurological   Pertaining to the brain and central nervous system.

neurophysiology   The study of brain activity that looks at neurological and physical abnormalities acquired during the fetal or perinatal stage, which is thought to control behaviour.

neurosis A syndrome in psychodynamic theory that posits that people suffer when they experience feelings of mental anguish and are afraid they are losing control of their personalities.

neuroticism A personality trait marked by unfounded anxiety, tension, and emotional instability.

neurotics People who fear that their primitive id impulses will dominate their personality.

neutralization theory Neutralization theory looks at the ability to overcome social norms and controls. This approach holds that offenders adhere to conventional values while drifting into periods of illegal behaviour by neutralizing legal and moral values.

niche A way of adapting to the prison community that stresses finding one's place (niche) in the system rather than fighting for one's individual rights.

nolo contendere No contest. An admission of guilt in a criminal case with the condition that the finding cannot be used against the defendant in any subsequent civil cases.

nonintervention A justice philosophy that emphasizes the least intrusive treatment possible. Among its central policies are decarceration, diversion, and decriminalization.

norm resistance In a branch of conflict theory, this refers to how interaction between authorities and subjects eventually produces open conflict between the two groups.

oath-helpers During the Middle Ages, groups of 12 to 25 people who would support the accused's innocence.

obitiatry According to Jack Kevorkian, the practice of helping people take their own lives.

obscenity According to current legal theory, sexually explicit material that lacks a serious purpose and appeals solely to the prurient interest of the viewer. While nudity per se is not usually considered obscene, open sexual behaviour, masturbation, and exhibition of the genitals is banned in most communities.

occasional criminal Unlike the professional criminal, does not derive a significant income from crime.

occupational crime Crime committed by employees for personal gain using the structural advantage provided by their employment.

offender-specific crime Criminals do not engage in random acts of antisocial behaviour; they analyze whether they have the prerequisites for committing a criminal act, including their skills, motives, needs, and fears.

offence-specific crime Offenders will react selectively to the characteristics of particular offences. This is particularly relevant to routine activities theory, where there is an assessment of opportunity, guardianship, and so on.

official crime Criminal behaviour that has been recorded by the police.

opportunist robber Someone who steals small amounts when a vulnerable target presents itself.

organized crime Crime committed by a gang, e.g., drug trafficking.

overt pathway In the study of the course of criminal careers, this refers to the escalation of aggressive acts beginning with aggression (annoying others, bullying) leading to physical (and gang) fighting and on to violence (attacking someone, strongarming, forced theft).

paraphilias Bizarre or abnormal sexual practices that may involve recurrent sexual urges focused on objects, humiliation, or children.

parens patriae Power of the state to act on behalf of the child and provide care and protection equivalent to that of a parent.

parricide The killing of a close relative by a child.

partial deterrent A legal measure designed to restrict or control rather than eliminate an undesirable act.

passive precipitation The view that some people become victims because of personal and social characteristics that make them "attractive" targets for predatory criminals.

paternalistic The way in which leaders in government or organizations are seen as father figures and others are treated as "children."

pathways The view that the path to a criminal career may have more than one route, beginning with mild misconduct and escalating to serious crimes.

patriarchy A male-dominated system. The patriarchal family is one dominated by the father.

patricide The murder of a father by his son or daughter.

peacemaking A branch of conflict theory that stresses humanism, mediation, and conflict resolution as a means to end crime.

percentage change Calculating the increase or decrease in crime rates over a period of years, for example, can tell the criminologist whether society is becoming more dangerous.

perceptual deterrence The perceived risk of getting caught or the threat of severe punishments can deter active criminal offenders.

peremptory challenge The dismissal of a potential juror by either the prosecution or the defence for unexplained, discretionary reasons.

persisters Those criminals who do not age out of crime; chronic delinquents who continue offending into their adulthood.

personality An idea used to explain how psychological conflict or underdevelopment may result in neurotic or psychotic behaviour patterns.

pilferage Theft by employees through stealth or deception.

plain view The doctrine that evidence that is in plain view to police officers may be seized without a search warrant.

plea An answer to formal charges by an accused. Possible pleas are guilty, not guilty, *nolo contendere,* and not guilty by reason of insanity. A guilty plea is a confession of the offence as charged. A not guilty plea is a denial of the charge and places the burden on the prosecution to prove the elements of the offence.

plea bargaining The discussion between the defence counsel and the prosecution by which the accused agrees to plead guilty for certain considerations. The advantage to the defendant may be a reduction of the charges, a lenient sentence, or (in the case of multiple charges) dropped charges. The advantage to the prosecution is that a conviction is obtained without the time and expense of lengthy trial proceedings.

pledge system An early method of law enforcement that relied on self-help and mutual aid.

police discretion The ability of police officers to enforce the law selectively. Police officers in the field have great latitude to use their discretion in deciding whether to invoke their arrest powers.

police officer style The belief that the bulk of police officers can be classified into ideal personality types. Popular style types include supercops, who desire to enforce only serious crimes, such as robbery and rape; professionals, who use a broad definition of police work; service-oriented officers, who see their job as a helping profession; and avoiders, who do as little as possible.

policing-sensitive crimes This is a category of crimes that are particularly sensitive to law enforcement; if drug crime, for example, was not proactively investigated by the police, it is unlikely that many drug transactions would come to the attention of the police.

poor laws Seventeenth-century laws that bound vagrants and abandoned children to masters as indentured servants.

population All people who share a particular personal characteristic, such as all high school students or all police officers.

pornography In feminism, this is distinguished from erotica, and involves the exploitation of women and children for male pleasure; it exists in a variety of forms and is usually defined in relation to community standards of obscenity.

positivism The branch of social science that uses the scientific method of the natural sciences and suggests that human behaviour is a product of social, biological, psychological, or economic forces.

poverty line A social indicator used to explain crime rates, usually felt to be a minimum standard of income that people need in order to survive.

power control According to Hagan, the power and standing each parent has in the economic structure, which determines the manner in which the parents exert control over their families and, in particular, adolescent behaviour.

power groups Criminal organizations that do not provide services or illegal goods but trade exclusively in violence and extortion.

power rape A rape motivated by the need for sexual conquest.

power syndicates Organized crime groups that use force and violence to extort money from legitimate businesses and other criminal groups engaged in illegal business enterprises.

predatory crime A violent, opportunistic crime, not usually familiar-related, such as stealing brand-name clothing from strangers.

preemptive deterrence An approach advocated by left realists in which community organization efforts can eliminate or reduce crime before it becomes necessary to use police forces.

preliminary hearings The step at which criminal charges initiated by an information are tested for probable cause; the prosecution presents enough evidence to establish probable cause—that is, a *prima facie* case. The hearing is public and may be attended by the accused and his or her attorney.

premeditation In a case of first-degree homicide, the prosecution must prove that the offence was thought out and planned.

premenstrual syndrome The biogenetic theory (unfortunately caricaturized as a stereotype) that several days prior to and during menstruation females are beset by irritability and poor judgment as a result of hormonal changes, and that this puts them at a greater risk for criminality.

preponderance of the evidence The level of proof in civil cases; more than half the evidence supports the allegations of one side.

presentence report An investigation performed by a probation officer attached to a trial court after the conviction of a defendant. The report contains information about the defendant's background, education, previous employment, and family; his or her own statement concerning the offence; the person's prior criminal record; interviews with neighbours or acquaintances; and his or her mental and physical condition (that is, information that would not be made in the case of a guilty plea or that would be inadmissible as evidence at a trial but could be influential and important at the sentencing state). After conviction, a judge sets a date for sentencing (usually ten days to two weeks from the date of conviction), during which time the presentence report is made. In the case of juvenile offenders, the presentence report is also known as a social history report.

presumptive sentences   Sentencing structures that provide an average sentence that should be served along with the option of extending or decreasing the punishment because of aggravating or mitigating circumstances.

preventive detention   The practice of holding dangerous suspects before trial without bail.

price fixing   A form of corporate crime, where companies conspire together to artificially inflate the price of goods.

primary deviance   According to Lemert, deviant acts that do not help redefine the self and public image of the offender.

primary sociopaths   People with an inherited trait that predisposes them to antisocial behaviour.

prison   A correctional institution for incarceration of offenders.

privilege   In conflict theory, this concept refers to the wealth and prestige enjoyed by some, which puts them in conflict with those less well-off in society.

pro bono   The practice by private attorneys of taking the cases of indigent offenders without fee as a service to the profession and the community.

probability sample   A randomly drawn sample in which each member of the population being tapped has an equal chance of being selected.

probable cause   The evidentiary criterion necessary to sustain an arrest or the issuance of an arrest or search warrant; less than absolute certainty or beyond a reasonable doubt but greater than mere suspicion or hunch. A set of facts, information, circumstances, or conditions that would lead a reasonable person to believe that an offence was committed and that the accused committed that offence. An arrest made without probable cause may be susceptible to prosecution as an illegal arrest under false imprisonment statutes.

probation   A sentence entailing the conditional release of a convicted offender into the community under the supervision of the court (in the form of a probation officer), subject to certain conditions for a specified time. The conditions are usually similar to those of parole. (Probation is a sentence, an alternative to incarceration; parole is administrative release from incarceration.) Violation of the conditions of probation may result in revocation of probation.

problem behaviour syndrome   In the life-course view of crime, antisocial behaviours cluster together and typically include family dysfunction, substance abuse, smoking, precocious sexuality and early pregnancy, educational underachievement, suicide attempts, sensation seeking, and unemployment.

problem-oriented policing   A style of police management that stresses proactive problem solving rather than reactive crime fighting.

procedural law   The rules that define the operation of criminal proceedings. Procedural law describes the methods that must be followed in obtaining warrants, investigating offences, effecting lawful arrests, using force, conducting trials, introducing evidence, sentencing convicted offenders, and reviewing cases by appellate courts (in general, legislatures have ignored postsentencing procedures). While the substantive law defines criminal offences, procedural law delineates how the substantive offences are to be enforced.

professional criminals   Make a significant portion of their income from crime.

progressives   Early 20th-century reformers who believed that state action could relieve human ills.

proletariat   In Marxist theory, the bourgeoisie controls the means of production, and the proletariat provides the labour; sometimes referred to as the working class.

proof beyond a reasonable doubt   The standard of proof needed to convict in a criminal case. The evidence offered in court does not have to amount to absolute certainty, but it should leave no reasonable doubt that the defendant committed the alleged crime.

property in service   The 18th-century practice of selling control of inmates to shipmasters who would then transport them to colonies for sale as indentured servants.

prosecutor   Representative of the state (executive branch) in criminal proceedings; advocate for the state's case in the adversary trial. The prosecutor participates in investigations both before and after arrest, prepares legal documents, participates in obtaining arrest or search warrants, decides whether to charge a suspect and, if so, with which offence. The prosecutor argues the state's case at trial, advises the police, participates in plea negotiations, and makes sentencing recommendations.

prosocial bonds   In the social development model, the way in which to control the risk of antisocial behaviour is to maintain prosocial bonds developed within the context of a family life; providing prosocial opportunities and consistent positive feedback.

prostitution The buying and selling of sex is technically not illegal in Canada, although there are various prostitution-related offences, such as pimping, brothel-keeping, and communication.

proximity hypothesis The view that people become crime victims because they live or work in areas with large criminal populations.

pseudo maturity Kids who mature faster have a greater chance of becoming life-course persisters; see *adolescent-limited*.

psychoanalytic (psychodynamic) approach Branch of psychology holding that the human personality is controlled by unconscious mental processes developed early in childhood.

psychodynamic theory This is also known as psychoanalytic psychology, and was originated by the famous Viennese doctor Sigmund Freud.

psychopath A person whose personality is characterized by a lack of warmth and feeling, inappropriate behaviour responses, and an inability to learn from experience. While some psychologists view psychopathy as a result of childhood trauma, others see it as a result of biological abnormality.

psychopharmacological A mood-altering substance has this effect when it produces a change in behaviour, including violence and aggression, e.g., alcohol, PCP, amphetamines.

psychosis This is what people who have lost total control and are dominated by their primitive id are said to be suffering from. They are referred to as psychotics, and their behaviour may be marked by bizarre episodes, hallucinations, and inappropriate responses to situations.

psychotics In Freudian theory, people whose id has broken free and now dominates their personality. Psychotics suffer from delusions and experience hallucinations and sudden mood shifts.

public order crimes Sometimes called victimless crimes, these acts interfere with public order, such as loitering for the purposes of prostitution.

Racketeer Influenced and Corrupt Organizations Act (RICO) U.S. federal legislation that enables prosecutors to bring additional criminal or civil charges against people whose multiple criminal acts constitute a conspiracy. RICO features monetary penalties that allow the government to confiscate all profits derived from criminal activities. Originally intended to be used against organized criminals, RICO has also been used against white-collar criminals.

r/k theory An evolutionary theory of crime that holds that k-oriented people are more cooperative and sensitive to others, while r-oriented people are more cunning and deceptive; corresponding to a female/male split in criminality.

radical feminists In this view, female crime is caused by male supremacy (patriarchy), the subsequent subordination of women, male aggression, and the efforts of men to control females sexually.

random sample A sample selected on the basis of chance so that each person in the population has an equal opportunity to be selected.

rational choice theory The view that crime is a function of a decision-making process in which the potential offender weighs the potential costs and benefits of an illegal act.

reaction formation According to Cohen, rejecting goals and standards that seem impossible to achieve. Because a boy cannot hope to get into college, for example, he considers higher education a waste of time.

reasonable competence The standard by which legal representation is judged: Did the defendant receive a reasonable level of legal aid?

reasonable doubt The possibility that a defendant did not commit the crime. A jury cannot find the defendant guilty if a reasonable doubt exists that he or she committed the crime. The level of proof needed to convict in a criminal trial is beyond a reasonable doubt.

recidivism Repetition of criminal behaviour; habitual criminality. Recidivism is measured by (1) criminal acts that result in conviction by a court when committed by individuals who are under correctional supervision or who had been released from correctional supervision within the previous three years, and (2) technical violations of probation or parole in which a sentencing or paroling authority has taken action resulting in an adverse change in the offender's legal status.

reflected appraisal According to Matsueda and Heimer, a youth's self-evaluation based on his or her perceptions of how others evaluate him or her.

reflective role-taking According to Matsueda and Heimer, the phenomenon that occurs when youths who view themselves as delinquents are giving an inner-voice to their perceptions how significant others feel about them.

reintegration The correctional philosophy that stresses reintroducing the inmate into the community.

reintegrative shaming A method of correction that encourages offenders to confront their misdeeds, experience shame because of the harm they caused, and then be reincluded in society.

relative deprivation The condition that exists when people of wealth and poverty live in close proximity to one another. Some criminologists attribute crime rate differentials to relative deprivation.

release on recognizance A nonmonetary condition for the pretrial release of an accused individual; an alternative to monetary bail that is granted after the court determines that the accused has ties in the community, has no prior record of default, and is likely to appear at subsequent proceedings.

report-sensitive crimes This is a category of crimes that are particularly sensitive to the willingness of victims to report them; if a victim of sexual assault, for example, does not report the crime, then it is unlikely that the police will ever know about it.

repression A process identified in psychodynamic theory that the unconscious mind contains feelings about sex and hostility, which people keep below the surface of consciousness.

restitution A condition of probation in which the offender repays society or the victim of crime for the trouble the offender caused. Monetary restitution involves a direct payment to the victim as a form of compensation. Community service restitution may be used in victimless crimes and involves work in the community in lieu of more severe criminal penalties.

restorative justice A restorative system of justice views crime as an injury to personal and community relations rather than as an abstract legal violation against society; it focuses on mediation and conflict resolution as an alternative to the more formalistic workings of the court system.

revocation An administrative act performed by a parole authority that removes a person from parole or a judicial order by a court removing a person from parole or probation, in response to a violation on the part of the parolee or probationer.

right to counsel The right of the accused to the assistance of defence counsel in all criminal prosecutions.

right to treatment The philosophy that offenders have a statutory right to treatment.

rights of defendant Powers and privileges that are constitutionally guaranteed to every defendant in a criminal trial.

robbery A crime of violence involving the use of force to obtain money or goods.

role diffusion According to Erikson, a phenomenon that occurs when youths spread themselves too thin, experience personal uncertainty, and place themselves at the mercy of leaders who promise to give them a sense of identity they cannot develop for themselves.

routine activities theory An approach that holds the view that crime is a "normal" function of the routine activities of modern living. Offences can be expected if there is a suitable target that is not protected by capable guardians.

Royal Commission on the Wrongful Incarceration of Donald Marshall Jr. This Nova Scotia report (1988), brought out at a cost of $6 million, established that racism, faulty police procedure, political interference, and judicial error were responsible for Marshall spending 11 years in prison for a murder he didn't commit.

sadistic rape A rape motivated by the offender's desire to torment or abuse the victim.

sample A limited number of people selected for study from a population.

schizophrenia A type of psychosis often marked by bizarre behaviour, hallucinations, loss of thought control, and inappropriate emotional responses. Schizophrenic types include catatonic, which characteristically involves impairment of motor activity; paranoid, which is characterized by delusions of persecution; and hebephrenic, which is characterized by immature behaviour and giddiness.

search and seizure The legal term that refers to the searching for and carrying away of evidence by police during a criminal investigation.

secondary deviance According to Lemert, accepting deviant labels as a personal identity. Acts become secondary when they form a basis for self-concept.

secondary sociopaths People who are constitutionally normal but whose life experiences influence their antisocial behaviour. Suspected influences include poor parenting, racial segregation, and social conflict.

seductions of crime According to Katz, the visceral and emotional appeal that the situation of crime has for those who engage in illegal acts.

selective incapacitation The policy of creating enhanced prison sentences for the relatively small group of dangerous chronic offenders.

self-fulfilling prophecy Deviant behaviour patterns that are a response to an earlier labelling experience. People act in synch with social labels, even if the labels are falsely bestowed.

self-rejection The consequence of successfully being labelled, where the negative stigma is internalized.

self-report survey A research approach that requires subjects to reveal their own participation in delinquent or criminal acts.

semiotics In this approach, language is studied as a set of signs that indicate more than the mere meaning of words; words are not mere descriptors, but convey a meaning understood by their audience.

sentence The criminal sanction imposed by the court on a convicted defendant, usually in the form of a fine, incarceration, or probation. Sentencing may be carried out by a judge, jury, or sentencing council (panel of judges), depending on the statutes of the jurisdiction.

sequester The insulation of jurors from the outside world so that their decision-making cannot be influenced or affected by extralegal events.

sexual abuse A form of violence, usually familiar-related, that can occur in wife abuse, child abuse, and elder abuse.

serial murder The killing of a large number of people over time by an offender who seeks to escape detection.

shield laws Laws designed to protect rape victims by prohibiting the defence attorney from inquiring about their previous sexual relationships.

shire An area in early England about the size of a county, where the senior law enforcement figure was the reeve, the forerunner of today's sheriff.

shock incarceration A short prison sentence served in boot camp-type facilities.

shock probation A sentence in which offenders serve a short prison term to impress them with the pains of imprisonment before they begin probation.

short-run hedonism According to Cohen, the desire of lower-class gang youths to engage in behaviour that will give them immediate gratification and excitement but in the long run will be dysfunctional and negative.

siege mentality A consequence and symptom of community disorganization, where community fear causes the development of belief that the outside world is an enemy out to destroy the neighbourhood.

situational crime prevention A method of crime prevention that stresses tactics and strategies to eliminate or reduce particular crimes in narrow settings, such as reducing burglaries in a housing project by increasing lighting and installing security alarms.

situational inducement Crimes such as occasional property crime occurs when there is an opportunity to commit crime; these are usually short-run influences on a person's behaviour that increase risk taking.

skeezers Prostitutes who trade sex for drugs, usually crack.

skinhead Member of a white supremacist gang, identified by a shaved skull and Nazi or Ku Klux Klan markings.

snitches Most shoplifters are amateur pilferers who think of themselves as respectable people.

social bond Ties a person has to the institutions and processes of society. According to Hirschi, elements of the social bond include commitment, attachment, involvement, and belief.

social capital Positive relations with individuals and institutions that are life sustaining.

social control theory An approach that looks at the ability of society and its institutions to control, manage, restrain, or direct human behaviour, sometimes called control theory.

social development model The attempt to integrate social control, social learning, and structural models of crime.

social deviant In labelling theory, the degree to which a person is perceived as a social deviant may affect his or her treatment at home, at work, at school, and in other social situations.

social disorganization theory An approach that looks at how neighbourhoods or areas are marked by culture conflict, lack of cohesiveness, transient population, insufficient social organizations, and anomie.

social distance In labelling theory, a person is labelled deviant primarily as a consequence of the differences in power between the labeller and the person labelled, differences located in race, class, and ethnicity.

social ecologists A modern variant of disorganization theory that looks at community-level indicators of social disorganization, including disorder, poverty, alienation, disassociation, and fear of crime.

social injustice In communities where the poor and wealthy live in close proximity, and people can see how poorly off they are, the consequent perception of injustice leads to a state of disorganization and anger; see *income inequality.*

social learning theory The view that human behaviour is modelled through observation of human social interactions, either directly from observing those who are close and from intimate contact, or indirectly through the media. Interactions that are rewarded are copied, while those that are punished are avoided.

social process theory An approach that looks at the operations of formal and informal social institutions. Elements of the social process include socialization within family and peer groups, the educational process, and the justice system.

social reality of crime Quinney's conflict theory about how power, society, and criminality are interrelated.

social structure theory An approach that looks at the various stratifications that characterize the fabric of postindustrial society.

socialization Process of human development and enculturation. Socialization is influenced by key social processes and institutions.

sociobiology Branch of science that views human behaviour as being motivated by inborn biological urges and desires. The urge to survive and preserve the species motivates human behaviour.

sociopath Person whose personality is characterized by lack of warmth and affection, inappropriate responses, and an inability to learn from experience. The term is used interchangeably with psychopath and antisocial personality disorder.

sodomy Illegal sexual intercourse. Sodomy has no single definition, and acts included within its scope include both oral and anal intercourse.

somatype An idea used in a system developed for categorizing people on the basis of their body build, associated with the work of William Sheldon.

specific deterrence A crime control policy suggesting that punishment be severe enough to convince convicted offenders never to repeat their criminal activity. It is based on the principle that an individual can be prevented from committing a crime if the cost outweighs the benefit; see *utilitarianism*.

specific intent The intent to accomplish a specific purpose as an element of crime, such as breaking into someone's house for the express purpose of stealing jewels.

spontaneous remission Another term for the aging-out process.

stalking Laws that make it a criminal offence to stalk or harass a victim even though no actual assault or battery has occurred.

standard of proof The level of proof needed to process a person at various stages of the justice system; the standard of proof for an arrest to be made is probable cause. The Supreme Court has made the "beyond a reasonable doubt" standard a due process and constitutional requirement for conviction at trial.

stare decisis To stand by decided cases; the legal principle by which the decision or holding in an earlier case becomes the standard by which subsequent similar cases are judged.

status frustration In subcultural theory, it is the view that because social conditions make lower-class youths incapable of achieving success legitimately, they experience a form of culture conflict that results in many of them joining in gangs and engaging in behaviour that is nonutilitarian, malicious, and negativistic.

statutory law Laws created by legislative bodies to meet changing social conditions, public opinion, and custom.

steroids Drugs used to gain muscle bulk and strength for athletics and body building.

stigmatize To create an enduring label that taints a person's identity and changes him or her in the eyes of others.

stimulants Synthetic drugs that stimulate action in the central nervous system. They produce an intense physical reaction: increased blood pressure, increased breathing rate, increased bodily activity, and elevated mood. One widely used set of stimulants, amphetamines, produces psychological effects such an increased confidence, euphoria, fearlessness, talkativeness, impulsive behaviour, and loss of appetite.

sting An undercover police operation in which police pose as criminals to trap the law violators.

stoopers Petty criminals who earn their living by retrieving winning tickets that are accidentally discarded by racetrack patrons.

stop and frisk The situation where police officers who are suspicious of an individual run their hands lightly over the suspect's outer garments to determine whether the person is carrying a concealed weapon; also called a "patdown" or "threshold inquiry."

strain theory An approach that looks at the emotional turmoil and conflict caused when people believe they cannot achieve their desires and goals through legitimate means. Members of the lower class might feel strain because they are denied access to adequate educational opportunities and social support.

stranger-related crime Unlike acquaintance-related crime, some crimes do not require or arise from a prior relationship between the offender and the victim; an example would be carjacking.

stratification Grouping according to social strata or levels. Canadian society is considered stratified on the basis of economic class and wealth.

street crime Illegal acts designed to prey on the public through theft, damage, and violence.

strict-liability crimes Illegal acts whose elements do not contain the need for intent, or *mens rea;* they are usually acts that endanger the public welfare, such as illegal dumping of toxic wastes.

structural Marxist theory The view that the law and the justice system are designed to maintain the capitalist system and that members of both the owner and worker classes whose behaviour threatens the stability of the system will be sanctioned.

structural violence A form of state-sponsored terrorism that involves physical harm caused by the unequal distribution of wealth; a set of social conditions from which flows poverty, disease, hunger, malnutrition, poor sanitation, premature death, and high infant mortality.

subculture A group that is loosely a part of the dominant culture but maintains a unique set of values, beliefs, and traditions; a subculture of violence focuses on violent criminality.

subpoena   A court order requiring the recipient to appear in court on an indicated time and date.

substantive criminal laws   A body of specific rules that declare what conduct is criminal and prescribe the punishment to be imposed for such conduct.

subterranean values   Important to neutralization theory, these are the morally tinged influences that have become entrenched in the culture but are publicly condemned by "right thinking" members of society.

suitable target   According to routine activities theory, a target for crime that is relatively valuable, easily transportable, and not capably guarded.

summary offence   Minor offences for which the penalty is restricted to a maximum of six months in jail, or a fine, or both.

summons   An alternative to arrest usually used for petty or traffic offences; a written order notifying an individual that he or she has been charged with an offence. A summons directs the person to appear in court to answer the charge. It is used primarily in instances of low risk, where the person will not be required to appear at a later date. The summons is advantageous to police officers in that they are freed from having to spend time on arrest and booking procedures; it is advantageous to the accused in that he or she is spared time in jail.

sureties   During the Middle Ages, people who made themselves responsible for the behaviour of offenders released in their care.

surplus value   The Marxist view that the labouring classes produce wealth that far exceeds their wages and goes to the capitalist class as profits.

suspended sentence   A prison term that is delayed while the defendant undergoes a period of community treatment. If the treatment is successful, the prison sentence is terminated.

swindling   Stealing through deception by individuals who have no legitimate job and whose entire purpose is to bilk people out of their money, e.g., door-to-door sale of faulty merchandise.

symbolic interaction theory   The sociological view that people communicate through symbols. People interpret symbolic communication and incorporate it within their personality. A person's view of reality, then, depends on his or her interpretation of symbolic gestures.

systematic forgers   Fraud artists who make a substantial living by passing bad cheques.

systemic link   Violent behaviour that results from the conflict inherent in the drug trade.

target hardening   Making one's home and business crime-proof through locks, bars, alarms, and other devices; this approach is based in routine activities theory, and is based on an analysis of potential risk factors.

target reduction strategies   See *target hardening.*

team policing   An experimental police technique in which groups of officers are assigned to a particular area of the city on a 24-hour basis.

technical parole violation   Revocation of parole because conditions set by correctional authorities have been violated.

technique of neutralization   According to neutralization theory, the ability of delinquent youth to neutralize moral constraints so they may drift into criminal acts.

temperance movement   An effort to prohibit the sale of liquor, largely seen as unsuccessful.

terrorism   Includes a wide variety of violent acts that have a political motivation, committed against a state, and also by a state.

testosterone   An androgen, or male hormone, which controls secondary sex characteristics and can alter behaviour.

thanatos   According to Freud, the instinctual drive toward aggression and violence.

threshold inquiry   A term used to describe a stop and frisk.

thrill killings   Impulsive violence motivated by the killer's decision to kill a stranger as an act of daring or recklessness.

tithings   During the Middle Ages, groups of about ten families who were responsible for maintaining order among themselves and dealing with disturbances, fires, wild animals, and so on.

tort law   The law of personal wrongs and damage. Tort actions include negligence, libel, slander, assault, and trespass.

totality of the circumstances   A legal doctrine mandating that a decision maker consider all the issues and circumstances of a case before judging the outcome. For example, before concluding whether a suspect understood his or her rights, a judge must consider the totality of the circumstances under which the warning was given. The suspect's age, intelligence, and competency may influence his or her understanding and judgment.

trait theories   This approach looks at the combination of biological or psychological attributes that might explain criminality. Each offender is considered unique, physically and mentally; consequently, there must be a unique explanation for each person's behaviour.

transferred intent   The principle that if an illegal yet unintended act results from the intent to commit a crime, that act is also considered illegal.

transitional neighbourhood An area undergoing a shift in population and structure, usually from middle-class residential to lower-class mixed use.

truly disadvantaged William Julius Wilson's description of the lowest levels of the underclass; socially isolated people who dwell in urban inner cities and occupy the bottom rung of the social ladder.

turning points According to Laub and Sampson, the life events that alter the development of a criminal career.

Twelve Tables Roman law formulated in 451 B.C. by a special commission of ten men in response to pressure from the lower classes.

underclass In Gunnar Myrdal's work, he described a world cut off from society, its members lacking the education and skills needed to survive in the modern world; this became a breeding ground for criminality.

Uniform Crime Report This is an aggregate census based on reports from about 420 different police forces across Canada; it is the official basis for criminological research in Canada.

utilitarianism A view that believes that the punishment of crime should be balanced and fair, which underlies the belief in classical criminology that even criminal behaviour must be seen as purposeful and reasonable.

uxoricide The killing of one's wife.

vagrancy Today vagrancy is a summary offence crime, but because it has been a capital offence in the past, it is a good example of historical changes in the law.

value conflict What occurs when the deviant values of teenage law-violating groups, an essential element of youthful misbehaviour in slum areas, come into conflict with existing middle-class norms, which demand strict obedience to the legal code.

variable This is a basic measurement tool used in social science; in criminology, it is a factor that either affects crime independently or is in turn influenced by it.

venire The group called for jury duty from which jury panels are selected.

vice squad Police officers assigned to enforce morally tinged laws, such as those governing prostitution, gambling, and pornography.

victim compensation Financial restitution to the victim of crime, usually provided by the state and funded by a surcharge levied in criminal cases.

victim-precipitation Refers to crime in which the victim's behaviour was the spark that ignited the subsequent offence, as when the victim abused the offender verbally or physically.

victimless crime Acts such as prostitution and drug transactions where there are two willing parties to the crime; enforcement has to be proactive.

victimization survey A crime measurement technique that surveys citizens to measure their experiences as victims of crime.

victimology The study of the victim's role in criminal transactions.

victimologist This type of criminologist looks at the role that the victim plays in the crime process.

vigilante Someone who takes the law into their own hands, who acts outside the law in the interest of justice.

virulency According to Athens, a stage in a violent career in which criminals develop a violent identity that makes them feared. They consequently enjoy hurting others.

voir dire The process in which a potential jury panel is questioned by the prosecution and the defence to select jurors who are unbiased and objective. It also refers to a "trial within a trial," where potential evidence is heard by the judge in the absence of the jury.

waiver The act of voluntarily relinquishing a right or advantage; often used in the context of waiving one's right to counsel, or waiving certain steps in the criminal justice process such as the preliminary hearing. Essential to waiver is the voluntary consent of the individual.

warrant A written court order issued by a magistrate authorizing and directing that an individual be taken into custody to answer criminal charges.

watch system In medieval England, men organized in church parishes to guard against disturbances and breaches of the peace at night; they were under the direction of the local constable.

watchman A style of policing that stresses reacting to calls for service rather than aggressively pursuing crime.

wergild Under medieval law, the money paid by the offender to compensate the victim and the state for a criminal offence.

white-collar crime Illegal acts that capitalize on a person's status in the marketplace. White-collar crimes can involve theft, embezzlement, fraud, market manipulation, restraint of trade, and false advertising.

widening the net The charge that programs designed to divert offenders from the justice system actually enmesh them further in the process by substituting more intrusive treatment programs for less intrusive punishment-oriented outcomes.

wite The portion of the wergild that went to the victim's family.

work furlough   A prison treatment program that allows inmates to leave during the day to work in the community and return to prison at night.

writ of *habeas corpus*   A judicial order requesting that a person detaining another produce the body of the prisoner and give reasons for his or her capture and detention. This is a legal device used to request that a judicial body review the reasons for a person's confinement and the conditions of confinement.

zero tolerance   A policy of not allowing any cases, e.g., schoolyard violence, to go unprosecuted.

Notes

Chapter 1

1. See, generally, Joel Milner, ed., "Special Issue: Physical Child Abuse," *Criminal Justice and Behavior* 18 (1991); Russell Dobash, R. Emerson Dobash, Margo Wilson, and Martin Daly, "The Myth of Sexual Symmetry in Marital Violence," *Social Problems* 39 (1992): 71–86; Martin Schwartz and Walter DeKeseredy, "The Return of the 'Battered Husband Syndrome': Typification of Women as Violent," *Crime, Law and Social Change* 4 (1993): 37–43.

2. For a thorough review, see Robin Malinosky-Rummell and David Hansen, "Long-Term Consequences of Childhood Physical Abuse," *Psychological Bulletin* 114 (1993): 68–79.

3. For a variety of daily polls in the Ottawa area, see www.ottawastart.com.

4. "Canada Needs to Get Back to Basics," a poll conducted by the Council for Canadian Unity, http://www.cric.ca/en_html/opinion/, May 25, 2000.

5. Edwin Sutherland and Donald Cressey, *Principles of Criminology*, 6th ed. (Philadelphia: J.B. Lippincott, 1960), p. 3.

6. For a review of the development of criminal justice as a field of study, see Frank Remington, "Development of Criminal Justice as an Academic Field," *Journal of Criminal Justice Education* 1 (1990): 9–20.

7. Marvin Zalman, *A Heuristic Model of Criminology and Criminal Justice* (Chicago: Joint Commission on Criminology Education and Standards, University of Illinois, Chicago Circle, 1981), pp. 9–11; John Ekstedt, "Canadian Justice Policy," in Margaret A. Jackson and Curt T. Griffiths, *Canadian Criminology: Perspectives on Crime and Criminality*, 2nd ed. (Toronto: Harcourt Brace and Co., 1995).

8. Charles McCaghy, *Deviant Behavior* (New York: Macmillan, 1976), pp. 2–3; Vincent F. Sacco, *Deviance: Conformity and Control in Canadian Society*, 2nd ed. (Scarborough: Prentice-Hall, 1992), pp. 4–7.

9. "The 1999 Canada Drug Poll," www.cyberpages.com/polls.

10. "Vancouver Residents Soften Views on Drugs," *Vancouver Sun*, January 31, 2001.

11. John Hagan, *The Disreputable Pleasures: Crime and Deviance in Canada*, 3rd ed. (Toronto: McGraw-Hill, 1991), p. 13.

12. Patricia Erickson, *Cannabis Criminals: The Social Effects of Punishment on Drug Users* (Toronto: ARF, 1980); Edward Brecher, *Licit and Illicit Drugs* (Boston: Little, Brown, 1972), pp. 413–16; Hagan, *The Disreputable Pleasures*, pp. 27–30.

13. Sacco, ed., *Deviance: Conformity and Control in Canadian Society*.

14. Cesare Beccaria, *On Crimes and Punishments* (originally published in 1764; Bobbs-Merrill, 1963).

15. Described in David Lykken, "Psychopathy, Sociopathy, and Crime," *Society* 34 (1996): 29–38.

16. See Peter Scott, "Henry Maudsley," in *Pioneers in Criminology*, ed. Hermann Mannheim (Montclair, NJ: Prentice-Hall, 1981).

17. Nicole Hahn Rafter, "Criminal Anthropology in the United States," *Criminology* 30 (1992): 525–47.

18. L.A.J. Quetelet, *A Treatise on Man and the Development of His Faculties* (Gainesville, FL: Scholars' Facsimiles and Reprints, 1969), pp. 82–96.

19. Piers Beirne, "The Invention of Positivist Criminology: An Introduction to Quetelet's Social Mechanics of Crime," in Brian C. MacLean, *Crime and Society: Readings in Critical Criminology* (Toronto: Copp Clark, 1996).

20. See, generally, Robert Nisbet, *The Sociology of Emile Durkheim* (New York: Oxford University Press, 1974), p. 209; Emile Durkheim, *Rules of the Sociological Method*, trans. S.A. Solvay and J.H. Mueller, ed. G. Catlin (New York: Free Press, 1966), pp. 65–73; Emile Durkheim, *De la division de travail social: Étude sur l'organisation des sociétés supérieures* (Paris: Félix Alcan, 1893); idem, *The Division of Labor in Society* (New York: Free Press, 1964); idem, *Suicide: A Study in Sociology* (Glencoe, IL: Free Press, 1951).

21. Robert Park and Ernest Burgess, *The City* (Chicago: University of Chicago Press, 1925).

22. Marlene Shore, *The Science of Social Redemption: McGill, the Chicago School, and the Origins of Social Research in Canada* (Toronto: University of Toronto Press, 1987).

23. Karl Marx and Friedrich Engels, *Capital: A Critique of Political Economy*, trans. E. Aveling (Chicago: Charles Kern, 1906); Karl Marx, *Selected Writings in Sociology and Social Philosophy*, trans. P.B. Bottomore (New York: McGraw-Hill, 1956). For a general discussion of Marxist thought, see Michael Lynch and W. Byron Groves, *A Primer in Radical Criminology* (New York: Harrow and Heston, 1986), pp. 6–26.

24. Willem Bonger, *Criminality and Economic Conditions* (1916, abridged ed., Bloomington: Indiana University Press, 1969); Ralf Dahrendorf, *Class and Class Conflict in Industrial Society* (Palo Alto, CA: Stanford University Press, 1959).

25. Marvin Wolfgang and Franco Ferracuti, *The Subculture of Violence* (London: Social Science Paperbacks, 1967), p. 20.

26. "Lawyer to Probe Rodriguez Suicide," *Globe and Mail*, January 11, 1995, p. A1.

27. Associated Press, "Michigan Senate Acts to Outlaw Aiding Suicides," *Boston Globe*, March 20, 1994, p. 22.

28. Marvin Wolfgang, *Patterns in Criminal Homicide* (Philadelphia: University of Pennsylvania Press, 1958).

29. Edwin H. Sutherland, "White-Collar Criminality," *American Sociological Review* 5, 1 (1940): 2–10.

30. Hans von Hentig, *The Criminal and His Victim* (New Haven, CT: Yale University Press, 1948); Stephen Schafer, *The Victim and His Criminal* (New York: Random House, 1968).

31. Sutherland and Cressey, *Principles of Criminology*, p. 8.

32. Eugene Doleschal and Nora Klapmuts, "Toward a New Criminology," *Crime and Delinquency* 5 (1973): 607.

33. Michael Lynch and W. Byron Groves, *A Primer in Radical Criminology* (Albany, NY: Harrow and Heston, 1989), p. 32.

34. See Herbert Blumer, *Symbolic Interactionism* (Englewood Cliffs, NJ: Prentice-Hall, 1969).

35. Howard Becker, *Outsiders* (New York: The Free Press, 1963), p. 9.

36. Michael Gottfredson and Travis Hirschi, "The Methodological Adequacy of Longitudinal Research on Crime," *Criminology* 25 (1987): 581–614.

37. See, generally, David Farrington, Lloyd Ohlin, and James Q. Wilson, *Understanding and Controlling Crime* (New York: Springer-Verlag, 1986), pp. 11–18.

38. Cathy Spaatz Widom, "Child Abuse, Neglect, and Adult Behavior," *American Journal of Orthopsychiatry* 15 (1989): pp. 355–67.

39. "Statscan Says More Drivers Staying Sober," *Globe and Mail*, November 18, 1997, p. A8.

40. Claire Sterck-Elifson, "Just for Fun? Cocaine Use among Middle-Class Women," *Journal of Drug Issues* 26 (1996): 63–76.

41. William F. Whyte, *Street Corner Society* (Chicago: University of Chicago Press, 1955).

42. Herman Schwendinger and Julia Schwendinger, *Adolescent Subcultures and Delinquency* (New York: Praeger, 1985).

43. For a review of these studies, see L. Rowell Huesmann and Neil Malamuth, eds., "Media Violence and Antisocial Behavior," *Journal of Social Issues* 42 (1986): 31–53.

44. Luis T. Garcia, "Exposure to Pornography and Attitudes About Women and Rape: A Correlational Study," *Journal of Sex Research* 23 (1986): 378–85; N.M. Malamuth and E. Donnerstein, "The Effects of Aggressive-Pornographic Mass Media Stimuli," in *Advances in Experimental Social Psychology*, ed L. Berkowitz (New York: Academic Press, 1982), pp. 104–36.

45. Don Clairmont, "In Defence of Liberal Models of Research and Policy," *Canadian Journal of Criminology* 41 (1999): 151–60.

46. See, for example, Michael Hindelang and Travis Hirschi, "Intelligence and Delinquency: A Revisionist Review," *American Sociological Review* 42 (1977): 471–86.

47. Richard Herrnstein and Charles Murray, *The Bell Curve* (New York: Free Press, 1994).

48. Alan Ryan, "Apocalypse Now?" in *The Bell Curve Debate: History, Documents, Opinions*, eds. Russell Jacoby and Naomi Glauberman (New York: Random, 1995), p. 21.

Chapter 2

1. The historical material in the following sections was derived from a number of sources. The most important include Rene Wormser, *The Story of Law*, rev. ed. (New York: Simon & Schuster, 1962); Jackson Spielvogel, *Western Civilization* (St. Paul: West Publishing, 1991); Eugen Weber, *A Modern History of Europe* (New York: W.W. Norton, 1971); James Heath, *Eighteenth-Century Penal Theory* (New York: Oxford University Press, 1963); David Jones, *History of Criminology* (Westport, CT: Greenwood Press, 1986); Fred Inbau, James Thompson, and James Zagel, *Criminal Law and Its Administration* (Mineola, NY: Foundation Press, 1974); Wayne LaFave and Austin Scott, *Criminal Law*, 2nd ed. (St. Paul: West Publishing, 1986); and Sanford Kadish and Monrad Paulsen, *Criminal Law and Its Processes* (Boston: Little, Brown, 1975).

2. Chris McCormick, "Matters of Record: Documenting Discipline in Nova Scotia Baptist Churches, circa 1800," paper presented to the 12th Church History Workshop, 2001.

3. Wayne LaFave and Austin Scott, *Handbook on Criminal Law* (St. Paul, MN: West Publishing, 1982), pp. 528–29.

4. Caldwell 397 (1784), cited in LaFave and Scott, *Handbook on Criminal Law*, p. 422.

5. 9 George I, C. 22, 1723, cited in Douglas Hay, "Crime and Justice in Eighteenth and Nineteenth Century England," in *Crime and Justice*, vol. 2, ed. Norval Norris and Michael Tonrey (Chicago: University of Chicago Press, 1980), p. 51.

6. See, generally, Alfred Lindesmith, *The Addict and the Law* (New York: Vintage Books, 1965), Chapter 1.

7. A. Elizabeth Comack, "The Origins of Canadian Drug Legislation: Labelling versus Class Analysis," in *The New Criminologies in Canada*, ed. Tom Fleming (Toronto: Oxford, 1985).

8. This section owes much to Alison J. Hatch, for her excellent review, "Historical Legacies of Crime and Criminal Justice in Canada," in *Canadian Criminology: Perspectives on Crime and Criminality*, eds., Margaret A. Jackson and Curt T. Griffiths (Toronto: Harcourt Brace, 1991, 1995).

9. Pierre Berton, *Klondike: The Last Great Gold Rush, 1896-1899* (Toronto: McClelland and Stewart, 1958, 1981).

10. L. Brown and C. Brown, *An Unauthorized History of the R.C.M.P.* (Toronto: James Lorimer, 1973).

11. G.H. Crouse, "A Critique of Canadian Criminal Legislation," *Canadian Bar Review*, 12 (1934): 545–78.

12. Edna Erez and Bankole Thompson, "Rape in Sierra Leone: Conflict between the Sexes and Conflict of Laws," *International Journal of Comparative and Applied Criminal Justice* 14 (1990): 201–10.

13. William Henry, "Did the Music Say 'Do It'?" *Time*, 30 July 1990, p. 65; Doug Ireland, "Press Sins," *Village Voice*, March 20, 1990; Linda B. Deutschmann, *Deviance and Social Control* (Scarborough, ON: Nelson, 1994), p. 91.

14. For example, see *Brinegar v. United States*, 388 U.S. 160 (1949); *Speiser v. Randall*, 357 U.S. 513 (1958); *In re Winship*, 397 U.S. 358 (1970).

15. Richard Barnhorst, Sherrie Barnhorst, and Kenneth L. Clarke, *Criminal Law and the Canadian Criminal Code*, 2nd ed. (Toronto: McGraw-Hill Ryerson, 1992).

16. Curt T. Griffiths and Simon N. Verdun-Jones, *Canadian Criminal Justice*, 2nd ed. (Toronto: Harcourt Brace, 1994); for a good example of the conflict model, see generally R.S. Ratner and John L. McMullan, *State Control: Criminal Justice Politics in Canada* (Vancouver: UBC Press, 1987).

17. Oliver Wendell Holmes, *The Common Law*, ed. Mark De Wolf (Boston: Little, Brown, 1881), p. 36.

18. William Chambliss, "A Sociological Analysis of the Law of Vagrancy," *Social Problems* 12 (1964): 67–77; idem, "On Trashing Marxist Criminology," *Criminology* 27 (1989): 231–39.

19. Jeffrey Adler, "A Historical Analysis of the Law of Vagrancy," *Criminology* 27 (1989): 209–30; "Vagging the Demons and Scoundrels: Vagrancy and the Growth of St. Louis, 1830–1861," *Journal of Urban History* 13 (1986): 3–30.

20. *Carrier's case*, Y.B. 13 Edw. 4, f. 9, pl. 5 (Star Chamber and Exchequer Chamber, 1473), discussed at length in Jerome Hall, *Theft, Law and Society* (Indianapolis: Bobbs-Merrill, 1952), Chapter 1.

21. *R. v. Parks* [1992] 2 S.C.R. 871 (S.C.C.); Online Available: http://www.droit.umontreal.ca/doc/.../1992/vol2/html/1992scr_0871.html.

22. 8 Eng. Rep. 718 (1843).

23. *Regina v. Dudley and Stephens*, 14 Q.B. 273 (1884).

24. "Canadian Rescue Pilot of Plane Lost a Month in Arctic," *New York Times*, December 10, 1972, p. 1; "Pilot Rescued

after 32-day Ordeal in Arctic," *Globe and Mail,* December 11, 1972, p. A1; "Pilot Resorted to Cannibalism to Keep Alive, Statement Says," *Globe and Mail,* March 1, 1973, p. A1; "Bush Pilot Tells of Cannibalism," *New York Times,* March 2, 1973, p. 5.

25. Zalman et al., "Michigan Assisted Suicide Three Ring Circus"; 1992 P.A. 270 as amended by 1993 P.A. 3, M.C. L. ss. 752.1021 to 752.1027.

26. Brian Bergman, "The Final Hours," *Maclean's,* March 9, 1998, pp. 46–49.

27. National Institute of Justice, Project to Develop a Model Anti-stalking Statute (Washington, DC: National Institute of Justice, 1994).

28. "Clinton Signs Tougher Megan's Law," CNN News Service, May 17, 1996.

29. Roger Fillion, "Cracking Down on Internet Crime," *Boston Globe,* December 28, 1995, p. 65.

Chapter 3

1. Timothy F. Hartnagel, "Crime among the Provinces: The Effect of Geographic Mobility," *Canadian Journal of Criminology,* October 1997: 387–402.

2. Statistics Canada, "Family Violence 1999," *The Daily,* July 25, 2000.

3. Craig Perkins and Patsy Klaus, *Criminal Victimization, 1994* (Washington, DC: Bureau of Justice Statistics, 1996) (hereinafter cited as NCVS, 1994); Rosemary Gartner and Anthony N. Doob, "Trends in Criminal Victimization: 1988–1993," *Juristat* 14 (1994).

4. *The 2000 British Crime Survey, England and Wales* (London: British Home Office, 2000).

5. Paul Tappan, *Crime, Justice and Corrections* (New York: McGraw-Hill, 1960); Daniel Bell, *The End of Ideology* (New York: Free Press, 1967), p. 152.

6. Jim Hackler and Wasanti Paranjape, "Juvenile Justice Statistics: Mythmaking or Measure of System Response," *Canadian Journal of Criminology* 25 (1983): 209–26.

7. Lawrence Sherman and Barry Glick, "The Quality of Arrest Statistics," *Police Foundation Reports* 2 (1984): 1–8; David Seidman and Michael Couzens, "Getting the Crime Rate Down: Political Pressure and Crime Reporting," *Law and Society Review* 8 (1974): 457; Robert O'Brien, "Police Productivity and Crime Rates: 1973–1992," *Criminology* 34 (1996): 183–207.

8. Duncan Chappell, Gilbert Geis, Stephen Schafer, and Larry Siegel, "Forcible Rape: A Comparative Study of Offenses Known to the Police in Boston and Los Angeles," in *Studies in the Sociology of Sex,* ed. James Henslin (New York: Appleton-Century-Crofts, 1971), pp. 169–93.

9. Patrick Jackson, "Assessing the Validity of Official Data on Arson," *Criminology* 26 (1988): 181–95.

10. Peter Carrington, "Factors Affecting Police Diversion of Young Offenders: A Statistical Analysis," Report to the Solicitor General Canada, 1998.

11. "Arson in Canada," *Juristat* 12 (1992).

12. "Youth Courts Hear Fewer Cases," *Daily News,* May 1, 1998.

13. R. P. Ericson, P.M. Baranek, and J. Chan, *Visualizing Deviance: A Study of News Sources* (Toronto: University of Toronto Press, 1989); R.P. Ericson, P.M. Baranek, and J. Chan, *Negotiating Control: A Study of News Sources*

(Toronto: University of Toronto Press, 1989); R. P. Ericson, P.M.Baranek, and J. Chan, *Representing Order* (Toronto: University of Toronto Press, 1991).

14. M. Maltz, "Crime Statistics: A Historical Perspective," *Crime and Delinquency* 23 (1977): 32–40.

15. A. Doyle and R. Ericson, "Breaking into Prison: News Sources and Correctional Institutions," *Canadian Journal of Criminology* 38: 155–90.

16. Leonard Savitz, "Official Statistics," in *Contemporary Criminology,* ed. Leonard Savitz and Norman Johnston (New York: Wiley, 1982), pp. 3–15.

17. A pioneering effort in self-report research is A.L. Porterfield, *Youth in Trouble* (Fort Worth, TX: Leo Potishman Foundation, 1946); for a review, see Robert Hardt and George Bodine, *Development of Self-Report Instruments in Delinquency Research: A Conference Report* (Syracuse, NY: Syracuse University Youth Development Center, 1965). See also Fred Murphy, Mary Shirley, and Helen Witner, "The Incidence of Hidden Delinquency," *American Journal of Orthopsychology* 16 (1946): 686–96.

18. Franklyn Dunford and Delbert Elliott, "Identifying Career Criminals Using Self-Reported Data," *Journal of Research in Crime and Delinquency* 21 (1983): 57–86.

19. For example, see E. Vaz, "Middle Class Delinquency: Self Reported Delinquency and Youth Culture," *Canadian Review of Sociology and Anthropology* 2 (1965): 52–70; M. LeBlanc, "Middle Class Delinquency," in *Crime in Canadian Society,* ed. Robert A. Silverman and James J. Teevan (Toronto: Butterworths, 1975); I.M. Gomme, Mary E. Morton, and W. Gordon West, "Rates, Types, and Patterns of Male and Female Delinquency in an Ontario County," *Canadian Journal of Criminology* 26 (1984): 313–24.

20. Thomas Gabor, "Methodological Orthodoxy or Eclecticism? The Case of Youth Violence," *Canadian Journal of Criminology* 42 (2000): 77–83.

21. See, for example, Spencer Rathus and Larry Siegel, "Crime and Personality Revisited: Effects of MMPI Sets on Self-Report Studies," *Criminology* 18 (1980): 245–51; John Clark and Larry Tifft, "Polygraph and Interview Validation of Self-Reported Deviant Behavior," *American Sociological Review* 31 (1966): 516–23.

22. See, for example, Harwin Voss, "Ethnic Differences in Delinquency in Honolulu," *Journal of Criminal Law, Criminology and Police Science* 54 (1963): 322–27; Maynard Erickson and LaMar Empey, "Court Records, Undetected Delinquency and Decision Making," *Journal of Criminal Law, Criminology and Police Science* 54 (1963): 456–59; H.B. Gibson, Sylvia Morrison, and D.J. West, "The Confession of Known Offenses in Response to a Self-Reported Delinquency Schedule," *British Journal of Criminology* 10 (1970): 277–80; John Blackmore, "The Relationship between Self-Reported Delinquency and Official Convictions amongst Adolescent Boys," *British Journal of Criminology* 14 (1974): 172–76; Clark and Tifft, "Polygraph and Interview Validation of Self-Reported Deviant Behavior"; Michael Hindelang, Travis Hirschi, and Joseph Weis, *Measuring Delinquency* (Beverly Hills, CA: Sage, 1981).

23. Terence Thornberry, Beth Bjerregaard, and William Miles, "The Consequences of Respondent Attrition in Panel Studies: A Simulation Based on the Rochester Youth

Development Study," *Journal of Quantitative Criminology* 9 (1993): 127–58.

24. Minu Mathur, Richard Dodder, and Harjit Sandhu, "Inmate Self-Report Data: A Study of Reliability," *Criminal Justice Review* 17 (1992): 258–67.

25. Thomas Gray and Eric Wish, *Maryland Youth at Risk: A Study of Drug Use in Juvenile Detainees* (College Park, MD: Center for Substance Abuse Research, 1993); Eric Wish and Christina Polsenberg, "Arrestee Urine Tests and Self-Reports of Drug Use: Which Is More Related to Rearrest?" paper presented at the annual meeting of the American Society of Criminology, Phoenix, AZ, November 1993.

26. L. Edward Wells and Joseph Rankin, "Juvenile Victimization: Convergent Validation of Alternative Measurements," *Journal of Research in Crime and Delinquency* 32 (1995): 287–307.

27. Alfred Blumstein, Jacqueline Cohen, and Richard Rosenfeld, "Trend and Deviation in Crime Rates: A Comparison of UCR and NCVS Data for Burglary and Robbery," *Criminology* 29 (1991): 237–48. See also Hindelang, Hirschi, and Weis, *Measuring Delinquency.*

28. For a critique, see Scott Menard, "Residual Gains, Reliability, and the UCR–NCVS Relationship: A Comment on Blumstein, Cohen and Rosenfeld (1991)," *Criminology* 30 (1992): 105–15; David McDowall and Colin Loftin, "Comparing the UCR and NCVS over Time," *Criminology* 30 (1992): 125–33.

29. Ontario, Report of the Commission on Systemic Racism in the Ontario Criminal Justice System. Queen's Printer for Ontario, 1995.

30. Nova Scotia. *Royal Commission into the Wrongful Incarceration of Donald Marshall, Jr.* (Halifax: Queen's Printer, 1989).

31. Alberta, *Justice on Trial: Report of the Task Force on the Criminal Justice System and Its Impact on the Indian and Metis People of Alberta* (Edmonton: The Task Force, 1991).

32. Manitoba, *Report of the Aboriginal Justice Inquiry* (Winnipeg: Queen's Printer. 1991).

33. Saskatchewan, *Report of the Saskatchewan Indian Justice Review Committee* (Regina: The Indian Justice Review Committee, 1992); Saskatchewan, *Report of Commission of Inquiry Into the Shooting Death of Leo Lachance* (Regina: Saskatchewan Justice, 1993).

34. Michael Harris, *The Royal Commission of Inquiry into the Response of the Newfoundland Criminal Justice System to Complaints* (St. John's: Queen's Printer, 1991).

35. The Honourable Stuart G. Stratton, Q.C., *Report of an Independent Investigation in Respect of Incidents and Allegations of Sexual and Other Physical Abuse at Five Nova Scotia Residential Institutions*, June 30, 1995.

36. Justice in Crisis: A Report on Canada's Criminal Justice System. Online: http://www.mennonitecc.ca/mcc/misc/justice-in-crisis.html.

37. Vincent F. Sacco and Leslie W. Kennedy, *The Criminal Event*, 2nd ed. (Toronto: ITP Nelson, 1998); M. Martin and L. Ogrodnik, "Canadian Crime Trends," in *Crime Counts*, ed. L.W. Kennedy and V.F. Sacco (Toronto: ITP Nelson, 1996).

38. L.W. Kennedy and D. Veitch, "Why Are the Crime Rates Going Down? A Case Study in Edmonton," *Canadian Journal of Criminology* 39 (1997): 51–69.

39. Glenn Pierce and James Alan Fox, *Recent Trends in Violent Crime: A Closer Look* (Boston: National Crime Analysis Program, Northeastern University, 1992).

40. Ron Logan, "Crime Statistics in Canada, 2000," *Juristat* 21 (2001).

41. Anthony N. Doob and Jane B. Sprott, "Is the 'Quality' of Youth Violence Becoming More Serious," *Canadian Journal of Criminology*, April 1998: 185-194; Thomas Gabor, "Trends in Youth Crime: Some Evidence Pointing to Increases in the Severity and Volume of Violence on the Part of Young People," *Canadian Journal of Criminology*, July 1999: 385–92.

42. Donald J. Auger, Anthony N. Doob, Raymond P. Auger, and Paul Driben, "Crime and Control in Three Nishnawbe-Aski Nation Communities: An Exploratory Investigation," *Canadian Journal of Criminology*, October 1992: 317–38; Carol LaPrairie, "The Role of Sentencing in the Over-Representation of Aboriginal People in Correctional Institutions," *Canadian Journal of Criminology* 32 (1990): 429–40.

43. Canadian Centre for Justice Statistics, *Aboriginal Peoples in Canada* (Ottawa: Statistics Canada, 2001).

44. National Crime Prevention Centre, *Aboriginal Canadians: Violence, Victimization and Prevention* (Ottawa: Department of Justice, 2001).

45. John McMullan, "A Social Economy of Arson," *Canadian Journal of Criminology* 31 (1989).

46. Rosemary Gartner, "Family Structure, Welfare Spending, and Child Homicide in Developed Democracies," *Journal of Marriage and the Family* 53 (1991): 231–40.

47. John Donohue and Steven Levitt, "The Impact of Legalized Abortion on Crime," National Bureau of Economic Research Working Paper, November 2000.

48. Rosemary Gartner and Robert Nash Parker, "Cross-National Evidence on Homicide and the Age Structure of the Population," *Social Forces* 69 (1990): 351–71.

49. John Braithwaite, *Crime, Shame and Reintegration* (Cambridge: Cambridge University Press, 1989).

50. Koichiro Ito, "Research on the Fear of Crime: Perceptions and Realities of Crime in Japan," *Crime and Delinquency* 39 (1993): 392–95; Joachim Kersten, "Street Youths, Bosozoku, and Yakuza: Subculture Formation and Social Reactions in Japan," *Crime and Delinquency* 39 (1993): 277–95; Michael Vaughn and Nobuho Tomita, "A Longitudinal Analysis of Japanese Crime from 1926–1987: The Pre-War, War and Post-War Eras," *International Journal of Comparative and Applied Criminal Justice* 14 (1990): 145–60; Ted Westermann and James Burfeind, *Crime and Justice in Two Societies: Japan and the United States* (Pacific Grove, CA: Brooks/Cole, 1991).

51. Joseph Sheley and James Wright, *In the Line of Fire: Youth, Guns, and Violence in Urban America* (New York: Aldine de Gruyter, 1995).

52. "The Justice Factfinder 1998," *Juristat* 20 (2000).

53. Thomas Gabor, "Canadians Rarely Use Firearms for Self-protection," *Canadian Journal of Criminology* 38 (1996): 217–20; Gary Mauser, "Do Canadians Use Firearms in Self-protection," *Canadian Journal of Criminology* 37 (1995): 556–62.

54. Alfred Blumstein, "Violence by Young People: Why the Deadly Nexus," *National Institute of Justice Journal* 229 (1995): 2–9.

55. Steven Dillingham, *Violent Crime in the United States* (Washington, DC: Bureau of Justice Statistics, 1991), p. 17; Bruce Johnson, Andrew Golub, and Jeffrey Fagan, "Careers in Crack, Drug Use, Drug Distribution, and Nondrug Criminality," *Crime and Delinquency* 41 (1995): 275–95.

56. J.Q. Wilson and G. Kelling, "Broken Windows: The Police and Neighbourhood Safety," *Atlantic Monthly* (March 19, 1996), pp. 29–38; and George L. Kelling and Catherine M. Coles, *Fixing Broken Windows: Reducing Order and Reducing Crime in Our Communities* (New York: Martin Kessler Books/Free Press, 1997).

57. Darrell Steffensmeier and Miles Harer, "Did Crime Rise or Fall during the Reagan Presidency? The Effects of an 'Aging' U.S. Population on the Nation's Crime Rate," *Journal of Research in Crime and Delinquency* 28 (1991): 330–39.

58. James A. Fox, *Trends in Juvenile Violence: A Report to the United States Attorney General on Current and Future Rates of Juvenile Offending* (Boston, MA: Northeastern University, 1996).

59. Ellen Cohn, "The Effect of Weather and Temporal Variations on Calls for Police Service," *American Journal of Police* 15 (1996): 23–43.

60. R.A. Baron, "Aggression as a Function of Ambient Temperature and Prior Anger Arousal," *Journal of Personality and Social Psychology* 21 (1972): 183–89; Ellen Cohn, "The Prediction of Police Calls for Service: The Influence of Weather and Temporal Variables on Rape and Domestic Violence," *Journal of Environmental Psychology* 13 (1993): 71–83; Derral Cheatwood, "The Effects of Weather on Homicide," *Journal of Quantitative Criminology* 11 (1995): 51–70; Ellen Cohn and James Rotton, "Assault as a Function of Time and Temperature: A Moderator-Variable Times-Series Analysis," paper presented at the annual meeting of the American Society of Criminology, Chicago, November 1996, p. 23.

61. Robert Nash Parker, "Bringing 'Booze' Back In: The Relationship between Alcohol and Homicide," *Journal of Research in Crime and Delinquency* 32 (1995): 3–38.

62. Victoria Brewer and M. Dwayne Smith, "Gender Inequality and Rates of Female Homicide Victimization Across U.S. Cities," *Journal of Research in Crime and Delinquency* 32 (1995): 175–90.

63. F. Ivan Nye, James Short, and Virgil Olsen, "Socio-economic Status and Delinquent Behavior," *American Journal of Sociology* 63 (1958): 381–89; Robert Dentler and Lawrence Monroe, "Social Correlates of Early Adolescent Theft," *American Sociological Review* 63 (1961): 733–43. See also Terence Thornberry and Margaret Farnworth, "Social Correlates of Criminal Involvement: Further Evidence of the Relationship between Social Status and Criminal Behavior," *American Sociological Review* 47 (1982): 505–18.

64. Charles Tittle, Wayne Villemez, and Douglas Smith, "The Myth of Social Class and Criminality: An Empirical Assessment of the Empirical Evidence," *American Sociological Review* 43 (1978): 643–56.

65. Charles Tittle and Robert Meier, "Specifying the SES/Delinquency Relationship," *Criminology* 28 (1990): 271–301.

66. Delbert Elliott and Suzanne Ageton, "Reconciling Race and Class Differences in Self-Reported and Official Estimates of Delinquency," *American Sociological Review* 45 (1980): 95–110.

67. See also Delbert Elliott and David Huizinga, "Social Class and Delinquent Behavior in a National Youth Panel: 1976–1980," *Criminology* 21 (1983): 149–77. For a similar view, see John Braithwaite, "The Myth of Social Class and Criminality Reconsidered," *American Sociological Review* 46 (1981): 35–58, and Hindelang, Hirschi, and Weis, *Measuring Delinquency*, p. 196.

68. David Brownfield, "Social Class and Violent Behavior," *Criminology* 24 (1986): 421–39.

69. Douglas Smith and Laura Davidson, "Interfacing Indicators and Constructs in Criminological Research: A Note on the Comparability of Self-Report Violence Data for Race and Sex Groups," *Criminology* 24 (1986): 473–88.

70. Sally Simpson and Lori Elis, "Doing Gender: Sorting Out the Case and Crime Conundrum," *Criminology* 33 (1995): 47–81.

71. Judith Blau and Peter Blau, "The Cost of Inequality: Metropolitan Structure and Violent Crime," *American Sociological Review* 147 (1982): 114–29; Richard Block, "Community Environment and Violent Crime," *Criminology* 17 (1979): 46–57; Robert Sampson, "Structural Sources of Variation in Race-Age-Specific Rates of Offending across Major U.S. Cities," *Criminology* 23 (1985): 647–73.

72. Chin-Chi Hsieh and M.D. Pugh, "Poverty, Income Inequality, and Violent Crime: A Meta-Analysis of Recent Aggregate Data Studies," *Criminal Justice Review* 18 (1993): 182–99.

73. Alan Lizotte, Terence Thornberry, Marvin Krohn, Deborah Chard-Wierschem, and David McDowall, "Neighborhood Context and Delinquency: A Longitudinal Analysis," in *Cross National Longitudinal Research on Human Development and Criminal Behavior*, ed. E.M. Weitekamp and H.J. Kerner (Stavernstr, Netherlands: Kluwer, 1994), pp. 217–27.

74. Travis Hirschi and Michael Gottfredson, "Age and the Explanation of Crime," *American Journal of Sociology* 89 (1983): 552–84.

75. Darrell Steffensmeier and Cathy Streifel, "Age, Gender, and Crime Across Three Historical Periods: 1935, 1960 and 1985," *Social Forces* 69 (1991): 869–94; John Laub, David Clark, Leslie Siegel, and James Garofolo, *Trends in Juvenile Crime in the United States: 1973–1983* (Albany, NY: Hindelang Research Center, 1987). On another note, for a comprehensive review of crime and the elderly, see Kyle Kercher, "Causes and Correlates of Crime Committed by the Elderly," in *Critical Issues in Aging Policy*, ed. E. Borgatta and R. Montgomery (Beverly Hills: Sage, 1987), pp. 254–306, and Darrell Steffensmeier, "The Invention of the 'New' Senior Citizen Criminal," *Research on Aging* 9 (1987): 281–311.

76. Hirschi and Gottfredson, "Age and the Explanation of Crime"; Michael Gottfredson and Travis Hirschi, "The True Value of Lambda Would Appear to Be Zero: An Essay on Career Criminals, Criminal Careers, Selective Incapacitation, Cohort Studies and Related Topics,"

Criminology 24 (1986): 213–34; further support for their position can be found in Lawrence Cohen and Kenneth Land, "Age Structure and Crime," *American Sociological Review* 52 (1987): 170–83.

77. Kyle Kercher, "Explaining the Relationship between Age and Crime: The Biological Versus Sociological Model," paper presented at the American Society of Criminology meeting, Montreal, November 1987; Alfred Blumstein, Jacqueline Cohen, and David Farrington, "Criminal Career Research: Its Value for Criminology," *Criminology* 26 (1988): 1–37; Sung Joon Jang and Marvin Krohn, "Developmental Patterns of Sex Differences in Delinquency among African American Adolescents: A Test of the Sex-Invariance Hypothesis," *Journal of Quantitative Criminology* 11 (1995): 195–220; Candace Kruttschnitt, "Violence by and against Women: A Comparative and Cross-National Analysis," *Violence and Victims* 8 (1994): 1–28.

78. David Greenberg, "Age, Crime, and Social Explanation," *American Journal of Sociology* 91 (1985): 1–21; Marvin Wolfgang, Robert Figlio, and Thorsten Sellin, *Delinquency in a Birth Cohort* (Chicago: University of Chicago Press, 1972); Lyle Shannon, *Assessing the Relationship of Adult Criminal Careers to Juvenile Careers: A Summary* (Washington, DC: U.S. Department of Justice, 1982); D.J. West and David P. Farrington, *The Delinquent Way of Life* (London: Hienemann, 1977); Donna Hamparian, Richard Schuster, Simon Dinitz, and John Conrad, *The Violent Few* (Lexington, MA: Lexington Books, 1978); Rolf Loeber, Magda Stouthamer-Loeber, and Stephanie Green, "Age at Onset of Problem Behaviour in Boys and Later Disruptive and Delinquent Behaviours," *Criminal Behaviour and Mental Health* 1 (1991): 229–46.

79. Darrell Steffensmeier, Emilie Andersen Allan, Miles Harer, and Cathy Streifel, "Age and the Distribution of Crime: Variant or Invariant?" paper presented at the American Society of Criminology meeting, Montreal, November 1987; Hilary Saner, Robert MacCoun, and Peter Reuter, "On the Ubiquity of Drug Selling among Youthful Offenders in Washington, DC, 1985–1991: Age, Period, or Cohort Effect?" *Journal of Quantitative Criminology* 11 (1995): 362–73.

80. Arnold Barnett, Alfred Blumstein, and David Farrington, "Probabilistic Models of Youthful Criminal Careers," *Criminology* 25 (1987): 83–107.

81. Peter Greenwood, "Differences in Criminal Behavior and Court Responses among Juvenile and Young Adult Defendants," in *Crime and Justice, An Annual Review of Research,* ed. Michael Tonry and Norval Morris (Chicago: University of Chicago Press, 1986), pp. 151–89.

82. John Hagan and Alberto Palloni, "Crimes as Social Events in the Life Course: Reconceiving a Criminological Controversy," *Criminology* 26 (1988): 87–101.

83. Travis Hirschi and Michael Gottfredson, "Age and Crime, Logic and Scholarship: Comment on Greenberg," *American Journal of Sociology* 91 (1985): 22–27; "All Wise after the Fact Learning Theory, Again: Reply to Baldwin," *American Journal of Sociology* 90 (1985): 1330–33; John Baldwin, "Thrill and Adventure Seeking and the Age Distribution of Crime: Comment on Hirschi and Gottfredson," *American Journal of Sociology* 90

(1985): 1326–29; Per-Olof Wikstrom, "Age and Crime in a Stockholm Cohort," *Journal of Quantitative Criminology* 6 (1990): 61–82.

84. Edward Mulvey and John LaRosa, "Delinquency Cessation and Adolescent Development: Preliminary Data," *American Journal of Orthopsychiatry* 56 (1986): 212–24.

85. Gordon Trasler, "Cautions for a Biological Approach to Crime," in *The Causes of Crime, New Biological Approaches,* ed. Sarnoff Mednick, Terrie Moffitt, and Susan Stack (Cambridge: Cambridge University Press, 1987), pp. 7–25.

86. James Q. Wilson and Richard Herrnstein, *Crime and Human Nature* (New York: Simon & Schuster, 1985), pp. 126–47.

87. Charles Tittle, "Two Empirical Regularities (Maybe) in Search of an Explanation: Commentary on the Age/Crime Debate," *Criminology* 26 (1988): 75–85.

88. Neal Shover and Carol Thompson, "Age, Differential Expectations and Crime Desistance," *Criminology* 30 (1992): 89–105.

89. Erich Labouvie, "Maturing Out of Substance Use: Selection and Self-Correction," *Journal of Drug Issues* 26 (1996): 457–74.

90. Walter Gove, "The Effect of Age and Gender on Deviant Behavior: A Biopsychosocial Perspective," in *Gender and the Life Course,* ed. A. Ross (Chicago: Aldine, 1985), p. 131.

91. Steven D. Levitt, "The Limited Role of Changing Age Structure in Explaining Aggregate Crime Rates," *Criminology* 37 (1999): 581–597.

92. Cesare Lombroso, *The Female Offender* (New York: Appleton Publishers, 1895/1920).

93. Otto Pollack, *The Criminality of Women* (Philadelphia: University of Pennsylvania, 1950).

94. For a review of this issue, see Darrell Steffensmeier, "Assessing the Impact of the Women's Movement on Sex-Based Differences in the Handling of Adult Criminal Defendants," *Crime and Delinquency* 26 (1980): 344–57.

95. Alan Booth and D. Wayne Osgood, "The Influence of Testosterone on Deviance in Adulthood: Assessing and Explaining the Relationship," *Criminology* 31 (1993): 93–118.

96. Darrell Steffensmeier and Robert Clark, "Sociocultural Versus Biological/Sexist Explanations of Sex Differences in Crime: A Survey of American Criminology Textbooks, 1918–1965," *American Sociologist* 15 (1980): 246–55.

97. Gisela Konopka, *The Adolescent Girl in Conflict* (Englewood Cliffs, NJ: Prentice-Hall, 1966); Clyde Vedder and Dora Somerville, *The Delinquent Girl* (Springfield, IL: Charles C Thomas, 1970).

98. John Mirowsky and Catherine Ross, "Sex Differences in Distress: Real or Artifact?" *American Sociological Review* 60 (1995): 449–68; for a review of this issue, see Anne Campbell, *Men, Women and Aggression* (New York: Basic Books, 1993).

99. Robert Hoge, D.A. Andrews, and Alan Leschied, "Tests of Three Hypotheses Regarding the Predictors of Delinquency," *Journal of Abnormal Child Psychology* 22 (1994): 547–59.

100. Freda Adler, *Sisters in Crime* (New York: McGraw-Hill, 1975); Rita James Simon, *The Contemporary Woman and Crime* (Washington, DC: U.S. Government Printing Office, 1975).

101. Timothy F. Hartnagel and Muhammad Mizanuddin, "Modernization, Gender Role Convergence, and Female Crime," *International Journal of Comparative Sociology* 27 (1986): 1-14.

102. David Rowe, Alexander Vazsonyi, and Daniel Flannery, "Sex Differences in Crime: Do Mean and Within-Sex Variation Have Similar Causes?" *Journal of Research in Crime and Delinquency* 32 (1995): 84-100; Michael Hindelang, "Age, Sex, and the Versatility of Delinquency Involvements," *Social Forces* 14 (1971): 525-34; Martin Gold, *Delinquent Behavior in an American City* (Belmont, CA: Brooks/Cole, 1970); Gary Jensen and Raymond Eve, "Sex Differences in Delinquency: An Examination of Popular Sociological Explanations," *Criminology* 13 (1976): 427-48.

103. Darrel Steffensmeier and Renee Hoffman Steffensmeier, "Trends in Female Delinquency," *Criminology* 18 (1980): 62-85; see also idem, "Crime and the Contemporary Woman: An Analysis of Changing Levels of Female Property Crime, 1960-1975," *Social Forces* 57 (1978): 566-84; Joseph Weis, "Liberation and Crime: The Invention of the New Female Criminal," *Crime and Social Justice* 1 (1976): 17-27; Carol Smart, "The New Female Offender: Reality or Myth," *British Journal of Criminology* 19 (1979): 50-59; Steven Box and Chris Hale, "Liberation/Emancipation, Economic Marginalization or Less Chivalry," *Criminology* 22 (1984): 473-78.

104. Meda Chesney-Lind, "Female Offenders: Paternalism Reexamined," in *Women, the Courts and Equality*, ed. Laura Crites and Winifred Hepperle (Newberry Park, CA: Sage, 1987), pp. 114-39.

105. Darrell Steffensmeier, Emilie Allan, and Cathy Streifel, "Development and Female Crime: A Cross-National Test of Alternative Explanations," *Social Forces* 68 (1989): 262-83.

106. Roy Austin, "Recent Trends in the Male and Female Crime Rate: The Convergence Controversy," *Journal of Criminal Justice* 21 (1993): 447-66.

107. Marvin Wolfgang, Robert Figlio, and Thorsten Sellin, *Delinquency in a Birth Cohort* (Chicago: University of Chicago Press, 1972).

108. See Thorsten Sellin and Marvin Wolfgang, *The Measurement of Delinquency* (New York: Wiley, 1964), p. 120.

109. Paul Tracy and Robert Figlio, "Chronic Recidivism in the 1950 Birth Cohort," paper presented at the American Society of Criminology meeting, Toronto, October 1982; Marvin Wolfgang, "Delinquency in Two Birth Cohorts," in *Perspective Studies of Crime and Delinquency*, ed. Katherine Teilmann Van Dusen and Sarnoff Mednick (Boston: Kluwer-Nijhoff, 1983), pp. 7-17. The following sections rely heavily on these sources.

110. Lyle Shannon, *Criminal Career Opportunity* (New York: Human Sciences Press, 1988); idem, *Assessing the Relationship of Adult Criminal Careers to Juvenile Careers.*

111. D.J. West and David P. Farrington, *The Delinquent Way of Life* (London: Heinemann, 1977); David Farrington and D.J. West, "Criminal, Penal and Life Histories of Chronic Offenders: Risk and Protective Factors and Early Identification," in *Integrating Individual and Ecological Aspects of Crime* (Stockholm: National Council for Crime Prevention, 1993).

112. See, generally, M. Wolfgang, T. Thornberry, and R. Figlio, eds. *From Boy to Man, from Delinquency to Crime* (Chicago: University of Chicago Press, 1987); Paul Tracy and Kimberly Kempf-Leonard, *Continuity and Discontinuity in Criminal Careers* (New York: Plenum Press, 1996).

113. R. Tremblay, R. Loeber, C. Gagnon, P. Charlebois, S. Larivee, and M. LeBlanc, "Disruptive Boys with Stable and Unstable High Fighting Behavior Patterns During Junior Elementary School," *Journal of Abnormal Child Psychology* 19 (1991): 285-300; Jennifer White, Terrie Moffitt, Felton Earls, Lee Robins, and Phil Silva, "How Early Can We Tell? Predictors of Childhood Conduct Disorder and Adolescent Delinquency," *Criminology* 28 (1990): 507-35; John Laub and Robert Sampson, "Unemployment, Marital Discord, and Deviant Behavior: The Long-Term Correlates of Childhood Misbehavior," paper presented at the annual meeting of the American Society of Criminology, Baltimore, November 1990; rev. version.

114. Jane B. Sprott and Anthony N. Doob, "Bad, Sad, and Rejected: The Lives of Aggressive Children," *Canadian Journal of Criminology* 42 (2000): 123-34.

115. David Farrington and J. David Hawkins, "Predicting Participation, Early Onset, and Later Persistence in Officially Recorded Offending," *Criminal Behavior and Mental Health* 1 (1991): 1-33; Daniel Nagin, David Farrington, and Terrie Moffitt, "Life-Course Trajectories of Different Types of Offenders," *Criminology* 33 (1995): 111-39.

116. Susan Martin, "Policing Career Criminals: An Examination of an Innovative Crime Control Program," *Journal of Criminal Law and Criminology* 77 (1986): 1159-82.

117. "A One-Day Snapshot of Inmates in Canada's Adult Correctional Facilities," *Juristat* 18 (1998).

Chapter 4

1. Arthur Lurigio, "Are All Victims Alike? The Adverse, Generalized, and Differential Impact of Crime," *Crime and Delinquency* 33 (1987): 452-67.

2. Ted Miller, Mark Cohen, and Brian Wiersema, *The Extent and Costs of Crime Victimization: A New Look* (Washington, DC: National Institute of Justice, 1996).

3. Peter Finn, *Victims* (Washington, DC: Bureau of Justice Statistics, 1988); Alison Hatch Cunningham and Curt T. Griffiths, *Canadian Criminal Justice: A Primer* (Toronto: Harcourt Brace, 1997).

4. Susan Leslie Bryant and Lillian Range, "Suicidality in College Women Who Were Sexually and Physically Abused and Physically Punished by Parents," *Violence and Victims* 10 (1995): 195-215.

5. Sally Davies-Netley, Michael Hurlburt, and Richard Hough, "Childhood Abuse as a Precursor to Homelessness for Homeless Women with Severe Mental Illness," *Violence and Victims* 11 (1996): 129-42.

6. See, generally, M.D. Pagelow, *Woman Battering: Victims and Their Experiences* (Beverly Hills, CA: Sage, 1981); Walter Gleason, "Mental Disorders in Battered Women," *Violence and Victims* 8 (1993): 53-66; Daniel Saunders, "Posttraumatic Stress Symptom Profiles of Battered Women: A Comparison of Survivors in Two Settings,"

Violence and Victims 9 (1994): 31–43.

7. Trevor Markesteyn, *The Psychological Impact of Nonsexual Criminal Offenses on Victims*, prepared for the Corrections Branch, Ministry of the Solicitor General of Canada. Report No. 1992-21.

8. Elizabeth Stanko and Kathy Hobdell, "Assault on Men, Masculinity and Male Victimization," *British Journal of Criminology* 33 (1993): 400–15.

9. John McKendy, "Dialogue and the Risk of Responsibility," *Humanity & Society*, 23 (1999): 238–53; see also, "Ideological Practices and the Management of Emotions: The Case of Wife Abusers," *Critical Sociology* 19 (1992): 61–80.

10. Robert Davis, Bruce Taylor, and Arthur Lurigio, "Adjusting to Criminal Victimization: The Correlates of Postcrime Distress," *Violence and Victimization* 11 (1996): 21–34.

11. James Anderson, Terry Grandison, and Laronistine Dyson, "Victims of Random Violence and the Public Health Implication: A Health Care of Criminal Justice Issue," *Journal of Criminal Justice* 24 (1996): 379–93.

12. Rosemary Gartner and Anthony Doob, "Trends in Criminal Victimization in 1988–1993," *Juristat* 14 (1994).

13. Paul Brantingham and Stephen Easton, *The Costs of Crime: Who Pays and How Much?* Fraser Institute Critical Issues Bulletin. 1998.

14. "Murder Rate Down for Fourth Year in a Row - TV Coverage Up," *The Fraser Institute's National Media Archive*, 1996.

15. Sandra Besserer and Catherine Trainor, "Criminal Victimization in Canada, 1999," *Juristat* 20 (2000).

16. For some interesting studies in this area, see Vincent F. Sacco, "The Effects of Mass Media on Perceptions of Crime," *Pacific Sociological Review* 25 (1982): 475–93; Julian V. Roberts and Michelle G. Grossman, "Crime Prevention and Public Opinion," *Canadian Journal of Criminology*, January (1990): 75–90; and "The Effect of Pretrial Publicity: The Bernardo Case," *Canadian Journal of Criminology*, July (1996): 253–70.

17. Timothy Ireland and Cathy Spatz Widom, *Childhood Victimization and Risk for Alcohol and Drug Arrests* (Washington, DC: National Institute of Justice, 1995).

18. Cathy Spatz Widom, *The Cycle of Violence* (Washington, DC: National Institute of Justice, 1992), p. 1; idem, "The Cycle of Violence," *Science* 244 (1989): 160–66.

19. Steve Spaccarelli, J. Douglas Coatsworth, and Blake Sperry Bowden, "Exposure to Serious Family Violence among Incarcerated Boys: Its Association with Violent Offending and Potential Mediating Variables," *Violence and Victims* 10 (1995): 163–80.

20. Jerome Kolbo, "Risk and Resilience among Children Exposed to Family Violence," *Violence and Victims* 11 (1996): 113–27.

21. P. Rock, *A View from the Shadows: The Ministry of the Solicitor General Canada and the Justice for Victims of Crime Initiative* (Oxford: Clarendon Press, 1986); Brian D. Maclean, "A Program of Local Crime-Survey Research for Canada," in *Crime in Society: Readings in Critical Criminology*, ed. Brian D. Maclean (Toronto: Copp Clark, 1996).

22. Solicitor General Canada, *Reported and Unreported Crimes: Canadian Urban Victimization Survey.* Bulletin 2 (Ottawa: Ministry Secretariat, 1984).

23. V.F. Sacco and H. Johnson, *Patterns of Criminal Victimization in Canada*, General Social Survey Analysis Services, Statistics Canada, Catalogue 11-612E, No. 2. (Ottawa: Ministry of Supply and Services, 1990).

24. Holly Johnson and Vincent F. Sacco, "The Risk of Criminal Victimization: Data from a National Study," in *Crime in Canadian Society*, 4th ed., ed. Robert A. Silverman, James J. Teevan, and Vincent F. Sacco (Toronto: Butterworths, 1991).

25. Ronet Bachman, *Violence against Women* (Washington, DC: Bureau of Justice Statistics, 1994).

26. Elizabeth Comack, *Women in Trouble: Connecting Women's Law Violations to Their Histories of Abuse* (Halifax: Fernwood, 1996).

27. Statistics Canada, "Criminal Harassment," *The Daily*, November 29, 2000.

28. Holly Johnson and Gary Lazarus, "The Impact of Age on Crime Victimization Rates," *Canadian Journal of Criminology* 31 (1989): 309–17.

29. William Meloff and Robert A. Silverman, "Canadian Kids Who Kill," *Canadian Journal of Criminology* (1992): 15-34.

30. Holly Johnson, "Children and Youths as Victims of Violent Crimes," *Juristat* 15 (1995).

31. N. Trocme, D. McPhee, and K. Kwon Tam, "Child Abuse and Neglect in Ontario: Incidence and Characteristics," *Child Welfare* 74 (1995): 563–86.

32. Murray Straus, Richard Gelles, and Suzanne Steinmentz, *Behind Closed Doors: Violence in the American Family* (Garden City, NY: Anchor Books, 1980); Richard Gelles and Murray Straus, "Violence in the American Family," *Journal of Social Issues* 35 (1979): 15–39; Richard Gelles and Murray Straus, *Is Violence toward Children Increasing? A Comparison of 1975 and 1985 National Survey Rates* (Durham, NH: Family Violence Research Program, 1985).

33. Ching-Tung Lung and Deborah Daro, *Current Trends in Child Abuse Reporting and Fatalities: The Results of the 1995 Annual Fifty-State Survey* (Chicago: National Committee to Prevent Child Abuse, 1996).

34. Nico Trocme and David Wolfe, *The Canadian Incidence Study of Reported Child Abuse and Neglect* (Ottawa: Health Canada, Spring 2001).

35. Walter S. Dekeseredy and Ronald Hinch, *Woman Abuse: Sociological Perspectives* (Toronto: Thompson, 1991); Karen Rodgers, "Wife Assault: The Findings of a National Survey," *Juristat* 14 (1990).

36. Yasmin Jiwani, "The 1999 General Social Survey on Spousal Violence: An Analysis," The FREDA Centre for Research on Violence against Women and Children, August 2000; also, Daisy Locke, "Family Homicide," in *Family Violence in Canada: A Statistical Profile* (Ottawa: Statistics Canada, 2000), pp. 39–44; Holly Johnson, *Dangerous Domains: Violence Against Women in Canada* (Scarborough, ON: Nelson Canada, 1996); and, Robin Fitzgerald, *Family Violence in Canada: A Statistical Profile* (Ottawa: Statistics Canada, 1999).

37. *R. v. Whynot* (1983), 9 C.C.C. 449 (N.S.C.A.).

38. Janet Lauritsen and Kenna Davis Quinet, "Repeat Victimizations among Adolescents and Young Adults," *Journal of Quantitative Criminology* 11 (1995): 143–63.

39. Denise Osborn, Dan Ellingworth, Tim Hope, and Alan Trickett, "Are Repeatedly Victimized Households Different?" *Journal of Quantitative Criminology* 12 (1996): 223–45.

40. Graham Farrell, "Predicting and Preventing Revictimization," in *Crime and Justice: An Annual Review of Research*, vol. 20, ed. Michael Tonry and David Farrington (Chicago: University of Chicago Press, 1995), pp. 61–126.

41. David Finkelhor and Nancy Asdigian, "Risk Factors for Youth Victimization: Beyond a Lifestyles/Routine Activities Theory Approach," *Violence and Victimization* 11 (1996): 3–19.

42. Lauritsen and Quinet, "Repeat Victimizations," p. 161.

43. Graham Farrell, Coretta Phillips, and Ken Pease, "Like Taking Candy, Why Does Repeat Victimization Occur?" *British Journal of Criminology* 35 (1995): 384–99.

44. A. Karmen, *Crime Victims: An Introduction to Victimology* (Pacific Grove, CA: Brooks/Cole, 1990).

45. Hans Von Hentig, *The Criminal and His Victim: Studies in the Sociobiology of Crime* (New Haven, CT: Yale University Press, 1948), p. 384.

46. Stephen Schafer, *The Victim and His Criminal* (New York: Random House, 1968), p. 152.

47. Marvin Wolfgang, *Patterns of Criminal Homicide* (Philadelphia: University of Pennsylvania Press, 1958).

48. Menachim Amir, *Patterns in Forcible Rape* (Chicago: University of Chicago Press, 1971).

49. Susan Estrich, *Real Rape* (Cambridge, MA: Harvard University Press, 1987), p. 69.

50. "McClung Letter Throws Canadian Legal Circles into Turmoil," *Globe and Mail*, March 1, 1999, p. A3.

51. Martin Yaqzan, "'Rape'–Yesterday and Today!" *The Brunswickan*, November 5, 1993; "Dispatch Case," *The Chronicle of Higher Education* (November 24, 1993), p. A34; "Date Rape Comments Cause Campus Furor: It's a Natural Outlet, Says Professor," *Globe and Mail*, November 9, 1993, p. A4.

52. L. Clark and D. Lewis, *Rape: The Price of Coercive Sexuality* (Toronto: Women's Press, 1977), p. 150.

53. E.A. Fattah, "Some Recent Theoretical Developments in Victimology," *Victimology: An International Journal* 4 (1979): 198–213; see also, idem, "Canada's Successful Experience with the Abolition of the Death Penalty," *Canadian Journal of Criminology*, 25 (1983): 421–31; idem, "Victimology: Past, Present and Future," *Criminologie* 33 (2000): 17–46.

54. Martin Daly and Margo Wilson, *Homicide* (New York: Aldine de Gruyter, 1988).

55. "Bill Won't Foster Gay Lifestyle, Rock Says," *Globe and Mail*, November 18, 1994, p. A3; "Bill C-41 (Sentencing Reform) Passes Third Reading in House of Commons," Parliamentary press release, June 15, 1995.

56. Rosemary Gartner and Bill McCarthy, "The Social Distribution of Femicide in Urban Canada, 1921–1988," *Law and Society Review* 25 (1991): 287–311.

57. Julian V. Roberts, "Disproportionate Harm: Hate Crime in Canada," Department of Justice Canada, Working Document 1995-11e, 1995.

58. "ADL Survey Analyzes Neo-Nazi Skinhead Menace and International Connections," *CJ International* 12 (1996): 7; FBI, news release, November 4, 1996.

59. Derek E. Janhevich, *Hate Crime in Canada: An Overview of Issues and Data Sources*, Canadian Centre for Justice Statistics Catalogue no. 85-551-XIE, January 2001.

60. James Garofalo, "Bias and Non-Bias Crimes in New York City: Preliminary Findings," paper presented at the annual meeting of the American Society of Criminology, Baltimore, November 1990.

61. Ronald Powers, "Bensonhurst Man Guilty," *Boston Globe*, May 18, 1990, p. 3.

62. "Boy Gets 18 Years in Fatal Park Beating of Transient," *Los Angeles Times*, December 24, 1987, p. 9B.

63. Mike McPhee, "In Denver, Attacks Stir Fears of Racism," *Boston Globe*, December 10, 1990, p. 3.

64. Jack McDevitt, "The Study of the Character of Civil Rights Crimes in Massachusetts (1983–1987)," paper presented at the annual meeting of the American Society of Criminology, Reno, NV, November 1989; see also, Jack Levin and Jack McDevitt, *Hate Crimes: The Rising Tide of Bigotry and Bloodshed* (New York: Plenum, 1993); Jack Levin and Jack McDevitt, *Hate Crimes: A Study of Offenders' Motivations* (Boston, MA: Northeastern University, 1993).

65. Lawrence Cohen and Marcus Felson, "Social Change and Crime Rate Trends: A Routine Activities Approach," *American Sociological Review* 44 (1979): 588–608; L. Cohen, James Kleugel, and Kenneth Land, "Social Inequality and Predatory Criminal Victimization: An Exposition and Test of a Formal Theory," *American Sociological Review* 46 (1981): 505–24; Steven Messner and Kenneth Tardiff, "The Social Ecology of Urban Homicide: An Application of the Routine Activities Approach," *Criminology* 23 (1985): 241–67.

66. See, generally, Gary Gottfredson and Denise Gottfredson, *Victimization in Schools* (New York: Plenum Press, 1985), and "Children as Victims of Violent Crime," *Juristat* 11 (1991).

67. Gary Jensen and David Brownfield, "Gender, Lifestyles, and Victimization: Beyond Routine Activity Theory," *Violence and Victims* 1 (1986): 85–99.

68. Less Whitbeck and Ronald Simons, "A Comparison of Adaptive Strategies and Patterns of Victimization among Homeless Adolescents and Adults," *Violence and Victims* 8 (1993): 135–51; Kevin Fitzpatrick, Mark La Gory, and Ferris Ritchey, "Criminal Victimization among the Homeless," *Justice Quarterly* 10 (1993): 353–68.

69. Joan McDermott, "Crime in the School and in the Community: Offenders, Victims and Fearful Youth," *Crime and Delinquency* 29 (1983): 270–83.

70. Simon Singer, "Homogeneous Victim–Offender Populations: A Review and Some Research Implications," *Journal of Criminal Law and Criminology* 72 (1981): 779–99.

71. Janet Lauritsen, John Laub, and Robert Sampson, "Conventional and Delinquent Activities: Implications for the Prevention of Violent Victimization Among Adolescents," *Violence and Victims* 7 (1992): 91–102.

72. Gary Jensen and David Brownfield, "Gender, Lifestyles and Victimization: Beyond Routine Activities," *Violence and Victims* 1 (1986): 85–101.

73. Ross Vasta, "Physical Child Abuse: A Dual Component Analysis," *Developmental Review* 2 (1982): 128–35.

74. Elise Lake, "An Exploration of the Violent Victim Experiences of Female Offenders," *Violence and Victims* 8 (1993): 41–50.

75. Jeffrey Fagan, Elizabeth Piper, and Yu-Teh Cheng, "Contributions of Victimization to Delinquency in Inner Cities," *The Journal of Criminal Law and Criminology* 78 (1987): 586–613.

76. M. Hindelang, M. Gottfredson, and J. Garofalo, *Victims of Personal Crime: An Empirical Foundation for a Theory of Personal Victimization* (Cambridge, MA: Ballinger, 1978).

77. James Garofalo, "Reassessing the Lifestyle Model of Criminal Victimization," in *Positive Criminology*, ed. Michael Gottfredson and Travis Hirschi (Newbury Park, CA: Sage Publications, 1987), pp. 23–42.

78. Terance Miethe and David McDowall, "Contextual Effects in Models of Criminal Victimization," *Social Forces* 71 (1993): 741–59.

79. Terance Miethe and Robert Meier, "Opportunity, Choice, and Criminal Victimization: A Test of a Theoretical Model," *Journal of Research in Crime and Delinquency* 27 (1990): 243–66.

80. Robert Sampson and Janet Lauritsen, "Deviant Lifestyles, Proximity to Crime and the Offender–Deviant Link in Personal Violence," *Journal of Research in Crime and Delinquency* 27 (1990): 110–39.

81. Rodney Stark, "Deviant Places: A Theory of the Ecology of Crime," *Criminology* 25 (1987): 893–911.

82. William Julius Wilson, *The Truly Disadvantaged* (Chicago: University of Chicago Press, 1987); Allen Liska and Paul Bellair, "Violent-Crime Rates and Racial Composition: Convergence over Time," *American Journal of Sociology* 101 (1995): 578–610.

83. Lawrence Cohen and Marcus Felson, "Social Change and Crime Rate Trends: A Routine Activities Approach," *American Sociological Review* 44 (1979): 588–608.

84. Lawrence Cohen, Marcus Felson, and Kenneth Land, "Property Crime Rates in the United States: A Macrodynamic Analysis, 1947–1977, with Ex-ante Forecasts for the Mid-1980s," *American Journal of Sociology* 86 (1980): 90–118.

85. Terance Miethe and Robert Meier, *Crime and Its Social Context: Toward an Integrated Theory of Offenders, Victims, and Situations* (Albany: State University of New York Press, 1994).

86. See Messner and Tardiff, "The Social Ecology of Urban Homicide"; Philip Cook, "The Demand and Supply of Criminal Opportunities," in *Crime and Justice*, vol. 7, ed. Michael Tonry and Norval Morris (Chicago: University of Chicago Press, 1986), pp. 1–28; Ronald Clarke and Derek Cornish, "Modeling Offender's Decisions: A Framework for Research and Policy," in *Crime and Justice*, vol. 6, ed. Michael Tonry and Norval Morris (Chicago: University of Chicago Press, 1985), pp. 147–87.

87. Michael Maxfield, "Household Composition, Routine Activity, and Victimization: A Comparative Analysis," *Journal of Quantitative Criminology* 3 (1987): 301–20.

88. James Lynch and David Cantor, "Ecological and Behavioral Influences on Property Victimization at Home: Implications for Opportunity Theory," *Journal of Research in Crime and Delinquency* 29 (1992): 335–62.

89. David Maume, "Inequality and Metropolitan Rape Rates: A Routine Activities Approach," *Justice Quarterly* 6 (1989): 513–27.

90. James Massey, Marvin Krohn, and Lisa Bonati, "Property Crime and the Routine Activities of Individuals," *Journal of Research in Crime and Delinquency* 26 (1989): 378–400.

91. Terance Miethe, Mark Stafford, and Douglas Stone, "Lifestyle Changes and Risks of Criminal Victimization," *Journal of Quantitative Criminology* 6 (1990): 357–75.

92. R.R. Corado, R. Roesch, W. Glackman, J.L. Evans, and G.J. Leger, "Lifestyles and Personal Victimization: A Test of the Model with Canadian Survey Data," *Journal of Crime and Justice* 3 (1980): 129–39.

93. Messner and Tardiff, "The Social Ecology of Urban Homicide."

94. James Lasley, "Drinking Routines, Lifestyles and Predatory Victimization: A Causal Analysis," *Justice Quarterly* 6 (1989): 529–42.

95. Richard R. Benett, "Development and Crime," *The Sociological Quarterly* 32 (1991): 343–63.

96. Christopher Birkbeck and Gary LaFree, "The Situational Analysis of Crime and Deviance," *Annual Review of Sociology* 19 (1993): 113–37.

97. T.D. Miethe, M.C. Stafford, and J.S. Long, "Routine Activities/Lifestyle and Victimization," *American Sociological Review* 52 (1987): 184–94.

98. Leslie Kennedy and Stephen Baron, "Routine Activities and a Subculture of Violence: A Study of Violence on the Street," *Journal of Research in Crime and Delinquency* 30 (1993): 88–112.

99. Marcus Felson, *Crime and Everday Life* (Thousand Oaks, CA: Pine Forge Press, 1994).

100. M. Hough and P. Matthew, *The British Crime Survey's First Report* (London: Her Majesty's Stationery Office, 1983).

101. Patricia Resnick, "Psychological Effects of Victimization: Implications for the Criminal Justice System," *Crime and Delinquency* 33 (1987): 468–78.

102. Dean Kilpatrick, Benjamin Saunders, Lois Veronen, Connie Best, and Judith Von, "Criminal Victimization: Lifetime Prevalence, Reporting to Police, and Psychological Impact," *Crime and Delinquency* 33 (1987): 479–89.

103. Mark Santello and Harold Leitenberg, "Sexual Aggression by an Acquaintance: Methods of Coping and Later Psychological Adjustment," *Violence and Victims* 8 (1993): 91–103.

104. U.S. Department of Justice, *Report of the President's Task Force on Victims of Crime* (Washington, DC: U.S. Government Printing Office, 1983).

105. Ibid., pp. 2–10; and "Review on Victims–Witnesses of Crime," *Massachusetts Lawyers Weekly*, April 25, 1983, p. 26; Robert Davis, *Crime Victims: Learning How to Help Them* (Washington, DC: National Institute of Justice, 1987).

106. John Howard Society of Alberta, *Victim Impact Statements*, 1997. Online: http://www.acinet.org.

107. Randall Schmidt, "Crime Victim Compensation Legislation: A Comparative Study," *Victimology* 5 (1980): 428–37.

108. A.C. Bowland, "Sexual Assault Trials and the Protection of 'Bad Girls': The Battle between the Courts and Parliament," in *Confronting Sexual Assault: A Decade of Legal and Social Change*, ed. Julian Roberts and R.M. Mohr (Toronto: University of Toronto Press, 1994).

109. Peter Jaffe, Marlies Sudermann, Deborah Reitzel, and Steve Killip, "An Evaluation of a Secondary School Primary Prevention Program on Violence in Intimate Relationships," *Violence and Victims* 7 (1992): 129–45; *Healthy Relationships: A Violence-Prevention Curriculum* (Halifax: Men for Change, 1994).

110. Vicki McNickel Rose, "Rape as a Social Problem: A By-Product of the Feminist Movement," *Social Problems* 25 (1977): 75–89.

111. Janet Gornick, Martha Burt, and Karen Pittman, "Structure and Activities of Rape Crisis Centers in the Early 1980s," *Crime and Delinquency* 31 (1985): 247–68.

112. Andrew Karmen, "Victim–Offender Reconciliation Programs: Pro and Con," *Perspectives of the American Probation and Parole Association* 20 (1996): 11–14.

113. See Frank Carrington, "Victim's Rights Litigation: A Wave of the Future," in *Perspectives on Crime Victims*, ed. Burt Galaway and Joe Hudson (St. Louis: Mosby, 1981).

114. Alison Hatch Cunningham and Curt T. Griffiths, *Canadian Criminal Justice: A Primer* (Toronto: Harcourt Brace, 1997).

115. Ontario Ministry of the Attorney General. "Victim's Bill of Rights" (Toronto: Queen's Printer, 1996). Online: http://www.gov.on.ca/ATG/english/plp/plpvbr.htm.

116. Pamela Wilcox Rountree and Kenneth Land, "Burglary Victimization, Perceptions of Crime Risk, and Routine Activities: A Multilevel Analysis across Seattle Neighborhoods and Census Tracts," *Journal of Research in Crime and Delinquency* 33 (1996): 1147–80.

117. Leslie Kennedy, "Going It Alone: Unreported Crime and Individual Self-Help," *Journal of Criminal Justice* 16 (1988): 403–13.

118. Rosemary Gartner and Anthony Doob, "Trends in Criminal Victimization: 1988–1993," *Juristat* 14 (1994).

119. Ronald Clarke, "Situational Crime Prevention: Its Theoretical Basis and Practical Scope," in *Annual Review of Criminal Justice Research*, ed. Michael Tonry and Norval Morris (Chicago: University of Chicago Press, 1983).

120. D.P. Rosenbaum, "Community Crime Protection, A Review and Synthesis of the Literature," *Justice Quarterly* 5 (1988): 323–95.

121. Andrew Buck, Simon Hakim, and George Rengert, "Burglar Alarms and the Choice Behavior of Burglars," *Journal of Criminal Justice* 21 (1993): 497–507; for an opposing view, see Lynch and Cantor, "Ecological and Behavioral Influences on Property Victimization at Home."

122. R. McNamara, *Crime Displacement: The Other Side of Prevention* (East Rockaway, NY: Cummings and Hathaway, 1994).

123. Alan Lizotte, "Determinants of Completing Rape and Assault," *Journal of Quantitative Criminology* 2 (1986): 213–17; Polly Marchbanks, Kung-Jong Lui, and James Mercy, "Risk of Injury from Resisting Rape," *American Journal of Epidemiology* 132 (1990): 540–49.

124. Caroline Wolf Harlow, *Robbery Victims* (Washington, DC: Bureau of Justice Statistics, 1987).

125. Gary Kleck, "Guns and Violence: An Interpretive Review of the Field," *Social Pathology* 1 (1995): 12–45.

126. James Fyfe, "Police Use of Deadly Force: Research and Reform," *Justice Quarterly* 5 (1988): 157–76.

127. Gary Kleck, "Rape and Resistance," *Social Problems* 37 (1990): 149–62.

128. Gary Mauser, "Armed Self Defense: The Canadian Case," *Journal of Criminal Justice* 24 (1996): 393–406; see also, Gary Mauser, "Canadians Do Use Firearms in Self-protection," *Canadian Journal of Criminology*, October (1996):

485–88; Gary Mauser, "Armed Self Defense: The Canadian Case," *Journal of Criminal Justice*, 24 (1996): 393–406; Gary Mauser and Richard Holmes, "An Evaluation of the 1977 Canadian Firearms Legislation," *Evaluation Review* 16 (1992): 603–617; Gary Mauser and Michael Margolis, "The Politics of Gun Control: Comparing Canadian and American Patterns," *Government and Policy* 10 (1992): 189–209.

129. Gary Green, "Citizen Gun Ownership and Criminal Deterrence: Theory, Research and Policy," *Criminology* 25 (1987): 63–81.

130. James Garofalo and Maureen McLeod, *Improving the Use and Effectiveness of Neighborhood Watch Programs* (Washington, DC: National Institute of Justice, 1988); Kevin D. Carriere and Richard V. Ericson, *CrimeStoppers: A Study in the Organization of Community Policing* (University of Toronto: Centre of Criminology, 1989); Dennis P. Forcese, *Policing Canadian Society* (Scarborough: Prentice Hall, 1992).

131. Peter Finn, *Block Watches Help Crime Victims in Philadelphia* (Washington, DC: National Institute of Justice, 1986).

Chapter 5

1. Cesare Beccaria, *On Crimes and Punishments*, excerpted in Joseph E. Jacoby, *Classics of Criminology*, 2nd ed. (Prospect Heights, IL: Waveland, 1994): 277–86; Francis Edward Devine, "Cesare Beccaria and the Theoretical Foundations of Modern Penal Jurisprudence," *New England Journal on Prison Law* 7 (1982): 8–21; Marcello Maestro, *Cesare Beccaria and the Origins of Penal Reform* (Philadelphia: Temple University, 1973).

2. Graeme Newman and Pietro Marongiu, "Penological Reform and the Myth of Beccaria," *Criminology* 28 (1990): 325–46.

3. Bob Roshier, *Controlling Crime* (Chicago: Lyceum Books, 1989), p. 10.

4. Jeremy Bentham, *A Fragment on Government and an Introduction to the Principle of Morals and Legislation*, ed. Wilfred Harrison (Oxford: Basil Blackwell, 1967).

5. Robert Martinson, "What Works?–Questions and Answers About Prison Reform," *Public Interest* 35 (1974): 22–54.

6. Charles Murray and Louis Cox, *Beyond Probation* (Beverly Hills, CA: Sage, 1979).

7. Ronald Bayer, "Crime, Punishment and the Decline of Liberal Optimism," *Crime and Delinquency* 27 (1981): 190.

8. James Q. Wilson, *Thinking About Crime*, rev. ed. (New York: Vintage Books, 1983), pp. 128, 260.

9. Frederick J. Desroches, *Force and Fear: Robbery in Canada* (Toronto: Nelson, 1995).

10. Phonse Jessome, *Murder at McDonald's: The Killers Next Door* (Halifax: Nimbus, 1994).

11. See, generally, Derek Cornish and Ronald Clarke, eds., *The Reasoning Criminal: Rational Choice Perspectives on Offending* (New York: Springer Verlag, 1986); Philip Cook, "The Demand and Supply of Criminal Opportunities," in *Crime and Justice*, vol. 7, ed. Michael Tonry and Norval Morris (Chicago: University of Chicago Press, 1986), pp. 1–28; Ronald Clarke and Derek Cornish, "Modeling Offender's Decisions: A Framework for Research and Policy," in *Crime and Justice*, vol. 6, ed. Michael Tonry

and Norval Morris (Chicago: University of Chicago Press, 1985), pp. 147–87; Morgan Reynolds, *Crime by Choice: An Economic Analysis* (Dallas: Fisher Institute, 1985).

12. George Rengert and John Wasilchick, *Suburban Burglary: A Time and Place for Everything* (Springfield, IL: Charles C Thomas, 1985).

13. John McIver, "Criminal Mobility: A Review of Empirical Studies," in *Crime Spillover*, ed. Simon Hakim and George Rengert (Beverly Hills, CA: Sage, 1981), pp. 110–121; Carol Kohfeld and John Sprague, "Demography, Police Behavior, and Deterrence," *Criminology* 28 (1990): 111–36.

14. Derek Cornish and Ronald Clarke, "Understanding Crime Displacement: An Application of Rational Choice Theory," *Criminology* 25 (1987): 933–47.

15. Lloyd Phillips and Harold Votey, "The Influence of Police Interventions and Alternative Income Sources on the Dynamic Process of Choosing Crime as a Career," *Journal of Quantitative Criminology* 3 (1987): 251–74.

16. Michael Gottfredson and Travis Hirschi, *A General Theory of Crime* (Stanford, CA: Stanford University Press, 1990).

17. Liliana Pezzin, "Earnings Prospects, Matching Effects, and the Decision to Terminate a Criminal Career," *Journal of Quantitative Criminology* 11 (1995): 29–50.

18. Neal Shover, *Aging Criminals* (Beverly Hills, CA: Sage, 1985).

19. Ronald Akers, "Rational Choice, Deterrence and Social Learning Theory in Criminology: The Path Not Taken," *Journal of Criminal Law and Criminology* 81 (1990): 653–76.

20. Robert Agnew, "Determinism, Indeterminism, and Crime: An Empirical Exploration," *Criminology* 33 (1995): 83–109.

21. Bruce Jacobs, "Crack Dealers' Apprehension Avoidance Techniques: A Case of Restrictive Deterrence," *Justice Quarterly* 13 (1996): 359–81.

22. Paul Cromwell, James Olson, and D'Aunn Wester Avery, *Breaking and Entering: An Ethnographic Analysis of Burglary* (Newbury Park, CA: Sage, 1989).

23. John Gibbs and Peggy Shelly, "Life in the Fast Lane: A Retrospective View by Commercial Thieves," *Journal of Research in Crime and Delinquency* 19 (1982): 229–30.

24. George Rengert and John Wasilchick, *Space, Time and Crime: Ethnographic Insights into Residential Burglary* (Washington, DC: National Institute of Justice, 1989); see also idem, *Suburban Burglary*.

25. Leanne Fiftal Alarid, James Marquart, Velmer Burton, Francis Cullen, and Steven Cuvelier, "Women's Roles in Serious Offenses: A Study of Adult Felons," *Justice Quarterly* 13 (1996): 431–54.

26. Ronald Clarke and Marcus Felson, "Introduction: Criminology, Routine Activity and Rational Choice," in *Routine Activity and Rational Choice* (New Brunswick, NJ: Transaction Publishers, 1993), pp. 1–14.

27. Andrew Buck, Simon Hakim, and George Rengert, "Burglar Alarms and the Choice Behavior of Burglars: A Suburban Phenomenon," *Journal of Criminal Justice* 21 (1993): 497–507.

28. Ralph Taylor and Stephen Gottfredson, "Environmental Design, Crime, and Prevention: An Examination of Community Dynamics," in *Communities and Crime*, ed. Albert Reiss and Michael Tonry (Chicago: University of Chicago Press, 1986), pp. 387–416.

29. Michael Costanzo, William Halperin, and Nathan Gale, "Criminal Mobility and the Directional Component in Journeys to Crime," in *Metropolitan Crime Patterns*, ed.

Robert Figlio, Simon Hakim, and George Rengert (Monsey, NY: Criminal Justice Press, 1986), pp. 73–95.

30. Garland White, "Neighborhood Permeability and Burglary Rates," *Justice Quarterly* 7 (1990): 57–67.

31. James Massey, Marvin Krohn, and Lisa Bonati, "Property Crime and the Routine Activities of Individuals," *Journal of Research in Crime and Delinquency* 26 (1989): 378–400; note, however, that the findings here generally disagree with routine activities theory.

32. Kenneth Tunnell, *Choosing Crime* (Chicago: Nelson-Hall, 1992), p. 105.

33. Robert Sampson and Jacqueline Cohen, "Deterrent Effects of the Police on Crime: A Replication and Theoretical Extension," *Law and Society Review* 22 (1988): 163–88.

34. Marcus Felson et al., "Preventing Crime at Newark Subway Stations," *Security Journal* 1 (1990): 137–40.

35. Simha Landau and Daniel Fridman, "The Seasonality of Violent Crime: The Case of Robbery and Homicide in Israel," *Journal of Research in Crime and Delinquency* 30 (1993): 163–91.

36. Tunnell, *Choosing Crime*, p. 67.

37. Angela Browne and Kirk Williams, "Exploring the Effect of Resource Availability and the Likelihood of Female-Perpetrated Homicides," *Law and Society Review* 23 (1989): 89–93.

38. Ronald Clarke, "Situational Crime Prevention," in *Building a Safer Society: Strategic Approaches to Crime Prevention*, vol. 19 of *Crime and Justice: A Review of Research*, ed. Michael Tonry and David Farrington (Chicago: University of Chicago Press, 1995): 91–151.

39. Mark Warr, "Parents, Peers, and Delinquency," *Social Forces* 72 (1993): 247–64.

40. John Hagan, "Destiny and Drift: Subcultural Preferences, Status Attainments, and the Risks and Rewards of Youth," *American Sociological Review* 56 (1991): 567–82.

41. D. Wayne Osgood, Janet Wilson, Patrick O'Malley, Jerald Bachman, and Lloyd Johnston, "Routine Activities and Individual Deviant Behavior," *American Sociological Review* 61 (1996): 635–55.

42. Associated Press, "Thrift Hearings Resume Today in Senate," *Boston Globe*, January 2, 1991, p. 10.

43. Ronald Clarke and Patricia Harris, "Auto Theft and Its Prevention," in *Crime and Justice: An Annual Edition*, ed. Michael Tonry and Norval Morris (Chicago: University of Chicago Press, 1992), pp. 1–54, at 20–21.

44. Lisa Maher, "Hidden in the Light: Occupational Norms Among Crack-Using Street-Level Sex Workers," *Journal of Drug Issues* 26 (1996): 143–73.

45. John Petraitis, Brian Flay, and Todd Miller, "Reviewing Theories of Adolescent Substance Use: Organizing Pieces in the Puzzle," *Psychological Bulletin* 117 (1995): 67–86.

46. Bruce Jacobs, "Crack Dealers' Apprehension Avoidance Techniques: A Case of Restrictive Deterrence," *Justice Quarterly* 13 (1996): 359–81.

47. Patricia Morgan and Karen Ann Joe, "Citizens and Outlaws: The Private Lives and Public Lifestyles of Women in the Illicit Drug Economy," *Journal of Drug Issues* 26 (1996): 125–42.

48. Richard Felson and Steven Messner, "To Kill or Not to Kill? Lethal Outcomes in Injurious Attacks," *Criminology* 34 (1996): 519–45.

49. James Wright and Peter Rossi, *Armed and Considered Dangerous: A Survey of Felons and Their Firearms* (Hawthorne, NY: Aldine, 1983), pp. 141–59.

50. Eric Hickey, *Serial Murderers and Their Victims* (Pacific Grove, CA: Brooks/Cole, 1991), p. 84.

51. Scott Decker, "Deviant Homicide: A New Look at the Role of Motives and Victim-Offender Relationships," *Journal of Research in Crime and Delinquency* 33 (1996): 427–49.

52. Felson and Messner, "To Kill or Not to Kill?"

53. Christopher Birkbeck and Gary LaFree, "The Situational Analysis of Crime and Deviance," *American Review of Sociology* 19 (1993): 113–37; Karen Heimer and Ross Matsueda, "Role-Taking, Role Commitment, and Delinquency: A Theory of Differential Social Control," *American Sociological Review* 59 (1994): 111–31.

54. Jack Katz, *Seductions of Crime* (New York: Basic Books, 1988).

55. Bill McCarthy and John Hagan, "Mean Streets: The Theoretical Significance of Situational Delinquency Among Homeless Youths," *American Journal of Sociology* 3 (1992): 597–627.

56. Bill McCarthy, "Not Just 'For the Thrill of It': An Instrumentalist Elaboration of Katz's Explanation of Sneaky Thrill Property Crime," *Criminology* 33 (1995): 519–39.

57. William O'Grady and Mark Ashbridge, "Illegal Tobacco Sales to Youth: A View from Rational Choice Theory," *Canadian Journal of Criminology* 42 (2000): 1–21.

58. George Rengert, "Spatial Justice and Criminal Victimization," *Justice Quarterly* 6 (1989): 543–64.

59. Oscar Newman, *Defensible Space: Crime Prevention through Urban Design* (New York: Macmillan, 1973).

60. C. Ray Jeffery, *Crime Prevention through Environmental Design* (Beverly Hills, CA: Sage, 1971).

61. See also Pochara Theerathorn, "Architectural Style, Aesthetic Landscaping, Home Value, and Crime Prevention," *International Journal of Comparative and Applied Criminal Justice* 12 (1988): 269–77.

62. Ronald Clarke, *Situational Crime Prevention: Successful Case Studies* (Albany, NY: Harrow and Heston, 1992).

63. Patricia Brantingham and Paul Brantingham, "The Relative Spatial Concentration on Criminality and Its Analysis: Toward a Revival of Environmental Criminology" (in French), *Criminologie* 27 (1994): 81–97; Paul Brantingham and Patricia Brantingham, "The Spatial Patterning of Burglary," *Howard Journal of Penology and Crime Prevention* 14 (1975): 11–23; Paul Brantingham and Patricia Brantingham, "How Public Transit Feeds Private Crime: Notes on the Vancouver 'Sky Train' Experience," *Security Journal* 2 (1991): 91–95; Patricia L. Brantingham and Paul J. Brantingham, "Situational Crime Prevention in British Columbia," *Journal of Security Administration* 11: 18–27; Paul Brantingham and Patricia Brantingham, , "Situational Crime Prevention in Practice," *Canadian Journal of Criminology* 32 (1990): 17–40.

64. Marcus Felson, "Routine Activities and Crime Prevention," in *Studies on Crime and Crime Prevention, Annual Review*, vol. 1, National Council for Crime Prevention (Stockholm: Scandinavian University Press, 1992), pp. 30–34.

65. Anthony A. Braga, David M. Kennedy, Elin J. Waring, and Anne Morrison Piehl, "Problem-oriented Policing, Deterrence, and Youth Violence: An Evaluation of Boston's Operation Ceasefire," *Journal of Research in Crime and Delinquency* 38 (2001).

66. Barry Webb, "Steering Column Locks and Motor Vehicle Theft: Evaluations for Three Countries," in *Crime Prevention Studies*, ed. Ronald Clarke (Monsey, NY: Criminal Justice Press, 1994), pp. 71–89.

67. Barbara Morse and Delbert Elliott, "Effects of Ignition Interlock Devices on DUI Recidivism: Findings from a Longitudinal Study in Hamilton County, Ohio," *Crime and Delinquency* 38 (1992): 131–57.

68. L. Blake and R.T. Coupe, "The Impact of Single and Two-officer Patrols on Catching Burglars in the Act," *British Journal of Criminology* 41 (2001): 381–96.

69. Nancy LaVigne, "Gasoline Drive-Offs: Designing a Less Convenient Environment," in *Crime Prevention Studies*, vol. 2, ed. Ronald Clarke (Monsey, NY: Criminal Justice Press, 1994), pp. 91–114.

70. Ronald Clark, "Deterring Obscene Phone Callers: The New Jersey Experience," *Situational Crime Prevention*, ed. Ronald Clark (Albany, NY: Harrow and Heston, 1992), pp. 124–32.

71. Marcus Felson, "Those Who Discourage Crime," in *Crime and Place, Crime Prevention Studies*, vol. 4, ed. John Eck and David Weisburd (Monsey, NY: Criminal Justice Press, 1995), pp. 53–66; John Eck, *Drug Markets and Drug Places: A Case-Control Study of the Spatial Structure of Illicit Drug Dealing*. Doctoral dissertation, University of Maryland, College Park, 1994.

72. Robert Barr and Ken Pease, "Crime Placement, Displacement, and Deflection," in *Crime and Justice: A Review of Research,* vol. 12, ed. Michael Tonry and Norval Morris (Chicago: University of Chicago Press, 1990), pp. 277–319.

73. Keith Harries, *Mapping Crime: Principle and Practice* (Washington, DC: U.S. Department of Justice, Office of Justice Programs, National Institute of Justice, 1999).

74. Thomas Gabor, "Crime Displacement and Situational Prevention: Toward the Development of Some Principles," *Canadian Journal of Criminology* 32 (1990): 41–71.

75. Ronald Clarke and David Weisburd, "Diffusion of Crime Control Benefits: Observations of the Reverse of Displacement," in *Crime Prevention Studies*, vol. 2, ed. Ronald Clarke (New York: Criminal Justice Press, 1994).

76. David Weisburd and Lorraine Green, "Policing Drug Hot Spots: The Jersey City Drug Market Analysis Experiment," *Justice Quarterly* 12 (1995): 711–34.

77. Lorraine Green, "Cleaning Up Drug Hot Spots in Oakland, California: The Displacement and Diffusion Effects," *Justice Quarterly* 12 (1995): 737–54.

78. R. Yeaman, *The Deterrent Effectiveness of Criminal Justice Sanction Strategies: Summary Report* (Washington, DC: U.S. Government Printing Office, 1972); see, generally, Jack Gibbs, "Crime Punishment and Deterrence," *Social Science Quarterly* 48 (1968): 515–30.

79. Charles Tittle and Alan Rowe, "Certainty of Arrest and Crime Rates: A Further Test of the Deterrence Hypothesis," *Social Forces* 52 (1974): 455–62.

80. Robert Bursik, Harold Grasmick, and Mitchell Chamlin, "The Effect of Longitudinal Arrest Patterns on the Development of Robbery Trends at the Neighborhood Level," *Criminology* 28 (1990): 431–50; Theodore Chiricos and Gordon Waldo, "Punishment and Crime: An Examination of Some Empirical Evidence," *Social Problems* 18 (1970): 200–17.

81. Jiang Wu and Allen Liska, "The Certainty of Punishment: A Reference Group Effect and Its Functional Form," *Criminology* 31 (1993): 447–64.

82. Edwin Zedlewski, "Deterrence Findings and Data Sources: A Comparison of the Uniform Crime Rates and the National Crime Surveys," *Journal of Research in Crime and Delinquency* 20 (1983): 262–76.

83. Kimberly N. Varma, and Anthony N. Doob, "Deterring Economic Crimes: The Case of Tax Evasion," *Canadian Journal of Criminology* 40 (1998): 165–84.

84. "First Marathon Fined $4-million," *Report on Business, Globe and Mail,* July 21, 1998, p. B1; "OSC to Hire More Investigators," *Report on Business, Globe and Mail,* July 18, 1998, p. B1.

85. "Mine Disaster Sparks Call for Corporate Liability in Criminal Code," *Edmonton Journal,* August 4, 1998; *The Westray Story: A Predictable Path to Disaster. Report of the Westray Mine Public Inquiry* (Halifax, NS: Province of Nova Scotia, 1997).

86. David Bayley, *Policing for the Future* (New York: Oxford, 1994).

87. For a review, see Thomas Marvell and Carlisle Moody, "Specification Problems, Police Levels, and Crime Rates," *Criminology* 34 (1996): 609–46.

88. Joseph P. Hornick, Barry N. Leighton, and Barbara A. Burrows, "Evaluating Community Policing: The Edmonton Project," in *Evaluating Justice: Canadian Policies and Programs,* ed. Joe Hudson and Julian Roberts (Toronto: Thompson Educational Publishing, 1993).

89. S.G. Walker, C. Walker, C. Johnson, J. Sauvageau, and S. Williams, *You Can Do It: A Practical Guide to Evaluating Police and Community Crime Prevention Programs* (Ottawa: National Crime Prevention Center, 2001).

90. George Kelling, Tony Pate, Duane Dieckman, and Charles Brown, *The Kansas City Preventive Patrol Experiment: A Summary Report* (Washington, DC: Police Foundation, 1974).

91. Lawrence Sherman, "Police Crackdowns," *NIJ Reports,* March/April 1990, pp. 2–6; George L. Kelling and Catherine M. Coles, *Fixing Broken Windows: Restoring Order and Reducing Crime in Our Communities* (New York: Martin Kessler, 1997).

92. Lawrence Sherman, "Police Crackdowns," *NIJ Reports,* March/April 1990: 3; "Local Radar," *Canadian Living,* August 1997, p. 15; "Ontario May Try Tough 'Big Apple' Approach to Crime," *Halifax Daily News,* December 10, 1997.

93. Gary Green, "General Deterrence and Television Cable Crime: A Field Experiment in Social Crime," *Criminology* 23 (1986): 629–45.

94. H. Laurence Ross, "Implications of Drinking-and-Driving Law Studies for Deterrence Research," in *Critique and Explanation: Essays in Honor of Gwynne Nettler,* ed. Timothy Hartnagel and Robert Silverman (New Brunswick, NJ: Transaction Books, 1986), pp. 159–71.

95. H. Laurence Ross, Richard McCleary, and Gary LaFree, "Can Mandatory Jail Laws Deter Drunk Driving? The Arizona Case," *Journal of Criminal Law and Criminology* 81 (1990): 156–67.

96. For a review, see Jeffrey Roth, *Firearms and Violence* (Washington, DC: National Institute of Justice, 1994).

97. Thomas Marvell and Carlisle Moody, "The Impact of Enhanced Prison Terms for Felonies Committed with Guns," *Criminology* 33 (1995): 247–81.

98. Robert Dann, "The Deterrent Effect of Capital Punishment," *Friends Social Service Series* 29 (1935).

99. William Bowers and Glenn Pierce, "Deterrence or Brutalization: What Is the Effect of Executions?" *Crime and Delinquency* 26 (1980): 453–84; John Cochran, Mitchell Chamlin, and Mark Seth, "Deterrence or Brutalization? An Impact Assessment of Oklahoma's Return to Capital Punishment," *Criminology* 32 (1994): 107–34.

100. David Phillips, "The Deterrent Effect of Capital Punishment," *American Journal of Sociology* 86 (1980): 139–48; Hans Zeisel, "A Comment on 'The Deterrent Effect of Capital Punishment' by Phillips," *American Journal of Sociology* 88 (1982): 167–69; see also Sam McFarland, "Is Capital Punishment a Short-Term Deterrent to Homicide? A Study of the Effects of Four Recent American Executions," *Journal of Criminal Law and Criminology* 74 (1984): 1014–32.

101. Steven Stack, "Publicized Executions and Homicide, 1950–1980," *American Sociological Review* 52 (1987): 532–40; for a study challenging Stack's methods, see William Bailey and Ruth Peterson, "Murder and Capital Punishment: A Monthly Time-Series Analysis of Execution Publicity," *American Sociological Review* 54 (1989): 722–43.

102. Karl Schuessler, "The Deterrent Influence of the Death Penalty," *Annals of the Academy of Political and Social Sciences* 284 (1952): 54–62; Thorsten Sellin, *The Death Penalty* (Philadelphia: American Law Institute, 1959); Walter Reckless, "Use of the Death Penalty," *Crime and Delinquency* 15 (1969): 43–51; Richard Lempert, "The Effect of Executions on Homicides: A New Look in an Old Light," *Crime and Delinquency* 29 (1983): 88–115; Derral Cheatwood, "Capital Punishment and the Deterrence of Violent Crime in Comparable Counties," *Criminal Justice Review* 18 (1993): 165–81.

103. Dane Archer, Rosemary Gartner, and Marc Beittel, "Homicide and the Death Penalty: A Cross-National Test of a Deterrence Hypothesis," *Journal of Criminal Law and Criminology* 74 (1983): 991–1014.

104. Isaac Ehrlich, "The Deterrent Effect on Capital Punishment: A Question of Life and Death," *American Economic Review* 65 (1975): 397–417.

105. James Fox and Michael Radelet, "Persistent Flaws in Econometric Studies of the Deterrent Effect of the Death Penalty," *Loyola of Los Angeles Law Review* 23 (1987): 29–44; William B. Bowers and Glenn Pierce, "The Illusion of Deterrence in Isaac Ehrlich's Research on Capital Punishment," *Yale Law Journal* 85 (1975): 187–208.

106. William Bailey, "Disaggregation in Deterrence and Death Penalty Research: The Case of Murder in Chicago," *Journal of Criminal Law and Criminology* 74 (1986): 827–59.

107. Steven Messner and Kenneth Tardiff, "Economic Inequality and Level of Homicide: An Analysis of Urban Neighborhoods," *Criminology* 24 (1986): 297–317.

108. Donald Green, "Past Behavior as a Measure of Actual Future Behavior: An Unresolved Issue in Perceptual Deterrence Research," *Journal of Criminal Law and Criminology* 80 (1989): 781–804.

109. Donna Bishop, "Deterrence: A Panel Analysis," *Justice Quarterly* 1 (1984): 311–28; Julie Horney and Ineke Haen Marshall, "Risk Perceptions Among Serious Offenders: The Role of Crime and Punishment," *Criminology* 30 (1992): 575–94.

110. Raymond Paternoster, "Decisions to Participate in and Desist from Four Types of Common Delinquency: Deterrence and the Rational Choice Perspective," *Law and*

Society Review 23 (1989): 7–29; idem, "Examining Three-Wave Deterrence Models: A Question of Temporal Order and Specification," *Journal of Criminal Law and Criminology* 79 (1988): 135–63; Raymond Paternoster, Linda Saltzman, Gordon Waldo, and Theodore Chiricos, "Estimating Perceptual Stability and Deterrent Effects: The Role of Perceived Legal Punishment in the Inhibition of Criminal Involvement," *Journal of Criminal Law and Criminology* 74 (1983): 270–97; M. William Minor and Joseph Harry, "Deterrent and Experiential Effects in Perceptual Deterrence Research: A Replication and Extension," *Journal of Research in Crime and Delinquency* 19 (1982): 190–203; Lonn Lanza-Kaduce, "Perceptual Deterrence and Drinking and Driving Among College Students," *Criminology* 26 (1988): 321–41.

111. Harold Grasmick and Robert Bursik, "Conscience, Significant Others, and Rational Choice: Extending the Deterrence Model," *Law and Society Review* 24 (1990): 837–61.

112. Steven Klepper and Daniel Nagin, "The Deterrent Effect of Perceived Certainty and Severity of Punishment Revisited," *Criminology* 27 (1989): 721–46.

113. Scott Decker, Richard Wright, and Robert Logie, "Perceptual Deterrence Among Active Residential Burglars: A Research Note," *Criminology* 31 (1993): 135–47.

114. Irving Piliavin, Rosemary Gartner, Craig Thornton, and Ross Matsueda, "Crime, Deterrence, and Rational Choice," *American Sociological Review* 51 (1986): 101–19.

115. Eleni Apospori, Geoffrey Alpert, and Raymond Paternoster, "The Effect of Involvement with the Criminal Justice System: A Neglected Dimension of the Relationship Between Experience and Perceptions," *Justice Quarterly* 9 (1992): 379–92.

116. Eleni Apospori and Geoffrey Alpert, "Research Note: The Role of Differential Experience with the Criminal Justice System in Changes in Perceptions of Severity of Legal Sanctions over Time," *Crime and Delinquency* 39 (1993): 184–94.

117. Harold Grasmick and George Bryjak, "The Deterrent Effect of Perceived Severity of Punishment," *Social Forces* 59 (1980): 471–91.

118. Harold Grasmick, Robert Bursik, and Karyl Kinsey, "Shame and Embarrassment as Deterrents to Noncompliance with the Law: The Case of an Anti-Littering Campaign," paper presented at the annual meeting of the American Society of Criminology, Baltimore, November 1990, p. 3.

119. Charles Tittle, *Sanctions and Social Deviance* (New York: Praeger, 1980).

120. For an opposite view, see Steven Burkett and David Ward, "A Note on Perceptual Deterrence, Religiously Based Moral Condemnation, and Social Control," *Criminology* 31 (1993): 119–34.

121. John Snortum, "Drinking-Driving Compliance in Great Britain: The Role of Law as a 'Threat' and as a 'Moral Eye-Opener,'" *Journal of Criminal Justice* 18 (1990): 479–99.

122. Green, "Past Behavior as a Measure of Actual Future Behavior," p. 803; Matthew Silberman, "Toward a Theory of Criminal Deterrence," *American Sociological Review* 41 (1976): 442–61; Linda Anderson, Theodore Chiricos, and Gordon Waldo, "Formal and Informal Sanctions: A Comparison of Deterrent Effects," *Social Problems* 25 (1977): 103–14; see also Maynard Erickson and Jack Gibbs, "Objective and Perceptual Properties of Legal Punishment and Deterrence Doctrine," *Social Problems* 25 (1978): 253–64.

123. Grasmick and Bursik, "Conscience, Significant Others, and Rational Choices," p. 854.

124. Grasmick, Bursik, and Kinsey, "Shame and Embarrassment as Deterrents to Noncompliance with the Law"; Harold Grasmick, Robert Bursik, and Bruce Arneklev, "Reduction in Drunk Driving as a Response to Increased Threats of Shame, Embarrassment, and Legal Sanctions," *Criminology* 31 (1993): 41–69.

125. Harold Grasmick, Brenda Sims Blackwell, and Robert Bursik, "Changes in the Sex Patterning of Perceived Threats of Sanctions," *Law and Society Review* 27 (1993): 679–99.

126. Daniel Nagin and Raymond Paternoster, "Enduring Individual Differences and Rational Choice Theories of Crime," *Law and Society Review* 27 (1993): 467–85.

127. Kirk Williams and Richard Hawkins, "The Meaning of Arrest for Wife Assault," *Criminology* 27 (1989): 163–81.

128. Thomas Peete, Trudie Milner, and Michael Welch, "Levels of Social Integration in Group Contexts and the Effects of Informal Sanction Threat on Deviance," *Criminology* 32 (1994): 85–105.

129. Ronet Bachman, Raymond Paternoster, and Sally Ward, "The Rationality of Sexual Offending: Testing a Deterrence/Rational Choice Conception of Sexual Assault," *Law and Society Review* 26 (1992): 343–58.

130. Scotland, *Crime and Criminal Justice Research Findings No. 8*, Central Research Office (1995).

131. Marcus Nieto, "Public Video Surveillance: Is It an Effective Crime Prevention Tool?", Sacramento, CA: California Research Bureau, 1997.

132. ICPC, *Crime Prevention Digest,* International Center for the Prevention of Crime, http://www.crime-prevention-intl.org/, 1997.

133. Robert D. Bickel, "Legal Issues Related to Silent Video Surveillance," paper presented to the Security Industry Association and the Private Sector Liaison Committee, 1999.

134. Nieto, "Public Video Surveillance: Is It an Effective Crime Prevention Tool?"

135. David H. Flaherty, "Investigation Report: Video Surveillance by Public Bodies," Investigation P98-012, March 31, 1998.

136. Roy Coleman and Joe Sim, "'You'll Never Walk Alone': CCTV Surveillance, Order and Neo-liberal Rule in Liverpool City Centre," *British Journal of Sociology* 51 (2000): 623–39.

137. Ernest Van Den Haag, "The Criminal Law as a Threat System," *Journal of Criminal Law and Criminology* 73 (1982): 709–85.

138. Thomas Feucht, *Drug Use Forecasting* (Washington, DC: National Institute of Justice, 1996).

139. David Lykken, "Psychopathy, Sociopathy, and Crime," *Society* 34 (1996): 30–38.

140. Ken Auletta, *The Under Class* (New York: Random House, 1982).

141. David Klinger, "Policing Spousal Assault," *Journal of Research in Crime and Delinquency* 32 (1995): 308–24.

142. Paternoster, "Decisions to Participate in and Desist from Four Types of Common Delinquency."

143. James Williams and Daniel Rodeheaver, "Processing of Criminal Homicide Cases in a Large Southern City," *Sociology and Social Research* 75 (1991): 80–88.

144. Wilson, *Thinking About Crime.*

145. James Q. Wilson and Richard Herrnstein, *Crime and Human Nature* (New York: Simon & Schuster, 1985), p. 494.

146. Paul Tracy and Kimberly Kempf-Leonard, *Continuity and Discontinuity in Criminal Careers* (New York: Plenum Press, 1996).

147. Solicitor General of Canada (Correctional Services of Canada), *Basic Facts about Corrections in Canada* (Ottawa: Public Works and Government Services, 1997), p. 26.

148. Lawrence Greenfeld, *Examining Recidivism* (Washington, DC: U.S. Government Printing Office, 1985); Allen Beck and Bernard Shipley, *Recidivism of Prisoners Released in 1983* (Washington, DC: Bureau of Justice Statistics, 1989).

149. David Weisburd, Elin Waring, and Ellen Chayet, "Specific Deterrence in a Sample of Offenders Convicted of White-Collar Crimes," *Criminology* 33 (1995): 587–607.

150. Raymond Paternoster and Alex Piquero, "Reconceptualizing Deterrence: An Empirical Test of Personal and Vicarious Experiences," *Journal of Research in Crime and Delinquency* 32 (1995): 201–28.

151. Charles Murray and Louis Cox, *Beyond Probation* (Beverly Hills, CA: Sage, 1979); Perry Shapiro and Harold Votey, "Deterrence and Subjective Probabilities of Arrest: Modeling Individual Decisions to Drink and Drive in Sweden," *Law and Society Review* 18 (1984): 111–49; Douglas Smith and Patrick Gartin, "Specifying Specific Deterrence: The Influence of Arrest on Future Criminal Activity," *American Sociological Review* 54 (1989): 94–105.

152. Graeme Newman, *Just and Painful* (New York: Macmillan, 1983), pp. 139–43.

153. John Braithwaite, *Crime, Shame and Reintegration* (Melbourne, Australia: Cambridge University Press, 1989).

154. For more on this approach, see Jane Mugford and Stephen Mugford, "Shame and Reintegration in the Punishment and Deterrence of Spouse Assault," paper presented at the annual meeting of the American Society of Criminology, San Francisco, 1991.

155. John Braithwaite and Stephen Mugford, "Conditions of Successful Reintegration Ceremonies: Dealing with Juvenile Offenders," *British Journal of Criminology* 34, 2 (1994): 129–71.

156. Mark Stafford and Mark Warr, "A Reconceptualization of General and Specific Deterrence," *Journal of Research on Crime and Delinquency* 30 (1993): 123–35.

157. Paternoster and Piquero, "Reconceptualizing Deterrence: An Empirical Test of Personal and Vicarious Experiences."

158. Andrew Karmen, "Why Is New York City's Murder Rate Dropping So Sharply?" John Jay College, New York City, preliminary draft, 1996.

159. See, generally, Raymond Paternoster, "Absolute and Restrictive Deterrence in a Panel of Youth: Explaining the Onset, Persistence/Desistance, and Frequency of Delinquent Offending," *Social Problems* 36 (1989): 289–307; idem, "The Deterrent Effect of Perceived Severity of Punishment: A Review of the Evidence and Issues," *Justice Quarterly* 42 (1987): 173–217.

160. David Greenberg, "The Incapacitative Effects of Imprisonment: Some Estimates," *Law and Society Review* 9 (1975): 541–80.

161. Isaac Ehrlich, "Participation in Illegitimate Activities: An Economic Analysis," *Journal of Political Economy* 81 (1973): 521–67; Lee Bowker, "Crime and the Use of Prisons in the United States: A Time Series Analysis," *Crime and Delinquency* 27 (1981): 206–12.

162. Reuel Shinnar and Shlomo Shinnar, "The Effects of the Criminal Justice System on the Control of Crime: A Quantitative Approach," *Law and Society Review* 9 (1975): 581–611.

163. Stephan Van Dine, Simon Dinitz, and John Conrad, *Restraining the Wicked: The Dangerous Offender Project* (Lexington, MA: Lexington Books, 1979).

164. For review of this issue, see James Austin and John Irwin, *Does Imprisonment Reduce Crime? A Critique of "Voodoo" Criminology* (San Francisco: National Council of Crime and Delinquency, 1993).

165. John Wallerstedt, *Returning to Prison*, Bureau of Justice Statistics Special Report (Washington, DC: U.S. Department of Justice, 1984).

166. *Justice Spending in Canada* (Ottawa: Canadian Centre for Justice Statistics, 1997), pp. 3, 17.

167. Peter Greenwood, *Selective Incapacitation* (Santa Monica, CA: Rand Corporation, 1982).

168. Paul Gendreau and Claire Coggin, *The Effect of Prison Sentences on Recidivism*, Report prepared for the Solicitor General of Canada, 1999.

169. Stephen Markman and Paul Cassell, "Protecting the Innocent: A Response to the Bedeau-Radelet Study," *Stanford Law Review* 41 (1988): 121–70 at 153.

170. James Stephan and Tracy Snell, *Capital Punishment, 1994* (Washington, DC: Bureau of Justice Statistics, 1996), p. 8.

171. Andrew Von Hirsch, *Doing Justice* (New York: Hill and Wang, 1976).

Chapter 6

1. Israel Nachshon, "Neurological Bases of Crime, Psychopathy and Aggression," in *Crime in Biological, Social and Moral Contexts*, ed. Lee Ellis and Harry Hoffman (New York: Praeger, 1990).

2. Raffaele Garofalo, *Criminology*, trans. Robert Miller (Boston: Little, Brown, 1914), p. 92.

3. Enrico Ferri, *Criminal Sociology* (New York: D. Appleton, 1909).

4. Richard Dugdale, *The Jukes: A Study in Crime, Pauperism, Disease, and Heredity* (New York: Putnam, 1910); Arthur Estabrook, *The Jukes in 1915* (Washington, DC: Carnegie Institute of Washington, 1916).

5. William Sheldon, *Varieties of Delinquent Youth* (New York: Harper Bros., 1949); William Sheldon, *Atlas of Men: A Guide for Somatyping the Adult Male at All Ages* (New York: Harper and Row, 1954).

6. Lee Ellis, "A Discipline in Peril: Sociology's Future Hinges on Curing Biophobia," *American Sociologist* 27 (1996): 21–41.

7. Pierre van den Bergle, "Bringing the Beast Back In: Toward a Biosocial Theory of Aggression," *American Sociological Review* 39 (1974): 779.

8. Edmund O. Wilson, *Sociobiology* (Cambridge: Harvard University Press, 1975).

9. See, generally, Lee Ellis, "Introduction: The Nature of the Biosocial Perspective," *Crime in Biological, Social and Moral Contexts*, pp. 3–18.

10. See, for example, Tracy Bennett Herbert and Sheldon Cohen, "Depression and Immunity: A Meta-Analytic Review," *Psychological Bulletin* 113 (1993): 472–86.

11. See, generally, Lee Ellis, *Theories of Rape* (New York: Hemisphere Publications, 1989).

12. Leonard Hippchen, "Some Possible Biochemical Aspects of Criminal Behavior," *Journal of Behavioral Ecology* 2 (1981): 1–6; Sarnoff Mednick and Jan Volavka, "Biology and Crime," in *Crime and Justice*, ed. Norval Morris and Michael Tonry (Chicago: University of Chicago Press, 1980), pp. 85–159; Saleem Shah and Loren Roth, "Biological and Psychophysiological Factors in Criminality," in *Handbook of Criminology*, ed. Daniel Glazer (Chicago: Rand McNally, 1974), pp. 125–40.

13. *Time*, May 28, 1979, p. 57.

14. Ulric Neisser et al., "Intelligence: Knowns and Unknowns," *American Psychologist* 51 (1996): 77–101.

15. Leonard Hippchen, ed., *Ecologic-Biochemical Approaches to Treatment of Delinquents and Criminals* (New York: Von Nostrand Reinhold, 1978), p. 14.

16. Michael Krassner, "Diet and Brain Function," *Nutrition Reviews* 44 (1986): 12–15.

17. J. Kershner and W. Hawke, "Megavitamins and Learning Disorders: A Controlled Double-Blind Experiment," *Journal of Nutrition* 109 (1979): 819–26.

18. Richard Knox, "Test Shows Smart People's Brains Use Nutrients Better," *Boston Globe*, February 16, 1988, p. 9; Ronald Prinz and David Riddle, "Associations between Nutrition and Behavior in 5-Year-Old Children," *Nutrition Reviews* Supplement 44 (1986): 151–58.

19. Stephen Schoenthaler and Walter Doraz, "Types of Offenses Which Can Be Reduced in an Institutional Setting Using Nutritional Intervention," *International Journal of Biosocial Research* 4 (1983): 74–84; idem, "Diet and Crime," *International Journal of Biosocial Research* 4 (1983): 85–94. See also A.G. Schauss, "Differential Outcomes among Probationers Comparing Orthomolecular Approaches to Conventional Casework Counseling," paper presented at the annual meeting of the American Society of Criminology, Dallas, November 9, 1978; A. Schauss and C. Simonsen, "A Critical Analysis of the Diets of Chronic Juvenile Offenders, Part I," *Journal of Orthomolecular Psychiatry* 8 (1979): 222–26; A. Hoffer, "Children with Learning and Behavioral Disorders," *Journal of Orthomolecular Psychiatry* 5 (1976): 229.

20. H. Bruce Ferguson, Clare Stoddart, and Jovan Simeon, "Double-Blind Challenge Studies of Behavioral and Cognitive Effects of Sucrose-Aspartame Ingestion in Normal Children," *Nutrition Reviews* Supplement 44 (1986): 144–58; Gregory Gray, "Diet, Crime and Delinquency: A Critique," *Nutrition Reviews* Supplement 44 (1986): 89–94.

21. Mark Wolraich, Scott Lindgren, Phyllis Stumbo, Lewis Stegink, Mark Appelbaum, and Mary Kiritsy, "Effects of Diets High in Sucrose or Aspartame on the Behavior and Cognitive Performance of Children," *The New England Journal of Medicine* 330 (1994): 303–6.

22. Dian Gans, "Sucrose and Unusual Childhood Behavior," *Nutrition Today* 26 (1991): 8–14.

23. D. Hill and W. Sargent, "A Case of Matricide," *Lancet* 244 (1943): 526–27; E. Podolsky, "The Chemistry of Murder," *Pakistan Medical Journal* 15 (1964): 9–14.

24. J.A. Yaryura-Tobias and F. Neziroglu, "Violent Behavior, Brain Dysrhythmia and Glucose Dysfunction: A New Syndrome," *Journal of Orthopsychiatry* 4 (1975): 182–88; Matti Virkkunen, "Reactive Hypoglycemic Tendency Among Habitually Violent Offenders," *Nutrition Reviews Supplement* 44 (1986): 94–103.

25. James Q. Wilson, *The Moral Sense* (New York: Free Press, 1993).

26. Walter Gove, "The Effect of Age and Gender on Deviant Behavior: A Biopsychosocial Perspective," in *Gender and the Life Course*, ed. A.S. Rossi (New York: Aldine, 1985), pp. 115–44.

27. Alan Booth and D. Wayne Osgood, "The Influence of Testosterone on Deviance in Adulthood: Assessing and Explaining the Relationship," *Criminology* 31 (1993): 93–118.

28. Christy Miller Buchanan, Jacquelynne Eccles, and Jill Becker, "Are Adolescents the Victims of Raging Hormones? Evidence for Activational Effects of Hormones on Moods and Behavior at Adolescence," *Psychological Bulletin* 111 (1992): 62–107.

29. Albert Reiss and Jeffrey Roth, eds., *Understanding and Preventing Violence* (Washington, DC: National Academy Press, 1993), p. 118. This report by the National Research Council Panel on the Understanding and Control of Violent Behavior is hereafter cited as *Understanding Violence.*

30. L.E. Kreuz and R.M. Rose, "Assessment of Aggressive Behavior and Plasma Testosterone in a Young Criminal Population," *Psychosomatic Medicine* 34 (1972): 321–32.

31. Anne McIlroy, "Must Men Fight? Probably," *Globe and Mail*, January 27, 2001.

32. Lee Ellis, "Evolutionary and Neurochemical Causes of Sex Differences in Victimizing Behavior: Toward a Unified Theory of Criminal Behavior and Social Stratification," *Social Science Information* 28 (1989): 605–36.

33. For a general review, see Lee Ellis and Phyllis Coontz, "Androgens, Brain Functioning, and Criminality: The Neurohormonal Foundations of Antisociality," in *Crime in Biological Contexts*, pp. 162–93. Also see Robert Rubin, "The Neuroendocrinology and Neurochemistry of Antisocial Behavior," in *The Causes of Crime, New Biological Appoaches*, ed. Sarnoff Mednick, Terrie Moffitt, and Susan Stack (Cambridge: Cambridge University Press, 1987), pp. 239–62.

34. J. Money, "Influence of Hormones on Psychosexual Differentiation," *Medical Aspects of Nutrition* 30 (1976): 165.

35. For a review of this concept see Anne E. Figert, "The Three Faces of PMS: The Professional, Gendered, and Scientific Structuring of a Psychiatric Disorder," *Social Problems* 42 (1995): 56–72.

36. Katharina Dalton, *The Premenstrual Syndrome* (Springfield, IL: Charles C Thomas, 1971).

37. Julie Horney, "Menstrual Cycles and Criminal Responsibility," *Law and Human Nature* 2 (1978): 25–36.

38. Diana Fishbein, "Selected Studies on the Biology of Antisocial Behavior," in *New Perspectives in Criminology*, ed. John Conklin (Needham Heights, MA: Allyn & Bacon, 1996), pp. 26–38.

39. Daniel J. Curran and Claire M. Renzetti, *Theories of Crime* (Boston: Allyn and Bacon, 1994); "Woman's Syndrome

Brings Leniency," *Vancouver Sun,* February 10, 1987; "Should PMT Be a Woman's All-Purpose Excuse?" *London Times,* November 12, 1981, p. 12. See also J.C. Chisler and K.B. Levy, "The Media Construct a Menstrual Monster: A Content Analysis of PMS Articles in the Popular Press," *Women and Health* (1990): 89–104.

40. Fishbein, "Selected Studies on the Biology of Antisocial Behavior"; Karen Paige, "Effects of Oral Contraceptives on Affective Fluctuations Associated with the Menstrual Cycle," *Psychosomatic Medicine* 33 (1971): 515–37.

41. H.E. Amos and J.J.P. Drake, "Problems Posed by Food Additives," *Journal of Human Nutrition* 30 (1976): 165.

42. Ray Wunderlich, "Neuroallergy as a Contributing Factor to Social Misfits: Diagnosis and Treatment," in *Ecologic-Biochemical Approaches,* pp. 229–53; Paul Marshall, "Allergy and Depression: A Neurochemical Threshold Model of the Relation Between the Illnesses," *Psychological Bulletin* 113 (1993): 23–39.

43. A.R. Mawson and K.J. Jacobs, "Corn Consumption, Tryptophan, and Cross-National Homicide Rates," *Journal of Orthomolecular Psychiatry* 7 (1978): 227–30.

44. Alexander Schauss, *Diet, Crime and Delinquency* (Berkeley, CA: Parker House, 1980).

45. C. Hawley and R.E. Buckley, "Food Dyes and Hyperkinetic Children," *Academy Therapy* 10 (1974): 27–32.

46. John Ott, "The Effects of Light and Radiation on Human Health and Behavior," in *Ecologic-Biochemical Approaches,* pp. 105–83. See also A. Kreuger and S. Sigel, "Ions in the Air," *Human Nature* (July 1978): 46–47; Harry Wohlfarth, "The Effect of Color Psychodynamic Environmental Modification on Discipline Incidents in Elementary Schools over One School Year: A Controlled Study," *International Journal of Biosocial Research* 6 (1984): 44–53.

47. Oliver David, Stanley Hoffman, Jeffrey Sverd, Julian Clark, and Kytja Voeller, "Lead and Hyperactivity, Behavior Response to Chelation: A Pilot Study," *American Journal of Psychiatry* 133 (1976): 1155–58.

48. Deborah Denno, "Considering Lead Poisoning as a Criminal Defense," *Fordham Urban Law Journal* 20 (1993): 377–400; Herbert Needleman, Julie Riess, Michael Tobin, Gretchen Biesecker, and Joel Greenohouse, "Bone Lead Levels and Delinquent Behavior," *Journal of the American Medical Association* 275 (1996): 363–69.

49. Ulric Neisser et al., "Intelligence: Knowns and Unknowns," *American Psychologist* 51 (1996): 77–101.

50. Terrie Moffitt, "The Neuropsychology of Juvenile Delinquency: A Critical Review," in *Crime and Justice: An Annual Review,* vol. 12, ed. Norval Morris and Michael Tonry (Chicago: University of Chicago Press, 1990), pp. 99–169; Terrie Moffitt, Donald Lyman, and Phil Silva, "Neuropsychological Tests Predicting Persistent Male Delinquency," *Criminology* 32 (1994): 277–300; Elizabeth Kandel and Sarnoff Mednick, "Perinatal Complications Predict Violent Offending," *Criminology* 29 (1991): 519–29; Sarnoff Mednick, Ricardo Machon, Matti Virkkunen, and Douglas Bonett, "Adult Schizophrenia Following Prenatal Exposure to an Influenza Epidemic," *Archives of General Psychiatry* 44 (1987): 35–46; C.A. Fogel, S.A. Mednick, and N. Michelson, "Hyperactive Behavior and Minor Physical Anomalies," *Acta Psychiatrica Scandinavia* 72 (1985): 551–56.

51. R. Johnson, *Aggression in Man and Animals* (Philadelphia: Saunders, 1972), p. 79.

52. Jean Seguin, Robert Pihl, Philip Harden, Richard Tremblay, and Bernard Boulerice, "Cognitive and Neuropsychological Characteristics of Physically Aggressive Boys," *Journal of Abnormal Psychology* 104 (1995): 614–24; Deborah Denno, "Gender, Crime and the Criminal Law Defenses," *Journal of Criminal Law and Criminology* 85 (1994): 80–180.

53. Deborah Denno, *Biology, Crime and Violence: New Evidence* (Cambridge: Cambridge University Press, 1989).

54. Diana Fishbein and Robert Thatcher, "New Diagnostic Methods in Criminology: Assessing Organic Sources of Behavioral Disorders," *Journal of Research in Crime and Delinquency* 23 (1986): 240–67.

55. Lorne Yeudall, "A Neuropsychosocial Perspective of Persistent Juvenile Delinquency and Criminal Behaviour," paper presented at the New York Academy of Sciences, September 26, 1979.

56. R.W. Aind and T. Yamamoto, "Behavior Disorders of Childhood," *Electroencephalography and Clinical Neurophysiology* 21 (1966): 148–56.

57. See, generally, Jan Volavka, "Electroencephalogram among Criminals," in *The Causes of Crime, New Biological Approaches,* ed. Sarnoff Mednick, Terrie Moffitt, and Susan Stack (Cambridge: Cambridge University Press, 1987), pp. 137–45.

58. Z.A. Zayed, S.A. Lewis, and R.P. Britain, "An Encephalographic and Psychiatric Study of 32 Insane Murderers," *British Journal of Psychiatry* 115 (1969): 1115–24.

59. D.R. Robin, R.M. Starles, T.J. Kenney, B.J. Reynolds, and F.P. Heald, "Adolescents Who Attempt Suicide," *Journal of Pediatrics* 90 (1977): 636–38.

60. R.R. Monroe, *Brain Dysfunction in Aggressive Criminals* (Lexington, MA: D.C. Heath, 1978).

61. L.T. Yeudall, *Childhood Experiences as Causes of Criminal Behavior* (Ottawa: Senate of Canada, 1977).

62. Stephen Faraone et al., "Intellectual Performance and School Failure in Children with Attention Deficit Hyperactivity Disorder and in Their Siblings," *Journal of Abnormal Psychology* 102 (1993): 616–23.

63. Terrie Moffitt and Phil Silva, "Self-Reported Delinquency, Neuropsychological Deficit, and History of Attention Deficit Disorder," *Journal of Abnormal Child Psychology* 16 (1988): 553–69.

64. Eugene Maguin, Rolf Loeber, and Paul LeMahieu, "Does the Relationship between Poor Reading and Delinquency Hold for Males of Different Ages and Ethnic Groups?" *Journal of Emotional and Behavioral Disorders* 1 (1993): 88–100.

65. Elizabeth Hart et al., "Developmental Change in Attention-Deficit Hyperactivity Disorder in Boys: A Four-Year Longitudinal Study," *Journal of Consulting and Clinical Psychology* 62 (1994): 472–91.

66. Yeudall, "A Neuropsychosocial Perspective of Persistent Juvenile Delinquency and Criminal Behavior," p. 4; F.A. Elliott, "Neurological Aspects of Antisocial Behavior," in *The Psychopath: A Comprehensive Study of Antisocial Disorders and Behaviors,* ed. W.H. Reid (New York: Brunner/Mazel, 1978), pp. 146–89.

67. Lorne Yeudall, Orestes Fedora, and Delee Fromm, "A Neuropsychosocial Theory of Persistent Criminality:

Implications for Assessment and Treatment," in *Advances in Forensic Psychology and Psychiatry*, ed. Robert Rieber (Norwood, NJ: Ablex Publishing, 1987), pp. 119–91.

68. H.K. Kletschka, "Violent Behavior Associated with Brain Tumor," *Minnesota Medicine* 49 (1966): 1853–55.

69. V.E. Krynicki, "Cerebral Dysfunction in Repetitively Assaultive Adolescents," *Journal of Nervous and Mental Disease* 166 (1978): 59–67.

70. C.E. Lyght, ed., *The Merck Manual of Diagnosis and Therapy* (West Point, FL: Merck, 1966).

71. M. Virkkunen, M.J. DeJong, J. Bartko, and M. Linnoila, "Psychobiological Concomitants of History of Suicide Attempts among Violent Offenders and Impulsive Fire Starters," *Archives of General Psychiatry* 46 (1989): 604–6; Matti Virkkunen, David Goldman, and Markku Linnoila, "Serotonin in Alcoholic Violent Offenders," *The Ciba Foundation Symposium, Genetics of Criminal and Antisocial Behavior* (Chichester, England: Wiley, 1995).

72. Lee Ellis, "Left- and Mixed-Handedness and Criminality: Explanations for a Probable Relationship," in *Left-Handedness: Behavioral Implications and Anomalies*, ed. S. Coren (Amsterdam: Elsevier, 1990): 485–507.

73. Lee Ellis, "Monoamine Oxidase and Criminality: Identifying an Apparent Biological Marker for Antisocial Behavior," *Journal of Research in Crime and Delinquency* 28 (1991): 227–51.

74. Walter Gove and Charles Wilmoth, "Risk, Crime and Neurophysiologic Highs: A Consideration of Brain Processes That May Reinforce Delinquent and Criminal Behavior," in *Crime in Biological Contexts*, pp. 261–93.

75. Jack Katz, *Seduction of Crime: Moral and Sensual Attractions of Doing Evil* (New York: Basic Books, 1988), pp. 12–15.

76. Lee Ellis, "Arousal Theory and the Religiosity–Criminality Relationship," in *Contemporary Criminological Theory*, ed. Peter Cordella and Larry Siegel (Boston, MA: Northeastern University, 1996), pp. 65–84.

77. For a general view, see Richard Lerner and Terryl Foch, *Biological-Psychosocial Interactions in Early Adolescence* (Hilldale, NJ: Lawrence Erlbaum Associates, 1987).

78. Kerry Jang, W. John Livesley, and Philip Vernon, "Heritability of the Big Five Personality Dimensions and Their Facets: A Twin Study," *Journal of Personality* 64 (1996): 577–89.

79. David Rowe, "As the Twig Is Bent: The Myth of Child-Rearing Influences on Personality Development," *Journal of Counseling and Development* 68 (1990): 606–11; David Rowe, Joseph Rogers, and Sylvia Meseck-Bushey, "Sibling Delinquency and the Family Environment: Shared and Unshared Influences," *Child Development* 63 (1992): 59–67.

80. Patricia Brennan, Sarnoff Mednick, and Bjorn Jacobsen, "Assessing the Role of Genetics in Crime Using Adoption Cohorts," *Genetics of Criminal and Antisocial Behavior*, pp. 115–28; Gregory Carey and David DiLalla, "Personality and Psychopathology: Genetic Perspectives," *Journal of Abnormal Psychology* 103 (1994): 32–43.

81. T.R. Sarbin and L.E. Miller, "Demonism Revisited: The XYY Chromosome Anomaly," *Issues in Criminology* 5 (1970): 195–207.

82. See Sarnoff A. Mednick and Karl O. Christiansen, eds., *Biosocial Bases in Criminal Behavior* (New York: Gardner Press, 1977).

83. David Rowe, "Genetic and Environmental Components of Antisocial Behavior: A Study of 265 Twin Pairs," *Criminology* 24 (1986): 513–32; David Rowe and D. Wayne Osgood, "Heredity and Sociological Theories of Delinquency: A Reconsideration," *American Sociological Review* 49 (1984): 526–40.

84. Edwin J.C.G. van den Oord, Frank Verhulst, and Dorret Boomsma, "A Genetic Study of Maternal and Paternal Ratings of Problem Behaviors in 3-Year-Old Twins," *Journal of Abnormal Psychology* 105 (1996): 349–57.

85. Michael Lyons, "A Twin Study of Self-Reported Criminal Behavior"; Judy Silberg, Joanne Meyer, Andrew Pickles, Emily Simonoff, Lindon Eaves, John Hewitt, Hermine Maes, and Michael Rutter, "Heterogeneity among Juvenile Antisocial Behaviors: Findings from the Virginia Twin Study of Adolescent Behavioral Development," in *The Ciba Foundation Symposium, Genetics of Criminal and Antisocial Behavior* (Chichester, England: Wiley, 1995).

86. Gregory Carey, "Twin Imitation for Antisocial Behavior: Implications for Genetic and Family Environment Research," *Journal of Abnormal Psychology* 101 (1992): 18–25; David Rowe and Joseph Rodgers, "The Ohio Twin Project and ADSEX Studies: Behavior Genetic Approaches to Understanding Antisocial Behavior," paper presented at the American Society of Criminology Meeting, Montreal, November 1987.

87. David Rowe, *The Limits of Family Influence: Genes, Experiences and Behavior* (New York: Guilford Press, 1995), p. 64.

88. R.J. Cadoret, C. Cain, and R.R. Crowe, "Evidence for a Gene-Environment Interaction in the Development of Adolescent Antisocial Behavior," *Behavior Genetics* 13 (1983): 301–10.

89. Barry Hutchings and Sarnoff A. Mednick, "Criminality in Adoptees and Their Adoptive and Biological Parents: A Pilot Study," in *Biological Bases in Criminal Behavior*, ed. S.A. Mednick and K.O. Christiansen (New York: Gardner Press, 1977).

90. For similar results, see Sarnoff Mednick, Terrie Moffitt, William Gabrielli, and Barry Hutchings, "Genetic Factors in Criminal Behavior: A Review," *Development of Antisocial and Prosocial Behavior* (New York: Academic Press, 1986), pp. 3–50; Sarnoff Mednick, William Gabrielli, and Barry Hutchings, "Genetic Influences in Criminal Behavior: Evidence from an Adoption Cohort," in *Perspective Studies of Crime and Delinquency*, ed. Katherine Teilmann Van Dusen and Sarnoff Mednick (Boston: Kluver-Nijhoff, 1983), pp. 39–57.

91. Michael Bohman, "Predisposition to Criminality: Swedish Adoption Studies in Retrospect," in *Genetics of Criminal and Antisocial Behavior*, pp. 99–114.

92. Glenn Walters, "A Meta-Analysis of the Gene-Crime Relationship," *Criminology* 30 (1992): 595–613.

93. Lawrence Cohen and Richard Machalek, "A General Theory of Expropriative Crime: An Evolutionary Ecological Approach," *American Journal of Sociology* 94 (1988): 465–501.

94. Lee Ellis, "The Evolution of Violent Criminal Behavior and Its Nonlegal Equivalent," *Crime in Biological Contexts*, pp. 63–65.

95. Lee Ellis and Anthony Walsh, "Gene-Based Evolutionary Theories of Criminology," *Criminology* 35 (1997): 229–76;

Lee Ellis, "Sex Differences in Criminality: An Explanation Based on the Concept of r/k Selection," *Mankind Quarterly* 30 (1990): 17–37; Ellis and Walsh, "Gene-Based Evolutionary Theories of Criminology"; Byron Roth, "Crime and Child Rearing," *Society* 34 (1996): 39–45.

96. Deborah Denno, "Sociological and Human Developmental Explanations of Crime: Conflict or Consensus," *Criminology* 23 (1985): 711–41.

97. Israel Nachshon and Deborah Denno, "Violence and Cerebral Function," in *The Causes of Crime, New Biological Approaches*, ed. Sarnoff Mednick, Terrie Moffitt, and Susan Stack (Cambridge: Cambridge University Press, 1987), pp. 185–217.

98. Avshalom Caspi, Donald Lyman, Terrie Moffitt, and Phil Silva, "Unraveling Girls' Delinquency: Biological, Dispositional, and Contextual Contributions to Adolescent Misbehavior," *Developmental Psychology* 29 (1993): 283–89.

99. Glenn Walters and Thomas White, "Heredity and Crime: Bad Genes or Bad Research," *Criminology* 27 (1989): 455–86.

100. Charles Goring, *The English Convict: A Statistical Study, 1913* (Montclair, NJ: Patterson Smith, 1972); Edwin Driver, "Charles Buckman Goring," in *Pioneers in Criminology*, ed. Hermann Mannheim (Montclair, NJ: Patterson Smith, 1970), p. 440.

101. Gabriel Tarde, *Penal Philosophy*, trans. R. Howell (Boston: Little, Brown, 1912).

102. See, generally, Donn Byrne and Kathryn Kelly, *An Introduction to Personality* (Englewood Cliffs, NJ: Prentice-Hall, 1981).

103. Frank R. Farnham, David V. James, and Paul Cantrell, "Association Between Violence, Psychosis, and Relationship to Victim in Stalkers," *The Lancet*, January 15, 2000: 199.

104. Sigmund Freud, "The Ego and the Id," in *Complete Psychological Works of Sigmund Freud,* vol. 19 (London: Hogarth, 1948), p. 52.

105. August Aichorn, *Wayward Youth* (New York: Viking Press, 1935).

106. David Abrahamsen, *Crime and the Human Mind* (New York: Columbia University Press, 1944), p. 137; see, generally, Fritz Redl and Hans Toch, "The Psychoanalytic Perspective," in *Psychology of Crime and Criminal Justice,* ed. Hans Toch (New York: Holt, Rinehart and Winston, 1979), pp. 193–95.

107. See, generally, D.A. Andrews and James Bonta, *The Psychology of Criminal Conduct* (Cincinnati: Anderson, 1994), pp. 72–75.

108. Robert Krueger, Avshalom Caspi, Phil Silva, and Rob McGee, "Personality Traits Are Differentially Linked to Mental Disorders: A Multitrait-Multidiagnosis Study of an Adolescent Birth Cohort," *Journal of Abnormal Psychology* 105 (1996): 299–312; Seymour Halleck, *Psychiatry and the Dilemmas of Crime* (Berkeley: University of California Press, 1971).

109. This discussion is based on three works by Albert Bandura: *Aggression: A Social Learning Analysis* (Englewood Cliffs, NJ: Prentice-Hall, 1973), *Social Learning Theory* (Englewood Cliffs, NJ: Prentice-Hall, 1977), and "The Social Learning Perspective: Mechanisms of Aggression," in *Psychology of Crime and Criminal Justice*, pp. 198–236.

110. David Phillips, "The Impact of Mass Media Violence on U.S. Homicides," *American Sociological Review* 48 (1983): 560–68.

111. See, generally, Jean Piaget, *The Moral Judgment of the Child* (London: Kegan Paul, 1932).

112. Lawrence Kohlberg, *Stages in the Development of Moral Thought and Action* (New York: Holt, Rinehart and Winston, 1969).

113. Lawrence Kohlberg, K. Kauffman, P. Scharf, and J. Hickey, *The Just Community Approach in Corrections: A Manual* (Niantic: Connecticut Department of Corrections, 1973); Scott Henggeler, *Delinquency in Adolescence* (Newbury Park, CA: Sage, 1989), p. 26.

114. Carol Veneziano and Louis Veneziano, "The Relationship between Deterrence and Moral Reasoning," *Criminal Justice Review* 17 (1992): 209–16.

115. K.A. Dodge, "A Social Information Processing Model of Social Competence in Children," in *Minnesota Symposium in Child Psychology*, vol. 18, ed. M. Perlmutter (Hillsdale, NJ: Lawrence Erlbaum, 1986), pp. 77–125.

116. L. Huesman and L. Eron, "Individual Differences and the Trait of Aggression," *European Journal of Personality* 3 (1989): 95–106.

117. J.E. Lochman, "Self and Peer Perceptions and Attributional Biases of Aggressive and Nonaggressive Boys in Dyadic Interactions," *Journal of Consulting and Clinical Psychology* 55 (1987): 404–10.

118. D. Lipton, E.C. McDonel, and R. McFall, "Heterosocial Perception in Rapists," *Journal of Consulting and Clinical Psychology* 55 (1987): 17–21.

119. James Sorrells, "Kids Who Kill," *Crime and Delinquency* 23 (1977): 312–20.

120. Richard Rosner, "Adolescents Accused of Murder and Manslaughter: A Five-Year Descriptive Study," *Bulletin of the American Academy of Psychiatry and the Law* 7 (1979): 342–51.

121. Richard Famularo, Robert Kinscherff, and Terence Fenton, "Psychiatric Diagnoses of Abusive Mothers: A Preliminary Report," *Journal of Nervous and Mental Disease* 180 (1992): 658–60.

122. Richard Wagner, Dawn Taylor, Joy Wright, Alison Sloat, Gwynneth Springett, Sandy Arnold, and Heather Weinberg, "Substance Abuse Among the Mentally Ill," *American Journal of Orthopsychiatry* 64 (1994): 30–38.

123. Bruce Link, Howard Andrews, and Francis Cullen, "The Violent and Illegal Behavior of Mental Patients Reconsidered," *American Sociological Review* 57 (1992): 275–92; Ellen Hochstedler Steury, "Criminal Defendants with Psychiatric Impairment: Prevalence, Probabilities and Rates," *Journal of Criminal Law and Criminology* 84 (1993): 354–74.

124. Marc Hillbrand, John Krystal, Kimberly Sharpe, and Hilliard Foster, "Clinical Predictors of Self-Mutilation in Hospitalized Patients," *Journal of Nervous and Mental Disease* 182 (1994): 9–13.

125. Carmen Cirincione, Henry Steadman, Pamela Clark Robbins, and John Monahan, *Mental Illness as a Factor in Criminality: A Study of Prisoners and Mental Patients* (Delmar, NY: Policy Research Associates, 1991). See also idem, *Schizophrenia as a Contingent Risk Factor for Criminal Violence* (Delmar, NY: Policy Research Associates, 1991).

126. John Monahan, *Mental Illness and Violent Crime* (Washington, DC: National Institute of Justice, 1996).

127. Howard Berenbaum and Frank Fujita, "Schizophrenia and Personality: Exploring the Boundaries and Connections between Vulnerability and Outcome," *Journal of Abnormal Psychology* 103 (1994): 148–58.

128. D.A. Andrews and J. Stephen Wormith, "Personality and Crime: Knowledge and Construction in Criminology," *Justice Quarterly* 6 (1989): 289–310; Donald Gibbons, "Comment—Personality and Crime: Non-Issues, Real Issues, and a Theory and Research Agenda," *Justice Quarterly* (1989): 311–24.

129. Sheldon Glueck and Eleanor Glueck, *Unraveling Juvenile Delinquency* (Cambridge: Harvard University Press, 1950).

130. See, generally, Hans Eysenck, *Personality and Crime* (London: Routledge & Kegan Paul, 1977).

131. Hans Eysenck and M.W. Eysenck, *Personality and Individual Differences* (New York: Plenum, 1985).

132. David Farrington, "Psychobiological Factors in the Explanation and Reduction of Delinquency," *Today's Delinquent* (1988): 37–51; Laurie Frost, Terrie Moffitt, and Rob McGee, "Neuropsychological Correlates of Psychopathology in an Unselected Cohort of Young Adolescents," *Journal of Abnormal Psychology* 98 (1989): 307–13.

133. David Lykken, "Psychopathy, Sociopathy, and Crime," *Society* 34 (1996): 30–38.

134. Lykken, "Psychopathy, Sociopathy, and Crime"; Lawrence Cohen and Bryan Vila, "Self-Control and Social Control: An Exposition of the Gottfredson-Hirschi/Sampson-Laub Debate," *Studies on Crime and Crime Prevention* 5 (1996): 1–21; Donald Lynam, "Early Identification of Chronic Offenders: Who Is the Fledgling Psychopath?" *Psychological Bulletin* 120 (1996): 209–34; James Ogloff and Stephen Wong, "Electrodermal and Cardiovascular Evidence of a Coping Response in Psychopaths," *Criminal Justice and Behaviour* 17 (1990): 231–45; Laurie Frost, Terrie Moffitt, and Rob McGee, "Neuropsychological Correlates of Psychopathology in an Unselected Cohort of Young Adolescents," *Journal of Abnormal Psychology* 98 (1989): 307–13; Hervey Cleckley, "Psychopathic States," in *American Handbook of Psychiatry*, ed. S. Aneti (New York: Basic Books, 1959), pp. 567–69; Spencer Rathus and Jeffrey Nevid, *Abnormal Psychology* (Englewood Cliffs, NJ: Prentice-Hall, 1991), pp. 310–16; Helene Raskin White, Erich Labouvie, and Marsha Bates, "The Relationship between Sensation Seeking and Delinquency: A Longitudinal Analysis," *Journal of Research in Crime and Delinquency* 22 (1985): 197–211.

135. Sheldon Glueck and Eleanor Glueck, *Delinquents and Nondelinquents in Perspective* (Cambridge, MA: Harvard University Press, 1968).

136. See, generally, R. Starke Hathaway and Elio Monachesi, *Analyzing and Predicting Juvenile Delinquency with the MMPI* (Minneapolis: University of Minnesota Press, 1953).

137. R. Starke Hathaway, Elio Monachesi, and Lawrence Young, "Delinquency Rates and Personality," *Journal of Criminal Law, Criminology, and Police Science* 51 (1960): 443–60; Michael Hindelang and Joseph Weis, "Personality and Self-Reported Delinquency: An Application of Cluster Analysis," *Criminology* 10 (1972): 268; Spencer Rathus and Larry Siegel, "Crime and Personality Revisited," *Criminology* 18 (1980): 245–51; see, generally, Edward Megargee, *The California Psychological Inventory Handbook* (San Francisco: Jossey-Bass, 1972).

138. Karl Schuessler and Donald Cressey, "Personality Characteristics of Criminals," *American Journal of Sociology* 55 (1950): 476–84; Gordon Waldo and Simon Dinitz, "Personality Attributes of the Criminal: An Analysis of Research Studies 1950–1965," *Journal of Research in Crime and Delinquency* 4 (1967): 185–201; David Tennenbaum, "Research Studies of Personality and Criminality," *Journal of Criminal Justice* 5 (1977): 1–19.

139. Edward Helmes and John Reddon, "A Perspective on Developments in Assessing Psychopathology: A Critical Review of the MMPI and MMPI-2," *Psychological Bulletin* 113 (1993): 453–71.

140. Avshalom Caspi, Terrie Moffitt, Phil Silva, Magda Stouthamer-Loeber, Robert Krueger, and Pamela Schmutte, "Are Some People Crime-Prone? Replications of the Personality-Crime Relationship Across Countries, Genders, Races and Methods," *Criminology* 32 (1994): 163–95.

141. Henry Goddard, *Efficiency and Levels of Intelligence* (Princeton, NJ: Princeton University Press, 1920); Edwin Sutherland, "Mental Deficiency and Crime," in *Social Attitudes*, ed. Kimball Young (New York: Henry Holt, 1931), chap. 15.

142. William Healy and Augusta Bronner, *Delinquency and Criminals: Their Making and Unmaking* (New York: Macmillan, 1926).

143. John Slawson, *The Delinquent Boys* (Boston: Budget Press, 1926).

144. Sutherland, "Mental Deficiency and Crime."

145. Travis Hirschi and Michael Hindelang, "Intelligence and Delinquency: A Revisionist Review," *American Sociological Review* 42 (1977): 471–586.

146. Deborah Denno, "Sociological and Human Developmental Explanations of Crime: Conflict or Consensus," *Criminology* 23 (1985): 711–41; Christine Ward and Richard McFall, "Further Validation of the Problem Inventory for Adolescent Girls: Comparing Caucasian and Black Delinquents and Nondelinquents," *Journal of Consulting and Clinical Psychology* 54 (1986): 732–33; L. Hubble and M. Groff, "Magnitude and Direction of WISC-R Verbal Performance IQ Discrepancies among Adjudicated Male Delinquents," *Journal of Youth and Adolescence* 10 (1981): 179–83; Robert Gordon, "IQ Commensurability of Black-White Differences in Crime and Delinquency," paper presented at the annual meeting of the American Psychological Association, Washington, DC, August 1986; idem, "Two Illustrations of the IQ-Surrogate Hypothesis: IQ Versus Parental Education and Occupational Status in the Race-IQ-Delinquency Model," paper presented at the annual meeting of the American Society of Criminology, Montreal, November 1987; Donald Lynam, Terrie Moffitt, and Magda Stouthamer-Loeber, "Explaining the Relation Between IQ and Delinquency: Class, Race, Test Motivation, School Failure or Self-Control," *Journal of Abnormal Psychology* 102 (1993): 187–96.

147. James Q. Wilson and Richard Herrnstein, *Crime and Human Nature* (New York: Simon & Schuster, 1985), p. 148.

148. Terrie Moffitt, William Gabrielli, Sarnoff Mednick, and Fini Schulsinger, "Socioeconomic Status, IQ, and

Delinquency," *Journal of Abnormal Psychology* 90 (1981): 152–56; for a similar finding, see Hubble and Groff, "Magnitude and Direction of WISC-R Verbal Performance IQ Discrepancies." See also Lorne Yeudall, Delee Fromm-Auch, and Priscilla Davies, "Neuropsychological Impairment of Persistent Delinquency," *Journal of Nervous and Mental Diseases* 170 (1982): 257–65. And, Hakan Stattin and Ingrid Klackenberg-Larsson, "Early Language and Intelligence Development and Their Relationship to Future Criminal Behavior," *Journal of Abnormal Psychology* 102 (1993): 369–78.

149. Scott Menard and Barbara Morse, "A Structuralist Critique of the IQ–Delinquency Hypothesis: Theory and Evidence," *American Journal of Sociology* 89 (1984): 1347–78; Denno, "Sociological and Human Developmental Explanations of Crime."

150. Ulric Neisser et al., "Intelligence: Knowns and Unknowns," *American Psychologist* 51 (1996): 77–101.

151. Richard Herrnstein and Charles Murray, *The Bell Curve: Intelligence and Class Structure in American Life* (New York: Free Press, 1994).

152. Susan Pease and Craig T. Love, "Optimal Methods and Issues in Nutrition Research in the Correctional Setting," *Nutrition Reviews Supplement* 44 (1986): 122–31.

153. Mark O'Callaghan and Douglas Carroll, "The Role of Psychosurgical Studies in the Control of Antisocial Behavior," in *The Causes of Crime, New Biological Approaches,* ed. Sarnoff Mednick, Terrie Moffitt, and Susan Stack (Cambridge: Cambridge University Press, 1987), pp. 312–28.

154. Mednick, Moffitt, Gabrielli, and Hutchings, "Genetic Factors in Criminal Behavior: A Review," pp. 47–48.

Chapter 7

1. Steven Messner and Richard Rosenfeld, *Crime and the American Dream* (Belmont, CA: Wadsworth, 1994), p. 11.

2. Robert Park, "The City: Suggestions for the Investigation of Behavior in the City Environment," *American Journal of Sociology* 20 (1915): 579–83.

3. Robert Park, Ernest Burgess, and Roderic McKenzie, *The City* (Chicago: University of Chicago Press, 1925).

4. Harvey Zorbaugh, *The Gold Coast and the Slum* (Chicago: University of Chicago Press, 1929); Frederick Thrasher, *The Gang* (Chicago: University of Chicago Press, 1927); Louis Wirth, *The Ghetto* (Chicago: University of Chicago Press, 1928).

5. Daniel Bell, *The Coming of Post-Industrial Society* (New York: Basic Books, 1973).

6. See, generally, Stephen Cernkovich and Peggy Giordano, "Family Relationships and Delinquency," *Criminology* 25 (1987): 295–321; Paul Howes and Howard Markman, "Marital Quality and Child Functioning: A Longitudinal Investigation," *Child Development* 60 (1989): 1044–51.

7. Emilie Andersen Allan and Darrell Steffensmeier, "Youth, Underemployment, and Property Crime: Differential Effects of Job Availability and Job Quality on Juvenile and Young Adult Arrest Rates," *American Sociological Review* 54 (1989): 107–23.

8. Edwin Lemert, *Human Deviance, Social Problems and Social Control* (Englewood Cliffs, NJ: Prentice-Hall, 1967).

9. Jonathan Crane, "The Epidemic Theory of Ghettos and Neighborhood Effects on Dropping Out and Teenage Childbearing," *American Journal of Sociology* 96 (1991): 1226–59; see also Rodrick Wallace, "Expanding Coupled Shock Fronts of Urban Decay and Criminal Behavior: How U.S. Cities Are Becoming 'Hollowed Out,'" *Journal of Quantitative Criminology* 7 (1991): 333–55.

10. Douglas Massey and Mitchell Eggers, "The Ecology of Inequality: Minorities and the Concentration of Poverty, 1970–1980," *American Journal of Sociology* 95 (1990): 1153–88; Melvin Thomas, "Race, Class and Personal Income: An Empirical Test of the Declining Significance of Race Thesis, 1968–1988," *Social Problems* 40 (1993): 328–39.

11. Oscar Lewis, "The Culture of Poverty," *Scientific American* 215 (1966): 19–25.

12. Gunnar Myrdal, *The Challenge of World Poverty* (New York: Vintage Books, 1970); Ken Auletta, *The Under Class* (New York: Random House, 1982).

13. Herbert Gans, "Deconstructing the Underclass: The Term's Danger as a Planning Concept," *Journal of the American Planning Association* 56 (1990): 271–77.

14. Laurence Lynn and Michael G.H. McGeary, eds., *Inner-City Poverty in the United States* (Washington, DC: National Academy Press, 1990), p. 3; Cynthia Rexroat, *Declining Economic Status of Black Children: Examining the Change* (Washington, DC: Joint Center for Political and Economic Studies, 1990), p. 1.

15. David Brownfield, "Social Class and Violent Behavior," *Criminology* 24 (1986): 421–38; Charles Tittle and Robert Meier, "Specifying the SES/Delinquency Relationship," *Criminology* 28 (1990): 271–95.

16. Ruth Kornhauser, *Social Sources of Delinquency* (Chicago: University of Chicago Press, 1978), p. 75.

17. Clifford R. Shaw and Henry D. McKay, *Juvenile Delinquency and Urban Areas*, rev. ed. (Chicago: University of Chicago Press, 1972).

18. Anthony Platt, *The Child Savers: The Invention of Delinquency* (Chicago: University of Chicago Press, 1968).

19. Shaw and McKay, *Juvenile Delinquency and Urban Areas*, p. 52.

20. For a discussion of these issues, see Robert Bursik, "Social Disorganization and Theories of Crime and Delinquency: Problems and Prospects," *Criminology* 26 (1988): 521–39.

21. Robert Sampson, "Effects of Socioeconomic Context of Official Reaction to Juvenile Delinquency," *American Sociological Review* 51 (1986): 876–85; Jeffrey Fagan, Ellen Slaughter, and Eliot Hartstone, "Blind Justice? The Impact of Race on the Juvenile Justice Process," *Crime and Delinquency* 33 (1987): 224–58; Merry Morash, "Establishment of a Juvenile Police Record," *Criminology* 22 (1984): 97–113.

22. Bernard Lander, *Towards an Understanding of Juvenile Delinquency* (New York: Columbia University Press, 1954); David Bordua, "Juvenile Delinquency and 'Anomie': An Attempt at Replication," *Social Problems* 6 (1958): 230–38; Roland Chilton, "Continuities in Delinquency Area Research: A Comparison of Studies in Baltimore, Detroit, and Indianapolis," *American Sociological Review* 29 (1964): 71–73.

23. For a general review, see James Byrne and Robert Sampson, eds., *The Social Ecology of Crime* (New York: Springer Verlag, 1985).

24. See, generally, Bursik, "Social Disorganization and Theories of Crime and Delinquency," pp. 519–51.

25. William Spelman, "Abandoned Buildings: Magnets for Crime?" *Journal of Criminal Justice* 21 (1993): 481–93.

26. Keith Harries and Andrea Powell, "Juvenile Gun Crime and Social Stress: Baltimore, 1980–1990," *Urban Geography* 15 (1994): 45–63.

27. Steven Messner and Kenneth Tardiff, "Economic Inequality and Levels of Homicide: An Analysis of Urban Neighborhoods," *Criminology* 24 (1986): 297–317.

28. G. David Curry and Irving Spergel, "Gang Homicide, Delinquency, and Community," *Criminology* 26 (1988): 381–407.

29. Per-Olof Wikstrom and Lars Dolmen, "Crime and Crime Trends in Different Urban Environments," *Journal of Quantitative Criminology* 6 (1990): 7–28.

30. Robert Sampson and W. Byron Groves, "Community Structure and Crime: Testing Social Disorganization Theory," *American Journal of Sociology* 94 (1989): 774–802.

31. Bursik, "Social Disorganization and Theories of Crime and Delinquency," p. 520.

32. Richard McGahey, "Economic Conditions, Organization, and Urban Crime," in *Communities and Crime,* ed. Albert Reiss and Michael Tonry (Chicago: University of Chicago Press, 1986), pp. 231–70; Scott Menard and Delbert Elliott, "Self-Reported Offending, Maturational Reform, and the Easterlin Hypothesis," *Journal of Quantitative Criminology* 6 (1990): 237–68.

33. Elijah Anderson, *Streetwise: Race, Class and Change in an Urban Community* (Chicago: University of Chicago Press, 1990), pp. 243–44.

34. Pamela Wilcox Rountree and Kenneth Land, "Burglary Victimization, Perceptions of Crime Risk, and Routine Activities: A Multilevel Analysis Across Seattle Neighborhoods and Census Tracts," *Journal of Research in Crime and Delinquency* 33 (1996): 147–80.

35. Randy LaGrange, Kenneth Ferraro, and Michael Supancic, "Perceived Risk and Fear of Crime: Role of Social and Physical Incivilities," *Journal of Research in Crime and Delinquency* 29 (1992): 311–34.

36. Ralph Taylor and Jeanette Covington, "Community Structural Change and Fear of Crime," *Social Problems* 40 (1993): 374–92.

37. Wesley Skogan, "Fear of Crime and Neighborhood Change," in *Communities and Crime*, ed. Reiss and Tonry, pp. 191–232.

38. Stephanie Greenberg, "Fear and Its Relationship to Crime, Neighborhood Deterioration and Informal Social Control," in *The Social Ecology of Crime*, ed. James Byrne and Robert Sampson (New York: Springer Verlag, 1985), pp. 47–62.

39. Anderson, *Streetwise: Race, Class and Change in an Urban Community,* p. 245.

40. Finn Aage-Esbensen and David Huizinga, "Community Structure and Drug Use: From a Social Disorganization Perspective," *Justice Quarterly* 7 (1990): 691–709; Allen Liska and Paul Bellair, "Violent-Crime Rates and Racial Composition: Convergence over Time," *American Journal of Sociology* 101 (1995): 578–610; Wesley Skogan, *Disorder and Decline: Crime and the Spiral of Decay in American Neighborhoods* (New York: Free Press, 1990), pp. 15–35.

41. Ralph Taylor and Jeanette Covington, "Neighborhood Changes in Ecology and Violence," *Criminology* 26 (1988): 553–89.

42. Leo Scheurman and Solomon Kobrin, "Community Careers in Crime," in *Communities and Crime*, ed. Reiss and Tonry, pp. 67–100.

43. See, generally, Robert Bursik, "Delinquency Rates as Sources of Ecological Change," in *The Social Ecology of Crime*, ed. Byrne and Sampson, pp. 63–77; Janet Heitgerd and Robert Bursik, "Extracommunity Dynamics and the Ecology of Delinquency," *American Journal of Sociology* 92 (1987): 775–87.

44. Carolyn Rebecca Block and Richard Block, *Street Gang Crime in Chicago* (Washington, DC: National Institute of Justice, 1993), p. 7.

45. Barbara Warner and Glenn Pierce, "Reexamining Social Disorganization Theory Using Calls to the Police as a Measure of Crime," *Criminology* 31 (1993): 493–519.

46. Donald Black, "Social Control as a Dependent Variable," in *Toward a General Theory of Social Control*, ed. D. Black (Orlando, FL: Academic Press, 1990).

47. Rodney Stark, "Deviant Places: A Theory of the Ecology of Crime," *Criminology* 25 (1987): 893–911.

48. Delbert Elliott, William Julius Wilson, David Huizinga, Robert Sampson, Amanda Elliott, and Bruce Rankin, "The Effects of Neighborhood Disadvantage on Adolescent Development," *Journal of Research in Crime and Delinquency* 33 (1996): 389–426.

49. Robert Bursik and Harold Grasmick, "Economic Deprivation and Neighborhood Crime Rates, 1960–1980," *Law and Society Review* 27 (1993): 263–78.

50. Skogan, *Disorder and Decline.*

51. Robert Sampson and W. Byron Groves, "Community Structure and Crime: Testing Social Disorganization Theory," *American Journal of Sociology* 94 (1989): 774–802; Denise Gottfredson, Richard McNeill, and Gary Gottfredson, "Social Area Influences on Delinquency: A Multilevel Analysis," *Journal of Research in Crime and Delinquency* 28 (1991): 197–206.

52. Mitchell Chamlin and John Cochran, "Social Altruism and Crime," *Criminology* 35 (1997): 203–28.

53. Robert Merton, *Social Theory and Social Structure*, enlarged ed. (New York: Free Press, 1968); for an analysis, see Richard Hilbert, "Durkheim and Merton on Anomie: An Unexplored Contrast in Its Derivatives," *Social Problems* 36 (1989): 242–56.

54. Ibid., p. 243.

55. Albert Cohen, "The Sociology of the Deviant Act: Anomie Theory and Beyond," *American Sociological Review* 30 (1965): 5–14.

56. See Robert Agnew, "The Contribution of Social Psychological Strain Theory to the Explanation of Crime and Delinquency," in *Advances in Criminological Theory* 6 (1995): 113–22.

57. These criticisms are in Steven Messner and Richard Rosenfeld, *Crime and the American Dream*, p. 60.

58. Scott Menard, "A Developmental Test of Mertonian Anomie Theory," *Journal of Research in Crime and Delinquency* 32 (1995): 136–74.

59. John Hagan, Hans Merkens, and Klaus Boehnke, "Delinquency and Disdain: Social Capital and Control of Right-Wing Extremism among East and West Berlin Youth," *American Journal of Sociology* 100 (1995): 1028–52.

60. Steven Messner and Richard Rosenfeld, "An Institutional-Anomie Theory of the Social Distribution of Crime,"

paper presented at the annual meeting of the American Society of Criminology, Phoenix, Arizona, November 1993.

61. Mitchell Chamlin and John Cochran, "Assessing Messner and Rosenfeld's Institutional Anomie Theory: A Partial Test," *Criminology* 33 (1995): 411–29.

62. John Braithwaite, "Poverty Power, White-Collar Crime and the Paradoxes of Criminological Theory," *Australian and New Zealand Journal of Criminology* 24 (1991): 40–58.

63. Judith Blau and Peter Blau, "The Cost of Inequality: Metropolitan Structure and Violent Crime," *American Sociological Review* 147 (1982): 114–29.

64. Peter Blau and Joseph Schwartz, *Crosscutting Social Circles* (New York: Academic Press, 1984).

65. Scott South and Steven Messner, "Structural Determinants of Intergroup Association," *American Journal of Sociology* 91 (1986): 1409–30; Steven Messner and Scott South, "Economic Deprivation, Opportunity Structure and Robbery Victimization," *Social Forces* 64 (1986): 975–91.

66. Richard Fowles and Mary Merva, "Wage Inequality and Criminal Activity: An Extreme Bounds Analysis for the United States, 1975–1990," *Criminology* 34 (1996): 163–82.

67. Taylor and Covington, "Neighborhood Changes in Ecology and Violence," p. 582; Richard Block, "Community Environment and Violent Crime," *Criminology* 17 (1979): 46–57; Robert Sampson, "Structural Sources of Variation in Race-Age-Specific Rates of Offending Across Major U.S. Cities," *Criminology* 23 (1985): 647–73; Richard Rosenfeld, "Urban Crime Rates: Effects of Inequality, Welfare Dependency, Region and Race," in *The Social Ecology of Crime,* ed. James Byrne and Robert Sampson (New York: Springer Verlag, 1985), pp. 116–30.

68. Fowles and Merva, "Wage Inequality and Criminal Activity"; Ruth Peterson and William Bailey, "Rape and Dimensions of Gender Socioeconomic Inequality in U.S. Metropolitan Areas," *Journal of Research in Crime and Delinquency* 29 (1992): 162–77; Gary LaFree, Kriss Drass, and Patrick O'Day, "Race and Crime in Postwar America: Determinants of African-American and White Rates, 1957–1988," *Criminology* 30 (1992): 157–88.

69. Kenneth Land, Patricia McCall, and Lawrence Cohen, "Structural Covariates of Homicide Rates: Are There Any Invariances Across Time and Social Space?" *American Journal of Sociology* 95 (1990): 922–63; Robert Bursik and James Webb, "Community Change and Patterns of Delinquency," *American Journal of Sociology* 88 (1982): 24–42.

70. Robert Agnew, "A Durkheimian Strain Theory of Delinquency," paper presented at the annual meeting of the American Society of Criminology, Baltimore, November 1990.

71. Jeanne Brooks-Gunn, Greg Duncan, Pamela Klato Klebanov, and Naomi Sealand, "Do Neighborhoods Influence Child and Adolescent Development?" *American Journal of Sociology* 99 (1993): 353–95.

72. Nikos Passas, "Anomie and Relative Deprivation," paper presented at the annual meeting of the Eastern Sociological Society, Boston, 1987.

73. Robert Agnew, "Foundation for a General Strain Theory of Crime and Delinquency," *Criminology* 30 (1992): 47–87.

74. Paul Mazerolle and Alex Piquero, "Linking General Strain with Anger: Investigating the Instrumental, Escapist, and Violent Adaptations to Strain," paper presented at the American Society of Criminology meeting, Boston, November 1995.

75. Robert Agnew, "Stability and Change in Crime over the Life Course: A Strain Theory Explanation," in *Advances in Criminological Theory,* vol. 7, *Developmental Theories of Crime and Delinquency,* ed. Terence Thornberry (New Brunswick, NJ: Transaction Books, 1995), pp. 113–37.

76. Lawrence Wu, "Effects of Family Instability, Income and Income Instability on the Risk of Premarital Birth," *American Sociological Review* 61 (1996): 386–406.

77. Robert Agnew and Helene Raskin White, "An Empirical Test of General Strain Theory," *Criminology* 30 (1992): 475–99.

78. John Hoffman and Alan Miller, "A Latent Variable Analysis of General Strain Theory," *Journal of Quantitative Criminology* (in press, 1997); Raymond Paternoster and Paul Mazerolle, "General Strain Theory and Delinquency: A Replication and Extension," *Journal of Research in Crime and Delinquency* 31 (1994): 235–63.

79. G. Roger Jarjoura, "The Conditional Effect of Social Class on the Dropout-Delinquency Relationship," *Journal of Research in Crime and Delinquency* 33 (1996): 232–55.

80. Teresa Lagrange and Robert Silverman, "Perceived Strain and Delinquency Motivation: An Empirical Evaluation of General Strain Theory," paper presented at the American Society of Criminology meeting, Boston, November 1995.

81. Thomas Ashby Wills, Donato Vaccaro, Grace McNamara, and A. Elizabeth Hirky, "Escalated Substance Use: A Longitudinal Grouping Analysis from Early to Middle Adolescence," *Journal of Abnormal Psychology* 105 (1996): 166–80.

82. Timothy Brezina, "Adapting to Strain: An Examination of Delinquent Coping Responses," *Criminology* 34 (1996): 39–61.

83. John Hoffman and S. Susan Su, "The Conditional Effects of Stress on Delinquency and Drug Use: A Strain Theory in Assessment of Sex Differences," *Journal of Research in Crime and Delinquency* 34 (1997): 46–78.

84. Lisa Broidy, "The Role of Gender in General Strain Theory," paper presented at the American Society of Criminology meeting, Boston, November 1995.

85. Robbin Ogle, Daniel Maier-Katkin, and Thomas Bernard, "A Theory of Homicidal Behavior Among Women," *Criminology* 33 (1995): 173–93.

86. Thorsten Sellin, *Culture Conflict and Crime,* bulletin no. 41 (New York: Social Science Research Council, 1938).

87. Walter Miller, "Lower-Class Culture as a Generating Milieu of Gang Delinquency," *Journal of Social Issues* 14 (1958): 5–19.

88. Albert Cohen, *Delinquent Boys* (New York: Free Press, 1955).

89. Clarence Schrag, *Crime and Justice American Style* (Washington, DC: U.S. Government Printing Office, 1971), p. 74.

90. J. Johnstone, "Social Class, Social Areas, and Delinquency," *Sociology and Social Research* 63 (1978): 49–72; Joseph Harry, "Social Class and Delinquency: One More Time," *Sociological Quarterly* 15 (1974): 294–301.

91. Stephen Baron and Leslie Kennedy, "Deterrence and Homeless Male Street Youths," *Canadian Journal of Criminology* 40 (1998): 27–52.

92. Richard Cloward and Lloyd Ohlin, *Delinquency and Opportunity* (New York: Free Press, 1960).

93. G. David Curry, Robert Fox, Richard Ball, and Daryl Stone, *National Assessment and Law Enforcement Anti-Gang Information Resources*, Final Report (Morgantown, WV: National Assessment Survey, 1992); G. David Curry, *Gang Crime and Law Enforcement Record Keeping* (Washington, DC: National Institute of Justice, 1994); G. David Curry, Richard Ball, and Scott Decker, "Estimating the National Scope of Gang Crime from Law Enforcement Data," in *Gangs in America*, 2nd ed., ed. C. Ronald Huff (Newbury Park, CA: Sage, 1996).

94. Malcolm Klein, *The American Street Gang, Its Nature, Prevalence and Control* (New York: Oxford University Press, 1995), pp. 31–35.

95. Finn-Aage Esbensen and David Huizinga, "Gangs, Drugs, and Delinquency in a Survey of Urban Youth," *Criminology* 31 (1993): 565–91; Malcom Klein, Cheryl Maxson, and Lea Cunningham, "Crack, Street Gangs, and Violence," *Criminology* 29 (1991): 623–50; see also Irving Spergel, "Youth Gangs: Continuity and Change," in *Crime and Justice*, vol. 12, ed. Michael Tonry and Norval Morris (Chicago: University of Chicago Press, 1990), pp. 171–277.

96. Felix Padilla, *The Gang as an American Enterprise* (New Brunswick, NJ: Rutgers University Press, 1992); see also Jeffery Fagan, "The Political Economy of Drug Dealing Among Urban Gangs," in *Drugs and the Community*, ed. Robert Davis, Arthur Lurigio, and Dennis Rosenbaum (Springfield, IL: Charles C Thomas, 1993), pp. 19–54.

97. Pamela Irving Jackson, "Crime, Youth Gangs, and Urban Transition: The Social Dislocations of Postindustrial Economic Development," *Justice Quarterly* 8 (1991): 379–97.

98. Robert Sampson and William Julius Wilson, "Toward a Theory of Race, Crime and Urban Inequality," in *Crime and Inequality*, ed. John Hagan and Ruth Peterson (Stanford, CA: Stanford University Press, 1995), pp. 37–54.

99. For a general criticism, see Kornhauser, *Social Sources of Delinquency*.

100. Charles Tittle, "Social Class and Criminal Behavior: A Critique of the Theoretical Foundations," *Social Forces* 62 (1983): 334–58.

101. James Q. Wilson and Richard Herrnstein, *Crime and Human Nature* (New York: Simon & Schuster, 1985).

102. Kenneth Polk and F. Lynn Richmond, "Those Who Fail," in *Schools and Delinquency*, ed. Kenneth Polk and Walter Schafer (Englewood Cliffs, NJ: Prentice-Hall, 1974), p. 67.

103. James DeFronzo, "Welfare and Burglary," *Crime and Delinquency* 42 (1996): 223–30.

104. Solomon Kobrin, "The Chicago Area Project—25-Year Assessment," *Annals of the American Academy of Political and Social Science* 322 (1959): 20–29.

Chapter 8

1. See, for example, James Q. Wilson and Allan Abrahamse, "Does Crime Pay?" *Justice Quarterly* 9 (1992): 359–78.

2. Alan Lizotte, Terence Thornberry, Marvin Krohn, Deborah Chard-Wierschem, and David McDowall, "Neighborhood Context and Delinquency: A Longitudinal Analysis," in *Cross-National Longitudinal Research on Human Development and Criminal Behavior*, ed. E.M. Weitekamp and H.J. Kerner (Netherlands: Kluwer, 1994), pp. 217–27.

3. Charles Tittle and Robert Meier, "Specifying the SES/Delinquency Relationship," *Criminology* 28 (1990): 271–99.

4. Lizotte, Thornberry, Krohn, Chard-Wierschem, and McDowall, "Neighborhood Context and Delinquency."

5. Denise Kandel, "The Parental and Peer Contexts of Adolescent Deviance: An Algebra of Interpersonal Influences," *Journal of Drug Issues* 26 (1996): 289–315; Ann Goetting, "The Parenting Crime Connection," *Journal of Primary Prevention* 14 (1994): 167–84.

6. Sheldon Glueck and Eleanor Glueck, *Unraveling Juvenile Delinquency* (Cambridge, MA: Harvard University Press, 1950); Ashley Weeks, "Predicting Juvenile Delinquency," *American Sociological Review* 8 (1943): 40–46.

7. For general reviews of the relationship between families and delinquency, see Alan Jay Lincoln and Murray Straus, *Crime and the Family* (Springfield, IL: Charles C Thomas, 1985); Rolf Loeber and Magda Stouthamer-Loeber, "Family Factors as Correlates and Predictors of Juvenile Conduct Problems and Delinquency," in *Crime and Justice, An Annual Review of Research*, vol. 7, ed. Michael Tonry and Norval Morris (Chicago: University of Chicago Press, 1986), pp. 29–151; Goetting, "The Parenting Crime Connection."

8. Joseph Weis, Katherine Worsley, and Carol Zeiss, "The Family and Delinquency: Organizing the Conceptual Chaos" (Center for Law and Justice, University of Washington, 1982, Monograph).

9. Susan Stern and Carolyn Smith, "Family Processes and Delinquency in an Ecological Context," *Social Service Review* 37 (1995): 707–31.

10. Lawrence Rosen and Kathleen Neilson, "Broken Homes," in *Contemporary Criminology*, ed. Leonard Savitz and Norman Johnston (New York: Wiley, 1982), pp. 126–35.

11. James Q. Wilson and Richard Herrnstein, *Crime and Human Nature* (New York: Simon & Schuster, 1985), p. 249.

12. L. Edward Wells and Joseph Rankin, "Families and Delinquency: A Meta-Analysis of the Impact of Broken Homes," *Social Problems* 38 (1991): 71–90.

13. Nan Marie Astone and Sara McLanahan, "Family Structure, Parental Practices and High School Completion," *American Sociological Review* 56 (1991): 309–20.

14. Mary Pat Traxler, "The Influence of the Father and Alternative Male Role Models on African-American Boys' Involvement in Antisocial Behavior," paper presented at the annual meeting of the American Society of Criminology, New Orleans, November 1992.

15. Paul Amato and Bruce Keith, "Parental Divorce and the Well-Being of Children: A Meta-Analysis," *Psychological Bulletin* 110 (1991): 26–46.

16. Joseph Rankin and L. Edward Wells, "The Effect of Parental Attachments and Direct Controls on Delinquency," *Journal of Research in Crime and Delinquency* 27 (1990): 140–65.

17. Robert Roberts and Vern Bengston, "Affective Ties to Parents in Early Adulthood and Self-Esteem Across 20 Years," *Social Psychology Quarterly* 59 (1996): 96–106.

18. Robert Johnson, S. Susan Su, Dean Gerstein, Hee-Choon Shin, and John Hoffman, "Parental Influences on Deviant Behavior in Early Adolescence: A Logistic Response Analysis of Age- and Gender-Differentiated Effects,"

Journal of Quantitative Criminology 11 (1995): 167–92.

19. Judith Brook and Li-Jng Tseng, "Influences of Parental Drug Use, Personality, and Child Rearing on the Toddler's Anger and Negativity," *Genetic, Social and General Psychology Monographs* 122 (1996): 107–28.

20. Thomas Ashby Wills, Donato Vaccaro, Grace McNamara, and A. Elizabeth Hirky, "Escalated Substance Use: A Longitudinal Grouping Analysis from Early to Middle Adolescence," *Journal of Abnormal Psychology* 105 (1996): 166–80.

21. John Laub and Robert Sampson, "Unraveling Families and Delinquency: A Reanalysis of the Gluecks' Data," *Criminology* 26 (1988): 355–80.

22. Richard Famularo, Karen Stone, Richard Barnum, and Robert Wharton, "Alcoholism and Severe Child Maltreatment," *American Journal of Orthopsychiatry* 56 (1987): 481–85; Richard Gelles, "Child Abuse and Violence in Single-Parent Families: Parent Absence and Economic Deprivation," *American Journal of Orthopsychiatry* 59 (1989): 492–501; Cecil Willis and Richard Wells, "The Police and Child Abuse: An Analysis of Police Decisions to Report Illegal Behavior," *Criminology* 26 (1988): 695–716; Carolyn Webster-Stratton, "Comparison of Abusive and Nonabusive Families with Conduct-Disordered Children," *American Journal of Orthopsychiatry* 55 (1985): 59–69.

23. Carolyn Smith and Terence Thornberry, "The Relationship between Childhood Maltreatment and Adolescent Involvement in Delinquency," *Criminology* 33 (1995): 451–79.

24. Herman Daldin, "The Fate of the Sexually Abused Child," *Clinical Social Work Journal* 16 (1988): 20–26; Gerald Ellenson, "Horror, Rage and Defenses in the Symptoms of Female Sexual Abuse Survivors," *Social Casework: The Journal of Contemporary Social Work* 70 (1989): 589–96.

25. Susan Zuravin, "The Ecology of Child Abuse and Neglect: Review of the Literature and Presentation of Data," *Violence and Victims* 4 (1989): 101–20.

26. Lening Zhang and Steven Messner, "Family Deviance and Delinquency in China," *Criminology* 33 (1995): 359–87.

27. *The Forgotten Half: Pathways to Success for America's Youth and Young Families* (Washington, DC: William T. Grant Foundation, 1988); Lee Jussim, "Teacher Expectations: Self-Fulfilling Prophecies, Perceptual Biases, and Accuracy," *Journal of Personality and Social Psychology* 57 (1989): 469–80.

28. Eugene Maguin and Rolf Loeber, "Academic Performance and Delinquency," in *Crime and Justice: A Review of Research*, vol. 20, ed. Michael Tonry (Chicago: University of Chicago Press, 1996), pp. 145–264.

29. Jeannie Oakes, *Keeping Track: How Schools Structure Inequality* (New Haven, CT: Yale University Press, 1985); Marc LeBlanc, Evelyne Valliere, and Pierre McDuff, "Adolescent's School Experience and Self-Reported Offending: A Longitudinal Test of Social Control Theory," paper presented at the annual meeting of the American Society of Criminology, Baltimore, November 1990.

30. G. Roger Jarjoura, "Does Dropping Out of School Enhance Delinquent Involvement? Results from a Large-Scale National Probability Sample," *Criminology* 31 (1993): 149–72; Terence Thornberry, Melanie Moore, and R.L. Christenson, "The Effect of Dropping Out of High School on Subsequent Criminal Behavior," *Criminology* 23 (1985): 3–18.

31. Carolyn Smith, Alan Lizotte, Terence Thornberry, and Marvin Krohn, *Resilient Youth: Identifying Factors That Prevent High-Risk Youth from Engaging in Delinquency and Drug Use* (Albany, NY: Rochester Youth Development Study, 1994), pp. 19–21.

32. Irving Janis, *Groupthink: Psychological Studies of Policy Decisions and Fiascoes* (Boston: Houghton Mifflin, 1982).

33. Lening Zhang and Steven Messner, "Family Deviance and Delinquency in China," *Criminology* 33 (1995): 359–87.

34. Thomas Berndt, "The Features and Effects of Friendships in Early Adolescence," *Child Development* 53 (1982): 1447–69; Thomas Berndt and T.B. Perry, "Children's Perceptions of Friendships as Supportive Relationships," *Developmental Psychology* 22 (1986): 640–48; Spencer Rathus, *Understanding Child Development* (New York: Holt, Rinehart and Winston, 1988), p. 462.

35. Peggy Giordano, "The Wider Circle of Friends in Adolescence," *American Journal of Sociology* 101 (1995): 661–97.

36. Delbert Elliott, David Huizinga, and Suzanne Ageton, *Explaining Delinquency and Drug Use* (Beverly Hills, CA: Sage, 1985); Helene Raskin White, Robert Padina, and Randy LaGrange, "Longitudinal Predictors of Serious Substance Use and Delinquency," *Criminology* 6 (1987): 715–40.

37. See, generally, John Hagedorn, *People and Folks: Gangs, Crime and the Underclass in a Rustbelt City* (Chicago: Lakeview Press, 1988).

38. Scott Menard, "Demographic and Theoretical Variables in the Age-Period Cohort Analysis of Illegal Behavior," *Journal of Research in Crime and Delinquency* 29 (1992): 178–99.

39. Patrick Jackson, "Theories and Findings About Youth Gangs," *Criminal Justice Abstracts*, June 1989, pp. 313–27.

40. Marvin Krohn and Terence Thornberry, "Network Theory: A Model for Understanding Drug Abuse among African-American and Hispanic Youth," in *Drug Abuse among Minority Youth: Advances in Research and Methodology*, ed. Mario De La Rosa and Juan-Luis Recio Adrados (Washington, DC: U.S. Department of Health and Human Services, 1993).

41. D. Wayne Osgood, Janet Wilson, Patrick O'Malley, Jerald Bachman, and Lloyd Johnston, "Routine Activities and Individual Deviant Behavior," *American Sociological Review* 61 (1996): 635–55.

42. Mark Warr, "Age, Peers, and Delinquency," *Criminology* 31 (1993): 17–40.

43. Mark Warr, "Organization and Instigation in Delinquent Groups," *Criminology* 34 (1996): 11–35.

44. Travis Hirschi and Rodney Stark, "Hellfire and Delinquency," *Social Problems* 17 (1969): 202–13.

45. T. David Evans, Francis Cullen, R. Gregory Dunaway, and Velmer Burton, Jr., "Religion and Crime Reexamined: The Impact of Religion, Secular Controls, and Social Ecology on Adult Criminality," *Criminology* 33 (1995): 195–224.

46. Lee Ellis and James Patterson, "Crime and Religion: An International Comparison Among Thirteen Industrial Nations," *Personal Individual Differences* 20 (1996): 761–68.

47. Walter Miller, *Violence by Youth Gangs and Youth Groups as a Crime Problem in Major American Cities* (Washington, DC: U.S. Government Printing Office, 1975).

48. Edwin Sutherland, Principles of *Criminology* (Philadelphia: Lippincott, 1939).

49. See, for example, Edwin Sutherland, "White-Collar Criminality," *American Sociological Review* 5 (1940): 2–10.

50. This section is adapted from Clarence Schrag, *Crime and Justice: American Style* (Washington, DC: U.S. Government Printing Office, 1971), p. 46.

51. See Edwin Sutherland and Donald Cressey, *Criminology*, 8th ed. (Philadelphia: Lippincott, 1970), pp. 77–79.

52. Sandra Brown, Vicki Creamer, and Barbara Stetson, "Adolescent Alcohol Expectancies in Relation to Personal and Parental Drinking Patterns," *Journal of Abnormal Psychology* 96 (1987): 117–21.

53. Ibid.

54. Ross Matsueda and Karen Heimer, "Race, Family Structure and Delinquency: A Test of Differential Association and Social Control Theories," *American Sociological Review* 52 (1987): 826–40.

55. James Short, "Differential Association as a Hypothesis: Problems of Empirical Testing," *Social Problems* 8 (1960): 14–25.

56. Albert Reiss and A. Lewis Rhodes, "The Distribution of Delinquency in the Social Class Structure," *American Sociological Review* 26 (1961): 732.

57. Douglas Smith, Christy Visher, and G. Roger Jarjoura, "Dimensions of Delinquency: Exploring the Correlates of Participation, Frequency, and Persistence of Delinquent Behavior," *Journal of Research in Crime and Delinquency* 28 (1991): 6–32.

58. Warr, "Age, Peers, and Delinquency."

59. Denise Kandel and Mark Davies, "Friendship Networks, Intimacy, and Illicit Drug Use in Young Adulthood: A Comparison of Two Competing Theories," *Criminology* 29 (1991): 441–67.

60. Kenneth Tunnell, "Inside the Drug Trade: Trafficking from the Dealer's Perspective," *Qualitative Sociology* 16 (1993): 361–81.

61. Krohn and Thornberry, "Network Theory," pp. 123–24.

62. Charles Tittle, *Sanctions and Social Deviance* (New York: Praeger, 1980).

63. Yuet-Wah Cheung and Agnes M.C. Ng, "Social Factors in Adolescent Deviant Behavior in Hong Kong: An Integrated Theoretical Approach," *International Journal of Comparative and Applied Criminal Justice* 12 (1988): 27–44.

64. Robert Burgess and Ronald Akers, "A Differential Association-Reinforcement Theory of Criminal Behavior," *Social Problems* 14 (1966): 128–47.

65. Ross Matsueda, "The Current State of Differential Association Theory," *Crime and Delinquency* 34 (1988): 277–306.

66. Burgess and Akers, "A Differential Association-Reinforcement Theory of Criminal Behavior."

67. Matsueda, "The Current State of Differential Association Theory."

68. Graham Ousey and David Aday, Jr., "The Interaction Hypothesis: A Test Using Social Control Theory and Social Learning Theory," paper presented at the American Society of Criminology meeting, Boston, November 1995.

69. Warr, "Age, Peers and Delinquency."

70. The most influential critique of differential association is contained in Ruth Kornhauser, *Social Sources of Delinquency* (Chicago: University of Chicago Press, 1978).

71. These misconceptions are derived from Donald Cressey, "Epidemiologies and Individual Conduct: A Case from Criminology," *Pacific Sociological Review* 3 (1960): 47–58.

72. Kornhauser, *Social Sources of Delinquency*; in contrast, see Matsueda, "The Current State of Differential Association Theory."

73. Ronald Akers, "Is Differential Association/Social Learning Cultural Deviance Theory?" *Criminology* 34 (1996): 229–47; for an opposing view, see Travis Hirschi, "Theory Without Ideas: Reply to Akers," *Criminology* 34 (1996): 249–56.

74. Craig Reinerman and Jeffrey Fagan, "Social Organization and Differential Association: A Research Note from a Longitudinal Study of Violent Juvenile Offenders," *Crime and Delinquency* 34 (1988): 307–27.

75. Sue Titus Reed, *Crime and Criminology*, 2nd ed. (New York: Holt, Rinehart and Winston, 1979), p. 234.

76. See, for example, Albert Bandura, *Social Learning and Personality Development* (New York: Holt, Rinehart and Winston, 1963).

77. Ronald Akers, *Deviant Behavior: A Social Learning Approach*, 2nd ed. (Belmont, CA: Wadsworth, 1977).

78. Ronald Akers, Marvin Krohn, Lonn Lonza-Kaduce, and Marcia Radosevich, "Social Learning and Deviant Behavior: A Specific Test of a General Theory," *American Sociological Review* 44 (1979): 638.

79. Ibid.

80. Marvin Krohn, William Skinner, James Massey, and Ronald Akers, "Social Learning Theory and Adolescent Cigarette Smoking: A Longitudinal Study," *Social Problems* 32 (1985): 455–71.

81. Ibid., pp. 636–55.

82. Ronald Akers and Gang Lee, "A Longitudinal Test of Social Learning Theory: Adolescent Smoking," *Journal of Drug Issues* 26 (1996): 317–43.

83. Gary Jensen and David Brownfield, "Parents and Drugs," *Criminology* 21 (1983): 543–54.

84. Ronald Akers, "Rational Choice, Deterrence and Social Learning Theory in Criminology: The Path Not Taken," *Journal of Criminal Law and Criminology* 81 (1990): 653–76.

85. Gresham Sykes and David Matza, "Techniques of Neutralization: A Theory of Delinquency," *American Sociological Review* 22 (1957): 664–70; David Matza, *Delinquency and Drift* (New York: Wiley, 1964).

86. Matza, *Delinquency and Drift*, p. 51.

87. Sykes and Matza, "Techniques of Neutralization," pp. 664–70; see also David Matza, "Subterranean Traditions of Youths," *Annals of the American Academy of Political and Social Science* 378 (1961): 116.

88. Sykes and Matza, "Techniques of Neutralization."

89. Ibid.

90. Michael Hindelang, "The Commitment of Delinquents to Their Misdeeds: Do Delinquents Drift?" *Social Problems* 17 (1970): 509.

91. Robert Regoli and Eric Poole, "The Commitment of Delinquents to Their Misdeeds: A Reexamination," *Journal of Criminal Justice* 6 (1978): 261–69.

92. Robert Agnew, "The Techniques of Neutralization and Violence," *Criminology* 32 (1994): 555–79.

93. Robert Ball, "An Empirical Exploration of Neutralization Theory," *Criminologica* 4 (1966): 22–32. For a similar

view, see M. William Minor, "The Neutralization of Criminal Offense," *Criminology* 18 (1980): 103–20.

94. Mark Pogrebin, Eric Poole, and Amos Martinez, "Accounts of Professional Misdeeds: The Sexual Exploitation of Clients by Psychotherapists," *Deviant Behavior* 13 (1992): 229–52.

95. Eric Wish, *Drug Use Forecasting 1990* (Washington, DC: National Institute of Justice, 1991).

96. Scott Briar and Irvin Piliavin, "Delinquency: Situational Inducements and Commitment to Conformity," *Social Problems* 13 (1965–1966): 35–45.

97. Lawrence Sherman and Douglas Smith, with Janell Schmidt and Dennis Rogan, "Crime, Punishment, and Stake in Conformity: Legal and Informal Control of Domestic Violence," *American Sociological Review* 57 (1992): 680–90.

98. Albert Reiss, "Delinquency as the Failure of Personal and Social Controls," *American Sociological Review* 16 (1951): 196–207.

99. Briar and Piliavin, "Delinquency: Situational Inducements and Commitment to Conformity."

100. John McCarthy and Dean Hoge, "The Dynamics of Self-Esteem and Delinquency," *American Journal of Sociology* 90 (1984): 396–410; Edward Wells and Joseph Rankin, "Self-Concept as a Mediating Concept in Delinquency," *Social Psychology Quarterly* 46 (1983): 11–22.

101. Howard Kaplan, *Deviant Behavior in Defense of Self* (New York: Academic Press, 1980); idem, "Self-Attitudes and Deviant Response," *Social Forces* 54 (1978): 788–801.

102. Howard Kaplan, Robert Johnson, and Carol Bailey, "Self-Rejection and the Explanation of Deviance: Refinement and Elaboration of a Latent Structure," *Social Psychology Quarterly* 49 (1986): 110–28.

103. L. Edward Wells, "Self-Enhancement through Delinquency: A Conditional Test of Self-Derogation Theory," *Journal of Research in Crime and Delinquency* 26 (1989): 226–52.

104. See, generally, Walter Reckless, *The Crime Problem* (New York: Appleton-Century-Crofts, 1967). Among the many research reports by Walter Reckless and his colleagues are Walter Reckless, Simon Dinitz, and Ellen Murray, "Self-Concept as an Insulator Against Delinquency," *American Sociological Review* 21 (1956): 744–46; Reckless, Dinitz, and Murray, "The Good Boy in a High Delinquency Area," *Journal of Criminal Law, Criminology, and Police Science* 48 (1957): 1826; Walter Reckless, Simon Dinitz, and Barbara Kay, "The Self-Component in Potential Delinquency and Potential Nondelinquency," *American Sociological Review* 22 (1957): 566–70; Reckless and Dinitz, "Pioneering with Self-Concept as a Vulnerability Factor in Delinquency," *Journal of Criminal Law, Criminology, and Police Science* 58 (1967): 515–23.

105. Travis Hirschi, *Causes of Delinquency* (Berkeley: University of California Press, 1969).

106. Ibid., p. 231.

107. Ibid., pp. 66–74.

108. Marc LeBlanc, "Family Dynamics, Adolescent Delinquency, and Adult Criminality," paper presented at the Society for Life History Research Conference, Keystone, CO, October 1990, p. 6.

109. Patricia Van Voorhis, Francis Cullen, Richard Mathers, and Connie Chenoweth Garner, "The Impact of Family Structure and Quality on Delinquency: A Comparative Assessment of Structural and Functional Factors," *Criminology* 26 (1988): 235–61.

110. Marc LeBlanc, Evelyne Valliere, and Pierre McDuff, "Adolescent's School Experience and Self-Reported Offending: A Longitudinal Test of Social Control Theory," paper presented at the annual meeting of the American Society of Criminology, Baltimore, November 1990.

111. Marianne Junger and Wim Polder, "Some Explanations of Crime Among Four Ethnic Groups in the Netherlands," *Journal of Quantitative Criminology* 8 (1992): 51–78.

112. John Cochran and Ronald Akers, "An Exploration of the Variable Effects of Religiosity on Adolescent Marijuana and Alcohol Use," *Journal of Research in Crime and Delinquency* 26 (1989): 198–225.

113. Robert Agnew and David Peterson, "Leisure and Delinquency," *Social Problems* 36 (1989): 332–48.

114. Josine Junger-Tas, "An Empirical Test of Social Control Theory," *Journal of Quantitative Criminology* 8 (1992): 18–29.

115. Teresa Lagrange and Robert Silverman, "Perceived Strain and Delinquency Motivation: An Empirical Evaluation of General Strain Theory," paper presented at the American Society of Criminology meeting, Boston, November 1995.

116. For a review of exciting research, see Kimberly Kempf, "The Empirical Status of Hirschi's Control Theory," in *Advances in Criminological Theory,* ed. Bill Laufer and Freda Adler (New Brunswick, NJ: Transaction Publishers, 1992).

117. Richard Lawrence, "Parents, Peers, School—and Delinquency," paper presented at the American Society of Criminology meeting, Boston, November 1995.

118. Peggy Giordano, Stephen Cernkovich, and M.D. Pugh, "Friendships and Delinquency," *American Journal of Sociology* 91 (1986): 1170–1202.

119. Denise Kandel and Mark Davies, "Friendship Networks, Intimacy, and Illicit Drug Use in Young Adulthood: A Comparison of Two Competing Theories," *Criminology* 29 (1991): 441–67.

120. Velmer Burton, Francis Cullen, T. David Evans, R. Gregory Dunaway, Sesha Kethineni, and Gary Payne, "The Impact of Parental Controls on Delinquency," *Journal of Criminal Justice* 23 (1995): 111–26.

121. Kimberly Kempf Leonard and Scott Decker, "The Theory of Social Control: Does It Apply to the Very Young?" *Journal of Criminal Justice* 22 (1994): 89–105.

122. Michael Hindelang, "Causes of Delinquency: A Partial Replication and Extension," *Social Problems* 21 (1973): 471–87.

123. Gary Jensen and David Brownfield, "Parents and Drugs," *Criminology* 21 (1983): 543–54. See also M. Wiatrowski, D. Griswold, and M. Roberts, "Social Control Theory and Delinquency," *American Sociological Review* 46 (1981): 525–41.

124. Leslie Samuelson, Timothy Hartnagel, and Harvey Krahn, "Crime and Social Control Among High School Dropouts," *Journal of Crime and Justice* 18 (1990): 129–61.

125. Mark Warr, "Parents, Peers, and Delinquency," *Social Forces* 72 (1993): 247–64.

126. Marvin Krohn and James Massey, "Social Control and Delinquent Behavior: An Examination of the Elements of the Social Bond," *Sociological Quarterly* 21 (1980): 529–43.

127. Jill Leslie Rosenbaum and James Lasley, "School, Community Context, and Delinquency: Rethinking the Gender Gap," *Justice Quarterly* 7 (1990): 493–513.

128. Randy LaGrange and Helene Raskin White, "Age Differences in Delinquency: A Test of Theory," *Criminology* 23 (1985): 19–45.

129. Robert Agnew, "Social Control Theory and Delinquency: A Longitudinal Test," *Criminology* 23 (1985): 47–61.

130. Alan E. Liska and M.D. Reed, "Ties to Conventional Institutions and Delinquency: Estimating Reciprocal Effects," *American Sociological Review* 50 (1985): 547–60.

131. Michael Wiatrowski, David Griswold, and Mary K. Roberts, "Social Control Theory and Delinquency," *American Sociological Review* 46 (1981): 525–41.

132. Ibid.

133. George Herbert Mead, *Mind, Self and Society* (Chicago: University of Chicago Press, 1934); idem, *The Philosophy of the Act* (Chicago: University of Chicago Press, 1938); Charles Horton Cooley, *Human Nature and the Social Order* (New York: Schocken, 1964, originally published 1902); Herbert Blumer, *Symbolic Interactionism: Perspective and Method* (Englewood Cliffs, NJ: Prentice-Hall, 1969).

134. Bruce Link, Elmer Streuning, Francis Cullen, Patrick Shrout, and Bruce Dohrenwend, "A Modified Labeling Theory Approach to Mental Disorders: An Empirical Assessment," *American Sociological Review* 54 (1989): 400–23.

135. Linda Jackson, John Hunter, and Carole Hodge, "Physical Attractiveness and Intellectual Competence: A Meta-Analytic Review," *Social Psychology Quarterly* 58 (1995): 108–22.

136. President's Commission on Law Enforcement and the Administration of Youth Crime, Task Force Report: Juvenile Delinquency and Youth (Washington, DC: U.S. Government Printing Office, 1967), p. 43.

137. Kai Erickson, "Notes on the Sociology of Deviance," *Social Problems* 9 (1962): 397–414.

138. Edwin Schur, *Labeling Deviant Behavior* (New York: Harper & Row, 1972), p. 21.

139. Howard Becker, *Outsiders: Studies in the Sociology of Deviance* (New York: Macmillan, 1963), p. 9.

140. Christy Visher, "Gender, Police Arrest Decision, and Notions of Chivalry," *Criminology* 21 (1983): 5–28.

141. Marjorie Zatz, "Race, Ethnicity and Determinate Sentencing," *Criminology* 22 (1984): 147–71.

142. Roland Chilton and Jim Galvin, "Race, Crime and Criminal Justice," *Crime and Delinquency* 31 (1985): 3–14.

143. Joan Petersilia, "Racial Disparities in the Criminal Justice System: A Summary," *Crime and Delinquency* 31 (1985): 15–34.

144. Walter Gove, *The Labeling of Deviance: Evaluating a Perspective* (New York: Wiley, 1975), p. 5.

145. Harold Garfinkle, "Conditions of Successful Degradation Ceremonies," *American Journal of Sociology* 61 (1956): 420–24.

146. John Lofland, *Deviance and Identity* (Englewood Cliffs, NJ: Prentice-Hall, 1969).

147. Frank Tannenbaum, *Crime and the Community* (New York: Columbia University Press, 1938), pp. 19–20.

148. Edwin Lemert, *Social Pathology* (New York: McGraw-Hill, 1951).

149. Ibid., p. 75.

150. See, for example, Howard Kaplan and Hiroshi Fukurai, "Negative Social Sanctions, Self-Rejection, and Drug Use," *Youth and Society* 23 (1992): 275–98.

151. Howard Kaplan, *Toward a General Theory of Deviance: Contributions from Perspectives on Deviance and Criminality* (College Station: Texas A&M University, n.d.).

152. Howard Kaplan and Robert Johnson, "Negative Social Sanctions and Juvenile Delinquency: Effects of Labeling in a Model of Deviant Behavior," *Social Science Quarterly* 72 (1991): 98–122; Howard Kaplan, Robert Johnson, and Carol Bailey, "Deviant Peers and Deviant Behavior: Further Elaboration of a Model," *Social Psychology Quarterly* 30 (1987): 277–84.

153. Karen Heimer and Ross Matsueda, "Role-Taking, Role-Commitment and Delinquency: A Theory of Differential Social Control," *American Sociological Review* 59 (1994): 400–37.

154. Karen Heimer, "Gender, Race, and the Pathways to Delinquency: An Interactionist Explanation," in *Crime and Inequality*, ed. John Hagan and Ruth Peterson (Stanford, CA: Stanford University Press, 1995).

155. National Minority Council on Criminal Justice, *The Inequality of Justice* (Washington, DC: National Minority Advisory Council on Criminal Justice, 1981), p. 200.

156. Carl Pope and William Feyerherm, "Minority Status and Juvenile Justice Processing," *Criminal Justice Abstracts* 22 (1990): 327–36; see also Carl Pope, "Race and Crime Revisited," *Crime and Delinquency* 25 (1979): 347–57.

157. Leslie Margolin, "Deviance on Record: Techniques for Labeling Child Abusers in Official Documents," *Social Problems* 39 (1992): 58–68.

158. Charles Corley, Stephen Cernkovich, and Peggy Giordano, "Sex and the Likelihood of Sanction," *Journal of Criminal Law and Criminology* 80 (1989): 540–53.

159. Kaplan and Johnson, "Negative Social Sanctions and Juvenile Delinquency: Effects of Labeling in a Model of Deviant Behavior."

160. Ruth Triplett, "The Conflict Perspective, Symbolic Interactionism, and the Status Characteristics Hypothesis," *Justice Quarterly* 10 (1993): 540–58.

161. Ross Matsueda, "Reflected Appraisals, Parental Labeling, and Delinquency: Specifying a Symbolic Interactionist Theory," *American Journal of Sociology* 97 (1992): 1577–1611.

162. Suzanne Ageton and Delbert Elliott, *The Effect of Legal Processing on Self-Concept* (Boulder, CO: Institute of Behavioral Science, 1973).

163. Christine Bowditch, "Getting Rid of Troublemakers: High School Disciplinary Procedures and the Production of Dropouts," *Social Problems* 40 (1993): 493–507.

164. Melvin Ray and William Downs, "An Empirical Test of Labeling Theory Using Longitudinal Data," *Journal of Research in Crime and Delinquency* 23 (1986): 169–94.

165. Sherman and Smith, with Schmidt and Rogan, "Crime, Punishment, and Stake in Conformity."

166. Charles Tittle, "Two Empirical Regularities (Maybe) in Search of an Explanation: Commentary on the Age/Crime Debate," *Criminology* 26 (1988): 75–85.

167. Douglas Smith and Robert Brame, "On the Initiation and Continuation of Delinquency," *Criminology* 4 (1994): 607–30.

168. Jack Gibbs, "Conceptions of Deviant Behavior: The Old and the New," *Pacific Sociological Review* 9 (1966): 11–13.

169. Schur, *Labeling Deviant Behavior*, p. 14.

170. Ronald Akers, "Problems in the Sociology of Deviance," *Social Problems* 46 (1968): 463.

171. Charles Wellford, "Labeling Theory and Criminology: An Assessment," *Social Problems* 22 (1975): 335–47.

172. Ibid., p. 337.

173. Alexander Liazos, "The Poverty of the Sociology of Deviance: Nuts, Sluts, and Perverts," *Social Problems* 20 (1971): 103–20.

174. Tittle, "Two Empirical Regularities (Maybe) in Search of an Explanation."

175. Paul Lipsett, "The Juvenile Offender's Perception," *Crime and Delinquency* 14 (1968): 49; Jack Foster, Simon Dinitz, and Walter Reckless, "Perception of Stigma Following Public Intervention for Delinquent Behavior," *Social Problems* 20 (1972): 202.

176. Charles Tittle, "Labeling and Crime: An Empirical Evaluation," in *The Labeling of Deviance: Evaluating a Perspective*, ed. Walter Gove (New York: Wiley, 1975), pp. 157–79.

177. David Farrington, "Early Predictors of Adolescent Aggression and Adult Violence," *Violence and Victims* 4 (1989): 79–100.

178. Raymond Paternoster and Leeann Iovanni, "The Labeling Perspective and Delinquency: An Elaboration of the Theory and an Assessment of the Evidence," *Justice Quarterly* 6 (1989): 358–94.

Chapter 9

1. Michael Lynch, "Rediscovering Criminology: Lessons from the Marxist Tradition," in *Marxist Sociology: Surveys of Contemporary Theory and Research*, ed. Donald McQuarie and Patrick McGuire (New York: General Hall Press, 1994).

2. Michael Lynch and W. Byron Groves, *A Primer in Radical Criminology*, 2nd ed. (Albany, NY: Harrow and Heston, 1989), pp. 32–33.

3. Ibid., p. 4.

4. See, generally, Karl Marx and Friedrich Engels, *Capital: A Critique of Political Economy*, trans. E. Aveling (Chicago: Charles Kern, 1906); Karl Marx, *Selected Writings in Sociology and Social Philosophy*, trans. P.B. Bottomore (New York: McGraw-Hill, 1956). For a general discussion of Marxist thought, see Lynch and Groves, *A Primer in Radical Criminology*, pp. 6–26.

5. Karl Marx, *Grundrisse: Introduction to the Critique of Political Economy*, trans. Martin Nicolaus (New York: Vintage, 1973), pp. 106–7.

6. Lynch, "Rediscovering Criminology."

7. Karl Marx, "Population, Crime and Pauperism," in Karl Marx and Friedrich Engels, *Ireland and the Irish Question* (Moscow: Progress, 1859, reprinted 1971), p. 92.

8. Friedrich Engels, *The Condition of the Working Class in England in 1844* (London: Allen & Unwin, 1950).

9. Lynch, "Rediscovering Criminology," p. 5.

10. Willem Bonger, *Criminality and Economic Conditions* (1916, abridged ed., Bloomington: Indiana University Press, 1969).

11. Ralf Dahrendorf, *Class and Class Conflict in Industrial Society* (Palo Alto, CA: Stanford University Press, 1959).

12. Ibid., p. 48.

13. George Vold, *Theoretical Criminology* (New York: Oxford University Press, 1958).

14. James Short and F. Ivan Nye, "Extent of Undetected Delinquency: Tentative Conclusions," *Journal of Criminal Law, Criminology, and Police Science* 49 (1958): 296–302.

15. For a general view, see David Friedrichs, "Crime, Deviance and Criminal Justice: In Search of a Radical Humanistic Perspective," *Humanity and Society* 6 (1982): 200–26.

16. Edwin Lemert, *Social Pathology* (New York: McGraw-Hill, 1951); Howard Becker, *Outsiders: Studies in the Sociology of Deviance* (New York: Macmillan, 1963).

17. Alexander Liazos, "The Poverty of the Sociology of Deviance: Nuts, Sluts and Perverts," *Social Problems* 20 (1972): 103–20.

18. See, generally, Robert Meier, "The New Criminology: Continuity in Criminological Theory," *Journal of Criminal Law and Criminology* 67 (1977): 461–69.

19. David Greenberg, ed., *Crime and Capitalism* (Palo Alto, CA: Mayfield Publishing, 1981), p. 3.

20. William Chambliss and Robert Seidman, *Law, Order and Power* (Reading, MA: Addison-Wesley, 1971), p. 503.

21. John Braithwaite, "Retributivism, Punishment and Privilege," in *Punishment and Privilege*, ed. W. Byron Groves and Graeme Newman (Albany, NY: Harrow and Heston, 1986), pp. 55–66.

22. Austin Turk, "Class, Conflict and Criminology," *Sociological Focus* 10 (1977): 209–20.

23. Daniel Georges-Abeyie, "Race, Ethnicity, and the Spatial Dynamic: Toward a Realistic Study of Black Crime, Crime Victimization, and Criminal Justice Processing of Blacks," *Social Justice* 16 (1989): 35–54.

24. John Hagan and Celesta Albonetti, "Race, Class and the Perception of Criminal Injustice in America," *American Journal of Sociology* 88 (1982): 329–55.

25. Richard Quinney, *The Social Reality of Crime* (Boston: Little, Brown, 1970), pp. 15–23.

26. Austin Turk, *Criminality and Legal Order* (Chicago: Rand McNally, 1969), p. 58.

27. Lynch and Groves, *A Primer in Radical Criminology*, 2nd ed., p. 38.

28. Austin Turk, *Criminality and Legal Order* (Chicago: Rand McNally, 1969).

29. David McDowall, "Poverty and Homicide in Detroit, 1926–1978," *Victims and Violence* 1 (1986): 23–34; David McDowall and Sandra Norris, "Poverty and Homicide in Baltimore, Cleveland, and Memphis, 1937–1980," paper presented at the annual meeting of the American Society of Criminology, Montreal, November 1987.

30. Judith Blau and Peter Blau, "The Cost of Inequality: Metropolitan Structure and Violent Crime," *American Sociological Review* 147 (1982): 114–29; Richard Block, "Community Environment and Violent Crime," *Criminology* 17 (1979): 46–57; Robert Sampson, "Structural Sources of Variation in Race-Age-Specific Rates of Offending across Major U.S. Cities," *Criminology* 23 (1985): 647–73.

31. David Jacobs and David Britt, "Inequality and Police Use of Deadly Force: An Empirical Assessment of a Conflict Hypothesis," *Social Problems* 26 (1979): 403–12.

32. Alan Lizotte, "Extra-Legal Factors in Chicago's Criminal Courts: Testing the Conflict Model of Criminal Justice," *Social Problems* 25 (1978): 564–80.

33. Terance Miethe and Charles Moore, "Racial Differences in Criminal Processing: The Consequences of Model Selection on Conclusions About Differential Treatment," *Sociological Quarterly* 27 (1987): 217–37.

34. Douglas Smith, Christy Visher, and Laura Davidson, "Equity and Discretionary Justice: The Influence of Race on Police Arrest Decisions," *Journal of Criminal Law and Criminology* 75 (1984): 234–49.

35. Thomas Arvanites, "Increasing Imprisonment: A Function of Crime or Socioeconomic Factors?" *American Journal of Criminal Justice* 17 (1992): 19–38.

36. Nancy Wonders, "Determinate Sentencing: A Feminist and Postmodern Story," *Justice Quarterly* 13 (1996): 610–48.

37. Michael Leiber, Anne Woodrick, and E. Michele Roudebush, "Religion, Discriminatory Attitudes and the Orientations of Juvenile Justice Personnel: A Research Note," *Criminology* 33 (1995): 431–47.

38. Michael Leiber and Katherine Jamieson, "Race and Decision Making Within Juvenile Justice: The Importance of Context," *Journal of Quantitative Criminology* 11 (1995): 363–88.

39. Dragan Milovanovic, "Postmodern Criminology: Mapping the Terrain," *Justice Quarterly* 13 (1996): 567–610.

40. Richard Greenleaf and Lonn Lanza-Kaduce, "Sophistication, Organization and Authority-Subject Conflict: Rediscovering and Unraveling Turk's Theory of Norm Resistance," *Criminology* 33 (1995): 565–85.

41. Jackson Toby, "The New Criminology Is the Old Sentimentality," *Criminology* 16 (1979): 513–26.

42. Kenneth Land and Marcus Felson, "A General Framework for Building Dynamic Macro Social Indicator Models: An Analysis of Changes in Crime Rates and Police Expenditures," *American Journal of Sociology* 82 (1976): 565–604.

43. Arvanites, "Increasing Imprisonment," p. 34.

44. See, generally, William Wilbanks, *The Myth of a Racist Criminal Justice System* (Monterey, CA: Brooks/Cole, 1987).

45. Theodore Chiricos and Gordon Waldo, "Socioeconomic Status and Criminal Sentencing: An Empirical Assessment of a Conflict Proposition," *American Sociological Review* 40 (1975): 753–72.

46. Stephen Klein, Joan Petersilia, and Susan Turner, "Race and Imprisonment Decisions in California," *Science* 247 (1990): 812–16.

47. Basil Owomero, "Crime in Tanzania: Contradictions of a Socialist Experiment," *International Journal of Comparative and Applied Criminal Justice* 12 (1988): 177–89.

48. Lynch and Groves, *A Primer in Radical Criminology,* 2nd ed., p. 6.

49. This section borrows heavily from Richard Sparks, "A Critique of Marxist Criminology," in *Crime and Justice,* vol. 2, ed. Norval Morris and Michael Tonry (Chicago: University of Chicago Press, 1980), pp. 159–208.

50. Jeffery Reiman, *The Rich Get Richer and the Poor Get Prison* (New York: Wiley, 1984), pp. 43–44.

51. For a general review of Marxist criminology, see Lynch and Groves, *A Primer in Radical Criminology,* 2nd ed.

52. Ian Taylor, Paul Walton, and Jock Young, *The New Criminology: For a Social Theory of Deviance* (London: Routledge & Kegan Paul, 1973).

53. Barry Krisberg, *Crime and Privilege: Toward a New Criminology* (Englewood Cliffs, NJ: Prentice-Hall, 1975), p. 167.

54. David Friedrichs, "Critical Criminology and Critical Legal Studies," *Critical Criminologist* 1 (1989): 7.

55. See, for example, Larry Tifft and Dennis Sullivan, *The Struggle to Be Human: Crime, Criminology and Anarchism* (Orkney Islands, Over-the-Water-Sanday: Cienfuegos Press, 1979); Dennis Sullivan, *The Mask of Love* (Port Washington, NY: Kennikat Press, 1980).

56. R.M. Bohm, "Radical Criminology: An Explication," *Criminology* 19 (1982): 565–89.

57. Robert Bohm, "Radical Criminology: Back to the Basics," paper presented at the annual meeting of the American Society of Criminology, Phoenix, AZ, November 1993, p. 2.

58. Ibid., p. 4.

59. Lynch and Groves, *A Primer in Radical Criminology,* 2nd ed., p. 7.

60. W. Byron Groves and Robert Sampson, "Critical Theory and Criminology," *Social Problems* 33 (1986): 58–80.

61. Gregg Barak, "'Crimes of the Homeless' or the 'Crime of Homelessness': A Self-Reflexive, New-Marxist Analysis of Crime and Social Control," paper presented at the annual meeting of the American Society of Criminology, Montreal, November 1987.

62. Michael Lynch, "Assessing the State of Radical Criminology: Toward the Year 2000," paper presented at the annual meeting of the American Society of Criminology, Phoenix, AZ, November 1993.

63. Bohm, "Radical Criminology," p. 5.

64. Gresham Sykes, "The Rise of Critical Criminology," *Journal of Criminal Law and Criminology* 65 (1974): 211.

65. David Jacobs, "Corporate Economic Power and the State: A Longitudinal Assessment of Two Explanations," *American Journal of Sociology* 93 (1988): 852–81.

66. Deanna Alexander, "Victims of the L.A. Riots: A Theoretical Consideration," paper presented at the annual meeting of the American Society of Criminology, Phoenix, AZ, November 1993.

67. Ibid., p. 2.

68. Richard Quinney, "Crime Control in Capitalist Society," in *Critical Criminology,* ed. Ian Taylor, Paul Walton, and Jock Young (London: Routledge and Kegan Paul, 1975), p. 199.

69. Herman Schwendinger and Julia Schwendinger, "Delinquency and Social Reform: A Radical Perspective," in *Juvenile Justice,* ed. Lamar Empey (Charlottesville: University of Virginia Press, 1979), pp. 246–90.

70. Krisberg, *Crime and* Privilege.

71. Elliott Currie, "A Dialogue with Anthony M. Platt," *Issues in Criminology* 8 (1973): 28.

72. Lynch, "Rediscovering Criminology," p. 14.

73. John Hagan, *Structural Criminology* (New Brunswick, NJ: Rutgers University Press, 1989), pp. 110–19.

74. Stephen Spitzer, "Toward a Marxian Theory of Deviance," *Social Problems* 22 (1975): 638–51.

75. Roy Bhaskar, "Empiricism," in *A Dictionary of Marxist Thought,* ed. T. Bottomore (Cambridge: Harvard University Press, 1983), pp. 149–50.

76. Byron Groves, "Marxism and Positivism," *Crime and Social Justice* 23 (1985): 129–50; Michael Lynch, "Quantitative Analysis and Marxist Criminology: Some Old Answers to a Dilemma in Marxist Criminology," *Crime and Social Justice* 29 (1987): 110–17.

77. Alan Lizotte, James Mercy, and Eric Monkkonen, "Crime and Police Strength in an Urban Setting: Chicago,

1947–1970," in *Quantitative Criminology*, ed. John Hagan (Beverly Hills, CA: Sage, 1982), pp. 129–48.

78. William Chambliss, "The State, the Law and the Definition of Behavior as Criminal or Delinquent," in *Handbook of Criminology*, ed. D. Glazer (Chicago: Rand McNally, 1974), pp. 7–44.

79. Timothy Carter and Donald Clelland, "A Neo-Marxian Critique, Formulation and Test of Juvenile Dispositions as a Function of Social Class," *Social Problems* 27 (1979): 96–108.

80. David Greenberg, "Socio-Economic Status and Criminal Sentences: Is There an Association?" *American Sociological Review* 42 (1977): 174–75; David Greenberg and Drew Humphries, "The Co-optation of Fixed Sentencing Reform," *Crime and Delinquency* 26 (1980): 206–25.

81. Steven Box, *Power, Crime and Mystification* (London: Tavistock, 1984); Gregg Barak, *In Defense of Whom? A Critique of Criminal Justice Reform* (Cincinnati: Anderson Publishing, 1980); for an opposing view, see Franklin Williams, "Conflict Theory and Differential Processing: An Analysis of the Research Literature," in *Radical Criminology: The Coming Crisis*, ed. J. Inciardi (Beverly Hills, CA: Sage, 1980), pp. 213–31.

82. Herman Schwendinger and Julia Schwendinger, "Rape Victims and the False Sense of Guilt," *Crime and Social Justice* 13 (1980): 4–17.

83. For more of their work, see Herman Schwendinger and Julia Schwendinger, *Adolescent Subcultures and Delinquency* (New York: Praeger, 1985); idem, "The Paradigmatic Crisis in Delinquency Theory," *Crime and Social Justice* 18 (1982): 70–78; idem, "The Collective Varieties of Youth," *Crime and Social Justice* 5 (1976): 7–25; idem, "Marginal Youth and Social Policy," *Social Problems* 24 (1976): 184–91.

84. Michael Rustigan, "A Reinterpretation of Criminal Law Reform in Nineteenth-Century England," in *Crime and Capitalism*, ed. D. Greenberg (Palo Alto, CA: Mayfield Publishing, 1981), pp. 255–78.

85. Rosalind Petchesky, "At Hard Labor: Penal Confinement and Production in Nineteenth-Century America," in *Crime and Capitalism*, ed. D. Greenberg, pp. 341–57; Paul Takagi, "The Walnut Street Jail: A Penal Reform to Centralize the Powers of the State," *Federal Probation* 49 (1975): 18–26.

86. Steven Spitzer and Andrew Scull, "Privatization and Capitalist Development: The Case of the Private Police," *Social Problems* 25 (1977): 18–29; Dennis Hoffman, "Cops and Wobblies" (Ph.D. diss., Portland State University, 1977).

87. Sidney Harring, "Policing a Class Society: The Expansion of the Urban Police in the Late Nineteenth and Early Twentieth Centuries," in *Crime and Capitalism*, ed. D. Greenberg, pp. 292–313.

88. Jack Gibbs, "An Incorrigible Positivist," *Criminologist* 12 (1987): 2–3.

89. Toby, "The New Criminology Is the Old Sentimentality."

90. Sparks, "A Critique of Marxist Criminology," pp. 198–99.

91. Carl Klockars, "The Contemporary Crises of Marxist Criminology," in *Radical Criminology: The Coming Crisis*, ed. J. Inciardi (Beverly Hills, CA: Sage, 1980), pp. 92–123.

92. Ibid., pp. 112–14.

93. Ibid.

94. Michael Lynch, W. Byron Groves, and Alan Lizotte, "The Rate of Surplus Value and Crime: A Theoretical and Empirical Examination of Marxian Economic Theory and Criminology," *Crime, Law and Social Change* 1 (1994): 1–11.

95. Anthony Platt, "Criminology in the 1980s: Progressive Alternatives to 'Law and Order,'" *Crime and Social Justice* 21–22 (1985): 191–99.

96. See, generally, Roger Matthews and Jock Young, eds., *Confronting Crime* (London: Sage, 1986); for a thorough review of left realism, see Martin Schwartz and Walter DeKeseredy, "Left Realist Criminology: Strengths, Weaknesses and the Feminist Critique," *Crime, Law and Social Change* 15 (1991): 51–72.

97. John Lea and Jock Young, *What Is to Be Done About Law and Order?* (Harmondsworth, England: Penguin, 1984).

98. Ibid., p. 88.

99. Richard Kinsey, John Lea, and Jock Young, *Losing the Fight against Crime* (London: Blackwell, 1986).

100. Martin Schwartz and Walter DeKeseredy, *Contemporary Criminology* (Belmont, CA: Wadsworth, 1996), p. 249.

101. Schwartz and DeKeseredy, "Left Realist Criminology."

102. Ibid., p. 54.

103. Ibid., p. 58.

104. For a general review of this issue, see Kathleen Daly and Meda Chesney-Lind, "Feminism and Criminology," *Justice Quarterly* 5 (1988): 497–538; Douglas Smith and Raymond Paternoster, "The Gender Gap in Theories of Deviance: Issues and Evidence," *Journal of Research in Crime and Delinquency* 24 (1987): 140–72; Pat Carlen, "Women, Crime, Feminism, and Realism," *Social Justice* 17 (1990): 106–23.

105. Julia Schwendinger and Herman Schwendinger, *Rape and Inequality* (Beverly Hills, CA: Sage, 1983).

106. Daly and Chesney-Lind, "Feminism and Criminology," p. 536.

107. James Messerschmidt, *Capitalism, Patriarchy and Crime* (Totowa, NJ: Rowman and Littlefield, 1986); for a critique of this work, see Herman Schwendinger and Julia Schwendinger, "The World According to James Messerschmidt," *Social Justice* 15 (1988): 123–45.

108. Kathleen Daly, "Gender and Varieties of White-Collar Crime," *Criminology* 27 (1989): 769–93.

109. Jane Roberts Chapman, "Violence against Women as a Violation of Human Rights," *Social Justice* 17 (1990): 54–71.

110. James Messerschmidt, *Masculinities and Crime: Critique and Reconceptualization of Theory* (Lanham, MD: Rowman and Littlefield, 1993).

111. For a review of feminist theory, see Sally Simpson, "Feminist Theory, Crime and Justice," *Criminology* 27 (1989): 605–32.

112. Suzie Dod Thomas and Nancy Stein, "Criminality, Imprisonment, and Women's Rights in the 1990s," *Social Justice* 17 (1990): 1–5.

113. Walter DeKeseredy and Martin Schwartz, "Male Peer Support and Woman Abuse: An Expansion of DeKeseredy's Model," *Sociological Spectrum* 13 (1993): 393–413.

114. Daly and Chesney-Lind, "Feminism and Criminology." See also Drew Humphries and Susan Caringella-MacDonald, "Murdered Mothers, Missing Wives: Reconsidering Female Victimization," *Social Justice* 17 (1990): 71–78.

115. Center for Research on Women, *Secrets in Public: Sexual Harassment in Our Schools* (Wellesley, MA: Wellesley College, 1993).

116. Jane Siegel and Linda Meyer Williams, "Aggressive Behavior among Women Sexually Abused as Children," paper presented at the American Society of Criminology meeting, Phoenix, AZ, 1993, rev. version.

117. Susan Ehrlich Martin and Nancy Jurik, *Doing Justice, Doing Gender* (Thousand Oaks, CA: Sage, 1996), p. 27.

118. Ruth Alexander, *The "Girl Problem": Female Sexual Delinquency in New York, 1900-1930* (Ithaca, NY: Cornell University Press, 1995).

119. Mary Odem and Steven Schlossman, "Guardians of Virtue: The Juvenile Court and Female Delinquency in Early 20th-Century Los Angeles," *Crime and Delinquency* 37 (1991): 186-203.

120. Meda Chesney-Lind, "Judicial Enforcement of the Female Sex Role: The Family Court and the Female Delinquent," *Issues in Criminology* 8 (1973): 51-69; see also idem, "Women and Crime: The Female Offender," *Signs: Journal of Women in Culture and Society* 12 (1986): 78-96; idem, "Female Offenders: Paternalism Reexamined," in *Women, the Courts, and Equality,* ed. Laura L. Crites and Winifred L. Hepperle (Newbury Park, CA: Sage, 1987): 114-39; idem, "Girls' Crime and a Woman's Place: Toward a Feminist Model of Female Delinquency," paper presented at a meeting of the American Society of Criminology, Montreal, 1987.

121. Hagan, *Structural Criminology.*

122. John Hagan, A.R. Gillis, and John Simpson, "The Class Structure and Delinquency: Toward a Power-Control Theory of Common Delinquent Behavior," *American Journal of Sociology* 90 (1985): 1151-78; John Hagan, John Simpson, and A.R. Gillis, "Class in the Household: A Power-Control Theory of Gender and Delinquency," *American Journal of Sociology* 92 (1987): 788-816.

123. Gary Jensen, "Power-Control versus Social-Control Theory: Identifying Crucial Differences for Future Research," paper presented at the annual meeting of the American Society of Criminology, Baltimore, November 1990.

124. Gary Jensen and Kevin Thompson, "What's Class Got to Do with It? A Further Examination of Power-Control Theory," *American Journal of Sociology* 95 (1990): 1009-23. For some critical research, see Simon Singer and Murray Levine, "Power Control Theory, Gender and Delinquency: A Partial Replication with Additional Evidence on the Effects of Peers," *Criminology* 26 (1988): 627-48.

125. For a lengthy review, see Hagan, *Structural Criminology.*

126. Kevin Thompson, "Gender and Adolescent Drinking Problems: The Effects of Occupational Structure," *Social Problems* 36 (1989): 30-38.

127. See, generally, Lynch, "Rediscovering Criminology," pp. 27-28.

128. Dragan Milovanovic, *A Primer in the Sociology of Law* (New York: Harrow and Heston, 1988) pp. 127-28.

129. Peter Cordella, *Restorative Justice* (unpublished paper, Manchester, NH: St. Anselm College, 1997); see also Herbert Bianchi, *Justice as Sanctuary* (Bloomington: Indiana University Press, 1994); Nils Christie, "Conflicts as Property," *The British Journal of Criminology* 17 (1977): 1-15; L. Hulsman, "Critical Criminology and the Concept of Crime," *Contemporary Crises* 10 (1986): 63-80.

130. Richard Quinney, "The Way of Peace: On Crime, Suffering and Service," in *Criminology as Peacemaking,* ed. Harold Pepinsky and Richard Quinney (Bloomington: Indiana University Press, 1991), pp. 8-9.

131. See, for example, Tifft and Sullivan, *The Struggle to Be Human*; and Sullivan, *The Mask of Love.*

132. Larry Tifft, Foreword, to Sullivan, *The Mask of Love*, p. 6.

133. Ibid., p. 141.

134. Pepinsky and Quinney, *Criminology as Peacemaking.*

Chapter 10

1. Emilie Andersen Allan, "Theory Is Not a Zero-Sum Game: The Quest for an Integrated Theory," paper presented at the annual meeting of the American Society of Criminology, Phoenix, AZ, November 1993.

2. Gerald Patterson and Karen Yoerger, "Developmental Models for Delinquent Behavior," in *Mental Disorder and Crime,* ed. Sheilagh Higdins (Newbury Park, CA: Sage, 1993), pp. 150-59.

3. David Rowe, D. Wayne Osgood, and W. Alan Nicewander, "A Latent Trait Approach to Unifying Criminal Careers," *Criminology* 28 (1990): 237-70.

4. David Rowe, Alexander Vazsonyi, and Daniel Flannery, "Sex Differences in Crime: Do Means and Within-Sex Variation Have Similar Causes?" *Journal of Research in Crime and Delinquency* 32 (1995): 84-100.

5. G.R. Patterson, Barbara DeBaryshe, and Elizabeth Ramsey, "A Developmental Perspective on Antisocial Behavior," *American Psychologist* 44 (1989): 329-35.

6. Kenneth Land and Daniel Nagin, "Micro-Models of Criminal Careers: A Synthesis of the Criminal Careers and Life-Course Approaches via Semiparametric Mixed Poisson Regression Models with Empirical Applications," *Journal of Quantitative Criminology* 12 (1996): 163-90.

7. Daniel Glazer, *Crime in Our Changing Society* (New York: Holt, Rinehart and Winston, 1978).

8. Ibid., p. 125.

9. Joseph Weis and J. David Hawkins, Reports of the National Juvenile Assessment Centers, *Preventing Delinquency* (Washington, DC: U.S. Department of Justice, 1981); Joseph Weis and John Sederstrom, Reports of the National Juvenile Justice Assessment Centers, *The Prevention of Serious Delinquency: What to Do* (Washington, DC: U.S. Department of Justice, 1981).

10. Julie O'Donnell, J. David Hawkins, and Robert Abbott, "Predicting Serious Delinquency and Substance Use among Aggressive Boys," *Journal of Consulting and Clinical Psychology* 63 (1995): 529-37.

11. Ibid., pp. 534-36; Richard Catalano, Rick Kosterman, J. David Hawkins, Michael Newcomb, and Robert Abbott, "Modeling the Etiology of Adolescent Substance Use: A Test of the Social Development Model," *Journal of Drug Issues* 26 (1996): 429-55.

12. David Brownfield, Kevin Thompson, and Ann Marie Sorenson, "Correlates of Gang Membership: A Test of Strain, Social Learning, and Control-Bonding Theories," paper presented at the annual meeting of the American Society of Criminology, Chicago, November 1996.

13. J. David Hawkins, Richard Catalano, Diane Morrison, Julie O'Donnell, Robert Abbott, and L. Edward Day, "The Seattle Social Development Project," in *The Prevention of Antisocial Behavior in Children,* ed. Joan McCord and Richard Tremblay (New York: Guilford, 1992), pp. 139-60.

14. Delbert Elliott, David Huizinga, and Suzanne Ageton, *Explaining Delinquency and Drug Use* (Beverly Hills, CA: Sage, 1985).

15. Scott Menard and Delbert Elliott, "Delinquent Bonding, Moral Beliefs, and Illegal Behavior: A Three Wave–Panel Model," *Justice Quarterly* 11 (1994): 173–88.

16. Ibid., p. 184.

17. Mark Colvin and John Pauly, "A Critique of Criminology: Toward an Integrated Structural-Marxist Theory of Delinquency Production," *American Journal of Sociology* 89 (1983): 513–51.

18. Ibid., p. 542.

19. Steven Messner and Marvin Krohn, "Class, Compliance Structures, and Delinquency: Assessing Integrated Structural-Marxist Theory," *American Journal of Sociology* 96 (1990): 300–28.

20. Lee Ellis, "Neurohormonal Bases of Varying Tendencies to Learn Delinquent and Criminal Behavior," in *Behavioral Approaches to Crime and Delinquency*, ed. E. Morris and C. Braukmann (New York: Plenum, 1988), pp. 499–518.

21. James Q. Wilson and Richard Herrnstein, *Crime and Human Nature* (New York: Simon & Schuster, 1985).

22. Ibid., p. 44.

23. Ibid., p. 171.

24. Ibid.

25. Ibid., p. 528.

26. Michael Gottfredson and Travis Hirschi, *A General Theory of Crime* (Stanford, CA: Stanford University Press, 1990).

27. Ibid., p. 27.

28. Ibid., p. 90.

29. Ibid., p. 89.

30. Alex Piquero and Stephen Tibbetts, "Specifying the Direct and Indirect Effects of Low Self-Control and Situational Factors in Offenders' Decision Making: Toward a More Complete Model of Rational Offending," *Justice Quarterly* 13 (1996): 481–508.

31. Ibid.

32. Ibid.

33. Dennis Giever, "An Empirical Assessment of the Core Elements of Gottfredson and Hirschi's General Theory of Crime," paper presented at the American Society of Criminology meeting, Boston, November 1995.

34. Robert Agnew, "The Contribution of Social-Psychological Strain Theory to the Explanation of Crime and Delinquency," *Advances in Criminological Theory* 6 (1994).

35. Travis Hirschi and Michael Gottfredson, "Rethinking the Juvenile Justice System," *Crime and Delinquency* 39 (1993): 262–71.

36. David Brownfield and Ann Marie Sorenson, "Self-Control and Juvenile Delinquency: Theoretical Issues and an Empirical Assessment of Selected Elements of a General Theory of Crime," *Deviant Behavior* 14 (1993): 243–64; Harold Grasmick, Charles Tittle, Robert Bursik, and Bruce Arneklev, "Testing the Core Empirical Implications of Gottfredson and Hirschi's General Theory of Crime," *Journal of Research in Crime and Delinquency* 30 (1993): 5–29; John Cochran, Peter Wood, and Bruce Arneklev, "Is the Religiosity-Delinquency Relationship Spurious? A Test of Arousal and Social Control Theories," *Journal of Research in Crime and Delinquency* 31 (1994): 92–123.

37. Carl Keane, Paul Maxim, and James Teevan, "Drinking and Driving, Self-Control, and Gender: Testing a General Theory of Crime," *Journal of Research in Crime and Delinquency* 30 (1993): 30–46.

38. Judith DeJong, Matti Virkkunen, and Marku Linnoila, "Factors Associated with Recidivism in a Criminal Population," *The Journal of Nervous and Mental Disease* 180 (1992): 543–50.

39. David Cantor, "Drug Involvement and Offending Among Incarcerated Juveniles," paper presented at the American Society of Criminology meeting, Boston, November 1995.

40. Brownfield and Sorenson, "Self-Control and Juvenile Delinquency."

41. Jon Gibbs and Dennis Giever, "Self-Control and Its Manifestations Among University Students: An Empirical Test of Gottfredson and Hirschi's General Theory," *Justice Quarterly* 12 (1995): 231–55.

42. Dennis Giever, "An Empirical Assessment of the Core Elements of Gottfredson and Hirschi's General Theory of Crime," paper presented at the American Society of Criminology meeting, Boston, November 1995.

43. Marc LeBlanc, Marc Ouimet, and Richard Tremblay, "An Integrative Control Theory of Delinquent Behavior: A Validation, 1976–1985," *Psychiatry* 51 (1988): 164–76.

44. See, for example, Douglas Longshore, Susan Turner, and Judith Stein, "Self-Control in a Criminal Sample: An Examination of Construct Validity," *Criminology* 34 (1996): 209–28; Grasmick et al., "Testing the Core Empirical Implications of Gottfredson and Hirschi's General Theory of Crime"; Daniel Nagin and Raymond Paternoster, "Enduring Individual Differences and Rational Choice Theories of Crime," *Law and Society Review* 27 (1993): 467–89.

45. Bruce Link, Elmer Streuning, Francis Cullen, Patrick Shrout, and Bruce Dohrenwend, "A Modified Labeling Theory Approach to Mental Disorders: An Empirical Assessment," *American Sociological Review* 54 (1989): 400–23.

46. Michael Benson and Elizabeth Moore, "Are White-Collar and Common Offenders the Same? An Empirical and Theoretical Critique of a Recently Proposed General Theory of Crime," *Journal of Research in Crime and Delinquency* 29 (1992): 251–72.

47. For a general review and critique, see Kenneth Polk's book review in *Crime and Delinquency* 37 (1991): 575–81.

48. Ronald Akers, "Self-Control as a General Theory of Crime," *Journal of Quantitative Criminology* 7 (1991): 201–11.

49. Gottfredson and Hirschi, *General Theory of Crime*, p. 88.

50. Samuel Yochelson and Clifford Samenow, *The Criminal Personality* (New York: Jason Aronson, 1977).

51. Gottfredson and Hirschi, *A General Theory of Crime*, p. 153.

52. Ann Marie Sorenson and David Brownfield, "Normative Concepts in Social Control," paper presented at the annual meeting of the American Society of Criminology, Phoenix, AZ, November 1993.

53. Scott Menard, Delbert Elliott, and Sharon Wofford, "Social Control Theories in Developmental Perspective," *Studies on Crime and Crime Prevention* 2 (1993): 69–87.

54. Delbert Elliott and Scott Menard, "Delinquent Friends and Delinquent Behavior: Temporal and Developmental Patterns," in *Current Theories of Crime and Deviance*, ed. J. David Hawkins (Cambridge: Cambridge University Press, in press).

55. Graham Ousey and David Aday, Jr., "The Interaction Hypothesis: A Test Using Social Control Theory and Social Learning Theory," paper presented at the American Society of Criminology meeting, Boston, November 1995.

56. Julie Horney, D. Wayne Osgood, and Ineke Haen Marshall, "Criminal Careers in the Short-Term: Intra-Individual Variability in Crime and Its Relations to Local Life Circumstances," *American Sociological Review* 60 (1995): 655–73.

57. Otwin Marenin and Michael Resig, "A General Theory of Crime and Patterns of Crime in Nigeria: An Exploration of Methodological Assumptions," *Journal of Criminal Justice* 23 (1995): 501–18.

58. Bruce Arneklev, Harold Grasmick, Charles Tittle, and Robert Bursik, "Low Self-Control and Imprudent Behavior," *Journal of Quantitative Criminology* 9 (1993): 225–46.

59. Kevin Thompson, "Sexual Harassment and Low Self-Control: An Application of Gottfredson and Hirschi's General Theory of Crime," paper presented at the annual meeting of the American Society of Criminology, Phoenix, AZ, November 1993.

60. R.E. Tremblay and L.C. Masse, "Cognitive Deficits, School Achievement, Disruptive Behavior and Juvenile Delinquency: A Longitudinal Look at Their Developmental Sequence," paper presented at the annual meeting of the American Society of Criminology, Phoenix, AZ, November 1993.

61. David Nurco, Timothy Kinlock, and Mitchell Balter, "The Severity of Preaddiction Criminal Behavior among Urban, Male Narcotic Addicts and Two Nonaddicted Control Groups," *Journal of Research in Crime and Delinquency* 30 (1993): 293–316.

62. G.R. Patterson and Karen Yoerger, "Differentiating Outcomes and Histories for Early and Late Onset Arrests," paper presented at the annual meeting of the American Society of Criminology, Phoenix, AZ, November 1993.

63. Joan McCord, "Family Relationships, Juvenile Delinquency, and Adult Criminality," *Criminology* 29 (1991): 397–417.

64. Robert Sampson and John Laub, "Crime and Deviance in the Life Course," *American Review of Sociology* 18 (1992): 63–84.

65. Gerald Patterson, J.B. Reid, and Thomas Dishion, *A Social Interactional Approach: Antisocial Boys* (Eugene, OR: Castalia Press, 1992).

66. Francois Poulin, Thomas Dishion, Mike Stoolmiller, and Gerald Patterson, "Modeling Growth in Adolescent Delinquency: The Combined Effect and Developmental Specificity of Parent Bonding and Deviant Peers," paper presented at the annual meeting of the American Society of Criminology, Chicago, November 1996.

67. See, generally, Sheldon Glueck and Eleanor Glueck, *500 Criminal Careers* (New York: Knopf, 1930); idem, *One Thousand Juvenile Delinquents* (Cambridge, MA: Harvard University Press, 1934); idem, *Predicting Delinquency and Crime* (Cambridge, MA: Harvard University Press, 1967), pp. 82–83.

68. Sheldon Glueck and Eleanor Glueck, *Unraveling Juvenile Delinquency* (Cambridge, MA: Harvard University Press, 1950).

69. See, generally, John Laub and Robert Sampson, "The Sutherland-Glueck Debate: On the Sociology of Criminological Knowledge," *American Journal of Sociology* 96 (1991): 1402–40; idem, "Unraveling Families and Delinquency: A Reanalysis of the Gluecks' Data," *Criminology* 26 (1988): 355–80.

70. Rolf Loeber and Marc LeBlanc, "Toward a Developmental Criminology," in *Crime and Justice*, vol. 12, ed. Norval Morris and Michael Tonry (Chicago: University of Chicago Press, 1990), pp. 375–473.

71. G.R. Patterson, L. Crosby, and S. Vuchinich, "Predicting Risk for Early Police Arrest," *Journal of Quantitative Criminology* 8 (1992): 335–55.

72. Patterson, DeBaryshe, and Ramsey, "A Developmental Perspective on Antisocial Behavior," pp. 331–33.

73. Rolf Loeber, Magda Southamer-Loeber, Welmoet Van Kammen, and David Farrington, "Initiation, Escalation and Desistance in Juvenile Offending and Their Correlates," *Journal of Criminal Law and Criminology* 82 (1991): 36–82.

74. Richard Jessor, John Donovan, and Francis Costa, *Beyond Adolescence: Problem Behavior and Young Adult Development* (New York: Cambridge University Press, 1991).

75. Richard Jessor, "Risk Behavior in Adolescence: A Psychosocial Framework for Understanding and Action," in *Adolescents at Risk: Medical and Social Perspectives*, ed. D.E. Rogers and E. Ginzburg (Boulder, CO: Westview, 1992).

76. Deborah Capaldi and Gerald Patterson, "Can Violent Offenders Be Distinguished from Frequent Offenders: Prediction from Childhood to Adolescence," *Journal of Research in Crime and Delinquency* 33 (1996): 206–31; D. Wayne Osgood, "The Covariation among Adolescent Problem Behaviors," paper presented at the annual meeting of the American Society of Criminology, Baltimore, November 1990.

77. Todd Miller, Timothy Smith, Charles Turner, Margarita Guijarro, and Amanda Hallet, "A Meta-Analytic Review of Research on Hostility and Physical Health," *Psychological Bulletin* 119 (1996): 322–48; Marianne Junger, "Accidents and Crime," in *The Generality of Deviance*, ed. T. Hirschi and M. Gottfredson (New Brunswick, NJ: Transaction Press, 1993).

78. Robert Johnson, S. Susan Su, Dean Gerstein, Hee-Choon Shin, and John Hoffman, "Parental Influences on Deviant Behavior in Early Adolescence: A Logistic Response Analysis of Age- and Gender-Differentiated Effects," *Journal of Quantitative Criminology* 11 (1995): 167–92; Judith Brooks, Martin Whiteman, and Patricia Cohen, "Stage of Drug Use, Aggression, and Theft/Vandalism," in *Drugs, Crime and Other Deviant Adaptations: Longitudinal Studies*, ed. Howard Kaplan (New York: Plenum Press, 1995), pp. 83–96; Robert Hoge, D.A. Andrews, and Alan Leschied, "Tests of Three Hypotheses Regarding the Predictors of Delinquency," *Journal of Abnormal Child Psychology* 22 (1994): 547–59.

79. David Huizinga, Rolf Loeber, and Terence Thornberry, "Longitudinal Study of Delinquency, Drug Use, Sexual Activity, and Pregnancy among Children and Youth in Three Cities," *Public Health Reports* 108 (1993): 90–96.

80. Jeanne Hernandez, "The Concurrence of Eating Disorders with Histories of Child Abuse among Adolescents," paper presented at the annual meeting of the American Society of *Criminology*, Phoenix, AZ, November 1993.

81. Candace Kruttschnitt, Jane McLeod, and Maude Dornfeld, "The Economic Environment of Child Abuse," *Social Problems* 41 (1994): 299–312.

82. Helene Raskin White, "Early Problem Behavior and Later Drug Problems," *Journal of Research in Crime and Delinquency* 29 (1992): 412–29.

83. Helene Raskin White and Erich Labouvie, "Generality Versus Specificity of Problem Behavior: Psychological and Functional Differences," *Journal of Drug Issues* 24 (1994): 55–74.

84. See, generally, Richard Dembo, Linda Williams, Werner Wothke, James Schmeidier, Alan Getreu, Estrellita Berry, and Eric Wish, "The Generality of Deviance: Replication of a Structural Model Among High-Risk Youths," *Journal of Research in Crime and Delinquency* 29 (1992): 200–16.

85. Rolf Loeber, Phen Wung, Kate Keenan, Bruce Giroux, Magda Stouthamer-Loeber, Wemoet Van Kammen, and Barbara Maughan, "Developmental Pathways in Disruptive Behavior," *Development and Psychopathology* (1993): 12–48.

86. Amy D'Unger, Kenneth Land, Patricia McCall, and Daniel Nagin, "How Many Latent Classes of Delinquent/Criminal Careers? Results from Mixed Poisson Regression Analyses of the London, Philadelphia, and Racine Cohort Studies," paper presented at the annual meeting of the American Society of Criminology, Chicago, November 1996.

87. Terrie Moffitt, "Natural Histories of Delinquency," in *Cross-National Longitudinal Research on Human Development and Criminal Behavior*, ed. Elmar Weitekamp and Hans-Jurgen Kerner (Dordrecht, Netherlands: Kluwer, 1994), pp. 3–65.

88. Terrie Moffitt, "Adolescence-Limited and Life-Course Persistent Antisocial Behavior: A Developmental Taxonomy," *Psychological Review* 100 (1993): 674–701.

89. Michael Newcomb, "Pseudomaturity among Adolescents: Construct Validation, Sex Differences, and Associations in Adulthood," *Journal of Drug Issues* 26 (1996): 477–504.

90. Paul Tracy and Kimberly Kempf-Leonard, *Continuity and Discontinuity in Criminal Careers* (New York: Plenum Press, 1996), p. 208.

91. Ronald Simons, Chyi-In Wu, Rand Conger, and Frederick Lorenz, "Two Routes to Delinquency: Differences Between Early and Later Starters in the Impact of Parenting and Deviant Careers," *Criminology* 32 (1994): 247–75.

92. Paul Mazerolle, "Understanding the Theoretical and Empirical Dimensions of Late Onset to Delinquent Behavior," paper presented at the annual meeting of the American Society of Criminology, Boston, November 1995.

93. Charles Dean, Robert Brame, and Alex Piquero, "Criminal Propensities, Discrete Groups of Offenders, and Persistence of Crime," *Criminology* 34 (1966): 547–73.

94. See, for example, the Rochester Youth Development Study, Hindelang Criminal Justice Research Center, 135 Western Avenue, Albany, New York 12222.

95. David Farrington, "The Development of Offending and Antisocial Behavior from Childhood to Adulthood," paper presented at the Congress on Rethinking Delinquency, University of Minho, Braga, Portugal, July 1992.

96. See, generally, D.J. West and David P. Farrington, *The Delinquent Way of Life* (London: Heinemann, 1977).

97. The material in the following sections is summarized from Farrington, "The Development of Offending and

Antisocial Behavior from Childhood to Adulthood"; idem, "Psychobiological Factors in the Explanation and Reduction of Delinquency," *Today's Delinquent* 7 (1988): 44–46; idem, "Childhood Origins of Teenage Antisocial Behaviour and Adult Social Dysfunction," *Journal of the Royal Society of Medicine* 86 (1993): 13–17; idem, "Psychosocial Influences on the Development of Antisocial Personality," paper presented at the annual meeting of the American Society of Criminology, Phoenix, AZ, November 1993.

98. Terence Thornberry, "Toward an Interactional Theory of Delinquency," *Criminology* 25 (1987): 863–91.

99. See, for example, Jean Piaget, *The Grasp of Consciousness* (Cambridge, MA: Harvard University Press, 1976).

100. Ibid., p. 386.

101. This research is known as the Rochester Youth Development Study. Thornberry's colleagues on the project include Alan Lizotte, Margaret Farnworth, Marvin Krohn, and Susan Stern.

102. Terence Thornberry, Alan Lizotte, Marvin Krohn, and Margaret Farnworth, "The Role of Delinquent Peers in the Initiation of Delinquent Behavior," working paper no. 6, rev., Rochester Youth Development Study (Albany, NY: Hindelang Criminal Justice Research Center, 1993).

103. Terence Thornberry, Alan Lizotte, Marvin Krohn, Margaret Farnworth, and Sung Joon Jang, "Delinquent Peers, Beliefs, and Delinquent Behavior: A Longitudinal Test of Interactional Theory," *Criminology* 32 (1994): 601–37.

104. Terence Thornberry, Alan Lizotte, Marvin Krohn, Margaret Farnworth, and Sung Joon Jang, "Delinquent Peers, Beliefs, and Delinquent Behavior: A Longitudinal Test of Interactional Theory," working paper no. 6, rev., Rochester Youth Development Study (Albany, NY: Hindelang Criminal Justice Research Center, 1992).

105. Terence Thornberry, Alan Lizotte, Marvin Krohn, Margaret Farnworth, and Sung Joon Jang, "Testing Interactional Theory: An Examination of Reciprocal Causal Relationships Among Family, School and Delinquency," *Journal of Criminal Law and Criminology* 82 (1991): 3–35.

106. Scott Menard and Delbert Elliott, "Delinquent Bonding, Moral Beliefs, and Illegal Behavior: A Three Wave-Panel Model," *Justice Quarterly* 11 (1994): 173–88.

107. Carolyn Smith, Alan Lizotte, Terence Thornberry, and Marvin Krohn, *Resilient Youth: Identifying Factors That Prevent High-Risk Youth from Engaging in Delinquency and Drug Use* (Albany, NY: Rochester Youth Development Study, 1994).

108. Thornberry et al., "Delinquent Peers, Beliefs, and Delinquent Behavior," pp. 628–29.

109. Robert Sampson and John Laub, *Crime in the Making: Pathways and Turning Points through Life* (Cambridge, MA: Harvard University Press, 1993); John Laub and Robert Sampson, "Turning Points in the Life Course: Why Change Matters to the Study of Crime," paper presented at the annual meeting of the American Society of Criminology, New Orleans, November 1992.

110. Terri Orbuch, James House, Richard Mero, and Pamela Webster, "Marital Quality over the Life Course," *Social Psychology Quarterly* 59 (1996): 162–71; Lee Lillard and Linda Waite, "'Til Death Do Us Part: Marital Disruption and Mortality," *American Journal of Sociology* 100 (1995): 1131–56.

111. Pamela Webster, Terri Orbuch, and James House, "Effects of Childhood Family Background on Adult Marital Quality and Perceived Stability," *American Journal of Sociology* 101 (1995): 404–32.

112. John Hagan, Ross MacMillan, and Blair Wheaton, "New Kid in Town: Social Capital and the Life Course Effects of Family Migration on Children," *American Sociological Review* 61 (1996): 368–85.

113. Sampson and Laub, *Crime in the Making*, p. 249.

114. Robert Hoge, D.A. Andrews, and Alan Leschied, "An Investigation of Risk and Protective Factors in a Sample of Youthful Offenders," *Journal of Child Psychology and Psychiatry* 37 (1996): 419–24.

115. For a discussion see Mark Collins and Don Weatherburn, "Unemployment and the Dynamics of Offender Populations," *Journal of Quantitative Criminology* 11 (1995): 231–45.

116. Erich Labouvie, "Maturing Out of Substance Use: Selection and Self-Correction," *Journal of Drug Issues* 26 (1996): 457–74.

117. Robert Sampson and John Laub, "Socioeconomic Achievement in the Life Course of Disadvantaged Men: Military Service as a Turning Point, circa 1940–1965," *American Sociological Review* 61 (1996): 347–67.

118. Daniel Nagin and Raymond Paternoster, "Personal Capital and Social Control: The Deterrence Implications of a Theory of Criminal Offending," *Criminology* 32 (1994): 581–606.

119. Eloise Dunlop and Bruce Johnson, "Family and Human Resources in the Development of a Female Crack-Seller Career: Case Study of a Hidden Population," *Journal of Drug Issues* 26 (1996): 175–198.

Chapter 11

1. Albert Reiss and Jeffrey Roth, *Understanding and Preventing Violence* (Washington, DC: National Academy Press, 1993); Jeffrey Ian Ross, ed., *Violence in Canada: Sociopolitical Perspectives* (Don Mills, ON: Oxford, 1995).

2. Doug Fischer, "Most Support Death Penalty: Backing Weakest in Atlantic Canada," *Daily News*, July 10, 1995, p. 8.

3. *Stanford v. Kentucky*, 109 Supreme Court, 2969 (1989).

4. Robert Nash Parker and Catherine Colony, "Relationships, Homicides, and Weapons: A Detailed Analysis," paper presented at the annual meeting of the American Society of Criminology, Montreal, November 1987.

5. Stryker McGuire, "The Dunblane Effect," *Newsweek*, October 28, 1996, p. 46; "Gunman Kills 14, Self. Letter Blames Feminists," *Mail Star* (Halifax), December 7, 1989, p. A1.

6. Laura Bender, "Children and Adolescents Who Have Killed," *American Journal of Psychiatry* 116 (1959): 510–16.

7. Dorothy Otnow Lewis, Ernest Moy, Lori Jackson, Robert Aaronson, Nicholas Restifo, Susan Serra, and Alexander Simos, "Biopsychosocial Characteristics of Children Who Later Murder," *American Journal of Psychiatry* 142 (1985): 1161–67.

8. Amy Holtzworth-Munroe and Gregory Stuart, "Typologies of Male Batterers: Three Subtypes and the Differences Among Them," *Psychological Bulletin* 116 (1994): 476–97.

9. "Jury Recommends Death for Florida Killer of Five," *New York Times*, March 25, 1994, p. A14.

10. Deborah Capaldi and Gerald Patterson, "Can Violent Offenders Be Distinguished from Frequent Offenders? Prediction from Childhood to Adolescence," *Journal of Research in Crime and Delinquency* 33 (1996): 206–31; see also, Pamela Lattimore, Christy Visher, and Richard Linster, "Predicting Rearrest for Violence Among Serious Youthful Offenders," *Journal of Research in Crime and Delinquency* 32 (1995): 54–83.

11. Robert Scudder, William Blount, Kathleen Heide, and Ira Silverman, "Important Links between Child Abuse, Neglect, and Delinquency," *International Journal of Offender Therapy* 37 (1993): 315–23.

12. Dorothy Lewis et al., "Neuropsychiatric, Psychoeducational, and Family Characteristics of 14 Juveniles Condemned to Death in the United States," *American Journal of Psychiatry* 145 (1988): 584–88.

13. Charles Patrick Ewing, *When Children Kill* (Lexington, MA: Lexington Books, 1990), p. 22.

14. Murray Straus, "Discipline and Deviance: Physical Punishment of Children and Violence and Other Crime in Adulthood," *Social Problems* 38 (1991): 133–54.

15. Lonnie Athens, *The Creation of Dangerous Violent Criminals* (Urbana: University of Illinois Press, 1992), pp. 27–80.

16. Cathy Spatz Widom, "Child Abuse, Neglect, and Violent Criminal Behavior," *Criminology* 27 (1989): 251–71; Beverly Rivera and Cathy Spatz Widom, "Childhood Victimization and Violent Offending," *Violence and Victims* 5 (1990): 19–34.

17. Sigmund Freud, *Beyond the Pleasure Principle* (London: Inter-Psychoanalytic Press, 1922).

18. Konrad Lorenz, *On Aggression* (New York: Harcourt Brace Jovanovich, 1966).

19. See, generally, Lee Ellis and Anthony Walsh, "Gene-Based Evolutionary Theories in Criminology," *Criminology* (1997, in press).

20. Paul Joubert and Craig Forsyth, "A Macro View of Two Decades of Violence in America," *American Journal of Criminal Justice* 13 (1988): 10–25; M. Dwayne Smith and Victoria Brewer, "A Sex-Specific Analysis of Correlates of Homicide Victimization in United States Cities," *Violence and Victims* 7 (1992): 279–85.

21. Marvin Wolfgang and Franco Ferracuti, *The Subculture of Violence* (London: Tavistock, 1967).

22. David Luckenbill and Daniel Doyle, "Structural Position and Violence: Developing a Cultural Explanation," *Criminology* 27 (1989): 419–36.

23. Steven Messner, "Regional and Racial Effects on the Urban Homicide Rate: The Subculture of Violence Revisited," *American Journal of Sociology* 88 (1983): 997–1007; Steven Messner and Kenneth Tardiff, "Economic Inequality and Levels of Homicide: An Analysis of Urban Neighborhoods," *Criminology* 24 (1986): 297–317.

24. Beth Bjerregaard and Alan Lizotte, "Gun Ownership and Gang Membership," *Journal of Criminal Law and Criminology* 86 (1995): 37–58.

25. Scott Decker, "Gangs and Violence: The Expressive Character of Collective Involvement," unpublished manuscript, University of Missouri–St. Louis, 1994.

26. Carolyn Rebecca Block, "Chicago Homicide from the Sixties to the Nineties: Have Patterns of Lethal Violence Changed?" paper presented at the annual meeting of the American Society of Criminology, Baltimore, November 1990.

27. Vincent F. Sacco and Leslie W. Kennedy, *The Criminal Event,* 2nd ed. (Toronto, ON: ITP Nelson, 1998).

28. See, generally, Kirk Williams and Robert Flewelling, "The Social Production of Criminal Homicide: A Comparative Study of Disaggregated Rates in American Cities," *American Sociological Review* 53 (1988): 421–31.

29. Raymond Gastil, "Homicide and the Regional Culture of Violence," *American Sociological Review* 36 (1971): 12–27; Keith Harries, *Serious Violence: Patterns of Homicide and Assault in America* (Springfield, IL: Charles C. Thomas, 1990).

30. Howard Erlanger, "Is There a Subculture of Violence in the South?" *Journal of Criminal Law and Criminology* 66 (1976): 483–90; Colin Loftin and Robert Hill, "Regional Subculture of Violence: An Examination of the Gastil-Hackney Thesis," *American Sociological Review* 39 (1974): 714–24; Raymond Gastil, "Comments," *Criminology* 16 (1975): 60–64; F. Frederick Hawley and Steven Messner, "The Southern Violence Construct: A Review of Arguments, Evidence, and the Normative Context," *Justice Quarterly* 6 (1989): 481–511.

31. T.F. Hartnagel, "The Effect of Age and Sex Compositions of Provincial Populations on Provincial Crime Rates," *Canadian Journal of Criminology* 20 (1978): 28–33; C. Lindsay, "Trends in the Crime Rate in Canada, 1970–1985," *Canadian Social Trends* (Autumn 1986): 33–38; L.W. Kennedy, R.A. Silverman, and D.R. Forde, "Homicide in Urban Canada," *Canadian Journal of Sociology* 16 (1991): 397–410; for the United States, see Gregory Kowalski and Thomas Petee, "Sunbelt Effects on Homicide Rates," *Sociology and Social Research* 76 (1991): 73–79.

32. Leslie Kennedy, Robert Silverman, and David Forde, "Homicide in Urban Canada: Testing the Impact of Economic Inequality and Social Disorganization," *Canadian Journal of Sociology* 16 (1991): 397.

33. Paul Goldstein, Henry Brownstein, and Patrick Ryan, "Drug-Related Homicide in New York: 1984–1988," *Crime and Delinquency* 38 (1992): 459–76.

34. James Collins and Pamela Messerschmidt, "Epidemiology of Alcohol-Related Violence," *Alcohol Health and Research World* 17 (1993): 93–100.

35. Thomas Feucht, *Drug Use Forecasting 1995* (Washington, DC: National Institute of Justice, 1996).

36. Christopher Innes, *Profile of State Prison Inmates 1986* (Washington, DC: Bureau of Justice Statistics, 1988).

37. Paul Goldstein, Patricia Bellucci, Barry Spunt, and Thomas Miller, "Volume of Cocaine Use and Violence: A Comparison between Men and Women," *Journal of Drug Issues* 21 (1991): 345–67; Paul Goldstein, Henry Brownstein, Patrick Ryan, and Patricia Bellucci, "Crack and Homicide in New York City, 1988: A Conceptually Based Event Analysis," unpublished paper, Narcotic and Drug Research, New York, 1989; Goldstein, Brownstein, and Ryan, "Drug-Related Homicide in New York: 1984–1988," p. 473.

38. Tracey Leesti, "Weapons and Violent Crime," *Juristat* 17 (1997); Orest Fedowycz, "Homicide in Canada - 1999," *Juristat* 20 (2000).

39. Federal Bureau of Investigation, *Crime in the United States, 1995* (Washington, DC: U.S. Government Printing Office, 1996).

40. David Brent, Joshua Perper, Christopher Allman, Grace Moritz, Mary Wartella, and Janice Zelenak, "The Presence and Accessibility of Firearms in the Home and Adolescent Suicides," *Journal of the American Medical Association* 266 (1991): 2989–95.

41. Linda Saltzman, James Mercy, Patrick O'Carroll, Mark Rosenberg, and Philip Rhodes, "Weapon Involvement and Injury Outcomes in Family and Intimate Assaults," *Journal of the American Medical Association* 267 (1992): 3043–47.

42. William Green, *Rape* (Lexington, MA: Lexington Books, 1988), p. 5.

43. Susan Randall and Vicki McNickle Rose, "Forcible Rape," in *Major Forms of Crime,* ed. Robert Meyer (Beverly Hills, CA: Sage, 1984), p. 47.

44. As cited in Chris McCormick, "Contemporary Sociological Thought," in *Canadian Criminology: Perspectives in Crime and Criminality,* 2nd ed., Margaret A. Jackson and Curt T. Griffiths (Toronto, ON: Harcourt Brace, 1995), p. 129.

45. Associated Press, "Judge Who Told Rape Suspect to Get a Girlfriend Orders Him into Custody," *Manchester Union Leader,* February 19, 1994, p. 2.

46. Susan Brownmiller, *Against Our Will: Men, Women and Rape* (New York: Simon & Schuster, 1975).

47. Gregory Vistica, "Rape in the Ranks," *Newsweek,* November 25, 1996, pp. 29–31.

48. Diego Ribadeneira, "In Haiti's Poorest Areas, Women Tell of Rape by Armed Men," *Boston Globe,* August 29, 1993, p. 6.

49. Canadian Centre for Justice Statistics, *Canadian Crime Statistics 1995,* Statistics Canada, catalogue no. 85-205 XPE, 1996.

50. Julian V. Roberts, "Criminal Justice Processing of Sexual Assault Cases," *Juristat* 14 (1994).

51. Robin Warshaw, *I Never Called It Rape: The Ms. Report on Recognizing, Fighting, and Surviving Date and Acquaintance Rape* (New York: Harper and Row, 1988), p. 26.

52. NCVS news release, "Victims Report 9 Percent Fewer Violent Crimes Last Year," September 17, 1996.

53. Angela Browne, "Violence against Women: Relevance for Medical Practitioners," *Journal of the American Medical Association* 267 (1992): 3184–89.

54. Roberts, "Criminal Justice Processing of Sexual Assault Cases."

55. *The Final Report of the Task Force on Sexual Abuse of Patients,* Ontario College of Physicians and Surgeons, November 25, 1991.

56. Mark Warr, "Rape, Burglary and Opportunity," *Journal of Quantitative Criminology* 4 (1988): 275–88.

57. James LeBeau, "Patterns of Stranger and Serial Rape Offending Factors Distinguishing Apprehended and At-Large Offenders," *Journal of Criminal Law and Delinquency* 78 (1987): 309–26.

58. A. Nicholas Groth and Jean Birnbaum, *Men Who Rape* (New York: Plenum Press, 1979).

59. Raymond Knight, "Validation of a Typology of Rapists," in *Sex Offender Research and Treatment: State-of-the-Art in North America and Europe,* ed. W.L. Marshall and J. Frenken (Beverly Hills, CA: Sage, 1997).

60. Julie Allison and Lawrence Wrightsman, *Rape: The Misunderstood Crime* (Newbury Park, CA: Sage, 1993), p. 51.

61. Roberts, "Criminal Justice Processing of Sexual Assault Cases."

62. Canadian Centre for Justice Statistics, *Canadian Crime Statistics 1995*, and *Canadian Crime Statistics 1999*, catalogue 85-205-XPE.

63. R. Lance Shotland, "A Model of the Causes of Date Rape in Developing and Close Relationships," in *Close Relationships,* ed. C. Hendrick (Newbury Park, CA: Sage, 1989), pp. 247–70.

64. Walter DeKeseredy, Martin Schwartz, and Karen Tait, "Sexual Assault and Stranger Aggression on a Canadian Campus," *Sex Roles* 28 (1993): 263–77; Thomas Meyer, "Date Rape: A Serious Campus Problem That Few Talk About," *Chronicle of Higher Education* 29 (December 1984): 15.

65. Martin Schwartz, "Humanist Sociology and Date Rape on the College Campus," *Humanity and Society* 15 (1991): 304–16.

66. Mark Starr, "The Writing on the Wall," *Newsweek,* November 26, 1990, p. 64.

67. Peggy Reeves Sanday, *Fraternity Gang Rape: Sex, Brotherhood, and Privilege on Campus* (New York: New York University, 1990); Sarah Elton, "McMaster: Rohypol [sic] and Sexual Assault," *The Brunswickan,* March 13, 1998, p. 4.

68. David Finkelhor and K. Yllo, *License to Rape: Sexual Abuse of Wives* (New York: Holt, Rinehart and Winston, 1985).

69. Cited in Diana Russell, "Wife Rape," in *Acquaintance Rape: The Hidden Crime,* ed. A. Parrot and L. Bechhofer (New York: Wiley, 1991).

70. Associated Press, "British Court Rejects Precedent, Finds a Man Guilty of Raping Wife," *Boston Globe,* March 15, 1991, p. 68.

71. Donald Symons, *The Evolution of Human Sexuality* (Oxford: Oxford University Press, 1979).

72. Lee Ellis, "A Synthesized (Biosocial) Theory of Rape," *Journal of Consulting and Clinical Psychology* 39 (1991): 631–42.

73. Diana Russell, *The Politics of Rape* (New York: Stein & Day, 1975).

74. Paul Gebhard, John Gagnon, Wardell Pomeroy, and Cornelia Christenson, *Sex Offenders: An Analysis of Types* (New York: Harper & Row, 1965), pp. 198–205; Richard Rada, ed., *Clinical Aspects of the Rapist* (New York: Grune & Stratton, 1978), pp. 122–30.

75. See, generally, Edward Donnerstein, Daniel Linz, and Steven Penrod, *The Question of Pornography* (New York: Free Press, 1987); Diana Russell, *Sexual Exploitation* (Beverly Hills, CA: Sage, 1985), pp. 115–16; Neil Malamuth and John Briere, "Sexual Violence in the Media: Indirect Effects on Aggression Against Women," *Journal of Social Issues* 42 (1986): 75–92.

76. Associated Press, "Trial on TV May Have Influenced Boy Facing Sexual-Assault Count," *Omaha World Herald,* April 18, 1984, p. 50.

77. Richard Felson and Marvin Krohn, "Motives for Rape," *Journal of Research in Crime and Delinquency* 27 (1990): 222–42.

78. Larry Baron and Murray Straus, "Four Theories of Rape: A Macrosociological Analysis," *Social Problems* 34 (1987): 467–89.

79. Julie Horney and Cassia Spohn, "The Influence of Blame and Believability Factors on the Processing of Simple versus Aggravated Rape Cases," *Criminology* 34 (1996): 135–63.

80. "Woman Urges Dotson's Release," *Omaha World Herald,* April 25, 1985, p. 3; Associated Press, "Apology Is Aired for Lie about Rape," *Boston Globe,* September 6, 1990, p. 12; Associated Press, "Protection Urged for Rape Suspects," *Boston Globe,* January 13, 1997, p. A5.

81. Gerald Robin, "Forcible Rape: Institutionalized Sexism in the Criminal Justice System," *Crime and Delinquency* 23 (1977): 136–53.

82. Associated Press, "Jury Stirs Furor by Citing Dress in Rape Acquittal," *Boston Globe,* October 6, 1989, p. 12.

83. *Michigan v. Lucas* 90-149 (1991); Comment, "The Rape Shield Paradox: Complainant Protection Amidst Oscillating Trends of State Judicial Interpretation," *Journal of Criminal Law and Criminology* 78 (1987): 644–98.

84. Andrew Karmen, *Crime Victims* (Pacific Grove, CA: Brooks/Cole, 1990), p. 252.

85. See, for example, Mich. Comp. Laws Ann. 750.5200-(1); Florida Statutes Annotated, Sec. 794.011. See, generally, Gary LaFree, "Official Reactions to Rape," *American Sociological Review* 45 (1980): 842–54; Martin Schwartz and Todd Clear, "Toward a New Law on Rape," *Crime and Delinquency* 26 (1980): 129–51; Susan Caringella-MacDonald, "The Comparability in Sexual and Nonsexual Assault Case Treatment: Did Statute Change Meet the Objective?" *Crime and Delinquency* 31 (1985): 206–23.

86. Linda Coates, "Causal Attributions in Sexual Assault Trial Judgments," *Journal of Language and Social Psychology* 16 (1997): 287–96; Linda Coates, Janet Bavelas and James Gibson, "Anomalous Language in Sexual Assault Trial Judgments," *Discourse and Society* 5 (1994): 189–206.

87. The legal principles here come from Wayne LaFave and Austin Scott, *Criminal Law* (St. Paul: West Publishing, 1986; updated, 1993).

88. Orest Fedorowycz, "Homicide in Canada—1994," *Juristat* 15 (11) (1995).

89. Marc Reidel and Margaret Zahn, *The Nature and Pattern of American Homicide* (Washington, DC: U.S. Government Printing Office, 1985); Orest Fedorowycz, "Homicide in Canada—1994," *Juristat* 15 (1995).

90. Angela Browne and Kirk Williams, "Gender, Intimacy, and Lethal Violence: Trends from 1976 through 1987," *Gender and Society* 7 (1993): 78–98. See also, Linda Saltzman and James Mercy, "Assaults between Intimates: The Range of Relationships Involved," in *Homicide, The Victim/ Offender Connection,* ed. Anna Victoria Wilson (Cincinnati: Anderson Publishing, 1993), pp. 65–74; Angela Browne and Kirk Williams, "Exploring the Effect of Resource Availability and the Likelihood of Female-Perpetrated Homicides," *Law and Society Review* 23 (1989): 75–94; Joseph A. Kuypers, *Man's Will to Hurt: Investigating the Causes, Supports and Varieties of His Violence* (Halifax: Fernwood, 1992).

91. Robert Silverman and Leslie Kennedy, "Women Who Kill Their Children," *Violence and Victims* 3 (1988): 113.

92. Robert Silverman and William Meloff, "Canadian Kids Who Kill," *Canadian Journal of Criminology*, January (1992): 15.

93. Margaret Zahn and Philip Sagi, "Stranger Homicides in Nine American Cities," *Journal of Criminal Law and Criminology* 78 (1987): 377–97.

94. David Luckenbill, "Criminal Homicide as a Situational Transaction," *Social Problems* 25 (1977): 176–86.

95. Leslie Kennedy and Robert Silverman, "The Elderly Victim of Homicide: An Application of the Routine Activities Approach," *Sociological Quarterly* 31 (1990): 308.

96. Stephen Baron, and Leslie Kennedy, "Routine Activities and a Subculture of Violence: A Study of Violence on the Street," *Journal of Research in Crime and Delinquency* 30 (1993): 88.

97. Michael Hazlett and Thomas Tomlinson, "Females Involved in Homicides: Victims and Offenders in Two Southern States," paper presented at the annual meeting of the American Society of Criminology, Montreal, November 1987; rev. 1988.

98. Scott Decker, "Deviant Homicide: A New Look at the Role of Motives and Victim-Offender Relationships," *Journal of Research in Crime and Delinquency* 33 (1996): 427–49.

99. Scott Decker, "Exploring Victim–Offender Relationships in Homicide: The Role of Individual and Event Characteristics," *Justice Quarterly* 10 (1993): 585–613.

100. James A. Fox and Jack Levin, *Mass Murder,* 2nd ed. (New York: Plenum Press, 1991).

101. Cindy Horswell, "Teen Held in Mom's Shooting Death: 'The Devil Made Me Do It,'" *Houston Chronicle*, May 19, 1993, p. 1.

102. Thomas Palmer, "A Doctor Smelled Arsenic, Leading to Arrest of Serial Killer," *Boston Globe*, August 20, 1987, p. 3.

103. "Police Suspect 'Something Snapped' to Ignite Wilder's Crime Spree," *Omaha World Herald*, April 15, 1984, p. 21A; Mark Starr, "The Random Killers," *Newsweek*, November 26, 1984, pp. 100–106; Thomas Palmer, "Ex-Hospital Aide Admits Killing 24 in Cincinnati," *Boston Globe*, August 19, 1987, p. 3.

104. Ronald Holmes and Stephen Homes, *Murder in America* (Thousand Oaks, CA: Sage, 1994), p. 6.

105. Jenkins, "Serial Murder in England, 1940–1985," p. 9.

106. Ronald Holmes and James DeBurger, *Serial Murder* (Newbury Park, CA: Sage, 1988), pp. 58–59.

107. Holmes and Homes, *Murder in America*, pp. 13–14.

108. Belea Keeney and Kathleen Heide, "Gender Differences in Serial Murderers: A Preliminary Analysis," *Journal of Interpersonal Violence* 9 (1994): 37–56.

109. "Violent Crime Linkage Analysis System," Online: http://www.rcmp-grc.gc.ca/html/viclas-e.htm; Jennifer Browdy, "VI-CAP System to Be Operational This Summer," *Law Enforcement News*, May 21, 1984, p. 1.

110. Philip Jenkins, "A Murder 'Wave'? Trends in American Serial Homicide 1940–1990," *Criminal Justice Review* 17 (1992): 1–18.

111. See, generally, Joel Milner, ed., "Special Issue: Physical Child Abuse," *Criminal Justice and Behavior* 18 (1991); see, generally, Ruth S. Kempe and C. Henry Kempe, *Child Abuse* (Cambridge, MA: Harvard University Press, 1978).

112. Holly Johnson, "Children and Youths as Victims of Violent Crimes," *Juristat* 15 (1995); for the United States, see David Wiese and Deborah Daro, *Current Trends in Child Abuse Reporting and Fatalities: The Results of the 1994 Annual Fifty-State Survey* (Chicago: National Committee to Prevent Child Abuse, 1995).

113. Richard Gelles and Murray Straus, "Violence in the American Family," *Journal of Social Issues* 35 (1979): 15–39.

114. Steve Geissinger, "Boy Scouts Dismissed 1,800 Suspected Molesters from 1971–91," *Boston Globe*, October 15, 1993, p. 3.

115. Diana Russell, "The Incidence and Prevalence of Intrafamilial and Extrafamilial Sexual Abuse of Female Children," *Child Abuse and Neglect* 7 (1983): 133–46; see also David Finkelhor, *Sexually Victimized Children* (New York: Free Press, 1979), p. 88.

116. Jeanne Hernandez, "Eating Disorders and Sexual Abuse in Adolescents," paper presented at the annual meeting of the American Psychosomatic Society, Charleston, SC, March 1993; Glenn Wolfner and Richard Gelles, "A Profile of Violence Toward Children: A National Study," *Child Abuse and Neglect* 17 (1993): 197–212.

117. Louanne Lawson and Mark Chaffin, "False Negatives in Sexual Abuse Disclosure Interviews," *Journal of Interpersonal Violence* 7 (1992): 532–42.

118. For a thorough review, see Kathleen Kendall-Tackett, Linda Meyer Williams, and David Finkelhor, "Impact of Sexual Abuse on Children: A Review and Synthesis of Recent Empirical Studies," *Psychological Bulletin* 133 (1993): 164–80.

119. Wolfner and Gelles, "A Profile of Violence Toward Children."

120. Brandt Steele, "Violence within the Family," in *Child Abuse and Neglect: The Family and the Community*, ed. R. Helfer and C.H. Kempe (Cambridge, MA: Ballinger Publishing, 1976), p. 12.

121. M. O'Keefe, "Predictors of Child Abuse in Maritally Violent Families," *Journal of Interpersonal Violence* 10 (1995): 3–25; as cited in Johnson, "Children and Youths as Victims of Violent Crimes."

122. Ruth Inglis, *Sins of the Fathers: A Study of the Physical and Emotional Abuse of Children* (New York: St. Martin's Press, 1978), p. 68.

123. Associated Press, "Lorena Freed," *Manchester Union Leader,* March 1, 1994, p. 44.

124. Russell Dobash, R. Emerson Dobash, Margo Wilson, and Martin Daly, "The Myth of Sexual Symmetry in Marital Violence," *Social Problems* 39 (1992): 71–86; Martin Schwartz and Walter DeKeseredy, "The Return of the 'Battered Husband Syndrome': Typification of Women as Violent," *Crime, Law and Social Change* 8 (1993): 11–27.

125. Schwartz and DeKeseredy, "The Return of the 'Battered Husband Syndrome.'"

126. R. Emerson Dobash and Russell Dobash, *Violence against Wives* (New York: Free Press, 1979); Julia O'Faolain and Laura Martines, eds., *Not in God's Image: Women in History* (Glasgow: Fontana/Collins, 1974); Laurence Stone, "The Rise of the Nuclear Family in Modern England: The Patriarchal Stage," in *The Family in History*, ed. Charles Rosenberg (Philadelphia: University of Pennsylvania Press, 1975), p. 53. See also John Braithwaite, "Inequality and Republican Criminology," paper presented at the annual meeting of the American Society of Criminology, San Francisco, November 1991, p. 20.

127. Merlin Brinkenhoff and Eugene Lupri, "Interspousal Violence," *Canadian Journal of Sociology* 13 (1988): 407.

128. Karen Rodgers, "Wife Assault: The Findings of a National Survey," *Juristat* 14 (1994).

129. James Makepeace, "Social Factor and Victim-Offender Differences in Courtship Violence," *Family Relations* 33 (1987): 87–91.

130. Graeme Newman, *Understanding Violence* (New York: Lippincott, 1979), pp. 145–46.

131. Gerald Hotaling and David Sugarman, "An Analysis of Risk Markers in Husband to Wife Violence," *Violence and Victims* 1 (1986): 101–24; Ronald Simons, Chyi-In Wu, Christine Johnson, and Rand Conger, "A Test of Various Perspectives on the Intergenerational Transmission of Domestic Violence," *Criminology* 33 (1995): 141–71.

132. Canadian Centre for Justice Statistics, *Canadian Crime Statistics 1996*, catalogue 85-205-XPE.

133. F.H. McClintock and Evelyn Gibson, *Robbery in London* (London: Macmillan, 1961), p. 15.

134. John Conklin, *Robbery and the Criminal Justice System* (New York: Lippincott, 1972), pp. 1–80.

135. James Calder and John Bauer, "Convenience Store Robberies: Security Measures and Store Robbery Incidents," *Journal of Criminal Justice* 20 (1992): 553–66.

136. John Scott Cameron, *Lessons from the Fabrikant File: A Report to the Board of Governors of Concordia University*, May 1994.

137. James Alan Fox and Jack Levin, "Firing Back: The Growing Threat of Workplace Homicide," *Annals* 536 (1994): 16–30.

138. Associated Press, "Gunman Wounds 3 Doctors in L.A. Hospital," *Cleveland Plain Dealer*, February 9, 1993, p. 1B.

139. Neil Boyd, "Violence in the Workplace in British Columbia: A Preliminary Investigation," *Canadian Journal of Criminology*, October (1995): 491.

140. Stephen Schafer, *The Political Criminal* (New York: Free Press, 1974), p. 1.

141. Robert Friedlander, *Terrorism* (Dobbs Ferry, NY: Oceana Publishers, 1979); Walter Laquer, *The Age of Terrorism* (Boston: Little, Brown, 1987), p. 72; National Advisory Commission on Criminal Justice Standards and Goals, *Report of the Task Force on Disorders and Terrorism* (Washington, DC: U.S. Government Printing Office, 1976), p. 3.

142. Paul Wilkinson, *Terrorism and the Liberal State* (New York: Wiley, 1977), p. 49.

143. Jack Gibbs, "Conceptualization of Terrorism," *American Sociological Review* 54 (1989): 329–40.

144. Daniel Georges-Abeyie, "Political Crime and Terrorism," in *Crime and Deviance: A Comparative Perspective*, ed. Graeme Newman (Beverly Hills, CA: Sage, 1980), pp. 313–33.

145. This section relies heavily on Friedlander, *Terrorism*, pp. 8–20.

146. For a general view, see Jonathan White, *Terrorism* (Pacific Grove, CA: Brooks/Cole, 1991).

147. Jonathan Kaufman, "Trauma of a German Slaying," *Boston Globe*, April 3, 1991, p. 2.

148. Claire Sterling, "Gen. Dozier and the International Terror Network," *Wall Street Journal*, December 29, 1981, p. 12.

149. Associated Press–Reuters, "Saudi Exile Is America's Most Wanted," *The Toronto Star*, August 21, 1998.

150. Peter Annin and Mark Hosenball, "A Showdown in Montana," *Newsweek*, April 8, 1996, p. 39.

151. Reuters, "Five White Separatists Indicted in Robberies," *Boston Globe*, January 31, 1997, p. A8.

152. William Smith, "Libya's Ministry of Fear," *Time*, April 30, 1984, pp. 36–38.

153. Reuters, "Nile Tour Boat Is Attacked; Blast Hits Egyptian Resort," *Boston Globe*, April 10, 1993, p. 5.

154. Associated Press, "31 Decapitated South of Algiers," *Boston Globe*, February 3, 1997, p. A5.

155. "Ottawa Is Prepared to Go Any Distance to Stop FLQ, Trudeau Says," *Globe and Mail*, October 14, 1970.

156. Charles Hillsinger and Mark Stein, "Militant Vegetarians Tied to Attacks on Livestock Industry," *Boston Globe*, November 23, 1989, p. A34.

157. Ted Robert Gurr, "Political Terrorism in the United States: Historical Antecedents and Contemporary Trends," in *The Politics of Terrorism*, ed. Michael Stohl (New York: Dekker, 1988); Martha Crenshaw, ed., *Terrorism, Legitimacy, and Power* (Middletown, CT: Wesleyan University Press, 1983), pp. 1–10.

158. Reuters, "New Haiti Police Have Executed 15, Rights Group Asserts," *Boston Globe*, January 24, 1997, p. A10.

159. Amnesty International, *Annual Report*, 1992 (Washington, DC), released July 1993.

160. This report on state action in Peru can be obtained on the Amnesty International Web site at http://www.amnesty.org/ailib/aipub/1996/AMR/2460396.html.

161. "Human Rights Watch/Americas Faults Ombudsman's First Year As President of Guatemala," Human Rights Watch news release, June 14, 1994.

162. Ronald Kramer, "Structural Violence and State Terrorism: Neglected Forms of Criminal Violence," paper presented at the annual meeting of the American Society of Criminology, Phoenix, AZ, November 1993.

163. Dick Ward, "The Nuclear Terror Threat," *CJ International* 12 (1996): 1–4.

164. Theodore Gurr, *Why Men Rebel* (Princeton, NJ: Princeton University Press, 1970).

165. M. Cherif Bassiouni, "Terrorism, Law Enforcement, and Mass Media: Perspectives, Problems and Proposals," *Journal of Criminal Law and Criminology* 72 (1981): 1–51.

166. Austin Turk, "Political Crime," in *Major Forms of Crime*, ed. R. Meier (Beverly Hills, CA: Sage, 1984), pp. 119–35.

167. Reuters, "18 Beheaded in Sri Lanka; Revenge for Slaying Seen," *Boston Globe*, October 6, 1989, p. 13.

168. The Special Senate Committee on the Subject-Matter of Bill C-36, 2001; "Justice Minister Preparing for Possible Changes to Anti-terrorism Bill," *National Post*, November 15, 2001.

Chapter 12

1. Andrew McCall, *The Medieval Underworld* (London: Hamish Hamilton, 1979), p. 86.

2. J.J. Tobias, *Crime and Police in England, 1700–1900* (London: Gill and Macmillan, 1979).

3. Marilyn Walsh, *The Fence* (Westport, CT: Greenwood Press, 1977), pp. 18–25.

4. Sandra Besserer and Catherine Trainor, "Criminal Victimization in Canada, 1999," *Juristat* 20 (2000): Figure 3; Rosemary Garter and Anthony N. Doob, "Trends in Criminal Victimization: 1988–1993," *Juristat* 14 (1994): Table 7.

5. John Hepburn, "Occasional Criminals," in *Major Forms of Crime*, ed. Robert Meier (Beverly Hills, CA: Sage, 1984), pp. 73–94.

6. P.F. Cromwell, J.N. Olson, and D.W. Avary, *Breaking and Entering: An Ethnographic Analysis of Burglary* (Newbury Park, CA: Sage, 1991).

7. Dianne Hendrick, "Theft," in *Crime Counts: A Criminal Event Analysis*, ed. Leslie W. Kennedy and Vincent F. Sacco (Toronto: ITP Nelson, 1996).

8. James Inciardi, "Professional Crime," in *Major Forms of Crime*, p. 223.

9. Harry King and William Chambliss, *Box Man: A Professional Thief's Journal* (New York: Harper & Row, 1972), p. 24.

10. Edwin Sutherland, "White-Collar Criminality," *American Sociological Review* 5 (1940): 2–10.

11. Gilbert Geis, "Avocational Crime," in *Handbook of Criminology*, ed. D. Glazer (Chicago: Rand McNally, 1974), p. 284.

12. Edwin Sutherland and Chic Conwell, *The Professional Thief* (Chicago: University of Chicago Press, 1937).

13. See, for example, Edwin Lemert, "The Behavior of the Systematic Check Forger," *Social Problems* 6 (1958): 141–48.

14. Carl Klockars, *The Professional Fence* (New York: Free Press, 1976); Darrell Steffensmeier, *The Fence: In the Shadow of Two Worlds* (Totowa, NJ: Rowman and Littlefield, 1986); Walsh, *The Fence*, pp. 25–28.

15. Walsh, *The Fence*, p. 34.

16. Paul Cromwell, James Olson, and D'Aunn Avary, "Who Buys Stolen Property? A New Look at Criminal Receiving," *Journal of Crime and Justice* 16 (1993): 75–95.

17. This section depends heavily on a classic book: Wayne LaFave and Austin Scott, *Handbook on Criminal Law* (St. Paul: West Publishing, 1972).

18. L.E. Cohen and M. Felson, "Social Change and Crime Rate Trends: A Routine Activity Approach," *American Sociological Review* 44 (1979): 588–608.

19. Paul McPhie, "Fraud," in *Crime Counts: A Criminal Event Analysis*, ed. Leslie W. Kennedy and Vincent F. Sacco (Toronto: Nelson, 1996).

20. D. Hartmann, D. Gelfand, B. Page, and P. Walder, "Rates of Bystander Observation and Reporting of Contrived Shoplifting Incidents," *Criminology* 10 (1972): 248.

21. Mary Owen Cameron, *The Booster and the Snitch* (New York: Free Press, 1964).

22. Lawrence Cohen and Rodney Stark, "Discriminatory Labeling and the Five-Finger Discount: An Empirical Analysis of Differential Shoplifting Dispositions," *Journal of Research on Crime and Delinquency* 11 (1974): 25–35.

23. Lloyd Klemke, "Does Apprehension for Shoplifting Amplify or Terminate Shoplifting Activity?" *Law and Society Review* 12 (1978): 390–403.

24. Hartmann et al., "Rates of Bystander Observation and Reporting," p. 267.

25. Erhard Blankenburg, "The Selectivity of Legal Sanctions: An Empirical Investigation of Shoplifting," *Law and Society Review* 11 (1976): 109–29.

26. Michael Hindelang, "Decisions of Shoplifting Victims to Invoke the Criminal Justice Process," *Social Problems* 21 (1974): 580–95.

27. George Keckeisen, *Retail Security versus the Shoplifter* (Springfield, IL: Charles C Thomas, 1993), pp. 31–32.

28. Melissa Davis, Richard Lundman, and Ramiro Martinez, Jr., "Private Corporate Justice: Store Police, Shoplifters, and Civil Recovery," *Social Problems* 38 (1991): 395–408.

29. Peter Morrison, "Motor-Vehicle Crimes," in *Crime Counts: A Criminal Event Analysis*, ed. Leslie W. Kennedy and Vincent F. Sacco (Toronto: Nelson, 1996).

30. "Challenges and Champions," Canadian Coalition Against Insurance Fraud, April 2001.

31. Charles McCaghy, Peggy Giordano, and Trudy Knicely Henson, "Auto Theft," *Criminology* 15 (1977): 367–81.

32. Donald Gibbons, *Society, Crime and Criminal Careers* (Englewood Cliffs, NJ: Prentice-Hall, 1977), p. 310.

33. Kim Hazelbaker, "Insurance Industry Analyses and the Prevention of Motor Vehicle Theft," in *Business and Crime Prevention*, ed. Marcus Felson and Ronald Clarke (Monsey, NY: Criminal Justice Press, 1997), pp. 283–93.

34. "Vehicle Crime Profits Can Be Used to Support Terrorist Organizations, Interpol's Chief Says," Interpol press release, November 19, 2000, at www.interpol.int.

35. Michael Rand, *Carjacking* (Washington, DC: Bureau of Justice Statistics, 1994), p. 1.

36. Frederick J. Desroches, *Force and Fear: Robbery in Canada* (Toronto: ITP Nelson, 1995).

37. Ronald Clarke and Patricia Harris, "Auto Theft and Its Prevention," in *Crime and Justice, An Annual Review*, ed. N. Morris and M. Tonry (Chicago: Chicago University Press, 1992).

38. R. Light, C. Nee, and H. Ingham, *Car Theft: The Offender's Perspective, Home Office Research Study No. 130* (London: Home Office, 1993); R.V. Clarke and P.M. Harris, "Auto Theft and Its Prevention," in *Crime and Justice: A Review of Research*, ed. M. Tonry (Chicago: University of Chicago Pess, 1992).

39. P.J. Brantingham and P.L. Brantingham, *Patterns in Crime* (New York: Macmillan, 1984).

40. La Fave and Scott, *Handbook on Criminal Law*, p. 655.

41. 30 Geo. III, C.24 (1975).

42. As described in Charles McCaghy, *Deviant Behavior* (New York: Macmillan, 1976), pp. 230–31.

43. Susan Gembrowski and Tim Dahlberg, "Over 100 Here Indicted after Telemarketing Fraud Probe around the U.S.," *San Diego Daily Transcript Online*, December 8, 1995: http://www.sddt.com/files/library/95headlines/DN95_12_08/DN95_12_08_02.html.

44. Edwin Lemert, "An Isolation and Closure Theory of Naive Check Forgery," *Journal of Criminal Law, Criminology and Police Science* 44 (1953): 297–98.

45. Online: http://www.cba.ca.

46. Jerome Hall, *Theft, Law and Society* (Indianapolis: Bobbs-Merrill, 1952), p. 36.

47. La Fave and Scott, *Handbook on Criminal Law*, p. 644.

48. E. Blackstone, *Commentaries on the Laws of England* (London: 1769), p. 224.

49. Frank Hoheimer, *The Home Invaders: Confessions of a Cat Burglar* (Chicago: Chicago Review, 1975).

50. Richard Wright, Robert Logie, and Scott Decker, "Criminal Expertise and Offender Decision Making: An Experimental Study of the Target Selection Process in Residential Burglary," *Journal of Research in Crime and Delinquency* 32 (1995): 39–53.

51. Richard Wright and Scott Decker, *Burglars on the Job: Streetlife and Residential Break-Ins* (Boston: Northeastern University Press, 1994).

52. See, generally, Neal Shover, "Structures and Careers in Burglary," *Journal of Criminal Law, Criminology and Police Science* 63 (1972): 540–49.

53. Paul Cromwell, James Olson, and D'Aunn Wester Avary, *Breaking and Entering: An Ethnographic Analysis of Burglary* (Newbury Park, CA: Sage, 1991), pp. 48–51.

54. See M. Taylor and C. Nee, "The Role of Cues in Simulated Residential Burglary: A Preliminary Investigation," *British Journal of Criminology* 28 (1988): 398–401; Julia MacDonald and Robert Gifford, "Territorial Cues and Defensible Space Theory: The Burglar's Point of View," *Journal of Environmental Psychology* 9 (1989): 193–205.

55. Roger Litton, "Crime Prevention and the Insurance Industry," in *Business and Crime Prevention*, ed. Marcus Felson and Ronald Clarke (Monsey, NY: Criminal Justice Press, 1997), p. 162.

56. Graham Farrell, Coretta Phillips, and Ken Pease, "Like Taking Candy, Why Does Repeat Victimization Occur?" *British Journal of Criminology* 35 (1995): 384–99.

57. Scott Decker, Richard Wright, Allison Redfern, and Dietrich Smith, "A Woman's Place Is in the Home: Females and Residential Burglary," *Justice Quarterly* 10 (1993): 143–63.

58. Eileen M. Garry, *Juvenile Firesetting and Arson* (Washington, DC: Office of Juvenile Justice and Delinquency Prevention, 1997).

59. Wayne Wooden, "Juvenile Firesetters in Cross-Cultural Perspective: How Should Society Respond," in *Official Responses to Problem Juveniles: Some International Reflections,* ed. James Hackler (Onati, Spain: Onati Publications, 1991), pp. 339–48.

60. Nancy Webb, George Sakheim, Luz Towns-Miranda, and Charles Wagner, "Collaborative Treatment of Juvenile Firestarters: Assessment and Outreach," *American Journal of Orthopsychiatry* 60 (1990): 305–10.

61. Vernon Quinsey, Terry Chaplin, and Douglas Unfold, "Arsonists and Sexual Arousal to Fire Setting: Correlations Unsupported," *Journal of Behavior Therapy and Experimental Psychiatry* 20 (1989): 203–9.

62. Leigh Edward Somers, *Economic Crimes* (New York: Clark Boardman, 1984), pp. 158–68.

63. Michael Rogers, "The Fire Next Time," *Newsweek,* November 26, 1990, p. 63.

Chapter 13

1. Dwight Smith, Jr., "White-Collar Crime, Organized Crime and the Business Establishment: Resolving a Crisis in Criminological Theory," in *White Collar and Economic Crime: A Multidisciplinary and Crossnational Perspective*, ed. P. Wickman and T. Dailey (Lexington, MA: Lexington Books, 1982), p. 53.

2. See, generally, Dwight Smith, Jr., "Organized Crime and Entrepreneurship," *International Journal of Criminology and Penology* 6 (1978): 161–77; idem, "Paragons, Pariahs, and Pirates: A Spectrum-Based Theory of Enterprise," *Crime and Delinquency* 26 (1980): 358–86; Dwight Smith, Jr., and Richard S. Alba, "Organized Crime and American Life," *Society* 16 (1979): 32–38.

3. Mark Haller, "Illegal Enterprise: A Theoretical and Historical Interpretation," *Criminology* 28 (1990): 207–35.

4. Nancy Frank and Michael Lynch, *Corporate Crime, Corporate Violence* (Albany, NY: Harrow and Heston, 1992), p. 7.

5. Nikos Passas and David Nelken, "The Thin Line between Legitimate and Criminal Enterprises: Subsidy Frauds in the European Community," *Crime, Law and Social Change* 19 (1993): 223–43.

6. For a thorough review, see David Friedrichs, *Trusted Criminals* (Belmont, CA: Wadsworth, 1996).

7. Kitty Calavita and Henry Pontell, "Savings and Loan Fraud as Organized Crime: Toward a Conceptual Typology of Corporate Illegality," *Criminology* 31 (1993): 519–48.

8. Edwin Sutherland, *White-Collar Crime: The Uncut Version* (New Haven, CT: Yale University Press, 1983).

9. Edwin Sutherland, "White-Collar Criminality," *American Sociological Review* 5 (1940): 2–10.

10. See, generally, Herbert Edelhertz, *The Nature, Impact and Prosecution of White-Collar Crime* (Washington, DC: U.S. Government Printing Office, 1970), pp. 73–75.

11. James Coleman, "What Is White Collar Crime? New Battles in the War of Definitions," in James Helmkamp, Richard Ball, and Kitty Townsend, Proceedings of the Academic Workshop, "Definitional Dilemma: Can and Should There Be a Universal Definition of White Collar Crime?" (Morgantown, WV: National White Collar Crime Center, 1996), pp. 77–86.

12. James Helmkamp and Richard Ball, "Progress in the Definition and Exploration of White-Collar Crime," paper presented at the annual meeting of the American Society of Criminology, Chicago, November 1996, p. 9.

13. David Weisburd and Kip Schlegel, "Returning to the Mainstream," in *White-Collar Crime Reconsidered*, ed. Kip Schlegel and David Weisburd (Boston: Northeastern University Press, 1992), pp. 352–65.

14. Gilbert Geis, "Avocational Crime," in *Handbook of Criminology*, ed. Daniel Glazer (Chicago: Rand McNally, 1974), p. 284.

15. Ronald Kramer and Raymond Michalowski, "State-Corporate Crime," paper presented at the annual meeting of the American Society of Criminology, Baltimore, November 1990.

16. Elizabeth Moore and Michael Mills, "The Neglected Victims and Unexamined Costs of White-Collar Crime," *Crime and Delinquency* 36 (1990): 408–18.

17. Stuart Traub, "Battling Employee Crime: A Review of Corporate Strategies and Programs," *Crime and Delinquency* 42 (1996): 244–56.

18. Laura Schrager and James Short, "Toward a Sociology of Organizational Crime," *Social Problems* 25 (1978): 415–25.

19. Gilbert Geis, "White-Collar and Corporate Crime," in *Major Forms of Crime*, ed. Robert Meier (Beverly Hills, CA: Sage, 1984), p. 145.

20. Bureau of Justice Statistics, *The Severity of Crime* (Washington, DC: U.S. Government Printing Office, 1984).

21. Xie Baogue, "The Function of the Chinese Procuratorial Organ in Combat Against Corruption," *Police Studies* 11 (1988): 38–43.

22. Dai Yisheng, "Expanding Economy and Growing Crime," *CJ International* 11 (1995): 916.

23. Jim Moran, "Thailand, Crime and Corruption Become Increasing Threat," *CJ International* 12 (1996): 5.

24. Sam Perry, "Economic Espionage and Corporate Responsibility," *CJ International* 11 (1995): 3–4.

25. Nikos Passas and David Nelkin, "The Fight against Fraud in the European Community: Cacophony Rather Than Harmony," *Corruption and Reform* 6 (1991): 237–66.

26. Ibid. See also Passas and Nelkin, "The Thin Blue Line between Legitimate and Criminal Enterprises."

27. Nikos Passas, "European Integration, Protectionism, and Criminogenesis: A Case Study on Farm Subsidy Frauds," *Mediterranean Quarterly* 5 (1994): 66–84.

28. Marshall Clinard and Richard Quinney, *Criminal Behavior Systems: A Typology* (New York: Holt, Rinehart and Winston, 1973), p. 117.

29. Edelhertz, *The Nature, Impact and Prosecution of White-Collar Crime.*

30. Mark Moore, "Notes Toward a National Strategy to Deal with White-Collar Crime," in *A National Strategy for Containing White-Collar Crime*, ed. Herbert Edelhertz and Charles Rogovin (Lexington, MA: Lexington Books, 1980), pp. 32–44.

31. For a general review, see John Braithwaite, "White-Collar Crime," *Annual Review of Sociology* 11 (1985): 1–25.

32. Scott Paltrow, "Goldblum Now in Consulting and on Parole," *Wall Street Journal*, March 22, 1982, p. 25.

33. Nikos Passas, "Structural Sources of International Crime: Policy Lessons from the BCCI Affair," *Crime, Law and Social Change* 19 (1994): 223–31.

34. Nikos Passas, "Accounting for Fraud: Auditors' Ethical Dilemmas in the BCCI Affair," in *The Ethics of Accounting and Finance*, ed. W. Michael Hoffman, Judith Brown Kamm, Robert Frederick, and Edward Petry (Westport, CT: Quorum Books, 1996), pp. 85–99.

35. Paul Nowell, "Bakker Convicted of Fraud," *Boston Globe*, October 6, 1989, p. 1.

36. Earl Gottschalk, "Churchgoers Are the Prey as Scams Rise," *Wall Street Journal*, August 7, 1989, p. C1.

37. Diana Henriques, "10 Percent of Fruit Juice Sold in U.S. Is Not All Juice, Regulators Say," *New York Times*, October 31, 1993, p. 1.

38. Richard Quinney, "Occupational Structure and Criminal Behavior: Prescription Violation of Retail Pharmacists," *Social Problems* 11 (1963): 179–85; see also John Braithwaite, *Corporate Crime in the Pharmaceutical Industry* (London: Routledge and Kegan Paul, 1984).

39. Amy Dockser Marcus, "Thievery by Lawyers Is on the Increase, with Duped Clients Losing Bigger Sums," *Wall Street Journal*, November 26, 1990, p. B1.

40. James Armstrong et al., "Securities Fraud," *American Criminal Law Review* 33 (1995): 973–1016.

41. Robert Rose and Jeff Bailey, "Traders in CBOT Soybean Pit Indicted," *Wall Street Journal*, August 3, 1989, p. A4.

42. Scott McMurray, "Futures Pit Trader Goes to Trial," *Wall Street Journal*, May 8, 1990, p. C1; idem, "Chicago Pits' Dazzling Growth Permitted a Free-for-All Mecca," *Wall Street Journal*, August 3, 1989, p. A4.

43. *Carpenter v. United States* 484 U.S. 19 (1987); also see John Boland, "The SEC Trims the First Amendment," *Wall Street Journal*, December 4, 1986, p. 28.

44. Tim Metz and Michael Miller, "Boesky's Rise and Fall Illustrate a Compulsion to Profit by Getting Inside Track on Market," *Wall Street Journal*, November 17, 1986, p. 28; Wade Lambert, "FDIC Receives Cooperation of Milken Aide," *Wall Street Journal*, April 25, 1991, p. A3.

45. This section depends heavily on Frank Browning and John Gerassi, *The American Way of Crime* (New York: Putnam, 1980), p. 151.

46. Edward Ranzal, "City Report Finds Building Industry Infested by Graft," *New York Times*, November 8, 1974, p. 1.

47. Rod Macdonell, "Tory Senator Must Pay Fine," *Halifax Daily News*, July 8, 1998; Toni Locy, "Former Lawmaker Gets Plea Deal," *Washington Post*, April 17, 1996.

48. Marshall Clinard and Peter Yeager, *Corporate Crime* (New York: Free Press, 1980), pp. 166–67.

49. *Fraud Update, The White Paper* (1991): 3–4.

50. United Press International, "Minority Leader in N.Y. Senate Is Charged," *Boston Globe*, September 17, 1987, p. 20.

51. "Now Williams—Last, Not Least of ABSCAM Trials," *New York Times*, April 5, 1982, p. E7.

52. Edward Pound, "Honored Employee Is a Key in Huge Fraud in Defense Purchasing," *Wall Street Journal*, March 2, 1988, p. 1.

53. Discussed in Friedrichs, *Trusted Criminals*, p. 147.

54. Larry Tye, "A Tide of State Corruption Sweeps from Coast to Coast," *Boston Globe*, March 25, 1991, p. 1.

55. *The Knapp Commission Report on Police Corruption* (New York: George Braziller, 1973), pp. 1–3, 170–82.

56. Michael Rezendes, "N.Y. Hears of Police Corrupted," *Boston Globe*, October 10, 1993, p. 1.

57. Cited in Hugh Barlow, *Introduction to Criminology*, 2nd ed. (Boston: Little, Brown, 1984).

58. Thomas Burton, "The More Baxter Hides Its Israeli Boycott Role, the More Flak It Gets," *Wall Street Journal*, April 25, 1991, p. 1.

59. "Newsbreaks," *Aviation Week and Space Technology*, July 10, 1995, p. 19.

60. Charles McCaghy, *Deviant Behavior* (New York: Macmillan, 1976), p. 178.

61. John Clark and Richard Hollinger, *Theft by Employees in Work Organizations* (Washington, DC: U.S. Government Printing Office, 1983), pp. 2–3.

62. "Business Fraud Prevails, May Worsen, Study Says," *Wall Street Journal*, August 17, 1993, p. A4.

63. J. Sorenson, H. Grove, and T. Sorenson, "Detecting Management Fraud: The Role of the Independent Auditor," in *White-Collar Crime, Theory and Research*, ed. G. Geis and E. Stotland (Beverly Hills, CA: Sage, 1980), pp. 221–51.

64. Teri Agins, "Report Is Said to Show Pervasive Fraud at Leslie Fay," *Wall Street Journal*, October 27, 1993, p. B4.

65. "Business Fraud Prevails," p. A4.

66. Henry Pontell, Kitty Calavita, and Robert Tillman, *Fraud in the Savings and Loan Industry: White-Collar Crime and Government Response* (Report to the National Institute of Justice, Washington, DC, 1994); Robert Tillman and Henry Pontell, "Organizations and Fraud in the Savings and Loan Industry," *Social Forces* 73 (1995): 1439–63; Kitty Calavita and Henry Pontell, "Savings and Loan Fraud as Organized Crime: Toward a Conceptual Typology of Corporate Illegality," *Criminology* 31 (1993): 519–48; idem, "'Heads I Win, Tails You Lose': Deregulation, Crime, and Crisis in the Savings and Loan Industry," *Crime and Delinquency* 36 (1990): 309–41; Rich Thomas, "Sit Down Taxpayers," *Newsweek*, June 4, 1990, p. 60; John Gallagher, "Good Old Bad Boy," *Time*, June

25, 1990, pp. 42–43; L. Gordon Crovitz, "Milken's Tragedy: Oh, How the Mighty Fall before RICO," *Wall Street Journal*, May 2, 1990, p. A17.

67. See Kristine DeBry, Bonny Harbinger, and Susan Rotkis, "Health Care Fraud," *American Criminal Law Review* 33 (1995): 818–38.

68. Bruce Lambert, "12 Chiropractors among 20 Arrested in Insurance Fraud Sting," *New York Times*, May 22, 1997, p. A30.

69. Laura Johannes and Wendy Bounds, "Corning Agrees to Pay $6.8 Million to Settle Medicare Billing Charges," *Wall Street Journal*, February 22, 1996, p. B2.

70. Carl Hartman, "Study Says Underground Economy May Represent 33 Percent of Production," *Boston Globe*, February 16, 1988, p. 38.

71. Alan Murray, "IRS in Losing Battle against Tax Evaders Despite Its New Gear," *Wall Street Journal*, April 10, 1984, p. 1; "The Police Perspective on Organized Crime," *RCMP Gazette*, n.d.

72. Paul Duke, "IRS Excels at Tracking the Average Earner but Not the Wealthy," *Wall Street Journal*, April 15, 1991, p. 1.

73. Nancy Frank and Michael Lynch, *Corporate Crime, Corporate Violence* (Albany, NY: Harrow and Heston), pp. 12–13.

74. Sutherland, "White-Collar Criminality," pp. 2–10.

75. Michael Maltz and Stephen Pollack, "Suspected Collusion Among Bidders," in *White-Collar Crime, Theory and Research*, ed. G. Geis and E. Stotland (Beverly Hills, CA: Sage, 1980), pp. 174–98.

76. Bruce Ingersoll and Alecia Swasy, "FDA Puts Squeeze on P&G over Citrus Hill Labeling," *Wall Street Journal*, April 25, 1991, p. B1.

77. Clinard and Yeager, *Corporate Crime*.

78. John Conklin, *Illegal but Not Criminal* (Englewood Cliffs, NJ: Prentice-Hall, 1972), pp. 45–46.

79. For an analysis of false claims, see Jonathan Kaye and John Patrick Sullivan, "False Claims," in *Eighth Survey of White-Collar Crime, American Criminal Law Review* 30 (1993): 643–57.

80. "Union Carbide Says Bhopal Plant Should Have Been Closed," *Wall Street Journal*, March 21, 1985, p. 18.

81. "Judge Rejects Exxon Alaska Spill Pact," *Wall Street Journal*, April 25, 1991, p. A3.

82. Roger Fillion, "Cracking Down on Internet Crime," *Boston Globe*, December 28, 1995, p. 65.

83. M. Swanson and J. Terriot, "Computer Crime: Dimensions, Types, Causes and Investigations," *Journal of Political Science and Administration* 8 (1980): 305–6; Donn Parker, "Computer-Related White-Collar Crime," in *White-Collar Crime, Theory and Research*, ed. G. Geis and E. Stotland (Beverly Hills, CA: Sage, 1980), pp. 199–220.

84. Anne Branscomb, "Rogue Computer Programs and Computer Rogues: Tailoring Punishment to Fit the Crime," *Rutgers Computer and Technology Law Journal* 16 (1990): 24–26.

85. David Stipp, "Computer Virus Maker Is Given Probation, Fine," *Wall Street Journal*, May 7, 1990, p. B3.

86. Erik Larson, "Computers Turn Out to Be Valuable Aid in Employee Crime," *Wall Street Journal*, January 14, 1985, p. 1.

87. Kathleen Daly, "Gender and Varieties of White-Collar Crime," *Criminology* 27 (1989): 769–93.

88. Quoted in Metz and Miller, "Boesky's Rise and Fall Illustrate a Compulsion to Profit by Getting Inside Track on Market," p. 28.

89. Donald Cressey, *Other People's Money: A Study of the Social Psychology of Embezzlement* (Glencoe, IL: Free Press, 1973).

90. Ronald Kramer, "Corporate Crime: An Organizational Perspective," in *White-Collar and Economic Crime: A Multidisciplinary and Crossnational Perspective*, ed. P. Wickman and T. Dailey (Lexington, MA: Lexington Books, 1982), pp. 75–94.

91. John Braithwaite, "Toward a Theory of Organizational Crime," paper presented at the annual meeting of the American Society of Criminology, Montreal, November 1987.

92. Travis Hirschi and Michael Gottfredson, "Causes of White-Collar Crime," *Criminology* 25 (1987): 949–74.

93. Michael Gottfredson and Travis Hirschi, *A General Theory of Crime* (Stanford, CA: Stanford University Press, 1990), p. 191.

94. David Weisburd, Ellen Chayet, and Elin Waring, "White-Collar and Criminal Careers: Some Preliminary Findings," *Crime and Delinquency* 36 (1990): 342–55.

95. Michael Benson and Elizabeth Moore, "Are White-Collar and Common Offenders the Same? An Empirical and Theoretical Critique of a Recently Proposed General Theory of Crime," *Journal of Research in Crime and Delinquency* 29 (1992): 251–72.

96. David Simon and D. Stanley Eitzen, *Elite Deviance* (Boston: Allyn & Bacon, 1982), p. 28.

97. Jesilow, Pontell, and Geis, "Physician Immunity from Prosecution and Punishment for Medical Program Fraud," p. 19.

98. Clinard and Yeager, *Corporate Crime*, p. 124.

99. Peter Yeager, "Structural Bias in Regulatory Law Enforcement: The Case of the U.S. Environmental Protection Agency," *Social Problems* 34 (1987): 330–44.

100. See, generally, Stanton Wheeler, David Weisburd, Elin Waring, and Nancy Bode, "White-Collar Crimes and Criminals," *American Criminal Law Review* 25 (1988): 331–57.

101. Susanne Schafer, "One General Fired, Two Punished for Mismanaging C-17 Plane," *Boston Globe*, May 1, 1993, p. 3.

102. Paul Blustein, "Disputes Arise over Value of Laws on Insider Trading," *Wall Street Journal*, November 17, 1986, p. 28.

103. Paul Barrett, "For Many Dalkon Shield Claimants Settlement Won't End the Trauma," *Wall Street Journal*, March 9, 1988, p. 29.

104. This section relies on Daniel Skoler, "White-Collar Crime and the Criminal Justice System: Problems and Challenges," in *A National Strategy for Containing White-Collar Crime*, ed. Herbert Edelhertz and Charles Rogovin (Lexington, MA: Lexington Books, 1980), pp. 57–76.

105. Michael Benson, Francis Cullen, and William Maakestad, "Local Prosecutors and Corporate Crime," *Crime and Delinquency* 36 (1990): 356–72.

106. Traub, "Battling Employee Crime: A Review of Corporate Strategies and Programs," pp. 248–52.

107. Alan Otten, "States Begin to Protect Employees Who Blow Whistle on Their Firms," *Wall Street Journal*, December 31, 1984, p. 11.

108. This section relies heavily on Albert Reiss, Jr., "Selecting Strategies of Social Control over Organizational Life," in *Enforcing Regulation*, ed. Keith Hawkins and John M. Thomas (Boston: Klowver Publications, 1984), pp. 25–37.

109. John Braithwaite, "The Limits of Economism in Controlling Harmful Corporate Conduct," *Law and Society Review* 16 (1981–1982): 481–504.

110. "EPA Sues Sherwin-Williams: Pattern of Pollution at Paint Factory Is Alleged," *Wall Street Journal*, July 19, 1993, p. 1; "Making Firms Liable for Cleaning Toxic Sites," *Wall Street Journal*, March 9, 1988, p. 29.

111. Rhonda Rundle, "Computer Sciences Will Pay $2.1 Million to Settle Charges by U.S. Government," *Wall Street Journal*, July 19, 1993, p. B8.

112. Wayne Gray and John Scholz, "Does Regulatory Enforcement Work? A Panel Analysis of OSHA Enforcement," *Law and Society Review* 27 (1993): 177–91.

113. Michael Benson, "Emotions and Adjudication: Status Degradation Among White-Collar Criminals," *Justice Quarterly* 7 (1990): 515–28; John Braithwaite, *Crime, Shame and Reintegration* (Sydney: Cambridge University Press, 1989).

114. John Braithwaite and Gilbert Geis, "On Theory and Action for Corporate Crime Control," *Crime and Delinquency* 28 (1982): 292–314.

115. Frank and Lynch, *Corporate Crime, Corporate Violence*, pp. 33–34.

116. James Miller, "U.S. Ban on Baxter International Bids Hurt Reputation More Than Business," *Wall Street Journal*, August 16, 1993, p. A3.

117. Kip Schlegel, "Desert, Retribution and Corporate Criminality," *Justice Quarterly* 5 (1988): 615–34.

118. Raymond Michalowski and Ronald Kramer, "The Space Between Laws: The Problem of Corporate Crime in a Transnational Context," *Social Problems* 34 (1987): 34–53.

119. Steven Klepper and Daniel Nagin, "The Deterrent Effect of Perceived Certainty and Severity of Punishment Revisited," *Criminology* 27 (1989): 721–46.

120. "The Follies Go On," *Time*, April 15, 1991, p. 45.

121. Bill Richards and Alex Kotlowitz, "Judge Finds Three Corporate Officials Guilty of Murder in Cyanide Death of Worker," *Wall Street Journal*, June 17, 1985, p. 2.

122. Donald Manson, *Tracking Offenders: White-Collar Crime* (Washington, DC: Bureau of Justice Statistics, 1986); Kenneth Carlson and Jan Chaiken, *White-Collar Crime* (Washington, DC: Bureau of Justice Statistics, 1987); Robert Bennett, "Foreword: Eighth Survey of White-Collar Crime," *American Criminal Law Review* 30 (1993).

123. David Weisburd, Elin Waring, and Stanton Wheeler, "Class, Status, and the Punishment of White-Collar Criminals," *Law and Social Inquiry* 15 (1990): 223–43.

124. Mark Cohen, "Environmental Crime and Punishment: Legal/Economic Theory and Empirical Evidence on Enforcement of Federal Environmental Statutes," *Journal of Criminal Law and Criminology* 82 (1992): 1054–1109.

125. See, generally, President's Commission on Organized Crime, Report to the President and the Attorney General, *The Impact: Organized Crime Today* (Washington, DC: U.S. Government Printing Office, 1986). Herein cited as *Organized Crime Today*.

126. Frederick Martens and Michele Cunningham-Niederer, "Media Magic, Mafia Mania," *Federal Probation* 49 (1985): 60–68.

127. Alan Block and William Chambliss, *Organizing Crime* (New York: Elsevier, 1981).

128. *Organized Crime Today*, p. 462.

129. Attorney General's Commission on Pornography, *Final Report* (Washington, DC: U.S. Government Printing Office, 1986), p. 1053.

130. Alan Block, *East Side/West Side* (New Brunswick, NJ: Transaction Books, 1983), pp. vii, 10–11; G.R. Blakey and M. Goldsmith, "Criminal Redistribution of Stolen Property: The Need for Law Reform," *Michigan Law Review* 81 (August 1976): 45–46.

131. Merry Morash, "Organized Crime," in *Major Forms of Crime*, ed. Robert Meier (Beverly Hills, CA: Sage, 1984), p. 198.

132. Stephen Koepp, "Dirty Cash and Tarnished Vaults," *Time*, February 25, 1985, p. 65; Roy Rowan, "The 50 Biggest Mafia Bosses," *Fortune*, November 10, 1986, p. 24.

133. Donald Cressey, *Theft of the Nation* (New York: Harper and Row, 1969).

134. Dwight Smith, Jr., *The Mafia Mystique* (New York: Basic Books, 1975).

135. *Organized Crime Today*, p. 489; Robert Rhodes, *Organized Crime: Crime Control versus Civil Liberties* (New York: Random House, 1984).

136. This section borrows heavily from Browning and Gerassi, *The American Way of Crime*, pp. 288–472; and August Bequai, *Organized Crime* (Lexington, MA: Lexington Books, 1979).

137. Jay Albanese, "God and the Mafia Revisited: From Valachi to Frantianno," paper presented at the annual meeting of the American Society of Criminology, Toronto, 1982.

138. Philip Jenkins and Gary Potter, "The Politics and Mythology of Organized Crime: A Philadelphia Case Study," *Journal of Criminal Justice* 15 (1987): 473–84.

139. Based on the 2001 Report on Organized Crime in Canada prepared by the Criminal Intelligence Service of Canada, available at http://www.cisc.gc.ca/AnnualReport2001/Cisc2001/front-page2001.html.

140. Omar Bartos, "Growth of Russian Organized Crime Poses Serious Threat," *CJ International* 11 (1995): 8–9; Francis Ianni, *Black Mafia: Ethnic Succession in Organized Crime* (New York: Pocket Books, 1975).

141. Robert Kelly and Rufus Schatzberg, "Types of Minority Organized Crime: Some Considerations," paper presented at the annual meeting of the American Society of Criminology, Montreal, November 1987.

142. Peter Kerr, "Chinese Now Dominate New York Heroin Trade," *New York Times*, August 9, 1987, p. 1; Ian McDermid Gomme, *The Shadow Line: Deviance and Crime in Canada*, 2nd ed. (Toronto: Harcourt Brace, 1998).

143. Jenkins and Potter, "The Politics and Mythology of Organized Crime."

144. William Chambliss, *On the Take* (Bloomington: Indiana University Press, 1978).

145. Russell Watson, "Death on the Spot," *Newsweek*, December 13, 1993, pp. 18–20.

146. Yumiko Ono, "Top Kirin Brewery Executives Resign Amid Reports of Paying Off Racketeers," *Wall Street Journal*, July 19, 1993, p. A6.

147. Michael Elliott, "Global Mafia," *Newsweek*, December 13, 1993, pp. 22–29.

148. Associated Press, "Gangland Violence Rises and Startles in Moscow," *Boston Globe*, July 22, 1993, p. 44.

149. George Vold, *Theoretical Criminology*, 2nd ed., rev. Thomas Bernard (New York: Oxford University Press, 1979).

150. Selwyn Raab, "A Battered and Ailing Mafia Is Losing Its Grip on America," *New York Times*, October 22, 1990, p. 1.

151. Jay Albanese, *Organized Crime in America*, 2nd ed. (Cincinnati: Anderson, 1989), p. 68.

Chapter 14

1. "Guess Found Guilty," *Globe and Mail*, June 20, 1998; "Prosecutor Says Juror Knew Affair Was Wrong," *Telegraph Journal*, June 18, 1998, p. D1; "Crown's Summation Brings Guess to Tears," *Halifax Herald*, June 18, 1998; "Off with Her Head, February 24, 1998, Regina v. Gillian Guess." Online: http://members.tripod.com/~gguess/witch.html.

2. Edwin Schur, *Crimes without Victims* (Englewood Cliffs, NJ: Prentice-Hall, 1965).

3. Andrea Dworkin, quoted in "Where Do We Stand on Pornography," *Ms*, January–February 1994, p. 34.

4. Jennifer Williard, *Juvenile Prostitution* (Washington, DC: National Victim Resource Center, 1991).

5. The Committee on Sexual Offences against Children and Youth (the Badgley Committee), 1984; and the *Report of the Special Committee on Pornography and Prostitution* (the Fraser Committee), 1985.

6. The Royal Commission on the Criminal Law Relating to Criminal Sexual Psychopaths, 1956.

7. Morris Cohen, "Moral Aspects of the Criminal Law," *Yale Law Journal* 49 (1940): 1017.

8. Sir Patrick Devlin, *The Enforcement of Morals* (New York: Oxford University Press, 1959), p. 20.

9. See Joel Feinberg, *Social Philosophy* (Englewood Cliffs, NJ: Prentice-Hall, 1973), chap. 2, 3.

10. *United States v. 12 200-ft Reels of Super 8mm Film*, 413 U.S. 123 (1973) at 137.

11. David Kaplan, "Is It Torture or Tradition?" *Newsweek*, December 20, 1993, p. 124.

12. H.L.A. Hart, "Immorality and Treason," *Listener* 62 (1959): 163.

13. Joseph Gusfield, "On Legislating Morals: The Symbolic Process of Designating Deviancy," *California Law Review* 56 (1968): 58–59.

14. E. Hatfield, S. Sprecher, and J. Traupman, "Men and Women's Reactions to Sexually Explicit Films: A Serendipitous Finding," *Archives of Sexual Behavior* 6 (1978): 583–92; Henry Lesieur and Joseph Sheley, "Illegal Appended Enterprises: Selling the Lines," *Social Problems* 34 (1987): 249–60.

15. Wayne LaFave and Austin Scott, Jr., *Criminal Law* (St. Paul, MN: West Publishing, 1986), p. 12.

16. Tina Loo and Lorna McLean, *Historical Perspectives on Law and Society in Canada* (Toronto: Copp Clark, 1994); Bryan D. Palmer, "Discordant Music: Charivaris and White-Capping in Nineteenth-Century North America," *Labour/Le Travail* 3 (1978): 5–62.

17. Howard Becker, *Outsiders* (New York: Macmillan, 1963), pp. 13–14.

18. Daniel Claster, *Bad Guys and Good Guys, Moral Polarization and Crime* (Westport, CT: Greenwood Press, 1992), pp. 28–29.

19. "Amsterdam Cafe Raided." Online at www.hempbc.com/library/bust/amsterdam.html.

20. Reuters, "Belgians Promise to Clean Up Courts," *Boston Globe*, October 22, 1996, p. A17.

21. See, generally, Spencer Rathus and Jeffery Nevid, *Abnormal Psychology* (Englewood Cliffs, NJ: Prentice-Hall, 1991), pp. 373–411.

22. *Canadian Crime Statistics 2000* (Ottawa: Canadian Centre for Crime Statistics, 2001).

23. G. Kinsman, "'Character Weaknesses' and 'Fruit Machines': Towards an Analysis of the Anti-homosexual Security Campaign in the Canadian Civil Service," *Labour / Le travail* 35 (1995): 133–61; Gary Kinsman and Patrizia Gentile, 'In the Interests of the State': The Anti-gay, Anti-lesbian National Security Campaign in Canada," unpublished report.

24. See, generally, V. Bullogh, *Sexual Variance in Society and History* (Chicago: University of Chicago Press, 1958), pp. 143–44; Spencer Rathus, *Human Sexuality* (New York: Holt, Rinehart and Winston), p. 463; Annette Jolin, "On the Backs of Working Prostitutes: Feminist Theory and Prostitution Policy," *Crime and Delinquency* 40 (1994): 60–83.

25. "The Court and the Soliciting Law," *Globe and Mail*, June 6, 1990; Richard Barnhorst, Sherrie Barnhorst, and Kenneth Clarke, *Criminal Law and the Canadian Criminal Code* (Toronto, McGraw-Hill Ryerson, 1992).

26. "NOW Charges Dropped. Alright!" *NOW*, September 27, 1990; "Crown Finds No Legal Basis, Drops NOW Charges," *NOW*, September 27, 1990, p. 15.

27. Charles McCaghy, *Deviant Behavior* (New York: Macmillan, 1976), pp. 348–49.

28. Information for the following section draws on various sources, including Charles Winick and Paul Kinsie, *The Lively Commerce* (Chicago: Quadrangle Books, 1971); Jennifer James, "Prostitutes and Prostitution," in *Deviants: Voluntary Action in a Hostile World*, ed. E. Sagarin and F. Montanino (New York: Scott, Foresman, 1977).

29. Mark-David Janus, Barbara Scanlon, and Virginia Price, "Youth Prostitution," in *Child Pornography and Sex Rings*, ed. Ann Wolbert Burgess (Lexington, MA: Lexington Books, 1989), pp. 127–46.

30. Paul Goldstein, "Occupational Mobility in the World of Prostitution: Becoming a Madam," *Deviant Behavior* 4 (1983): 267–79.

31. Goldstein, "Occupational Mobility in the World of Prostitution," pp. 267–70.

32. Described in Rathus, *Human Sexuality*, p. 468.

33. Paul Goldstein, Lawrence Ouellet, and Michael Fendrich, "From Bag Brides to Skeezers: A Historical Perspective on Sex-for-Drugs Behavior," *Journal of Psychoactive Drugs* 24 (1992): 349–61; Lisa Maher and Kathleen Daly, "Women in the Street-Level Drug Economy: Continuity or Change?" *Criminology* 34 (1996): 465–91.

34. D. Kelly Weisberg, *Children of the Night: A Study of Adolescent Prostitution* (Lexington, MA: Lexington Books, 1985), pp. 44–55.

35. Gerald Hotaling and David Finkelhor, *The Sexual Exploitation of Missing Children* (Washington, DC: U.S. Department of Justice, 1988).

36. N. Jackman, Richard O'Toole, and Gilbert Geis, "The Self-Image of the Prostitute," in *Sexual Deviance,* ed. J. Gagnon and W. Simon (New York: Harper & Row, 1967), pp. 152–53.

37. Paul Gebhard, "Misconceptions about Female Prostitutes," *Medical Aspects of Human Sexuality* 3 (July 1969): 28–30.

38. Reuters, "UN Cites Sharp Rise in Child Labour, Prostitution," *Boston Globe,* November 12, 1996, p. A6.

39. Dorothy Bracey, *"Baby Pros": Preliminary Profiles of Juvenile Prostitutes* (New York: JohnJay Press, 1979).

40. A. Brannigan, L. Knafla, and C. Levy, *Street Prostitution. Assessing the Impact of the Law: Calgary* (Ottawa: Department of Justice, 1989); N. Crook, *A Report on Prostitution in the Atlantic Provinces,* Working Papers on Pornography and Prostitution, Report No. 12 (Ottawa: Department of Justice, 1984); J. Lowman, *Vancouver Field Study of Prostitution,* Working Papers on Pornography and Prostitution, Report No. 8 (Ottawa: Department of Justice, 1984).

41. Andrea Dworkin, *Pornography* (New York: Dutton, 1989).

42. Jolin, "On the Backs of Working Prostitutes," pp. 76–77.

43. *Merriam-Webster Dictionary* (New York: Pocket Books, 1974), p. 484.

44. Albert Belanger et al., "Typology of Sex Rings Exploiting Children," in *Child Pornography and Sex Rings,* ed. Ann Wolbert Burgess (Lexington, MA: Lexington Books, 1984), pp. 51–81.

45. *The Report of the Commission on Obscenity and Pornography* (Washington, DC: U.S. Government Printing Office, 1970).

46. *Pornography Commission,* pp. 837–902.

47. Berl Kutchinsky, "The Effect of Easy Availability of Pornography on the Incidence of Sex Crimes," *Journal of Social Issues* 29 (1973): 95–112.

48. Michael Goldstein, "Exposure to Erotic Stimuli and Sexual Deviance," *Journal of Social Issues* 29 (1973): 197–219.

49. John Court, "Sex and Violence: A Ripple Effect," *Pornography and Aggression,* ed. Neal Malamuth and Edward Donnerstein (Orlando, FL: Academic Press, 1984).

50. See Edward Donnerstein, Daniel Linz, and Steven Penrod, *The Question of Pornography* (New York: Free Press, 1987).

51. Edward Donnerstein, "Pornography and Violence against Women," *Annals of the New York Academy of Science* 347 (1980): 277–88; E. Donnerstein and J. Hallam, "Facilitating Effects of Erotica on Aggression against Women," *Journal of Personality and Social Psychology* 36 (1977): 1270–77; Seymour Fishbach and Neil Malamuth, "Sex and Aggression: Proving the Link," *Psychology Today* 12 (1978): 111–22.

52. Don Smith, "Sexual Aggression in American Pornography: The Stereotype of Rape," paper presented at the annual meeting of the American Sociological Association, 1976.

53. Associated Press, "N.Y. Firm Fined for Broadcasting Pornographic Films by Satellite," *Boston Globe,* February 16, 1991, p. 12.

54. Jared Sandberg, "U.S. Cracks Down on On-Line Child Pornography," *Wall Street Journal,* September 14, 1995, p. A3.

55. Ralph Weisheit, "Studying Drugs in Rural Areas: Notes from the Field," *Journal of Research in Crime and Delinquency* 30 (1993): 213–32.

56. Arnold Trebach, *The Heroin Solution* (New Haven, CT: Yale University Press, 1982).

57. James Inciardi, *The War on Drugs* (Palo Alto, CA: Mayfield, 1986), p. 2.

58. See, generally, David Pittman, "Drug Addiction and Crime," in *Handbook of Criminology,* ed. D. Glazer (Chicago: Rand McNally, 1974), pp. 209–32; Board of Directors, National Council on Crime and Delinquency, "Drug Addiction: A Medical, Not a Law Enforcement, Problem," *Crime and Delinquency* 20 (1974): 4–9.

59. Associated Press, "Records Detail Royals' Turn-of-Century Drug Use," *Boston Globe,* August 29, 1993, p. 13.

60. James Inciardi, *Reflections on Crime* (New York: Holt, Rinehart and Winston, 1978), p. 15.

61. William Bates and Betty Crowther, "Drug Abuse," in *Deviants: Voluntary Actors in a Hostile World,* ed. E. Sagarin and F. Montanino (New York: Foresman and Co., 1977), p. 269.

62. A. Elizabeth Comack, "The Origins of Canadian Drug Legislation: Labelling versus Class Analysis," in *The New Criminologies in Canada,* ed. Brian Fleming (Toronto: Oxford, 1985).

63. Inciardi, *Reflections on Crime,* pp. 8–10; see also A. Greeley, William McCready, and Gary Theisen, *Ethnic Drinking Subcultures* (New York: Praeger, 1980); Joseph Gusfield, *Symbolic Crusade* (Urbana: University of Illinois Press, 1963), chap. 3.

64. John Phyne, "Prohibition's Legacy: The Emergence of Provincial Policing in Nova Scotia, 1921–1932," *Canadian Journal of Law and Society* 7 (1992): 157–84.

65. This section relies heavily on the descriptions in Kenneth Jones, Louis Shainberg, and Curtin Byer, *Drugs and Alcohol* (New York: Harper & Row, 1979), pp. 57–114.

66. Canadian Press, "Pot-Smoking Cleric Seeks Tory Leadership," July 16, 1998.

67. Glenn F. Murray, "Cocaine Use in the Era of Social Reform: The Natural History of a Social Problem in Canada, 1880–1911," *Canadian Journal of Law and Society* 2 (1987): 29–43; Jeffrey Fagan and Ko-Lin Chin, "Initiation into Crack and Powdered Cocaine: A Tale of Two Epidemics," *Contemporary Drug Problems* 16 (1989): 579–617.

68. Thomas Mieczkowski, "The Damage Done: Cocaine Methods in Detroit," *International Journal of Comparative and Applied Criminal Justice* 12 (1988): 261–67.

69. *RCMP National Drug Intelligence Estimate 1994* (Ottawa: Minister of Supply and Services, 1994).

70. The Metro Toronto Research Group on Drug Use. July 31, 1996, at www.toronto.on.ca.

71. John Hagedorn, "Homeboys, Dope Fiends, Legits, and New Jacks," *Criminology* 32 (1994): 197–220.

72. Charles Winick, "Physician Narcotics Addicts," *Social Problems* 9 (1961): 174–86.

73. *Commission of Inquiry into the Use of Drugs and Banned Practices Intended to Increase Athletic Performance* (Ottawa: Supply and Services Canada, 1990).

74. "Deaths Due to Alcohol," Addiction Research Foundation–Statistical Information Service. Online: http://www.arf.org/isd/stats/alcdeath.html.

75. D.J. Rohsenow, "Drinking Habits and Expectancies about Alcohol's Effects for Self Versus Others," *Journal of Consulting and Clinical Psychology* 51 (1983): 752–56.

76. Spencer Rathus, *Psychology*, 4th ed. (New York: Holt, Rinehart and Winston, 1990), p. 161.

77. G. Kolata, "Study Backs Heart Benefits in Light Drinking," *New York Times*, August 3, 1988, p. A24.

78. Eric Wish, *Drug Use Forecasting Program, Annual Report 1990* (Washington, DC: National Institute of Justice, 1990).

79. Thomas Gray and Eric Wish, *Maryland Youth at Risk: A Study of Drug Use in Juvenile Detainees* (College Park, MD: Center for Substance Abuse Research, 1993); Eric Wish and Christina Polsenberg, "Arrestee Urine Tests and Self-Reports of Drug Use: Which Is More Related to Rearrest?" paper presented at the annual meeting of the American Society of Criminology, Phoenix AZ, November 1993.

80. "Canadian Crime Statistics, 1996," *Juristat* 17 (1997); "Drug Offences in Canada," *Juristat* 10 (1990).

81. Subtance Abuse among Manitoba High School Students, online at www.afm.mb.ca/HSSU.pdf; Centre for Addiction and Mental Health's 1999 Ontario Student Drug Use Survey, online at www.camh.net/press_releases/student_drug_use_151199.html.

82. Hilary Saner, Robert MacCoun, Peter Reuter, "On the Ubiquity of Drug Selling among Youthful Offenders in Washington, DC, 1985–1991: Age, Period, or Cohort Effect?" *Journal of Quantitative Criminology* 11 (1995): 362–73.

83. See, generally, Mark Blumberg, ed., *AIDS: The Impact on the Criminal Justice System* (Columbus, OH: Merrill Publishing, 1990).

84. Scott Decker and Richard Rosenfeld, "Intravenous Drug Use and the AIDS Epidemic: Findings for a Twenty-City Sample of Arrestees," paper presented at the annual meeting of the American Society of Criminology, Baltimore, November 1990.

85. HIV and AIDS in Canada. Surveillance Report to June 30, 2000. Health Canada. Online at www.hc-sc.gc.ca.

86. Douglas Longshore, "Prevalence and Circumstances of Drug Injection at Los Angeles Shooting Galleries," *Crime and Delinquency* 42 (1996): 21–35.

87. Mark Blumberg, "AIDS and the Criminal Justice System: An Overview," in *AIDS: The Impact on the Criminal Justice System*, p. 11.

88. Bruce Johnson, Andrew Golub, and Jeffrey Fagan, "Careers in Crack, Drug Use, Drug Distribution, and Nondrug Criminality," *Crime and Delinquency* 41 (1995): 275–95.

89. "Women's AIDS Blamed on Men," *Toronto Star*, September 30, 1994, p. A1.

90. "Where Death Gets a Double Shot. The Call to Clean Up a Hotbed of Heroin and HIV in Canada's Poorest Ghetto," *Globe and Mail*, October 8, 1997.

91. C. Bowden, "Determinants of Initial Use of Opioids," *Comprehensive Psychiatry* 12 (1971): 136–40.

92. Marvin Krohn, Alan Lizotte, Terence Thornberry, Carolyn Smith, and David McDowall, "Reciprocal Causal Relationships among Drug Use, Peers, and Beliefs: A Five-Wave Panel Model," *Journal of Drug Issues* 26 (1996): 205–428; R. Cloward and L. Ohlin, *Delinquency and Opportunity: A Theory of Delinquent Gangs* (Glencoe, IL: Free Press, 1960).

93. Kellie Barr, Michael Farrell, Grace Barnes, and John Welte, "Race, Class, and Gender Differences in Substance Abuse: Evidence of Middle-Class/Underclass Polarization among Black Males," *Social Problems* 40 (1993): 314–26.

94. Alison Bass, "Mental Ills, Drug Abuse Linked," *Boston Globe*, November 21, 1990, p. 3.

95. D.W. Goodwin, "Alcoholism and Genetics," *Archives of General Psychiatry* 42 (1985): 171–74.

96. For a thorough review of this issue, see John Petraitis, Brian Flay, and Todd Miller, "Reviewing Theories of Adolescent Substance Use: Organizing Pieces in the Puzzle," *Psychological Bulletin* 117 (1995): 67–86.

97. Judith Brooks and Li-Jung Tseng, "Influences of Parental Drug Use, Personality, and Child Rearing on the Toddler's Anger and Negativity," *Genetic, Social and General Psychology Monographs* 122 (1996): 107–28; Thomas Ashby Wills, Donato Vaccaro, Grace McNamara, and A. Elizabeth Hirky, "Escalated Substance Use: A Longitudinal Grouping Analysis from Early to Middle Adolescence," *Journal of Abnormal Psychology* 105 (1996): 166–80.

98. Denise Kandel and Mark Davies, "Friendship Networks, Intimacy and Illicit Drug Use in Young Adulthood: A Comparison of Two Competing Theories," *Criminology* 29 (1991): 441–71.

99. J.S. Mio, G. Nanjundappa, D.E. Verlur, and M.D. DeRios, "Drug Abuse and the Adolescent Sex Offender: A Preliminary Analysis," *Journal of Psychoactive Drugs* 18 (1986): 65–72.

100. D. Baer and J. Corrado, "Heroin Addict Relationships with Parents during Childhood and Early Adolescent Years," *Journal of Genetic Psychology* 124 (1974): 99–103.

101. James Inciardi, Ruth Horowitz, and Anne Pottieger, *Street Kids, Street Drugs, Street Crime: An Examination of Drug Use and Serious Delinquency in Miami* (Belmont, CA: Wadsworth, 1993), p. 43.

102. John Wallace and Jerald Bachman, "Explaining Racial/Ethnic Differences in Adolescent Drug Use: The Impact of Background and Lifestyle," *Social Problems* 38 (1991): 333–57.

103. John Donovan, "Problem-Behavior Theory and the Explanation of Adolescent Marijuana Use," *Journal of Drug Issues* 26 (1996): 379–404.

104. A. Christiansen, G.T. Smith, P.V. Roehling, and M.S. Goldman, "Using Alcohol Expectancies to Predict Adolescent Drinking Behavior after One Year," *Journal of Counseling and Clinical Psychology* 57 (1989): 93–99.

105. Claire Sterck-Elifson, "Just for Fun? Cocaine Use among Middle-Class Women," *Journal of Drug Issues* 26 (1996): 63–76.

106. Icek Ajzen, *Attitudes, Personality and Behavior* (Homewood, IL: Dorsey Press, 1988).

107. Lester Grinspoon and James B. Bakalar, *Cocaine: A Drug and Its Social Evolution*, rev. ed. (New York: Basic Books, 1985).

108. Judith Brook, Martin Whiteman, Elinor Balka, and Beatrix Hamburg, "African-American and Puerto Rican Drug Use: Personality, Familial, and Other Environmental Risk Factors," *Genetic, Social, and General Psychology Monographs* 118 (1992): 419–38.

109. Carolyn Rebecca Block and Antigone Christakos, "Intimate Partner Homicide in Chicago over 29 Years," *Crime and Delinquency* 41 (1995): 496–526.

110. Douglas Smith and Christina Polsenberg, "Specifying the Relationship between Arrestee Drug Test Results and

Recidivism," *Journal of Criminal Law and Criminology* 83 (1992): 364–77.

111. George Speckart and M. Douglas Anglin, "Narcotics Use and Crime: An Overview of Recent Research Advances," *Contemporary Drug Problems* 13 (1986): 741–69; Charles Faupel and Carl Klockars, "Drugs-Crime Connections: Elaborations from the Life Histories of Hard-Core Heroin Addicts," *Social Problems* 34 (1987): 54–68.

112. Speckart and Anglin, "Narcotics Use and Crime: An Overview of Recent Research Advances," p. 752.

113. Helene Raskin White and Stephen Hansell, "The Moderating Effects of Gender and Hostility on the Alcohol-Aggression Relationship," *Journal of Research in Crime and Delinquency* 33 (1996): 450–70; James Inciardi, "Heroin Use and Street Crime," *Crime and Delinquency* 25 (1979): 335–46; see also W. McGlothlin, M. Anglin, and B. Wilson, "Narcotic Addiction and Crime," *Criminology* 16 (1978): 293–311; M. Douglas Anglin and George Speckart, "Narcotics Use and Crime: A Multisample, Multimethod Analysis," *Criminology* 26 (1988): 197–235; David Nurco, Ira Cisin, and John Ball, "Crime as a Source of Income for Narcotics Addicts," *Journal of Substance Abuse Treatment* 2 (1985): 113–15.

114. Allen Beck, Darrell Gilliard, Lawrence Greenfeld, Caroline Harlow, Thomas Hester, Lewis Jankowski, Tracy Snell, James Stephen, and Danielle Morton, *Survey of State Prison Inmates, 1991* (Washington, DC: Bureau of Justice Statistics, 1993). The survey of prison inmates is conducted by the Bureau of Justice Statistics every five to seven years.

115. Paul Goldstein, "The Drugs-Violence Nexus: A Tripartite Conceptual Framework," *Journal of Drug Issues* 15 (1985): 493–506.

116. Charles Faupel, "Heroin Use, Crime and Unemployment Status," *Journal of Drug Issues* 18 (1988): 467–79.

117. Royal Commission on Disturbances in a Portion of the City of Vancouver known as "Gastown," as cited in Royal Commissions and Commissions of Inquiry in British Columbia, 1943–1980 (BC Legislative Library, 1982).

118. Eric Jensen, Jurg Gerber, and Ginna Babcock, "The New War on Drugs: Grass Roots Movement or Political Construction?" *Journal of Drug Issues* 21 (1991): 651–67.

119. *RCMP National Drug Intelligence Estimate, 1994* (Ottawa: Minister of Supply and Services, 1994).

120. Christopher Wren, "U.S. Is Certifying Mexico as an Ally in Fighting Drugs," *New York Times*, March 1, 1997, p. 1; Diego Ribadneira, "In Escobar Death, No Curb in Drugs Seen," *Boston Globe*, December 4, 1993, p. 2.

121. Bureau for International Narcotics and Law Enforcement Affairs, *International Narcotics Control Strategy Report, 1996* (Washington, DC: U.S. Department of State, 1997).

122. Walter Shapiro, "Going After the Hell's Angels," *Newsweek*, May 13, 1985, p. 41.

123. David Hayeslip, "Local-Level Drug Enforcement: New Strategies," *NIJ Reports*, March/April 1989.

124. Mark Moore, *Drug Trafficking* (Washington, DC: National Institute of Justice, 1988).

125. "Why It Took 30 Years to Bust a Crime Family," *Globe and Mail*, July 17, 1998, p. A1.

126. Robert Davis, Arthur Lurigio, and Dennis Rosenbaum, eds., *Drugs and the Community* (Springfield, IL: Charles C. Thomas, 1993), pp. xii–xv.

127. Saul Weingart, "A Typology of Community Responses to Drugs," in *Drugs and the Community,* ed. Davis, Lurigio, and Rosenbaum, pp. 85–105.

128. Davis, Lurigio, and Rosenbaum, *Drugs and the Community,* pp. xii–xiii.

129. Bureau of Justice Statistics, *Drugs, Crime and the Justice System* (Washington, DC: Bureau of Justice Statistics, 1992), pp. 109–12.

130. "TD's Drug-Testing Policy Wrong, Court Rules," *Globe and Mail*, July 25, 1998, p. A3; "Drug Testing in the Workplace," *Daily News*, August 21, 1994, p. 19; "Just Say No to Testing," *Toronto Star*, August 23, 1994, p. A12; Submission on Mandatory Drug Testing in the Workplace, Canadian Civil Liberties Association. Online: http://www.ccla.org/pos/briefs/drugtest.html.

131. "Infants' Hair Tested without Moms Knowing," *Toronto Star*, April 15, 1995, p. A1.

132. Ethan Nadelmann, "America's Drug Problem," *Bulletin of the American Academy of Arts and Sciences* 65 (1991): 24–40.

133. Ethan Nadelmann, "Should We Legalize Drugs? History Answers Yes," *American Heritage* (February/March 1993): 41–56.

134. See, generally, Ralph Weisheit, *Drugs, Crime and the Criminal Justice System* (Cincinnati: Anderson, 1990).

135. David Courtwright, "Should We Legalize Drugs? History Answers No," *American Heritage* (February/March 1993): 43–56; James Inciardi and Duane McBride, "Legalizing Drugs: A Gormless, Naive Idea," *Criminologist* 15 (1990): 1–4.

136. Kathryn Ann Farr, "Revitalizing the Drug Decriminalization Debate," *Crime and Delinquency* 36 (1990): 223–37.

137. "Nancy B's Gift," *Mail Star*, January 8, 1992, p. C1; "Nancy B.'s Right to Die," *Montreal Gazette*, January 7, 1992, p. B2; "Exercising the Right to Die," *Globe and Mail*, November 29, 1991, p. A18.

138. "The Government as Bookie," *Globe and Mail*, May 23, 1995, p. A18.

139. "Bernie Bets Big on Gambling Gains," *Halifax Herald*, April 12, 1995, p. A1; "A Sure Bet Industry," *Perspectives* 8 3–6 (1996).

140. "RCMP Fears Fuel N.S. Casino Debate," *Globe and Mail*, April 27, 1994, p. A3; "Casino Will Boost Crime, Windsor Police Report Says," *Globe and Mail*, August 4, 1993, p. A4; "Mobsters Bet on Niagara Falls to Win Casino," *Toronto Star*, May 16, 1994, p. A1.

Copyright Acknowledgments

Chapter One

p. 7, Figure 1.1: © "The Varieties of Deviance" from Hagan, John, *The Disreputable Pleasures: Crime and Deviance in Canada*, 3rd ed. (1991). Toronto: McGraw-Hill Ryerson Ltd., p. 13. Reprinted by permission.

p. 10, Figure 1.3: Boston College http://www.bc.edu/bc_org/ avp/cas/fnart/phrenology/phrenology1.html

Chapter Two

p. 29, Exhibit 2.1: ©*The Internet Medieval Sourcebook.*

p. 33, Table 2.1: "Outdated Canadian Crimes" from the Criminal Code of Canada.

p. 33, Figure 2.2: As used in Gerald L. Gall, *The Canadian Legal System*, 4th edition, p.36. Reprinted by permission of Carswell, a division of Thomson Canada Limited.

p. 35, Figure 2.3: "The Divisions of Law" from Gerald L. Gall, *The Canadian Legal System*, 4th edition, Ch. 2 Reprinted by permission of Carswell, a division of Thomson Canada Limited.

p. 45, Table 2.3: "Constitution Act, 1982–Canadian Charter of Rights and Freedoms–Legal Rights" from the Constitution Act, 1982.

p. 48, Exhibit 2.3: "Quick Code: Criminal Harassment Section 264" from the Criminal Code of Canada.

Chapter Three

p. 53, Table 3.1: "Incidence, Rate, and Clearance Status of Selected Crimes, Canada, 1996" adapted from the Statistics Canada publication *Canadian Crime Statistics*, Catalogue No. 85-205, 1995.

p. 54, Figure 3.1: "Crime Rates by Province and Territory" adapted from the Statistics Canada publication *The Daily*, Catalogue No.11-00, July 19, 2001.

p. 56, Figure 3.2: "Arson Incidents, 1987 to 1993" adapted from the Statistics Canada publication *Canadian Crime Statistics*, Catalogue No. 85-205, 1993.

p. 57, Table 3.2: "Understanding public views of crime and the youth justice system" from Sprott, Jane B., *Canadian Journal of Criminology* (July 1996): pp. 271-290. Reprinted with permission. Copyright of the Canadian Criminal Justice Association.

p. 62, Report: © Reprinted by permission of the Edmonton Police Service.

p. 63, Cartoon: Mike Graston/*Windsor Star.*

p. 63, Figure 3.4: "Crime Rates" adapted from the Statistics Canada publication *The Daily*, Catalogue No.11-001, July 19, 2001.

p. 64, Table 3.4: Offender Management System, CSC, March 31, 1997 from *Basic Facts about Corrections in Canada*, Solicitor General, 1997: p.19.

p. 74, Figure 3.5: "Crime Rate and Selected Demographics, Canada, 1962-2000" adapted from Statistics Canada's *Uniform Crime Reporting Survey*, January 2001, and Statistics Canada's *Annual Demographic Statistics*, April 2001.

p. 75, Exhibit 3.2: "Profile of Women and the Criminal Justice System" adapted from the Statistics Canada publication *Women in Canada, Canadian Centre for Justice Statistics Profile Series*, Catalogue 85F0033MIE, June 14,2001.

Chapter Four

p. 83, Table 4.1: © 1998 Reprinted with permission of The Fraser Institute.

p. 84, Figure 4.1: © 1997 Reprinted with permission of The National Media Archive.

p. 86, Table 4.2: © 2000 Times Newspapers Limited.

pp. 88-89, Table 4.3: "Personal Victimization Rates, by Victim Characteristics, 1999" adapted from the Statistics Canada publication *Juristat*, Catalogue No. 85-002, 1997, Vol. 20, No. 10.

p. 95, Exhibit 4.1: Criminal Code of Canada 718.2.

p. 102, Exhibit 4.2: © 1995, Reprinted by permission of Ken Pence, Nashville Police Department.

Chapter Five

p. 120, Figure 5.1: © "Situational Crime Prevention" from Clarke, Ronald, *Building a Safer Society: Strategic Approaches to Crime Prevention*, Vol. 19 of *Crime and Justice, A Review of Research*, eds. Michael Tonry and David Farrington. Chicago: University of Chicago Press (1995), p.103. Reprinted with permission.

p. 122, Figure 5.2: Reprinted with permission–The Toronto Star Syndicate.

p. 127, Table 5.2: © "Crime Discouragers" from Marcus Felon, "Those who discourage Crime," in John Eck and David Weisburd, *Crime and Place*. Monsey, N.Y: Criminal Justice Press, (1995), p.59. Reprinted with permission.

p. 134, Crime in the News: The National Post Online © 2000.

Chapter Six

p. 150, © The Canadian Press (1987).

p. 159, Table 6.2: © "Association between violence, psychosis, and relationship to victim in stalkers" by Frank R. Farnham, David V. James, and Paul Cantrell, *The Lancet*, January 15, 2000:199. Reprinted by permission of Elsevier Science.

Chapter Seven

p. 184, Figure 7.4: © "Diagram II: The Pattern of Expansion as Displayed by Montreal" from C.A. Dawson and W.E. Gettys, *An Introduction to Sociology*. New York: Ronald Press 1929, 1935, p.130.

p. 187, Famous Canadian Criminals: Reprinted with permission of *The Globe and Mail.*

p. 189, Table 7.1: Reprinted with the permission of The Free Press, a Division of Simon & Schuster Inc., from *Social Theory and Social Structure* by Robert K. Merton. Copyright © 1957 by The Free Press; copyright renewed 1985 by Robert K. Merton.

Chapter Nine

p. 246, Crime in the News: Copyright © 2001 by Parker Donham.

Chapter Ten

p. 269, Famous Canadian Criminals: © The Canadian Press.

p. 273, Figure 10.7: Reprinted by permission of the publisher from Robert Samson and John Laub, *Crime in the Making: Pathways and Turning Points Through Life*, pp. 244-45, Cambridge, MA: Harvard University Press. Copyright © 1993. All Rights Reserved.

Chapter Eleven

p. 282, Figure 11.2: Adapted from Statistics Canada, "National Longitudinal Survey of Children and Youth", 1998-1999, Cycle 3.

p. 285, Exhibit 11.1: Adapted from the Statistics Canada publication, *Juristat*: Catalogue 85-002, Vol. 17, No. 7, 1997.

p. 285, Exhibit 11.2: © Harcourt Canada.

p. 286, Exhibit 11.3: Reprinted with permission of *The Globe and Mail*.

p. 290, Exhibit 11.4: Adapted from the Statistics Canada publication, *Juristat*: Catalogue 85-002, Vol. 20, No. 9, 2000.

p. 293, Culture, Gender, Ethnicity, and Criminology: © Telegraph Group Limited, 1996.

p. 295, Exhibit 11.5: Adapted from the Statistics Canada publication, *Juristat*: Catalogue 85-002, Vol. 15, No. 15, 1995.

p. 302, Crime in the News: Reprinted with permission of *The Globe and Mail*.

Chapter Twelve

p. 312, Figure 12.1: © Edwin Sutherland and Chic Conwell, *The Professional Thief* (Chicago: University of Chicago Press, 1937).

p. 313, Exhibit 12.1: © Pocket Criminal Code (Scarborough, ON: Carswell, 1995).

p. 317, Exhibit 12.3 © Pocket Criminal Code (Scarborough, ON: Carswell, 1995).

p. 320, Crime in the News: Reprinted with permission of *The Daily Gleaner*.

p. 324, Exhibit 12.6: Reprinted with permission of Toronto Police Service, Fraud and Forgery Squad.

p. 326, Exhibit 12.8: © Pocket Criminal Code (Scarborough, ON: Carswell, 1995).

p. 327, Exhibit 12.9: © Richard Wright and Scott Decker, *Burglars on the Job: Streetlife and Residential Break-ins* (Boston, MA: Northeastern University Press, 1994).

p. 328, © Scott Decker, Richard Wright, Allison Redfern and Dietrich Smith, "A Woman's Place is in the Home: Females and Residential Burglary," *Justice Quarterly 10* (1993): 143-63. Reprinted with permission of the Academy of Criminal Justice Sciences.

Chapter Thirteen

p. 337, Famous Canadian Criminals: © *National Post*, December 8, 2001, p. A16.

p. 346, Box 13.2: © People's Tribune, November 2000, vol. 26, No. 11 by Anthony Prince. Reprinted with permission of The League of Revolutionaries for a New America.

p. 349, Figure 13.1: © *The Toronto Star*, May 11, 1992, p. A1.

p. 352, Culture, Gender, Ethnicity, and Criminology: © Paul Palango, "Mountie Misery" *Maclean's*, July 28, 1997, pp. 10-15.

p. 358, Figure 13.2: "Crimes Most Frequently Committed by Organized Crime Groups" from the Statistics Canada survey "Organized Crime Activity in Canada, 1998: Results of a Pilot Survey of 16 Police Services," Catalogue 85-548, May 1999.

p. 360, Exhibit 13.7: © "The Fight Against Organized Crime," Solicitor General of Canada. Reproduced with permission of the Minister of Public Works and Government Services Canada, 2002.

Chapter Fourteen

p. 369, Crime in the News: © "The Fruit Machine," by Dean Bibby, *The Canadian Press*, 24 April 1992.

p. 369, Exhibit 14.1: © "Quick Code on Prostitution" from the Criminal Code of Canada.

p. 370, Figure 14.1: © "Overview of Persons Charged with Communication in 1995" from the Statistics Canada publication *Juristat*, Catalogue No. 85-002, 17 (2), February, 1997.

p. 375, Crime in the News: © "The Sinking of I'm Alone" from *The New York Times*, 29 March 1929. Reprinted with permission.

p. 376, Figure 14.2: © "Major Cannabis Trafficking Routes into Canada, 1993" from RCMP National Drug Intelligence Estimate, 1994. Reprinted by permission of the RCMP.

p. 381, Famous Canadian Criminals: © "The High Life of Brian O'Dea" by Charlie Gillis from *The National Post*, 8 December 2001.

p. 388, Exhibit 14.2: "Quick Code: Permitted Lotteries" from the Criminal Code of Canada.

p. 389, Figure 14.4: "Lottery Play is tied to Household Income" from the Statistics Canada publication *Perspectives on Labour and Income*, Catalogue 75-001, Vol. 8, No.3, September 1996.

Photo Credits

This page constitutes an extension of the copyright page. We have made every effort to trace the ownership of all copyrighted material and to secure permissions from copyright holders. In the event of any questions arising as to the use of any material, we will be pleased to make the necessary corrections in future printings. Thanks are due to the following authors, publishers, and agents for permission to use the material indicated.

Chapter 1

3: © *The Toronto Star*/P. Power; 4: © CP Picture Archive/ Frank Gunn; 8: © T. Mattheson, 'The Trial of George Jacobs, August 5, 1692.' Oil on canvas, 39 x 53 inches. #1246. Peabody Essex Museum, Salem, MA. 21: Copyright © 2000 Province of British Columbia. All Rights Reserved. Reprinted with permission of the Province of British Columbia.

Chapter 2

27: © CP Picture Archive/Ron Poling; 31: © Internet Medieval Sourcebook; 37: CP Picture Archive/Kevin Frayer; 42: CP Picture Archive/ Andrew Vaughan.

Chapter 3

51: © CP Picture Archive; 62: © CP Picture Archive/ *Fredericton Daily Gleaner*/ Bob Wilson; 71: © CP Picture Archive/Joe Bryska/ AP; 78: Stoddart/ Katz/ Corbis SABA.

Chapter 4

81: © CP Picture Archive/ Moe Doiron; 82: © *The Toronto Star*/ Ron Bull; 93: © Provincial Archives of Alberta, Photo Collection OB2562; 106: © Reprinted with permission of Pete Wagner.

Chapter 5

113: © *The Toronto Star*/Stan Behal; 133: Thomson Nelson; 137: © Image courtesy of David L. Getchell, http://getchwood.com.

Chapter 6

143: Cartoon by Daumier, 1839. CORBIS/MAGMA; 146: From The Encyclopedia of Sociology: New and Updated, 2nd edition, by DPG Reference Publishing, Inc., Guilford, CT. Reprinted by permission of McGraw Hill/Dushkin, a division of McGraw-Hill Companies, Guilford, CT, 06437. 164: © Rick Kopstein 169: © Matrix/Alex Quesada.

Chapter 7

173: © CP Picture Archive/ Frank Gunn; 176: © Archive Photos/ Leo Vals; 189: © CP Picture Archive/ Fred Thornhill; 198: © *The Toronto Star*/ K. Faught.

Chapter 8

204: © CP Picture Archive/ Cheryl Hnatiuk; 217: Stockphoto.com/ Black Star/ Todd Yates; 223: © Brooks Kraft/CORBIS/ MAGMA; 225: © CP Picture Archive/ Kevin Frayer.

Chapter 9

231: © CP Picture Archive/ Ryan Remiorz; 236: © CP Picture Archive/ Paul Chiasson; 243: © CP Picture Archive/ Kevin Frayer; 244: © Saskatchewan Archives Board.

Chapter 10

254: © The Image Works/B. Daemmrich Photography, Inc; 269: © CP Picture Archive/ *Calgary Herald*/ Rob Galbraith; 271: © *Montreal Gazette*/ John Kenney; 274: © Matrix International, Inc.

Chapter 11

279: © CP Picture Archive/ Tom Hanson; 293: © Press Association; 301: © CP Picture Archive/ Moshe Bursurker/ AP; 303: © CP Picture Archive/ Chuck Mitchell.

Chapter 12

308: Siede Preis/ PhotoDisc; 315: © Courtesy of Toronto and Regional Crime Stoppers; 322: © CP Picture Archive/*Hamilton Spectator*; 329: © *The Toronto Star*/ J. Mahler.

Chapter 13

332: © Mark Sherman Photography; 335: © CP Picture Archive/ Daniel Beltra/ AP; 338: © Chuck Burton/ Sygma/ MAGMA.

Chapter 14

363: © Halifax Herald Ltd. 365: © *Toronto Sun*/ Cassese; 374: © Bettman/CORBIS.

Index